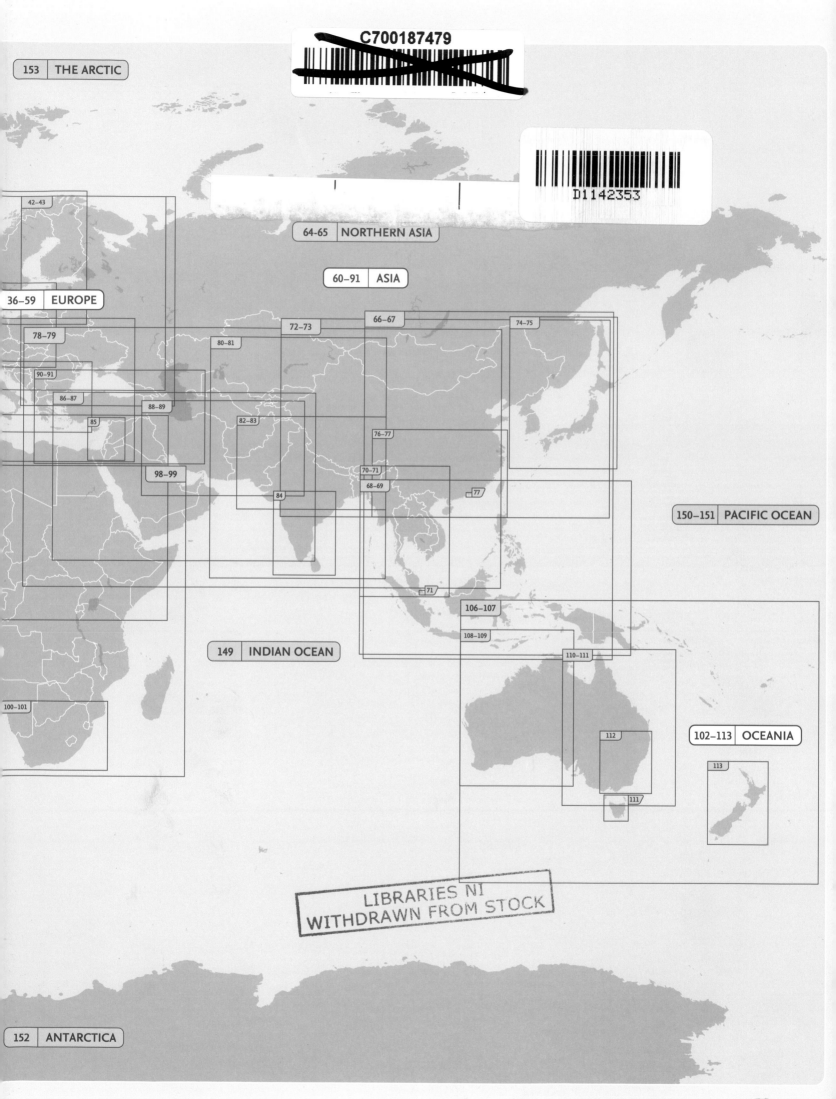

153 | THE ARCTIC

C700187479

D1142353

42–43

64-65 | NORTHERN ASIA

60–91 | ASIA

36–59 | EUROPE

78–79

66–67

72–73

80–81

74–75

90–91

86–87

88–89

85

82–83

76–77

98–99

84

70–71

68–69

77

150–151 | PACIFIC OCEAN

71

149 | INDIAN OCEAN

106–107

108–109

110–111

100–101

112

102–113 | OCEANIA

113

111

152 | ANTARCTICA

Find your map

COLLINS WORLD ATLAS
CONCISE EDITION

Collins
An imprint of HarperCollins Publishers
77–85 Fulham Palace Road
London
W6 8JB

First Published 2006
Originally published as Collins World Atlas Illustrated Edition 2003

Second edition 2009

Copyright © HarperCollins Publishers 2009
Maps © Collins Bartholomew Ltd 2009

Printed in Hong Kong

British Library Cataloguing in Publication Data.
A catalogue record for this book is available from the British Library.

ISBN 978-0-00-728902-8

Imp 001

All mapping in this atlas is generated from Collins
Bartholomew™ digital databases. Collins Bartholomew™,
the UK's leading independent geographical information
supplier, can provide a digital, custom, and premium
mapping service to a variety of markets.
For further information:
Tel: +44 (0) 141 306 3752
e-mail: collinsbartholomew@harpercollins.co.uk

We also offer a choice of books, atlases and maps that
can be customized to suit a customer's own requirements.
For further information:
Tel +44 (0) 1242 258155
e-mail: business.gifts@harpercollins.co.uk

or visit our website at: www.collinsbartholomew.com

Cover image: Planetary Visions/Science Photo Library

Collins World Atlas

Collins

Contents

Contents

Southern Europe | Japan | Antarctica

Settlements

Population	National capital	Administrative capital	Other city or town
over 10 million	BEIJING ⊛	Karachi ◉	New York ◉
5 million to 10 million	JAKARTA ✪	Tianjin ◉	Nova Iguaçu ◉
1 million to 5 million	KĀBUL ✪	Sydney ◉	Kaohsiung ◉
500 000 to 1 million	BANGUI ✪	Trujillo ◎	Jeddah ◎
100 000 to 500 000	WELLINGTON ✿	Mansa ◉	Apucarana ◎
50 000 to 100 000	PORT OF SPAIN ✿	Potenza ◎	Arecibo ◌
10 000 to 50 000	MALABO ✿	Chinhoyi ◌	Ceres ◌
under 10 000	VALLETTA ✿	Ati ◌	Venta ◌

⬬ Built-up area

Boundaries

— International boundary

–·–·– Disputed international boundary or alignment unconfirmed

— Administrative boundary

········ Ceasefire line

Miscellaneous

---------- National park

············· Reserve or Regional park

✳ Site of specific interest

⬬⬬⬬⬬⬬ Wall

Land and sea features

Desert

⌄ Oasis

Lava field

Marsh

1234 △ Volcano height in metres

Ice cap or Glacier

Escarpment

Coral reef

ᴧ 1234 Pass height in metres

Lakes and rivers

Lake

Impermanent lake

Salt lake or lagoon

Impermanent salt lake

Dry salt lake or salt pan

123 Lake height surface height above sea level, in metres

— River

— Impermanent river or watercourse

‖ Waterfall

| Dam

| Barrage

Relief

Contour intervals and layer colours

Height metres		feet
5000		16404
3000		9843
2000		6562
1000		3281
500		1640
200		656
0		0
below sea level		
0		0
200		656
2000		6562
4000		13124
6000		19686

Depth

1234 △ Summit height in metres

-123 Spot height height in metres

123 Ocean deep depth in metres

Transport

⟶ ·······	Motorway (tunnel; under construction)
⟶ -----	Main road (tunnel; under construction)
⟶ -----	Secondary road (tunnel; under construction)
·············	Track
⊢⊢⊢ -----	Main railway (tunnel; under construction)
⟶ -----	Secondary railway (tunnel; under construction)
⟶ -----	Other railway (tunnel; under construction)
—	Canal
✈	Main airport
✈	Regional airport

Satellite imagery - The thematic pages in the atlas contain a wide variety of photographs and images. These are a mixture of terrestrial and aerial photographs and satellite imagery. All are used to illustrate specific themes and to give an indication of the variety of imagery available today. The main types of imagery used in the atlas are described in the table below. The sensor for each satellite image is detailed on the acknowledgements page.

Main satellites/sensors

Satellite/sensor name	Launch dates	Owner	Aims and applications	Internet links	Additional internet links
Landsat 1, 2, 3, 4, 5, 7	July 1972–April 1999	National Aeronautics and Space Administration (NASA), USA	The first satellite to be designed specifically for observing the Earth's surface. Originally set up to produce images of use for agriculture and geology. Today is of use for numerous environmental and scientific applications.	landsat.gsfc.nasa.gov	asterweb.jpl.nasa.gov
					earth.jsc.nasa.gov
					earthnet.esrin.esa.it
SPOT 1, 2, 3, 4, 5 (Satellite Pour l'Observation de la Terre)	February 1986–March 1998	Centre National d'Etudes Spatiales (CNES) and Spot Image, France	Particularly useful for monitoring land use, water resources research, coastal studies and cartography.	www.spotimage.fr	earthobservatory.nasa.gov
					eol.jsc.nasa.gov
					gs.mdacorporation.com
Space Shuttle	Regular launches from 1981	NASA, USA	Each shuttle mission has separate aims. Astronauts take photographs with high specification hand held cameras. The Shuttle Radar Topography Mission (SRTM) in 2000 obtained the most complete near-global high-resolution database of the earth's topography.	science.ksc.nasa.gov/shuttle/countdown www.jpl.nasa.gov/srtm	modis.gsfc.nasa.gov
					seawifs.gsfc.nasa.gov
					topex-www.jpl.nasa.gov
IKONOS	September 1999	GeoEye	First commercial high-resolution satellite. Useful for a variety of applications mainly Cartography, Defence, Urban Planning, Agriculture, Forestry and Insurance.	www.geoeye.com	visibleearth.nasa.gov
					www.usgs.gov

Amsterdam, Netherlands

The Alps

Europe		Area sq km	Area sq miles	Population	Capital	Languages	Religions	Currency
ALBANIA		28 748	11 100	3 190 000	Tirana	Albanian, Greek	Sunni Muslim, Albanian Orthodox, Roman Catholic	Lek
ANDORRA		465	180	75 000	Andorra la Vella	Spanish, Catalan, French	Roman Catholic	Euro
AUSTRIA		83 855	32 377	8 361 000	Vienna	German, Croatian, Turkish	Roman Catholic, Protestant	Euro
BELARUS		207 600	80 155	9 689 000	Minsk	Belorussian, Russian	Belorussian Orthodox, Roman Catholic	Belarus rouble
BELGIUM		30 520	11 784	10 457 000	Brussels	Dutch (Flemish), French (Walloon), German	Roman Catholic, Protestant	Euro
BOSNIA-HERZEGOVINA		51 130	19 741	3 935 000	Sarajevo	Bosnian, Serbian, Croatian	Sunni Muslim, Serbian Orthodox, Roman Catholic, Protestant	Marka
BULGARIA		110 994	42 855	7 639 000	Sofia	Bulgarian, Turkish, Romany, Macedonian	Bulgarian Orthodox, Sunni Muslim	Lev
CROATIA		56 538	21 829	4 555 000	Zagreb	Croatian, Serbian	Roman Catholic, Serbian Orthodox, Sunni Muslim	Kuna
CZECH REPUBLIC		78 864	30 450	10 186 000	Prague	Czech, Moravian, Slovak	Roman Catholic, Protestant	Czech koruna
DENMARK		43 075	16 631	5 442 000	Copenhagen	Danish	Protestant	Danish krone
ESTONIA		45 200	17 452	1 335 000	Tallinn	Estonian, Russian	Protestant, Estonian and Russian Orthodox	Kroon
FINLAND		338 145	130 559	5 277 000	Helsinki	Finnish, Swedish	Protestant, Greek Orthodox	Euro
FRANCE		543 965	210 026	61 647 000	Paris	French, Arabic	Roman Catholic, Protestant, Sunni Muslim	Euro
GERMANY		357 022	137 849	82 599 000	Berlin	German, Turkish	Protestant, Roman Catholic	Euro
GREECE		131 957	50 949	11 147 000	Athens	Greek	Greek Orthodox, Sunni Muslim	Euro
HUNGARY		93 030	35 919	10 030 000	Budapest	Hungarian	Roman Catholic, Protestant	Forint
ICELAND		102 820	39 699	301 000	Reykjavík	Icelandic	Protestant	Icelandic króna
IRELAND		70 282	27 136	4 301 000	Dublin	English, Irish	Roman Catholic, Protestant	Euro
ITALY		301 245	116 311	58 877 000	Rome	Italian	Roman Catholic	Euro
KOSOVO		10 908	4 212	2 070 000	Prishtinë (Priština)	Albanian, Serbian	Sunni Muslim, Serbian Orthodox	Euro
LATVIA		63 700	24 595	2 277 000	Rīga	Latvian, Russian	Protestant, Roman Catholic, Russian Orthodox	Lats
LIECHTENSTEIN		160	62	35 000	Vaduz	German	Roman Catholic, Protestant	Swiss franc
LITHUANIA		65 200	25 174	3 390 000	Vilnius	Lithuanian, Russian, Polish	Roman Catholic, Protestant, Russian Orthodox	Litas
LUXEMBOURG		2 586	998	467 000	Luxembourg	Letzeburgish, German, French	Roman Catholic	Euro
MACEDONIA (F.Y.R.O.M.)		25 713	9 928	2 038 000	Skopje	Macedonian, Albanian, Turkish	Macedonian Orthodox, Sunni Muslim	Macedonian denar
MALTA		316	122	407 000	Valletta	Maltese, English	Roman Catholic	Euro
MOLDOVA		33 700	13 012	3 794 000	Chişinău	Romanian, Ukrainian, Gagauz, Russian	Romanian Orthodox, Russian Orthodox	Moldovan leu
MONACO		2	1	33 000	Monaco-Ville	French, Monegasque, Italian	Roman Catholic	Euro
MONTENEGRO		13 812	5 333	598 000	Podgorica	Serbian (Montenegrin), Albanian	Montenegrin Orthodox, Sunni Muslim	Euro
NETHERLANDS		41 526	16 033	16 419 000	Amsterdam/The Hague	Dutch, Frisian	Roman Catholic, Protestant, Sunni Muslim	Euro
NORWAY		323 878	125 050	4 698 000	Oslo	Norwegian	Protestant, Roman Catholic	Norwegian krone
POLAND		312 683	120 728	38 082 000	Warsaw	Polish, German	Roman Catholic, Polish Orthodox	Złoty
PORTUGAL		88 940	34 340	10 623 000	Lisbon	Portuguese	Roman Catholic, Protestant	Euro
ROMANIA		237 500	91 699	21 438 000	Bucharest	Romanian, Hungarian	Romanian Orthodox, Protestant, Roman Catholic	Romanian leu
RUSSIAN FEDERATION		17 075 400	6 592 849	142 499 000	Moscow	Russian, Tatar, Ukrainian, local languages	Russian Orthodox, Sunni Muslim, Protestant	Russian rouble
SAN MARINO		61	24	31 000	San Marino	Italian	Roman Catholic	Euro
SERBIA		77 453	29 904	7 788 000	Belgrade	Serbian, Hungarian	Serbian Orthodox, Roman Catholic, Sunni Muslim	Serbian dinar
SLOVAKIA		49 035	18 933	5 390 000	Bratislava	Slovak, Hungarian, Czech	Roman Catholic, Protestant, Orthodox	Euro
SLOVENIA		20 251	7 819	2 002 000	Ljubljana	Slovene, Croatian, Serbian	Roman Catholic, Protestant	Euro
SPAIN		504 782	194 897	44 279 000	Madrid	Castilian, Catalan, Galician, Basque	Roman Catholic	Euro
SWEDEN		449 964	173 732	9 119 000	Stockholm	Swedish	Protestant, Roman Catholic	Swedish krona
SWITZERLAND		41 293	15 943	7 484 000	Bern	German, French, Italian, Romansch	Roman Catholic, Protestant	Swiss franc
UKRAINE		603 700	233 090	46 205 000	Kiev	Ukrainian, Russian	Ukrainian Orthodox, Ukrainian Catholic, Roman Catholic	Hryvnia
UNITED KINGDOM		243 609	94 058	60 769 000	London	English, Welsh, Gaelic	Protestant, Roman Catholic, Muslim	Pound sterling
VATICAN CITY		0.5	0.2	557	Vatican City	Italian	Roman Catholic	Euro

Dependent territories		Territorial status	Area sq km	Area sq miles	Population	Capital	Languages	Religions	Currency
Azores		Autonomous Region of Portugal	2 300	888	242 000	Ponta Delgada	Portuguese	Roman Catholic, Protestant	Euro
Faroe Islands		Self-governing Danish Territory	1 399	540	49 000	Tórshavn	Faroese, Danish	Protestant	Danish krone
Gibraltar		United Kingdom Overseas Territory	7	3	29 000	Gibraltar	English, Spanish	Roman Catholic, Protestant, Sunni Muslim	Gibraltar pound
Guernsey		United Kingdom Crown Dependency	78	30	64 000	St Peter Port	English, French	Protestant, Roman Catholic	Pound sterling
Isle of Man		United Kingdom Crown Dependency	572	221	79 000	Douglas	English	Protestant, Roman Catholic	Pound sterling
Jersey		United Kingdom Crown Dependency	116	45	88 000	St Helier	English, French	Protestant, Roman Catholic	Pound sterling

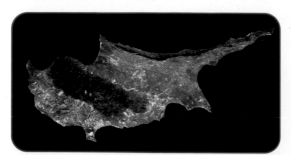

Cyprus, eastern Mediterranean

Bhutan, Himalayas

Asia		Area sq km	Area sq miles	Population	Capital	Languages	Religions	Currency
AFGHANISTAN		652 225	251 825	27 145 000	Kābul	Dari, Pushtu, Uzbek, Turkmen	Sunni Muslim, Shi'a Muslim	Afghani
ARMENIA		29 800	11 506	3 002 000	Yerevan	Armenian, Azeri	Armenian Orthodox	Dram
AZERBAIJAN		86 600	33 436	8 467 000	Baku	Azeri, Armenian, Russian, Lezgian	Shi'a Muslim, Sunni Muslim, Russian and Armenian Orthodox	Azerbaijani manat
BAHRAIN		691	267	753 000	Manama	Arabic, English	Shi'a Muslim, Sunni Muslim, Christian	Bahrain dinar
BANGLADESH		143 998	55 598	158 665 000	Dhaka	Bengali, English	Sunni Muslim, Hindu	Taka
BHUTAN		46 620	18 000	658 000	Thimphu	Dzongkha, Nepali, Assamese	Buddhist, Hindu	Ngultrum, Indian rupee
BRUNEI		5 765	2 226	390 000	Bandar Seri Begawan	Malay, English, Chinese	Sunni Muslim, Buddhist, Christian	Brunei dollar
CAMBODIA		181 035	69 884	14 444 000	Phnom Penh	Khmer, Vietnamese	Buddhist, Roman Catholic, Sunni Muslim	Riel
CHINA		9 584 492	3 700 593	1 313 437 000	Beijing	Mandarin, Wu, Cantonese, Hsiang, regional languages	Confucian, Taoist, Buddhist, Christian, Sunni Muslim	Yuan, HK dollar**, Macau pataca
CYPRUS		9 251	3 572	855 000	Nicosia	Greek, Turkish, English	Greek Orthodox, Sunni Muslim	Euro
EAST TIMOR		14 874	5 743	1 155 000	Dili	Portuguese, Tetun, English	Roman Catholic	United States dollar
GEORGIA		69 700	26 911	4 395 000	T'bilisi	Georgian, Russian, Armenian, Azeri, Ossetian, Abkhaz	Georgian Orthodox, Russian Orthodox, Sunni Muslim	Lari
INDIA		3 064 898	1 183 364	1 169 016 000	New Delhi	Hindi, English, many regional languages	Hindu, Sunni Muslim, Shi'a Muslim, Sikh, Christian	Indian rupee
INDONESIA		1 919 445	741 102	231 627 000	Jakarta	Indonesian, local languages	Sunni Muslim, Protestant, Roman Catholic, Hindu, Buddhist	Rupiah
IRAN		1 648 000	636 296	71 208 000	Tehrān	Farsi, Azeri, Kurdish, regional languages	Shi'a Muslim, Sunni Muslim	Iranian rial
IRAQ		438 317	169 235	28 993 000	Baghdād	Arabic, Kurdish, Turkmen	Shi'a Muslim, Sunni Muslim, Christian	Iraqi dinar
ISRAEL		20 770	8 019	6 928 000	Jerusalem (Yerushalayim) (El Quds)*	Hebrew, Arabic	Jewish, Sunni Muslim, Christian, Druze	Shekel
JAPAN		377 727	145 841	127 967 000	Tōkyō	Japanese	Shintoist, Buddhist, Christian	Yen
JORDAN		89 206	34 443	5 924 000	'Ammān	Arabic	Sunni Muslim, Christian	Jordanian dinar
KAZAKHSTAN		2 717 300	1 049 155	15 422 000	Astana	Kazakh, Russian, Ukrainian, German, Uzbek, Tatar	Sunni Muslim, Russian Orthodox, Protestant	Tenge
KUWAIT		17 818	6 880	2 851 000	Kuwait	Arabic	Sunni Muslim, Shi'a Muslim, Christian, Hindu	Kuwaiti dinar
KYRGYZSTAN		198 500	76 641	5 317 000	Bishkek	Kyrgyz, Russian, Uzbek	Sunni Muslim, Russian Orthodox	Kyrgyz som
LAOS		236 800	91 429	5 859 000	Vientiane	Lao, local languages	Buddhist, traditional beliefs	Kip
LEBANON		10 452	4 036	4 099 000	Beirut	Arabic, Armenian, French	Shi'a Muslim, Sunni Muslim, Christian	Lebanese pound
MALAYSIA		332 965	128 559	26 572 000	Kuala Lumpur/Putrajaya	Malay, English, Chinese, Tamil, local languages	Sunni Muslim, Buddhist, Hindu, Christian, traditional beliefs	Ringgit
MALDIVES		298	115	306 000	Male	Divehi (Maldivian)	Sunni Muslim	Rufiyaa
MONGOLIA		1 565 000	604 250	2 629 000	Ulan Bator	Khalka (Mongolian), Kazakh, local languages	Buddhist, Sunni Muslim	Tugrik (tögrög)
MYANMAR		676 577	261 228	48 798 000	Nay Pyi Taw/Rangoon	Burmese, Shan, Karen, local languages	Buddhist, Christian, Sunni Muslim	Kyat
NEPAL		147 181	56 827	28 196 000	Kathmandu	Nepali, Maithili, Bhojpuri, English, local languages	Hindu, Buddhist, Sunni Muslim	Nepalese rupee
NORTH KOREA		120 538	46 540	23 790 000	P'yŏngyang	Korean	Traditional beliefs, Chondoist, Buddhist	North Korean won
OMAN		309 500	119 499	2 595 000	Muscat	Arabic, Baluchi, Indian languages	Ibadhi Muslim, Sunni Muslim	Omani riyal
PAKISTAN		803 940	310 403	163 902 000	Islamabad	Urdu, Punjabi, Sindhi, Pushtu, English	Sunni Muslim, Shi'a Muslim, Christian, Hindu	Pakistani rupee
PALAU		497	192	20 000	Melekeok	Palauan, English	Roman Catholic, Protestant, traditional beliefs	United States dollar
PHILIPPINES		300 000	115 831	87 960 000	Manila	English, Filipino, Tagalog, Cebuano, local languages	Roman Catholic, Protestant, Sunni Muslim, Aglipayan	Philippine peso
QATAR		11 437	4 416	841 000	Doha	Arabic	Sunni Muslim	Qatari riyal
RUSSIAN FEDERATION		17 075 400	6 592 849	142 499 000	Moscow	Russian, Tatar, Ukrainian, local languages	Russian Orthodox, Sunni Muslim, Protestant	Russian rouble
SAUDI ARABIA		2 200 000	849 425	24 735 000	Riyadh	Arabic	Sunni Muslim, Shi'a Muslim	Saudi Arabian riyal
SINGAPORE		639	247	4 436 000	Singapore	Chinese, English, Malay, Tamil	Buddhist, Taoist, Sunni Muslim, Christian, Hindu	Singapore dollar
SOUTH KOREA		99 274	38 330	48 224 000	Seoul	Korean	Buddhist, Protestant, Roman Catholic	South Korean won
SRI LANKA		65 610	25 332	19 299 000	Sri Jayewardenepura Kotte	Sinhalese, Tamil, English	Buddhist, Hindu, Sunni Muslim, Roman Catholic	Sri Lankan rupee
SYRIA		185 180	71 498	19 929 000	Damascus	Arabic, Kurdish, Armenian	Sunni Muslim, Shi'a Muslim, Christian	Syrian pound
TAIWAN*		36 179	13 969	22 880 000	T'aipei	Mandarin, Min, Hakka, local languages	Buddhist, Taoist, Confucian, Christian	Taiwan dollar
TAJIKISTAN		143 100	55 251	6 736 000	Dushanbe	Tajik, Uzbek, Russian	Sunni Muslim	Somoni
THAILAND		513 115	198 115	63 884 000	Bangkok	Thai, Lao, Chinese, Malay, Mon-Khmer languages	Buddhist, Sunni Muslim	Baht
TURKEY		779 452	300 948	74 877 000	Ankara	Turkish, Kurdish	Sunni Muslim, Shi'a Muslim	Lira
TURKMENISTAN		488 100	188 456	4 965 000	Aşgabat	Turkmen, Uzbek, Russian	Sunni Muslim, Russian Orthodox	Turkmen manat
UNITED ARAB EMIRATES		77 700	30 000	4 380 000	Abu Dhabi	Arabic, English	Sunni Muslim, Shi'a Muslim	United Arab Emirates dirham
UZBEKISTAN		447 400	172 742	27 372 000	Toshkent	Uzbek, Russian, Tajik, Kazakh	Sunni Muslim, Russian Orthodox	Uzbek som
VIETNAM		329 565	127 246	87 375 000	Ha Nôi	Vietnamese, Thai, Khmer, Chinese, local languages	Buddhist, Taoist, Roman Catholic, Cao Dai, Hoa Hao	Dong
YEMEN		527 968	203 850	22 389 000	Şan'ā'	Arabic	Sunni Muslim, Shi'a Muslim	Yemeni rial

Dependent and disputed territories		Territorial status	Area sq km	Area sq miles	Population	Capital	Languages	Religions	Currency
Christmas Island		Australian External Territory	135	52	1 500	The Settlement	English	Buddhist, Sunni Muslim, Protestant, Roman Catholic	Australian dollar
Cocos Islands		Australian External Territory	14	5	621	West Island	English	Sunni Muslim, Christian	Australian dollar
Gaza		Semi-autonomous region	363	140	1 586 000	Gaza	Arabic	Sunni Muslim, Shi'a Muslim	Israeli shekel
Jammu and Kashmir		Disputed territory (India/Pakistan)	222 236	85 806	13 000 000	Srinagar			
West Bank		Disputed territory	5 860	2 263	2 676 000		Arabic, Hebrew	Sunni Muslim, Jewish, Shi'a Muslim, Christian	Jordanian dinar, Israeli shekel

*China claims Taiwan as its 23rd province   *De facto capital. Disputed   **Hong Kong dollar

Victoria Falls, Zambia/Zimbabwe

Africa		Area sq km	Area sq miles	Population	Capital	Languages	Religions	Currency
ALGERIA		2 381 741	919 595	33 858 000	Algiers	Arabic, French, Berber	Sunni Muslim	Algerian dinar
ANGOLA		1 246 700	481 354	17 024 000	Luanda	Portuguese, Bantu, local languages	Roman Catholic, Protestant, traditional beliefs	Kwanza
BENIN		112 620	43 483	9 033 000	Porto-Novo	French, Fon, Yoruba, Adja, local languages	Traditional beliefs, Roman Catholic, Sunni Muslim	CFA franc*
BOTSWANA		581 370	224 468	1 882 000	Gaborone	English, Setswana, Shona, local languages	Traditional beliefs, Protestant, Roman Catholic	Pula
BURKINA		274 200	105 869	14 784 000	Ouagadougou	French, Moore (Mossi), Fulani, local languages	Sunni Muslim, traditional beliefs, Roman Catholic	CFA franc*
BURUNDI		27 835	10 747	8 508 000	Bujumbura	Kirundi (Hutu, Tutsi), French	Roman Catholic, traditional beliefs, Protestant	Burundian franc
CAMEROON		475 442	183 569	18 549 000	Yaoundé	French, English, Fang, Bamileke, local languages	Roman Catholic, traditional beliefs, Sunni Muslim, Protestant	CFA franc*
CAPE VERDE		4 033	1 557	530 000	Praia	Portuguese, creole	Roman Catholic, Protestant	Cape Verde escudo
CENTRAL AFRICAN REPUBLIC		622 436	240 324	4 343 000	Bangui	French, Sango, Banda, Baya, local languages	Protestant, Roman Catholic, traditional beliefs, Sunni Muslim	CFA franc*
CHAD		1 284 000	495 755	10 781 000	Ndjamena	Arabic, French, Sara, local languages	Sunni Muslim, Roman Catholic, Protestant, traditional beliefs	CFA franc*
COMOROS		1 862	719	839 000	Moroni	Comorian, French, Arabic	Sunni Muslim, Roman Catholic	Comoros franc
CONGO		342 000	132 047	3 768 000	Brazzaville	French, Kongo, Monokutuba, local languages	Roman Catholic, Protestant, traditional beliefs, Sunni Muslim	CFA franc*
CONGO, DEM. REP. OF THE		2 345 410	905 568	62 636 000	Kinshasa	French, Lingala, Swahili, Kongo, local languages	Christian, Sunni Muslim	Congolese franc
CÔTE D'IVOIRE		322 463	124 504	19 262 000	Yamoussoukro	French, creole, Akan, local languages	Sunni Muslim, Roman Catholic, traditional beliefs, Protestant	CFA franc*
DJIBOUTI		23 200	8 958	833 000	Djibouti	Somali, Afar, French, Arabic	Sunni Muslim, Christian	Djibouti franc
EGYPT		1 000 250	386 199	75 498 000	Cairo	Arabic	Sunni Muslim, Coptic Christian	Egyptian pound
EQUATORIAL GUINEA		28 051	10 831	507 000	Malabo	Spanish, French, Fang	Roman Catholic, traditional beliefs	CFA franc*
ERITREA		117 400	45 328	4 851 000	Asmara	Tigrinya, Tigre	Sunni Muslim, Coptic Christian	Nakfa
ETHIOPIA		1 133 880	437 794	83 099 000	Addis Ababa	Oromo, Amharic, Tigrinya, local languages	Ethiopian Orthodox, Sunni Muslim, traditional beliefs	Birr
GABON		267 667	103 347	1 331 000	Libreville	French, Fang, local languages	Roman Catholic, Protestant, traditional beliefs	CFA franc*
THE GAMBIA		11 295	4 361	1 709 000	Banjul	English, Malinke, Fulani, Wolof	Sunni Muslim, Protestant	Dalasi
GHANA		238 537	92 100	23 478 000	Accra	English, Hausa, Akan, local languages	Christian, Sunni Muslim, traditional beliefs	Cedi
GUINEA		245 857	94 926	9 370 000	Conakry	French, Fulani, Malinke, local languages	Sunni Muslim, traditional beliefs, Christian	Guinea franc
GUINEA-BISSAU		36 125	13 948	1 695 000	Bissau	Portuguese, crioulo, local languages	Traditional beliefs, Sunni Muslim, Christian	CFA franc*
KENYA		582 646	224 961	37 538 000	Nairobi	Swahili, English, local languages	Christian, traditional beliefs	Kenyan shilling
LESOTHO		30 355	11 720	2 008 000	Maseru	Sesotho, English, Zulu	Christian, traditional beliefs	Loti, S. African rand
LIBERIA		111 369	43 000	3 750 000	Monrovia	English, creole, local languages	Traditional beliefs, Christian, Sunni Muslim	Liberian dollar
LIBYA		1 759 540	679 362	6 160 000	Tripoli	Arabic, Berber	Sunni Muslim	Libyan dinar
MADAGASCAR		587 041	226 658	19 683 000	Antananarivo	Malagasy, French	Traditional beliefs, Christian, Sunni Muslim	Malagasy ariary, Malagasy franc
MALAWI		118 484	45 747	13 925 000	Lilongwe	Chichewa, English, local languages	Christian, traditional beliefs, Sunni Muslim	Malawian kwacha
MALI		1 240 140	478 821	12 337 000	Bamako	French, Bambara, local languages	Sunni Muslim, traditional beliefs, Christian	CFA franc*
MAURITANIA		1 030 700	397 955	3 124 000	Nouakchott	Arabic, French, local languages	Sunni Muslim	Ouguiya
MAURITIUS		2 040	788	1 262 000	Port Louis	English, creole, Hindi, Bhojpurī, French	Hindu, Roman Catholic, Sunni Muslim	Mauritius rupee
MOROCCO		446 550	172 414	31 224 000	Rabat	Arabic, Berber, French	Sunni Muslim	Moroccan dirham
MOZAMBIQUE		799 380	308 642	21 397 000	Maputo	Portuguese, Makua, Tsonga, local languages	Traditional beliefs, Roman Catholic, Sunni Muslim	Metical
NAMIBIA		824 292	318 261	2 074 000	Windhoek	English, Afrikaans, German, Ovambo, local languages	Protestant, Roman Catholic	Namibian dollar
NIGER		1 267 000	489 191	14 226 000	Niamey	French, Hausa, Fulani, local languages	Sunni Muslim, traditional beliefs	CFA franc*
NIGERIA		923 768	356 669	148 093 000	Abuja	English, Hausa, Yoruba, Ibo, Fulani, local languages	Sunni Muslim, Christian, traditional beliefs	Naira
RWANDA		26 338	10 169	9 725 000	Kigali	Kinyarwanda, French, English	Roman Catholic, traditional beliefs, Protestant	Rwandan franc
SÃO TOMÉ AND PRÍNCIPE		964	372	158 000	São Tomé	Portuguese, creole	Roman Catholic, Protestant	Dobra
SENEGAL		196 720	75 954	12 379 000	Dakar	French, Wolof, Fulani, local languages	Sunni Muslim, Roman Catholic, traditional beliefs	CFA franc*
SEYCHELLES		455	176	87 000	Victoria	English, French, creole	Roman Catholic, Protestant	Seychelles rupee
SIERRA LEONE		71 740	27 699	5 866 000	Freetown	English, creole, Mende, Temne, local languages	Sunni Muslim, traditional beliefs	Leone
SOMALIA		637 657	246 201	8 699 000	Mogadishu	Somali, Arabic	Sunni Muslim	Somali shilling
SOUTH AFRICA, REPUBLIC OF		1 219 090	470 693	48 577 000	Pretoria/Cape Town	Afrikaans, English, nine official local languages	Protestant, Roman Catholic, Sunni Muslim, Hindu	Rand
SUDAN		2 505 813	967 500	38 560 000	Khartoum	Arabic, Dinka, Nubian, Beja, Nuer, local languages	Sunni Muslim, traditional beliefs, Christian	Sudanese pound (Sudani)
SWAZILAND		17 364	6 704	1 141 000	Mbabane	Swazi, English	Christian, traditional beliefs	Emalangeni, South African rand
TANZANIA		945 087	364 900	40 454 000	Dodoma	Swahili, English, Nyamwezi, local languages	Shi'a Muslim, Sunni Muslim, traditional beliefs, Christian	Tanzanian shilling
TOGO		56 785	21 925	6 585 000	Lomé	French, Ewe, Kabre, local languages	Traditional beliefs, Christian, Sunni Muslim	CFA franc*
TUNISIA		164 150	63 379	10 327 000	Tunis	Arabic, French	Sunni Muslim	Tunisian dinar
UGANDA		241 038	93 065	30 884 000	Kampala	English, Swahili, Luganda, local languages	Roman Catholic, Protestant, Sunni Muslim, traditional beliefs	Ugandan shilling
ZAMBIA		752 614	290 586	11 922 000	Lusaka	English, Bemba, Nyanja, Tonga, local languages	Christian, traditional beliefs	Zambian kwacha
ZIMBABWE		390 759	150 873	13 349 000	Harare	English, Shona, Ndebele	Christian, traditional beliefs	Zimbabwean dollar

Dependent and disputed territories		Territorial status	Area sq km	Area sq miles	Population	Capital	Languages	Religions	Currency
Canary Islands		Autonomous Community of Spain	7 447	2 875	1 996 000	Santa Cruz de Tenerife/Las Palmas	Spanish	Roman Catholic	Euro
Madeira		Autonomous Region of Portugal	779	301	245 000	Funchal	Portuguese	Roman Catholic, Protestant	Euro
Mayotte		French Territorial Collectivity	373	144	186 000	Dzaoudzi	French, Mahorian	Sunni Muslim, Christian	Euro
Réunion		French Overseas Department	2 551	985	807 000	St-Denis	French, creole	Roman Catholic	Euro
St Helena and Dependencies		United Kingdom Overseas Territory	121	47	7 000	Jamestown	English	Protestant, Roman Catholic	St Helena pound
Western Sahara		Disputed territory (Morocco)	266 000	102 703	480 000	Laâyoune	Arabic	Sunni Muslim	Moroccan dirham

*Communauté Financière Africaine franc

Sydney, Australia

Uluṟu (Ayers Rock), Australia

Oceania		Area sq km	Area sq miles	Population	Capital	Languages	Religions	Currency
AUSTRALIA		7 692 024	2 969 907	20 743 000	Canberra	English, Italian, Greek	Protestant, Roman Catholic, Orthodox	Australian dollar
FIJI		18 330	7 077	839 000	Suva	English, Fijian, Hindi	Christian, Hindu, Sunni Muslim	Fiji dollar
KIRIBATI		717	277	95 000	Bairiki	Gilbertese, English	Roman Catholic, Protestant	Australian dollar
MARSHALL ISLANDS		181	70	59 000	Delap-Uliga-Djarrit	English, Marshallese	Protestant, Roman Catholic	United States dollar
MICRONESIA, FEDERATED STATES OF		701	271	111 000	Palikir	English, Chuukese, Pohnpeian, local languages	Roman Catholic, Protestant	United States dollar
NAURU		21	8	10 000	Yaren	Nauruan, English	Protestant, Roman Catholic	Australian dollar
NEW ZEALAND		270 534	104 454	4 179 000	Wellington	English, Maori	Protestant, Roman Catholic	New Zealand dollar
PAPUA NEW GUINEA		462 840	178 704	6 331 000	Port Moresby	English, Tok Pisin (creole), local languages	Protestant, Roman Catholic, traditional beliefs	Kina
SAMOA		2 831	1 093	187 000	Apia	Samoan, English	Protestant, Roman Catholic	Tala
SOLOMON ISLANDS		28 370	10 954	496 000	Honiara	English, creole, local languages	Protestant, Roman Catholic	Solomon Islands dollar
TONGA		748	289	100 000	Nuku'alofa	Tongan, English	Protestant, Roman Catholic	Pa'anga
TUVALU		25	10	11 000	Vaiaku	Tuvaluan, English	Protestant	Australian dollar
VANUATU		12 190	4 707	226 000	Port Vila	English, Bislama (creole), French	Protestant, Roman Catholic, traditional beliefs	Vatu

Dependent territories		Territorial status	Area sq km	Area sq miles	Population	Capital	Languages	Religions	Currency
American Samoa		United States Unincorporated Territory	197	76	67 000	Fagatogo	Samoan, English	Protestant, Roman Catholic	United States dollar
Cook Islands		Self-governing New Zealand Territory	293	113	13 000	Avarua	English, Maori	Protestant, Roman Catholic	New Zealand dollar
French Polynesia		French Overseas Country	3 265	1 261	263 000	Papeete	French, Tahitian, Polynesian languages	Protestant, Roman Catholic	CFP franc*
Guam		United States Unincorporated Territory	541	209	173 000	Hagåtña	Chamorro, English, Tapalog	Roman Catholic	United States dollar
New Caledonia		French Overseas Collectivity	19 058	7 358	242 000	Nouméa	French, local languages	Roman Catholic, Protestant, Sunni Muslim	CFP franc*
Niue		Self-governing New Zealand Territory	258	100	2 000	Alofi	English, Niuean	Christian	New Zealand dollar
Norfolk Island		Australian External Territory	35	14	2 500	Kingston	English	Protestant, Roman Catholic	Australian Dollar
Northern Mariana Islands		United States Commonwealth	477	184	84 000	Capitol Hill	English, Chamorro, local languages	Roman Catholic	United States dollar
Pitcairn Islands		United Kingdom Overseas Territory	45	17	48	Adamstown	English	Protestant	New Zealand dollar
Tokelau		New Zealand Overseas Territory	10	4	1 000		English, Tokelauan	Christian	New Zealand dollar
Wallis and Futuna Islands		French Overseas Collectivity	274	106	15 000	Matā'utu	French, Wallisian, Futunian	Roman Catholic	CFP franc*

*Franc des Comptoirs Français du Pacifique

Aoraki (Mount Cook), New Zealand

	Currency
	East Caribbean dollar
	Bahamian dollar
	Barbados dollar
	Belize dollar
	Canadian dollar
	Costa Rican colón
	Cuban peso
	East Caribbean dollar
	Dominican peso
	El Salvador colón, United States dollar
	East Caribbean dollar
	Quetzal, United States dollar
	Gourde
	Lempira
	Jamaican dollar
	Mexican peso
	Córdoba
	Balboa
	East Caribbean dollar
	East Caribbean dollar
	East Caribbean dollar
	Trinidad and Tobago dollar
	United States dollar

	Currency
an Catholic	East Caribbean dollar
, Protestant	Arubian florin
an Catholic	Bermuda dollar
an Catholic	Cayman Islands dollar
	Danish krone
	Euro
, traditional beliefs	Euro
an Catholic	East Caribbean dollar
, Protestant	Neth. Antilles guilder
, Protestant	United States dollar
	Euro
	United States dollar
an Catholic	United States dollar
an Catholic	United States dollar

	Currency
	Argentinian peso
	Boliviano
	Real
	Chilean peso
	Colombian peso
	US dollar
ni Muslim	Guyana dollar
	Guaraní
	Sol
ni Muslim	Suriname guilder
	Uruguayan peso
	Bolívar fuerte

	Currency
holic	Falkland Islands pound
	Euro

World
Countries

The current pattern of the [...]
conflict and politics. The fa[...]
Kosovo, only being created[...]
since 1950 when there we[...]
over the last fifty years, alt[...]

The shapes of countries ar[...]
reflect both physical and p[...]
follow natural features – ri[...]
others are defined accordi[...]
agreement or as a result o[...]
are still subject to dispute[...]
two or more countries, an[...]
many remain undefined
on the ground.

40°

Tropic of Cancer

Hawaiian Islands
(U.S.A.)

20°

PAC[...]

Line Islands

INTERNATIONAL DATE LINE

Equator 0°

OCE[...]

KIRIBATI

Marque[...]
Islands

American
Samoa

Cook
Islands

Niue Islands
(N.Z.) (N.Z.)

Tahiti

Society
Islands

Tuamotu Islands

French
Polynesia

Rarotonga
Tropic of Capricorn

Tubuai Islands

20°

40°

Facts

- **The longest single continuous land border st[...]
  6 416 kilometres between Canada and the US[...]**

- **Both China and the Russian Federation have[...]
  borders with 14 different countries**

- **Vatican City, the smallest independent country,[...]
  in 1929 as an enclave within Rome, the capita[...]**

- **All countries of the world are members of th[...]
  United Nations except Kosovo, Taiwan and Va[...]**

A.	ANDORRA	HUN.	HUNGARY	R.F.	RUSSIAN FEDERATION
AL.	ALBANIA	ISR.	ISRAEL	ROM.	ROMANIA
ARM.	ARMENIA	JOR.	JORDAN	S.	SERBIA
AUST.	AUSTRIA	K.	KOSOVO	SL.	SLOVENIA
AZER.	AZERBAIJAN	L.	LUXEMBOURG	SLA.	SLOVAKIA
B.	BURUNDI	LAT.	LATVIA	SUR.	SURINAME
BE.	BENIN	LEB.	LEBANON	SW.	SWITZERLAND
BEL.	BELGIUM	LITH.	LITHUANIA	T.	TOGO
B.H.	BOSNIA-HERZEGOVINA	M.	MONTENEGRO	TAJIK.	TAJIKISTAN
BULG.	BULGARIA	MA.	MACEDONIA	TURKM.	TURKMENISTAN
CR.	CROATIA	MOL.	MOLDOVA	U.A.E.	UNITED ARAB EMIRATES
CZ.R.	CZECH REPUBLIC	NETH.	NETHERLANDS	U.K.	UNITED KINGDOM
EST.	ESTONIA	N.Z.	NEW ZEALAND	U.S.A.	UNITED STATES OF AMERICA
GEOR.	GEORGIA	R.	RWANDA	UZBEK.	UZBEKISTAN

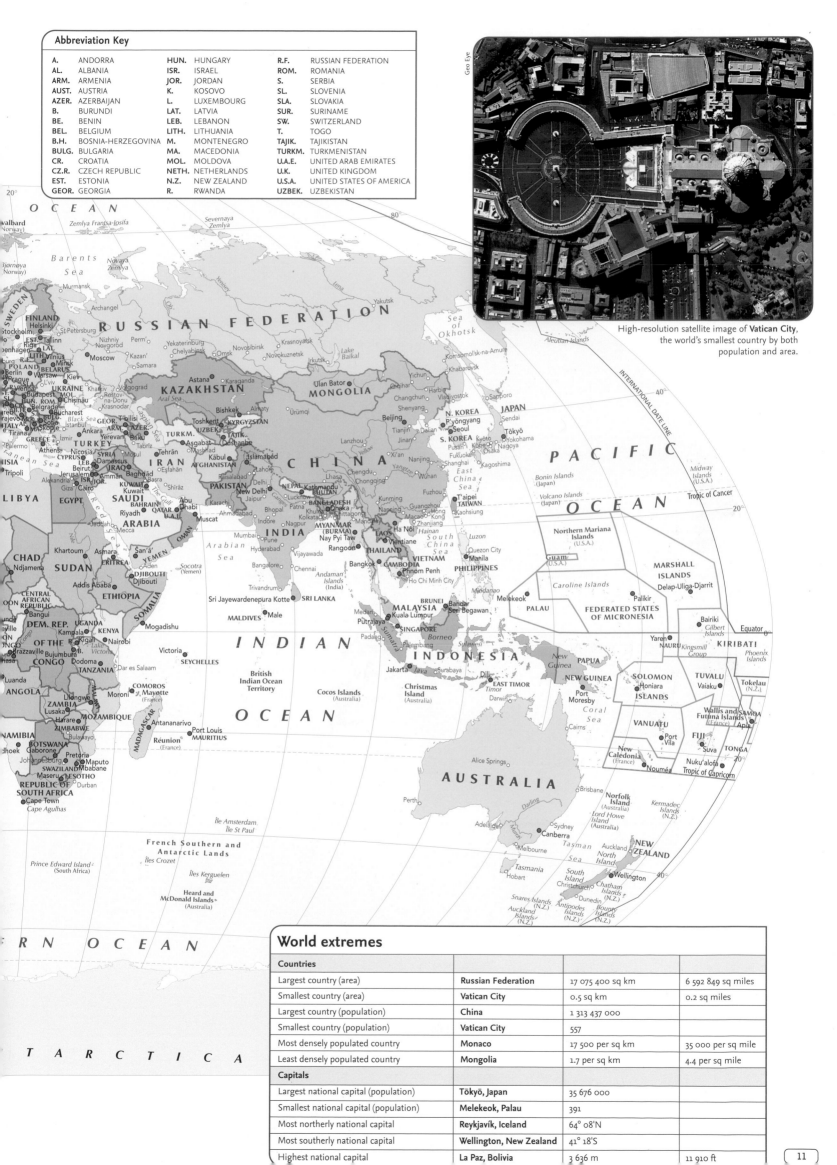

High-resolution satellite image of **Vatican City**, the world's smallest country by both population and area.

World extremes

Countries			
Largest country (area)	**Russian Federation**	17 075 400 sq km	6 592 849 sq miles
Smallest country (area)	**Vatican City**	0.5 sq km	0.2 sq miles
Largest country (population)	**China**	1 313 437 000	
Smallest country (population)	**Vatican City**	557	
Most densely populated country	**Monaco**	17 500 per sq km	35 000 per sq mile
Least densely populated country	**Mongolia**	1.7 per sq km	4.4 per sq mile
Capitals			
Largest national capital (population)	**Tōkyō, Japan**	35 676 000	
Smallest national capital (population)	**Melekeok, Palau**	391	
Most northerly national capital	**Reykjavík, Iceland**	64° 08'N	
Most southerly national capital	**Wellington, New Zealand**	41° 18'S	
Highest national capital	**La Paz, Bolivia**	3 636 m	11 910 ft

World
Landscapes

The Earth's physical features, both on land and on the sea bed, closely reflect its geological structure. The current shapes of the continents and oceans have evolved over millions of years. Movements of the tectonic plates which make up the Earth's crust have created some of the best-known and most spectacular features. The processes which have shaped the Earth continue today with earthquakes, volcanoes, erosion, climatic variations and man's activities all affecting the Earth's landscapes.

The total topographic range of the Earth's surface is nearly 20 000 metres, from the highest point Mount Everest, to the lowest point in the Mariana Trench. Major mountain ranges include the Himalaya, the Andes and the Rocky Mountains, each of which give rise to some of the world's greatest rivers. In contrast, the deserts of the Sahara, Australia, the Arabian Peninsula and the Gobi cover vast areas and each provide unique landscapes.

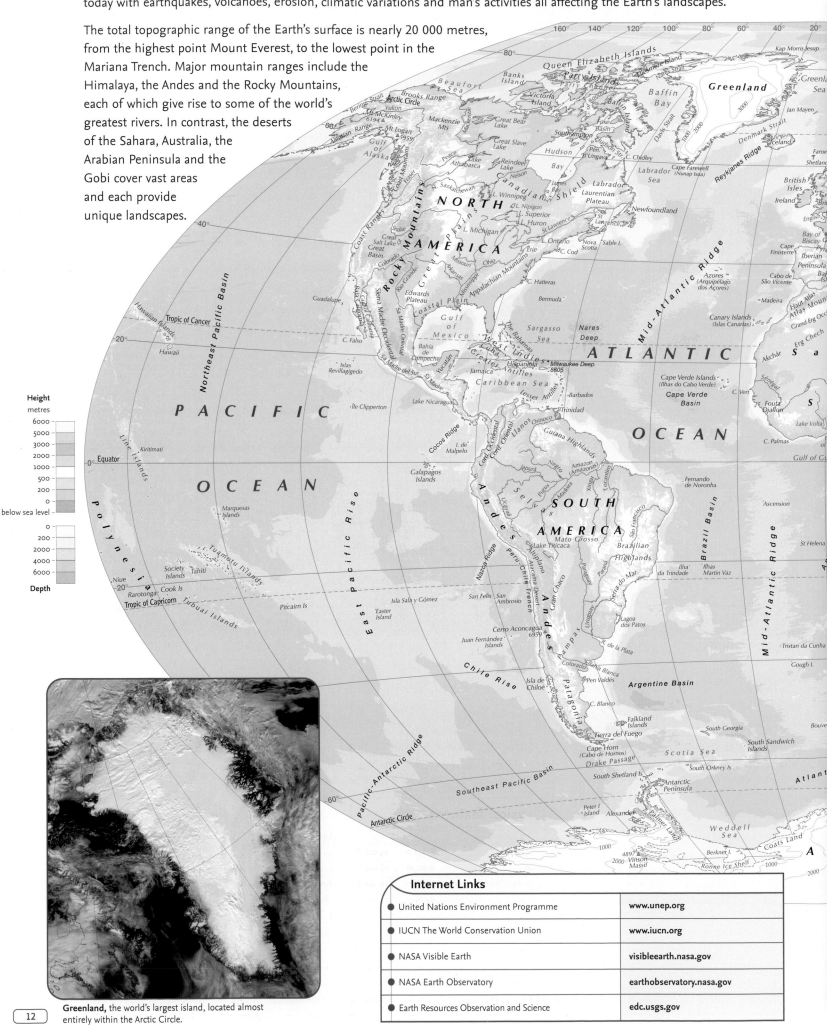

Height

metres

6000
5000
3000
2000
1000
500
200
0

below sea level

0
200
2000
4000
6000

Depth

Greenland, the world's largest island, located almost entirely within the Arctic Circle.

Internet Links	
● United Nations Environment Programme	**www.unep.org**
● IUCN The World Conservation Union	**www.iucn.org**
● NASA Visible Earth	**visibleearth.nasa.gov**
● NASA Earth Observatory	**earthobservatory.nasa.gov**
● Earth Resources Observation and Science	**edc.usgs.gov**

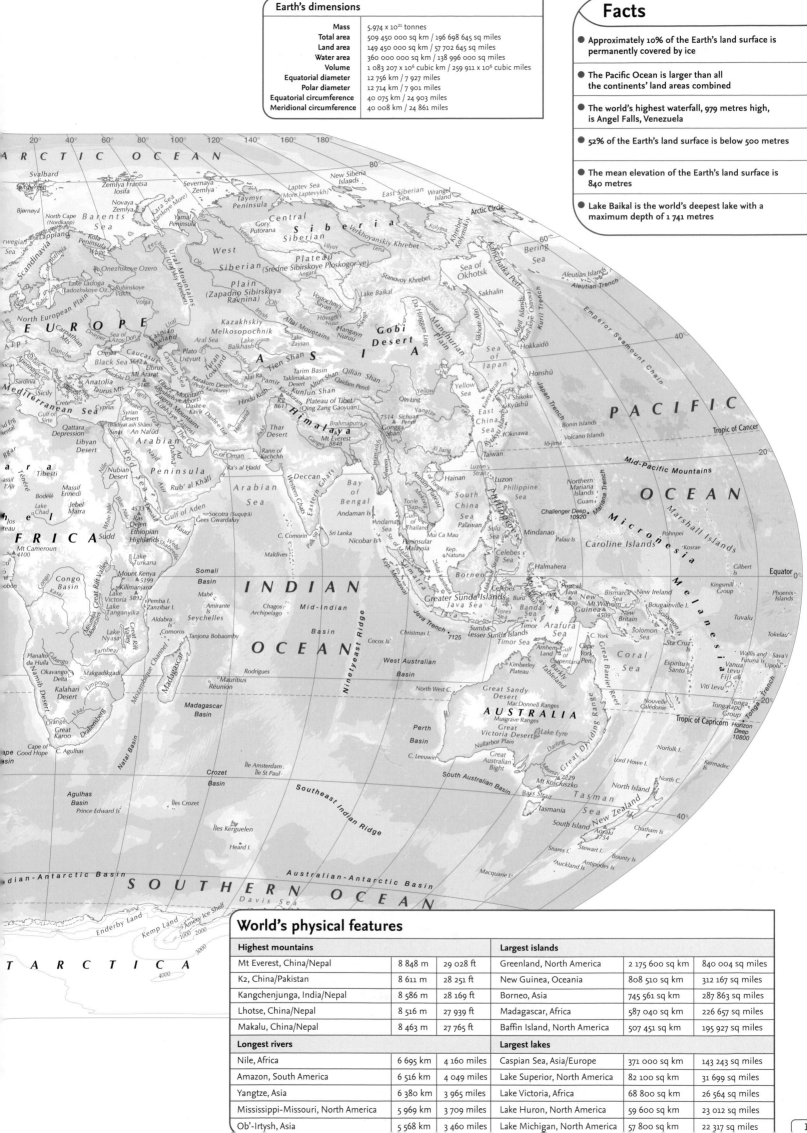

Earth's dimensions	
Mass	5.974 x 10²¹ tonnes
Total area	509 450 000 sq km / 196 698 645 sq miles
Land area	149 450 000 sq km / 57 702 645 sq miles
Water area	360 000 000 sq km / 138 996 000 sq miles
Volume	1 083 207 x 10⁶ cubic km / 259 911 x 10⁶ cubic miles
Equatorial diameter	12 756 km / 7 927 miles
Polar diameter	12 714 km / 7 901 miles
Equatorial circumference	40 075 km / 24 903 miles
Meridional circumference	40 008 km / 24 861 miles

Facts

- Approximately 10% of the Earth's land surface is permanently covered by ice

- The Pacific Ocean is larger than all the continents' land areas combined

- The world's highest waterfall, 979 metres high, is Angel Falls, Venezuela

- 52% of the Earth's land surface is below 500 metres

- The mean elevation of the Earth's land surface is 840 metres

- Lake Baikal is the world's deepest lake with a maximum depth of 1 741 metres

World's physical features

Highest mountains			Largest islands		
Mt Everest, China/Nepal	8 848 m	29 028 ft	Greenland, North America	2 175 600 sq km	840 004 sq miles
K2, China/Pakistan	8 611 m	28 251 ft	New Guinea, Oceania	808 510 sq km	312 167 sq miles
Kangchenjunga, India/Nepal	8 586 m	28 169 ft	Borneo, Asia	745 561 sq km	287 863 sq miles
Lhotse, China/Nepal	8 516 m	27 939 ft	Madagascar, Africa	587 040 sq km	226 657 sq miles
Makalu, China/Nepal	8 463 m	27 765 ft	Baffin Island, North America	507 451 sq km	195 927 sq miles
Longest rivers			**Largest lakes**		
Nile, Africa	6 695 km	4 160 miles	Caspian Sea, Asia/Europe	371 000 sq km	143 243 sq miles
Amazon, South America	6 516 km	4 049 miles	Lake Superior, North America	82 100 sq km	31 699 sq miles
Yangtze, Asia	6 380 km	3 965 miles	Lake Victoria, Africa	68 800 sq km	26 564 sq miles
Mississippi-Missouri, North America	5 969 km	3 709 miles	Lake Huron, North America	59 600 sq km	23 012 sq miles
Ob'-Irtysh, Asia	5 568 km	3 460 miles	Lake Michigan, North America	57 800 sq km	22 317 sq miles

Earthquakes and volcanoes hold a constant fascination because of their power, their beauty, and the fact that they cannot be controlled or accurately predicted. Our understanding of these phenomena relies mainly on the theory of plate tectonics. This defines the Earth's surface as a series of 'plates' which are constantly moving relative to each other, at rates of a few centimetres per year. As plates move against each other enormous pressure builds up and when the rocks can no longer bear this pressure they fracture, and energy is released as an earthquake. The pressures involved can also melt the rock to form magma which then rises to the Earth's surface to form a volcano. The distribution of earthquakes and volcanoes therefore relates closely to plate boundaries. In particular, most active volcanoes and much of the Earth's seismic activity are centred on the 'Ring of Fire' around the Pacific Ocean.

Facts

- Over 900 earthquakes of magnitude 5.0 or greater occur every year
- An earthquake of magnitude 8.0 releases energy equivalent to 1 billion tons of TNT explosive
- Ground shaking during an earthquake in Alaska in 1964 lasted for 3 minutes
- Indonesia has more than 120 volcanoes and over 30% of the world's active volcanoes
- Volcanoes can produce very fertile soil and important industrial materials and chemicals

Earthquakes

Earthquakes are caused by movement along fractures or 'faults' in the Earth's crust, particularly along plate boundaries. There are three types of plate boundary: constructive boundaries where plates are moving apart; destructive boundaries where two or more plates collide; conservative boundaries where plates slide past each other. Destructive and conservative boundaries are the main sources of earthquake activity.

The epicentre of an earthquake is the point on the Earth's surface directly above its source. If this is near to large centres of population, and the earthquake is powerful, major devastation can result. The size, or magnitude, of an earthquake is generally measured on the Richter Scale.

Earthquake magnitude – the Richter Scale
The scale measures the energy released by an earthquake. It is a logarithmic scale: an earthquake measuring 5 is thirty times more powerful than one measuring 4.

2.5 – Recorded, not felt
3.5 – Recorded, tremor felt
4.5 – Quake easily felt, local damage caused
6.0 – Destructive earthquake
7.0 – Major earthquake
9.5 – Most powerful earthquake recorded

Plate boundaries

Constructive boundary
Destructive boundary
Conservative boundary

Volcanoes

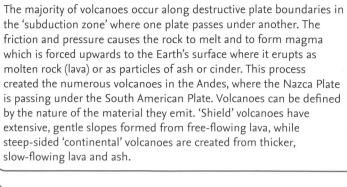

The majority of volcanoes occur along destructive plate boundaries in the 'subduction zone' where one plate passes under another. The friction and pressure causes the rock to melt and to form magma which is forced upwards to the Earth's surface where it erupts as molten rock (lava) or as particles of ash or cinder. This process created the numerous volcanoes in the Andes, where the Nazca Plate is passing under the South American Plate. Volcanoes can be defined by the nature of the material they emit. 'Shield' volcanoes have extensive, gentle slopes formed from free-flowing lava, while steep-sided 'continental' volcanoes are created from thicker, slow-flowing lava and ash.

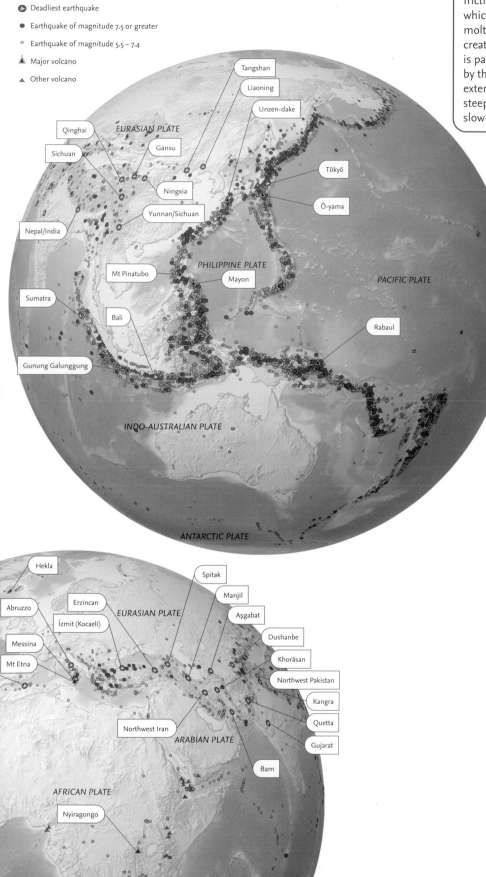

Legend:
- Deadliest earthquake
- Earthquake of magnitude 7.5 or greater
- Earthquake of magnitude 5.5 – 7.4
- ▲ Major volcano
- ▲ Other volcano

Major volcanic eruptions since 1980

Volcano	Country	Date
Mt St Helens	USA	1980
El Chichónal	Mexico	1982
Gunung Galunggung	Indonesia	1982
Kilauea	Hawaii, USA	1983
Ō-yama	Japan	1983
Nevado del Ruiz	Colombia	1985
Mt Pinatubo	Philippines	1991
Unzen-dake	Japan	1991
Mayon	Philippines	1993
Volcán Galeras	Colombia	1993
Volcán Llaima	Chile	1994
Rabaul	Papua New Guinea	1994
Soufrière Hills	Montserrat	1997
Hekla	Iceland	2000
Mt Etna	Italy	2001
Nyiragongo	Democratic Republic of the Congo	2002

Deadliest earthquakes since 1900

Year	Location	Deaths
1905	Kangra, India	19 000
1907	west of Dushanbe, Tajikistan	12 000
1908	Messina, Italy	110 000
1915	Abruzzo, Italy	35 000
1917	Bali, Indonesia	15 000
1920	Ningxia Province, China	200 000
1923	Tōkyō, Japan	142 807
1927	Qinghai Province, China	200 000
1932	Gansu Province, China	70 000
1933	Sichuan Province, China	10 000
1934	Nepal/India	10 700
1935	Quetta, Pakistan	30 000
1939	Chillán, Chile	28 000
1939	Erzincan, Turkey	32 700
1948	Aşgabat, Turkmenistan	19 800
1962	northwest Iran	12 225
1970	Huánuco Province, Peru	66 794
1974	Yunnan and Sichuan Provinces, China	20 000
1975	Liaoning Province, China	10 000
1976	central Guatemala	22 778
1976	Tangshan, Hebei Province, China	255 000
1978	Khorāsan Province, Iran	20 000
1980	Chlef, Algeria	11 000
1988	Spitak, Armenia	25 000
1990	Manjil, Iran	50 000
1999	İzmit (Kocaeli), Turkey	17 000
2001	Gujarat, India	20 000
2003	Bam, Iran	26 271
2004	off Sumatra, Indian Ocean	225 000
2005	northwest Pakistan	74 648
2008	Sichuan Province, China	> 60 000

Internet Links

USGS National Earthquake Hazards Program	earthquake.usgs.gov/regional/neic
USGS Volcano Hazards Program	volcanoes.usgs.gov
British Geological Survey	www.bgs.ac.uk
NASA Natural Hazards	earthobservatory.nasa.gov/NaturalHazards
Volcano World	volcano.und.nodak.edu

World
Climate and Weather

The climate of a region is defined by its long-term prevailing weather conditions. Classification of Climate Types is based on the relationship between temperature and humidity and how these factors are affected by latitude, altitude, ocean currents and winds. Weather is the specific short term condition which occurs locally and consists of events such as thunderstorms, hurricanes, blizzards and heat waves. Temperature and rainfall data recorded at weather stations can be plotted graphically and the graphs shown here, typical of each climate region, illustrate the various combinations of temperature and rainfall which exist worldwide for each month of the year. Data used for climate graphs are based on average monthly figures recorded over a minimum period of thirty years.

World Statistics: see pages 154–160

Major climate regions, ocean currents and sea surface temperatures

Ice cap	Humid subtropical
Tundra	Mediterranean
Subarctic	Steppe
Continental cool summer	Desert
Continental warm summer	Savanna
Temperate	Rain forest

YUMA ★ Weather extreme location
Moscow • Weather station
→ Warm current
→ Cold current
→ Seasonal drift during northern winter

Sea surface temperature — 30°C / 20 / 0

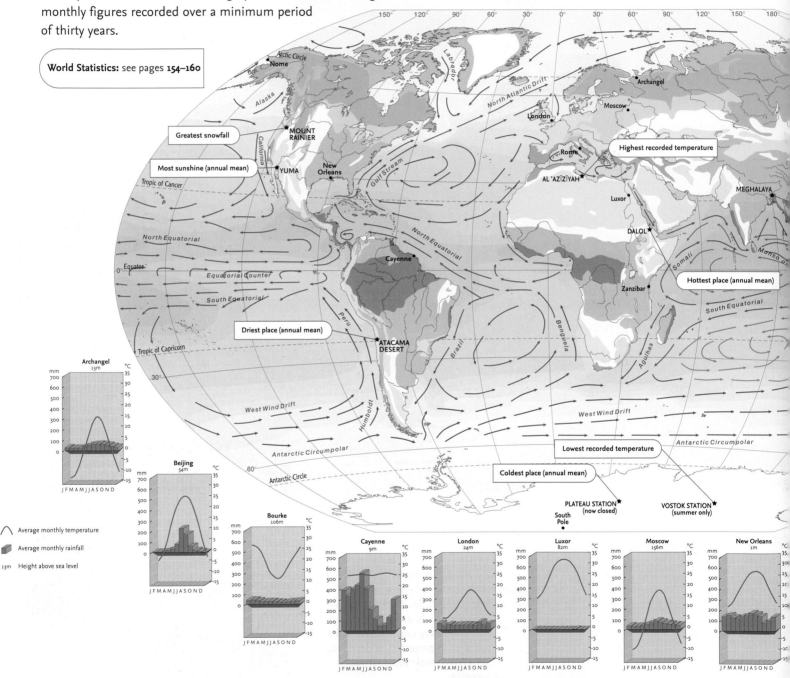

Average monthly temperature

Average monthly rainfall

13m Height above sea level

Climate change

In 2004 the global mean temperature was over 0.6°C higher than that at the end of the nineteenth century. Most of this warming is caused by human activities which result in a build-up of greenhouse gases, mainly carbon dioxide, allowing heat to be trapped within the atmosphere. Carbon dioxide emissions have increased since the beginning of the industrial revolution due to burning of fossil fuels, increased urbanization, population growth, deforestation and industrial pollution.

Annual climate indicators such as number of frost-free days, length of growing season, heat wave frequency, number of wet days, length of dry spells and frequency of weather extremes are used to monitor climate change. The map opposite shows how future changes in temperature will not be spread evenly around the world. Some regions will warm faster than the global average, while others will warm more slowly.

…ckness has declined …0 years
…Niña episodes occur at …s of 2–7 years
…ing by one centimetre
…he northern hemisphere
…ncreased in frequency …parts of Asia and Africa

Projection of global temperatures 2090–2099

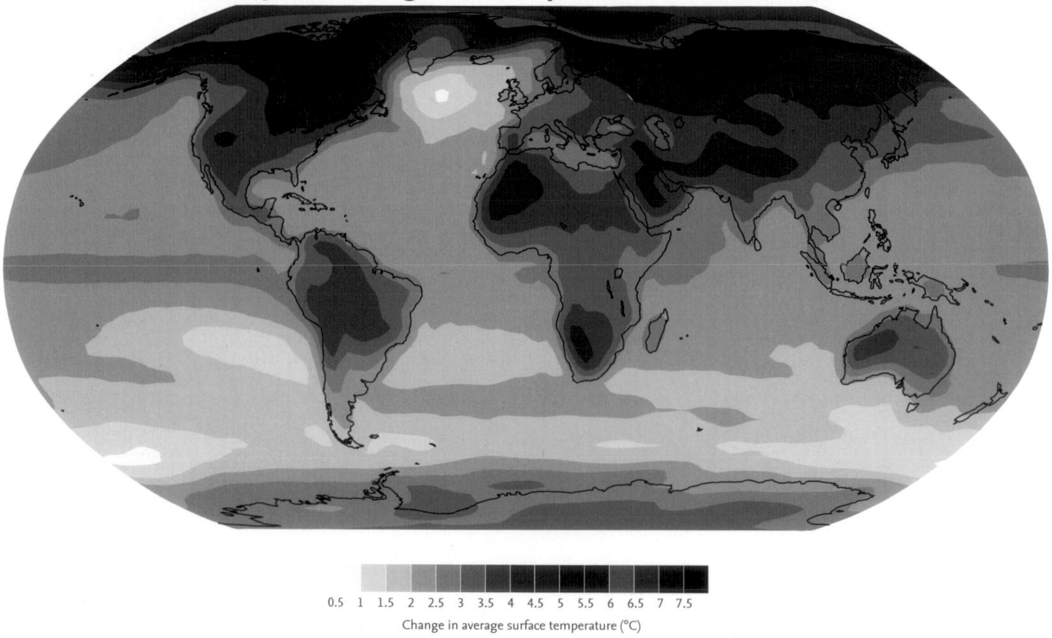

0.5 1 1.5 2 2.5 3 3.5 4 4.5 5 5.5 6 6.5 7 7.5
Change in average surface temperature (°C)

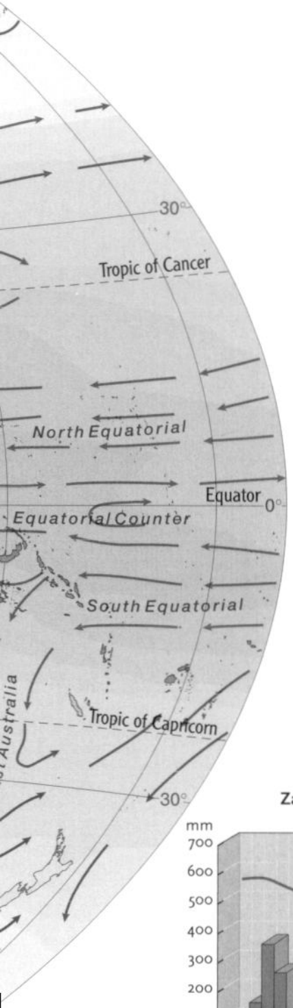

30°
Tropic of Cancer
North Equatorial
Equator 0°
Equatorial Counter
South Equatorial
Australia
Tropic of Capricorn
30°

Tracks of tropical storms

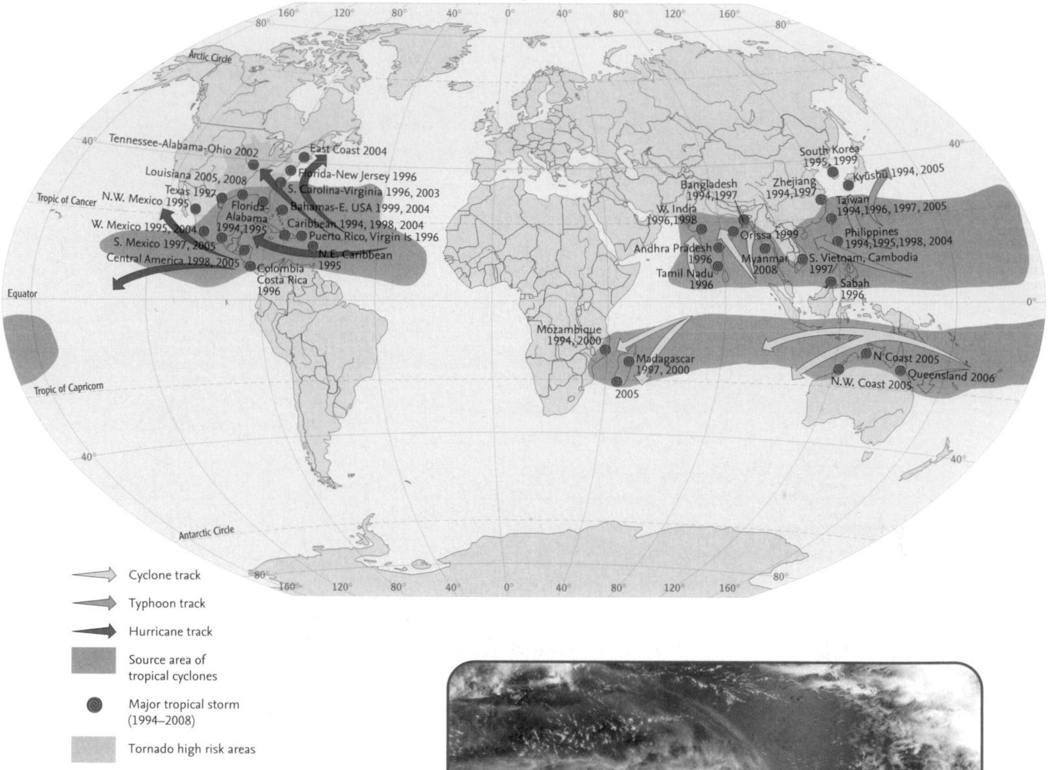

Arctic Circle
Tropic of Cancer
Equator
Tropic of Capricorn
Antarctic Circle
Tennessee-Alabama-Ohio 2002
East Coast 2004
Louisiana 2005, 2008
Florida-New Jersey 1996
Texas 1997
S. Carolina-Virginia 1996, 2003
N.W. Mexico 1995
Florida-Alabama 1994,1995
Bahamas-E. USA 1999, 2004
W. Mexico 1995, 2004
Caribbean 1994, 1998, 2004
Puerto Rico, Virgin Is 1996
S. Mexico 1997, 2005
N.E. Caribbean 1995
Central America 1998, 2005
Colombia Costa Rica 1996
South Korea 1995, 1999
Kyushu 1994, 2005
Zhejiang 1994,1997
Bangladesh 1994,1997
W. India 1996,1998
Taiwan 1994,1996, 1997, 2005
Orissa 1999
Philippines 1994,1995,1998, 2004
Andhra Pradesh 1996
Myanmar 2008
S. Vietnam, Cambodia 1997
Tamil Nadu 1996
Sabah 1996
Mozambique 1994, 2000
Madagascar 1997, 2000
2005
N. Coast 2005
Queensland 2006
N.W. Coast 2005
Cyclone track
Typhoon track
Hurricane track
Source area of tropical cyclones
Major tropical storm (1994–2008)
Tornado high risk areas

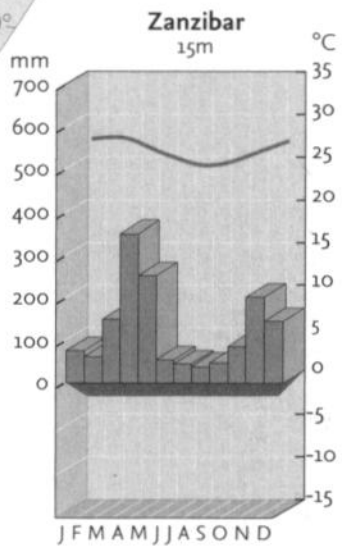

Zanzibar
15m
mm
°C
J F M A M J J A S O N D

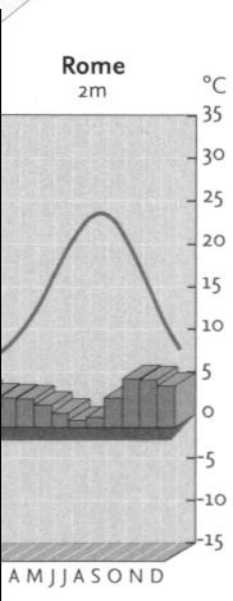

Rome
2m
°C
A M J J A S O N D

Tropical storms

Tropical storms are among the most powerful and destructive weather systems on Earth. Of the eighty to one hundred which develop annually over the tropical oceans, many make landfall and cause considerable damage to property and loss of life as a result of high winds and heavy rain. Although the number of tropical storms is projected to decrease, their intensity, and therefore their destructive power, is likely to increase.

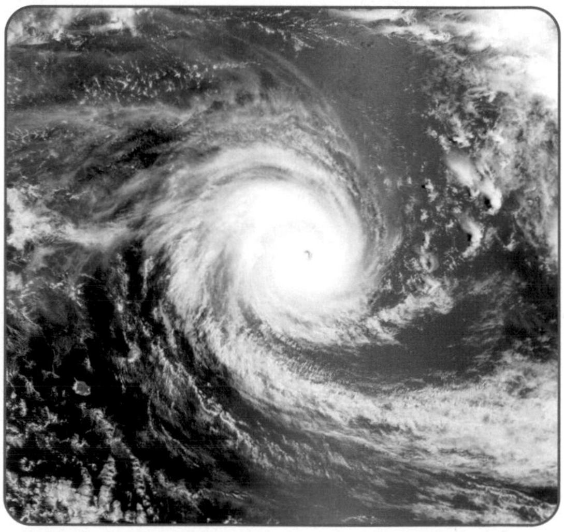

Tropical storm Dina, January 2002.

…s

…perature	**57.8°C/136°F** Al'Azīzīyah, Libya (September 1922)
…al mean	**34.4°C/93.9°F** Dalol, Ethiopia
…al mean	**0.1mm/0.004 inches** Atacama Desert, Chile
…al mean	**90%** Yuma, Arizona, USA (over 4000 hours)
…perature	**-89.2°C/-128.6°F** Vostok Station, Antarctica (July 1983)
…al mean	**-56.6°C/-69.9°F** Plateau Station, Antarctica
…al mean	**11 873 mm/467.4 inches** Meghalaya, India
…snowfall	**31 102 mm/1 224.5 inches** Mount Rainier, Washington, USA (February 1971 – February 1972)
…est place	**322 km per hour/200 miles per hour** (in gales) Commonwealth Bay, Antarctica

Internet Links

● Met Office	**www.metoffice.gov.uk**
● BBC Weather Centre	**www.bbc.co.uk/weather**
● National Oceanic and Atmospheric Administration	**www.noaa.gov**
● National Climatic Data Center	**www.ncdc.noaa.gov**
● United Nations World Meteorological Organization	**www.wmo.ch**

World
Land Cover

The oxygen- and water-rich environment of the Earth has helped create a wide range of habitats. Forest and woodland ecosystems form the predominant natural land cover over most of the Earth's surface. Tropical rainforests are part of an intricate land-atmosphere relationship that is disturbed by land cover changes. Forests in the tropics are believed to hold most of the world's bird, animal, and plant species. Grassland, shrubland and deserts collectively cover most of the unwooded land surface, with tundra on frozen subsoil at high northern latitudes. These areas tend to have lower species diversity than most forests, with the notable exception of Mediterranean shrublands, which support some of the most diverse floras on the Earth. Humans have extensively altered most grassland and shrubland areas, usually through conversion to agriculture, burning and introduction of domestic livestock. They have had less immediate impact on tundra and true desert regions, although these remain vulnerable to global climate change.

World land cover

Evergreen needleleaf forest	Grasslands
Evergreen broadleaf forest	Permanent wetlands
Deciduous needleleaf forest	Croplands
Deciduous broadleaf forest	Urban and built-up
Mixed forest	Cropland/Natural vegetation mosaic
Closed shrublands	Snow and Ice
Open shrublands	Barren or sparsely vegetated
Woody savannas	Water bodies
Savannas	

Land cover

The land cover map shown here was developed at Boston University in Boston, M.A., U.S.A. using data from the Moderate-resolution Imaging-Spectroradiometer (MODIS) instrument aboard NASA's Terra satellite. The high resolution (ground resolution of 1km) of the imagery used to compile the data set and map allows detailed interpretation of land cover patterns across the world. Important uses include managing forest resources, improving estimates of the Earth's water and energy cycles, and modelling climate change.

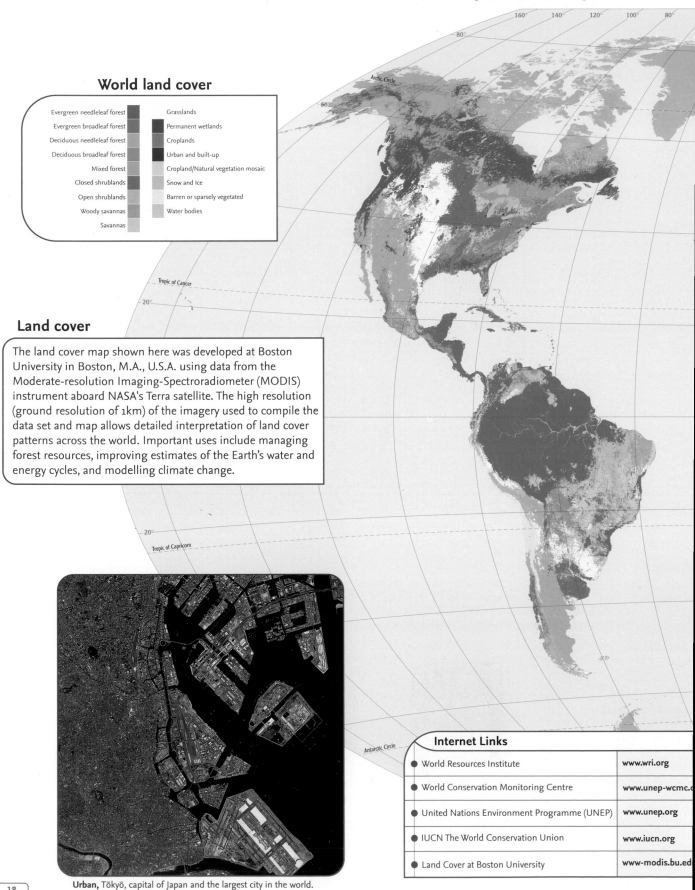

Urban, Tōkyō, capital of Japan and the largest city in the world.

Internet Links

● World Resources Institute	www.wri.org
● World Conservation Monitoring Centre	www.unep-wcmc.c
● United Nations Environment Programme (UNEP)	www.unep.org
● IUCN The World Conservation Union	www.iucn.org
● Land Cover at Boston University	www-modis.bu.ed

Cropland, near Consuegra, Spain.

Barren/Shrubland, Mojave Desert, California, United States of America.

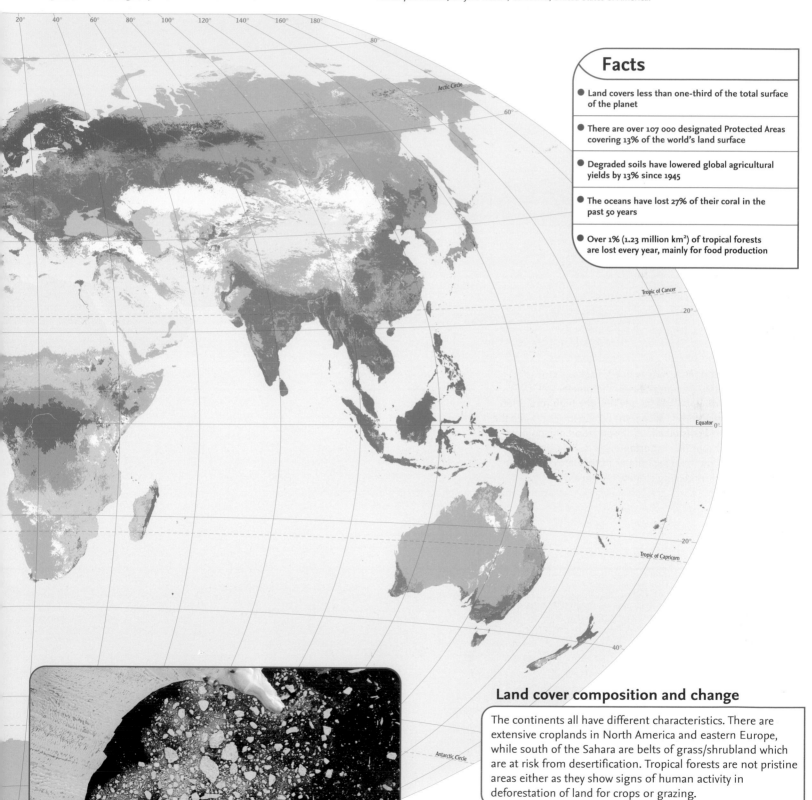

Facts

- Land covers less than one-third of the total surface of the planet

- There are over 107 000 designated Protected Areas covering 13% of the world's land surface

- Degraded soils have lowered global agricultural yields by 13% since 1945

- The oceans have lost 27% of their coral in the past 50 years

- Over 1% (1.23 million km²) of tropical forests are lost every year, mainly for food production

Land cover composition and change

The continents all have different characteristics. There are extensive croplands in North America and eastern Europe, while south of the Sahara are belts of grass/shrubland which are at risk from desertification. Tropical forests are not pristine areas either as they show signs of human activity in deforestation of land for crops or grazing.

Snow and ice, Larsen Ice Shelf, Antarctica.

World
Population

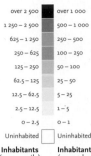

After increasing very slowly for most of human history, world population more than doubled in the last half century. Whereas world population did not pass the one billion mark until 1804 and took another 123 years to reach two billion in 1927, it then added the third billion in 33 years, the fourth in 14 years and the fifth in 13 years. Just twelve years later on October 12, 1999 the United Nations announced that the global population had reached the six billion mark. It is expected that another 2.5 billion people will have been added to the world's population by 2050.

World Statistics: see pages 154–160

World population distribution
Population density, continental populations (2005) and continental population change (2000–2005)

Inhabitants (per sq mile)	Inhabitants (per sq km)
over 2 500	over 1 000
1 250 – 2 500	500 – 1 000
625 – 1 250	250 – 500
250 – 625	100 – 250
125 – 250	50 – 100
62.5 – 125	25 – 50
12.5 – 62.5	5 – 25
2.5 – 12.5	1 – 5
0 – 2.5	0 – 1
Uninhabited	Uninhabited

World population change

Population growth since 1950 has been spread very unevenly between the continents. While overall numbers have been growing rapidly since 1950, a massive 89 per cent increase has taken place in the less developed regions, especially southern and eastern Asia. In contrast, Europe's population level has been almost stationary and is expected to decrease in the future. India and China alone are responsible for over one-third of current growth. Most of the highest rates of growth are to be found in Sub-Saharan Africa and, until population growth is brought under tighter control, the developing world in particular will continue to face enormous problems of supporting a rising population.

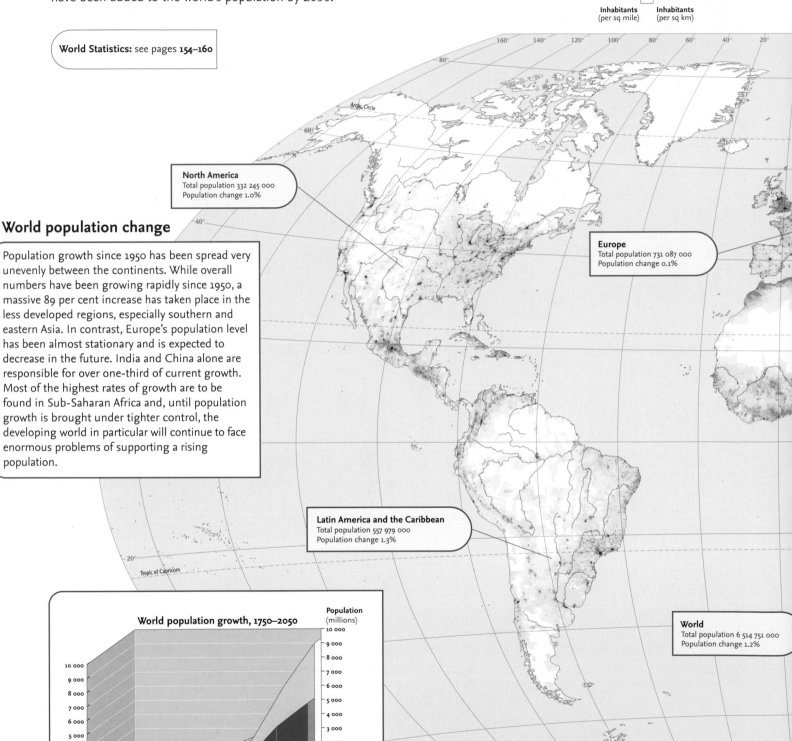

North America
Total population 332 245 000
Population change 1.0%

Europe
Total population 731 087 000
Population change 0.1%

Latin America and the Caribbean
Total population 557 979 000
Population change 1.3%

World
Total population 6 514 751 000
Population change 1.2%

World population growth, 1750–2050

Population (millions)

Legend: World, Asia, Africa, Latin America and the Caribbean, Europe, North America, Oceania

Top 10 countries by population, 2007

Rank	Country	Population
1	China	1 313 437 000
2	India	1 169 016 000
3	United States of America	305 826 000
4	Indonesia	231 627 000
5	Brazil	191 791 000
6	Pakistan	163 902 000
7	Bangladesh	158 669 000
8	Nigeria	148 093 000
9	Russian Federation	142 499 000
10	Japan	127 967 000

The island nation of **Singapore,** the world's second most densely populated country.

Kuna Indians inhabit this congested island off the north coast of Panama.

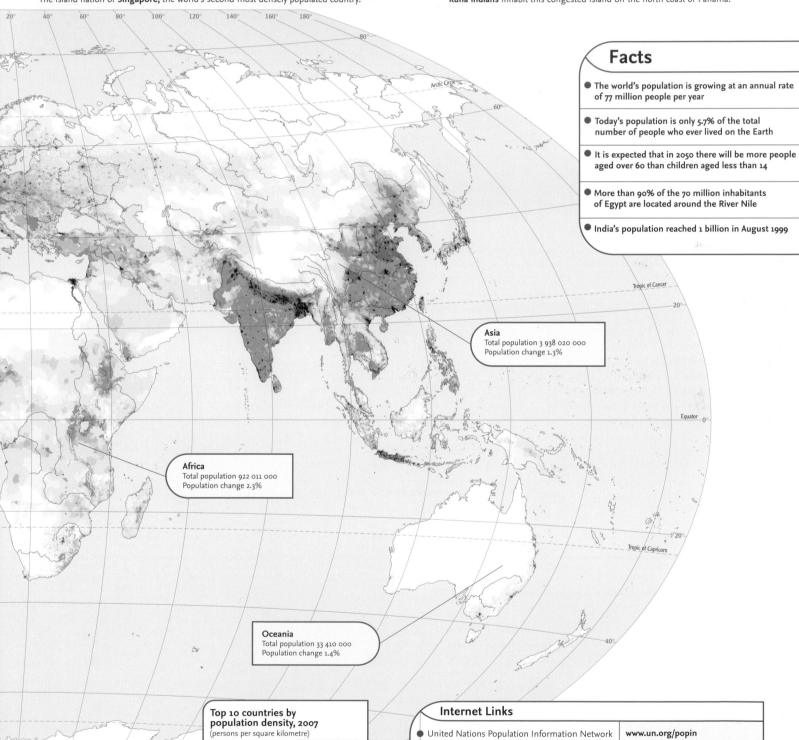

Facts

- The world's population is growing at an annual rate of 77 million people per year

- Today's population is only 5.7% of the total number of people who ever lived on the Earth

- It is expected that in 2050 there will be more people aged over 60 than children aged less than 14

- More than 90% of the 70 million inhabitants of Egypt are located around the River Nile

- India's population reached 1 billion in August 1999

Asia
Total population 3 938 020 000
Population change 1.3%

Africa
Total population 922 011 000
Population change 2.3%

Oceania
Total population 33 410 000
Population change 1.4%

Top 10 countries by population density, 2007
(persons per square kilometre)

Rank	Country*	Population density
1	**Bangladesh**	1 102
2	**Taiwan**	632
3	**South Korea**	486
4	**Netherlands**	395
5	**India**	381
6	**Belgium**	343
7	**Japan**	339
8	**Sri Lanka**	294
9	**Philippines**	293
10	**Vietnam**	265

*Only countries with a population of over 10 million are considered

Internet Links

United Nations Population Information Network	**www.un.org/popin**
US Census Bureau	**www.census.gov**
UK Census	**www.statistics.gov.uk/census2001**
Population Reference Bureau Popnet	**www.prb.org**
Socioeconomic Data and Applications Center	**sedac.ciesin.columbia.edu**

World
Urbanization and Cities

The world is becoming increasingly urban but the level of urbanization varies greatly between and within continents. At the beginning of the twentieth century only fourteen per cent of the world's population was urban and by 1950 this had increased to thirty per cent. In the more developed regions and in Latin America and the Caribbean over seventy per cent of the population is urban while in Africa and Asia the figure is forty per cent. In recent decades urban growth has increased rapidly to fifty per cent and there are now nearly 400 cities with over 1 000 000 inhabitants. It is in the developing regions that the most rapid increases are taking place and it is expected that by 2030 over half of urban dwellers worldwide will live in Asia. Migration from the countryside to the city in the search for better job opportunities is the main factor in urban growth.

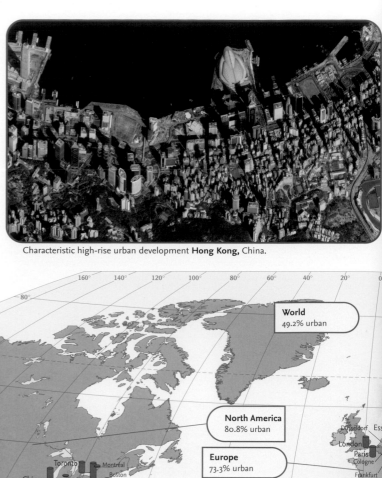

Characteristic high-rise urban development **Hong Kong,** China.

World Statistics: see pages **154–160**

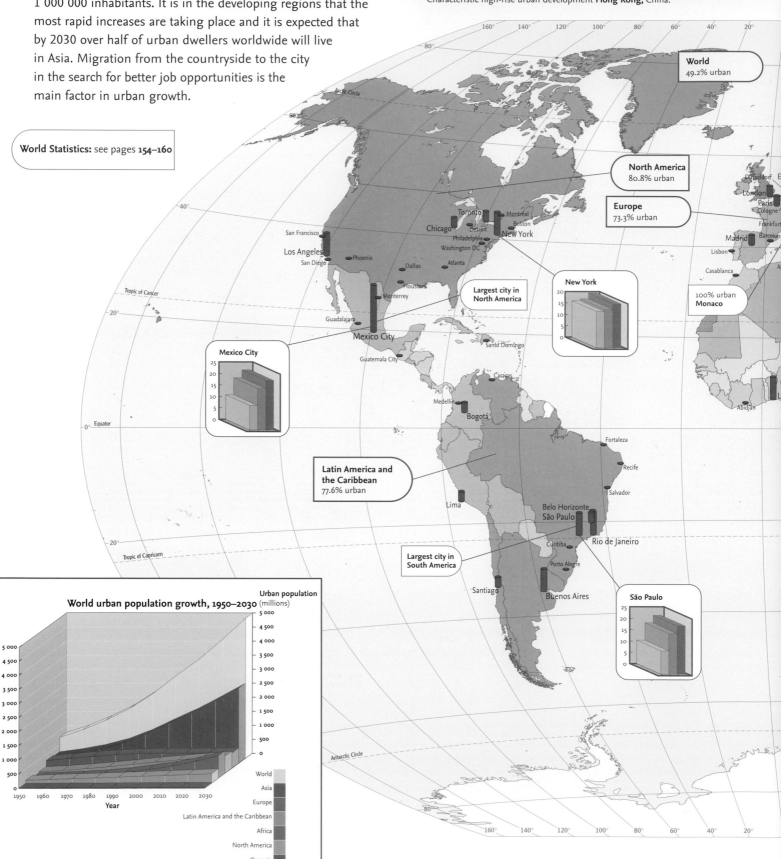

World
49.2% urban

North America
80.8% urban

Europe
73.3% urban

New York

Largest city in North America

100% urban
Monaco

Mexico City

Largest city in South America

Latin America and the Caribbean
77.6% urban

São Paulo

World urban population growth, 1950–2030

Urban population (millions)

World
Asia
Europe
Latin America and the Caribbean
Africa
North America
Oceania

Year

Level of urbanization and the world's largest cities

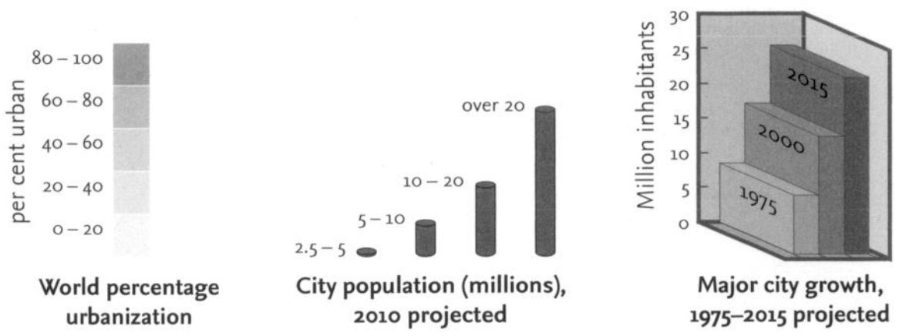

Megacities

There are currently forty-nine cities in the world with over 5 000 000 inhabitants. Nineteen of these, often referred to as megacities, have over 10 000 000 inhabitants and one has over 30 000 000. Tōkyō, with 35 467 000 inhabitants, has remained the world's largest city since 1970 and is likely to remain so for the next decade. Other cities expected to grow to over 20 000 000 by 2015 are Mumbai, São Paulo, Delhi and Mexico City. Eleven of the world's megacities are in Asia, all of them having over 10 000 000 inhabitants.

Facts

- From 2008, cities occupying less than 2% of the Earth's land surface will house over 50% of the human population

- Urban growth rates in Asia are the highest in the world

- Antarctica is uninhabited and most settlements in the Arctic regions have less than 5 000 inhabitants

- By 2010 India will have 48 cities with over one million inhabitants

- London was the first city to reach a population of over 5 million

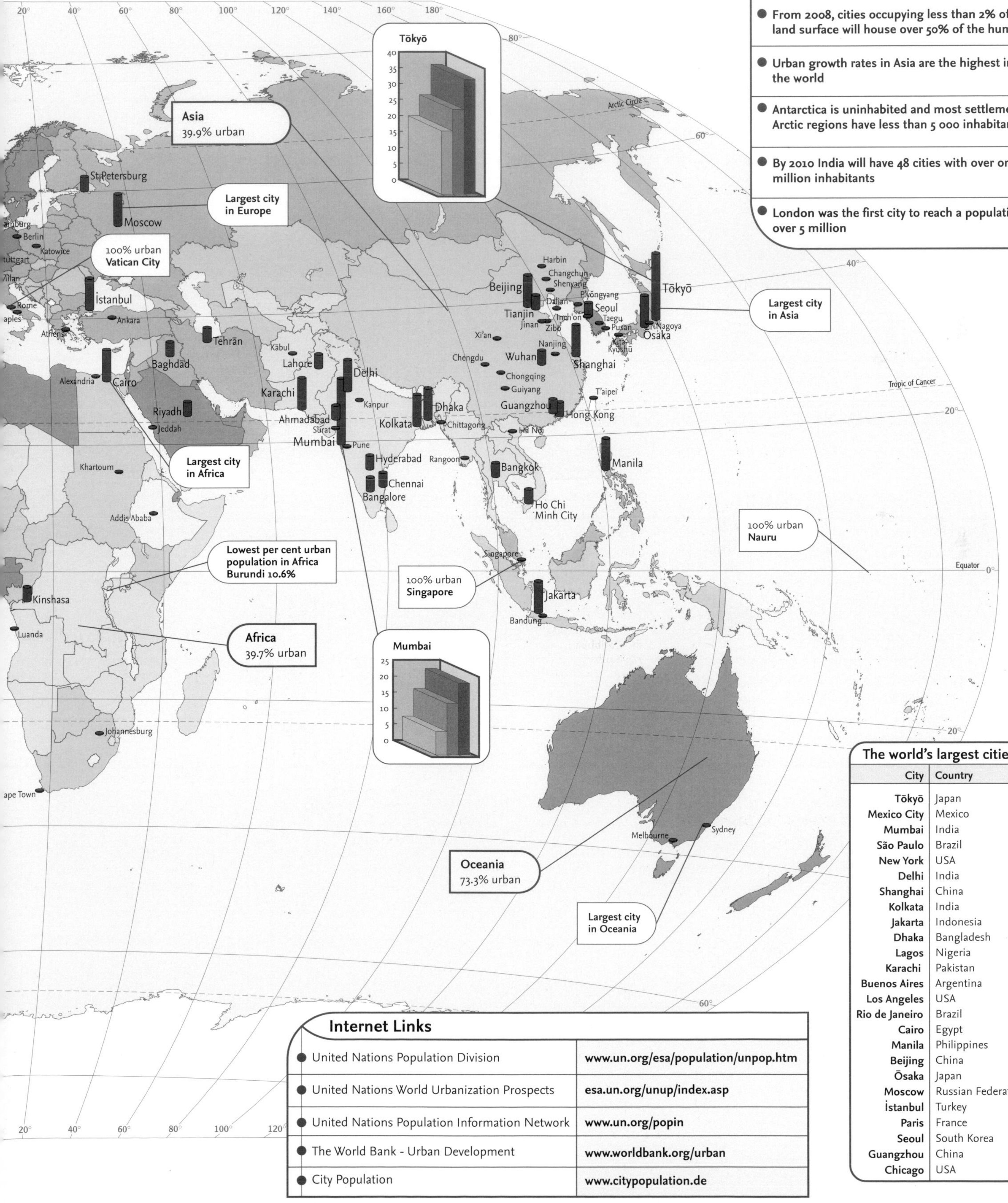

Asia
39.9% urban

Largest city in Europe

100% urban
Vatican City

Largest city in Asia

Tōkyō

Mumbai

Largest city in Africa

Lowest per cent urban population in Africa
Burundi 10.6%

100% urban
Singapore

100% urban
Nauru

Africa
39.7% urban

Oceania
73.3% urban

Largest city in Oceania

The world's largest cities, 2010

City	Country	Population
Tōkyō	Japan	35 467 000
Mexico City	Mexico	20 688 000
Mumbai	India	20 036 000
São Paulo	Brazil	19 582 000
New York	USA	19 388 000
Delhi	India	16 983 000
Shanghai	China	15 790 000
Kolkata	India	15 548 000
Jakarta	Indonesia	15 206 000
Dhaka	Bangladesh	14 625 000
Lagos	Nigeria	13 717 000
Karachi	Pakistan	13 252 000
Buenos Aires	Argentina	13 067 000
Los Angeles	USA	12 738 000
Rio de Janeiro	Brazil	12 170 000
Cairo	Egypt	12 041 000
Manila	Philippines	11 799 000
Beijing	China	11 741 000
Ōsaka	Japan	11 305 000
Moscow	Russian Federation	10 967 000
İstanbul	Turkey	10 546 000
Paris	France	9 856 000
Seoul	South Korea	9 554 000
Guangzhou	China	9 447 000
Chicago	USA	9 186 000

Increased availability and ownership of telecommunications equipment since the beginning of the 1970s has aided the globalization of the world economy. Over half of the world's fixed telephone lines have been installed since the mid-1980s and the majority of the world's internet hosts have come on line since 1997. There are now over one billion fixed telephone lines in the world. The number of mobile cellular subscribers has grown dramatically from sixteen million in 1991 to well over one billion today.

The internet is the fastest growing communications network of all time. It is relatively cheap and now links over 140 million host computers globally. Its growth has resulted in the emergence of hundreds of Internet Service Providers (ISPs) and internet traffic is now doubling every six months. In 1993 the number of internet users was estimated to be just under ten million, there are now over half a billion.

Facts

- The first transatlantic telegraph cable came into operation in 1858
- Fibre-optic cables can now carry approximately 20 million simultaneous telephone calls
- The internet is the fastest growing communications network of all time and now has over 267 million host computers
- Bermuda has the world's highest density of internet and broadband subscribers
- Sputnik, the world's first artificial satellite, was launched in 1957

Internet users and major Internet routes

Internet users per 10 000 inhabitants 2006

	3 000 – 11 000
	1 000 – 2 999
	400 – 999
	200 – 399
	0 – 199
	no data

Gigabytes per second

© TeleGeography Research   www.telegeography.com

Aggregate international internet capacity 2007

The Internet

The Internet is a global network of millions of computers around the world, all capable of being connected to each other. Internet Service Providers (ISPs) provide access via 'host' computers, of which there are now over 267 million. It has become a vital means of communication and data transfer for businesses, governments and financial and academic institutions, with a steadily increasing proportion of business transactions being carried out on-line. Personal use of the Internet – particularly for access to the World Wide Web information network, and for e-mail communication – has increased enormously and there are now estimated to be over half a billion users worldwide.

Top Broadband Economies 2006
Countries with the highest broadband penetration rate – subscribers per 100 inhabitants

	Top Economies	Rate
1	Denmark	29.3
2	Netherlands	28.8
3	Iceland	27.3
4	South Korea	26.4
5	Switzerland	26.2
6	Finland	25.0
7	Norway	24.6
8	Sweden	22.7
9	Canada	22.4
10	United Kingdom	19.4
11	Belgium	19.3
12	USA	19.2
13	Japan	19.0
14	Luxembourg	17.9
15	France	17.7
16	Austria	17.7
17	Australia	17.4
18	Germany	15.1
19	Spain	13.6
20	Italy	13.2

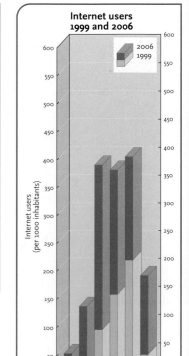

Internet users 1999 and 2006

Internet users (per 1000 inhabitants)

Africa, Asia, Europe, Americas, Oceania, World

2006
1999

Internet Links

OECD Information and Communication Technologies	www.oecd.org
TeleGeography Research	www.telegeography.com
International Telecommunication Union	www.itu.int

communications

l telecommunications use either fibre-optic cables or satellites as
n media. Although cables carry the vast majority of traffic around the world,
tions satellites are important for person-to-person communication,
llular telephones, and for broadcasting. The positions of communications
critical to their use, and reflect the demand for such communications in
the world. Such satellites are placed in 'geostationary' orbit 36 000 km
quator. This means that they move at the same speed as the Earth and
above a single point on the Earth's surface.

e phone subscribers and
unications satellites

- In service
- Inclined orbit
- Planned

Geostationary communications satellites

obile subscribers
habitants 2006

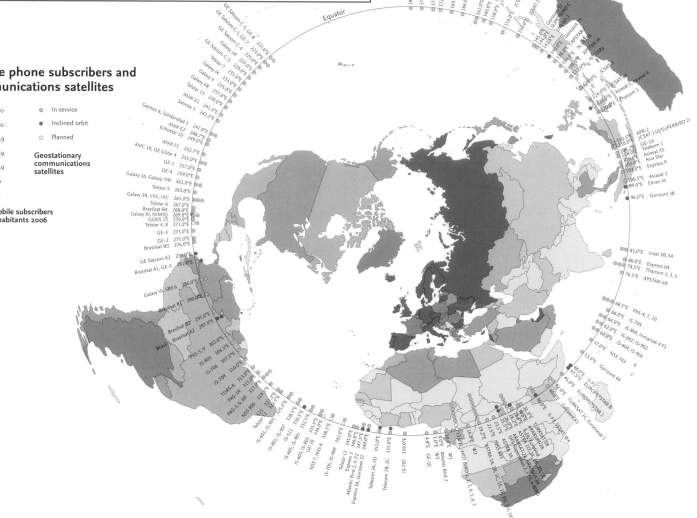

onal telecommunications traffic

Each band is proportional to the total annual TDM (Time
Division Multiplexed) traffic on the public telephone network
in both directions between each pair of countries.

15 000   7 500   2 500

The main projection depicts
inter-continental flows greater than 100
Mbps.

**Millions of minutes of
telecommunications traffic**

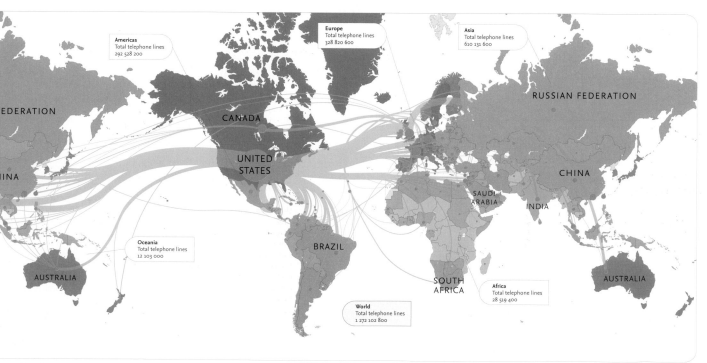

| Americas
Total telephone lines
292 528 200 |
| Europe
Total telephone lines
328 820 600 |
| Asia
Total telephone lines
610 131 600 |
| Oceania
Total telephone lines
12 103 000 |
| Africa
Total telephone lines
28 519 400 |
| World
Total telephone lines
1 272 102 800 |

The area of each circle is
proportional to the volume of the
total annual outgoing TDM traffic
from each country.

- 10 001 – 20 000
- 5 001 – 10 000
- 1 001 – 5 000
- 101 – 1000
- > 100

over 50.0	5.0 – 9.9
35.0 – 50.0	1.0 – 4.9
15.0 – 34.9	0 – 0.9
10.0 – 14.9	no data

Telephone lines per 100 inhabitants 2006

Countries are often judged on their level of economic development, but national and personal wealth are not the only measures of a country's status. Numerous other indicators can give a better picture of the overall level of development and standard of living achieved by a country. The availability and standard of health services, levels of educational provision and attainment, levels of nutrition, water supply, life expectancy and mortality rates are just some of the factors which can be measured to assess and compare countries.

While nations strive to improve their economies, and hopefully also to improve the standard of living of their citizens, the measurement of such indicators often exposes great discrepancies between the countries of the 'developed' world and those of the 'less developed' world. They also show great variations within continents and regions and at the same time can hide great inequalities within countries.

World Statistics: see pages 154–160

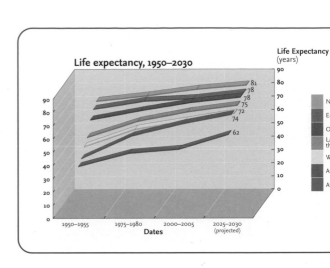

Life expectancy, 1950–2030

Life Expectancy (years)

81
78
78
75
72
74
62

1950–1955   1975–1980   2000–2005   2025–2030 (projected)
Dates

Under-five mortality rate, 2006 and life expectancy by continent, 2005–2010

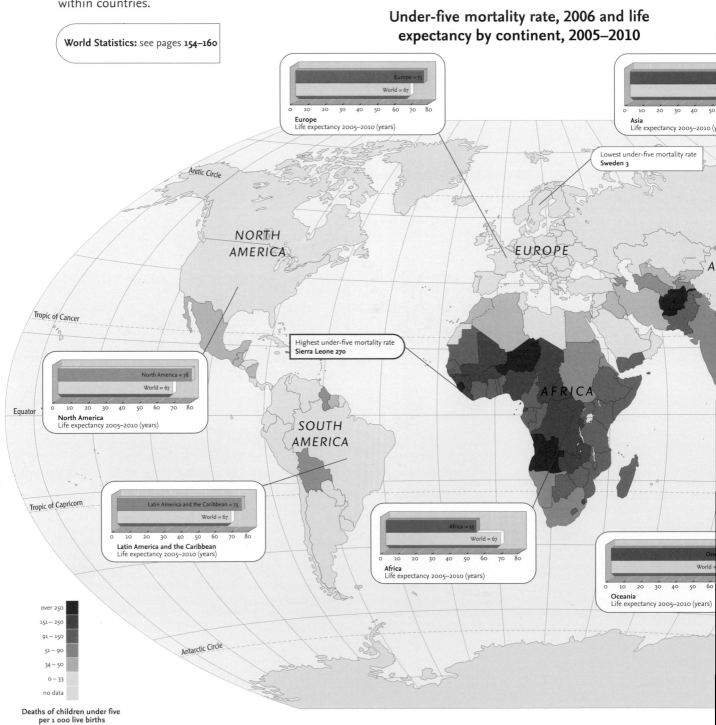

Europe = 75
World = 67
0 10 20 30 40 50 60 70 80
Europe
Life expectancy 2005–2010 (years)

Asia
0 10 20 30 40 50
Asia
Life expectancy 2005–2010 (y

Lowest under-five mortality rate
Sweden 3

North America = 78
World = 67
0 10 20 30 40 50 60 70 80
North America
Life expectancy 2005–2010 (years)

Highest under-five mortality rate
Sierra Leone 270

Latin America and the Caribbean = 73
World = 67
0 10 20 30 40 50 60 70 80
Latin America and the Caribbean
Life expectancy 2005–2010 (years)

Africa = 53
World = 67
0 10 20 30 40 50 60 70 80
Africa
Life expectancy 2005–2010 (years)

Oce
World =
0 10 20 30 40 50 60
Oceania
Life expectancy 2005–2010 (years)

Arctic Circle
NORTH AMERICA
EUROPE
Tropic of Cancer
Equator
SOUTH AMERICA
AFRICA
Tropic of Capricorn
Antarctic Circle

over 250
151 – 250
91 – 150
51 – 90
34 – 50
0 – 33
no data

Deaths of children under five per 1 000 live births

Health and education

Perhaps the most important indicators used for measuring the level of national development are those relating to health and education. Both of these key areas are vital to the future development of a country, and if there are concerns in standards attained in either (or worse, in both) of these, then they may indicate fundamental problems within the country concerned. The ability to read and write (literacy) is seen as vital in educating people and encouraging development, while easy access to appropriate health services and specialists is an important requirement in maintaining satisfactory levels of basic health.

Literacy rate

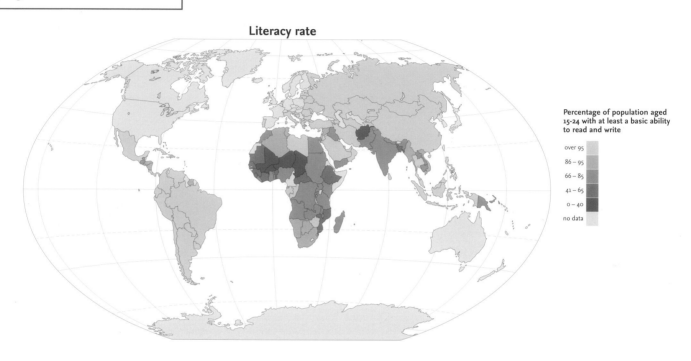

Percentage of population aged 15-24 with at least a basic ability to read and write

- over 95
- 86 – 95
- 66 – 85
- 41 – 65
- 0 – 40
- no data

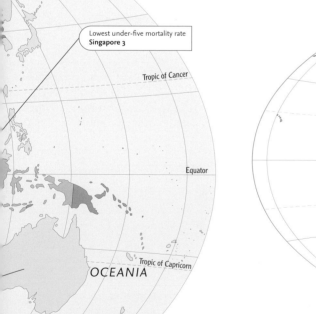

Lowest under-five mortality rate
Singapore 3

Tropic of Cancer

Equator

Tropic of Capricorn

OCEANIA

Arctic Circle

Antarctic Circle

Doctors per 100 000 people

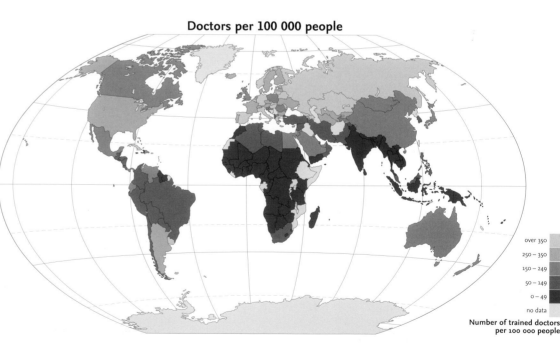

- over 350
- 250 – 350
- 150 – 249
- 50 – 149
- 0 – 49
- no data

Number of trained doctors per 100 000 people

UN Millennium Development Goals
From the Millennium Declaration, 2000

Goal 1	Eradicate extreme poverty and hunger
Goal 2	Achieve universal primary education
Goal 3	Promote gender equality and empower women
Goal 4	Reduce child mortality
Goal 5	Improve maternal health
Goal 6	Combat HIV/AIDS, malaria and other diseases
Goal 7	Ensure environmental sustainability
Goal 8	Develop a global partnership for development

Internet Links

United Nation Development Programme	**www.undp.org**
World Health Organization	**www.who.int**
United Nations Statistics Division	**unstats.un.org**
United Nations Millennium Development Goals	**www.un.org/millenniumgoals**

World
Economy and Wealth

The globalization of the economy is making the world appear a smaller place. However, this shrinkage is an uneven process. Countries are being included in and excluded from the global economy to differing degrees. The wealthy countries of the developed world, with their market-led economies, access to productive new technologies and international markets, dominate the world economic system. Great inequalities exist between and within countries. There may also be discrepancies between social groups within countries due to gender and ethnic divisions. Differences between countries are evident by looking at overall wealth on a national and individual level.

World Statistics: see pages 154–160

Facts

- The City, one of 33 London boroughs, is the world's largest financial centre and contains Europe's biggest stock market

- Half the world's population earns only 5% of the world's wealth

- During the second half of the 20th century rich countries gave over US$1 trillion in aid

- For every £1 in grant aid to developing countries, more than £13 comes back in debt repayments

- On average, The World Bank distributes US$30 billion each year between 100 countries

Personal wealth

A poverty line set at $1 a day has been accepted as the working definition of extreme poverty in low-income countries. It is estimated that a total of 1.2 billion people live below that poverty line. This indicator has also been adopted by the United Nations in relation to their Millennium Development Goals. The United Nations goal is to halve the proportion of people living on less than $1 a day in 1990 to 14.5 per cent by 2015. Today, over 80 per cent of the total population of Ethiopia, Uganda and Nicaragua live on less than this amount.

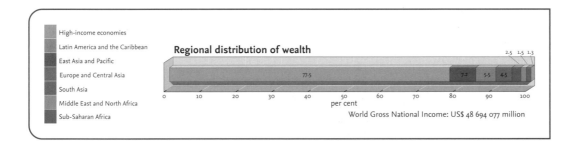

High-income economies
Latin America and the Caribbean
East Asia and Pacific
Europe and Central Asia
South Asia
Middle East and North Africa
Sub-Saharan Africa

Regional distribution of wealth

77.5   7.2   5.5   4.5   2.5 1.5 1.3

0   10   20   30   40   50   60   70   80   90   100
per cent

World Gross National Income: US$ 48 694 077 million

Percentage of population living on less than $1 a day

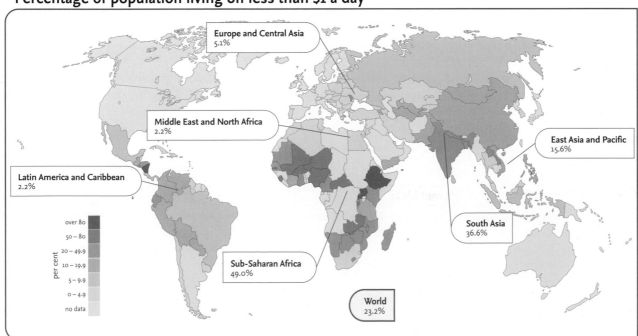

Europe and Central Asia
5.1%

Middle East and North Africa
2.2%

East Asia and Pacific
15.6%

Latin America and Caribbean
2.2%

South Asia
36.6%

Sub-Saharan Africa
49.0%

World
23.2%

per cent
over 80
50 – 80
20 – 49.9
10 – 19.9
5 – 9.9
0 – 4.9
no data

The world's biggest companies		
Rank	Name	Sales (US$ millions)
1	Wal-Mart Stores	351 139
2	ExxonMobil	347 254
3	Royal Dutch/Shell Group	318 845
4	BP	274 316
5	General Motors	207 349
6	Toyota Motor	204 746
7	Chevron	200 567
8	DaimlerChrysler	190 191
9	ConocoPhillips	172 451
10	Total	168 357

Rural homesteads, **Sudan** – most of the world's poorest countries are in Africa.

Gross National Income per capita

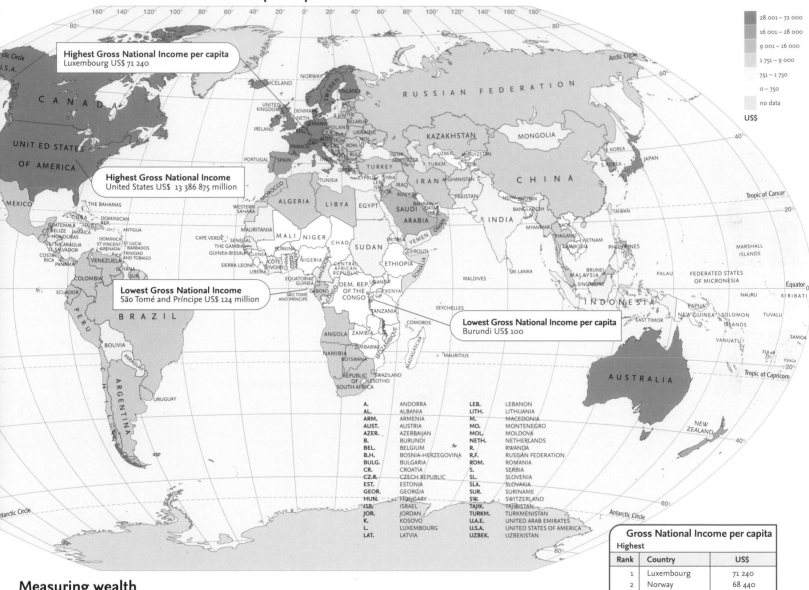

Highest Gross National Income per capita
Luxembourg US$ 71 240

Highest Gross National Income
United States US$ 13 386 875 million

Lowest Gross National Income
São Tomé and Príncipe US$ 124 million

Lowest Gross National Income per capita
Burundi US$ 100

28 001 – 72 000
16 001 – 28 000
9 001 – 16 000
1 751 – 9 000
751 – 1 750
0 – 750
no data

US$

A.	ANDORRA	LEB.	LEBANON
AL.	ALBANIA	LITH.	LITHUANIA
ARM.	ARMENIA	M.	MACEDONIA
AUST.	AUSTRIA	MO.	MONTENEGRO
AZER.	AZERBAIJAN	MOL.	MOLDOVA
B.	BURUNDI	NETH.	NETHERLANDS
BEL.	BELGIUM	R.	RWANDA
B.H.	BOSNIA-HERZEGOVINA	R.F.	RUSSIAN FEDERATION
BULG.	BULGARIA	ROM.	ROMANIA
CR.	CROATIA	S.	SERBIA
CZ.R.	CZECH REPUBLIC	SL.	SLOVENIA
EST.	ESTONIA	SLA.	SLOVAKIA
GEOR.	GEORGIA	SUR.	SURINAME
HUN.	HUNGARY	SW.	SWITZERLAND
ISR.	ISRAEL	TAJIK.	TAJIKISTAN
JOR.	JORDAN	TURKM.	TURKMENISTAN
K.	KOSOVO	U.A.E.	UNITED ARAB EMIRATES
L.	LUXEMBOURG	U.S.A.	UNITED STATES OF AMERICA
LAT.	LATVIA	UZBEK.	UZBEKISTAN

Measuring wealth

One of the indicators used to determine a country's wealth is its Gross National Income (GNI). This gives a broad measure of an economy's performance. This is the value of the final output of goods and services produced by a country plus net income from non-resident sources. The total GNI is divided by the country's population to give an average figure of the GNI per capita. From this it is evident that the developed countries dominate the world economy with the United States having the highest GNI. China is a growing world economic player with the fourth highest GNI figure and a relatively high GNI per capita (US$2 000) in proportion to its huge population.

Internet Links	
● United Nations Statistics Division	**unstats.un.org**
● The World Bank	**www.worldbank.org**
● International Monetary Fund	**www.imf.org**
● Organisation for Economic Co-operation and Development	**www.oecd.org**

Gross National Income per capita		
Highest		
Rank	Country	US$
1	Luxembourg	71 240
2	Norway	68 440
3	Switzerland	58 050
4	Denmark	52 110
5	Iceland	49 960
6	San Marino	45 130
7	Ireland	44 830
8	United States	44 710
9	Sweden	43 530
10	Netherlands	43 050
Lowest		
Rank	Country	US$
156	Niger	270
157	Rwanda	250
158	Sierra Leone	240
159	Malawi	230
160=	Eritrea	190
160=	Guinea-Bissau	190
161	Ethiopia	170
162=	Dem. Rep. Congo	130
162=	Liberia	130
163	Burundi	100

Geo-political issues shape the countries of the world and the current political situation in many parts of the world reflects a long history of armed conflict. Since the Second World War conflicts have been fairly localized, but there are numerous 'flash points' where factors such as territorial claims, ideology, religion, ethnicity and access to resources can cause friction between two or more countries. Such factors also lie behind the recent growth in global terrorism.

Military expenditure can take up a disproportionate amount of a country's wealth – Eritrea, with a Gross National Income (GNI) per capita of only US$190 spends twenty-four per cent of its total GDP on military activity. There is an encouraging trend towards wider international cooperation, mainly through the United Nations (UN) and the North Atlantic Treaty Organization (NATO), to prevent escalation of conflicts and on peacekeeping missions.

Military spending, 2006 and conflicts, 1946–2003

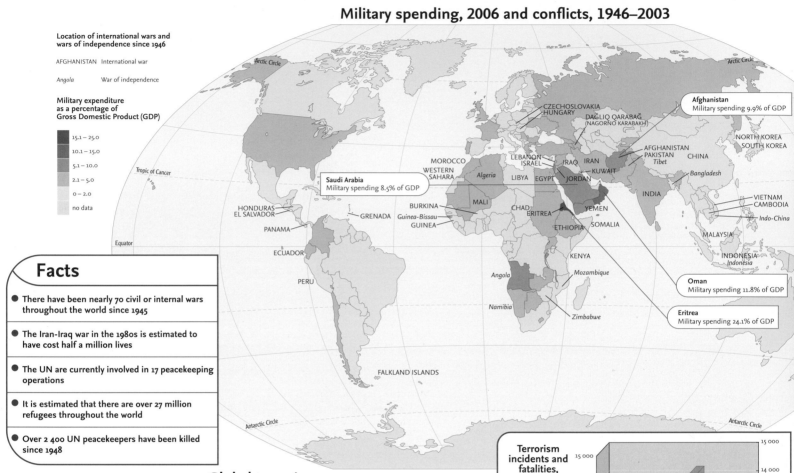

Location of international wars and wars of independence since 1946

AFGHANISTAN   International war

Angola   War of independence

Military expenditure as a percentage of Gross Domestic Product (GDP)

- 15.1 – 25.0
- 10.1 – 15.0
- 5.1 – 10.0
- 2.1 – 5.0
- 0 – 2.0
- no data

Afghanistan Military spending 9.9% of GDP

Saudi Arabia Military spending 8.5% of GDP

Oman Military spending 11.8% of GDP

Eritrea Military spending 24.1% of GDP

Facts

- There have been nearly 70 civil or internal wars throughout the world since 1945
- The Iran-Iraq war in the 1980s is estimated to have cost half a million lives
- The UN are currently involved in 17 peacekeeping operations
- It is estimated that there are over 27 million refugees throughout the world
- Over 2 400 UN peacekeepers have been killed since 1948

Global terrorism

Terrorism is defined by the United Nations as "All criminal acts directed against a State and intended or calculated to create a state of terror in the minds of particular persons or a group of persons or the general public". The world has become increasingly concerned about terrorism and the possibility that terrorists could acquire and use nuclear, chemical and biological weapons. One common form of terrorist attack is suicide bombing. Pioneered by Tamil secessionists in Sri Lanka, it has been widely used by Palestinian groups fighting against Israeli occupation of the West Bank and Gaza. In recent years it has also been used by the Al Qaida network in its attacks on the western world.

Internet Links

United Nations Peace and Security	www.un.org/peace
United Nations Refugee Agency	www.unhcr.org
NATO	www.nato.int
BBC News	news.bbc.co.uk
International Boundaries Research Unit	www.dur.ac.uk/ibru
International Peace Research Institute	www.prio.no

Terrorism incidents and fatalities, 2007

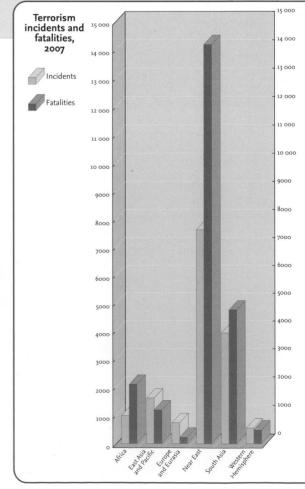

Incidents

Fatalities

United Nations peacekeeping

United Nations peacekeeping was developed by the Organization as a way to help countries torn by conflict create the conditions for lasting peace. The first UN peacekeeping mission was established in 1948, when the Security Council authorized the deployment of UN military observers to the Middle East to monitor the Armistice Agreement between Israel and its Arab neighbours. Since then, there have been a total of 63 UN peacekeeping operations around the world.

UN peacekeeping goals were primarily limited to maintaining ceasefires and stabilizing situations on the ground, so that efforts could be made at the political level to resolve the conflict by peaceful means. Today's peacekeepers undertake a wide variety of complex tasks, from helping to build sustainable institutions of governance, to human rights monitoring, to security sector reform, to the disarmament, demobilization and reintegration of former combatants.

United Nations peacekeeping operations 1948–2008
Current peacekeeping operations are named on the map

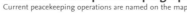

Refugees from **Darfur** in Iridmi refugee camp, Sudan.

Major terrorist incidents

Date	Location	Summary	Killed	Injured
December 1988	**Lockerbie, Scotland**	Airline bombing	270	5
March 1995	**Tōkyō, Japan**	Sarin gas attack on subway	12	5 510
April 1995	**Oklahoma City, USA**	Bomb in the Federal building	168	over 800
August 1998	**Nairobi, Kenya and Dar es Salaam, Tanzania**	US Embassy bombings	225	over 4 000
August 1998	**Omagh, Northern Ireland**	Town centre bombing	29	220
September 2001	**New York and Washington D.C., USA**	Airline hijacking and crashing	3 018	over 6 200
October 2002	**Bali, Indonesia**	Car bomb outside nightclub	202	over 200
October 2002	**Moscow, Russian Federation**	Theatre siege	170	over 600
March 2004	**Bāghdad and Karbalā', Iraq**	Suicide bombing of pilgrims	181	over 400
March 2004	**Madrid, Spain**	Train bombings	191	1 800
September 2004	**Beslan, Russian Federation**	School siege	385	over 700
July 2005	**London, UK**	Underground and bus bombings	56	700
July 2005	**Sharm ash Shaykh, Egypt**	Bombs at tourist sites	88	200
July 2006	**Mumbai, India**	Train bombings	209	700
August 2007	**Qahtaniya, Iraq**	Suicide bombing in town centres	796	over 1 500

Terrorist incidents

Number of terrorist incidents 2000-2006

- over 600
- 200–600
- 50–199
- 5–49
- 0–4
- no data

⭐ Major terrorist incident location

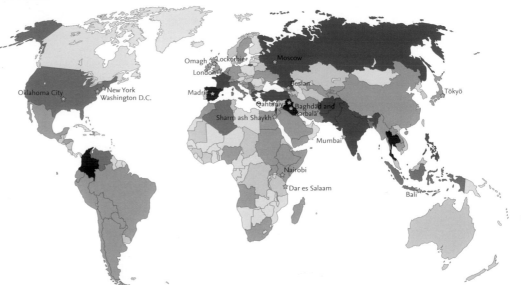

World
Global Issues

With the process of globalization has come an increased awareness of, and direct interest in, issues which have global implications. Social issues can now affect large parts of the world and can impact on large sections of society. Perhaps the current issues of greatest concern are those of national security, including the problem of international terrorism, health, crime and natural resources. The three issues highlighted here reflect this and are of immediate concern.

The international drugs trade, and the crimes commonly associated with it, can impact on society and individuals in devastating ways; scarcity of water resources and lack of access to safe drinking water can have major economic implications and cause severe health problems; and the AIDS epidemic is having disastrous consequences in large parts of the world, particularly in sub-Saharan Africa.

The drugs trade

The international trade in illegal drugs is estimated to be worth over US$400 billion. While it may be a lucrative business for the criminals involved, the effects of the drugs on individual users and on society in general can be devastating. Patterns of drug production and abuse vary, but there are clear centres for the production of the most harmful drugs – the opiates (opium, morphine and heroin) and cocaine. The 'Golden Triangle' of Laos, Myanmar and Thailand, and western South America respectively are the main producing areas for these drugs. Significant efforts are expended to counter the drugs trade, and there have been signs recently of downward trends in the production of heroin and cocaine.

Soldiers in **Colombia**, a major producer of cocaine, destroy an illegal drug processing laboratory.

The international drugs trade

Main producers and trafficking routes for opiates (opium, morphine, heroin) and cocaine

- Cocaine producer
- Opiate producer

→ Cocaine trafficking route
→ Opiate trafficking route

Afghanistan
Opiate production 2006:
6 100 metric tonnes

Colombia
Cocaine production 2006:
610 metric tonnes

Peru
Cocaine production 2006:
280 metric tonnes

Myanmar
Opiate production 2006:
315 metric tonnes

World
Opiate production 2006: 6 610 metric tonnes
Cocaine production 2006: 984 metric tonnes

ARCTIC CIRCLE · ARCTIC CIRCLE · UNITED STATES OF AMERICA · MEXICO · CARIBBEAN · CENTRAL AMERICA · COLOMBIA · PERU · BOLIVIA · SOUTH AMERICA · WEST AFRICA · SOUTH AFRICA · WESTERN EUROPE · EASTERN EUROPE · AFGHANISTAN · PAKISTAN · INDIA · MYANMAR · LAOS · THAILAND · VIETNAM · JAPAN · AUSTRALIA · Tropic of Cancer · Equator · Tropic of Capricorn · Antarctic Circle

AIDS epidemic

With over 30 million people living with HIV/AIDS (Human Immunodeficiency Virus/Acquired Immune Deficiency Syndrome) and more than 20 million deaths from the disease, the AIDS epidemic poses one of the biggest threats to public health. The UNAIDS project estimated that 2.5 million people were newly infected in 2007 and that 2.1 million AIDS sufferers died. Estimates into the future look bleak, especially for poorer developing countries where an additional 45 million people are likely to become infected by 2010. The human cost is huge. As well as the death count itself, more than 11 million African children, half of whom are between the ages of 10 and 14, have been orphaned as a result of the disease.

Facts

- The majority of people infected with **HIV**, if not treated, develop signs of AIDS within 8 to 10 years
- One in five developing countries will face water shortages by 2030
- Over 5 million people die each year from water-related diseases such as cholera and dysentery
- Estimates suggest that 200 million people consume illegal drugs around the world

Population living with HIV/AIDS, 2005

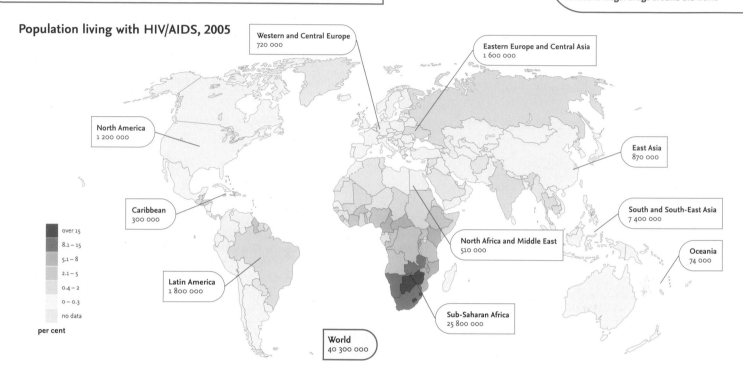

Western and Central Europe
720 000

Eastern Europe and Central Asia
1 600 000

North America
1 200 000

East Asia
870 000

Caribbean
300 000

South and South-East Asia
7 400 000

North Africa and Middle East
510 000

Oceania
74 000

Latin America
1 800 000

Sub-Saharan Africa
25 800 000

World
40 300 000

over 15
8.1 – 15
5.1 – 8
2.1 – 5
0.4 – 2
0 – 0.3
no data

per cent

Water resources

Water is one of the fundamental requirements of life, and yet in some countries it is becoming more scarce due to increasing population and climate change. Safe drinking water, basic hygiene, health education and sanitation facilities are often virtually nonexistent for impoverished people in developing countries throughout the world. WHO/UNICEF estimate that the combination of these conditions results in 6 000 deaths every day, most of these being children. Currently over 1.2 billion people drink untreated water and expose themselves to serious health risks, while political struggles over diminishing water resources are increasingly likely to be the cause of international conflict.

Domestic use of **untreated water** in Kathmandu, Nepal

Access to safe water, 2004
Percentage of population with access to improved drinking water

91 – 100
66 – 90
51 – 65
31 – 50
0 – 30
no data

per cent

Internet Links

UNESCO	**www.unesco.org**
UNAIDS	**www.unaids.org**
WaterAid	**www.wateraid.org.uk**
World Health Organization	**www.who.int**
United Nations Office on Drugs and Crime	**www.unodc.org**

The Earth has a rich and diverse environment which is under threat from both natural and man-induced forces. Forests and woodland form the predominant natural land cover with tropical rain forests – currently disappearing at alarming rates – believed to be home to the majority of animal and plant species. Grassland and scrub tend to have a lower natural species diversity but have suffered the most impact from man's intervention through conversion to agriculture, burning and the introduction of livestock. Wherever man interferes with existing biological and environmental processes degradation of that environment occurs to varying degrees. This interference also affects inland water and oceans where pollution, over-exploitation of marine resources and the need for fresh water has had major consequences on land and sea environments.

Facts

- The Sundarbans stretching across the Ganges delta is the largest area of mangrove forest in the world, covering 10 000 square kilometres (3 861 square miles) and forming an important ecological area, home to 260 species of birds, the Bengal tiger and other threatened species

- Over 90 000 square kilometres of precious tropical forest and wetland habitats are lost each year

- The surface level of the Dead Sea has fallen by more than 25 metres over the last 50 years

- Climate change and mismanagement of land areas can lead to soils becoming degraded and semi-arid grasslands becoming deserts – a process known as desertification

Environmental change

Whenever natural resources are exploited by man, the environment is changed. Approximately half the area of post-glacial forest has been cleared or degraded, and the amount of old-growth forest continues to decline. Desertification caused by climate change and the impact of man can turn semi-arid grasslands into arid desert. Regions bordering tropical deserts, such as the Sahel region south of the Sahara and regions around the Thar Desert in India, are most vulnerable to this process. Coral reefs are equally fragile environments, and many are under threat from coastal development, pollution and over-exploitation of marine resources.

Water resources in certain parts of the world are becoming increasingly scarce and competition for water is likely to become a common cause of conflict. The Aral Sea in central Asia was once the world's fourth largest lake but it now ranks only sixteenth after shrinking by almost 40 000 square kilometres. This shrinkage has been due to climatic change and to the diversion, for farming purposes, of the major rivers which feed the lake. The change has had a devastating effect on the local fishing industry and the exposure of chemicals on the lake bed has caused health problems for the local population.

Deforestation and the creation of the **Itaipu Dam** on the Paraná river in Brazil have had a dramatic effect on the landscape and ecosystems of this part of South America. Some forest on the right of the images lies within Iguaçu National Park and has been protected from destruction.

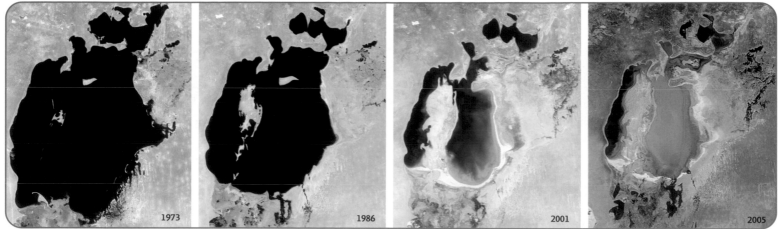

Aral Sea, Kazakhstan/Uzbekistan 1973-2005 Climate change and the diversion of rivers have caused its dramatic shrinkage.

Environmental Impacts

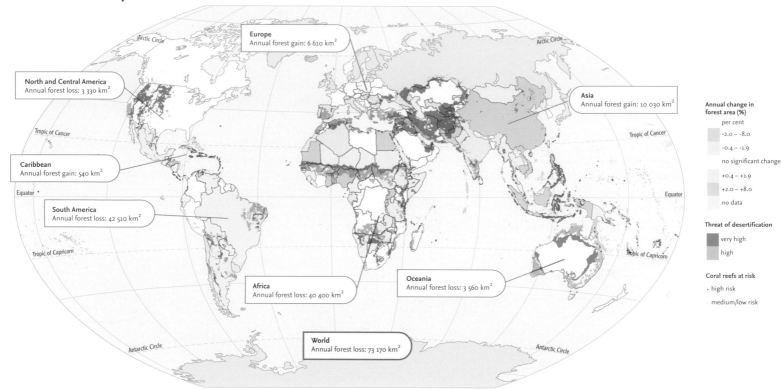

Europe
Annual forest gain: 6 610 km²

North and Central America
Annual forest loss: 3 330 km²

Asia
Annual forest gain: 10 030 km²

Caribbean
Annual forest gain: 540 km²

South America
Annual forest loss: 42 510 km²

Africa
Annual forest loss: 40 400 km²

Oceania
Annual forest loss: 3 560 km²

World
Annual forest loss: 73 170 km²

Annual change in
forest area (%)
per cent

	-2.0 – -8.0
	-0.4 – -1.9
	no significant change
	+0.4 – +1.9
	+2.0 – +8.0
	no data

Threat of desertification

	very high
	high

Coral reefs at risk

· high risk

- medium/low risk

Internet links

● UN Environment Programme	www.unep.org
● IUCN World Conservation Union	www.iucn.org
● UNESCO World Heritage Sites	whc.unesco.org

Environmental protection

Top 10 protected areas by size

Rank	Protected area	Country	Size (sq km)	Designation
1	Northeast Greenland	Greenland	972 000	National Park
2	Rub' al-Khālī	Saudi Arabia	640 000	Wildlife Management Area
3	Phoenix Islands	Kiribati	410 500	Protected Area
4	Great Barrier Reef	Australia	344 400	Marine Park
5	Papahānaumokuākea Marine National Monument	United States	341 362	Coral Reef Ecosystem Reserve
6	Qiangtang	China	298 000	Nature Reserve
7	Macquarie Island	Australia	162 060	Marine Park
8	Sanjiangyuan	China	152 300	Nature Reserve
9	Galápagos	Ecuador	133 000	Marine Reserve
10	Northern Wildlife Management Zone	Saudi Arabia	100 875	Wildlife Management Area

Great Barrier Reef, Australia, the world's third largest protected area.

Europe
Landscapes

Europe, the westward extension of the Asian continent and the second smallest of the world's continents, has a remarkable variety of physical features and landscapes. The continent is bounded by mountain ranges of varying character – the highlands of Scandinavia and northwest Britain, the Pyrenees, the Alps, the Carpathian Mountains, the Caucasus and the Ural Mountains. Two of these, the Caucasus and Ural Mountains, define the eastern limits of Europe, with the Black Sea and the Bosporus defining its southeastern boundary with Asia.

Across the centre of the continent stretches the North European Plain, broken by some of Europe's greatest rivers, including the Volga and the Dnieper and containing some of its largest lakes. To the south, the Mediterranean Sea divides Europe from Africa. The Mediterranean region itself has a very distinct climate and landscape.

Facts

- The Danube flows through 7 countries and has 7 different name forms

- Lakes cover almost 10% of the total land area of Finland

- The Strait of Gibraltar, separating the Atlantic Ocean from the Mediterranean Sea and Europe from Africa, is only 13 kilometres wide at its narrowest point

- The highest mountain in the Alps is Mont Blanc, 4 808 metres, on the France/Italy border

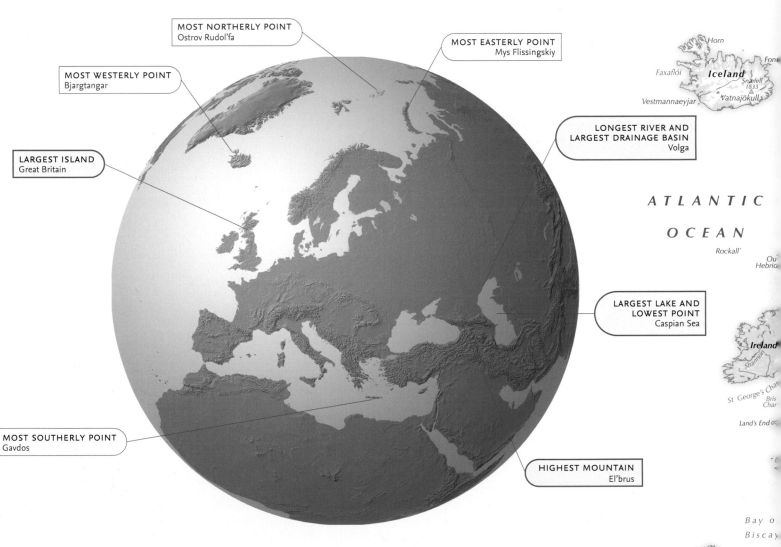

Europe's greatest physical features

Highest mountain	El'brus, Russian Federation	5 642 metres	18 510 feet
Longest river	Volga, Russian Federation	3 688 km	2 292 miles
Largest lake	Caspian Sea	371 000 sq km	143 243 sq miles
Largest island	Great Britain, United Kingdom	218 476 sq km	84 354 sq miles
Largest drainage basin	Volga, Russian Federation	1 380 000 sq km	532 818 sq miles

Europe's extent

TOTAL LAND AREA	9 908 599 sq km / 3 825 710 sq miles
Most northerly point	Ostrov Rudol'fa, Russian Federation
Most southerly point	Gavdos, Crete, Greece
Most westerly point	Bjargtangar, Iceland
Most easterly point	Mys Flissingskiy, Russian Federation

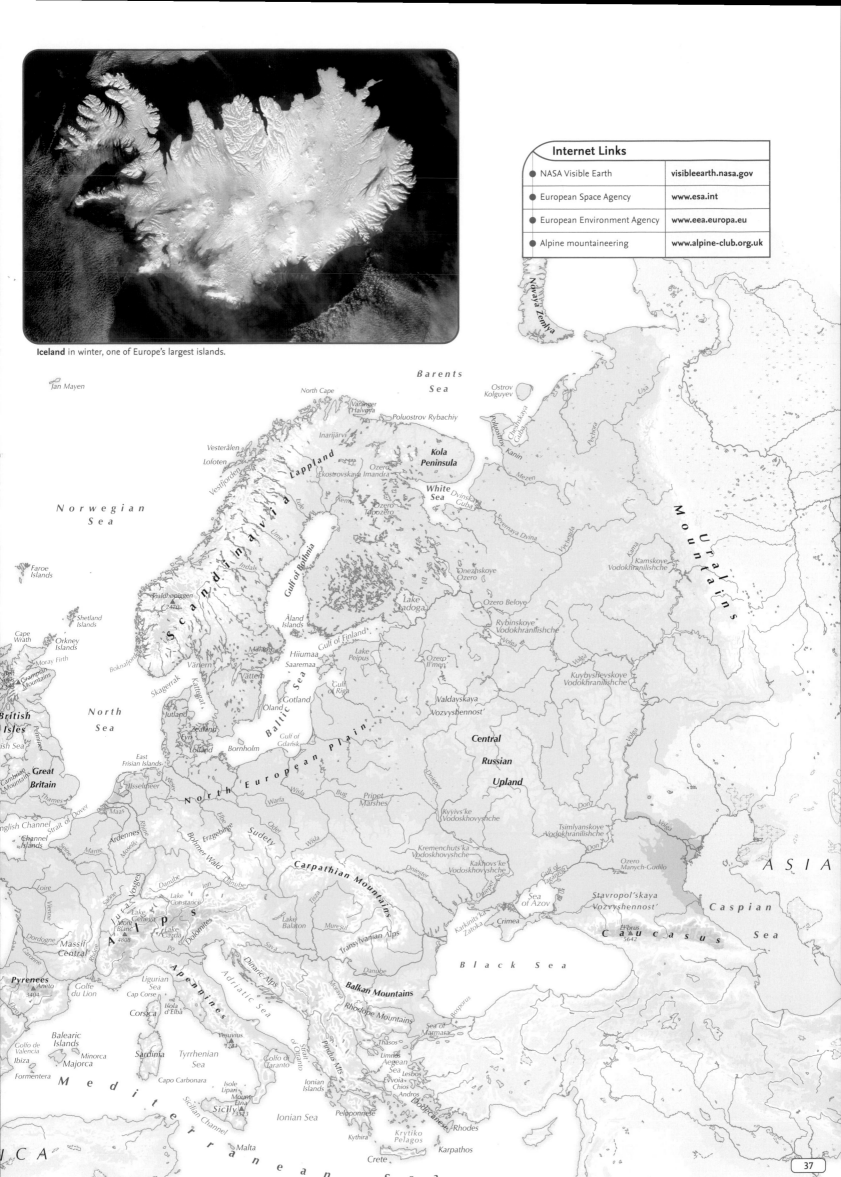

Iceland in winter, one of Europe's largest islands.

Jan Mayen

Barents Sea

North Cape
Varanger Halvøya
Poluostrov Rybachiy
Ostrov Kolguyev
Poluostrov Kanin
Cheshskaya Guba
Usa
Pechora

Novaya Zemlya

Inarijärvi
Vesterålen
Lofoten
Vestfjorden

Lappland

Ozero Imandra
Ekostrovskaya Imandra

Kola Peninsula

Mezen

Norwegian Sea

Scandinavia

Kemi
Ume
Jule
Indals

White Sea
Dvinskaya Guba
Severnaya Dvina
Vychegda

Ozero Topozero

Ural Mountains

Galdhøpiggen
2470

Gulf of Bothnia

Onezhskoye Ozero

Ozero Beloye

Kamskoye Vodokhranilishche

Faroe Islands

Indals

Åland Islands

Lake Ladoga

Rybinskoye Vodokhranilishche

Kama

Shetland Islands

Vänern

Malaren

Hiiumaa
Saaremaa

Gulf of Finland

Lake Peipus

Ozero Il'men'

Volga

Kuybyshevskoye Vodokhranilishche

Cape Wrath
Orkney Islands

Moray Firth
Grampian Mountains

Vättern

Baltic Sea

Gotland

Öland

Gulf of Riga

Valdayskaya Vozvyshennost'

Volga

Skagerrak
Kattegat
Jutland
Zealand
Fyn
Lolland
Bornholm

Gulf of Gdańsk

Central Russian Upland

North Sea

British Isles
ish Sea

Pennines

East Frisian Islands
IJsselmeer

North European Plain

Wisla
Bug
Pripet Marshes

Dnieper

Kyiyvs'ke Vodoskhovyshche

Don

Tsimlyanskoye Vodokhranilishche

Volga

Great Britain

Thames

Warta
Oder

Kremenchuts'ka Vodoskhovyshche

Cambrian Mountains

Strait of Dover

Elbe

Wisla

Dniester

Kakhovs'ke Vodoskhovyshche

ASIA

English Channel
Channel Islands

Seine
Marne
Moselle
Rhine
Ardennes
Maas
Erzgebirge
Böhmer Wald
Sudety

Tisza

Dnieper

Gulf of Taganrog

Sea of Azov

Stavropol'skaya Vozvyshennost'

Caspian Sea

Loire
Vienne
Saône

Vosges
Jura
Danube
Inn
Danube

Lake Constance

Carpathian Mountains

Dniester

Crimea

Karkinits'ka Zatoka

Elbrus
5642

Dordogne

Mont Blanc
4808

Lake Geneva
Alps
Lake Garda
Dolomites

Lake Balaton
Mureşul

Transylvanian Alps

Danube

Caucasus

Massif Central
Rhône
Po

Sava

Pyrenees
Aneto
3404

Golfe du Lion

Ligurian Sea
Cap Corse
Isola d'Elba

Apennines

Adriatic Sea

Dinaric Alps

Morava

Black Sea

Bosporus

Balkan Mountains

Rhodope Mountains

Sea of Marmara

Corsica

Pindus Mts.

Thasos

Balearic Islands

Golfo de Valencia
Minorca
Majorca
Ibiza
Formentera

Sardinia

Tyrrhenian Sea

Vesuvius
1281

Golfo di Taranto

Strait of Otranto

Ionian Islands

Limnos
Aegean Sea
Lesbos
Evvoia
Chios
Andros

Mediterranean Sea

Capo Carbonara

Isole Lipari
Mount Etna
3323

Sicily

Sicilian Channel

Ionian Sea

Peloponnese

Dodecanese

Rhodes

Krytiko Pelagos

Kythira

Karpathos

Malta

Crete

ICA

Europe
Countries

The predominantly temperate climate of Europe has led to it becoming the most densely populated of the continents. It is highly industrialized, and has exploited its great wealth of natural resources and agricultural land to become one of the most powerful economic regions in the world.

The current pattern of countries within Europe is a result of numerous and complicated changes throughout its history. Ethnic, religious and linguistic differences have often been the cause of conflict, particularly in the Balkan region which has a very complex ethnic pattern. Current boundaries reflect, to some extent, these divisions which continue to be a source of tension. The historic distinction between 'Eastern' and 'Western' Europe is no longer made, following the collapse of Communism and the break up of the Soviet Union in 1991.

Facts

- The European Union was founded by six countries: Belgium, France, Germany, Italy, Luxembourg, and the Netherlands. It now has 27 members

- The newest members of the European Union, Bulgaria and Romania joined in 2007

- Europe has the 2 smallest independent countries in the world – Vatican City and Monaco

- Vatican City is an independent country entirely within the city of Rome, and is the centre of the Roman Catholic Church

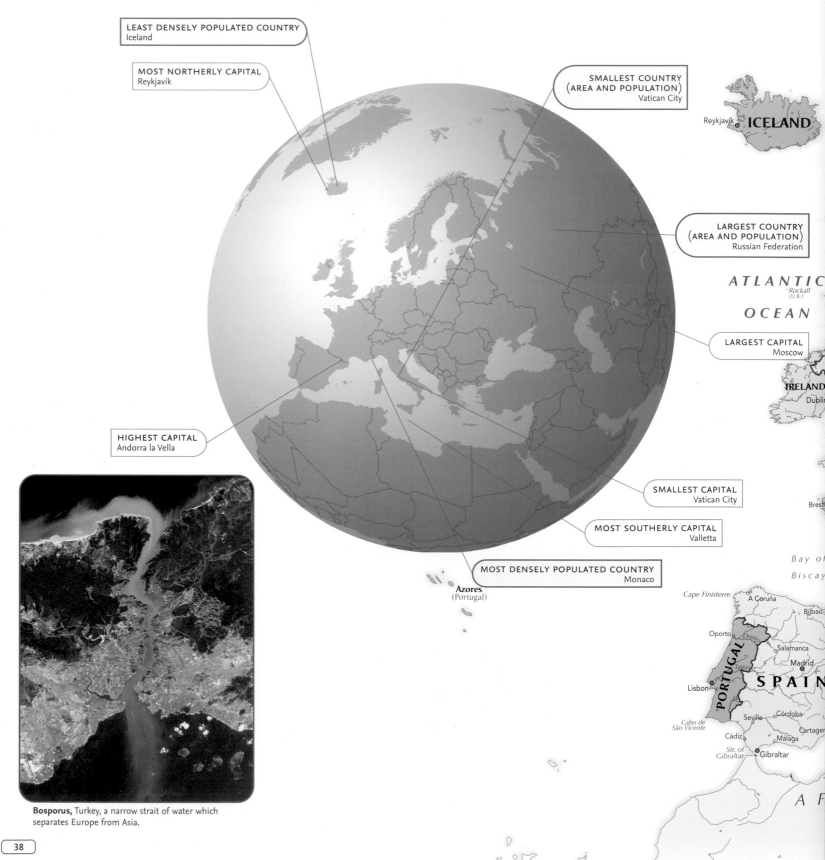

LEAST DENSELY POPULATED COUNTRY
Iceland

MOST NORTHERLY CAPITAL
Reykjavík

SMALLEST COUNTRY (AREA AND POPULATION)
Vatican City

Reykjavík • **ICELAND**

LARGEST COUNTRY (AREA AND POPULATION)
Russian Federation

ATLANTIC
·Rockall (U.K.)

OCEAN

LARGEST CAPITAL
Moscow

IRELAND
Dublin

HIGHEST CAPITAL
Andorra la Vella

Brest

SMALLEST CAPITAL
Vatican City

MOST SOUTHERLY CAPITAL
Valletta

Bay of

MOST DENSELY POPULATED COUNTRY
Monaco

Biscay

Azores
(Portugal)

Cape Finisterre • A Coruña

Bilbao

Oporto
Douro
Salamanca
Madrid

Lisbon • **PORTUGAL**
Tagus
SPAIN

Cabo de
São Vicente
Seville • Córdoba

Cádiz • Málaga
Cartagen

Str. of
Gibraltar • Gibraltar

A F

Bosporus, Turkey, a narrow strait of water which separates Europe from Asia.

Europe's capitals

Largest capital (population)	Moscow, Russian Federaton	10 452 000
Smallest capital (population)	Vatican City	557
Most northerly capital	Reykjavík, Iceland	64° 39'N
Most southerly capital	Valletta, Malta	35° 54'N
Highest capital	Andorra la Vella, Andorra	1 029 metres 3 376 feet

Europe's countries

Largest country (area)	Russian Federation	17 075 400 sq km	6 592 849 sq miles
Smallest country (area)	Vatican City	0.5 sq km	0.2 sq miles
Largest country (population)	Russian Federation	143 202 000	
Smallest country (population)	Vatican City	557	
Most densely populated country	Monaco	17 000 per sq km	34 000 per sq mile
Least densely populated country	Iceland	3 per sq km	7 per sq mile

Conic Equidistant Projection

1:10 000 000

| 0 | 100 | 200 | 300 | 400 miles |

| 0 | 100 | 200 | 300 | 400 | 500 | 600 | km |

Europe
Western Russian Federation

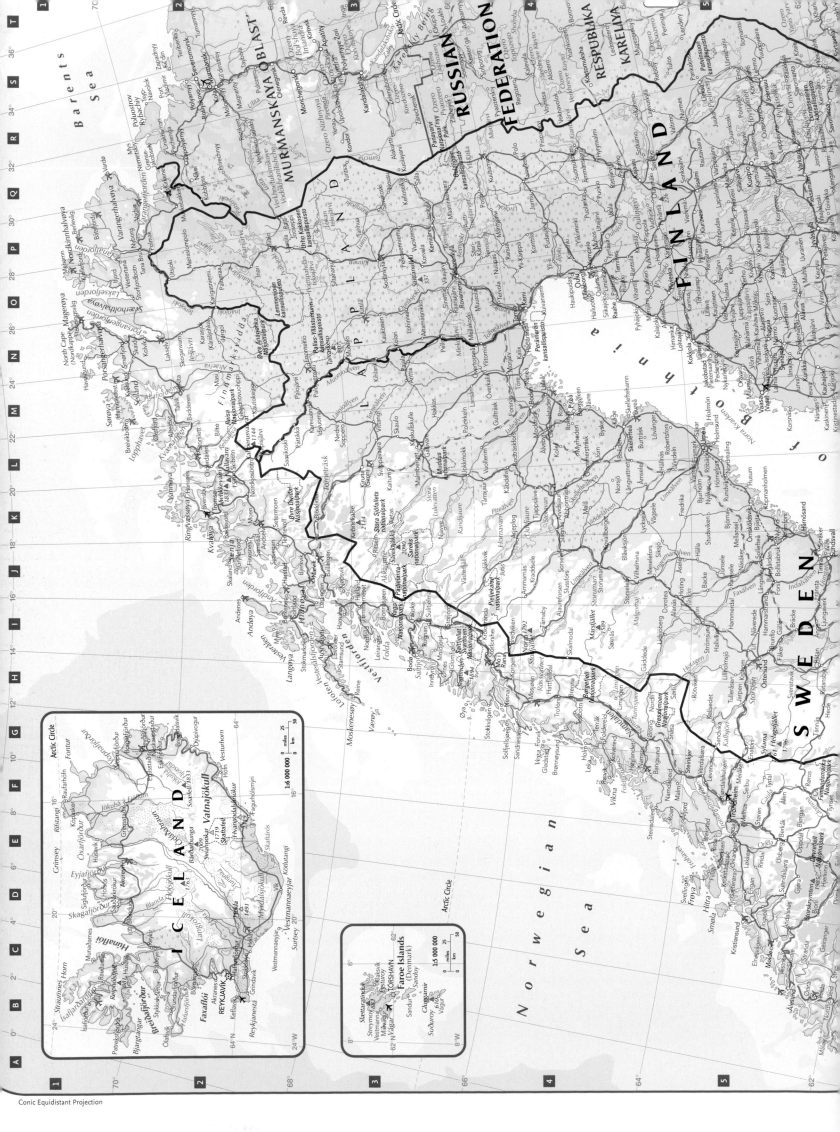

Conic Equidistant Projection

1:5 000 000

Europe

Scandinavia and the Baltic States

Conic Equidistant Projection

1:5 000 000

0   50   100   150 miles

0   50   100   150   200   250 km

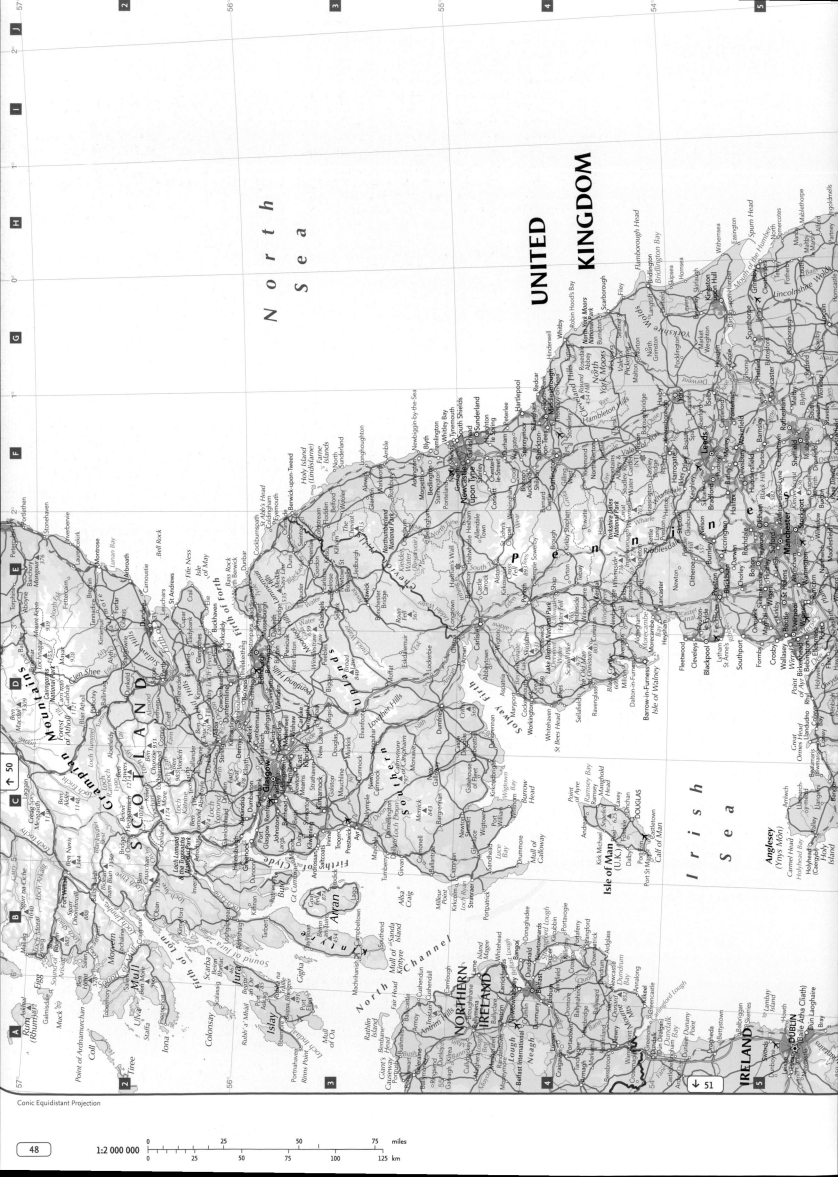

Conic Equidistant Projection

1:2 000 000

0   25   50   75   miles
0   25   50   75   100   125 km

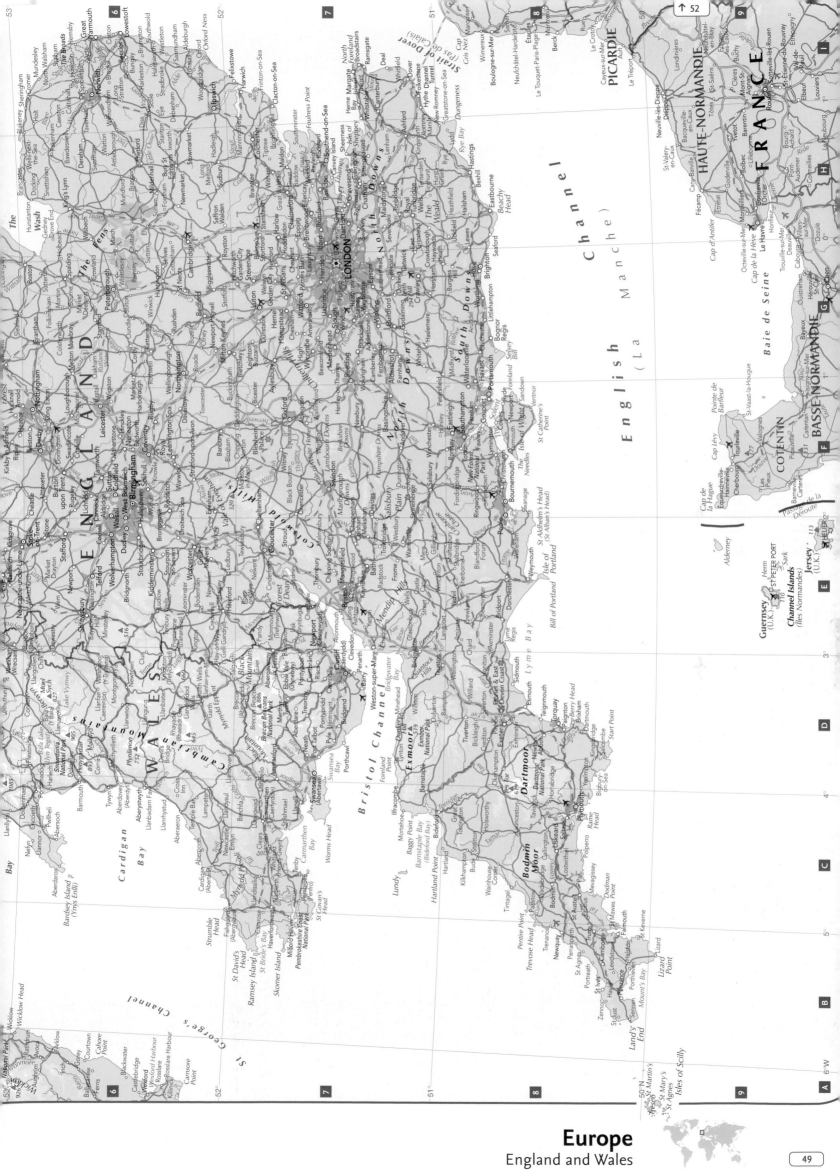

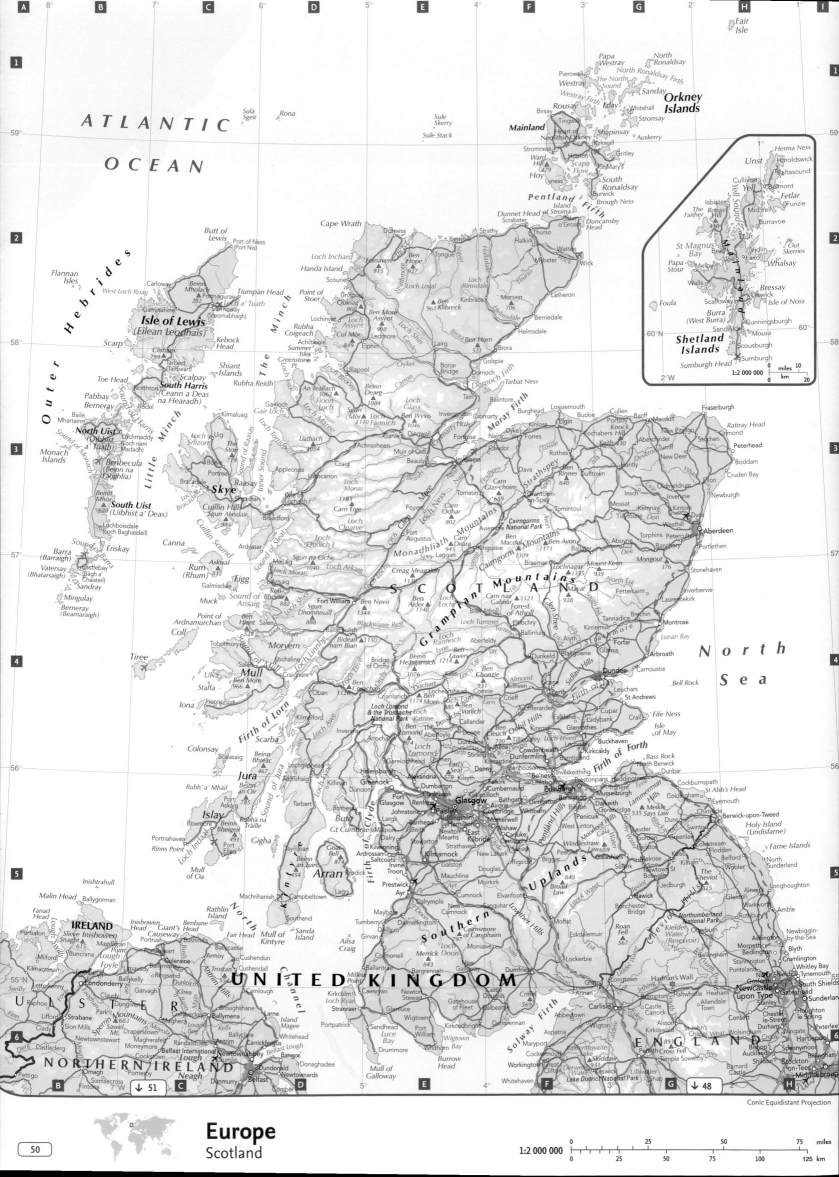

ATLANTIC

OCEAN

Fair
Isle

Papa
Westray
Pierowall   North Ronaldsay
Westray   The North Ronaldsay Firth
Westray   Sound   Sanday
Rousay   Eday   Whitehall
Birsay   Stronsay   Orkney
Tingwall   Shapinsay   Islands
Mainland   Heart of   Auskerry
Neolithic Orkney   Kirkwall
Stromness   Houton   Gritley
Ward   Scapa   St Mary's
Hill   Flow   South
Hoy   Lyness   Ronaldsay
Burwick   Brough Ness

Pentland   Duncansby
Firth   Head
Dunnet Head   Island of   John
Cape Wrath   Scrabster   Stroma   o'Groats
Durness   Strathy   Thurso
Loch Eriboll   Bettyhill   Halkirk   Wick
Ben Hope   Tongue   Halladale   Watten
915   Loch Loyal   Mybster

Flannan
Isles

Butt of
Lewis
Port of Ness
(Port Nis)

Sula
Sgeir   Rona

Sule
Skerry

Sule Stack

59°

58°

57°

56°

55°N

United Kingdom

North
Sea

Shetland Islands inset:

Herma Ness
Haroldswick
Unst   Baltasound
The   Burrafirth   Belmont
Faither   Muckle Flugga   Fetlar
Isbister   Mid Yell   Funzie
Brae   Yell   Laxo
St Magnus   Yell Sound   Out
Bay   Melby   Vidlin   Skerries
Papa   Walls   Whalsay
Stour   Lerwick
Foula   Scalloway   Isle of Noss
Burra   Bressay
(West Burra)   Mousa
Sandwick   Gulberwick
Shetland   Scousburgh
Islands   Sumburgh
Sumburgh Head

Conic Equidistant Projection

Europe
Scotland

1:2 000 000

Europe
Ireland

51

Europe
Southern Europe and the Mediterranean

Conic Equidistant Projection

Europe
France

1:5 000 000

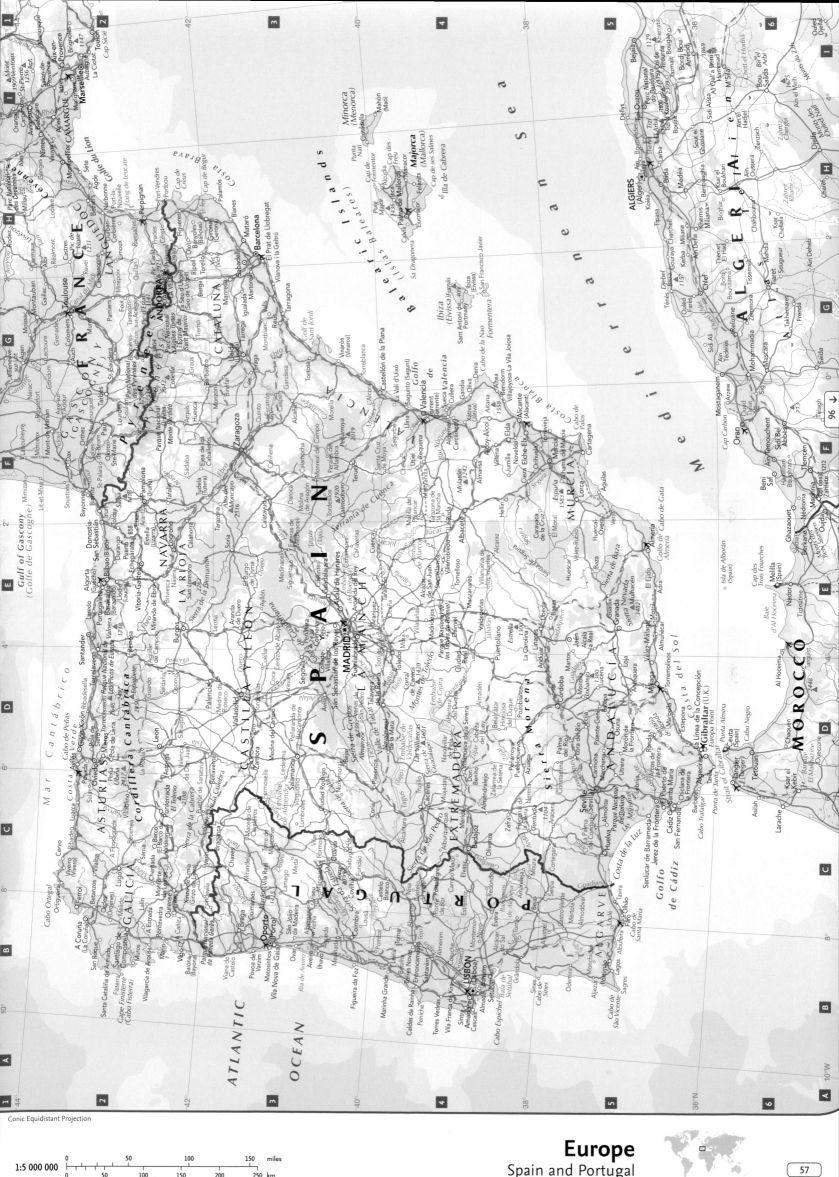

Europe
Spain and Portugal

1:5 000 000

| 0 | 50 | 100 | 150 | miles |
| 0 | 50 | 100 | 150 | 200 | 250 km |

Conic Equidistant Projection

1:5 000 000

Asia
Landscapes

Asia is the world's largest continent and occupies almost one-third of the world's total land area. Stretching across approximately 165° of longitude from the Mediterranean Sea to the easternmost point of the Russian Federation on the Bering Strait, it contains the world's highest and lowest points and some of the world's greatest physical features. Its mountain ranges include the Himalaya, Hindu Kush, Karakoram and the Ural Mountains and its major rivers – including the Yangtze, Tigris-Euphrates, Indus, Ganges and Mekong – are equally well-known and evocative.

Asia's deserts include the Gobi, the Taklimakan, and those on the Arabian Peninsula, and significant areas of volcanic and tectonic activity are present on the Kamchatka Peninsula, in Japan, and on Indonesia's numerous islands. The continent's landscapes are greatly influenced by climatic variations, with great contrasts between the islands of the Arctic Ocean and the vast Siberian plains in the north, and the tropical islands of Indonesia.

The **Yangtze**, China, Asia's longest river, flowing into the East China Sea near Shanghai.

Asia's physical features

Highest mountain	Mt Everest, China/Nepal	8 848 metres	29 028 feet
Longest river	Yangtze, China	6 380 km	3 965 miles
Largest lake	Caspian Sea	371 000 sq km	143 243 sq miles
Largest island	Borneo	745 561 sq km	287 861 sq miles
Largest drainage basin	Ob'-Irtysh, Kazakhstan/Russian Federation	2 990 000 sq km	1 154 439 sq miles
Lowest point	Dead Sea	-421 metres	-1 381 feet

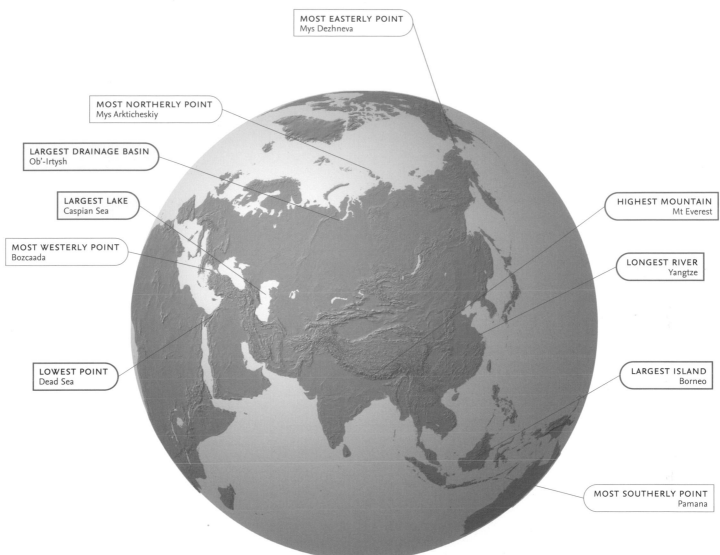

MOST EASTERLY POINT
Mys Dezhneva

MOST NORTHERLY POINT
Mys Arkticheskiy

LARGEST DRAINAGE BASIN
Ob'-Irtysh

LARGEST LAKE
Caspian Sea

MOST WESTERLY POINT
Bozcaada

LOWEST POINT
Dead Sea

HIGHEST MOUNTAIN
Mt Everest

LONGEST RIVER
Yangtze

LARGEST ISLAND
Borneo

MOST SOUTHERLY POINT
Pamana

Hahajima-retto
Bonin Islands
Volcano Islands

PACIFIC OCEAN

Palau Islands

zirah oberai
Puncak Jaya
5030
New Guinea

Kepulauan Aru
Kepulauan Tanimbar
Arafura Sea

Asia's extent

TOTAL LAND AREA	45 036 492 sq km / 17 388 686 sq miles
Most northerly point	Mys Arkticheskiy, Russian Federation
Most southerly point	Pamana, Indonesia
Most westerly point	Bozcaada, Turkey
Most easterly point	Mys Dezhneva, Russian Federation

Facts

● 90 of the world's 100 highest mountains are in Asia

● The Indonesian archipelago is made up of over 13 500 islands

● The height of the land in Nepal ranges from 60 metres to 8 848 metres

● The deepest lake in the world is Lake Baikal, Russian Federation, with a maximum depth of 1 741 metres

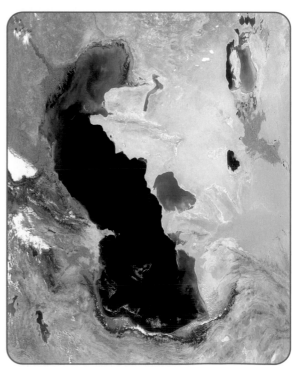

Caspian Sea, Europe/Asia, the world's largest expanse of inland water.

Asia
Countries

With approximately sixty per cent of the world's population, Asia is home to numerous cultures, people groups and lifestyles. Several of the world's earliest civilizations were established in Asia, including those of Sumeria, Babylonia and Assyria. Cultural and historical differences have led to a complex political pattern, and the continent has been, and continues to be, subject to numerous territorial and political conflicts – including the current disputes in the Middle East and in Jammu and Kashmir.

Separate regions within Asia can be defined by the cultural, economic and political systems they support. The major regions are: the arid, oil-rich, mainly Islamic southwest; southern Asia with its distinct cultures, isolated from the rest of Asia by major mountain ranges; the Indian- and Chinese-influenced monsoon region of southeast Asia; the mainly Chinese-influenced industrialized areas of eastern Asia; and Soviet Asia, made up of most of the former Soviet Union.

Timor island in southeast Asia, on which East Timor, Asia's newest independent state, is located.

Internet Links

● UK Foreign and Commonwealth Office	**www.fco.gov.uk**
● CIA World Factbook	**www.cia.gov/library/publicaions/ the-world-factfile/index.html**
● Asian Development Bank	**www.adb.org**
● Association of Southeast Asian Nations (ASEAN)	**www.aseansec.org**
● Asia-Pacific Economic Cooperation	**www.apecsec.org**

Asia's countries

Largest country (area)	Russian Federation	17 075 400 sq km	6 592 849 sq miles
Smallest country (area)	Maldives	298 sq km	115 sq miles
Largest country (population)	China	1 313 437 000	
Smallest country (population)	Palau	20 000	
Most densely populated country	Singapore	6 770 per sq km	17 534 per sq mile
Least densely populated country	Mongolia	2 per sq km	5 per sq mile

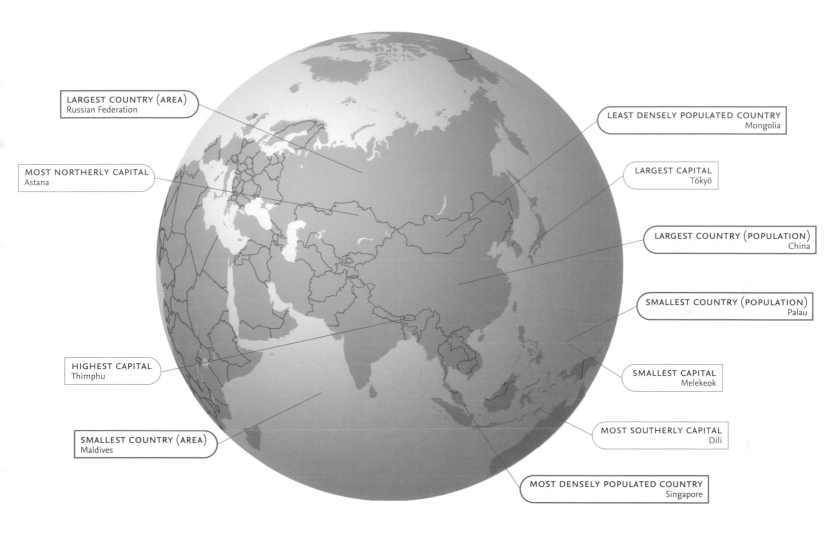

LARGEST COUNTRY (AREA)
Russian Federation

MOST NORTHERLY CAPITAL
Astana

HIGHEST CAPITAL
Thimphu

SMALLEST COUNTRY (AREA)
Maldives

LEAST DENSELY POPULATED COUNTRY
Mongolia

LARGEST CAPITAL
Tōkyō

LARGEST COUNTRY (POPULATION)
China

SMALLEST COUNTRY (POPULATION)
Palau

SMALLEST CAPITAL
Melekeok

MOST SOUTHERLY CAPITAL
Dili

MOST DENSELY POPULATED COUNTRY
Singapore

Asia's capitals

Largest capital (population)	Tōkyō, Japan	35 676 000
Smallest capital (population)	Melekeok, Palau	391
Most northerly capital	Astana, Kazakhstan	51° 10'N
Most southerly capital	Dili, East Timor	8° 35'S
Highest capital	Thimphu, Bhutan	2 423 metres 7 949 feet

Facts

- ● Over 60% of the world's population live in Asia

- ● Asia has 11 of the world's 20 largest cities

- ● The Korean peninsula was divided into North Korea and South Korea in 1948 approximately along the 38th parallel

onin
ands
(Japan)

lcano
lands
(Japan)

Melekeok
PALAU

Jayapura

New Guinea

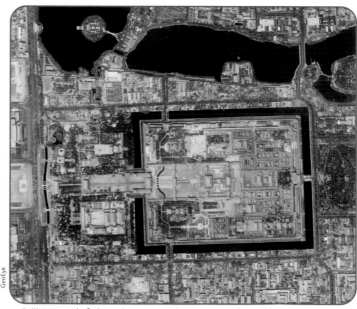

GeoEye

Beijing, capital of China, the most populous country in the world.

Asia
Northern Asia

Albers Conic Equal Area Projection

1:20 000 000

| 0 | 200 | 400 | 600 | miles |

| 0 | 200 | 400 | 600 | 800 | 1000 km |

Asia

Eastern and Southeast Asia

T'AIPEI
Chilung
Ilan
Fengyüan
Hualien
Sakishima-shotō
Yaeyama-rettō
Ryukyu Islands
(Nansei-shotō) *(Japan)*
Ishigaki
Chiai
Yü Shan
3997
TAIWAN
The People's Republic
of China claims Taiwan
as its 23rd province
T'aitung
Lan Yü
Bashi *Channel*
Kaohsiung
ainan

Okino-Daitō-jima

Kita-Iō-jima
Volcano Islands
(Kazan-rettō)
(Japan)
Minami-Iō-jima

Tropic of Cancer

Luzon Strait
Calayan
Babuyan
Babuyan Islands
Fuga
Babuyan Channel
Itbayat
Batan Islands
Batan

Okino-Tori-shima (Japan)

Farallon de Pajaros (Uracas)
Maug Islands
Asuncion

20°

Bangued
Tuguegarao
Bontoc
Ilagan
Fernando
2922
Santiago
Baguio
Dagupan
Cabanatuan

MANILA
Quezon City
San Pablo
Lucena
Calapan
Iriga
Naga
Loper
Daet
Catanduanes
Virac
Legaspi
Sorsogon
Irosin

Polillo Islands

PHILIPPINES

P A C I F I C

O C E A N

Agrihan
Pagan
Alamagan
Guguan

Northern Mariana Islands
(U.S.A.)

Sarigan
Anatahan
Farallon de Medinilla

CAPITOL HILL
Saipan
Tinian
Aguijan
Rota

Mindoro
Roxas
Romblon
Looc
Semirara Is
Cuyo Islands
San Jose de Buenavista
Caluya

Laoang
Catarman
Calbayog
Catbalogan
Samar
Tacloban
Ormoc
Leyte
Danao
Baybay
Maasin
Dinagat
Siargao

Masbate
Masbate
Visayan Sea

Bacolod
Talisay
Cebu
Carcar
Tanjay
Dumaguete
Cebu
Bohol Sea
Bohol
Tandag
Bislig

HAGÅTÑA
Guam
(U.S.A.)

Ulithi

Colonia **Yap**
Fais

FEDERATED STATES

15°

10°

Dipolog
Oroquieta
Ozamiz
Pagadian
Iligan
Malaybalay
Cagayan de Oro
Butuan

Faraulep
West Fayu
Pikelot
Namonuito

Sorol

OF MICRONESIA

Ngeruangel
Ngulu
Woleai
Olimarao
Lamotrek
Elato
Satawal
Puluwat

PALAU
Koror
MELEKEOK
Palau Islands
Eil Malk
Angaur

Eauripik
Ifalik
Caroline Islands
Pulusuk

Pulap
Pulo

5°

Cotabato
293?
Davao
Mindanao
Davao
Mati
Davao Gulf
Norala
Digos
Malita
Cape San Agustin
General Santos
Sarangani Islands

Kepulauan Nanusa

Sonsorol Islands

Pulo Anna
Merir

Zamboanga
Basilan
Isabela
Jolo
Sulu Archipelago

Kepulauan Talaud
Karakelong
Tahuna
Niampak
Kaburuang

Equator

0°

C e l e b e s

S e a

Salibabu

Siau
1784
Kepulauan Sangir
Tahulandang

Tobi
Helen

Helen Reef

Manado
Bitung
Tondano
Semenanjung Minahasa
Tolitoli
ntung
pamas
Gorontalo
Taman Nasional Bogani Nani Wartabone

Tanjung Sopi
Susupu
Morotai
Daruba
Tanjung Lelai
Lolodo
1635
Akelamo
Ternate
Halmahera

Asia

Myanmar, Thailand, Peninsular Malaysia and Indo-China

Albers Conic Equal Area Projection

1:15 000 000

0   200   400   miles

0   200   400   600   800   km

Asia
Eastern Asia

Conic Equidistant Projection

1:7 000 000

Asia

Japan, North Korea and South Korea

Conic Equidistant Projection

1:7 000 000

Asia
Southeast China

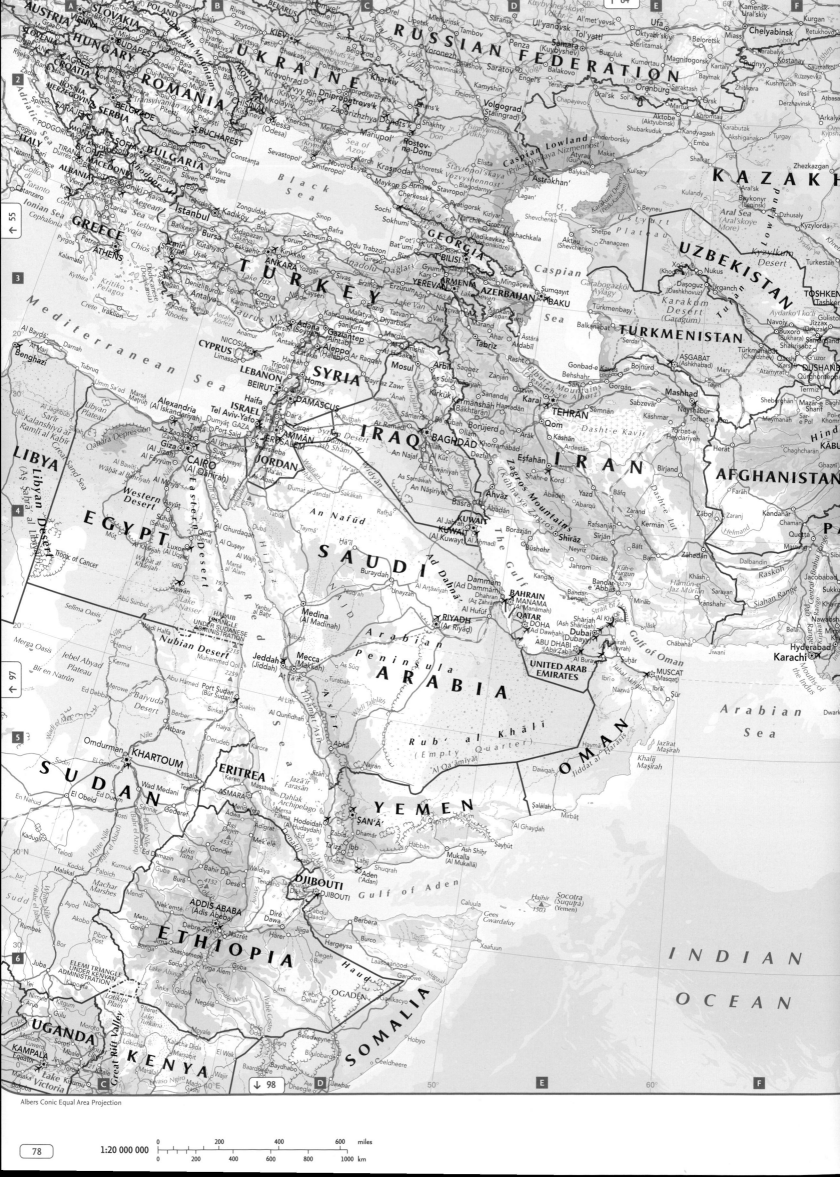

Albers Conic Equal Area Projection

1:20 000 000

Asia

Central and Southern Asia

Albers Equal Area Conic Projection

1:13 000 000

0 100 200 300 400 500 miles

0 100 200 300 400 500 600 700 800 km

Conic Equidistant Projection

1:7 000 000

Administrative divisions in India numbered on the map:

1. DADRA AND NAGAR HAVELI (C5)
2. DAMAN AND DIU (B5, C5)

Asia
Northern India, Nepal, Bhutan and Bangladesh

Asia
Southern India and Sri Lanka

1:7 000 000

Conic Equidistant Projection

Administrative divisions in India
numbered on the map:

1. DADRA AND NAGAR HAVELI (B1)
2. DAMAN AND DIU (A1, B1)
3. PUDUCHERRY (C4)

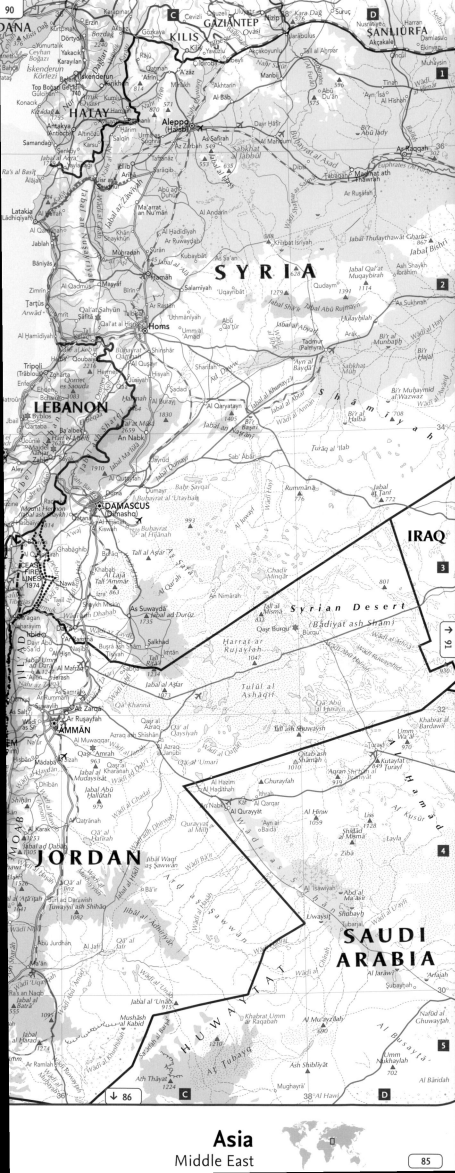

Asia
Middle East

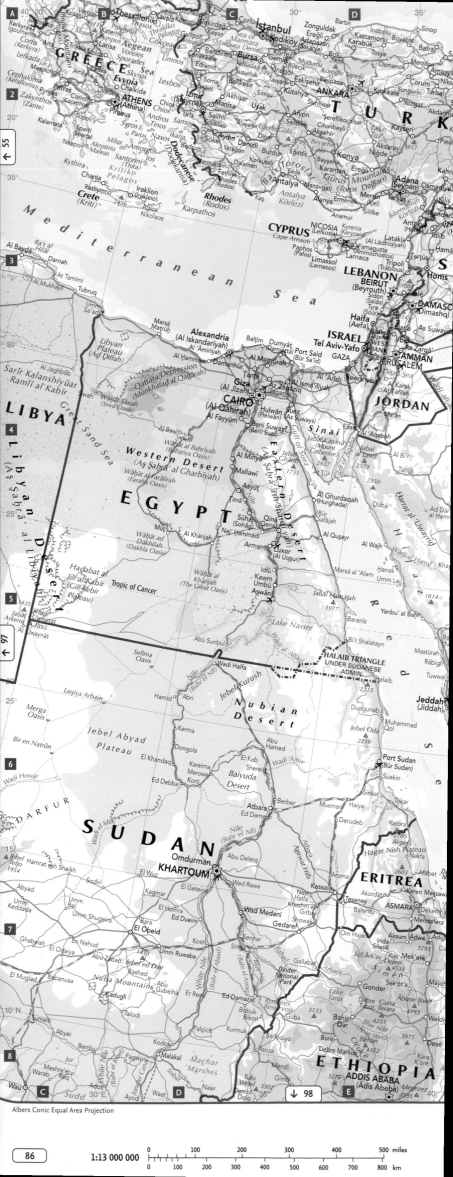

Black Sea

SERBIA
KOSOVO
MACEDONIA
(F.Y.R.O.M.)
ROMANIA
BUCHAREST
BULGARIA
SOFIA
UKRAINE
Crimea

GREECE
THRACE
Istanbul
ANKARA
ANADOLU
(ANATOLIA)
TURKEY
PISIDIA
Thessaloniki
ATHENS
Evvoia
Cyclades
(Kyklades)
Dodecanese
Crete
(Kriti)
Lesbos
(Lesvos)
Izmir
Smyrna
Bursa
Rhodes
(Rodos)
Taurus Mountains

Mediterranean Sea

CYPRUS
NICOSIA
(Lefkosia)
Aleppo
(Halab)
SYRIA
LEBANON
BEIRUT
(Beyrouth)
DAMASCUS
(Dimashq)
Homs

Haifa
(Hefa)
Tel Aviv-Yafo
WEST
BANK
JERUSALEM
GAZA
ISRAEL
AMMAN
JORDAN

LIBYA
Alexandria
(Al Iskandariyah)
Port Said
(Bur Sa'id)
CAIRO
(Al Qahirah)
Suez
(As Suways)
Giza
(Al Jizah)

EGYPT

Western Desert
(Aş Şaḥrāʾ al Gharbīyah)

Great Sand Sea

Qattara Depression
(Munkhafaḍ Qaṭṭārah)

Sinai
(Shibh Jazirat Sina')

Gulf of Suez

Gulf of Aqaba

Red Sea

SAUDI

Eastern Desert
(Aş Şaḥrāʾ ash Sharqīyah)

SYRIA

HUWAIMAT

0   100   200   miles
0   100   200   300   400   km

Africa
Landscapes

Some of the world's greatest physical features are in Africa, the world's second largest continent. Variations in climate and elevation give rise to the continent's great variety of landscapes. The Sahara, the world's largest desert, extends across the whole continent from west to east, and covers an area of over nine million square kilometres. Other significant African deserts are the Kalahari and the Namib. In contrast, some of the world's greatest rivers flow in Africa, including the Nile, the world's longest, and the Congo.

The Great Rift Valley is perhaps Africa's most notable geological feature. It stretches for nearly 3 000 kilometres from Jordan, through the Red Sea and south to Mozambique, and contains many of Africa's largest lakes. Significant mountain ranges on the continent are the Atlas Mountains and the Ethiopian Highlands in the north, the Ruwenzori in east central Africa, and the Drakensberg in the far southeast.

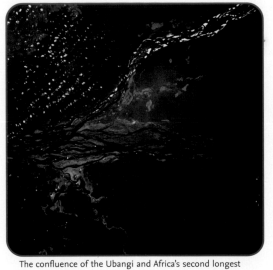

The confluence of the Ubangi and Africa's second longest river, the **Congo**.

Africa's extent

TOTAL LAND AREA	30 343 578 sq km / 11 715 655 sq miles
Most northerly point	La Galite, Tunisia
Most southerly point	Cape Agulhas, South Africa
Most westerly point	Santo Antão, Cape Verde
Most easterly point	Raas Xaafuun, Somalia

Internet Links

● NASA Visible Earth	**visibleearth.nasa.gov**
● NASA Astronaut Photography	**eol.jsc.nasa.gov**
● Peace Parks Foundation	**www.peaceparks.org**

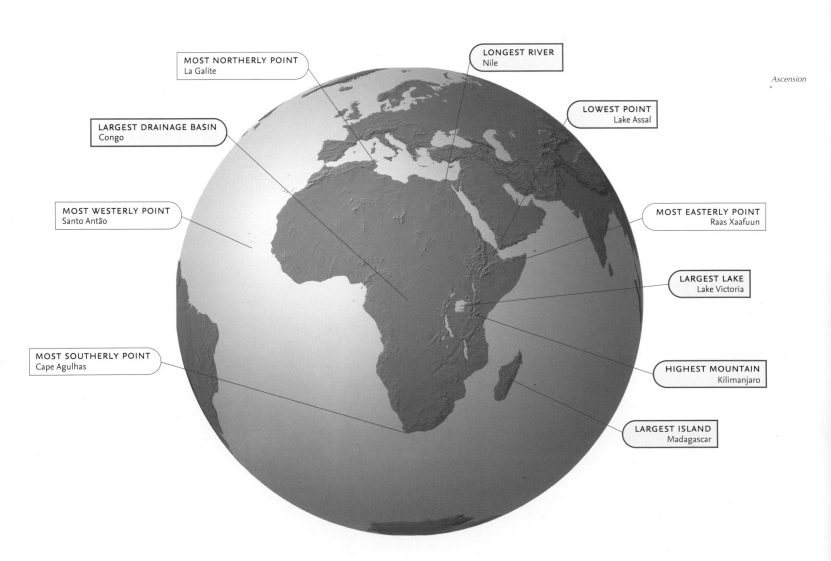

MOST NORTHERLY POINT
La Galite

LONGEST RIVER
Nile

LARGEST DRAINAGE BASIN
Congo

LOWEST POINT
Lake Assal

MOST WESTERLY POINT
Santo Antão

MOST EASTERLY POINT
Raas Xaafuun

MOST SOUTHERLY POINT
Cape Agulhas

LARGEST LAKE
Lake Victoria

HIGHEST MOUNTAIN
Kilimanjaro

LARGEST ISLAND
Madagascar

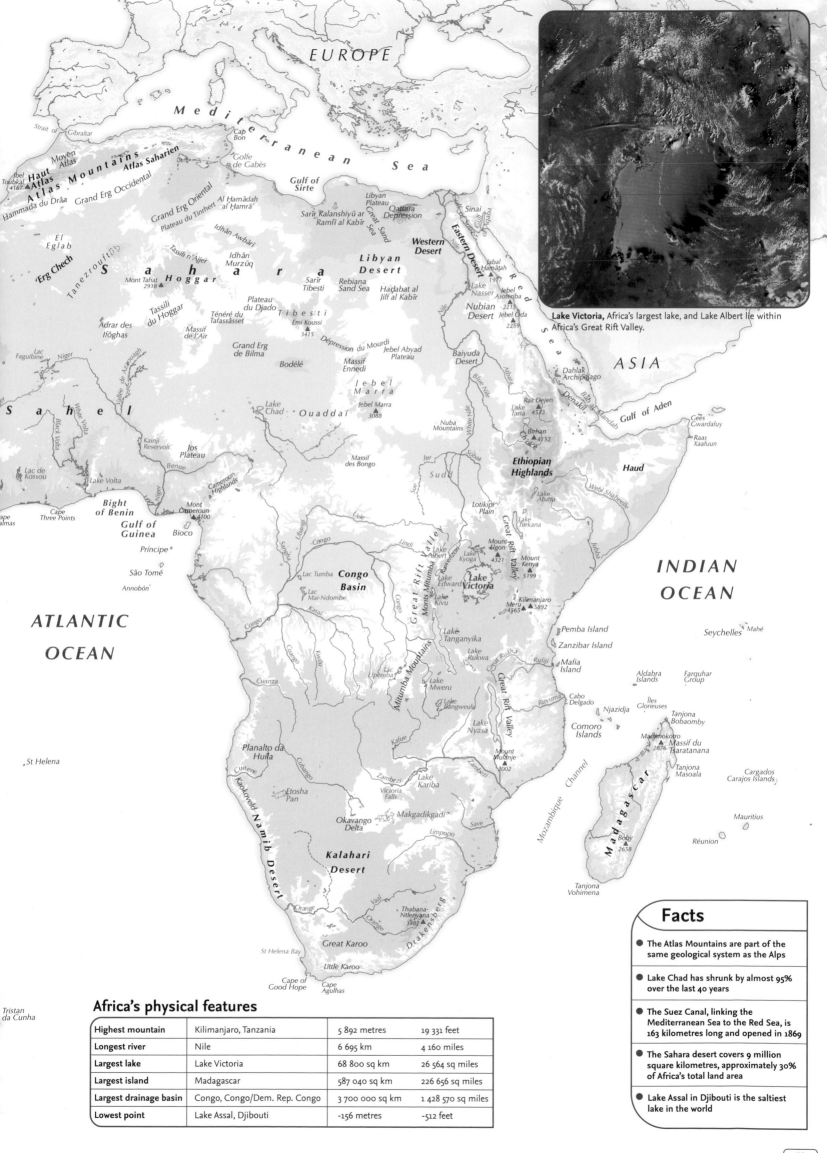

Lake Victoria, Africa's largest lake, and Lake Albert lie within Africa's Great Rift Valley.

Africa's physical features

Highest mountain	Kilimanjaro, Tanzania	5 892 metres	19 331 feet
Longest river	Nile	6 695 km	4 160 miles
Largest lake	Lake Victoria	68 800 sq km	26 564 sq miles
Largest island	Madagascar	587 040 sq km	226 656 sq miles
Largest drainage basin	Congo, Congo/Dem. Rep. Congo	3 700 000 sq km	1 428 570 sq miles
Lowest point	Lake Assal, Djibouti	-156 metres	-512 feet

Facts

- The Atlas Mountains are part of the same geological system as the Alps

- Lake Chad has shrunk by almost 95% over the last 40 years

- The Suez Canal, linking the Mediterranean Sea to the Red Sea, is 163 kilometres long and opened in 1869

- The Sahara desert covers 9 million square kilometres, approximately 30% of Africa's total land area

- Lake Assal in Djibouti is the saltiest lake in the world

Africa
Countries

Africa is a complex continent, with over fifty independent countries and a long history of political change. It supports a great variety of ethnic groups, with the Sahara creating the major divide between Arab and Berber groups in the north and a diverse range of groups, including the Yoruba and Masai, in the south.

The current pattern of countries in Africa is a product of a long and complex history, including the colonial period, which saw European control of the vast majority of the continent from the fifteenth century until widespread moves to independence began in the 1950s. Despite its great wealth of natural resources, Africa is by far the world's poorest continent. Many of its countries are heavily dependent upon foreign aid and many are also subject to serious political instability.

Facts

- Africa has over 1 000 linguistic and cultural groups

- Only Liberia and Ethiopia have remained free from colonial rule throughout their history

- Over 30% of the world's minerals, and over 50% of the world's diamonds, come from Africa

- 9 of the 10 poorest countries in the world are in Africa

Madeira (Portugal)

Canary Islands (Spain)

Laâyoune

WESTERN SAHARA

Nouâdhibou

MAURITANIA
Nouakchott

CAPE VERDE

St-Louis

Sénégal

Dakar
Kaolack
Banjul
THE GAMBIA
Bissau
GUINEA-BISSAU

Praia

SENEGAL
Kayes

GUINEA
Kank

Conakry
Freetown
SIERRA LEONE
Monrovia
LIBERI

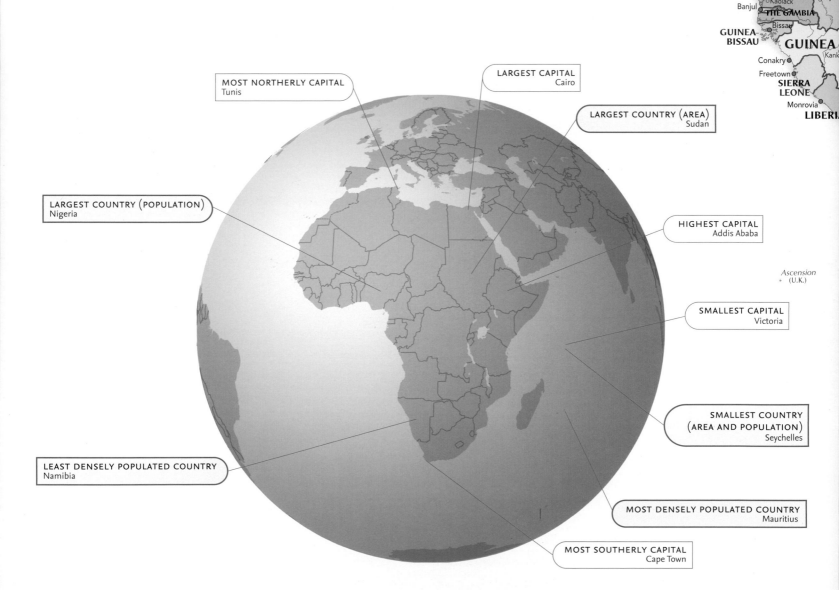

MOST NORTHERLY CAPITAL
Tunis

LARGEST CAPITAL
Cairo

LARGEST COUNTRY (AREA)
Sudan

LARGEST COUNTRY (POPULATION)
Nigeria

HIGHEST CAPITAL
Addis Ababa

Ascension (U.K.)

SMALLEST CAPITAL
Victoria

SMALLEST COUNTRY (AREA AND POPULATION)
Seychelles

LEAST DENSELY POPULATED COUNTRY
Namibia

MOST DENSELY POPULATED COUNTRY
Mauritius

MOST SOUTHERLY CAPITAL
Cape Town

Internet Links

UK Foreign and Commonwealth Office	www.fco.gov.uk
CIA World Factbook	www.cia.gov/library/publications/the-world-factbook/index.html
Southern African Development Community	www.sadc.int
GeoEye	www.GeoEye.com

Cape Town, legislative capital of the Republic of South Africa and the most southerly African capital city.

Africa's capitals

Largest capital (population)	Cairo, Egypt	11 893 000
Smallest capital (population)	Victoria, Seychelles	25 500
Most northerly capital	Tunis, Tunisia	36° 46'N
Most southerly capital	Cape Town, Republic of South Africa	33° 57'S
Highest capital	Addis Ababa, Ethiopia	2 408 metres 7 900 feet

Africa's countries

Largest country (area)	Sudan	2 505 813 sq km	967 500 sq miles
Smallest country (area)	Seychelles	455 sq km	176 sq miles
Largest country (population)	Nigeria	131 530 000	
Smallest country (population)	Seychelles	81 000	
Most densely populated country	Mauritius	599 per sq km	1 549 per sq mile
Least densely populated country	Namibia	2 per sq km	6 per sq mile

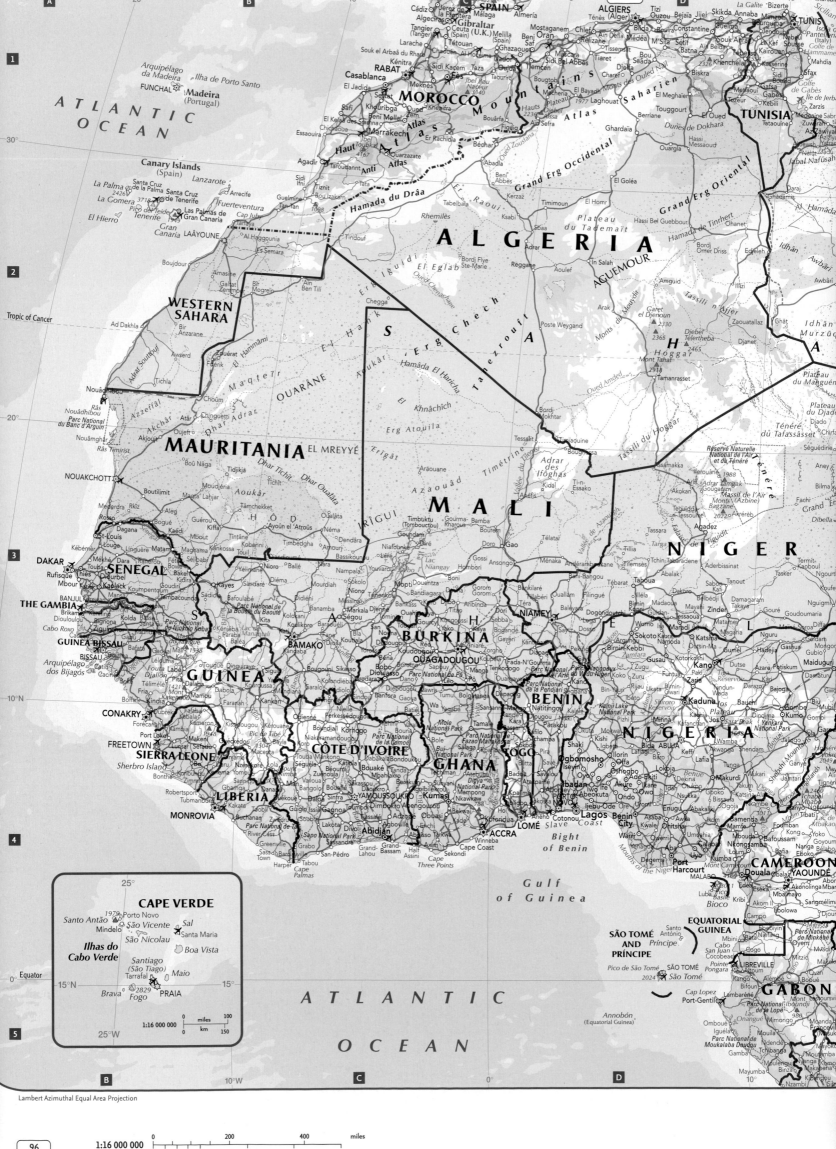

Lambert Azimuthal Equal Area Projection

1:16 000 000

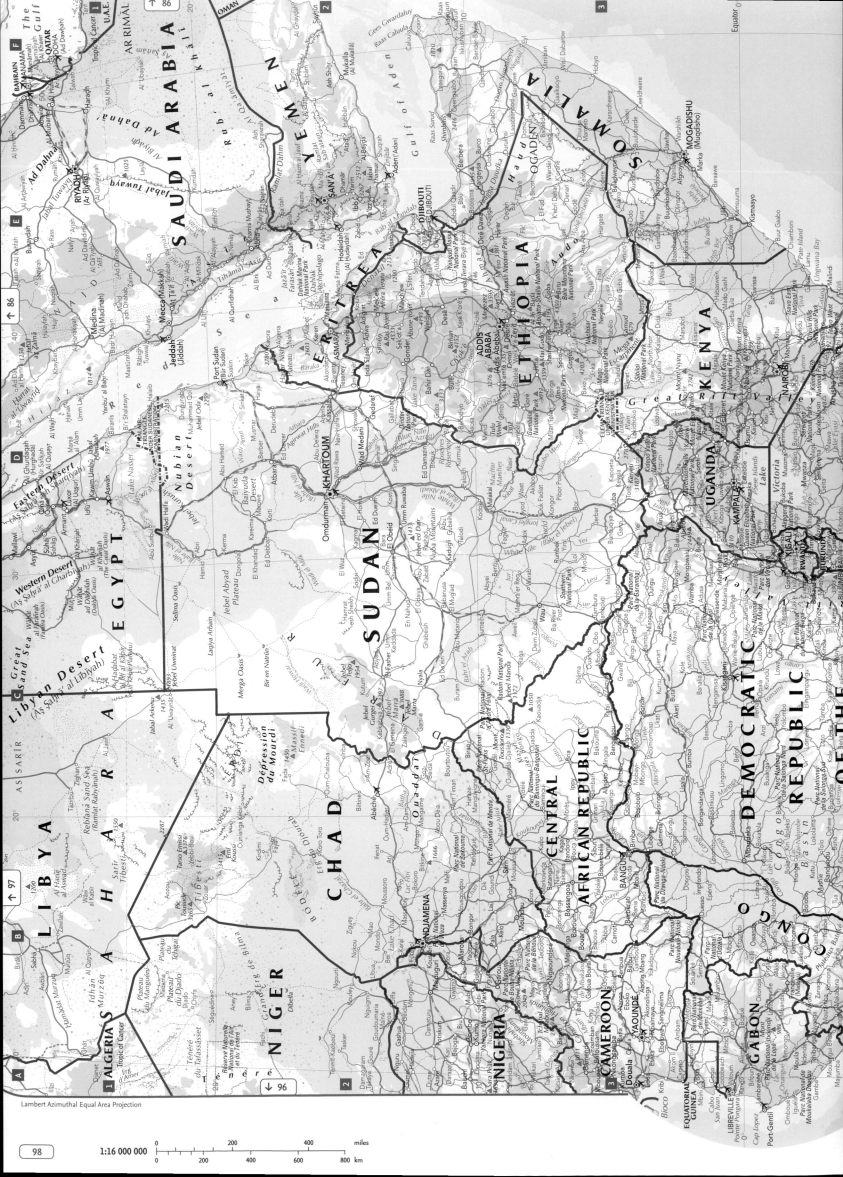

Lambert Azimuthal Equal Area Projection

1:16 000 000

0   200   400   miles
0   200   400   600   800 km

Africa

Central and Southern Africa

Lambert Azimuthal Equal Area Projection

1:5 000 000

| 0 | | 50 | | 100 | | 150 | miles |

| 0 | 50 | 100 | 150 | 200 | 250 | km |

Africa
Republic of South Africa

101

Oceania
Landscapes

Oceania comprises Australia, New Zealand, New Guinea and the islands of the Pacific Ocean. It is the smallest of the world's continents by land area. Its dominating feature is Australia, which is mainly flat and very dry. Australia's western half consists of a low plateau, broken in places by higher mountain ranges, which has very few permanent rivers or lakes. The narrow, fertile coastal plain of the east coast is separated from the interior by the Great Dividing Range, which includes the highest mountain in Australia.

The numerous Pacific islands of Oceania are generally either volcanic in origin or consist of coral. They can be divided into three main regions - Micronesia, north of the equator between Palau and the Gilbert islands; Melanesia, stretching from mountainous New Guinea to Fiji; and Polynesia, covering a vast area of the eastern and central Pacific Ocean.

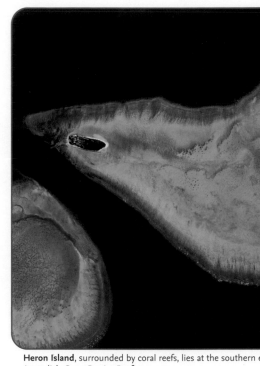

Heron Island, surrounded by coral reefs, lies at the southern e Australia's Great Barrier Reef.

Facts

- Australia's Great Barrier Reef is the world's largest coral reef and stretches for over 2 000 kilometres

- The highest point of Tuvalu is only 5 metres above sea level

- New Zealand lies directly on the boundary between the Pacific and Indo-Australian tectonic plates

- The Mariana Trench in the Pacific Ocean contains the earth's deepest point – Challenger Deep, 10 920 metres below sea level

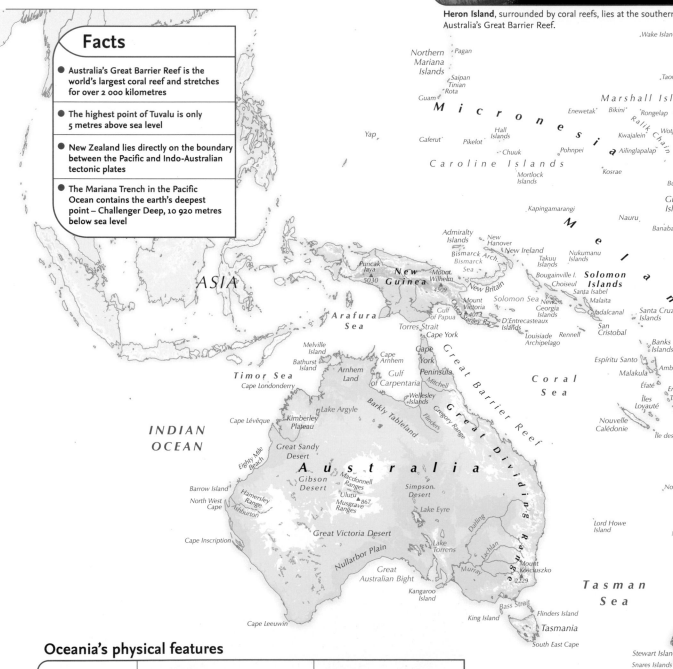

Oceania's physical features

Highest mountain	Puncak Jaya, Indonesia	5 030 metres	16 502 feet
Longest river	Murray-Darling, Australia	3 750 km	2 330 miles
Largest lake	Lake Eyre, Australia	0–8 900 sq km	0–3 436 sq miles
Largest island	New Guinea, Indonesia/Papua New Guinea	808 510 sq km	312 166 sq miles
Largest drainage basin	Murray-Darling, Australia	1 058 000 sq km	408 494 sq miles
Lowest point	Lake Eyre, Australia	-16 metres	-53 feet

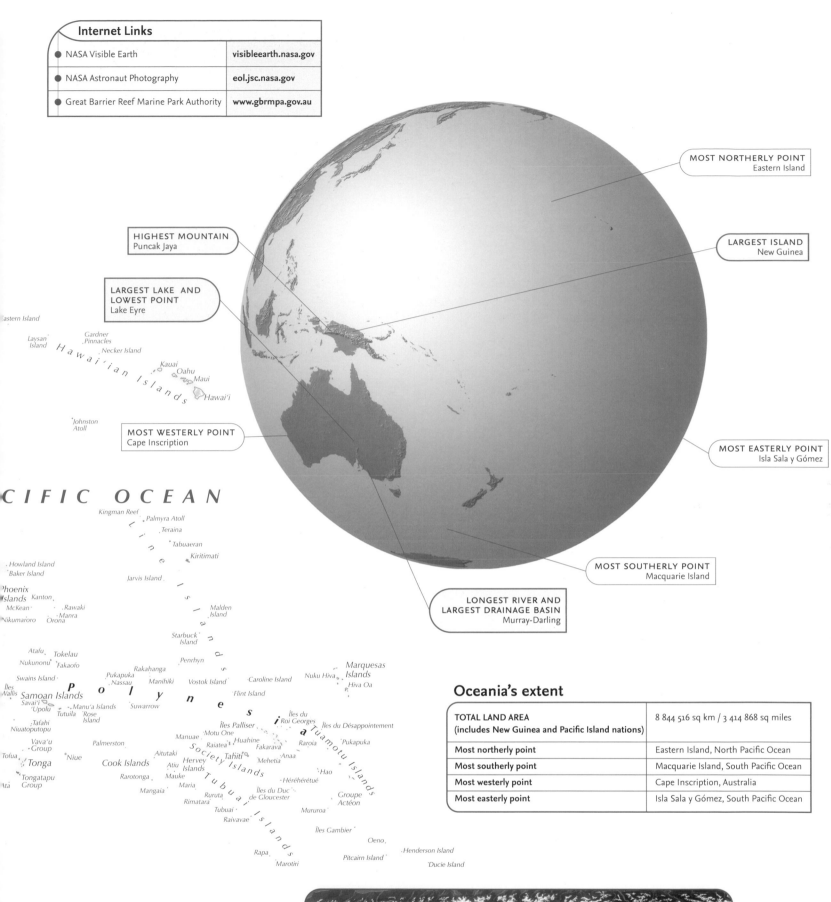

MOST NORTHERLY POINT
Eastern Island

LARGEST ISLAND
New Guinea

HIGHEST MOUNTAIN
Puncak Jaya

LARGEST LAKE AND LOWEST POINT
Lake Eyre

MOST EASTERLY POINT
Isla Sala y Gómez

MOST WESTERLY POINT
Cape Inscription

MOST SOUTHERLY POINT
Macquarie Island

LONGEST RIVER AND LARGEST DRAINAGE BASIN
Murray-Darling

Eastern Island

Laysan Island
Gardner Pinnacles
Necker Island
Hawai'ian Islands
Kauai
Oahu
Maui
Hawai'i
Johnston Atoll

CIFIC OCEAN

Kingman Reef
Palmyra Atoll
Teraina
Tabuaeran
Kiritimati
Line Islands

Howland Island
Baker Island
Jarvis Island

Phoenix Islands
Kanton
McKean
Rawaki
Manra
Nikumaroro
Orona
Malden Island
Starbuck Island

Atafu
Tokelau
Nukunonu
Fakaofo
Penrhyn
Rakahanga
Pukapuka
Manihiki
Vostok Island
Caroline Island
Nuku Hiva
Marquesas Islands
Hiva Oa
Nassau
Flint Island
P o l y n e s i a
Îles Wallis
Swains Island
Samoan Islands
Savai'i
'Upolu
Manu'a Islands
Tutuila
Rose Island
Suwarrow
Niuatoputopu
Manuae
Motu One
Îles Palliser
Îles du Roi Georges
Îles du Désappointement
Raiatea
Huahine
Fakarava
Raroia
Pukapuka
Vava'u Group
Palmerston
Aitutaki
Tahiti
Anaa
Tuamotu Islands
Tofua
Tonga
Niue
Cook Islands
Atiu
Hervey Islands
Mehetia
Hao
Tongatapu Group
Rarotonga
Mauke
Society Islands
Héréhérétué
Ata
Mangaia
Maria
Rurutu
Îles du Duc de Gloucester
Groupe Actéon
Rimatara
Mururoa
Tubuai
Tubuai Islands
Raivavae
Îles Gambier
Oeno
Henderson Island
Rapa
Pitcairn Island
Ducie Island
Marotiri

Chatham Islands
Pitt Island

HERN OCEAN

Oceania's extent

TOTAL LAND AREA (includes New Guinea and Pacific Island nations)	8 844 516 sq km / 3 414 868 sq miles
Most northerly point	Eastern Island, North Pacific Ocean
Most southerly point	Macquarie Island, South Pacific Ocean
Most westerly point	Cape Inscription, Australia
Most easterly point	Isla Sala y Gómez, South Pacific Ocean

Banks Peninsula, Canterbury Plains and the **Southern Alps**, South Island, New Zealand.

Oceania
Countries

Stretching across almost the whole width of the Pacific Ocean, Oceania has a great variety of cultures and an enormously diverse range of countries and territories. Australia, by far the largest and most industrialized country in the continent, contrasts with the numerous tiny Pacific island nations which have smaller, and more fragile economies based largely on agriculture, fishing and the exploitation of natural resources.

The division of the Pacific island groups into the main regions of Micronesia, Melanesia and Polynesia – often referred to as the South Sea islands – broadly reflects the ethnological differences across the continent. There is a long history of colonial influence in the region, which still contains dependent territories belonging to Australia, France, New Zealand, the UK and the USA.

Nouméa, capital of the French dependency of New Caledonia in the southern Pacific Ocean.

Facts

- Over 91% of Australia's population live in urban areas

- The Maori name for New Zealand is Aotearoa, meaning 'land of the long white cloud'

- Auckland, New Zealand, has the largest Polynesian population of any city in Oceania

- Over 800 different languages are spoken in Papua New Guinea

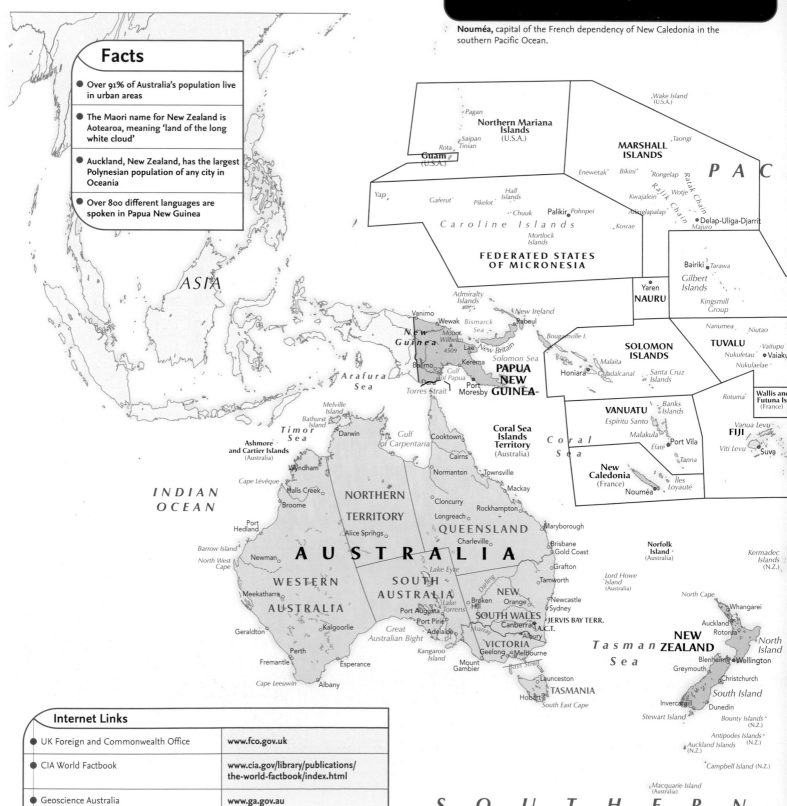

Internet Links

UK Foreign and Commonwealth Office	www.fco.gov.uk
CIA World Factbook	www.cia.gov/library/publications/the-world-factbook/index.html
Geoscience Australia	www.ga.gov.au

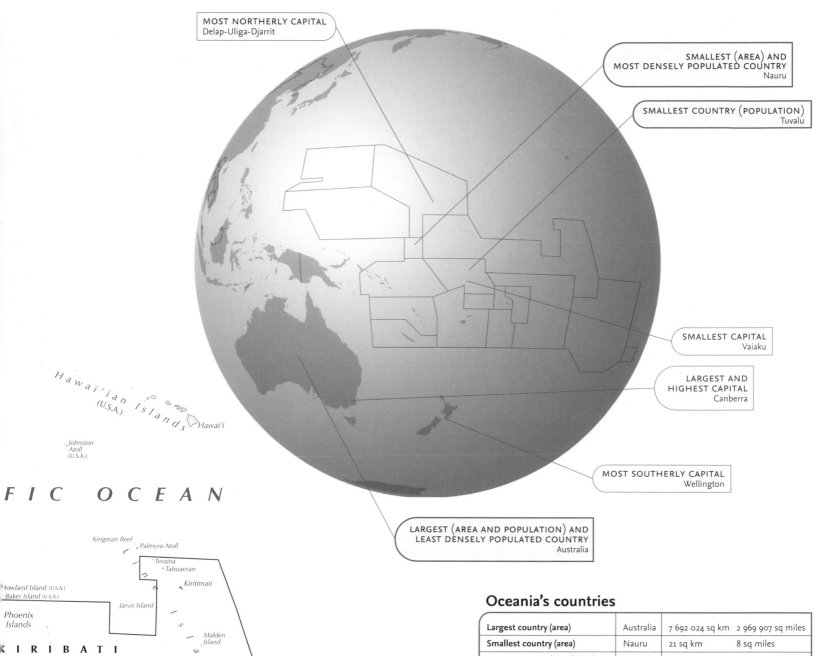

MOST NORTHERLY CAPITAL
Delap-Uliga-Djarrit

SMALLEST (AREA) AND
MOST DENSELY POPULATED COUNTRY
Nauru

SMALLEST COUNTRY (POPULATION)
Tuvalu

SMALLEST CAPITAL
Vaiaku

LARGEST AND
HIGHEST CAPITAL
Canberra

MOST SOUTHERLY CAPITAL
Wellington

LARGEST (AREA AND POPULATION) AND
LEAST DENSELY POPULATED COUNTRY
Australia

FIC OCEAN

Hawai'ian Islands (U.S.A.)

Hawai'i

Johnston Atoll (U.S.A.)

Kingman Reef
Palmyra Atoll
Teraina
Tabuaeran
Kiritimati

Howland Island (U.S.A.)
Baker Island (U.S.A.)

Phoenix Islands

Jarvis Island

Malden Island

K I R I B A T I

Starbuck Island

Tokelau (N.Z.)

Penrhyn

Nuku Hiva
Marquesas Islands
Hiva Oa

Samoan Islands

SAMOA
Savai'i Apia
'Upolu
Manu'a Islands

American Samoa (U.S.A.)

Vava'u Group

Alofi
Niue (N.Z.)

Cook Islands (N.Z.)

Aitutaki

TONGA
Nuku'alofa

Tongatapu Group

Rarotonga

Îles du Roi Georges
Tuamotu Islands
Îles Palliser
Society Islands
Tahiti Moorea
Hervey Islands

French

Tubuai Islands

Îles du Duc de Gloucester

Tubuai

Mururoa

Groupe Actéon

Polynesia

Îles Gambier

Pitcairn Is (U.K.)
Henderson Island
Pitcairn Island

Rapa

Chatham Islands (N.Z.)

Oceania's countries

Largest country (area)	Australia	7 692 024 sq km	2 969 907 sq miles
Smallest country (area)	Nauru	21 sq km	8 sq miles
Largest country (population)	Australia	20 155 000	
Smallest country (population)	Tuvalu	10 000	
Most densely populated country	Nauru	619 per sq km	1 625 per sq mile
Least densely populated country	Australia	3 per sq km	7 per sq mile

Oceania's capitals

Largest capital (population)	Canberra, Australia	381 000
Smallest capital (population)	Vaiaku, Tuvalu	516
Most northerly capital	Delap-Uliga-Djarrit, Marshall Islands	7° 7'N
Most southerly capital	Wellington, New Zealand	41° 18'S
Highest capital	Canberra, Australia	581 metres 1 906 feet

Wellington, capital of New Zealand.

O C E A N

INDONESIA

Borneo

Celebes Sea

Laut Maluku (Molucca Sea)

PAPUA

NEW GUINEA

New Guinea

PORT MORESBY

Torres Strait

INDIAN OCEAN

Timor Sea

Arafura Sea

Gulf of Carpentaria

Arnhem Land

Cape York Peninsula

Kimberley Plateau

Great Sandy Desert

NORTHERN TERRITORY

Tanami Desert

QUEENSLAND

Great Barrier Reef

Cairns

Townsville

WESTERN AUSTRALIA

Gibson Desert

Great Victoria Desert

SOUTH AUSTRALIA

Simpson Desert

Alice Springs

Uluru (Ayers Rock)

Coral Sea Islands Territory (Australia)

Mackay

Rockhampton

Brisbane

Gold Coast

NEW SOUTH WALES

Nullarbor Plain

Tropic of Capricorn

Perth

Great Australian Bight

Adelaide

VICTORIA

Melbourne

Sydney

Wollongong

Canberra A.C.T.

Bass Strait

TASMANIA

Hobart

Lambert Azimuthal Equal Area Projection

1:20 000 000

0   200   400   600 miles

0   200   400   600   800   1000 km

Aranuka
Howland Island (U.S.A.)
Banaba
(Ocean Island)
Nonouti
Baker Island (U.S.A.)
0°

Nauru
YAREN
Tabiteuea
Beru
Nikunau
K I R I B A T I

NAURU
Onotoa
Kingsmill Group
Tamana
Arorae

Phoenix
Islands
Kanton

Takuu
Islands
Nukumanu
Islands
McKean
Rawaki

Ontong
Java Atoll
Roncador
Reef
Nanumea
Nikumaroro
Orona
Manra
2

Choiseul
Santa
Isabel
Stewart
Islands
Nanumanga
Niutao

New
Georgia Sound
Buala
Malu'u
Nui
Vaitupu

New
Georgia
Islands
Florida
Islands
Malaita
TUVALU
Nukufetau

Guadalcanal
HONIARA
Auvuu
Maramasike
Ulawa Island
Funafuti
VAIAKU

San Cristobal
(Makira)
Santa
Ana
Duff
Islands
Nukulaelae
Tokelau
(New Zealand)
Atafu

al Sea
Rennell
Kirakira
Nupani
Swallow Islands
Santa Cruz Islands
(Solomon Islands)
Niulakita
Nukunonu
10°

Indispensable
Reefs
Ndeni
Utupua
Mitre
Island
Swains Island
Fakaofo

Torres Islands
Vanikoro
Islands
Cherry
Island
Rotuma
(Fiji)
Pukapuka
(Danger Islands)
Nassau

Uréparapara
Tikopia
Îles
Wallis
SAMOA

Banks
Islands
Vanua Lava
Santa María Island
**Wallis and
Futuna Islands**
(France)
MATA'UTU
Savai'i
**American
Samoa**
(U.S.A.)
Suwarrow

Espíritu Santo
Mount
Tabwémasana
Aoba
Maéwo
Îles de Hoorn
'Upolu
APIA
Manu'a
Islands

1879
Pentecost Island
Niuafo'ou
Tutuila
FAGATOGO
Rose
Island

VANUATU
Norsup
Ambrym
210
Tafahi
Niuatoputapu
Cook Islands
(New Zealand)
3

Malakula
1270
Epi
Émaé
Shepherd
Islands
Yasawa
Group
Great Sea Reef
Vanua Levu

Récifs
d'Entrecasteaux
PORT VILA
Éfaté
Bligh
Water
Cobia
(Lomosa)
Taveuni
Northern
Lau Group

Îles Chesterfield
(France)
Grand Passage
Erromango
Lautoka
Mt Victoria
Koro
Vava'u
Group

Grand Récif
de Cook
Tanna
361
Futuna
FIJI
Viti Levu
SUVA
Koro
Sea
Gau
Lakeba

Îles Belep
Récif des
Français
Anatom
(Aneityum)
Kadavu Passage
Moala
Southern
Lau Group

New Caledonia
(France)
Koumac
Nouvelle Calédonie
Îles Loyauté
Kadavu
Matuku
Vatoa

Bourail
Lifou
Maré
Ceva-i-Ra
(Conway Reef)
Doi
Ono-i-Lau
Tofua
500
Ha'apai
Group
Niue
(New Zealand)

NOUMÉA
Île des Pins
Hunter
Island
100
TONGA
ALOFI
Niue

Grand Récif
du Sud
NUKU'ALOFA
Tongatapu
Group
20°

Ata
Minerva Reefs
Palmerston

P A C I F I C
Tropic of Capricorn
160°

O C E A N

Norfolk Island
(Australia)
KINGSTON
Raoul Island
4

Lord Howe Island
(Australia)
Kermadec Islands
(New Zealand)
Macauley Island
Curtis Island

Havre Rock
L'Espérance Rock

Three Kings
Islands
North
Cape
30°

man Sea
Cape
Maria van Diemen
Awanui
Whangarei
Great Barrier Island

Takapuna
Auckland
Manukau

North Island
Hamilton
Tauranga
East Cape

**NEW
ZEALAND**
Te Kuiti
Tokoroa
Taupo
Whakatane
Gisborne

New
Plymouth
Mount Taranaki
(Mount Egmont)
2518
Mount
Ruapehu
Wairoa
Mahia Peninsula

Hawera
Wanganui
Napier
Hastings
5

Cape Farewell
Palmerston North
Levin

South
Island
Nelson
Tasman
Bay
Masterton
Lower Hutt

Westport
Blenheim
WELLINGTON

Hokitika
Greymouth

Aoraki
(Mount Cook)
3754
Christchurch
Banks Peninsula

Mount
Aspiring
3030
Southern Alps
Ashburton

Cape Providence
Mount
Christina
2502
Queenstown
Timaru
Chatham Islands
(New Zealand)

Gore
Oamaru
Chatham Island

Foveaux
Strait
Invercargill
Dunedin
Waitangi
Pitt Island
40°

Stewart Island
South West Cape
Bounty Islands
(New Zealand)

Snares
Islands
6

Auckland Islands
(New Zealand)
Antipodes Islands
(New Zealand)

Oceania
Australia, New Zealand and Southwest Pacific

Lambert Azimuthal Equal Area Projection

1:8 000 000

| 0 | 100 | 200 | 300 | miles |

| 0 | 100 | 200 | 300 | 400 | 500 km |

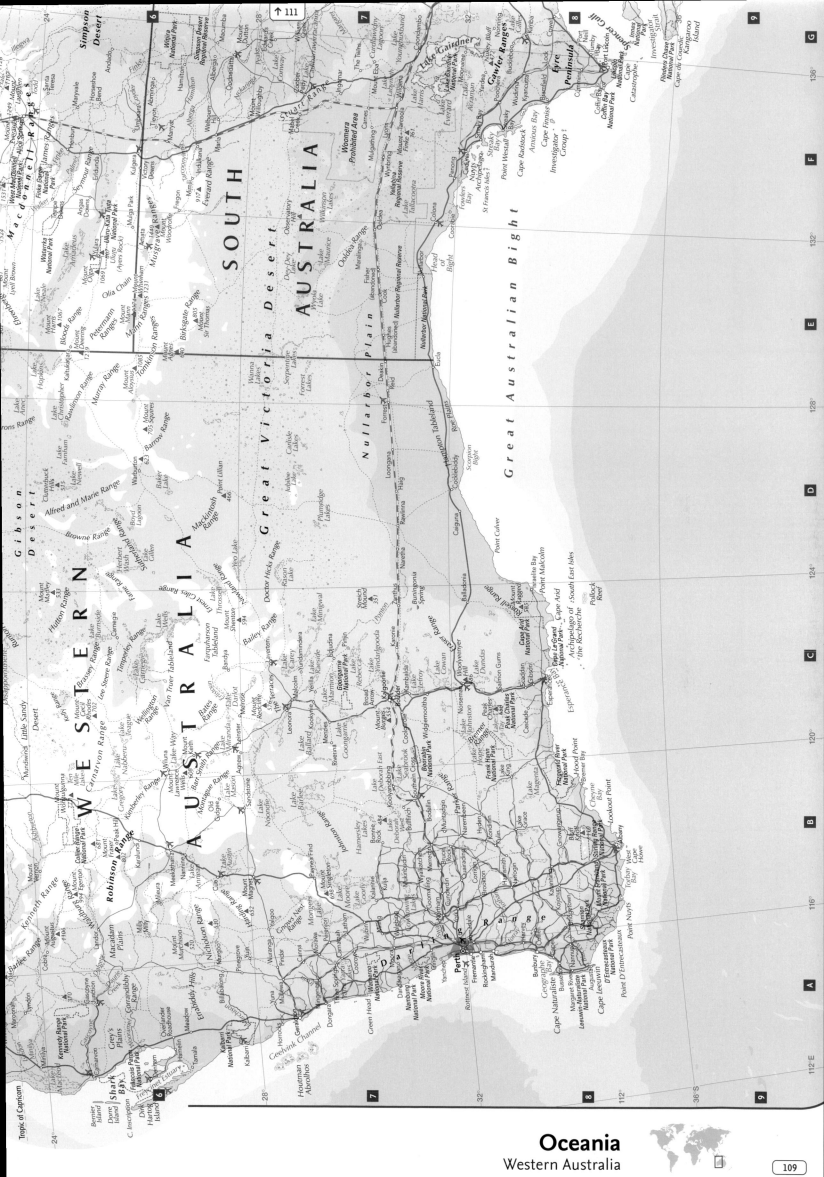

Oceania
Western Australia

Lambert Azimuthal Equal Area Projection

1:8 000 000

0   100   200   300   miles

0   100   200   300   400   500 km

PAPUA NEW GUINEA

Coral Sea

Coral Sea Islands Territory (Australia)

Arafura Sea

Gulf

of

Carpentaria

Arnhem Land

Cape York Peninsula

NORTHERN

TERRITORY

QUEENSLAND

Great Dividing Range

Gregory Range

Simpson Desert

← 106

↓ 108

↓ 108

Oceania
Eastern Australia

Oceania
Southeast Australia

Lambert Azimuthal Equal Area Projection

1:5 000 000

NEW

ZEALAND

Tasman

Sea

North Island

South Island

Tasman Sea

PACIFIC

OCEAN

Conic Equidistant Projection

1:5 250 000

| 0 | 50 | 100 | 150 | miles |

| 0 | 50 | 100 | 150 | 200 | 250 km |

North America

Landscapes

North America, the world's third largest continent, supports a wide range of landscapes from the Arctic north to sub-tropical Central America. The main physiographic regions of the continent are the mountains of the west coast, stretching from Alaska in the north to Mexico and Central America in the south; the vast, relatively flat Canadian Shield; the Great Plains which make up the majority of the interior; the Appalachian Mountains in the east; and the Atlantic coastal plain.

These regions contain some significant physical features, including the Rocky Mountains, the Great Lakes – three of which are amongst the five largest lakes in the world – and the Mississippi-Missouri river system which is the world's fourth longest river. The Caribbean Sea contains a complex pattern of islands, many volcanic in origin, and the continent is joined to South America by the narrow Isthmus of Panama.

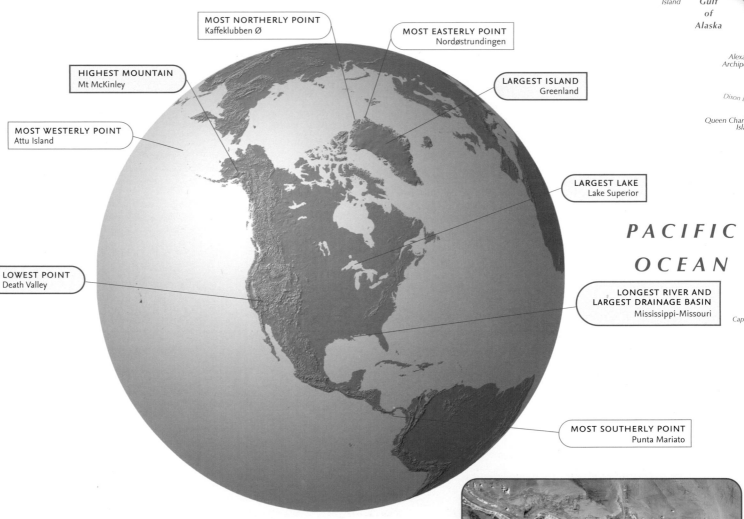

MOST NORTHERLY POINT
Kaffeklubben Ø

MOST EASTERLY POINT
Nordøstrundingen

HIGHEST MOUNTAIN
Mt McKinley

LARGEST ISLAND
Greenland

MOST WESTERLY POINT
Attu Island

LARGEST LAKE
Lake Superior

LOWEST POINT
Death Valley

LONGEST RIVER AND
LARGEST DRAINAGE BASIN
Mississippi-Missouri

MOST SOUTHERLY POINT
Punta Mariato

PACIFIC

OCEAN

North America's physical features

Highest mountain	Mt McKinley, USA	6 194 metres	20 321 feet
Longest river	Mississippi-Missouri, USA	5 969 km	3 709 miles
Largest lake	Lake Superior, Canada/USA	82 100 sq km	31 699 sq miles
Largest island	Greenland	2 175 600 sq km	839 999 sq miles
Largest drainage basin	Mississippi-Missouri, USA	3 250 000 sq km	1 254 825 sq miles
Lowest point	Death Valley, USA	-86 metres	-282 feet

North America's longest river system, the **Mississippi-Missouri**, flows into the Gulf of Mexico through the Mississippi Delta.

North America's extent

TOTAL LAND AREA (including Hawai'ian Islands)	24 680 331 sq km / 9 529 076 sq miles
Most northerly point	Kaffeklubben Ø, Greenland
Most southerly point	Punta Mariato, Panama
Most westerly point	Attu Island, USA
Most easterly point	Nordøstrundingen, Greenland

The **Panama Canal,** Panama, linking the Pacific Ocean to the Atlantic Ocean.

Facts

- Devon Island, Canada, is the world's largest uninhabited island

- Canada has the longest coastline of any country in the world

- Lake Superior is the world's largest freshwater lake

- Over 320 000 square kilometres of the USA is protected for conservation purposes

North America
Countries

North America has been dominated economically and politically by the USA since the nineteenth century. Before that, the continent was subject to colonial influences, particularly of Spain in the south and of Britain and France in the east. The nineteenth century saw the steady development of the western half of the continent. The wealth of natural resources and the generally temperate climate were an excellent basis for settlement, agriculture and industrial development which has led to the USA being the richest nation in the world today.

Although there are twenty-three independent countries and fourteen dependent territories in North America, Canada, Mexico and the USA have approximately eighty-five per cent of the continent's population and eighty-eight per cent of its land area. Large parts of the north remain sparsely populated, while the most densely populated areas are in the northeast USA, and the Caribbean.

North America's capitals

Largest capital (population)	Mexico City, Mexico	19 028 000
Smallest capital (population)	Belmopan, Belize	13 500
Most northerly capital	Ottawa, Canada	45° 25'N
Most southerly capital	Panama City, Panama	8° 56'N
Highest capital	Mexico City, Mexico	2 300 metres 7 546 feet

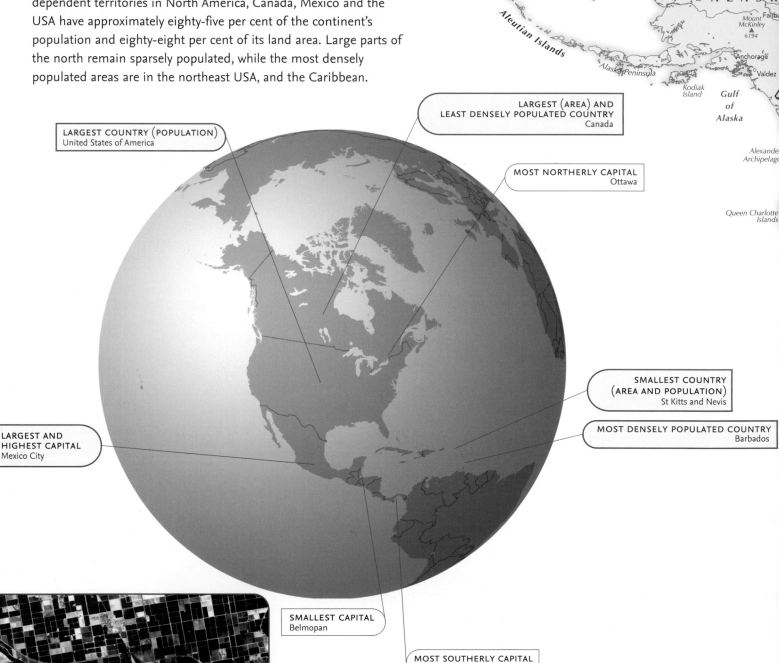

LARGEST COUNTRY (POPULATION)
United States of America

LARGEST (AREA) AND LEAST DENSELY POPULATED COUNTRY
Canada

MOST NORTHERLY CAPITAL
Ottawa

SMALLEST COUNTRY (AREA AND POPULATION)
St Kitts and Nevis

MOST DENSELY POPULATED COUNTRY
Barbados

LARGEST AND HIGHEST CAPITAL
Mexico City

SMALLEST CAPITAL
Belmopan

MOST SOUTHERLY CAPITAL
Panama City

Point Hope
Bering Strait
St Lawrence Island
Nome
U.S
Yukon
ALASK
Mount McKinley 6194
Fairban
Anchorage
Valdez
Kodiak Island
Gulf of Alaska
Aleutian Islands
Alaska Peninsula
Alexander Archipelago
Queen Charlotte Islands

False-colour satellite image of the **Mexico-USA** boundary at Mexicali.

North America's countries

Largest country (area)	Canada	9 984 670 sq km	3 855 103 sq miles
Smallest country (area)	St Kitts and Nevis	261 sq km	101 sq miles
Largest country (population)	United States of America	298 213 000	
Smallest country (population)	St Kitts and Nevis	43 000	
Most densely populated country	Barbados	628 per sq km	1 627 per sq mile
Least densely populated country	Canada	3 per sq km	8 per sq mile

Internet Links

● UK Foreign and Commonwealth Office	www.fco.gov.uk
● CIA World Factbook	www.cia.gov/library/publications/the-world-factbook/index.html
● U.S. Board on Geographic Names	geonames.usgs.gov
● NASA Astronaut Photography	eol.jsc.nasa.gov

The Bahamas, a chain of islands in the North Atlantic Ocean, lying southeast of Florida, USA.

Facts

- The Panama Canal, opened in 1914, cut the journey between the Atlantic and the Pacific by over 14 000 km

- Mexico City is the highest city in North America and houses approximately 18% of Mexico's population

- The state of Alaska was bought by the USA from Russia in 1867

- The territory of Nunavut is Canada's newest administrative division, created in 1999 from the eastern part of Northwest Territories

Lambert Conformal Conic Projection

1:16 000 000

North America

Canada

Conic Equidistant Projection

1:7 000 000

North America
Western Canada

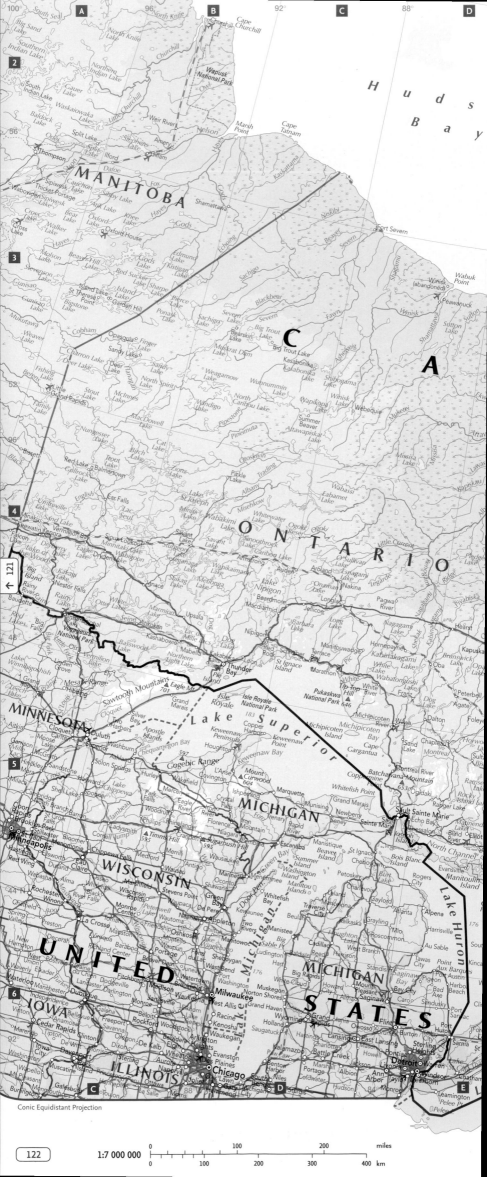

Conic Equidistant Projection

1:7 000 000

North America

Eastern Canada

Lambert Conformal Conic Projection

126

1:7 000 000

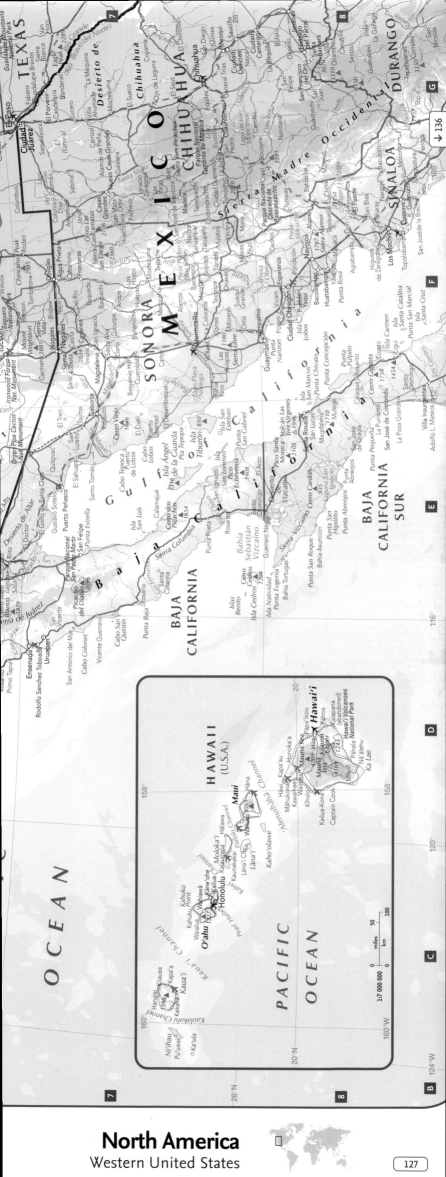

North America
Western United States

PACIFIC

OCEAN

Lambert Conformal Conic Projection

1:3 500 000

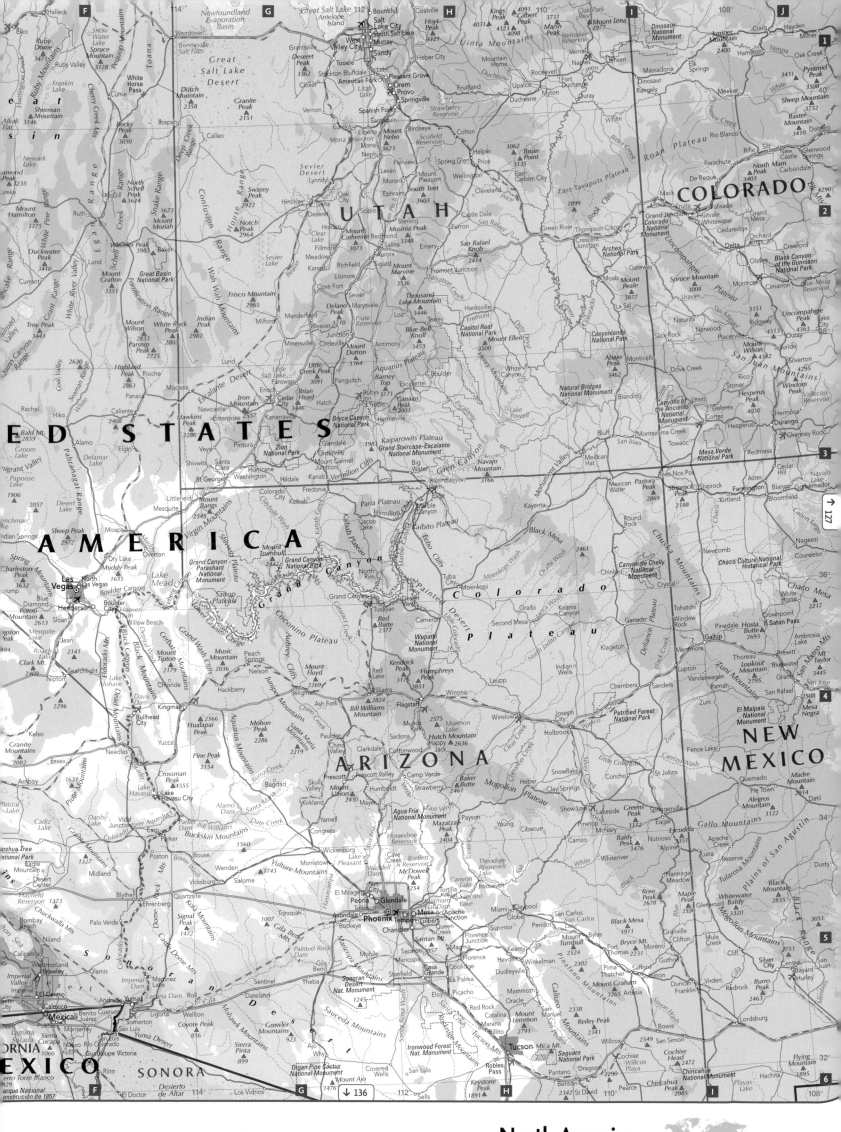

Lambert Conformal Conic Projection

1:7 000 000

| 0 | | 100 | | 200 | miles |
| 0 | 100 | 200 | 300 | 400 km | |

↓ 127

↓ 136

North America
Central United States

States in the U.S.A.
numbered on the map:
1. CONNECTICUT (F3)
2. DELAWARE (F4)
3. MASSACHUSETTS (F3)
4. RHODE ISLAND (G3)

CANADA

QUÉBEC

ONTARIO

NEW BRUNSWICK

MAINE

VERMONT

NEW HAMPSHIRE

NEW YORK

PENNSYLVANIA

OHIO

MICHIGAN

WISCONSIN

ILLINOIS

INDIANA

KENTUCKY

TENNESSEE

MISSOURI

IOWA

MINNESOTA

WEST VIRGINIA

VIRGINIA

MARYLAND

NEW JERSEY

NORTH CAROLINA

UNITED STATES

Lake Superior

Lake Michigan

Lake Huron

Lake Erie

Lake Ontario

Georgian Bay

Gulf of Maine

Long Island

Cape Cod

Chesapeake Bay

Montreal

Ottawa

Toronto

Buffalo

Rochester

Boston

New York

Philadelphia

Baltimore

WASHINGTON D.C.

Richmond

Virginia Beach

Pittsburgh

Cleveland

Columbus

Cincinnati

Detroit

Chicago

Milwaukee

Indianapolis

Louisville

St. Louis

Lambert Conformal Conic Projection

1:7 000 000

0   100   200   miles

0   100   200   300   400   km

Tropic of Cancer

G

Turks and Caicos
Island (U.K.)

ATLANTIC

OCEAN

F

THE
BAHAMAS

Great Abaco

Grand
Bahama

NASSAU

Andros

E

Great Bahama Bank

MEXICO

OF AMERICA

NORTH CAROLINA

Charlotte

Wilmington

Cape Hatteras

Cape Lookout

Cape Fear

Myrtle Beach

SOUTH CAROLINA

Charleston

North Charleston

GEORGIA

Savannah

Atlanta

Columbus

ALABAMA

Montgomery

Birmingham

MISSISSIPPI

FLORIDA

Jacksonville

Orlando

Tampa

St Petersburg

Clearwater

Daytona Beach

Cape Canaveral

Melbourne

West Palm
Beach

Fort Lauderdale

Hollywood

Miami

Miami Beach

Everglades
National Park

Key West

Gulf

of

Mexico

Straits of Florida

HAVANA
(La Habana)

CUBA

Yucatan Channel

Tropic of Cancer

24°N

↓ 131

↓ 137

North America
Eastern United States

Lambert Conformal Conic Projection

1:3 500 000

North America
Northeast United States

Lambert Conformal Conic Projection

1:14 000 000

	miles	
0	200	400
0 200 400 600	800 km	

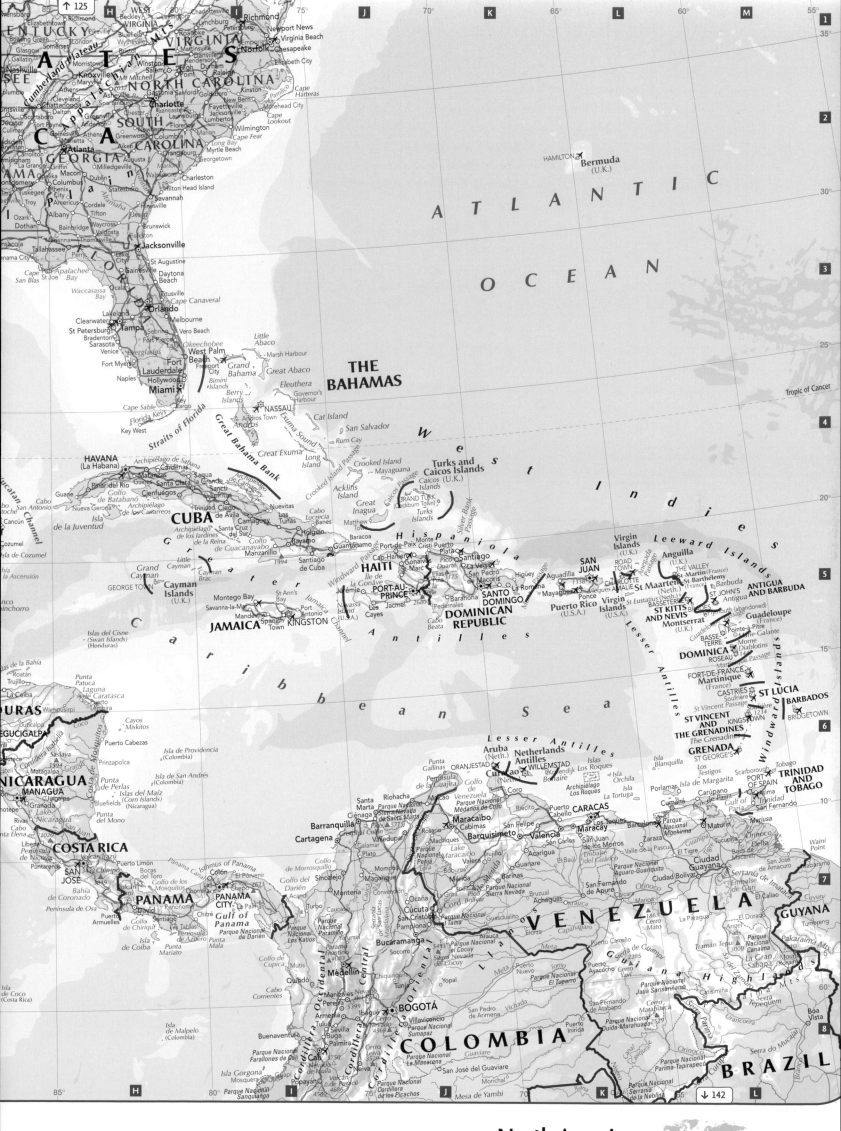

ATLANTIC

OCEAN

HAMILTON ✈
Bermuda
(U.K.)

Tropic of Cancer

THE
BAHAMAS

West Indies

Leeward Islands

Lesser Antilles

Windward Islands

Caribbean Sea

Lesser Antilles

VENEZUELA

COLOMBIA

BRAZIL

North America
Central America and the Caribbean

137

South America
Landscapes

South America is a continent of great contrasts, with landscapes varying from the tropical rainforests of the Amazon Basin, to the Atacama Desert, the driest place on earth, and the sub-Antarctic regions of southern Chile and Argentina. The dominant physical features are the Andes, stretching along the entire west coast of the continent and containing numerous mountains over 6 000 metres high, and the Amazon, which is the second longest river in the world and has the world's largest drainage basin.

The Altiplano is a high plateau lying between two of the Andes ranges. It contains Lake Titicaca, the world's highest navigable lake. By contrast, large lowland areas dominate the centre of the continent, lying between the Andes and the Guiana and Brazilian Highlands. These vast grasslands stretch from the Llanos of the north through the Selvas and the Gran Chaco to the Pampas of Argentina.

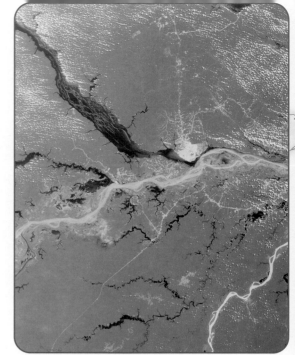

Confluence of the **Amazon** and **Negro** rivers at Manaus, northern Brazil.

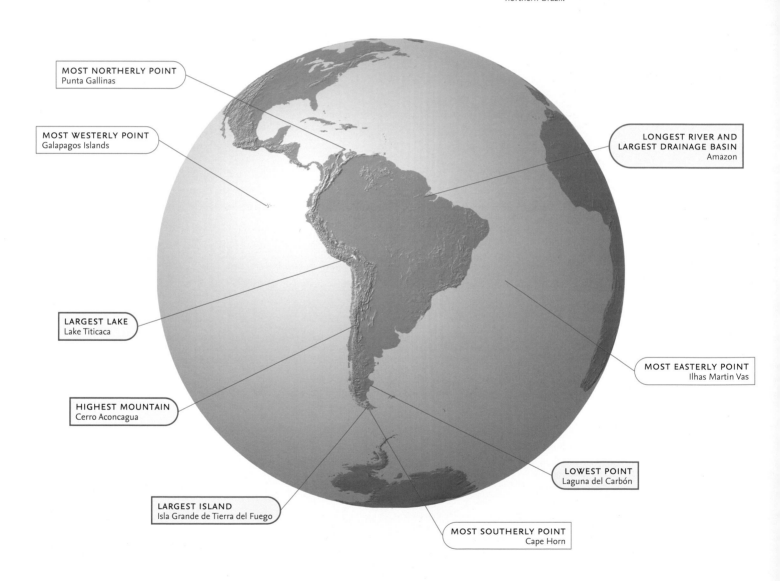

MOST NORTHERLY POINT
Punta Gallinas

MOST WESTERLY POINT
Galapagos Islands

LONGEST RIVER AND
LARGEST DRAINAGE BASIN
Amazon

LARGEST LAKE
Lake Titicaca

MOST EASTERLY POINT
Ilhas Martin Vas

HIGHEST MOUNTAIN
Cerro Aconcagua

LOWEST POINT
Laguna del Carbón

LARGEST ISLAND
Isla Grande de Tierra del Fuego

MOST SOUTHERLY POINT
Cape Horn

South America's physical features

Highest mountain	Cerro Aconcagua, Argentina	6 959 metres	22 831 feet
Longest river	Amazon	6 516 km	4 049 miles
Largest lake	Lake Titicaca, Bolivia/Peru	8 340 sq km	3 220 sq miles
Largest island	Isla Grande de Tierra del Fuego, Argentina/Chile	47 000 sq km	18 147 sq miles
Largest drainage basin	Amazon	7 050 000 sq km	2 722 005 sq miles
Lowest point	Laguna del Carbón, Argentina	-105 metres	-345 feet

Internet Links

Internet Links	
NASA Visible Earth	visibleearth.nasa.gov
NASA Astronaut Photography	eol.jsc.nasa.gov
World Rainforest Information Portal	www.rainforestweb.org
Peakware World Mountain Encyclopedia	www.peakware.com

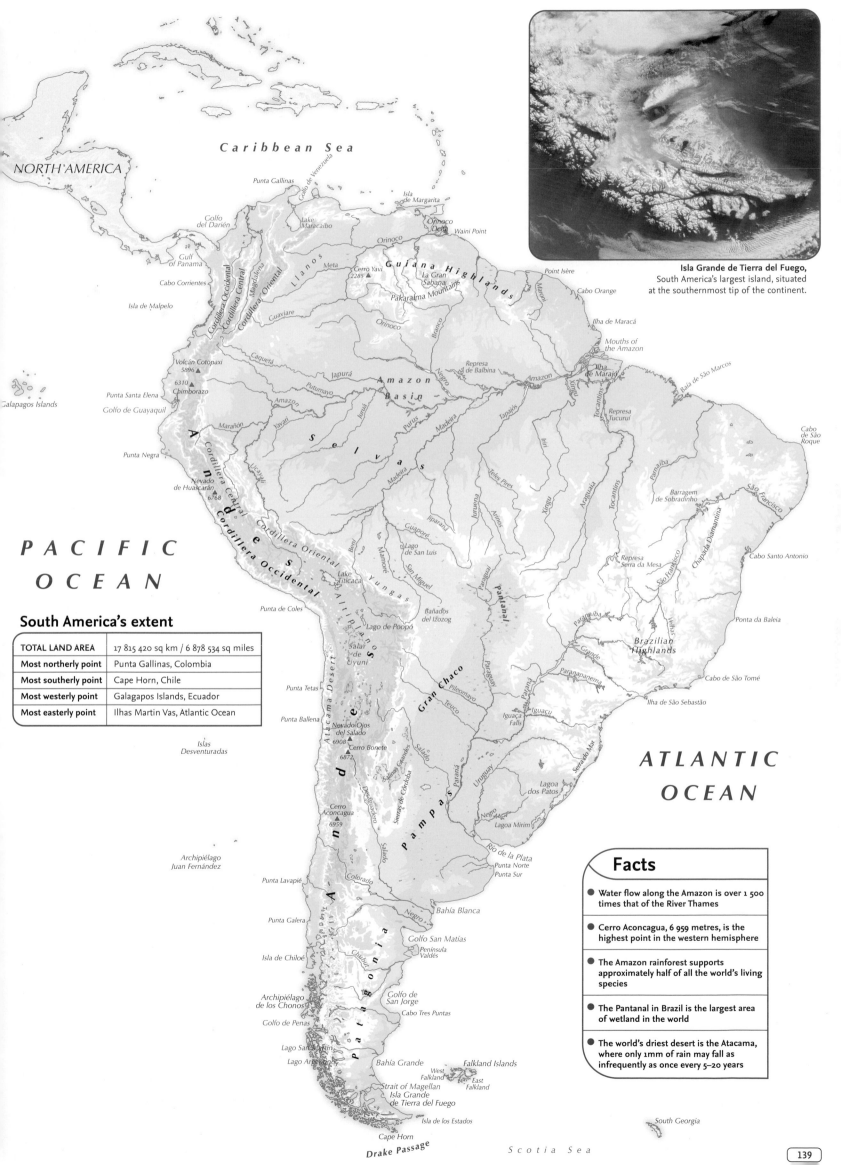

Isla Grande de Tierra del Fuego, South America's largest island, situated at the southernmost tip of the continent.

South America's extent

TOTAL LAND AREA	17 815 420 sq km / 6 878 534 sq miles
Most northerly point	Punta Gallinas, Colombia
Most southerly point	Cape Horn, Chile
Most westerly point	Galapagos Islands, Ecuador
Most easterly point	Ilhas Martin Vas, Atlantic Ocean

Facts

- Water flow along the Amazon is over 1 500 times that of the River Thames
- Cerro Aconcagua, 6 959 metres, is the highest point in the western hemisphere
- The Amazon rainforest supports approximately half of all the world's living species
- The Pantanal in Brazil is the largest area of wetland in the world
- The world's driest desert is the Atacama, where only 1mm of rain may fall as infrequently as once every 5–20 years

South America
Countries

French Guiana, a French Department, is the only remaining territory under overseas control on a continent which has seen a long colonial history. Much of South America was colonized by Spain in the sixteenth century, with Britain, Portugal and the Netherlands each claiming territory in the northeast of the continent. This colonization led to the conquering of ancient civilizations, including the Incas in Peru. Most countries became independent from Spain and Portugal in the early nineteenth century.

The population of the continent reflects its history, being composed primarily of indigenous Indian peoples and mestizos – reflecting the long Hispanic influence. There has been a steady process of urbanization within the continent, with major movements of the population from rural to urban areas. The majority of the population now lives in the major cities and within 300 kilometres of the coast.

Galapagos Islands, an island territory of Ecuador which lies on the equator in the eastern Pacific Ocean over 900 kilometres west of the coast of Ecuador.

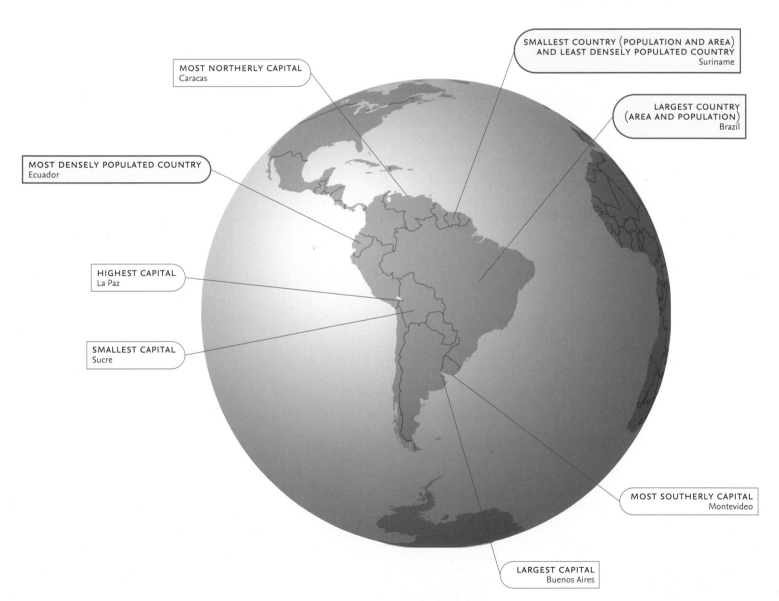

SMALLEST COUNTRY (POPULATION AND AREA) AND LEAST DENSELY POPULATED COUNTRY
Suriname

MOST NORTHERLY CAPITAL
Caracas

LARGEST COUNTRY (AREA AND POPULATION)
Brazil

MOST DENSELY POPULATED COUNTRY
Ecuador

HIGHEST CAPITAL
La Paz

SMALLEST CAPITAL
Sucre

MOST SOUTHERLY CAPITAL
Montevideo

LARGEST CAPITAL
Buenos Aires

South America's countries

Largest country (area)	Brazil	8 514 879 sq km	3 287 613 sq miles
Smallest country (area)	Suriname	163 820 sq km	63 251 sq miles
Largest country (population)	Brazil	186 405 000	
Smallest country (population)	Suriname	449 000	
Most densely populated country	Ecuador	48 per sq km	124 per sq mile
Least densely populated country	Suriname	3 per sq km	7 per sq mile

Internet Links

UK Foreign and Commonwealth Office	www.fco.gov.uk
CIA World Factbook	www.cia.gov/library/publications/the-world-factbook/index.html
Caribbean Community (Caricom)	www.caricom.org
Latin American Network Information Center	lanic.utexas.edu

South America's capitals

Largest capital (population)	Buenos Aires, Argentina	13 349 000
Smallest capital (population)	Sucre, Bolivia	231 000
Most northerly capital	Caracas, Venezuela	10° 28'N
Most southerly capital	Montevideo, Uruguay	34° 52'S
Highest capital	La Paz, Bolivia	3 630 metres 11 909 feet

NORTH AMERICA

Caribbean Sea

VENEZUELA

GUYANA

SURINAME **French Guiana**

COLOMBIA

ECUADOR

PERU

B R A Z I L

BOLIVIA

PARAGUAY

PACIFIC OCEAN

Galapagos Islands (Ecuador)

Islas Desventuradas (Chile)

Archipiélago Juan Fernández (Chile)

CHILE

ARGENTINA

URUGUAY

ATLANTIC OCEAN

Patagonia

Archipiélago de los Chonos

Isla de Chiloé

Isla Grande de Tierra del Fuego

Cape Horn

Falkland Islands (U.K.)

South Georgia (U.K.)

Facts

- South America is often referred to as 'Latin America', reflecting the historic influences of Spain and Portugal

- The largest city in each South American country is the capital, except in Brazil and Ecuador

- South America has only two landlocked countries – Bolivia and Paraguay

- Chile is over 4 000 kilometres long but has an average width of only 177 kilometres

Falkland Islands, an overseas UK territory in the South Atlantic Ocean.

Lambert Azimuthal Equal Area Projection

1:14 000 000

Galapagos Islands (Islas Galápagos) (Ecuador)

1:14 000 000

South America
Northern South America

South America
Southern South America

1:14 000 000

Lambert Azimuthal Equal Area Projection

South America
Southeast Brazil

Between them, the world's oceans and polar regions cover approximately seventy per cent of the Earth's surface. The oceans contain ninety-six per cent of the Earth's water and a vast range of flora and fauna. They are a major influence on the world's climate, particularly through ocean currents. The Arctic and Antarctica are the coldest and most inhospitable places on the Earth. They both have vast amounts of ice which, if global warming continues, could have a major influence on sea level across the globe.

Our understanding of the oceans and polar regions has increased enormously over the last twenty years through the development of new technologies, particularly that of satellite remote sensing, which can generate vast amounts of data relating to, for example, topography (both on land and the seafloor), land cover and sea surface temperature.

Pacific Ocean
World's largest ocean: 166 241 000 sq km
Average depth: 4 200m

Challenger Deep: 10 920 metres
Mariana Trench
Deepest point

PACIFIC

OCEAN

AUSTRALIA

South Pacific Ocean
Average depth: 3 935 metres

The oceans

The world's major oceans are the Pacific, the Atlantic and the Indian Oceans. The Arctic Ocean is generally considered as part of the Atlantic, and the Southern Ocean, which stretches around the whole of Antarctica is usually treated as an extension of each of the three major oceans.

One of the most important factors affecting the earth's climate is the circulation of water within and between the oceans. Differences in temperature and surface winds create ocean currents which move enormous quantities of water around the globe. These currents re-distribute heat which the oceans have absorbed from the sun, and so have a major effect on the world's climate system. El Niño is one climatic phenomenon directly influenced by these ocean processes.

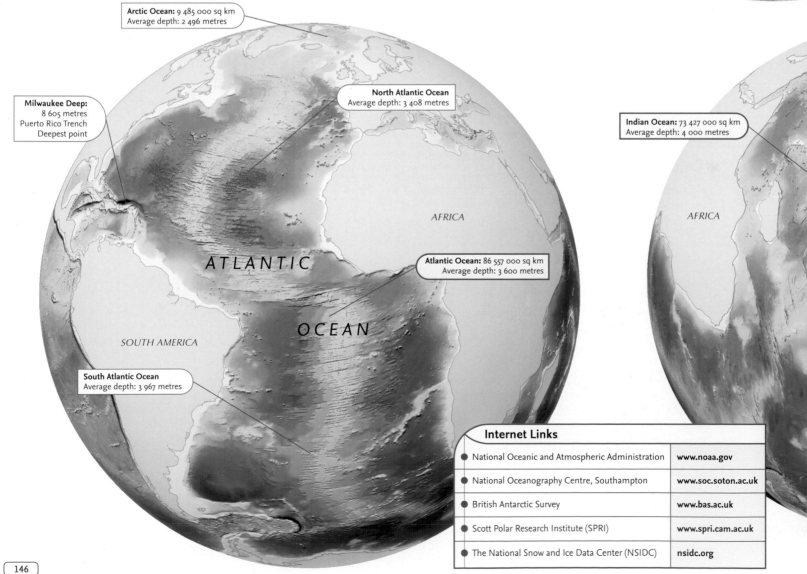

Arctic Ocean: 9 485 000 sq km
Average depth: 2 496 metres

Milwaukee Deep:
8 605 metres
Puerto Rico Trench
Deepest point

North Atlantic Ocean
Average depth: 3 408 metres

Indian Ocean: 73 427 000 sq km
Average depth: 4 000 metres

AFRICA

ATLANTIC

AFRICA

Atlantic Ocean: 86 557 000 sq km
Average depth: 3 600 metres

OCEAN

SOUTH AMERICA

South Atlantic Ocean
Average depth: 3 967 metres

Internet Links

National Oceanic and Atmospheric Administration	**www.noaa.gov**
National Oceanography Centre, Southampton	**www.soc.soton.ac.uk**
British Antarctic Survey	**www.bas.ac.uk**
Scott Polar Research Institute (SPRI)	**www.spri.cam.ac.uk**
The National Snow and Ice Data Center (NSIDC)	**nsidc.org**

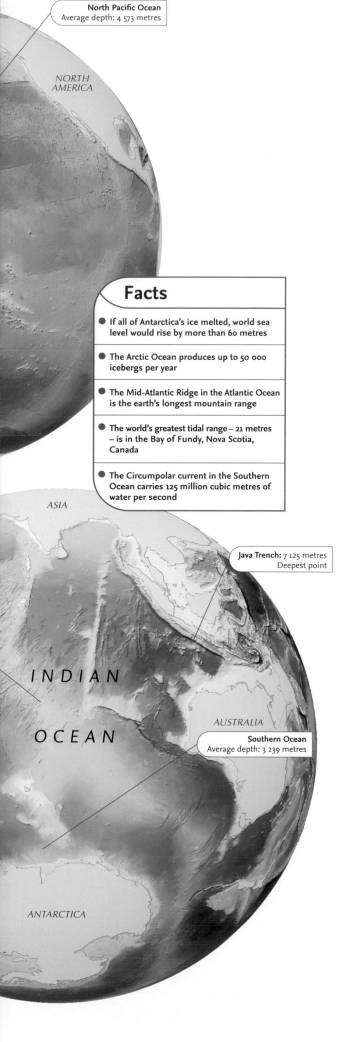

North Pacific Ocean
Average depth: 4 573 metres

*NORTH
AMERICA*

Facts

- If all of Antarctica's ice melted, world sea level would rise by more than 60 metres

- The Arctic Ocean produces up to 50 000 icebergs per year

- The Mid-Atlantic Ridge in the Atlantic Ocean is the earth's longest mountain range

- The world's greatest tidal range – 21 metres – is in the Bay of Fundy, Nova Scotia, Canada

- The Circumpolar current in the Southern Ocean carries 125 million cubic metres of water per second

ASIA

Java Trench: 7 125 metres
Deepest point

INDIAN

OCEAN

AUSTRALIA

Southern Ocean
Average depth: 3 239 metres

ANTARCTICA

Polar regions

Although a harsh climate is common to the two polar regions, there are major differences between the Arctic and Antarctica. The North Pole is surrounded by the Arctic Ocean, much of which is permanently covered by sea ice, while the South Pole lies on the huge land mass of Antarctica. This is covered by a permanent ice cap which reaches a maximum thickness of over four kilometres. Antarctica has no permanent population, but Europe, Asia and North America all stretch into the Arctic region which is populated by numerous ethnic groups. Antarctica is subject to the Antarctic Treaty of 1959 which does not recognize individual land claims and protects the continent in the interests of international scientific cooperation.

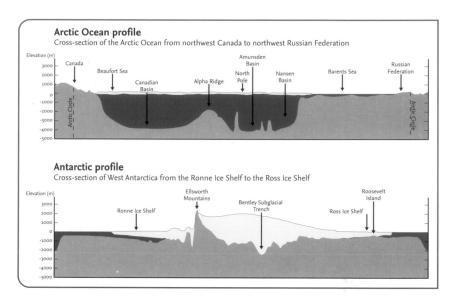

Arctic Ocean profile
Cross-section of the Arctic Ocean from northwest Canada to northwest Russian Federation

Antarctic profile
Cross-section of West Antarctica from the Ronne Ice Shelf to the Ross Ice Shelf

Antarctica's physical features

Highest mountain: Vinson Massif	4 897 m	16 066 ft
Total land area (excluding ice shelves)	12 093 000 sq km	4 669 107 sq miles
Ice shelves	1 559 000 sq km	601 930 sq miles
Exposed rock	49 000 sq km	18 919 sq miles
Lowest bedrock elevation (Bentley Subglacial Trench)	2 496 m below sea level	8 189 ft below sea level
Maximum ice thickness (Astrolabe Subglacial Basin)	4 776 m	15 669 ft
Mean ice thickness (including ice shelves)	1 859 m	6 099 ft
Volume of ice sheet (including ice shelves)	25 400 000 cubic km	6 094 628 cubic miles

The **Antarctic Peninsula** and the **Larsen Ice Shelf** in western Antarctica.

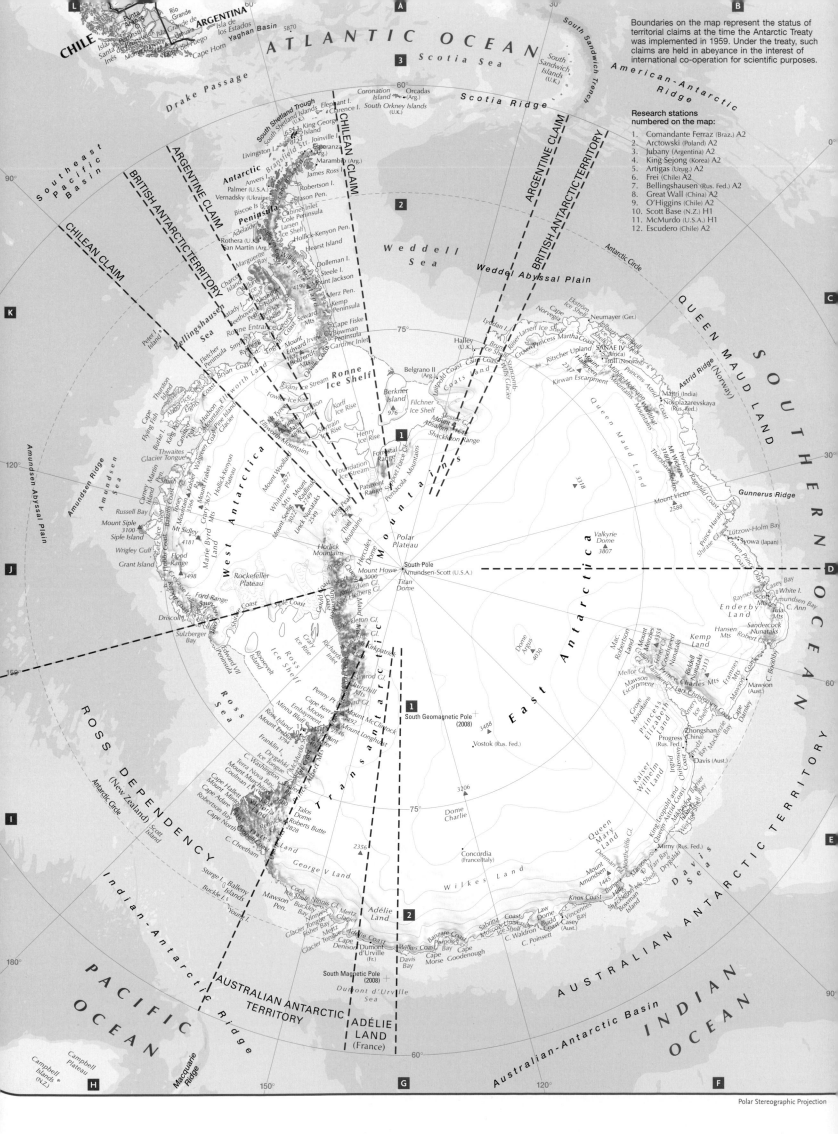

L

Río Grande
CHILE ARGENTINA Isla de
los Estados
Punta Grande de
Arenas Tierra del Fuego
Ushuaia
Cape Horn Yaghan Basin 5870

30

B

ATLANTIC OCEAN
Scotia Sea

South Sandwich Trench

South Sandwich Islands (U.K.)

3

Boundaries on the map represent the status of
territorial claims at the time the Antarctic Treaty
was implemented in 1959. Under the treaty, such
claims are held in abeyance in the interest of
international co-operation for scientific purposes.

Drake Passage

Scotia Ridge

American-Antarctic Ridge

60°

Coronation
Island Orcadas
(Arg.)

South Orkney Islands
(U.K.)

Research stations
numbered on the map:

Southeast Pacific Basin

90°

ARGENTINE CLAIM

BRITISH ANTARCTIC TERRITORY

South Shetland Trough Elephant I.
King George I. Clarence I.
6534 8823
Livingston I.
Joinville I.
Esperanza (Arg.)
Marambio (Arg.)
Antarctic
Anvers I.
Palmer (U.S.A.) Robertson I.
Vernadsky (Ukraine) James Ross I.
Biscoe Is. Cabinet Inlet Larsen
Adelaide I. Cole Peninsula Ice Shelf
Rothera (U.K.) Hollick-Kenyon Pen.
San Martín Hearst Island

ARGENTINE CLAIM

BRITISH ANTARCTIC TERRITORY

2

0°

1. Comandante Ferraz (Braz.) A2
2. Arctowski (Poland) A2
3. Jubany (Argentina) A2
4. King Sejong (Korea) A2
5. Artigas (Urug.) A2
6. Frei (Chile) A2
7. Bellingshausen (Rus. Fed.) A2
8. Great Wall (China) A2
9. O'Higgins (Chile) A2
10. Scott Base (N.Z.) H1
11. McMurdo (U.S.A.) H1
12. Escudero (Chile) A2

Antarctic Circle

QUEEN MAUD LAND

SOUTHERN

CHILEAN CLAIM

K

Peninsula

Weddell Sea

Weddell Abyssal Plain

Ekström Ice Shelf Neumayer (Ger.)

Cape Norvegia

Lyddan I.
Riiser-Larsen Ice Shelf
Halley (U.K.)
SANAE IV (S. Africa)
Troll (Norway)
Maitri (India)

C

Bellingshausen Sea

Marguerite Bay
Dolleman I.
Steele I.
Charcot Mount Jackson
Island 4190

Merz Pen.
Kemp Peninsula
Cape Fiske
Bowman Peninsula
Gardner Inlet

75°

Belgrano II (Arg.)

Berkner Island

Filchner Ice Shelf
976

Ronne Ice Shelf

Coats Land

Wills Glacier

Ritscher Upland Princess Martha Coast
Kirwan Escarpment

Novolazarevskaya (Rus. Fed.)

Astrid Ridge

OCEAN

0°

120°

Peter I Island

Fletcher Peninsula
Cape Flying Fish

Thurston Island

Cape Adams
Abbot Ice Shelf
Eights Coast

Hudson Mountains
Pine Island
Bear Peninsula

Carney Martin Pen.
Island

Russell Bay

Mount Siple
3100
Siple Island

Amundsen Sea

Amundsen Ridge

Amundsen Abyssal Plain

Walgreen Coast
Mt Frakes

Mt Sidley
4181

Wrigley Gulf

Grant Island

Flood Range

3498

Executive Committee Range

Ronne Entrance
Smyley I.
English Coast

Ellsworth Land

Ellsworth Mountains

Evans Ice Stream
Fowler Ice Rise

Thiel Mountains

West Antarctica

Marie Byrd Land

Rockefeller Plateau

Ford Range

Saunders Coast

Edward Irvine
Mts
Behrendt Mts

Korff Ice Rise

Carlson Inlet

Skytrain Ice Rise
Henry Ice Rise

Foundation Ice Stream

Support Force Gl.

Mount Woollard
3677
Whitmore Mount
Mts Seelig
3022
Radliwe
2749
Linck Nunataks
2599

King Peak
4199

Hercules Dome

Horlick Mountains

Mount Howe
3000

Amundsen Gl.
Liv Gl.
Reedy Gl.
Scott Gl.
Leverett Gl.

Siple Coast

Ross Ice Shelf

Shirase Coast

Edward VII Peninsula

Roosevelt Island

Steller
Absalom Hills
Shackleton Range

Patuxent Range
Pensacola Mountains

3318

Queen Maud Land

Wohlthat Mountains
2347 Princess Astrid Coast

Sør Rondane Mountains

3891 Mt Widerøe
Thorshammer

Mount Victor
2588

Mount Jensen
Mühlig-Hofmann Mts

Gunnerus Ridge

Prince Harald Coast
Lützow-Holm Bay

Syowa (Japan)

Princess Ragnhild Coast
Crown Prince Olav Coast

Casey Bay
Rayner White I.
Scott Amundsen Bay
Mts C. Ann

Enderby Land

Transantarctic Mountains

Polar Plateau

South Pole
Amundsen-Scott (U.S.A.)

Titan Dome

Valkyrie Dome
3807

East Antarctica

Dome Argus
4030

Vostok (Rus. Fed.)

Hansen Mts
Sandercock Nunataks

Robert Gl.

Kemp Land

Mawson (Aust.)

C. Blofeldy

60°

D

J

D

150°

Driscoll I.

Sulzberger Bay

Ross Sea

Gray Ice Rise

Richards Inlet

Kirkpatrick

Nimrod Gl.
Churchill Mts
Byrd Gl.
Mount McClintock
2492

Shackleton Gl.

South Geomagnetic Pole (2008)

3488

Mac. Robertson Land
Mount Menzies
3355
Goodspeed Nunataks

Mellor Gl.
Mawson Escarpment
Grove Mountains

Prince Charles Mts
2313
Mawson Coast

Frannes Mts

Mawson (Aust.)

Lars Christensen Coast

60°

E

ROSS DEPENDENCY (New Zealand)

I

Antarctic Circle

Scott Island

Ross Island

Penny Pt.
Cape Kerr
Minna Bluff
Mount Erebus
3794
Franklin I.
Terra Nova Bay
Mount Murchison
Drygalski Ice Tongue
Cape Washington
Coulman I.
Cape Hallett
Cape Adare
Robertson Bay
Cape North

Embayment
Moore
Hillary Coast

McMurdo

Victoria Land

Oates Land

Talos Dome
Roberts Butte
2828

2356

Zhongshan (China)

Progress (Rus. Fed.)

Kaiser Wilhelm II Land

Ingrid Christensen Coast

Princess Elizabeth Land

Ice Shelf

Davis (Aust.)

3206

Dome Charlie

Queen Mary Land

Denman Gl.

75°

Davis Sea

I

E

George V Land

Balleny Islands

Cook Ice Shelf

Buckle I.
Young I.
Sturge I.
Ninnis Gl.
Mertz Gl.
Mawson Pen.

Ninnis Gl.

Glacier Tongue

Adélie Coast
Cape Denison
Dumont d'Urville (Fr.)

Adélie Land

2

Wilkes Land

Concordia (France/Italy)

Mount Amundsen
1445

Bunger Hills
Shackleton Ice Shelf
Bowman Island

Knox Coast

Sabrina Coast
Moscow University Ice Shelf

Budd Coast
Casey (Aust.)
Law Dome

Vincennes Bay
C. Poinsett

Mirny (Rus. Fed.)
Drygalski Is.

Barr Bay
Farr Bay

180°

PACIFIC OCEAN

Macquarie Ridge

H

Campbell Plateau

Campbell Islands (N.Z.)

150°

AUSTRALIAN ANTARCTIC TERRITORY

Indian-Antarctic Ridge

G

South Magnetic Pole (2008)

Dumont d'Urville Sea

ADÉLIE LAND (France)

60°

120°

Banzare Coast
Clarie Coast

Davis Bay

C. Morse
Goodenough
Cape

Wilkes Coast

Australian-Antarctic Basin

AUSTRALIAN ANTARCTIC TERRITORY

INDIAN OCEAN

90°

F

Polar Stereographic Projection

Antarctica

1:26 000 000

0 200 400 600 800 1000 miles

0 200 400 600 800 1000 1200 1400 1600 km

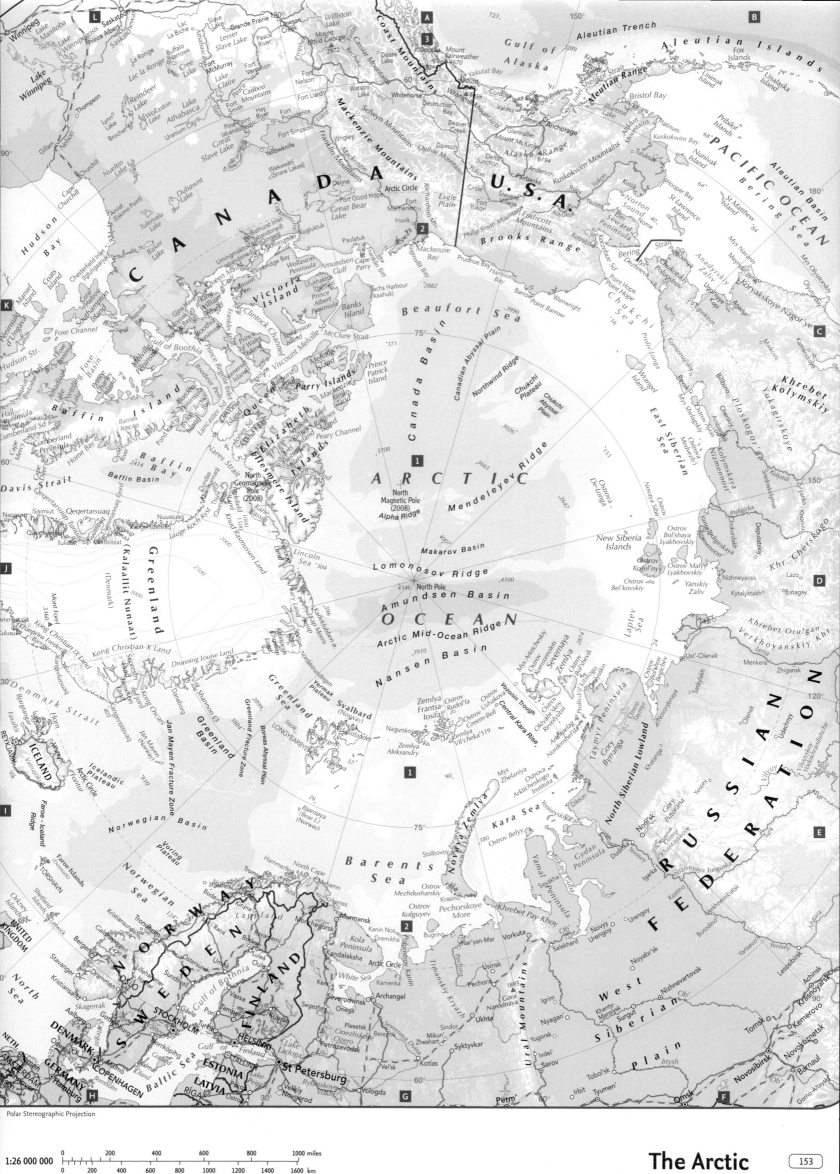

The Arctic

153

Polar Stereographic Projection

1:26 000 000

World
Statistics

See page 160 for explanatory table and sources

	Population							Economy					
	Total population	Population change (%)	% urban	Total fertility	Population by age (%)		2050 projected population	Total Gross National Income (GNI) (US$M)	GNI per capita (US$)	Debt service ratio (% GNI)	Total debt service (US$)	Aid receipts (% GNI)	Military spending (% GDP)
					0–14	60 or over							
WORLD	6 671 226 000	1.2	49.2	2.6	28.2	10.4	9 075 903 000	48 694 077	7 448	...	...	...	2.5
AFGHANISTAN	27 145 000	3.9	24.3	7.1	46.5	4.4	97 324 000	8 092	...	0.1	9 260 000	35.7	9.9
ALBANIA	3 190 000	0.6	45.0	2.1	27.0	12.0	3 458 000	9 295	2 930	1.4	132 034 000	3.5	1.6
ALGERIA	33 858 000	1.5	60.0	2.4	29.6	6.5	49 500 000	101 206	3 030	12.4	13 351 425 000	0.2	2.7
ANDORRA	75 000	0.4	91.1	...	...	...	58 000	...	...	...	...	...	...
ANGOLA	17 024 000	2.8	37.2	6.4	46.5	3.9	43 501 000	32 646	1 970	10.8	4 296 094 000	0.4	5.4
ANTIGUA AND BARBUDA	85 000	1.2	38.4	...	...	...	112 000	929	11 050	...	...	0.4	...
ARGENTINA	39 531 000	1.0	90.6	2.3	26.4	13.9	51 382 000	201 347	5 150	9.1	18 993 819 000	0.1	0.9
ARMENIA	3 002 000	-0.2	64.1	1.4	20.8	14.5	2 506 000	5 788	1 920	2.6	167 008 000	3.3	2.8
AUSTRALIA	20 743 000	1.0	92.7	1.8	19.6	17.3	27 940 000	742 254	35 860	...	...	...	1.8
AUSTRIA	8 361 000	0.4	65.8	1.4	15.5	22.7	8 073 000	329 183	39 750	...	...	...	0.8
AZERBAIJAN	8 467 000	0.8	49.9	1.8	25.8	9.2	9 631 000	15 639	1 840	1.4	241 872 000	1.2	3.3
THE BAHAMAS	331 000	1.2	90.0	2.0	28.3	9.3	466 000	...	...	...	...	...	0.7
BAHRAIN	753 000	1.8	90.2	2.3	27.1	4.5	1 155 000	14 022	19 350	...	...	...	3.0
BANGLADESH	158 665 000	1.7	25.0	2.8	35.5	5.7	242 937 000	70 475	450	1.0	684 513 000	1.9	1.1
BARBADOS	294 000	0.3	52.9	1.5	18.9	13.2	255 000	...	...	...	...	...	...
BELARUS	9 689 000	-0.6	71.6	1.2	15.2	18.6	7 017 000	33 760	3 470	2.0	733 327 000	0.2	1.7
BELGIUM	10 457 000	0.2	97.3	1.7	16.8	22.4	10 302 000	405 419	38 460	...	...	...	1.1
BELIZE	288 000	2.1	48.6	2.9	36.8	5.9	442 000	1 114	3 740	12.3	134 775 000	0.7	...
BENIN	9 033 000	3.0	46.1	5.4	44.2	4.3	22 123 000	4 665	530	1.8	82 763 000	8.0	...
BHUTAN	658 000	1.4	9.1	2.2	38.4	7.0	4 393 000	928	1 430	1.1	10 105 000	10.2	...
BOLIVIA	9 525 000	1.8	64.4	3.5	38.1	6.7	14 908 000	10 293	1 100	4.0	430 341 000	5.4	1.5
BOSNIA-HERZEGOVINA	3 935 000	0.1	45.3	1.2	16.5	19.2	3 170 000	12 689	3 230	4.6	589 095 000	4.2	1.6
BOTSWANA	1 882 000	1.2	52.5	2.9	37.6	5.1	1 658 000	10 358	5 570	0.6	54 861 000	0.7	3.0
BRAZIL	191 791 000	1.3	84.2	2.3	27.9	8.8	253 105 000	892 639	4 710	6.0	62 144 534 000	0.0	1.5
BRUNEI	390 000	2.1	77.6	2.3	29.6	4.7	681 000	10 287	26 930	...	...	...	2.4
BULGARIA	7 639 000	-0.7	70.5	1.3	13.8	22.4	5 065 000	30 669	3 990	8.7	2 743 215 000	...	2.3
BURKINA	14 784 000	2.9	18.6	6.0	47.2	4.2	39 093 000	6 249	440	0.8	51 765 000	14.0	1.4
BURUNDI	8 508 000	3.9	10.6	6.8	45.0	4.2	25 812 000	815	100	4.5	39 523 000	52.8	5.5
CAMBODIA	14 444 000	1.7	19.7	3.2	37.1	5.6	25 972 000	6 990	490	0.4	30 584 000	7.7	1.7
CAMEROON	18 549 000	2.0	52.9	4.3	41.2	5.6	26 891 000	18 060	990	2.9	518 897 000	9.3	1.4
CANADA	32 876 000	0.9	81.1	1.5	17.6	17.9	42 844 000	1 196 626	36 650	...	...	...	1.2
CAPE VERDE	530 000	2.2	57.6	3.4	39.5	5.5	1 002 000	1 105	2 130	2.9	31 361 000	12.6	0.7
CENTRAL AFRICAN REPUBLIC	4 343 000	1.8	43.8	4.6	43.0	6.1	6 747 000	1 499	350	4.7	70 406 000	9.0	1.1
CHAD	10 781 000	2.9	25.8	6.2	47.3	4.7	31 497 000	4 708	450	1.3	67 834 000	5.5	0.9
CHILE	16 635 000	1.0	87.7	1.9	24.9	11.6	20 657 000	111 869	6 810	10.9	13 792 891 000	0.1	3.6
CHINA	1 313 437 000	0.6	40.5	1.7	21.4	10.9	1 402 062 000	2 620 951	2 000	1.0	27 876 906 000	0.1	1.9
COLOMBIA	46 156 000	1.3	77.4	2.2	31.0	7.5	65 679 000	141 982	3 120	7.2	10 639 506 000	0.8	3.5
COMOROS	839 000	2.5	36.3	4.3	42.0	4.3	1 781 000	406	660	0.9	3 616 000	7.6	...
CONGO	3 768 000	2.1	54.4	4.5	47.1	4.5	13 721 000	3 806	1 050	2.7	101 220 000	...	1.1
CONGO, DEM. REPUBLIC OF THE	62 636 000	3.2	32.7	6.7	47.3	4.3	177 271 000	7 742	130	3.9	319 345 000	25.2	0.0
COSTA RICA	4 468 000	1.5	61.7	2.1	28.4	8.3	6 426 000	21 894	4 980	2.8	597 316 000	0.1	...
CÔTE D'IVOIRE	19 262 000	1.8	45.8	4.5	41.9	5.3	33 959 000	16 578	880	0.8	126 329 000	1.6	1.6
CROATIA	4 555 000	-0.1	59.9	1.4	15.5	22.1	3 686 000	41 348	9 310	18.5	7 680 306 000	0.5	1.6
CUBA	11 268 000	0.0	76.0	1.5	19.1	15.3	9 749 000	...	...	...	...	...	...
CYPRUS	855 000	1.1	69.5	1.6	19.9	16.8	1 174 000	17 948	23 270	...	...	...	1.4
CZECH REPUBLIC	10 186 000	0.0	74.5	1.2	14.6	20.0	8 452 000	131 404	12 790	...	...	...	1.7
DENMARK	5 442 000	0.2	85.5	1.8	18.8	21.1	5 851 000	283 316	52 110	...	...	...	1.4
DJIBOUTI	833 000	1.7	84.6	4.0	41.5	4.7	1 547 000	864	1 060	2.6	22 564 000	14.0	...
DOMINICA	67 000	-0.3	72.7	...	...	...	98 000	300	4 160	6.9	21 255 000	7.0	...
DOMINICAN REPUBLIC	9 760 000	1.5	60.1	2.8	32.7	6.2	12 668 000	27 954	2 910	4.5	1 345 913 000	0.2	0.5
EAST TIMOR	1 155 000	3.5	7.8	6.5	41.1	5.0	3 265 000	865	840	...	...	24.7	...
ECUADOR	13 341 000	1.1	62.8	2.6	32.4	8.3	19 214 000	38 481	2 910	10.5	4 157 073 000	0.5	2.3
EGYPT	75 498 000	1.8	42.3	2.9	33.6	7.1	125 916 000	100 912	1 360	2.1	2 201 406 000	0.8	2.7
EL SALVADOR	6 857 000	1.4	60.1	2.7	34.0	7.6	10 823 000	18 096	2 680	6.2	1 133 017 000	0.9	0.6
EQUATORIAL GUINEA	507 000	2.4	50.0	5.4	44.4	6.0	1 146 000	4 216	8 510	0.1	4 307 000	0.5	...
ERITREA	4 851 000	3.2	20.8	5.1	44.8	4.0	11 229 000	888	190	1.2	12 682 000	12.0	24.1
ESTONIA	1 335 000	-0.4	69.6	1.5	15.2	21.6	1 119 000	15 302	11 400	...	...	...	1.4
ETHIOPIA	83 099 000	2.5	16.2	5.3	44.5	4.7	170 190 000	12 874	170	1.2	163 799 000	14.7	2.6
FIJI	839 000	0.6	53.2	2.8	31.7	6.4	934 000	3 098	3 720	0.5	16 360 000	2.0	1.2
FINLAND	5 277 000	0.3	60.9	1.8	17.3	21.3	5 329 000	217 803	41 360	...	...	...	1.4
FRANCE	61 647 000	0.5	76.7	1.9	18.2	21.1	63 116 000	2 306 714	36 560	...	...	...	2.4
GABON	1 331 000	1.5	85.2	3.1	40.0	6.2	2 279 000	7 032	5 360	1.1	84 901 000	0.4	1.2
THE GAMBIA	1 709 000	2.6	26.1	4.7	40.1	6.0	3 106 000	488	290	6.6	33 137 000	14.8	0.5
GEORGIA	4 395 000	-0.8	51.5	1.4	18.9	17.9	2 985 000	7 008	1 580	3.6	268 375 000	4.9	3.1

	Social Indicators				Environment				Communications				
Child mortality rate	Life expectancy	Literacy rate (%)	Access to safe water (%)	Doctors per 100 000 people	Forest area (%)	Annual change in forest area (%)	Protected land area (%)	CO$_2$ emissions (metric tonnes per capita)	Main telephone lines per 100 people	Cellular phone subscribers per 100 people	Internet users per 10 000 people	International dialling code	Time zone
72	67.2	87.6	83	152	30.3	0.2	10.8	4.3	19.7	42.0	1 853	...	...
257	43.8	34.3	39	19	1.3	-3.1	0.3	...	0.3	8.1	172	93	+4.5
17	76.4	99.4	96	139	29.0	0.6	0.7	1.2	11.3	60.4	1 498	355	+1
38	72.3	90.1	85	85	1.0	1.2	5.1	6.0	8.5	63.0	738	213	+1
3	...	...	100	259	35.6	0.0	9.7	...	51.3	96.9	3 257	376	+1
260	42.7	72.2	53	8	47.4	-0.2	10.0	0.5	0.6	14.3	60	244	+1
11	...	...	91	17	21.4	0.0	0.0	5.1	45.5	133.6	6 424	1 268	-4
16	75.3	98.9	96	301	12.1	-0.4	6.3	3.7	24.2	80.5	2 091	54	-3
24	72.0	99.8	92	353	10.0	-1.5	8.1	1.2	19.7	10.5	575	374	+4
6	81.2	...	100	249	21.3	-0.1	9.5	16.2	48.8	97.0	4 713	61	+8 to +10.5
5	79.8	...	100	324	46.7	0.1	28.3	8.5	43.4	112.8	5 131	43	+1
88	67.5	99.9	77	354	11.3	0.0	2.4	3.8	14.0	39.2	979	994	+4
14	73.5	...	97	106	51.5	0.0	0.1	6.3	40.2	77.3	3 188	1 242	-5
10	75.6	97.0	...	160	0.6	3.8	3.4	23.8	26.3	122.9	2 844	973	+3
69	64.1	63.6	74	23	6.7	-0.3	0.7	0.2	0.8	13.3	31	880	+6
12	77.3	...	100	121	4.0	0.0	0.1	4.4	50.1	87.8	5 948	1 246	-4
13	69.0	99.8	100	450	38.0	0.1	5.2	6.6	34.7	61.4	5 647	375	+2
4	79.4	...	...	418	22.0	0.0	3.2	9.7	45.2	92.6	5 260	32	+1
16	76.1	...	91	105	72.5	0.0	36.0	2.8	12.3	44.1	1 236	501	-6
148	56.7	45.3	67	6	21.3	-2.5	22.0	0.3	0.9	12.1	144	229	+1
70	65.6	...	62	5	68.0	0.3	31.5	0.7	3.8	9.8	357	975	+6
61	65.6	97.3	85	73	54.2	-0.5	20.0	0.8	7.1	30.8	620	591	-4
15	74.9	99.8	97	134	43.1	0.0	0.5	4.0	25.3	48.3	2 428	387	+1
124	50.7	94.0	95	29	21.1	-1.0	30.1	2.4	7.8	46.8	455	267	+2
20	72.4	96.8	90	206	57.2	-0.6	17.8	1.8	20.5	52.9	2 255	55	-2 to -5
9	77.1	98.9	...	101	52.8	-0.7	53.3	24.1	21.0	78.9	4 169	673	+8
14	73.0	98.2	99	338	32.8	1.4	10.0	5.5	31.3	107.6	2 166	359	+2
204	52.3	33.0	61	4	29.0	-0.3	14.0	0.1	0.7	7.5	59	226	GMT
181	49.6	73.3	79	5	5.9	-5.2	5.7	0.0	0.4	2.0	77	257	+2
82	59.7	83.4	41	16	59.2	-2.0	22.8	0.0	0.2	7.9	31	855	+7
149	50.4	...	66	7	45.6	-1.0	8.6	0.2	0.8	18.9	223	237	+1
6	80.7	...	100	209	33.6	0.0	4.8	20.0	64.5	57.6	6 789	1	-3.5 to -8
34	71.7	96.3	80	17	20.7	0.4	...	0.6	13.8	21.0	636	238	-1
175	44.7	58.5	75	4	36.5	-0.1	15.3	0.1	0.3	2.5	32	236	+1
209	50.7	37.6	42	3	9.5	-0.7	9.0	0.0	0.1	4.7	60	235	+1
9	78.6	99.0	95	109	21.5	0.4	3.9	3.9	20.2	75.6	2 524	56	-4
24	73.0	98.9	77	164	21.2	2.2	15.3	3.9	27.8	34.8	1 035	86	+8
21	72.9	98.0	93	135	58.5	-0.1	24.7	1.2	17.0	64.3	1 449	57	-5
68	65.2	...	86	7	2.9	-7.4	...	0.1	2.3	4.5	256	269	+3
126	55.3	97.4	58	25	65.8	-0.1	14.1	1.0	0.4	12.3	170	242	+1
205	46.5	70.4	46	7	58.9	-0.2	8.4	0.0	0.0	7.4	30	243	+1 to +2
12	78.8	97.6	97	172	46.8	0.1	21.1	1.5	30.7	32.8	2 761	506	-6
127	48.3	60.7	84	9	32.7	0.1	12.1	0.3	1.4	22.0	163	225	GMT
6	75.7	99.6	100	237	38.2	0.1	5.9	5.3	40.1	96.5	3 698	385	+1
7	78.3	100.0	91	591	24.7	2.2	1.4	2.3	8.6	1.4	213	53	-5
4	79.0	99.8	100	298	18.9	0.2	9.0	9.1	48.3	102.8	4 222	357	+2
4	76.5	...	100	343	34.3	0.1	15.9	11.5	28.3	116.4	3 469	420	+1
5	78.3	...	100	366	11.8	0.6	6.0	9.8	56.9	107.0	5 823	45	+1
130	54.8	...	73	13	0.2	0.0	...	0.5	1.6	6.4	136	253	+3
15	...	...	97	49	61.3	-0.6	46.8	1.5	29.4	58.7	3 722	1 767	-4
29	72.2	94.2	95	188	28.4	0.0	25.0	2.1	9.9	51.1	2 217	1 809	-4
55	60.8	...	58	...	53.7	-1.3	6.1	0.2	0.2	4.9	12	670	+9
24	75.0	96.4	94	148	39.2	-1.7	24.6	2.3	13.1	63.2	1 154	593	-5
35	71.3	84.9	98	212	0.1	2.6	5.3	2.2	14.3	23.9	795	20	+2
25	71.9	88.5	84	127	14.4	-1.7	1.0	0.9	14.8	55.0	1 000	503	-6
206	51.6	94.9	43	25	58.2	-0.9	17.1	11.5	2.0	19.3	155	240	+1
74	58.0	...	60	3	15.4	-0.3	4.2	0.2	0.8	1.4	219	291	+3
7	71.4	99.8	100	316	53.9	0.4	43.9	14.0	34.1	125.2	5 736	372	+2
123	52.9	49.9	22	3	11.9	-1.1	16.4	0.1	0.9	1.1	21	251	+3
18	68.8	...	47	34	54.7	0.0	0.9	1.3	13.3	15.9	936	679	+12
4	79.3	...	100	311	73.9	...	8.9	12.6	36.3	107.8	5 560	358	+2
4	80.7	...	100	329	28.3	0.3	10.2	6.2	55.8	85.1	4 957	33	+1
91	56.7	96.0	88	29	84.5	...	13.3	1.1	2.6	54.4	576	241	+1
113	59.4	...	82	4	41.7	0.4	...	0.2	3.0	26.0	529	220	GMT
32	71.0	...	82	391	39.7	...	3.9	0.9	12.5	38.4	749	995	+4

	Population						Economy					
	Total population	Population change (%)	% urban	Total fertility	Population by age (%) 0 – 14	Population by age (%) 60 or over	2050 projected population	Total Gross National Income (GNI) (US$M)	GNI per capita (US$)	Debt service ratio (% GNI)	Total debt service (US$)	Aid receipts (% GNI)	Military spending (% GDP)
GERMANY	82 599 000	-0.1	88.5	1.4	14.3	25.1	78 765 000	3 032 617	36 810	...	...	...	1.3
GHANA	23 478 000	2.0	46.3	3.8	39.0	5.7	40 573 000	11 778	510	2.0	261 043 000	9.2	0.7
GREECE	11 147 000	0.2	61.4	1.3	14.3	23.0	10 742 000	305 308	27 390	...	...	...	3.2
GRENADA	106 000	0.0	42.2	2.3	...	...	157 000	495	4 650	2.2	15 321 000	5.6	...
GUATEMALA	13 354 000	2.5	47.2	4.2	43.2	6.1	25 612 000	33 725	2 590	1.6	550 958 000	1.4	0.4
GUINEA	9 370 000	2.2	36.5	5.4	43.7	5.6	22 987 000	3 713	400	5.0	164 764 000	5.0	2.0
GUINEA-BISSAU	1 695 000	3.0	35.6	7.1	47.5	4.7	5 312 000	307	190	11.5	33 831 000	27.9	4.0
GUYANA	738 000	-0.2	38.5	2.3	29.3	7.4	488 000	849	1 150	3.8	32 940 000	20.1	...
HAITI	9 598 000	1.6	38.8	3.5	37.5	6.0	12 996 000	4 044	430	1.3	56 732 000	13.4	...
HONDURAS	7 106 000	2.0	46.4	3.3	39.2	5.6	12 776 000	8 844	1 270	3.6	325 235 000	6.6	0.6
HUNGARY	10 030 000	-0.3	65.9	1.3	15.7	20.8	8 262 000	109 461	10 870	29.4	30 827 896 000	...	1.2
ICELAND	301 000	0.8	93.0	2.1	22.0	15.8	370 000	15 078	49 960	...	...	...	0.0
INDIA	1 169 016 000	1.5	28.7	2.8	32.1	7.9	1 592 704 000	909 138	820	2.0	17 878 568 000	0.2	2.7
INDONESIA	231 627 000	1.2	47.9	2.2	28.3	8.4	284 640 000	315 845	1 420	5.9	20 434 246 000	0.4	1.2
IRAN	71 208 000	1.4	68.1	2.0	28.7	6.4	101 944 000	205 040	2 930	1.2	2 555 530 000	0.1	4.8
IRAQ	28 993 000	1.8	66.8	4.3	41.0	4.5	63 693 000	...	...	...	...	...	...
IRELAND	4 301 000	1.8	60.4	2.0	20.2	15.1	5 762 000	191 315	44 830	...	...	...	0.5
ISRAEL	6 928 000	1.7	91.7	2.8	27.8	13.3	10 403 000	142 199	20 170	...	...	...	8.4
ITALY	58 877 000	0.1	67.5	1.4	14.0	25.6	50 912 000	1 882 544	31 990	...	...	...	1.7
JAMAICA	2 714 000	0.5	52.2	2.4	31.2	10.2	2 586 000	9 504	3 560	8.8	824 547 000	0.4	0.6
JAPAN	127 967 000	0.0	65.7	1.3	14.0	26.3	112 198 000	4 934 676	38 630	...	...	...	0.9
JORDAN	5 924 000	3.0	79.3	3.1	37.2	5.1	10 225 000	14 653	2 650	4.7	688 206 000	3.9	4.9
KAZAKHSTAN	15 422 000	0.7	55.9	2.3	23.1	11.3	13 086 000	59 175	3 870	20.3	14 531 967 000	0.3	0.9
KENYA	37 538 000	2.7	41.6	5.0	42.8	4.1	83 073 000	21 335	580	1.9	432 974 000	4.5	1.6
KIRIBATI	95 000	1.6	50.2	...	...	...	177 000	124	1 240	...	...	-37.6	...
KOSOVO*	2 069 989	...	...	...	...	...	...	...	...	...	...	...	...
KUWAIT	2 851 000	2.4	96.4	2.2	24.3	3.1	5 279 000	77 660	30 630	...	...	...	4.8
KYRGYZSTAN	5 317 000	1.1	33.7	2.5	31.5	7.6	6 664 000	2 609	500	3.5	96 608 000	11.8	3.1
LAOS	5 859 000	1.7	21.6	3.2	40.9	5.3	11 586 000	2 890	500	5.6	169 326 000	12.1	...
LATVIA	2 277 000	-0.5	65.9	1.3	14.7	22.5	1 678 000	18 525	8 100	16.9	3 279 260 000	...	1.6
LEBANON	4 099 000	1.1	88.0	2.2	28.6	10.3	4 702 000	22 640	5 580	19.8	4 433 178 000	3.2	4.1
LESOTHO	2 008 000	0.6	18.2	3.4	38.6	7.5	1 601 000	1 957	980	2.5	47 040 000	4.0	2.4
LIBERIA	3 750 000	4.5	47.9	6.8	47.1	3.6	10 653 000	469	130	0.2	809 000	54.4	...
LIBYA	6 160 000	2.0	86.9	2.7	30.1	6.5	9 553 000	44 011	7 290	...	...	0.1	1.5
LIECHTENSTEIN	35 000	0.9	21.8	...	...	...	44 000	...	...	...	...	...	...
LITHUANIA	3 390 000	-0.5	66.6	1.3	16.7	20.7	2 565 000	26 917	7 930	15.3	4 215 870 000	...	1.2
LUXEMBOURG	467 000	1.1	92.4	1.7	18.9	18.3	721 000	32 904	71 240	...	...	...	0.8
MACEDONIA (F.Y.R.O.M.)	2 038 000	0.1	59.7	1.4	19.6	15.5	1 884 000	6 260	3 070	8.4	522 292 000	3.2	2.0
MADAGASCAR	19 683 000	2.7	27.0	4.8	44.0	4.8	43 508 000	5 343	280	1.2	67 571 000	13.9	1.0
MALAWI	13 925 000	2.6	17.2	5.6	47.3	4.7	29 452 000	3 143	230	2.9	90 044 000	30.5	0.5
MALAYSIA	26 572 000	1.7	65.1	2.6	32.4	7.0	38 924 000	146 754	5 620	5.2	7 630 086 000	0.2	2.0
MALDIVES	306 000	1.8	29.7	2.6	40.7	5.1	682 000	903	3 010	3.9	34 588 000	4.4	...
MALI	12 337 000	3.0	33.7	6.5	48.2	4.2	41 976 000	5 546	460	1.5	80 175 000	13.4	2.2
MALTA	407 000	0.4	92.1	1.4	17.6	18.8	428 000	6 216	15 310	...	...	...	0.6
MARSHALL ISLANDS	59 000	2.2	66.7	...	...	...	150 000	195	2 980	...	...	28.5	...
MAURITANIA	3 124 000	2.5	64.3	4.4	43.0	5.3	7 497 000	2 325	760	3.5	97 426 000	6.8	2.5
MAURITIUS	1 262 000	0.8	43.8	1.9	24.6	9.6	1 465 000	6 812	5 430	4.8	308 955 000	0.3	0.2
MEXICO	106 535 000	1.1	76.0	2.2	31.0	7.8	139 015 000	815 741	7 830	6.8	56 068 050 000	0.0	0.4
MICRONESIA, FED. STATES OF	111 000	0.5	30.0	3.7	39.0	4.9	99 000	264	2 390	...	...	41.4	...
MOLDOVA	3 794 000	-0.9	46.3	1.4	18.3	13.7	3 312 000	3 650	1 080	8.9	334 842 000	6.0	0.3
MONACO	33 000	0.3	100.0	...	...	...	55 000	...	...	...	...	...	...
MONGOLIA	2 629 000	1.0	57.0	1.9	30.5	5.7	3 625 000	2 576	1 000	1.6	48 462 000	7.8	1.3
MONTENEGRO*	598 000	-0.3	...	1.8	...	...	...	2 481	4 130	0.5	13 260 000	4.2	...
MOROCCO	31 224 000	1.2	58.8	2.4	31.1	6.8	46 397 000	65 793	2 160	5.3	3 404 801 000	1.8	3.7
MOZAMBIQUE	21 397 000	2.0	38.0	5.1	44.0	5.2	37 604 000	6 453	310	0.9	55 018 000	23.3	0.0
MYANMAR	48 798 000	0.9	30.6	2.1	29.5	7.5	63 657 000	...	...	...	86 428 000	...	...
NAMIBIA	2 074 000	1.3	33.5	3.2	41.5	5.3	3 060 000	6 573	3 210	...	...	2.3	2.9
NAURU	10 000	0.3	100.0	...	...	...	18 000	...	...	...	...	...	...
NEPAL	28 196 000	2.0	15.8	3.3	39.0	5.8	51 172 000	8 790	320	1.6	139 842 000	6.3	1.9
NETHERLANDS	16 419 000	0.2	66.8	1.7	18.2	19.2	17 139 000	703 484	43 050	...	...	...	1.5
NEW ZEALAND	4 179 000	0.9	86.0	2.0	21.3	16.7	4 790 000	111 958	26 750	...	...	...	1.0
NICARAGUA	5 603 000	1.3	58.1	2.8	38.9	4.9	9 371 000	5 163	930	2.4	122 997 000	13.9	0.7
NIGER	14 226 000	3.5	23.3	7.2	49.0	3.3	50 156 000	3 665	270	5.0	181 178 000	11.0	1.1
NIGERIA	148 093 000	2.3	48.3	5.3	44.3	4.8	258 108 000	90 025	620	6.8	6 805 053 000	11.1	0.7
NORTH KOREA	23 790 000	0.3	61.7	1.9	25.0	11.2	24 192 000	...	...	...	...	...	...

* See Serbia for figures prior to formation of independent states

	Social Indicators					Environment				Communications			
Child mortality rate	Life expectancy	Literacy rate (%)	Access to safe water (%)	Doctors per 100 000 people	Forest area (%)	Annual change in forest area (%)	Protected land area (%)	CO_2 emissions (metric tonnes per capita)	Main telephone lines per 100 people	Cellular phone subscribers per 100 people	Internet users per 10 000 people	International dialling code	Time zone
4	79.4	...	100	362	31.7	0.0	21.3	9.8	65.9	103.6	4 667	49	+1
120	60.0	70.7	75	9	24.2	-2.0	15.1	0.3	1.6	23.1	270	233	GMT
4	79.5	98.9	...	440	29.1	0.8	3.2	8.7	55.4	98.6	1 838	30	+2
20	68.7	...	95	50	12.2	0.0	3.5	2.0	26.7	44.6	1 864	1 473	-4
41	70.3	82.2	95	90	36.3	-1.3	32.2	1.0	10.5	55.6	1 022	502	-6
161	56.0	46.6	50	9	27.4	-0.5	6.1	0.2	0.3	2.4	52	224	GMT
200	46.4	...	59	17	73.7	-0.5	9.1	0.2	0.4	9.2	226	245	GMT
62	66.8	...	83	48	76.7	0.0	2.3	2.0	14.7	37.5	2 130	592	-4
80	60.9	...	54	25	3.8	-0.7	0.3	0.2	1.7	13.9	751	509	-5
27	70.2	88.9	87	83	41.5	-3.1	19.4	1.1	9.7	30.4	467	504	-6
7	73.3	...	99	316	21.5	0.7	5.7	5.7	33.4	99.0	3 475	36	+1
3	81.8	...	100	347	0.5	3.9	3.9	7.6	63.5	108.7	6 530	354	GMT
76	64.7	76.4	86	51	22.8	...	4.8	1.2	3.6	14.8	1 072	91	+5.5
34	70.7	98.7	77	16	48.8	-2.0	11.0	1.7	6.6	28.3	469	62	+7 to +9
34	71.0	97.4	94	105	6.8	0.0	6.2	6.4	31.2	21.8	2 554	98	+3.5
46	59.5	84.8	81	54	1.9	0.1	...	...	4.0	15.5	16	964	+3
5	78.9	...	...	237	9.7	1.9	1.2	10.4	49.9	112.6	3 423	353	GMT
5	80.7	99.8	100	391	8.3	0.8	14.9	10.5	43.9	122.7	2 774	972	+2
4	80.5	99.8	...	606	33.9	1.1	6.4	7.7	46.3	135.1	5 291	39	+1
31	72.6	...	93	85	31.3	-0.1	14.8	4.0	12.9	93.7	2 942	1 876	-5
4	82.6	...	100	201	68.2	...	9.3	9.8	43.0	79.3	6 827	81	+9
25	72.5	99.0	97	205	0.9	0.0	10.7	3.1	10.5	74.4	1 365	962	+2
29	67.0	99.8	86	330	1.2	-0.2	2.7	13.3	19.8	52.9	842	7	+5 to +6
121	54.1	80.3	61	13	6.2	-0.3	11.8	0.3	0.8	20.9	789	254	+3
64	...	...	65	30	3.0	0.0	...	0.3	5.1	0.7	215	686	+12 to +14
...	...	...	...	...	...	...	...	...	...	...	...	381	+1
11	77.6	99.7	...	153	0.3	2.7	0.0	40.4	18.7	91.5	2 953	965	+3
41	65.9	99.7	77	268	4.5	0.3	3.1	1.1	8.6	23.7	560	996	+6
75	64.4	78.5	51	59	69.9	-0.5	16.3	0.2	1.5	16.7	116	856	+7
9	72.7	99.8	99	291	47.4	0.4	16.1	3.1	28.6	95.1	4 665	371	+2
30	72.0	...	100	325	13.3	0.8	0.4	4.1	18.9	30.6	2 628	961	+2
132	42.6	...	79	5	0.3	2.7	0.2	...	3.0	20.0	287	266	+2
235	45.7	67.4	61	2	32.7	-1.8	15.9	0.1	0.2	4.9	...	231	GMT
18	74.0	98.0	...	129	0.1	0.0	0.1	10.3	8.1	65.8	436	218	+2
3	...	...	...	...	43.1	0.0	57.4	...	57.2	81.8	6 398	423	+1
8	73.0	99.7	...	403	33.5	0.8	5.5	3.9	23.2	138.1	3 169	370	+2
4	78.7	...	100	255	33.5	0.0	16.7	24.9	52.4	116.8	7 201	352	+1
17	74.2	98.7	...	219	35.8	0.0	7.2	5.1	24.1	69.6	1 315	389	+1
115	59.4	70.2	50	9	22.1	-0.3	2.6	0.2	0.7	5.5	58	261	+3
120	48.3	76.0	73	1	36.2	-0.9	15.7	0.1	0.8	3.3	45	265	+2
12	74.2	97.2	99	70	63.6	-0.7	18.2	7.0	16.8	75.5	5 423	60	+8
30	68.5	98.2	83	78	3.0	0.0	...	2.5	10.9	87.9	664	960	+5
217	54.5	24.2	50	4	10.3	-0.8	2.1	0.1	0.6	10.9	64	223	GMT
6	79.4	96.0	100	293	1.1	0.0	21.4	6.1	50.1	86.0	3 173	356	+1
56	...	...	87	47	...	0.0	...	...	8.3	1.1	...	692	+12
125	64.2	61.3	53	14	0.3	-3.4	...	0.9	1.1	33.6	95	222	GMT
14	72.8	94.5	100	85	18.2	-0.5	4.8	2.6	28.5	61.5	2 548	230	+4
35	76.2	97.6	97	171	33.7	-0.4	5.2	4.3	18.3	52.6	1 898	52	-6 to -8
41	68.5	...	94	60	90.6	0.0	32.7	...	11.2	12.7	1 439	691	+10 to +11
19	68.9	99.7	92	269	10.0	0.2	1.4	2.0	24.3	32.4	1 735	373	+2
4	...	...	100	586	0.0	0.0	...	...	96.8	51.6	5 634	377	+1
43	66.8	97.7	62	267	6.5	-0.8	14.0	3.4	5.9	28.9	1 157	976	+8
10	74.5	...	...	...	...	...	...	...	58.9	107.3	4 434	382	+1
37	71.2	70.5	81	48	9.8	0.2	1.2	1.4	4.1	52.1	1 985	212	GMT
138	42.1	47.0	43	2	24.6	-0.3	5.7	0.1	0.3	11.6	90	258	+2
104	62.1	94.5	78	30	49.0	-1.4	5.4	0.2	0.9	0.4	18	95	+6.5
61	52.9	92.3	87	30	9.3	-0.9	5.2	1.2	6.8	24.4	397	264	+1
30	...	...	...	...	0.0	0.0	...	...	...	...	...	674	+12
59	63.8	70.1	90	5	25.4	-1.4	15.4	0.1	2.2	4.2	114	977	+5.75
5	79.8	...	100	329	10.8	0.3	12.4	8.7	46.6	106.9	10 998	31	+1
6	80.2	...	...	223	31.0	0.2	24.2	7.7	44.1	94.0	7 877	64	+12
36	72.9	86.2	79	164	42.7	-1.3	16.4	0.7	4.4	32.7	277	505	-6
253	56.9	36.5	46	3	1.0	-1.0	7.1	0.1	0.2	3.4	28	227	+1
191	46.9	84.2	48	27	12.2	-3.3	6.2	0.8	1.3	24.1	595	234	+1
55	67.3	...	100	297	51.4	-1.9	2.6	3.4	4.4	...	...	850	+9

World
Statistics

See page 160 for explanatory table and sources

	Population							Economy					
	Total population	Population change (%)	% urban	Total fertility	Population by age (%) 0 – 14	Population by age (%) 60 or over	2050 projected population	Total Gross National Income (GNI) (US$M)	GNI per capita (US$)	Debt service ratio (% GNI)	Total debt service (US$)	Aid receipts (% GNI)	Military spending (% GDP)
NORWAY	4 698 000	0.6	80.5	1.9	19.6	20.0	5 435 000	318 919	68 440	...	...	...	1.5
OMAN	2 595 000	2.0	78.6	3.0	34.5	4.2	4 958 000	27 887	11 120	5.1	310 065 000	...	11.8
PAKISTAN	163 902 000	1.8	34.8	3.5	38.3	5.8	304 700 000	126 711	800	1.8	2 282 421 000	1.7	3.8
PALAU	20 000	0.4	68.2	...	...	...	21 000	161	7 990	...	...	23.5	...
PANAMA	3 343 000	1.7	57.8	2.6	30.4	8.8	5 093 000	16 442	5 000	21.5	3 458 784 000	0.2	...
PAPUA NEW GUINEA	6 331 000	2.0	13.2	3.8	40.3	3.9	10 619 000	4 603	740	5.8	293 913 000	5.5	0.5
PARAGUAY	6 127 000	1.8	58.5	3.1	37.6	5.6	12 095 000	8 461	1 410	4.5	420 751 000	0.6	0.8
PERU	27 903 000	1.2	74.6	2.5	32.2	7.8	42 552 000	82 201	2 980	4.4	3 745 566 000	0.6	1.2
PHILIPPINES	87 960 000	1.9	62.6	3.2	35.1	6.1	127 068 000	120 190	1 390	10.7	13 680 640 000	0.4	0.9
POLAND	38 082 000	-0.2	62.0	1.2	16.3	16.8	31 916 000	312 994	8 210	11.1	36 044 403 000	...	2.0
PORTUGAL	10 623 000	0.4	55.6	1.5	15.9	22.3	10 723 000	189 017	17 850	...	...	...	2.1
QATAR	841 000	2.1	92.3	2.7	21.7	2.6	1 330 000	...	...	...	...	...	...
ROMANIA	21 438 000	-0.5	54.7	1.3	15.4	19.3	16 757 000	104 382	4 830	7.3	8 678 183 000	...	1.9
RUSSIAN FEDERATION	142 499 000	-0.5	73.3	1.3	15.3	17.1	111 752 000	822 328	5 770	5.2	50 222 974 000	...	4.0
RWANDA	9 725 000	2.8	21.8	5.9	43.5	3.9	18 153 000	2 341	250	1.2	30 612 000	23.6	2.7
SAMOA	187 000	0.9	22.5	3.9	40.7	6.5	157 000	421	2 270	7.0	29 506 000	11.3	...
SAN MARINO	31 000	0.8	88.7	...	...	...	30 000	1 291	45 130	...	...	...	...
SÃO TOMÉ AND PRÍNCIPE	158 000	1.6	37.9	3.9	39.5	5.7	295 000	124	800	7.8	9 337 000	18.0	...
SAUDI ARABIA	24 735 000	2.2	88.5	3.4	37.3	4.6	49 464 000	331 041	13 980	...	...	...	8.5
SENEGAL	12 379 000	2.5	51.0	4.7	42.6	4.9	23 108 000	9 117	760	2.2	202 197 000	9.3	1.6
SERBIA	7 788 448	0.1	52.3*	1.8	18.3*	18.5*	9 426 000*	29 961	4 030	8.5	2 679 730 000	5.1	2.1
SEYCHELLES	87 000	0.5	50.2	...	...	...	99 000	751	8 870	24.8	181 083 000	2.0	1.8
SIERRA LEONE	5 866 000	2.0	40.2	6.5	42.8	5.5	13 786 000	1 353	240	2.4	33 899 000	25.7	1.0
SINGAPORE	4 436 000	1.2	100.0	1.3	19.5	12.2	5 213 000	128 816	28 730	...	...	...	4.7
SLOVAKIA	5 390 000	0.0	58.0	1.3	16.7	16.2	4 612 000	51 807	9 610	7.8	4 125 305 000	...	1.7
SLOVENIA	2 002 000	0.0	50.8	1.3	13.9	20.5	1 630 000	37 445	18 660	...	...	...	1.7
SOLOMON ISLANDS	496 000	2.3	17.1	3.9	40.6	4.2	921 000	333	690	1.3	4 276 000	60.6	...
SOMALIA	8 699 000	2.9	35.9	6.0	44.1	4.2	21 329 000	...	...	...	19 000	...	...
SOUTH AFRICA, REPUBLIC OF	48 577 000	0.6	57.9	2.6	32.6	6.8	48 660 000	255 389	5 390	2.2	5 472 200 000	0.3	1.4
SOUTH KOREA	48 224 000	0.3	80.8	1.2	18.6	13.7	44 629 000	856 565	17 690	...	...	...	2.7
SPAIN	44 279 000	0.8	76.7	1.4	14.3	21.4	42 541 000	1 206 169	27 340	...	...	...	1.0
SRI LANKA	19 299 000	0.5	21.0	1.9	24.1	10.7	23 554 000	26 001	1 310	3.6	957 927 000	3.0	2.4
ST KITTS AND NEVIS	50 000	1.3	31.9	...	...	...	59 000	406	8 460	12.3	46 585 000	1.2	...
ST LUCIA	165 000	1.1	31.3	2.2	28.8	9.7	188 000	833	5 060	4.1	34 456 000	2.2	...
ST VINCENT AND THE GRENADINES	120 000	0.5	60.5	2.2	29.2	8.9	105 000	395	3 320	7.0	35 627 000	1.0	...
SUDAN	38 560 000	2.2	40.8	4.2	39.2	5.6	66 705 000	30 086	800	0.8	292 431 000	6.0	2.2
SURINAME	458 000	0.6	77.2	2.4	30.1	9.0	429 000	1 918	4 210	...	...	4.1	...
SWAZILAND	1 141 000	0.6	23.9	3.5	41.0	5.4	1 026 000	2 737	2 400	1.7	44 704 000	1.3	1.9
SWEDEN	9 119 000	0.5	83.4	1.8	17.5	23.4	10 054 000	395 411	43 530	...	...	...	1.4
SWITZERLAND	7 484 000	0.4	67.5	1.4	16.5	21.8	7 252 000	434 844	58 050	...	...	...	0.9
SYRIA	19 929 000	2.5	50.3	3.1	36.9	4.7	35 935 000	30 333	1 560	0.6	186 679 000	0.1	3.8
TAIWAN	22 880 000	...	...	...	19.8	9.2*	...	...	...	...	...	...	...
TAJIKISTAN	6 736 000	1.5	24.2	3.4	39.0	5.1	10 423 000	2 572	390	5.0	136 859 000	8.8	2.2
TANZANIA	40 454 000	2.5	37.5	5.2	42.6	5.1	66 845 000	13 404	350	0.9	113 148 000	14.5	1.1
THAILAND	63 884 000	0.7	32.5	1.9	23.8	10.5	74 594 000	193 734	3 050	7.3	14 685 762 000	-0.1	1.1
TOGO	6 585 000	2.7	36.3	4.8	43.5	4.9	13 544 000	2 265	350	0.7	15 432 000	3.6	1.6
TONGA	100 000	0.5	34.0	3.8	35.9	8.8	75 000	225	2 250	1.4	3 203 000	9.6	1.1
TRINIDAD AND TOBAGO	1 333 000	0.4	76.2	1.6	21.5	10.7	1 230 000	16 612	12 500	...	...	0.1	...
TUNISIA	10 327 000	1.1	64.4	1.9	25.9	8.6	12 927 000	30 091	2 970	8.8	2 520 202 000	1.5	1.4
TURKEY	74 877 000	1.3	67.3	2.1	29.2	8.0	101 208 000	393 903	5 400	10.1	40 511 288 000	0.1	2.9
TURKMENISTAN	4 965 000	1.3	45.8	2.5	31.8	6.2	6 780 000	...	...	2.6	254 770 000	0.3	...
TUVALU	11 000	0.4	57.0	...	...	...	12 000	...	...	...	...	...	...
UGANDA	30 884 000	3.2	12.4	6.5	50.5	3.8	126 950 000	8 996	300	1.2	114 694 000	16.9	2.1
UKRAINE	46 205 000	-0.8	67.3	1.2	14.9	20.9	26 393 000	90 740	1 940	9.0	9 388 953 000	0.5	2.1
UNITED ARAB EMIRATES	4 380 000	2.9	85.5	2.3	22.0	1.6	9 056 000	...	...	...	...	...	2.0
UNITED KINGDOM	60 769 000	0.4	89.2	1.8	17.9	21.2	67 143 000	2 455 691	40 560	...	...	...	2.6
UNITED STATES OF AMERICA	305 826 000	1.0	80.8	2.1	20.8	16.7	394 976 000	13 386 875	44 710	...	...	...	4.1
URUGUAY	3 340 000	0.3	93.0	2.1	24.3	17.4	4 043 000	17 591	5 310	30.3	5 689 614 000	0.1	1.2
UZBEKISTAN	27 372 000	1.4	36.4	2.5	33.2	6.2	38 665 000	16 179	610	5.4	923 830 000	0.9	0.5
VANUATU	226 000	2.4	23.7	3.7	39.9	5.1	375 000	373	1 690	1.0	3 725 000	13.6	...
VATICAN CITY	557	0.1	100.0	...	...	...	1 000	...	...	...	...	...	...
VENEZUELA	27 657 000	1.7	88.1	2.6	31.2	7.6	41 991 000	163 959	6 070	5.5	9 964 936 000	0.0	1.1
VIETNAM	87 375 000	1.3	26.7	2.1	29.5	7.5	116 654 000	58 506	700	1.5	918 307 000	3.1	...
YEMEN	22 389 000	3.0	26.3	5.5	46.4	3.6	59 454 000	16 444	760	1.3	225 869 000	1.6	6.0
ZAMBIA	11 922 000	1.9	36.5	5.2	45.8	4.6	22 781 000	7 413	630	1.6	153 699 000	14.3	2.3
ZIMBABWE	13 349 000	1.0	35.9	3.2	40.0	5.4	15 805 000	4 466	340	7.0	83 389 000	...	0.0

* Figures are for Serbia and Montenegro (including Kosovo) prior to formation of independent states

Social Indicators					Environment				Communications				
Child mortality rate	Life expectancy	Literacy rate (%)	Access to safe water (%)	Doctors per 100 000 people	Forest area (%)	Annual change in forest area (%)	Protected land area (%)	CO_2 emissions (metric tonnes per capita)	Main telephone lines per 100 people	Cellular phone subscribers per 100 people	Internet users per 10 000 people	International dialling code	Time zone
4	80.2	...	100	356	30.7	0.2	5.1	19.1	44.3	108.6	8 168	47	+1
12	75.6	97.3	...	126	0.0	0.0	0.1	12.5	10.3	69.6	1 222	968	+4
97	65.5	65.1	91	66	2.5	-2.1	7.4	0.8	3.3	22.0	764	92	+5
11	...	...	85	109	87.6	0.4	0.0	11.9	...	...	...	680	+9
23	75.5	96.1	90	168	57.7	-0.1	10.3	1.8	14.9	66.1	669	507	-5
73	57.2	66.7	39	5	65.0	-0.5	7.9	0.4	1.1	1.3	183	675	+10
22	71.8	95.9	86	117	46.5	-0.9	5.8	0.7	5.3	51.3	413	595	-4
25	71.4	97.1	83	117	53.7	-0.1	13.6	1.2	8.5	30.9	2 581	51	-5
32	71.7	95.1	85	116	24.0	-2.1	10.7	1.0	4.3	50.8	548	63	+8
7	75.6	...	...	220	30.0	0.3	24.2	8.0	29.8	95.5	3 658	48	+1
5	78.1	99.6	...	324	41.3	1.1	5.1	5.6	40.2	116.0	3 025	351	GMT
21	75.6	95.9	100	221	0.0	0.0	0.0	69.2	27.2	109.6	3 455	974	+3
18	72.5	97.8	57	189	27.7	...	2.2	4.2	19.4	80.5	5 224	40	+2
16	65.5	99.7	97	417	47.9	...	6.6	10.6	30.8	105.7	1 802	7	+2 to +12
160	46.2	77.6	74	2	19.5	6.9	8.0	0.1	0.2	3.4	55	250	+2
28	71.5	99.3	88	70	60.4	0.0	2.8	0.8	10.9	25.4	446	685	-11
3	...	...	...	251	1.6	0.0	...	...	77.8	64.4	5 704	378	+1
96	65.5	95.4	79	47	28.4	0.0	...	0.6	4.7	11.5	1 811	239	GMT
25	72.8	95.8	...	140	1.3	0.0	42.3	13.7	15.7	78.1	1 866	966	+3
116	63.1	49.1	76	8	45.0	-0.5	10.9	0.4	2.4	25.0	545	221	GMT
8	74.0	99.4*	...	...	26.4*	...	3.2*	...	25.9	63.3	1 334	381	+1
13	...	99.1	88	132	88.9	0.0	17.2	6.6	25.4	86.5	3 567	248	+4
270	42.6	47.9	57	7	38.5	-0.7	4.0	0.2	0.5	2.2	19	232	GMT
3	80.0	99.5	100	140	3.4	0.0	7.3	12.3	42.3	109.3	4 362	65	+8
8	74.7	...	100	325	40.1	0.1	19.8	6.7	21.6	90.6	4 176	421	+1
4	77.9	99.8	...	219	62.8	0.4	6.5	8.1	42.6	92.6	6 362	386	+1
73	63.6	...	70	13	77.6	-1.7	1.0	0.4	1.6	1.3	163	677	+11
145	48.2	...	29	4	11.4	-1.0	0.3	...	1.2	6.1	111	252	+3
69	49.3	93.9	88	69	7.6	0.0	6.0	9.4	10.0	83.3	1 075	27	+2
5	78.6	...	92	181	63.5	-0.1	3.7	9.7	49.8	83.8	7 275	82	+9
4	80.9	...	100	320	35.9	1.7	8.2	7.7	42.4	106.4	4 283	34	+1
13	72.4	95.6	79	43	29.9	-1.5	17.5	0.6	9.0	25.9	169	94	+5.5
19	...	...	100	118	14.7	0.0	0.1	2.7	59.3	23.7	2 428	1 869	-4
14	73.7	...	98	518	27.9	0.0	29.3	2.3	32.6	65.7	6 169	1 758	-4
20	71.6	...	...	88	27.4	0.8	18.6	1.7	19.0	73.6	840	1 784	-4
89	58.6	77.2	70	16	28.4	-0.8	4.6	0.3	1.7	12.7	946	249	+3
39	70.2	94.9	92	45	94.7	0.0	12.9	5.1	18.0	70.8	712	597	-3
164	39.6	88.4	62	18	31.5	0.9	3.2	0.9	4.3	24.3	408	268	+2
3	80.9	...	100	305	66.9	...	9.6	5.9	59.5	105.9	7 697	46	+1
5	81.7	...	100	352	30.9	0.4	28.2	5.5	66.9	99.0	5 807	41	+1
14	74.1	92.5	93	140	2.5	1.3	0.7	3.7	16.6	24.0	794	963	+2
...	...	...	...	...	...	...	...	...	63.6	102.0	6 368	886	+8
68	66.7	99.8	59	218	2.9	0.0	13.6	0.8	4.3	4.1	30	992	+5
118	52.5	78.4	62	2	39.9	-1.1	36.4	0.1	0.4	14.8	100	255	+3
8	70.6	98.0	99	30	28.4	-0.4	19.7	4.3	10.9	62.9	1 307	66	+7
108	58.4	74.4	52	6	7.1	-4.5	10.7	0.4	1.3	11.2	507	228	GMT
24	73.3	99.3	100	34	5.0	0.0	24.4	1.2	13.7	29.8	302	676	+13
38	69.8	99.5	91	79	44.1	-0.2	5.5	24.7	24.9	126.4	1 248	1 868	-4
23	73.9	94.3	93	70	6.8	1.9	1.5	2.3	12.4	71.9	1 268	216	+1
26	71.8	95.6	96	124	13.2	0.2	1.6	3.2	25.4	71.0	1 773	90	+2
51	63.2	99.8	72	317	8.8	0.0	2.3	8.7	8.2	4.4	132	993	+5
38	...	...	100	...	33.3	0.0	...	...	10.3	15	4 673	688	+12
134	51.5	76.6	60	5	18.4	-2.2	25.6	0.1	0.4	6.7	251	256	+3
24	67.9	99.8	96	297	16.5	0.1	3.3	6.9	26.8	106.7	1 206	380	+2
8	78.7	97.0	100	202	3.7	0.1	0.3	37.8	28.1	118.5	3 669	971	+4
6	79.4	...	100	166	11.8	0.4	20.0	9.8	56.2	116.6	6 316	44	GMT
8	78.2	...	100	549	33.1	0.1	14.6	20.6	57.2	77.4	6 983	1	-5 to -10
12	76.4	98.6	100	365	8.6	1.3	0.3	1.7	28.3	66.8	2 055	598	-3
43	67.2	...	82	289	8.0	0.5	2.0	5.3	6.7	9.3	630	998	+5
36	70.0	...	60	11	36.1	0.0	1.0	0.4	3.2	5.9	346	678	+11
...	...	...	...	...	0.0	0.0	...	CO_2	...	...	...	39	+1
21	73.7	97.2	83	194	54.1	-0.6	69.9	6.6	15.8	69.0	1 521	58	-4.5
17	74.2	93.9	85	53	39.7	2.0	5.0	1.2	18.8	18.2	1 721	84	+7
100	62.7	75.2	67	22	1.0	0.0	0.0	1.0	4.5	13.8	125	967	+3
182	42.4	69.5	58	7	57.1	-1.0	39.9	0.2	0.8	14.0	422	260	+2
105	43.5	97.7	81	6	45.3	-1.7	14.6	0.8	2.6	6.5	932	263	+2

Definitions

Indicator	Definition
Population	
Total population	Interpolated mid-year population, 2005.
Population change	Percentage average annual rate of change, 2005–2010.
% urban	Urban population as a percentage of the total population, 2005.
Total fertility	Average number of children a woman will have during her child-bearing years, 2005–2010.
Population by age	Percentage of population in age groups 0–14 and 60 or over, 2005.
2050 projected population	Projected total population for the year 2050.
Economy	
Total Gross National Income (GNI)	The sum of value added to the economy by all resident producers plus taxes, less subsidies, plus net receipts of primary income from abroad. Data are in U.S. dollars (millions), 2006. Formerly known as Gross National Product (GNP).
GNI per capita	Gross National Income per person in U.S. dollars using the World Bank Atlas method, 2006.
Debt service ratio	Debt service as a percentage of GNI, 2006.
Total debt service	Sum of principal repayments and interest paid on long-term debt, interest paid on short-term debt and repayments to the International Monetary Fund (IMF), 2006.
Aid receipts	Aid received as a percentage of GNI from the Development Assistance Committee (DAC) countries of the Organization for Economic Co-operation and Development (OECD), 2006.
Military spending	Military-related spending, including recruiting, training, construction and the purchase of military supplies and equipment, as a percentage of Gross National Income, 2006.
Social Indicators	
Child mortality rate	Number of deaths of children aged under 5 per 1 000 live births, 2006.
Life expectancy	Average life expectancy, at birth in years, male and female, 2005–2010.
Literacy rate	Percentage of population aged 15–24 with at least a basic ability to read and write, 2005.
Access to safe water	Percentage of population using improved drinking water, 2004.
Doctors	Number of trained doctors per 100 000 people, 2004.
Environment	
Forest area	Percentage of total land area covered by forest, 2005.
Change in forest area	Average annual percentage change in forest area, 2000-2005.
Protected land area	Percentage of total land area designated as protected land, 2006.
CO_2 emissions	Emissions of carbon dioxide from the burning of fossil fuels and the manufacture of cement, divided by the population, expressed in metric tons per capita, 2004.
Communications	
Telephone lines	Main (fixed) telephone lines per 100 inhabitants, 2006.
Cellular phone subscribers	Cellular mobile subscribers per 100 inhabitants, 2006.
Internet users	Internet users per 10 000 inhabitants, 2006.
International dialling code	The country code prefix to be used when dialling from another country.
Time zone	Time difference in hours between local standard time and Greenwich Mean Time.

Main Statistical Sources	Internet Links
United Nations Department of Economic and Social Affairs (UDESA) World Population Prospects: The 2006 Revision. World Urbanization Prospects: The 2005 Revision.	www.un.org/esa/population/unpop
UNESCO Education Data Centre	stats.uis.unesco.org
UN Human Development Report 2004	hdr.undp.org
World Bank World Development Indicators online	www.worldbank.org/data
OECD: Development Co-operation Report 2007	www.oecd.org
UNICEF: The State of the World's Children 2008	www.unicef.org
Food and Agriculture Organization (FAO) of the UN: Global Forest Resources Assessment 2005	www.fao.org
World Resources Institute Biodiversity and Protected Areas Database	www.wri.org
International Telecommunications Union (ITU)	www.itu.int

Introduction to the index

The index includes all names shown on the reference maps in the atlas. Each entry includes the country or geographical area in which the feature is located, a page number and an alphanumeric reference. Additional entry details and aspects of the index are explained below.

Name forms
The names policy in this atlas is generally to use local name forms which are officially recognized by the governments of the countries concerned. Rules established by the Permanent Committee on Geographical Names for British Official Use (PCGN) are applied to the conversion of non-roman alphabet names, for example in the Russian Federation, into the roman alphabet used in English.

However, English conventional name forms are used for the most well-known places for which such a form is in common use. In these cases, the local form is included in brackets on the map and appears as a cross-reference in the index. Other alternative names, such as well-known historical names or those in other languages, may also be included in brackets on the map and as cross-references in the index. All country names and those for international physical features appear in their English forms. Names appear in full in the index, although they may appear in abbreviated form on the maps.

Referencing
Names are referenced by page number and by grid reference. The grid reference relates to the alphanumeric values which appear on the edges of each map. These reflect the graticule on the map – the letter relates to longitude divisions, the number to latitude divisions. Names are generally referenced to the largest scale map page on which they appear. For large geographical features, including countries, the reference is to the largest scale map on which the feature appears in its entirety, or on which the majority of it appears.

Rivers are referenced to their lowest downstream point – either their mouth or their confluence with another river. The river name will generally be positioned as close to this point as possible.

Alternative names
Alternative names appear as cross-references and refer the user to the index entry for the form of the name used on the map.

For rivers with multiple names - for example those which flow through several countries - all alternative name forms are included within the main index entries, with details of the countries in which each form applies.

Administrative qualifiers
Administrative divisions are included in entries to differentiate duplicate names - entries of exactly the same name and feature type within the one country - where these division names are shown on the maps. In such cases, duplicate names are alphabetized in the order of the administrative division names.

Additional qualifiers are included for names within selected geographical areas, to indicate more clearly their location.

Descriptors
Entries, other than those for towns and cities, include a descriptor indicating the type of geographical feature. Descriptors are not included where the type of feature is implicit in the name itself, unless there is a town or city of exactly the same name.

Insets
Where relevant, the index clearly indicates [inset] if a feature appears on an inset map.

Alphabetical order
The Icelandic characters Þ and þ are transliterated and alphabetized as 'Th' and 'th'. The German character ß is alphabetized as 'ss'. Names beginning with Mac or Mc are alphabetized exactly as they appear. The terms Saint, Sainte, etc, are abbreviated to St, Ste, etc, but alphabetized as if in the full form.

Numerical entries
Entries beginning with numerals appear at the beginning of the index, in numerical order. Elsewhere, numerals are alphabetized before 'a'.

Permuted terms
Names beginning with generic geographical terms are permuted - the descriptive term is placed after, and the index alphabetized by, the main part of the name. For example, Mount Everest is indexed as Everest, Mount; Lake Superior as Superior, Lake. This policy is applied to all languages. Permuting has not been applied to names of towns, cities or administrative divisions beginning with such geographical terms. These remain in their full form, for example, Lake Isabella, USA.

Gazetteer entries
Selected entries have been extended to include gazetteer-style information. Important geographical facts which relate specifically to the entry are included within the entry.

Abbreviations

admin. dist.	administrative district	IL	Illinois	plat.	plateau
admin. div.	administrative division	imp. l.	impermanent lake	P.N.G.	Papua New Guinea
admin. reg.	administrative region	IN	Indiana	Port.	Portugal
Afgh.	Afghanistan	Indon.	Indonesia	pref.	prefecture
AK	Alaska	Kazakh.	Kazakhstan	prov.	province
AL	Alabama	KS	Kansas	pt	point
Alg.	Algeria	KY	Kentucky	Qld	Queensland
AR	Arkansas	Kyrg.	Kyrgyzstan	Que.	Québec
Arg.	Argentina	l.	lake	r.	river
aut. comm.	autonomous community	LA	Louisiana	reg.	region
aut. reg.	autonomous region	lag.	lagoon	res.	reserve
aut. rep.	autonomous republic	Lith.	Lithuania	resr	reservoir
AZ	Arizona	Lux.	Luxembourg	RI	Rhode Island
Azer.	Azerbaijan	MA	Massachusetts	Rus. Fed.	Russian Federation
b.	bay	Madag.	Madagascar	S.	South, Southern
Bangl.	Bangladesh	Man.	Manitoba	S.A.	South Australia
B.C.	British Columbia	MD	Maryland	salt l.	salt lake
Bol.	Bolivia	ME	Maine	Sask.	Saskatchewan
Bos.-Herz.	Bosnia-Herzegovina	Mex.	Mexico	SC	South Carolina
Bulg.	Bulgaria	MI	Michigan	SD	South Dakota
c.	cape	MN	Minnesota	sea chan.	sea channel
CA	California	MO	Missouri	Sing.	Singapore
Cent. Afr. Rep.	Central African Republic	Moz.	Mozambique	Switz.	Switzerland
CO	Colorado	MS	Mississippi	Tajik.	Tajikistan
Col.	Colombia	MT	Montana	Tanz.	Tanzania
CT	Connecticut	mt.	mountain	Tas.	Tasmania
Czech Rep.	Czech Republic	mts	mountains	terr.	territory
DC	District of Columbia	N.	North, Northern	Thai.	Thailand
DE	Delaware	nat. park	national park	TN	Tennessee
Dem. Rep. Congo	Democratic Republic of the Congo	N.B.	New Brunswick	Trin. and Tob.	Trinidad and Tobago
depr.	depression	NC	North Carolina	Turkm.	Turkmenistan
des.	desert	ND	North Dakota	TX	Texas
Dom. Rep.	Dominican Republic	NE	Nebraska	U.A.E.	United Arab Emirates
E.	East, Eastern	Neth.	Netherlands	U.K.	United Kingdom
Equat. Guinea	Equatorial Guinea	NH	New Hampshire	Ukr.	Ukraine
esc.	escarpment	NJ	New Jersey	U.S.A.	United States of America
est.	estuary	NM	New Mexico	UT	Utah
Eth.	Ethiopia	N.S.	Nova Scotia	Uzbek.	Uzbekistan
Fin.	Finland	N.S.W.	New South Wales	VA	Virginia
FL	Florida	N.T.	Northern Territory	Venez.	Venezuela
for.	forest	NV	Nevada	Vic.	Victoria
Fr. Guiana	French Guiana	N.W.T.	Northwest Territories	vol.	volcano
F.Y.R.O.M.	Former Yugoslav Republic of Macedonia	NY	New York	vol. crater	volcanic crater
g.	gulf	N.Z.	New Zealand	VT	Vermont
GA	Georgia	OH	Ohio	W.	West, Western
Guat.	Guatemala	OK	Oklahoma	WA	Washington
HI	Hawaii	OR	Oregon	W.A.	Western Australia
H.K.	Hong Kong	PA	Pennsylvania	WI	Wisconsin
Hond.	Honduras	Para.	Paraguay	WV	West Virginia
i.	island	P.E.I.	Prince Edward Island	WY	Wyoming
IA	Iowa	pen.	peninsula	Y.T.	Yukon Territory
ID	Idaho	Phil.	Philippines		

1

1st Three Mile Opening sea chan. Australia 110 D2
2nd Three Mile Opening sea chan. Australia 110 C2
3-y Severnyy Rus. Fed. 41 S3
5 de Outubro Angola see Xá-Muteba
9 de Julio Arg. 144 D5
25 de Mayo Buenos Aires Arg. 144 D5
25 de Mayo La Pampa Arg. 144 C5
70 Mile House Canada 120 F5
100 Mile House Canada 120 F5
150 Mile House Canada 120 F4

A

Aabenraa Denmark 45 F9
Aachen Germany 52 G4
Aalborg Denmark 45 F8
Aalborg Bugt b. Denmark 45 G8
Aalen Germany 53 K6
Aalesund Norway see Ålesund
Aaley Lebanon see Aley
Aalst Belgium 52 E4
Aanaar Fin. see Inari
Aarhus Denmark see Århus
Aarlen Belgium see Arlon
Aars Denmark 45 F8
Aarschot Belgium 52 E4
Aasiaat Greenland 119 M3
Aath Belgium see Ath
Aba China 76 D1
Aba Dem. Rep. Congo 98 D3
Aba Nigeria 96 D4
Abacaxis r. Brazil 143 G4
Ābādān Iran 88 C4
Abadan Turkm. 88 E2
Ābādeh Iran 88 D4
Ābādeh Ţashk Iran 88 D4
Abadla Alg. 54 D5
Abaeté Brazil 145 B2
Abaetetuba Brazil 143 I4
Abagnar Qi China see Xilinhot
Abaiang atoll Kiribati 150 H5
Abajo Peak U.S.A. 129 I3
Abakaliki Nigeria 96 D4
Abakan Rus. Fed. 72 G2
Abakanskiy Khrebet mts Rus. Fed. 72 F2
Abalak Niger 96 D3
Abana Turkey 90 D2
Abancay Peru 142 D6
Abariringa atoll Kiribati see Kanton
Abarkūh, Kavīr-e des. Iran 88 D4
Abarqū Iran 88 D4
Abarshahr Iran see Neyshābūr
Abashiri Japan 74 G3
Abashiri-wan b. Japan 74 G3
Abasolo Mex. 131 D7
Abau P.N.G. 110 E1
Abaya, Lake Eth. 98 D3
Ābaya Hāyk' l. Eth. see Abaya, Lake
Ābay Wenz r. Eth./Sudan 98 D2 see Blue Nile
Abaza Rus. Fed. 72 G2
Abba Cent. Afr. Rep. 98 B3
'Abbāsābād Iran 88 D3
'Abbāsābād Iran 88 E2
Abbasanta Sardinia Italy 58 C4
Abbatis Villa France see Abbeville
Abbe, Lake Djibouti/Eth. 86 F7
Abbeville France 52 B4
Abbeville AL U.S.A. 133 C6
Abbeville GA U.S.A. 133 D6
Abbeville LA U.S.A. 131 E6
Abbeville SC U.S.A. 133 D5
Abbey Canada 121 I5
Abbeyfeale Ireland 51 C5
Abbeytown U.K. 48 D4
Abborrträsk Sweden 44 K4
Abbot, Mount Australia 110 D4
Abbot Ice Shelf Antarctica 152 K2
Abbotsford Canada 120 F5
Abbott NM U.S.A. 127 G5
Abbott VA U.S.A. 134 E5
Abbottabad Pak. 89 I3
'Abd al 'Azīz, Jabal hill Syria 91 F3
'Abd al Kūrī i. Yemen 86 H7
'Abd Allah, Khawr sea chan. Iraq/Kuwait 88 C4
Abd al Ma'asīr well Saudi Arabia 85 D4
Ābdānān Iran 88 B3
'Abdollāhābād Iran 88 D3
Abdulino Rus. Fed. 41 Q5
Abéché Chad 97 F3
Abellinum Italy see Avellino
Abel Tasman National Park N.Z. 113 D5
Abengourou Côte d'Ivoire 96 C4
Åbenrå Denmark see Aabenraa
Abensberg Germany 53 L6
Abeokuta Nigeria 96 D4
Aberaeron U.K. 49 C6
Aberchirder U.K. 50 G3
Abercorn Zambia see Mbala
Abercrombie r. Australia 112 D4
Aberdare U.K. 49 D7
Aberdaron U.K. 49 C6
Aberdaugleddau U.K. see Milford Haven
Aberdeen Australia 112 E4
Aberdeen H.K. China 77 [inset]
Aberdeen S. Africa 100 G7
Aberdeen U.K. 50 G3
Aberdeen U.S.A. 130 D2
Aberdeen Lake Canada 121 L1
Aberdovey U.K. 49 C6
Aberdyfi Wales U.K. see Aberdovey
Aberfeldy U.K. 50 F4
Aberford U.K. 48 F5
Aberfoyle U.K. 50 E4
Abergavenny U.K. 49 D7
Abergwaun U.K. see Fishguard
Aberhonddu U.K. see Brecon
Abermaw U.K. see Barmouth
Abernathy U.S.A. 131 C5
Aberporth U.K. 49 C6
Abersoch U.K. 49 C6
Abertawe U.K. see Swansea
Aberteifi U.K. see Cardigan
Aberystwyth U.K. 49 C6
Abeshr Chad see Abéché
Abez' Rus. Fed. 41 S2
Āb Gāh Iran 89 E5
Abhā Saudi Arabia 86 F6
Abhar Iran 88 C2
Abiad, Bahr el r. Sudan/Uganda 86 D6 see White Nile

▶Abidjan Côte d'Ivoire 96 C4
Former capital of Côte d'Ivoire.

Abijatta-Shalla National Park Eth. 98 D3
Ab-i-Kavīr salt flat Iran 88 E3
Abilene KS U.S.A. 130 D4
Abilene TX U.S.A. 131 D5
Abingdon U.K. 49 F7
Abingdon U.S.A. 134 D5
Abington Reef Australia 110 E3
Abinsk Rus. Fed. 90 E1
Abitau Lake Canada 121 J2
Abitibi, Lake Canada 122 E4
Ab Khūr Iran 88 E3
Abminga Australia 109 F6
Abnūb Egypt 90 C6
Åbo Fin. see Turku
Abohar India 82 C3
Aboisso Côte d'Ivoire 96 C4
Aboite U.S.A. 134 C3
Abomey Benin 96 D4
Abongabong, Gunung mt. Indon. 71 B6
Abong Mbang Cameroon 96 E4
Abou Déia Chad 97 E3
Abovyan Armenia 91 G2
Aboyne U.K. 50 G3
Abqaiq Saudi Arabia 88 C5
Abraham's Bay Bahamas 133 F8
Abramov, Mys pt Rus. Fed. 42 I2
Abrantes Port. 57 B4
Abra Pampa Arg. 144 C2
Abreojos, Punta pt Mex. 127 E8
'Abri Sudan 86 D5
Abrolhos Bank sea feature S. Atlantic Ocean 148 F7
Abruzzo, Parco Nazionale d' nat. park Italy 58 E4
Absalom, Mount Antarctica 152 B1
Absaroka Range mts U.S.A. 126 F3
Abtar, Jabal al hills Syria 85 C2
Abtsgmünd Germany 53 J6
Abū aḑ Ḑuhūr Syria 85 C2
Abū al Abyaḑ i. U.A.E. 88 D5
Abū al Ḩusayn, Qā' imp. l. Jordan 85 D3
Abū 'Alī i. Saudi Arabia 88 C5
Abū 'Āmūd, Wādī watercourse Jordan 85 C4
Abū 'Arīsh Saudi Arabia 86 F6
Abu 'Aweigîla well Egypt see Abū 'Uwayqilah
Abu Deleiq Sudan 86 D6

▶Abu Dhabi U.A.E. 88 D5
Capital of the United Arab Emirates.

Abū Du'ān Syria 85 D1
Abu Gubeiha Sudan 86 D7
Abū Ḩafnah, Wādī watercourse Jordan 85 D3
Abu Haggag Egypt see Ra's al Ḩikmah
Abū Ḩallūfah, Jabal hill Jordan 85 C4
Abu Hamed Sudan 86 D6

▶Abuja Nigeria 96 D4
Capital of Nigeria.

Abū Jifān well Saudi Arabia 88 B5
Abū Jurdhān Jordan 85 B4
Abū Kamāl Syria 91 F4
Abu Matariq Sudan 97 F3
Abumombazi Dem. Rep. Congo 98 C3
Abu Musa i. The Gulf 88 D5
Abū Mūsá, Jazīreh-ye i. The Gulf see Abu Musa
Abunã r. Bol. 142 E5
Abunã Brazil 142 E5
Ābune Yosēf mt. Eth. 86 E7
Abū Nujaym Libya 97 E1
Abū Qa'ţūr Syria 85 C2
Abū Rawthah, Jabal mt. Egypt 85 B5
Aburo mt. Dem. Rep. Congo 98 D3
Abu Road India 79 G4
Abū Rujmayn, Jabal mts Syria 85 D2
Abu Rûtha, Gebel mt. Egypt see Abū Rawthah, Jabal
Abū Sawādah well Saudi Arabia 88 C5
Abu Simbil Egypt see Abū Sunbul
Abū Sunbul Egypt 86 D5
Abū Ţarfā', Wādī watercourse Egypt 85 A5
Abut Head hd N.Z. 113 C6
Abū 'Uwayqilah well Egypt 85 B4
Abu Zabad Sudan 86 C7
Abū Ẓabī U.A.E. see Abu Dhabi
Abūzam Iran 88 C4
Abū Zanīmah Egypt 90 D5
Abu Zenîma Egypt see Abū Zanīmah
Abyad Sudan 86 C7
Abyaḑ, Jabal al mts Syria 85 C2
Abyār al Hakīm well Libya 90 A5
Abydos Australia 108 B5
Abyei Sudan 86 C8
Abyssinia country Africa see Ethiopia
Academician Vernadskiy research station Antarctica see Vernadsky
Academy Bay Rus. Fed. see Akademii, Zaliv
Acadia prov. Canada see Nova Scotia
Acadia National Park U.S.A. 132 G2
Açailândia Brazil 143 I5
Acamarachi mt. Chile see Pili, Cerro
Acampamento de Caça do Mucusso Angola 99 C5
Acandí Col. 142 C2
A Cañiza Spain 57 B2
Acaponeta Mex. 136 C4
Acapulco Mex. 136 E5
Acapulco de Juárez Mex. see Acapulco
Acará Brazil 143 I4
Acarai Mountains hills Brazil/Guyana 143 G3
Acaraú Brazil 143 J4
Acaray, Represa de resr Para. 144 E3
Acarigua Venez. 142 E2
Acatlán Mex. 136 E5
Accho Israel see 'Akko
Accomac U.S.A. 135 H5
Accomack U.S.A. see Accomac

▶Accra Ghana 96 C4
Capital of Ghana.

Accrington U.K. 48 E5
Ach r. Germany 53 L6
Achacachi Bol. 142 E7
Achaguas Venez. 142 E2
Achalpur India 82 D5
Achampet India 84 C2
Achan Rus. Fed. 74 E2
Achayvayam Rus. Fed. 65 S3
Acheng China 74 B3
Achhota India 84 D1
Achicourt France 52 C4
Achill Ireland 51 C4
Achillbeg Island Ireland 51 C4
Achill Island Ireland 51 B4
Achiltibuie U.K. 50 D2
Achim Germany 53 J1
Achinsk Rus. Fed. 64 K4
Achit Rus. Fed. 41 R4
Achit Nuur l. Mongolia 80 H2
Achkhoy-Martan Rus. Fed. 91 G2
Achna Cyprus 85 A2
Achnasheen U.K. 50 D3
Acıgöl l. Turkey 59 M6
Acıpayam Turkey 59 M6
Acireale Sicily Italy 58 F6
Ackerman U.S.A. 131 F5
Ackley U.S.A. 130 E3
Acklins Island Bahamas 133 F8
Acle U.K. 49 I6

▶Aconcagua, Cerro mt. Arg. 144 B4
Highest mountain in South America.

Acopiara Brazil 143 K5
A Coruña Spain 57 B2
Acqui Terme Italy 58 C2
Acra U.S.A. 135 H2
Acragas Sicily Italy see Agrigento
Acraman, Lake salt flat Australia 111 A7
Acre r. Brazil 142 E6
Acre Israel see 'Akko
Acre, Bay of Israel see Haifa, Bay of
Acri Italy 58 G5
Ács Hungary 47 Q7
Actaeon Group is Fr. Polynesia see Actéon, Groupe
Actéon, Groupe is Fr. Polynesia 151 K7
Acton Canada 134 E2
Acton U.S.A. 128 D4
Acungui Brazil 145 A4
Acunum Acusio France see Montélimar
Ada MN U.S.A. 130 D2
Ada OH U.S.A. 134 D3
Ada OK U.S.A. 131 D5
Ada WI U.S.A. 134 B2
Adabazar Sakarya Turkey see Adapazarı
Adaja r. Spain 57 D3
Adalia Turkey see Antalya
Adam Oman 87 I5
Adam, Mount hill Falkland Is 144 E8
Adamantina Brazil 145 A3
Adams IN U.S.A. 134 C4
Adams KY U.S.A. 134 D4
Adams MA U.S.A. 135 I2
Adams NY U.S.A. 135 G2
Adams, Mount U.S.A. 126 C3
Adams Center U.S.A. 135 G2
Adams Lake Canada 120 G5
Adams Mountain U.S.A. 120 D4
Adam's Peak Sri Lanka 84 D5
Adams Peak U.S.A. 128 C2

▶Adamstown Pitcairn Is 151 L7
Capital of the Pitcairn Islands.

'Adan Yemen see Aden
Adana Turkey 85 B1
Adana prov. Turkey 85 B1
Adana Yemen see Aden
Adapazarı Turkey 59 N4
Adare Ireland 51 D5
Adare, Cape Antarctica 152 H2
Adavale Australia 111 D5
Adban Afgh. 89 H2
Ad Dabbah Sudan see Ed Debba
Ad Ḑabbīyah well Saudi Arabia 88 C5
Ad Dafīnah Saudi Arabia 86 F5
Ad Dahnā' des. Saudi Arabia 86 G5
Ad Dakhla W. Sahara 96 B2
Ad Damir Sudan see Ed Damer
Ad Dammām Saudi Arabia see Dammam
Addanki India 84 C3
Ad Dār al Ḩamrā' Saudi Arabia 86 E4
Ad Darb Saudi Arabia 86 F6
Ad Dawādimī Saudi Arabia 86 F5
Ad Dawḩah Qatar see Doha
Ad Dawr Iraq 91 F4
Ad Daww plain Syria 85 C2
Ad Dayr Iraq 91 G5
Ad Dibdibah plain Saudi Arabia 88 B5
Aḑ Ḑiffah plat. Egypt see Libyan Plateau

▶Addis Ababa Eth. 98 D3
Capital of Ethiopia.

Addison U.S.A. 135 G2
Ad Dīwānīyah Iraq 91 G5
Addlestone U.K. 49 G7
Addo Elephant National Park S. Africa 101 G7
Addoo Atoll Maldives see Addu Atoll
Addu Atoll Maldives 81 D12
Ad Duwayd well Saudi Arabia 91 F5
Ad Duwaym Sudan see Ed Dueim
Ad Duwayris well Saudi Arabia 88 C6
Adegaon India 82 D5
Adel GA U.S.A. 133 D6
Adel IA U.S.A. 130 E3

▶Adelaide Australia 111 B7
Capital of South Australia.

Adelaide r. Australia 108 E3
Adelaide Bahamas 133 E7
Adelaide Island Antarctica 152 L2
Adelaide River Australia 108 E3
Adele Island Australia 108 C3
Adélie Coast Antarctica 152 G2
Adélie Land reg. Antarctica 152 G2
Adelong Australia 112 D5
Aden Yemen 86 F7
Aden, Gulf of Somalia/Yemen 86 G7
Adena U.S.A. 134 E3
Adenau Germany 52 G4
Adendorf Germany 53 K1
Aderbissinat Niger 96 D3
Aderno Sicily Italy see Adrano
Adesar India 82 B5
Adhan, Jabal mt. U.A.E. 88 E5
Adh Dhāyūf well Saudi Arabia 91 G6
'Adhfā' well Saudi Arabia 91 F5
'Ādhirīyāt, Jibāl al mts Jordan 85 C4
Adi i. Indon. 69 I7
Ādī Ārk'ay Eth. 86 E7
Adige r. Italy 58 E2
Ādīgrat Eth. 98 D2
Adilabad India 84 C2
Adilcevaz Turkey 91 F3
Adin U.S.A. 126 C4
Adīrī Libya 97 E2
Adirondack Mountains U.S.A. 135 H1
Ādīs Ābeba Eth. see Addis Ababa
Adi Ugri Eritrea see Mendefera
Adıyaman Turkey 90 E3
Adjud Romania 59 L1
Adlavik Islands Canada 123 K3
Admiralty Island Canada 119 H3
Admiralty Island U.S.A. 120 C3
Admiralty Island National Monument-Kootznoowoo Wilderness nat. park U.S.A. 120 C3
Admiralty Islands P.N.G. 69 L7
Ado-Ekiti Nigeria 96 D4
Adok Sudan 86 D8
Adolfo L. Mateos Mex. 127 E8
Adolphus U.S.A. 134 B5
Adonara i. Indon. 108 C2
Adoni India 84 C3
Adorf Germany 53 M4
Adorf (Diemelsee) Germany 53 I3
Ado-Tymovo Rus. Fed. 74 F2
Adour r. France 56 D5
Adra Spain 57 E5
Adramyttium Turkey see Edremit
Adramyttium, Gulf of Turkey see Edremit Körfezi
Adrano Sicily Italy 58 F6
Adrar Alg. 96 C2
Adrar hills Mali see Ifôghas, Adrar des
Adraskand r. Afgh. 89 F3
Adré Chad 97 F3
Adrian MI U.S.A. 134 C3
Adrian TX U.S.A. 131 C5
Adrianople Turkey see Edirne
Adrianopolis Turkey see Edirne
Adriatic Sea Europe 58 E2
Adua Eth. see Ādwa
Adunara i. Indon. see Adonara
Adusa Dem. Rep. Congo 98 C3
Aduwa Eth. see Ādwa
Adverse Well Australia 108 C5
Ādwa Eth. 98 D2
Adycha r. Rus. Fed. 65 O3
Adyk Rus. Fed. 43 J7
Adzopé Côte d'Ivoire 96 C4
Aegean Sea Greece/Turkey 59 K5
Aegina i. Greece see Aigina
Aegyptus country Africa see Egypt
Aela Jordan see Al 'Aqabah
Aelana Jordan see Al 'Aqabah
Aelia Capitolina Israel/West Bank see Jerusalem
Aelōnlaplap atoll Marshall Is see Ailinglaplap
Aenus Turkey see Enez
Aerzen Germany 53 J2
Aesernia Italy see Isernia
A Estrada Spain 57 B2
Afabet Eritrea 86 E6
Afanas'yevo Rus. Fed. 42 L4
Affreville Alg. see Khemis Miliana
Afghānestān country Asia see Afghanistan
Afghanistan country Asia 89 G3
Afgooye Somalia 98 E3
'Afīf Saudi Arabia 86 F5
Afiun Karahissar Turkey see Afyon
Åfjord Norway 44 G5
Aflou Alg. 54 E5
Afmadow Somalia 98 E3
Afogados da Ingazoira Brazil 143 K5
A Fonsagrada Spain 57 C2
Afonso Cláudio Brazil 145 C3
Āfrēra Terara vol. Eth. 86 F7
Africa Nova country Africa see Tunisia
'Afrīn Syria 85 C1
'Afrīn, Nahr r. Syria/Turkey 85 C1
Afşin Turkey 90 E3
Afsluitdijk barrage Neth. 52 F2
Afton U.S.A. 126 F4
Afuá Brazil 143 H4
'Afula Israel 85 B3
Afyon Turkey 59 N5
Afyonkarahisar Turkey see Afyon
Aga Germany 53 M4
Agadès Niger see Agadez
Agadez Niger 96 D3
Agadir Morocco 96 C1
Agadyr' Kazakh. 80 D2
Agalega Islands Mauritius 149 L6
Agana Guam see Hagåtña
Agara Georgia 91 F2
Agartala India 83 G5
Agashi India 84 B2
Agate Canada 122 E4
Agathe France see Agde
Agathonisi i. Greece 59 L6
Agats Indon. 69 J8
Agatti i. India 84 B4
Agboville Côte d'Ivoire 96 C4
Ağcabädi Azer. 91 G2
Ağdam Azer. 91 G3
Ağdaş Azer. 91 G2
Agdash Azer. see Ağdaş
Agde France 56 F5
Agdzhabedi Azer. see Ağcabädi
Agedabia Libya see Ajdābiyā
Agen France 56 E4
Aggeneys S. Africa 100 D5
Aggteleki nat. park Hungary 47 R6
Aghil Pass China 82 D1
Agiabampo Mex. 127 F8
Agiguan i. N. Mariana Is see Aguijan
Ağın Turkey 90 E3
Aginskoye Rus. Fed. 72 G1
Aginum France see Agen
Agios Dimitrios Greece 59 J6
Agios Efstratios i. Greece 59 K5
Agios Georgios i. Greece 59 J6
Agios Nikolaos Greece 59 K7
Agios Theodoros Cyprus 85 B2
Agiou Orous, Kolpos b. Greece 59 J4
Agirwat Hills Sudan 86 E6
Agisanang S. Africa 101 G4
Agnes, Mount hill Australia 109 E6
Agnew Australia 109 C6
Agnibilékrou Côte d'Ivoire 96 C4
Agnita Romania 59 K2
Agniye-Afanas'yevsk Rus. Fed. 74 E2
Agra India 82 D4
Agrakhanskiy Poluostrov pen. Rus. Fed. 91 G2
Agram Croatia see Zagreb
Ağrı Turkey 91 F3
Agria Gramvousa i. Greece 59 J7
Agrigan i. N. Mariana Is see Agrihan
Agrigento Sicily Italy 58 E6
Agrigentum Sicily Italy see Agrigento
Agrihan i. N. Mariana Is 69 L3
Agrinio Greece 59 I5
Agropoli Italy 58 F4
Agryz Rus. Fed. 41 Q4
Ağsu Azer. 91 H2
Agua, Volcán de vol. Guat. 136 F6
Água Clara Brazil 144 F2
Aguadilla Puerto Rico 137 K5
Agua Escondida Arg. 144 C5
Agua Fria r. U.S.A. 129 G5
Agua Fria National Monument nat. park U.S.A. 129 G4
Aguanaval r. Mex. 131 C7
Aguanga U.S.A. 128 E5
Aguanish r. Canada 123 J4
Aguapeí r. Brazil 145 A3
Agua Prieta Mex. 127 F7
Aguaro-Guariquito, Parque Nacional nat. park Venez. 142 E2
Aguascalientes Mex. 136 D4
Agudos Brazil 145 A3
Águeda Port. 57 B3
Aguemour reg. Alg. 96 D2
Aguié Niger 96 D3
Aguijan i. N. Mariana Is 69 L4
Aguilar U.S.A. 127 G5
Aguilar de Campóo Spain 57 D2
Águilas Spain 57 F5

▶Agulhas, Cape S. Africa 100 E8
Most southerly point of Africa.

Agulhas Basin sea feature Southern Ocean 149 J9
Agulhas Negras mt. Brazil 145 B3
Agulhas Plateau sea feature Southern Ocean 149 J8
Agulhas Ridge sea feature S. Atlantic Ocean 148 I8
Ağva Turkey 59 M4
Agvali Rus. Fed. 91 G2
Ahaggar plat. Alg. see Hoggar
Āhangarān Iran 89 F3
Ahar Iran 88 B2
Ahaura N.Z. 113 C6
Ahaus Germany 52 H2
Ahipara Bay N.Z. 113 D2
Ahiri India 84 D2
Ahklun Mountains U.S.A. 118 B4
Ahlen Germany 53 H3
Ahmadabad India 82 C5
Aḩmadābād Iran 89 E3
Aḩmad al Bāqir, Jabal mt. Jordan 85 B5
Ahmadī Iran 88 E5
Ahmadnagar India 84 B2
Ahmadpur East Pak. 89 H4
Ahmar mts Eth. 98 E3
Ahmar Mountains Eth. see Ahmar
Ahmedabad India see Ahmadabad
Ahmednagar India see Ahmadnagar
Ahorn Germany 53 K4
Ahr r. Germany 52 H4
Ahram Iran 88 C4
Ahrensburg Germany 53 K1
Āhtäri Fin. 44 N5
Ahtme Estonia 45 O7
Ahu China 77 H1
Āhū Iran 88 C4
Ahun France 56 F3
Ahuzhen China see Ahu
Ahvāz Iran 88 C4
Ahwa India 84 B1
Ahwāz Iran see Ahvāz
Ai-Ais Namibia 100 C4
Ai-Ais Hot Springs Game Park nature res. Namibia 100 C4
Aichwara India 82 D4
Aid U.S.A. 134 D4
Aigialousa Cyprus 85 B2
Aigina i. Greece 59 J6
Aigio Greece 59 J5
Aigle de Chambeyron mt. France 56 H4
Aigües Tortes i Estany de Sant Maurici, Parc Nacional d' nat. park Spain 57 G2
Ai He r. China 74 B4
Aihua China see Yunxian
Aihui China see Heihe
Aijal India see Aizawl
Aikawa Japan 75 E5
Aiken U.S.A. 133 D5
Ailao Shan mts China 76 D3
Aileron Australia 108 F5
Ailinglabelab atoll Marshall Is see Ailinglaplap
Ailinglaplap atoll Marshall Is 150 H5
Ailly-sur-Noye France 52 C5
Ailsa Craig Canada 134 E2
Ailsa Craig i. U.K. 50 D5
Ailt an Chorráin Ireland 51 D3
Aimangala India 84 C3
Aimorés, Serra dos hills Brazil 145 C2
Aïn Beïda Alg. 58 B7
'Aïn Ben Tili Mauritania 96 C2
'Ain Dâlla spring Egypt see 'Ayn Dāllah
Aïn Defla Alg. 57 H5
Aïn Deheb Alg. 57 G6
Aïn el Hadjel Alg. 57 H6
'Ain el Maqfi spring Egypt see 'Ayn al Maqfī
Aïn el Melh Alg. 57 I6
Aïn Mdila well Alg. 58 B7
Aïn-M'Lila Alg. 54 F4
Aïn Oussera Alg. 57 H6
Ain Salah Alg. see In Salah
Aïn Sefra Alg. 54 D5
Ainsworth U.S.A. 130 D3
Aintab Turkey see Gaziantep
Aïn Taya Alg. 57 H5
Aïn Tédélès Alg. 57 G6
Aïn Temouchent Alg. 57 F6
'Ain Tibaghbagh spring Egypt see 'Ayn Tabaghbugh
'Ain Timeira spring Egypt see 'Ayn Tumayrah
'Ain Zeitûn Egypt see 'Ayn Zaytūn
Aiquile Bol. 142 E7
Air i. Indon. 71 D7
Airaines France 52 B5
Airdrie Canada 120 H5
Airdrie U.K. 50 F5
Aire r. France 52 E5
Aire, Canal d' France 52 C4
Aire-sur-l'Adour France 56 D5
Air Force Island Canada 119 K3
Airpanas Indon. 108 D1
Aisatung Mountain Myanmar 70 A2
Aisch r. Germany 53 L5
Aishihik Canada 120 B2
Aishihik Lake Canada 120 B2
Aisne r. France 52 C5
Aïssa, Djebel mt. Alg. 54 D5
Aitamännikkö Fin. 44 N3
Aitana mt. Spain 57 F4
Aït Benhaddou tourist site Morocco 54 C5
Aiterach r. Germany 53 M6
Aitkin U.S.A. 130 E2
Aiud Romania 59 J1
Aix France see Aix-en-Provence
Aix-en-Provence France 56 G5
Aix-la-Chapelle Germany see Aachen
Aix-les-Bains France 56 G4
Aíyina i. Greece see Aigina
Aíyion Greece see Aigio
Aizawl India 83 H5
Aizkraukle Latvia 45 N8
Aizpute Latvia 45 L8
Aizu-Wakamatsu Japan 75 E5
Ajaccio Corsica France 56 I6
Ajanta India 84 B1
Ajanta Range hills India see Sahyadriparvat Range
Ajaureforsen Sweden 44 I4
Ajax Canada 134 F2
Ajayameru India see Ajmer
Ajban U.A.E. 88 D5
Aj Bogd Uul mt. Mongolia 80 I3
Ajdābiyā Libya 97 F1
a-Jiddét des. Oman see Ḩarāsīs, Jiddat al
'Ajlūn Jordan 85 B3
'Ajman U.A.E. 88 D5
Ajmer India 82 C4
Ajmer-Merwara India see Ajmer
Ajnala India 82 C3
Ajo U.S.A. 129 G5
Ajo, Mount U.S.A. 129 G5
Ajrestan Afgh. 89 G3
Ajyyap Turkm. 88 D2
Akademii, Zaliv b. Rus. Fed. 74 E1
Akademii Nauk, Khrebet mt. Tajik. see Akademiyai Fanho, Qatorkŭhi
Akademiyai Fanho, Qatorkŭhi mt. Tajik. 89 H2
Akagera National Park Rwanda 98 D4
Akalkot India 84 C2
Akama, Akra c. Cyprus see Arnauti, Cape
Akamagaseki Japan see Shimonoseki
Akan Kokuritsu-kōen nat. park Japan 74 G4
Akaroa N.Z. 113 D6
Akas reg. India 76 B3
Akāshat Iraq 91 E4
Akbarābād Iran 91 I5
Akbarpur Uttar Prad. India 82 E4
Akbarpur Uttar Prad. India 83 E4
Akbaytal, Pereval pass Tajik. 89 I2
Akbaytal Pass Tajik. see Akbaytal, Pereval
Akbez Turkey 85 C1
Akçadağ Turkey 90 E3
Akçakale Turkey 85 D1
Akçakoca Turkey 59 N4
Akçakoca Dağları mts Turkey 59 N4
Akçakoyunlu Turkey 85 C1
Akçalı Dağları mts Turkey 85 A1
Akchâr reg. Mauritania 96 B3
Akchi Kazakh. see Akshiy
Akdağlar mts Turkey 59 M6
Akdağmadeni Turkey 90 D3
Akdere Turkey 85 A1
Akelamo Indon. 69 H6
Åkersberga Sweden 45 K7
Akersloot Neth. 52 E2
Aketi Dem. Rep. Congo 98 C3
Akgyr Erezi hills Turkm. 88 D1
Akhali-Afoni Georgia see Akhali Ap'oni
Akhali Ap'oni Georgia 91 F2
Akhḑar, Al Jabal al mts Libya 97 F1
Akhḑar, Jabal mts Oman 88 E6
Akhisar Turkey 59 L5
Akhnoor India 82 C2
Akhsu Azer. see Ağsu
Akhta Armenia see Hrazdan
Akhtarīn Syria 85 C1
Akhtubinsk Rus. Fed. 43 J6
Akhty Rus. Fed. 91 G2
Akhtyrka Ukr. see Okhtyrka
Aki Japan 75 D6
Akiéni Gabon 98 B4
Akimiski Island Canada 122 E3
Akishma r. Rus. Fed. 74 D1
Akita Japan 75 F5
Akjoujt Mauritania 96 B3
Akkajaure l. Sweden 44 J3
Akkerman Ukr. see Bilhorod-Dnistrovs'kyy
Akkeshi Japan 74 G4
'Akko Israel 85 B3
Akkol' Akmolinskaya Oblast' Kazakh. 80 D1
Akkol' Atyrauskaya Oblast' Kazakh. 43 K7

Akku Kazakh. **80** E1
Akkul' Kazakh. *see* **Akkol'**
Akkuş Turkey **90** E2
Akkyr, Gory *hills* Turkm. *see* **Akgyr Erezi**
Aklavik Canada **118** E3
Aklera India **82** D4
Ak-Mechet Kazakh. *see* **Kyzylorda**
Akmeņrags *pt* Latvia **45** L8
Akmeqit China **82** D1
Akmola Kazakh. *see* **Astana**
Akmolinsk Kazakh. *see* **Astana**
Akobo Sudan **97** G4
Akobo Wenz *r.* Eth./Sudan **98** D3
Akokan Niger **96** D3
Akola India **84** C1
Akom II Cameroon **96** E4
Akonolinga Cameroon **96** E4
Akordat Eritrea **86** E6
Akören Turkey **90** D3
Akot India **82** D5
Akpatok Island Canada **123** I1
Akqi China **80** E3
Akra, Jabal *mt.* Syria/Turkey *see* **Aqra', Jabal al**
Akranes Iceland **44** [inset]
Åkrehamn Norway **45** D7
Akréréb Niger **96** D3
Akron *CO* U.S.A. **130** C3
Akron *IN* U.S.A. **134** B3
Akron *OH* U.S.A. **134** E3
Akrotiri Bay Cyprus **85** A2
Akrotirion Bay Cyprus *see* **Akrotiri Bay**
Akrotiriou, Kolpos *b.* Cyprus *see* **Akrotiri Bay**
Akrotiri Sovereign Base Area *military base* Cyprus **85** A2

▶**Aksai Chin** *terr.* Asia **82** D2
Disputed territory (China/India).

Aksaray Turkey **90** D3
Aksay China **80** H4
Aksay Kazakh. **41** Q5
Ak-Say *r.* Kyrg. **87** M1
Aksay Rus. Fed. **43** H7
Akşehir Turkey **59** N5
Akşehir Gölü *l.* Turkey **59** N5
Akseki Turkey **90** C3
Aksha Rus. Fed. **73** K2
Akshiganak Kazakh. **80** B2
Akshiy Kazakh. **80** E3
Akshukur Kazakh. **91** H2
Aksu China **80** F3
Aksu Kazakh. **80** E1
Aksu *r.* Tajik. *see* **Oqsu**
Aksu *r.* Turkey **59** N6
Aksuat Kazakh. **80** F2
Aksu-Ayuly Kazakh. **80** D2
Aksubayevo Rus. Fed. **43** K5
Āksum Eth. **86** E7
Aktag *mt.* China **83** F1
Aktas Dağı *mt.* Turkey **91** G3
Aktau Kazakh. **78** E2
Akto China **89** J2
Aktobe Kazakh. **78** E1
Aktogay *Karagandinskaya Oblast'* Kazakh. **80** E2
Aktogay *Vostochnyy Kazakhstan* Kazakh. **80** E2
Aktsyabrski Belarus **43** F5
Aktyubinsk Kazakh. *see* **Aktobe**
Akulivik Canada **119** K3
Akune Japan **75** C6
Akure Nigeria **96** D4
Akuressa Sri Lanka **84** D5
Akureyri Iceland **44** [inset]
Akusha Rus. Fed. **43** J8
Akwanga Nigeria **96** D4
Akxokesay China **83** G1
Akyab Myanmar *see* **Sittwe**
Akyatan Gölü *salt l.* Turkey **85** B1
Akyazı Turkey **59** N4
Akzhaykyn, Ozero *salt l.* Kazakh. **80** C3
Ål Norway **45** F6
'Alā, Jabal al *hills* Syria **85** C2
Alabama *r.* U.S.A. **133** C6
Alabama *state* U.S.A. **133** C5
Alabaster *AL* U.S.A. **133** C5
Alabaster *MI* U.S.A. **134** D1
Al 'Abṭīyah *well* Iraq **91** G5
Alaca Turkey **90** D2
Alacahan Turkey **90** E3
Alaçam Turkey **90** D2
Alaçam Dağları *mts* Turkey **59** M5
Alacant *Valencia* Spain *see* **Alicante**
Alaçatı Turkey **59** L5
Aladağ Turkey **90** B3
Ala Dağlar *mts* Turkey **91** F3
Ala Dağları *mts* Turkey **90** D3
Al 'Adam Libya **90** A5
Ala'er China **80** F3
Al Aflāj *reg.* Saudi Arabia **88** B6
Alag Hu *l.* China **76** C1
Alagir Rus. Fed. **91** G2
Alagoinhas Brazil **145** D1
Alahärmä Fin. **44** M5
Al Aḥmadī Kuwait **88** C4
Alai Range *mts* Asia **89** H2
Ālaivān Iran **88** D3
Ālājah Syria **85** B2
Alajärvi Fin. **44** M5
Al 'Ajrūd *well* Egypt **85** B4
Alakanuk U.S.A. **118** B3
Al Akhḍar Saudi Arabia **90** E5
Alakol', Ozero *salt l.* Kazakh. **80** F2
Ala Kul *salt l.* Kazakh. *see* **Alakol', Ozero**
Alakurtti Rus. Fed. **44** Q3
Al 'Alamayn Egypt **90** C5
Al 'Alayyah Saudi Arabia **86** F6
Alama Somalia **98** E3
Al 'Amādīyah Iraq **91** F3
Alamagan *i.* N. Mariana Is **69** L3
Alamaguan *i.* N. Mariana Is *see* **Alamagan**
Al 'Amārah Iraq **91** G5
'Alam ar Rūm, Ra's *pt* Egypt **90** B5
'Alāmarvdasht *watercourse* Iran **88** D4
Alameda U.S.A. **128** B3
'Alam el Rûm, Râs *pt* Egypt *see* **'Alam ar Rūm, Ra's**
Al Amghar *waterhole* Iraq **91** G5
Al 'Āmirīyah Egypt **90** C5
Alamítos, Sierra de los *mt.* Mex. **131** C7
Alamo *GA* U.S.A. **133** D5
Alamo *NV* U.S.A. **129** F3
Alamo Dam U.S.A. **129** G4
Alamogordo U.S.A. **127** G6
Alamo Heights U.S.A. **131** D6
Alamos *Sonora* Mex. **127** F7
Alamos *Sonora* Mex. **127** F8
Alamos *r.* Mex. **131** C7
Alamos, Sierra *mts* Mex. **127** F8
Alamosa U.S.A. **127** G5
Alamos de Peña Mex. **127** G7
Alampur India **84** C3
Alan Myanmar *see* **Aunglan**
Alanäs Sweden **44** I4
Åland *is* Fin. *see* **Åland Islands**
Aland *r.* Germany **53** L1
Aland India **84** C2
Al Andarīn Syria **85** C2
Åland Islands Fin. **45** K6
Alando China **76** B2
Alandur India **84** D3
Alanson U.S.A. **134** C1
Alanya Turkey **90** D3
Alapli Turkey **59** N4
Alappuzha India *see* **Alleppey**
Alapuzha India *see* **Alleppey**
Al 'Aqabah Jordan **85** B5
Al 'Aqīq Saudi Arabia **86** F5
Al 'Arabīyah as Sa'ūdīyah *country* Asia *see* **Saudi Arabia**
Alarcón, Embalse de *resr* Spain **57** E4
Al 'Arīsh Egypt **85** A4
Al Arṭāwīyah Saudi Arabia **86** G4
Alas, Selat *sea chan.* Indon. **108** B2
Alaşehir Turkey **59** M5
Alashiya *country* Asia *see* **Cyprus**
Al Ashmūnayn Egypt **90** C6
Alaska *state* U.S.A. **118** D3
Alaska, Gulf of U.S.A. **118** D4
Alaska Highway Canada/U.S.A. **120** A2
Alaska Peninsula U.S.A. **118** B4
Alaska Range *mts* U.S.A. **118** D3
Älät Azer. **91** H3
Alat Uzbek. *see* **Olot**
Alataw Shankou *pass* China/Kazakh. *see* **Dzungarian Gate**
Al Atwā' *well* Saudi Arabia **91** F5
Alatyr' Rus. Fed. **43** J5
Alatyr' *r.* Rus. Fed. **43** J5
Alausí Ecuador **142** C4
Alaverdi Armenia **91** G2
'Alavī Iran **88** C3
Alavieska Fin. **44** N4
Alavus Fin. **44** M5
Alawbum Myanmar **70** B1
Alawoona Australia **111** C7
Alay Kyrka Toosu *mts* Asia *see* **Alai Range**
Al 'Ayn Oman **88** E6
Al 'Ayn U.A.E. **88** D5
Alayskiy Khrebet *mts* Asia *see* **Alai Range**
Al 'Azīzīyah Iraq **91** G4

▶**Al 'Azīzīyah** Libya **55** G5
Highest recorded shade temperature in the world.

Al Azraq al Janūbī Jordan **85** C4
Alba Italy **58** C2
Alba U.S.A. **134** C1
Al Bāb Syria **85** C1
Albacete Spain **57** F4
Al Badī' Saudi Arabia **88** B6
Al Bādiyah al Janūbīyah *hill* Iraq **91** G5
Al Bahrayn *country* Asia *see* **Bahrain**
Alba Iulia Romania **59** J1
Al Bajā' *well* U.A.E. **88** C5
Albājī Iran **88** C4
Al Bakhrā *well* Saudi Arabia **88** B5
Albanel, Lac *l.* Canada **123** G4
Albania *country* Europe **59** H4
Albany Australia **109** B8
Albany *r.* Canada **122** E3
Albany *GA* U.S.A. **133** C6
Albany *IN* U.S.A. **134** C3
Albany *KY* U.S.A. **134** C5
Albany *MO* U.S.A. **130** E3

▶**Albany** *NY* U.S.A. **135** I2
Capital of New York state.

Albany *OH* U.S.A. **134** D4
Albany *OR* U.S.A. **126** C3
Albany *TX* U.S.A. **131** D5
Albany Downs Australia **112** D1
Albardão do João Maria *coastal area* Brazil **144** F4
Al Bardī Libya **90** B5
Al Bārīdah *hills* Saudi Arabia **85** D5
Al Başrah Iraq *see* **Basra**
Al Baṭḥa' *marsh* Iraq **91** G5
Al Bāṭinah *reg.* Oman **88** E5
Albatross Bay Australia **110** C2
Albatross Island Australia **111** [inset]
Al Bawītī Egypt **90** C5
Al Bayḍā' Libya **86** B3
Al Bayḍā' Yemen **86** G7
Albemarle U.S.A. **133** D5
Albemarle Island *Galápagos* Ecuador *see* **Isabela, Isla**
Albemarle Sound *sea chan.* U.S.A. **132** E5
Albenga Italy **58** C2
Alberche *r.* Spain **57** D4
Alberga Australia **111** A5
Alberga *watercourse* Australia **111** A5
Albergaria-a-Velha Port. **57** B3
Albert Australia **112** C4
Albert France **52** C5
Albert, Lake Dem. Rep. Congo/Uganda **98** D3
Albert, Parc National *nat. park* Dem. Rep. Congo *see* **Virunga, Parc National des**
Alberta *prov.* Canada **120** H4
Alberta U.S.A. **135** G5
Albert Kanaal *canal* Belgium **52** F4
Albert Lea U.S.A. **130** E3
Albert Nile *r.* Sudan/Uganda **97** G4
Alberto de Agostini, Parque Nacional *nat. park* Chile **144** B8
Alberton S. Africa **101** I4
Alberton U.S.A. **126** E3
Albert Town Bahamas **133** F8
Albertville Dem. Rep. Congo *see* **Kalemie**
Albertville France **56** H4
Albertville U.S.A. **133** C5
Albestroff France **52** G6
Albi France **56** F5
Albia U.S.A. **130** E3
Al Bīḍah *des.* Saudi Arabia **88** C5
Albina Suriname **143** H2
Albino Italy **58** C2
Albion *CA* U.S.A. **128** B2
Albion *IL* U.S.A. **130** F4
Albion *IN* U.S.A. **134** C3
Albion *MI* U.S.A. **134** C2
Albion *NE* U.S.A. **130** D3
Albion *NY* U.S.A. **135** F2
Albion *PA* U.S.A. **134** E3
Al Biqā' *valley* Lebanon *see* **El Béqaa**
Al Bi'r Saudi Arabia **90** E5
Al Birk Saudi Arabia **86** F6
Al Biyāḍh *reg.* Saudi Arabia **86** G5
Alborán, Isla de *i.* Spain **57** E6
Ålborg Denmark *see* **Aalborg**
Ålborg Bugt *b.* Denmark *see* **Aalborg Bugt**
Albro Australia **110** D4
Al Budayyi' Bahrain **88** C5
Albufeira Port. **57** B5
Al Buḥayrāt al Murrah *lakes* Egypt *see* **Bitter Lakes**
Albuquerque U.S.A. **127** G6
Al Burayj Syria **85** C2
Al Buraymī Oman **88** D5
Al Burj Jordan **85** B5
Alburquerque Spain **57** C4
Albury Australia **112** C6
Al Buşayrah Syria **91** F4
Al Busayṭā' *plain* Saudi Arabia **85** D4
Al Bushūk *well* Saudi Arabia **88** B4
Alcácer do Sal Port. **57** B4
Alcalá de Henares Spain **57** E3
Alcalá la Real Spain **57** E5
Alcamo *Sicily* Italy **58** E6
Alcañiz Spain **57** F3
Alcántara Spain **57** C4
Alcantara Lake Canada **121** I2
Alcaraz Spain **57** E4
Alcázar de San Juan Spain **57** E4
Alcazarquivir Morocco *see* **Ksar el Kebir**
Alchevs'k Ukr. **43** H6
Alcobaça Brazil **145** D2
Alcoi Spain *see* **Alcoy-Alcoi**
Alcoota Australia **108** F5
Alcova U.S.A. **126** G4
Alcoy Spain *see* **Alcoy-Alcoi**
Alcoy-Alcoi Spain **57** F4
Alcúdia Spain **57** H4
Aldabra Islands Seychelles **99** E4
Aldan Rus. Fed. **65** N4
Aldan *r.* Rus. Fed. **65** N3
Alde *r.* U.K. **49** I6
Aldeboarn Neth. **52** F1
Aldeburgh U.K. **49** I6
Alder Creek U.S.A. **135** H2
Alderney *i.* Channel Is **49** E9
Alder Peak U.S.A. **128** C4
Aldershot U.K. **49** G7
Al Dhafrah *reg.* U.A.E. **88** D6
Aldingham U.K. **48** D4
Aldridge U.K. **49** F6
Aleg Mauritania **96** B3
Alegre *Espírito Santo* Brazil **145** C3
Alegre *Minas Gerais* Brazil **145** B2
Alegrete Brazil **144** E3
Alegros Mountain U.S.A. **129** I4
Aleksandra, Mys *hd* Rus. Fed. **74** E1
Aleksandriya Ukr. *see* **Oleksandriya**
Aleksandro-Nevskiy Rus. Fed. **43** I5
Aleksandropol Armenia *see* **Gyumri**
Aleksandrov Rus. Fed. **42** H4
Aleksandrov Gay Rus. Fed. **43** K6
Aleksandrovsk Rus. Fed. **41** R4
Aleksandrovsk Ukr. *see* **Zaporizhzhya**
Aleksandrovsky Rus. Fed. *see* **Aleksandrovsk**
Aleksandrovskoye Rus. Fed. **91** F1
Aleksandrovsk-Sakhalinskiy Rus. Fed. **74** F2
Aleksandry, Zemlya *i.* Rus. Fed. **64** F1
Alekseyevka *Akmolinskaya Oblast'* Kazakh. *see* **Akkol'**
Alekseyevka *Vostochnyy Kazakhstan* Kazakh. *see* **Terekty**
Alekseyevka *Amurskaya Oblast'* Rus. Fed. **74** B1
Alekseyevka *Belgorodskaya Oblast'* Rus. Fed. **43** H6
Alekseyevka *Belgorodskaya Oblast'* Rus. Fed. **43** H6
Alekseyevskaya Rus. Fed. **43** I6
Alekseyevskoye Rus. Fed. **42** K5
Aleksin Rus. Fed. **43** H5
Aleksinac Serbia **59** I3
Alèmbé Gabon **98** B4
Ålen Norway **44** G5
Alençon France **56** E2
Alenquer Brazil **143** H4
'Alenuihāhā Channel U.S.A. **127** [inset]
Alep Syria *see* **Aleppo**
Aleppo Syria **85** C1
Alert Canada **119** L1
Alerta Peru **142** D6
Alès France **56** G4
Aleşd Romania **59** J1
Aleshki Ukr. *see* **Tsyurupyns'k**
Aleşkirt Turkey *see* **Eleşkirt**
Alessandria Italy **58** C2
Alessio Albania *see* **Lezhë**
Ålesund Norway **44** E5
Aleutian Basin *sea feature* Bering Sea **150** H2
Aleutian Islands U.S.A. **118** A4
Aleutian Range *mts* U.S.A. **118** C4
Aleutian Trench *sea feature* N. Pacific Ocean **150** I2
Alevina, Mys *c.* Rus. Fed. **65** Q4
Alevişik Turkey *see* **Samandağı**
Alexander U.S.A. **130** C2
Alexander, Kap *c.* Greenland *see* **Ullersuaq**
Alexander, Mount *hill* Australia **110** B2
Alexander Archipelago *is* U.S.A. **120** B3
Alexander Bay *b.* Namibia/S. Africa **100** C5
Alexander Bay S. Africa **100** C5
Alexander City U.S.A. **133** C5
Alexander Island Antarctica **152** L2
Alexandra Australia **112** B6
Alexandra N.Z. **113** B7
Alexandra, Cape S. Georgia **144** I8
Alexandra Channel India **71** A4
Alexandra Land *i.* Rus. Fed. *see* **Aleksandry, Zemlya**
Alexandreia Greece **59** J4
Alexandretta Turkey *see* **İskenderun**
Alexandria Afgh. *see* **Ghaznī**
Alexandria Canada **135** H1

▶**Alexandria** Egypt **90** C5
5th most populous city in Africa.

Alexandria Romania **59** K3
Alexandria S. Africa **101** H7
Alexandria Turkm. *see* **Mary**
Alexandria U.K. **50** E5
Alexandria *IN* U.S.A. **134** C3
Alexandria *KY* U.S.A. **134** C4
Alexandria *LA* U.S.A. **131** E6
Alexandria *VA* U.S.A. **135** G4
Alexandria Arachoton Afgh. *see* **Kandahār**
Alexandria Areion Afgh. *see* **Herāt**
Alexandria Bay U.S.A. **135** H1
Alexandria Prophthasia Afgh. *see* **Farāh**
Alexandrina, Lake Australia **111** B7
Alexandroupoli Greece **59** K4
Alexis *r.* Canada **123** K3
Alexis Creek Canada **120** F4
Aley Lebanon **85** B3
Aleyak Iran **88** E2
Aleysk Rus. Fed. **72** E2
Alf Germany **52** H4
Al Farwānīyah Kuwait **88** B4
Al Fas Morocco *see* **Fès**
Al Fatḥah Iraq **91** F4
Al Fāw Iraq **91** H5
Al Fayyūm Egypt **90** C5
Alfeld (Leine) Germany **53** J3
Alfenas Brazil **145** B3
Alford U.K. **48** H5
Alfred *ME* U.S.A. **135** J2
Alfred *NY* U.S.A. **135** G2
Alfred and Marie Range *hills* Australia **109** D6
Al Fujayrah U.A.E. *see* **Fujairah**
Al Fuqahā' Libya **97** E2
Al Furāt *r.* Asia **85** D2 *see* **Euphrates**
Alga Kazakh. **80** A2
Ålgård Norway **45** D7
Algarrobo del Aguilla Arg. **144** C5
Algarve *reg.* Port. **57** B5
Algeciras Spain **57** D5
Algemesí Spain **57** F4
Algena Eritrea **86** E6
Alger Alg. *see* **Algiers**
Alger U.S.A. **134** C1

▶**Algeria** *country* Africa **96** C2
2nd largest country in Africa.

Algérie *country* Africa *see* **Algeria**
Algermissen Germany **53** J2
Algha Kazakh. *see* **Alga**
Al Ghāfāt Oman **88** E6
Al Ghammās Iraq **91** G5
Al Ghardaqah Egypt *see* **Al Ghurdaqah**
Al Ghawr *plain* Jordan/West Bank **85** B4
Al Ghayḍah Yemen **86** H6
Alghero *Sardinia* Italy **58** C4
Al Ghurdaqah Egypt **86** D4
Al Ghuwayr *well* Qatar **88** C5

▶**Algiers** Alg. **57** H5
Capital of Algeria.

Algoa Bay S. Africa **101** G7
Algoma U.S.A. **134** B1
Algona U.S.A. **130** E3
Algonac U.S.A. **134** D2
Algonquin Park Canada **135** F1
Algonquin Provincial Park Canada **135** F1
Algorta Spain **57** E2
Algueirao Moz. *see* **Hacufera**
Al Habakah *well* Saudi Arabia **91** F5
Al Ḥabbānīyah Iraq **91** F4
Al Ḥadaqah *well* Saudi Arabia **88** B4
Al Ḥadd Bahrain **88** C5
Al Hadhālīl *plat.* Saudi Arabia **91** F5
Al Ḥadīdīyah Syria **85** C2
Al Ḥadīthah Iraq **91** F4
Al Hadīthah Saudi Arabia **85** C4
Al Ḥaḍr Iraq *see* **Hatra**
Al Ḥafār *well* Saudi Arabia **91** F5
Al Ḥaffah Syria **85** C2
Al Haggounia W. Sahara **96** B2
Al Ḥajar al Gharbī *mts* Oman **88** E5
Al Ḥajar ash Sharqī *mts* Oman **88** E6
Al Ḥamād *plain* Asia **90** E5
Al Ḥamādah al Ḥamrā' *plat.* Libya **96** E2
Alhama de Murcia Spain **57** F5
Al Ḥamar Saudi Arabia **88** B6
Al Ḥamīdīyah Syria **85** B2
Al Ḥammām Egypt **90** C5
Al Ḥanākīyah Saudi Arabia **86** F5
Al Haniyah *esc.* Iraq **91** G5
Al Hariq Saudi Arabia **88** B6
Al Ḥarrah Egypt **90** C5
Al Ḥarūj al Aswad *hills* Libya **97** E2
Al Hasa *reg.* Saudi Arabia **88** C5
Al Ḥasakah Syria **91** F3
Al Hawi *salt pan* Saudi Arabia **85** D5
Al Hawjā' Saudi Arabia **90** E5
Al Ḥawṭah *reg.* Saudi Arabia **88** B6
Al Ḥayy Iraq **91** G4
Al Ḥayz Egypt **90** C5
Al Hazīm Jordan **85** C4
Al Ḥazm Saudi Arabia **90** E5
Al Ḥazm al Jawf Yemen **86** F6
Al Ḥibāk *des.* Saudi Arabia **87** H6
Al Hījānah Syria **85** C3
Al Ḥillah Iraq *see* **Hillah**
Al Ḥillah Saudi Arabia **86** G5
Al Ḥinnāh Saudi Arabia **98** E1
Al Ḥinw *mt.* Saudi Arabia **85** D4
Al Hirrah *well* Saudi Arabia **88** C6
Al Hīshah Syria **85** D1
Al Ḥismā *plain* Saudi Arabia **90** D5
Al Ḥiṣn Jordan **85** B3
Al Hoceima Morocco **57** E6
Al Ḥudaydah Yemen *see* **Hodeidah**
Al Ḥufrah *reg.* Saudi Arabia **90** E5
Al Hūj *hills* Saudi Arabia **90** E5
Al Husayfin Oman **88** E5
Al Huwwah Saudi Arabia **88** B6
Ali China **82** D2
'Alīābād Afgh. **89** H2
'Alīābād *Golestān* Iran **88** D2
'Alīābād *Hormozgan* Iran **88** D4
'Alīābād *Khorāsān* Iran **89** F4
'Alīābād *Kordestān* Iran **88** B2
'Alīābād, Kūh-e *mt.* Iran **88** C3
Aliağa Turkey **59** L5
Aliakmonas *r.* Greece **59** J4
Alibag India **84** B2
Äli Bayramlı Azer. **91** H3
Alicante Spain **57** F4
Alice *r.* Australia **110** C2
Alice *watercourse* Australia **110** D5
Alice U.S.A. **131** D7
Alice, Punta *pt* Italy **58** G5
Alice Springs Australia **109** F5
Alice Town Bahamas **133** E7
Aliceville U.S.A. **131** F5
Alichur Tajik. **89** I2
Alichur *r.* Tajik. **89** I2
Alick Creek *r.* Australia **110** C4
Alifu Atoll Maldives *see* **Ari Atoll**
Al Ifzī'iyyah *i.* U.A.E. **88** C5
Aliganj India **82** D4
Aligarh *Rajasthan* India **82** D4
Aligarh *Uttar Prad.* India **82** D4
Alīgūdarz Iran **88** C3
Alihe China **74** A2
Alījūq, Kūh-e *mt.* Iran **88** C4
'Alī Kheyl Afgh. **89** H3
Al Imārāt al 'Arabīyah at Muttaḥidah *country* Asia *see* **United Arab Emirates**
Alimia *i.* Greece **59** L6
Alindao Cent. Afr. Rep. **98** C3
Alingsås Sweden **45** H8
Aliova *r.* Turkey **59** M5
Alipura India **82** D4
Alipur Duar India **83** G4
Alirajpur India **82** C5
Al 'Irāq *country* Asia *see* **Iraq**
Al 'Īsāwīyah Saudi Arabia **85** C4
Al Iskandarīyah Egypt *see* **Alexandria**
Al Iskandarīyah Iraq **91** G4
Al Ismā'īlīyah Egypt **90** D5
Al Ismā'īlīyah *governorate* Egypt **85** A4
Aliveri Greece **59** K5
Aliwal North S. Africa **101** H6
Alix Canada **120** H4
Al Jafr Jordan **85** C4
Al Jāfūrah *des.* Saudi Arabia **88** C5
Al Jaghbūb Libya **90** B5
Al Jahrah Kuwait **88** B4
Al Jamalīyah Qatar **88** C5
Al Jarāwī *well* Saudi Arabia **85** D4
Al Jauf Saudi Arabia *see* **Dumat al Jandal**
Al Jawb *reg.* Saudi Arabia **88** C6
Al Jawf Libya **97** F2
Al Jawsh Libya **96** E1
Al Jaza'ir *country* Africa *see* **Algeria**
Al Jaza'ir Alg. *see* **Algiers**
Aljezur Port. **57** B5
Al Jībān *reg.* Saudi Arabia **88** C5
Al Jil *well* Iraq **91** F5
Al Jilh *esc.* Saudi Arabia **88** B5
Al Jithāmīyah Saudi Arabia **91** F6
Al Jīzah Egypt *see* **Giza**
Al Jīzah Jordan **85** B4
Al Jubayl *hills* Saudi Arabia **88** B5
Al Jubaylah Saudi Arabia **88** B5
Al Jufrah Libya **97** E2
Al Julayqah *well* Saudi Arabia **88** C5
Aljustrel Port. **57** B5
Al Juwayf *depr.* Syria **85** C3
Al Kahfah *Al Qaşīm* Saudi Arabia **86** F4
Al Kahfah *Ash Sharqīyah* Saudi Arabia **88** C5
Alkali Lake Canada **120** F5
Al Karak Jordan **85** B4
Al Khābūrah Oman **88** E6
Al Khalīl West Bank *see* **Hebron**
Al Khāliş Iraq **91** G4
Al Khārijah Egypt **86** D4
Al Kharj *reg.* Saudi Arabia **88** B6
Al Kharrārah Qatar **88** C5
Al Kharrūbah Egypt **85** A4
Al Khaşab Oman **88** E5
Al Khatam *reg.* U.A.E. **88** D5
Al Khawkhah Yemen **86** F7
Al Khawr Qatar **88** C5
Al Khizāmī *well* Saudi Arabia **88** C5
Al Khums Libya **97** E1
Al Khunfah *sand area* Saudi Arabia **90** E5
Al Khunn Saudi Arabia **98** E1
Al Kifl Iraq **91** G4
Al Kir'ānah Qatar **88** C5
Al Kiswah Syria **85** C3
Alkmaar Neth. **52** E2
Al Kūbrī Egypt **85** A4
Al Kumayt Iraq **91** G4
Al Kuntillah Egypt **85** B5
Al Kusūr *hills* Saudi Arabia **85** D4
Al Kūt Iraq **91** G4
Al Kuwayt *country* Asia *see* **Kuwait**
Al Kuwayt Kuwait *see* **Kuwait**
Al Labbah *plain* Saudi Arabia **91** F5
Al Lādhiqīyah Syria *see* **Latakia**
Allagadda India **84** C3
Allahabad India **83** E4
Al Lajā *lava field* Syria **85** C3
Allakaket U.S.A. **118** C3
Allakh-Yun' Rus. Fed. **65** O3
Allanmyo Myanmar *see* **Aunglan**
Allanridge S. Africa **101** H4
Allapalli India **84** D2
'Allāqī, Wādī al *watercourse* Egypt **86** D5
'Allāqi, Wâdi el *watercourse* Egypt *see* **'Allāqī, Wādī al**
Allardville Canada **123** I5
Alldays S. Africa **101** I2
Allegan U.S.A. **134** C2
Allegheny *r.* U.S.A. **134** F3
Allegheny Mountains U.S.A. **134** D5
Allegheny Reservoir U.S.A. **135** F3
Allen, Lough *l.* Ireland **51** D3
Allendale U.S.A. **133** D5
Allendale Town U.K. **48** E4
Allende *Coahuila* Mex. **131** C6
Allende *Nuevo León* Mex. **131** C7
Allendorf (Lumda) Germany **53** I4
Allenford Canada **134** E1
Allenstein Poland *see* **Olsztyn**
Allensville U.S.A. **134** B5
Allentown U.S.A. **135** H3
Alleppey India **84** C4
Aller *r.* Germany **53** J2
Alliance *NE* U.S.A. **130** C3
Alliance *OH* U.S.A. **134** E3
Al Lībīyah *country* Africa *see* **Libya**
Allier *r.* France **56** F3
Al Lihābah *well* Saudi Arabia **88** B5
Allinge-Sandvig Denmark **45** I9
Al Lişāfah *well* Saudi Arabia **88** B5
Al Lisān *pen.* Jordan **85** B4
Alliston Canada **134** F1
Al Līth Saudi Arabia **86** F5
Al Liwā' *oasis* U.A.E. **88** D6
Alloa U.K. **50** F4
Allons U.S.A. **134** C5
Allora Australia **112** F2
Allur India **84** D3
Alluru Kottapatnam India **84** D3
Al Lussuf *well* Iraq **91** F5
Alma Canada **123** H4
Alma *MI* U.S.A. **134** C2
Alma *NE* U.S.A. **130** D3
Alma *WI* U.S.A. **130** F2
Al Ma'ānīyah Iraq **91** F5
Alma-Ata Kazakh. *see* **Almaty**
Almada Port. **57** B4
Al Madāfi' *plat.* Saudi Arabia **90** E5
Al Ma'danīyāt *well* Iraq **91** G5
Almaden Australia **110** D3
Almadén Spain **57** D4
Al Madīnah Saudi Arabia *see* **Medina**
Al Mafraq Jordan **85** C3
Al Maghrib *country* Africa *see* **Morocco**
Al Maghrib *reg.* U.A.E. **88** D6
Al Mahākīk *reg.* Saudi Arabia **88** C6
Al Mahdum Syria **85** C1
Al Maḥiā *depr.* Saudi Arabia **90** E6
Al Maḥwīt Yemen **86** F6
Al Malsūnīyah *reg.* Saudi Arabia **88** C5
Almalyk Uzbek. *see* **Olmaliq**
Al Manadir *reg.* Oman **88** D6
Al Manāmah Bahrain *see* **Manama**
Al Manjūr *well* Saudi Arabia **88** B6
Almanor, Lake U.S.A. **128** C1
Almansa Spain **57** F4
Al Manşūrah Egypt **90** C5
Almanzor *mt.* Spain **57** D3
Al Mariyyah U.A.E. **88** D6
Al Marj Libya **97** F1
Almas, Rio das *r.* Brazil **145** A1
Al Maṭarīyah Egypt **90** D5

▶**Almaty** Kazakh. **80** E3
Former capital of Kazakhstan.

Al Mawşil Iraq *see* **Mosul**
Al Mayādīn Syria **91** F4
Al Mazār Egypt **85** A4
Almaznyy Rus. Fed. **65** M3
Almeirim Brazil **143** H4
Almeirim Port. **57** B4
Almelo Neth. **52** G2
Almenara Brazil **145** C2
Almendra, Embalse de *resr* Spain **57** C3
Almendralejo Spain **57** C4
Almere Neth. **52** F2
Almería Spain **57** E5
Almería, Golfo de *b.* Spain **57** E5
Al'met'yevsk Rus. Fed. *see* **Al'met'yevsk**
Al'met'yevsk Rus. Fed. **41** Q5
Älmhult Sweden **45** I8
Almina, Punta *pt* Spain **57** D6
Al Mindak Saudi Arabia **86** F5
Al Minyā Egypt **90** C5
Almirós Greece *see* **Almyros**
Al Mish'āb Saudi Arabia **88** C4
Almodôvar Port. **57** B5
Almond *r.* U.K. **50** F4
Almont U.S.A. **134** D2
Almonte Spain **57** C5
Almora India **82** D3
Al Mu'ayzīlah *hill* Saudi Arabia **85** D5
Al Mubarrez Saudi Arabia **86** G4
Al Muḍaibī Oman **87** I5
Al Muḍairib Oman **88** E6
Al Muḥarraq Bahrain **88** C5
Al Mukallā Yemen *see* **Mukalla**
Al Mukhā Yemen *see* **Mocha**
Al Mukhaylī Libya **86** B3
Al Munbaṭiḥ *des.* Saudi Arabia **88** C6
Almuñécar Spain **57** E5
Al Muqdādīyah Iraq **91** G4
Al Mūrītānīyah *country* Africa *see* **Mauritania**
Al Murūt *well* Saudi Arabia **91** E5
Almus Turkey **90** E2
Al Musannāh *ridge* Saudi Arabia **88** B4
Al Musayyib Iraq **88** B3
Al Muwaqqar Jordan **85** C4
Almyros Greece **59** J5
Almyrou, Ormos *b.* Greece **59** K7
Alnwick U.K. **48** F3

▶**Alofi** Niue **107** J3
Capital of Niue.

Aloja Latvia **45** N8
Alon Myanmar **70** A2
Along India **83** H3
Alongshan China **74** A2
Alonnisos *i.* Greece **59** J5
Alor *i.* Indon. **108** D2
Alor, Kepulauan *is* Indon. **108** D2
Alor Setar Malaysia **71** C6
Alor Star Malaysia *see* **Alor Setar**
Alost Belgium *see* **Aalst**
Aloysius, Mount Australia **109** E6
Alozero Rus. Fed. **44** Q4
Alpen Germany **52** G3
Alpena U.S.A. **134** D1
Alpercatas, Serra das *hills* Brazil **143** J5
Alpha Australia **110** D4
Alpha Ridge *sea feature* Arctic Ocean **153** A1
Alpine *AZ* U.S.A. **129** I5

Alpine NY U.S.A. 135 G2
Alpine TX U.S.A. 131 C6
Alpine WY U.S.A. 126 F4
Alpine National Park Australia 112 C6
Alps mts Europe 56 H4
Al Qa'āmīyāt reg. Saudi Arabia 86 G6
Al Qaddāḥīyah Libya 97 E1
Al Qadmūs Syria 85 C2
Al Qaffāy i. U.A.E. 88 D5
Al Qāhirah Egypt see Cairo
Al Qā'īyah Saudi Arabia 86 F5
Al Qā'īyah well Saudi Arabia 88 B5
Al Qal'a Beni Hammad tourist site Alg. 57 I6
Al Qalībah Saudi Arabia 90 E5
Al Qāmishlī Syria 91 F3
Al Qar'ah Libya 90 B5
Al Qar'ah well Saudi Arabia 88 B5
Al Qar'ah lava field Syria 85 C3
Al Qardāḥah Syria 85 C2
Al Qarqar Saudi Arabia 85 C4
Al Qaryatayn Syria 85 C2
Al Qaṣab Ar Riyāḍ Saudi Arabia 88 B5
Al Qaṣab Ash Sharqīyah Saudi Arabia 88 C6
Al Qaṭīf Saudi Arabia 88 C5
Al Qaṭn Yemen 86 G6
Al Qaṭrānah Jordan 85 C4
Al Qaṭrūn Libya 97 E2
Al Qāyṣūmah well Saudi Arabia 91 F5
Alqueva, Barragem de resr 57 C4
Al Qumur country Africa see Comoros
Al Qunayṭirah Syria 85 B3
Al Qunfidhah Saudi Arabia 86 F6
Al Qurayyāt Saudi Arabia 85 C4
Al Qurnah Iraq 91 G5
Al Quṣaymah Egypt 85 B4
Al Quṣayr Egypt 86 D4
Al Quṣayr Syria 85 C2
Al Qūṣīyah Egypt 90 C6
Al Qūṣūrīyah Saudi Arabia 88 B6
Al Quṭayfah Syria 85 C3
Al Quwayi' Saudi Arabia 88 B6
Al Quwayīyah Saudi Arabia 86 G5
Al Quwayrah Jordan 85 B5
Al Rabbād reg. U.A.E. 88 D6
Alroy Downs Australia 110 B3
Alsace admin. reg. France 53 H6
Alsace reg. France 56 H2
Alsager U.K. 49 E5
Al Samīt well Iraq 91 F5
Alsask Canada 121 I5
Alsatia reg. France see Alsace
Alsek r. U.S.A. 120 B3
Alsfeld Germany 53 J4
Alsleben (Saale) Germany 53 L3
Alston U.K. 48 E4
Alstonville Australia 112 F2
Alsunga Latvia 45 L8
Alta Norway 44 M2
Alta, Mount N.Z. 113 B7
Altaelva r. Norway 44 M2
Altafjorden sea chan. Norway 44 M1
Alta Floresta Brazil 143 G5
Altai Mountains Asia 72 F3
Altamaha r. U.S.A. 133 D6
Altamira Brazil 143 H4
Altamura Italy 58 G4
Altan Shiret China 73 J5
Altan Xiret China see Altan Shiret
Alta Paraiso de Goiás Brazil 145 B1
Altar r. Mex. 127 F7
Altar, Desierto de des. Mex. 129 F6
Altavista U.S.A. 134 F5
Altay China 80 G2
Altay Mongolia 80 H3
Altay Mongolia 80 I2
Altayskiy Rus. Fed. 80 G1
Altayskiy Khrebet mts Asia see Altai Mountains
Altdorf Switz. 56 I3
Altea Spain 57 F4
Alteidet Norway 44 M1
Altenahr Germany 52 G4
Altenberge Germany 53 H2
Altenburg Germany 53 M4
Altenkirchen (Westerwald) Germany 53 H4
Altenqoke China 83 H1
Altin Köprü Iraq 91 G4
Altınoluk Turkey 59 L5
Altınözü Turkey 85 C1
Altıntaş Turkey 59 N5
Altiplano plain Bol. 142 E7
Altmark reg. Germany 53 L2
Altmühl r. Germany 53 L6
Alto, Monte hill Italy 58 D2
Alto Chicapa Angola 99 B5
Alto del Moncayo mt. Spain 57 F3
Alto de Pencoso hills Arg. 144 C4
Alto Garças Brazil 143 H7
Alto Madidi, Parque Nacional nat. park Bol. 142 E6
Alton CA U.S.A. 128 A1
Alton IL U.S.A. 130 F4
Alton MO U.S.A. 131 F4
Alton NH U.S.A. 135 J2
Altona Canada 120 F3
Altoona U.S.A. 135 F3
Alto Parnaíba Brazil 143 I5
Alto Taquarí Mato Grosso Brazil 143 H7
Altötting Germany 47 N6
Altrincham U.K. 48 E5
Alt Schwerin Germany 53 M1
Altūn Kūbrī Iraq see Altin Köprü
Altun Shan mts China 80 G4
Alturas U.S.A. 126 C4
Altus U.S.A. 131 D5
Al 'Ubaylah Saudi Arabia 98 F1
Alucra Turkey 90 E2
Alūksne Latvia 45 O8
Alūm Iran 88 C3
Alum Bridge U.S.A. 134 E4
Al 'Uqaylah Libya 97 E1
Al 'Uqaylah Saudi Arabia see An Nabk
Al Uqṣur Egypt see Luxor
Alur India 84 C3
Al 'Urayq des. Saudi Arabia 90 E5
Al 'Urdun country Asia see Jordan
Alur Setar Malaysia see Alor Setar
'Alūt Iran 88 B3
Aluva India see Alwaye
Al 'Uwayjā' well Saudi Arabia 88 C6
Al 'Uwaynāt Libya 86 B5
Al 'Uwayqīlah Saudi Arabia 91 F5
Al 'Uzayr Iraq 91 G5
Alva U.S.A. 131 D4
Alvand, Kūh-e mt. Iran 88 C3
Alvarães Brazil 142 F4
Alvaton U.S.A. 134 B5
Alvdal Norway 44 G5
Älvdalen Sweden 45 I6
Alvesta Sweden 45 I8
Ålvik Norway 45 E6
Alvik Sweden 44 J5
Alvin U.S.A. 131 E6
Alvorada do Norte Brazil 145 B1
Älvsbyn Sweden 44 L4
Al Wafrah Kuwait 88 B4
Al Wajh Saudi Arabia 86 E4
Al Wakrah Qatar 88 C5
Al Waqbá well Saudi Arabia 88 B4
Alwar India 82 D4
Al Warī'ah Saudi Arabia 86 G4
Al Wāṭiyah well Egypt 90 B5
Alwaye India 84 C4
Al Widyān plat. Iraq/Saudi Arabia 91 F4
Al Wusayṭ well Saudi Arabia 88 B4
Alxa Youqi China see Ehen Hudag
Alxa Zuoqi China see Bayan Hot
Al Yamāmah Saudi Arabia 88 B5
Al Yaman country Asia see Yemen
Alyangula Australia 110 B2
Al Yāsāt i. U.A.E. 88 C5
Alyth U.K. 50 F4
Alytus Lith. 45 N9
Alzette r. Lux. 52 G5
Alzey Germany 53 I5
Amacayacu, Parque Nacional nat. park Col. 142 D4
Amadeus, Lake salt flat Australia 109 E6
Amadjuak Lake Canada 119 K3
Amadora Port. 57 B4
Amakusa-nada b. Japan 75 C6
Åmål Sweden 45 H7
Amalia S. Africa 101 G4
Amaliada Greece 59 I6
Amalner India 82 C5
Amamapare Indon. 69 J7
Amambaí Brazil 144 E2
Amambaí, Serra de hills Brazil/Para. 144 E2
Amami-Ō-shima i. Japan 75 C7
Amami-shotō is Japan 75 C8
Amamula Dem. Rep. Congo 98 C4
Amanab P.N.G. 69 K7
Amangel'dy Kazakh. 80 C1
Amankeldi Kazakh. see Amangel'dy
Amantea Italy 58 G5
Amanzimtoti S. Africa 101 J6
Amapá Brazil 143 H3
Amarante Brazil 143 J5
Amarapura Myanmar 70 B2
Amareleja Port. 57 C4
Amargosa Brazil 145 D1
Amargosa watercourse U.S.A. 128 E3
Amargosa Desert U.S.A. 128 E3
Amargosa Range mts U.S.A. 128 E3
Amargosa Valley U.S.A. 128 E3
Amarillo U.S.A. 131 C5
Amarillo, Cerro mt. Arg. 144 C4
Amarkantak India 83 E5
Amarpur Madh. Prad. India 82 E5
Amasia Turkey see Amasya
Amasine W. Sahara 96 B2
Amasra Turkey 90 D2
Amasya Turkey 90 D2
Amata Australia 109 E6
Amatulla India 83 H4
Amau P.N.G. 110 E1
Amay Belgium 52 F4
Amazar Rus. Fed. 74 A1
Amazar r. Rus. Fed. 74 A1

▶Amazon r. S. America 142 F4
Longest river and largest drainage basin in South America and 2nd longest river in the world.
Also known as Amazonas or Solimões

Amazon, Mouths of the Brazil 143 I3
Amazonas r. S. America 142 F4 see Amazon
Amazon Cone sea feature S. Atlantic Ocean 148 E5
Amazónia, Parque Nacional nat. park Brazil 143 G4
Ambajogai India 84 C2
Ambala India 82 D3
Ambalangoda Sri Lanka 84 D5
Ambalavao Madag. 99 E6
Ambam Cameroon 98 B3
Ambar Iran 88 E4
Ambarchik Rus. Fed. 65 R3
Ambarnyy Rus. Fed. 44 R4
Ambasa India see Ambassa
Ambasamudram India 84 C4
Ambassa India 83 G5
Ambathala Australia 111 D5
Ambato Ecuador 142 C4
Ambato Boeny Madag. 99 E5
Ambato Finandrahana Madag. 99 E6
Ambatolampy Madag. 99 E5
Ambatomainty Madag. 99 E5
Ambatondrazaka Madag. 99 E5
Ambejogai India see Ambajogai
Ambelau i. Indon. 69 H7
Ambeno enclave East Timor see Ocussi
Amberg Germany 53 L5
Ambergris Cay i. Belize 136 G5
Ambérieu-en-Bugey France 56 G4
Amberley Canada 134 E1
Ambgaon India 84 D1
Ambianum France see Amiens
Ambikapur India 83 E5
Ambilobe Madag. 99 E5
Ambition, Mount Canada 120 D3
Amble U.K. 48 F3
Ambler U.S.A. 118 C3
Ambleside U.K. 48 E4
Amblève r. Belgium 52 F4
Ambo India 83 F5
Amboasary Madag. 99 E6
Ambodifotatra Madag. 99 E5
Ambohimahasoa Madag. 99 E6
Ambohitra mt. Madag. 99 E5
Amboina Indon. see Ambon
Ambon Indon. 69 H7
Ambon i. Indon. 69 H7
Amboró, Parque Nacional nat. park Bol. 142 F7
Ambositra Madag. 99 E6
Ambovombe Madag. 99 E6
Amboy U.S.A. 129 F4
Ambre, Cap d' c. Madag. see Bobaomby, Tanjona
Ambrim i. Vanuatu see Ambrym
Ambriz Angola 99 B4
Ambrizete Angola see N'zeto
Ambrosia Lake U.S.A. 129 J4
Ambrym i. Vanuatu 107 G3
Ambunti P.N.G. 69 K7
Ambur India 84 C3
Am-Dam Chad 97 F3
Amded, Oued watercourse Alg. 96 D2
Amdo China see Lharigarbo
Ameland i. Neth. 52 F1
Amelia Court House U.S.A. 135 G5
Amenia U.S.A. 135 I3
Amer, Erg d' des. Alg. 98 A1
Amereli India see Amreli
American, North Fork r. U.S.A. 128 C2
Americana Brazil 145 B3
American-Antarctic Ridge sea feature S. Atlantic Ocean 148 G9
American Falls U.S.A. 126 E4
American Falls Reservoir U.S.A. 126 E4
American Fork U.S.A. 129 H1

▶American Samoa terr. S. Pacific Ocean 107 J3
United States Unincorporated Territory.

Americus U.S.A. 133 C5
Amersfoort Neth. 52 F2
Amersfoort S. Africa 101 I4
Amersham U.K. 49 G7
Amery Canada 121 M3
Amery Ice Shelf Antarctica 152 E2
Ames U.S.A. 130 E3
Amesbury U.K. 49 F7
Amesbury U.S.A. 135 J2
Amet India 82 C4
Amethi India 83 E4
Amfissa Greece 59 J5
Amga Rus. Fed. 65 O3
Amgalang China 73 L3
Amgu Rus. Fed. 74 E3
Amguid Alg. 96 D2
Amgun' r. Rus. Fed. 74 E1
Amherst Canada 123 I5
Amherst Myanmar see Kyaikkami
Amherst MA U.S.A. 135 I2
Amherst OH U.S.A. 134 D3
Amherst VA U.S.A. 134 F5
Amherstburg Canada 134 D2
Amherst Island Canada 135 G1
Amiata, Monte mt. Italy 58 D3
Amida Turkey see Diyarbakır
Amidon U.S.A. 130 C2
Amiens France 52 C5
'Amīj, Wādī watercourse Iraq 91 F4
Amik Ovası marsh Turkey 85 C1
'Amīnābād Iran 88 D4
Amindivi atoll India see Amini
Amindivi Islands India 84 B4
Amini atoll India 84 B4
Amino Eth. 98 E3
Aminuis Namibia 100 D2
Amīrābād Iran 88 B3
Amirante Islands Seychelles 149 L6
Amirante Trench sea feature Indian Ocean 149 L6
Amisk Lake Canada 121 K4
Amistad, Represa de resr Mex./U.S.A. see Amistad Reservoir
Amistad Reservoir Mex./U.S.A. 131 C6
Amisus Turkey see Samsun
Amite U.S.A. 131 F6
Amity Point Australia 112 F1
Amla India 82 D5
Amlapura Indon. see Karangasem
Amlash Iran 88 C2
Amlekhganj Nepal 83 F4
Åmli Norway 45 F7
Amlia Island U.S.A. 118 A4
Amlwch U.K. 48 C5

▶'Ammān Jordan 85 B4
Capital of Jordan.

Ammanazar Turkm. 88 D2
Ammanford U.K. 49 D7
Ämmänsaari Fin. 44 P4
'Ammār, Tall hill Syria 85 C3
Ammarnäs Sweden 44 J4
Ammaroo Australia 110 A4
Ammassalik Greenland 153 J2
Ammerland reg. Germany 53 H1
Ammern Germany 53 K3
Ammochostos Cyprus see Famagusta
Ammochostos Bay Cyprus 85 B2
Am Nābiyah Yemen 86 F7
Amne Machin Range mts China see A'nyêmaqên Shan
Amnok-kang r. China/N. Korea see Yalu Jiang
Amo Jiang r. China 76 D4
Amol Iran 88 D2
Amorbach Germany 53 J5
Amorgos i. Greece 59 K6
Amory U.S.A. 131 F5
Amos Canada 122 F4
Amourj Mauritania 96 C3
Amoy China see Xiamen
Ampani India 84 D2
Ampanihy Madag. 99 E6
Amparai Sri Lanka 84 D5
Amparo Brazil 145 B3
Ampasimanolotra Madag. 99 E5
Amphitheatre Australia 112 A6
Amphitrite Group is Paracel Is 68 E3
Ampoa Indon. 69 G7
Amraoti India see Amravati
Amravati India 84 C1
Amrawad India 82 D5
Amreli India 82 B5
Amri Pak. 89 H5
Amring India 83 H4
'Amrīt Syria 85 B2
Amritsar India 82 C3
Amroha India 82 D3
Amsden U.S.A. 134 D3
Åmsele Sweden 44 K4
Amstelveen Neth. 52 E2

▶Amsterdam Neth. 52 E2
Official capital of the Netherlands.

Amsterdam S. Africa 101 J4
Amsterdam U.S.A. 135 H2
Amsterdam, Île i. Indian Ocean 149 N8
Amstetten Austria 47 O6
Am Timan Chad 97 F3
Amudar'ya r. Asia 89 F2
Amudaryo r. Asia see Amudar'ya
Amund Ringnes Island Canada 119 I2
Amundsen, Mount Antarctica 152 F2
Amundsen Abyssal Plain sea feature Southern Ocean 152 J2
Amundsen Basin sea feature Arctic Ocean 153 H1
Amundsen Bay Antarctica 152 D2
Amundsen Coast Antarctica 152 J1
Amundsen Glacier Antarctica 152 I1
Amundsen Gulf Canada 118 F2
Amundsen Ridges sea feature Southern Ocean 152 J2
Amundsen-Scott research station Antarctica 152 C1
Amundsen Sea Antarctica 152 K2
Amuntai Indon. 68 F7
Amur r. China/Rus. Fed. 74 D2
also known as Heilong Jiang (China)
Amur r. Rus. Fed. 74 F1
'Amur, Wadi watercourse Sudan 86 D6
Amur Oblast admin. div. Rus. Fed. see Amurskaya Oblast'
Amursk Rus. Fed. 74 E2
Amurskaya Oblast' admin. div. Rus. Fed. 74 C1
Amurskiy Liman strait Rus. Fed. 74 F1
Amurzet Rus. Fed. 74 C3
Amvrosiyivka Ukr. 43 H7
Amyderya r. Asia see Amudar'ya
Am-Zoer Chad 97 F3
An Myanmar 70 A3
Anaa atoll Fr. Polynesia 151 K7
Anabanua Indon. 69 G7
Anabar r. Rus. Fed. 65 M2
Anacapa Islands U.S.A. 128 D4
Anaconda U.S.A. 126 E3
Anacortes U.S.A. 126 C2
Anadarko U.S.A. 131 D5
Anadolu reg. Turkey 90 D3
Anadolu Dağları mts Turkey 90 E2
Anadyr' Rus. Fed. 65 S3
Anadyr, Gulf of Rus. Fed. see Anadyrskiy Zaliv
Anadyrskiy Zaliv b. Rus. Fed. 65 T3
Anafi i. Greece 59 K6
Anagé Brazil 145 C1
'Ānah Iraq 91 F4
Anaheim U.S.A. 128 E5
Anahim Lake Canada 120 E4
Anáhuac Mex. 131 C7
Anahuac U.S.A. 131 E6
Anaimalai Hills India 84 C4
Anaiteum i. Vanuatu see Anatom
Anajás Brazil 143 I4
Anakie Australia 110 D4
Analalava Madag. 99 E5
Anamã Brazil 142 F4
Anambas, Kepulauan is Indon. 71 D7
Anamosa U.S.A. 130 F3
Anamur Turkey 85 A1
Anan Japan 75 D6
Anand India 82 C5
Anandapur India 83 F5
Anantapur India 84 C3
Ananthapur India see Anantapur
Anantnag India 82 C2
Anant Peth India 82 D4
Anantpur India see Anantapur
Ananyev Ukr. see Anan'yiv
Anan'yiv Ukr. 43 F7
Anapa Rus. Fed. 90 E1
Anápolis Brazil 145 A2
Anār Fin. see Inari
Anār Iran 88 D4
Anardara Afgh. 89 F3
Anatahan i. N. Mariana Is 69 L3
Anatajan i. N. Mariana Is see Anatahan
Anatom i. Vanuatu 107 G4
Añatuya Arg. 144 D3
Anaypazari Turkey see Gülnar
An Baile Breac Ireland 51 B6
An Bun Beag Ireland 51 D2
Anbūr-e Kālārī Iran 88 D5
Anbyon N. Korea 75 B5
Ancenis France 56 D3
Anchorage U.S.A. 118 D3
Anchorage Island atoll Cook Is see Suwarrow
Anchor Bay U.S.A. 134 D2
Anchuthengu India see Anjengo
Anci China see Langfang
An Clochán Liath Ireland 51 D3
An Cóbh Ireland see Cobh
Ancona Italy 58 E3
Ancud, Golfo de g. Chile 144 B6
Ancyra Turkey see Ankara
Anda Heilong. China see Daqing
Anda Heilong. China 74 B3
Andacollo Chile 144 B4
Andado Australia 110 A5
Andahuaylas Peru 142 D6
An Daingean Ireland 51 B5
Andal India 83 F5
Åndalsnes Norway 44 E5
Andalucía aut. comm. Spain 57 D5
Andalusia aut. comm. Spain see Andalucía
Andalusia U.S.A. 133 C6
Andaman Basin sea feature Indian Ocean 149 O5
Andaman Islands India 71 A4
Andaman Sea Indian Ocean 71 A5
Andaman Strait India 71 A4
Andamooka Australia 111 B6
Andapa Madag. 99 E5
Andarāb reg. Afgh. 89 H3
Ande China 76 E4
Andegavum France see Angers
Andelle r. France 52 B5
Andenes Norway 44 J2
Andenne Belgium 52 F4
Andéramboukane Mali 96 D3
Anderlecht Belgium 52 E4
Andermatt Switz. 56 I3
Andernos-les-Bains France 56 D4
Anderson r. Canada 118 F3
Anderson AK U.S.A. 118 D3
Anderson IN U.S.A. 134 C3
Anderson SC U.S.A. 133 D5
Anderson TX U.S.A. 131 E6
Anderson Bay Australia 111 [inset]
Anderson Lake Canada 120 F5
Andes mts S. America 144 C4
Andfjorden sea chan. Norway 44 J2
Andhíparos i. Greece see Antiparos
Andhra Lake India 84 B2
Andhra Pradesh state India 84 C2
Andijon Uzbek. 80 D3
Andikithira i. Greece see Antikythira
Andilamena Madag. 99 E5
Andilanatoby Madag. 99 E5
Andīmeshk Iran 88 C3
Andímilos i. Greece see Antimilos
Andípsara i. Greece see Antipsara
Andırın Turkey 90 E3
Andirlangar China 83 E1
Andizhan Uzbek. see Andijon
Andkhvoy Afgh. 89 G2
Andoany Madag. 99 E5
Andoas Peru 142 C4
Andogskaya Gryada hills Rus. Fed. 42 H4
Andol India 84 C2
Andong China see Dandong
Andong S. Korea 75 C5
Andongwei China 77 H1
Andoom Australia 110 C2
Andorra country Europe 57 G2

▶Andorra la Vella Andorra 57 G2
Capital of Andorra.

Andorra la Vieja Andorra see Andorra la Vella
Andover U.K. 49 F7
Andover NY U.S.A. 135 G2
Andover OH U.S.A. 134 E3
Andøya i. Norway 44 I2
Andrade U.S.A. 129 F5
Andradina Brazil 145 A3
Andranomavo Madag. 99 E5
Andranopasy Madag. 99 E6
Andreanof Islands U.S.A. 150 I2
Andreapol' Rus. Fed. 42 G4
Andreas Isle of Man 48 C4
André Félix, Parc National d' nat. park Cent. Afr. Rep. 98 C3
Andrelândia Brazil 145 B3
Andrew Canada 121 H4
Andrew Bay Myanmar 70 A3
Andrews SC U.S.A. 133 E5
Andrews TX U.S.A. 131 C5
Andria Italy 58 G4
Androka Madag. 99 E6
Andropov Rus. Fed. see Rybinsk
Andros i. Bahamas 133 E7
Andros i. Greece 59 K6
Androscoggin r. U.S.A. 135 K2
Andros Town Bahamas 133 E7
Androtti i. India 84 B4
Andselv Norway 44 K2
Andújar Spain 57 D4
Andulo Angola 99 B5
Anec, Lake salt flat Australia 109 E5
Ǟneen-Kio terr. N. Pacific Ocean see Wake Island
Anéfis Mali 96 D3
Anegada, Bahía b. Arg. 144 D6
Anegada Passage Virgin Is (U.K.) 137 L5
Aného Togo 96 D4
Aneityum i. Vanuatu see Anatom
'Aneiza, Jabal hill Iraq see 'Unayzah, Jabal
Anemourion tourist site Turkey 85 A1
Anepmete P.N.G. 69 L8
Anet France 52 B6
Anetchom, Île i. Vanuatu see Anatom
Aneto mt. Spain 57 G2
Änewetak atoll Marshall Is see Enewetak
Aney Niger 96 E3
Aneytioum, Île i. Vanuatu see Anatom
Anfu China 77 G3
Angalarri r. Australia 108 E3
Angamos, Punta pt Chile 144 B2
Ang'angxi China 74 A3

▶Angara r. Rus. Fed. 72 G1
Part of the Yenisey-Angara-Selenga, 3rd longest river in Asia.

Angarsk Rus. Fed. 72 I2
Angas Downs Australia 109 F6
Angatuba Brazil 145 A3
Angaur i. Palau 69 I5
Ånge Sweden 44 I5
Angel, Salto waterfall Venez. see Angel Falls
Ángel de la Guarda, Isla i. Mex. 127 E7

▶Angel Falls waterfall Venez. 142 F2
Highest waterfall in the world.

Ängelholm Sweden 45 H8
Angellala Creek r. Australia 112 C1
Angels Camp U.S.A. 128 C2
Ångermanälven r. Sweden 44 J5
Angers France 56 D3
Angikuni Lake Canada 121 L2
Angiola U.S.A. 128 D4
Angkor tourist site Cambodia 71 C4
Anglesea Australia 112 B7
Anglesey i. U.K. 48 C5
Angleton U.S.A. 131 E6
Anglo-Egyptian Sudan country Africa see Sudan
Angmagssalik Greenland see Ammassalik
Ang Mo Kio Sing. 71 [inset]
Ango Dem. Rep. Congo 98 C3
Angoche Moz. 99 D5
Angohrān Iran 88 E5
Angol Chile 144 B5
Angola country Africa 99 B5
Angola IN U.S.A. 134 C3
Angola NY U.S.A. 134 F2
Angola Basin sea feature S. Atlantic Ocean 148 H7
Angora Turkey see Ankara
Angostura Mex. 127 F8
Angoulême France 56 E4
Angra dos Reis Brazil 145 B3
Angren Uzbek. 80 D3
Ang Thong Thai. 71 C4
Anguang China 74 A3

▶Anguilla terr. West Indies 137 L5
United Kingdom Overseas Territory.

Anguilla Cays is Bahamas 133 E8
Anguille, Cape Canada 123 K5
Angul India 84 E1
Angus Canada 134 F1
Angutia Char i. Bangl. 83 G5
Anholt i. Denmark 45 G8
Anhua China 77 F2
Anhui prov. China 77 H1
Anhumas Brazil 143 H7
Anhwei prov. China see Anhui
Aniak U.S.A. 118 C3
Aniakchak National Monument and Preserve nat. park U.S.A. 118 C4
Anin Myanmar 70 B4
Anitápolis Brazil 145 A4
Anıtlı Turkey 85 A1
Aniva Rus. Fed. 74 F3
Aniva, Mys c. Rus. Fed. 74 F3
Aniva, Zaliv b. Rus. Fed. 74 F3
Anizy-le-Château France 52 D5
Anjadip i. India 84 B3
Anjalankoski Fin. 45 O6
Anjengo India 84 C4
Anji China 77 H2
Anjir Avand Iran 88 D3
Anjoman Iran 88 E3
Anjou reg. France 56 D3
Anjouan i. Comoros see Nzwani
Anjozorobe Madag. 99 E5
Anjuman reg. Afgh. 89 H3
Anjuthengu India see Anjengo
Ankang China 77 F1

▶Ankara Turkey 90 D3
Capital of Turkey.

Ankaratra mt. Madag. 99 E5
Ankazoabo Madag. 99 E6
Ankeny U.S.A. 130 E3
An Khê Vietnam 71 E4
Ankleshwar India 82 C5
Anklesvar India see Ankleshwar
Ankola India 84 B3
Ankouzhen China 76 E1
An Lôc Vietnam 71 D5
Anlong China 76 E3
Anlu China 77 G2
Anmoore U.S.A. 134 E4
An Muileann gCearr Ireland see Mullingar
Anmyŏn-do i. S. Korea 75 B5
Ann, Cape Antarctica 152 D2
Ann, Cape U.S.A. 135 J2
Anna Rus. Fed. 43 I6
Anna, Lake U.S.A. 135 G4
Annaba Alg. 58 B6
Annaberg-Buchholtz Germany 53 N4
An Nabk Saudi Arabia 85 C4
An Nabk Syria 85 C2
An Nafūd des. Saudi Arabia 91 F5
Annalee r. Ireland 51 E3
Annalong U.K. 51 G3
Annam reg. Vietnam 68 D3
Annam Highlands mts Laos/Vietnam 70 D3
Annan U.K. 50 F6
Annan r. U.K. 50 F6
'Annān, Wādī al watercourse Syria 85 D2
Annandale U.S.A. 135 G4
Anna Plains Australia 108 C4

▶Annapolis U.S.A. 135 G4
Capital of Maryland.

Annapurna Conservation Area nature res. Nepal 83 F3

▶Annapurna I mt. Nepal 83 E3
10th highest mountain in the world and in Asia.

Ann Arbor U.S.A. 134 D2
Anna Regina Guyana 143 G2
An Nás Ireland see Naas
An Naṣrānī, Jabal mts Syria 85 C3
Annean, Lake salt flat Australia 109 B6
Anne Arundel Town U.S.A. see Annapolis
Annecy France 56 H4
Anne Marie Lake Canada 123 J3
Annen Neth. 52 G1
Annette Island U.S.A. 120 D4
An Nimārah Syria 85 C3
An Nimāṣ Saudi Arabia 86 F6
Anning China 76 D3
Anniston U.S.A. 133 C5
Annobón i. Equat. Guinea 96 D5
Annonay France 56 G4
An Nu'mānīyah Iraq 91 G4
An Nuṣayrīyah, Jabal mts Syria 85 C2
Anonima atoll Micronesia see Namonuito
Anoón de Sardinas, Bahía de b. Col. 142 C3
Anorontany, Tanjona hd Madag. 99 E5
Ano Viannos Kriti Greece see Viannos
Anpu Gang b. China 77 F4
Anqing China 77 H2
Anren China 77 G3
Ans Belgium 52 F4
Ansbach Germany 53 K5
Anser Group is Australia 112 C7
Anshan China 74 A4
Anshun China 76 E3
Anshunchang China 76 D2
An Sirhān, Wādī watercourse Saudi Arabia 90 E5
Ansley U.S.A. 130 D3
Anson U.S.A. 131 D5
Anson Bay Australia 108 E3

Ansongo Mali 96 D3
Ansonville Canada 122 E4
Ansted U.S.A. 134 E4
Ansudu Indon. 69 J7
Antabamba Peru 142 D6
Antakya Turkey 85 C1
Antalaha Madag. 99 F5
Antalya Turkey 59 N6
Antalya prov. Turkey 85 A1
Antalya Körfezi g. Turkey 59 N6

▶Antananarivo Madag. 99 E5
Capital of Madagascar.

An tAonach Ireland see Nenagh

▶Antarctica 152
Most southerly and coldest continent, and the continent with the highest average elevation.

Antarctic Peninsula Antarctica 152 L2
Antas r. Brazil 145 A5
An Teallach mt. U.K. 50 D3
Antelope Island U.S.A. 129 G1
Antelope Range mts U.S.A. 128 E2
Antequera Spain 57 D5
Anthony Lagoon Australia 110 A3
Anti Atlas mts Morocco 54 C6
Antibes France 56 H5
Anticosti, Île d' i. Canada 123 J4
Anticosti Island Canada see Anticosti, Île d'
Antifer, Cap d' c. France 49 H9
Antigo U.S.A. 130 F2
Antigonish Canada 123 J5
Antigua i. Antigua and Barbuda 137 L5
Antigua country West Indies see Antigua and Barbuda
Antigua and Barbuda country West Indies 137 L5
Antikythira i. Greece 59 J7
Antikythiro, Steno sea chan. Greece 59 J7
Anti Lebanon mts Lebanon/Syria see Sharqī, Jabal ash
Antimilos i. Greece 59 K6
Antimony U.S.A. 129 H2
An tInbhear Mór Ireland see Arklow
Antioch Turkey see Antakya
Antioch U.S.A. 128 C2
Antiocheia ad Cragum tourist site Turkey 85 A1
Antiochia Turkey see Antakya
Antiparos i. Greece 59 K6
Antipodes Islands N.Z. 107 H6
Antipsara i. Greece 59 K5
Antium Italy see Anzio
Antlers U.S.A. 131 E5
Antofagasta Chile 144 B2
Antofagasta de la Sierra Arg. 144 C3
Antofalla, Volcán vol. Arg. 144 C3
Antoing Belgium 52 D4
António Enes Moz. see Angoche
Antri India 82 D4
Antrim U.K. 51 F3
Antrim Hills U.K. 51 F2
Antrim Plateau Australia 108 E4
Antropovo Rus. Fed. 42 I4
Antsalova Madag. 99 E5
Antseranana Madag. see Antsirañana
Antsirabe Madag. 99 E5
Antsirañana Madag. 99 E5
Antsla Estonia 45 O8
Antsohihy Madag. 99 E5
Anttis Sweden 44 M3
Anttola Fin. 45 O6
An Tuc Vietnam see An Khê
Antwerp Belgium 52 E3
Antwerp U.S.A. 135 H1
Antwerpen Belgium see Antwerp
An Uaimh Ireland see Navan
Anuc, Lac l. Canada 122 G2
Anuchino Rus. Fed. 74 D4
Anugul India see Angul
Anupgarh India 82 C3
Anuradhapura Sri Lanka 84 D4
Anveh Iran 88 D5
Anvers Island Antarctica 152 L2
Anvik U.S.A. 118 B3
Anvil Range mts Canada 120 C2
Anxi Fujian China 77 H3
Anxi Gansu China 80 I3
Anxiang China 77 G2
Anxious Bay Australia 109 F8
Anyang Guangxi China see Du'an
Anyang Henan China 73 K5
Anyang S. Korea 75 B5
A'nyêmaqên Shan mts China 76 C1
Anyuan Jiangxi China 77 G3
Anyuan Jiangxi China 77 G3
Anyue China 76 E2
Anyuy r. Rus. Fed. 74 E2
Anyuysk Rus. Fed. 65 R3
Anzac Alta Canada 121 I3
Anzac B.C. Canada 120 F4
Anzhero-Sudzhensk Rus. Fed. 64 J4
Anzi Dem. Rep. Congo 98 C4
Anzio Italy 58 E4
Aoba i. Vanuatu 107 G3
Aoga-shima i. Japan 75 E6
Ao Kham, Laem pt Thai. 71 B5
Aomen China see Macao
Aomen Tebie Xingzhengqu aut. reg. China see Macao
Aomori Japan 74 F4
Ao Phang Nga National Park Thai. 71 B5

▶Aoraki mt. N.Z. 113 C6
Highest mountain in New Zealand.

Aoraki/Mount Cook National Park N.Z. 113 C6
Aôral, Phnum mt. Cambodia 71 D4
Aorangi mt. N.Z. see Aoraki
Aorangi mt. N.Z. see Aoraki
Aosta Italy 58 B2
Aotearoa country Oceania see New Zealand
Aouk, Bahr r. Cent. Afr. Rep./Chad 97 E4
Aoukâr reg. Mali/Mauritania 96 C2
Aoulef Alg. 96 D2
Aozou Chad 97 E2
Apa r. Brazil 144 E2
Apache Creek U.S.A. 129 I5
Apache Junction U.S.A. 129 H5
Apaiang atoll Kiribati see Abaiang
Apalachee Bay U.S.A. 133 C6
Apalachicola U.S.A. 133 C6
Apalachicola r. U.S.A. 133 C6
Apalachin U.S.A. 135 G2
Apamea Turkey see Dinar
Apaporis r. Col. 142 E4
Aparecida do Tabuado Brazil 145 A3
Aparima N.Z. see Riverton
Aparri Phil. 150 E4
Apatity Rus. Fed. 44 R3
Apatzingán Mex. 136 D5
Ape Latvia 45 O8
Apeldoorn Neth. 52 F2
Apelern Germany 53 J2
Apennines mts Italy 58 D2
Apensen Germany 53 J1
Apex Mountain Canada 120 B2
Api mt. Nepal 82 E3
Api i. Vanuatu see Epi
Apia atoll Kiribati see Abaiang

▶Apia Samoa 107 I3
Capital of Samoa.

Apiacas, Serra dos hills Brazil 143 G6
Apiaí Brazil 145 A4
Apishapa r. U.S.A. 130 C4
Apiti N.Z. 113 E4
Apizolaya Mex. 131 C7
Aplao Peru 142 D7
Apo, Mount vol. Phil. 69 H5
Apoera Suriname 143 G2
Apolda Germany 53 L3
Apollo Bay Australia 112 A7
Apollonia Bulg. see Sozopol
Apolo Bol. 142 E6
Aporé Brazil 145 A2
Aporé r. Brazil 145 A2
Apostle Islands U.S.A. 130 F2
Apostolens Tommelfinger mt. Greenland 119 N3
Apostolos Andreas, Cape Cyprus 85 B2
Apoteri Guyana 143 G3
Apozai Pak. 89 H4
Appalachian Mountains U.S.A. 134 D5
Appalla i. Fiji see Kabara
Appennino mts Italy see Apennines
Appennino Abruzzese mts Italy 58 E3
Appennino Tosco-Emiliano mts Italy 58 D3
Appennino Umbro-Marchigiano mts Italy 58 E3
Appingedam Neth. 52 G1
Applecross U.K. 50 D3
Appleton MN U.S.A. 130 D2
Appleton WI U.S.A. 134 A1
Apple Valley U.S.A. 128 E4
Appomattox U.S.A. 135 F5
Aprilia Italy 58 E4
Aprunyi India 76 B2
Apsheronsk Rus. Fed. 91 E1
Apsheronskaya Rus. Fed. see Apsheronsk
Apsley Canada 135 F1
Apt France 56 G5
Apucarana Brazil 145 A3
Apucarana, Serra da hills Brazil 145 A3
Apulum Romania see Alba Iulia
Aq"a Georgia see Sokhumi
'Aqaba Jordan see Al 'Aqabah
Aqaba, Gulf of Asia 90 D5
'Aqaba, Wâdi el watercourse Egypt see 'Aqabah, Wādī al
'Aqabah, Birkat al well Iraq 88 A4
'Aqabah, Wādī al watercourse Egypt 85 A4
Aqadyr Kazakh. see Agadyr'
Aqdoghmish r. Iran 88 B2
Aqköl Akmolinskaya Oblast' Kazakh. see Akkol'
Aqköl Atyrauskaya Oblast' Kazakh. see Akkol'
Aqmola Kazakh. see Astana
Aqqan China 83 F1
Aqqikkol Hu salt l. China 83 G1
'Aqra', Jabal al mt. Syria/Turkey 85 B2
'Aqran hill Saudi Arabia 85 D4
Aqsay Kazakh. see Aksay
Aqsayqin Hit terr. Asia see Aksai Chin
Aqshī Kazakh. see Akshiy
Aqshuqyr Kazakh. see Akshukur
Aqsū Kazakh. see Aksu
Aqsūat Kazakh. see Aksuat
Aqsū-Ayuly Kazakh. see Aksu-Ayuly
Aqtaū Kazakh. see Aktau
Aqtöbe Kazakh. see Aktobe
Aqtoghay Kazakh. see Aktogay
Aquae Grani Germany see Aachen
Aquae Gratianae France see Aix-les-Bains
Aquae Sextiae France see Aix-en-Provence
Aquae Statiellae Italy see Acqui Terme
Aquarius Mountains U.S.A. 129 G4
Aquarius Plateau U.S.A. 129 H3
Aquaviva delle Fonti Italy 58 G4
Aquidauana Brazil 144 E2
Aquiles Mex. 127 G7
Aquincum Hungary see Budapest
Aquiry r. Brazil see Acre
Aquisgranum Germany see Aachen
Aquitaine reg. France 56 D5
Aquitania reg. France see Aquitaine
Aqzhayqyn Köli salt l. Kazakh. see Akzhaykyn, Ozero
Ara India 83 F4
Āra Ārba Eth. 98 E3
Arab Afgh. 89 G4
Arab, Bahr el watercourse Sudan 97 F4
'Arab, Khalîg el b. Egypt see 'Arab, Khalīj al
'Arab, Khalīj al b. Egypt 90 C5
'Arabah, Wādī al watercourse Israel/Jordan 85 B5
Arabian Basin sea feature Indian Ocean 149 M5
Arabian Gulf Asia see The Gulf
Arabian Peninsula Asia 86 G5
Arabian Sea Indian Ocean 87 K6
Araç Turkey 90 D2
Araça r. Brazil 142 F4
Aracaju Brazil 143 K6
Aracati Brazil 143 K4
Aracatu Brazil 145 C1
Araçatuba Brazil 145 A3
Aracena Spain 57 C5
Aracruz Brazil 145 C2
Araçuaí Brazil 145 C2
Araçuaí r. Brazil 145 C2
'Arad Israel 85 B4
Arad Romania 59 I1
'Arādah U.A.E. 88 D6
Arafura Sea Australia/Indon. 106 D2
Arafura Shelf sea feature Australia/Indon. 150 E6
Aragarças Brazil 143 H7
Aragón r. Spain 57 F2
Araguaçu Brazil 145 A1
Araguaia r. Brazil 145 A1
Araguaia, Parque Nacional do nat. park Brazil 143 H6
Araguaiana Brazil 145 A1
Araguaína Brazil 143 I5
Araguari Brazil 145 A2
Araguari r. Brazil 143 H3
Araguatins Brazil 143 I5
Arai Brazil 145 B1
'Arâif el Naga, Gebel hill Egypt see 'Urayf an Nāqah, Jabal
Araiosos Brazil 143 J4
Arak Alg. 96 D2
Arāk Iran 88 C3
Arak Syria 85 D2
Arakan reg. Myanmar 70 A2
Arakan Yoma mts Myanmar 70 A2
Arakkonam India 84 C3
Araks r. Azer. see Araz
Araku India 84 D2
Aral Kazakh. see Aral'sk
Aral Tajik. see Vose

▶Aral Sea salt l. Kazakh./Uzbek. 80 B2
4th largest lake in Asia.

Aral'sk Kazakh. 80 B2
Aral'skoye More salt l. Kazakh./Uzbek. see Aral Sea
Aralsor, Ozero l. Kazakh. 43 K6
Aral Tengizi salt l. Kazakh./Uzbek. see Aral Sea
Aramac Australia 110 D4
Aramac Creek watercourse Australia 110 D4
Aramah plat. Saudi Arabia 88 B5
Aramberri Mex. 131 D7
Aramia r. P.N.G. 69 K8
Aran r. India 84 C2
Aranda de Duero Spain 57 E3
Arandai Indon. 69 I7
Aranđelovac Serbia 59 I2
Arandis Namibia 100 B2
Arang India 83 E5
Arani India 84 C3
Aran Islands Ireland 51 C4
Aranjuez Spain 57 E3
Aranos Namibia 100 D3
Aransas Pass U.S.A. 131 D7
Arantangi India 84 C4
Aranuka atoll Kiribati 107 H1
Aranyaprathet Thai. 71 C4
Arao Japan 75 C6
Araouane Mali 96 C3
Arapaho U.S.A. 131 D5
Arapgir Turkey 90 E3
Arapiraca Brazil 143 K5
Arapis, Akra pt Greece see Arapis, Akrotirio
Arapis, Akrotirio pt Greece 59 K4
Arapkir Turkey see Arapgir
Arapongas Brazil 145 A3
Araquari Brazil 145 A4
'Ar'ar Saudi Arabia 91 F5
Araracuara Col. 142 D4
Araranguá Brazil 145 A5
Araraquara Brazil 145 A3
Araras Brazil 143 H5
Ararat Armenia 91 G3
Ararat Australia 112 A6
Ararat, Mount Turkey 91 G3
Araria India 83 F4
Araripina Brazil 143 J5
Aras r. Azer. see Araz
Aras Turkey 91 F3
Arataca Brazil 145 D1
Arauca Col. 142 D2
Arauca r. Venez. 142 E2
Aravalli Range mts India 82 C4
Aravete Estonia 45 N7
Arawa P.N.G. 106 F2
Araxá Brazil 145 B2
Araxes r. Azer. see Araz
Arayıt Dağı mt. Turkey 59 N5
Araz r. Azer. 91 H2
also spelt Araks (Armenia), Aras (Turkey), formerly known as Araxes
Arbailu Iraq see Arbīl
Arbat Iraq 91 G4
Arbela Iraq see Arbīl
Arberth U.K. see Narberth
Arbīl Iraq 91 G3
Arboga Sweden 45 I7
Arborfield Canada 121 K4
Arborg Canada 121 L5
Arbroath U.K. 50 G4
Arbuckle U.S.A. 128 B2
Arbu Lut, Dasht-e des. Afgh. 89 F4
Arcachon France 56 D4
Arcade U.S.A. 135 F2
Arcadia FL U.S.A. 133 D7
Arcadia LA U.S.A. 131 E5
Arcadia MI U.S.A. 134 B1
Arcanum U.S.A. 134 C4
Arcata U.S.A. 126 B4
Arc Dome mt. U.S.A. 128 E2
Arcelia Mex. 136 D5
Archangel Rus. Fed. 42 I2
Archer r. Australia 67 G9
Archer Bend National Park Australia 110 C2
Archer City U.S.A. 131 D5
Arches National Park U.S.A. 129 I2
Archipiélago Los Roques nat. park Venez. 142 E1
Ärçivan Azer. 91 H3
Arckaringa watercourse Australia 111 A6
Arco U.S.A. 126 E4
Arcos Brazil 145 B3
Arcos de la Frontera Spain 57 D5
Arctic Bay Canada 119 J2
Arctic Institute Islands Rus. Fed. see Arkticheskogo Instituta, Ostrova
Arctic Mid-Ocean Ridge sea feature Arctic Ocean 153 H1
Arctic Ocean 153 B1
Arctic Red r. Canada 118 E3
Arctowski research station Antarctica 152 A2
Arda r. Bulg. 59 L4
also known as Ardas (Greece)
Ardabīl Iran 88 C2
Ardahan Turkey 91 F2
Ardakān Iran 88 D3
Årdalstangen Norway 45 E6
Ardara Ireland 51 D3
Ardas r. Bulg. see Arda
Ard aş Şawwān plain Jordan 85 C4
Ardatov Nizhegorodskaya Oblast' Rus. Fed. 43 I5
Ardatov Respublika Mordoviya Rus. Fed. 43 J5
Ardee Ireland 51 F4
Ardennes plat. Belgium 52 E5
Ardennes, Canal des France 52 E5
Arden Town U.S.A. 128 C2
Arderin hill Ireland 51 E4
Ardestān Iran 88 D3
Ardglass U.K. 51 G3
Ardila r. Port. 57 C4
Ardlethan Australia 112 C5
Ardmore U.S.A. 131 D5
Ardnamurchan, Point of U.K. 50 C4
Ardon Rus. Fed. 91 G2
Ardrishaig U.K. 50 D4
Ardrossan U.K. 50 E5
Ardvasar U.K. 50 D3
Areia Branca Brazil 143 K4
Arel Belgium see Arlon
Arelas France see Arles
Arelate France see Arles
Aremberg hill Germany 52 G4
Arena, Point U.S.A. 128 B2
Arenas de San Pedro Spain 57 D3
Arendal Norway 45 F7
Arendsee (Altmark) Germany 53 L2
Areopoli Greece 59 J6
Arequipa Peru 142 D7
Arere Brazil 143 H4
Arévalo Spain 57 D3
Arezzo Italy 58 D3
'Arfajah well Saudi Arabia 85 D4
Argadargada Australia 110 B4
Arganda del Rey Spain 57 E3
Argel Alg. see Algiers
Argentan France 56 D2
Argentario, Monte hill Italy 58 D3
Argentera, Cima dell' mt. Italy 58 B2
Argenthal Germany 53 H5

▶Argentina country S. America 144 C5
2nd largest and 3rd most populous country in South America, and 8th largest in the world.

Argentine Abyssal Plain sea feature S. Atlantic Ocean 148 E9
Argentine Basin sea feature S. Atlantic Ocean 148 F8
Argentine Republic country S. America see Argentina
Argentine Rise sea feature S. Atlantic Ocean 148 E8
Argentino, Lago l. Arg. 144 B8
Argenton-sur-Creuse France 56 E3
Argentoratum France see Strasbourg
Argeş r. Romania 59 L2
Arghandab r. Afgh. 89 G4
Argi r. Rus. Fed. 74 C1
Argolikos Kolpos b. Greece 59 J6
Argos Greece 59 J6
Argos U.S.A. 134 B3
Argostoli Greece 59 I5
Arguís Spain 57 F2
Argun' r. China/Rus. Fed. 73 M2
Argun Rus. Fed. 91 G2
Argungu Nigeria 96 D3
Argus Range mts U.S.A. 128 E4
Argyle Canada 123 I6
Argyle, Lake Australia 108 E4
Argyrokastron Albania see Gjirokastër
Ar Horqin Qi China see Tianshan
Århus Denmark 45 G8
Ariah Park Australia 112 C5
Ariamsvlei Namibia 100 D5
Ariana Tunisia see L'Ariana
Ariano Irpino Italy 58 F4
Ari Atoll Maldives 81 D11
Aribinda Burkina 96 C3
Arica Chile 142 D7
Arid, Cape Australia 109 C8
Arigza China 76 C1
Arīḩā Syria 85 C2
Arīḩā West Bank see Jericho
Arikaree r. U.S.A. 130 C3
Arima Trin. and Tob. 137 L6
Ariminum Italy see Rimini
Arinos Brazil 145 B1
Aripuanã Brazil 143 G6
Aripuanã r. Brazil 142 F5
Ariquemes Brazil 142 F5
Aris Namibia 100 C2
Arisaig U.K. 50 D4
Arisaig, Sound of sea chan. U.K. 50 D4
'Arīsh, Wādī al watercourse Egypt 85 A4
Aristazabal Island Canada 120 D4
Arixang China see Wenquan
Ariyalur India 84 C4
Arizaro, Salar de salt flat Arg. 144 C2
Arizona Arg. 144 C5
Arizona state U.S.A. 127 F6
Arizpe Mex. 127 F7
'Arjah Saudi Arabia 86 F5
Arjasa Indon. 68 F8
Arjeplog Sweden 44 J3
Arjuni Chhattisgarh India 84 D1
Arjuni India 82 E5
Arkadak Rus. Fed. 43 I6
Arkadelphia U.S.A. 131 E5
Arkaig, Loch l. U.K. 50 D4
Arkalyk Kazakh. 80 C1
Arkansas r. U.S.A. 131 F5
Arkansas state U.S.A. 131 E5
Arkansas City AR U.S.A. 131 F5
Arkansas City KS U.S.A. 131 D4
Arkatag Shan mts China 83 G1
Arkell, Mount Canada 120 C2
Arkenu, Jabal mt. Libya 86 B5
Arkhangel'sk Rus. Fed. see Archangel
Arkhara Rus. Fed. 74 C2
Arkhipovka Rus. Fed. 74 D4
Árki i. Greece see Arkoi
Arklow Ireland 51 F5
Arkoi i. Greece 59 L6
Arkona Canada 134 E2
Arkona, Kap c. Germany 47 N3
Arkonam India see Arakkonam
Arkport U.S.A. 135 G2
Arkticheskogo Instituta, Ostrova is Rus. Fed. 64 J2
Arkul' Rus. Fed. 42 K4
Arlandag mt. Turkm. 88 D2
Arles France 56 G5
Arlington S. Africa 101 H5
Arlington NY U.S.A. 135 I3
Arlington OH U.S.A. 134 D3
Arlington SD U.S.A. 130 D2
Arlington VA U.S.A. 135 G4
Arlington Heights U.S.A. 134 A2
Arlit Niger 96 D3
Arlon Belgium 52 F5
Arm r. Canada 121 J5
Armadale Australia 109 A8
Armagh U.K. 51 F3
Armant Egypt 86 D4
Armavir Armenia 91 G2
Armavir Rus. Fed. 91 F1
Armenia country Asia 91 G2
Armenia Col. 142 C3
Armenopolis Romania see Gherla
Armeria Mex. 136 D5
Armidale Australia 112 E3
Armington U.S.A. 126 F3
Armit Lake Canada 121 N1
Armori India 84 D1
Armour U.S.A. 130 D3
Armoy U.K. 51 F2
Armstrong r. Australia 108 E4
Armstrong Canada 122 C4
Armstrong, Mount Canada 120 C2
Armstrong Island Cook Is see Rarotonga
Armu r. Rus. Fed. 74 E3
Armur India 84 C2
Armutçuk Dağı mts Turkey 59 L5
Armyanskaya S.S.R. country Asia see Armenia
Arnaoutis, Cape Cyprus see Arnauti, Cape
Arnaud r. Canada 123 H2
Arnauti, Cape Cyprus 85 A2
Årnes Norway 45 G6
Arnett U.S.A. 131 D4
Arnhem Neth. 52 F3
Arnhem, Cape Australia 110 B2
Arnhem Land reg. Australia 108 F3
Arno r. Italy 58 D3
Arno Bay Australia 111 B7
Arnold U.K. 49 F5
Arnold's Cove Canada 123 L5
Arnon r. Jordan see Mawjib, Wādī al
Arnprior Canada 135 G1
Arnsberg Germany 53 I3
Arnstadt Germany 53 K4
Arnstein Germany 53 J5
Arnstorf Germany 53 M6
Aroab Namibia 100 D4
Aroland Canada 122 D4
Arolsen Germany 53 J3
Aroma Sudan 86 E6
Arona Italy 58 C2
Arorae i. Kiribati 107 H2
Arore i. Kiribati see Arorae
Aros r. Mex. 127 F7
Arossi i. Solomon Is see San Cristobal
Arqalyq Kazakh. see Arkalyk
Arquipélago da Madeira aut. reg. Port. 96 B1
Arrabury Australia 111 C5
Arrah India see Ara
Arraias Brazil 145 B1
Arraias, Serra de hills Brazil 145 B1
Ar Ramlah Jordan 85 B5
Ar Ramthā Jordan 85 C3
Arran i. U.K. 50 D5
Arranmore Island Ireland 51 D3
Ar Raqqah Syria 85 D2
Arras France 52 C4
Ar Rass Saudi Arabia 86 F4
Ar Rastān Syria 85 C2
Ar Rayyān Qatar 88 C5
Arrecife Canary Is 96 B2
Arretium Italy see Arezzo
Arriagá Mex. 136 F5
Ar Rifā'ī Iraq 91 G5
Ar Rihāb salt flat Iraq 91 G5
Ar Rimāl reg. Saudi Arabia 98 F1
Arrington U.S.A. 135 F5
Ar Riyāḑ Saudi Arabia see Riyadh
Arrochar U.K. 50 E4
Arrojado r. Brazil 145 B1
Arrow, Lough l. Ireland 51 D3
Arrowsmith, Mount N.Z. 113 C6
Arroyo Grande U.S.A. 128 C4
Ar Rubay'iyah Saudi Arabia 88 B5
Ar Rummān Jordan 85 B3
Ar Ruq'ī well Saudi Arabia 88 B4
Ar Ruşāfah Syria 85 D2
Ar Ruşayfah Jordan 85 C3
Ar Rustāq Oman 88 E6
Ar Ruţbah Iraq 91 F4
Ar Ruwaydah Saudi Arabia 88 B5
Ar Ruwaydah Saudi Arabia 88 B6
Ar Ruwayḑah Syria 85 C2
Års Denmark see Aars
Ars Iran 88 B2
Arseno Lake Canada 120 H1
Arsen'yev Rus. Fed. 74 D3
Arsk Rus. Fed. 42 K4
Arta Greece 59 I5
Artem Rus. Fed. 74 D4
Artemisa Cuba 133 D8
Artemivs'k Ukr. 43 H6
Artemovsk Ukr. see Artemivs'k
Artenay France 56 E2
Artesia AZ U.S.A. 129 I5
Artesia NM U.S.A. 127 G6
Arthur Canada 134 E2
Arthur NE U.S.A. 130 C3
Arthur TN U.S.A. 134 D5
Arthur, Lake U.S.A. 134 E3
Arthur's Pass National Park N.Z. 113 C6
Arthur's Town Bahamas 133 F7
Arti Rus. Fed. 41 R4
Artigas research station Antarctica 152 A2
Artigas Uruguay 144 E4
Art'ik Armenia 91 F2
Artillery Lake Canada 121 I2
Artisia Botswana 101 H3
Artois reg. France 52 B4
Artois, Collines d' hills France 52 B4
Artos Dağı mt. Turkey 91 F3
Artova Turkey 90 E2
Artsakh aut. reg. Azer. see Dağlıq Qarabağ
Artsiz Ukr. see Artsyz
Artsyz Ukr. 59 M2
Artur de Paiva Angola see Kuvango
Artux China 80 E4
Artvin Turkey 91 F2
Artyk Turkm. 88 E2
Aru, Kepulauan is Indon. 108 F1
Arua Uganda 98 D3
Aruanã Brazil 145 A1

▶Aruba terr. West Indies 137 K6
Self-governing Netherlands territory.

Arunachal Pradesh state India 83 H4
Arundel U.K. 49 G8
Arun Gol r. China 74 B3
Arun He r. China see Arun Gol
Arun Qi China see Naji
Aruppukkottai India 84 C4
Arusha Tanz. 98 D4
Aruwimi r. Dem. Rep. Congo 98 C3
Arvada U.S.A. 126 G5
Arvagh Ireland 51 E4
Arvayheer Mongolia 80 J2
Arviat Canada 121 M2
Arvidsjaur Sweden 44 K4
Arvika Sweden 45 H7
Arvonia U.S.A. 135 F5
Arwā' Saudi Arabia 88 B6
Arwād i. Syria 85 B2
Arwala Indon. 108 D1
Arxan China 73 L3
Aryanah Tunisia see L'Ariana
Arys' Kazakh. 80 C3
Arzamas Rus. Fed. 43 I5
Arzanah i. U.A.E. 88 D5
Arzberg Germany 53 M4
Arzew Alg. 57 F6
Arzgir Rus. Fed. 91 G1
Arzila Morocco see Asilah
Aš Czech Rep. 53 M4
Asaba Nigeria 96 D4
Asad, Buḩayrat al resr Syria 85 D1
Asadābād Afgh. 89 H3
Asadābād Iran 88 C3
Asahi-dake vol. Japan 74 F4
Asahikawa Japan 74 F4
'Asal Egypt 85 A5
Āsalē l. Eth. 98 E2
Asālem Iran 88 C2
'Asalūyeh Iran 88 D5
Asan-man b. S. Korea 75 B5
Asansol India 83 F5
Āsayita Eth. 98 E2
Asbach Germany 53 H4
Asbestos Mountains S. Africa 100 F5
Asbury Park U.S.A. 135 H3
Ascalon Israel see Ashqelon
Ascea Italy 58 F4
Ascensión Bol. 142 F7
Ascensión Mex. 127 G7
Ascension atoll Micronesia see Pohnpei

▶Ascension i. S. Atlantic Ocean 148 H6
Dependency of St Helena.

Aschaffenburg Germany 53 J5
Ascheberg Germany 53 H3
Aschersleben Germany 53 L3
Ascoli Piceno Italy 58 E3
Asculum Italy see Ascoli Piceno
Asculum Picenum Italy see Ascoli Piceno
Ascutney U.S.A. 135 I2
Āseb Eritrea see Assab
Āseda Sweden 45 I8
Āsele Sweden 44 J4
Asenovgrad Bulg. 59 K3
Aşfar, Jabal al mt. Jordan 85 C3
Aşfar, Tall al hill Syria 85 C3

▶Aşgabat Turkm. 88 E2
Capital of Turkmenistan.

Asha Rus. Fed. 41 R5
Ashburn U.S.A. 133 D6
Ashburton watercourse Australia 108 A5
Ashburton N.Z. 113 C6
Ashburton Range hills Australia 108 F4
Ashdod Israel 85 B4
Ashdown U.S.A. 131 E5
Asheboro U.S.A. 132 E5
Asher U.S.A. 131 D5
Ashern Canada 121 L5
Asheville U.S.A. 132 D5
Asheweig r. Canada 122 D3
Ashford Australia 112 E2
Ashford U.K. 49 H7
Ash Fork U.S.A. 129 G4
Ashgabat Turkm. see Aşgabat
Ashibetsu Japan 74 F4
Ashikaga Japan 75 E5
Ashington U.K. 48 F3
Ashizuri-misaki pt Japan 75 D6
Ashkelon Israel see Ashqelon
Ashkhabad Turkm. see Aşgabat
Ashkum U.S.A. 134 B3
Ashkun reg. Afgh. 89 H3
Ashland AL U.S.A. 133 C5
Ashland ME U.S.A. 132 G2
Ashland NH U.S.A. 135 J2
Ashland OH U.S.A. 134 D3
Ashland OR U.S.A. 126 C4
Ashland VA U.S.A. 135 G5
Ashland WI U.S.A. 130 F2
Ashland City U.S.A. 134 B5
Ashley Australia 112 D2
Ashley MI U.S.A. 134 C2
Ashley ND U.S.A. 130 D2

Bacobampo Mex. 127 F8
Bacolod Phil. 69 G4
Bacqueville, Lac l. Canada 122 G2
Bacqueville-en-Caux France 49 H9
Bacubirito Mex. 127 G8
Bād Iran 88 D3
Bada China see Xilin
Bada mt. Eth. 98 D3
Bada i. Myanmar 71 B5
Badabaýhan Turkm. 89 F2
Bad Abbach Germany 53 M6
Badagara India 84 B4
Badain Jaran Shamo des. China 80 J3
Badajoz Spain 57 C4
Badami India 84 B3
Badampaharh India 83 F5
Badanah Saudi Arabia 91 F5
Badanjilin Shamo des. China see Badain Jaran Shamo
Badaojiang China see Baishan
Badarpur India 83 H4
Badaun India see Budaun
Bad Axe U.S.A. 134 D2
Bad Bederkesa Germany 53 I1
Bad Bergzabern Germany 53 H5
Bad Berleburg Germany 53 I3
Bad Bevensen Germany 53 K1
Bad Blankenburg Germany 53 L4
Bad Camberg Germany 53 I4
Badderen Norway 44 M2
Bad Driburg Germany 53 J3
Bad Düben Germany 53 M3
Bad Dürkheim Germany 53 I5
Bad Dürrenberg Germany 53 M3
Bademli Turkey see Aladağ
Bademli Geçidi pass Turkey 90 C3
Bad Ems Germany 53 H4
Baden Austria 47 P6
Baden Switz. 56 I3
Baden-Baden Germany 53 I6
Baden-Württemberg land Germany 53 I6
Bad Essen Germany 53 I2
Bad Grund (Harz) Germany 53 K3
Bad Harzburg Germany 53 K3
Bad Hersfeld Germany 53 J4
Bad Hofgastein Austria 47 N7
Bad Homburg vor der Höhe Germany 53 I4
Badia Polesine Italy 58 D2
Badin Pak. 89 H5
Bad Ischl Austria 47 N7
Bādiyat ash Shām des. Asia see Syrian Desert
Bad Kissingen Germany 53 K4
Bad Königsdorff Poland see Jastrzębie-Zdrój
Bad Kösen Germany 53 L3
Bad Kreuznach Germany 53 H5
Bad Laasphe Germany 53 I4
Badlands reg. ND U.S.A. 130 C2
Badlands reg. SD U.S.A. 130 C3
Badlands National Park U.S.A. 130 C3
Bad Langensalza Germany 53 K3
Bad Lauterberg im Harz Germany 53 K3
Bad Liebenwerda Germany 53 N3
Bad Lippspringe Germany 53 I3
Bad Marienberg (Westerwald) Germany 53 H4
Bad Mergentheim Germany 53 J5
Bad Nauheim Germany 53 I4
Badnawar India 82 C5
Badnera India 84 C1
Bad Neuenahr-Ahrweiler Germany 52 H4
Bad Neustadt an der Saale Germany 53 K4
Badnor India 82 C4
Badong China 77 F2
Ba Đông Vietnam 71 D5
Badou Togo 96 D4
Bad Pyrmont Germany 53 J3
Badrah Iraq 91 G4
Bad Reichenhall Germany 47 N7
Badr Ḥunayn Saudi Arabia 86 E5
Bad Sachsa Germany 53 K3
Bad Salzdetfurth Germany 53 K2
Bad Salzuflen Germany 53 I2
Bad Salzungen Germany 53 K4
Bad Schwalbach Germany 53 I4
Bad Schwartau Germany 47 M4
Bad Segeberg Germany 47 M4
Bad Sobernheim Germany 53 H5
Badu Island Australia 110 C1
Badulla Sri Lanka 84 D5
Bad Vilbel Germany 53 I4
Bad Wilsnack Germany 53 L2
Bad Windsheim Germany 53 K5
Badzhal Rus. Fed. 74 D2
Badzhal'skiy Khrebet mts Rus. Fed. 74 D2
Bad Zwischenahn Germany 53 I1
Bae Colwyn U.K. see Colwyn Bay
Baesweiler Germany 52 G4
Baeza Spain 57 E5
Bafatá Guinea-Bissau 96 B3
Baffa Pak. 89 I3
Baffin Bay sea Canada/Greenland 119 L2

▶Baffin Island Canada 119 L3
2nd largest island in North America, and 5th in the world.

Bafia Cameroon 96 E4
Bafilo Togo 96 D4
Bafing r. Africa 96 B3
Bafoulabé Mali 96 B3
Bafoussam Cameroon 96 E4
Bāfq Iran 88 D4
Bafra Turkey 90 D2
Bafra Burnu pt Turkey 90 D2
Bāft Iran 88 E4
Bafwaboli Dem. Rep. Congo 98 C3
Bafwasende Dem. Rep. Congo 98 C3
Bagaha India 83 F4
Bagalkot India 84 B2
Bagalkote India see Bagalkot
Bagamoyo Tanz. 99 D4
Bagan China 76 C1
Bagan Datoh Malaysia see Bagan Datuk
Bagan Datuk Malaysia 71 C7
Bagansiapiapi Indon. 71 C7
Bagata Dem. Rep. Congo 98 B4
Bagdad U.S.A. 129 G4
Bagdarin Rus. Fed. 73 K2
Bagé Brazil 144 F4
Bagenalstown Ireland 51 F5
Bagerhat Bangl. 83 G5
Bageshwar India 82 D3
Baggs U.S.A. 126 G4
Baggy Point U.K. 49 C7
Bagh India 82 C5
Bàgh a' Chaisteil U.K. see Castlebay
Baghak Pak. 89 G4
Baghbaghū Iran 89 F2

▶Baghdād Iraq 91 G4
Capital of Iraq.

Bāgh-e Malek Iran 88 C4
Bagherhat Bangl. see Bagerhat
Bāghīn Iran 88 E4
Baghlān Afgh. 89 H2
Baghrān Afgh. 89 G3
Bağırsak r. Turkey 85 C1
Bağırsak Deresi r. Syria/Turkey see Sājūr, Nahr
Bagley U.S.A. 130 E2
Baglung Nepal 83 E3
Bagnères-de-Luchon France 56 E5
Bago Myanmar see Pegu
Bago Phil. 69 G4
Bagong China see Sansui
Bagor India 89 I5
Bagrationovsk Rus. Fed. 45 L9
Bagrax China see Bohu
Bagrax Hu l. China see Bosten Hu
Baguio Phil. 69 G3
Bagur, Cabo c. Spain see Begur, Cap de
Bagzane, Monts mts Niger 96 D3
Bahādorābād-e Bālā Iran 88 E4
Bahalda India 83 F5
Bahāmābād Iran see Rafsanjān
Bahamas, The country West Indies 133 E7
Bahara Pak. 89 G5
Baharampur India 83 G4
Bahardipur Pak. 89 H5
Bahariya Oasis oasis Egypt see Bahrīyah, Wāḥāt al
Bahau Malaysia 71 C7
Bahawalnagar Pak. 89 I4
Bahawalpur Pak. 89 H4
Bahçe Adana Turkey 85 B1
Bahçe Osmaniye Turkey 90 E3
Baher Dar Eth. see Bahir Dar
Baheri India 82 D3
Bahia Brazil see Salvador
Bahia state Brazil 145 C1
Bahía, Islas de la is Hond. 137 G5
Bahía Asunción Mex. 127 E8
Bahía Blanca Arg. 144 D5
Bahía Kino Mex. 127 F7
Bahía Laura Arg. 144 C7
Bahía Negra Para. 144 E2
Bahía Tortugas Mex. 127 E8
Bahir Dar Eth. 98 D2
Bahl India 82 C3
Bahlā Oman 88 E6
Bahomonte Indon. 69 G7
Bahraich India 83 E4
Bahrain country Asia 88 C5
Bahrain, Gulf of Asia 88 C5
Bahrām Beyg Iran 88 C2
Bahrāmjerd Iran 88 E4
Bahrīyah, Wāḥāt al oasis Egypt 90 C6
Bahuaja-Sonene, Parque Nacional nat. park Peru 142 E6
Baia Mare Romania 59 J1
Baiazeh Iran 88 D3
Baicang China 83 G3
Baicheng Henan China see Xiping
Baicheng Jilin China 74 A3
Baicheng Xinjiang China 80 F3
Baidoa Somalia see Baydhabo
Baidoi Co l. China 83 F2
Baidu China 77 H3
Baie-aux-Feuilles Canada see Tasiujaq
Baie-Comeau Canada 123 H4
Baie-du-Poste Canada see Mistissini
Baie-St-Paul Canada 123 H5
Baie-Trinité Canada 123 I4
Baie Verte Canada 123 K4
Baiguan China see Shangyu
Baiguo Hubei China 77 G2
Baiguo Hunan China 77 G3
Baihanchang China 76 C3
Baihar India 82 E5
Baihe Jilin China 74 C4
Baihe Shaanxi China 77 F1
Baiji Iraq see Bayjī

▶Baikal, Lake Rus. Fed. 72 J2
Deepest and 2nd largest lake in Asia, and 8th largest in the world.

Baikunthpur India 83 E5
Baile Átha Cliath Ireland see Dublin
Baile Átha Luain Ireland see Athlone
Baile Mhartainn U.K. 50 B3
Baile na Finne Ireland 51 D3
Băileşti Romania 59 J2
Bailey Range hills Australia 109 C7
Bailianhe Shuiku resr China 77 G2
Bailieborough Ireland 51 F4
Bailleul France 52 C4
Baillie r. Canada 121 J1
Bailong China see Hadapu
Bailong Jiang r. China 76 E1
Baima Qinghai China 76 D1
Baima Xizang China see Baxoi
Baima Jian mt. China 77 H2
Baimuru P.N.G. 69 K8
Bain r. U.K. 48 G5
Bainang China see Norkyung
Bainbridge GA U.S.A. 133 C6
Bainbridge IN U.S.A. 134 B4
Bainbridge NY U.S.A. 135 H2
Bainduru India 84 B3
Baingoin China see Porong
Baini China see Yuqing
Baiona Spain 57 B2
Baiqên China 76 D1
Baiquan China 74 B3
Bā'ir Jordan 85 C4
Bā'ir, Wādī watercourse Jordan/Saudi Arabia 85 C4
Bairab Co l. China 83 E2
Bairat India 82 D4
Baird U.S.A. 131 D5
Baird Mountains U.S.A. 118 C3

▶Bairiki Kiribati 150 H5
Capital of Kiribati, on Tarawa atoll.

Bairin Youqi China see Daban
Bairnsdale Australia 112 C6
Baisha Chongqing China 76 E2
Baisha Hainan China 77 F5
Baisha Sichuan China 77 F2
Baishan Guangxi China see Mashan
Baishan Jilin China 74 B4
Baishan Jilin China see Baishanzhen
Baishanzhen China 74 B4
Baishui Shaanxi China 77 F1
Baishui Sichuan China 76 E1
Baishui Jiang r. China 76 E1
Baisogala Lith. 45 M9
Baitadi Nepal 82 E3
Baitang China 76 C1
Bai Thường Vietnam 70 D3
Baixi China see Yibin
Baiyashi China see Dong'an
Baiyin China 72 I5
Baiyü China 76 C2
Baiyuda Desert Sudan 86 D6
Baja Hungary 58 H1
Baja, Punta pt Mex. 127 E7
Baja California pen. Mex. 127 E7
Baja California state Mex. 127 E7
Baja California Norte state Mex. see Baja California
Baja California Sur state Mex. 127 E8
Bajan Mex. 131 C7
Bajau i. Indon. 71 D7
Bajaur reg. Pak. 89 H3
Bajawa Indon. 108 C2
Baj Baj India 83 G5
Bājgīrān Iran 88 E2
Bājil Yemen 86 F7
Bajo Caracoles Arg. 144 B7
Bajoga Nigeria 96 E3
Bajoi China 76 D2
Bajrakot India 83 F5
Bakala Cent. Afr. Rep. 97 F4
Bakanas Kazakh. 80 E3
Bakar Pak. 89 H5
Bakel Senegal 96 B3
Baker CA U.S.A. 128 E4
Baker ID U.S.A. 126 E3
Baker LA U.S.A. 131 F6
Baker MT U.S.A. 126 G3
Baker NV U.S.A. 129 F2
Baker OR U.S.A. 126 D3
Baker WV U.S.A. 135 F4
Baker, Mount vol. U.S.A. 126 C2
Baker Butte mt. U.S.A. 129 H4

▶Baker Island terr. N. Pacific Ocean 107 I1
United States Unincorporated Territory.

Baker Island U.S.A. 120 C4
Baker Lake salt flat Australia 109 D6
Baker Lake Canada 121 M1
Baker Lake l. Canada 121 M1
Baker's Dozen Islands Canada 122 F2
Bakersfield U.S.A. 128 D4
Bakersville U.S.A. 132 D4
Bâ Kêv Cambodia 71 D4
Bakhardok Turkm. see Bokurdak
Bākharz mts Iran 89 F3
Bakhasar India 82 B4
Bakhirevo Rus. Fed. 74 C2
Bakhmach Ukr. 43 G6
Bakhma Dam Iraq see Bēkma, Sadd
Bakhmut Ukr. see Artemivs'k
Bākhtarān Iran see Kermānshāh
Bakhtegan, Daryācheh-ye l. Iran 88 D4
Bakhtiari Country reg. Iran 88 C3
Bakı Azer. see Baku
Baki Awdal 98 E2
Bakırköy Turkey 59 M4
Bakkejord Norway 44 K2
Bakloh India 82 C2
Bako Eth. 98 D3
Bakongan Indon. 71 B7
Bakouma Cent. Afr. Rep. 98 C3
Baksan Rus. Fed. 91 F2

▶Baku Azer. 91 H2
Capital of Azerbaijan.

Baku Dem. Rep. Congo 98 D3
Bakutis Coast Antarctica 152 J2
Baky Azer. see Baku
Balâ Turkey 90 D3
Bala U.K. 49 D6
Bala, Cerros de mts Bol. 142 E6
Balabac i. Phil. 68 F5
Balabac Strait Malaysia/Phil. 68 F5
Baladeh Māzandarān Iran 88 C2
Baladeh Māzandarān Iran 88 C2
Baladek Rus. Fed. 74 D1
Balaghat India 82 E5
Balaghat Range hills India 84 B2
Bālā Ḥowz Iran 88 E4
Balaka Malawi 99 D5
Balakän Azer. 91 G2
Balakhna Rus. Fed. 42 I4
Balakhta Rus. Fed. 72 G1
Balaklava Australia 111 B7
Balaklava Ukr. 90 D1
Balakleya Ukr. see Balakliya
Balakliya Ukr. 43 H6
Balakovo Rus. Fed. 43 J5
Bala Lake l. U.K. 49 D6
Balaman India 82 E4
Balan India 82 B4
Balanda Rus. Fed. see Kalininsk
Balanda r. Rus. Fed. 43 J6
Balan Dağ hill Turkey 59 M6
Balanga Phil. 69 G4
Balangir India see Bolangir
Balaözen r. Kazakh./Rus. Fed. see Malyy Uzen'
Balarampur India see Balrampur
Balashov Rus. Fed. 43 I6
Balasore India see Baleshwar
Balaton, Lake Hungary 58 G1
Balatonboglár Hungary 58 G1
Balatonfüred Hungary 58 G1
Balbina Brazil 143 G4
Balbina, Represa de resr Brazil 143 G4
Balbriggan Ireland 51 F4
Balchik Bulg. 59 M3
Balclutha N.Z. 113 B8
Balcones Escarpment U.S.A. 131 C6
Bald Knob U.S.A. 134 E5
Bald Mountain U.S.A. 129 F3
Baldock Lake Canada 121 L3
Baldwin Canada 134 F1
Baldwin FL U.S.A. 133 D6
Baldwin MI U.S.A. 134 C2
Baldwin PA U.S.A. 134 F3
Baldy Mount Canada 126 D2
Baldy Mountain hill Canada 121 K5
Baldy Peak U.S.A. 129 I5
Bale Indon. 68 C7
Bâle Switz. see Basel
Baléa Mali 96 B3
Baleares is Spain see Balearic Islands
Baleares, Islas is Spain see Balearic Islands
Baleares Insulae is Spain see Balearic Islands
Balearic Islands is Spain 57 G4
Balears is Spain see Balearic Islands
Balears, Illes is Spain see Balearic Islands
Baleia, Ponta da pt Brazil 145 D2
Bale Mountains National Park Eth. 98 D3
Baler Phil. 69 G3
Baleshwar India 83 F5
Balestrand Norway 45 E6
Baléyara Niger 96 D3
Balezino Rus. Fed. 41 Q4
Balfe's Creek Australia 110 D4
Balfour Downs Australia 108 C5
Balgo Australia 108 D5
Balguntay China 80 G3
Bali India 82 C4
Bali i. Indon. 108 A2
Bali, Laut sea Indon. 108 A1
Balia India see Ballia
Baliapal India 83 F5
Balige Indon. 71 B7
Baliguda India 84 D1
Balıkesir Turkey 59 L5
Balīkh r. Syria/Turkey 85 D2
Balikpapan Indon. 68 F7
Balimila Reservoir India 84 D2
Balimo P.N.G. 69 K8
Balin China 74 A2
Baling Malaysia 71 C6
Balingen Germany 47 L6
Balintore U.K. 50 F3
Bali Sea Indon. see Bali, Laut
Balk Neth. 52 F2
Balkanabat Turkm. 88 D2
Balkan Mountains Bulg./Serbia 59 J3
Balkassar Pak. 89 I3
Balkhash Kazakh. 80 D2

▶Balkhash, Lake Kazakh. 80 D2
3rd largest lake in Asia.

Balkhash, Ozero l. Kazakh. see Balkhash, Lake
Balkuduk Kazakh. 43 J7
Ballachulish U.K. 50 D4
Balladonia Australia 109 C8
Balladoran Australia 112 D3
Ballaghaderreen Ireland 51 D4
Ballan Australia 112 B6
Ballangen Norway 44 J2
Ballantine U.S.A. 126 F3
Ballantrae U.K. 50 E5
Ballarat Australia 112 A6
Ballard, Lake salt flat Australia 109 C7
Ballarpur India 84 C2
Ballater U.K. 50 F3
Ballé Mali 96 C3
Ballena, Punta pt Chile 144 B3
Balleny Islands Antarctica 152 H2
Ballia India 83 F4
Ballina Australia 112 F2
Ballina Ireland 51 C3
Ballinafad Ireland 51 D3
Ballinalack Ireland 51 E4
Ballinamore Ireland 51 E3
Ballinasloe Ireland 51 D4
Ballindine Ireland 51 D4
Ballinger U.S.A. 131 D6
Ballinluig U.K. 50 F4
Ballinrobe Ireland 51 C4
Ballston Spa U.S.A. 135 I2
Ballybay Ireland 51 F3
Ballybunion Ireland 51 C5
Ballycanew Ireland 51 F5
Ballycastle Ireland 51 C3
Ballycastle U.K. 51 F2
Ballyclare U.K. 51 G3
Ballyconnell Ireland 51 E3
Ballygar Ireland 51 D4
Ballygawley U.K. 51 E3
Ballygorman Ireland 51 E2
Ballyhaunis Ireland 51 D4
Ballyheigue Ireland 51 C5
Ballykelly U.K. 51 E2
Ballylynan Ireland 51 E5
Ballymacmague Ireland 51 E5
Ballymahon Ireland 51 E4
Ballymena U.K. 51 F3
Ballymoney U.K. 51 F2
Ballymote Ireland 51 D3
Ballynahinch U.K. 51 G3
Ballyshannon Ireland 51 D3
Ballyteige Bay Ireland 51 F5
Ballyvaughan Ireland 51 C4
Ballyward U.K. 51 F3
Balmartin U.K. see Baile Mhartainn
Balmer India see Barmer
Balmertown Canada 121 M5
Balmorhea U.S.A. 131 C6
Balochistan prov. Pak. 89 G4
Balombo Angola 99 B5
Balonne r. Australia 112 D2
Balotra India 82 C4
Balqash Kazakh. see Balkhash
Balqash Köli l. Kazakh. see Balkhash, Lake
Balrampur India 83 E4
Balranald Australia 112 A5
Balş Romania 59 K2
Balsam Lake Canada 135 F1
Balsas Brazil 143 I5
Balta Ukr. 43 F7
Baltasound U.K. 50 [inset]
Baltay Rus. Fed. 43 J5
Bălţi Moldova 43 E7
Baltic U.S.A. 134 E3
Baltic Sea g. Europe 45 J9
Balṭīm Egypt 90 C5
Balṭīm Egypt see Balṭīm
Baltimore S. Africa 101 I2
Baltimore MD U.S.A. 135 G4
Baltimore OH U.S.A. 134 D4
Baltinglass Ireland 51 F5
Baltistan reg. Pak. 82 C2
Baltiysk Rus. Fed. 45 K9
Balu India 76 B3
Baluarte, Arroyo watercourse U.S.A. 131 D7
Baluch Ab well Iran 88 E4
Balumundam Indon. 71 B7
Balurghat India 83 G4
Balve Germany 53 H3
Balvi Latvia 45 O8
Balya Turkey 59 L5
Balykchy Kyrg. 80 E3
Balykshi Kazakh. 78 E2
Balyqshy Kazakh. see Balykshi
Bam Iran 88 E4
Bām Iran 88 E2
Bama China 76 E3

▶Bamako Mali 96 C3
Capital of Mali.

Bamba Mali 96 C3
Bambari Cent. Afr. Rep. 98 C3
Bambel Indon. 71 B7
Bamberg Germany 53 K5
Bamberg U.S.A. 133 D5
Bambili Dem. Rep. Congo 98 C3
Bambio Cent. Afr. Rep. 98 B3
Bamboesberg mts S. Africa 101 H6
Bamboo Creek Australia 108 C5
Bambouti Cent. Afr. Rep. 98 C3
Bambuí Brazil 145 B3
Bamda China 76 C2
Bamenda Cameroon 96 E4
Bāmīān Afgh. 89 G3
Bamiantong China see Muling
Bamingui Cent. Afr. Rep. 98 C3
Bamingui-Bangoran, Parc National du nat. park Cent. Afr. Rep. 98 B3
Bâmnak Cambodia 71 D4
Bamnet Narong Thai. 70 C4
Bamor India 82 D4
Bamori India 84 C1
Bam Posht reg. Iran 89 F5
Bam Posht, Kūh-e mts Iran 89 F5
Bampton U.K. 49 D8
Bampūr Iran 89 F5
Bampūr watercourse Iran 89 E5
Bamrūd Iran 89 F3
Bam Tso l. China 83 G3
Bamyili Australia 108 F3
Banaba i. Kiribati 107 G2
Banabuiu, Açude resr Brazil 143 K5
Bañados del Izozog swamp Bol. 142 F7
Banagher Ireland 51 E4
Banalia Dem. Rep. Congo 98 C3
Banamana, Lagoa l. Moz. 101 K2
Banamba Mali 96 C3
Banámichi Mex. 127 F7
Banana Australia 110 E5
Bananal, Ilha do i. Brazil 143 H6
Bananga India 71 A6
Banapur India 84 E2
Banas r. India 82 D4
Banaz Turkey 59 M5
Ban Ban Laos 70 C3
Banbar China see Domartang
Ban Bo Laos 70 C3
Banbridge U.K. 51 F3
Ban Bua Chum Thai. 70 C4
Ban Bua Yai Thai. 70 C4
Ban Bungxai Laos 70 D4
Banbury U.K. 49 F6
Ban Cang Vietnam 70 C2
Banc d'Arguin, Parc National du nat. park Mauritania 96 B2
Ban Channabot Thai. 70 C3
Banchory U.K. 50 G3
Bancroft Canada 135 G1
Bancroft Zambia see Chililabombwe
Banda Dem. Rep. Congo 98 C3
Banda India 82 E4
Banda, Kepulauan is Indon. 69 H7
Banda, Laut sea Indon. 69 H8
Banda Aceh Indon. 71 A6
Banda Banda, Mount Australia 112 F3
Banda Daud Shah Pak. 89 H3
Bandahara, Gunung mt. Indon. 71 B7
Bandama r. Côte d'Ivoire 96 C4
Bandān Kūh mts Iran 89 F4
Bandar India see Machilipatnam
Bandar Moz. 99 D5
Bandar Abbas Iran see Bandar-e 'Abbās
Bandarban Bangl. 83 H5
Bandar-e 'Abbās Iran 88 E5
Bandar-e Anzalī Iran 88 C2
Bandar-e Deylam Iran 88 C4
Bandar-e Emām Khomeynī Iran 88 C4
Bandar-e Lengeh Iran 88 D5
Bandar-e Ma'shur Iran 88 C4
Bandar-e Nakhīlū Iran 88 D5
Bandar-e Pahlavī Iran see Bandar-e Anzalī
Bandar-e Shāh Iran see Bandar-e Torkeman
Bandar-e Shāhpūr Iran see Bandar-e Emām Khomeynī
Bandar-e Shīū' Iran 88 D5
Bandar-e Torkeman Iran 88 D2
Bandar Labuan Malaysia see Labuan
Bandar Lampung Indon. 68 D8
Bandarpunch mt. India 82 D3

▶Bandar Seri Begawan Brunei 68 E6
Capital of Brunei.

Banda Sea sea Indon. see Banda, Laut
Band-e Amīr l. Afgh. 89 G3
Band-e Amīr, Daryā-ye r. Afgh. 89 G2
Band-e Bābā mts Afgh. 89 F3
Bandeira Brazil 145 C1
Bandeirante Brazil 145 A1
Bandeiras, Pico de mt. Brazil 145 C3
Bandelierkop S. Africa 101 I2
Banderas Mex. 131 B6
Banderas, Bahía de b. Mex. 136 C4
Band-e Sar Qom Iran 88 D3
Band-e Torkestān mts Afgh. 89 F3
Bandhi Pak. 89 H5
Bandhogarh India 82 E5
Bandi r. India 82 C4
Bandiagara Mali 96 C3
Bandikui India 82 D4
Bandipur National Park India 84 C4
Bandırma Turkey 59 L4
Bandjarmasin Indon. see Banjarmasin
Bandon Ireland 51 D6
Bandon r. Ireland 51 D6
Ban Don Thai. see Surat Thani
Bandon U.S.A. 126 B4
Band Qīr Iran 88 C4
Bandra India 84 B2
Bandundu Dem. Rep. Congo 98 B4
Bandung Indon. 68 D8
Bandya Australia 109 C6
Bāneh Iran 88 B3
Banera India 82 C4
Banes Cuba 137 I4
Banff Canada 120 H5
Banff U.K. 50 G3
Banff National Park Canada 120 G5
Banfora Burkina 96 C3
Banga Dem. Rep. Congo 99 C4
Bangalore India 84 C3
Bangalow Australia 112 F2
Bangaon India 83 G5
Bangar Brunei 68 F6
Bangassou Cent. Afr. Rep. 98 C3
Bangdag Co salt l. China 83 E2
Banggai Indon. 69 G7
Banggai, Kepulauan is Indon. 69 G7
Banggi i. Malaysia 68 F5
Banghāzī Libya see Benghazi
Banghiang, Xé r. Laos 70 D3
Bangka i. Indon. 68 D7
Bangka, Selat sea chan. Indon. 68 D7
Bangkalan Indon. 68 E8
Bangkaru i. Indon. 71 B7
Bangko Indon. 68 C7

▶Bangkok Thai. 71 C4
Capital of Thailand.

Bangkok, Bight of b. Thai. 71 C4
Bangkor China 83 F3
Bangla state India see West Bengal

▶Bangladesh country Asia 83 G4
7th most populous country in the world.

Bangma Shan mts China 76 C4
Bang Mun Nak Thai. 70 C3
Ba Ngoi Vietnam 71 E5
Bangolo Côte d'Ivoire 96 C4
Bangong Co salt l. China/India 82 D2
Bangor Ireland 51 C3
Bangor Northern Ireland U.K. 51 G3
Bangor Wales U.K. 48 C5
Bangor ME U.S.A. 132 G2
Bangor MI U.S.A. 134 B2
Bangor PA U.S.A. 135 H3
Bangs, Mount U.S.A. 129 G3
Bang Saphan Yai Thai. 71 B5
Bangsund Norway 44 G4
Bangued Phil. 69 G3

▶Bangui Cent. Afr. Rep. 98 B3
Capital of the Central African Republic.

Bangweulu, Lake Zambia 99 C5
Banhā Egypt 90 C5
Banhine, Parque Nacional de nat. park Moz. 101 K2
Ban Hin Heup Laos 70 C3
Ban Houei Sai Laos see Huayxay
Ban Huai Khon Thai. 70 C3
Ban Huai Yang Thai. 71 B5
Bani, Jbel ridge Morocco 54 C6
Bania Cent. Afr. Rep. 98 B3
Bani-Bangou Niger 96 D3
Banifing r. Mali 96 C3
Banī Forūr, Jazīreh-ye i. Iran 88 D5
Banihal Pass and Tunnel India 82 C2
Banister r. U.S.A. 134 F5
Banī Suwayf Egypt 90 C5
Banī Walīd Libya 97 E1
Banī Wuṭayfān well Saudi Arabia 88 C5
Bāniyās Al Qunayṭirah Syria 85 B3
Bāniyās Ṭarṭūs Syria 85 B2
Bani Yas reg. U.A.E. 88 D6
Banja Luka Bos.-Herz. 58 G2
Banjarmasin Indon. 68 E7
Banjes, Liqeni i resr Albania 59 I4

▶Banjul Gambia 96 B3
Capital of The Gambia.

Banka India 83 F4
Banka Banka Australia 108 F4
Bankapur India 84 B3
Bankass Mali 96 C3
Ban Kengkabao Laos 70 D3
Ban Khao Yoi Thai. 71 B4
Ban Khok Kloi Thai. 71 B5
Bankilaré Niger 96 D3
Banks Island B.C. Canada 120 D4
Banks Island N.W.T. Canada 118 F2
Banks Islands Vanuatu 107 G3
Banks Lake Canada 121 M2
Banks Lake U.S.A. 126 D3
Banks Peninsula N.Z. 113 D6
Banks Strait Australia 111 [inset]
Bankura India 83 F5
Ban Lamduan Thai. 71 C4
Banlan China 77 F3
Ban Mae La Luang Thai. 70 B3
Banmaw Myanmar see Bhamo
Banmo Myanmar see Bhamo
Bann r. Ireland 51 F5
Bann r. U.K. 51 F2
Ban Nakham Laos 70 D3
Bannerman Town Bahamas 133 E7
Banning U.S.A. 128 E5
Banningville Dem. Rep. Congo see Bandundu

Ban Noi Myanmar 70 B3
Ban Nong Kung Thai. 70 D3
Bannu Pak. 89 H3
Bano India 83 F5
Bañolas Spain see Banyoles
Ban Phai Thai. 70 C3
Ban Phôn Laos see Lamam
Ban Phôn-Hông Laos 70 C3
Banqiao Yunnan China 76 C3
Banqiao Yunnan China 76 E3
Bansi Bihar India 83 F4
Bansi Rajasthan India 82 C4
Bansi Uttar Prad. India 82 D4
Bansi Uttar Prad. India 83 E4
Bansihari India 83 G4
Banská Bystrica Slovakia 47 Q6
Banspani India 83 F5
Bansur India 82 D4
Ban Sut Ta Thai. 70 B3
Ban Suwan Wari Thai. 70 D4
Banswara India 82 C5
Banteer Ireland 51 D5
Ban Tha Song Yang Thai. 70 B3
Banthat mts Cambodia/Thai. see Cardamom Range
Ban Tha Tum Thai. 70 C4
Ban Tôp Laos 70 D3
Bantry Ireland 51 C6
Bantry Bay Ireland 51 C6
Bantval India 84 B3
Ban Wang Chao Thai. 70 B3
Ban Woen Laos 70 C3
Ban Xepian Laos 70 D4
Banyak, Pulau-pulau is Indon. 71 B7
Ban Yang Yong Thai. 71 B4
Banyo Cameroon 96 E4
Banyoles Spain 57 H2
Banyuwangi Indon. 108 A2
Banzare Coast Antarctica 152 G2
Banzare Seamount sea feature Indian Ocean 149 N9
Banzart Tunisia see Bizerte
Banzkow Germany 53 L1
Banzyville Dem. Rep. Congo see Mobayi-Mbongo
Bao'an China see Shenzhen
Baochang China 73 L4
Baocheng China 76 E1
Baoding China 73 L5
Baofeng China 77 G1
Baohe China see Weixi
Baoji Shaanxi China 76 E1
Baoji Shaanxi China 76 E1
Baokang Hubei China 77 F2
Baokang Nei Mongol China 74 A3
Bao Lac Vietnam 70 D2
Baolin China 74 C3
Bao Lôc Vietnam 71 D5
Baoqing China 74 D3
Baoro Cent. Afr. Rep. 98 B3
Baoshan China 76 C3
Baotou China 73 K4
Baotou Shan mt. China/N. Korea 74 C4
Baoulé r. Mali 96 C3
Baoxing China 76 D2
Baoying China 77 H1
Baoyou China see Ledong
Bap India 82 C4
Bapatla India 84 D3
Bapaume France 52 C4
Baptiste Lake Canada 135 F1
Bapu China see Meigu
Baq'ā' oasis Saudi Arabia 91 F6
Baqbaq Egypt see Buqbuq
Baqên Xizang China 76 B1
Baqên Xizang China 76 B2
Baqiu China 77 G3
Ba'qūbah Iraq 91 G4
Bar Montenegro 59 H3
Bara Sudan 86 D7
Baraawe Somalia 98 E3
Bara Banki India see Barabanki
Barabanki India 82 E4
Baraboo U.S.A. 130 F3
Baracaju r. Brazil 145 A1
Baracaldo Spain see Barakaldo
Baracoa Cuba 137 J4
Baradá, Nahr r. Syria 85 C3
Baradine Australia 112 D3
Baradine r. Australia 112 D3
Baragarh India see Bargarh
Barahona Dom. Rep. 137 J5
Barail Range mts India 83 H4
Baraka watercourse Eritrea/Sudan 97 G3
Barakaldo Spain 57 E2
Barakī Barak Afgh. 89 H3
Baralaba Australia 110 E5
Bara Lacha Pass India 82 D2
Baralzon Lake Canada 121 L3
Baram India 83 F5
Baram r. Malaysia 68 E6
Baramati India 84 B2
Baramula India see Baramulla
Baramulla India 82 C2
Baran India 82 D4
Baran r. Pak. 89 H5
Bārān, Kūh-e mts Iran 89 F3
Baranavichy Belarus 45 O10
Barang, Dasht-i des. Afgh. 89 F3
Baranikha Rus. Fed. 65 R3
Baranīs Egypt 86 E5
Baranīs Egypt see Baranīs
Barannda India 82 E4
Baranof Island U.S.A. 120 C3
Baranovichi Belarus see Baranavichy
Baranowicze Belarus see Baranavichy
Baraouéli Mali 96 C3
Baraque de Fraiture hill Belgium 52 F4
Barasat India 83 G5
Barat Daya, Kepulauan is Indon. 108 D1
Baraut India 82 D3
Barbacena Brazil 145 C3
Barbados country West Indies 137 M6
Barbar, Gebel el mt. Egypt see Barbar, Jabal
Barbar, Jabal mt. Egypt 85 A5
Barbara Lake Canada 122 D4
Barbastro Spain 57 G2
Barbate Spain 57 D5
Barberton S. Africa 101 J3
Barberton U.S.A. 134 E3
Barbezieux-St-Hilaire France 56 D4
Barbour Bay Canada 121 M2
Barbourville U.S.A. 134 D5
Barboza Phil. 69 G4
Barbuda i. Antigua and Barbuda 137 L5
Barby (Elbe) Germany 53 L3
Barcaldine Australia 110 D4
Barce Libya see Al Marj
Barcelona Spain 57 H3
Barcelona Venez. 142 F1
Barcelonnette France 56 H4
Barcelos Brazil 142 F4
Barchfeld Germany 53 K4
Barcino Spain see Barcelona
Barclay de Tolly atoll Fr. Polynesia see Raroia
Barclayville Liberia 96 C4
Barcoo watercourse Australia 110 C5
Barcoo Creek watercourse Australia see Cooper Creek
Barcoo National Park Australia see Welford National Park
Barcs Hungary 58 G2
Bärdä Azer. 91 G2
Bárðarbunga mt. Iceland 44 [inset]
Bardaskan Iran 88 E3
Bardawil, Khabrat al salt pan Saudi Arabia 85 D4
Bardawīl, Sabkhat al lag. Egypt 85 A4
Barddhaman India 83 F5
Bardejov Slovakia 43 D6
Bardera Somalia see Baardheere
Bardhaman India see Barddhaman
Bardsey Island U.K. 49 C6
Bardsīr Iran 88 E4
Barðsneshorn pt Iceland 40 D2
Bardstown U.S.A. 134 C5
Barduli Italy see Barletta
Bardwell U.S.A. 131 F4
Bareilly India 82 D3
Barellan Australia 112 C5
Barentin France 49 H9
Barentsburg Svalbard 64 C2
Barents Sea Arctic Ocean 42 I1
Barentu Eritrea 86 E6
Barfleur, Pointe de pt France 49 F9
Bārgāh Iran 88 E5
Bargarh India 83 E5
Barghamad Iran 88 E2
Bargrennan U.K. 50 E5
Bargteheide Germany 53 K1
Barguna Bangl. 83 G5
Barhaj India 83 E4
Barham Australia 112 B5
Bari Italy 58 G4
Bari Doab lowland Pak. 89 I4
Barika Alg. 54 F4
Barinas Venez. 142 D2
Baripada India 83 F5
Bariri Brazil 145 A3
Bari Sadri India 82 C4
Barisal Bangl. 83 G5
Barisan, Pegunungan mts Indon. 68 C7
Barito r. Indon. 68 E7
Barium Italy see Bari
Barkal Bangl. 83 H5
Barkam China 76 D2
Barkan, Ra's-e pt Iran 88 C4
Barkava Latvia 45 O8
Bark Lake Canada 135 G1
Barkly East S. Africa 101 H6
Barkly Homestead Australia 110 A3
Barkly-Oos S. Africa see Barkly East
Barkly Tableland reg. Australia 110 A3
Barkly-Wes S. Africa see Barkly West
Barkly West S. Africa 100 G5
Barkol China 80 H3
Barla Turkey 59 N5
Bârlad Romania 59 L1
Bar-le-Duc France 52 F6
Barlee, Lake salt flat Australia 109 B7
Barlee Range hills Australia 109 A5
Barletta Italy 58 G4
Barlow Canada 120 B2
Barlow Lake Canada 121 K2
Barmah Forest Australia 112 B5
Barmedman Australia 112 C5
Barmen-Elberfeld Germany see Wuppertal
Barmer India 82 B4
Barm Fīrūz, Kūh-e mt. Iran 88 C4
Barmouth U.K. 49 C6
Barnala India 82 C3
Barnard Castle U.K. 48 F4
Barnato Australia 112 B3
Barnaul Rus. Fed. 72 E2
Barnegat Bay U.S.A. 135 H4
Barnes Icecap Canada 119 K2
Barnesville GA U.S.A. 133 D5
Barnesville MN U.S.A. 130 D2
Barneveld Neth. 52 F2
Barneville-Carteret France 49 F9
Barneys Lake imp. l. Australia 112 B4
Barney Top mt. U.S.A. 129 H3
Barnsley U.K. 48 F5
Barnstable U.S.A. 135 J3
Barnstaple U.K. 49 C7
Barnstaple Bay U.K. 49 C7
Barnstorf Germany 53 I2
Baro Nigeria 96 D4
Baroda Gujarat India see Vadodara
Baroda Madh. Prad. India 82 D4
Barong China 76 C2
Barons Range hills Australia 109 D6
Barowghīl, Kowtal-e Afgh. 89 I2
Barpathar India 76 B3
Barpeta India 83 G4
Bar Pla Soi Thai. see Chon Buri
Barques, Point Aux U.S.A. 134 D1
Barquisimeto Venez. 142 E1
Barra Brazil 143 J6
Barra i. U.K. 50 B4
Barra, Ponta da pt Moz. 101 L2
Barra, Sound of sea chan. U.K. 50 B3
Barraba Australia 112 E3
Barra Bonita Brazil 145 A3
Barracão do Barreto Brazil 143 G5
Barra do Bugres Brazil 143 G7
Barra do Corda Brazil 143 I5
Barra do Cuieté Brazil 145 C2
Barra do Garças Brazil 143 H7
Barra do Piraí Brazil 145 C3
Barra do São Manuel Brazil 143 G5
Barra do Turvo Brazil 145 A4
Barra Falsa, Ponta da pt Moz. 101 L2
Barraigh i. U.K. see Barra
Barra Mansa Brazil 145 B3
Barrana Pak. 89 I4
Barranca Peru 142 C4
Barranqueras Arg. 144 E3
Barranquilla Col. 142 D1
Barre MA U.S.A. 135 I2
Barre VT U.S.A. 135 I1
Barre des Écrins mt. France 56 H4
Barreiras Brazil 143 J6
Barreirinha Brazil 143 G4
Barreirinhas Brazil 143 J4
Barreiro Port. 57 B4
Barreiros Brazil 143 K5
Barren Island India 71 A4
Barren Island Kiribati see Starbuck Island
Barren River Lake U.S.A. 134 B5
Barretos Brazil 145 A3
Barrett, Mount hill Australia 108 D4
Barrhead Canada 120 H4
Barrhead U.K. 50 E5
Barrie Canada 134 F1
Barrier Bay Antarctica 152 E2
Barrière Canada 120 F5
Barrier Range hills Australia 111 C6
Barrington Canada 123 I6
Barrington, Mount Australia 112 E4
Barrington Tops National Park Australia 112 E4
Barringun Australia 112 B2
Barro Alto Brazil 145 A1
Barrocão Brazil 145 C2
Barron U.S.A. 130 F2
Barrow r. Ireland 51 F5
Barrow U.S.A. 118 C2
Barrow, Point U.S.A. 118 C2
Barrow Creek Australia 108 F5
Barrow-in-Furness U.K. 48 D4
Barrow Island Australia 108 A5
Barrow Range hills Australia 109 D6
Barrow Strait Canada 119 I2
Barr Smith Range hills Australia 109 C6
Barry U.K. 49 D7
Barrydale S. Africa 100 E7
Barry Mountains Australia 112 C6
Barrys Bay Canada 135 G1
Barryville U.S.A. 135 H3
Barsalpur India 82 C3
Barshatas Kazakh. 80 E2
Barshi India see Barsi
Barsi India 84 B2
Barsinghausen Germany 53 J2
Barstow U.S.A. 128 E4
Barsur India 84 D2
Bar-sur-Aube France 56 G2
Bartang Tajik. 89 H2
Barth Germany 47 N3
Bartica Guyana 143 G2
Bartın Turkey 90 D2
Bartle Frere, Mount Australia 110 D3
Bartlett U.S.A. 130 D3
Bartlett Reservoir U.S.A. 129 H5
Barton U.S.A. 135 I1
Barton-upon-Humber U.K. 48 G5
Bartoszyce Poland 47 R3
Bartow U.S.A. 133 D7
Barú, Volcán vol. Panama 137 H7
Barung i. Indon. 68 E8
Barunga Australia see Bamyili
Barun-Torey, Ozero l. Rus. Fed. 73 L2
Barus Indon. 71 B7
Baruunturuun Mongolia 80 H2
Baruun-Urt Mongolia 73 K3
Baruva India 84 E2
Barwani India 82 C5
Barwéli Mali see Baraouéli
Barwon r. Australia 112 C3
Barygaza India see Bharuch
Barysaw Belarus 45 P9
Barysh Rus. Fed. 43 J5
Basaga Turkm. 89 G2
Basāk, Tônlé r. Cambodia 71 D5
Basalt r. Australia 110 D3
Basalt Island H.K. China 77 [inset]
Basankusu Dem. Rep. Congo 98 B3
Basar India 84 C2
Basarabi Romania 59 M2
Basargechar Armenia see Vardenis
Bascuñán, Cabo c. Chile 144 B3
Basel Switz. 56 H3
Bashākerd, Kūhhā-ye mts Iran 88 E5
Bashanta Rus. Fed. see Gorodovikovsk
Bashaw Canada 120 H4
Bashee r. S. Africa 101 I7
Bāshī Iran 88 C4
Bashi Channel Phil./Taiwan 69 G2
Bashmakovo Rus. Fed. 43 I5
Bāsht Iran 88 C4
Bashtanka Ukr. 43 G7
Basi Punjab India 82 D3
Basi Rajasthan India 82 D4
Basia India 83 F5
Basilan i. Phil. 69 G5
Basildon U.K. 49 H7
Basile, Pico mt. Equat. Guinea 96 D4
Basin U.S.A. 126 F3
Basingstoke U.K. 49 F7
Basin Lake Canada 121 J4
Basirhat India 83 G5
Basīţ, Ra's al pt Syria 85 B2
Başkale Turkey 91 G3
Baskatong, Réservoir resr Canada 122 G5
Baskerville, Cape Australia 108 C4
Başkomutan Tarıhı Milli Parkı nat. park Turkey 59 N5
Başköy Turkey 85 A1
Baskunchak, Ozero l. Rus. Fed. 43 J6
Basle Switz. see Basel
Basmat India 84 C2
Basoko Dem. Rep. Congo 98 C3
Basra Iraq 91 G5
Bassano Canada 121 H5
Bassano del Grappa Italy 58 D2
Bassar Togo 96 D4
Bassas da India reef Indian Ocean 99 D6
Bassas de Pedro Padua Bank sea feature India 84 B3
Bassein Myanmar 70 A3
Bassein r. Myanmar 70 A3
Basse-Normandie admin. reg. France 49 F9
Bassenthwaite Lake U.K. 48 D4
Basse Santa Su Gambia 96 B3
▶Basse-Terre Guadeloupe 137 L5
Capital of Guadeloupe.
▶Basseterre St Kitts and Nevis 137 L5
Capital of St Kitts and Nevis.
Bassett NE U.S.A. 130 D3
Bassett VA U.S.A. 134 F5
Bassikounou Mauritania 96 C3
Bass Rock i. U.K. 50 G4
Bass Strait Australia 111 D8
Bassum Germany 53 I2
Basswood Lake Canada 122 C4
Båstad Sweden 45 H8
Bāstānābād Iran 88 B2
Bastheim Germany 53 K4
Basti India 83 E4
Bastia Corsica France 56 I5
Bastioes r. Brazil 143 K5
Bastogne Belgium 52 F4
Bastrop LA U.S.A. 131 F5
Bastrop TX U.S.A. 131 D6
Basul r. Pak. 89 G5
Basuo China see Dongfang
Basutoland country Africa see Lesotho
Başyayla Turkey 85 A1
Bata Equat. Guinea 96 D4
Batabanó, Golfo de b. Cuba 137 H4
Batagay Rus. Fed. 65 O3
Batala India 82 C3
Batalha Port. 57 B4
Batam i. Indon. 71 D7
Batamay Rus. Fed. 65 N3
Batamshinskiy Kazakh. 80 A1
Batamshy Kazakh. see Batamshinskiy
Batan Jiangsu China 77 I1
Batan Qinghai China 76 D1
Batan i. Phil. 69 G2
Batan is Phil. 69 G2
Batang China 76 C2
Batangafo Cent. Afr. Rep. 98 B3
Batangas Phil. 69 G4
Batangtoru Indon. 71 B7
Batan Islands Phil. 69 G2
Batavia Indon. see Jakarta
Batavia NY U.S.A. 135 F2
Batavia OH U.S.A. 134 C4
Bataysk Rus. Fed. 43 H7
Batchawana Mountain hill Canada 122 D5
Bătdâmbâng Cambodia 71 C4
Bateemeucica, Gunung mt. Indon. 71 A6
Batéké, Plateaux Congo 98 B4
Batemans Bay Australia 112 E5
Bates Range hills Australia 109 C6
Batesville AR U.S.A. 131 F5
Batesville IN U.S.A. 134 C4
Batesville MS U.S.A. 131 F5
Batetskiy Rus. Fed. 42 F4
Bath N.B. Canada 123 I5
Bath Ont. Canada 135 G1
Bath U.K. 49 E7
Bath ME U.S.A. 135 K2
Bath NY U.S.A. 135 G2
Bath PA U.S.A. 135 H3
Batha watercourse Chad 97 E3
Bathgate U.K. 50 F5
Bathinda India 82 C3
Bathurst Australia 112 D4
Bathurst Canada 123 I5
Bathurst Gambia see Banjul
Bathurst S. Africa 101 H7
Bathurst, Cape Canada 118 F2
Bathurst, Lake Australia 112 D5
Bathurst Inlet inlet Canada 118 H3
Bathurst Inlet (abandoned) Canada 118 H3
Bathurst Island Australia 108 E2
Bathurst Island Canada 119 I2
Bathyz Döwlet Gorugy nature res. Turkm. 89 F3
Batié Burkina 96 C4
Batı Menteşe Dağları mts Turkey 59 L6
Batı Toroslar mts Turkey 59 N6
Batken Kyrg. 80 D4
Batkes Indon. 108 E1
Bāţlāq-e Gavkhūnī marsh Iran 88 D3
Batley U.K. 48 F5
Batlow Australia 112 D5
Batman Turkey 91 F3
Batna Alg. 54 F4
Batok, Bukit hill Sing. 71 [inset]
▶Baton Rouge U.S.A. 131 F6
Capital of Louisiana.
Batopilas Mex. 127 G8
Batouri Cameroon 97 E4
Batrā' tourist site Jordan see Petra
Batrā', Jabal al mt. Jordan 85 B5
Batroûn Lebanon 85 B2
Båtsfjord Norway 44 P1
Battambang Cambodia see Bătdâmbâng
Batticaloa Sri Lanka 84 D5
Batti Malv i. India 71 A5
Battipaglia Italy 58 F4
Battle r. Canada 121 I4
Battle Creek U.S.A. 134 C2
Battleford Canada 121 I4
Battle Mountain U.S.A. 128 E1
Battle Mountain mt. U.S.A. 128 E1
Battura Glacier Pak. 82 C1
Batu mt. Eth. 98 D3
Batu, Pulau-pulau is Indon. 68 B7
Batudaka i. Indon. 69 G7
Batu Gajah Malaysia 71 C6
Batum Georgia see Bat'umi
Bat'umi Georgia 91 F2
Batu Pahat Malaysia 71 C7
Batu Putih, Gunung mt. Malaysia 71 C6
Baturaja Indon. 68 C7
Baturité Brazil 143 K4
Batyrevo Rus. Fed. 43 J5
Batys Qazaqstan admin. div. Kazakh. see Zapadnyy Kazakhstan
Bau Sarawak Malaysia 68 E6
Baubau Indon. 69 G8
Baucau East Timor 108 D2
Bauchi Nigeria 96 D3
Bauda India see Boudh
Baudette U.S.A. 130 E1
Baudh India see Boudh
Baugé France 56 D3
Bauhinia Australia 110 E5
Baukau East Timor see Baucau
Bauld, Cape Canada 123 L4
Baume-les-Dames France 56 H3
Baunach r. Germany 53 K5
Baundal India 82 C2
Baura Bangl. 83 G4
Bauru Brazil 145 A3
Bausendorf Germany 52 G4
Bauska Latvia 45 N8
Bautino Kazakh. 91 H1
Bautzen Germany 47 O5
Bavānāt Iran 88 D4
Bavaria land Germany see Bayern
Bavaria reg. Germany 53 L6
Bavda India 84 B2
Baviaanskloofberge mts S. Africa 100 F7
Bavispe r. Mex. 127 F7
Bavla India 82 C5
Bavly Rus. Fed. 41 Q5
Baw Myanmar 70 A2
Bawal India 82 D3
Baw Baw National Park Australia 112 C6
Bawdeswell U.K. 49 I6
Bawdwin Myanmar 70 B2
Bawean i. Indon. 68 E8
Bawinkel Germany 53 H2
Bawlake Myanmar 70 B3
Bawolung China 76 D2
Baxi China 76 D1
Baxley U.S.A. 133 D6
Baxoi China 76 C2
Baxter Mountain U.S.A. 129 J2
Bay China see Baicheng
Bayamo Cuba 137 I4
Bayan Heilong. China 74 B3
Bayan Qinghai China 76 C1
Bayana India 82 D4
Bayan-Adraga Mongolia 73 K3
Bayanaul Kazakh. 80 E1
Bayanbulak China 80 F3
Bayanday Rus. Fed. 72 J2
Bayan Gol China see Dengkou
Bayan Har Shan mts China 76 B1
Bayan Har Shankou pass China 76 C1
Bayanhongor Mongolia 80 J2
Bayan Hot China 72 J5
Bayan Mod China 72 I4
Bayan Obo China 73 J4
Bayantsagaan Mongolia 80 I2
Bayan Ul Hot China 73 L4
Bayan-Uul Mongolia 73 K3
Bayard U.S.A. 129 I5
Bayat Turkey 59 N5
Bayāz Iran 88 E4
Baybay Phil. 69 G4
Bayboro U.S.A. 133 E5
Bayburt Turkey 91 F2
Bay Canh, Hon i. Vietnam 71 D5
Bay City MI U.S.A. 134 D2
Bay City TX U.S.A. 131 D6
Baydaratskaya Guba Rus. Fed. 64 H3
Baydhabo Somalia 98 E3
Bayerischer Wald mts Germany 53 M5
Bayerischer Wald nat. park Germany 53 M5
Bayerischer Wald, Nationalpark nat. park Germany 47 N6
Bayern land Germany 53 L6
Bayeux France 49 G9
Bayfield Canada 134 E2
Bayındır Turkey 59 L5
Bay Islands is Hond. see Bahía, Islas de la
Bayizhen China 76 B2
Bayjī Iraq 91 F4
Baykal, Ozero l. Rus. Fed. see Baikal, Lake
Baykal-Amur Magistral Rus. Fed. 74 C1
Baykal Range mts Rus. Fed. see Baykal'skiy Khrebet
Baykal'skiy Khrebet mts Rus. Fed. 73 J2
Baykan Turkey 91 F3
Bay-Khaak Rus. Fed. 80 H1
Baykibashevo Rus. Fed. 41 R4
Baykonur Kazakh. see Baykonyr
Baykonyr Kazakh. 80 B2
Baymak Rus. Fed. 64 G4
Bay Minette U.S.A. 133 C6
Baynūna'h reg. U.A.E. 88 D6
Bayombong Phil. 69 G3
Bayona Spain see Baiona
Bayonne France 56 D5
Bayonne U.S.A. 135 H3
Bay Port U.S.A. 134 D2
Bayqongyr Kazakh. see Baykonyr
Bayram-Ali Turkm. see Baýramaly
Baýramaly Turkm. 89 F2
Bayramiç Turkey 59 L5
Bayreuth Germany 53 L5
Bayrūt Lebanon see Beirut
Bays, Lake of Canada 134 F1
Bayshore U.S.A. 134 C1
Bay Shore U.S.A. 135 I3
Bay Springs U.S.A. 131 F6
Bayston Hill U.K. 49 E6
Baysun Uzbek. see Boysun
Bayt Lahm West Bank see Bethlehem
Baytown U.S.A. 131 E6
Bay View N.Z. 113 F4
Bayy al Kabīr, Wādī watercourse Libya 97 E1
Baza Spain 57 E5
Baza, Sierra de mts Spain 57 E5
Bāzārak Afgh. 89 G3
Bazardüzü Dağı mt. Azer./Rus. Fed. see Bazardyuzyu, Gora
Bazardyuzyu, Gora mt. Azer./Rus. Fed. 91 G2
Bāzār-e Māsāl Iran 88 C2
Bazarnyy Karabulak Rus. Fed. 43 J5
Bazaruto, Ilha do i. Moz. 99 D6
Bazdar Pak. 89 G5
Bazhong China 76 E2
Bazhou China see Bazhong
Bazin r. Canada 122 G5
Bazmān Iran 89 F5
Bazmān, Kūh-e mt. Iran 89 F4
Bcharré Lebanon 85 C2
Be, Sông r. Vietnam 71 D5
Beach U.S.A. 130 C2
Beachy Head hd U.K. 49 H8
Beacon U.S.A. 135 I3
Beacon Bay S. Africa 101 H7
Beaconsfield U.K. 49 G7
Beagle, Canal sea chan. Arg. 144 C8
Beagle Bank reef Australia 108 C3
Beagle Bay Australia 108 C4
Beagle Gulf Australia 108 E3
Bealanana Madag. 99 E5
Béal an Átha Ireland see Ballina
Béal an Mhuirthead Ireland 51 C3
Béal Átha na Sluaighe Ireland see Ballinasloe
Beale, Lake India 84 B2
Beaminster U.K. 49 E8
Bear r. U.S.A. 126 E4
Bearalváhki Norway see Berlevåg
Bear Cove Point Canada 121 O2
Beardmore Canada 122 D4
Beardmore Glacier Antarctica 152 H1
Bear Island Arctic Ocean see Bjørnøya
Bear Island Canada 122 E3
Bear Lake l. Canada 122 A3
Bear Lake U.S.A. 134 B1
Bear Lake l. U.S.A. 126 F4
Bearma r. India 82 D4
Bear Mountain U.S.A. 130 C3
Bearnaraigh i. U.K. see Berneray
Bear Paw Mountain U.S.A. 126 F2
Bearpaw Mountains U.S.A. 126 F2
Bearskin Lake Canada 121 N4
Beas Dam India 82 C3
Beata, Cabo c. Dom. Rep. 137 J5
Beatrice U.S.A. 130 D3
Beatrice, Cape Australia 110 B2
Beatton r. Canada 120 F3
Beatton River Canada 120 F3
Beatty U.S.A. 128 E3
Beattyville Canada 122 F4
Beattyville U.S.A. 134 D5
Beaucaire France 56 G5
Beauchene Island Falkland Is 144 E8
Beaufort Australia 112 A6
Beaufort NC U.S.A. 133 E5
Beaufort SC U.S.A. 133 D5
Beaufort Island H.K. China 77 [inset]
Beaufort Sea Canada/U.S.A. 118 D2
Beaufort West S. Africa 100 F7
Beaulieu r. Canada 121 H2
Beauly U.K. 50 E3
Beauly r. U.K. 50 E3
Beaumaris U.K. 48 C5
Beaumont Belgium 52 E4
Beaumont N.Z. 113 B7
Beaumont MS U.S.A. 131 F6
Beaumont TX U.S.A. 131 E6
Beaune France 56 G3
Beaupréau France 56 D3
Beauquesne France 52 C4
Beauraing Belgium 52 E4
Beauséjour Canada 121 L5
Beauvais France 52 C5
Beauval France 52 C4
Beaver r. Alberta/Saskatchewan Canada 121 J4
Beaver r. Ont. Canada 122 D3
Beaver r. Y.T. Canada 120 E3
Beaver OK U.S.A. 131 C4
Beaver PA U.S.A. 134 E3
Beaver UT U.S.A. 129 G2
Beaver r. U.S.A. 129 G2
Beaver Creek Canada 153 A2
Beavercreek U.S.A. 134 C4
Beaver Creek r. MT U.S.A. 130 B1
Beaver Creek r. ND U.S.A. 130 C2
Beaver Dam KY U.S.A. 134 B5
Beaver Dam WI U.S.A. 130 F3
Beaver Falls U.S.A. 134 E3
Beaverhead Mountains U.S.A. 126 E3
Beaverhill Lake Alta Canada 121 H4
Beaver Hill Lake Canada 121 M4
Beaverhill Lake N.W.T. Canada 121 J2
Beaver Island U.S.A. 132 C2
Beaverlodge Canada 120 G4
Beaverton Canada 134 F1
Beaverton MI U.S.A. 134 C2
Beaverton OR U.S.A. 126 C3
Beawar India 82 C4
Beazley Arg. 144 C4
Bebedouro Brazil 145 A3
Bebington U.K. 48 D5
Bebra Germany 53 J4
Bêca China 76 C2
Bécard, Lac l. Canada 123 G1
Beccles U.K. 49 I6
Bečej Serbia 59 I2
Becerreá Spain 57 C2
Béchar Alg. 54 D5
Bechhofen Germany 53 K5
Bechuanaland country Africa see Botswana
Beckley U.S.A. 134 E5
Beckum Germany 53 I3
Becky Peak U.S.A. 129 F2
Bečov nad Teplou Czech Rep. 53 M4
Bedale U.K. 48 F4
Bedburg Germany 52 G4
Bedelē Eth. 98 D3
Bedford N.S. Canada 123 J5
Bedford Que. Canada 135 I1
Bedford E. Cape S. Africa 101 H7
Bedford Kwazulu-Natal S. Africa 101 J5
Bedford U.K. 49 G6
Bedford IN U.S.A. 134 B4
Bedford KY U.S.A. 134 C4
Bedford PA U.S.A. 135 F3
Bedford VA U.S.A. 134 F5
Bedford, Cape Australia 110 D2
Bedford Downs Australia 108 D4
Bedgerebong Australia 112 C4
Bedi India 82 B5
Bedla India 82 C4
Bedlington U.K. 48 F3
Bedok Sing. 71 [inset]
Bedok Jetty Sing. 71 [inset]
Bedok Reservoir Sing. 71 [inset]
Bedou China 77 F3
Bedourie Australia 110 B5
Bedum Neth. 52 G1
Bedworth U.K. 49 F6
Beechworth Australia 112 C6
Beechy Canada 121 J5
Beecroft Peninsula Australia 112 E5
Beed India see Bid
Beelitz Germany 53 M2
Beenleigh Australia 112 F1

Beernem Belgium 52 D3
Beersheba Israel 85 B4
Be'ér Sheva' Israel see Beersheba
Be'ér Sheva' *watercourse* Israel 85 B4
Beervlei Dam S. Africa 100 F7
Beerwah Australia 112 F1
Beetaloo Australia 108 F4
Beethoven Peninsula Antarctica 152 L2
Beeville U.S.A. 131 D6
Befori Dem. Rep. Congo 98 C3
Beg, Lough *l.* U.K. 51 F3
Bega Australia 112 D6
Begari *r.* Pak. 89 H4
Begicheva, Ostrov *i.* Rus. Fed. *see* Bol'shoy Begichev, Ostrov
Begur, Cap de *c.* Spain 57 H3
Begusarai India 83 F4
Béhague, Pointe *pt* Fr. Guiana 143 H3
Behbehān Iran 88 C4
Behchokǫ̀ Canada 120 G2
Behrendt Mountains Antarctica 152 L2
Behrūsī Iran 88 D4
Behshahr Iran 88 D2
Behsūd Afgh. 89 G3
Bei'an China 74 B2
Bei'ao China *see* Dongtou
Beibei China 76 E2
Beichuan China 76 E2
Beida Libya *see* Al Bayḍā'
Beigang Taiwan *see* Peikang
Beiguan China *see* Anyang
Beihai China 77 F4
Bei Hulsan Hu *salt l.* China 83 H1
▶Beijing China 73 L5
Capital of China.
Beijing *municipality* China 73 L4
Beik Myanmar *see* Myeik
Beilen Neth. 52 G2
Beiliu China 77 F4
Beilngries Germany 53 L5
Beiluheyan China 76 B1
Beinn an Oir *hill* U.K. 50 D5
Beinn an Tuirc *hill* U.K. 50 D5
Beinn Bheigeir *hill* U.K. 50 C5
Beinn Bhreac *hill* U.K. 50 D4
Beinn Dearg *mt.* U.K. 50 E3
Beinn Heasgarnich *mt.* U.K. 50 E4
Beinn Mholach *hill* U.K. 50 C2
Beinn Mhòr *hill* U.K. 50 B3
Beinn na Faoghlia *i.* U.K. *see* Benbecula
Beipan Jiang *r.* China 76 E3
Beipiao China 73 M4
Beira Moz. 99 D5
▶Beirut Lebanon 85 B3
Capital of Lebanon.
Bei Shan *mts* China 80 I3
Beitbridge Zimbabwe 99 C6
Beith U.K. 50 E5
Beit Jālā West Bank 85 B4
Beja Port. 57 C4
Béja Tunisia 58 C6
Bejaïa Alg. 57 I5
Béjar Spain 57 D3
Beji *r.* Pak. 80 C6
Bekaa *valley* Lebanon *see* El Béqaa
Békés Hungary 59 I1
Békéscsaba Hungary 59 I1
Bekily Madag. 99 E6
Bekkai Japan 74 G4
Bēkma, Sadd *dam* Iraq 91 G3
Bekovo Rus. Fed. 43 I5
Bekwai Ghana 96 C4
Bela India 83 E4
Bela Pak. 89 G5
Belab *r.* Pak. 89 H4
Bela-Bela S. Africa 101 I3
Bélabo Cameroon 96 E4
Bela Crkva Serbia 59 I2
Bel Air U.S.A. 135 G4
Belalcázar Spain 57 D4
Bělá nad Radbuzou Czech Rep. 53 M5
Belapur India 84 B2
Belarus *country* Europe 43 E5
Belau *country* N. Pacific Ocean *see* Palau
Bela Vista Brazil 144 E2
Bela Vista Moz. 101 K4
Bela Vista de Goiás Brazil 145 A2
Belawan Indon. 71 B7
Belaya *r.* Rus. Fed. 65 S3
also known as Bila
Belaya Glina Rus. Fed. 43 I7
Belaya Kalitva Rus. Fed. 43 I6
Belaya Kholunitsa Rus. Fed. 42 K4
Belaya Tserkva Ukr. *see* Bila Tserkva
Belbédji Niger 96 D3
Bełchatów Poland 47 Q5
Belcher U.S.A. 134 D5
Belcher Islands Canada 122 F2
Belchiragh Afgh. 89 G3
Belcoo U.K. 51 E3
Belden U.S.A. 128 C1
Belding U.S.A. 134 C2
Beleapani *reef* India *see* Cherbaniani Reef
Belebey Rus. Fed. 41 Q5
Beledweyne Somalia 98 E3
Belém Brazil 143 I4
Belém Novo Brazil 145 A5
Belén Arg. 144 C3
Belen *Antalya* Turkey 85 A1
Belen *Hatay* Turkey 85 C1
Belen U.S.A. 127 G6
Belep, Îles *is* New Caledonia 107 G3
Belev Rus. Fed. 43 H5
Belfast S. Africa 101 J3
▶Belfast U.K. 51 G3
Capital of Northern Ireland.
Belfast U.S.A. 132 G2
Belfast Lough *inlet* U.K. 51 G3
Bēlfodiyo Eth. 98 D2
Belford U.K. 48 F3
Belfort France 56 H3
Belgaum India 84 B3
Belgern Germany 53 N3
Belgian Congo *country* Africa *see* Congo, Democratic Republic of the
België *country* Europe *see* Belgium
Belgique *country* Europe *see* Belgium
Belgium *country* Europe 52 E4
Belgorod Rus. Fed. 43 H6
Belgorod-Dnestrovskyy Ukr. *see* Bilhorod-Dnistrovs'kyy
▶Belgrade Serbia 59 I2
Capital of Serbia.
Belgrade *ME* U.S.A. 135 K1
Belgrade *MT* U.S.A. 126 F3
Belgrano II *research station* Antarctica 152 A1
Belice *r. Sicily* Italy 58 E6
Belinskiy Rus. Fed. 43 I5
Belinyu Indon. 68 D7
Belitung *i.* Indon. 68 D7
Belize Angola 99 B4
▶Belize Belize 136 G5
Former capital of Belize.
Belize *country* Central America 136 G5
Beljak Austria *see* Villach
Belkina, Mys *pt* Rus. Fed. 74 E3
Bel'kovskiy, Ostrov *i.* Rus. Fed. 65 O2
Bell Australia 112 E1
Bell *r.* Australia 112 D4
Bell *r.* Canada 122 F4
Bella Bella Canada 120 D4
Bellac France 56 E3
Bella Coola Canada 120 E4
Bellaire U.S.A. 134 C1
Bellary India 84 C3
Bellata Australia 112 D2
Bella Unión Uruguay 144 E4
Bella Vista U.S.A. 128 B1
Bellbrook Australia 112 F3
Bell Cay *reef* Australia 110 E4
Belledonne *mts* France 56 G4
Bellefontaine U.S.A. 134 D3
Bellefonte U.S.A. 135 G3
Belle Fourche U.S.A. 130 C2
Belle Fourche *r.* U.S.A. 130 C2
Belle Glade U.S.A. 133 D7
Belle-Île *i.* France 56 C3
Belle Isle *i.* Canada 123 L4
Belle Isle, Strait of Canada 123 K4
Belleville Canada 135 G1
Belleville *IL* U.S.A. 130 F4
Belleville *KS* U.S.A. 130 D4
Bellevue *IA* U.S.A. 130 F3
Bellevue *MI* U.S.A. 134 C2
Bellevue *OH* U.S.A. 134 D3
Bellevue *WA* U.S.A. 126 C3
Bellin Canada *see* Kangirsuk
Bellingham U.K. 48 E3
Bellingham U.S.A. 126 C2
Bellingshausen *research station* Antarctica 152 A2
Bellingshausen Sea Antarctica 152 L2
Bellinzona Switz. 56 I3
Bellows Falls U.S.A. 135 I2
Bellpat Pak. 89 H4
Belluno Italy 58 E1
Belluru India 84 C3
Bell Ville Arg. 144 D4
Bellville S. Africa 100 D7
Belm Germany 53 I2
Belmont Australia 112 E4
Belmont U.K. 50 [inset]
Belmont U.S.A. 135 F2
Belmonte Brazil 145 D1
▶Belmopan Belize 136 G5
Capital of Belize.
Belmore, Mount *hill* Australia 112 F2
Belo Madag. 99 E6
Belo Campo Brazil 145 C1
Belœil Belgium 52 D4
Belogorsk Rus. Fed. 74 C2
Belogorsk Ukr. *see* Bilohirs'k
Beloha Madag. 99 E6
Belo Horizonte Brazil 145 C2
Beloit *KS* U.S.A. 130 D4
Beloit *WI* U.S.A. 130 F3
Belokurikha Rus. Fed. 80 F1
Belo Monte Brazil 143 H4
Belomorsk Rus. Fed. 42 G2
Belonia India 83 G5
Belorechensk Rus. Fed. 91 E1
Belorechenskaya Rus. Fed. *see* Belorechensk
Belören Turkey 90 D3
Beloretsk Rus. Fed. 64 G4
Belorussia *country* Europe *see* Belarus
Belorusskaya S.S.R. *country* Europe *see* Belarus
Belostok Poland *see* Białystok
Belot, Lac *l.* Canada 118 F3
Belo Tsiribihina Madag. 99 E5
Belovo Rus. Fed. 72 F2
Beloyarskiy Rus. Fed. 41 T3
Beloye, Ozero *l.* Rus. Fed. 42 H3
Beloye More *sea* Rus. Fed. *see* White Sea
Belozersk Rus. Fed. 42 H3
Belpre U.S.A. 134 E4
Beltana Australia 111 B6
Belted Range *mts* U.S.A. 128 E3
Belton U.S.A. 131 D6
Bel'ts' Moldova *see* Bălţi
Bel'tsy Moldova *see* Bălţi
Belukha, Gora *mt.* Kazakh./Rus. Fed. 80 G2
Belush'ye Rus. Fed. 42 J2
Belvidere *IL* U.S.A. 130 F3
Belvidere *NJ* U.S.A. 135 H3
Belyando *r.* Australia 110 D4
Belyayevka Ukr. *see* Bilyayivka
Belyy Rus. Fed. 42 G5
Belyy, Ostrov *i.* Rus. Fed. 64 I2
Belzig Germany 53 M2
Belzoni U.S.A. 131 F5
Bemaraha, Plateau du Madag. 99 E5
Bembe Angola 99 B4
Bemidji U.S.A. 130 E2
Béna Burkina 96 C3
Bena Dibele Dem. Rep. Congo 98 C4
Ben Alder *mt.* U.K. 50 E4
Benalla Australia 112 B6
Benares India *see* Varanasi
Ben Arous Tunisia 58 D6
Benavente Spain 57 D2
Ben Avon *mt.* U.K. 50 F3
Benbane Head *hd* U.K. 51 F2
Benbecula *i.* U.K. 50 B3
Ben Boyd National Park Australia 112 E6
Benburb U.K. 51 F3
Bencha China 77 I1
Ben Chonzie *hill* U.K. 50 F4
Ben Cleuch *hill* U.K. 50 F4
Ben Cruachan *mt.* U.K. 50 D4
Bend U.S.A. 126 C3
Bendearg *mt.* S. Africa 101 H6
Bender Moldova *see* Tighina
Bender-Bayla Somalia 98 F3
Bendery Moldova *see* Tighina
Bendigo Australia 112 B6
Bendoc Australia 112 D6
Bene Moz. 99 D5
Benedict, Mount *hill* Canada 123 K3
Benenitra Madag. 99 E6
Benešov Czech Rep. 47 O6
Bénestroff France 52 G6
Benevento Italy 58 F4
Beneventum Italy *see* Benevento
Benezette U.S.A. 135 F3
Beng, Nam *r.* Laos 70 C3
Bengal, Bay of *sea* Indian Ocean 81 G8
Bengamisa Dem. Rep. Congo 98 C3
Bengbu China 77 H1
Benghazi Libya 97 F1
Bengkalis Indon. 71 C7
Bengkalis *i.* Indon. 71 C7
Bengkulu Indon. 68 C7
Bengtsfors Sweden 45 H7
Benguela Angola 99 B5
Benha Egypt *see* Banhā
Ben Hiant *hill* U.K. 50 C4
Ben Hope *hill* U.K. 50 E2
Ben Horn *hill* U.K. 50 E2
Beni *r.* Bol. 142 E6
Beni Dem. Rep. Congo 98 C3
Beni Nepal 83 E3
Beni Abbès Alg. 54 D5
Beniah Lake Canada 121 H2
Benidorm Spain 57 F4
Beni Mellal Morocco 54 C5
Benin *country* Africa 96 D4
Benin, Bight of *g.* Africa 96 D4
Benin City Nigeria 96 D4
Beni Saf Alg. 57 F6
Beni Snassen, Monts des *mts* Morocco 57 E6
Beni Suef Egypt *see* Banī Suwayf
Benito, Islas *is* Mex. 127 E7
Benito Juárez Arg. 144 E5
Benito Juárez Mex. 129 F5
Benjamim Constant Brazil 142 E4
Benjamin U.S.A. 131 D5
Benjamín Hill Mex. 127 F7
Benjina Indon. 69 I8
Benkelman U.S.A. 130 C3
Ben Klibreck *hill* U.K. 50 E2
Ben Lavin Nature Reserve S. Africa 101 I2
Ben Lawers *mt.* U.K. 50 E4
Ben Lomond *mt.* Australia 112 E3
Ben Lomond *hill* U.K. 50 E4
Ben Lomond National Park Australia 111 [inset]
Ben Macdui *mt.* U.K. 50 F3
Benmara Australia 110 B3
Ben More *hill* U.K. 50 C4
Ben More *mt.* U.K. 50 E4
Benmore, Lake N.Z. 113 C7
Ben More Assynt *hill* U.K. 50 E2
Bennetta, Ostrov *i.* Rus. Fed. 65 P2
Bennett Island Rus. Fed. *see* Bennetta, Ostrov
Bennett Lake Canada 120 C3
Bennettsville U.S.A. 133 E5
Ben Nevis *mt.* U.K. 50 D4
Bennington *NH* U.S.A. 135 J2
Bennington *VT* U.S.A. 135 I2
Benoni S. Africa 101 I4
Ben Rinnes *hill* U.K. 50 F3
Bensheim Germany 53 I5
Benson *AZ* U.S.A. 129 H6
Benson *MN* U.S.A. 130 E2
Benta Seberang Malaysia 71 C6
Benteng Indon. 69 G8
Bentinck Island Myanmar 71 B5
Bentiu Sudan 86 C8
Bent Jbaïl Lebanon 85 B3
Bentley U.K. 48 F5
Bento Gonçalves Brazil 145 A5
Benton *AR* U.S.A. 131 E5
Benton *CA* U.S.A. 128 D3
Benton *IL* U.S.A. 130 F4
Benton *KY* U.S.A. 131 F4
Benton *LA* U.S.A. 131 E5
Benton *MO* U.S.A. 131 F4
Benton *PA* U.S.A. 135 G3
Bentong Malaysia *see* Bentung
Benton Harbor U.S.A. 134 B2
Bentonville U.S.A. 131 E4
Bên Tre Vietnam 71 D5
Bentung Malaysia 71 C7
Benue *r.* Nigeria 96 D4
Benum, Gunung *mt.* Malaysia 71 C7
Ben Vorlich *hill* U.K. 50 E4
Benwee Head *hd* Ireland 51 C3
Benwood U.S.A. 134 E3
Ben Wyvis *mt.* U.K. 50 E3
Benxi *Liaoning* China 74 A4
Benxi *Liaoning* China 74 B4
Beograd Serbia *see* Belgrade
Béoumi Côte d'Ivoire 96 C4
Beppu Japan 75 C6
Béqaa *valley* Lebanon *see* El Béqaa
Berach *r.* India 82 C4
Beraketa Madag. 99 E6
Bérard, Lac *l.* Canada 123 H2
Berasia India 82 D5
Berat Albania 59 H4
Beravina Madag. 99 E5
Berbak, Taman Nasional Indon. 68 C7
Berber Sudan 86 D6
Berbera Somalia 98 E2
Berbérati Cent. Afr. Rep. 98 B3
Berchtesgaden, Nationalpark *nat. park* Germany 47 N7
Berck France 52 B4
Berdichev Ukr. *see* Berdychiv
Berdigestyakh Rus. Fed. 65 N3
Berdyans'k Ukr. 43 H7
Berdychiv Ukr. 43 F6
Berea *KY* U.S.A. 134 C5
Berea *OH* U.S.A. 134 E3
Beregovo Ukr. *see* Berehove
Beregovoy Rus. Fed. 74 B1
Berehove Ukr. 43 D6
Bereina P.N.G. 69 L8
Bere Island Ireland 51 C6
Bereket Turkm. 88 D2
Berekum Ghana 96 C4
Berenice Egypt *see* Baranīs
Berenice Libya *see* Benghazi
Berens *r.* Canada 121 L4
Berens Island Canada 121 L4
Berens River Canada 121 L4
Beresford U.S.A. 130 D3
Bereza Belarus *see* Byaroza
Berezino Belarus *see* Byerazino
Berezivka Ukr. 43 F7
Berezne Ukr. 43 E6
Bereznik Rus. Fed. 42 I3
Berezniki Rus. Fed. 41 R4
Berezov Rus. Fed. *see* Berezovo
Berezovka Rus. Fed. 74 B2
Berezovka Ukr. *see* Berezivka
Berezovo Rus. Fed. 41 T3
Berezovyy Rus. Fed. 74 D2
Berga Germany 53 L3
Berga Spain 57 G2
Bergama Turkey 59 L5
Bergamo Italy 58 C2
Bergby Sweden 45 J6
Bergen *Mecklenburg-Vorpommern* Germany 47 N3
Bergen *Niedersachsen* Germany 53 J2
Bergen Norway 45 D6
Bergen U.S.A. 135 G2
Bergen op Zoom Neth. 52 E3
Bergerac France 56 E4
Bergères-lès-Vertus France 52 E6
Bergheim (Erft) Germany 52 G4
Bergisches Land *reg.* Germany 53 H4
Bergisch Gladbach Germany 52 H4
Bergland Namibia 100 C2
Bergomum Italy *see* Bergamo
Bergoo U.S.A. 134 E4
Bergsjö Sweden 45 J6
Bergsviken Sweden 44 L4
Bergtheim Germany 53 K5
Bergues France 52 C4
Bergum Neth. *see* Burgum
Bergville S. Africa 101 I5
Berhampur India *see* Baharampur
Beringa, Ostrov *i.* Rus. Fed. 65 R4
Beringen Belgium 52 F3
Beringovskiy Rus. Fed. 65 S3
Bering Sea N. Pacific Ocean 65 S4
Bering Strait Rus. Fed./U.S.A. 65 U3
Berīs, Ra's *pt* Iran 89 F5
Berislav Ukr. *see* Beryslav
Berkåk Norway 44 G5
Berkane Morocco 57 E6
Berkel *r.* Neth. 52 G2
Berkeley U.S.A. 128 B3
Berkeley Springs U.S.A. 135 F4
Berkhout Neth. 52 F2
Berkner Island Antarctica 152 A1
Berkovitsa Bulg. 59 J3
Berkshire Downs *hills* U.K. 49 F7
Berkshire Hills U.S.A. 135 I2
Berland *r.* Canada 120 G4
Berlare Belgium 52 E3
Berlevåg Norway 44 P1
▶Berlin Germany 53 N2
Capital of Germany.
Berlin *land* Germany 53 N2
Berlin *MD* U.S.A. 135 H4
Berlin *NH* U.S.A. 135 J1
Berlin *PA* U.S.A. 135 F4
Berlin Lake U.S.A. 134 E3
Bermagui Australia 112 E6
Bermejo *r.* Arg./Bol. 144 E3
Bermejo Bol. 142 F8
Bermen, Lac *l.* Canada 123 H3
▶Bermuda *terr.* N. Atlantic Ocean 137 L2
United Kingdom Overseas Territory.
north america 9, 116–117
Bermuda Rise *sea feature* N. Atlantic Ocean 148 D4
▶Bern Switz. 56 H3
Capital of Switzerland.
Bernalillo U.S.A. 127 G6
Bernardino de Campos Brazil 145 A3
Bernardo O'Higgins, Parque Nacional *nat. park* Chile 144 B7
Bernasconi Arg. 144 D5
Bernau Germany 53 N2
Bernburg (Saale) Germany 53 L3
Berne Germany 53 I1
Berne Switz. *see* Bern
Berne U.S.A. 134 C3
Berner Alpen *mts* Switz. 56 H3
Berneray *i. Scotland* U.K. 50 B3
Berneray *i. Scotland* U.K. 50 B4
Bernier Island Australia 109 A6
Bernina Pass Switz. 56 J3
Bernkastel-Kues Germany 52 H5
Beroea Greece *see* Veroia
Beroea Syria *see* Aleppo
Beroroha Madag. 99 E6
Beroun Czech Rep. 47 O6
Berounka *r.* Czech Rep. 47 O6
Berovina Madag. *see* Beravina
Berri Australia 111 C7
Berriane Alg. 54 E5
Berridale Australia 112 D6
Berriedale U.K. 50 F2
Berrigan Australia 112 B5
Berrima Australia 112 E5
Berrouaghia Alg. 57 H5
Berry Australia 112 E5
Berry U.S.A. 134 C4
Berryessa, Lake U.S.A. 128 B2
Berry Head *hd* U.K. 49 D8
Berry Islands Bahamas 133 E7
Berryville U.S.A. 135 G4
Berseba Namibia 100 C4
Bersenbrück Germany 53 H2
Bertam Malaysia 71 C6
Berté, Lac *l.* Canada 123 H4
Berthoud Pass U.S.A. 126 G5
Bertolínia Brazil 143 J5
Bertoua Cameroon 96 E4
Bertraghboy Bay Ireland 51 C4
Beru *atoll* Kiribati 107 H2
Beruri Brazil 142 F4
Beruwala Sri Lanka 84 C5
Berwick Australia 112 B7
Berwick U.S.A. 135 G3
Berwick-upon-Tweed U.K. 48 E3
Berwyn *hills* U.K. 49 D6
Beryslav Ukr. 59 O1
Berytus Lebanon *see* Beirut
Besalampy Madag. 99 E5
Besançon France 56 H3
Besar, Gunung *mt.* Malaysia 71 C7
Besbay Kazakh. 80 A2
Beserah Malaysia 71 C7
Beshkent Uzbek. 89 G2
Beshneh Iran 88 D4
Besikama Indon. 108 D2
Besitang Indon. 71 B6
Beskra Alg. *see* Biskra
Beslan Rus. Fed. 91 G2
Besnard Lake Canada 121 J4
Besni Turkey 90 E3
Besor *watercourse* Israel 85 B4
Beşparmak Dağları *mts* Cyprus *see* Pentadaktylos Range
Bessbrook U.K. 51 F3
Bessemer U.S.A. 133 C5
Besshoky, Gora *hill* Kazakh. 91 I1
Besskorbnaya Rus. Fed. 43 I7
Bessonovka Rus. Fed. 43 J5
Betanzos Spain 57 B2
Bethal S. Africa 101 I4
Bethanie Namibia 100 C4
Bethany U.S.A. 130 E3
Bethel U.S.A. 123 H5
Bethel Park U.S.A. 134 E3
Bethesda U.K. 48 C5
Bethesda *MD* U.S.A. 135 G4
Bethesda *OH* U.S.A. 134 E3
Bethlehem S. Africa 101 I5
Bethlehem U.S.A. 135 H3
Bethlehem West Bank 85 B4
Bethulie S. Africa 101 G6
Béthune France 52 C4
Beti Pak. 89 H4
Betim Brazil 145 B2
Bet Lehem West Bank *see* Bethlehem
Betma India 82 C5
Betong Thai. 71 C6
Betoota Australia 110 C5
Betpak-Dala *plain* Kazakh. 80 D2
Betroka Madag. 99 E6
Bet She'an Israel 85 B3
Betsiamites Canada 123 H4
Betsiamites *r.* Canada 123 H4
Bettiah India 83 F4
Bettyhill U.K. 50 E2
Bettystown Ireland 51 F4
Betul India 82 D5
Betung Kerihun, Taman Nasional Indon. 68 E6
Betwa *r.* India 82 D4
Betws-y-coed U.K. 49 D5
Betzdorf Germany 53 H4
Beulah Australia 111 C7
Beulah *MI* U.S.A. 134 B1
Beulah *ND* U.S.A. 130 C2
Beult *r.* U.K. 49 H7
Beuthen Poland *see* Bytom
Bever *r.* Germany 53 H2
Beverley U.K. 48 G5
Beverly *MA* U.S.A. 135 J2
Beverly *OH* U.S.A. 134 E4
Beverly Hills U.S.A. 128 D4
Beverly Lake Canada 121 K1
Beverstedt Germany 53 I1
Beverungen Germany 53 J3
Beverwijk Neth. 52 E2
Bewani P.N.G. 69 K7
Bexbach Germany 53 H5
Bexhill U.K. 49 H8
Bexley, Cape Canada 118 G3
Beyānlū Iran 88 B3
Beyce Turkey *see* Orhaneli
Bey Dağları *mts* Turkey 59 N6
Beykoz Turkey 59 M4
Beyla Guinea 96 C4
Beylagan Azer. *see* Beyläqan
Beyläqan Azer. 91 G3
Beyneu Kazakh. 78 E2
Beypazarı Turkey 59 N4
Beypınarı Turkey 90 E3
Beypore India 84 B4
Beyrouth Lebanon *see* Beirut
Beyşehir Turkey 90 C3
Beyşehir Gölü *l.* Turkey 90 C3
Beytonovo Rus. Fed. 74 B1
Beytüşşebap Turkey 91 F3
Bezameh Iran 88 E3
Bezbozhnik Rus. Fed. 42 K4
Bezhanitsy Rus. Fed. 42 F4
Bezhetsk Rus. Fed. 42 H4
Béziers France 56 F5
Bezmein Turkm. *see* Abadan
Bezwada India *see* Vijayawada
Bhabha India *see* Bhabhua
Bhabhar India 82 B4
Bhabhua India 83 E4
Bhabua India *see* Bhabhua
Bhachau India 82 B5
Bhachbhar India 82 B4
Bhadgaon Nepal *see* Bhaktapur
Bhadohi India 83 E4
Bhadra India 82 C3
Bhadrachalam Road Station India *see* Kottagudem
Bhadrak India 83 F5
Bhadrakh India *see* Bhadrak
Bhadravati India 84 B3
Bhag Pak. 89 G4
Bhagalpur India 83 F4
Bhainsa India 84 C2
Bhainsdehi India 82 D5
Bhairab Bazar Bangl. 83 G4
Bhairi Hol *mt.* Pak. 89 G5
Bhaktapur Nepal 83 F4
Bhalki India 84 C2
Bhamo Myanmar 70 B1
Bhamragarh India 84 D2
Bhandara India 82 D5
Bhanjanagar India 84 E2
Bhanrer Range *hills* India 82 D5
Bhaptiahi India 83 F4
Bharat *country* Asia *see* India
Bharatpur India 82 D4
Bhareli *r.* India 83 H4
Bharuch India 82 C5
Bhatapara India 83 E5
Bhatarsaigh *i.* U.K. *see* Vatersay
Bhatghar Lake India 84 B2
Bhatinda India *see* Bathinda
Bhatnair India *see* Hanumangarh
Bhatpara India 83 G5
Bhaunagar India *see* Bhavnagar
Bhavani *r.* India 84 C4
Bhavani Sagar *l.* India 84 C4
Bhavnagar India 82 C5
Bhawana Pak. 89 I4
Bhawanipatna India 84 D2
Bhearnaraigh, Eilean *i.* U.K. *see* Berneray
Bheemavaram India *see* Bhimavaram
Bhekuzulu S. Africa 101 J4
Bhera Pak. 89 I3
Bhigvan India 84 B2
Bhikhna Thori Nepal 83 F4
Bhilai India 82 E5
Bhildi India 82 C4
Bhilwara India 82 C4
Bhima *r.* India 84 C2
Bhimar India 82 B4
Bhimavaram India 84 D2
Bhimlath India 82 E5
Bhind India 82 D4
Bhinga India 83 E4
Bhisho S. Africa 101 H7
Bhiwandi India 84 B2
Bhiwani India 82 D3
Bhogaipur India 82 D4
Bhojpur Nepal 83 F4
Bhola Bangl. 83 G5
Bhongweni S. Africa 101 I6
Bhopal India 82 D5
Bhopalpatnam India 84 D2
Bhrigukaccha India *see* Bharuch
Bhuban India 84 E1
Bhubaneshwar India 84 E1
Bhubaneswar India *see* Bhubaneshwar
Bhuj India 82 B5
Bhusawal India 82 C5
Bhutan *country* Asia 83 G4
Bhuttewala India 82 B4
Bia *r.* Ghana 96 C4
Bia, Phou *mt.* Laos 70 C3
Bīābān *mts* Iran 88 E5
Biafo Glacier Pak. 82 C2
Biafra, Bight of *g.* Africa *see* Benin, Bight of
Biak Indon. 69 J7
Biak *i.* Indon. 69 J7
Biała Podlaska Poland 43 D5
Białogard Poland 47 O4
Białystok Poland 43 D5
Bianco, Monte *mt.* France/Italy *see* Mont Blanc
Biandangang Kou *r. mouth* China 77 I1
Bianzhao China 74 A3
Bianzhuang China *see* Cangshan
Biaora India 82 D5
Biarritz France 56 D5
Bi'ār Tabrāk *well* Saudi Arabia 88 B5
Bibai Japan 74 F4
Bibbenluke Australia 112 D6
Bibbiena Italy 58 D3
Bibby Island Canada 121 M2
Biberach an der Riß Germany 47 L6
Bibile Sri Lanka 84 D5
Biblis Germany 53 I5
Biblos Lebanon *see* Jbail
Bicas Brazil 145 C3
Biçer Turkey 59 N5
Bicester U.K. 49 F7
Bichabhera India 82 C4
Bicheng China *see* Bishan
Bichevaya Rus. Fed. 74 D3
Bichi *r.* Rus. Fed. 74 E1
Bickerton Island Australia 110 B2
Bickleigh U.K. 49 D8
Bicknell U.S.A. 134 B4
Bicuari, Parque Nacional do *nat. park* Angola 99 B5
Bid India 84 B2
Bida Nigeria 96 D4
Bidar India 84 C2
Biddeford U.S.A. 135 J2
Biddinghuizen Neth. 52 F2
Bidean nam Bian *mt.* U.K. 50 D4
Bideford U.K. 49 C7
Bideford Bay U.K. *see* Barnstaple Bay
Bidokht Iran 88 E3
Bidzhan Rus. Fed. 74 C3
Bié Angola *see* Kuito
Bié, Planalto do Angola 99 B5
Biebrzański Park Narodowy *nat. park* Poland 45 M10
Biedenkopf Germany 53 I4
Biel Switz. 56 H3
Bielawa Poland 47 P5
Bielefeld Germany 53 I2
Bielitz Poland *see* Bielsko-Biała
Biella Italy 58 C2
Bielsko-Biała Poland 47 Q6
Bielstein *hill* Germany 53 J3
Bienenbüttel Germany 53 K1
Biên Hoa Vietnam 71 D5
Bienne Switz. *see* Biel
Bienville, Lac *l.* Canada 123 G3
Bierbank Australia 112 B1
Biesiesvlei S. Africa 101 G4
Bietigheim-Bissingen Germany 53 J6
Bièvre Belgium 52 F5
Bifoun Gabon 98 B4
Big *r.* Canada 123 K3
Biga Turkey 59 L4
Bigadiç Turkey 59 M5

Biga Yarımadası pen. Turkey 59 L5
Big Baldy Mountain U.S.A. 126 F3
Big Bar Creek Canada 120 F5
Big Bear Lake U.S.A. 128 E4
Big Belt Mountains U.S.A. 126 F3
Big Bend Swaziland 101 J4
Big Bend National Park U.S.A. 131 C6
Bigbury-on-Sea U.K. 49 D8
Big Canyon watercourse U.S.A. 131 C6
Biger Nuur salt l. Mongolia 80 I2
Big Falls U.S.A. 130 E1
Big Fork r. U.S.A. 130 E1
Biggar Canada 121 J4
Biggar U.K. 50 F5
Biggar, Lac l. Canada 122 G4
Bigge Island Australia 108 D3
Biggenden Australia 111 F5
Bigger, Mount Canada 120 B3
Biggesee l. Germany 53 H3
Biggleswade U.K. 49 G6
Biggs CA U.S.A. 128 C2
Biggs OR U.S.A. 126 C3
Big Hole r. U.S.A. 126 E3
Bighorn r. U.S.A. 126 G3
Bighorn Mountains U.S.A. 126 G3
Big Island Nunavut Canada 119 K3
Big Island N.W.T. Canada 120 G2
Big Island Ont. Canada 121 M5
Big Kalzas Lake Canada 120 C2
Big Lake l. Canada 121 H1
Big Lake U.S.A. 131 C6
Bignona Senegal 96 B3
Big Pine U.S.A. 128 D3
Big Pine Peak U.S.A. 128 D4
Big Raccoon r. U.S.A. 134 B4
Big Rapids U.S.A. 134 C2
Big River Canada 121 J4
Big Sable Point U.S.A. 134 B1
Big Salmon r. Canada 120 C2
Big Sand Lake Canada 121 L3
Big Sandy r. U.S.A. 126 F4
Big Sandy Lake Canada 121 J4
Big Smokey Valley U.S.A. 128 E2
Big South Fork National River and Recreation Area park U.S.A. 134 C5
Big Spring U.S.A. 131 C5
Big Stone Canada 121 I5
Big Stone Gap U.S.A. 134 D5
Bigstone Lake Canada 121 M4
Big Timber U.S.A. 126 F3
Big Trout Lake Canada 121 N4
Big Trout Lake l. Canada 121 N4
Big Valley Canada 121 H4
Big Water U.S.A. 129 H3
Bihać Bos.-Herz. 58 F2
Bihar state India 83 F4
Bihariganj India 83 F4
Bihar Sharif India 83 F4
Bihor, Vârful mt. Romania 59 J1
Bihoro Japan 74 G4
Bijagós, Arquipélago dos is Guinea-Bissau 96 B3
Bijaipur India 82 D4
Bijapur India 84 B2
Bījār Iran 88 B3
Bijbehara India 82 C2
Bijeljina Bos.-Herz. 59 H2
Bijelo Polje Montenegro 59 H3
Bijeraghogarh India 82 E5
Bijiang China see Zhiziluo
Bijie China 76 E3
Bijji India 84 D2
Bijnor India 82 D3
Bijnore India see Bijnor
Bijnot Pak. 89 H4
Bijrān well Saudi Arabia 88 C5
Bijrān, Khashm hill Saudi Arabia 88 C5
Bikampur India 82 C4
Bikaner India 82 C3
Bīkhūyeh Iran 88 D5
Bikin Rus. Fed. 74 D3
Bikin r. Rus. Fed. 74 D3
Bikini atoll Marshall Is 150 H5
Bikori Sudan 86 D7
Bikoro Dem. Rep. Congo 98 B4
Bikou China 76 E1
Bikramganj India 83 F4
Bilād Banī Bū 'Alī Oman 87 I5
Bilaigarh India 84 D1
Bilara India 82 C4
Bilaspur Chhattisgarh India 83 E5
Bilaspur Hima. Prad. India 82 D3
Biläsuvar Azer. 91 H3
Bila Tserkva Ukr. 43 F6
Bilauktaung Range mts Myanmar/Thai. 71 B4
Bilbao Spain 57 E2
Bilbays Egypt 90 C5
Bilbeis Egypt see Bilbays
Bilbo Spain see Bilbao
Bilecik Turkey 59 M4
Biłgoraj Poland 43 D6
Bilharamulo Tanz. 98 D4
Bilhaur India 82 E4
Bilhorod-Dnistrovs'kyy Ukr. 59 N1
Bili Dem. Rep. Congo 98 C3
Bilibino Rus. Fed. 65 R3
Bilin Myanmar 70 B3
Bill U.S.A. 126 G4
Billabalong Australia 109 A6
Billabong Creek r. Australia see Moulamein Creek
Billericay U.K. 49 H7
Billiluna Australia 108 D4
Billingham U.K. 48 F4
Billings U.S.A. 126 F3
Billiton i. Indon. see Belitung
Bill of Portland hd U.K. 49 E8
Bill Williams r. U.S.A. 129 F4
Bill Williams Mountain U.S.A. 129 G4
Bilma Niger 96 E3
Bilo r. Rus. Fed. see Belaya
Biloela Australia 110 E5
Bilohirs'k Ukr. 90 D1
Bilohir"ya Ukr. 43 E6
Biloku Guyana 143 G3
Biloli India 84 C2
Bilovods'k Ukr. 43 H6
Biloxi U.S.A. 131 F6
Bilpa Morea Claypan salt flat Australia 110 B5
Bilston U.K. 50 F5
Biltine Chad 97 F3
Bilto Norway 44 L2
Bilugyun Island Myanmar 70 B3
Bilyayivka Ukr. 59 N1
Bilzen Belgium 52 F4
Bima Indon. 108 B2
Bimberi, Mount Australia 112 D5
Bimbo Ombella-Mpoko 97 E4
Bimini Islands Bahamas 133 E7
Bimlipatam India 84 D2
Bīnāb Iran 88 C2
Bina-Etawa India 82 D4
Binaija, Gunung mt. Indon. 67 E8
Bīnālūd, Kūh-e mts Iran 88 E2
Binboğa Daği mt. Turkey 90 E3
Bincheng China see Binzhou
Binchuan China 76 D3
Bindebango Australia 112 C1
Bindle Australia 112 D1
Bindu Dem. Rep. Congo 99 B4
Bindura Zimbabwe 99 D5
Binefar Spain 57 G3
Binga Zimbabwe 99 C5
Binga, Monte mt. Moz. 99 D5
Bingara Australia 112 E2
Bingaram i. India 84 B4
Bing Bong Australia 110 B2
Bingen am Rhein Germany 53 H5
Bingham U.S.A. 135 K1
Binghamton U.S.A. 135 H2
Bingmei China see Congjiang
Bingöl Turkey 91 F3
Bingol Dağı mt. Turkey 91 F3
Bingxi China see Yushan
Bingzhongluo China 76 C2
Binh Gia Vietnam 70 D2
Binika India 83 E5
Binjai Indon. 71 B7
Bin Mürkhan well U.A.E. 88 D5
Binnaway Australia 112 D3
Binpur India 83 F5
Bintan i. Indon. 71 D7
Bint Jbeil Lebanon see Bent Jbaïl
Bintulu Sarawak Malaysia 68 E6
Binxian Heilong. China 74 B3
Binxian Shaanxi China 77 F1
Binya Australia 112 C5
Binyang China 77 F4
Bin-Yauri Nigeria 96 D3
Binzhou Guangxi China see Binyang
Binzhou Heilong. China see Binxian
Binzhou Shandong China 73 L5
Bioco i. Equat. Guinea 96 D4
Biograd na Moru Croatia 58 F3
Bioko i. Equat. Guinea see Bioco
Biokovo mts Croatia 58 G3
Biquinhas Brazil 145 B2
Bir India see Bid
Bira Rus. Fed. 74 D2
Bi'r Abū Jady oasis Syria 85 D1
Birag, Kūh-e mts Iran 89 F5
Birāk Libya 97 E2
Birakan Rus. Fed. 74 C2
Bi'r al 'Abd Egypt 85 A4
Bi'r al Ḥalbā well Syria 85 D2
Bi'r al Jifjāfah well Egypt 85 A4
Bi'r al Khamsah well Egypt 90 B5
Bi'r al Māliḥah well Egypt 85 A5
Bi'r al Mulūsi Iraq 91 F4
Bi'r al Munbaṭiḥ well Syria 85 D2
Bi'r al Qaṭrānī well Egypt 90 B5
Bi'r al Ubbayiḍ well Egypt 90 B6
Birandozero Rus. Fed. 42 H3
Bi'r an Nuṣf well Egypt see Bi'r an Nuṣṣ
Bi'r an Nuṣṣ well Egypt 90 B5
Bir Anzarane W. Sahara 96 B2
Birao Cent. Afr. Rep. 98 C2
Bi'r ar Rābiyah well Egypt 90 B5
Birata Turkm. 89 F1
Biratnagar Nepal 83 F4
Bi'r aṭ Ṭarfāwī well Libya 90 B5
Bi'r Başīrī well Syria 85 C2
Bi'r Bayḍā' well Egypt 85 B4
Bi'r Baylī well Egypt 90 B5
Bîr Beiḍa well Egypt see Bi'r Bayḍā'
Bi'r Buṭaymān Syria 91 E3
Birch r. Canada 121 H3
Birch Hills Canada 121 J4
Birch Island Canada 120 G5
Birch Lake N.W.T. Canada 120 G2
Birch Lake Ont. Canada 121 M5
Birch Lake Sask. Canada 121 I4
Birch Mountains Canada 120 H3
Birch River U.S.A. 134 E4
Birch Run U.S.A. 134 D2
Bircot Eth. 98 E3
Birdaard Neth. see Burdaard
Bîr Dignâsh well Egypt see Bi'r Diqnāsh
Bi'r Diqnāsh well Egypt 90 B5
Bird Island N. Mariana Is see Farallon de Medinilla
Birdseye U.S.A. 129 H2
Birdsville Australia 111 B5
Birecik Turkey 90 E3
Bîr el 'Abd Egypt see Bi'r al 'Abd
Bir el Arbi well Alg. 57 I6
Bîr el Istabl well Egypt see Bi'r Iṣṭabl
Bîr el Khamsa well Egypt see Bi'r al Khamsah
Bîr el Nuṣṣ well Egypt see Bi'r an Nuṣṣ
Bîr el Obeiyiḍ well Egypt see Bi'r al Ubbayiḍ
Bîr el Qaṭrâni well Egypt see Bi'r al Qaṭrānī
Bîr el Râbia well Egypt see Bi'r ar Rābiyah
Birendranagar Nepal see Surkhet
Bir en Natrûn well Sudan 86 C6
Bireun Indon. 71 B6
Bi'r Fāḍil well Saudi Arabia 88 C6
Bi'r Fajr well Saudi Arabia 90 E5
Bi'r Fu'ād well Egypt 90 B5
Bîr Gifgâfa well Egypt see Bi'r al Jifjāfah
Bi'r Ḥajal well Syria 85 D2
Birhan mt. Eth. 98 D2
Bi'r Ḥasanah well Egypt 85 A4
Bi'r Ḥayzān well Saudi Arabia 90 E6
Bi'r Ibn Hirmās Saudi Arabia see Al Bi'r
Bir Ibn Juhayyim Saudi Arabia 88 C6
Birigüi Brazil 145 A3
Bīrīn Syria 85 C2
Bi'r Iṣṭabl well Egypt 90 B5
Bīrjand Iran 88 E3
Bi'r Jubnī well Libya 90 B5
Birkát Hamad well Iraq 91 G5
Birkenfeld Germany 53 H5
Birkenhead U.K. 48 D5
Birkirkara Malta 58 F7
Birksgate Range hills Australia 109 E6
Bîrlad Romania see Bârlad
Bi'r Lahfān well Egypt 85 A4
Birlik Kazakh. 80 D3
Birmal reg. Afgh. 89 H3
Birmingham U.K. 49 F6
Birmingham U.S.A. 133 C5
Bîr Mogreïn Mauritania 96 B2
Bi'r Muḥaymid al Wazwaz well Syria 85 D2
Bi'r Nāḥid oasis Egypt 90 C5
Birnin-Gwari Nigeria 96 D3
Birnin-Kebbi Nigeria 96 D3
Birnin Konni Niger 96 D3
Birobidzhan Rus. Fed. 74 D2
Bi'r Qaşīr as Sirr well Egypt 90 B5
Birr Ireland 51 E4
Bi'r Rawḍ Sālim well Egypt 85 A4
Birrie r. Australia 112 C2
Birrindudu Australia 108 E4
Bîr Rôḍ Sâlim well Egypt see Bi'r Rawḍ Sālim
Birsay U.K. 50 F1
Bi'r Shalatayn Egypt 86 E5
Bîr Shalatein Egypt see Bi'r Shalatayn
Birsk Rus. Fed. 41 R4
Birstall U.K. 49 F6
Birstein Germany 53 J4
Bir Ṭalḥah well Saudi Arabia 88 B6
Birthday Mountain hill Australia 110 C2
Birtle Canada 121 K5
Biru China 76 B2
Birur India 84 B3
Bi'r Usaylilah well Saudi Arabia 88 B6
Biruxiong China see Biru
Biržai Lith. 45 N8
Bisa India 70 A1
Bisa i. Indon. 69 H7
Bisalpur India 82 D3
Bisau India 82 C3
Bisbee U.S.A. 127 F7
Biscay, Bay of sea France/Spain 56 B4
Biscay Abyssal Plain sea feature N. Atlantic Ocean 148 H3
Biscayne National Park U.S.A. 133 D7
Biscoe Islands Antarctica 152 L2
Biscotasi Lake Canada 122 E5
Biscotasing Canada 122 E5
Bisezhai China 76 D4
Bishan China 76 E2
Bishbek Kyrg. see Bishkek
Bishenpur India see Bishnupur

▶Bishkek Kyrg. 80 D3
Capital of Kyrgyzstan.

Bishnath India 76 B3
Bishnupur Manipur India 83 H4
Bishnupur W. Bengal India 83 F5
Bishop U.S.A. 128 D3
Bishop Auckland U.K. 48 F4
Bishop Lake Canada 120 G1
Bishop's Stortford U.K. 49 H7
Bishopville U.S.A. 133 D5
Bishrī, Jabal hills Syria 85 D2
Bishui Heilong. China 74 A1
Bishui Henan China see Biyang
Biskra Alg. 54 F5
Bislig Phil. 69 H5

▶Bismarck U.S.A. 130 C2
Capital of North Dakota.

Bismarck Archipelago is P.N.G. 69 L7
Bismarck Range mts P.N.G. 69 K7
Bismarck Sea P.N.G. 69 L7
Bismark (Altmark) Germany 53 L2
Bismil Turkey 91 F3
Bismo Norway 44 F6
Bison U.S.A. 130 C2
Bispgården Sweden 44 J5
Bispingen Germany 53 K1
Bissa, Djebel mt. Alg. 57 G5
Bissamcuttak India 84 D2

▶Bissau Guinea-Bissau 96 B3
Capital of Guinea-Bissau.

Bissaula Nigeria 96 E4
Bissett Canada 121 M5
Bistcho Lake Canada 120 G3
Bistrița Romania 59 K1
Bistrița r. Romania 59 L1
Bitburg Germany 52 G5
Bitche France 53 H5
Bithur India 82 E4
Bithynia reg. Turkey 59 M4
Bitkine Chad 97 E3
Bitlis Turkey 91 F3
Bitola Macedonia 59 I4
Bitolj Macedonia see Bitola
Bitonto Italy 58 G4
Bitrān, Jabal hill Saudi Arabia 88 B6
Bitra Par reef India 84 B4
Bitter Creek r. U.S.A. 129 I2
Bitterfeld Germany 53 M3
Bitterfontein S. Africa 100 D6
Bitter Lakes Egypt 90 D5
Bitterroot r. U.S.A. 126 E3
Bitterroot Range mts U.S.A. 126 E3
Bitterwater U.S.A. 128 C3
Bittkau Germany 53 L2
Bitung Indon. 69 H6
Biu Nigeria 96 E3
Biwa-ko l. Japan 75 D6
Biwmaris U.K. see Beaumaris
Biyang China 77 G1
Bīye K'obē Eth. 98 E2
Biysk Rus. Fed. 72 F2
Bizana S. Africa 101 I6
Bizerta Tunisia see Bizerte
Bizerte Tunisia 58 C6
Bīzhanābād Iran 88 E5

▶Bjargtangar hd Iceland 44 [inset]
Most westerly point of Europe.

Bjästa Sweden 44 K5
Bjelovar Croatia 58 G2
Bjerkvik Norway 44 J2
Bjerringbro Denmark 45 F8
Bjørgan Norway 44 G5
Björkliden Sweden 44 K2
Björklinge Sweden 45 J6
Bjorli Norway 44 F5
Björna Sweden 44 K5
Björneborg Fin. see Pori

▶Bjørnøya i. Arctic Ocean 64 C2
Part of Norway.

Bjurholm Sweden 44 K5
Bla Mali 96 C3
Black r. Man. Canada 121 L5
Black r. Ont. Canada 122 E4
Black r. AR U.S.A. 131 F5
Black r. AR U.S.A. 131 F5
Black r. AZ U.S.A. 129 H5
Black r. Vietnam 70 D2
Blackadder Water r. U.K. 50 G5
Blackall Australia 110 D5
Blackbear r. Canada 121 N4
Black Birch Lake Canada 121 J3
Black Bourton U.K. 49 F7
Blackbull Australia 110 C3
Blackburn U.K. 48 E5
Blackbutt Australia 112 F1
Black Butte mt. U.S.A. 128 B2
Black Butte Lake U.S.A. 128 B2
Black Canyon gorge U.S.A. 129 F4
Black Canyon of the Gunnison National Park U.S.A. 129 J2
Black Combe hill U.K. 48 D4
Black Creek watercourse U.S.A. 129 I4
Black Donald Lake Canada 135 G1
Blackdown Tableland National Park Australia 110 E4
Blackduck U.S.A. 130 E2
Blackfalds Canada 120 H4
Blackfoot U.S.A. 126 E4
Black Foot r. U.S.A. 126 E3
Black Forest mts Germany 47 L7
Black Hill hill U.K. 48 F5
Black Hills SD U.S.A. 124 G3
Black Hills SD U.S.A. 126 G3
Black Island Canada 121 L5
Black Lake Canada 121 J3
Black Lake l. Canada 121 J3
Black Lake l. U.S.A. 134 C1
Black Mesa mt. U.S.A. 129 I5
Black Mesa ridge U.S.A. 129 H3
Black Mountain Pak. 89 I3
Black Mountain hill U.K. 49 D7
Black Mountain AK U.S.A. 118 B3
Black Mountain CA U.S.A. 128 E4
Black Mountain KY U.S.A. 134 D5
Black Mountain NM U.S.A. 129 I5
Black Mountains hills U.K. 49 D7
Black Mountains U.S.A. 129 F4
Black Nossob watercourse Namibia 100 D2
Black Pagoda India see Konarka
Blackpool U.K. 48 D5
Black Range mts U.S.A. 129 I5
Black River MI U.S.A. 134 D1
Black River NY U.S.A. 135 H1
Black River Falls U.S.A. 130 F2
Black Rock hill Jordan see 'Unāb, Jabal al
Black Rock Desert U.S.A. 126 D4
Blacksburg U.S.A. 134 E5
Black Sea Asia/Europe 43 H8
Blacks Fork r. U.S.A. 126 F4
Blackshear U.S.A. 133 D6
Blacksod Bay Ireland 51 B3
Black Springs U.S.A. 128 D2
Blackstairs Mountains hills Ireland 51 F5
Blackstone U.S.A. 135 F5
Black Sugarloaf mt. Australia 112 E3
Black Tickle Canada 123 L3
Blackville Australia 112 E3
Blackwater Australia 110 E4
Blackwater Ireland 51 F5
Blackwater r. Ireland 51 E5
Blackwater r. Ireland/U.K. 51 F3
Blackwater watercourse U.S.A. 131 C5
Blackwater Lake Canada 120 F2
Blackwater Reservoir U.K. 50 E4
Blackwood r. Australia 109 A8
Blackwood National Park Australia 110 D4
Bladensburg National Park Australia 110 C4
Blaenavon U.K. 49 D7
Blagodarnyy Rus. Fed. 91 F1
Blagoevgrad Bulg. 59 J3
Blagoveshchensk Amurskaya Oblast' Rus. Fed. 74 B2
Blagoveshchensk Respublika Bashkortostan Rus. Fed. 41 R4
Blaikiston, Mount Canada 120 H5
Blaine Lake Canada 121 J4
Blair U.S.A. 130 D3
Blair Athol Australia 110 D4
Blair Atholl U.K. 50 F4
Blairgowrie U.K. 50 F4
Blairsden U.S.A. 128 C2
Blairsville U.S.A. 133 D5
Blakang Mati, Pulau i. Sing. see Sentosa
Blakely U.S.A. 133 C6
Blakeney U.K. 49 I6

▶Blanc, Mont mt. France/Italy 56 H4
5th highest mountain in Europe.

Blanca, Bahía b. Arg. 144 D5
Blanca, Sierra mt. U.S.A. 127 G6
Blanca Peak U.S.A. 127 G5
Blanche, Lake salt flat S.A. Australia 111 B6
Blanche, Lake salt flat W.A. Australia 108 C5
Blanchester U.S.A. 134 D4
Blanc Nez, Cap c. France 52 B4
Blanco r. Bol. 142 F6
Blanco U.S.A. 129 J3
Blanco, Cape U.S.A. 126 B4
Blanc-Sablon Canada 123 K4
Bland r. Australia 112 C4
Bland U.S.A. 134 E5
Blanda r. Iceland 44 [inset]
Blandford Forum U.K. 49 E8
Blanding U.S.A. 129 I3
Blanes Spain 57 H3
Blangah, Telok Sing. 71 [inset]
Blangkejeren Indon. 71 B7
Blangpidie Indon. 71 B7
Blankenberge Belgium 52 D3
Blankenheim Germany 52 G4
Blanquilla, Isla i. Venez. 142 F1
Blansko Czech Rep. 47 P6
Blantyre Malawi 99 D5
Blarney Ireland 51 D6
Blaufelden Germany 53 J5
Blåviksjön Sweden 44 K4
Blaye France 56 D4
Blayney Australia 112 D4
Blaze, Point Australia 108 E3
Bleckede Germany 53 K1
Bleilochtalsperre resr Germany 53 L4
Blenheim Canada 134 E2
Blenheim N.Z. 113 D5
Blenheim Palace tourist site U.K. 49 F7
Blerick Neth. 52 G3
Blessington Lakes Ireland 51 F4
Bletchley U.K. 49 G6
Blida Alg. 57 H5
Blies r. Germany 53 H5
Bligh Water b. Fiji 107 H3
Blind River Canada 122 E5
Bliss U.S.A. 126 E4
Blissfield U.S.A. 134 D3
Blitta Togo 96 D4
Blocher U.S.A. 134 C4
Block Island U.S.A. 135 J3
Block Island Sound sea chan. U.S.A. 135 J3
Bloemfontein S. Africa 101 H5
Bloemhof S. Africa 101 G4
Bloemhof Dam S. Africa 101 G4
Bloemhof Dam Nature Reserve S. Africa 101 G4
Blomberg Germany 53 J3
Blönduós Iceland 44 [inset]
Blongas Indon. 108 B2
Bloods Range mts Australia 109 E6
Bloodsworth Island U.S.A. 135 G4
Bloodvein r. Canada 121 L5
Bloody Foreland pt Ireland 51 D2
Bloomer U.S.A. 130 F2
Bloomfield Canada 135 G2
Bloomfield IA U.S.A. 130 E3
Bloomfield IN U.S.A. 134 B4
Bloomfield MO U.S.A. 131 F4
Bloomfield NM U.S.A. 129 J3
Blooming Prairie U.S.A. 130 E3
Bloomington IL U.S.A. 130 F3
Bloomington IN U.S.A. 134 B4
Bloomington MN U.S.A. 130 E2
Bloomsburg U.S.A. 135 G3
Blossburg U.S.A. 135 G3
Blosseville Kyst coastal area Greenland 119 P3
Blouberg S. Africa 101 I2
Blouberg Nature Reserve S. Africa 101 I2
Blountstown U.S.A. 133 C6
Blountville U.S.A. 134 D5
Bloxham U.K. 49 F6
Blue r. Canada 120 D3
Blue watercourse U.S.A. 129 I5
Blue Bell Knoll mt. U.S.A. 129 H2
Blueberry r. Canada 120 F3
Blue Diamond U.S.A. 129 F3
Blue Earth U.S.A. 130 E3
Bluefield VA U.S.A. 132 D4
Bluefield WV U.S.A. 134 E5
Bluefields Nicaragua 137 H6
Blue Hills Turks and Caicos Is 133 F8
Blue Knob hill U.S.A. 135 F3
Blue Mesa Reservoir U.S.A. 129 J2
Blue Mountain hill Canada 123 K4
Blue Mountain India 83 H5
Blue Mountain Lake U.S.A. 135 H2
Blue Mountain Pass Lesotho 101 H5
Blue Mountains Australia 112 D4
Blue Mountains U.S.A. 126 D3
Blue Mountains National Park Australia 112 E4
Blue Nile r. Eth./Sudan 86 D6
also known as Ābay Wenz (Ethiopia), Bahr el Azraq (Sudan)
Bluenose Lake Canada 118 G3
Blue Ridge GA U.S.A. 133 C5
Blue Ridge VA U.S.A. 134 F5
Blue Ridge mts U.S.A. 134 E5
Blue Stack hill Ireland 51 D3
Blue Stack Mts hills Ireland 51 D3
Bluestone Lake U.S.A. 134 E5
Bluewater U.S.A. 129 J4
Bluff N.Z. 113 B8
Bluff U.S.A. 129 I3
Bluffdale U.S.A. 129 H1
Bluff Island H.K. China 77 [inset]
Bluff Knoll mt. Australia 109 B8
Bluffton IN U.S.A. 134 C3
Bluffton OH U.S.A. 134 D3
Blumenau Brazil 145 A4
Blustry Mountain Canada 126 C2
Blyde River Canyon Nature Reserve S. Africa 101 J3
Blyth Canada 134 E2
Blyth England U.K. 48 F3
Blyth England U.K. 48 F5
Blythe U.S.A. 129 F5
Blytheville U.S.A. 131 F5
Bø Norway 45 F7
Bo Sierra Leone 96 B4
Boa Esperança Brazil 145 B3
Bo'ai Henan China 77 G1
Bo'ai Yunnan China 76 E4
Boali Cent. Afr. Rep. 98 B3
Boalsert Neth. see Bolsward
Boane Moz. 101 K4
Boa Nova Brazil 145 C1
Boardman U.S.A. 134 E3
Boatlaname Botswana 101 G2
Boa Viagem Brazil 143 K5
Boa Vista Brazil 142 F3
Boa Vista i. Cape Verde 96 [inset]
Bobadah Australia 112 C4
Bobai China 77 F4
Bobaomby, Tanjona c. Madag. 99 E5
Bobbili India 84 D2
Bobcaygeon Canada 135 F1
Bobo-Dioulasso Burkina 96 C3
Bobotov Kuk mt. Montenegro see Durmitor
Bobriki Rus. Fed. see Novomoskovsk
Bobrinets Ukr. see Bobrynets'
Bobrov Rus. Fed. 43 I6
Bobrovitsa Ukr. see Bobrovytsya
Bobrovytsya Ukr. 43 F6
Bobruysk Belarus see Babruysk
Bobrynets' Ukr. 43 G6
Bobs Lake Canada 135 G1
Bobuk Sudan 86 D7
Bobures Venez. 142 D2
Boby mt. Madag. 99 E6
Boca de Macareo Venez. 142 F2
Boca do Acre Brazil 142 E5
Boca do Jari Brazil 143 H4
Bocaiúva Brazil 145 C2
Bocaranga Cent. Afr. Rep. 98 B3
Boca Raton U.S.A. 133 D7
Bocas del Toro Panama 137 H7
Bochnia Poland 47 R6
Bocholt Germany 52 G3
Bochum Germany 53 H3
Bockenem Germany 53 K2
Bocoio Angola 99 B5
Bocoyna Mex. 127 G8
Boda Cent. Afr. Rep. 98 B3
Bodalla Australia 112 E6
Bodallin Australia 109 B7
Bodaybo Rus. Fed. 65 M4
Boddam U.K. 50 H3
Bode r. Germany 53 L3
Bodega Head hd U.S.A. 128 B2
Bodélé reg. Chad 97 E3
Boden Sweden 44 L4
Bodenham U.K. 49 E6
Bodensee l. Germany/Switz. see Constance, Lake
Bodenteich Germany 53 K2
Bodenwerder Germany 53 J3
Bodie (abandoned) U.S.A. 128 D2
Bodinayakkanur India 84 C4
Bodmin U.K. 49 C8
Bodmin Moor moorland U.K. 49 C8
Bodø Norway 44 I3
Bodoquena Brazil 143 G7
Bodoquena, Serra da hills Brazil 144 E2
Bodrum Turkey 59 L6
Bodträskfors Sweden 44 L3
Boechout Belgium 52 E3
Boende Dem. Rep. Congo 97 F5
Boerne U.S.A. 131 D6
Boeuf r. U.S.A. 131 F6
Boffa Guinea 96 B3
Bogalay Myanmar see Bogale
Bogale Myanmar 70 A3
Bogale r. Myanmar 70 A4
Bogalusa U.S.A. 131 F6
Bogan r. Australia 112 C2
Bogandé Burkina 96 C3
Bogan Gate Australia 112 C4
Bogani Nani Wartabone, Taman Nasional Indon. 69 G6
Boğazlıyan Turkey 90 D3
Bogcang Zangbo r. China 83 F3
Bogd Övörhangay Mongolia 80 J3
Bogda Shan mts China 80 G3
Boggabilla Australia 112 E2
Boggabri Australia 112 E3
Boggeragh Mts hills Ireland 51 C5
Boghar Alg. 57 H6
Boghari Alg. see Ksar el Boukhari
Bognor Regis U.K. 49 G8
Bogodukhov Ukr. see Bohodukhiv
Bog of Allen reg. Ireland 51 E4
Bogong, Mount Australia 112 C6
Bogopol' Rus. Fed. 74 D3
Bogor Indon. 68 D8
Bogoroditsk Rus. Fed. 43 H5
Bogorodsk Rus. Fed. 42 I4
Bogorodskoye Khabarovskiy Kray Rus. Fed. 74 F1
Bogorodskoye Kirovskaya Oblast' Rus. Fed. 42 K4

▶Bogotá Col. 142 D3
Capital of Colombia. 4th most populous city in South America.

Bogotol Rus. Fed. 64 J4
Bogoyavlenskoye Rus. Fed. see Pervomayskiy
Bogra Bangl. 83 G4
Boguchany Rus. Fed. 65 K4
Boguchar Rus. Fed. 43 I6
Bogué Mauritania 96 B3
Bo Hai g. China 73 L5
Bohain-en-Vermandois France 52 D5
Bohai Wan b. China 66 D4
Bohemian Forest mts Germany see Böhmer Wald
Böhlen Germany 53 M3
Bohlokong S. Africa 101 I5
Böhme r. Germany 53 J2
Böhmer Wald mts Germany 53 M5
Bohmte Germany 53 I2
Bohodukhiv Ukr. 43 G6
Bohol i. Phil. 69 G5
Bohol Sea Phil. 69 G5
Bohu China 80 G3
Boiaçu Brazil 142 F4
Boichoko S. Africa 100 F5
Boigu Island Australia 69 K8
Boikhutso S. Africa 101 H4
Boileau, Cape Australia 108 C4
Boim Brazil 143 G4
Boipeba, Ilha i. Brazil 145 D1
Bois r. Brazil 145 A2
Bois Blanc Island U.S.A. 132 C2

▶Boise U.S.A. 126 D4
Capital of Idaho.

Boise City U.S.A. 131 C4
Boissevain Canada 121 K5
Boitumelong S. Africa 101 G4
Boizenburg Germany 53 K1
Bojd Iran 88 E3
Bojnūrd Iran 88 E2
Bokaak atoll Marshall Is see Taongi
Bokajan India 83 H4
Bokaro India 83 F5

Bokaro Reservoir India 83 F5
Bokatola Dem. Rep. Congo 98 B4
Boké Guinea 96 B3
Bokele Dem. Rep. Congo 98 C4
Bokhara r. Australia 112 C2
Bo Kheo Cambodia see Bâ Kêv
Boknafjorden sea chan. Norway 45 D7
Bokoko Dem. Rep. Congo 98 C3
Bokoro Chad 97 E3
Bokovskaya Rus. Fed. 43 I6
Bokspits S. Africa 100 E4
Boktor Rus. Fed. 74 E2
Bokurdak Turkm. 88 E2
Bol Chad 97 E3
Bolaiti Dem. Rep. Congo 97 F5
Bolama Guinea-Bissau 96 B3
Bolangir India 84 D1
Bolan Pass Pak. 89 G4
Bolavén, Phouphiang plat. Laos 70 D4
Bolbec France 56 E2
Bole China 80 F3
Bole Ghana 96 C4
Boleko Dem. Rep. Congo 98 B4
Bolen Rus. Fed. 74 D2
Bolgar Rus. Fed. 43 K5
Bolgatanga Ghana 96 C3
Bolgrad Ukr. see Bolhrad
Bolhrad Ukr. 59 M2
Boli China 74 C3
Bolia Dem. Rep. Congo 98 B4
Boliden Sweden 44 L4
Bolingbrook U.S.A. 134 A3
Bolintin-Vale Romania 59 K2
Bolívar Peru 142 C5
Bolivar NY U.S.A. 135 F2
Bolivar TN U.S.A. 131 F5
Bolívar, Pico mt. Venez. 142 D2
Bolivia Cuba 133 E8

▶Bolivia country S. America 142 E7
5th largest country in South America.

Bolkhov Rus. Fed. 43 H5
Bollène France 56 G4
Bollnäs Sweden 45 J6
Bollon Australia 112 C2
Bollstabruk Sweden 44 J5
Bolmen l. Sweden 45 H8
Bolobo Dem. Rep. Congo 98 B4
Bologna Italy 58 D2
Bolognesi Peru 142 D5
Bologoye Rus. Fed. 42 G4
Bolokanang S. Africa 101 G5
Bolomba Dem. Rep. Congo 98 B3
Bolon' Rus. Fed. see Achan
Bolpur India 83 F5
Bolsena, Lago di l. Italy 58 D3
Bol'shakovo Rus. Fed. 45 L9
Bol'shaya Chernigovka Rus. Fed. 41 Q5
Bol'shaya Glushitsa Rus. Fed. 43 K5
Bol'shaya Imandra, Ozero l. Rus. Fed. 44 R3
Bol'shaya Martinovka Rus. Fed. 43 I7
Bol'shaya Tsarevshchina Rus. Fed. see Volzhskiy
Bol'shenarymskoye Kazakh. 80 F2
Bol'shevik, Ostrov i. Rus. Fed. 65 L2
Bol'shezemel'skaya Tundra lowland Rus. Fed. 42 L2
Bol'shiye Barsuki, Peski des. Kazakh. 80 A2
Bol'shiye Chirki Rus. Fed. 42 J3
Bol'shiye Kozly Rus. Fed. 42 H2
Bol'shoy Begichev, Ostrov i. Rus. Fed. 153 E2
Bol'shoye Murashkino Rus. Fed. 42 J5
Bol'shoy Irgiz r. Rus. Fed. 43 J6
Bol'shoy Kamen' Rus. Fed. 74 D4
Bol'shoy Kavkaz mts Asia/Europe see Caucasus
Bol'shoy Kundysh r. Rus. Fed. 42 J4
Bol'shoy Lyakhovskiy, Ostrov i. Rus. Fed. 65 P2
Bol'shoy Tokmak Kyrg. see Tokmok
Bol'shoy Tokmak Ukr. see Tokmak
Bolsón de Mapimí des. Mex. 131 B7
Bolsward Neth. 52 F1
Bolton Canada 134 F2
Bolton U.K. 48 E5
Bolu Turkey 59 N4
Boluntay China 83 H1
Boluo China 77 G4
Bolus Head hd Ireland 51 B6
Bolvadin Turkey 59 N5
Bolzano Italy 58 D1
Boma Dem. Rep. Congo 99 B4
Bomaderry Australia 112 E5
Bombala Australia 112 D6
Bombay India see Mumbai
Bombay Beach U.S.A. 129 F5
Bomberai, Semenanjung pen. Indon. 69 I7
Bomboma Dem. Rep. Congo 98 B3
Bom Comércio Brazil 142 E5
Bomdila India 83 H4
Bomi China 76 B2
Bomili Dem. Rep. Congo 98 C3
Bom Jardim Brazil 145 D1
Bom Jardim de Goiás Brazil 145 A2
Bom Jesus Brazil 145 A5
Bom Jesus da Gurgueia, Serra do hills Brazil 143 J5
Bom Jesus da Lapa Brazil 145 C1
Bom Jesus do Norte Brazil 145 C3
Bømlo i. Norway 45 D7
Bomokandi r. Dem. Rep. Congo 98 C3
Bom Retiro Brazil 145 A4
Bom Sucesso Brazil 145 B3
Bon, Cap c. Tunisia 58 D6
Bon, Ko i. Thai. 71 B5
Bona Alg. see Annaba
Bona, Mount U.S.A. 120 A2
Bonāb Iran 88 B2
Bon Air U.S.A. 135 G5
Bonaire i. Neth. Antilles 137 K6
Bonanza Peak U.S.A. 126 C2
Bonaparte Archipelago is Australia 108 D3
Bonaparte Lake Canada 120 F5
Bonar Bridge U.K. 50 E3
Bonavista Canada 123 L4
Bonavista Bay Canada 123 L4
Bonchester Bridge U.K. 50 G5
Bondo Dem. Rep. Congo 98 C3
Bondokodi Indon. 68 F8
Bondoukou Côte d'Ivoire 96 C4
Bonduel U.S.A. 134 A1
Bondyuzhskiy Rus. Fed. see Mendeleyevsk
Bône Alg. see Annaba
Bone, Teluk b. Indon. 69 G8
Bönen Germany 53 H3
Bonerate, Kepulauan is Indon. 108 C1
Bo'ness U.K. 50 F4

▶Bonete, Cerro mt. Arg. 144 C3
3rd highest mountain in South America.

Bonga Eth. 98 D3
Bongaigaon India 83 G4
Bongandanga Dem. Rep. Congo 98 C3
Bongani S. Africa 100 F5
Bongao Phil. 68 F5
Bongba China 82 E2
Bong Co l. China 83 G3
Bongo, Massif des mts Cent. Afr. Rep. 98 C3
Bongo, Serra do mts Angola 99 B4
Bongolava mts Madag. 99 E5
Bongor Chad 97 E3
Bông Sơn Vietnam 71 E4
Bonham U.S.A. 131 D5
Bonheiden Belgium 52 E3
Boni Mali 96 C3
Bonifacio Corsica France 56 I6
Bonifacio, Bocche di strait France/Italy see Bonifacio, Strait of
Bonifacio, Bouches de strait France/Italy see Bonifacio, Strait of
Bonifacio, Strait of France/Italy 56 I6

▶Bonin Islands Japan 75 F8
Part of Japan.

▶Bonn Germany 52 H4
Former capital of Germany.

Bonna Germany see Bonn
Bonnåsjøen Norway 44 I3
Bonners Ferry U.S.A. 126 D2
Bonnet, Lac du resr Canada 121 M5
Bonneville France 56 H3
Bonneville Salt Flats U.S.A. 129 G1
Bonnières-sur-Seine France 52 B5
Bonnie Rock Australia 109 B7
Bonnieville U.S.A. 134 C5
Bonnyrigg U.K. 50 F5
Bonnyville Canada 121 I4
Bonobono Phil. 68 F5
Bononia Italy see Bologna
Bonorva Sardinia Italy 58 C4
Bonshaw Australia 112 E2
Bontebok National Park S. Africa 100 E8
Bonthe Sierra Leone 96 B4
Bontoc Phil. 77 I5
Bontosunggu Indon. 68 F8
Bontrug S. Africa 101 G7
Bonvouloir Islands P.N.G. 110 E1
Bonwapitse Botswana 101 H2
Boo, Kepulauan is Indon. 69 H7
Book Cliffs ridge U.S.A. 129 I2
Booker U.S.A. 131 C4
Boolba Australia 112 D2
Booligal Australia 112 B4
Boomer U.S.A. 134 E4
Boomi Australia 112 D2
Boon U.S.A. 134 C1
Boonah Australia 112 F1
Boone CO U.S.A. 127 G5
Boone IA U.S.A. 130 E3
Boone NC U.S.A. 132 D4
Boone Lake U.S.A. 134 D5
Boones Mill U.S.A. 134 F5
Booneville AR U.S.A. 131 E5
Booneville KY U.S.A. 134 D5
Booneville MS U.S.A. 131 F5
Böön Tsagaan Nuur salt l. Mongolia 80 I2
Boonville CA U.S.A. 128 B2
Boonville IN U.S.A. 134 B4
Boonville MO U.S.A. 130 E4
Boonville NY U.S.A. 135 H2
Boorabin National Park Australia 109 C7
Boorama Somalia 98 E3
Booroorban Australia 112 B5
Boorowa Australia 112 D5
Boort Australia 112 A6
Boothby, Cape Antarctica 152 D2
Boothia, Gulf of Canada 119 J3
Boothia Peninsula Canada 119 I2
Bootle U.K. 48 E5
Booué Gabon 98 B4
Boppard Germany 53 H4
Boqê China 83 G3
Boqueirão, Serra do hills Brazil 143 J6
Bor Czech Rep. 53 M5
Bor Rus. Fed. 42 J4
Bor Serbia 59 J2
Bor Sudan 97 G4
Bor Turkey 90 D3
Boraha, Nosy i. Madag. 99 F5
Borah Peak U.S.A. 126 E3
Borai India 84 D1
Borakalalo Nature Reserve S. Africa 101 H3
Boran Kazakh. see Buran
Boraphet, Bung l. Thai. 70 C4
Boraphet, Nong l. Thai. see Boraphet, Bung
Borås Sweden 45 H8
Borasambar India 84 D1
Borāzjān Iran 88 C4
Borba Brazil 143 G4
Borba China 76 C1
Borborema, Planalto da plat. Brazil 143 K5
Borchen Germany 53 I3
Borçka Turkey 91 F2
Bor Dağı mt. Turkey 59 M6
Bordeaux France 56 D4
Borden Island Canada 119 G2
Borden Peninsula Canada 119 J2
Border Ranges National Park Australia 112 F2
Borðeyri Iceland 44 [inset]
Bordj Bou Arréridj Alg. 57 I5
Bordj Bounaama Alg. 57 G6
Bordj Flye Ste-Marie Alg. 96 C2
Bordj Messaouda Alg. 54 F5
Bordj Mokhtar Alg. 96 D2
Bordj Omar Driss Alg. see Bordj Omer Driss
Bordj Omer Driss Alg. 96 D2
Boreas Abyssal Plain sea feature Arctic Ocean 153 H1
Borel r. Canada 123 H2
Borgå Fin. see Porvoo
Borgarfjörður Iceland 44 [inset]
Borgarnes Iceland 44 [inset]
Børgefjell Nasjonalpark nat. park Norway 44 H4
Borger U.S.A. 131 C5
Borgholm Sweden 45 J8
Borgne, Lake b. U.S.A. 131 F6
Borgo San Lorenzo Italy 58 D3
Bori India 84 C1
Bori r. India 82 C5
Borikhan Laos 70 C3
Borislav Ukr. see Boryslav
Borisoglebsk Rus. Fed. 43 I6
Borisov Belarus see Barysaw
Borisovka Rus. Fed. 43 H6
Borispol' Ukr. see Boryspil'
Bo River Post Sudan 97 F4
Borja Peru 142 C4
Borken Germany 52 G3
Borkenes Norway 44 J2
Borkovskaya Rus. Fed. 42 K2
Borkum Germany 52 G1
Borkum i. Germany 52 G1
Borlänge Sweden 45 I6
Borlaug Norway 45 E6
Borlu Turkey 59 M5
Borna Germany 53 M3
Born-Berge hill Germany 53 K3
Borndiep sea chan. Neth. 52 F1
Borne Neth. 52 G2

▶Borneo i. Asia 68 E6
Largest island in Asia, and 3rd in the world.

Bornholm county Denmark 153 H3
Bornholm i. Denmark 45 I9
Bornova Turkey 59 L5
Borodino Rus. Fed. 64 J3
Borodinskoye Rus. Fed. 45 P6
Borogontsy Rus. Fed. 65 O3
Borohoro Shan mts China 80 F3
Borok-Sulezhskiy Rus. Fed. 42 H4
Boromo Burkina 96 C3
Boron U.S.A. 128 E4
Borondi India 84 D2
Boroughbridge U.K. 48 F4
Borovichi Rus. Fed. 42 G4
Borovoy Kirovskaya Oblast' Rus. Fed. 42 K4
Borovoy Respublika Kareliya Rus. Fed. 44 R4
Borovoy Respublika Komi Rus. Fed. 42 L3
Borpeta India see Barpeta
Borrisokane Ireland 51 D5
Borroloola Australia 110 B3
Børsa Norway 44 G5
Borşa Romania 43 E7
Borsakelmas sho'rxogi salt marsh Uzbek. 91 J2
Borshchiv Ukr. 43 E6
Borshchovochnyy Khrebet mts Rus. Fed. 73 J3
Bortala China see Bole
Borton U.S.A. 134 B4
Borūjen Iran 88 C4
Borūjerd Iran 88 C3
Borun Iran 88 E3
Borve U.K. 50 C3
Boryslav Ukr. 43 D6
Boryspil' Ukr. 43 F6
Borzna Ukr. 43 G6
Borzya Rus. Fed. 73 L2
Bosanska Dubica Bos.-Herz. 58 G2
Bosanska Gradiška Bos.-Herz. 58 G2
Bosanska Krupa Bos.-Herz. 58 G2
Bosanski Novi Bos.-Herz. 58 G2
Bosansko Grahovo Bos.-Herz. 58 G2
Boscawen Island Tonga see Niuatoputopu
Bose China 76 E4
Boshof S. Africa 101 G5
Boshruyeh Iran 88 E3
Bosna i Hercegovina country Europe see Bosnia-Herzegovina
Bosna Saray Bos.-Herz. see Sarajevo
Bosnia-Herzegovina country Europe 58 G2
Bosobogolo Pan salt pan Botswana 100 F3
Bosobolo Dem. Rep. Congo 98 B3
Bōsō-hantō pen. Japan 75 F6
Bosporus strait Turkey 59 M4
Bossaga Turkm. see Basaga
Bossangoa Cent. Afr. Rep. 98 B3
Bossembélé Cent. Afr. Rep. 98 B3
Bossier City U.S.A. 131 E5
Bossiesvlei Namibia 100 C3
Bossut, Cape Australia 108 C4
Bostan China 83 F1
Bostān Iran 88 B4
Bostan Pak. 89 G4
Bostāneh, Ra's-e pt Iran 88 D5
Bosten Hu l. China 80 G3
Boston U.K. 49 G6

▶Boston U.S.A. 135 J2
Capital of Massachusetts.

Boston Mountains U.S.A. 131 E5
Boston Spa U.K. 48 F5
Boswell U.S.A. 134 B3
Botad India 82 B5
Botany Bay Australia 112 E4
Botev mt. Bulg. 59 K3
Botevgrad Bulg. 59 J3
Bothaville S. Africa 101 H4
Bothnia, Gulf of Fin./Sweden 45 K6
Bothwell Canada 134 E2
Botkins U.S.A. 134 C3
Botlikh Rus. Fed. 91 G2
Botoşani Romania 43 E7
Botou China 73 L5
Botshabelo S. Africa 101 H5
Botswana country Africa 99 C6
Botte Donato, Monte mt. Italy 58 G5
Bottesford U.K. 48 G5
Bottrop Germany 52 G3
Botucatu Brazil 145 A3
Botuporã Brazil 145 C1
Botwood Canada 123 L4
Bouaflé Côte d'Ivoire 96 C4
Bouaké Côte d'Ivoire 96 C4
Bouar Cent. Afr. Rep. 98 B3
Bouârfa Morocco 54 D5
Bouba Ndjida, Parc National de nat. park Cameroon 97 E4
Bouca Cent. Afr. Rep. 98 B3
Boucaut Bay Australia 108 F3
Bouchain France 52 D4
Bouctouche Canada 123 I5
Boudh India 84 E1
Bougaa Alg. 57 I5
Bougainville, Cape Australia 108 D3
Bougainville Island P.N.G. 106 F2
Bougainville Reef Australia 110 D2
Boughessa Mali 96 D3
Bougie Alg. see Bejaïa
Bougouni Mali 96 C3
Bougtob Alg. 54 E5
Bouillon Belgium 52 F5
Bouira Alg. 57 H5
Bou Izakarn Morocco 96 C2
Boujdour W. Sahara 96 B2
Boulder Australia 109 C7
Boulder CO U.S.A. 126 G4
Boulder MT U.S.A. 126 E3
Boulder UT U.S.A. 129 H3
Boulder Canyon gorge U.S.A. 129 F3
Boulder City U.S.A. 129 F4
Boulevard U.S.A. 128 E5
Boulia Australia 110 B4
Boulogne France see Boulogne-sur-Mer
Boulogne-Billancourt France 52 C6
Boulogne-sur-Mer France 52 B4
Boumerdes Alg. 57 H5
Bouna Côte d'Ivoire 96 C4
Bou Naceur, Jbel mt. Morocco 54 D5
Boû Nâga Mauritania 96 B3
Boundary Mountains U.S.A. 135 J1
Boundary Peak U.S.A. 128 D3
Boundiali Côte d'Ivoire 96 C4
Boundji Congo 98 B4
Boun Nua Laos 70 C2
Bountiful U.S.A. 129 H1
Bounty Islands N.Z. 107 H6
Bounty Trough sea feature S. Pacific Ocean 150 H9
Bourail New Caledonia 107 G4
Bourbon reg. France see Bourbonnais
Bourbon terr. Indian Ocean see Réunion
Bourbon U.S.A. 134 B3
Bourbonnais reg. France 56 F3
Bourem Mali 96 C3
Bouressa Mali see Boughessa
Bourg-Achard France 49 H9
Bourganeuf France 56 E4
Bourg-en-Bresse France 56 G3
Bourges France 56 F3
Bourget Canada 135 H1
Bourgogne reg. France see Burgundy
Bourgogne, Canal de France 56 G3
Bourke Australia 112 B3
Bourne U.K. 49 G6
Bournemouth U.K. 49 F8
Bourtoutou Chad 97 F3
Bou Saâda Alg. 57 I6
Bou Salem Tunisia 58 C6
Bouse U.S.A. 129 F5
Bouse Wash watercourse U.S.A. 129 F4
Boussu Belgium 52 D4
Boutilimit Mauritania 96 B3
Bouvet Island terr. S. Atlantic Ocean see Bouvetøya

▶Bouvetøya terr. S. Atlantic Ocean 148 I9
Dependency of Norway.

Bouy France 52 E5
Bova Marina Italy 58 F6
Bovenden Germany 53 J3
Bow r. Alta Canada 121 I5
Bow r. Alta Canada 126 F2
Bowa China see Muli
Bowbells U.S.A. 130 C1
Bowden U.S.A. 134 F4
Bowditch atoll Tokelau see Fakaofo
Bowen Australia 110 E4
Bowen, Mount Australia 112 D6
Bowenville Australia 112 E1
Bowers Ridge sea feature Bering Sea 150 H2
Bowie Australia 110 D4
Bowie AZ U.S.A. 129 I5
Bowie TX U.S.A. 131 D5
Bow Island Canada 121 I5
Bowling Green KY U.S.A. 134 B5
Bowling Green MO U.S.A. 130 F4
Bowling Green OH U.S.A. 134 D3
Bowling Green VA U.S.A. 135 G4
Bowling Green Bay National Park Australia 110 D3
Bowman U.S.A. 130 C2
Bowman, Mount Canada 126 C2
Bowman Island Antarctica 152 F2
Bowman Peninsula Antarctica 152 L2
Bowmore U.K. 50 C5
Bowo China see Bomi
Bowral Australia 112 E5
Bowser Lake Canada 120 D3
Boxberg Germany 53 J5
Box Elder U.S.A. 130 C2
Box Elder r. U.S.A. 130 C2
Boxtel Neth. 52 F3
Boyabat Turkey 90 D2
Boyana tourist site Bulg. 59 J3
Boyang China 77 H2
Boyd r. Australia 112 F2
Boyd Lagoon salt flat Australia 109 D6
Boyd Lake Canada 121 K2
Boydton U.S.A. 135 F5
Boyers U.S.A. 134 F3
Boykins U.S.A. 135 G5
Boyle Canada 121 H4
Boyle Ireland 51 D4
Boyne r. Ireland 51 F4
Boyne City U.S.A. 134 C1
Boysen Reservoir U.S.A. 126 F4
Boysun Uzbek. 89 G2
Boyuibe Bol. 142 F8
Böyük Qafqaz mts Asia/Europe see Caucasus

▶Bozcaada i. Turkey 59 L5
Most westerly point of Asia.

Bozdağ mt. Turkey 59 L5
Bozdağ mt. Turkey 85 C1
Boz Dağları mts Turkey 59 L5
Bozdoğan Turkey 59 M6
Bozeat U.K. 49 G6
Bozeman U.S.A. 126 F3
Bozen Italy see Bolzano
Bozhou China 77 G1
Bozoum Cent. Afr. Rep. 98 B3
Bozova Turkey 90 E3
Bozqūsh, Kūh-e mts Iran 88 B2
Bozüyük Turkey 59 N5
Bozyazı Turkey 85 A1
Bra Italy 58 B2
Brač i. Croatia 58 G3
Bracadale U.K. 50 C3
Bracadale, Loch b. U.K. 50 C3
Bracara Port. see Braga
Bracciano, Lago di l. Italy 58 E3
Bracebridge Canada 134 F1
Bräcke Sweden 44 I5
Brackenheim Germany 53 J5
Brackettville U.S.A. 131 C6
Bracknell U.K. 49 G7
Bradano r. Italy 58 G4
Bradenton U.S.A. 133 D7
Bradford Canada 134 F1
Bradford U.K. 48 F5
Bradford OH U.S.A. 134 C3
Bradford PA U.S.A. 135 F3
Bradley U.S.A. 134 B3
Brady U.S.A. 131 D6
Brady Glacier U.S.A. 120 B3
Brae U.K. 50 [inset]
Braemar U.K. 50 F3
Braga Port. 57 B3
Bragado Arg. 144 D5
Bragança Brazil 143 I4
Bragança Port. 57 C3
Bragança Paulista Brazil 145 B3
Brahin Belarus 43 F6
Brahlstorf Germany 53 K1
Brahmanbaria Bangl. 83 G5
Brahmapur India 84 E2
Brahmaputra r. Asia 83 H4
also known as Dihang (India) or Jamuna (Bangladesh) or Siang (India) or Yarlung Zangbo (China)
Brahmaur India 82 D2
Brăila Romania 59 L2
Braine France 52 D5
Braine-le-Comte Belgium 52 E4
Brainerd U.S.A. 130 E2
Braintree U.K. 49 H7
Braithwaite Point Australia 108 F2
Brak r. S. Africa 101 I2
Brake (Unterweser) Germany 53 I1
Brakel Belgium 52 D4
Brakel Germany 53 J3
Brakwater Namibia 100 C2
Bramfield Australia 109 F8
Bramming Denmark 45 F9
Brämön i. Sweden 44 J5
Brampton Canada 134 F2
Brampton England U.K. 48 E4
Brampton England U.K. 49 I6
Bramsche Germany 53 I2
Bramwell Australia 110 C2
Brancaster U.K. 49 H6
Branch Canada 123 L5
Branco r. Brazil 142 F4
Brandberg mt. Namibia 99 B6
Brandbu Norway 45 G6
Brande Denmark 45 F9
Brandenburg Germany 53 M2
Brandenburg land Germany 53 N2
Brandenburg U.S.A. 134 B5
Brandfort S. Africa 101 H5
Brandis Germany 53 N3
Brandon Canada 121 L5
Brandon U.K. 49 H6
Brandon MS U.S.A. 131 F5
Brandon VT U.S.A. 135 I2
Brandon Head hd Ireland 51 B5
Brandon Mountain hill Ireland 51 B5
Brandvlei S. Africa 100 E6
Braniewo Poland 47 Q3
Bransfield Strait Antarctica 152 L2
Branson U.S.A. 131 E4
Brantford Canada 134 E2
Branxton Australia 112 E4
Bras d'Or Lake Canada 123 J5
Brasil country S. America see Brazil
Brasileia Brazil 142 E6

▶Brasília Brazil 145 B1
Capital of Brazil.

Brasília de Minas Brazil 145 B2
Braslav Belarus see Braslaw
Braslaw Belarus 45 O9
Braşov Romania 59 K2
Brassey, Mount Australia 109 F5
Brassey Range hills Australia 109 C6
Brasstown Bald mt. U.S.A. 133 D5

▶Bratislava Slovakia 47 P6
Capital of Slovakia.

Bratsk Rus. Fed. 72 I1
Bratskoye Vodokhranilishche resr Rus. Fed. 72 I1
Brattleboro U.S.A. 135 I2
Braunau am Inn Austria 47 N6
Braunfels Germany 53 I4
Braunlage Germany 53 K3
Braunsbedra Germany 53 L3
Braunschweig Germany 53 K2
Brava i. Cape Verde 96 [inset]
Brave U.S.A. 134 E4
Bråviken inlet Sweden 45 J7
Bravo, Cerro mt. Bol. 142 F7
Bravo del Norte, Río r. Mex./U.S.A. 127 G7 see Rio Grande
Brawley U.S.A. 129 F5
Bray Ireland 51 F4
Bray Island Canada 119 K3
Brazeau r. Canada 120 H4
Brazeau, Mount Canada 120 G4

▶Brazil country S. America 143 G5
Largest and most populous country in South America, and 5th largest and 5th most populous in the world.

Brazil U.S.A. 134 B4
Brazil Basin sea feature S. Atlantic Ocean 148 G7
Brazilian Highlands plat. Brazil 143 J7
Brazos r. U.S.A. 131 E6

▶Brazzaville Congo 99 B4
Capital of Congo.

Brčko Bos.-Herz. 58 H2
Bré Ireland see Bray
Breadalbane Australia 110 B4
Breaksea Sound inlet N.Z. 113 A7
Bream Bay N.Z. 113 E2
Brechfa U.K. 49 C7
Brechin U.K. 50 G4
Brecht Belgium 52 E3
Breckenridge MI U.S.A. 134 C2
Breckenridge MN U.S.A. 130 D2
Breckenridge TX U.S.A. 131 D5
Břeclav Czech Rep. 47 P6
Brecon U.K. 49 D7
Brecon Beacons reg. U.K. 49 D7
Brecon Beacons National Park U.K. 49 D7
Breda Neth. 52 E3
Bredasdorp S. Africa 100 E8
Bredbo Australia 112 D5
Breddin Germany 53 M2
Bredevoort Neth. 52 G3
Bredviken Sweden 44 I3
Bree Belgium 52 F3
Breed U.S.A. 134 A1
Bregenz Austria 47 L7
Breiðafjörður b. Iceland 44 [inset]
Breiðdalsvík Iceland 44 [inset]
Breidenbach Germany 53 I4
Breien U.S.A. 130 C2
Breitenfelde Germany 53 K1
Breitengüßbach Germany 53 K5
Breiter Luzinsee l. Germany 53 N1
Breivikbotn Norway 44 M1
Breizh reg. France see Brittany
Brejo Velho Brazil 145 C1
Brekstad Norway 44 F5
Bremen Germany 53 I1
Bremen land Germany 53 I1
Bremen IN U.S.A. 134 B3
Bremen OH U.S.A. 134 D4
Bremer Bay Australia 109 B8
Bremerhaven Germany 53 I1
Bremer Range hills Australia 109 C8
Bremersdorp Swaziland see Manzini
Bremervörde Germany 53 J1
Bremm Germany 52 H4
Brenham U.S.A. 131 D6
Brenna Norway 44 H4
Brennero, Passo di pass Austria/Italy see Brenner Pass
Brennerpaß pass Austria/Italy see Brenner Pass
Brenner Pass Austria/Italy 58 D1
Brentwood U.K. 49 H7
Brescia Italy 58 D2
Breslau Poland see Wrocław
Bresle r. France 52 B4
Brésolles, Lac l. Canada 123 H3
Bressanone Italy 58 D1
Bressay i. U.K. 50 [inset]
Bressuire France 56 D3
Brest Belarus 45 M10
Brest France 56 B2
Brest-Litovsk Belarus see Brest
Bretagne reg. France see Brittany
Breteuil France 52 C5
Brétigny-sur-Orge France 52 C6
Breton Canada 120 H4
Breton Sound b. U.S.A. 131 F6
Brett, Cape N.Z. 113 E2
Bretten Germany 53 I5
Bretton U.K. 48 E5
Breueh, Pulau i. Indon. 71 A6
Brevard U.S.A. 133 D5
Breves Brazil 143 H4
Brewarrina Australia 112 C2
Brewer U.S.A. 132 G2
Brewster NE U.S.A. 130 D3
Brewster OH U.S.A. 134 E3
Brewster, Kap c. Greenland see Kangikajik
Brewster, Lake imp. l. Australia 112 B4
Brewton U.S.A. 133 C6
Breyten S. Africa 101 I4
Breytovo Rus. Fed. 42 H4
Brezhnev Rus. Fed. see Naberezhnyye Chelny
Brezno Slovakia 47 Q6
Brezovo Bulg. 59 K3
Brezovo Polje hill Croatia 58 G2
Bria Cent. Afr. Rep. 98 C3
Briançon France 56 H4
Brian Head mt. U.S.A. 129 G3
Bribbaree Australia 112 C5
Bribie Island Australia 112 F1
Briceni Moldova 43 E6
Brichany Moldova see Briceni
Brichen' Moldova see Briceni
Bridgend U.K. 49 D7
Bridge of Orchy U.K. 50 E4
Bridgeport CA U.S.A. 128 D2
Bridgeport CT U.S.A. 135 I3
Bridgeport IL U.S.A. 134 B4
Bridgeport NE U.S.A. 130 C3
Bridger Peak U.S.A. 126 G4
Bridgeton U.S.A. 135 H4
Bridgetown Australia 109 B8

▶Bridgetown Barbados 137 M6
Capital of Barbados.

Cabinda Angola 99 B4
Cabinda prov. Angola 99 B5
Cabinet Inlet Antarctica 152 L2
Cabinet Mountains U.S.A. 126 E2
Cabistra Turkey see Ereğli
Cabo Frio Brazil 145 C3
Cabo Frio, Ilha do i. Brazil 145 C3
Cabonga, Réservoir resr Canada 122 F5
Cabool U.S.A. 131 E4
Caboolture Australia 112 F1
Cabo Orange, Parque Nacional de nat. park Brazil 143 H3
Cabo Pantoja Peru 142 C4
Cabora Bassa, Lake resr Moz. 99 D5
Cabo Raso Arg. 144 C6
Caborca Mex. 127 E7
Cabot Head hd Canada 134 E1
Cabot Strait Canada 123 J5
Cabourg France 49 G9
Cabo Verde country N. Atlantic Ocean see Cape Verde
Cabo Verde, Ilhas do is N. Atlantic Ocean 96 [inset]
Cabo Yubi Morocco see Tarfaya
Cabral, Serra do mts Brazil 145 B2
Cäbrayıl Azer. 91 G3
Cabrera, Illa de i. Spain 57 H4
Cabri Canada 121 I5
Cabullona Mex. 127 F7
Caçador Brazil 145 A4
Cacagoin China see Qagca
Čačak Serbia 59 I3
Caccia, Capo c. Sardinia Italy 58 C4
Çäçe Turkm. 89 F2
Cacequi Brazil 144 F3
Cáceres Brazil 143 G7
Cáceres Spain 57 C4
Cache Creek Canada 120 F5
Cache Peak U.S.A. 126 E4
Cacheu Guinea-Bissau 96 B3
Cachi, Nevados de mts Arg. 144 C2
Cachimbo, Serra do hills Brazil 143 H5
Cachoeira Brazil 145 D1
Cachoeira Alta Brazil 145 A2
Cachoeira de Goiás Brazil 145 A2
Cachoeira do Arari Brazil 143 I4
Cachoeiro de Itapemirim Brazil 145 C3
Cacine Guinea-Bissau 96 B3
Caciporé, Cabo c. Brazil 143 H3
Cacolo Angola 99 B5
Cacongo Angola 99 B4
Cactus U.S.A. 131 C4
Caçu Brazil 145 A2
Caculé Brazil 145 C1
Čadca Slovakia 47 Q6
Cadereyta Mex. 131 C7
Cadibarrawirracanna, Lake salt flat Australia 111 A6
Cadillac Canada 121 J5
Cadillac U.S.A. 134 C1
Cadiz Phil. 69 G4
Cádiz Spain 57 C5
Cadiz IN U.S.A. 134 C4
Cadiz KY U.S.A. 132 C4
Cadiz OH U.S.A. 134 E3
Cádiz, Golfo de g. Spain 57 C5
Cadiz Lake U.S.A. 129 F4
Cadomin Canada 120 G4
Cadotte r. Canada 120 G3
Cadotte Lake Canada 120 G3
Caen France 56 D2
Caerdydd U.K. see Cardiff
Caerffili U.K. see Caerphilly
Caerfyrddin U.K. see Carmarthen
Caergybi U.K. see Holyhead
Caernarfon U.K. 49 C5
Caernarfon Bay U.K. 49 C5
Caernarvon U.K. see Caernarfon
Caerphilly U.K. 49 D7
Caesaraugusta Spain see Zaragoza
Caesarea Alg. see Cherchell
Caesarea Cappadociae Turkey see Kayseri
Caesarea Philippi Syria see Bāniyās
Caesarodunum France see Tours
Caesaromagus U.K. see Chelmsford
Caetité Brazil 145 C1
Cafayate Arg. 144 C3
Cafelândia Brazil 145 A3
Caffa Ukr. see Feodosiya
Cagayan de Oro Phil. 69 G5
Cagayan de Tawi-Tawi i. Phil. 68 F5
Cagles Mill Lake U.S.A. 134 B4
Cagli Italy 58 E3
Cagliari Sardinia Italy 58 C5
Cagliari, Golfo di b. Sardinia Italy 58 C5
Çagyl Turkm. 91 I2
Cahama Angola 99 B5
Caha Mts hills Ireland 51 C6
Cahermore Ireland 51 B6
Cahersiveen Ireland see Cahirsiveen
Cahir Ireland 51 E5
Cahirsiveen Ireland 51 B6
Cahora Bassa, Lago de resr Moz. see Cabora Bassa, Lake
Cahore Point Ireland 51 F5
Cahors France 56 E4
Cahuapanas Peru 142 C5
Cahul Moldova 59 M2
Caia Moz. 99 D5
Caiabis, Serra dos hills Brazil 143 G6
Caianda Angola 99 C5
Caiapó r. Brazil 145 A1
Caiapó, Serra do mts Brazil 145 A2
Caiapônia Brazil 145 A2
Caibarién Cuba 133 E8
Cai Bâu, Đao i. Vietnam 70 D2
Caicara Venez. 142 E2
Caicos Islands Turks and Caicos Is 137 J4
Caicos Passage Bahamas/Turks and Caicos Is 133 F8
Caidian China 77 G2
Caiguna Australia 109 D8
Caimodorro mt. Spain 57 F3
Cainnyigoin China 76 D1
Cains Store U.S.A. 134 C5
Caipe Arg. 144 C2
Caird Coast Antarctica 152 B1
Cairngorm Mountains U.K. 50 F3
Cairngorms National Park nat. park Scotland 46 F2
Cairngorms National Park nat. park Scotland 48 D2
Cairngorms National Park nat. park Scotland 50 F3
Cairnryan U.K. 50 D6
Cairns Australia 110 D3
Cairnsmore of Carsphairn hill U.K. 50 E5

▶Cairo Egypt 90 C5
Capital of Egypt. 2nd most populous city in Africa.

Cairo U.S.A. 133 C6
Caisleán an Bharraigh Ireland see Castlebar
Caiundo Angola 99 B5
Caiwarro (abandoned) Australia 112 B2
Caiyuanzhen China see Shengsi
Caizi Hu l. China 77 H2
Cajamarca Peru 142 C5
Cajati Brazil 145 A4
Cajuru Brazil 145 B3
Caka'lho China see Yanjing
Čakovec Croatia 58 G1
Çal Denizli Turkey 59 M5
Çal Hakkâri Turkey see Çukurca
Cala S. Africa 101 H6
Calabar Nigeria 96 D4
Calabogie Canada 135 G1
Calabria, Parco Nazionale della nat. park Italy 58 G5
Calafat Romania 59 J3
Calagua Mex. 127 F8
Calagurris Spain see Calahorra
Calahorra Spain 57 F2
Calai Angola 99 B5
Calais France 52 B4
Calais U.S.A. 123 I5
Calalasteo, Sierra de mts Arg. 144 C3
Calama Brazil 142 F5
Calama Chile 144 C2
Calamajué Mex. 127 E7
Calamar Col. 142 D1
Calamian Group is Phil. 68 F4
Calamocha Spain 57 F3
Calandula Angola 99 B4
Calang Indon. 71 A6
Calapan Phil. 69 G4
Călărași Romania 59 L2
Calatayud Spain 57 F3
Calayan i. Phil. 69 G3
Calbayog Phil. 69 G4
Calbe (Saale) Germany 53 L3
Calçoene Brazil 143 H3
Calcutta India see Kolkata
Caldas da Rainha Port. 57 B4
Caldas Novas Brazil 143 I7
Calden Germany 53 J3
Calder r. Canada 120 G1
Caldera Chile 144 B3
Caldervale Australia 110 D5
Caldew r. U.K. 48 E4
Caldwell ID U.S.A. 126 D4
Caldwell KS U.S.A. 131 D4
Caldwell OH U.S.A. 134 E4
Caldwell TX U.S.A. 131 D6
Caledon r. Lesotho/S. Africa 101 H6
Caledon S. Africa 100 D8
Caledon Bay Australia 110 B2
Caledonia Canada 134 F2
Caledonia admin. div. U.K. see Scotland
Caledonia U.S.A. 135 G2
Caleta el Cobre Chile 144 B2
Calexico U.S.A. 129 F5
Calf of Man i. Isle of Man 48 C4
Calgary Canada 120 H5
Calhoun U.S.A. 134 B5
Cali Col. 142 C3
Calicut India 84 B4
Caliente U.S.A. 129 F3
California U.S.A. 134 F3
California state U.S.A. 127 C4
California, Gulf of Mex. 127 E7
California Aqueduct canal U.S.A. 128 C3
Cälilabad Azer. 91 H3
Calingasta Arg. 144 C4
Calipatria U.S.A. 129 F5
Calistoga U.S.A. 128 B2
Calkiní Mex. 136 F4
Callabonna, Lake salt flat Australia 111 C6
Callaghan, Mount U.S.A. 128 E2
Callan Ireland 51 E5
Callan r. U.K. 51 F3
Callander Canada 122 F5
Callander U.K. 50 E4
Callang Phil. 77 I5
Callao Peru 142 C6
Callao U.S.A. 129 G2
Callicoon U.S.A. 135 H3
Calling Lake Canada 120 H4
Callington U.K. 49 C8
Calliope Australia 110 E5
Callipolis Turkey see Gallipoli
Calmar U.S.A. 130 F3
Caloosahatchee r. U.S.A. 133 D7
Caloundra Australia 112 F1
Caltagirone Sicily Italy 58 F6
Caltanissetta Sicily Italy 58 F6
Calucinga Angola 99 B5
Calulo Angola 99 B4
Calunga Angola 99 B5
Caluquembe Angola 99 B5
Caluula Somalia 98 F2
Caluula, Raas pt Somalia 98 F2
Calvert Hills Australia 110 B3
Calvert Island Canada 120 D5
Calvi Corsica France 56 I5
Calvià Spain 57 H4
Calvinia S. Africa 100 D6
Calvo, Monte mt. Italy 58 F4
Cam r. U.K. 49 H6
Camaçari Brazil 145 D1
Camache Reservoir U.S.A. 128 C2
Camachigama r. Canada 122 F5
Camacho Mex. 131 C7
Camacuio Angola 99 B5
Camacupa Angola 99 B5
Camagüey Cuba 137 I4
Camagüey, Archipiélago de is Cuba 137 I4
Camamu Brazil 145 D1
Camana Peru 142 D7
Camanongue Angola 99 C5
Camapuã Brazil 143 H7
Camaquã Brazil 144 F4
Çamardı Turkey 90 D3
Camargo Bol. 142 E8
Camargue reg. France 56 G5
Camarillo U.S.A. 128 D4
Camarones Arg. 144 C6
Camarones, Bahía b. Arg. 144 C6
Camas r. U.S.A. 126 E4
Ca Mau Vietnam 71 D5
Cambay India see Khambhat
Cambay, Gulf of India see Khambhat, Gulf of
Camberley U.K. 49 G7
Cambodia country Asia 71 D4
Camboriú Brazil 145 A4
Camborne U.K. 49 B8
Cambrai France 52 D4
Cambria admin. div. U.K. see Wales
Cambrian Mountains hills U.K. 49 D6
Cambridge Canada 134 E2
Cambridge N.Z. 113 E3
Cambridge U.K. 49 H6
Cambridge MA U.S.A. 135 J2
Cambridge MD U.S.A. 135 G4
Cambridge MN U.S.A. 130 E2
Cambridge NY U.S.A. 135 I2
Cambridge OH U.S.A. 134 E3
Cambridge Bay Canada 119 H3
Cambridge City U.S.A. 134 C4
Cambridge Springs U.S.A. 134 E3
Cambrien, Lac l. Canada 123 H2
Cambulo Angola 99 C4
Cambundi-Catembo Angola 99 B5
Cambuquira Brazil 145 B3
Cam Co l. China 83 E2
Camdeboo National Park S. Africa 100 G7
Camden AL U.S.A. 133 C5
Camden AR U.S.A. 131 E5
Camden NJ U.S.A. 135 H4
Camden NY U.S.A. 135 H2
Camden SC U.S.A. 133 D5
Camdenton U.S.A. 130 E4
Cameia Angola 99 C5
Cameia, Parque Nacional da nat. park Angola 99 C5
Cameron AZ U.S.A. 129 H4
Cameron LA U.S.A. 131 E6
Cameron MO U.S.A. 130 E4
Cameron TX U.S.A. 131 D6
Cameron Highlands mts Malaysia 71 C6
Cameron Hills Canada 120 G3
Cameron Island Canada 119 H2
Cameron Park U.S.A. 128 C2
Cameroon country Africa 96 E4
Cameroon, Mount vol. Cameroon see Cameroun, Mont
Cameroon Highlands slope Cameroon/Nigeria 96 E4
Caméroun country Africa see Cameroon
Cameroun, Mont vol. Cameroon 96 D4
Cametá Brazil 143 I4
Camiña Chile 142 E7
Camiri Bol. 142 F8
Camisea Peru 142 D6
Camocim Brazil 143 J4
Camooweal Australia 110 B3
Camooweal Caves National Park Australia 110 B4
Camorta i. India 81 H10
Campana Mex. 131 C7
Campana, Isla i. Chile 144 A7
Campania Island Canada 120 D4
Campbell S. Africa 100 F5
Campbell, Cape N.Z. 113 E5
Campbell, Mount hill Australia 108 E5
Campbellford Canada 135 G1
Campbell Hill hill U.S.A. 134 D3
Campbell Island N.Z. 150 H9
Campbell Lake Canada 121 J2
Campbell Plateau sea feature S. Pacific Ocean 150 H9
Campbell Range hills Australia 108 D3
Campbell River Canada 120 E5
Campbellsville U.S.A. 134 C5
Campbellton Canada 123 I5
Campbelltown Australia 112 E5
Campbeltown U.K. 50 D5
Campeche Mex. 136 F5
Campeche, Bahía de g. Mex. 136 F5
Camperdown Australia 112 A7
Câmpina Romania 59 K2
Campina Grande Brazil 143 K5
Campinas Brazil 145 B3
Campina Verde Brazil 145 A2
Campo Cameroon 96 D4
Campobasso Italy 58 F4
Campo Belo Brazil 145 B3
Campo Belo do Sul Brazil 145 A4
Campo de Diauarum Brazil 143 H6
Campo Florido Brazil 145 A2
Campo Gallo Arg. 144 D3
Campo Grande Brazil 144 F2
Campo Largo Brazil 145 A4
Campo Maior Brazil 143 J4
Campo Maior Port. 57 C4
Campo Mourão Brazil 144 F2
Campos Brazil 145 C3
Campos Altos Brazil 145 B2
Campos Novos Brazil 145 A4
Campos Sales Brazil 143 J5
Campton U.S.A. 134 D5
Câmpulung Romania 59 K2
Câmpulung Moldovenesc Romania 59 K1
Camp Verde U.S.A. 129 H4
Camrose Canada 121 H4
Camrose U.K. 49 B7
Camsell Lake Canada 121 I2
Camsell Portage Canada 121 I3
Camsell Range mts Canada 120 F2
Camulodunum U.K. see Colchester
Çan Turkey 59 L4
Ca Na, Mui hd Vietnam 71 E5
Canaan r. Canada 123 I5
Canaan U.S.A. 135 I2
Canaan Peak U.S.A. 129 H3
Canabrava Brazil 145 B2
Canacona India 84 B3

▶Canada country N. America 118 H4
Largest country in North America and 2nd in the world. 3rd most populous country in North America.

Canada Basin sea feature Arctic Ocean 153 A1
Canadian U.S.A. 131 C5
Canadian r. U.S.A. 131 E5
Canadian Abyssal Plain sea feature Arctic Ocean 153 A1
Cañadon Grande, Sierra mts Arg. 144 C7
Canaima, Parque Nacional nat. park Venez. 142 F2
Çanakkale Turkey 59 L4
Çanakkale Boğazı strait Turkey see Dardanelles
Canalejas Arg. 144 C5
Cañamares Spain 57 E3
Canandaigua U.S.A. 135 G2
Cananea Mex. 127 F7
Cananéia Brazil 145 B4
Canápolis Brazil 145 A2
Cañar Ecuador 142 C4
Canarias terr. N. Atlantic Ocean see Canary Islands
Canárias, Ilha das i. Brazil 143 J4
Canarias, Islas terr. N. Atlantic Ocean see Canary Islands

▶Canary Islands terr. N. Atlantic Ocean 96 B2
Autonomous Community of Spain.

Canaseraga U.S.A. 135 G2
Canastota U.S.A. 135 H2
Canastra, Serra da mts Brazil 145 B2
Canastra, Serra da mts Brazil 145 A1
Canatiba Brazil 145 C1
Canatlán Mex. 131 B7
Canaveral, Cape U.S.A. 133 D6
Cañaveras Spain 57 E3
Canavieiras Brazil 145 D1
Canbelego Australia 112 C3

▶Canberra Australia 112 D5
Capital of Australia and Australian Capital Territory.

Cancún Mex. 137 G4
Çandar Turkey see Kastamonu
Çandarlı Turkey 59 L5
Candela Mex. 131 C7
Candela r. Mex. 131 C7
Candelaria Mex. 127 G7
Candia Greece see Iraklion
Cândido de Abreu Brazil 145 A4
Çandır Turkey 90 D2
Candle Lake Canada 121 J4
Candlewood, Lake U.S.A. 135 I3
Cando U.S.A. 130 D1
Candon Phil. 77 I5
Cane r. Australia 108 A5
Canea Greece see Chania
Canela Brazil 145 A5
Canelones Uruguay 144 E4
Cane Valley U.S.A. 134 C5
Cangallo Peru 142 D6
Cangamba Angola 99 B5
Cangandala, Parque Nacional de nat. park Angola 99 B4
Cango Caves S. Africa 100 F7
Cangola Angola 99 B4
Cangshan China 77 H1
Canguaretama Brazil 143 K5
Canguçu Brazil 144 F4
Canguçu, Serra do hills Brazil 144 F4
Cangwu China 77 F4
Cangzhou China 73 L5
Caniapiscau Canada 123 H3
Caniapiscau r. Canada 123 H2
Caniapiscau, Réservoir de l. Canada 123 H3
Caniçado Moz. see Guija
Canicattì Sicily Italy 58 E6
Canim Lake Canada 120 F5
Canindé Brazil 143 K4
Canisteo U.S.A. 135 G2
Canisteo r. U.S.A. 135 G2
Canisteo Peninsula Antarctica 152 K2
Cañitas de Felipe Pescador Mex. 131 C8
Çankırı Turkey 90 D2
Canna Australia 109 A7
Canna i. U.K. 50 C3
Cannanore India 84 B4
Cannanore Islands India 84 B4
Cannelton U.S.A. 134 B5
Cannes France 56 H5
Cannock U.K. 49 E6
Cannon Beach U.S.A. 126 C3
Cann River Australia 112 D6
Canoas Brazil 145 A5
Canõas, Rio das r. Brazil 145 A4
Canoeiros Brazil 145 B2
Canoe Lake Canada 121 I4
Canoe Lake l. Canada 121 I4
Canoinhas Brazil 145 A4
Canon City U.S.A. 127 G5
Cañon Largo watercourse U.S.A. 129 J3
Canoona Australia 110 E4
Canora Canada 121 K5
Canowindra Australia 112 D4
Canso Canada 123 J5
Canso, Cape Canada 123 J5
Cantabrian Mountains Spain see Cantábrica, Cordillera
Cantábrica, Cordillera mts Spain 57 D2
Cantábrico, Mar sea Spain 57 C2
Canterbury U.K. 49 I7
Canterbury Bight b. N.Z. 113 C7
Canterbury Plains N.Z. 113 C6
Cân Thơ Vietnam 71 D5
Cantil U.S.A. 128 E4
Canton GA U.S.A. 133 C5
Canton IL U.S.A. 130 F3
Canton MO U.S.A. 130 F3
Canton MS U.S.A. 131 F5
Canton NY U.S.A. 135 H1
Canton OH U.S.A. 134 E3
Canton PA U.S.A. 135 G3
Canton SD U.S.A. 130 D3
Canton TX U.S.A. 131 E5
Canton Island atoll Kiribati see Kanton
Cantuaria U.K. see Canterbury
Canunda National Park Australia 111 C8
Canutama Brazil 142 F5
Canutillo Mex. 131 B7
Canvey Island U.K. 49 H7
Canwood Canada 121 J4
Cany-Barville France 49 H9
Canyon U.S.A. 131 C5
Canyon (abandoned) Canada 120 B2
Canyon City U.S.A. 126 D3
Canyondam U.S.A. 128 C1
Canyon de Chelly National Monument nat. park U.S.A. 129 I3
Canyon Ferry Lake U.S.A. 126 F3
Canyon Lake U.S.A. 129 H5
Canyonlands National Park U.S.A. 129 I2
Canyon Ranges mts Canada 120 E2
Canyons of the Ancients National Monument nat. park U.S.A. 129 I3
Canyonville U.S.A. 126 C4
Cao Băng Vietnam 70 D2
Caocheng China see Caoxian
Caohai China see Weining
Caohe China see Qichun
Caohu China 80 F3
Caojiahe China see Qichun
Caojian China 76 C3
Caoshi China 74 B4
Caoxian China 77 G1
Caozhou China see Heze
Capac U.S.A. 134 D2
Çapakçur Turkey see Bingöl
Capanaparo r. Venez. 142 E2
Capanema Brazil 143 I4
Capão Bonito Brazil 145 A4
Caparaó, Serra do mts Brazil 145 C3
Cap-aux-Meules Canada 123 J5
Cap-de-la-Madeleine Canada 123 G5
Cape r. Australia 110 D4
Cape Arid National Park Australia 109 C8
Cape Barren Island Australia 111 [inset]
Cape Basin sea feature S. Atlantic Ocean 148 I8
Cape Breton Highlands National Park Canada 123 J5
Cape Breton Island Canada 123 J5
Cape Charles Canada 123 L3
Cape Charles U.S.A. 135 G5
Cape Coast Ghana 96 C4
Cape Coast Castle Ghana see Cape Coast
Cape Cod Bay U.S.A. 135 J3
Cape Cod National Seashore nature res. U.S.A. 135 K3
Cape Coral U.S.A. 133 D7
Cape Crawford Australia 110 A3
Cape Dorset Canada 119 K3
Cape Fanshaw U.S.A. 120 C3
Cape Fear r. U.S.A. 133 E5
Cape George Canada 123 J5
Cape Girardeau U.S.A. 131 F4
Cape Johnson Depth sea feature N. Pacific Ocean 150 E5
Cape Juby Morocco see Tarfaya
Cape Krusenstern National Monument nat. park U.S.A. 118 B3
Capel Australia 109 A8
Cape Le Grand National Park Australia 109 C8
Capelinha Brazil 145 C2
Capella Australia 110 E4
Capelle aan de IJssel Neth. 52 E3
Capelongo Angola see Kuvango
Cape May U.S.A. 135 H4
Cape May Court House U.S.A. 135 H4
Cape May Point U.S.A. 135 H4
Cape Melville National Park Australia 110 D2
Capenda-Camulemba Angola 99 B4
Cape Palmerston National Park Australia 110 E4
Cape Range National Park Australia 108 A5
Cape St George Canada 123 K4

▶Cape Town S. Africa 100 D7
Legislative capital of South Africa.

Cape Tribulation National Park Australia 110 D2
Cape Upstart National Park Australia 110 D3
Cape Verde country N. Atlantic Ocean 96 [inset]
Cape Verde Basin sea feature N. Atlantic Ocean 148 F5
Cape Verde Plateau sea feature N. Atlantic Ocean 148 F4
Cape Vincent U.S.A. 135 G1
Cape York Peninsula Australia 110 C2
Cap-Haïtien Haiti 137 J5
Capim r. Brazil 143 I4
Capitán Arturo Prat research station Antarctica 152 A2

▶Capitol Hill N. Mariana Is 69 L3
Capital of the Northern Mariana Islands, on Saipan.

Capitol Reef National Park U.S.A. 129 H2
Capivara, Represa resr Brazil 145 A3
Čapljina Bos.-Herz. 58 G3
Cappoquin Ireland 51 E5
Capraia, Isola di i. Italy 58 C3
Caprara, Punta pt Sardinia Italy 58 C4
Capri, Isola di i. Italy 58 F4
Capricorn Channel Australia 110 E4
Capricorn Group atolls Australia 110 F4
Caprivi Strip reg. Namibia 99 C5
Cap Rock Escarpment U.S.A. 131 C5
Capsa Tunisia see Gafsa
Captain Cook U.S.A. 127 [inset]
Captina r. U.S.A. 134 E4
Capuava Brazil 145 B4
Caquetá r. Col. 142 E4
Caracal Romania 59 K2

▶Caracas Venez. 142 E1
Capital of Venezuela.

Caraguatatuba Brazil 145 B3
Caraí Brazil 145 C2
Carajás Brazil 143 H5
Carajás, Serra dos hills Brazil 143 H5
Carales Sardinia Italy see Cagliari
Caralis Sardinia Italy see Cagliari
Carandaí Brazil 145 C3
Caransebeș Romania 59 J2
Caraquet Canada 123 I5
Caratasca, Laguna de lag. Hond. 137 H5
Caratinga Brazil 145 C2
Carauari Brazil 142 E4
Caravaca de la Cruz Spain 57 F4
Caravelas Brazil 145 D2
Carberry Canada 121 L5
Carbó Mex. 127 F7
Carbon, Cap hd Alg. 57 F6

▶Carbón, Laguna del Arg. 144 C7
Lowest point in South America.

Carbonara, Capo c. Sardinia Italy 58 C5
Carbondale CO U.S.A. 129 J2
Carbondale PA U.S.A. 135 H3
Carboneras Mex. 131 D7
Carbonia Sardinia Italy 58 C5
Carbonita Brazil 145 C2
Carcaixent Spain 57 F4
Carcajou Canada 120 G3
Carcajou r. Canada 120 D1
Carcar Phil. 69 G4
Carcassonne France 56 F5
Cardamomes, Chaîne des mts Cambodia/Thai. see Cardamom Range
Cardamom Hills India 84 C4
Cardamom Range mts Cambodia/Thai. 71 C4
Cárdenas Cuba 137 H4
Cárdenas Mex. 136 E4
Cardenyabba watercourse Australia 112 A2
Çardi Turkey see Harmancık
Cardiel, Lago l. Arg. 144 B7

▶Cardiff U.K. 49 D7
Capital of Wales.

Cardiff U.S.A. 135 G4
Cardigan U.K. 49 C6
Cardigan Bay U.K. 49 C6
Cardinal Lake Canada 120 G3
Cardington U.S.A. 134 D3
Cardón, Cerro hill Mex. 127 E8
Cardoso Brazil 145 A3
Cardoso, Ilha do i. Brazil 145 B4
Cardston Canada 120 H5
Careen Lake Canada 121 I3
Carei Romania 59 J1
Carentan France 56 D2
Carey U.S.A. 134 D3
Carey, Lake salt flat Australia 109 C7
Carey Lake Canada 121 K2
Cargados Carajos Islands Mauritius 149 L7
Carhaix-Plouguer France 56 C2
Cariacica Brazil 145 C3
Cariamanga Ecuador 142 C4
Caribbean Sea N. Atlantic Ocean 137 H5
Cariboo Mountains Canada 120 F4
Caribou r. Man. Canada 121 M3
Caribou r. N.W.T. Canada 120 E2
Caribou U.S.A. 132 G2
Caribou Lake Canada 119 J4
Caribou Mountains Canada 120 H3
Carichic Mex. 127 G8
Carignan France 52 F5
Carinda Australia 112 C3
Cariñena Spain 57 F3
Carinhanha r. Brazil 145 C1
Carlabhagh U.K. see Carloway
Carleton U.S.A. 134 D2
Carleton, Mount hill Canada 123 I5
Carletonville S. Africa 101 H4
Carlin U.S.A. 128 E1
Carlingford Lough inlet Ireland/U.K. 51 F3
Carlinville U.S.A. 130 F4
Carlisle U.K. 48 E4
Carlisle IN U.S.A. 134 B4
Carlisle KY U.S.A. 134 C4
Carlisle NY U.S.A. 135 H2
Carlisle PA U.S.A. 135 G3
Carlisle Lakes salt flat Australia 109 D7
Carlit, Pic mt. France 56 E5
Carlos Chagas Brazil 145 C2
Carlow Ireland 51 F5
Carloway U.K. 50 C2
Carlsbad Czech Rep. see Karlovy Vary
Carlsbad CA U.S.A. 128 E5
Carlsbad NM U.S.A. 127 G6
Carlsbad Caverns National Park U.S.A. 127 G6
Carlsberg Ridge sea feature Indian Ocean 149 L5
Carlson Inlet Antarctica 152 L1
Carlton U.S.A. 130 E2
Carlton Hill Australia 108 E3
Carluke U.K. 50 F5
Carlyle Canada 121 K5
Carmacks Canada 120 B2
Carmagnola Italy 58 B2
Carman Canada 121 L5
Carmana Iran see Kermān
Carmarthen U.K. 49 C7
Carmarthen Bay U.K. 49 C7
Carmaux France 56 F4
Carmel IN U.S.A. 134 B4
Carmel NY U.S.A. 135 I3
Carmel, Mount hill Israel 85 B3
Carmel Head hd U.K. 48 C5
Carmel Valley U.S.A. 128 C3
Carmen r. Mex. 131 B6
Carmen U.S.A. 127 F7
Carmen, Isla i. Mex. 127 F8
Carmen de Patagones Arg. 144 D6
Carmi U.S.A. 130 F4
Carmichael U.S.A. 128 C2
Carmo da Cachoeira Brazil 145 B3
Carmo do Paranaíba Brazil 145 B2
Carmona Angola see Uíge
Carmona Spain 57 D5
Carnac France 56 C3
Carnamah Australia 109 A7
Carnarvon Australia 109 A6
Carnarvon S. Africa 100 F6
Carnarvon National Park Australia 110 D5
Carnarvon Range hills Australia 109 C6
Carnarvon Range mts Australia 110 E5
Carn Dearg hill U.K. 50 E3
Carndonagh Ireland 51 E2
Carnegie Australia 109 C6
Carnegie, Lake salt flat Australia 109 C6
Carn Eige mt. U.K. 50 D3

175

Chongqing China 76 E2
Chongqing *municipality* China 76 E2
Chonguene Moz. 101 K3
Chŏngŭp S. Korea 75 B6
Chongyang China 77 G2
Chongyi China 77 G3
Chongzuo China 76 E4
Chŏnju S. Korea 75 B6

▶Cho Oyu *mt.* China/Nepal 83 F3
6th highest mountain in the world and in Asia.

Chopda India 82 C5
Chor Pak. 89 H5
Chora Sfakion Greece 59 K7
Chorley U.K. 48 E5
Chornobyl' Ukr. 43 F6
Chornomors'ke Ukr. 59 O2
Chortkiv Ukr. 43 E6
Ch'osan N. Korea 74 B4
Chōshi Japan 75 F6
Chosŏn *country* Asia *see* South Korea
Chosŏn-minjujuŭi-inmin-konghwaguk *country* Asia *see* North Korea
Choszczno Poland 47 O4
Chota Peru 142 C5
Chota Sinchula *hill* India 83 G4
Choteau U.S.A. 126 E3
Choti Pak. 89 H4
Choûm Mauritania 96 B2
Chowchilla U.S.A. 128 C3
Chowghat India 84 B4
Chown, Mount Canada 120 G4
Choybalsan Mongolia 73 K3
Choyr Mongolia 73 J3
Chrétiens, Île aux *i.* Canada *see* Christian Island
Chřiby *hills* Czech Rep. 47 P6
Chrisman U.S.A. 134 B4
Chrissiesmeer S. Africa 101 J4
Christchurch N.Z. 113 D6
Christchurch U.K. 49 F8
Christian, Cape Canada 119 L2
Christiana S. Africa 101 G4
Christiania Norway *see* Oslo
Christian Island Canada 134 E1
Christiansburg U.S.A. 134 E5
Christianshåb Greenland *see* Qasigiannguit
Christie Bay Canada 121 I2
Christie Island Myanmar 71 B5
Christina *r.* Canada 121 I3
Christina, Mount N.Z. 113 B7

▶Christmas Island *terr.* Indian Ocean 68 D9
Australian External Territory.

Christopher, Lake *salt flat* Australia 109 D6
Chrudim Czech Rep. 47 O6
Chrysi *i. Kriti* Greece *see* Gaïdouronisi
Chrysochou Bay Cyprus 85 A2
Chrysochous, Kolpos *b.* Cyprus *see* Chrysochou Bay
Chu Kazakh. *see* Shu
Chu *r.* Kazakh./Kyrg. 80 C3
Chuadanga Bangl. 83 G5
Chuali, Lago *l.* Moz. 101 K3
Chuanhui China *see* Zhoukou
Chuansha China 77 I2
Chubalung China 76 C2
Chubarovka Ukr. *see* Polohy
Chubartau Kazakh. *see* Barshatas
Chūbu-Sangaku Kokuritsu-kōen *nat. park* Japan 75 E5
Chu-ching China *see* Zhujing
Chuchkovo Rus. Fed. 43 I5
Chuckwalla Mountains U.S.A. 129 F5
Chudniv Ukr. 43 F6
Chudovo Rus. Fed. 42 F4
Chudskoye, Ozero *l.* Estonia/Rus. Fed. *see* Peipus, Lake
Chugach Mountains U.S.A. 118 D3
Chūgoku-sanchi *mts* Japan 75 D6
Chugqênsumdo China *see* Jigzhi
Chuguchak China *see* Tacheng
Chuguyev Ukr. *see* Chuhuyiv
Chuguyevka Rus. Fed. 74 D3
Chugwater U.S.A. 126 G4
Chuhai China *see* Zhuhai
Chuhuyiv Ukr. 43 H6
Chu-Iliyskiye Gory *mts* Kazakh. 80 D3
Chujiang China *see* Shimen
Chukai Malaysia *see* Cukai
Chukchagirskoye, Ozero *l.* Rus. Fed. 74 E1
Chukchi Abyssal Plain *sea feature* Arctic Ocean 153 B1
Chukchi Peninsula Rus. Fed. *see* Chukotskiy Poluostrov
Chukchi Plateau *sea feature* Arctic Ocean 153 B1
Chukchi Sea Rus. Fed./U.S.A. 65 T3
Chukhloma Rus. Fed. 42 I4
Chukotskiy, Mys *c.* Rus. Fed. 118 A3
Chukotskiy Poluostrov *pen.* Rus. Fed. 65 T3
Chulakkurgan Kazakh. *see* Sholakkorgan
Chulaktau Kazakh. *see* Karatau
Chulasa Rus. Fed. 42 J2
Chula Vista U.S.A. 128 E5
Chulucanas Peru 142 B5
Chulung Pass Pak. 82 D2
Chulym Rus. Fed. 64 J4
Chumar India 82 D2
Chumbicha Arg. 144 C3
Chumda China 76 C1
Chumikan Rus. Fed. 65 O4
Chum Phae Thai. 70 C3
Chumphon Thai. 71 B5
Chum Saeng Thai. 70 C4
Chunar India 83 E4
Ch'unch'ŏn S. Korea 75 B5
Chunchura India 83 G5
Chundzha Kazakh. 80 E3
Chunga Zambia 99 C5
Chung-hua Jen-min Kung-ho-kuo *country* Asia *see* China
Chung-hua Min-kuo *country* Asia *see* Taiwan
Ch'ungju S. Korea 75 B5
Chungking China *see* Chongqing
Ch'ungmu S. Korea *see* T'ongyŏng
Chŭngsan N. Korea 75 B5
Chungyang Shanmo *mts* Taiwan 77 I4
Chunskiy Rus. Fed. 72 H1
Chunya *r.* Rus. Fed. 65 K3
Chuồi, Hon *i.* Vietnam 71 D5
Chuosijia China *see* Guanyinqiao
Chupa Rus. Fed. 44 R3
Chūplū Iran 88 B2
Chuquicamata Chile 144 C2
Chur Switz. 56 I3
Churachandpur India 83 H4
Chūrān Iran 88 D4
Churapcha Rus. Fed. 65 O3
Churchill Canada 121 M3
Churchill *r. Man.* Canada 121 M3
Churchill *r. Nfld. and Lab.* Canada 123 J3
Churchill, Cape Canada 121 M3
Churchill Falls Canada 123 J3
Churchill Lake Canada 121 I4
Churchill Mountains Antarctica 152 H1
Churchill Sound *sea chan.* Canada 122 F2
Churchs Ferry U.S.A. 130 D1
Churchville U.S.A. 134 F4
Churia Ghati Hills Nepal 83 F4
Churu India 82 C3
Churubusco U.S.A. 134 C3
Churún-Merú *waterfall* Venez. *see* Angel Falls
Chushul India 82 D2
Chuska Mountains U.S.A. 129 I3
Chusovaya *r.* Rus. Fed. 41 R4
Chusovoy Rus. Fed. 41 R4
Chust Ukr. *see* Khust
Chute-des-Passes Canada 123 H4
Chutia *Assam* India 83 H4
Chutia *Jharkhand* India 83 F5
Chutung Taiwan 77 I3
Chuuk *is* Micronesia 150 G5
Chuxiong China 76 D3
Chüy *r.* Kazakh./Kyrg. *see* Chu
Chư Yang Sin *mt.* Vietnam 71 E4
Chuzhou *Anhui* China 77 H1
Chuzhou *Jiangsu* China 77 H1
Chymyshliya Moldova *see* Cimişlia
Chyulu Hills National Park Kenya 98 D4
Ciadâr-Lunga Moldova *see* Ciadîr-Lunga
Ciadîr-Lunga Moldova 59 M1
Ciamis Indon. 68 D8
Cianjur Indon. 68 D8
Cianorte Brazil 144 F2
Cibecue U.S.A. 129 H4
Cibolo Creek *r.* U.S.A. 131 D6
Cibuta, Sierra *mt.* Mex. 127 F7
Čićarija *mts* Croatia 58 E2
Cicero U.S.A. 134 B3
Cide Turkey 90 D2
Ciechanów Poland 47 R4
Ciego de Ávila Cuba 137 I4
Ciénaga Col. 142 D1
Ciénega Mex. 131 C7
Ciénega de Flores Mex. 131 C7
Cienfuegos Cuba 137 H4
Cieza Spain 57 F4
Çiftlik Turkey *see* Kelkit
Cifuentes Spain 57 E3
Cigüela *r.* Spain 57 E4
Cihanbeyli Turkey 90 D3
Cijara, Embalse de *resr* Spain 57 D4
Cilacap Indon. 68 D8
Çıldır Turkey 91 F2
Çıldır Gölü *l.* Turkey 91 F2
Çıldıroba Turkey 85 C1
Cilento e del Vallo di Diano, Parco Nazionale del *nat. park* Italy 58 F4
Cili China 77 F2
Cilician Gates *pass* Turkey *see* Gülek Boğazı
Cill Airne Ireland *see* Killarney
Cill Chainnigh Ireland *see* Kilkenny
Cill Mhantáin Ireland *see* Wicklow
Çilmämmetgum *des.* Turkm. 88 D1
Cilo Dağı *mt.* Turkey 91 G3
Çilov Adası *i.* Azer. 91 H2
Cimarron *CO* U.S.A. 129 J2
Cimarron *KS* U.S.A. 130 C4
Cimarron *NM* U.S.A. 127 G5
Cimarron *r.* U.S.A. 131 D4
Cimişlia Moldova 59 M1
Cimone, Monte *mt.* Italy 58 D2
Cîmpina Romania *see* Câmpina
Cîmpulung Romania *see* Câmpulung
Cîmpulung Moldovenesc Romania *see* Câmpulung Moldovenesc
Cina, Tanjung *c.* Indon. 68 C8
Çınar Turkey 91 F3
Cinaruco-Capanaparo, Parque Nacional *nat. park* Venez. 142 E2
Cinca *r.* Spain 57 G3
Cincinnati U.S.A. 134 C4
Cinco de Outubro Angola *see* Xá-Muteba
Cinderford U.K. 49 E7
Çine Turkey 59 M6
Ciney Belgium 52 F4
Cintalapa Mex. 136 F5
Cinto, Monte *mt.* France 56 I5
Ciping China *see* Jinggangshan
Circeo, Parco Nazionale del *nat. park* Italy 58 E4
Circle *AK* U.S.A. 118 D3
Circle *MT* U.S.A. 126 G3
Circleville *OH* U.S.A. 134 D4
Circleville *UT* U.S.A. 129 G2
Cirebon Indon. 68 D8
Cirencester U.K. 49 F7
Cirò Marina Italy 58 G5
Cirta Alg. *see* Constantine
Cisco U.S.A. 129 I2
Cisne, Islas del *is* Caribbean Sea 137 H5
Citlaltépetl *vol.* Mex. *see* Orizaba, Pico de
Čitluk Bos.-Herz. 58 G3
Citronelle U.S.A. 131 F6
Citrus Heights U.S.A. 128 C2
Città di Castello Italy 58 E3
Ciucaş, Vârful *mt.* Romania 59 K2
Ciudad Acuña Mex. 131 C6
Ciudad Altamirano Mex. 136 D5
Ciudad Bolívar Venez. 142 F2
Ciudad Camargo Mex. 131 B7
Ciudad Constitución Mex. 136 B3
Ciudad del Carmen Mex. 136 F5
Ciudad Delicias Mex. 131 B6
Ciudad de Panamá Panama *see* Panama City
Ciudad de Valles Mex. 136 E4
Ciudad Flores Guat. *see* Flores
Ciudad Guayana Venez. 142 F2
Ciudad Guerrero Mex. 127 G7
Ciudad Guzmán Mex. 136 D5
Ciudad Juárez Mex. 127 G7
Ciudad Lerdo Mex. 131 C7
Ciudad Mante Mex. 136 E4
Ciudad Obregón Mex. 127 F8
Ciudad Real Spain 57 E4
Ciudad Río Bravo Mex. 131 D7
Ciudad Rodrigo Spain 57 C3
Ciudad Trujillo Dom. Rep. *see* Santo Domingo
Ciudad Victoria Mex. 131 D8
Ciutadella Spain 57 H3
Civa Burnu *pt* Turkey 90 E2
Cividale del Friuli Italy 58 E1
Civitanova Marche Italy 58 E3
Civitavecchia Italy 58 D3
Çivril Turkey 59 M5
Cixi China 77 I2
Cizre Turkey 91 F3
Clacton-on-Sea U.K. 49 I7
Clady U.K. 51 E3
Claire, Lake Canada 121 H3
Clairfontaine Alg. *see* El Aouinet
Clamecy France 56 F3
Clane Ireland 51 F4
Clanton U.S.A. 133 C5
Clanwilliam Dam S. Africa 100 D7
Clara Ireland 51 E4
Clara Island Myanmar 71 B5
Claraville Australia 110 C3
Clare *N.S.W.* Australia 112 A4
Clare *S.A.* Australia 111 B7
Clare *r.* Ireland 51 C4
Clare U.S.A. 134 C2
Clarecastle Ireland 51 D5
Clare Island Ireland 51 B4
Claremont U.S.A. 135 I2
Claremore U.S.A. 131 E4
Claremorris Ireland 51 D4
Clarence *r.* Australia 112 F2
Clarence N.Z. 113 D6
Clarence Island Antarctica 152 A2
Clarence Strait Iran *see* Khūran
Clarence Strait U.S.A. 120 C3
Clarence Town Bahamas 133 F8
Clarendon *AR* U.S.A. 131 F5
Clarendon *PA* U.S.A. 134 F3
Clarendon *TX* U.S.A. 131 C5
Clarenville Canada 123 L4
Claresholm Canada 120 H5
Clarie Coast Antarctica *see* Wilkes Coast
Clarinda U.S.A. 130 E3
Clarington U.S.A. 134 E4
Clarion *IA* U.S.A. 130 E3
Clarion *PA* U.S.A. 134 F3
Clarion *r.* U.S.A. 134 F3
Clarión, Isla *i.* Mex. 136 B5
Clark U.S.A. 130 D2
Clark, Mount Canada 120 F1
Clarkdale U.S.A. 129 G4
Clarkebury S. Africa 101 I6
Clarke Range *mts* Australia 110 D4
Clarke River Australia 110 D3
Clarke's Head Canada 123 L4
Clark Mountain U.S.A. 129 F4
Clark Point Canada 134 E1
Clarksburg U.S.A. 134 E4
Clarksdale U.S.A. 131 F5
Clarks Hill U.S.A. 134 B3
Clarksville *AR* U.S.A. 131 E5
Clarksville *TN* U.S.A. 134 B5
Clarksville *TX* U.S.A. 131 E5
Clarksville *VA* U.S.A. 135 F5
Claro *r. Goiás* Brazil 145 A2
Claro *r. Mato Grosso* Brazil 145 A1
Clashmore Ireland 51 E5
Claude U.S.A. 131 C5
Claudy U.K. 51 E3
Clavier Belgium 52 F4
Claxton U.S.A. 133 D5
Clay U.S.A. 134 E4
Clayburg U.S.A. 135 I1
Clay Center *KS* U.S.A. 130 D4
Clay Center *NE* U.S.A. 130 D3
Clay City *IN* U.S.A. 134 B4
Clay City *KY* U.S.A. 134 D5
Clayhole Wash *watercourse* U.S.A. 129 G3
Claypool U.S.A. 129 H5
Clay Springs U.S.A. 129 H4
Clayton *DE* U.S.A. 135 H4
Clayton *GA* U.S.A. 133 D5
Clayton *MI* U.S.A. 134 C3
Clayton *MO* U.S.A. 130 F4
Clayton *NM* U.S.A. 131 C4
Clayton *NY* U.S.A. 135 G1
Claytor Lake U.S.A. 134 E5
Clay Village U.S.A. 134 C4
Clear, Cape Ireland 51 C6
Clearco U.S.A. 134 E4
Clear Creek Canada 134 E2
Clear Creek *r.* U.S.A. 129 H4
Cleare, Cape U.S.A. 118 D4
Clearfield *PA* U.S.A. 135 F3
Clearfield *UT* U.S.A. 126 E4
Clear Fork Brazos *r.* U.S.A. 131 D5
Clear Hills Canada 120 G3
Clear Island Ireland 51 C6
Clear Lake *IA* U.S.A. 130 E3
Clear Lake *SD* U.S.A. 130 D2
Clear Lake *l. CA* U.S.A. 128 B2
Clear Lake *l. UT* U.S.A. 129 G2
Clearmont U.S.A. 126 G3
Clearwater Canada 120 G5
Clearwater *r. Alberta/Saskatchewan* Canada 121 I3
Clearwater *r. Alta* Canada 120 H4
Clearwater U.S.A. 133 D7
Clearwater Lake Canada 121 K4
Clearwater Mountains U.S.A. 126 E3
Cleaton U.S.A. 134 B5
Cleburne U.S.A. 131 D5
Cleethorpes U.K. 48 G5
Clementi Sing. 71 [inset]
Clendenin U.S.A. 134 E4
Clendening Lake U.S.A. 134 E3
Clères France 52 B5
Clerf Lux. *see* Clervaux
Clerke Reef Australia 108 B4
Clermont Australia 110 D4
Clermont France 52 C5
Clermont-en-Argonne France 52 F5
Clermont-Ferrand France 56 F4
Clervaux Lux. 52 G4
Cles Italy 58 D1
Clevedon U.K. 49 E7
Cleveland *MS* U.S.A. 131 F5
Cleveland *OH* U.S.A. 134 E3
Cleveland *TN* U.S.A. 133 C5
Cleveland *UT* U.S.A. 129 H2
Cleveland *WI* U.S.A. 134 B2
Cleveland, Cape Australia 110 D3
Cleveland, Mount U.S.A. 126 E2
Cleveland Heights U.S.A. 134 E3
Cleveland Hills U.K. 48 F4
Cleveleys U.K. 48 D5
Cleves Germany *see* Kleve
Clew Bay Ireland 51 C4
Clifden Ireland 51 B4
Cliff U.S.A. 129 I5
Cliffoney Ireland 51 D3
Clifton Australia 112 E1
Clifton U.S.A. 129 I5
Clifton Beach Australia 110 D3
Clifton Forge U.S.A. 134 F5
Clifton Park U.S.A. 135 I2
Climax Canada 121 I5
Climax U.S.A. 134 C2
Clinch Mountain *mts* U.S.A. 134 D5
Cline River Canada 120 G4
Clinton *B.C.* Canada 120 F5
Clinton *Ont.* Canada 134 E2
Clinton *IA* U.S.A. 130 F3
Clinton *IL* U.S.A. 130 F3
Clinton *IN* U.S.A. 134 B4
Clinton *KY* U.S.A. 131 F4
Clinton *MI* U.S.A. 134 D2
Clinton *MO* U.S.A. 130 E4
Clinton *MS* U.S.A. 131 F5
Clinton *NC* U.S.A. 133 E5
Clinton *OK* U.S.A. 131 D5
Clinton-Colden Lake Canada 121 J1
Clintwood U.S.A. 134 D5

▶Clipperton, Île *terr.* N. Pacific Ocean 151 M5
French Overseas Territory. Most easterly point of Oceania.

Clisham *hill* U.K. 50 C3
Clitheroe U.K. 48 E5
Clive Lake Canada 120 G2
Cliza Bol. 142 E7
Clocolan S. Africa 101 H5
Cloghan Ireland 51 E4
Clonakilty Ireland 51 D6
Clonbern Ireland 51 D4
Cloncurry Australia 110 C4
Cloncurry *r.* Australia 110 C3
Clones Ireland 51 E3
Clonmel Ireland 51 E5
Clonygowan Ireland 51 E4
Cloonbannin Ireland 51 C5
Clooneagh Ireland 51 E4
Cloppenburg Germany 53 I2
Cloquet U.S.A. 130 E2
Cloquet *r.* U.S.A. 130 E2
Cloud Peak *WY* U.S.A. 124 F3
Cloud Peak *WY* U.S.A. 126 G3
Clova Canada 122 G4
Clover U.S.A. 129 G1
Cloverdale *CA* U.S.A. 128 B2
Cloverdale *IN* U.S.A. 134 B4
Cloverport U.S.A. 134 B5
Clovis *CA* U.S.A. 128 D3
Clovis *NM* U.S.A. 131 C5
Cloyne Canada 135 G1
Cluain Meala Ireland *see* Clonmel
Cluanie, Loch *l.* U.K. 50 D3
Cluff Lake Mine Canada 121 I3
Cluj-Napoca Romania 59 J1
Clun U.K. 49 D6
Clunes Australia 112 A6
Cluny Australia 110 B5
Cluses France 56 H3
Cluster Springs U.S.A. 135 F5
Clut Lake Canada 120 G1
Clutterbuck Head *hd* Canada 123 H1
Clutterbuck Hills *hill* Australia 109 D6
Clwydian Range *hills* U.K. 48 D5
Clyde Canada 120 H4
Clyde *r.* U.K. 50 E5
Clyde *NY* U.S.A. 135 G2
Clyde *OH* U.S.A. 134 D3
Clyde, Firth of *est.* U.K. 50 E5
Clydebank U.K. 50 E5
Clyde River Canada 119 L2
Côa *r.* Port. 57 C3
Coachella U.S.A. 128 E5
Coahuila *state* Mex. 131 C7
Coahuila de Zaragoza *state* Mex. *see* Coahuila
Coal *r.* Canada 120 E3
Coal City U.S.A. 134 A3
Coaldale U.S.A. 128 E2
Coalgate U.S.A. 131 D5
Coal Harbour Canada 120 E5
Coalinga U.S.A. 128 C3
Coalport U.S.A. 135 F3
Coal River Canada 120 E3
Coal Valley U.S.A. 129 F3
Coalville U.K. 49 F6
Coalville U.S.A. 129 H1
Coari Brazil 142 F4
Coari *r.* Brazil 142 F4
Coarsegold U.S.A. 128 D3
Coastal Plain U.S.A. 131 E6
Coast Mountains Canada 120 E4
Coast Range *hills* Australia 111 E5
Coast Ranges *mts* U.S.A. 128 B1
Coatbridge U.K. 50 E5
Coatesville U.S.A. 135 H4
Coaticook Canada 135 J1
Coats Island Canada 119 J3
Coats Land *reg.* Antarctica 152 A1
Coatzacoalcos Mex. 136 F5
Cobar Australia 112 B3
Cobargo Australia 112 D6
Cobden Australia 112 A7
Cobh Ireland 51 D6
Cobham *r.* Canada 121 M4
Cobija Bol. 142 E6
Coblenz Germany *see* Koblenz
Cobleskill U.S.A. 135 H2
Cobourg Peninsula Australia 108 F2
Cobra Australia 109 B6
Cobram Australia 112 B5
Coburg Germany 53 K4
Coburg Island Canada 119 K2
Coca Ecuador 142 C4
Coca Spain 57 D3
Cocalinho Brazil 145 A1
Cocanada India *see* Kakinada
Cochabamba Bol. 142 E7
Cochem Germany 53 H4
Cochin India 84 C4
Cochin *reg.* Vietnam 71 D5
Cochinos, Bahía de *b.* Cuba *see* Pigs, Bay of
Cochise U.S.A. 129 I5
Cochise Head *mt.* U.S.A. 129 I5
Cochrane *Alta* Canada 120 H5
Cochrane *Ont.* Canada 122 E4
Cochrane *r.* Canada 121 K3
Cockburn Australia 111 C7
Cockburnspath U.K. 50 G5
Cockburn Town Bahamas 133 F7
Cockburn Town Turks and Caicos Is *see* Grand Turk
Cockermouth U.K. 48 D4
Cocklebiddy Australia 109 D8
Cockscomb *mt.* S. Africa 100 G7
Coco *r.* Hond./Nicaragua 137 H6
Coco, Cayo *i.* Cuba 133 E8
Coco, Isla de *i.* N. Pacific Ocean 137 G7
Cocobeach Gabon 98 A3
Coco Channel India 71 A4
Cocomórachic Mex. 127 G7
Coconino Plateau U.S.A. 129 G4
Cocopara National Park Australia 112 C5
Cocos Brazil 145 B1
Cocos Basin *sea feature* Indian Ocean 149 O5

▶Cocos Islands *terr.* Indian Ocean 68 B9
Australian External Territory.

Cocos Ridge *sea feature* N. Pacific Ocean 151 O5
Cocuy, Sierra Nevada del *mt.* Col. 142 D2
Cod, Cape U.S.A. 135 J3
Codajás Brazil 142 F4
Coderre Canada 121 J5
Codfish Island N.Z. 113 A8
Codigoro Italy 58 E2
Cod Island Canada 123 J2
Codlea Romania 59 K2
Codó Brazil 143 J4
Codsall U.K. 49 E6
Cod's Head *hd* Ireland 51 B6
Cody U.S.A. 126 F3
Coeburn U.S.A. 134 D5
Coen Australia 110 C2
Coesfeld Germany 53 H3
Coeur d'Alene U.S.A. 126 D3
Coeur d'Alene Lake U.S.A. 126 D3
Coevorden Neth. 52 G2
Coffee Bay S. Africa 101 I6
Coffeyville U.S.A. 131 E4
Coffin Bay Australia 111 A7
Coffin Bay National Park Australia 111 A7
Coffs Harbour Australia 112 F3
Cofimvaba S. Africa 101 H7
Cognac France 56 D4
Cogo Equat. Guinea 96 D4
Coguno Moz. 101 L3
Cohoes U.S.A. 135 I2
Cohuna Australia 112 B5
Coiba, Isla de *i.* Panama 137 H7
Coigeach, Rubha *pt* U.K. 50 D2
Coihaique Chile 144 B7
Coimbatore India 84 C4
Coimbra Port. 57 B3
Coipasa, Salar de *salt flat* Bol. 142 E7
Coire Switz. *see* Chur
Colac Australia 112 A7
Colair Lake India *see* Kolleru Lake
Colatina Brazil 145 C2
Colbitz Germany 53 L2
Colborne Canada 135 G2
Colby U.S.A. 130 C4
Colchester U.K. 49 H7
Colchester U.S.A. 135 I3
Cold Bay U.S.A. 118 B4
Coldingham U.K. 50 G5
Colditz Germany 53 M3
Cold Lake Canada 121 I4
Cold Lake *l.* Canada 121 I4
Coldspring U.S.A. 131 E6
Coldstream Canada 120 G5
Coldstream U.K. 50 G5
Coldwater Canada 134 F1
Coldwater *KS* U.S.A. 131 D4
Coldwater *MI* U.S.A. 134 C3
Coldwater *r.* U.S.A. 131 F5
Coleambally Australia 112 B5
Colebrook U.S.A. 135 J1
Coleman *r.* Australia 110 C2
Coleman U.S.A. 131 D6
Çölemerik Turkey *see* Hakkârı
Colenso S. Africa 101 I5
Cole Peninsula Antarctica 152 L2
Coleraine Australia 111 C8
Coleraine U.K. 51 F2
Coles, Punta de *pt* Peru 142 D7
Coles Bay Australia 111 [inset]
Colesberg S. Africa 101 G6
Coleville Canada 121 I5
Colfax *CA* U.S.A. 128 C2
Colfax *LA* U.S.A. 131 E6
Colfax *WA* U.S.A. 126 D3
Colhué Huapí, Lago *l.* Arg. 144 C7
Coligny S. Africa 101 H4
Colima Mex. 136 D5
Colima, Nevado de *vol.* Mex. 136 D5
Coll *i.* U.K. 50 C4
Collado Villalba Spain 57 E3
Collarenebri Australia 112 D2
College Station U.S.A. 131 D6
Collerina Australia 112 C2
Collie *N.S.W.* Australia 112 D3
Collie *W.A.* Australia 109 B8
Collier Bay Australia 108 D4
Collier Range National Park Australia 109 B6
Collingwood Canada 134 E1
Collingwood N.Z. 113 D5
Collins U.S.A. 131 F6
Collins Glacier Antarctica 152 E2
Collinson Peninsula Canada 119 H2
Collipulli Chile 144 B5
Collmberg *hill* Germany 53 N3
Collooney Ireland 51 D3
Colmar France 56 H2
Colmenar Viejo Spain 57 E3
Colmonell U.K. 50 E5
Colne *r.* U.K. 49 H7
Cologne Germany 52 G4
Coloma U.S.A. 134 B2
Colomb-Béchar Alg. *see* Béchar
Colômbia Brazil 145 A3
Colombia Mex. 131 D7

▶Colombia *country* S. America 142 D3
2nd most populous and 4th largest country in South America.

Colombian Basin *sea feature* S. Atlantic Ocean 148 C5

▶Colombo Sri Lanka 84 C5
Former capital of Sri Lanka.

Colomiers France 56 E5
Colón *Buenos Aires* Arg. 144 D4
Colón *Entre Ríos* Arg. 144 E4
Colón Cuba 133 D8
Colón Panama 137 I7
Colon U.S.A. 134 C3
Colón, Archipiélago de *is* Ecuador *see* Galapagos Islands
Colona Australia 109 F7
Colonelganj India 83 E4
Colonel Hill Bahamas 133 F8
Colonet, Cabo *c.* Mex. 127 D7
Colônia *r.* Brazil 145 D1
Colonia Micronesia 69 J5
Colonia Agrippina Germany *see* Cologne
Colonia Díaz Mex. 127 F7
Colonia Julia Fenestris Italy *see* Fano
Colonia Las Heras Arg. 144 C7
Colonial Heights U.S.A. 135 G5
Colonna, Capo *c.* Italy 58 G5
Colonsay *i.* U.K. 50 C4
Colorado *r.* Arg. 144 D5
Colorado *r.* Mex./U.S.A. 127 E7
Colorado *r.* U.S.A. 131 D6
Colorado *state* U.S.A. 126 G5
Colorado City *AZ* U.S.A. 129 G3
Colorado City *TX* U.S.A. 131 C5
Colorado Desert U.S.A. 128 E5
Colorado National Monument *nat. park* U.S.A. 129 I2
Colorado Plateau U.S.A. 129 I3
Colorado River Aqueduct *canal* U.S.A. 129 F4
Colorado Springs U.S.A. 126 G5
Colossae Turkey *see* Honaz
Colotlán Mex. 136 D4
Cölpin Germany 53 N1
Colquiri Bol. 142 E7
Colquitt U.S.A. 133 C6
Colson U.S.A. 134 D5
Colsterworth U.K. 49 G6
Colstrip U.S.A. 126 G3
Coltishall U.K. 49 I6
Colton *CA* U.S.A. 128 E4
Colton *NY* U.S.A. 135 H1
Colton *UT* U.S.A. 129 H2
Columbia *KY* U.S.A. 134 C5
Columbia *LA* U.S.A. 131 E5
Columbia *MD* U.S.A. 135 G4
Columbia *MO* U.S.A. 130 E4
Columbia *MS* U.S.A. 131 F6
Columbia *NC* U.S.A. 132 E5
Columbia *PA* U.S.A. 135 G3

▶Columbia *SC* U.S.A. 133 D5
Capital of South Carolina.

Columbia *TN* U.S.A. 132 C5
Columbia *r.* U.S.A. 126 C3
Columbia, District of *admin. dist.* U.S.A. 135 G4
Columbia, Mount Canada 120 G4
Columbia, Sierra *mts* Mex. 127 E7
Columbia City U.S.A. 134 C3
Columbia Lake Canada 120 H5
Columbia Mountains Canada 120 F4
Columbia Plateau U.S.A. 126 D3
Columbine, Cape S. Africa 100 C7
Columbus *GA* U.S.A. 133 C5
Columbus *IN* U.S.A. 134 C4
Columbus *MS* U.S.A. 131 F5
Columbus *MT* U.S.A. 126 F3
Columbus *NC* U.S.A. 133 D5
Columbus *NE* U.S.A. 130 D3
Columbus *NM* U.S.A. 127 G7

▶Columbus *OH* U.S.A. 134 D4
Capital of Ohio.

Columbus *TX* U.S.A. 131 D6
Columbus Grove U.S.A. 134 C3
Columbus Salt Marsh U.S.A. 128 D2
Colusa U.S.A. 128 B2
Colville N.Z. 113 E3
Colville U.S.A. 126 D2
Colville *r.* U.S.A. 118 C2
Colville Channel N.Z. 113 E3
Colville Lake Canada 118 F3
Colwyn Bay U.K. 48 D5
Comacchio Italy 58 E2
Comacchio, Valli di *lag.* Italy 58 E2
Comai China 83 G3
Comalcalco Mex. 136 F5
Comanche U.S.A. 131 D6
Comandante Ferraz *research station* Antarctica 152 A2
Comandante Salas Arg. 144 C4
Comănești Romania 59 L1
Combahee *r.* U.S.A. 133 D5
Combarbalá Chile 144 B4
Comber U.K. 51 G3
Combermere Bay Myanmar 70 A3
Combles France 52 C4
Combol *i.* Indon. 71 C7

Combomune Moz. **101** K2
Comboyne Australia **112** F3
Comencho, Lac *l.* Canada **122** G4
Comendador Dom. Rep. *see* **Elías Piña**
Comendador Gomes Brazil **145** A2
Comeragh Mountains *hills* Ireland **51** E5
Comercinho Brazil **145** C2
Cometela Moz. **101** L1
Comfort U.S.A. **131** D6
Comilla Bangl. **83** G5
Comines Belgium **52** C4
Comino, Capo *c. Sardinia* Italy **58** C4
Comitán de Domínguez Mex. **136** F5
Commack U.S.A. **135** I3
Commentry France **56** F3
Committee Bay Canada **119** J3
Commonwealth Territory *admin. div.* Australia *see* **Jervis Bay Territory**
Como Italy **58** C2
Como, Lago di Italy *see* **Como, Lake**
Como, Lake Italy **58** C2
Como Chamling *l.* China **83** G3
Comodoro Rivadavia Arg. **144** C7
Comores *country* Africa *see* **Comoros**
Comorin, Cape India **84** C4
Comoro Islands *country* Africa *see* **Comoros**
Comoros *country* Africa **99** E5
Compiègne France **52** C5
Comprida, Ilha *i.* Brazil **145** B4
Comrat Moldova **59** M1
Comrie U.K. **50** F4
Comstock U.S.A. **131** C6
Côn, Sông *r.* Vietnam **71** E4
Cona China **83** G4

▶**Conakry** Guinea **96** B4
Capital of Guinea.

Cona Niyeo Arg. **144** C6
Conceição *r.* Brazil **145** B2
Conceição da Barra Brazil **145** D2
Conceição do Araguaia Brazil **143** I5
Conceição do Mato Dentro Brazil **145** C2
Concepción Chile **144** B5
Concepción Mex. **131** C7
Concepción *r.* Mex. **127** E7
Concepción Para. **144** E2
Concepción, Punta *pt* Mex. **127** F8
Concepción de la Vega Dom. Rep. *see* **La Vega**
Conception, Point U.S.A. **128** C4
Conception Island Bahamas **133** F8
Conchas U.S.A. **127** G6
Conchas Lake U.S.A. **127** G6
Concho U.S.A. **129** I4
Conchos *r. Nuevo León/Tamaulipas* Mex. **131** D7
Conchos *r.* Mex. **131** B6
Concord *CA* U.S.A. **128** B3
Concord *NC* U.S.A. **133** D5

▶**Concord** *NH* U.S.A. **135** J2
Capital of New Hampshire.

Concord *VT* U.S.A. **135** J1
Concordia Arg. **144** E4
Concordia Mex. **131** B8
Concordia Peru **142** D4
Concordia S. Africa **100** C5
Concordia *KS* U.S.A. **130** D4
Concordia *KY* U.S.A. **134** B4
Concordia *research stn* **152** G2
Concord Peak Afgh. **89** I2
Con Cuông Vietnam **70** D3
Condamine Australia **112** E1
Condamine *r.* Australia **112** D1
Côn Đao Vietnam **71** D5
Condeúba Brazil **145** C1
Condobolin Australia **112** C4
Condom France **56** E5
Condon U.S.A. **126** C3
Condor, Cordillera del *mts* Ecuador/Peru **142** C4
Condroz *reg.* Belgium **52** E4
Conecuh *r.* U.S.A. **133** C6
Conègliano Italy **58** E2
Conejos Mex. **131** C7
Conejos U.S.A. **127** G5
Conemaugh *r.* U.S.A. **134** F3
Conestogo Lake Canada **134** E2
Conesus Lake U.S.A. **135** G2
Conflict Group *is* P.N.G. **110** E1
Confoederatio Helvetica *country* Europe *see* **Switzerland**
Confusion Range *mts* U.S.A. **129** G2
Congdü China **83** F3
Conghua China **77** G4
Congjiang China **77** F3
Congleton U.K. **48** E5
Congo *country* Africa **98** B4

▶**Congo** *r.* Congo/Dem. Rep. Congo **98** B4
2nd longest river in Africa, and 8th in the world.
Formerly known as Zaïre.

Congo (Brazzaville) *country* Africa *see* **Congo**
Congo (Kinshasa) *country* Africa *see* **Congo, Democratic Republic of the**

▶**Congo, Democratic Republic of the** *country* Africa **98** C4
3rd largest and 4th most populous country in Africa.

Congo, Republic of *country* Africa *see* **Congo**
Congo Basin Dem. Rep. Congo **98** C4
Congo Cone *sea feature* S. Atlantic Ocean **148** I6
Congo Free State *country* Africa *see* **Congo, Democratic Republic of the**
Congonhas Brazil **145** C3
Congress U.S.A. **129** G4
Conimbla National Park Australia **112** D4
Coningsby U.K. **49** G5
Coniston Canada **122** E5
Coniston U.K. **48** D4
Conjuboy Australia **110** D3
Conklin Canada **121** I4
Conn *r.* Canada **122** F3
Conn, Lough *l.* Ireland **51** C3
Connacht *reg.* Ireland *see* **Connaught**
Connaught *reg.* Ireland **51** C4
Conneaut U.S.A. **134** E3
Connecticut *state* U.S.A. **135** I3
Connemara *reg.* Ireland **51** C4
Connemara National Park Ireland **51** C4
Connersville U.S.A. **134** C4
Connolly, Mount Canada **120** C2
Connors Range *hills* Australia **110** E4
Conoble Australia **112** B4
Conquista Brazil **145** B2
Conrad U.S.A. **126** F2
Conrad Rise *sea feature* Southern Ocean **149** K9
Conroe U.S.A. **131** E6
Conselheiro Lafaiete Brazil **145** C3
Consett U.K. **48** F4
Consolación del Sur Cuba **133** D8
Côn Sơn, Đao *i.* Vietnam **71** D5
Consort Canada **121** I4
Constance Germany *see* **Konstanz**
Constance, Lake Germany/Switz. **47** L7
Constância dos Baetas Brazil **142** F5
Constanța Romania **59** M2
Constantia *tourist site* Cyprus *see* **Salamis**
Constantia Germany *see* **Konstanz**
Constantina Spain **57** D5
Constantine Alg. **54** F4
Constantine, Cape U.S.A. **118** C4
Constantinople Turkey *see* **İstanbul**
Constitución de 1857, Parque Nacional *nat. park* Mex. **129** F5
Consul Canada **121** I5
Contact U.S.A. **126** E4
Contagalo Brazil **145** C3
Contamana Peru **142** C5
Contas *r.* Brazil **145** D1
Contoy, Isla *i.* Mex. **133** C8
Contria Brazil **145** B2
Contwoyto Lake Canada **121** I1
Convención Col. **142** D2
Convent U.S.A. **131** F6
Conway U.K. *see* **Conwy**
Conway *AR* U.S.A. **131** E5
Conway *ND* U.S.A. **130** D1
Conway *NH* U.S.A. **135** J2
Conway *SC* U.S.A. **133** E5
Conway, Cape Australia **110** E4
Conway, Lake *salt flat* Australia **111** A6
Conway National Park Australia **110** E4
Conway Reef Fiji *see* **Ceva-i-Ra**
Conwy U.K. **48** D5
Conwy *r.* U.K. **49** D5
Coober Pedy Australia **109** F7
Cooch Behar India *see* **Koch Bihar**
Coochbehar India *see* **Koch Bihar**
Cook Australia **109** E7
Cook, Cape Canada **120** E5
Cook, Grand Récif de *reef* New Caledonia **107** G3
Cook, Mount *mt.* N.Z. *see* **Aoraki**
Cookes Peak U.S.A. **127** G6
Cookeville U.S.A. **132** C4
Cookhouse S. Africa **101** G7
Cook Ice Shelf Antarctica **152** H2
Cook Inlet *sea chan.* U.S.A. **118** C3

▶**Cook Islands** *terr.* S. Pacific Ocean **150** J7
Self-governing New Zealand Territory.

Cooksburg U.S.A. **135** H2
Cooks Passage Australia **110** D2
Cookstown U.K. **51** F3
Cook Strait N.Z. **113** E5
Cooktown Australia **110** D2
Coolabah Australia **112** C3
Cooladdi Australia **112** B1
Coolah Australia **112** D3
Coolamon Australia **112** C5
Coolgardie Australia **109** C7
Coolibah Australia **108** E3
Coolidge U.S.A. **129** H5
Cooloola National Park Australia **111** F5
Coolum Beach Australia **111** F5
Cooma Australia **112** D6
Coombah Australia **111** C7
Coonabarabran Australia **112** D3
Coonamble Australia **112** D3
Coondambo Australia **111** A6
Coondapoor India *see* **Kundapura**
Coongoola Australia **112** B1
Coon Rapids U.S.A. **130** E2
Cooper Creek *watercourse* Australia **111** B6
Cooper Mountain Canada **120** G5
Coopernook Australia **112** F3
Cooper's Town Bahamas **133** E7
Cooperstown *ND* U.S.A. **130** D2
Cooperstown *NY* U.S.A. **135** H2
Coopracambra National Park Australia **112** D6
Coorabie Australia **109** F7
Coorong National Park Australia **111** B8
Coorow Australia **109** B7
Coosa *r.* U.S.A. **133** C5
Coos Bay U.S.A. **126** B4
Coos Bay *b.* U.S.A. **126** B4
Cootamundra Australia **112** D5
Cootehill Ireland **51** E3
Cooyar Australia **112** E1
Copala Mex. **136** E5
Cope U.S.A. **130** C4
Copemish U.S.A. **134** C1

▶**Copenhagen** Denmark **45** H9
Capital of Denmark.

Copenhagen U.S.A. **135** H2
Copertino Italy **58** H4
Copeton Reservoir Australia **112** E2
Cô Pi, Phou *mt.* Laos/Vietnam **70** D3
Copiapó Chile **144** B3
Copley Australia **111** B6
Copparo Italy **58** D2
Copper Cliff Canada **122** E5
Copper Harbor U.S.A. **132** C2
Coppermine Canada *see* **Kugluktuk**
Coppermine *r.* Canada **120** H1
Coppermine Point Canada **122** D5
Copperton S. Africa **100** F5
Copp Lake Canada **120** H2
Coqên China **83** F3
Coqên *Xizang* China **83** F3
Coquilhatville Dem. Rep. Congo *see* **Mbandaka**
Coquille *i.* Micronesia *see* **Pikelot**
Coquille U.S.A. **126** B4
Coquimbo Chile **144** B3
Coquitlam Canada **120** F5
Corabia Romania **59** K3
Coração de Jesus Brazil **145** B2
Coracesium Turkey *see* **Alanya**
Coraki Australia **112** F2
Coral Bay Australia **109** A5
Coral Harbour Canada **119** J3
Coral Sea S. Pacific Ocean **106** F3
Coral Sea Basin S. Pacific Ocean **150** G6

▶**Coral Sea Islands Territory** *terr.* Australia **106** F3
Australian External Territory.

Corangamite, Lake Australia **112** A7
Corat Azer. **91** H2
Corbeny France **52** D5
Corbett Inlet Canada **121** M2
Corbett National Park India **82** D3
Corbie France **52** C5
Corbin U.S.A. **134** C5
Corby U.K. **49** G6
Corcaigh Ireland *see* **Cork**
Corcoran U.S.A. **128** D3
Corcovado, Golfo de *sea chan.* Chile **144** B6
Corcyra *i.* Greece *see* **Corfu**
Cordele U.S.A. **133** D6
Cordelia U.S.A. **128** B2
Cordell U.S.A. **131** D5
Cordilheiras, Serra das *hills* Brazil **143** I5
Cordillera Azul, Parque Nacional *nat. park* Peru **142** C5
Cordillera de los Picachos, Parque Nacional *nat. park* Col. **142** D3
Cordillo Downs Australia **111** C5
Cordisburgo Brazil **145** B2
Córdoba Arg. **144** D4
Córdoba *Durango* Mex. **131** C7
Córdoba *Veracruz* Mex. **136** E5
Córdoba Spain **57** D5
Córdoba, Sierras de *mts* Arg. **144** D4
Cordova Spain *see* **Córdoba**
Cordova U.S.A. **118** D3
Corduba Spain *see* **Córdoba**
Corfu *i.* Greece **59** H5
Coria Spain **57** C4
Coribe Brazil **145** B1
Coricudgy *mt.* Australia **112** E4
Corigliano Calabro Italy **58** G5
Coringa Islands Australia **110** E3
Corinium U.K. *see* **Cirencester**
Corinth Greece **59** J6
Corinth *KY* U.S.A. **134** C4
Corinth *MS* U.S.A. **131** F5
Corinth *NY* U.S.A. **135** I2
Corinth, Gulf of *sea chan.* Greece **59** J5
Corinthus Greece *see* **Corinth**
Corinto Brazil **145** B2
Cork Ireland **51** D6
Corleone *Sicily* Italy **58** E6
Çorlu Turkey **59** L4
Cormeilles France **49** H9
Cornelia S. Africa **101** I4
Cornélio Procópio Brazil **145** A3
Cornélios Brazil **145** A5
Cornell U.S.A. **130** F2
Corner Brook Canada **123** K4
Corner Inlet *b.* Australia **112** C7
Corner Seamounts *sea feature* N. Atlantic Ocean **148** E3
Corneto Italy *see* **Tarquinia**
Cornillet, Mont *hill* France **52** E5
Corning *AR* U.S.A. **131** F4
Corning *CA* U.S.A. **128** B2
Corning *NY* U.S.A. **135** G2
Cornish *watercourse* Australia **110** D4
Corn Islands *is* Nicaragua *see* **Maíz, Islas del**
Corno, Monte *mt.* Italy **58** E3
Corno di Campo *mt.* Italy/Switz. **56** J3
Cornwall Canada **135** H1
Cornwallis Island Canada **119** I2
Cornwall Island Canada **119** I2
Coro Venez. **142** E1
Coroaci Brazil **145** C2
Coroatá Brazil **143** J4
Corofin Ireland **51** C5
Coromandel Brazil **145** B2
Coromandel Coast India **84** D4
Coromandel Peninsula N.Z. **113** E3
Coromandel Range *hills* N.Z. **113** E3
Corona *CA* U.S.A. **128** E5
Corona *NM* U.S.A. **127** G6
Coronado U.S.A. **128** E5
Coronado, Bahía de *b.* Costa Rica **137** H7
Coronation Canada **121** I4
Coronation Gulf Canada **118** G3
Coronation Island S. Atlantic Ocean **152** A2
Coronda Arg. **144** D4
Coronel Fabriciano Brazil **145** C2
Coronel Oviedo Para. **144** E3
Coronel Pringles Arg. **144** D5
Coronel Suárez Arg. **144** D5
Çorovodë Albania **59** I4
Corowa Australia **112** C5
Corpus Christi U.S.A. **131** D7
Corque Bol. **142** E7
Corral de Cantos *mt.* Spain **57** D4
Corrales Mex. **131** B7
Corralilla Cuba **133** D8
Corrandibby Range *hills* Australia **109** A6
Corrente Brazil **143** I6
Corrente *r. Bahia* Brazil **145** C1
Corrente *r. Minas Gerais* Brazil **145** A2
Correntes Brazil **143** H7
Correntina Brazil **145** B1
Correntina *r.* Brazil *see* **Éguas**
Corrib, Lough *l.* Ireland **51** C4
Corrientes Arg. **144** E3
Corrientes, Cabo *c.* Col. **142** C2
Corrientes, Cabo *c.* Cuba **133** C8
Corrientes, Cabo *c.* Mex. **136** C4
Corrigin Australia **109** B8
Corris U.K. **49** D6
Corry U.S.A. **134** F3
Corse *i.* France *see* **Corsica**
Corse, Cap *c. Corsica* France **56** I5
Corsham U.K. **49** E7
Corsica *i.* France **56** I5
Corsicana U.S.A. **131** D5
Corte *Corsica* France **56** I5
Cortegana Spain **57** C5
Cortes, Sea of *g.* Mex. *see* **California, Golfo de**
Cortez U.S.A. **129** I3
Cortina d'Ampezzo Italy **58** E1
Cortland U.S.A. **135** G2
Corton U.K. **49** I6
Cortona Italy **58** D3
Coruche Port. **57** B4
Çoruh Turkey *see* **Artvin**
Çoruh *r.* Turkey **91** F2
Çorum Turkey **90** D2
Corumbá Brazil **143** G7
Corumbá *r.* Brazil **145** A2
Corumbá de Goiás Brazil **145** A1
Corumbaíba Brazil **145** A2
Corumbaú, Ponta *pt* Brazil **145** D2
Corunna Spain *see* **A Coruña**
Corunna U.S.A. **134** C2
Corvallis U.S.A. **126** C3
Corwen U.K. **49** D6
Corydon *IA* U.S.A. **130** E3
Corydon *IN* U.S.A. **134** B4
Coryville U.S.A. **135** F3
Cos *i.* Greece *see* **Kos**
Cosentia Italy *see* **Cosenza**
Cosenza Italy **58** G5
Coshocton U.S.A. **134** E3
Cosne-Cours-sur-Loire France **56** F3
Costa Blanca *coastal area* Spain **57** F4
Costa Brava *coastal area* Spain **57** H3
Costa de la Luz *coastal area* Spain **57** C5
Costa del Sol *coastal area* Spain **57** D5
Costa de Miskitos *coastal area* Nicaragua *see* **Costa de Mosquitos**
Costa de Mosquitos *coastal area* Nicaragua **137** H6
Costa Marques Brazil **142** F6
Costa Rica Brazil **143** H7
Costa Rica *country* Central America **137** H6
Costa Rica Mex. **136** C4
Costa Verde *coastal area* Spain **57** C2
Costermansville Dem. Rep. Congo *see* **Bukavu**
Costești Romania **59** K2
Costigan Lake Canada **121** J3
Coswig Germany **53** M3
Cotabato Phil. **69** G5
Cotagaita Bol. **142** E8
Cotahuasi Peru **142** D7
Cote, Mount U.S.A. **120** D3
Coteau des Prairies *slope* U.S.A. **130** D2
Coteau du Missouri *slope ND* U.S.A. **130** C1
Coteau du Missouri *slope SD* U.S.A. **130** C2
Côte d'Azur *coastal area* France **56** H5
Côte d'Ivoire *country* Africa **96** C4
Côte Française de Somalis *country* Africa *see* **Djibouti**
Cotentin *pen.* France **49** F9
Côtes de Meuse *ridge* France **52** E5
Cothi *r.* U.K. **49** C7
Cotiaeum Turkey *see* **Kütahya**
Cotiella *mt.* Spain **57** G2
Cotonou Benin **96** D4
Cotopaxi, Volcán *vol.* Ecuador **142** C4
Cotswold Hills U.K. **49** E7
Cottage Grove U.S.A. **126** C4
Cottbus Germany **47** O5
Cottenham U.K. **49** H6
Cottian Alps *mts* France/Italy **56** H4
Cottica Suriname **143** H3
Cottiennes, Alpes *mts* France/Italy *see* **Cottian Alps**
Cottonwood *AZ* U.S.A. **129** G4
Cottonwood *CA* U.S.A. **128** B1
Cottonwood *r.* U.S.A. **130** D4
Cottonwood Falls U.S.A. **130** D4
Cotulla U.S.A. **131** D6
Coudersport U.S.A. **135** F3
Couedic, Cape du Australia **111** B8
Coulee City U.S.A. **126** D3
Coulee Dam U.S.A. **126** D3
Coulman Island Antarctica **152** H2
Coulogne France **52** B4
Coulommiers France **52** D6
Coulonge *r.* Canada **122** F5
Coulterville U.S.A. **128** C3
Council U.S.A. **126** D3
Council Bluffs U.S.A. **130** E3
Council Grove U.S.A. **130** D4
Councillor Island Australia **111** [inset]
Counselor U.S.A. **129** J3
Coupeville U.S.A. **126** C2
Courageous Lake Canada **121** I1
Courland Lagoon *b.* Lith./Rus. Fed. **45** L9
Courtenay Canada **120** E5
Courtland U.S.A. **135** G5
Courtmacsherry Ireland **51** D6
Courtmacsherry Bay Ireland **51** D6
Courtown Ireland **51** F5
Courtrai Belgium *see* **Kortrijk**
Coushatta U.S.A. **131** E5
Coutances France **56** D2
Coutts Canada **121** I5
Couture, Lac *l.* Canada **122** G2
Couvin Belgium **52** E4
Cove Fort U.S.A. **129** G2
Cove Island Canada **134** E1
Cove Mountains *hills* U.S.A. **135** F4
Coventry U.K. **49** F6
Covered Wells U.S.A. **129** G5
Covesville U.S.A. **135** F5
Covilhã Port. **57** C3
Covington *GA* U.S.A. **133** D5
Covington *IN* U.S.A. **134** B3
Covington *KY* U.S.A. **134** C4
Covington *LA* U.S.A. **131** F6
Covington *MI* U.S.A. **130** F2
Covington *TN* U.S.A. **131** F5
Covington *VA* U.S.A. **134** E5
Cowal, Lake *dry lake* Australia **112** C4
Cowan, Lake *salt flat* Australia **109** C7
Cowansville Canada **135** I1
Cowargarzê China **76** C1
Cowcowing Lakes *salt flat* Australia **109** B7
Cowdenbeath U.K. **50** F4
Cowell Australia **111** B7
Cowes U.K. **49** F8
Cowichan Lake Canada **120** E5
Cowley Australia **112** B1
Cowper Point Canada **119** G2
Cowra Australia **112** D4
Cox *r.* Australia **110** A2
Coxá *r.* Brazil **145** B1
Coxen Hole Hond. *see* **Roatán**
Coxilha de Santana *hills* Brazil/Uruguay **144** E4
Coxilha Grande *hills* Brazil **144** F3
Coxim Brazil **143** H7
Cox's Bazar Bangl. **83** G5
Coyame Mex. **131** B6
Coyhaique Chile *see* **Coihaique**
Coyote Lake U.S.A. **128** E4
Coyote Peak *hill* U.S.A. **129** F5
Cozhê China **83** F2
Cozie, Alpi *mts* France/Italy *see* **Cottian Alps**
Cozumel Mex. **137** G4
Cozumel, Isla de *i.* Mex. **137** G4
Craboon Australia **112** D4
Cracovia Poland *see* **Kraków**
Cracow Australia **110** E5
Cracow Poland *see* **Kraków**
Cradle Mountain Lake St Clair National Park Australia **111** [inset]
Cradock S. Africa **101** G7
Craig U.K. **50** D3
Craig *AK* U.S.A. **120** C4
Craig *CO* U.S.A. **129** J1
Craigavon U.K. **51** F3
Craigieburn Australia **112** B6
Craig Island Taiwan *see* **Mienhua Yü**
Craignure U.K. **50** D4
Craigsville U.S.A. **134** E4
Crail U.K. **50** G4
Crailsheim Germany **53** K5
Craiova Romania **59** J2
Cramlington U.K. **48** F3
Cranberry Lake U.S.A. **135** H1
Cranberry Portage Canada **121** K4
Cranborne Chase *for.* U.K. **49** E8
Cranbourne Australia **112** B7
Cranbrook Canada **120** H5
Crandon U.S.A. **130** F2
Crane Lake Canada **121** I5
Cranston *KY* U.S.A. **134** D4
Cranston *RI* U.S.A. **135** J3
Cranz Rus. Fed. *see* **Zelenogradsk**
Crary Ice Rise Antarctica **152** I1
Crary Mountains Antarctica **152** J1
Crater Lake National Park U.S.A. **126** C4
Crater Peak U.S.A. **128** C1
Craters of the Moon National Monument *nat. park* U.S.A. **126** E4
Crateús Brazil **143** J5
Crato Brazil **143** K5
Crawford *CO* U.S.A. **129** J2
Crawford *NE* U.S.A. **130** C3
Crawfordsville U.S.A. **134** B3
Crawfordville *FL* U.S.A. **133** C6
Crawfordville *GA* U.S.A. **133** D5
Crawley U.K. **49** G7
Crazy Mountains U.S.A. **126** F3
Creag Meagaidh *mt.* U.K. **50** E4
Crécy-en-Ponthieu France **52** B4
Credenhill U.K. **49** E6
Crediton U.K. **49** D8
Cree *r.* Canada **121** J3
Creel Mex. **127** G8
Cree Lake Canada **121** J3
Creemore Canada **134** E1
Creighton Canada **121** K4
Creil France **52** C5
Creil Neth. **52** F2
Crema Italy **58** C2
Cremlingen Germany **53** K2
Cremona Canada **120** H5
Cremona Italy **58** D2
Crépy-en-Valois France **52** C5
Cres *i.* Croatia **58** F2
Crescent U.S.A. **126** C4
Crescent City *CA* U.S.A. **126** B4
Crescent City *FL* U.S.A. **133** D6
Crescent Group *is* Paracel Is **68** E3
Crescent Head Australia **112** F3
Crescent Junction U.S.A. **129** I2
Crescent Valley U.S.A. **128** E1
Cressy Australia **112** A7
Crest Hill *hill H.K.* China **77** [inset]
Crestline U.S.A. **134** D3
Creston Canada **120** G5
Creston *IA* U.S.A. **130** E3
Creston *WY* U.S.A. **126** G4
Crestview U.S.A. **133** C6
Creswick Australia **112** A6
Creta *i.* Greece *see* **Crete**
Crete *i.* Greece **59** K7
Crete U.S.A. **130** D3
Creus, Cap de *c.* Spain **57** H2
Creuse *r.* France **56** E3
Creußen Germany **53** L5
Creutzwald France **52** G5
Creuzburg Germany **53** K3
Crevasse Valley Glacier Antarctica **152** J1
Crewe U.K. **49** E5
Crewe U.S.A. **135** F5
Crewkerne U.K. **49** E8
Crianlarich U.K. **50** E4
Criccieth U.K. **49** C6
Criciúma Brazil **145** A5
Crieff U.K. **50** F4
Criffel *hill* U.K. **50** F6
Criffell *hill* U.K. *see* **Criffel**
Crikvenica Croatia **58** F2
Crillon, Mount U.S.A. **120** B3
Crimea *pen.* Ukr. **90** D1
Crimmitschau Germany **53** M4
Crimond U.K. **50** H3
Crisfield U.S.A. **135** H5
Cristalândia Brazil **143** I6
Cristalina Brazil **145** B2
Cristalino *r.* Brazil *see* **Mariembero**
Cristóbal Colón, Pico *mt.* Col. **142** D1
Crixás Brazil **145** A1
Crixás Açu *r.* Brazil **145** A1
Crixás Mirim *r.* Brazil **145** A1
Crna Gora *country* Europe *see* **Montenegro**
Crni Vrh *mt.* Serbia **59** J2
Črnomelj Slovenia **58** F2
Croagh Patrick *hill* Ireland **51** C4
Croajingolong National Park Australia **112** D6
Croatia *country* Europe **58** G2
Crocker, Banjaran *mts* Malaysia **68** E6
Crockett U.S.A. **131** E6
Crofton *KY* U.S.A. **134** B5
Crofton *NE* U.S.A. **130** D3
Croghan U.S.A. **135** H2
Croisilles France **52** C4
Croker, Cape Canada **134** E1
Croker Island Australia **108** F2
Cromarty U.K. **50** E3
Cromarty Firth *est.* U.K. **50** E3
Cromer U.K. **49** I6
Crook U.K. **48** F4
Crooked Harbour *b. H.K.* China **77** [inset]
Crooked Island Bahamas **133** F8
Crooked Island *H.K.* China **77** [inset]
Crooked Island Passage Bahamas **133** F8
Crookston U.S.A. **130** D2
Crooksville U.S.A. **134** D4
Crookwell Australia **112** D5
Croom Ireland **51** D5
Croppa Creek Australia **112** E2
Crosby U.K. **48** D5
Crosby *MN* U.S.A. **130** E2
Crosby *ND* U.S.A. **130** C1
Crosbyton U.S.A. **131** C5
Cross Bay Canada **121** M2
Cross City U.S.A. **133** D6
Cross Fell *hill* U.K. **48** E4
Crossfield Canada **120** H5
Crossgar U.K. **51** G3
Crosshaven Ireland **51** D6
Cross Inn U.K. **49** C6
Cross Lake Canada **121** L4
Cross Lake *l.* Canada **121** L4
Cross Lake *l.* U.S.A. **135** G2
Crossmaglen U.K. **51** F3
Crossman Peak U.S.A. **129** F4
Crossville U.S.A. **132** C5
Crotch Lake Canada **135** G1
Croton Italy *see* **Crotone**
Crotone Italy **58** G5
Crouch *r.* U.K. **49** H7
Crow *r.* Canada **120** E3
Crow Agency U.S.A. **126** G3
Crowal *watercourse* Australia **112** C3
Crowborough U.K. **49** H7
Crowdy Bay National Park Australia **112** F3
Crowell U.S.A. **131** D5
Crowland U.K. **49** G6
Crowley U.S.A. **131** E6
Crowley, Lake U.S.A. **128** D3
Crown Point *IN* U.S.A. **134** B3
Crownpoint U.S.A. **129** I4
Crown Point *NY* U.S.A. **135** I2
Crown Prince Olav Coast Antarctica **152** D2
Crown Princess Martha Coast Antarctica **152** B1
Crows Nest Australia **112** F1
Crowsnest Pass Canada **120** H5
Crowsnest Pass *pass* Canada **120** H5
Crow Wing *r.* U.S.A. **130** E2
Croydon Australia **110** C3
Crozet U.S.A. **135** F4
Crozet, Îles *is* Indian Ocean **149** L9
Crozet Basin *sea feature* Indian Ocean **149** M8
Crozet Plateau *sea feature* Indian Ocean **149** K8
Crozon France **56** B2
Cruces Cuba **133** D8
Cruden Bay U.K. **50** H3
Cruillas Mex. **131** D7
Crum U.S.A. **134** D5
Crumlin U.K. **51** F3
Crusheen Ireland **51** D5
Cruz Alta Brazil **144** F3
Cruz del Eje Arg. **144** D4
Cruzeiro Brazil **145** B3
Cruzeiro do Sul Brazil **142** D5
Cry Lake Canada **120** D3
Crysdale, Mount Canada **120** F4
Crystal U.S.A. **129** I3
Crystal City Canada **121** L5
Crystal City U.S.A. **131** D6
Crystal Falls U.S.A. **130** F2
Crystal Lake U.S.A. **134** A2
Crystal River U.S.A. **133** D6
Csongrád Hungary **59** I1
Cửa Lớn, Sông *r.* Vietnam **71** D5
Cuamba Moz. **99** D5
Cuando *r.* Angola/Zambia **99** C5
Cuangar Angola **99** B5
Cuango Angola **99** B4
Cuanza *r.* Angola **99** B4
Cuatro Ciénegas Mex. **131** C7
Cuauhtémoc Mex. **127** G7
Cuba *NM* U.S.A. **127** G5
Cuba *NY* U.S.A. **135** F2

▶**Cuba** *country* West Indies **137** H4
5th largest island and 5th most populous country in North America.

Cubal Angola **99** B5
Cubango *r.* Angola/Namibia **99** C5
Cubatão Brazil **145** B3
Cub Hills Canada **121** J4
Çubuk Turkey **90** D2
Cucapa, Sierra *mts* Mex. **129** F5
Cuchi Angola **99** B5
Cuchilla Grande *hills* Uruguay **144** E4
Cucuí Brazil **142** E3
Cucurpe Mex. **127** F7
Cúcuta Col. **142** D2
Cudal Australia **112** D4
Cuddalore India **84** C4
Cuddapah India **84** C3
Cuddeback Lake U.S.A. **128** E4
Cue Australia **109** B6
Cuéllar Spain **57** D3
Cuemba Angola **99** B5
Cuenca Ecuador **142** C4
Cuenca Spain **57** E3

Cuenca, Serranía de mts Spain 57 E3
Cuencamé Mex. 131 C7
Cuernavaca Mex. 136 E5
Cuero U.S.A. 131 D6
Cuervos Mex. 129 F5
Cugir Romania 59 J2
Cuiabá Amazonas Brazil 143 G5
Cuiabá Mato Grosso Brazil 143 G7
Cuiabá r. Brazil 143 G7
Cuihua China see Daguan
Cuijiang China see Ninghua
Cuijk Neth. 52 F3
Cuilcagh hill Ireland/U.K. 51 E3
Cuillin Hills U.K. 50 C3
Cuillin Sound sea chan. U.K. 50 C3
Cuilo Angola 99 B4
Cuiluan China 74 C3
Cuité r. Brazil 145 C2
Cuito r. Angola 99 C5
Cuito Cuanavale Angola 99 B5
Cukai Malaysia 71 C6
Çukurca Turkey 88 A2
Çukurova plat. Turkey 85 B1
Cu Lao Cham i. Vietnam 70 E4
Cu Lao Xanh i. Vietnam 71 E4
Culcairn Australia 112 C5
Culfa Azer. 91 G3
Culgoa r. Australia 112 C2
Culiacán Mex. 136 C4
Culiacán Rosales Mex. see Culiacán
Culion Phil. 69 F4
Culion i. Phil. 68 F4
Cullen U.K. 50 G3
Cullen Point Australia 110 C1
Cullera Spain 57 F4
Cullivoe U.K. 50 [inset]
Cullman U.S.A. 133 C5
Cullybackey U.K. 51 F3
Cul Mòr hill U.K. 50 D2
Culpeper U.S.A. 135 G4
Culuene r. Brazil 143 H6
Culver, Point Australia 109 D8
Culverden N.Z. 113 D6
Cumaná Venez. 142 F1
Cumari Brazil 145 A2
Cumbal, Nevado de vol. Col. 142 C3
Cumberland KY U.S.A. 134 D5
Cumberland MD U.S.A. 135 F4
Cumberland VA U.S.A. 135 F5
Cumberland r. U.S.A. 132 C4
Cumberland, Lake U.S.A. 134 C5
Cumberland Lake Canada 121 K4
Cumberland Mountains U.S.A. 134 D5
Cumberland Peninsula Canada 119 L3
Cumberland Plateau U.S.A. 132 C5
Cumberland Point U.S.A. 130 F2
Cumberland Sound sea chan. Canada 119 L3
Cumbernauld U.K. 50 F5
Cumbres de Majalca, Parque Nacional nat. park Mex. 127 G7
Cumbres de Monterey, Parque Nacional nat. park Mex. 131 C7
Cumbum India 84 C3
Cumlosen Germany 53 L1
Cummings U.S.A. 128 B2
Cummins Australia 111 A7
Cummins Range hills Australia 108 D4
Cumnock Australia 112 D4
Cumnock U.K. 50 E5
Çumra Turkey 90 D3
Cumuruxatiba Brazil 145 D2
Cunagua Cuba see Bolivia
Cunderdin Australia 109 B7
Cunene r. Angola 99 B5
also known as Kunene
Cuneo Italy 58 B2
Cung Sơn Vietnam 71 E4
Cunnamulla Australia 112 B2
Cunningsburgh U.K. 50 [inset]
Cupar U.K. 50 F4
Cupica, Golfo de b. Col. 142 C2
Curaçá Brazil 143 K5
Curaçá r. Brazil 142 D4
Curaçao i. Neth. Antilles 137 K6
Curaray r. Ecuador 142 D4
Curdlawidny Lagoon salt flat Australia 111 B6
Curia Switz. see Chur
Curicó Chile 144 B4
Curitiba Brazil 145 A4
Curitibanos Brazil 145 A4
Curlewis Australia 112 E3
Curnamona Australia 111 B6
Currabubula Australia 112 E3
Currais Novos Brazil 143 K5
Curran U.S.A. 134 D1
Currane, Lough l. Ireland 51 B6
Currant U.S.A. 129 F2
Curranyalpa Australia 112 B3
Currawilla Australia 110 C5
Currawinya National Park Australia 112 B2
Currie Australia 106 E5
Currie U.S.A. 129 F1
Currituck U.S.A. 135 G5
Currockbilly, Mount Australia 112 E5
Curtis Channel Australia 110 F5
Curtis Island Australia 110 E4
Curtis Island N.Z. 107 I5
Curuá r. Brazil 143 H5
Curup Indon. 68 C7
Curupira, Serra mts Brazil/Venez. 142 F3
Cururupu Brazil 143 J4
Curvelo Brazil 145 B2
Curwood, Mount hill U.S.A. 130 F2
Cusco Peru 142 D6
Cushendall U.K. 51 F2
Cushendun U.K. 51 F2
Cushing U.S.A. 131 D4
Cusseta U.S.A. 133 C5
Custer MT U.S.A. 126 G3
Custer SD U.S.A. 130 C3
Cut Bank U.S.A. 126 E2
Cuthbert U.S.A. 133 C6
Cuthbertson Falls Australia 108 F3
Cut Knife Canada 121 I4
Cutler Ridge U.S.A. 133 D7
Cuttaburra Creek r. Australia 112 B2
Cuttack India 84 E1
Cuvelai Angola 99 B5
Cuxhaven Germany 47 L4
Cuya Chile 142 D7
Cuyahoga Falls U.S.A. 134 E3
Cuyama U.S.A. 128 D4
Cuyama r. U.S.A. 128 C4
Cuyo Islands Phil. 69 G4
Cuyuni r. Guyana 143 G2
Cuzco Peru see Cusco
Cwmbrân U.K. 49 D7
Cyangugu Rwanda 98 C4
Cyclades is Greece 59 K6
Cydonia Greece see Chania
Cygnet U.S.A. 134 D3
Cymru admin. div. U.K. see Wales
Cynthiana U.S.A. 134 C4
Cypress Hills Canada 121 I5
Cyprus country Asia 85 A2
Cyrenaica reg. Libya 97 F2
Cythera i. Greece see Kythira
Czar Canada 121 I4
Czechia country Europe see Czech Republic

▶Czechoslovakia
Divided in 1993 into the Czech Republic and Slovakia.

Czech Republic country Europe 47 O6
Czernowitz Ukr. see Chernivtsi
Czersk Poland 47 P4
Częstochowa Poland 47 Q5

D

Đa, Sông r. Vietnam see Black
Da'an China 74 B3
Ḑabāb, Jabal aḑ mt. Jordan 85 B4
Dabakala Côte d'Ivoire 96 C4
Daban China 73 L4
Dabao China 76 D2
Daba Shan mts China 77 F1
Dabba China see Daocheng
Dabein Myanmar 70 B3
Dabhoi India 82 C5
Ḑab'ī, Wādī aḑ watercourse Jordan 85 C4
Dabie Shan mts China 77 G2
Dablana India 82 C4
Dabola Guinea 96 B3
Dabqig China 73 J5
Dąbrowa Górnicza Poland 47 Q5
Dabsan Hu salt l. China 83 H1
Dabs Nur l. China 74 A3
Dabu Guangdong China 77 H3
Dabu Guangxi China see Liucheng
Dabusu Pao l. China see Dabs Nur
Dacca Bangl. see Dhaka
Dachau Germany 47 M6
Dachuan China see Dazhou
Dacre Canada 135 G1
Daday Turkey 90 D2
Dade City U.S.A. 133 D6
Dadeville U.S.A. 133 C5
Dādkān Iran 89 F5
Dadong China see Donggang
Dadra India see Achalpur
Dadu Pak. 89 G5
Daegu S. Korea see Taegu
Daejŏn S. Korea see Taejŏn
Daet Phil. 69 G4
Dafang China 76 E3
Dafeng China 77 I1
Dafengman China 74 B4
Dafla Hills India 83 H4
Dafoe Canada 121 J5
Dafoe r. Canada 121 M4
Dagana Senegal 96 B3
Dagcagoin China see Zoigê
Dagcanglhamo China 76 D1
Daghmar Oman 88 E6
Dağlıq Qarabağ aut. reg. Azer. 91 G3
Daglung China 83 G3
Dagö i. Estonia see Hiiumaa
Dagon Myanmar see Rangoon
Daguan China 76 D3
Daguokui Shan hill China 74 C3
Dagupan Phil. 69 G3
Dagxoi Sichuan China see Yidun
Dagxoi Sichuan China see Sowa
Dagzê China 83 G3
Dagzê Co salt l. China 83 F3
Dahadinni r. Canada 120 E2
Dahalach, Isole is Eritrea see Dahlak Archipelago
Dahana des. Saudi Arabia see Ad Dahnā'
Dahe China see Ziyuan
Daheiding Shan mt. China 74 C3
Dahei Shan mts China 74 B4
Dahej India 82 C5
Daheng China 77 H3
Dahezhen China 74 D3
Da Hinggan Ling mts China 74 A2
Dahlak Archipelago is Eritrea 86 F6
Dahlak Marine National Park Eritrea 86 F6
Daḩl al Furayy well Saudi Arabia 88 B5
Dahlem Germany 52 G4
Dahlenburg Germany 53 K1
Dahm, Ramlat des. Saudi Arabia/Yemen 86 G6
Dahmani Tunisia 58 C7
Dahme Germany 53 N3
Dahn Germany 53 H5
Dahnā' plain Saudi Arabia 88 B5
Dahod India 82 C5
Dahomey country Africa see Benin
Dahongliutan Aksai Chin 82 D2
Dahra Senegal see Dara
Dähre Germany 53 K2
Dahūk Iraq 91 F3
Dai i. Indon. 108 E1
Daik Indon. 68 C7
Daik-U Myanmar 70 B3
Đai Lanh, Mui pt Vietnam 71 E4
Dailekh Nepal 83 E3
Dailly U.K. 50 E5
Daimiel Spain 57 E4
Dainkog China 76 C1
Dainkognubma China 76 C1
Daintree National Park Australia 110 D3
Dair, Jebel ed mt. Sudan 86 D7
Dairen China see Dalian
Dai-sen vol. Japan 75 D6
Daisetsu-zan Kokuritsu-kōen nat. park Japan 74 F4
Daishan China 77 I2
Daiyun Shan mts China 77 H3
Dajarra Australia 110 B4
Dajin Chuan r. China 76 D2
Da Juh China 83 H1

▶Dakar Senegal 96 B3
Capital of Senegal.

Dākhilah, Wāḩāt ad oasis Egypt 86 C4
Dakhla W. Sahara see Ad Dakhla
Dakhla Oasis oasis Egypt see Dākhilah, Wāḩāt ad
Đâk Lăk, Cao Nguyên plat. Vietnam 71 E4
Dakoank India 71 A6
Dakol'ka r. Belarus 43 F5
Dakor India 82 C5
Dakoro Niger 96 D3
Dakota City IA U.S.A. 130 E3
Dakota City NE U.S.A. 130 D3
Đakovica Kosovo see Gjakovë
Đakovo Croatia 58 H2
Daktuy Rus. Fed. 74 B1
Dala Angola 99 C5
Dalaba Guinea 96 B3
Dalai China see Da'an
Dalain Hob China 80 J3
Dālakī Iran 88 C4
Dalälven r. Sweden 45 J6
Dalaman Turkey 59 M6
Dalandzadgad Mongolia 72 I4
Dalap-Uliga-Darrit Marshall Is see Delap-Uliga-Djarrit
Đa Lat Vietnam 71 E5
Dalatando Angola see N'dalatando
Dalaud India 82 C5
Dalauda India 82 C5
Dalbandin Pak. 89 G4
Dalbeattie U.K. 50 F6
Dalbeg Australia 110 D4
Dalby Australia 112 E1
Dalby Isle of Man 48 C4
Dale Hordaland Norway 45 D6
Dale Sogn og Fjordane Norway 45 D6
Dale City U.S.A. 135 G4
Dale Hollow Lake U.S.A. 134 C5
Dalen Neth. 52 G2
Dalet Myanmar 70 A3
Daletme Myanmar 70 A2
Dalfors Sweden 45 I6
Dalgān Iran 88 E5
Dalgety Australia 112 D6
Dalgety r. Australia 109 A6
Dalhart U.S.A. 131 C4
Dalhousie Canada 123 I4
Dalhousie, Cape Canada 118 F2
Dali Shaanxi China 77 F1
Dali Yunnan China 76 D3
Dalian China 73 M5
Daliang China see Shunde
Daliang Shan mts China 76 D2
Daliji China 77 H1
Dalin China 74 A4
Dalizi China 74 B4
Dalkeith U.K. 50 F5
Dallas OR U.S.A. 126 C3
Dallas TX U.S.A. 131 D5
Dalles City U.S.A. see The Dalles
Dall Island U.S.A. 120 C4
Dalmā i. U.A.E. 88 D5
Dalmacija reg. Bos.-Herz./Croatia see Dalmatia
Dalmas, Lac l. Canada 123 H3
Dalmatia reg. Bos.-Herz./Croatia 78 A2
Dalmau India 82 E4
Dalmellington U.K. 50 E5
Dalmeny Canada 121 J4
Dalmi India 83 F5
Dal'negorsk Rus. Fed. 74 D3
Dal'nerechensk Rus. Fed. 74 D3
Dal'niye Zelentsy Rus. Fed. 42 H1
Dalny China see Dalian
Daloa Côte d'Ivoire 96 C4

▶Dalol Eth. 86 F7
Highest recorded annual mean temperature in the world.

Daloloia Group is P.N.G. 110 E1
Dalou Shan mts China 76 E3
Dalqān well Saudi Arabia 88 B5
Dalry U.K. 50 E5
Dalrymple U.K. 50 E5
Dalrymple, Lake Australia 110 D4
Daltenganj India 83 F4
Dalton Canada 122 D4
Dalton S. Africa 101 J5
Dalton GA U.S.A. 133 C5
Dalton MA U.S.A. 135 I2
Dalton PA U.S.A. 135 H3
Daltonganj India see Daltenganj
Dalton-in-Furness U.K. 48 D4
Daludalu Indon. 71 C7
Daluo China 76 D4
Daly r. Australia 108 E3
Daly City U.S.A. 128 B3
Daly River Australia 108 E3
Daly Waters Australia 108 F4
Damagaram Takaya Niger 96 D3
Daman India 84 B1
Daman and Diu union terr. India 84 A1
Damanhūr Egypt 90 C5
Damanhûr Egypt see Damanhūr
Damant Lake Canada 121 J2
Damão India see Daman
Damar i. Indon. 108 E1
Damara Cent. Afr. Rep. 98 B3
Damaraland reg. Namibia 99 B6
Damas Syria see Damascus

▶Damascus Syria 85 C3
Capital of Syria.

Damascus U.S.A. 134 E5
Damaturu Nigeria 96 E3
Damāvand Iran 88 D3
Damāvand, Qolleh-ye mt. Iran 88 D3
Dambulla Sri Lanka 84 D5
Damdy Kazakh. 80 B1
Damghan Iran 88 D2
Damianópolis Brazil 145 B1
Damietta Egypt see Dumyāţ
Daming Shan mt. China 77 F4
Dāmiyā Jordan 85 B3
Damjong China 76 B1
Damlasu Turkey 85 D1
Dammam Saudi Arabia 86 H4
Damme Belgium 52 D3
Damme Germany 53 I2
Damoh India 82 D5
Damour Lebanon 85 B3
Dampar, Tasik l. Malaysia 71 C7
Dampier Archipelago is Australia 108 B5
Dampier Island P.N.G. see Karkar Island
Dampier Land reg. Australia 108 C4
Dampier Strait P.N.G. 69 L8
Dampir, Selat sea chan. Indon. 69 I7
Damqoq Zangbo r. China see Maquan He
Dam Qu r. China 76 B1
Dâmrei, Chuŏr Phnum mts Cambodia 71 D5
Damroh India 76 B2
Damwâld Neth. see Damwoude
Damwoude Neth. 52 G1
Damxoi China see Comai
Damxung China 83 G3
Ḑanā Jordan 85 B4
Dana Nepal 83 E3
Danakil reg. Africa see Denakil
Danané Côte d'Ivoire 96 C4
Đa Nẵng Vietnam 70 E3
Đa Nẵng, Vung b. Vietnam 70 E3
Danao Phil. 69 G4
Danata Turkm. 88 D2
Danba China 76 D2
Danbury CT U.S.A. 135 I3
Danbury NC U.S.A. 132 D4
Danby U.S.A. 135 I2
Danby Lake U.S.A. 129 F4
Dandaragan Australia 109 A7
Dande Eth. 98 D3
Dandeldhura Nepal 82 E3
Dandeli India 84 B3
Dandong China 75 B4
Dandot Pak. 89 I3
Dandridge U.S.A. 132 D4
Dane r. U.K. 48 E5
Daneborg Greenland 153 I2
Danese U.S.A. 134 E5
Danfeng China see Shizong
Dangan Liedao i. China 77 G4
Dangara Tajik. see Danghara
Dangbizhen Rus. Fed. 74 C3
Dangchang China 76 E1
Dangchengwan China see Subei
Danger Islands atoll Cook Is see Pukapuka
Danger Point S. Africa 100 D8
Danghara Tajik. 89 H2
Danghe Nanshan mts China 80 H4
Dang La pass China see Tanggula Shankou
Dangla Shan mts China see Tanggula Shan
Dangqên China 83 G3
Dângrêk, Chuŏr Phnum mts Cambodia/Thai. see Phanom Dong Rak, Thiu Khao
Dangriga Belize 136 G5
Dangshan China 77 H1
Dangtu China 77 H2
Daniel's Harbour Canada 123 K4
Daniëlskuil S. Africa 100 F5
Danilov Rus. Fed. 42 I4
Danilovka Rus. Fed. 43 J6
Danilovskaya Vozvyshennost' hills Rus. Fed. 42 H4
Danjiang China see Leishan
Danjiangkou China 77 F1
Danjiangkou Shuiku resr China 77 F1
Danjo-guntō is Japan 75 C6
Ḑank Oman 88 E6
Dankhar India 82 D2
Dankov Rus. Fed. 43 H5
Danlí Hond. 137 G6
Danmark country Europe see Denmark
Dannebrog Ø i. Greenland see Qillak
Dannenberg (Elbe) Germany 53 L1
Dannenwalde Germany 53 N1
Dannevirke N.Z. 113 F5
Dannhauser S. Africa 101 J5
Dano Burkina 96 C3
Danshui Taiwan see Tanshui
Dansville U.S.A. 135 G2
Danta India 82 C4
Dantan India 83 F5
Dantevada India see Dantewara
Dantewada India see Dantewara
Dantewara India 84 D2
Dantu China see Zhenjiang

▶Danube r. Europe 47 P6
2nd longest river in Europe.
Also spelt Donau (Austria/Germany) or Duna (Hungary) or Dunaj (Slovakia) or Dunărea (Romania) or Dunav (Bulgaria/Croatia/Serbia) or Dunay (Ukraine).

Danube Delta Romania/Ukr. 59 M2
Danubyu Myanmar 70 A3
Danville IL U.S.A. 134 B3
Danville IN U.S.A. 134 B4
Danville KY U.S.A. 134 C5
Danville OH U.S.A. 134 D3
Danville PA U.S.A. 135 G3
Danville VA U.S.A. 134 F5
Danville VT U.S.A. 135 I1
Danxian China see Danzhou
Danzhai China 76 E3
Danzhou Guangxi China 77 F3
Danzhou Hainan China 77 F5
Danzig Poland see Gdańsk
Danzig, Gulf of Poland/Rus. Fed. see Gdańsk, Gulf of
Daocheng China 76 D2
Daokou China see Huaxian
Dao Tay Sa is S. China Sea see Paracel Islands
Daoud Alg. see Aïn Beïda
Daoukro Côte d'Ivoire 96 C4
Daozhen China 76 E2
Dapaong Togo 96 D3
Dapeng Wan b. H.K. China see Mirs Bay
Daphabum mt. India 83 I4
Dapitan Phil. 69 G5
Daporijo India 83 H4
Dapu China see Liucheng
Da Qaidam Zhen China 80 I4
Daqiao China 76 D3
Daqing China 74 B3
Daqiu China 77 H3
Dāq Mashī Iran 88 E3
Daqq-e Patargān salt flat Iran 89 F3
Daqq-e Sorkh, Kavīr-e salt flat Iran 88 D3
Daqq-e Tundi, Dasht-e imp. l. Afgh. 89 F3
Daqu Shan i. China 77 I2
Dara Senegal 96 B3
Dar'ā Syria 85 C3
Dāra, Gebel mt. Egypt see Dārah, Jabal
Dārāb Iran 88 D4
Darāgāh Iran 88 D4
Dārah, Jabal mt. Egypt 90 D6
Daraj Libya 96 E1
Dārākūyeh Iran 88 D4
Dārān Iran 88 C3
Daraut-Korgon Kyrg. 89 I2
Darazo Nigeria 96 E3
Darband, Kūh-e mt. Iran 88 E4
Darband-e Hajjī Boland Turkm. 89 F2
Darbhanga India 83 F4
Darcang China 76 C1
Dardanelle U.S.A. 131 E5
Dardanelles strait Turkey 59 L4
Dardania prov. Europe see Kosovo
Dardesheim Germany 53 K3
Dardo China see Kangding
Dar el Beida Morocco see Casablanca
Darende Turkey 90 E3

▶Dar es Salaam Tanz. 99 D4
Former capital of Tanzania.

Darfo Boario Terme Italy 58 D2
Dargai Pak. 89 H3
Dargaville N.Z. 113 D2
Dargo Australia 112 C6
Dargo Zangbo r. China 83 F3
Darhan Mongolia 72 J3
Darien U.S.A. 133 D6
Darién, Golfo del g. Col. 142 C2
Darién, Parque Nacional de nat. park Panama 137 I7
Dariga Pak. 89 G5
Darīganga Mongolia 73 K3
Darjeeling India see Darjiling
Darjiling India 83 G4
Darkhazīneh Iran 88 C4
Darlag China 76 C1

▶Darling r. Australia 112 B3
2nd longest river in Oceania, and a major part of the longest (Murray-Darling)

Darling Downs hills Australia 112 D1
Darling Range hills Australia 109 A8
Darlington U.K. 48 F4
Darlington U.S.A. 130 F3
Darlington Point Australia 112 C5
Darlot, Lake salt flat Australia 109 C6
Darłowo Poland 47 P3
Darma Pass China/India 82 E3
Darmstadt Germany 53 I5
Darnah Libya 90 A4
Darnall S. Africa 101 J5
Darnick Australia 112 A4
Darnley, Cape Antarctica 152 E2
Daroca Spain 57 F3
Daroot-Korgon Kyrg. see Daraut-Korgon
Darovskoy Rus. Fed. 42 J4
Darr watercourse Australia 110 C4
Darreh Bīd Iran 88 E3
Darreh-ye Bāhābād Iran 88 D4
Darreh-ye Shahr Iran 88 B3
Darsi India 84 C3
Dart r. U.K. 49 D8
Dartang China see Baqên
Dartford U.K. 49 H7
Dartmoor Australia 111 C8
Dartmoor hills U.K. 49 C8
Dartmoor National Park U.K. 49 D8
Dartmouth Canada 123 J5
Dartmouth U.K. 49 D8
Dartmouth, Lake salt flat Australia 111 D5
Dartmouth Reservoir Australia 112 C6
Darton U.K. 48 F5
Daru P.N.G. 69 K8
Daru Sierra Leone 96 B4
Daruba Indon. 69 H6
Darvaza Turkm. see Derweze
Darvoz, Qatorkŭhi mts Tajik. 89 H2
Darwazgai Afgh. 89 G4
Darwen U.K. 48 E5
Darweshan Afgh. 89 G4

▶Darwin Australia 108 E3
Capital of Northern Territory.

Darwin, Monte mt. Chile 144 C8
Daryācheh-ye Orūmīyeh salt l. Iran see Urmia, Lake
Dar'yalyktakyr, Ravnina plain Kazakh. 80 B2
Dar"yoi Amu r. Asia see Amudar'ya
Dārzīn Iran 88 E4
Dās i. U.A.E. 88 D5
Dasada India 82 B5
Dashennongjia mt. China see Shennong Ding
Dashhowuz Daşoguz Turkm. see Daşoguz
Dashkesan Azer. see Daşkäsän
Dashkhovuz Daşoguz Turkm. see Daşoguz
Dashköpri Turkm. see Daşköpri
Dashoguz Daşoguz Turkm. see Daşoguz
Dasht Iran 88 E2
Dashtiari Iran 89 F5
Daska Pak. 89 I3
Daşkäsän Azer. 91 G2
Daşköpri Turkm. 89 F2
Daşoguz Turkm. 87 I1
Daşoguz Turkm. see Daşoguz
Dasongshu China 76 E3
Daspar mt. Pak. 89 I2
Dassel Germany 53 J3
Dastgardān Iran 88 E3
Datadian Indon. 68 F6
Datça Turkey 59 L6
Date Japan 74 F4
Date Creek watercourse U.S.A. 129 G4
Dateland U.S.A. 129 G5
Datha India 82 C5
Datia India 82 D4
Datian China 77 H3
Datian Ding mt. China 77 F4
Datil U.S.A. 129 J4
Datong Anhui China 77 H2
Datong Heilong. China 74 B3
Datong Shanxi China 73 K4
Datong He r. China 72 I5
Dattapur India 84 C1
Datu, Tanjung c. Indon./Malaysia 71 E7
Daudkandi Bangl. 83 G5
Daugava r. Latvia 45 N8
Daugavpils Latvia 45 O9
Daulatabad India 84 B2
Daulatabad Iran see Malāyer
Daulatpur Bangl. 83 G5
Daun Germany 52 G4
Daungyu r. Myanmar 70 A2
Dauphin Canada 121 K5
Dauphiné reg. France 56 G4
Dauphiné, Alpes du mts France 56 G4
Dauphin Lake Canada 121 L5
Daurie Creek r. Australia 109 A6
Dausa India 82 D4
Dâu Tiêng, Hô resr Vietnam 71 D5
Dava U.K. 50 F3
Däväçi Azer. 91 H2
Davanagere India see Davangere
Davangere India 84 B3
Davao Phil. 69 H5
Davao Gulf Phil. 69 H5
Dāvarī Iran 88 E5
Dāvarzan Iran 88 E2
Davel S. Africa 101 I4
Davenport IA U.S.A. 130 F3
Davenport WA U.S.A. 126 D3
Davenport Downs Australia 110 C5
Davenport Range hills Australia 108 F5
Daventry U.K. 49 F6
Daveyton S. Africa 101 I4
David Panama 137 H7
David City U.S.A. 130 D3
Davidson Canada 121 J5
Davidson, Mount hill Australia 108 E5
Davis research station Antarctica 152 E2
Davis r. Australia 108 C5
Davis i. Myanmar see Than Kyun
Davis CA U.S.A. 128 C2
Davis WV U.S.A. 134 F4
Davis, Mount hill U.S.A. 134 F4
Davis Bay Antarctica 152 G2
Davis Dam U.S.A. 129 F4
Davis Inlet (abandoned) Canada 123 J3
Davis Sea Antarctica 152 F2
Davis Strait Canada/Greenland 119 M3
Davlekanovo Rus. Fed. 41 Q5
Davos Switz. 56 I3
Davy Lake Canada 121 I3
Dawa Co l. China 83 F3
Dawa Wenz r. Eth. 98 E3
Dawaxung China 83 F3
Dawê China 76 D2
Dawei Myanmar see Tavoy
Dawei r. mouth Myanmar see Tavoy
Dawera i. Indon. 108 E1
Dawna Range mts Myanmar/Thai. 70 B3
Dawna Taungdan mts Myanmar/Thai. see Dawna Range
Dawo China see Maqên
Dawqah Oman 87 H6
Dawson r. Australia 110 E4
Dawson Canada 120 B1
Dawson GA U.S.A. 133 C6
Dawson ND U.S.A. 130 D2
Dawson, Mount Canada 120 G5
Dawson Bay Canada 121 K4
Dawson Creek Canada 120 F4
Dawson Inlet Canada 121 M2
Dawson Range mts Canada 120 A2
Dawsons Landing Canada 120 E5
Dawu Hubei China 77 G2
Dawu Qinghai China see Maqên
Dawu Taiwan see Tawu
Dawukou China see Shizuishan
Dawu Shan hill China 77 G2
Dax France 56 D5
Daxian China see Dazhou
Daxiang Ling mts China 76 D2
Daxin China 76 E4
Daxing Yunnan China see Ninglang
Daxing Yunnan China see Lüchun
Daxing'an Ling mts China see Da Hinggan Ling
Da Xueshan mts China 76 D2
Dayan China see Lijiang
Dayangshu China 74 B2
Dayao China 76 D3
Dayao Shan mts China 77 F4
Daye China 77 G2
Daying China 76 E2
Daying Jiang r. China 76 C3
Dayishan China see Guanyun
Dāykundī Afgh. 89 G3
Daylesford Australia 112 B6
Daylight Pass U.S.A. 128 E3
Dayong China see Zhangjiajie
Dayr Abū Sa'īd Jordan 85 B3
Dayr az Zawr Syria 91 F4
Dayr Ḩāfir Syria 85 C1
Daysland Canada 121 H4
Dayton OH U.S.A. 134 C4
Dayton TN U.S.A. 132 C5
Dayton VA U.S.A. 135 F4
Dayton WA U.S.A. 126 D3
Daytona Beach U.S.A. 133 D6
Dayu Ling mts China 77 G3
Da Yunhe canal China 77 H1
Dayyer Iran 88 C5
Dayyīna i. U.A.E. 88 D5
Dazhongji China see Dafeng
Dazhou China 76 E2
Dazhou Dao i. China 77 F5
Dazhu China 76 E2
Dazu China 76 E2
Dazu Rock Carvings tourist site China 76 E2
De Aar S. Africa 100 G6
Dead r. Ireland 51 D5
Deadman Lake U.S.A. 128 E4
Deadman's Cay Bahamas 133 F8

Dixon IL U.S.A. 130 F3
Dixon KY U.S.A. 134 B5
Dixon MT U.S.A. 126 E3
Dixon Entrance sea chan. Canada/U.S.A. 120 C4
Dixonville Canada 120 G3
Dixville Canada 135 J1
Diyadin Turkey 91 F3
Diyarbakır Turkey 91 F3
Diz Pak. 89 F5
Diz Chah Iran 88 D3
Dize Turkey see Yüksekova
Dizney U.S.A. 134 D5
Djado Niger 96 E2
Djado, Plateau du Niger 96 E2
Djaja, Puntjak mt. Indon. see Jaya, Puncak
Djakarta Indon. see Jakarta
Djakovica Kosovo see Gjakovë
Djakovo Croatia see Đakovo
Djambala Congo 98 B4
Djanet Alg. 96 D2
Djarrit-Uliga-Dalap Marshall Is see Delap-Uliga-Djarrit
Djelfa Alg. 57 H6
Djéma Cent. Afr. Rep. 98 C3
Djenné Mali 96 C3
Djerdap nat. park Serbia 59 J2
Djibo Burkina 96 C3
Djibouti country Africa 86 F7

▶Djibouti Djibouti 86 F7
Capital of Djibouti.

Djidjelli Alg. see Jijel
Djizak Uzbek. see Jizzax
Djougou Benin 96 D4
Djoum Cameroon 96 E4
Djourab, Erg du des. Chad 97 E3
Djúpivogur Iceland 44 [inset]
Djurås Sweden 45 I6
Djurdjura, Parc National du Alg. 57 I5
Dmitriya Lapteva, Proliv sea chan. Rus. Fed. 65 P2
Dmitriyev-L'govskiy Rus. Fed. 43 G5
Dmitriyevsk Ukr. see Makiyivka
Dmitrov Rus. Fed. 42 H4
Dmytriyevs'k Ukr. see Makiyivka
Dnepr r. Europe 43 F5 see Dnieper
Dneprodzerzhinsk Ukr. see Dniprodzerzhyns'k
Dnepropetrovsk Ukr. see Dnipropetrovs'k

▶Dnieper r. Europe 43 G7
3rd longest river in Europe. Also spelt Dnepr (Rus. Fed.) or Dnipro (Ukraine) or Dnyapro (Belarus).

Dniester r. Ukr. 43 F6
also spelt Dnister (Ukraine) or Nistru (Moldova)
Dnipro r. Europe 43 G7 see Dnieper
Dniprodzerzhyns'k Ukr. 43 G6
Dnipropetrovs'k Ukr. 43 G6
Dnister r. Ukr. 43 F6 see Dniester
Dno Rus. Fed. 42 F4
Dnyapro r. Europe 43 F6 see Dnieper
Doāb Afgh. 89 G3
Doaba Pak. 89 H3
Doan Hung Vietnam 70 D2
Doba Chad 97 E4
Doba China see Toiba
Dobele Latvia 45 M8
Döbeln Germany 53 N3
Doberai, Jazirah pen. Indon. 69 I7
Doberai Peninsula Indon. see Doberai, Jazirah
Dobo Indon. 69 I8
Doboj Bos.-Herz. 58 H2
Do Borjī Iran 88 D4
Döbraberg hill Germany 53 L4
Dobrich Bulg. 59 L3
Dobrinka Rus. Fed. 43 I5
Dobroye Rus. Fed. 43 H5
Dobrudja reg. Romania see Dobruja
Dobruja reg. Romania 59 L3
Dobrush Belarus 43 F5
Dobryanka Rus. Fed. 41 R4
Dobzha China 83 G3
Doce r. Brazil 145 D2
Dochart r. U.K. 50 E4
Do China Qala Afgh. 89 H4
Docking U.K. 49 H6
Doctor Hicks Range hills Australia 109 D7
Doctor Pedro P. Peña Para. 144 D2
Doda India 82 C2
Doda Betta mt. India 84 C4
Dod Ballapur India 84 C3
Dodecanese is Greece 59 L7
Dodekanisa is Greece see Dodecanese
Dodekanisos is Greece see Dodecanese
Dodge City U.S.A. 130 C4
Dodgeville U.S.A. 130 F3
Dodman Point U.K. 49 C8

▶Dodoma Tanz. 99 D4
Capital of Tanzania.

Dodsonville U.S.A. 134 D4
Doetinchem Neth. 52 G3
Dog r. Canada 122 C4
Dogai Coring salt l. China 83 G2
Dogaicoring Qangco salt l. China 83 G2
Doğanşehir Turkey 90 E3
Dogên Co l. Xizang China 83 G3
Dogên Co l. Xizang China see Bam Tso
Doghārūn Iran 89 F3
Dog Island Canada 123 J2
Dog Lake Man. Canada 121 L5
Dog Lake Ont. Canada 122 C4
Dog Lake Ont. Canada 122 D4
Dōgo i. Japan 75 D5
Dogondoutchi Niger 96 D3
Dog Rocks is Bahamas 133 E7
Doğubeyazıt Turkey 91 G3
Doğu Menteşe Dağları mts Turkey 59 M6
Dogxung Zangbo r. China 83 F3
Do'gyaling China 83 G3

▶Doha Qatar 88 C5
Capital of Qatar.

Dohad India see Dahod
Dohazari Bangl. 83 H5
Dohrighat India 83 E4
Doi i. Fiji 107 I4
Doi Inthanon National Park Thai. 70 B3
Doi Luang National Park Thai. 70 B3
Doire U.K. see Londonderry
Doi Saket Thai. 70 B3
Dois Irmãos, Serra dos hills Brazil 143 J5
Dokan, Sadd Iraq 91 G4
Dok-do i. Asia see Liancourt Rocks
Dokhara, Dunes de des. Alg. 54 F5
Dokka Norway 45 G6
Dokkum Neth. 52 F1
Dokog He r. China 76 D2
Dokri Pak. 89 H5
Dokshukino Rus. Fed. see Nartkala
Dokshytsy Belarus 45 O9
Dokuchayeva, Mys c. Rus. Fed. 74 G3
Dokuchayevka Kazakh. see Karamendy
Dokuchayevs'k Ukr. 43 H7
Dolbeau-Mistassini Canada 123 G4
Dolbenmaen U.K. 49 C6
Dol-de-Bretagne France 56 D2
Dole France 56 G3
Dolgellau U.K. 49 D6
Dolgen Germany 53 N1
Dolgiy, Ostrov i. Rus. Fed. 42 L1
Dolgorukovo Rus. Fed. 43 H5
Dolina Ukr. see Dolyna
Dolinsk Rus. Fed. 74 F3
Dolisie Congo see Loubomo
Dolleman Island Antarctica 152 L2
Dollnstein Germany 53 L6
Dolok, Pulau i. Indon. 69 J8
Dolomites mts Italy 58 D2
Dolomiti mts Italy see Dolomites
Dolomiti Bellunesi, Parco Nazionale delle nat. park Italy 58 D1
Dolomitiche, Alpi mts Italy see Dolomites
Dolonnur China 73 L4
Dolo Odo Eth. 98 E3
Dolores Arg. 144 E5
Dolores Uruguay 144 E4
Dolores U.S.A. 129 I3
Dolphin and Union Strait Canada 118 G3
Dolphin Head hd Namibia 100 B3
Đô Lương Vietnam 70 D3
Dolyna Ukr. 43 D6
Domaila India 82 D3
Domaniç Turkey 59 M5
Domar China 80 F5
Domartang China 76 B2
Domažlice Czech Rep. 53 M5
Domba China 76 B1
Dom Bākh Iran 88 B3
Dombås Norway 44 F5
Dombóvár Hungary 58 H1
Dombrau Poland see Dąbrowa Górnicza
Dombrovitsa Ukr. see Dubrovytsya
Dombrowa Poland see Dąbrowa Górnicza
Domda China see Qingshuihe
Dome Argus ice feature Antarctica 152 E1
Dome Charlie ice feature Antarctica 152 F2
Dome Creek Canada 120 F4
Dome Rock Mountains U.S.A. 129 F5
Domeyko Chile 144 B3
Domfront France 56 D2
Dominica country West Indies 137 L5
Dominicana, República country West Indies see Dominican Republic
Dominican Republic country West Indies 137 J5
Dominion, Cape Canada 119 K3
Dominique i. Fr. Polynesia see Hiva Oa
Dömitz Germany 53 L1
Dom Joaquim Brazil 145 C2
Dommel r. Neth. 52 F3
Domo Eth. 98 E3
Domokos Greece 59 J5
Dompu Indon. 108 B2
Domula China see Duomula
Domuyo, Volcán vol. Arg. 144 B5
Domville, Mount hill Australia 112 E2
Don Mex. 127 F8

▶Don r. Rus. Fed. 43 H7
5th longest river in Europe.

Don r. U.K. 50 G3
Don, Xé r. Laos 70 D4
Donaghadee U.K. 51 G3
Donaghmore U.K. 51 F3
Donald Australia 112 A6
Donaldsonville U.S.A. 131 F6
Donalsonville U.S.A. 133 C6
Doñana, Parque Nacional de nat. park Spain 57 C5
Donau r. Europe 47 P6 see Danube
Donauwörth Germany 53 K6
Don Benito Spain 57 D4
Doncaster U.K. 48 F5
Dondo Angola 99 B4
Dondo Moz. 99 D5
Dondra Head hd Sri Lanka 84 D5
Donegal Ireland 51 D3
Donegal Bay Ireland 51 D3
Donets'k Ukr. 43 H7
Donetsko-Amrovsiyevka Ukr. see Amvrosiyivka
Donets'kyy Kryazh hills Rus. Fed./Ukr. 43 H6
Donga r. Cameroon/Nigeria 96 D4
Dong'an China 77 F3
Dongane, Lagoa lag. Moz. 101 L3
Dongara Australia 109 A7
Dongbo China see Mêdog
Dongchuan Yunnan China 76 D3
Dongchuan Yunnan China see Yao'an
Dongco China 83 F2
Dong Co l. China 83 F2
Dongfang China 77 F5
Dongfanghong China 74 D3
Donggang China 75 B5
Donggang Shandong China 77 H1
Donggi Conag l. China 76 C1
Donggou China see Donggang
Donggu China 77 G3
Dongguan China 77 G4
Dong Hai sea N. Pacific Ocean see East China Sea
Đông Hơi Vietnam 70 D3
Donghuang China see Xishui
Dongjiang Shuiku resr China 77 G3
Dongjug China 76 B2
Dongkou China 77 F3
Donglan China 76 E3
Dongliao He r. China 74 A4
Dongmen China see Luocheng
Dongminzhutun China 74 A3
Dongning China 74 C3
Dongo Angola 99 B5
Dongo Dem. Rep. Congo 98 B3
Dongola Sudan 86 D6
Dongou Congo 98 B3
Dong Phraya Yen esc. Thai. 70 C4
Dongping Guangdong China 77 G4
Dongping Hunan China see Anhua
Dongpo China see Meishan
Dongqiao China 83 G3
Dongshan Fujian China 77 H4
Dongshan Jiangsu China 77 I2
Dongshan Jiangxi China see Shangyou
Dongshao China 77 G3
Dongsha Qundao is China 68 F2
Dongsheng Nei Mongol China see Ordos
Dongsheng Sichuan China see Shuangliu
Dongshuan China see Tangdan
Dongtai China 77 I1
Dongting Hu l. China 77 G2
Dongtou China 77 I3
Đông Triều Vietnam 70 D2
Dong Ujimqin Qi China see Uliastai
Đông Văn Vietnam 70 D2
Dongxiang China 77 H2
Dongxi Liandao i. China 77 H1
Dongxing Guangxi China 76 E4
Dongxing Heilong. China 74 B3
Dongyang China 77 I2
Dongying China 73 L5
Dongzhi China 77 H2
Donkerbroek Neth. 52 G1
Donnacona Canada 123 H5
Donnellys Crossing N.Z. 113 D2
Donner Pass U.S.A. 128 C2
Donnersberg hill Germany 53 H5
Donostia-San Sebastián Spain 57 F2
Donousa i. Greece 59 K6
Donoussa i. Greece see Donousa
Donskoye Rus. Fed. 43 I7
Donyztau, Sor dry lake Kazakh. 80 A2
Dooagh Ireland 51 B4
Doomadgee Australia 110 B3
Doon r. U.K. 50 E5
Doon, Loch l. U.K. 50 E5
Doonbeg r. Ireland 51 C5
Doorn Neth. 52 F2
Door Peninsula U.S.A. 134 B1
Doorwerth Neth. 52 F3
Dooxo Nugaaleed valley Somalia 98 E3
Doqêmo China 76 B2
Dor watercourse Afgh. 89 F4
Dor Israel 85 B3
Dora U.S.A. 131 C5
Dora, Lake salt flat Australia 108 C5
Dorado Mex. 131 B7
Dorah Pass Pak. 89 H2
Doran Lake Canada 121 I2
Dorbiljin China see Emin
Dorbod China see Taikang
Dorbod Qi China see Ulan Hua
Dorchester U.K. 49 E8
Dordabis Namibia 100 C2
Dordogne r. France 56 D4
Dordrecht Neth. 52 E3
Dordrecht S. Africa 101 H6
Doreenville Namibia 100 D2
Doré Lake Canada 121 J4
Doré Lake l. Canada 121 J4
Dores do Indaiá Brazil 145 B2
Dorgê Co l. China 83 H2
Dori r. Afgh. 89 G4
Dori Burkina 96 C3
Doring r. S. Africa 100 D6
Dorisvale Australia 108 E3
Dorking U.K. 49 G7
Dormagen Germany 52 G3
Dormans France 52 D5
Dormidontovka Rus. Fed. 74 D3
Dornoch U.K. 50 E3
Dornoch Firth est. U.K. 50 E3
Dornum Germany 53 H1
Doro Mali 96 C3
Dorogobuzh Rus. Fed. 43 G5
Dorogorskoye Rus. Fed. 42 J2
Dorohoi Romania 43 E7
Döröö Nuur salt l. Mongolia 80 H2
Dorostol Bulg. see Silistra
Dorotea Sweden 44 J4
Dorpat Estonia see Tartu
Dorre Island Australia 109 A6
Dorrigo Australia 112 F3
Dorris U.S.A. 126 C4
Dorset Canada 135 F1
Dorsoidong Co l. China 83 G2
Dortmund Germany 53 H3
Dörtyol Turkey 85 C1
Dorum Germany 53 I1
Doruma Dem. Rep. Congo 98 C3
Dorüneh, Küh-e mts Iran 88 E3
Dörverden Germany 53 J2
Dorylaeum Turkey see Eskişehir
Dos Bahías, Cabo c. Arg. 144 C6
Dos de Mayo Peru 142 C5
Doshakh, Koh-i- mt. Afgh. see Do Shākh, Kūh-e
Do Shākh, Kūh-e mt. Afgh. 89 F3
Đo Sơn Vietnam 70 D2
Dos Palos U.S.A. 128 C3
Dosse r. Germany 53 M2
Dosso Niger 96 D3
Dothan U.S.A. 133 C6
Dotsero U.S.A. 129 J2
Douai France 52 D4
Douala Cameroon 96 D4
Douarnenez France 56 B2
Double Headed Shot Cays is Bahamas 133 D8
Double Island H.K. China 77 [inset]
Double Island Point Australia 111 F5
Double Mountain Fork r. U.S.A. 131 C5
Double Peak U.S.A. 128 D4
Double Point Australia 110 D3
Double Springs U.S.A. 133 C5
Doubs r. France/Switz. 56 G3
Doubtful Sound inlet N.Z. 113 A7
Doubtless Bay N.Z. 113 D2
Douentza Mali 96 C3
Dougga tourist site Tunisia 58 C6

▶Douglas Isle of Man 48 C4
Capital of the Isle of Man.

Douglas S. Africa 100 F5
Douglas U.K. 50 F5
Douglas AZ U.S.A. 127 F7
Douglas GA U.S.A. 133 D6
Douglas WY U.S.A. 126 G4
Douglas Reef i. Japan see Okino-Tori-shima
Douglasville U.S.A. 133 C5
Douhudi China see Gong'an
Doulatpur Bangl. see Daulatpur
Douliu Taiwan see Touliu
Doullens France 52 C4
Douna Mali 96 C3
Doune U.K. 50 E4
Doupovské hory mts Czech Rep. 53 N4
Dourada, Serra hills Brazil 145 A2
Dourada, Serra mts Brazil 145 A1
Dourados Brazil 144 F2
Douro r. Port. 57 B3
also known as Duero (Spain)
Doushi China see Gong'an
Doushui Shuiku resr China 77 G3
Douve r. France 49 F9
Douzy France 52 F5
Dove r. U.K. 49 F6
Dove Brook Canada 123 K3
Dove Creek U.S.A. 129 I3
Dover U.K. 49 I7

▶Dover DE U.S.A. 135 H4
Capital of Delaware.

Dover NH U.S.A. 135 J2
Dover NJ U.S.A. 135 H3
Dover OH U.S.A. 134 E3
Dover TN U.S.A. 132 C4
Dover, Strait of France/U.K. 56 E1
Dover-Foxcroft U.S.A. 135 K1
Dovey r. U.K. 49 D6
Dovrefjell Nasjonalpark nat. park Norway 44 F5
Dowagiac U.S.A. 134 B3
Dowi, Tanjung pt Indon. 71 B7
Dowlaiswaram India 84 D2
Dowlatābād Afgh. 89 F3
Dowlatābād Fārs Iran 88 C4
Dowlatābād Fārs Iran 88 D4
Dowlatābād Khorāsān Iran 88 E2
Dowlatābād Khorāsān Iran 89 F2
Dowl at Yār Afgh. 89 G3
Downieville U.S.A. 128 C2
Downpatrick U.K. 51 G3
Downsville U.S.A. 135 H2
Dow Rūd Iran 88 C3
Doyle U.S.A. 128 C1
Doylestown U.S.A. 135 H3
Dozdān r. Iran 88 E5
Dōzen is Japan 75 D5
Dozois, Réservoir resr Canada 122 F5
Dozulé France 49 G9
Drâa, Hamada du plat. Alg. 54 C6
Dracena Brazil 145 A3
Drachten Neth. 52 G1
Drăgănești-Olt Romania 59 K2
Drăgășani Romania 59 K2
Dragonera, Isla i. Spain see Sa Dragonera
Dragoon U.S.A. 129 H5
Dragsfjärd Fin. 45 M6
Draguignan France 56 H5
Drahichyn Belarus 45 N10
Drake Australia 112 F2
Drake U.S.A. 130 C2
Drakensberg mts S. Africa 101 I3
Drake Passage S. Atlantic Ocean 148 D9
Drakes Bay U.S.A. 128 B3
Drama Greece 59 K4
Drammen Norway 45 G7
Drang, Prêk r. Cambodia 71 D4
Drangedal Norway 45 F7
Dransfeld Germany 53 J3
Draper, Mount U.S.A. 120 B3
Draperstown U.K. 51 F3
Drapsaca Afgh. see Kunduz
Dras India 82 C2
Drasan Pak. 89 I2
Drau r. Europe 47 O7 see Drava
Drava r. Europe 58 H2
also known as Drau (Austria), Drave or Drava (Slovenia and Croatia), Dráva (Hungary)
Dráva r. Europe see Drava
Drave r. Europe see Drava
Drayton Valley Canada 120 H4
Drazinda Pak. 89 H4
Dréan Alg. 58 B6
Dreistelzberge hill Germany 53 J4
Drentse Hoofdvaart canal Neth. 52 G2
Drepano, Akra pt Greece see Laimos, Akrotirio
Dresden Canada 134 D2
Dresden Germany 47 N5
Dreux France 52 B6
Drevsjø Norway 45 H6
Drewryville U.S.A. 135 G5
Dri China 76 C2
Driffield U.K. 48 G4
Driftwood U.S.A. 135 F3
Driggs U.S.A. 126 F4
Drillham Australia 112 E1
Drimoleague Ireland 51 C6
Drina r. Bosnia-Herzegovina/Serbia 59 H2
Driscoll Island Antarctica 152 J1
Drissa Belarus see Vyerkhnyadzvinsk
Drniš Croatia 58 G3
Drobeta-Turnu Severin Romania 59 J2
Drochtersen Germany 53 J1
Drogheda Ireland 51 F4
Drogichin Belarus see Drahichyn
Drogobych Ukr. see Drohobych
Drohobych Ukr. 43 D6
Droichead Átha Ireland see Drogheda
Droichead Nua Ireland see Newbridge
Droitwich U.K. see Droitwich Spa
Droitwich Spa U.K. 49 E6
Dromedary, Cape Australia 112 E6
Dromod Ireland 51 E4
Dromore Northern Ireland U.K. 51 E3
Dromore Northern Ireland U.K. 51 F3
Dronfield U.K. 48 F5
Dronning Louise Land reg. Greenland 153 I1
Dronning Maud Land reg. Antarctica see Queen Maud Land
Dronten Neth. 52 F2
Druk-Yul country Asia see Bhutan
Drumheller Canada 121 H5
Drummond atoll Kiribati see Tabiteuea
Drummond U.S.A. 126 E3
Drummond, Lake U.S.A. 135 G5
Drummond Island Kiribati see McKean
Drummond Range hills Australia 110 D5
Drummondville Canada 123 G5
Drummore U.K. 50 E6
Drury Lake Canada 120 C2
Druskieniki Lith. see Druskininkai
Druskininkai Lith. 45 N10
Druzhina Rus. Fed. 65 P3
Druzhnaya Gorka Rus. Fed. 45 Q7
Dry r. Australia 108 F3
Dryanovo Bulg. 59 K3
Dryberry Lake Canada 121 M5
Dryden Canada 121 M5
Dryden U.S.A. 135 G2
Dry Fork r. U.S.A. 126 G4
Drygalski Ice Tongue Antarctica 152 H1
Drygalski Island Antarctica 152 F2
Dry Lake U.S.A. 129 F3
Dry Lake l. U.S.A. 130 D1
Drymen U.K. 50 E4
Dry Ridge U.S.A. 134 C4
Drysdale r. Australia 108 D3
Drysdale River National Park Australia 108 D3
Dry Tortugas is U.S.A. 133 D7
Du'an China 77 F4
Duaringa Australia 110 E4
Duarte, Pico mt. Dom. Rep. 137 J5
Duartina Brazil 145 A3
Ḍubā Saudi Arabia 86 E4
Dubai U.A.E. 88 D5
Dubakella Mountain U.S.A. 128 B1
Dubawnt r. Canada 121 L2
Dubawnt Lake Canada 121 K2
Dubayy U.A.E. see Dubai
Dubbo Australia 112 D4

▶Dublin Ireland 51 F4
Capital of Ireland.

Dublin U.S.A. 133 D5
Dubna Rus. Fed. 42 H4
Dubno Ukr. 43 E6
Dubois ID U.S.A. 126 E3
Dubois IN U.S.A. 134 B4
Du Bois U.S.A. 135 F3
Dubovka Rus. Fed. 43 J6
Dubovskoye Rus. Fed. 43 I7
Dubréka Guinea 96 B4
Dubris U.K. see Dover
Dubrovnik Croatia 58 H3
Dubrovytsya Ukr. 43 E6
Dubuque U.S.A. 130 F3
Dubysa r. Lith. 45 M9
Đức Bôn Vietnam 71 D5
Duc de Gloucester, Îles du is Fr. Polynesia 151 K7
Duchang China 77 H2
Ducheng China see Yunan
Duchesne U.S.A. 129 H1
Duchesne r. U.S.A. 129 I1
Duchess Australia 110 B4
Duchess Canada 121 I5
Ducie Island atoll Pitcairn Is 151 L7
Duck Bay Canada 121 K4
Duck Creek r. Australia 108 B5
Duck Lake Canada 121 J4
Duckwater Peak U.S.A. 129 F2
Duc Tho Vietnam 70 D3
Dudelange Lux. 52 G5
Duderstadt Germany 53 K3
Dudhi India 83 E4
Dudhwa India 82 E3
Dudinka Rus. Fed. 64 J3
Dudley U.K. 49 E6
Dudleyville U.S.A. 129 H5
Dudna r. India 84 C2
Dudu India 82 C4
Duékoué Côte d'Ivoire 96 C4
Duen, Bukit vol. Indon. 68 C7
Duero r. Spain 57 C3
also known as Douro (Portugal)
Duffel Belgium 52 E3
Dufferin, Cape Canada 122 F2
Duffer Peak U.S.A. 126 D4
Duff Islands Solomon Is 107 G2
Duffreboy, Lac l. Canada 123 H2
Dufftown U.K. 50 F3
Dufourspitze mt. Italy/Switz. 56 H4
Dufrost, Pointe pt Canada 122 F1
Dugi Otok i. Croatia 58 F2
Dugi Rat Croatia 58 G3
Du He r. China 77 F1
Duida-Marahuaca, Parque Nacional nat. park Venez. 142 E3
Duisburg Germany 52 G3
Duiwelskloof S. Africa 101 J2
Dujiangyan China 76 D2
Dukathole S. Africa 101 H6
Duke Island U.S.A. 120 D4
Duke of Clarence atoll Tokelau see Nukunonu
Duke of Gloucester Islands Fr. Polynesia see Duc de Gloucester, Îles du
Duke of York atoll Tokelau see Atafu
Duk Fadiat Sudan 97 G4
Dukhovnitskoye Rus. Fed. 43 K5
Duki Pak. 89 H4
Duki Rus. Fed. 74 D2
Duki r. Rus. Fed. 74 D2
Dukou China see Panzhihua
Dūkštas Lith. 45 O9
Dulac U.S.A. 131 F6
Dulan China 80 I4
Dulce r. Arg. 144 D4
Dulce U.S.A. 127 G5
Dul'durga Rus. Fed. 73 K2
Dulhunty r. Australia 110 C1
Dulishi Hu salt l. China 83 E2
Duliu Jiang r. China 77 F3
Dullewala Pak. 89 H4
Dullstroom S. Africa 101 J3
Dülmen Germany 53 H3
Dulmera India 82 C3
Dulovo Bulg. 59 L3
Duluth U.S.A. 130 E2
Dulverton U.K. 49 D7
Dūmā Syria 85 C3
Dumaguete Phil. 69 G5
Dumai Indon. 71 C7
Dumaran i. Phil. 68 G4
Dumaresq r. Australia 112 E2
Dumas U.S.A. 131 C5
Dumat al Jandal Saudi Arabia 91 E5
Ḍumayr Syria 85 C3
Ḍumayr, Jabal mts Syria 85 C3
Dumbakh Iran see Dom Bākh
Dumbarton U.K. 50 E5
Dumbe S. Africa 101 J4
Ďumbier mt. Slovakia 47 Q6
Dumchele India 82 D2
Dumdum i. Indon. 71 D7
Dum Duma India 83 H4
Dumfries U.K. 50 F5
Dumka India 83 F4
Dumont d'Urville research station Antarctica 152 G2
Dumont d'Urville Sea Antarctica 152 G2
Dümpelfeld Germany 52 G4
Dumyāṭ Egypt 90 C5
Dumyâț Egypt see Dumyāṭ
Duna r. Europe 58 H2 see Danube
Dünaburg Latvia see Daugavpils
Dunaj r. Europe see Danube
Dunajská Streda Slovakia 47 P7
Dunakeszi Hungary 59 H1
Dunany Point Ireland 51 F4
Dunărea r. Europe 59 L2 see Danube
Dunării, Delta Romania/Ukr. see Danube Delta
Dunaújváros Hungary 58 H1
Dunav r. Europe 58 L2 see Danube
Dunay r. Europe see Danube
Dunayivtsi Ukr. 43 E6
Dunbar Australia 110 C3
Dunbar U.K. 50 G4
Dunblane U.K. 50 F4
Dunboyne Ireland 51 F4
Duncan Canada 120 F5
Duncan AZ U.S.A. 129 I5
Duncan OK U.S.A. 131 D5
Duncan, Cape Canada 122 E3
Duncan, Lac l. Canada 122 F3
Duncan Lake Canada 120 H2
Duncan Passage India 71 A5
Duncansby Head hd U.K. 50 F2
Duncan Town Bahamas 133 F8
Duncormick Ireland 51 F5
Dundaga Latvia 45 M8
Dundalk Ireland 51 F3
Dundalk U.S.A. 135 G4
Dundalk Bay Ireland 51 F4
Dundas Canada 134 F2
Dundas Greenland 119 L2
Dundas, Lake salt flat Australia 109 C8
Dundas Island Canada 120 D4
Dundas Strait Australia 108 E2
Dún Dealgan Ireland see Dundalk
Dundee S. Africa 101 J5
Dundee U.K. 50 G4
Dundee MI U.S.A. 134 D3
Dundee NY U.S.A. 135 G2
Dundonald U.K. 51 G3
Dundoo Australia 112 B1
Dundrennan U.K. 50 F6
Dundrum U.K. 51 G3
Dundrum Bay U.K. 51 G3
Dundwa Range mts India/Nepal 83 E4
Dune, Lac l. Canada 122 G2
Dunedin N.Z. 113 C7
Dunedin U.S.A. 133 D6
Dunfermline U.K. 50 F4
Dungannon U.K. 51 F3
Dún Garbhán Ireland see Dungarvan
Dungarpur India 82 C5
Dungarvan Ireland 51 E5
Dung Co l. China 83 G3
Dungeness hd U.K. 49 H8
Dungeness, Punta pt Arg. 144 C8
Düngenheim Germany 53 H4
Dungiven U.K. 51 F3
Dungog Australia 112 E4
Dungu Dem. Rep. Congo 98 C3
Dungun Malaysia 71 C6
Dungunab Sudan 86 E5
Dunhua China 74 C4
Dunhuang China 80 H3
Dunkeld Australia 112 D1
Dunkeld U.K. 50 F4
Dunkellin r. Ireland 51 D4
Dunkerque France see Dunkirk
Dunkery Hill hill U.K. 49 D7
Dunkirk France 52 C3
Dunkirk U.S.A. 134 F2
Dún Laoghaire Ireland 51 F4
Dunlap IA U.S.A. 130 E3
Dunlap TN U.S.A. 132 C5
Dunlavin Ireland 51 F4
Dunleer Ireland 51 F4
Dunloy U.K. 51 F2
Dunmanway Ireland 51 C6
Dunmarra Australia 108 F4
Dunmor U.S.A. 134 B5
Dunmore Ireland 51 D4
Dunmore U.S.A. 135 H3
Dunmore Town Bahamas 133 E7
Dunmurry U.K. 51 G3
Dunnet Head hd U.K. 50 F2
Dunnigan U.S.A. 128 C2
Dunning U.S.A. 130 C3
Dunnville Canada 134 F2
Dunnville U.S.A. 134 C5
Dunolly Australia 112 A6
Dunoon U.K. 50 E5
Dunphy U.S.A. 128 E1
Duns U.K. 50 G5
Dunseith U.S.A. 130 C1
Dunstable U.K. 49 G7
Dunstan Mountains N.Z. 113 B7
Dun-sur-Meuse France 52 F5

Duntroon N.Z. 113 C7
Dunvegan Lake Canada 121 J2
Dunyapur Pak. 89 H4
Duolun Nei Mongol China see Dolonnur
Duomula China 83 E2
Dupang Ling mts China 77 F3
Duperré Alg. see Aïn Defla
Dupnitsa Bulg. 59 J3
Dupree U.S.A. 130 C2
Duque de Bragança Angola see Calandula
Dūrā West Bank 85 B4
Durack r. Australia 108 D3
Durack Range hills Australia 108 D4
Dura Europos Syria see Aş Şāliḩīyah
Durağan Turkey 90 D2
Durance r. France 56 G5
Durand U.S.A. 130 F2
Durango Mex. 131 B7
Durango state Mex. 131 B7
Durango Spain 57 E2
Durango U.S.A. 129 J3
Durani reg. Afgh. 89 G4
Durant U.S.A. 131 D5
Durazno Uruguay 144 E4
Durazzo Albania see Durrës
Durban S. Africa 101 J5
Durban-Corbières France 56 F5
Durbanville S. Africa 100 D7
Durbin U.S.A. 134 F4
Durbun Pak. 89 G4
Durbuy Belgium 52 F4
Düren Germany 52 G4
Düren Iran 88 E3
Duren, Kūh-e mt. Iran 88 E3
Durg India 82 E5
Durgapur Bangl. 83 G4
Durgapur India 83 F5
Durham Canada 134 E1
Durham U.K. 48 F4
Durham U.S.A. 132 E5
Durham Downs Australia 111 C5
Duri Indon. 71 C7
Durlas Ireland see Thurles
Durleşti Moldova 59 M1
Durmersheim Germany 53 I6
Durmitor mt. Montenegro 59 H3
Durmitor nat. park Montenegro 58 H3
Durness U.K. 50 E2
Durocortorum France see Reims
Durong South Australia 111 E5
Durostorum Bulg. see Silistra
Durour Island P.N.G. see Aua Island
Durovernum U.K. see Canterbury
Durrës Albania 59 H4
Durrie Australia 110 C5
Durrington U.K. 49 F7
Dursey Island Ireland 51 B6
Dursunbey Turkey 59 M5
Duru China see Wuchuan
Dūruḩ Iran 89 F3
Durukhsi Somalia 98 E3
Durusu Gölü l. Turkey 59 M4
Durūz, Jabal ad mt. Syria 85 C3
D'Urville, Tanjung pt Indon. 69 J7
D'Urville Island N.Z. 113 D5
Durzab Afgh. 89 G3
Duşak Turkm. 89 E2
Dushai Pak. 89 G4
Dushan China 76 E3

▶Dushanbe Tajik. 89 H2
Capital of Tajikistan.

Dushet'i Georgia 91 G2
Dushore U.S.A. 135 G3
Dusse-Alin', Khrebet mts Rus. Fed. 74 D2
Düsseldorf Germany 52 G3
Dusty NM U.S.A. 129 J5
Dusty WA U.S.A. 126 D3
Dutch East Indies country Asia see Indonesia
Dutch Guiana country S. America see Suriname
Dutch Mountain U.S.A. 129 G1
Dutch West Indies terr. West Indies see Netherlands Antilles
Dutlwe Botswana 100 F2
Dutse Nigeria 96 D3
Dutsin-Ma Nigeria 96 D3
Dutton r. Australia 110 C4
Dutton Canada 134 E2
Dutton U.S.A. 126 F3
Dutton, Lake salt flat Australia 111 B6
Dutton, Mount U.S.A. 129 G2
Duval Canada 121 J5
Duvert, Lac l. Canada 123 H2
Duvno Bos.-Herz. see Tomislavgrad
Duwin Iraq 91 G3
Düxanbibazar China 82 E1
Duyun China 76 E3
Duzab Pak. 89 F5
Düzce Turkey 59 N4
Duzdab Iran see Zāhedān
Dvina r. Europe see Zapadnaya Dvina
Dvina r. Rus. Fed. see Severnaya Dvina
Dvinsk Latvia see Daugavpils
Dvinskaya Guba g. Rus. Fed. 42 H2
Dwarka India 82 B5
Dwarsberg S. Africa 101 H3
Dwingelderveld, Nationaal Park nat. park Neth. 52 G2
Dworshak Reservoir U.S.A. 126 E3
Dwyka S. Africa 100 E7
Dyat'kovo Rus. Fed. 43 G5
Dyce U.K. 50 G3
Dyer, Cape Canada 119 L3
Dyer Bay Canada 134 E1
Dyersburg U.S.A. 131 F4
Dyffryn U.K. see Valley
Dyfi r. U.K. see Dovey
Dyfrdwy r. U.K. see Dee
Dyfrdwy r. England/Wales U.K. see Dee
Dyje r. Austria/Czech Rep. 47 P6
Dyke U.K. 50 F3

▶Dykh-Tau, Gora mt. Rus. Fed. 91 F2
2nd highest mountain in Europe.

Dyle r. Belgium 52 E4
Dyleň hill Czech Rep. 53 M5
Dylewska Góra hill Poland 47 Q4
Dymytrov Ukr. 43 H6
Dynevor Downs Australia 112 B2
Dyoki S. Africa 101 I6
Dyrrhachium Albania see Durrës
Dysart Australia 110 E4
Dysselsdorp S. Africa 100 F7
Dyurtyuli Rus. Fed. 41 Q4
Dzamīn Üüd Mongolia 73 K4
Dzanga-Ndoki, Parc National de nat. park Cent. Afr. Rep. 98 B3

▶Dzaoudzi Mayotte 99 E5
Capital of Mayotte.

Dzaudzhikau Rus. Fed. see Vladikavkaz
Dzavhan Mongolia 80 H2
Dzerzhinsk Belarus see Dzyarzhynsk
Dzerzhinsk Rus. Fed. 42 I4
Dzhagdy, Khrebet mts Rus. Fed. 74 C1
Dzhaki-Unakhta Yakbyyana, Khrebet mts Rus. Fed. 74 D2
Dzhalalabad Azer. see Cälilabad
Dzhalal-Abad Kyrg. see Jalal-Abad
Dzhalil' Rus. Fed. 41 Q4
Dzhalinda Rus. Fed. 74 A1
Dzhaltyr Kazakh. see Zhaltyr
Dzhambeyty Kazakh. see Zhympity
Dzhambul Kazakh. see Taraz
Dzhangala Kazakh. 41 Q6
Dzhankoy Ukr. 43 G7
Dzhanybek Kazakh. see Zhanibek
Dzharkent Kazakh. see Zharkent
Dzhava Georgia see Java
Dzhetygara Kazakh. see Zhitikara
Dzhezkazgan Kazakh. see Zhezkazgan
Dzhidinskiy, Khrebet mts Mongolia/Rus. Fed. 80 J1
Dzhirgatal' Tajik. see Jirgatol
Dzhizak Uzbek. see Jizzax
Dzhokhar Ghala Rus. Fed. see Groznyy
Dzhubga Rus. Fed. 90 E1
Dzhugdzhur, Khrebet mts Rus. Fed. 65 O4
Dzhul'fa Azer. see Culfa
Dzhuma Uzbek. see Juma
Dzhungarskiy Alatau, Khrebet mts China/Kazakh. 80 E3
Dzhusaly Kazakh. 80 B2
Działdowo Poland 47 R4
Dzūkija nat. park Lith. 45 N9
Dzungarian Basin China see Junggar Pendi
Dzungarian Gate pass China/Kazakh. 80 F2
Dzüünharaa Mongolia 72 J3
Dzuunmod Mongolia 72 J3
Dzyaniskavichy Belarus 45 O10
Dzyarzhynsk Belarus 45 O10
Dzyatlavichy Belarus 45 O10

E

Eabamet Lake Canada 122 D4
Eads U.S.A. 130 C4
Eagar U.S.A. 129 I4
Eagle r. Canada 123 K3
Eagle AK U.S.A. 118 D3
Eagle CO U.S.A. 126 G5
Eagle Cap mt. U.S.A. 126 D3
Eagle Crags mt. U.S.A. 128 E4
Eagle Creek r. Canada 121 J4
Eagle Lake Canada 121 M5
Eagle Lake CA U.S.A. 128 C1
Eagle Lake ME U.S.A. 132 G2
Eagle Mountain U.S.A. 129 F5
Eagle Mountain hill U.S.A. 130 F2
Eagle Pass U.S.A. 131 C6
Eagle Peak U.S.A. 127 G7
Eagle Plain Canada 118 E3
Eagle River U.S.A. 130 F2
Eagle Rock U.S.A. 134 F5
Eaglesham Canada 120 G4
Eap i. Micronesia see Yap
Ear Falls Canada 121 M5
Earlimart U.S.A. 128 D4
Earl's Seat hill U.K. 50 E4
Earlston U.K. 50 G5
Earn r. U.K. 50 F4
Earn, Loch l. U.K. 50 E4
Earp U.S.A. 129 F4
Earth U.S.A. 131 C5
Easington U.K. 48 H5
Easley U.S.A. 133 D5
East Alligator r. Australia 108 F3
East Antarctica reg. Antarctica 152 F1
East Ararat U.S.A. 135 H3
East Aurora U.S.A. 135 F2
East Bay inlet U.S.A. 133 C6
East Bengal country Asia see Bangladesh
Eastbourne U.K. 49 H8
East Branch Clarion River Reservoir U.S.A. 135 F3
East Caicos i. Turks and Caicos Is 133 G8
East Cape N.Z. 113 G3
East Carbon City U.S.A. 129 H2
East Caroline Basin sea feature N. Pacific Ocean 150 F5
East China Sea N. Pacific Ocean 73 N6
East Coast Bays N.Z. 113 E3
East Dereham England U.K. see Dereham
Eastend Canada 121 I5

▶Easter Island S. Pacific Ocean 151 M7
Part of Chile.

Eastern Cape prov. S. Africa 101 H6
Eastern Desert Egypt 86 D4
Eastern Fields reef Australia 110 D1
Eastern Ghats mts India 84 C4

▶Eastern Island U.S.A. 150 I4
Most northerly point of Oceania.

Eastern Nara canal Pak. 89 H5
Eastern Samoa terr. S. Pacific Ocean see American Samoa
Eastern Sayan Mountains Rus. Fed. see Vostochnyy Sayan
Eastern Taurus plat. Turkey see Güneydoğu Toroslar
Eastern Transvaal prov. S. Africa see Mpumalanga
Easterville Canada 121 L4
Easterwâlde Neth. see Oosterwolde
East Falkland i. Falkland Is 144 E8
East Falmouth U.S.A. 135 J3
East Frisian Islands Germany 47 K4
Eastgate U.S.A. 128 E2
East Greenwich U.S.A. 135 J3
East Grinstead U.K. 49 G7
Easthampton U.S.A. 135 I2
East Hampton U.S.A. 135 I3
East Hartford U.S.A. 135 I3
East Indiaman Ridge sea feature Indian Ocean 149 O7
East Jordan U.S.A. 134 C1
East Kilbride U.K. 50 E5
Eastlake U.S.A. 134 E3
East Lamma Channel H.K. China 77 [inset]
Eastland U.S.A. 131 D5
East Lansing U.S.A. 134 C2
Eastleigh U.K. 49 F8
East Liverpool U.S.A. 134 E3
East London S. Africa 101 H7
East Lynn Lake U.S.A. 134 D4
Eastmain Canada 122 F3
Eastmain r. Canada 122 F3
Eastman U.S.A. 133 D5
East Mariana Basin sea feature N. Pacific Ocean 150 G5
Eastmere Australia 110 D4
East Naples U.S.A. 133 D7
Easton MD U.S.A. 135 G4
Easton PA U.S.A. 135 H3
East Orange U.S.A. 135 H3
East Pacific Rise sea feature N. Pacific Ocean 151 M4
East Pakistan country Asia see Bangladesh
East Palestine U.S.A. 134 E3
East Park Reservoir U.S.A. 128 B2
East Point Canada 123 J5
Eastport U.S.A. 132 H2
East Providence U.S.A. 135 J3
East Range mts U.S.A. 128 E1
East Retford U.K. see Retford
East St Louis U.S.A. 130 F4
East Sea N. Pacific Ocean see Japan, Sea of
East Shoal Lake Canada 121 L5
East Siberian Sea Rus. Fed. 65 P2
East Side Canal r. U.S.A. 128 D4
East Stroudsburg U.S.A. 135 H3
East Tavaputs Plateau U.S.A. 129 I2

▶East Timor country Asia 108 D2
Former Portuguese territory. Gained independence from Indonesia in 2002.

East Toorale Australia 112 B3
East Troy U.S.A. 134 A2
East Verde r. U.S.A. 129 H4
Eastville U.S.A. 135 H5
East-Vlylân Neth. see Oost-Vlieland
East York Canada 134 F2
Eaton U.S.A. 134 C4
Eatonia Canada 121 I5
Eaton Rapids U.S.A. 134 C2
Eatonton U.S.A. 133 D5
Eau Claire U.S.A. 130 F2
Eauripik atoll Micronesia 69 K5
Eauripik Rise-New Guinea Rise sea feature N. Pacific Ocean 150 F5
Eauripypg atoll Micronesia see Eauripik
Ebbw Vale U.K. 49 D7
Ebebiyin Equat. Guinea 96 E4
Ebenerde Namibia 100 C3
Ebensburg U.S.A. 135 F3
Eber Gölü l. Turkey 59 N5
Ebergötzen Germany 53 K3
Eberswalde-Finow Germany 47 N4
Ebetsu Japan 74 F4
Ebian China 76 D2
Ebi Nor salt l. China see Ebinur Hu
Ebinur Hu salt l. China 80 F3
Eboli Italy 58 F4
Ebolowa Cameroon 96 E4
Ebony Namibia 100 B2
Ebre r. Spain see Ebro
Ebro r. Spain 57 G3
Ebstorf Germany 53 K1
Eburacum U.K. see York
Ebusus i. Spain see Ibiza
Ecbatana Iran see Hamadān
Eceabat Turkey 59 L4
Ech Chélif Alg. see Chlef
Echegárate, Puerto pass Spain 57 E2
Echeng China see Ezhou
Echeverria, Pico mt. Mex. 127 E7
Echmiadzin Armenia see Ejmiatsin
Echo U.S.A. 126 D3
Echo Bay N.W.T. Canada 120 G1
Echo Bay Ont. Canada 122 D5
Echo Cliffs U.S.A. 129 H3
Echoing r. Canada 121 M4
Echt Neth. 52 F3
Echternach Lux. 52 G5
Echuca Australia 112 B6
Echzell Germany 53 I4
Écija Spain 57 D5
Eckental Germany 53 L5
Eckernförde Germany 47 L3
Eclipse Sound sea chan. Canada 119 J2
Écrins, Parc National des nat. park France 56 H4
Ecuador country S. America 142 B4
Écueils, Pointe aux pt Canada 122 F2
Ed Eritrea 86 F7
Ed Sweden 45 G7
Edam Neth. 52 F2
Eday i. U.K. 50 G1
Ed Da'ein Sudan 97 F3
Ed Damazin Sudan 86 D7
Ed Damer Sudan 86 D6
Ed Debba Sudan 86 D6
Eddies Cove Canada 123 K4
Ed Dueim Sudan 86 D7
Eddystone Point Australia 111 [inset]
Eddyville U.S.A. 131 F4
Ede Neth. 52 F2
Edéa Cameroon 96 E4
Edehon Lake Canada 121 L2
Edéia Brazil 145 A2
Eden Australia 112 D6
Eden r. U.K. 48 D4
Eden NC U.S.A. 134 F5
Eden TX U.S.A. 131 D6
Edenburg S. Africa 101 G5
Edendale N.Z. 113 B8
Edenderry Ireland 51 E4
Edenton U.S.A. 132 E4
Edenville S. Africa 101 H4
Eder r. Germany 53 J3
Eder-Stausee resr Germany 53 I3
Edessa Greece 59 J4
Edessa Turkey see Şanlıurfa
Edewecht Germany 53 H1
Edfu Egypt see Idfū
Edgar Ranges hills Australia 108 C4
Edgartown U.S.A. 135 J3
Edgecumbe Island Solomon Is see Utupua
Edgefield U.S.A. 133 D5
Edge Island Svalbard see Edgeøya
Edgemont U.S.A. 130 C3
Edgeøya i. Svalbard 64 D2
Edgerton Canada 121 I4
Edgerton U.S.A. 134 C3
Edgeworthstown Ireland 51 E4
Edina U.S.A. 130 E3
Edinboro U.S.A. 134 E3
Edinburg TX U.S.A. 131 D7
Edinburg VA U.S.A. 135 F4

▶Edinburgh U.K. 50 F5
Capital of Scotland.

Edirne Turkey 59 L4
Edith, Mount U.S.A. 126 F3
Edith Cavell, Mount Canada 120 G4
Edith Ronne Land ice feature Antarctica see Ronne Ice Shelf
Edjeleh Libya 96 D2
Edjudina Australia 109 C7
Edku Egypt see Idkū
Edmond U.S.A. 131 D5
Edmonds U.S.A. 126 C3

▶Edmonton Canada 120 H4
Capital of Alberta.

Edmonton U.S.A. 134 C5
Edmore MI U.S.A. 134 C2
Edmore ND U.S.A. 130 D1
Edmund Lake Canada 121 M4
Edmundston Canada 123 H5
Edna U.S.A. 131 D6
Edna Bay U.S.A. 120 C4
Edo Japan see Tōkyō
Edom reg. Israel/Jordan 85 B4
Édouard, Lac l. Dem. Rep. Congo/Uganda see Edward, Lake
Edremit Turkey 59 L5
Edremit Körfezi b. Turkey 59 L5
Edrengiyn Nuruu mts Mongolia 80 I3
Edsbyn Sweden 45 I6
Edson Canada 120 G4
Eduni, Mount Canada 120 D1
Edward r. N.S.W. Australia 112 B5
Edward r. Qld Australia 110 C2
Edward, Lake Dem. Rep. Congo/Uganda 98 C4
Edward, Mount Antarctica 152 L1
Edwardesabad Pak. see Bannu
Edwards U.S.A. 135 H1
Edward's Creek Australia 111 A6
Edwards Plateau U.S.A. 131 C6
Edwardsville U.S.A. 130 F4
Edward VII Peninsula Antarctica 152 I1
Edziza, Mount Canada 120 D3
Edzo Canada see Behchokô
Eeklo Belgium 52 D3
Eel r. U.S.A. 128 A1
Eel, South Fork r. U.S.A. 128 B1
Eem r. Neth. 52 F2
Eemshaven pt Neth. 52 G1
Eenrum Neth. 52 G1
Eenzamheid Pan salt pan S. Africa 100 E4
Eesti country Europe see Estonia
Éfaté i. Vanuatu 107 G3
Effingham U.S.A. 130 F4
Efsus Turkey see Afşin
Egadi, Isole is Sicily Italy 58 D5
Egan Range mts U.S.A. 129 F2
Eganville Canada 135 G1
Egedesminde Greenland see Aasiaat
Eger r. Germany 53 M4
Eger Hungary 47 R7
Egersund Norway 45 E7
Egerton, Mount hill Australia 109 B6
Eggegebirge hills Germany 53 I3
Egg Lake Canada 121 J4
Eggolsheim Germany 53 L5
Eghezée Belgium 52 E4
Egilsstaðir Iceland 44 [inset]
Eğin Turkey see Kemaliye
Eğirdir Turkey 59 N6
Eğirdir Gölü l. Turkey 59 N6
Eglinton U.K. 51 E2
Egmond aan Zee Neth. 52 E2
Egmont, Cape N.Z. 113 D4
Egmont, Mount vol. N.Z. see Taranaki, Mount
Egmont National Park N.Z. 113 E4
eGoli S. Africa see Johannesburg
Eğrigöz Dağı mts Turkey 59 M5
Egton U.K. 48 G4
Éguas r. Brazil 145 B1
Egvekinot Rus. Fed. 65 T3

▶Egypt country Africa 86 C4
3rd most populous country in Africa.

Ehden Lebanon 85 B2
Ehen Hudag China 72 I5
Ehingen (Donau) Germany 47 L6
Ehle r. Germany 53 L2
Ehra-Lessien Germany 53 K2
Ehrenberg U.S.A. 129 F5
Ehrenberg Range hills Australia 109 E5
Eibelstadt Germany 53 K5
Eibergen Neth. 52 G2
Eichenzell Germany 53 J4
Eichstätt Germany 53 L6
Eidfjord Norway 45 E6
Eidsvold Australia 110 E5
Eidsvoll Norway 45 G6
Eifel hills Germany 52 G4
Eigg i. U.K. 50 C4
Eight Degree Channel India/Maldives 84 B5
Eights Coast Antarctica 152 K2
Eighty Mile Beach Australia 108 C4
Eilat Israel 85 B5
Eildon Australia 112 B6
Eildon, Lake Australia 112 C6
Eileen Lake Canada 121 J2
Eilenburg Germany 53 M3
Eil Malk i. Palau 69 I5
Eimke Germany 53 K2
Einasleigh Australia 110 D3
Einasleigh r. Australia 110 C3
Einbeck Germany 53 J3
Eindhoven Neth. 52 F3
Einme Myanmar 70 A3
Einsiedeln Switz. 56 I3
Eirik Ridge sea feature N. Atlantic Ocean 148 F2
Eiriosgaigh i. U.K. see Eriskay
Eirunepé Brazil 142 E5
Eisberg hill Germany 53 J3
Eiseb watercourse Namibia 99 C5
Eisenach Germany 53 K4
Eisenberg Germany 53 L4
Eisenhower, Mount Canada see Castle Mountain
Eisenhüttenstadt Germany 47 O4
Eisenstadt Austria 47 P7
Eisfeld Germany 53 K4
Eisleben Lutherstadt Germany 53 L3
Eite, Loch inlet U.K. see Etive, Loch
Eiterfeld Germany 53 J4
Eivissa Spain see Ibiza
Eivissa i. Spain see Ibiza
Ejea de los Caballeros Spain 57 F2
Ejeda Madag. 99 E6
Ejin Horo Qi China see Altan Shiret
Ejin Qi China see Dalain Hob
Ejmiadzin Armenia see Ejmiatsin
Ejmiatsin Armenia 91 G2
Ekalaka U.S.A. 126 G3
Ekenäs Fin. 45 M7
Ekerem Turkm. 88 D2
Ekeren Belgium 52 E3
Eketahuna N.Z. 113 E5
Ekibastuz Kazakh. 80 E1
Ekimchan Rus. Fed. 74 D1
Ekinyazı Turkey 85 D1
Ekonda Rus. Fed. 65 L3
Ekostrovskaya Imandra, Ozero l. Rus. Fed. 44 R3
Ekshärad Sweden 45 H6
Eksjö Sweden 45 I8
Eksteenfontein S. Africa 100 C5
Ekström Ice Shelf Antarctica 152 B2
Ekwan r. Canada 122 E3
Ekwan Point Canada 122 E3
Ela Myanmar 70 B3
El Aaiún W. Sahara see Laâyoune
Elafonisou, Steno sea chan. Greece 59 J6
El 'Agrûd well Egypt see Al 'Ajrūd
Elaia, Cape Cyprus 85 B2
El 'Alamein Egypt see Al 'Alamayn
El 'Âmirîya Egypt see Al 'Āmirīyah
Elands r. S. Africa 101 I3
Elandsdoorn S. Africa 101 I3
El Aouinet Alg. 58 B7
Elar Armenia see Abovyan
El Araïche Morocco see Larache
El Arco Mex. 127 E7
El Ariana Tunisia see L'Ariana
El Aricha Alg. 54 D5
El 'Arîsh Egypt see Al 'Arīsh
El Arrouch Alg. 58 B6
El Ashmûnein Egypt see Al Ashmūnayn
El Asnam Alg. see Chlef
Elassona Greece 59 J5
Elat Israel see Eilat
Elato atoll Micronesia 69 L5
Elazığ Turkey 91 E3
Elba U.S.A. 133 C6
Elba, Isola d' i. Italy 58 D3
El'ban Rus. Fed. 74 E2
El Barco de Valdeorras Spain see O Barco
El Barreal salt l. Mex. 127 G7
Elbasan Albania 59 I4
El Batroun Lebanon see Batroûn
El Baúl Venez. 142 E2
El Bawîti Egypt see Al Bawītī
El Bayadh Alg. 54 E5
Elbe r. Germany 53 J1
also known as Labe (Czech Republic)
Elbe-Havel-Kanal canal Germany 53 L2
El Béqaa valley Lebanon 85 C2
Elbert, Mount U.S.A. 126 G5
Elberta U.S.A. 129 H2
Elberton U.S.A. 133 D5
Elbeuf France 56 E2
Elbeyli Turkey 85 C1
Elbing Poland see Elbląg
Elbistan Turkey 90 E3
Elbląg Poland 47 Q3
El Boulaïda Alg. see Blida
Elbow Canada 121 J5
Elbow Lake U.S.A. 130 D2
El Bozal Mex. 131 C8
El Brasil Mex. 131 C7

▶El'brus mt. Rus. Fed. 91 F2
Highest mountain in Europe.

Elburg Neth. 52 F2
El Burgo de Osma Spain 57 E3
Elburz Mountains Iran 88 C2
El Cajon U.S.A. 128 E5
El Callao Venez. 142 F2
El Campo U.S.A. 131 D6
El Capitan Mountain U.S.A. 127 G6
El Capulín r. Mex. 131 C7
El Casco Mex. 131 B7
El Centro U.S.A. 129 F5
El Cerro Bol. 142 F7
Elche Spain see Elche-Elx
Elche-Elx Spain 57 F4
El Chilicote Mex. 131 B6
Elcho Island Australia 110 A1
El Coca Orellana Ecuador see Coca
El Coca Ecuador see Coca
El Cocuy, Parque Nacional nat. park Col. 142 D2
El Cuyo Mex. 133 C8
Elda Spain 57 F4
El Dátil Mex. 127 E7
El Desemboque Mex. 127 E7
El Diamante Mex. 131 C6
El'dikan Rus. Fed. 65 O3
El Djezair country Africa see Algeria
El Djezair Alg. see Algiers
El Doctor Mex. 129 F6
Eldon U.S.A. 130 E4
Eldorado Arg. 144 F3
Eldorado Brazil 145 A4
El Dorado Col. 142 D3
El Dorado Mex. 124 F7
El Dorado AR U.S.A. 131 E5
El Dorado KS U.S.A. 130 D4
Eldorado U.S.A. 131 C6
El Dorado Venez. 142 F2
Eldorado Mountains U.S.A. 129 F4
Eldoret Kenya 98 D3
Elea, Cape Cyprus see Elaia, Cape
Eleanor U.S.A. 134 E4
Electric Peak U.S.A. 126 F3
Elefantes r. Moz./S. Africa see Olifants
El Eglab plat. Alg. 96 C2
El Ejido Spain 57 E5

▶Elemi Triangle terr. Africa 98 D3
Disputed territory (Ethiopia/Kenya/Sudan) administered by Kenya.

El Encanto Col. 142 D4
Elend Germany 53 K3
Elephanta Caves tourist site India 84 B2
Elephant Butte Reservoir U.S.A. 127 G6
Elephant Island Antarctica 152 A2
Elephant Pass Sri Lanka 84 D4
Elephant Point Bangl. 83 H5
Eleşkirt Turkey 91 F3
El Eulma Alg. 54 F4
Eleuthera i. Bahamas 133 E7
Eleven Point r. U.S.A. 131 F4
El Fahs Tunisia 58 C6
El Faiyûm Egypt see Al Fayyūm
El Fasher Sudan 97 F3
El Ferrol Spain see Ferrol
El Ferrol del Caudillo Spain see Ferrol
Elfershausen Germany 53 J4
El Fud Eth. 98 E3
El Fuerte Mex. 127 F8
El Gara Egypt see Qārah
El Geneina Sudan 97 F3
El Geteina Sudan 86 D7
El Ghardaqa Egypt see Al Ghurdaqah
El Ghor plain Jordan/West Bank see Al Ghawr
Elgin U.K. 50 F3
Elgin IL U.S.A. 130 F3
Elgin ND U.S.A. 130 C2
Elgin NV U.S.A. 129 F3
Elgin TX U.S.A. 131 D6
El'ginskiy Rus. Fed. 65 P3
El Gîza Egypt see Giza
El Goléa Alg. 54 E5
El Golfo de Santa Clara Mex. 127 E7
Elgon, Mount Kenya/Uganda 78 C6
El Hadjar Alg. 58 B6
El Ḥammâm Egypt see Al Ḥammām
El Ḥammâmi reg. Mauritania 96 B2
El Ḥank esc. Mali/Mauritania 96 C2
El Ḥarra Egypt see Al Ḥarrah
El Hazim Jordan see Al Hazīm
El Ḥeiz Egypt see Al Ḥayz
El Hierro i. Canary Is 96 B2
El Homr Alg. 54 E6
El Homra Sudan 86 D7
Eliase Indon. 108 E2
Elías Piña Dom. Rep. 137 J5
Elichpur India see Achalpur
Elida U.S.A. 134 C3
Elie U.K. 50 G4
Elila r. Dem. Rep. Congo 98 C4
Elim U.S.A. 118 B3
Elimberrum France see Auch
Eling China see Yinjiang
Elingampangu Dem. Rep. Congo 98 C4
Eliot, Mount Canada 123 J2
Élisabethville Dem. Rep. Congo see Lubumbashi
Eliseu Martins Brazil 143 J5
El Iskandarîya Egypt see Alexandria
Elista Rus. Fed. 43 J7
Elizabeth NJ U.S.A. 135 H3
Elizabeth WV U.S.A. 134 E4
Elizabeth, Mount hill Australia 108 D4
Elizabeth Bay Namibia 100 B4
Elizabeth City U.S.A. 132 E4
Elizabeth Island Pitcairn Is see Henderson Island
Elizabeth Point Namibia 100 B4
Elizabethton U.S.A. 132 D4
Elizabethtown IL U.S.A. 130 F4
Elizabethtown KY U.S.A. 134 C5
Elizabethtown NC U.S.A. 133 E5
Elizabethtown NY U.S.A. 135 I1
El Jadida Morocco 54 C5
El Jaralito Mex. 131 B7
El Jem Tunisia 58 D7
Elk r. Canada 120 H5
Ełk Poland 47 S4
Elk r. U.S.A. 135 H4
El Kaa Lebanon see Qaa
El Kab Sudan 86 D6
Elkader U.S.A. 130 F3
El Kala Alg. 58 C6
Elk City U.S.A. 131 D5
Elkedra Australia 110 A4
Elkedra watercourse Australia 110 B4
El Kef Tunisia see Le Kef
El Kelaâ des Srarhna Morocco 54 C5
Elkford Canada 120 H5
Elk Grove U.S.A. 128 C2
El Khalil West Bank see Hebron
El Khandaq Sudan 86 D6
El Khârga Egypt see Al Khārijah
El Kharrûba Egypt see Al Kharrūbah

Elkhart IN U.S.A. 134 C3
Elkhart KS U.S.A. 131 C4
El Khartûm Sudan see Khartoum
El Khenachich esc. Mali see El Khnâchîch
El Khnâchîch esc. Mali 96 C2
Elkhorn U.S.A. 130 F3
Elkhorn City U.S.A. 134 D5
Elkhovo Bulg. 59 L3
Elki Turkey see Beytüşşebap
Elkin U.S.A. 132 D4
Elkins U.S.A. 134 F4
Elk Island National Park Canada 121 H4
Elk Lake Canada 122 E5
Elk Lake l. U.S.A. 134 C1
Elkland U.S.A. 135 G3
Elk Mountain U.S.A. 126 G4
Elk Mountains U.S.A. 129 J2
Elko Canada 120 H5
Elko U.S.A. 129 F1
Elk Point Canada 121 I4
Elk Point U.S.A. 130 D3
Elk Springs U.S.A. 129 I1
Elkton MD U.S.A. 135 H4
Elkton VA U.S.A. 135 F4
El Kûbri Egypt see Al Kūbrī
El Kuntilla Egypt see Al Kuntillah
Elkview U.S.A. 134 E4
Ellas country Europe see Greece
Ellaville U.S.A. 133 C5
Ell Bay Canada 121 O1
Ellef Ringnes Island Canada 119 H2
Ellen, Mount U.S.A. 129 H2
Ellenburg Depot U.S.A. 135 I1
Ellendale U.S.A. 130 D2
Ellensburg U.S.A. 126 C3
Ellenville U.S.A. 135 H3
El León, Cerro mt. Mex. 131 B7
Ellesmere, Lake N.Z. 113 D6

▶Ellesmere Island Canada 119 J2
4th largest island in North America, and 10th in the world.

Ellesmere Island National Park Reserve Canada see Quttinirpaaq National Park
Ellesmere Port U.K. 48 E5
Ellettsville U.S.A. 134 B4
Ellice r. Canada 121 K1
Ellice Island atoll Tuvalu see Funafuti
Ellice Islands country S. Pacific Ocean see Tuvalu
Ellicott City U.S.A. 135 G4
Ellijay U.S.A. 133 C5
Ellingen Germany 53 K5
Elliot S. Africa 101 H6
Elliot, Mount Australia 110 D3
Elliotdale S. Africa 101 I6
Elliot Knob mt. U.S.A. 134 F4
Elliot Lake Canada 122 E5
Elliott Australia 108 F4
Elliston U.S.A. 134 E5
Ellon U.K. 50 G3
Ellora Caves tourist site India 84 B1
Ellsworth KS U.S.A. 130 D4
Ellsworth ME U.S.A. 132 G2
Ellsworth NE U.S.A. 130 C3
Ellsworth WI U.S.A. 130 E2
Ellsworth Land reg. Antarctica 152 K1
Ellsworth Mountains Antarctica 152 L1
Ellwangen (Jagst) Germany 53 K6
El Maghreb country Africa see Morocco
Elmakuz Dağı mt. Turkey 85 A1
Elmalı Turkey 59 M6
El Malpais National Monument nat. park U.S.A. 129 J4
El Manşûra Egypt see Al Manşūrah
El Maţarîya Egypt see Al Maţarīyah
El Mazâr Egypt see Al Mazār
El Meghaïer Alg. 54 F5
El Milia Alg. 54 F4
El Minya Egypt see Al Minyā
Elmira Ont. Canada 134 E2
Elmira P.E.I. Canada 123 J5
Elmira MI U.S.A. 134 C1
Elmira NY U.S.A. 135 G2
El Mirage U.S.A. 129 G5
El Moral Spain 57 E5
Elmore Australia 112 B6
El Mreyyé reg. Mauritania 96 C3
Elmshorn Germany 53 J1
El Muglad Sudan 86 C7
Elmvale Canada 134 F1
Elnesvågen Norway 44 E5
El Nevado, Cerro mt. Col. 142 D3
El Oasis Mex. 129 F5
El Obeid Sudan 86 D7
El Odaiya Sudan 86 C7
El Oro Mex. 131 C7
Elorza Venez. 142 E2
El Oued Alg. 54 F5
Eloy U.S.A. 129 H5
El Palmito Mex. 131 B7
El Paso IL U.S.A. 130 F3
El Paso KS U.S.A. see Derby
El Paso TX U.S.A. 127 G7
Elphin U.K. 50 D2
Elphinstone i. Myanmar see Thayawthadangyi Kyun
El Portal U.S.A. 128 D3
El Porvenir Mex. 131 B6
El Porvenir Panama 137 I7
El Prat de Llobregat Spain 57 H3
El Progreso Hond. 136 G5
El Puerto de Santa María Spain 57 C5
El Qâhira Egypt see Cairo
El Qasimiye r. Lebanon 85 B3
El Quds Israel/West Bank see Jerusalem
El Quşeima Egypt see Al Quşaymah
El Quşeir Egypt see Al Quşayr
El Qûşîya Egypt see Al Qūşīyah
El Regocijo Mex. 131 B8
El Reno U.S.A. 131 D5
Elrose Canada 121 I5
Elsa Canada 120 C2
El Şaff Egypt see Aş Şaff
El Sahuaro Mex. 127 E7
El Salado Mex. 131 C7
El Salto Mex. 131 B8
El Salvador country Central America 136 G6
El Salvador Chile 144 C3
El Salvador Mex. 131 C7
Elsass reg. France see Alsace
El Sauz Mex. 127 G7
Else r. Germany 53 I2
El Sellûm Egypt see As Sallūm
Elsey Australia 108 F3
El Shallûfa Egypt see Ash Shallūfah
El Sharana Australia 108 F3
El Shaţţ Egypt see Ash Shaţţ
Elsie U.S.A. 134 C2
Elsinore Denmark see Helsingør
Elsinore CA U.S.A. 128 E5
Elsinore UT U.S.A. 129 G2
Elsinore Lake U.S.A. 128 E5
El Sueco Mex. 127 G7
El Suweis Egypt see Suez
El Suweis governorate Egypt see As Suways
El Tama, Parque Nacional nat. park Venez. 142 D2
El Tarf Alg. 58 C6
El Teleno mt. Spain 57 C2
El Temascal Mex. 131 D7
El Ter r. Spain 57 H2
El Thamad Egypt see Ath Thamad
El Tigre Venez. 142 F2
Eltmann Germany 53 K5
El'ton Rus. Fed. 43 J6
El'ton, Ozero l. Rus. Fed. 43 J6
El Tren Mex. 127 E7
El Tuparro, Parque Nacional nat. park Col. 142 E2
El Ţûr Egypt see Aţ Ţūr
El Turbio Arg. 144 B8
El Uqsur Egypt see Luxor
Eluru India 84 D2
Elva Estonia 45 O7
Elvanfoot U.K. 50 F5
Elvas Port. 57 C4
Elverum Norway 45 G6
Elvira Brazil 142 D5
El Wak Kenya 98 E3
El Wâtya well Egypt see Al Wāţiyah
Elwood IN U.S.A. 134 C3
Elwood NE U.S.A. 130 D3
El Wuz Sudan 86 D7
Elx Spain see Elche-Elx
Elxleben Germany 53 K3
Ely U.K. 49 H6
Ely MN U.S.A. 130 F2
Ely NV U.S.A. 129 F2
Elyria U.S.A. 134 D3
Elz Germany 53 I4
El Zagâzîg Egypt see Az Zaqāzīq
Elze Germany 53 J2
Émaé i. Vanuatu 107 G3
Emāmrūd Iran 88 D2
Emām Şaḩeb Afgh. 89 H2
Emām Taqī Iran 88 E2
Emån r. Sweden 45 J8
Emas, Parque Nacional das nat. park Brazil 143 H7
Emba Kazakh. 80 A2
Emba r. Kazakh. 80 A2
Embalenhle S. Africa 101 I4
Embarcación Arg. 144 D2
Embarras Portage Canada 121 I3
Embi Kazakh. see Emba
Embira r. Brazil see Envira
Emborcação, Represa de resr Brazil 145 B2
Embrun Canada 135 H1
Embu Kenya 98 D4
Emden Germany 53 H1
Emden Deep sea feature N. Pacific Ocean see Cape Johnson Depth
Emei China see Emeishan
Emeishan China 76 D2
Emei Shan mt. China 76 D2
Emerald Australia 110 E4
Emeril Canada 123 I3
Emerita Augusta Spain see Mérida
Emerson Canada 121 L5
Emerson U.S.A. 134 D4
Emery U.S.A. 129 H2
Emesa Syria see Homs
Emet Turkey 59 M5
eMgwenya S. Africa 101 J3
Emigrant Pass U.S.A. 128 E1
Emigrant Valley U.S.A. 129 F3
Emi Koussi mt. Chad 97 E3
Emile r. Canada 120 G2
Emiliano Zapata Mex. 136 F5
Emin China 80 F2
Emine, Nos pt Bulg. 59 L3
Eminence U.S.A. 134 C4
Eminska Planina hills Bulg. 59 L3
Emirdağ Turkey 59 N5
Emir Dağı mt. Turkey 59 N5
Emir Dağları mts Turkey 59 N5
eMjindini S. Africa 101 J3
Emmaboda Sweden 45 I8
Emmaste Estonia 45 M7
Emmaville Australia 112 E2
Emmeloord Neth. 52 F2
Emmelshausen Germany 53 H4
Emmen Neth. 52 G2
Emmen Switz. 56 I3
Emmerich Germany 52 G3
Emmet Australia 110 D5
Emmetsburg U.S.A. 130 E3
Emmett U.S.A. 126 D4
Emmiganuru India 84 C3
Emo Canada 121 M5
Emona Slovenia see Ljubljana
Emory Peak U.S.A. 131 C6
Empalme Mex. 127 F8
Empangeni S. Africa 101 J5
Emperor Seamount Chain sea feature N. Pacific Ocean 150 H2
Emperor Trough sea feature N. Pacific Ocean 150 H2
Empingham Reservoir U.K. see Rutland Water
Emplawas Indon. 108 E2
Empoli Italy 58 D3
Emporia KS U.S.A. 130 D4
Emporia VA U.S.A. 135 G5
Emporium U.S.A. 135 F3
Empress Canada 121 I5
Empty Quarter des. Saudi Arabia see Rub' al Khālī
Ems r. Germany 53 H1
Emsdale Canada 134 F1
Emsdetten Germany 53 H2
Ems-Jade-Kanal canal Germany 53 H1
eMzinoni S. Africa 101 I4
Enafors Sweden 44 H5
Encantadas, Serra das hills Brazil 144 F4
Encarnación Para. 144 E3
Enchi Ghana 96 C4
Encinal U.S.A. 131 D6
Encinitas U.S.A. 128 E5
Encino U.S.A. 127 G6
Encruzilhada Brazil 145 C1
Endako Canada 120 E4
Endau-Rompin National Park nat. park Malaysia 71 C7
Ende Indon. 108 C2
Endeavour Strait Australia 110 C1
Endeh Indon. see Ende
Enderby Canada 120 G5
Enderby atoll Micronesia see Puluwat
Enderby Land reg. Antarctica 152 D2
Endicott U.S.A. 135 G2
Endicott Mountains U.S.A. 118 C3
EnenKio terr. N. Pacific Ocean see Wake Island
Energodar Ukr. see Enerhodar
Enerhodar Ukr. 43 G7
Enewetak atoll Marshall Is 150 G5
Enez Turkey 59 L4
Enfe Lebanon 85 B2
Enfião, Ponta do pt Angola 99 B5
Enfidaville Tunisia 58 D6
Enfield U.S.A. 132 E4
Engan Norway 44 F5
Engaru Japan 74 F3
Engcobo S. Africa 101 H6
En Gedi Israel 85 B4
Engelhard U.S.A. 132 F5
Engel's Rus. Fed. 43 J6
Engelschmangat sea chan. Neth. 52 E1
Enggano i. Indon. 68 C8
Enghien Belgium 52 E4
England admin. div. U.K. 49 E6
Englee Canada 123 L4
Englehart Canada 122 F5
Englewood FL U.S.A. 133 D7
Englewood OH U.S.A. 134 C4
English r. Canada 121 M5
English U.S.A. 134 B4
English Bazar India see Ingraj Bazar
English Channel France/U.K. 49 F9
English Coast Antarctica 152 L2
Engozero Rus. Fed. 42 G2
Enhlalakahle S. Africa 101 J5
Enid U.S.A. 131 D4
Eniwa Japan 74 F4
Eniwetok atoll Marshall Is see Enewetak
Enjiang China see Yongfeng
Enkeldoorn Zimbabwe see Chivhu
Enkhuizen Neth. 52 F2
Enköping Sweden 45 J7
Enna Sicily Italy 58 F6
Ennadai Lake Canada 121 K2
En Nahud Sudan 86 C7
Ennedi, Massif mts Chad 97 F3
Ennell, Lough l. Ireland 51 E4
Enngonia Australia 112 B2
Enning U.S.A. 130 C2
Ennis Ireland 51 D5
Ennis MT U.S.A. 126 F3
Ennis TX U.S.A. 131 D5
Enniscorthy Ireland 51 F5
Enniskillen U.K. 51 E3
Ennistymon Ireland 51 C5
Enn Nâqoûra Lebanon 85 B3
Enns r. Austria 47 O6
Eno Fin. 44 Q5
Enoch U.S.A. 129 G3
Enontekiö Fin. 44 M2
Enosburg Falls U.S.A. 135 I1
Enosville U.S.A. 134 B4
Enping China 77 G4
Ens Neth. 52 F2
Ensay Australia 112 C6
Enschede Neth. 52 G2
Ense Germany 53 I3
Ensenada Mex. 127 D7
Enshi China 77 F2
Ensley U.S.A. 133 C6
Entebbe Uganda 98 D3
Enterprise Canada 120 G2
Enterprise AL U.S.A. 133 C6
Enterprise OR U.S.A. 126 D3
Enterprise UT U.S.A. 129 G3
Entre Ríos Bol. 142 F8
Entre Rios Brazil 143 H5
Entre Rios de Minas Brazil 145 B3
Entroncamento Port. 57 B4
Enugu Nigeria 96 D4
Enurmino Rus. Fed. 65 T3
Envira Brazil 142 D5
Envira r. Brazil 142 D5
'En Yahav Israel 85 B4
Enyamba Dem. Rep. Congo 98 C4
Eochaill Ireland see Youghal
Epe Neth. 52 F2
Epéna Congo 98 B3
Épernay France 52 D5
Ephraim U.S.A. 129 H2
Ephrata U.S.A. 135 G3
Epi i. Vanuatu 107 G3
Epidamnus Albania see Durrës
Épinal France 56 H2
Episkopi Bay Cyprus 85 A2
Episkopis, Kolpos b. Cyprus see Episkopi Bay
ePitoli S. Africa see Pretoria
Epomeo, Monte hill Italy 58 E4
Epping U.K. 49 H7
Epping Forest National Park Australia 110 D4
Eppstein Germany 53 I4
Eppynt, Mynydd hills U.K. 49 D6
Epsom U.K. 49 G7
Epte r. France 52 B5
Eqlīd Iran 88 D4
Equatorial Guinea country Africa 96 D4
Équeurdreville-Hainneville France 49 F9
Erac Creek watercourse Australia 112 B1
Erandol India 84 B1
Erawadi r. Myanmar see Irrawaddy
Erawan National Park Thai. 71 B4
Erbaa Turkey 90 E2
Erbendorf Germany 53 M5
Erbeskopf hill Germany 52 H5
Ercan airport Cyprus 85 A2
Erciş Turkey 91 F3
Erciyes Dağı mt. Turkey 90 D3
Érd Hungary 58 H1
Erdaobaihe China see Baihe
Erdaogou China 76 B1
Erdao Jiang r. China 74 B4
Erdek Turkey 59 L4
Erdemli Turkey 85 B1
Erdenedalay Mongolia 72 I3
Erdenet Mongolia 80 J2
Erdenetsagaan Mongolia 73 L3
Erdi reg. Chad 97 F3
Erdniyevskiy Rus. Fed. 43 J7

▶Erebus, Mount vol. Antarctica 152 H1
Highest active volcano in Antarctica.

Erechim Brazil 144 F3
Ereentsav Mongolia 73 L3
Ereğli Konya Turkey 90 D3
Ereğli Zonguldak Turkey 59 N4
Erego Moz. see Errego
Erei, Monti mts Sicily Italy 58 F6
Erementaū Kazakh. see Yereymentau
Erenhot China 73 K4
Erepucu, Lago de l. Brazil 143 G4
Erevan Armenia see Yerevan
Erfurt Germany 53 L4
Erfurt airport Germany 53 K4
Ergani Turkey 91 E3
'Erg Chech des. Alg./Mali 96 C2
Ergene r. Turkey 59 L4
Ērgli Latvia 45 N8
Ergu China 74 C3
Ergun China 73 M2
Ergun He r. China/Rus. Fed. see Argun'
Ergun Youqi China see Ergun
Ergun Zuoqi China see Genhe
Er Hai l. China 76 D3
Erhulai China 74 B4
Eriboll, Loch inlet U.K. 50 E2
Ericht r. U.K. 50 F4
Ericht, Loch l. U.K. 50 E4
Erickson Canada 121 L5
Erie KS U.S.A. 131 E4
Erie PA U.S.A. 134 E2
Erie, Lake Canada/U.S.A. 134 E2
'Erîgât des. Mali 96 C3
Erik Eriksenstretet sea chan. Svalbard 64 D2
Eriksdale Canada 121 L5
Erimo-misaki c. Japan 74 F4
Erin Canada 134 E2
Erinpura Road India 82 C4
Eriskay i. U.K. 50 B3
Eritrea country Africa 86 E6
Erlangen Germany 53 L5
Erlangping China 77 F1
Erldunda Australia 109 F6
Erlistoun watercourse Australia 109 C6
Erlong Shan mt. China 74 C4
Erlongshan Shuiku resr China 74 B4
Ermak Kazakh. see Aksu
Ermelo Neth. 52 F2
Ermelo S. Africa 101 I4
Ermenek Turkey 85 A1
Ermenek r. Turkey 85 A1
Ermont Egypt see Armant
Ermoupoli Greece 59 K6
Ernakulam India 84 C4
Erne r. Ireland/U.K. 51 D3
Ernest Giles Range hills Australia 109 C6
Erode India 84 C4
Eromanga Australia 111 C5
Erongo admin. reg. Namibia 100 B1
Erp Neth. 52 F3
Erqu China see Zhouzhi
Errabiddy Hills Australia 109 A6
Er Rachidia Morocco 54 D5
Er Raoui des. Alg. 54 D6
Errego Moz. 99 D5
Er Remla Tunisia 58 D7
Er Renk Sudan 86 D7
Errigal hill Ireland 51 D2
Errinundra National Park Australia 112 D6
Erris Head hd Ireland 51 B3
Errol U.S.A. 135 J1
Erromango i. Vanuatu 107 G3
Erronan i. Vanuatu see Futuna
Erseka Albania see Ersekë
Ersekë Albania 59 I4
Erskine U.S.A. 130 D2
Ersmark Sweden 44 L5
Ertai China 80 H2
Ertil' Rus. Fed. 43 I6
Ertis r. Kazakh./Rus. Fed. see Irtysh
Ertix He r. China/Kazakh. 80 G2
Ērtra country Africa see Eritrea
Eruh Turkey 91 F3
Erwin U.S.A. 132 D4
Erwitte Germany 53 I3
Erxleben Sachsen-Anhalt Germany 53 L2
Erxleben Sachsen-Anhalt Germany 53 L2
Eryuan China 76 C3
Erzerum Turkey see Erzurum
Erzgebirge mts Czech Rep./Germany 53 N4
Erzhan China 74 B2
Erzin Turkey 85 C1
Erzincan Turkey 91 E3
Erzurum Turkey 91 F3
Esa-ala P.N.G. 110 E1
Esan-misaki pt Japan 74 F4
Esashi Japan 74 F3
Esbjerg Denmark 45 F9
Esbo Fin. see Espoo
Escalante U.S.A. 129 H3
Escalante r. U.S.A. 129 H3
Escalante Desert U.S.A. 129 G3
Escalón Mex. 131 B7
Escambia r. U.S.A. 133 C6
Escanaba U.S.A. 132 C2
Escárcega Mex. 136 F5
Escatrón Spain 57 F3
Escaut r. Belgium 52 D4
Esch Neth. 52 F3
Eschede Germany 53 K2
Eschscholtz atoll Marshall Is see Bikini
Esch-sur-Alzette Lux. 52 F5
Eschwege Germany 53 K3
Eschweiler Germany 52 G4
Escondido r. Mex. 131 C6
Escondido U.S.A. 128 E5
Escudilla mt. U.S.A. 129 I5
Escuinapa Mex. 136 C4
Escuintla Guat. 136 F6
Eséka Cameroon 96 E4
Eşen Turkey 59 M6
Esenguly Turkm. 88 D2
Esenguly Döwlet Gorugy nature res. Turkm. 88 D2
Esens Germany 53 H1
Eşfahān Iran 88 C3
Esfarayen, Reshteh-ye mts Iran 88 E2
Esfideh Iran 89 E3
Eshan China 76 D3
Eshāqābād Iran 88 E3
Eshkamesh Afgh. 89 H2
Eshkanān Iran 88 D5
Eshowe S. Africa 101 J5
Esikhawini S. Africa 101 K5
Esil Kazakh. see Yesil'
Esil r. Kazakh./Rus. Fed. see Ishim
Esk Australia 112 F1
Esk r. Australia 111 [inset]
Esk r. U.K. 48 D4
Eskdalemuir U.K. 50 F5
Esker Canada 123 I3
Eskifjörður Iceland 44 [inset]
Eski Gediz Turkey 59 M5
Eskilstuna Sweden 45 J7
Eskimo Lakes Canada 118 E3
Eskimo Point Canada see Arviat
Eskipazar Turkey 90 D2
Eskişehir Turkey 59 N5
Eski-Yakkabog' Uzbek. 89 G2
Esla r. Spain 57 C3
Eslāmābād-e Gharb Iran 88 B3
Esler Dağı mt. Turkey 59 M6
Eslohe (Sauerland) Germany 53 I3
Eslöv Sweden 45 H9
Esmā'īlī-ye Soflá Iran 88 E4
Eşme Turkey 59 M5
Esmeraldas Ecuador 142 C3
Esmont U.S.A. 135 F5
Esnagami Lake Canada 122 D4
Esnes France 52 D4
Espakeh Iran 89 F5
Espalion France 56 F4
España country Europe see Spain
Espanola Canada 122 E5
Espanola U.S.A. 131 B4
Espelkamp Germany 53 I2
Esperance Australia 109 C8
Esperance Bay Australia 109 C8
Esperanza research station Antarctica 152 A2
Esperanza Arg. 144 B8
Esperanza Mex. 127 F8
Espichel, Cabo c. Port. 57 B4
Espigão, Serra do mts Brazil 145 A4
Espigüete mt. Spain 57 D2
Espinazo Mex. 131 C7
Espinhaço, Serra do mts Brazil 145 C2
Espinosa Brazil 145 C1
Espírito Santo Brazil see Vila Velha
Espírito Santo state Brazil 145 C2
Espíritu Santo i. Vanuatu 107 G3
Espíritu Santo, Isla i. Mex. 124 E7
Espoo Fin. 45 N6
Espuña mt. Spain 57 F5
Esqueda Mex. 127 F7
Esquel Arg. 144 B6
Esquimalt Canada 120 F5
Essaouira Morocco 96 C1
Es Semara W. Sahara 96 B2
Essen Belgium 52 E3
Essen Germany 52 H3
Essen (Oldenburg) Germany 53 H2
Essequibo r. Guyana 143 G2
Essex Canada 134 D2
Essex CA U.S.A. 129 F4
Essex MD U.S.A. 135 G4
Essex NY U.S.A. 135 I1
Essexville U.S.A. 134 D2
Esslingen am Neckar Germany 53 J6
Esso Rus. Fed. 65 Q4
Essoyla Rus. Fed. 42 G3
Eşţahbān Iran 88 D4
Estância Brazil 143 K6
Estancia U.S.A. 127 G6
Estand, Kūh-e mt. Iran 89 F4
Estats, Pic d' mt. France/Spain 56 E5
Estcourt S. Africa 101 I5
Este r. Germany 53 J1
Estelí Nicaragua 137 G6
Estella Spain 57 E2
Estepa Spain 57 D5
Estepona Spain 57 D5
Esteras de Medinaceli Spain 57 E3
Esterhazy Canada 121 K5
Estero Bay U.S.A. 128 C4
Esteros Para. 144 D2
Estevan Canada 121 K5
Estevan Group is Canada 120 D4
Estherville U.S.A. 130 E3
Estill U.S.A. 133 D5
Eston Canada 121 I5
Estonia country Europe 45 N7
Estonskaya S.S.R. country Europe see Estonia
Estrées-St-Denis France 52 C5
Estrela Brazil 145 A5
Estrela, Serra da mts Port. 57 C3
Estrela do Sul Brazil 145 B2
Estrella mt. Spain 57 E4
Estrella, Punta pt Mex. 127 E7
Estremoz Port. 57 C4
Estrondo, Serra hills Brazil 143 I5
Etadunna Australia 111 B6
Etah India 82 D4
Étain France 52 F5
Étamamiou Canada 123 K4
Étampes France 56 F2
Étaples France 52 B4
Etawah Rajasthan India 82 D4
Etawah Uttar Prad. India 82 D4
Ethandakukhanya S. Africa 101 J4
Ethelbert Canada 121 K5
Ethel Creek Australia 109 C5
E'Thembini S. Africa 100 F5

▶Ethiopia country Africa 98 D3
2nd most populous country in Africa.

Etimesğut Turkey 90 D3
Etive, Loch inlet U.K. 50 D4

▶Etna, Mount vol. Sicily Italy 58 F6
Highest active volcano in Europe.

Etne Norway 45 D7
Etobicoke Canada 134 F2
Etolin Strait U.S.A. 118 B3
Etorofu-tō i. Rus. Fed. see Iturup, Ostrov
Etosha National Park Namibia 99 B5
Etosha Pan salt pan Namibia 99 B5
Etoumbi Congo 98 B3
Etrek r. Iran/Turkm. see Atrek
Etrek Turkm. 88 D2
Étrépagny France 52 B5
Étretat France 49 H9
Ettelbruck Lux. 52 G5
Etten-Leur Neth. 52 E3
Ettlingen Germany 53 I6
Ettrick Water r. U.K. 50 F5
Euabalong Australia 112 C4
Euboea i. Greece see Evvoia
Eucla Australia 109 E7
Euclid U.S.A. 134 E3
Euclides da Cunha Brazil 143 K6
Eucumbene, Lake Australia 112 D6
Eudistes, Lac des l. Canada 123 I4
Eudora U.S.A. 131 F5
Eudunda Australia 111 B7
Eufaula AL U.S.A. 133 C6
Eufaula OK U.S.A. 131 E5
Eufaula Lake resr U.S.A. 131 E5
Eugene U.S.A. 126 C3
Eugenia, Punta pt Mex. 127 E8
Eugowra Australia 112 D4
Eulo Australia 112 B2
Eumungerie Australia 112 D3
Eungella Australia 110 E4
Eungella National Park Australia 110 E4
Eunice LA U.S.A. 131 E6
Eunice NM U.S.A. 131 C5
Eupen Belgium 52 G4

▶Euphrates r. Asia 91 G5
Longest river in western Asia. Also known as Al Furāt (Iraq/Syria) or Firat (Turkey).

Eura Fin. 45 M6
Eure r. France 52 B5
Eureka CA U.S.A. 126 B4
Eureka KS U.S.A. 130 D4
Eureka MT U.S.A. 126 E2
Eureka NV U.S.A. 129 F2
Eureka OH U.S.A. 134 D4
Eureka SD U.S.A. 130 D2
Eureka UT U.S.A. 129 G2
Eureka Sound sea chan. Canada 119 J2
Eureka Springs U.S.A. 131 E4
Eureka Valley U.S.A. 128 E3
Euriowie Australia 111 C6
Euroa Australia 112 B6
Eurombah Australia 111 E5
Eurombah Creek r. Australia 111 E5
Europa, Île i. Indian Ocean 99 E6
Europa, Punta de pt Gibraltar see Europa Point
Europa Point Gibraltar 57 D5
Euskirchen Germany 52 G4
Eutaw U.S.A. 133 C5
Eutsuk Lake Canada 120 E4
Eutzsch Germany 53 M3
Eva Downs Australia 108 F4
Evans, Lac l. Canada 122 F4
Evans, Mount U.S.A. 126 G5
Evansburg Canada 120 H4
Evans City U.S.A. 134 E3
Evans Head Australia 112 F2
Evans Head hd Australia 112 F2
Evans Ice Stream Antarctica 152 L1
Evans Strait Canada 121 P2
Evanston IL U.S.A. 134 B2
Evanston WY U.S.A. 126 F4
Evansville Canada 122 E5
Evansville IN U.S.A. 134 B5
Evansville WY U.S.A. 126 G4
Evant U.S.A. 131 D6
Eva Perón Arg. see La Plata
Evart U.S.A. 134 C2
Evaton S. Africa 101 H4
Evaz Iran 88 D5
Evening Shade U.S.A. 131 F4
Evensk Rus. Fed. 65 Q3
Everard, Lake salt flat Australia 111 A6
Everard, Mount Australia 109 F5
Everard Range hills Australia 109 F6
Everdingen Neth. 52 F3
Everek Turkey see Develi

▶Everest, Mount China/Nepal 83 F4
Highest mountain in the world and in Asia.

Everett PA U.S.A. 135 F3
Everett WA U.S.A. 126 C3
Evergem Belgium 52 D3
Everglades swamp U.S.A. 133 D7
Everglades National Park U.S.A. 133 D7
Evergreen U.S.A. 133 C6
Evesham Australia 110 C4
Evesham U.K. 49 F6
Evesham, Vale of valley U.K. 49 F6
Evijärvi Fin. 44 M5
Evje Norway 45 E7
Évora Port. 57 C4
Evoron, Ozero l. Rus. Fed. 74 E2
Évreux France 52 B5
Evros r. Bulg. see Maritsa
Evros r. Turkey see Meriç
Evrotas r. Greece 59 J6
Évry France 52 C6
Evrychou Cyprus 85 A2
Evrykhou Cyprus see Evrychou
Evvoia i. Greece 59 K5
Ewan Australia 110 D3
Ewaso Ngiro r. Kenya 98 E3
Ewe, Loch b. U.K. 50 D3

Ewing U.S.A. 134 D5
Ewo Congo 98 B4
Exaltación Bol. 142 E6
Excelsior S. Africa 101 H5
Excelsior Mountain U.S.A. 128 D2
Excelsior Mountains U.S.A. 128 D2
Exe r. U.K. 49 D8
Exeter Australia 112 E5
Exeter Canada 134 E2
Exeter U.K. 49 D8
Exeter CA U.S.A. 128 D3
Exeter NH U.S.A. 135 J2
Exeter Lake Canada 121 I1
Exloo Neth. 52 G2
Exminster U.K. 49 D8
Exmoor hills U.K. 49 D7
Exmoor National Park U.K. 49 D7
Exmore U.S.A. 135 H5
Exmouth Australia 108 A5
Exmouth U.K. 49 D8
Exmouth, Mount Australia 112 D3
Exmouth Gulf Australia 108 A5
Exmouth Lake Canada 120 H1
Exmouth Plateau sea feature Indian Ocean 149 P7
Expedition National Park Australia 110 E5
Expedition Range mts Australia 110 E5
Exploits r. Canada 123 L4
Exton U.S.A. 135 H3
Extremadura aut. comm. Spain 57 D4
Exuma Cays is Bahamas 133 E7
Exuma Sound sea chan. Bahamas 133 F7
Eyasi, Lake salt l. Tanz. 98 D4
Eyawadi r. Myanmar see Irrawaddy
Eye U.K. 49 I6
Eyeberry Lake Canada 121 J2
Eyelenoborsk Rus. Fed. 41 S3
Eyemouth U.K. 50 G5
Eyjafjörður inlet Iceland 44 [inset]
Eyl Somalia 98 E3
Eylau Rus. Fed. see Bagrationovsk
Eynsham U.K. 49 F7
Eyre (North), Lake Australia 111 B6
Eyre (South), Lake Australia 111 B6

▶Eyre, Lake Australia 111 B6
Largest lake in Oceania and lowest point.

Eyre Creek watercourse Australia 110 B5
Eyre Mountains N.Z. 113 B7
Eyre Peninsula Australia 111 A7
Eystrup Germany 53 J2
Eysturoy i. Faroe Is 44 [inset]
Ezakheni S. Africa 101 J5
Ezel U.S.A. 134 D5
Ezenzeleni S. Africa 101 I4
Ezequiel Ramos Mexía, Embalse resr Arg. 144 C5
Ezhou China 77 G2
Ezhva Rus. Fed. 42 K3
Ezine Turkey 59 L5
Ezo i. Japan see Hokkaidō
Ezousa r. Cyprus 85 A2

F

Faaborg Denmark 45 G9
Faadhippolhu Atoll Maldives 84 B5
Faafxadhuun Somalia 98 E3
Fabens U.S.A. 127 G7
Faber, Mount hill Sing. 71 [inset]
Faber Lake Canada 120 G2
Fåborg Denmark see Faaborg
Fabriano Italy 58 E3
Faches-Thumesnil France 52 D4
Fachi Niger 96 E3
Fada Chad 97 F3
Fada-N'Gourma Burkina 96 D3
Fadghāmī Syria 91 F4
Fadiffolu Atoll Maldives see Faadhippolhu Atoll
Fadippolu Atoll Maldives see Faadhippolhu Atoll
Faenza Italy 58 D2
Færoerne terr. N. Atlantic Ocean see Faroe Islands
Faeroes terr. N. Atlantic Ocean see Faroe Islands
Făgăraş Romania 59 K2

▶Fagatogo American Samoa 107 I3
Capital of American Samoa.

Fagersta Sweden 45 I7
Fagne reg. Belgium 52 E4
Fagurhólsmýri Iceland 44 [inset]
Fagwir Sudan 86 D8
Fahraj Iran 88 D4
Fā'id Egypt 90 D5
Fairbanks U.S.A. 118 D3
Fairborn U.S.A. 134 C4
Fairbury U.S.A. 130 D3
Fairchance U.S.A. 134 F4
Fairfax U.S.A. 135 G4
Fairfield CA U.S.A. 128 B2
Fairfield IA U.S.A. 130 F3
Fairfield ID U.S.A. 126 E4
Fairfield IL U.S.A. 130 F4
Fairfield OH U.S.A. 134 C4
Fairfield TX U.S.A. 131 D6
Fair Haven U.S.A. 135 I2
Fair Head hd U.K. 51 F2
Fair Isle i. U.K. 50 H1
Fairlee U.S.A. 135 I2
Fairlie Canterbury 113 C7
Fairmont MN U.S.A. 130 E3
Fairmont WV U.S.A. 134 E4
Fair Oaks U.S.A. 134 B3
Fairview Australia 110 D2
Fairview Canada 120 G3
Fairview MI U.S.A. 134 C1
Fairview OK U.S.A. 131 D4
Fairview PA U.S.A. 134 E2
Fairview UT U.S.A. 129 H2
Fairview Park H.K. China 77 [inset]
Fairweather, Cape U.S.A. 120 B3
Fairweather, Mount Canada/U.S.A. 120 B3
Fais i. Micronesia 69 K5
Faisalabad Pak. 89 I4
Faissault France 52 E5
Faith U.S.A. 130 C2
Faizabad Afgh. see Feyzābād
Faizabad India 83 E4
Fakaofo atoll Tokelau 107 I2
Fakaofu atoll Tokelau see Fakaofo
Fakenham U.K. 49 H6
Fåker Sweden 44 I5
Fakfak Indon. 69 I7
Fakhrābād Iran 88 D4
Fakiragram India 83 G4
Fako vol. Cameroon see Cameroun, Mont
Fal r. U.K. 49 C8
Falaba Sierra Leone 96 B4
Falaise Lake Canada 120 G2
Falam Myanmar 70 A2
Falavarjan Iran 88 C3
Falcon Lake Canada 121 M5
Falcon Lake l. Mex./U.S.A. 131 D7
Falenki Rus. Fed. 42 K4
Falfurrias U.S.A. 131 D7
Falher Canada 120 G4
Falkenberg Germany 53 N3
Falkenberg Sweden 45 H8
Falkenhagen Germany 53 M1
Falkenhain Germany 53 M3
Falkensee Germany 53 N2
Falkenstein Germany 53 M5
Falkirk U.K. 50 F5
Falkland U.K. 50 F4
Falkland Escarpment sea feature S. Atlantic Ocean 148 E9

▶Falkland Islands terr. S. Atlantic Ocean 144 E8
United Kingdom Overseas Territory.

Falkland Plateau sea feature S. Atlantic Ocean 148 E9
Falkland Sound sea chan. Falkland Is 144 D8
Falköping Sweden 45 H7
Fallbrook U.S.A. 128 E5
Fallieres Coast Antarctica 152 L2
Fallingbostel Germany 53 J2
Fallon U.S.A. 128 D2
Fall River U.S.A. 135 J3
Fall River Pass U.S.A. 126 G4
Falls City U.S.A. 130 E3
Falmouth U.K. 49 B8
Falmouth KY U.S.A. 134 C4
Falmouth VA U.S.A. 135 G4
False r. Canada 123 H2
False Bay S. Africa 100 D8
False Point India 83 F5
Falster i. Denmark 45 G9
Fălticeni Romania 43 E7
Falun Sweden 45 I6
Famagusta Cyprus 85 A2
Famagusta Bay Cyprus see Ammochostos Bay
Fameck France 52 G5
Famenin Iran 88 C3
Fame Range hills Australia 109 C6
Family Lake Canada 121 M5
Family Well Australia 108 D5
Fāmūr, Daryācheh-ye l. Iran 88 C4
Fana Mali 96 C3
Fanad Head hd Ireland 51 E2
Fandriana Madag. 99 E6
Fane r. Ireland 51 F4
Fang Thai. 70 B3
Fangcheng Guangxi China see Fangchenggang
Fangcheng Henan China 77 G1
Fangchenggang China 77 F4
Fangdou Shan mts China 77 F2
Fangliao Taiwan 77 I4
Fangshan Taiwan 77 I4
Fangxian China 77 F1
Fangzheng China 74 C3
Fankuai China 77 F2
Fankuaidian China see Fankuai
Fanling H.K. China 77 [inset]
Fannich, Loch l. U.K. 50 D3
Fannūj Iran 89 E5
Fano Italy 58 E3
Fanshan Anhui China 77 H2
Fanshan Zhejiang China 77 I3
Fanum Fortunae Italy see Fano
Faqīh Aḥmadān Iran 88 C4
Farab Turkm. see Farap
Faraba Mali 96 B3
Faradofay Madag. see Tôlañaro
Farafangana Madag. 99 E6
Farāfirah, Wāḥāt al oasis Egypt 86 C4
Farafra Oasis oasis Egypt see Farāfirah, Wāḥāt al
Farāh Afgh. 89 F3
Farahābād Iran see Khezerābād
Farallon de Medinilla i. N. Mariana Is 69 L3
Farallon de Pajaros vol. N. Mariana Is 69 K2
Farallones de Cali, Parque Nacional nat. park Col. 142 C3
Faranah Guinea 96 B3
Farap Turkm. 89 F2
Fararah Oman 87 I6
Farasān, Jazā'ir is Saudi Arabia 86 F6
Faraulep atoll Micronesia 69 K5
Fareham U.K. 49 F8
Farewell, Cape Greenland 119 N3
Farewell, Cape N.Z. 113 D5
Farewell Spit N.Z. 113 D5
Färgelanda Sweden 45 H7
Farghona Uzbek. see Farg'ona
Fargo U.S.A. 130 D2
Farg'ona Uzbek. 87 L1
Faribault U.S.A. 130 E2
Faribault, Lac l. Canada 123 H2
Faridabad India 82 D3
Faridkot India 82 C3
Faridpur Bangl. 83 G5
Farīmān Iran 89 E3
Farkhar Afgh. see Farkhato
Farkhato Afgh. 89 H2
Farkhor Tajik. 89 H2
Farmahin Iran 88 C3
Farmer Island Canada 122 E2
Farmerville U.S.A. 131 E5
Farmington Canada 120 F4
Farmington ME U.S.A. 135 J1
Farmington MO U.S.A. 130 F4
Farmington NH U.S.A. 135 J2
Farmington NM U.S.A. 129 I3
Farmington Hills U.S.A. 134 D2
Far Mountain Canada 120 E4
Farmville U.S.A. 135 F5
Farnborough U.K. 49 G7
Farne Islands U.K. 48 F3
Farnham U.K. 49 G7
Farnham, Lake salt flat Australia 109 D6
Farnham, Mount Canada 120 G5
Faro Brazil 143 G4
Faro Canada 120 C2
Faro Port. 57 C5
Fårö i. Sweden 45 K8
Faroe - Iceland Ridge sea feature Arctic Ocean 153 I2

▶Faroe Islands terr. N. Atlantic Ocean 44 [inset]
Self-governing Danish territory.

Fårösund Sweden 45 K8
Farquhar Group is Seychelles 99 F5
Farquharson Tableland hills Australia 109 C6
Farrāshband Iran 88 D4
Farr Bay Antarctica 152 F2
Farristown U.S.A. 134 C5
Farrukhabad India see Fatehgarh
Fārsī Afgh. 89 F3
Farsund Norway 45 E7
Fārūj Iran 88 E2
Farwell MI U.S.A. 134 C2
Farwell TX U.S.A. 131 C5
Fasā Iran 88 D4
Fasano Italy 58 G4
Faşikan Geçidi pass Turkey 85 A1
Faßberg Germany 53 K2
Fastiv Ukr. 43 F6
Fastov Ukr. see Fastiv
Fatehabad India 82 C3
Fatehgarh India 82 D4
Fatehpur Rajasthan India 82 C4
Fatehpur Uttar Prad. India 82 E4
Fatick Senegal 96 B3
Fattoilep atoll Micronesia see Faraulep
Faughan r. U.K. 51 E2
Faulkton U.S.A. 130 D2
Faulquemont France 52 G5
Fauresmith S. Africa 101 G5
Fauske Norway 44 I3
Faust Canada 120 H4
Fawcett Canada 120 H4
Fawley U.K. 49 F8
Fawn r. Canada 121 N4
Faxaflói b. Iceland 44 [inset]
Faxälven r. Sweden 44 J5
Faya Chad 97 E3
Fayette AL U.S.A. 133 C5
Fayette MO U.S.A. 130 E4
Fayette MS U.S.A. 131 F6
Fayette OH U.S.A. 134 C3
Fayetteville AR U.S.A. 131 E4
Fayetteville NC U.S.A. 133 E5
Fayetteville TN U.S.A. 133 C5
Fayetteville WV U.S.A. 134 E4
Fāyid Egypt see Fā'id
Faylakah i. Kuwait 88 C4
Fazao Malfakassa, Parc National de nat. park Togo 96 D4
Fazilka India 82 C3
Fazrān, Jabal hill Saudi Arabia 88 C5
Fdérik Mauritania 96 B2
Fead Group is P.N.G. see Nuguria Islands
Feale r. Ireland 51 C5
Fear, Cape U.S.A. 133 E5
Featherston N.Z. 113 E5
Feathertop, Mount Australia 112 C6
Fécamp France 56 E2
Federal District admin. dist. Brazil see Distrito Federal
Federalsburg U.S.A. 135 H4
Federated Malay States country Asia see Malaysia
Fedusar India 82 C4
Fehet Lake Canada 121 M1
Fehmarn i. Germany 47 M3
Fehrbellin Germany 53 M2
Feia, Lagoa lag. Brazil 145 C3
Feicheng China see Feixian
Feijó Brazil 142 D5
Feilding N.Z. 113 E5
Fei Ngo Shan hill H.K. China see Kowloon Peak
Feio r. Brazil see Aguapeí
Feira de Santana Brazil 145 D1
Feixi China 77 H2
Feixian China 77 H1
Fejd el Abiod pass Alg. 58 B6
Feke Turkey 90 D3
Felanitx Spain 57 H4
Feldberg Germany 53 N1
Feldberg mt. Germany 47 L7
Feldkirch Austria 47 L7
Feldkirchen in Kärnten Austria 47 O7
Felidhu Atoll Maldives 81 D11
Felidu Atoll Maldives see Felidhu Atoll
Felipe C. Puerto Mex. 136 G5
Felixlândia Brazil 145 B2
Felixstowe U.K. 49 I7
Felixton S. Africa 101 J5
Fellowsville U.S.A. 134 F4
Felsina Italy see Bologna
Felton U.S.A. 135 H4
Feltre Italy 58 D1
Femunden l. Norway 44 G5
Femundsmarka Nasjonalpark nat. park Norway 44 H5
Fenaio, Punta del pt Italy 58 D3
Fence Lake U.S.A. 129 I4
Fener Burnu hd Turkey 85 B1
Fénérive Madag. see Fenoarivo Atsinanana
Fengari mt. Greece 59 K4
Fengcheng Fujian China see Lianjiang
Fengcheng Fujian China see Yongding
Fengcheng Fujian China see Anxi
Fengcheng Guangdong China see Xinfeng
Fengcheng Guangxi China see Fengshan
Fengcheng Guizhou China see Tianzhu
Fengcheng Jiangxi China 77 G2
Fenggang Fujian China see Shaxian
Fenggang Guizhou China 76 E3
Fenggang Jiangxi China see Yihuang
Fengguang China 74 B3
Fenghuang China 77 F3
Fengjiaba China see Wangcang
Fengjie China 77 F2
Fengkai China 77 F4
Fenglin Taiwan 77 I4
Fengming Shaanxi China see Qishan
Fengming Sichuan China see Pengshan
Fengqing China 76 C3
Fengshan Fujian China see Luoyuan
Fengshan Guangxi China 76 E3
Fengshan Hubei China see Luotian
Fengshan Yunnan China see Fengqing
Fengshuba Shuiku resr China 77 G3
Fengshui Shan mt. China 74 A1
Fengtongzhai Giant Panda Reserve nature res. China 76 D2
Fengxian China 76 E1
Fengxiang Heilong. China see Luobei
Fengxiang Yunnan China see Lincang
Fengyang China 77 H1
Fengyüan Taiwan 77 I3
Fengzhen China 73 K4
Feni Bangl. 83 G5
Feni Islands P.N.G. 106 F2
Fennville U.S.A. 134 B2
Feno, Capo di c. Corsica France 56 I6
Fenoarivo Atsinanana Madag. 99 E5
Fenshui Guan pass China 77 H3
Fenton U.S.A. 134 D2
Fenua Ura atoll Fr. Polynesia see Manuae
Fenyi China 77 G3
Feodosiya Ukr. 90 D1
Fer, Cap de c. Alg. 58 B6
Férai Greece see Feres
Ferdows Iran 88 E3
Fère-Champenoise France 52 D6
Feres Greece 59 L4
Fergus Canada 134 E2
Fergus Falls U.S.A. 130 D2
Ferguson Lake Canada 121 L2
Fergusson Island P.N.G. 106 F2
Fériana Tunisia 58 C7
Ferijaz Kosovo 59 I3
Ferkessédougou Côte d'Ivoire 96 C4
Fermo Italy 58 E3
Fermont Canada 123 I3
Fermoselle Spain 57 C3
Fermoy Ireland 51 D5
Fernandina, Isla i. Galápagos Ecuador 142 [inset]
Fernandina Beach U.S.A. 133 D6
Fernando de Magallanes, Parque Nacional nat. park Chile 144 B8
Fernando de Noronha i. Brazil 148 F6
Fernandópolis Brazil 145 A3
Fernando Poó i. Equat. Guinea see Bioco
Fernão Dias Brazil 145 B2
Ferndale U.S.A. 128 A1
Ferndown U.K. 49 F8
Fernlee Australia 112 C2
Fernley U.S.A. 128 D2
Ferns Ireland 51 F5
Ferozepore India see Firozpur
Ferrara Italy 58 D2
Ferreira-Gomes Brazil 143 H3
Ferro, Capo c. Sardinia Italy 58 C4
Ferrol Spain 57 B2
Ferron U.S.A. 129 H2
Ferros Brazil 145 C2
Ferryland Canada 123 L5
Ferryville Tunisia see Menzel Bourguiba
Fertő-tavi nat. park Hungary 58 G1
Ferwerd Neth. see Ferwert
Ferwert Neth. 52 F1
Fès Morocco 54 D5
Feshi Dem. Rep. Congo 99 B4
Fessenden U.S.A. 130 D2
Festus U.S.A. 130 F4
Fété Bowé Senegal 96 B3
Fethard Ireland 51 E5
Fethiye Malatya Turkey see Yazıhan
Fethiye Muğla Turkey 59 M6
Fethiye Körfezi b. Turkey 59 M6
Fetisovo Kazakh. 91 I2
Fetlar i. U.K. 50 [inset]
Fettercairn U.K. 50 G4
Feucht Germany 53 L5
Feuchtwangen Germany 53 K5
Feuilles, Rivière aux r. Canada 123 H2
Fevral'sk Rus. Fed. 74 C1
Fevzipaşa Turkey 90 E3
Feyzābād Afgh. 89 H2
Feyzābād Kermān Iran 88 D4
Feyzābād Khorāsān Iran 88 E3
Fez Morocco see Fès
Ffestiniog U.K. 49 D6
Fianarantsoa Madag. 99 E6
Fichē Eth. 98 D3
Fichtelgebirge hills Germany 53 M4
Field U.S.A. 134 D5
Fier Albania 59 H4
Fiery Creek r. Australia 110 B3
Fife Lake U.S.A. 134 C1
Fife Ness pt U.K. 50 G4
Fifield Australia 112 C4
Fifth Meridian Canada 120 H3
Figeac France 56 F4
Figueira da Foz Port. 57 B3
Figueras Spain see Figueres
Figueres Spain 57 H2
Figuig Morocco 54 D5
Figuil Cameroon 97 E4

▶Fiji country S. Pacific Ocean 107 H3
4th most populous and 5th largest country in Oceania.

Fīk' Eth. 98 E3
Filadelfia Para. 144 D2
Filchner Ice Shelf Antarctica 152 A1
Filey U.K. 48 G4
Filibe Bulg. see Plovdiv
Filingué Niger 96 D3
Filipinas country Asia see Philippines
Filippiada Greece 59 I5
Filipstad Sweden 45 I7
Fillan Norway 44 F5
Fillmore CA U.S.A. 128 D4
Fillmore UT U.S.A. 129 G2
Fils r. Germany 53 J6
Filtu Eth. 98 E3
Fimbull Ice Shelf Antarctica 152 C2
Fin Iran 88 C3
Finch Canada 135 H1
Findhorn r. U.K. 50 F3
Fındık Turkey 88 A2
Findlay U.S.A. 134 D3
Fine U.S.A. 135 H1
Finger Lake Canada 121 M4
Finger Lakes U.S.A. 135 G2
Finike Turkey 59 N6
Finike Körfezi b. Turkey 59 N6
Finisterre Spain see Fisterra
Finisterre, Cabo c. Spain see Finisterre, Cape
Finisterre, Cape Spain 57 B2
Finke watercourse Australia 110 A5
Finke, Mount hill Australia 109 F7
Finke Bay Australia 108 E3
Finke Gorge National Park Australia 109 F6
Finland country Europe 44 O5
Finland, Gulf of Europe 45 M7

▶Finlay r. Canada 120 E3
Part of the Mackenzie-Peace-Finlay, the 2nd longest river in North America.

Finlay, Mount Canada 120 E3
Finlay Forks Canada 120 F4
Finley U.S.A. 130 D2
Finn r. Ireland 51 E3
Finne ridge Germany 53 L3
Finnigan, Mount Australia 110 D2
Finniss, Cape Australia 109 F8
Finnmarksvidda reg. Norway 44 H2
Finnsnes Norway 44 J2
Fins Oman 88 E6
Finschhafen P.N.G. 69 L8
Finspång Sweden 45 I7
Fintona U.K. 51 E3
Finucane Range hills Australia 110 C4
Fionn Loch l. U.K. 50 D3
Fionnphort U.K. 50 C4
Fiordland National Park N.Z. 113 A7
Fir reg. Saudi Arabia 88 B4
Fırat r. Asia 90 E3 see Euphrates
Firebaugh U.S.A. 128 C3
Firedrake Lake Canada 121 J2
Firenze Italy see Florence
Fireside Canada 120 E3
Firk, Sha'īb watercourse Iraq 91 G5
Firmat Arg. 144 D4
Firminy France 56 G4
Firmum Italy see Fermo
Firmum Picenum Italy see Fermo
Firovo Rus. Fed. 42 G4
Firozabad India 82 D4
Firozkoh reg. Afgh. 89 G3
Firozpur India 82 C3
Fīrūzābād Iran 88 D4
Fīrūzkūh Iran 88 D3
Firyuza Turkm. see Pöwrize
Fischbach Germany 53 H5
Fischersbrunn Namibia 100 B3
Fish watercourse Namibia 100 C5
Fisher (abandoned) Australia 109 E7
Fisher Bay Antarctica 152 G2
Fisher Glacier Antarctica 152 E2
Fisher River Canada 121 L5
Fishers U.S.A. 134 B4
Fishers Island U.S.A. 135 J3
Fisher Strait Canada 119 J3
Fishguard U.K. 49 C7
Fishing Creek U.S.A. 135 G4
Fishing Lake Canada 121 M4
Fish Lake Canada 120 F2
Fish Point U.S.A. 134 D2
Fish Ponds H.K. China 77 [inset]
Fiske, Cape Antarctica 152 L2
Fiskenæsset Greenland see Qeqertarsuatsiaat
Fismes France 52 D5
Fisterra Spain 57 B2
Fisterra, Cabo c. Spain see Finisterre, Cape
Fitchburg U.S.A. 130 F3
Fitri, Lac l. Chad 97 E3
Fitzgerald Canada 121 I3
Fitzgerald U.S.A. 133 D6
Fitzgerald River National Park Australia 109 B8
Fitz Hugh Sound sea chan. Canada 120 D5
Fitz Roy Arg. 144 C7
Fitzroy r. Australia 108 C4
Fitz Roy, Cerro mt. Arg. 144 B7
Fitzroy Crossing Australia 108 D4
Fitzwilliam Island Canada 134 E1
Fiume Croatia see Rijeka
Fivemiletown U.K. 51 E3
Five Points U.S.A. 128 C3
Fizi Dem. Rep. Congo 99 C4
Fizuli Azer. see Füzuli
Flå Norway 45 F6
Flagstaff S. Africa 101 I6
Flagstaff U.S.A. 129 H4
Flagstaff Lake U.S.A. 132 G2
Flaherty Island Canada 122 F2
Flambeau r. U.S.A. 130 F2
Flamborough Head hd U.K. 48 G4
Fläming hills Germany 53 M2
Flaming Gorge Reservoir U.S.A. 126 F4
Flaminksvlei salt pan S. Africa 100 E6
Flanagan r. Canada 121 M4
Flandre reg. France 52 C4
Flannagan Lake U.S.A. 134 D5
Flannan Isles U.K. 50 B2
Flåsjön l. Sweden 44 I4
Flat r. Canada 120 E2
Flat r. U.S.A. 134 C2
Flat Creek Canada 120 B2
Flathead r. U.S.A. 124 E2
Flathead Lake U.S.A. 126 E3
Flatiron mt. U.S.A. 126 E3
Flat Island S. China Sea 68 F4
Flat Lick U.S.A. 134 D5
Flattery, Cape Australia 110 D2
Flattery, Cape U.S.A. 126 B2
Flat Top mt. Canada 120 B2
Flatwillow Creek r. U.S.A. 126 G3
Flatwoods U.S.A. 134 E4
Fleetmark Germany 53 L2
Fleetwood Australia 110 D4
Fleetwood U.K. 48 D5
Fleetwood U.S.A. 135 H3
Flekkefjord Norway 45 E7
Flemingsburg U.S.A. 134 D4
Flemington U.S.A. 135 H3
Flen Sweden 45 J7
Flensburg Germany 47 L3
Flers France 56 D2
Flesherton Canada 134 E1
Fletcher Lake Canada 121 I2
Fletcher Peninsula Antarctica 152 L2
Fleur de Lys Canada 123 K4
Fleur-de-May, Lac l. Canada 123 I4
Flinders r. Australia 110 C3
Flinders Chase National Park Australia 111 B7
Flinders Group National Park Australia 110 D2
Flinders Island Australia 111 [inset]
Flinders Passage Australia 110 E3
Flinders Ranges mts Australia 111 B7
Flinders Ranges National Park Australia 111 B6
Flinders Reefs Australia 110 E3
Flin Flon Canada 121 K4
Flint U.K. 48 D5
Flint U.S.A. 134 D2
Flint r. U.S.A. 133 C6
Flint Island Kiribati 151 J6
Flinton Australia 112 D1
Flisa Norway 45 H6

▶Flissingskiy, Mys c. Rus. Fed. 64 H2
Most easterly point of Europe.

Flixecourt France 52 C4
Flodden U.K. 48 E3
Flöha Germany 53 N4
Flood Range mts Antarctica 152 J1
Flora r. Australia 108 E3
Flora U.S.A. 134 B3
Florac France 56 F4
Florala U.S.A. 133 C6
Florange France 52 G5
Flora Reef Australia 110 D3
Florence Italy 58 D3
Florence AL U.S.A. 133 C5
Florence AZ U.S.A. 129 H5
Florence CO U.S.A. 127 G5
Florence OR U.S.A. 126 B4
Florence SC U.S.A. 133 E5
Florence WI U.S.A. 130 F2
Florence Junction U.S.A. 129 H5
Florencia Col. 142 C3
Florennes Belgium 52 E4
Florentia Italy see Florence
Florentino Ameghino, Embalse resr Arg. 144 C6
Flores r. Arg. 144 E5
Flores Guat. 136 G5
Flores i. Indon. 108 C2
Flores, Laut sea Indon. 108 B1
Flores Island Canada 120 E5
Flores Sea Indon. see Flores, Laut
Floresta Brazil 143 K5
Floresville U.S.A. 131 D6
Floriano Brazil 143 J5
Florianópolis Brazil 145 A4
Florida Uruguay 144 E4
Florida state U.S.A. 133 D6
Florida, Straits of Bahamas/U.S.A. 133 D8
Florida Bay U.S.A. 133 D7
Florida City U.S.A. 133 D7
Florida Islands Solomon Is 107 G2
Florida Keys is U.S.A. 133 D7
Florin U.S.A. 128 C2
Florina Greece 59 I4
Florissant U.S.A. 130 F4
Florø Norway 45 D6
Flour Lake Canada 123 I3
Floyd U.S.A. 134 E5
Floyd, Mount U.S.A. 129 G4
Floydada U.S.A. 131 C5
Fluessen l. Neth. 52 F2
Flushing Neth. see Vlissingen
Fly r. P.N.G. 69 K8
Flying Fish, Cape Antarctica 152 K2
Flying Mountain U.S.A. 129 I6
Flylân i. Neth. see Vlieland
Foam Lake Canada 121 K5
Foča Bos.-Herz. 58 H3
Foça Turkey 59 L5
Fochabers U.K. 50 F3
Focşani Romania 59 L2
Fogang China 77 G4
Foggia Italy 58 F4
Fogi Indon. 69 H7
Fogo i. Cape Verde 96 [inset]
Fogo Island Canada 123 L4
Foinaven hill U.K. 50 E2
Foix France 56 E5
Folda sea chan. Norway 44 I3
Foldereid Norway 44 H4
Foldfjorden sea chan. Norway 44 G4
Folegandros i. Greece 59 K6
Foleyet Canada 122 E4
Foley Island Canada 119 K3
Foligno Italy 58 E3
Folkestone U.K. 49 I7
Folkingham U.K. 49 G6
Folkston U.S.A. 133 D6
Folldal Norway 44 G5
Follonica Italy 58 D3
Folsom Lake U.S.A. 128 C2
Fomboni Comoros 99 E5
Fomento Cuba 133 E8
Fomin Rus. Fed. 43 I7
Fominskaya Rus. Fed. 42 K2
Fominskoye Rus. Fed. 42 I4
Fonda U.S.A. 135 H2
Fond-du-Lac Canada 121 J3
Fond du Lac r. Canada 121 J3
Fond du Lac U.S.A. 134 A2
Fondevila Spain 57 B3
Fondi Italy 58 E4
Fonni Sardinia Italy 58 C4
Fonsagrada Spain see A Fonsagrada
Fonseca, Golfo do b. Central America 136 G6

G

Girâ, Wâdi watercourse Egypt see Jirā', Wādī
Gīrān Rīg mt. Iran 88 E4
Girard U.S.A. 134 E2
Girardin, Lac l. Canada 123 I2
Girdab Iran 88 E3
Giresun Turkey 90 E2
Girgenti Sicily Italy see Agrigento
Giridh India see Giridih
Giridih India 83 F4
Girilambone Australia 112 C3
Girna r. India 82 C5
Gir National Park India 82 B5
Girne Cyprus see Kyrenia
Girón Ecuador 142 C4
Giron Sweden see Kiruna
Girona Spain 57 H3
Gironde est. France 56 D4
Girot Pak. 89 I3
Girral Australia 112 C4
Girraween National Park Australia 112 E2
Girvan U.K. 50 E5
Girvas Rus. Fed. 42 G3
Gisborne N.Z. 113 G4
Giscome Canada 120 F4
Gislaved Sweden 45 H8
Gisors France 52 B5
Gissar Tajik. see Hisor
Gissar Range mts Tajik./Uzbek. 89 G2
Gissarskiy Khrebet mts Tajik./Uzbek. see Gissar Range
Gitarama Rwanda 98 C4
Gitega Burundi 98 C4
Giuba r. Somalia see Jubba
Giulianova Italy 58 E3
Giurgiu Romania 59 K3
Giuvala, Pasul pass Romania 59 K2
Givar Iran 88 E2
Givet France 52 E4
Givors France 56 G4
Givry-en-Argonne France 52 E6
Giyani S. Africa 101 J2
Giza Egypt 90 C5
Gizhiga Rus. Fed. 65 R3
Gjakovë Kosovo 59 I3
Gjilan Kosovo 59 I3
Gjirokastër Albania 59 I4
Gjirokastra Albania see Gjirokastër
Gjoa Haven Canada 119 I3
Gjøra Norway 44 F5
Gjøvik Norway 45 G6
Gkinas, Akrotirio pt Greece 59 M6
Glace Bay Canada 123 K5
Glacier Bay National Park and Preserve U.S.A. 120 B3
Glacier National Park Canada 120 G5
Glacier National Park U.S.A. 126 E2
Glacier Peak vol. U.S.A. 126 C2
Gladstad Norway 44 G4
Gladstone Australia 110 E4
Gladstone Canada 121 L5
Gladwin U.S.A. 134 C2
Gladys U.S.A. 134 F5
Gladys Lake Canada 120 C3
Glamis U.K. 50 F4
Glamis U.S.A. 129 F5
Glamoč Bos.-Herz. 58 G2
Glan r. Germany 53 H5
Glandorf Germany 53 I2
Glanton U.K. 48 F3
Glasgow U.K. 50 E5
Glasgow KY U.S.A. 134 C5
Glasgow MT U.S.A. 126 G2
Glasgow VA U.S.A. 134 F5
Glaslyn Canada 121 I4
Glass, Loch l. U.K. 50 E3
Glass Mountain U.S.A. 128 D3
Glastonbury U.K. 49 E7
Glauchau Germany 53 M4
Glazov Rus. Fed. 42 L4
Gleiwitz Poland see Gliwice
Glen U.S.A. 135 J1
Glen Allen U.S.A. 135 G5
Glen Alpine Dam S. Africa 101 I2
Glenamaddy Ireland 51 D4
Glenamoy r. Ireland 51 C3
Glen Arbor U.S.A. 134 C1
Glenbawn, Lake Australia 112 E4
Glenboro Canada 121 L5
Glen Canyon gorge U.S.A. 129 H3
Glen Canyon Dam U.S.A. 129 H3
Glencoe Canada 134 E2
Glencoe S. Africa 101 J5
Glencoe U.S.A. 130 E2
Glendale AZ U.S.A. 129 G5
Glendale CA U.S.A. 128 D4
Glendale UT U.S.A. 129 G3
Glendale Lake U.S.A. 135 F3
Glen Davis Australia 112 E4
Glenden Australia 110 E4
Glendive U.S.A. 126 G3
Glendon Canada 121 I4
Glendo Reservoir U.S.A. 126 G4
Glenfield U.S.A. 135 H2
Glengavlen Ireland 51 E3
Glengyle Australia 110 B5
Glen Innes Australia 112 E2
Glenluce U.K. 50 E6
Glen Lyon U.S.A. 135 G3
Glenlyon Peak Canada 120 C2
Glen More valley U.K. 50 E3
Glenmorgan Australia 112 D1
Glenn U.S.A. 128 B2
Glennallen U.S.A. 118 D3
Glennie U.S.A. 134 D1
Glenns Ferry U.S.A. 126 E4
Glenora Canada 120 D3
Glenore Australia 110 C3
Glenormiston Australia 110 B4
Glenreagh Australia 112 F3
Glen Rose U.S.A. 131 D5
Glenrothes U.K. 50 F4
Glens Falls U.S.A. 135 I2
Glen Shee valley U.K. 50 F4
Glenties Ireland 51 D3
Glenveagh National Park Ireland 51 E2
Glenville U.S.A. 134 E4
Glenwood AR U.S.A. 131 E5
Glenwood IA U.S.A. 130 E3
Glenwood MN U.S.A. 130 E2
Glenwood NM U.S.A. 129 I5
Glenwood Springs U.S.A. 129 J2
Glevum U.K. see Gloucester
Glinde Germany 53 K1
Glittertinden mt. Norway 45 F6
Gliwice Poland 47 Q5
Globe U.S.A. 129 H5
Glogau Poland see Głogów
Głogów Poland 47 P5
Glomfjord Norway 44 H3
Glomma r. Norway 44 G7
Glommersträsk Sweden 44 K4
Glorieuses, Îles is Indian Ocean 99 E5
Glorioso Islands Indian Ocean see Glorieuses, Îles
Gloster U.S.A. 131 F6
Gloucester Australia 112 E3
Gloucester U.K. 49 E7
Gloucester MA U.S.A. 135 J2
Gloucester VA U.S.A. 135 G5
Gloversville U.S.A. 135 H2
Glovertown Canada 123 L4
Glöwen Germany 53 M2
Glubinnoye Rus. Fed. 74 D3
Glubokiy Krasnoyarskiy Kray Rus. Fed. 72 H2
Glubokiy Rostovskaya Oblast' Rus. Fed. 43 I6
Glubokoye Belarus see Hlybokaye
Glubokoye Kazakh. 80 F1
Gluggarnir hill Faroe Is 44 [inset]
Glukhov Ukr. see Hlukhiv
Glusburn U.K. 48 F5
Glynebwy U.K. see Ebbw Vale
Gmelinka Rus. Fed. 43 J6
Gmünd Austria 47 O6
Gmunden Austria 47 N7
Gnarp Sweden 45 J5
Gnarrenburg Germany 53 J1
Gnesen Poland see Gniezno
Gniezno Poland 47 P4
Gnjilane Kosovo see Gjilan
Gnowangerup Australia 109 B8
Gnows Nest Range hills Australia 109 B7
Goa India 84 B3
Goa state India 84 B3
Goageb Namibia 100 C4
Goalen Head hd Australia 112 E6
Goalpara India 83 G4
Goat Fell hill U.K. 50 D5
Goba Eth. 98 E3
Gobabis Namibia 100 D2
Gobannium U.K. see Abergavenny
Gobas Namibia 100 D4
Gobi Desert des. China/Mongolia 72 J4
Gobindpur India 83 F5
Gobles U.S.A. 134 C2
Gobō Japan 75 D6
Goch Germany 52 G3
Gochas Namibia 100 D3
Go Công Vietnam 71 D5
Godalming U.K. 49 G7
Godavari r. India 84 D2
Godavari, Cape India 84 D2
Godda India 83 F4
Godē Eth. 98 E3
Godere Eth. 98 E3
Goderich Canada 134 E2
Goderville France 49 H9
Godhavn Greenland see Qeqertarsuaq
Godhra India 82 C5
Godia Creek b. India 89 H6
Gods r. Canada 121 M3
Gods Lake Canada 121 M4
God's Mercy, Bay of Canada 121 O2
Godthåb Greenland see Nuuk
Godwin-Austen, Mount China/Pakistan see K2
Goedereede Neth. 52 D3
Goedgegun Swaziland see Nhlangano
Goegap Nature Reserve S. Africa 100 D5
Goélands, Lac aux l. Canada 123 J3
Goes Neth. 52 D3
Gogama Canada 122 E5
Gogebic Range hills U.S.A. 130 F2
Gogra r. India see Ghaghara
Goiana Brazil 143 L5
Goiandira Brazil 145 A2
Goianésia Brazil 145 A1
Goiânia Brazil 145 A2
Goiás Brazil 145 A1
Goiás state Brazil 145 A2
Goinsargoin China 76 C2
Goio-Erê Brazil 144 F2
Gojra Pak. 89 I4
Gokak India 84 B2
Gokarn India 84 B3
Gök Çay r. Turkey 85 A1
Gökçeada i. Turkey 59 K4
Gökdepe Turkm. see Gëkdepe
Gökdere r. Turkey 85 A1
Goklenkuy, Solonchak salt l. Turkm. 88 E1
Gökova Körfezi b. Turkey 59 L6
Gokprosh Hills Pak. 89 F5
Göksun Turkey 90 E3
Goksu Parkı Turkey 85 A1
Gokteik Myanmar 70 B2
Gokwe Zimbabwe 99 C5
Gol Norway 45 F6
Golaghat India 83 H4
Golbāf Iran 88 E4
Gölbaşı Turkey 90 E3
Golconda U.S.A. 128 E1
Gölcük Turkey 59 M4
Gold U.S.A. 135 G3
Gołdap Poland 47 S3
Gold Beach U.S.A. 126 B4
Goldberg Germany 53 M1
Gold Coast country Africa see Ghana
Gold Coast Australia 112 F2
Golden U.S.A. 126 G5
Golden Bay N.Z. 113 D5
Goldendale U.S.A. 126 C3
Goldene Aue reg. Germany 53 K3
Golden Gate Highlands National Park S. Africa 101 I5
Golden Hinde mt. Canada 120 E5
Golden Lake Canada 135 G1
Golden Prairie Canada 121 I5
Goldenstedt Germany 53 I2
Goldfield U.S.A. 128 E3
Goldsand Lake Canada 121 K3
Goldsboro U.S.A. 133 E5
Goldstone Lake U.S.A. 128 E4
Goldsworthy (abandoned) Australia 108 B5
Goldthwaite U.S.A. 131 D6
Goldvein U.S.A. 135 G4
Göle Turkey 91 F2
Golestān Afgh. 89 F3
Goleta U.S.A. 128 D4
Golets-Davydov, Gora mt. Rus. Fed. 73 J2
Golfo di Orosei Gennargentu e Asinara, Parco Nazionale del nat. park Sardinia Italy 58 C4
Gölgeli Dağları mts Turkey 59 M6
Goliad U.S.A. 131 D6
Golingka China see Gongbo'gyamda
Gölköy Turkey 90 E2
Gollel Swaziland see Lavumisa
Golm Germany 53 M2
Golmberg hill Germany 53 N2
Golmud China 80 H4
Golovnino Rus. Fed. 74 G4
Golpāyegān Iran 88 C3
Gölpazarı Turkey 59 N4
Golspie U.K. 50 F3
Gol Vardeh Iran 89 F3
Golyama Syutkya mt. Bulg. 59 K4
Golyam Persenk mt. Bulg. 59 K4
Golyshi Rus. Fed. see Vetluzhskiy
Golzow Germany 53 M2
Goma Dem. Rep. Congo 98 C4
Gomang Co salt l. China 83 G3
Gomati r. India 87 N4
Gombak, Bukit hill Sing. 71 [inset]
Gombe Nigeria 96 E3
Gombe r. Tanz. 99 D4
Gombi Nigeria 96 E3
Gombroon Iran see Bandar-e 'Abbās
Gomel' Belarus see Homyel'
Gómez Palacio Mex. 131 C7
Gomīshān Iran 88 D2
Gommern Germany 53 L2
Gomo Co salt l. China 83 F2
Gonābād Iran 88 E2
Gonaïves Haiti 137 J5
Gonarezhou National Park Zimbabwe 99 D6
Gonbad-e Kavus Iran 88 D2
Gonda India 83 E4
Gondal India 82 B5
Gondar Eth. see Gonder
Gonder Eth. 98 D2
Gondia India 82 E5
Gondiya India see Gondia
Gönen Turkey 59 L4
Gonfreville-l'Orcher France 49 H9
Gong'an China 77 G2
Gongbalou China 83 G3
Gongbo'gyamda China 76 B2
Gongchang China see Longxi
Gongcheng China 77 F3
Gongga Shan mt. China 76 D2
Gonghe Qinghai China 80 J4
Gonghe Yunnan China see Mouding
Gongjiang China see Yudu
Gongogi r. Brazil 145 D1
Gongolgon Australia 112 C3
Gongpoquan China 80 I3
Gongquan China 76 E2
Gongtang China see Damxung
Gongwang Shan mts China 76 D3
Gongxian China see Gongquan
Gonjo China see Kasha
Gonjog China see Coqên
Gonzales CA U.S.A. 128 C3
Gonzales TX U.S.A. 131 D6
Gonzha Rus. Fed. 74 B1
Goochland U.S.A. 135 G5
Goodenough, Cape Antarctica 152 G2
Goodenough Island P.N.G. 106 F2
Gooderham Canada 135 F1
Good Hope, Cape of S. Africa 100 D8
Good Hope Mountain Canada 126 B2
Gooding U.S.A. 126 E4
Goodland IN U.S.A. 134 B3
Goodland KS U.S.A. 130 C4
Goodlettsville U.S.A. 134 B5
Goodooga Australia 112 C2
Goodspeed Nunataks Antarctica 152 E2
Goole U.K. 48 G5
Goolgowi Australia 112 B5
Goolma Australia 112 D4
Gooloogong Australia 112 D4
Goomalling Australia 109 B7
Goombalie Australia 112 B2
Goondiwindi Australia 112 E2
Goongarrie, Lake salt flat Australia 109 C7
Goongarrie National Park Australia 109 C7
Goonyella Australia 110 D4
Goorly, Lake salt flat Australia 109 B7
Goose Bay Canada see Happy Valley-Goose Bay
Goose Creek U.S.A. 133 D5
Goose Lake U.S.A. 126 C4
Gooty India 84 C3
Gopalganj Bangl. 83 G5
Gopalganj India 83 F4
Gopeshwar India 82 D3
Göppingen Germany 53 J6
Gorakhpur India 83 E4
Goražde Bos.-Herz. 58 H3
Gorbernador U.S.A. 129 J3
Gorczański Park Narodowy nat. park Poland 47 R6
Gorda, Punta pt U.S.A. 128 A1
Gördes Turkey 59 M5
Gordil Cent. Afr. Rep. 98 C3
Gordon r. Canada 121 O1
Gordon U.K. 50 G5
Gordon U.S.A. 130 C3
Gordon, Lake Australia 111 [inset]
Gordon Downs (abandoned) Australia 108 E4
Gordon Lake Canada 121 I3
Gordon Lake U.S.A. 135 F4
Gordonsville U.S.A. 135 F4
Goré Chad 97 E4
Gorē Eth. 98 D3
Gore N.Z. 113 B8
Gore U.S.A. 135 F4
Gorebridge U.K. 50 F5
Gore Point U.S.A. 118 C4
Gorey Ireland 51 F5
Gorg Iran 89 E4
Gorgān Iran 88 D2
Gorgān, Khalīj-e Iran 88 D2
Gorge Range hills Australia 108 B5
Gorgona, Isla i. Col. 142 C3
Gorham U.S.A. 135 J1
Gori Georgia 86 F1
Gorinchem Neth. 52 E3
Goris Armenia 91 G3
Gorizia Italy 58 E2
Gorki Belarus see Horki
Gor'kiy Rus. Fed. see Nizhniy Novgorod
Gor'kovskoye Vodokhranilishche resr Rus. Fed. 42 I4
Gorlice Poland 43 D6
Görlitz Germany 47 O5
Gorlovka Ukr. see Horlivka
Gorna Dzhumaya Bulg. see Blagoevgrad
Gorna Oryakhovitsa Bulg. 59 K3
Gornji Milanovac Serbia 59 I2
Gornji Vakuf Bos.-Herz. 58 G3
Gorno-Altaysk Rus. Fed. 80 G1
Gornotrakiyska Nizina lowland Bulg. 59 K3
Gornozavodsk Permskaya Oblast' Rus. Fed. 41 R4
Gornozavodsk Sakhalinskaya Oblast' Rus. Fed. 74 F3
Gornyak Rus. Fed. 80 F1
Gornyy Rus. Fed. 43 K6
Gornyye Klyuchi Rus. Fed. 74 D3
Goro i. Fiji see Koro
Gorodenka Ukr. see Horodenka
Gorodets Rus. Fed. 42 I4
Gorodishche Penzenskaya Oblast' Rus. Fed. 43 J5
Gorodishche Volgogradskaya Oblast' Rus. Fed. 43 J6
Gorodok Belarus see Haradok
Gorodok Rus. Fed. see Zakamensk
Gorodok Khmel'nyts'ka Oblast' Ukr. see Horodok
Gorodok L'vivs'ka Oblast' Ukr. see Horodok
Gorodovikovsk Rus. Fed. 43 I7
Goroka P.N.G. 69 L8
Gorokhovets Rus. Fed. 42 I4
Gorom Gorom Burkina 96 C3
Gorong, Kepulauan is Indon. 69 I7
Gorongosa mt. Moz. 99 D5
Gorongosa, Parque Nacional de nat. park Moz. 99 D5
Gorontalo Indon. 69 G6
Gorshechnoye Rus. Fed. 43 H6
Gort Ireland 51 D4
Gort an Choirce Ireland 51 D2
Gorutuba r. Brazil 145 C1
Gorveh Iran 88 E4
Goryachiy Klyuch Rus. Fed. 91 E1
Görzke Germany 53 M2
Gorzów Wielkopolski Poland 47 O4
Gosainthan mt. China see Xixabangma Feng
Gosforth U.K. 48 F3
Goshen CA U.S.A. 128 D3
Goshen IN U.S.A. 134 C3
Goshen NH U.S.A. 135 I2
Goshen NY U.S.A. 135 H3
Goshen VA U.S.A. 134 F5
Goshoba Turkm. see Goşoba
Goslar Germany 53 K3
Goşoba Turkm. 91 I2
Gospić Croatia 58 F2
Gosport U.K. 49 F8
Gossi Mali 96 C3
Gostivar Macedonia 59 I4
Gosu China 76 C1
Göteborg Sweden see Gothenburg
Götene Sweden 45 H7
Gotenhafen Poland see Gdynia
Gotha Germany 53 K4
Gothenburg Sweden 45 G8
Gothenburg U.S.A. 130 C3
Gotland i. Sweden 45 K8
Gotō-rettō is Japan 75 C6
Gotse Delchev Bulg. 59 J4
Gotska Sandön i. Sweden 45 K7
Gōtsu Japan 75 D6
Göttingen Germany 53 J3
Gott Peak Canada 120 F5
Gottwaldow Czech Rep. see Zlín
Gouda Neth. 52 E2
Goudiri Senegal 96 B3
Goudoumaria Niger 96 E3
Goûgaram Niger 96 D3
▶Gough Island S. Atlantic Ocean 148 H8
Dependency of St Helena.
Gouin, Réservoir resr Canada 122 G4
Goulburn Australia 112 D5
Goulburn r. N.S.W. Australia 112 E4
Goulburn r. Vic. Australia 112 B6
Goulburn Islands Australia 108 F2
Goulburn River National Park Australia 112 E4
Gould Coast Antarctica 152 J1
Goulou atoll Micronesia see Ngulu
Goundam Mali 96 C3
Goundi Chad 97 E4
Goupil, Lac l. Canada 123 H3
Gouraya Alg. 57 G5
Gourcy Burkina 96 C3
Gourdon France 56 E4
Gouré Niger 96 E3
Gouripur Bangl. 83 G4
Gourits r. S. Africa 100 E8
Gourma-Rharous Mali 96 C3
Gournay-en-Bray France 52 B5
Goussainville France 52 C5
Gouverneur U.S.A. 135 H1
Governador Valadares Brazil 145 C2
Governor's Harbour Bahamas 133 E7
Govĭ Altayn Nuruu mts Mongolia 80 I3
Govind Ballash Pant Sagar resr India 83 E4
Gowanda U.S.A. 135 F2
Gowan Range hills Australia 110 D5
Gowārān Afgh. 89 G4
Gowd-e Mokh l. Iran 88 D4
Gowd-e Zereh plain Afgh. 89 F4
Gowmal Kalay Afgh. 89 H3
Gowna, Lough l. Ireland 51 E4
Goya Arg. 144 E3
Göyçay Azer. 91 G2
Goyder watercourse Australia 109 F6
Goýmatdag hills Turkm. 88 D1
Goymatdag hills Turkm. see Goýmatdag
Göynük Turkey 59 N4
Goyoum Cameroon 96 E4
Gozareh Afgh. 89 F3
Goz-Beïda Chad 97 F3
Gozha Co salt l. China 82 E2
Gözkaya Turkey 85 C1
Gozo i. Malta 58 F6
Graaff-Reinet S. Africa 100 G7
Grabfeld plain Germany 53 K4
Grabo Côte d'Ivoire 96 C4
Grabouw S. Africa 100 D8
Grabow Germany 53 L1
Gračac Croatia 58 F2
Gracefield Canada 122 F5
Gracey U.S.A. 134 B5
Gradaús, Serra dos hills Brazil 143 H5
Gradiška Bos.-Herz. see Bosanska Gradiška
Grady U.S.A. 131 C5
Gräfenhainichen Germany 53 M3
Grafenwöhr Germany 53 L5
Grafton Australia 112 F2
Grafton ND U.S.A. 130 D1
Grafton WI U.S.A. 134 B2
Grafton WV U.S.A. 134 E4
Grafton, Cape Australia 110 D3
Grafton, Mount U.S.A. 129 F2
Grafton Passage Australia 110 D3
Graham NC U.S.A. 132 E4
Graham TX U.S.A. 131 D5
Graham, Mount U.S.A. 129 I5
Graham Bell Island Rus. Fed. see Greem-Bell, Ostrov
Graham Island B.C. Canada 120 C4
Graham Island Nunavut Canada 119 I2
Graham Land reg. Antarctica 152 L2
Grahamstown S. Africa 101 H7
Grahovo Bos.-Herz. see Bosansko Grahovo
Graigue Ireland 51 F5
Grajaú Brazil 143 I5
Grajaú r. Brazil 143 J4
Grammont Belgium see Geraardsbergen
Grammos mt. Greece 59 I4
Grampian Mountains U.K. 50 E4
Grampians National Park Australia 111 C8
Granada Nicaragua 137 G6
Granada Spain 57 E5
Granada U.S.A. 130 C4
Granard Ireland 51 E4
Granbury U.S.A. 131 D5
Granby Canada 123 G5
Gran Canaria i. Canary Is 96 B2
Gran Chaco reg. Arg./Para. 144 D3
Grand r. MO U.S.A. 134 B2
Grand r. SD U.S.A. 130 C2
Grand Atlas mts Morocco see Haut Atlas
Grand Bahama i. Bahamas 133 E7
Grand Ballon mt. France 47 K7
Grand Bank Canada 123 L5
Grand Banks of Newfoundland sea feature N. Atlantic Ocean 148 E3
Grand-Bassam Côte d'Ivoire 96 C4
Grand Bay-Westfield Canada 123 I5
Grand Bend Canada 134 E2
Grand Blanc U.S.A. 134 D2
Grand Canal Ireland 51 E4
Grand Canary i. Canary Is see Gran Canaria
Grand Canyon U.S.A. 129 G3
Grand Canyon gorge U.S.A. 129 G3
Grand Canyon National Park U.S.A. 129 G3
Grand Canyon - Parashant National Monument nat. park U.S.A. 129 G3
Grand Cayman i. Cayman Is 137 H5
Grand Drumont mt. France 47 K7
Grande r. Bahia Brazil 145 B1
Grande r. São Paulo Brazil 145 A3
Grande r. Nicaragua 137 H6
Grande, Bahía b. Arg. 144 C8
Grande, Ilha i. Brazil 145 B3
Grande Cache Canada 120 G4
Grande Comore i. Comoros see Njazidja
Grande Prairie Canada 120 G4
Grand Erg de Bilma des. Niger 96 E3
Grand Erg Occidental des. Alg. 54 D5
Grand Erg Oriental des. Alg. 54 F6
Grande-Rivière Canada 123 I4
Grandes, Salinas salt marsh Arg. 144 C4
Grande-Vallée Canada 123 I4
Grand Falls N.B. Canada 123 I5
Grand Falls-Windsor Nfld. and Lab. Canada 123 L4
Grand Forks Canada 120 G5
Grand Forks U.S.A. 130 D2
Grand Gorge U.S.A. 135 H2
Grand Haven U.S.A. 134 B2
Grandin, Lac l. Canada 120 G1
Grandioznyy, Pik mt. Rus. Fed. 72 H2
Grand Island U.S.A. 130 D3
Grand Isle U.S.A. 131 F6
Grand Junction U.S.A. 129 I2
Grand Lac Germain l. Canada 123 I4
Grand-Lahou Côte d'Ivoire 96 C4
Grand Lake N.B. Canada 123 I5
Grand Lake Nfld. and Lab. Canada 123 J3
Grand Lake Nfld. and Lab. Canada 123 K4
Grand Lake LA U.S.A. 131 E6
Grand Lake MI U.S.A. 134 D1
Grand Lake St Marys U.S.A. 134 C3
Grand Ledge U.S.A. 134 C2
Grand Manan Island Canada 123 I5
Grand Marais MI U.S.A. 132 C2
Grand Marais MN U.S.A. 130 F2
Grand-Mère Canada 123 G5
Grand Mesa U.S.A. 129 J2
Grândola Port. 57 B4
Grand Passage New Caledonia 107 G3
Grand Rapids Canada 121 L4
Grand Rapids MI U.S.A. 134 C2
Grand Rapids MN U.S.A. 130 E2
Grand-Sault Canada see Grand Falls
Grand St-Bernard, Col du pass Italy/Switz. see Great St Bernard Pass
Grand Teton mt. U.S.A. 126 F4
Grand Teton National Park U.S.A. 126 F4
Grand Traverse Bay U.S.A. 134 C1
▶Grand Turk Turks and Caicos Is 137 J4
Capital of the Turks and Caicos Islands.
Grandville U.S.A. 134 C2
Grandvilliers France 52 B5
Grand Wash Cliffs mts U.S.A. 129 F4
Grange Ireland 51 E6
Grängesberg Sweden 45 I6
Grangeville U.S.A. 126 D3
Granisle Canada 120 E4
Granite Falls U.S.A. 130 E2
Granite Mountain U.S.A. 128 E1
Granite Mountains CA U.S.A. 129 F4
Granite Mountains CA U.S.A. 129 F5
Granite Peak MT U.S.A. 126 F3
Granite Peak UT U.S.A. 129 G1
Granite Range mts AK U.S.A. 120 A3
Granite Range mts NV U.S.A. 128 D1
Granitola, Capo c. Sicily Italy 58 E6
Granja Brazil 143 J4
Gran Laguna Salada l. Arg. 144 C6
Gränna Sweden 45 I7
Gran Paradiso mt. Italy 58 B2
Gran Paradiso, Parco Nazionale del nat. park Italy 58 B2
Gran Pilastro mt. Austria/Italy 47 M7
Gran San Bernardo, Colle del pass Italy/Switz. see Great St Bernard Pass
Gran Sasso e Monti della Laga, Parco Nazionale del nat. park Italy 58 E3
Granschütz Germany 53 M3
Gransee Germany 53 N1
Grant U.S.A. 130 C3
Grant, Mount U.S.A. 128 E2
Grantham U.K. 49 G6
Grant Island Antarctica 152 J2
Grant Lake Canada 120 G1
Grantown-on-Spey U.K. 50 F3
Grant Range mts U.S.A. 129 F2
Grants U.S.A. 129 J4
Grants Pass U.S.A. 126 C4
Grantsville UT U.S.A. 129 G1
Grantsville WV U.S.A. 134 E4
Granville France 56 D2
Granville AZ U.S.A. 129 I5
Granville NY U.S.A. 135 I2
Granville TN U.S.A. 134 C5
Granville (abandoned) Canada 120 B2
Granville Lake Canada 121 K3
Grão Mogol Brazil 145 C2
Grapevine Mountains U.S.A. 128 E3
Gras, Lac de l. Canada 121 I1
Graskop S. Africa 101 J3
Grasplatz Namibia 100 B4
Grass r. Canada 121 L3
Grass r. U.S.A. 135 H1
Grasse France 56 H5
Grassflat U.S.A. 135 F3
Grassington U.K. 48 F4
Grasslands National Park Canada 121 J5
Grassrange U.S.A. 126 F3
Grass Valley U.S.A. 128 C2
Grassy Butte U.S.A. 130 C2
Grästorp Sweden 45 H7
Gratz U.S.A. 134 C4
Graudenz Poland see Grudziądz
Graus Spain 57 G2
Gravataí Brazil 145 A5
Grave, Pointe de pt France 56 D4
Gravelbourg Canada 121 J5
Gravel Hill Lake Canada 121 K2
Gravelines France 52 C4
Gravelotte S. Africa 101 J2
Gravenhurst Canada 134 F1
Grave Peak U.S.A. 126 E3
Gravesend Australia 112 E2
Gravesend U.K. 49 H7
Gravina in Puglia Italy 58 G4
Grawn U.S.A. 134 C1
Gray France 56 G3
Gray GA U.S.A. 133 D5
Gray KY U.S.A. 134 C5
Gray ME U.S.A. 135 J2
Grayback Mountain U.S.A. 126 C4
Gray Lake Canada 121 I2
Grayling r. Canada 120 E3
Grayling U.S.A. 134 C1
Grays U.K. 49 H7
Grays Harbor inlet U.S.A. 126 B3
Grays Lake U.S.A. 126 F4
Grayson U.S.A. 134 D4
Graz Austria 47 O7
Greasy Lake Canada 120 F2
Great Abaco i. Bahamas 133 E7
Great Australian Bight g. Australia 109 E8
Great Baddow U.K. 49 H7
Great Bahama Bank sea feature Bahamas 133 E7
Great Barrier Island N.Z. 113 E3
Great Barrier Reef Australia 110 D1
Great Barrier Reef Marine Park (Cairns Section) Australia 110 D3
Great Barrier Reef Marine Park (Capricorn Section) Australia 110 E4
Great Barrier Reef Marine Park (Central Section) Australia 110 E3
Great Barrier Reef Marine Park (Far North Section) Australia 110 D2
Great Barrington U.S.A. 135 I2
Great Basalt Wall National Park Australia 110 D3
Great Basin U.S.A. 128 E2
Great Basin National Park U.S.A. 129 F2
Great Bear r. Canada 120 E1
▶Great Bear Lake Canada 120 G1
4th largest lake in North America, and 7th in the world.
Great Belt sea chan. Denmark 45 G9
Great Bend U.S.A. 130 D4
Great Bitter Lake Egypt 85 A4
Great Blasket Island Ireland 51 B5
▶Great Britain i. U.K. 46 G4
Largest island in Europe, and 8th in the world.
Great Clifton U.K. 48 D4
Great Coco Island Cocos Is 68 A4
Great Cumbrae i. U.K. 50 E5

Great Dismal Swamp National Wildlife Refuge nature res. U.S.A. 135 G5
Great Dividing Range mts Australia 112 B6
Great Eastern Erg des. Alg. see Grand Erg Oriental
Greater Antarctica reg. Antarctica see East Antarctica
Greater Antilles is Caribbean Sea 137 H4
Greater Khingan Mountains China see Da Hinggan Ling
Greater Tunb i. The Gulf 88 D5
Great Exuma i. Bahamas 133 F8
Great Falls U.S.A. 126 F3
Great Fish r. S. Africa 101 H7
Great Fish Point S. Africa 101 H7
Great Fish River Reserve Complex nature res. S. Africa 101 H7
Great Gandak r. India 83 F4
Great Ganges atoll Cook Is see Manihiki
Great Guana Cay i. Bahamas 133 E7
Great Inagua i. Bahamas 137 J4
Great Karoo plat. S. Africa 100 F7
Great Kei r. S. Africa 101 I7
Great Lake Australia 111 [inset]
Great Limpopo Transfrontier Park 101 J2
Great Malvern U.K. 49 E6
Great Meteor Tablemount sea feature N. Atlantic Ocean 148 G4
Great Namaqualand reg. Namibia 100 C4
Great Nicobar i. India 71 A6
Great Ormes Head hd U.K. 48 D5
Great Ouse r. U.K. 49 H6
Great Oyster Bay Australia 111 [inset]
Great Palm Islands Australia 110 D3
Great Plain of the Koukdjuak Canada 119 K3
Great Plains U.S.A. 130 C3
Great Point U.S.A. 135 J3
Great Rift Valley Africa 98 D4
Great Ruaha r. Tanz. 99 D4
Great Sacandaga Lake U.S.A. 135 H2
Great St Bernard Pass Italy/Switz. 58 B2
Great Salt Lake U.S.A. 129 G1
Great Salt Lake Desert U.S.A. 129 G1
Great Sand Hills Canada 121 I5
Great Sand Sea des. Egypt/Libya 90 B5
Great Sandy Desert Australia 108 C5
Great Sandy Island Australia see Fraser Island
Great Sea Reef Fiji 107 H3

▶Great Slave Lake Canada 120 H2
Deepest and 5th largest lake in North America and 10th largest in the world.

Great Smoky Mountains U.S.A. 133 C5
Great Smoky Mountains National Park U.S.A. 132 D5
Great Snow Mountain Canada 120 E3
Greatstone-on-Sea U.K. 49 H8
Great Stour r. U.K. 49 I7
Great Torrington U.K. 49 C8
Great Victoria Desert Australia 109 E7
Great Wall research station Antarctica 152 A2
Great Wall tourist site China 73 L4
Great Waltham U.K. 49 H7
Great Western Erg des. Alg. see Grand Erg Occidental
Great West Torres Islands Myanmar 71 B5
Great Whernside hill U.K. 48 F4
Great Yarmouth U.K. 49 I6
Grebenkovskiy Ukr. see Hrebinka
Grebyonka Ukr. see Hrebinka
Greco, Cape Cyprus see Greko, Cape
Gredos, Sierra de mts Spain 57 D3
Greece country Europe 59 I5
Greece U.S.A. 135 G2
Greeley U.S.A. 126 G4
Greely Center U.S.A. 130 D3
Greem-Bell, Ostrov i. Rus. Fed. 64 H1
Green r. KY U.S.A. 134 B5
Green r. WY U.S.A. 129 I2
Green Bay U.S.A. 134 A1
Green Bay b. U.S.A. 134 B1
Greenbrier U.S.A. 134 B5
Greenbrier r. U.S.A. 134 E5
Green Cape Australia 112 E6
Greencastle Bahamas 133 E7
Greencastle U.K. 51 F3
Greencastle U.S.A. 134 B4
Green Cove Springs U.S.A. 133 D6
Greene ME U.S.A. 135 J1
Greene NY U.S.A. 135 H2
Greeneville U.S.A. 132 D4
Greenfield CA U.S.A. 128 C3
Greenfield IN U.S.A. 134 C4
Greenfield MA U.S.A. 135 I2
Greenfield OH U.S.A. 134 D4
Green Head hd Australia 109 A7
Greenhill Island Australia 108 F2
Green Island Taiwan see Lü Tao
Green Lake Canada 121 J4

▶Greenland terr. N. America 119 N3
Self-governing Danish territory. Largest island in North America and in the world, and 3rd largest political entity in North America.

Greenland Basin sea feature Arctic Ocean 153 I2
Greenland Fracture Zone sea feature Arctic Ocean 153 I1
Greenland Sea Greenland/Svalbard 64 A2
Greenlaw U.K. 50 G5
Green Mountains U.S.A. 135 I1
Greenock U.K. 50 E5
Greenore Ireland 51 F3
Greenport U.S.A. 135 I3
Green River P.N.G. 69 K7
Green River UT U.S.A. 129 H2
Green River WY U.S.A. 126 F4
Green River Lake U.S.A. 134 C5
Greensboro U.S.A. 133 D5
Greensburg IN U.S.A. 134 C4
Greensburg KS U.S.A. 130 D4
Greensburg KY U.S.A. 134 C5
Greensburg LA U.S.A. 131 F6
Greensburg PA U.S.A. 134 F3
Greens Peak U.S.A. 129 I4
Greenstone Point U.K. 50 D3
Green Swamp U.S.A. 133 E5
Greentown U.S.A. 134 C3
Greenup IL U.S.A. 130 F4
Greenup KY U.S.A. 134 D4
Green Valley Canada 135 H1
Greenville Liberia 96 C4
Greenville AL U.S.A. 133 C6
Greenville IL U.S.A. 130 F4
Greenville KY U.S.A. 134 B5
Greenville ME U.S.A. 132 G2
Greenville MI U.S.A. 134 C2
Greenville MS U.S.A. 131 F5
Greenville NC U.S.A. 132 E5
Greenville NH U.S.A. 135 J2
Greenville OH U.S.A. 134 C3
Greenville PA U.S.A. 134 E3
Greenville SC U.S.A. 133 D5
Greenville TX U.S.A. 131 D5
Greenwich atoll Micronesia see Kapingamarangi
Greenwich CT U.S.A. 135 I3
Greenwich OH U.S.A. 134 D3
Greenwood AR U.S.A. 131 E5
Greenwood IN U.S.A. 134 B4
Greenwood MS U.S.A. 131 F5
Greenwood SC U.S.A. 133 D5
Gregory r. Australia 110 B3
Gregory, Lake salt flat S.A. Australia 111 B6
Gregory, Lake salt flat W.A. Australia 108 D5
Gregory, Lake salt flat W.A. Australia 109 B6
Gregory Downs Australia 110 B3
Gregory National Park Australia 108 E4
Gregory Range hills Qld Australia 110 C3
Gregory Range hills W.A. Australia 108 C5
Greifswald Germany 47 N3
Greiz Germany 53 M4
Greko, Cape Cyprus 85 B2
Gremikha Rus. Fed. 153 G2
Gremyachinsk Rus. Fed. 41 R4
Grenå Denmark 45 G8
Grenaa Denmark see Grenå
Grenada U.S.A. 131 F5
Grenada country West Indies 137 L6
Grenade France 56 E5
Grenen spit Denmark 45 G8
Grenfell Australia 112 D4
Grenfell Canada 121 K5
Grenoble France 56 G4
Grense-Jakobselv Norway 44 Q2
Grenville, Cape Australia 110 C1
Grenville Island Fiji see Rotuma
Greshak Pak. 89 G5
Gresham U.S.A. 126 C3
Gressåmoen Nasjonalpark nat. park Norway 44 H4
Greta r. U.K. 48 E4
Gretna U.K. 50 F6
Gretna LA U.S.A. 131 F6
Gretna VA U.S.A. 134 F5
Greußen Germany 53 K3
Grevelingen sea chan. Neth. 52 D3
Greven Germany 53 H2
Grevena Greece 59 I4
Grevenbicht Neth. 52 F3
Grevenbroich Germany 52 G3
Grevenmacher Lux. 52 G5
Grevesmühlen Germany 47 M4
Grey, Cape Australia 110 B2
Greybull U.S.A. 126 F3
Greybull r. U.S.A. 126 F3
Grey Hunter Peak Canada 120 C2
Grey Islands Canada 123 L4
Greylock, Mount U.S.A. 135 I2
Greymouth N.Z. 113 C6
Grey Range hills Australia 112 A2
Grey's Plains Australia 109 A6
Greytown S. Africa 101 J5
Grez-Doiceau Belgium 52 E4
Gribanovskiy Rus. Fed. 43 I6
Gridley U.S.A. 128 C2
Griffin U.S.A. 133 C5
Griffith Australia 112 C5
Grigan i. N. Mariana Is see Agrihan
Grik Malaysia see Gerik
Grim, Cape Australia 111 [inset]
Grimari Cent. Afr. Rep. 98 C3
Grimma Germany 53 M3
Grimmen Germany 47 N3
Grimnitzsee l. Germany 53 N2
Grimsby U.K. 48 G5
Grímsey i. Iceland 44 [inset]
Grimshaw Canada 120 G3
Grímsstaðir Iceland 44 [inset]
Grimstad Norway 45 F7
Grindavík Iceland 44 [inset]
Grindsted Denmark 45 F9
Grind Stone City U.S.A. 134 D1
Grindul Chituc spit Romania 59 M2
Grinnell Peninsula Canada 119 I2
Griqualand East reg. S. Africa 101 I6
Griqualand West reg. S. Africa 100 F5
Griquatown S. Africa 100 F5
Grise Fiord Canada 119 J2
Grishino Ukr. see Krasnoarmiys'k
Gris Nez, Cap c. France 52 B4
Gritley U.K. 50 G2
Grizzly Bear Mountain hill Canada 120 F1
Grmeč mts Bos.-Herz. 58 G2
Grobbendonk Belgium 52 E3
Groblersdal S. Africa 101 I3
Groblershoop S. Africa 100 F5
Grodno Belarus see Hrodna
Groen watercourse S. Africa 100 F6
Groen watercourse S. Africa 100 C6
Groix, Île de i. France 56 C3
Grombalia Tunisia 58 D6
Gronau (Westfalen) Germany 52 H2
Grong Norway 44 H4
Groningen Neth. 52 G1
Groninger Wad tidal flat Neth. 52 G1
Grønland terr. N. America see Greenland
Groom Lake U.S.A. 129 F3
Groot-Aar Pan salt pan S. Africa 100 E4
Groot Berg r. S. Africa 100 D7
Groot Brakrivier S. Africa 100 F8
Grootdraaidam dam S. Africa 101 I4
Grootdrink S. Africa 100 E5
Groote Eylandt i. Australia 110 B2
Grootfontein Namibia 99 B5
Groot Karas Berg plat. Namibia 100 D4
Groot Letaba r. S. Africa 101 J2
Groot Marico S. Africa 101 H3
Groot Swartberge mts S. Africa 100 E7
Grootvloer salt pan S. Africa 100 E5
Groot Winterberg mt. S. Africa 101 H7
Gros Morne National Park Canada 123 K4
Gross Barmen Namibia 100 C2
Große Aue r. Germany 53 J2
Große Laaber r. Germany 53 M6
Großengottern Germany 53 K3
Großenkneten Germany 53 I2
Großenlüder Germany 53 J4
Großer Arber mt. Germany 53 N5
Großer Beerberg hill Germany 53 K4
Großer Eyberg hill Germany 53 H5
Großer Gleichberg hill Germany 53 K4
Großer Kornberg hill Germany 53 M4
Großer Osser mt. Czech Rep./Germany 53 N5
Großer Rachel mt. Germany 47 N6
Grosser Speikkogel mt. Austria 47 O7
Grosseto Italy 58 D3
Grossevichi Rus. Fed. 74 E3
Groß-Gerau Germany 53 I5
Großglockner mt. Austria 47 N7
Groß Oesingen Germany 53 K2
Großrudestedt Germany 53 L3
Groß Schönebeck Germany 53 N2
Gross Ums Namibia 100 D2
Großvenediger mt. Austria 47 N7
Gros Ventre Range mts U.S.A. 126 F4
Groswater Bay Canada 123 K3
Groton U.S.A. 130 D2
Grottoes U.S.A. 135 F4
Grou Neth. 52 F1
Groundhog r. Canada 122 E4
Grouw Neth. see Grou
Grove U.S.A. 131 E4
Grove City U.S.A. 134 D4
Grove Hill U.S.A. 133 C6
Grove Mountains Antarctica 152 E2
Grover Beach U.S.A. 128 C4
Grovertown U.S.A. 134 B3
Groveton NH U.S.A. 135 J1
Groveton TX U.S.A. 131 E6
Growler Mountains U.S.A. 129 G5
Groznyy Rus. Fed. 91 G2
Grubišno Polje Croatia 58 G2
Grudovo Bulg. see Sredets
Grudziądz Poland 47 Q4
Grünau Namibia 100 D4
Grünberg Poland see Zielona Góra
Grundarfjörður Iceland 44 [inset]
Grundy U.S.A. 134 D5
Gruñidora Mex. 131 C7
Grünstadt Germany 53 I5
Gruver U.S.A. 131 C4
Gruzinskaya S.S.R. country Asia see Georgia
Gryazi Rus. Fed. 43 H5
Gryazovets Rus. Fed. 42 I4
Gryfice Poland 47 O4
Gryfino Poland 47 O4
Gryfów Śląski Poland 47 O5
Gryllefjord Norway 44 J2
Grytviken S. Georgia 144 I8
Gua India 83 F5
Guacanayabo, Golfo de b. Cuba 137 I4
Guachochi Mex. 127 G8
Guadajoz r. Spain 57 D5
Guadalajara Mex. 136 D4
Guadalajara Spain 57 E3
Guadalcanal i. Solomon Is 107 G2
Guadalete r. Spain 57 C5
Guadalope r. Spain 57 F3
Guadalquivir r. Spain 57 C5
Guadalupe Mex. 131 C7
Guadalupe i. Mex. 127 D7
Guadalupe watercourse Mex. 128 E5
Guadalupe U.S.A. 128 C4
Guadalupe, Sierra de mts Spain 57 D4
Guadalupe Aguilera Mex. 131 B7
Guadalupe Bravos Mex. 127 G7
Guadalupe Mountains National Park U.S.A. 127 G7
Guadalupe Peak U.S.A. 127 G7
Guadalupe Victoria Baja California Mex. 129 F5
Guadalupe Victoria Durango Mex. 131 B7
Guadarrama, Sierra de mts Spain 57 D3

▶Guadeloupe terr. West Indies 137 L5
French Overseas Department.

Guadeloupe Passage Caribbean Sea 137 L5
Guadiana r. Port./Spain 57 C5
Guadix Spain 57 E5
Guafo, Isla i. Chile 144 B6
Guaíba Brazil 145 A5
Guaiçuí Brazil 145 B2
Guaíra Brazil 144 F2
Guajaba, Cayo i. Cuba 133 E8
Guaje, Llano de plain Mex. 131 C7
Gualala U.S.A. 128 B2
Gualeguay Arg. 144 E4
Gualeguaychu Arg. 144 E4
Gualicho, Salina salt flat Arg. 144 C6

▶Guam terr. N. Pacific Ocean 69 K4
United States Unincorporated Territory.

Guamblin, Isla i. Chile 144 A6
Guampí, Sierra de mts Venez. 142 E2
Guamúchil Mex. 127 F8
Guanabacoa Cuba 133 D8
Guanacevi Mex. 131 B7
Guanahacabibes, Península de pen. Cuba 133 C8
Guanajay Cuba 133 D8
Guanajuato Mex. 136 D4
Guanambi Brazil 145 C1
Guanare Venez. 142 E2
Guandu China 77 G3
Guane Cuba 137 H4
Guang'an China 76 E2
Guangchang China 77 H3
Guangdong prov. China 77 [inset]
Guanghai China 77 G4
Guanghan China 76 E2
Guanghua China see Laohekou
Guangming China see Xide
Guangming Ding mt. China 77 H2
Guangnan China 76 E3
Guangshan China 77 G2
Guangxi aut. reg. China see Guangxi Zhuangzu Zizhiqu
Guangxi Zhuangzu Zizhiqu aut. reg. China 76 F4
Guangyuan China 76 E1
Guangze China 77 H3
Guangzhou China 77 G4
Guanhães Brazil 145 C2
Guanhe Kou r. mouth China 77 H1
Guanipa r. Venez. 142 F2
Guanling China 76 E3
Guanmian Shan mts China 77 F2
Guannan China 77 H1
Guanpo China 77 F1
Guanshui China 74 B4
Guansuo China see Guanling
Guantánamo Cuba 137 I4
Guanxian China see Dujiangyan
Guanyang China 77 F3
Guanyinqiao China 76 D2
Guanyun China 77 H1
Guapé Brazil 145 B3
Guapí Col. 142 C3
Guaporé r. Bol./Brazil 142 E6
Guaporé Brazil 145 A5
Guaqui Bol. 142 E7
Guará r. Brazil 145 B1
Guarabira Brazil 143 K5
Guaranda Ecuador 142 C4
Guarapari Brazil 145 C3
Guarapuava Brazil 145 A4
Guararapes Brazil 145 A3
Guaratinguetá Brazil 145 B3
Guaratuba Brazil 145 A4
Guaratuba, Baía de b. Brazil 145 A4
Guarda Port. 57 C3
Guardafui, Cape Somalia see Gwardafuy, Gees
Guardiagrele Italy 58 F3
Guardo Spain 57 D2
Guárico, del Embalse resr Venez. 142 E2
Guarujá Brazil 145 B3
Guasave Mex. 127 F8
Guasdualito Venez. 142 D2

▶Guatemala country Central America 136 F5
4th most populous country in North America.

▶Guatemala City Guat. 136 F6
Capital of Guatemala.

Guaviare r. Col. 142 E3
Guaxupé Brazil 145 B3
Guayaquil Ecuador 142 C4
Guayaquil, Golfo de g. Ecuador 142 B4
Guaymas Mex. 127 F8
Guba Eth. 98 D2
Gubakha Rus. Fed. 41 R4
Gubbi India 84 C3
Gubio Nigeria 96 E3
Gubkin Rus. Fed. 43 H6
Gucheng China 77 F1
Gudari India 84 D2
Gudbrandsdalen valley Norway 45 F6
Gudermes Rus. Fed. 91 G2
Gudivada India 84 D2
Gudiyattam India 84 C3
Gudur Andhra Prad. India 84 C3
Gudur Andhra Prad. India 84 C3
Gudvangen Norway 45 E6
Gudzhal r. Rus. Fed. 74 D2
Gué, Rivière du r. Canada 123 H2
Guecho Spain see Algorta
Guéckédou Guinea 96 B4
Guelma Alg. 58 B6
Guelmine Morocco 96 B2
Guelph Canada 134 E2
Guémez Mex. 131 D8
Guénange France 52 G5
Guerara Alg. 54 E5
Guérard, Lac l. Canada 123 I2
Guercif Morocco 54 D5
Guéret France 56 E3

▶Guernsey terr. Channel Is 49 E9
United Kingdom Crown Dependency.

Guernsey U.S.A. 126 G4
Guérou Mauritania 96 B3
Guerrah Et-Tarf salt pan Alg. 58 B7
Guerrero Negro Mex. 127 E8
Guers, Lac l. Canada 123 I2
Gueugnon France 56 G3
Gufeng China see Pingnan
Gufu China see Xingshan
Gugë mt. Eth. 98 D3
Gügerd, Kūh-e mts Iran 88 D3
Guguan i. N. Mariana Is 69 L3
Guhakolak, Tanjung pt Indon. 68 D8
Guhe China 77 H2
Güh Küh mt. Iran 88 E5
Guhuai China see Pingyu
Guiana Basin sea feature N. Atlantic Ocean 148 E5
Guiana Highlands mts S. America 142 E2
Guichi China see Chizhou
Guidan-Roumji Niger 96 D3
Guider Cameroon 97 E4
Guiding China 76 E3
Guidong China 77 G3
Guidonia-Montecelio Italy 58 E4
Guigang China 77 F4
Guiglo Côte d'Ivoire 96 C4
Guignicourt France 52 D5
Guija Moz. 101 K3
Guiji Shan mts China 77 I2
Guildford U.K. 49 G7
Guilford U.S.A. 132 G2
Guilherme Capelo Angola see Cacongo
Guilin China 77 F3
Guillaume-Delisle, Lac l. Canada 122 F2
Guimarães Brazil 143 J4
Guimarães Port. 57 B3
Guinan China 76 D1
Guinea country Africa 96 B3
Guinea, Gulf of Africa 96 D4
Guinea Basin sea feature N. Atlantic Ocean 148 H5
Guinea-Bissau country Africa 96 B3
Guinea-Conakry country Africa see Guinea
Guinea Ecuatorial country Africa see Equatorial Guinea
Guiné-Bissau country Africa see Guinea-Bissau
Guinée country Africa see Guinea
Güines Cuba 137 H4
Guînes France 52 B4
Guines, Lac l. Canada 123 J3
Guingamp France 56 C2
Guipavas France 56 B2
Guiping China 77 F4
Güira de Melena Cuba 133 D8
Guiratinga Brazil 143 H7
Guiscard France 52 D5
Guise France 52 D5
Guishan China see Xinping
Guishun China 76 E3
Guixi Chongqing China see Dianjiang
Guixi Jiangxi China 77 H2
Guiyang Guizhou China 76 E3
Guiyang Hunan China 77 G3
Guizhou prov. China 76 E3
Guizi China 77 F4
Gujarat state India 82 C5
Gujar Khan Pak. 89 I3
Gujerat state India see Gujarat
Gujranwala Pak. 89 I3
Gujrat Pak. 89 I3
Gukovo Rus. Fed. 43 H6
Gulabgarh India 82 D2
Gulbarga India 84 C2
Gulbene Latvia 45 O8
Gul'cha Kyrg. see Gülchö
Gülchö Kyrg. 80 D3
Gülcihan Turkey 85 B1
Gülek Boğazı pass Turkey 90 D3
Gulf, The Asia 88 C4
Gulfport U.S.A. 131 F6
Gulian China 74 A1
Gulin China 76 E3
Gulistan Uzbek. see Guliston
Guliston Uzbek. 80 C3
Gülitz Germany 53 L1
Guliya Shan mt. China 74 A2
Gulja China see Yining
Gul Kach Pak. 89 H4
Gul'kevichi Rus. Fed. 91 F1
Gull Lake Canada 121 I5
Gullrock Lake Canada 121 M5
Gullträsk Sweden 44 L3
Güllük Körfezi b. Turkey 59 L6
Gülnar Turkey 85 A1
Gulü China see Xincai
Gulu Uganda 98 D3
Guluwuru Island Australia 110 B1
Gulyayevskiye Koshki, Ostrova is Rus. Fed. 42 L1
Guma China see Pishan
Gumal r. Pak. 89 H4
Gumare Botswana 99 C5
Gumbaz Pak. 89 H4
Gumbinnen Rus. Fed. see Gusev
Gumdag Turkm. 88 D2
Gumel Nigeria 96 D3
Gümgüm Turkey see Varto
Gumla India 83 F5
Gummersbach Germany 53 H3
Gümüşhacıköy Turkey 90 D2
Gümüşhane Turkey 91 E2
Guna India 82 D4
Gunan China see Qijiang
Guna Terara mt. Eth. 86 E7
Gunbar Australia 112 B5
Gunbower Australia 112 B5
Güncang China 76 B2
Gund r. Tajik. see Gunt
Gundagai Australia 112 D5
Gundelsheim Germany 53 J5
Güney Turkey 59 M5
Güneydoğu Toroslar plat. Turkey 90 F3
Gunglilap Myanmar 70 B1
Gungu Dem. Rep. Congo 99 B4
Gunib Rus. Fed. 91 G2
Gunisao r. Canada 121 L4
Gunisao Lake Canada 121 L4
Gunnaur India 82 D3
Gunnbjørn Fjeld nunatak Greenland 119 P3
Gunnedah Australia 112 E3
Gunning Australia 112 D5
Gunnison U.S.A. 127 G5
Gunnison r. U.S.A. 129 I2
Güns Hungary see Kőszeg
Gunt r. Tajik. 89 H2
Guntakal India 84 C3
Güntersberge Germany 53 K3
Guntur India 84 D2
Gunung Gading National Park Malaysia 71 E7
Gunung Leuser, Taman Nasional Indon. 71 B7
Gunung Niyut, Suaka Margasatwa nature res. Indon. 71 E7
Gunung Palung, Taman Nasional Indon. 68 E7
Gunungsitoli Indon. 71 B7
Günyüzü Turkey 90 C3
Gunza Angola see Porto Amboim
Günzburg Germany 47 M6
Gunzenhausen Germany 53 K5
Guo He r. China 77 H1
Guovdageaidnu Norway see Kautokeino
Guozhen China see Baoji
Gupis Pak. 82 C1
Gurbantünggüt Shamo des. China 80 G3
Gurdaspur India 82 C2
Gurdon U.S.A. 131 E5
Gurdzhaani Georgia see Gurjaani
Güre Turkey 59 M5
Gurgan Iran see Gorgān
Gurgaon India 82 D3
Gurgei, Jebel mt. Sudan 97 F3
Gurha India 82 B4
Guri, Embalse de resr Venez. 142 F2
Gurig National Park Australia 108 F2
Gurinhatã Brazil 145 A2
Gurjaani Georgia 91 G2
Gur Khar Iran 89 E4
Guro Moz. 99 D5
Gurşunmagdan Kārhanasy Turkm. 89 G2
Guru China 83 G3
Gürün Turkey 90 E3
Gurupá Brazil 143 H4
Gurupi Brazil 143 I6
Gurupi r. Brazil 143 I4
Gurupi, Serra do hills Brazil 143 I4
Guru Sikhar mt. India 82 C4
Guruzala India 84 C2
Gur'yev Kazakh. see Atyrau
Gur'yevsk Rus. Fed. 45 L9
Gur'yevskaya Oblast' admin. div. Kazakh. see Atyrauskaya Oblast'
Gurz Afgh. 89 G3
Gusau Nigeria 96 D3
Güsen Germany 53 L2
Gusev Rus. Fed. 45 M9
Gushan China 75 A5
Gushgy Turkm. see Serhetabat
Gushi China 77 G1
Gusino Rus. Fed. 43 F5
Gusinoozersk Rus. Fed. 72 J2
Gus'-Khrustal'nyy Rus. Fed. 42 I5
Guspini Sardinia Italy 58 C5
Gustav Holm, Kap c. Greenland see Tasiilap Karra
Gustavo Sotelo Mex. 127 E7
Güsten Germany 53 L3
Gustine U.S.A. 128 C3
Güstrow Germany 47 N4
Güterfelde Germany 53 N2
Gütersloh Germany 53 I3
Guthrie AZ U.S.A. 129 I5
Guthrie KY U.S.A. 134 B5
Guthrie OK U.S.A. 131 D5
Guthrie TX U.S.A. 131 C5
Gutian Fujian China 77 H3
Gutian Fujian China 77 H3
Gutian Shuiku resr China 77 H3
Guting China see Yutai
Gutsuo China 83 F3
Guwahati India 83 G4
Guwēr Iraq 91 F3
Guwlumaýak Turkm. 88 D1
Guwlumayak Turkm. see Guwlumaýak
Guxhagen Germany 53 J3
Guxian China 77 G3
Guyana country S. America 143 G2
Guyane Française terr. S. America see French Guiana
Guyang Hunan China see Guzhang
Guyang Nei Mongol China 73 K4
Guyenne reg. France 56 D4
Guy Fawkes River National Park Australia 112 F3
Guyi China see Sanjiang
Guymon U.S.A. 131 C4
Guyra Australia 112 E3
Guysborough Canada 123 J5
Guyuan Hebei China 73 L4
Guyuan Ningxia China 72 J5
Güzelolük Turkey 85 B1
Güzelyurt Cyprus see Morfou
Guzhang China 77 F2
Guzhen China 77 H1
Guzhou China see Rongjiang
Guzmán Mex. 127 G7
Guzmán, Lago de l. Mex. 127 G7
G'uzor Uzbek. 89 G2
Gvardeysk Rus. Fed. 45 L9
Gvasyugi Rus. Fed. 74 E3
Gwa Myanmar 70 A3
Gwabegar Australia 112 D3
Gwadar West Bay Pak. 89 F5
Gwaii Haanas National Park Reserve Canada 120 D4
Gwal Haidarzai Pak. 89 H4
Gwalior India 82 D4
Gwanda Zimbabwe 99 C6
Gwane Dem. Rep. Congo 98 C3
Gwardafuy, Gees c. Somalia 98 F2
Gwash Pak. 89 G4
Gwatar Bay Pak. 89 F5
Gwedaukkon Myanmar 70 A1
Gweebarra Bay Ireland 51 D3
Gwelo Zimbabwe see Gweru
Gweru Zimbabwe 99 C5
Gweta Botswana 99 C6
Gwinner U.S.A. 130 D2
Gwoza Nigeria 96 E3
Gwydir r. Australia 112 D2
Gyablung China 76 B2
Gyaca China 76 B2
Gyagartang China 76 D1
Gya'gya China see Saga
Gyaijêpozhanggê China see Zhidoi
Gyai Qu r. China 76 B2
Gyairong China 76 C1
Gyaisi China see Jiulong
Gyali i. Greece 59 L6
Gyamotang China see Dêngqên
Gyamug China 82 E2
Gyandzha Azer. see Gäncä
Gyangkar China see Dinngyê
Gyangnyi Caka salt l. China 83 F2
Gyangrang China 83 F3
Gyangtse China see Gyangzê
Gyangzê China 83 G3
Gyaring China 76 C1
Gyaring Co l. China 83 G3
Gyaring Hu l. China 76 C1
Gyarishing India 76 B2
Gyaros i. Greece 59 K6
Gyarubtang China 76 B2
Gydan, Khrebet mts Rus. Fed. see Kolymskiy, Khrebet
Gydan Peninsula Rus. Fed. 64 I2
Gydanskiy Poluostrov pen. Rus. Fed. see Gydan Peninsula
Gyêgu China see Yushu
Gyêmdong China 76 B2
Gyigang China 76 C2
Gyimda China 76 B2
Gyirong Xizang China 83 F3
Gyirong Xizang China 83 F3

Havelock Swaziland see Bulembu
Havelock U.S.A. 133 E5
Havelock Falls Australia 108 F3
Havelock Island India 71 A5
Havelock North N.Z. 113 F4
Haverfordwest U.K. 49 C7
Haverhill U.S.A. 135 J2
Haveri India 84 B3
Haversin Belgium 52 F4
Havixbeck Germany 53 H3
Havlíčkův Brod Czech Rep. 47 O6
Havøysund Norway 44 N1
Havran Turkey 59 L5
Havre U.S.A. 126 F2
Havre Aubert, Île du i. Canada 123 J5
Havre Rock i. Kermadec Is 107 I5
Havre-St-Pierre Canada 123 J4
Havza Turkey 90 D2
Hawai'i i. U.S.A. 127 [inset]
Hawai'ian Islands N. Pacific Ocean 150 I4
Hawaiian Ridge sea feature N. Pacific Ocean 150 I4
Hawai'i Volcanoes National Park U.S.A. 127 [inset]
Ḩawallī Kuwait 88 C4
Hawar i. Bahrain see Ḩuwār
Hawarden U.K. 48 D5
Hawea, Lake N.Z. 113 B7
Hawera N.Z. 113 E4
Hawes U.K. 48 E4
Hawesville U.S.A. 134 B5
Hāwī U.S.A. 127 [inset]
Hawick U.K. 50 F5
Ḩawīzah, Hawr al imp. l. Iraq 91 G5
Hawkdun Range mts N.Z. 113 B7
Hawke Bay N.Z. 113 F4
Hawkes Bay Canada 123 K4
Hawkins Peak U.S.A. 129 G3
Hawlēr Iraq see Arbīl
Hawley U.S.A. 135 H3
Hawng Luk Myanmar 70 B2
Ḩawrān, Wādī watercourse Iraq 91 F4
Ḩawshah, Jibāl al mts Saudi Arabia 88 B6
Hawston S. Africa 100 D8
Hawthorne U.S.A. 128 D2
Haxat China 74 B3
Haxby U.K. 48 F4
Hay Australia 112 B5
Hay watercourse Australia 110 B5
Hay r. Canada 120 H2
Hayachine-san mt. Japan 75 F5
Hayastan country Asia see Armenia
Haydān, Wādī al r. Jordan 85 B4
Hayden AZ U.S.A. 129 H5
Hayden CO U.S.A. 129 J1
Hayden IN U.S.A. 134 C4
Hayes r. Man. Canada 121 M3
Hayes r. Nunavut Canada 119 I3
Hayes Halvø pen. Greenland 119 L2
Hayfield Reservoir U.S.A. 129 F5
Hayfork U.S.A. 128 B1
Hayl, Wādī al watercourse Syria 85 C3
Hayl, Wādī al watercourse Syria 85 D2
Hayle U.K. 49 B8
Haymā' Oman 87 I6
Haymana Turkey 90 D3
Haymarket U.S.A. 135 G4
Hay-on-Wye U.K. 49 D6
Hayrabolu Turkey 59 L4
Hay River Canada 118 G3
Hay River Reserve Canada 120 H2
Hays KS U.S.A. 130 D4
Hays MT U.S.A. 126 F2
Ḩays Yemen 86 F7
Haysville U.S.A. 131 D4
Haysyn Ukr. 43 F6
Ḩaytān, Jabal hill Egypt 85 A4
Hayward CA U.S.A. 128 B3
Hayward WI U.S.A. 130 F2
Haywards Heath U.K. 49 G8
Hazar Turkm. 88 D2
Hazarajat reg. Afgh. 89 G3
Hazard U.S.A. 134 D5
Hazaribag India see Hazaribagh
Hazaribagh India 83 F5
Hazaribagh Range mts India 83 E5
Hazār Masjed, Kūh-e mts Iran 88 E2
Hazebrouck France 52 C4
Hazelton Canada 120 E4
Hazen Strait Canada 119 G2
Hazerswoude-Rijndijk Neth. 52 E2
Hazhdanahr reg. Afgh. 89 G2
Hazleton IN U.S.A. 134 B4
Hazleton PA U.S.A. 135 H3
Hazlett, Lake salt flat Australia 108 E5
Ḩazrat-e Solṭān Afgh. 89 G2
H. Bouchard Arg. 144 D4
Headford Ireland 51 C4
Headingly Australia 110 B4
Head of Bight b. Australia 109 E7
Healdsburg U.S.A. 128 B2
Healesville Australia 112 B6
Healy U.S.A. 118 D3
Heanor U.K. 49 F5

▶Heard and McDonald Islands terr. Indian Ocean 149 M9
Australian External Territory.

Heard Island Indian Ocean 149 M9
Hearne U.S.A. 131 D6
Hearne Lake Canada 121 H2
Hearrenfean Neth. see Heerenveen
Hearst Canada 122 E4
Hearst Island Antarctica 152 L2
Heart r. U.S.A. 130 C2
Heart of Neolithic Orkney tourist site U.K. 50 F1
Heathcote Australia 112 B6
Heathfield U.K. 49 H8
Heathsville U.S.A. 135 G5
Hebbardsville U.S.A. 134 B5
Hebbronville U.S.A. 131 D7
Hebei prov. China 73 L5
Hebel Australia 112 C2
Heber U.S.A. 129 H4
Heber City U.S.A. 129 H1
Heber Springs U.S.A. 131 E5
Hebi China 73 K5
Hebron Canada 123 J2
Hebron U.S.A. 130 D3
Hebron West Bank 85 B4
Hecate Strait Canada 120 D4
Hecheng Jiangxi China see Zixi
Hecheng Zhejiang China see Qingtian
Hechi China 77 F3
Hechuan Chongqing China 76 E2
Hechuan Jiangxi China see Yongxing
Hecla Island Canada 121 L5
Hede China see Sheyang
Hede Sweden 44 H5
Hedemora Sweden 45 I6
He Devil Mountain U.S.A. 126 D3
Hedi Shuiku resr China 77 F4
Heech Neth. see Heeg
Heeg Neth. 52 F2
Heek Germany 52 H2
Heer Belgium 52 E4
Heerde Neth. 52 G2
Heerenveen Neth. 52 F2
Heerhugowaard Neth. 52 E2
Heerlen Neth. 52 F4
Ḩefa Israel see Haifa
Ḩefa, Mifraz Israel see Haifa, Bay of
Hefei China 77 H2
Hefeng China 77 F2
Heflin U.S.A. 133 C5
Hegang China 74 C3
Heho Myanmar 70 B2
Heidan r. Jordan see Haydān, Wādī al
Heidberg hill Germany 53 L3
Heide Germany 47 L3
Heide Namibia 100 C2
Heidelberg Germany 53 I5
Heidelberg S. Africa 101 I4
Heidenheim an der Brenz Germany 53 K6
Heihe China 74 B2
Heilbron S. Africa 101 H4
Heilbronn Germany 53 J5
Heiligenhafen Germany 47 M3
Hei Ling Chau i. H.K. China 77 [inset]
Heilongjiang prov. China 74 C3
Heilong Jiang r. China/Rus. Fed. 74 D2 also known as Amur (Rus. Fed.)
Heilong Jiang r. Rus. Fed. see Amur
Heilsbronn Germany 53 K5
Heilungkiang prov. China see Heilongjiang
Heinola Fin. 45 O6
Heinze Islands Myanmar 71 B4
Heirnkut Myanmar 70 A1
Heishi Beihu l. China 83 E2
Heishui China 76 D1
Heisker Islands U.K. see Monach Islands
Heist-op-den-Berg Belgium 52 E3
Ḩeiṭân, Gebel hill Egypt see Ḩayṭān, Jabal
Hejaz reg. Saudi Arabia see Hijaz
Hejiang China 76 E2
He Jiang r. China 77 F4
Hejing China 80 G3
Hekimhan Turkey 90 E3
Hekla vol. Iceland 44 [inset]
Hekou Gansu China 72 I5
Hekou Hubei China 77 G2
Hekou Jiangxi China see Yanshan
Hekou Sichuan China see Yajiang
Hekou Yunnan China 76 D4
Helagsfjället mt. Sweden 44 H5
Helam India 76 B3
Helan Shan mts China 72 J5
Helbra Germany 53 L3
Helen atoll Palau 69 I6
Helena AR U.S.A. 131 F5

▶Helena MT U.S.A. 126 E3
Capital of Montana.

Helen Reef Palau 69 I6
Helensburgh U.K. 50 E4
Helen Springs Australia 108 F4
Ḩelez Israel 85 B4
Helgoland i. Germany 47 K3
Helgoländer Bucht g. Germany 47 L3
Heligoland i. Germany see Helgoland
Heligoland Bight g. Germany see Helgoländer Bucht
Heliopolis Lebanon see Ba'albek
Helixi China see Ningguo
Hella Iceland 44 [inset]
Helland Norway 44 J2
Hellas country Europe see Greece
Helleh r. Iran 88 C4
Hellespont strait Turkey see Dardanelles
Hellevoetsluis Neth. 52 E3
Hellhole Gorge National Park Australia 110 D5
Hellín Spain 57 F4
Hellinikon tourist site Greece 90 A3
Hells Canyon gorge U.S.A. 126 D3
Hell-Ville Madag. see Andoany
Helmand r. Afgh. 89 F4
Helmantica Spain see Salamanca
Helmbrechts Germany 53 L4
Helme r. Germany 53 L3
Helmeringhausen Namibia 100 C3
Helmond Neth. 52 F3
Helmsdale U.K. 50 F2
Helmsdale r. U.K. 50 F2
Helmstedt Germany 53 L2
Helong China 74 C4
Helper U.S.A. 129 H2
Helpter Berge hills Germany 53 N1
Helsingborg Sweden 45 H8
Helsingfors Fin. see Helsinki
Helsingør Denmark 45 H8

▶Helsinki Fin. 45 N6
Capital of Finland.

Helston U.K. 49 B8
Helvécia Brazil 145 D2
Helvetic Republic country Europe see Switzerland
Ḩelwân Egypt see Ḩulwān
Hemel Hempstead U.K. 49 G7
Hemet U.S.A. 128 E5
Hemingford U.S.A. 130 C3
Hemlock Lake U.S.A. 135 G2
Hemmingen Germany 53 J2
Hemmingford Canada 135 I1
Hemmoor Germany 53 J1
Hempstead U.S.A. 131 D6
Hemsby U.K. 49 I6
Hemse Sweden 45 K8
Henan China 76 D1
Henan prov. China 77 G1
Henares r. Spain 57 E3
Henashi-zaki pt Japan 75 E4
Henbury Australia 109 F6
Hendek Turkey 59 N4
Henderson KY U.S.A. 134 B5
Henderson NC U.S.A. 132 E4
Henderson NV U.S.A. 129 F3
Henderson NY U.S.A. 135 G2
Henderson TN U.S.A. 131 F5
Henderson TX U.S.A. 131 E5
Henderson Island Pitcairn Is 151 L7
Hendersonville NC U.S.A. 133 D5
Hendersonville TN U.S.A. 134 B5
Henderville atoll Kiribati see Aranuka
Hendon U.K. 49 G7
Hendorābī i. Iran 88 D5
Hendy-Gwyn U.K. see Whitland
Hengām Iran 89 E5
Hengduan Shan mts China 76 C2
Hengelo Neth. 52 G2
Hengfeng China 77 H2
Hengnan China see Hengyang
Hengshan China 74 C3
Heng Shan mt. China 77 G3
Hengshui Hebei China 73 L5
Hengshui Jiangxi China see Chongyi
Hengxian China 77 F4
Hengyang Hunan China 77 G3
Hengyang Hunan China 77 G3
Hengzhou China see Hengxian
Heniches'k Ukr. 43 G7
Henley N.Z. 113 C7
Henley-on-Thames U.K. 49 G7
Henlopen, Cape U.S.A. 135 H4
Hennef (Sieg) Germany 53 H4
Hennenman S. Africa 101 H4
Hennepin U.S.A. 130 F3
Hennessey U.S.A. 131 D4
Hennigsdorf Berlin Germany 53 N2
Henniker U.S.A. 135 J2
Henning U.S.A. 134 B3
Henrietta U.S.A. 131 D5
Henrietta Maria, Cape Canada 122 E3
Henrieville U.S.A. 129 H3
Henrique de Carvalho Angola see Saurimo
Henry, Cape U.S.A. 135 G5
Henry Ice Rise Antarctica 152 A1
Henryk Arctowski research station Antarctica see Arctowski
Henry Kater, Cape Canada 119 L3
Henry Mountains U.S.A. 129 H2
Hensall Canada 134 E2
Henshaw, Lake U.S.A. 128 E5
Hentiesbaai Namibia 100 B2
Henty Australia 112 C5
Henzada Myanmar see Hinthada
Heping Guangdong China 77 G3
Heping Guizhou China see Huishui
Heping Guizhou China see Yanhe
Hepo China see Jiexi
Heppner U.S.A. 126 D3
Heptanesus is Ionia Nisia Greece see Ionian Islands
Heptanesus is Greece see Ionian Islands
Hepu China 77 F4
Heqing China 76 D3
Heraclea Turkey see Ereğli
Heraclea Pontica Turkey see Ereğli
Heraklion Greece see Iraklion
Herald Cays atolls Australia 110 E3
Herāt Afgh. 89 F3
Hérault r. France 56 F5
Herbertabad India 71 A5
Herbert Downs Australia 110 B4
Herbert River Falls National Park Australia 110 D3
Herbert Wash salt flat Australia 109 D6
Herborn Germany 53 I4
Herbstein Germany 53 J4
Hercules Dome ice feature Antarctica 152 K1
Herdecke Germany 53 H3
Herdorf Germany 53 H4
Hereford U.K. 49 E6
Hereford U.S.A. 131 C5
Héréhérétué atoll Fr. Polynesia 151 K7
Herent Belgium 52 E4
Herford Germany 53 I2
Heringen (Werra) Germany 53 K4
Herington U.S.A. 130 D4
Herīs Iran 88 B2
Herisau Switz. 56 I3
Herkimer U.S.A. 135 H2
Herlen Gol r. China/Mongolia 73 L3
Herlen He r. China/Mongolia see Herlen Gol
Herleshausen Germany 53 K3
Herlong U.S.A. 128 C1
Herm i. Channel Is 49 E9
Hermanas Mex. 131 C7
Herma Ness hd U.K. 50 [inset]
Hermann U.S.A. 130 F4
Hermannsburg Germany 53 K2
Hermanus S. Africa 100 D8
Hermel Lebanon 85 C2
Hermes, Cape S. Africa 101 I6
Hermidale Australia 112 C3
Hermiston U.S.A. 126 D3
Hermitage MO U.S.A. 130 E4
Hermitage PA U.S.A. 134 E3
Hermitage Bay Canada 123 K5
Hermite, Islas is Chile 144 C9
Hermit Islands P.N.G. 69 L7
Hermon, Mount Lebanon/Syria 85 B3
Hermonthis Egypt see Armant
Hermopolis Magna Egypt see Al Ashmūnayn
Hermosa U.S.A. 129 J3
Hermosillo Mex. 127 F7
Hernandarias Para. 144 F3
Hernando U.S.A. 131 F5
Herndon CA U.S.A. 128 D3
Herndon PA U.S.A. 135 G3
Herndon WV U.S.A. 134 E5
Herne Germany 53 H3
Herne Bay U.K. 49 I7
Herning Denmark 45 F8
Heroica Nogales Mex. see Nogales
Heroica Puebla de Zaragoza Mex. see Puebla
Hérouville-St-Clair France 49 G9
Herowābād Iran see Khalkhāl
Herrera del Duque Spain 57 D4
Herrieden Germany 53 K5
Hershey U.S.A. 135 G3
Hertford U.K. 49 G7
Hertzogville S. Africa 101 G5
Herve Belgium 52 F4
Hervé, Lac l. Canada 123 H3
Hervey Islands Cook Is 151 J7
Herzberg Brandenburg Germany 53 M2
Herzberg Brandenburg Germany 53 N3
Herzlake Germany 53 H2
Herzliyya Israel 85 B3
Herzogenaurach Germany 53 K5
Herzsprung Germany 53 M1
Ḩeṣār Iran 88 C4
Ḩeṣār Iran 88 E5
Hesdin France 52 C4
Hesel Germany 53 H1
Heshan China 77 F4
Heshengqiao China 77 G2
Hesperia U.S.A. 128 E4
Hesperus U.S.A. 129 I3
Hesperus Peak U.S.A. 129 I3
Hesquiat Canada 120 E5
Hess r. Canada 120 C2
Heßdorf Germany 53 K5
Hesse land Germany see Hessen
Hesselberg hill Germany 53 K5
Hessen land Germany 53 J4
Hessisch Lichtenau Germany 53 J3
Hess Mountains Canada 120 C2
Het r. Laos 70 D2
Heteren Neth. 52 F3
Hetou China 77 F4
Hettinger U.S.A. 130 C2
Hetton U.K. 48 E4
Hettstedt Germany 53 L3
Heung Kong Tsai H.K. China see Aberdeen
Ḩevron West Bank see Hebron
Hexham U.K. 48 E4
Hexian Anhui China 77 H2
Hexian Guangxi China see Hezhou
Heyang China 77 F1
Ḩeydarābād Iran 88 B2
Ḩeydarābād Iran 89 F4
Heydebreck Poland see Kędzierzyn-Koźle
Heysham U.K. 48 E4
Heyshope Dam S. Africa 101 J4
Heyuan China 77 G4
Heywood U.K. 48 E5
Heze China 77 G1
Hezhang China 76 E3
Hezheng China 76 D1
Hezhou China 77 F3
Hezuo China 76 D1
Hezuozhen China see Hezuo
Hialeah U.S.A. 133 D7
Hiawassee U.S.A. 133 D5
Hiawatha U.S.A. 130 E4
Hibbing U.S.A. 130 E2
Hibbs, Point Australia 111 [inset]
Hibernia Reef Australia 108 C3
Hīchān Iran 89 F5
Hicks, Point Australia 112 D6
Hicks Bay N.Z. 113 G3
Hicks Lake Canada 121 K2
Hicksville U.S.A. 134 C3
Hico U.S.A. 131 D5
Hidaka-sanmyaku mts Japan 74 F4
Hidalgo Mex. 131 D7
Hidalgo del Parral Mex. 131 B7
Hidrolândia Brazil 145 A2
Hierosolyma Israel/West Bank see Jerusalem
Higashi-suidō sea chan. Japan 75 C6
Higgins U.S.A. 131 C4
Higgins Bay U.S.A. 135 H2
Higgins Lake U.S.A. 134 C1
High Atlas mts Morocco see Haut Atlas
High Desert U.S.A. 126 C4
High Island i. H.K. China 77 [inset]
High Island U.S.A. 131 E6
High Island Reservoir H.K. China 77 [inset]
Highland Peak CA U.S.A. 128 D2
Highland Peak NV U.S.A. 129 F3
Highlands U.S.A. 135 I3
Highland Springs U.S.A. 135 G5
High Level Canada 120 G3
Highmore U.S.A. 130 D2
High Point U.S.A. 132 E5
High Point hill U.S.A. 135 H3
High Prairie Canada 120 G4
High River Canada 120 H5
Highrock Lake Man. Canada 121 K4
Highrock Lake Sask. Canada 121 J3
High Springs U.S.A. 133 D6
High Tatras mts Poland/Slovakia see Tatra Mountains
High Wycombe U.K. 49 G7
Higuera de Zaragoza Mex. 127 F8
Higüey Dom. Rep. 137 K5
Hiiumaa i. Estonia 45 M7
Hijānah, Buḩayrat al imp. l. Syria 85 C3
Hijaz reg. Saudi Arabia 86 E4
Ḩikmah, Ra's al pt Egypt 90 B5
Hiko U.S.A. 129 F3
Hikone Japan 75 E6
Hikurangi mt. N.Z. 113 G3
Hila Indon. 108 D1
Hilāl, Jabal hill Egypt 85 A4
Hilāl, Ra's al pt Libya 86 B3
Hilary Coast Antarctica 152 H1
Hildale U.S.A. 129 G3
Hildburghausen Germany 53 K4
Hilders Germany 53 K4
Hildesheim Germany 53 J2
Hillah Iraq 91 G4
Hill City U.S.A. 130 D4
Hillegom Neth. 52 E2
Hill End Australia 112 D4
Hillerød Denmark 45 H9
Hillgrove Australia 110 D3
Hill Island Lake Canada 121 I2
Hillman U.S.A. 134 D1
Hillsboro ND U.S.A. 130 D2
Hillsboro NM U.S.A. 127 G6
Hillsboro OH U.S.A. 134 D4
Hillsboro OR U.S.A. 126 C3
Hillsboro TX U.S.A. 131 D5
Hillsdale IN U.S.A. 134 B4
Hillsdale MI U.S.A. 134 C3
Hillside Australia 108 B5
Hillston Australia 112 B4
Hillsville U.S.A. 134 E5
Hilo U.S.A. 127 [inset]
Hilton Australia 110 B4
Hilton S. Africa 101 J5
Hilton U.S.A. 135 G2
Hilton Head Island U.S.A. 133 D5
Hilvan Turkey 90 E3
Hilversum Neth. 52 F2
Himachal Pradesh state India 82 D3
Himalaya mts Asia 82 D2
Himalchul mt. Nepal 83 F3
Himanka Fin. 44 M4
Ḩimār, Wādī al watercourse Syria/Turkey 85 D1
Himarë Albania 59 H4
Himatnagar India 82 C5
Himeji Japan 75 D6
Ḩimş Syria see Homs
Ḩimş, Baḩrat resr Syria see Qaṭṭīnah, Buḩayrat
Hinchinbrook Island Australia 110 D3
Hinckley U.K. 49 F6
Hinckley MN U.S.A. 130 E2
Hinckley UT U.S.A. 129 G2
Hinckley Reservoir U.S.A. 135 H2
Hindaun India 82 D4
Hinderwell U.K. 48 G4
Hindley U.K. 48 E5
Hindman U.S.A. 134 D5
Hindmarsh, Lake dry lake Australia 111 C8
Hindu Kush mts Afgh./Pak. 89 G3
Hindupur India 84 C3
Hines Creek Canada 120 G3
Hinesville U.S.A. 133 D6
Hinganghat India 84 C1
Hingoli India 84 C2
Hınıs Turkey 91 F3
Hinnøya i. Norway 44 I2
Hinojosa del Duque Spain 57 D4
Hinsdale U.S.A. 135 I2
Hinte Germany 53 H1
Hinthada Myanmar 70 A3
Hinton Canada 120 G4
Hinton U.S.A. 134 E5
Hiort i. U.K. see St Kilda
Hippolytushoef Neth. 52 E2
Hipponium Italy see Vibo Valentia
Hippo Regius Alg. see Annaba
Hippo Zarytus Tunisia see Bizerte
Hirabit Dağ mt. Turkey 91 G3
Hirakud Dam India 83 E5
Hirakud Reservoir India 83 E5
Hirapur India 82 D4
Hiriyur India 84 C3
Hirosaki Japan 74 F4
Hiroshima Japan 75 D6
Hirschaid Germany 53 L5
Hirschberg Germany 53 L4
Hirschberg mt. Germany 47 M7
Hirschberg Poland see Jelenia Góra
Hirschenstein mt. Germany 53 M6
Hirson France 52 E5
Hîrşova Romania see Hârşova
Hirta is U.K. see St Kilda
Hirtshals Denmark 45 F8
Hisar India 82 C3
Hisar Iran 88 C2
Hisarköy Turkey see Domaniç
Hisarönü Turkey 59 O4
Ḩisb, Sha'īb watercourse Iraq 91 G5
Ḩisbān Jordan 85 B4
Hisiu P.N.G. 69 L8
Hisor Tajik. 89 H2
Hisor Tizmasi mts Tajik./Uzbek. see Gissar Range
Hispalis Spain see Seville
Hispania country Europe see Spain

▶Hispaniola i. Caribbean Sea 137 J4
Consists of the Dominican Republic and Haiti.

Hispur Glacier Pak. 82 C1
Hissar India see Hisar
Hisua India 83 F4
Ḩisyah Syria 85 C2
Hīt Iraq 91 F4
Hitachi Japan 75 F5
Hitachinaka Japan 75 F5
Hitra i. Norway 44 F5
Hitzacker Germany 53 L1
Hiva Oa i. Fr. Polynesia 151 K6
Hixon Canada 120 F4
Hixson Cay reef Australia 110 F4
Hiyyon watercourse Israel 85 B4
Hizan Turkey 91 F3
Hjälmaren l. Sweden 45 I7
Hjerkinn Norway 44 F5
Hjo Sweden 45 I7
Hjørring Denmark 45 G8
Hkakabo Razi mt. China/Myanmar 76 C2
Hlaingdet Myanmar 70 B2
Hlako Kangri mt. China see Lhagoi Kangri
Hlane Royal National Park Swaziland 101 J4
Hlatikulu Swaziland 101 J4
Hlegu Myanmar 70 B3
Hlohlowane S. Africa 101 H5
Hlotse Lesotho 101 I5
Hluhluwe-Umfolozi Park nature res. S. Africa 101 J5
Hlukhiv Ukr. 43 G6
Hlung-Tan Myanmar 70 B2
Hlusha Belarus 43 F5
Hlybokaye Belarus 45 O9
Ho Ghana 96 D4
Hoa Binh Vietnam 70 D2
Hoa Binh Vietnam 70 D3
Hoachanas Namibia 100 D2
Hoagland U.S.A. 134 C3
Hoang Liên Sơn mts Vietnam 70 C2
Hoang Sa is S. China Sea see Paracel Islands
Hoan Lao Vietnam 70 D3

▶Hobart Australia 111 [inset]
Capital of Tasmania.

Hobart U.S.A. 131 D5
Hobbs U.S.A. 131 C5
Hobbs Coast Antarctica 152 J1
Hobe Sound U.S.A. 133 D7
Hobiganj Bangl. see Habiganj
Hobro Denmark 45 F8
Hobyo Somalia 98 E3
Hoceima, Baie d'Al b. Morocco 57 E6
Höchberg Germany 53 J5
Hochfeiler mt. Austria/Italy see Gran Pilastro
Hochfeld Namibia 99 B6
Hochharz nat. park Germany 53 K3
Hô Chi Minh Vietnam see Ho Chi Minh City
Ho Chi Minh City Vietnam 71 D5
Hochschwab mt. Austria 47 O7
Hochschwab mts Austria 47 O7
Hockenheim Germany 53 I5
Ḩôḑ reg. Mauritania 96 C3
Hoddesdon U.K. 49 G7
Hodeidah Yemen 86 F7
Hodgenville U.S.A. 134 C5
Hodgson Downs Australia 108 F3
Hódmezővásárhely Hungary 59 I1
Hodna, Chott el salt l. Alg. 57 I6
Hodo-dan pt N. Korea 75 B5
Hoek van Holland Neth. see Hook of Holland
Hoensbroek Neth. 52 F4
Hoeryŏng N. Korea 74 C4
Hof Germany 53 L4
Hoffman Mountain U.S.A. 135 I2
Hofheim in Unterfranken Germany 53 K4
Hofmeyr S. Africa 101 G6
Höfn Iceland 44 [inset]
Hofors Sweden 45 J6
Hofsjökull ice cap Iceland 44 [inset]
Hofsós Iceland 44 [inset]
Hōfu Japan 75 C6
Hofūf Saudi Arabia 86 G4
Höganäs Sweden 45 H8
Hogan Group is Australia 112 C7
Hogansburg U.S.A. 135 H1
Hogback Mountain U.S.A. 130 C3
Hoge Vaart canal Neth. 52 F2
Hogg, Mount Canada 120 C2
Hoggar plat. Alg. 96 D2
Hog Island U.S.A. 135 H5
Högsby Sweden 45 J8
Hohenloher Ebene plain Germany 53 J5
Hohenmölsen Germany 53 M3
Hohennauen Germany 53 M2
Hohensalza Poland see Inowrocław
Hohenwald U.S.A. 132 C5
Hohenwartetalsperre resr Germany 53 L4
Hoher Dachstein mt. Austria 47 N7
Hohe Rhön mts Germany 53 J4
Hohe Tauern mts Austria 47 N7
Hohe Venn moorland Belgium 52 G4
Hohhot China 73 K4
Höhmorít Mongolia 80 H2
Hohneck mt. France 56 H2
Hoh Sai Hu l. China 83 H2
Hoh Xil Hu salt l. China 83 G2
Hoh Xil Shan mts China 83 G2
Hôi An Vietnam 70 E4
Hoima Uganda 98 D3
Hojagala Turkm. 88 E2
Hojai India 83 H4
Hojambaz Turkm. 89 G2
Højryggen mts Greenland 119 M2
Hokitika N.Z. 113 C6
Hokkaidō i. Japan 74 F4
Hokksund Norway 45 F7
Hol Norway 45 F6
Holbæk Denmark 45 G9
Holbeach U.K. 49 H6
Holbrook Australia 112 C5
Holbrook U.S.A. 129 H4
Holden U.S.A. 129 G2
Holdenville U.S.A. 131 D5
Holdrege U.S.A. 130 D3
Holgate U.S.A. 134 C3
Holguín Cuba 137 I4
Höljes Sweden 45 H6
Holland country Europe see Netherlands
Holland MI U.S.A. 134 B2
Holland NY U.S.A. 135 F2
Hollandia Indon. see Jayapura
Hollick-Kenyon Peninsula Antarctica 152 L2
Hollick-Kenyon Plateau Antarctica 152 K1
Hollidaysburg U.S.A. 135 F3
Hollis AK U.S.A. 120 C4
Hollis OK U.S.A. 131 D5
Hollister U.S.A. 128 C3
Holly U.S.A. 134 D2
Hollyhill U.S.A. 134 C5
Holly Springs U.S.A. 131 F5
Hollywood CA U.S.A. 129 D4
Hollywood FL U.S.A. 133 D7
Holm Norway 44 H4
Holmes Reef Australia 110 D3
Holmestrand Norway 45 G7
Holmgard Rus. Fed. see Velikiy Novgorod
Holm Ø i. Greenland see Kiatassuaq
Holmön i. Sweden 44 L5
Holmsund Sweden 44 L5
Ḩolon Israel 85 B3
Holoog Namibia 100 C4
Holothuria Banks reef Australia 108 D3
Holroyd r. Australia 110 C2
Holstebro Denmark 45 F8
Holstein U.S.A. 130 E3
Holsteinsborg Greenland see Sisimiut
Holston r. U.S.A. 132 D4
Holsworthy U.K. 49 C8
Holt U.K. 49 I6
Holt U.S.A. 134 C2
Holton U.S.A. 134 B2
Holwerd Neth. 52 F1
Holwert Neth. see Holwerd
Holycross Ireland 51 E5
Holy Cross U.S.A. 118 C3
Holy Cross, Mount of the U.S.A. 126 G5
Holyhead U.K. 48 C5
Holyhead Bay U.K. 48 C5
Holy Island England U.K. 48 F3
Holy Island Wales U.K. 48 C5
Holyoke U.S.A. 130 C3
Holy See Europe see Vatican City
Holywell U.K. 48 D5

Holzhausen Germany 53 M3
Holzkirchen Germany 47 M7
Holzminden Germany 53 J3
Homand Iran 89 E3
Homāyūnshahr Iran see Khomeynīshahr
Homberg (Efze) Germany 53 J3
Hombori Mali 96 C3
Homburg Germany 53 H5
Home Bay Canada 119 L3
Homécourt France 52 F5
Homer GA U.S.A. 133 D5
Homer LA U.S.A. 131 E5
Homer MI U.S.A. 134 C2
Homer NY U.S.A. 135 G2
Homerville U.S.A. 133 D6
Homestead Australia 110 D4
Homnabad India 84 C2
Homoine Moz. 101 L2
Homs Libya see Al Khums
Homs Syria 85 C2
Homyel' Belarus 43 F5
Honan prov. China see Henan
Honavar India 84 B3
Honaz Turkey 59 M6
Hon Chông Vietnam 71 D5
Hondeklipbaai S. Africa 100 C6
Hondo U.S.A. 131 D6
Hondsrug reg. Neth. 52 G1
▶Honduras country Central America 137 G6
5th largest country in Central and North America.
Hønefoss Norway 45 G6
Honesdale U.S.A. 135 H3
Honey Lake salt l. U.S.A. 128 C1
Honeyoye Lake U.S.A. 135 G2
Honfleur France 56 E2
Hong, Mouths of the Vietnam see Red River, Mouths of the
Hông, Sông r. Vietnam see Red
Hongchuan China see Hongya
Hongguo China see Panxian
Honghai Wan b. China 77 G4
Honghe China 76 D4
Hong He r. China 77 G1
Honghu China 77 G2
Hongjiang Hunan China 77 F3
Hongjiang Sichuan China see Wangcang
Hong Kong H.K. China 77 [inset]
Hong Kong aut. reg. China 77 [inset]
Hong Kong Harbour sea chan. H.K. China 77 [inset]
Hong Kong Island H.K. China 77 [inset]
Hongliuwan China see Aksay
Hongliuyuan China 80 I3
Hongqiao China see Qidong
Hongqizhen China see Wuzhishan
Hongqizhen Hainan China see Wuzhishan
Hongshi China 74 B4
Hongshui He r. China 76 F4
Honguedo, Détroit d' sea chan. Canada 123 I4
Hongwŏn N. Korea 75 B4
Hongxing China 74 A3
Hongya China 76 D2
Hongyuan China 76 D1
Hongze China 77 H1
Hongze Hu l. China 77 H1
▶Honiara Solomon Is 107 F2
Capital of the Solomon Islands.
Honiton U.K. 49 D8
Honjō Japan 75 F5
Honkajoki Fin. 45 M6
Honningsvåg Norway 44 N1
Honoka'a U.S.A. 127 [inset]
▶Honolulu U.S.A. 127 [inset]
Capital of Hawaii.
▶Honshū i. Japan 75 D6
Largest island in Japan, 3rd largest in Asia and 7th in the world.
Honwad India 84 B2
Hood, Mount vol. U.S.A. 126 C3
Hood Point Australia 109 B8
Hood Point P.N.G. 110 D1
Hood River U.S.A. 126 C3
Hoogeveen Neth. 52 G2
Hoogezand-Sappemeer Neth. 52 G1
Hooghly r. mouth India see Hugli
Hooker U.S.A. 131 C4
Hook Head hd Ireland 51 F5
Hook of Holland Neth. 52 E3
Hook Reef Australia 110 E3
Hoonah U.S.A. 120 C3
Hooper Bay U.S.A. 153 B2
Hooper Island U.S.A. 135 G4
Hoopeston U.S.A. 134 B3
Hoopstad S. Africa 101 G4
Höör Sweden 45 H9
Hoorn Neth. 52 F2
Hoorn, Îles de is Wallis and Futuna Is 107 I3
Hoosick U.S.A. 135 I2
Hoover Dam U.S.A. 129 F3
Hoover Memorial Reservoir U.S.A. 134 D3
Hopa Turkey 91 F2
Hope Canada 120 F5
Hope r. N.Z. 113 D6
Hope AR U.S.A. 131 E5
Hope IN U.S.A. 134 C4
Hope, Lake salt flat Australia 109 C8
Hope, Point U.S.A. 118 B3
Hopedale Canada 123 J3
Hopefield S. Africa 100 D7
Hopei prov. China see Hebei
Hope Mountains Canada 123 J3
Hope Saddle pass N.Z. 113 D5
Hopes Advance, Baie b. Canada 123 H2
Hopes Advance, Cap c. Canada 119 L3
Hopes Advance Bay Canada see Aupaluk
Hopetoun Australia 111 C7
Hopetown S. Africa 100 G5
Hopewell U.S.A. 135 G5
Hopewell Islands Canada 122 F2
Hopin Myanmar 70 B1
Hopkins r. Australia 111 C8
Hopkins, Lake salt flat Australia 109 E6
Hopkinsville U.S.A. 134 B5
Hopland U.S.A. 128 B2
Hoquiam U.S.A. 126 C3
Hor China 76 D1
Horasan Turkey 91 F2
Hörby Sweden 45 H9
▶Horizon Deep sea feature S. Pacific Ocean 150 I7
Deepest point in the Tonga Trench, and 2nd in the world.
Horki Belarus 43 F5
Horlick Mountains Antarctica 152 K1
Horlivka Ukr. 43 H6
Hormoz i. Iran 88 E5
Hormoz, Kūh-e mt. Iran 88 D5
Hormuz, Strait of Iran/Oman 88 E5
Horn Austria 47 O6
Horn r. Canada 120 G2
Horn c. Iceland 44 [inset]
▶Horn, Cape Chile 144 C9
Most southerly point of South America.
Hornavan l. Sweden 44 J3
Hornbrook U.S.A. 126 C4
Hornburg Germany 53 K2
Horncastle U.K. 48 G5
Horndal Sweden 45 J6
Horne, Îles de is Wallis and Futuna Is see Hoorn, Îles de
Horneburg Germany 53 J1
Hörnefors Sweden 44 K5
Hornell U.S.A. 135 G2
Hornepayne Canada 122 D4
Hornillos Mex. 127 F8
Hornisgrinde mt. Germany 47 L6
Hornkranz Namibia 100 C2
Horn Mountains Canada 120 F2
Hornos, Cabo de Chile see Horn, Cape
Hornoy-le-Bourg France 52 B5
Horn Peak Canada 120 D2
Hornsby Australia 112 E4
Hornsea U.K. 48 G5
Hornslandet pen. Sweden 45 J6
Horodenka Ukr. 43 E6
Horodnya Ukr. 43 F6
Horodok Khmel'nyts'ka Oblast' Ukr. 43 E6
Horodok L'vivs'ka Oblast' Ukr. 43 D6
Horokanai Japan 74 F3
Horoshiri-dake mt. Japan 74 F4
Horqin Youyi Qianqi China see Ulanhot
Horqin Zuoyi Houqi China see Ganjig
Horqin Zuoyi Zhongqi China see Baokang
Horrabridge U.K. 49 C8
Horrocks Australia 109 A7
Horru China 83 G3
Horse Cave U.S.A. 134 C5
Horsefly Canada 120 F4
Horseheads U.S.A. 135 G2
Horse Islands Canada 123 L4
Horseleap Ireland 51 D4
Horsens Denmark 45 F9
Horseshoe Bend Australia 109 F6
Horseshoe Reservoir U.S.A. 129 H4
Horseshoe Seamounts sea feature N. Atlantic Ocean 148 G3
Horsham Australia 111 C8
Horsham U.K. 49 G7
Horšovský Týn Czech Rep. 53 M5
Horst hill Germany 53 J4
Hörstel Germany 53 H2
Horten Norway 45 G7
Hortobágyi nat. park Hungary 59 I1
Horton r. Canada 118 F3
Horwood Lake Canada 122 E4
Hösbach Germany 53 J4
Hose, Pegunungan mts Malaysia 68 E6
Ḥoseynābād Iran 88 B3
Ḥoseynīyeh Iran 88 C4
Hoshab Pak. 89 F5
Hoshangabad India 82 D5
Hoshiarpur India 82 C3
Hospet India 84 C3
Hospital Ireland 51 D5
Hosséré Vokre mt. Cameroon 96 E4
Hosta Butte mt. U.S.A. 129 I4
Hotagen r. Sweden 44 I5
Hotahudo East Timor see Hatudo
Hotan China 82 E1
Hotazel S. Africa 100 F4
Hot Creek Range mts U.S.A. 128 E2
Hotgi India 84 C2
Hotham r. Australia 109 B8
Hoting Sweden 44 J4
Hot Springs AR U.S.A. 131 E5
Hot Springs NM U.S.A. see Truth or Consequences
Hot Springs SD U.S.A. 130 C3
Hot Sulphur Springs U.S.A. 126 G4
Hottah Lake Canada 120 G1
Hottentots Bay Namibia 100 B4
Hottentots Point Namibia 100 B4
Houdan France 52 B6
Houffalize Belgium 52 F4
Hougang Sing. 71 [inset]
Houghton MI U.S.A. 130 F2
Houghton NY U.S.A. 135 F2
Houghton Lake U.S.A. 134 C1
Houghton Lake l. U.S.A. 134 C1
Houghton le Spring U.K. 48 F4
Houie Moc, Phou mt. Laos 70 C2
Houlton U.S.A. 132 H2
Houma China 77 F1
Houma U.S.A. 131 F6
Houmen China 77 G4
House Range mts U.S.A. 129 G2
Houston Canada 120 E4
Houston MO U.S.A. 131 F4
Houston MS U.S.A. 131 F5
Houston TX U.S.A. 131 E6
Hout r. S. Africa 101 I2
Houtman Abrolhos is Australia 109 A7
Houton U.K. 50 F2
Houwater S. Africa 100 F6
Hovd Hovd Mongolia 80 H2
Hove U.K. 49 G8
Hoveton U.K. 49 I6
Hovmantorp Sweden 45 I8
Hövsgöl Nuur l. Mongolia 80 J1
Howar, Wadi watercourse Sudan 86 C6
Howard Australia 110 F5
Howard PA U.S.A. 135 G3
Howard SD U.S.A. 130 D2
Howard WI U.S.A. 134 A1
Howard City U.S.A. 134 C2
Howard Lake Canada 121 J2
Howden U.K. 48 G5
Howe, Cape Australia 112 D6
Howe, Mount Antarctica 152 J1
Howell U.S.A. 134 D2
Howick Canada 135 I1
Howick S. Africa 101 J5
Howland U.S.A. 132 G2
▶Howland Island terr. N. Pacific Ocean 107 I1
United States Unincorporated Territory.
Howlong Australia 112 C5
Howrah India see Haora
Howth Ireland 51 F4
Ḥowz well Iran 88 E3
Ḥowz-e Khān well Iran 88 E3
Ḥowz-e Panj Iran 88 E4
Ḥowz-e Panj waterhole Iran 88 D3
Howz i-Mian i-Tak Iran 88 D3
Hô Xa Vietnam 70 D3
Höxter Germany 53 J3
Hoy i. U.K. 50 F2
Hoya Germany 53 J2
Høyanger Norway 45 E6
Hoyerswerda Germany 47 O5
Høylandet Norway 44 H4
Hoym Germany 53 L3
Höytiäinen l. Fin. 44 P5
Hoyt Peak U.S.A. 129 H1
Hpa-an Myanmar 70 B3
Hpapun Myanmar 70 B3
Hradec Králové Czech Rep. 47 O5
Hradiště hill Czech Rep. 53 N4
Hrasnica Bos.-Herz. 58 H3
Hrazdan Armenia 91 G2
Hrebinka Ukr. 43 G6
Hrodna Belarus 45 M10
Hrvatska country Europe see Croatia
Hrvatsko Grahovo Bos.-Herz. see Bosansko Grahovo
Hsenwi Myanmar 70 B2
Hsiang Chang i. H.K. China see Hong Kong Island
Hsiang Kang H.K. China see Hong Kong
Hsi-hseng Myanmar 70 B2
Hsin-chia-p'o country Asia see Singapore
Hsin-chia-p'o Sing. see Singapore
Hsinchu Taiwan 77 I3
Hsinking China see Changchun
Hsinying Taiwan 77 I4
Hsipaw Myanmar 70 B2
Hsi-sha Ch'ün-tao is S. China Sea see Paracel Islands
Hsiyüp'ing Yü i. Taiwan 77 H4
Hsü-chou Jiangsu China see Xuzhou
Hsüeh Shan mt. Taiwan 77 I3
Huab watercourse Namibia 99 B6
Huachinera Mex. 127 F7
Huacho Peru 142 C6
Huachuan China 74 C3
Huade China 73 K4
Huadian China 74 B4
Huadu China 77 G4
Hua Hin Thai. 71 B4
Huai'an Jiangsu China 77 H1
Huai'an Jiangsu China see Chuzhou
Huaibei China 77 H1
Huaibin China 77 G1
Huaicheng Guangdong China see Huaiji
Huaicheng Jiangsu China see Chuzhou
Huaidezhen China 74 B4
Huaidian China see Shenqiu
Huai Had National Park Thai. 70 D3
Huaihua China 77 F3
Huaiji China 77 G4
Huai Kha Khaeng Wildlife Reserve nature res. Thai. 70 B4
Huaillilas mt. Peru 142 C5
Huainan China 77 H1
Huaining Anhui China 77 H2
Huaining Anhui China see Shipai
Huaiyang China 77 G1
Huaiyin Jiangsu China see Huai'an
Huaiyin Jiangsu China 77 H1
Huaiyuan China 77 H1
Huajialing China 76 E1
Huajuápan de León Mex. 136 E5
Hualapai Peak U.S.A. 129 G4
Hualian Taiwan see Hualien
Hualien Taiwan 77 I3
Huallaga r. Peru 142 C5
Huambo Angola 99 B5
Huanan China 74 C3
Huancane Peru 142 E7
Huancavelica Peru 142 C6
Huancayo Peru 142 C6
Huangbei China 77 G3
Huangcaoba China see Xingyi
Huang-chou Hubei China see Huanggang
Huangchuan China 77 G1
Huanggang China 77 G2
Huang Hai sea N. Pacific Ocean see Yellow Sea
Huang He r. China see Yellow River
Huangjiajian China 77 I1
Huang-kang Hubei China see Huanggang
Huangling China 77 F1
Huangliu China 77 F5
Huanglongsi China see Kaifeng
Huangmao Jian mt. China 77 H3
Huangmei China 77 G2
Huangpu China 77 G4
Huangqi China 77 H3
Huangshan China 77 H2
Huangshi China 77 G2
Huangtu Gaoyuan plat. China 73 J5
Huangyan China 77 I2
Huangzhou Hubei China see Huanggang
Huaning China 76 D3
Huanjiang China 77 F3
Huanren China 74 B4
Huanshan China see Yuhuan
Huánuco Peru 142 C5
Huaping China 76 D3
Huap'ing Yü i. Taiwan 77 I3
Huaqiao China 76 E2
Huaqiaozhen China see Huaqiao
Huaráz Peru 142 C5
Huarmey Peru 142 C6
Huarong China 77 G2
Huascarán, Nevado de mt. Peru 142 C5
Huasco Chile 144 B3
Hua Shan mt. China 77 F1
Huashixia China 76 C1
Huashugou China see Jingtieshan
Huashulinzi China 74 B4
Huatabampo Mex. 127 F8
Huaxian Guangdong China see Huadu
Huaxian Henan China 77 G1
Huayang China see Jixi
Huayin China 77 F1
Huayuan China 77 F2
Huayxay Laos 70 C2
Huazangsi China see Tianzhu
Hubbard, Mount Canada/U.S.A. 120 B2
Hubbard, Pointe pt Canada 123 I2
Hubbard Lake U.S.A. 134 D1
Hubbart Point Canada 121 M3
Hubei prov. China 77 G2
Hubli India 84 B3
Hückelhoven Germany 52 G3
Hucknall U.K. 49 F5
Huddersfield U.K. 48 F5
Huder China 74 A2
Hudiksvall Sweden 45 J6
Hudson MA U.S.A. 135 J2
Hudson MD U.S.A. 135 G4
Hudson MI U.S.A. 134 C3
Hudson NH U.S.A. 135 J2
Hudson NY U.S.A. 135 I2
Hudson r. U.S.A. 135 I3
Hudson, Baie d' sea Canada see Hudson Bay
Hudson, Détroit d' strait Canada see Hudson Strait
Hudson Bay Canada 121 K4
Hudson Bay sea Canada 119 J4
Hudson Falls U.S.A. 135 I2
Hudson Island Tuvalu see Nanumanga
Hudson Mountains Antarctica 152 K2
Hudson's Hope Canada 120 F3
Hudson Strait Canada 119 K3
Huê Vietnam 70 D3
Huehuetenango Guat. 136 F5
Huehueto, Cerro mt. Mex. 131 B7
Huelva Spain 57 C5
Huentelauquén Chile 144 B4
Huépac Mex. 127 F7
Huércal-Overa Spain 57 F5
Huertecillas Mex. 131 C7
Huesca Spain 57 F2
Huéscar Spain 57 E5
Hughenden Australia 110 D4
Hughes r. Canada 121 K3
Hughes (abandoned) Australia 109 E7
Hughson U.S.A. 128 C3
Hugli r. mouth India 83 F5
Hugo CO U.S.A. 130 C4
Hugo OK U.S.A. 131 E5
Hugo Lake U.S.A. 131 E5
Hugoton U.S.A. 131 C4
Huhehot China see Hohhot
Huhhot China see Hohhot
Huhudi S. Africa 100 G4
Hui'an China 77 H3
Hui'anpu China 72 J5
Huiarau Range mts N.Z. 113 F4
Huib-Hoch Plateau Namibia 100 C4
Huichang China 77 G3
Huicheng Anhui China see Shexian
Huicheng Guangdong China see Huilai
Huidong China 76 D3
Huijbergen Neth. 52 E3
Huila, Nevado de vol. Col. 142 C3
Huíla, Planalto da Angola 99 B5
Huilai China 77 H4
Huili China 76 D3
Huimanguillo Mex. 136 F5
Huinan China see Nanhui
Huining China 76 E1
Huishi China see Huining
Huishui China 76 E3
Huiten Nur l. China 83 G2
Huitong China 77 F3
Huittinen Fin. 45 M6
Huixian Gansu China 76 E1
Huixian Henan China 77 G1
Huiyang China see Huizhou
Huize China 76 D3
Huizhou China 77 G4
Hujr Saudi Arabia 86 F4
Hukawng Valley Myanmar 70 B1
Hukuntsi Botswana 100 E2
Hulan China 74 B3
Hulan Ergi China 74 A3
Ḥulayfah Saudi Arabia 86 F4
Ḥulayḥilah well Syria 85 D2
Huliao China see Dabu
Hulilan Iran 88 B3
Hulin China 74 D3
Hulin Gol r. China 74 B3
Hull Canada 135 H1
Hull U.K. see Kingston upon Hull
Hull Island atoll Kiribati see Orona
Hultsfred Sweden 45 I8
Hulun China see Hulun Buir
Hulun Nei Mongol China see Hulun Buir
Hulun Buir China 73 L3
Hulun Nur l. China 73 L3
Ḥulwān Egypt 90 C5
Huma China 74 B2
Humahuaca Arg. 144 C2
Humaitá Brazil 142 F5
Humaya r. Mex. 127 G8
Humaym well U.A.E. 88 D6
Humayyān, Jabal hill Saudi Arabia 88 B5
Humber, Mouth of the U.K. 48 H5
Humboldt Canada 121 J4
Humboldt AZ U.S.A. 129 G4
Humboldt NE U.S.A. 130 E3
Humboldt NV U.S.A. 128 D1
Humboldt r. U.S.A. 128 D1
Humboldt Bay U.S.A. 126 B4
Humboldt Range mts U.S.A. 128 D1
Humbolt Salt Marsh U.S.A. 128 E2
Hume r. Canada 120 D1
Humeburn Australia 112 B1
Hu Men sea chan. China 77 G4
Hume Reservoir Australia 112 C5
Humphrey Island atoll Cook Is see Manihiki
Humphreys, Mount U.S.A. 128 D3
Humphreys Peak U.S.A. 129 H4
Hūn Libya 97 E2
Húnaflói b. Iceland 44 [inset]
Hunan prov. China 77 F3
Hundeluft Germany 53 M3
Hunedoara Romania 59 J2
Hünfeld Germany 53 J4
Hungary country Europe 55 H2
Hungerford Australia 112 B2
Hung Fa Leng hill H.K. China see Robin's Nest
Hŭngnam N. Korea 75 B5
Hung Shui Kiu H.K. China 77 [inset]
Hưng Yên Vietnam 70 D2
Hunjiang China see Baishan
Huns Mountains Namibia 100 C4
Hunstanton U.K. 49 H6
Hunte r. Germany 53 I1
Hunter r. Australia 112 E4
Hunter Island Australia 111 [inset]
Hunter Island Canada 120 D5
Hunter Island S. Pacific Ocean 107 H4
Hunter Islands Australia 111 [inset]
Huntingburg U.S.A. 134 B4
Huntingdon Canada 135 H1
Huntingdon U.K. 49 G6
Huntingdon PA U.S.A. 135 G3
Huntingdon TN U.S.A. 131 F4
Huntington IN U.S.A. 134 C3
Huntington OR U.S.A. 126 D3
Huntington WV U.S.A. 134 D4
Huntington Beach U.S.A. 128 D5
Huntington Creek r. U.S.A. 129 F1
Huntly N.Z. 113 E3
Huntly U.K. 50 G3
Hunt Mountain U.S.A. 126 G3
Huntsville Canada 134 F1
Huntsville AL U.S.A. 133 C5
Huntsville AR U.S.A. 131 E4
Huntsville TN U.S.A. 134 C5
Huntsville TX U.S.A. 131 E6
Hunza reg. Pak. 82 C1
Huolin He r. China see Hulin Gol
Huolongmen China 74 B2
Hương Khê Vietnam 70 D3
Huonville Australia 111 [inset]
Huoqiu China 77 H1
Huoshan China 77 H2
Huo Shan mt. China see Baima Jian
Huoshao Tao i. Taiwan see Lü Tao
Hupeh prov. China see Hubei
Hupnik r. Turkey 85 C1
Hupu India 76 B2
Ḥūr Iran 88 E4
Hurault, Lac l. Canada 123 H3
Ḥuraydīn, Wādī watercourse Egypt 85 A4
Huraysān reg. Saudi Arabia 88 B6
Hurd, Cape Canada 134 E1
Hurd Island Kiribati see Arorae
Hurghada Egypt see Al Ghurdaqah
Hurler's Cross Ireland 51 D5
Hurley NM U.S.A. 129 I5
Hurley WI U.S.A. 130 F2
Hurmagai Pak. 89 G4
Huron CA U.S.A. 128 C3
Huron SD U.S.A. 130 D2
▶Huron, Lake Canada/U.S.A. 134 D1
2nd largest lake in North America, and 4th in the world.
Hurricane U.S.A. 129 G3
Hursley U.K. 49 F7
Hurst Green U.K. 49 H7
Husain Nika Pak. 89 H4
Húsavík Norðurland eystra Iceland 44 [inset]
Húsavík Vestfirðir Iceland 44 [inset]
Huseyinabat Turkey see Alaca
Huseyinli Turkey see Kızılırmak
Hushan Zhejiang China 77 H2
Hushan Zhejiang China see Wuyi
Hushan Zhejiang China see Cixi
Huşi Romania 59 M1
Huskvarna Sweden 45 I8
Husn Jordan see Al Ḥiṣn
Ḥuṣn Āl 'Abr Yemen 86 G6
Husnes Norway 45 D7
Husum Germany 47 L3
Husum Sweden 44 K5
Hutag-Öndör Mongolia 80 J2
Hutchinson KS U.S.A. 130 D4
Hutchinson MN U.S.A. 130 E2
Hutch Mountain U.S.A. 129 H4
Hutou China 74 D3
Hutsonville U.S.A. 134 B4
Hutton, Mount hill Australia 111 E5
Hutton Range hills Australia 109 C6
Huvadhu Atoll Maldives 81 D11
Hüvek Turkey see Bozova
Hūvīān, Kūh-e mts Iran 89 E5
Ḥuwār i. Bahrain 88 C5
Huwaytat reg. Saudi Arabia 85 C5
Huxi China 77 G3
Huzhong China 74 A2
Huzhou China 77 I2
Hvannadalshnúkur vol. Iceland 44 [inset]
Hvar i. Croatia 58 G3
Hvide Sande Denmark 45 F8
Hvíta r. Iceland 44 [inset]
Hwange Zimbabwe 99 C5
Hwange National Park Zimbabwe 99 C5
Hwang Ho r. China see Yellow River
Hwedza Zimbabwe 99 D5
Hwlffordd U.K. see Haverfordwest
Hyannis MA U.S.A. 135 J3
Hyannis NE U.S.A. 130 C3
Hyargas Nuur salt l. Mongolia 80 H2
Hyco Lake U.S.A. 134 F5
Hyde N.Z. 113 C7
Hyden Australia 109 B8
Hyden U.S.A. 134 D5
Hyde Park U.S.A. 135 I1
Hyderabad India 84 C2
Hyderabad Pak. 89 H5
Hydra i. Greece see Ydra
Hyères France 56 H5
Hyères, Îles d' is France 56 H5
Hyesan N. Korea 74 C4
Hyland, Mount Australia 112 F3
Hyland Post Canada 120 D3
Hyllestad Norway 45 D6
Hyltebruk Sweden 45 H8
Hyndman Peak U.S.A. 126 E4
Hyōno-sen mt. Japan 75 D6
Hyrcania Iran see Gorgān
Hyrynsalmi Fin. 44 P4
Hysham U.S.A. 126 G3
Hythe Canada 120 G4
Hythe U.K. 49 I7
Hyūga Japan 75 C6
Hyvinkää Fin. 45 N6

I

Iaciara Brazil 145 B1
Iaco r. Brazil 142 E5
Iaçu Brazil 145 C1
Iadera Croatia see Zadar
Iaeger U.S.A. 134 E5
Iakora Madag. 99 E6
Ialomiţa r. Romania 59 L2
Ianca Romania 59 L2
Iaşi Romania 59 L1
Iba Phil. 69 F3
Ibadan Nigeria 96 D4
Ibagué Col. 142 C3
Ibaiti Brazil 145 A3
Ibapah U.S.A. 129 G1
Ibarra Ecuador 142 C3
Ibb Yemen 86 F7
Ibbenbüren Germany 53 H2
Iberá, Esteros del marsh Arg. 144 E3
Iberia Peru 142 E6
▶Iberian Peninsula Europe 57
Consists of Portugal, Spain and Gibraltar.
Iberville, Lac d' l. Canada 123 G3
Ibeto Nigeria 96 D3
iBhayi S. Africa see Port Elizabeth
Ibi Indon. 71 B6
Ibi Nigeria 96 D4
Ibiá Brazil 145 B2
Ibiaí Brazil 145 B2
Ibiapaba, Serra da hills Brazil 143 J4
Ibiassucê Brazil 145 C1
Ibicaraí Brazil 145 D1
Ibiquera Brazil 145 C1
Ibirama Brazil 145 A4
Ibiranhém Brazil 145 C2
Ibitinga Brazil 145 A3
Ibiza Spain 57 G4
Ibiza i. Spain 57 G4
Iblei, Monti mts Sicily Italy 58 F6
Ibn Buşayyiş well Saudi Arabia 88 B5
Ibotirama Brazil 143 J6
Iboundji, Mont hill Gabon 98 B4
Ibrā' Oman 88 E6
İbradı Turkey 90 C3
Ibrī Oman 88 E6
Ica r. Col. see Putumayo
Ica Peru 142 C6
Içana Brazil 142 E3
Içana r. Brazil 142 E3
Icaria i. Greece see Ikaria
Icatu Brazil 143 J4
Iceberg Canyon gorge U.S.A. 129 F3
İçel Mersin Turkey see Mersin
▶Iceland country Europe 44 [inset]
2nd largest island in Europe.
Iceland Basin sea feature N. Atlantic Ocean 148 G2
Icelandic Plateau sea feature N. Atlantic Ocean 153 I2
Ichalkaranji India 84 B2
Ichifusa-yama mt. Japan 75 C6
Ichinomiya Japan 75 E6
Ichinoseki Japan 75 F5
Ichinskaya Sopka vol. Rus. Fed. 65 Q4
Ichkeul, Parc National de l' Tunisia 58 C6
Ichnya Ukr. 43 G6
Ichtegem Belgium 52 D3
Ichtershausen Germany 53 K4
Icó Brazil 143 K5
Iconha Brazil 145 C3
Iconium Turkey see Konya
Icosium Alg. see Algiers
Iculisma France see Angoulême
Icy Cape U.S.A. 118 B2
İd Turkey see Narman
Idabel U.S.A. 131 E5
Ida Grove U.S.A. 130 E3
Idah Nigeria 96 D4
Idaho state U.S.A. 126 E3
Idaho City U.S.A. 126 E4
Idaho Falls U.S.A. 126 E4
Idalia National Park Australia 110 D5
Idar India 82 C5
Idar-Oberstein Germany 53 H5
Ideriyn Gol r. Mongolia 80 J2
Idfū Egypt 86 D5
Idhān Awbārī des. Libya 96 E2
Idhān Murzūq des. Libya 96 E2
Idhra i. Greece see Ydra
Idi Amin Dada, Lake Dem. Rep. Congo/Uganda see Edward, Lake
Idiofa Dem. Rep. Congo 99 B4
Idivuoma Sweden 44 M2
Idkū Egypt 90 C5
Idle r. U.K. 48 G5
Idlewild airport U.S.A. see John F. Kennedy
Idlib Syria 85 C2
Idra i. Greece see Ydra

Idre Sweden 45 H6
Idstein Germany 53 I4
Idutywa S. Africa 101 I7
Idzhevan Armenia see Ijevan
Iecava Latvia 45 N8
Iepê Brazil 145 A3
Ieper Belgium 52 C4
Ierapetra Greece 59 K7
Ierissou, Kolpos b. Greece 59 J4
Iešjávri l. Norway 44 N2
Ifakara Tanz. 99 D4
Ifalik atoll Micronesia 69 K5
Ifaluk atoll Micronesia see Ifalik
Ifanadiana Madag. 99 E6
Ife Nigeria 96 D4
Ifenat Chad 97 E3
Iferouâne Niger 96 D3
Iffley Australia 110 C3
Ifjord Norway 44 O1
Ifôghas, Adrar des hills Mali 96 D3
Iforas, Adrar des hills Mali see Ifôghas, Adrar des
Igan Sarawak Malaysia 68 E6
Iganga Uganda 97 G4
Igarapava Brazil 145 B3
Igarka Rus. Fed. 64 J3
Igatpuri India 84 B2
Igbeti Nigeria see Igbetti
Igbetti Nigeria 96 D4
Igdir Iran 88 B2
Iğdır Turkey 91 G3
Iggesund Sweden 45 J6
Igikpak, Mount U.S.A. 118 C3
Igizyar China 89 J2
Iglesias Sardinia Italy 58 C5
Iglesiente reg. Sardinia Italy 58 C5
Igloolik Canada 119 J3
Igluligaarjuk Canada see Chesterfield Inlet
Ignace Canada 121 N5
Ignacio Zaragosa Mex. 127 G7
Ignacio Zaragoza Mex. 131 C8
Ignalina Lith. 45 O9
İğneada Turkey 59 L4
İğneada Burnu pt Turkey 59 M4
Ignoitijala India 71 A5
iGoli S. Africa see Johannesburg
Igoumenitsa Greece 59 I5
Igra Rus. Fed. 41 Q4
Igrim Rus. Fed. 41 S3
Iguaçu r. Brazil 145 A4
Iguaçu, Saltos do waterfall Arg./Brazil see Iguaçu Falls
Iguaçu Falls Arg./Brazil 144 F3
Iguaí Brazil 145 C1
Iguala Mex. 136 E5
Igualada Spain 57 G3
Iguape Brazil 145 B4
Iguaraçu Brazil 145 A3
Iguatama Brazil 145 B3
Iguatemi Brazil 144 F2
Iguatu Brazil 143 K5
Iguazú, Cataratas do waterfall Arg./Brazil see Iguaçu Falls
Iguéla Gabon 98 A4
Iguidi, Erg des. Alg./Mauritania 96 C2
Igunga Tanz. 99 D4
Iharaña Madag. 99 E5
Ihavandhippolhu Atoll Maldives 84 B5
Ihavandiffulu Atoll Maldives see Ihavandhippolhu Atoll
Ih Bogd Uul mt. Mongolia 80 J3
Ihosy Madag. 99 E6
Iide-san mt. Japan 75 E5
Iijärvi l. Fin. 44 O2
Iijoki r. Fin. 44 N4
Iisalmi Fin. 44 O5
Iizuka Japan 75 C6
Ijebu-Ode Nigeria 96 D4
Ijevan Armenia 91 G2
IJmuiden Neth. 52 E2
IJssel r. Neth. 52 F2
IJsselmeer l. Neth. 52 F2
IJzer r. France see Yser
Ikaahuk Canada see Sachs Harbour
Ikaalinen Fin. 45 M6
Ikageleng S. Africa 101 H3
Ikageng S. Africa 101 H4
iKapa S. Africa see Cape Town
Ikare Nigeria 96 D4
Ikaria i. Greece 59 L6
Ikast Denmark 45 F8
Ikeda Japan 74 F4
Ikela Dem. Rep. Congo 98 C4
Ikhtiman Bulg. 59 J3
Ikhutseng S. Africa 100 G5
Iki-Burul Rus. Fed. 43 J7
Ikom Nigeria 96 D4
Iksan S. Korea 75 B6
Ikungu Tanz. 99 D4
Ilagan Phil. 77 I5
Ilaisamis Kenya 98 D3
Īlām Iran 88 B3
Ilam Nepal 83 F4
Ilan Taiwan 77 I3
Ilave Peru 142 E7
Iława Poland 47 Q4
Ilazārān, Kūh-e mt. Iran 88 E4
Île-à-la-Crosse Canada 121 J4
Île-à-la-Crosse, Lac l. Canada 121 J4
Ilebo Dem. Rep. Congo 99 C4
Île-de-France admin. reg. France 52 C6
Île Europa i. Indian Ocean see Europa, Île
Ilek Kazakh. 41 Q5
Ilen r. Ireland 51 C6
Ileret Kenya 98 D3
Ileza Rus. Fed. 42 I3
Ilfeld Germany 53 K3
Ilford Canada 121 M3
Ilford U.K. 49 H7
Ilfracombe Australia 110 D4
Ilfracombe U.K. 49 C7
Ilgaz Turkey 90 D2
Ilgın Turkey 90 C3
Ilha Grande, Represa resr Brazil 144 F2
Ilha Solteíra, Represa resr Brazil 145 A3
Ílhavo Port. 57 B3
Ilhéus Brazil 145 D1
Ili Kazakh. see Kapchagay
Iliamna Lake U.S.A. 118 C4
İliç Turkey 90 E3
Il'ichevsk Azer. see Şărur
Il'ichevsk Ukr. see Illichivs'k
Ilici Spain see Elche-Elx
Iligan Phil. 69 G5
Ilimananngip Nunaa i. Greenland 119 P2
Il'inka Rus. Fed. 43 J7
Il'inskiy Permskaya Oblast' Rus. Fed. 41 R4
Il'inskiy Sakhalinskaya Oblast' Rus. Fed. 74 F3
Il'insko-Podomskoye Rus. Fed. 42 J3
Ilion U.S.A. 135 H2
Ilium tourist site Turkey see Troy
Iliysk Kazakh. see Kapchagay
Ilkal India 84 C3
Ilkeston U.K. 49 F6
Ilkley U.K. 48 F5
Illapel Chile 144 B4
Illéla Niger 96 D3
Iller r. Germany 47 L6
Illichivs'k Ukr. 59 N1
Illimani, Nevado de mt. Bol. 142 E7
Illinois r. U.S.A. 130 F4
Illinois state U.S.A. 134 A3
Illizi Alg. 96 D2
Illogwa watercourse Australia 110 A5
Ilm r. Germany 53 L3
Ilmajoki Fin. 44 M5
Il'men', Ozero l. Rus. Fed. 42 F4
Ilmenau Germany 53 K4
Ilmenau r. Germany 53 K1
Ilminster U.K. 49 E8
Ilo Peru 142 D7
Iloilo Phil. 69 G4
Ilomantsi Fin. 44 Q5
Ilong India 76 B3
Ilorin Nigeria 96 D4
Ilovlya Rus. Fed. 43 I6
Ilsede Germany 53 K2
Iluka Australia 112 F2
Ilulissat Greenland 119 M3
Iluppur India 84 C4
Ilva i. Italy see Elba, Isola d'
Imabari Japan 75 D6
Imaichi Japan 75 E5
Imala Moz. 99 D5
Imam-baba Turkm. 89 F2
İmamoğlu Turkey 90 D3
Iman Rus. Fed. see Dal'nerechensk
Iman r. Rus. Fed. 74 D3
Imari Japan 75 C6
Imaruí Brazil 145 A5
Imataca, Serranía de mts Venez. 142 F2
Imatra Fin. 45 P6
Imbituva Brazil 145 A4
imeni 26 Bakinskikh Komissarov Azer. see Uzboy
imeni Babushkina Rus. Fed. 42 I4
imeni Chapayevka Turkm. see S. A. Nyýazow Adyndaky
imeni Kalinina Tajik. see Cheshtebe
imeni Kirova Kazakh. see Kopbirlik
imeni Petra Stuchki Latvia see Aizkraukle
imeni Poliny Osipenko Rus. Fed. 74 E1
imeni Tel'mana Rus. Fed. 74 D2
Īmī Eth. 98 E3
Imishli Azer. see İmişli
İmişli Azer. 91 H3
Imit Pak. 82 C1
Imja-do i. S. Korea 75 B6
Imlay U.S.A. 128 D1
Imlay City U.S.A. 134 D2
Imola Italy 58 D2
iMonti S. Africa see East London
Impendle S. Africa 101 I5
Imperatriz Brazil 143 I5
Imperia Italy 58 C3
Imperial CA U.S.A. 129 F5
Imperial NE U.S.A. 130 C3
Imperial Beach U.S.A. 128 E5
Imperial Dam U.S.A. 129 F5
Imperial Valley plain U.S.A. 129 F5
Imperieuse Reef Australia 108 B4
Impfondo Congo 98 B3
Imphal India 83 H4
İmralı Adası i. Turkey 59 M4
İmroz Turkey 59 K4
İmroz i. Turkey see Gökçeada
Imtān Syria 85 C3
Imuris Mex. 127 F7
In r. Rus. Fed. 74 D2
Ina Japan 75 E6
Inambari r. Peru 142 E6
Inari Fin. 44 O2
Inarijärvi l. Fin. 44 O2
Inarijoki r. Fin./Norway 44 N2
Inca Spain 57 H4
İnce Burnu pt Turkey 59 L4
İnce Burun pt Turkey 90 D2
Inch Ireland 51 F5
Inchard, Loch b. U.K. 50 D2
Incheon S. Korea see Inch'ŏn
Inchicronan Lough l. Ireland 51 D5
Inch'ŏn S. Korea 75 B5
Incirli Turkey see Karasu
Indaal, Loch b. U.K. 50 C5
Indalsälven r. Sweden 44 J5
Indalstø Norway 45 D6
Inda Silasē Eth. 98 D2
Indaw Myanmar 70 A2
Indawgyi, Lake Myanmar 76 C3
Indé Mex. 131 B7
Indefatigable Island Galápagos Ecuador see Santa Cruz, Isla
Independence CA U.S.A. 128 D3
Independence IA U.S.A. 130 F3
Independence KS U.S.A. 131 E4
Independence KY U.S.A. 134 C4
Independence MO U.S.A. 130 E4
Independence VA U.S.A. 134 E5
Independence Mountains U.S.A. 126 D4
Inder China 74 A3
Inderborskiy Kazakh. 78 E2
Indi India 84 C2

▶India country Asia 81 E7
2nd most populous country in the world and in Asia. 3rd largest country in Asia, and 7th in the world.

Indian r. Canada 120 B2
Indiana U.S.A. 134 F3
Indiana state U.S.A. 134 B3
Indian-Antarctic Ridge sea feature Southern Ocean 150 D9

▶Indianapolis U.S.A. 134 B4
Capital of Indiana.

Indian Cabins Canada 120 G3
Indian Desert India/Pak. see Thar Desert
Indian Harbour Canada 123 K3
Indian Head Canada 121 K5
Indian Lake U.S.A. 135 H2
Indian Lake l. NY U.S.A. 135 H2
Indian Lake l. OH U.S.A. 134 D3
Indian Lake l. PA U.S.A. 135 F3

▶Indian Ocean 149
3rd largest ocean in the world.

Indianola IA U.S.A. 130 E3
Indianola MS U.S.A. 131 F5
Indian Peak U.S.A. 129 G2
Indian Springs IN U.S.A. 134 B4
Indian Springs NV U.S.A. 129 F3
Indian Wells U.S.A. 129 H4
Indiga Rus. Fed. 42 K2
Indigirka r. Rus. Fed. 65 P2
Indigskaya Guba b. Rus. Fed. 42 K2
Inđija Serbia 59 I2
Indin Lake Canada 120 H1
Indio U.S.A. 128 E5
Indira Point India see Pygmalion Point
Indira Priyadarshini Pench National Park India 82 D5
Indispensable Reefs Solomon Is 107 G3
Indjija Serbia see Inđija
Indo-China reg. Asia 70 D3

▶Indonesia country Asia 68 E7
4th most populous country in the world and 3rd in Asia.

Indore India 82 C5
Indrapura, Gunung vol. Indon. see Kerinci, Gunung
Indravati r. India 84 D2
Indre r. France 56 E3
Indulkana Australia 109 F6
Indur India see Nizamabad
Indus r. China/Pakistan 89 G6
also known as Sênggê Zangbo (China) or Shiquan He (China)
Indus, Mouths of the Pak. 89 G5
Indus Cone sea feature Indian Ocean 149 M4
Indwe S. Africa 101 H6
İnebolu Turkey 90 D2
İnegöl Turkey 59 M4
Inevi Turkey see Cihanbeyli
Inez U.S.A. 134 D5
Infantes Spain see Villanueva de los Infantes
Infiernillo, Presa resr Mex. 136 D5
Ing, Nam Mae r. Thai. 70 C2
Inga Rus. Fed. 44 S3
Ingalls, Mount U.S.A. 128 C2
Ingelmunster Belgium 52 D4
Ingenika r. Canada 120 E3
Ingersoll Canada 134 E2
Ingham Australia 110 D3
Ingichka Uzbek. 89 G2
Ingleborough hill U.K. 48 E4
Inglefield Land reg. Greenland 119 K2
Ingleton U.K. 48 E4
Inglewood Qld Australia 112 E2
Inglewood Vic. Australia 112 A6
Inglewood U.S.A. 128 D5
Ingoka Pum mt. Myanmar 70 B1
Ingoldmells U.K. 48 H5
Ingolstadt Germany 53 L6
Ingomar Australia 109 F7
Ingomar U.S.A. 126 G3
Ingonish Canada 123 J5
Ingraj Bazar India 83 G4
Ingram U.S.A. 134 F5
Ingray Lake Canada 120 G1
Ingrid Christensen Coast Antarctica 152 E2
Ingwavuma S. Africa 101 K4
Ingwavuma r. S. Africa/Swaziland see Ngwavuma
Ingwiller France 53 H6
Inhaca Moz. 101 K3
Inhaca, Península pen. Moz. 101 K4
Inhambane Moz. 101 L2
Inhambane prov. Moz. 101 L2
Inhaminga Moz. 99 D5
Inharrime Moz. 101 L3
Inhassoro Moz. 99 D6
Inhaúmas Brazil 145 B1
Inhobim Brazil 145 C1
Inhumas Brazil 145 A2
Inis Ireland see Ennis
Inis Córthaidh Ireland see Enniscorthy
Inishark i. Ireland 51 B4
Inishbofin i. Ireland 51 B4
Inisheer i. Ireland 51 C4
Inishkea North i. Ireland 51 B3
Inishkea South i. Ireland 51 B3
Inishmaan i. Ireland 51 C4
Inishmore i. Ireland 51 C4
Inishmurray i. Ireland 51 D3
Inishowen pen. Ireland 51 E2
Inishowen Head hd Ireland 51 F2
Inishtrahull i. Ireland 51 E2
Inishturk i. Ireland 51 B4
Injune Australia 111 E5
Inkerman Australia 110 C3
Inklin Canada 120 C3
Inklin r. Canada 120 C3
Inkylap Turkm. 89 F2
Inland Kaikoura Range mts N.Z. 113 D6
Inland Sea Japan see Seto-naikai
Inlet U.S.A. 135 H2
Inn r. Europe 47 M7
Innaanganeq c. Greenland 119 L2
Innamincka Australia 111 C5
Innamincka Regional Reserve nature res. Australia 111 C5
Inndyr Norway 44 I3
Inner Sound sea chan. U.K. 50 D3
Innes National Park Australia 111 B7
Innisfail Australia 110 D3
Innisfail Canada 120 H4
Innokent'yevka Rus. Fed. 74 C2
Innoko r. U.S.A. 118 C3
Innsbruck Austria 47 M7
Innuksuak r. Canada 122 F2
Inny r. Ireland 51 E4
Inocência Brazil 145 A2
Inongo Dem. Rep. Congo 98 B4
İnönü Turkey 59 N5
Inoucdjouac Canada see Inukjuak
Inowrocław Poland 47 Q4
In Salah Alg. 96 D2
Insch U.K. 50 G3

▶Inscription, Cape Australia 110 B3
Most westerly point of Oceania.

Insein Myanmar 70 B3
Insterburg Rus. Fed. see Chernyakhovsk
Inta Rus. Fed. 41 S2
Interamna Italy see Teramo
Interlaken Switz. 56 H3
International Falls U.S.A. 130 E1
Interview Island India 71 A4
Intracoastal Waterway canal U.S.A. 131 E6
Intutu Peru 142 D4
Inubō-zaki pt Japan 75 F6
Inukjuak Canada 122 F2
Inuvik Canada 118 E3
Inveraray U.K. 50 D4
Inverbervie U.K. 50 G4
Invercargill N.Z. 113 B8
Inverell Australia 112 E2
Invergordon U.K. 50 E3
Inverkeithing U.K. 50 F4
Inverleigh Australia 110 C3
Invermay Canada 121 K5
Inverness Canada 123 J5
Inverness U.K. 50 E3
Inverness CA U.S.A. 128 B2
Inverness FL U.S.A. 133 D6
Inverurie U.K. 50 G3
Investigator Channel Myanmar 71 B4
Investigator Group is Australia 109 F8
Investigator Ridge sea feature Indian Ocean 149 O6
Investigator Strait Australia 111 B7
Inwood U.S.A. 135 F4
Inya Rus. Fed. 80 G1
Inyanga Zimbabwe see Nyanga
Inyangani mt. Zimbabwe 99 D5
Inyokern U.S.A. 128 E4
Inyo Mountains U.S.A. 128 D3
Inyonga Tanz. 99 D4
Inza Rus. Fed. 43 J5
Inzhavino Rus. Fed. 43 I5
Ioannina Greece 59 I5
Iokanga r. Rus. Fed. 42 H2
Iola U.S.A. 130 E4
Iolgo, Khrebet mts Rus. Fed. 80 G1
Iolotan' Turkm. see Ýolöten
Iona Canada 123 J5
Iona i. U.K. 50 C4
Iona, Parque Nacional do nat. park Angola 99 B5
Ione U.S.A. 128 E2
Iongo Angola 99 B4
Ionia U.S.A. 134 C2
Ionia Nisia is Ionia Nisia Greece see Ionian Islands
Ionian Islands Greece 59 H5
Ionian Sea Greece/Italy 58 H5
Ionioi Nisoi is Ionia Nisia Greece see Ionian Islands
Ionioi Nisoi is Greece see Ionian Islands
Ios i. Greece 59 K6
Iowa state U.S.A. 130 E3
Iowa City U.S.A. 130 F3
Iowa Falls U.S.A. 130 E3
Ipameri Brazil 145 A2
Ipanema Brazil 145 C2
Iparía Peru 142 D5
Ipatinga Brazil 145 C2
Ipatovo Rus. Fed. 43 I7
Ipelegeng S. Africa 101 G4
Ipiales Col. 142 C3
Ipiaú Brazil 145 D1
Ipirá Brazil 145 D1
Ipiranga Brazil 145 A4
iPitoli S. Africa see Pretoria
Ipixuna r. Brazil 142 F5
Ipoh Malaysia 71 C6
Iporá Brazil 145 A2
Ippy Cent. Afr. Rep. 98 C3
İpsala Turkey 59 L4
Ipswich Australia 112 F1
Ipswich U.K. 49 I6
Ipswich U.S.A. 130 D2
Ipu Brazil 143 J4

▶Iqaluit Canada 119 L3
Capital of Nunavut.

Iquique Chile 144 B2
Iquiri r. Brazil see Ituxi
Iquitos Peru 142 D4
Īrafshān reg. Iran 89 F5
Irai Brazil 144 F3
Irakleio Greece see Iraklion
Iraklion Greece 59 K7
Iramaia Brazil 145 C1
Iran country Asia 88 D3
Iran, Pegunungan mts Indon. 68 E6
Īrānshahr Iran 89 F5
Irapuato Mex. 136 D4
Iraq country Asia 91 F4
Irara Brazil 145 D1
Irati Brazil 145 A4
Irayel' Rus. Fed. 42 L2
Irazú, Volcán vol. Costa Rica 137 H7
Irbid Jordan 85 B3
Irbil Iraq see Arbīl
Irbit Rus. Fed. 64 H4
Irecê Brazil 143 J6
Ireland country Europe 51 E4

▶Ireland i. Ireland/U.K. 51
4th largest island in Europe.

Irema Dem. Rep. Congo 98 C4
Irgiz Kazakh. 80 B2
Irgiz r. Kazakh. 80 B2
Iri S. Korea see Iksan
Irian, Teluk b. Indon. see Cenderawasih, Teluk
Iriba Chad 97 F3
Īrī Dāgh mt. Iran 88 B2
Iriga Phil. 69 G4
Irîgui reg. Mali/Mauritania 96 C3
Iringa Tanz. 99 D4
Iriri r. Brazil 143 H4
Irish Sea Ireland/U.K. 51 G4
Irituia Brazil 143 I4
'Irj well Saudi Arabia 88 C5
Irkutsk Rus. Fed. 72 I2
Irma Canada 121 I4
Irmak Turkey 90 D3
Irminger Basin sea feature N. Atlantic Ocean 148 F2
Iron Baron Australia 111 B7
Irondequoit U.S.A. 135 G2
Iron Mountain U.S.A. 130 F2
Iron Mountain mt. U.S.A. 129 G3
Iron Range National Park Australia 110 C2
Iron River U.S.A. 130 F2
Ironton MO U.S.A. 130 F4
Ironton OH U.S.A. 134 D4
Ironwood Forest National Monument nat. park U.S.A. 129 H5
Iroquois r. U.S.A. 134 B3
Iroquois Falls Canada 122 E4
Irosin Phil. 69 G4
Irpen' Ukr. see Irpin'
Irpin' Ukr. 43 F6
'Irq al Ḩarūrī des. Saudi Arabia 88 B5
'Irq Banbān des. Saudi Arabia 88 B5
Irrawaddy r. Myanmar 70 A4
Irrawaddy, Mouths of the Myanmar 70 A4
Irshad Pass Afgh./Pak. 89 I2
Irta Rus. Fed. 42 K3
Irthing r. U.K. 48 E4

▶Irtysh r. Kazakh./Rus. Fed. 80 E1
5th longest river in Asia and 10th in the world, and a major part of the 2nd longest in Asia (Ob'-Irtysh).

Irun Spain 57 F2
Iruña Spain see Pamplona
Iruñea Spain see Pamplona
Irvine U.K. 50 E5
Irvine CA U.S.A. 128 E5
Irvine KY U.S.A. 134 D5
Irvine Glacier Antarctica 152 L2
Irving U.S.A. 131 D5
Irvington U.S.A. 134 B5
Irwin r. Australia 109 A7
Irwinton U.S.A. 133 D5
Isa Nigeria 96 D3
Isaac r. Australia 110 E4
Isabel U.S.A. 130 C2
Isabela Phil. 69 G5
Isabela, Isla i. Galápagos Ecuador 142 [inset]
Isabelia, Cordillera mts Nicaragua 137 G6
Isabella Lake U.S.A. 128 D4
Isachsen, Cape Canada 119 H2
Ísafjarðardjúp est. Iceland 44 [inset]
Ísafjörður Iceland 44 [inset]
Isa Khel Pak. 89 H3
Isar r. Germany 53 M6
Isbister U.K. 50 [inset]
Ischia, Isola d' i. Italy 58 E4
Ise Japan 75 E6
Isère r. France 56 G4
Isère, Pointe pt Fr. Guiana 143 H2
Iserlohn Germany 53 H3
Isernhagen Germany 53 J2
Isernia Italy 58 F4
Ise-shima Kokuritsu-kōen nat. park Japan 75 E6
Ise-wan b. Japan 75 E6
Iseyin Nigeria 96 D4
Isfahan Iran see Eşfahān
Isfana Kyrg. 89 H2
Isheyevka Rus. Fed. 43 K5
Ishigaki Japan 73 M8
Ishikari-wan b. Japan 74 F4
Ishim r. Kazakh./Rus. Fed. 80 D1
Ishinomaki Japan 75 F5
Ishinomaki-wan b. Japan 73 Q5
Ishioka Japan 75 F5
Ishkoshim Tajik. 89 H2
Ishpeming U.S.A. 132 C2
Ishtikhon Uzbek. see Ishtixon
Ishtixon Uzbek. 89 G2
Ishtragh Afgh. 89 H2
Ishurdi Bangl. 83 G4
Ishwardi Bangl. see Ishurdi
Isiboro Sécure, Parque Nacional nat. park Bol. 142 E7
Isigny-sur-Mer France 49 F9
Işıklar Dağı mts Turkey 59 L4
Işıklı Turkey 59 M5
Isil'kul' Rus. Fed. 64 I4
Isimangaliso Wetland Park nature res. S. Africa 101 K4
Isipingo S. Africa 101 J5
Isiro Dem. Rep. Congo 98 C3
Isisford Australia 110 D5
Iskateley Rus. Fed. 42 L2
İskenderun Turkey 85 C1
İskenderun Körfezi b. Turkey 85 B1
İskilip Turkey 90 D2
Iskitim Rus. Fed. 64 J4
Iskür r. Bulg. 59 K3
Iskushuban Somalia 98 F2
Isla r. Scotland U.K. 50 F4
Isla r. Scotland U.K. 50 G3
Isla Gorge National Park Australia 110 E5
İslahiye Turkey 90 E3
Islamabad India see Anantnag

▶Islamabad Pak. 89 I3
Capital of Pakistan.

Islamgarh Pak. 89 H5
Islamkot Pak. 89 H5
Island r. Canada 120 F2
Ísland country Europe see Iceland
Island U.S.A. 134 B5
Island Falls U.S.A. 132 G2
Island Lagoon salt flat Australia 111 B6
Island Lake Canada 121 M4
Island Lake l. Canada 121 M4
Island Magee pen. U.K. 51 G3
Island Pond U.S.A. 135 J1
Islands, Bay of N.Z. 113 E2
Islay i. U.K. 50 C5

▶Isle of Man terr. Irish Sea 48 C4
United Kingdom Crown Dependency.

Isle of Wight U.S.A. 135 G5
Isle Royale National Park U.S.A. 130 F2
Ismail Ukr. see Izmayil
Ismâ'ilîya Egypt see Al Ismā'īlīyah
Ismâ'ilîya governorate Egypt see Al Ismā'īlīyah
Ismailly Azer. see İsmayıllı
İsmayıllı Azer. 91 H2
Isojoki Fin. 44 L5
Isoka Zambia 99 D5
Isokylä Fin. 44 O3
Isokyrö Fin. 44 M5
Isola di Capo Rizzuto Italy 58 G5
Ispahan Iran see Eşfahān
Isparta Turkey 59 N6
Isperikh Bulg. 59 L3
Ispikan Pak. 89 F5
İspir Turkey 91 F2
Ispisar Tajik. see Khŭjand
Isplinji Pak. 89 G4
Israel country Asia 85 B4
Israelite Bay Australia 109 C8
Isra'īl country Asia see Israel
Isselburg Germany 52 G3
Issia Côte d'Ivoire 96 C4
Issoire France 56 F4
Issyk-Kul' Kyrg. see Balykchy
Issyk-Kul', Ozero salt l. Kyrg. see Ysyk-Köl
Istalif Afgh. 89 H3

▶İstanbul Turkey 59 M4
2nd most populous city in Europe.

İstanbul Boğazı strait Turkey see Bosporus
Īstgāh-e Eznā Iran 88 C3
Istiaia Greece 59 J5
Istik r. Tajik. 89 I2
Istočni Drvar Bos.-Herz. 58 G2
Istra pen. Croatia see Istria
Istres France 56 G5
Istria pen. Croatia 58 E2
Iswardi Bangl. see Ishurdi
Itabapoana r. Brazil 145 C3
Itaberá Brazil 145 A3
Itaberaba Brazil 145 C1
Itaberaí Brazil 145 A2
Itabira Brazil 145 C2
Itabirito Brazil 145 C3
Itabuna Brazil 145 D1
Itacajá Brazil 143 I5
Itacarambi Brazil 145 B1
Itacoatiara Brazil 143 G4
Itaetê Brazil 145 C1
Itagmatana Iran see Hamadān
Itaguaçu Brazil 145 C2
Itaí Brazil 145 A3
Itaiópolis Brazil 145 A4
Itäisen Suomenlahden kansallispuisto nat. park Fin. 45 O6
Itaituba Brazil 143 G4
Itajaí Brazil 145 A4
Itajubá Brazil 145 B3
Itajuipe Brazil 145 D1
Italia country Europe see Italy
Italia, Laguna l. Bol. 142 F6

▶Italy country Europe 58 E3
5th most populous country in Europe.

Itamarandiba Brazil 145 C2
Itambé Brazil 145 C1
Itambé, Pico de mt. Brazil 145 C2
It Amelân i. Neth. see Ameland
Itampolo Madag. 99 E6
Itanagar India 83 H4
Itanguari r. Brazil 145 B1
Itanhaém Brazil 145 B4
Itanhém Brazil 145 C2
Itanhém r. Brazil 145 D2
Itaobím Brazil 145 C2
Itapaci Brazil 145 A1
Itapajipe Brazil 145 A2
Itapebi Brazil 145 D1
Itapecerica Brazil 145 B3
Itapemirim Brazil 145 C3
Itaperuna Brazil 145 C3
Itapetinga Brazil 145 C1
Itapetininga Brazil 145 A3
Itapeva Brazil 145 A3
Itapeva, Lago l. Brazil 145 A5
Itapicuru Brazil 143 J6
Itapicuru, Serra de hills Brazil 143 I5
Itapicuru Mirim Brazil 143 J4
Itapipoca Brazil 143 K4
Itapira Brazil 145 B3
Itaporanga Brazil 145 A3
Itapuã Brazil 145 A5
Itaqui Brazil 144 E3
Itararé Brazil 145 A4
Itarsi India 82 D5
Itarumã Brazil 145 A2
Itatiba Brazil 145 B3
Itatuba Brazil 142 F5
Itaúnas Brazil 145 D2
Itbayat i. Phil. 69 G2
Itchen Lake Canada 121 H1
Itea Greece 59 J5
Ithaca MI U.S.A. 134 C2
Ithaca NY U.S.A. 135 G2
It Hearrenfean Neth. see Heerenveen
iThekweni S. Africa see Durban
Ith Hils ridge Germany 53 J2
Ithrah Saudi Arabia 85 C4
Itilleq Greenland 119 M3
Itimbiri r. Dem. Rep. Congo 98 C3
Itinga Brazil 145 C2
Itiquira Brazil 143 H7
Itiruçu Brazil 145 C1
Itiúba, Serra de hills Brazil 143 K6
Itō Japan 75 E6
iTswane S. Africa see Pretoria
Ittiri Sardinia Italy 58 C4

Kamenskoye Ukr. see Dniprodzerzhyns'k
Kamensk-Shakhtinskiy Rus. Fed. 43 I6
Kamensk-Ural'skiy Rus. Fed. 64 H4
Kamet mt. China 82 D3
Kamiesberge mts S. Africa 100 D6
Kamieskroon S. Africa 100 C6
Kamileroi Australia 110 C3
Kamilukuak Lake Canada 121 K2
Kamina Dem. Rep. Congo 99 C4
Kaminak Lake Canada 121 M2
Kaminuriak Lake Canada see Qamanirjuaq Lake
Kamishihoro Japan 74 F4
Kamloops Canada 120 F5
Kamo Armenia see Gavarr
Kamoke Pak. 89 I4
Kamonia Dem. Rep. Congo 99 C4

▶Kampala Uganda 98 D3
Capital of Uganda.

Kampar r. Indon. 68 C6
Kampar Malaysia 71 C6
Kampara India 84 D1
Kampen Neth. 52 F2
Kampene Dem. Rep. Congo 98 C4
Kamphaeng Phet Thai. 70 B3
Kampinoski Park Narodowy nat. park Poland 47 R4
Kâmpóng Cham Cambodia 71 D5
Kâmpóng Chhnăng Cambodia 71 D4
Kâmpóng Khleăng Cambodia 71 D4
Kâmpóng Saôm Cambodia see Sihanoukville
Kâmpóng Spœ Cambodia 71 D5
Kâmpóng Thum Cambodia 71 D4
Kâmpóng Trâbêk Cambodia 71 D5
Kâmpôt Cambodia 71 D5
Kampuchea country Asia see Cambodia
Kamrau, Teluk b. Indon. 69 I7
Kamsack Canada 121 K5
Kamskoye Vodokhranilishche resr Rus. Fed. 41 R4
Kamsuuma Somalia 98 E3
Kamuchawie Lake Canada 121 K3
Kamuli Uganda 98 D3
Kam"yanets'-Podil's'kyy Ukr. 43 E6
Kam"yanka-Buz'ka Ukr. 43 E6
Kamyanyets Belarus 45 M10
Kāmyārān Iran 88 B3
Kamyshin Rus. Fed. 43 J6
Kamystybas, Ozero l. Kazakh. 80 B2
Kamyzyak Rus. Fed. 43 K7
Kamzar Oman 88 E5
Kanaaupscow r. Canada 122 F3
Kanab U.S.A. 129 G3
Kanab Creek r. U.S.A. 129 G3
Kanairiktok r. Canada 123 K3
Kanak Pak. 89 G4
Kananga Dem. Rep. Congo 99 C4
Kanangio, Mount vol. P.N.G. 69 L7
Kanangra-Boyd National Park Australia 112 E4
Kanarak India see Konarka
Kanarraville U.S.A. 129 G3
Kanas watercourse Namibia 100 C4
Kanash Rus. Fed. 42 J5
Kanauj India see Kannauj
Kanazawa Japan 75 E5
Kanbalu Myanmar 70 A2
Kanchanaburi Thai. 71 B4
Kanchanjanga mt. India/Nepal see Kangchenjunga
Kanchipuram India 84 C3
Kand mt. Pak. 89 G4
Kanda Pak. 89 G4
Kandahār Afgh. 89 G4
Kandalaksha Rus. Fed. 44 R3
Kandalakshskiy Zaliv g. Rus. Fed. 44 R3
Kandang Indon. 71 B7
Kandar Indon. 108 E2
Kandavu i. Fiji see Kadavu
Kandavu Passage Fiji see Kadavu Passage
Kandé Togo 96 D4
Kandh Kot Pak. 89 H4
Kandi Benin 96 D3
Kandi India 84 C2
Kandiaro Pak. 89 H5
Kandıra Turkey 59 N4
Kandos Australia 112 D4
Kandreho Madag. 99 E5
Kandrian P.N.G. 69 L8
Kandukur India 84 C3
Kandy Sri Lanka 84 D5
Kandyagash Kazakh. 80 A2
Kane U.S.A. 135 F3
Kane Bassin b. Greenland 153 K1
Kaneh watercourse Iran 88 D5
Kāne'ohe U.S.A. 127 [inset]
Kaneti Pak. 89 G4
Kanevskaya Rus. Fed. 43 H7
Kang Afgh. 89 F4
Kang Botswana 100 F2
Kangaamiut Greenland 119 M3
Kangaarsussuaq c. Greenland 119 K2
Kangaba Mali 96 C3
Kangal Turkey 90 E3
Kangān Būshehr Iran 88 D5
Kangān Hormozgan Iran 88 E5
Kangandala, Parque Nacional de nat. park Angola see Cangandala, Parque Nacional de
Kangar Malaysia 71 C6
Kangaroo Island Australia 111 B7
Kangaroo Point Australia 110 B3
Kangaslampi Fin. 44 P5
Kangasniemi Fin. 44 O6
Kangāvar Iran 88 B3

▶Kangchenjunga mt. India/Nepal 83 G4
3rd highest mountain in Asia and in the world.

Kangding China 76 D2
Kangean, Kepulauan is Indon. 68 F8
Kangen r. Sudan 97 G4
Kangerlussuaq Greenland 119 M3
Kangerlussuaq inlet Greenland 119 M3
Kangerlussuaq inlet Greenland 153 J2
Kangersuatsiaq Greenland 119 M2
Kangertittivaq sea chan. Greenland 119 P2
Kanggye N. Korea 74 B4
Kanghwa S. Korea 75 B5
Kangikajik c. Greenland 119 P2
Kangiqsualujjuaq Canada 123 I2
Kangirsuk Canada 123 H1
Kang Krung National Park Thai. 71 B5
Kangle Gansu China 76 D1
Kangle Jiangxi China see Wanzai
Kanglong China 76 C1
Kangmar China 83 F3
Kangnŭng S. Korea 75 C5
Kango Gabon 98 B3
Kangping China 74 A4
Kangri Karpo Pass China/India 83 I3
Kangrinboqê Feng mt. China 82 E3
Kangsangdobdê China see Xainza
Kangto mt. China/India 83 H4
Kangtog China 83 F2
Kangxian China 76 E1
Kanibongan Sabah Malaysia 68 F5
Kanifing Gambia 96 B3
Kanigiri India 84 C3
Kanin, Poluostrov pen. Rus. Fed. 42 J2
Kanin Nos Rus. Fed. 153 G2
Kanin Nos, Mys c. Rus. Fed. 42 I1
Kaninskiy Bereg coastal area Rus. Fed. 42 I2
Kanjiroba mt. Nepal 83 E3
Kankaanpää Fin. 45 M6
Kankakee U.S.A. 134 B3
Kankan Guinea 96 C3
Kanker India 84 D1
Kankesanturai Sri Lanka 84 D4
Kankossa Mauritania 96 B3
Kanmaw Kyun i. Myanmar 71 B5
Kannauj India 82 D4
Kanniya Kumari c. India see Comorin, Cape
Kannonkoski Fin. 44 N5
Kannur India see Cannanore
Kannus Fin. 44 M5
Kano Nigeria 96 D3
Kanonpunt pt S. Africa 100 E8
Kanosh U.S.A. 129 G2
Kanovlei Namibia 99 B5
Kanoya Japan 75 C7
Kanpur Orissa India 84 E1
Kanpur Uttar Prad. India 82 E4
Kanrach reg. Pak. 89 G5
Kansai airport Japan 75 D6
Kansas U.S.A. 134 B4
Kansas r. U.S.A. 130 E4
Kansas state U.S.A. 130 D4
Kansas City KS U.S.A. 130 E4
Kansas City MO U.S.A. 130 E4
Kansk Rus. Fed. 65 K4
Kansu prov. China see Gansu
Kantang Thai. 71 B6
Kantara hill Cyprus 85 A2
Kantaralak Thai. 71 D4
Kantavu i. Fiji see Kadavu
Kantchari Burkina 96 D3
Kantemirovka Rus. Fed. 43 H6
Kanthi India 83 F5
Kantishna r. U.S.A. 118 C3
Kanton atoll Kiribati 107 I2
Kantulong Myanmar 70 B3
Kanturk Ireland 51 D5
Kanuku Mountains Guyana 143 G3
Kanur India 84 C3
Kanus Namibia 100 D4
Kanyakubja India see Kannauj
Kanyamazane S. Africa 101 J3
Kanye Botswana 101 G3
Kaôh Pring i. Cambodia 71 C5
Kaohsiung Taiwan 77 I4
Kaôh Smăch i. Cambodia 71 C5
Kaôh Tang i. Cambodia 71 C5
Kaokoveld plat. Namibia 99 B5
Kaolack Senegal 96 B3
Kaoma Zambia 99 C5
Kaouadja Cent. Afr. Rep. 98 C3
Kapa S. Africa see Cape Town
Kapa'a U.S.A. 127 [inset]
Kapa'au U.S.A. 127 [inset]
Kapan Armenia 91 G3
Kapanga Dem. Rep. Congo 99 C4
Kaparhā Iran 88 C4
Kapatu Zambia 99 D4
Kapchagay Kazakh. 80 E3
Kapchagayskoye Vodokhranilishche resr Kazakh. 80 E3
Kap Dan Greenland see Kulusuk
Kapellen Belgium 52 E3
Kapello, Akra pt Attiki Greece see Kapello, Akrotirio
Kapello, Akrotirio pt Greece 59 J6
Kapellskär Sweden 45 K7
Kapelskär Sweden see Kapellskär
Kapili r. India 83 G4
Kapingamarangi atoll Micronesia 150 G5
Kapingamarangi Rise sea feature N. Pacific Ocean 150 G5
Kapıorman Dağları mts Turkey 59 N4
Kapip Pak. 89 H4
Kapiri Mposhi Zambia 99 C5
Kapisillit Greenland 119 M3
Kapiskau r. Canada 122 E3
Kapit Sarawak Malaysia 68 E6
Kapiti Island N.Z. 113 E5
Kaplankyr, Chink hills Asia 91 I2
Kaplankyr Döwlet Gorugy nature res. Turkm. 88 E1
Kapoeta Sudan 97 G4
Kapondai, Tanjung pt Indon. 69 G8
Kaposvár Hungary 58 G1
Kappel Germany 53 H5
Kappeln Germany 47 L3
Kapsukas Lith. see Marijampolė
Kaptai Bangl. 83 H5
Kapuas r. Indon. 68 D7
Kapuriya India 82 C4
Kapurthala India 82 C3
Kapuskasing Canada 122 E4
Kapustin Yar Rus. Fed. 43 J6
Kaputar mt. Australia 112 E3
Kaputir Kenya 98 D3
Kapuvár Hungary 58 G1
Kapydzhik, Gora mt. Armenia/Azer. see Qazangödağ
Kapyl' Belarus 45 O10
Kaqung China 89 J2
Kara India 82 E4
Kara Togo 96 D4
Kara r. Turkey 91 F3
Kara Art Pass China 89 I2
Kara-Balta Kyrg. 80 D3
Karabalyk Kazakh. 78 F1
Karabekaul' Turkm. see Garabekewül
Karabiga Turkey 59 L4
Karabil', Vozvyshennost' hills Turkm. see Garabil Belentligi
Kara-Bogaz-Gol, Proliv sea chan. Turkm. see Garabogazköl Bogazy
Kara-Bogaz-Gol'skiy Zaliv b. Turkm. see Garabogazköl Aýlagy
Karabük Turkey 90 D2
Karaburun Turkey 59 L5
Karabutak Kazakh. 80 B2
Karacabey Turkey 59 M4
Karacaköy Turkey 59 M4
Karacalı Dağ mt. Turkey 91 E3
Karaçal Tepe mt. Turkey 85 A1
Karacasu Turkey 59 M6
Karaca Yarımadası pen. Turkey 59 N6
Karachayevsk Rus. Fed. 91 F2
Karachev Rus. Fed. 43 G5
Karachi Pak. 89 G5
Karacurun Turkey see Hilvan
Karad India 84 B2
Kara Dağ hill Turkey 85 D1
Kara Dağ mt. Turkey 90 D3
Kara-Dar'ya Uzbek. see Payshanba
Kara Deniz sea Asia/Europe see Black Sea
Karagan Rus. Fed. 74 A1
Karaganda Kazakh. 80 D2
Karagayly Kazakh. 80 E2
Karaginskiy Zaliv b. Rus. Fed. 65 R4
Karagiye, Vpadina depr. Kazakh. 91 H2
Karagola India 83 F4
Karahallı Turkey 59 M5
Karahasanlı Turkey 90 D3
Karaikal India 84 C4
Karaikkudi India 84 C4
Karaisalı Turkey 90 D3
Karaj Iran 88 C3
Karak Jordan see Al Karak
Karakalli Turkey see Özalp
Karakax China see Moyu
Karakax He r. China 82 E1
Karakax Shan mts China 82 E2
Karakelong i. Indon. 69 H6
Karaki China 82 E1
Karaklis Armenia see Vanadzor
Karakoçan Turkey 91 F3
Kara-Köl Kyrg. 79 G2
Karakol Kyrg. 80 E3
Karakoram Pass China/India 82 D2
Karakoram Range mts Asia 79 G3
Karakoram Range mts Asia 89 I2
Kara K'orē Eth. 98 D2
Karakorum Range mts Asia see Karakoram Range
Karakorum Range mts Asia see Karakoram Range
Karaköse Turkey see Ağrı
Kara Kul' Kyrg. see Kara-Köl
Karakul', Ozero l. Tajik. see Qarokŭl
Kara Kum des. Turkm. see Garagum
Kara Kum des. Turkm. see Karakum Desert
Karakum, Peski Kazakh. see Karakum Desert
Karakum Desert Kazakh. 78 E2
Karakum Desert Turkm. see Garagum
Karakum Desert Turkm. 88 F2
Karakumskiy Kanal canal Turkm. see Garagum Kanaly
Kara Kumy des. Turkm. see Garagum
Karakurt Turkey 91 F2
Karakuş Dağı ridge Turkey 59 N5
Karal Chad 97 E3
Karala Estonia 45 L7
Karalundi Australia 109 B6
Karama r. Indon. 68 F7
Karaman Turkey 90 D3
Karaman prov. Turkey 85 A1
Karamanlı Turkey 59 M6
Karamay China 80 F2
Karambar Pass Afgh./Pak. 89 I2
Karamea N.Z. 113 D5
Karamea Bight b. N.Z. 113 C5
Karamendy Kazakh. 80 B1
Karamiran China 83 F1
Karamiran Shankou pass China 83 F1
Karamürsel Turkey 59 M4
Karamyshevo Rus. Fed. 45 P8
Karān i. Saudi Arabia 88 C5
Karangasem Indon. 108 A2
Karanja India 84 C1
Karanjia India 82 E5
Karapınar Gaziantep Turkey 85 C1
Karapınar Konya Turkey 90 D3
Karas admin. reg. Namibia 100 C4
Karasay China 83 E1
Karasburg Namibia 100 D5
Kara Sea Rus. Fed. 64 I2
Kárášjohka Finnmark Norway see Karasjok
Karasjok Norway 44 N2
Kara Strait Rus. Fed. see Karskiye Vorota, Proliv
Karasu r. Syria/Turkey 85 C1
Karasu Bitlis Turkey see Hizan
Karasu Sakarya Turkey 59 N4
Karasu r. Turkey 91 F3
Karasubazar Ukr. see Bilohirs'k
Karasuk Rus. Fed. 64 I4
Karāt Iran 89 F3
Karataş Turkey 85 B1
Karataş Burnu hd Turkey see Fener Burnu
Karatau Kazakh. 80 D3
Karatau, Khrebet mts Kazakh. 80 C3
Karatepe Turkey 85 A1
Karathuri Myanmar 71 B5
Karativu i. Sri Lanka 84 C4
Karatsu Japan 75 C6
Karaudanawa Guyana 143 G3
Karauli India 82 D4
Karavan Kyrg. see Kerben
Karavostasi Cyprus 85 A2
Karawang Indon. 68 D8
Karayılan Turkey 85 C1
Karayulgan China 80 F3
Karazhal Kazakh. 80 D2
Karbalā' Iraq 91 G4
Karben Germany 53 I4
Karcag Hungary 59 I1
Karden Germany 53 H4
Kardhítsa Greece see Karditsa
Karditsa Greece 59 I5
Kärdla Estonia 45 M7
Karee S. Africa 101 H5
Kareeberge mts S. Africa 100 E6
Kareima Sudan 86 D6
Kareli India 82 D5
Karelia aut. rep. Rus. Fed. see Kareliya, Respublika
Kareliya, Respublika aut. rep. Rus. Fed. 44 R5
Karel'skaya A.S.S.R. aut. rep. Rus. Fed. see Kareliya, Respublika
Karel'skiy Bereg coastal area Rus. Fed. 44 R3
Karema Tanz. 99 D4
Karera India 82 D4
Karesuando Sweden 44 M2
Kārevāndar Iran 89 F5
Kargalinskaya Rus. Fed. 91 G2
Kargalinski Rus. Fed. see Kargalinskaya
Kargapazarı Dağları mts Turkey 91 F3
Karghalik China see Yecheng
Kargı Turkey 90 D2
Kargil India 82 D2
Kargilik China see Yecheng
Kargıpınarı Turkey 85 B1
Kargopol' Rus. Fed. 42 H3
Kari Nigeria 96 E3
Karīān Iran 88 E5
Kariba Zimbabwe 99 C5
Kariba, Lake resr Zambia/Zimbabwe 99 C5
Kariba Dam Zambia/Zimbabwe 99 C5
Kariba-yama vol. Japan 74 E4
Karibib Namibia 100 B1
Karigasniemi Fin. 44 N2
Karijini National Park Australia 109 B5
Karijoki Fin. 44 L5
Karikachi-tōge pass Japan 74 F4
Karikari, Cape N.Z. 113 D2
Karimata, Pulau-pulau is Indon. 68 D7
Karimata, Selat strait Indon. 68 D7
Karimganj India 83 H4
Karimnagar India 84 C2
Karimun Besar i. Indon. 71 C7
Karimunjawa, Pulau-pulau is Indon. 68 E8
Káristos Greece see Karystos
Karjat Mahar. India 84 B2
Karjat Mahar. India 84 B2
Karkaralinsk Kazakh. 80 E2
Karkar Island P.N.G. 69 L7
Karkh Pak. 89 G5
Karkinits'ka Zatoka g. Ukr. 59 O2
Kärkölä Fin. 45 N6
Karkonoski Park Narodowy nat. park Czech Rep./Poland see Krkonošský národní park
Karksi-Nuia Estonia 45 N7
Karkūk Iraq see Kirkūk
Karlachi Pak. 89 H3
Karlholmsbruk Sweden 45 J6
Karlik Shan mt. China 80 H3
Karlıova Turkey 91 F3
Karlivka Ukr. 43 G6
Karl Marks, Qullai mt. Tajik. 89 I2
Karl-Marx-Stadt Germany see Chemnitz
Karlovac Croatia 58 F2
Karlovka Ukr. see Karlivka
Karlovo Bulg. 59 K3
Karlovy Vary Czech Rep. 53 M4
Karlsbad Germany 53 I6
Karlsborg Sweden 45 I7
Karlsburg Romania see Alba Iulia
Karlshamn Sweden 45 I8
Karlskoga Sweden 45 I7
Karlskrona Sweden 45 I8
Karlsruhe Germany 53 I5
Karlstad Sweden 45 H7
Karlstad U.S.A. 130 D1
Karlstadt Germany 53 J5
Karluk U.S.A. 118 C4
Karlyk Turkm. 89 G2
Karmala India 84 B2
Karmel, Har hill Israel see Carmel, Mount
Karmona Spain see Córdoba
Karmøy i. Norway 45 D7
Karmpur Pak. 89 I4
Karnafuli Reservoir Bangl. 83 H5
Karnal India 82 D3
Karnataka state India 84 B3
Karnavati India see Ahmadabad
Karnes City U.S.A. 131 D6
Karnobat Bulg. 59 L3
Karodi Pak. 89 G5
Karoi Zimbabwe 99 C5
Karokpi Myanmar 70 B4
Karo La pass China 83 G3
Karong India 83 H4
Karonga Malawi 99 D4
Karonie Australia 109 C7
Karoo National Park S. Africa 100 F7
Karoonda Australia 111 B7
Karora Eritrea 86 E6
Káros i. Greece see Keros
Karossa Indon. 68 F7
Karossa, Tanjung pt Indon. 108 B2
Karow Germany 53 M1
Karpasia pen. Cyprus 85 B2
Karpas Peninsula Cyprus see Karpasia
Karpathos i. Greece 59 L7
Karpathou, Steno sea chan. Greece 59 L6
Karpaty mts Europe see Carpathian Mountains
Karpenisi Greece 59 I5
Karpilovka Belarus see Aktsyabrski
Karpinsk Rus. Fed. 41 S4
Karpogory Rus. Fed. 42 J2
Karpuz r. Turkey 85 A1
Karratha Australia 108 B5
Karroo plat. S. Africa see Great Karoo
Karrychirla Turkm. see Garryçyrla
Kars Turkey 91 F2
Kärsämäki Fin. 44 N5
Kārsava Latvia 45 O8
Karshi Qashqadaryo Uzbek. see Qarshi
Karskiye Vorota, Proliv strait Rus. Fed. 64 G3
Karskoye More sea Rus. Fed. see Kara Sea
Karstädt Germany 53 L1
Karstula Fin. 44 N5
Karsu Turkey 85 C1
Karsun Rus. Fed. 43 J5
Kartal Turkey 59 M4
Kartaly Rus. Fed. 64 H4
Kartayel' Rus. Fed. 42 L2
Karttula Fin. 44 O5
Karumba Australia 110 C3
Karumbhar Island India 82 B5
Karun, Kūh-e hill Iran 88 C4
Kārūn, Rūd-e r. Iran 88 C4
Karuni Indon. 108 B2
Karur India 84 C4
Karvia Fin. 44 M5
Karviná Czech Rep. 47 Q6
Karwar India 84 B3
Karyagino Azer. see Füzuli
Karymskoye Rus. Fed. 73 K2
Karynzharyk, Peski des. Kazakh. 91 I2
Karystos Greece 59 K5
Kaş Turkey 59 M6
Kasa India 84 B2
Kasaba Turkey see Turgutlu
Kasabonika Canada 122 C3
Kasabonika Lake Canada 122 C3
Kasaï r. Dem. Rep. Congo 98 B4
also known as Kwa
Kasaï, Plateau du Dem. Rep. Congo 99 C4
Kasaji Dem. Rep. Congo 99 C5
Kasama Zambia 99 D5
Kasan Uzbek. see Koson
Kasane Botswana 99 C5
Kasaragod India 84 B3
Kasargod India see Kasaragod
Kasargode India see Kasaragod
Kasatkino Rus. Fed. 74 C2
Kasba Lake Canada 121 K2
Kasba Tadla Morocco 54 C5
Kasenga Dem. Rep. Congo 99 C5
Kasengu Dem. Rep. Congo 99 C4
Kasese Dem. Rep. Congo 98 C4
Kasese Uganda 98 D3
Kasevo Rus. Fed. see Neftekamsk
Kasganj India 82 D4
Kasha China 76 C2
Kashabowie Canada 122 C4
Kāshān Iran 88 C3
Kashary Rus. Fed. 43 I6
Kashechewan Canada 122 E3
Kashgar China see Kashi
Kashi China 80 E4
Kashihara Japan 75 D6
Kashima-nada b. Japan 75 F5
Kashin Rus. Fed. 42 H4
Kashipur India 82 D3
Kashira Rus. Fed. 43 H5
Kashiwazaki Japan 75 E5
Kashkarantsy Rus. Fed. 42 H2
Kashku'iyeh Iran 88 D4
Kāshmar Iran 88 E3
Kashmir terr. Asia see Jammu and Kashmir
Kashmir, Vale of reg. India 82 C2
Kashyukulu Dem. Rep. Congo 99 C4
Kasi India see Varanasi
Kasigar Afgh. 89 H3
Kasimov Rus. Fed. 43 I5
Kaskattama r. Canada 121 N3
Kaskinen Fin. 44 L5
Kas Klong i. Cambodia see Kŏng, Kaôh
Kaskö Fin. see Kaskinen
Kaslo Canada 120 G5
Kasmere Lake Canada 121 K3
Kasongo Dem. Rep. Congo 99 C4
Kasongo-Lunda Dem. Rep. Congo 99 B4
Kasos i. Greece 59 L7
Kaspiy Mangy Oypaty lowland Kazakh./Rus. Fed. see Caspian Lowland
Kaspiysk Rus. Fed. 91 G2
Kaspiyskiy Rus. Fed. see Lagan'
Kaspiyskoye More l. Asia/Europe see Caspian Sea
Kassa Slovakia see Košice
Kassala Sudan 86 E6
Kassandras, Akra pt Greece see Kassandras, Akrotirio
Kassandras, Akrotirio pt Greece 59 J5
Kassandras, Kolpos b. Greece 59 J4
Kassel Germany 53 J3
Kasserine Tunisia 58 C7
Kastag Pak. 89 F5
Kastamonu Turkey 90 D2
Kastellaun Germany 53 H4
Kastelli Kriti Greece see Kissamos
Kastéllion Greece see Kissamos
Kastéllion Kriti Greece see Kissamos
Kastellorizon i. Greece see Megisti
Kasterlee Belgium 52 E3
Kastoria Greece 59 I4
Kastornoye Rus. Fed. 43 H6
Kastsyukovichy Belarus 43 G5
Kasulu Tanz. 99 D4
Kasumkent Rus. Fed. 91 H2
Kasungu Malawi 99 D5
Kasungu National Park Malawi 99 D5
Kasur Pak. 89 I4
Katādtlit Nunāt terr. N. America see Greenland
Katahdin, Mount U.S.A. 132 G2
Kataklik India 82 D2
Katako-Kombe Dem. Rep. Congo 98 C4
Katakwi Uganda 98 D3
Katana India 82 C5
Katangi India 82 D5
Katanning Australia 109 B8
Katavi National Park Tanz. 99 D4
Katawaz reg. Afgh. 89 G3
Katchall i. India 71 A6
Katea Dem. Rep. Congo 99 C4
Katerini Greece 59 J4
Katesh Tanz. 99 D4
Kate's Needle mt. Canada/U.S.A. 120 C3
Katete Zambia 99 D5
Katherîna, Gebel mt. Egypt see Kātrīnā, Jabal
Katherine Australia 108 F3
Katherine Gorge National Park Australia see Nitmiluk National Park
Kathi India 89 I6
Kathiawar pen. India 82 B5
Kathihar India see Katihar
Kathiraveli Sri Lanka 84 D4
Kathiwara India 82 C5
Kathleen Falls Australia 108 E3

▶Kathmandu Nepal 83 F4
Capital of Nepal.

Kathu S. Africa 100 F4
Kathua India 82 C2
Kati Mali 96 C3
Katihar India 83 F4
Katikati S. Africa 101 H7
Katima Mulilo Namibia 99 C5
Katimik Lake Canada 121 L4
Katiola Côte d'Ivoire 96 C4
Kā Tiritiri o te Moana mts N.Z. see Southern Alps
Katkop Hills S. Africa 100 E6
Katlehong S. Africa 101 I4
Katmai National Park and Preserve U.S.A. 118 C4
Katmandu Nepal see Kathmandu
Kato Achaïa Greece 59 I5
Kat O Chau H.K. China see Crooked Island
Kat O Hoi b. H.K. China see Crooked Harbour
Katoomba Australia 112 E4
Katowice Poland 47 Q5
Katoya India 83 G5
Katrancık Dağı mts Turkey 59 M6
Kātrīnā, Jabal mt. Egypt 90 D5
Katrine, Loch l. U.K. 50 E4
Katrineholm Sweden 45 J7
Katse Dam Lesotho 101 I5
Katsina Nigeria 96 D3
Katsina-Ala Nigeria 96 D4
Katsuura Japan 75 F6
Kattaktoc, Cap c. Canada 123 I2
Kattamudda Well Australia 108 D5
Kattaqo'rg'on Uzbek. 89 G2
Kattaqŭrghon Uzbek. see Kattaqo'rg'on
Kattasang Hills Afgh. 89 G3
Kattegat strait Denmark/Sweden 45 G8
Kattowitz Poland see Katowice
Katumbar India 82 D4
Katunino Rus. Fed. 42 J4
Katuri Pak. 89 H4
Katwa India see Katoya
Katwijk aan Zee Neth. 52 E2
Katzenbuckel hill Germany 53 J5
Kaua'i i. U.S.A. 127 [inset]
Kaua'i Channel U.S.A. 127 [inset]
Kaub Germany 53 H4
Kaufungen Germany 53 J3
Kauhajoki Fin. 44 M5
Kauhava Fin. 44 M5
Kaukauna U.S.A. 134 A1
Kaukkwè Hills Myanmar 70 B1
Kaukonen Fin. 44 N3
Ka'ula i. U.S.A. 127 [inset]
Kaulakahi Channel U.S.A. 127 [inset]
Kaumajet Mountains Canada 123 J2
Kaunakakai U.S.A. 127 [inset]
Kaunas Lith. 45 M9
Kaunata Latvia 45 O8
Kaundy, Vpadina depr. Kazakh. 91 I2
Kaunia Bangl. 83 G4
Kaura-Namoda Nigeria 96 D3
Kau Sai Chau i. H.K. China 77 [inset]
Kaustinen Fin. 44 M5
Kautokeino Norway 44 M2
Kau-ye Kyun i. Myanmar 71 B5
Kavadarci Macedonia 59 J4
Kavak Turkey 90 E2
Kavaklıdere Turkey 59 M6
Kavala Greece 59 K4
Kavalas, Kolpos b. Greece 59 K4
Kavalerovo Rus. Fed. 74 D3
Kavali India 84 D3
Kavār Iran 88 D4
Kavaratti India 84 B4
Kavaratti atoll India 84 B4
Kavarna Bulg. 59 M3
Kavendou, Mont mt. Guinea 96 B3
Kaveri r. India 84 C4
Kavīr Iran 88 C3
Kavīr, Dasht-e des. Iran 88 D3
Kavīr Kūshk well Iran 88 E3
Kavkasioni mts Asia/Europe see Caucasus
Kawa Myanmar 70 B3
Kawagama Lake Canada 135 F1
Kawagoe Japan 75 E6
Kawaguchi Japan 75 E6
Kawaihae U.S.A. 127 [inset]
Kawaikini U.S.A. 127 [inset]
Kawakawa N.Z. 113 E2
Kawambwa Zambia 99 C4
Kawana Zambia 99 C5
Kawardha India 82 E5
Kawartha Lakes Canada 135 F1
Kawasaki Japan 75 E6
Kawau Island N.Z. 113 E3
Kawawachikamach Canada 123 I3
Kawdut Myanmar 70 B4
Kawerau N.Z. 113 F4
Kawhia N.Z. 113 E4
Kawhia Harbour N.Z. 113 E4
Kawich Peak U.S.A. 128 E3
Kawich Range mts U.S.A. 128 E3
Kawinaw Lake Canada 121 L4
Kaw Lake U.S.A. 131 D4
Kawlin Myanmar 70 A2
Kawm Umbū Egypt 86 D5
Kawngmeum Myanmar 70 B2
Kawthaung Myanmar 71 B5
Kaxgar China see Kashi
Kaxgar He r. China 80 E4
Kax He r. China 80 F3
Kaxtax Shan mts China 83 E1
Kaya Burkina 96 C3

Kayadibi Turkey 90 E3
Kayan r. Indon. 68 F6
Kayankulam India 84 C4
Kayar India 84 C2
Kaycee U.S.A. 126 G4
Kaydak, Sor dry lake Kazakh. 91 I1
Kaydanovo Belarus see Dzyarzhynsk
Kayembe-Mukulu Dem. Rep. Congo 99 C4
Kayenta U.S.A. 129 H3
Kayes Mali 96 B3
Kaymaz Turkey 59 N5
Kaynar Kazakh. 80 E2
Kaynar Turkey 90 E3
Kayseri Turkey 90 D3
Kayuyu Dem. Rep. Congo 98 C4
Kayyngdy Kyrg. 80 D3
Kazach'ye Rus. Fed. 65 O2
Kazakh Azer. see Qazax
Kazakhskaya S.S.R. country Asia see Kazakhstan
Kazakhskiy Melkosopochnik plain Kazakh. 80 D1
Kazakhskiy Zaliv b. Kazakh. 91 I2

▶Kazakhstan country Asia 78 F2
4th largest country in Asia, and 9th in the world.

Kazakhstan Kazakh. see Aksay
Kazakstan country Asia see Kazakhstan
Kazan r. Canada 121 M2
Kazan' Rus. Fed. 42 K5
Kazandzhik Turkm. see Bereket
Kazanka r. Rus. Fed. 42 K5
Kazanlı Turkey 85 B1
Kazanlŭk Bulg. 59 K3
Kazan-rettō is Japan see Volcano Islands
Kazatin Ukr. see Kozyatyn

▶Kazbek mt. Georgia/Rus. Fed. 43 J8
4th highest mountain in Europe.

Kaz Dağı mts Turkey 59 L5
Kāzerūn Iran 88 C4
Kazhim Rus. Fed. 42 K3
Kazidi Tajik. see Qozideh
Kazi Magomed Azer. see Qazımämmäd
Kazincbarcika Hungary 43 D6
Kaziranga National Park India 83 H4
Kazret'i Georgia 91 G2
Kaztalovka Kazakh. 41 P6
Kazy Turkm. 88 E2
Kazym r. Rus. Fed. 41 T3
Kazymskiy Mys Rus. Fed. 41 T3
Kea i. Notio Aigaio Greece see Tzia
Kea i. Notio Aigaio Greece see Tzia
Keady U.K. 51 F3
Keams Canyon U.S.A. 129 H4
Kéamu i. Vanuatu see Anatom
Kearney U.S.A. 130 D3
Kearny U.S.A. 129 H5
Keban Turkey 90 E3
Keban Barajı resr Turkey 90 E3
Kébémèr Senegal 96 B3
Kebili Tunisia 54 F5
Kebīr, Nahr al r. Lebanon/Syria 85 B2
Kebkabiya Sudan 97 F3
Kebnekaise mt. Sweden 44 K3
Kebock Head hd U.K. 50 C2
K'ebrī Dehar Eth. 98 E3
Kech reg. Pak. 89 F5
Kechika r. Canada 120 E3
Keçiborlu Turkey 59 N6
Kecskemét Hungary 59 H1
K'eda Georgia 91 F2
Kėdainiai Lith. 45 M9
Kedairu Passage Fiji see Kadavu Passage
Kedgwick Canada 123 I5
Kedian China 77 G2
Kedong China 74 B3
Kedva r. Rus. Fed. 42 L2
Kędzierzyn-Koźle Poland 47 Q5
Keele r. Canada 120 E1
Keele Peak Canada 120 D2
Keeler U.S.A. 128 E3
Keeley Lake Canada 121 I4
Keeling Islands terr. Indian Ocean see Cocos Islands
Keen, Mount hill U.K. 50 G4
Keene CA U.S.A. 128 D4
Keene KY U.S.A. 134 C5
Keene NH U.S.A. 135 I2
Keene OH U.S.A. 134 E3
Keeper Hill hill Ireland 51 D5
Keepit, Lake resr Australia 112 E3
Keep River National Park Australia 108 E3
Keerbergen Belgium 52 E3
Keer-weer, Cape Australia 110 C2
Keetmanshoop Namibia 100 D4
Keewatin Canada 121 M5
Kefallinía i. Greece see Cephalonia
Kefallonia i. Greece see Cephalonia
Kefamenanu Indon. 108 D2
Kefe Ukr. see Feodosiya
Keffi Nigeria 96 D4
Keflavík Iceland 44 [inset]
Kê Ga, Mui pt Vietnam 71 E5
Kegalla Sri Lanka 84 D5
Kegen Kazakh. 80 E3
Keglo, Baie de b. Canada 123 I2
Keg River Canada 120 G3
Kegul'ta Rus. Fed. 43 J7
Kehra Estonia 45 N7
Kehsi Mansam Myanmar 70 B2
Keighley U.K. 48 F5
Keila Estonia 45 N7
Keimoes S. Africa 100 E5
Keitele Fin. 44 O5
Keitele l. Fin. 44 O5
Keith Australia 111 C8
Keith U.K. 50 G3
Keith Arm b. Canada 120 F1
Kejimkujik National Park Canada 123 I5
Kekaha U.S.A. 127 [inset]
Kékes mt. Hungary 47 R7
Kekri India 82 C4
K'elafo Eth. 98 E3
Kelai i. Maldives 84 B5
Kelberg Germany 52 G4
Kelheim Germany 53 L6
Kelibia Tunisia 58 D6
Kelif Uzboýy marsh Turkm. 89 F2
Kelīrī Iran 88 E5
Kelkheim (Taunus) Germany 53 I4
Kelkit Turkey 91 E2
Kelkit r. Turkey 90 E2
Kéllé Congo 98 B4
Keller Lake Canada 120 F2
Kellett, Cape Canada 118 F2
Kelleys Island U.S.A. 134 D3
Kelliher Canada 121 K5
Kelloselkä Fin. 44 P3
Kells Ireland 51 F4
Kells r. U.K. 51 F3
Kelly U.S.A. 134 B5
Kelly Lake Canada 120 E1
Kelly Range hills Australia 109 C6
Kelmė Lith. 45 M9
Kelmis Belgium 52 G4
Kélo Chad 97 E4
Kelowna Canada 120 G5
Kelp Head hd Canada 120 E5
Kelseyville U.S.A. 128 B2
Kelso U.K. 50 G5
Kelso CA U.S.A. 129 F4
Kelso WA U.S.A. 126 C3
Keluang Malaysia 71 C7
Kelvington Canada 121 K4
Kem' Rus. Fed. 42 G2
Kem' r. Rus. Fed. 42 G2
Ke Macina Mali see Massina
Kemah Turkey 90 E3
Kemaliye Turkey 90 E3
Kemalpaşa Turkey 59 L5
Kemano (abandoned) Canada 120 E4
Kembé Cent. Afr. Rep. 98 C3
Kemeneshát hills Hungary 58 G1
Kemer Antalya Turkey 59 N6
Kemer Muğla Turkey 59 M6
Kemer Barajı resr Turkey 59 M6
Kemerovo Rus. Fed. 64 J4
Kemi Fin. 44 N4
Kemijärvi Fin. 44 O3
Kemijärvi l. Fin. 44 O3
Kemijoki r. Fin. 44 N4
Kemiö Fin. see Kimito
Kemir Turkm. see Keymir
Kemmerer U.S.A. 126 F4
Kemnath Germany 53 L5
Kemnay U.K. 50 G3
Kemp Coast reg. Antarctica see Kemp Land
Kempele Fin. 44 N4
Kempen Germany 52 G3
Kempisch Kanaal canal Belgium 52 F3
Kemp Land reg. Antarctica 152 D2
Kemp Peninsula Antarctica 152 A2
Kemp's Bay Bahamas 133 E7
Kempsey Australia 112 F3
Kempt, Lac l. Canada 122 G5
Kempten (Allgäu) Germany 47 M7
Kempton U.S.A. 134 B3
Kempton Park S. Africa 101 I4
Kemptville Canada 135 H1
Kemujan i. Indon. 68 E8
Ken r. India 82 E4
Kenai U.S.A. 118 C3
Kenai Fiords National Park U.S.A. 118 C4
Kenai Mountains U.S.A. 118 C4
Kenamu r. Canada 123 K3
Kenansville U.S.A. 133 E5
Kenâyis, Râs el pt Egypt see Ḥikmah, Ra's al
Kenbridge U.S.A. 135 F5
Kendal U.K. 48 E4
Kendall Australia 112 F3
Kendall, Cape Canada 119 J3
Kendallville U.S.A. 134 C3
Kendari Indon. 69 G7
Kendawangan Indon. 68 E7
Kendégué Chad 97 E3
Kendrapara India 83 F5
Kendraparha India see Kendrapara
Kendrick Peak U.S.A. 129 H4
Kendujhar India see Keonjhar
Kendujhargarh India see Keonjhar
Kendyrli-Kayasanskoye, Plato plat. Kazakh. 91 I2
Kendyrlisor, Solonchak salt l. Kazakh. 91 I2
Kenebri Australia 112 D3
Kenedy U.S.A. 131 D6
Kenema Sierra Leone 96 B4
Kenge Dem. Rep. Congo 99 B4
Keng Lap Myanmar 70 C2
Kengtung Myanmar 70 B2
Kenhardt S. Africa 100 E5
Kéniéba Mali 96 B3
Kénitra Morocco 54 C5
Kenmare Ireland 51 C6
Kenmare U.S.A. 130 C1
Kenmare River inlet Ireland 51 B6
Kenmore U.S.A. 135 F2
Kenn Germany 52 G5
Kenna U.S.A. 131 C5
Kennebec U.S.A. 130 D3
Kennebec r. U.S.A. 132 G2
Kennebunkport U.S.A. 135 J2
Kennedy, Cape U.S.A. see Canaveral, Cape
Kennedy Range National Park Australia 109 A6
Kennedy Town H.K. China 77 [inset]
Kenner U.S.A. 131 F6
Kennet r. U.K. 49 G7
Kenneth Range hills Australia 109 B5
Kennett U.S.A. 131 F4
Kennewick U.S.A. 126 D3
Kenn Reef Australia 110 F4
Kenogami r. Canada 122 D4
Keno Hill Canada 120 C2
Kenora Canada 121 M5
Kenosha U.S.A. 134 B2
Kenozero, Ozero l. Rus. Fed. 42 H3
Kent r. U.K. 48 E4
Kent OH U.S.A. 134 E3
Kent TX U.S.A. 131 B6
Kent VA U.S.A. 134 E5
Kent WA U.S.A. 126 C3
Kentani S. Africa 101 I7
Kent Group is Australia 111 [inset]
Kentland U.S.A. 134 B3
Kenton U.S.A. 134 D3
Kent Peninsula Canada 118 H3
Kentucky state U.S.A. 134 C5
Kentucky Lake U.S.A. 131 F4
Kenya country Africa 98 D3

▶Kenya, Mount Kenya 98 D4
2nd highest mountain in Africa.

Kenyir, Tasik resr Malaysia 71 C6
Keokuk U.S.A. 130 F3
Keoladeo National Park India 82 D4
Keonjhar India 83 F5
Keonjhargarh India see Keonjhar
Keosauqua U.S.A. 130 F3
Keowee, Lake resr U.S.A. 133 D5
Kepina r. Rus. Fed. 42 I2
Keppel Bay Australia 110 E4
Kepsut Turkey 59 M5
Kera India 83 F5
Kerāh Iran 88 E4
Kerala state India 84 B4
Kerang Australia 112 A5
Kerava Fin. 45 N6
Kerba Alg. 57 G5
Kerbela Iraq see Karbalā'
Kerben Kyrg. 80 D3
Kerbi r. Rus. Fed. 74 E1
Kerbodot, Lac l. Canada 123 I3
Kerch Ukr. 90 E1
Kerchem'ya Rus. Fed. 42 L3
Kerema P.N.G. 69 L8
Keremeos Canada 120 G5
Kerempe Burun pt Turkey 90 D2
Keren Eritrea 86 E6
Kerewan Gambia 96 B3
Kergeli Turkm. 88 E2
Kerguélen, Îles is Indian Ocean 149 M9
Kerguelen Islands Indian Ocean see Kerguélen, Îles
Kerguelen Plateau sea feature Indian Ocean 149 M9
Kericho Kenya 98 D4
Kerikeri N.Z. 113 D2
Kerimäki Fin. 44 P6
Kerinci, Gunung vol. Indon. 68 C7
Kerinci Seblat, Taman Nasional Indon. 68 C7
Kerintji vol. Indon. see Kerinci, Gunung
Keriya He watercourse China 72 E5
Keriya Shankou pass China 83 E2
Kerken Germany 52 G3
Kerkennah, Îles is Tunisia 58 D7
Kerkiçi Turkm. 89 G2
Kerkini, Limni l. Greece 59 J4
Kerkinitis, Limni l. Greece see Kerkini, Limni
Kérkira i. Greece see Corfu
Kerkouane tourist site Tunisia 58 D6
Kerkyra Greece 59 H5
Kerkyra i. Greece see Corfu
Kerma Sudan 86 D6
Kermadec Islands S. Pacific Ocean 107 I5

▶Kermadec Trench sea feature S. Pacific Ocean 150 I8
4th deepest trench in the world.

Kermān Iran 88 E4
Kerman U.S.A. 128 C3
Kermān, Bīābān-e Iran 88 E4
Kermānshāh Iran 88 B3
Kermānshāhān Iran 88 D4
Kermine Uzbek. see Navoiy
Kermit U.S.A. 131 C6
Kern r. U.S.A. 128 D4
Kernertut, Cap c. Canada 123 I2
Keros i. Greece 59 K6
Keros Rus. Fed. 42 L3
Kérouané Guinea 96 C4
Kerpen Germany 52 G4
Kerr, Cape Antarctica 152 H1
Kerrobert Canada 121 I5
Kerrville U.S.A. 131 D6
Kerry Head hd Ireland 51 C5
Kerteminde Denmark 45 G9
Kerulen r. China/Mongolia see Herlen Gol
Kerur India 84 B2
Keryneia Cyprus see Kyrenia
Kerzaz Alg. 96 C2
Kerzhenets r. Rus. Fed. 42 J4
Kesagami Lake Canada 122 E4
Kesälahti Fin. 44 P6
Keşan Turkey 59 L4
Keşap Turkey 43 H8
Kesariya India 83 F4
Kesennuma Japan 75 F5
Keshan China 74 B2
Keshem Afgh. 89 H2
Keshena U.S.A. 134 A1
Keshendeh-ye Bala Afgh. 89 G2
Keshod India 82 B5
Keshvar Iran 88 C3
Keskin Turkey 90 D3
Keskozero Rus. Fed. 42 G3
Kesova Gora Rus. Fed. 42 H4
Kessel Neth. 52 G3
Kestell S. Africa 101 I5
Kesten'ga Rus. Fed. 44 Q4
Kestilä Fin. 44 O4
Keswick Canada 134 F1
Keswick U.K. 48 D4
Keszthely Hungary 58 G1
Ketapang Indon. 68 E7
Ketchikan U.S.A. 120 D4
Keti Bandar Pak. 89 G5
Ketmen', Khrebet mts China/Kazakh. 80 F3
Kettering U.K. 49 G6
Kettering U.S.A. 134 C4
Kettle r. Canada 120 G5
Kettle Creek r. U.S.A. 135 G3
Kettle Falls U.S.A. 126 D2
Kettleman City U.S.A. 128 D3
Kettle River Range mts U.S.A. 126 D2
Keuka U.S.A. 135 G2
Keuka Lake U.S.A. 135 G2
Keumgang, Mount N. Korea see Kumgang-san
Keumsang, Mount N. Korea see Kumgang-san
Keuruu Fin. 44 N5
Kew Turks and Caicos Is 133 F8
Kewanee U.S.A. 130 F3
Kewaunee U.S.A. 134 B1
Keweenaw Bay U.S.A. 130 F2
Keweenaw Peninsula U.S.A. 130 F2
Keweenaw Point U.S.A. 132 C2
Key, Lough l. Ireland 51 D3
Keyala Sudan 97 G4
Keyano Canada 123 G3
Keya Paha r. U.S.A. 130 D3
Key Harbour Canada 122 E5
Keyihe China 74 A2
Key Largo U.S.A. 133 D7
Keymir Turkm. 88 D2
Keynsham U.K. 49 E7
Keyser U.S.A. 135 F4
Keystone Lake U.S.A. 131 D4
Keystone Peak U.S.A. 129 H6
Keysville U.S.A. 135 F5
Keytesville U.S.A. 130 E4
Keyvy, Vozvyshennost' hills Rus. Fed. 42 H2
Key West U.S.A. 133 D7
Kez Rus. Fed. 41 Q4
Kezi Zimbabwe 99 C6
Kgalagadi admin. dist. Botswana 100 E3
Kgalagadi Transfrontier National Park 101 D2
Kgalazadi admin. dist. Botswana see Kgalagadi
Kgatlen admin. dist. Botswana see Kgatleng
Kgatleng admin. dist. Botswana 101 H3
Kgomofatshe Pan salt pan Botswana 100 E2
Kgoro Pan salt pan Botswana 100 G3
Kgotsong S. Africa 101 H4
Khabab Syria 85 C3
Khabar Iran 88 D4
Khabarikha Rus. Fed. 42 L2
Khabarovsk Rus. Fed. 74 D2
Khabarovskiy Kray admin. div. Rus. Fed. 74 D2
Khabarovsk Kray admin. div. Rus. Fed. see Khabarovskiy Kray
Khabary Rus. Fed. 72 D2
Khabis Iran see Shahdād
Khabody Pass Afgh. 89 F3
Khachmas Azer. see Xaçmaz
Khadar, Jabal mt. Oman 88 E6
Khadro Pak. 89 H5
Khadzhiolen Turkm. 88 E2
Khafs Banbān well Saudi Arabia 88 B5
Khagaria India 83 F4
Khagrachari Bangl. 83 G5
Khagrachhari Bangl. see Khagrachari
Khairgarh Pak. 89 H4
Khairpur Punjab Pak. 89 I4
Khairpur Sindh Pak. 89 H5
Khāīz, Kūh-e mt. Iran 88 C4
Khaja Du Koh hill Afgh. 89 G2
Khajuha India 82 E4
Khāk-e Jabbar Afgh. 89 H3
Khakhea Botswana 100 F3
Khak-rēz Afgh. 89 G4
Khakriz reg. Afgh. 89 G4
Khalajestan reg. Iran 88 C3
Khalatse India 82 D2
Khalifat mt. Pak. 89 G4
Khalīj Surt g. Libya see Sirte, Gulf of
Khalilabad India 83 E4
Khalīlī Iran 88 D5
Khalkabad Turkm. 89 F1
Khalkhāl Iran 88 C2
Khálki i. Greece see Chalki
Khalkís Greece see Chalkida
Khallikot India 84 E2
Khalturin Rus. Fed. see Orlov
Khamar-Daban, Khrebet mts Rus. Fed. 72 I2
Khamaria India 84 D1
Khambhat India 82 C5
Khambhat, Gulf of India 84 A2
Khamgaon India 84 C1
Khamir Yemen 86 F6
Khamis Mushayṭ Saudi Arabia 86 F6
Khamkkeut Laos 70 D3
Khamma well Saudi Arabia 88 B5
Khammam India 84 D2
Khammouan Laos see Thakèk
Khamra Rus. Fed. 65 M3
Khamseh reg. Iran 88 C3
Khan Afgh. 89 H3
Khan, Nam r. Laos 70 C3
Khānābād Afgh. 89 H2
Khān al Baghdādī Iraq 91 F4
Khān al Mashāhidah Iraq 91 G4
Khān al Muşallá Iraq 91 G4
Khanapur India 84 B2
Khān ar Raḥbah Iraq 91 G5
Khanasur Pass Iran/Turkey 91 G3
Khanbalik China see Beijing
Khānch Iran 88 B2
Khandu India 89 I6
Khandwa India 82 D5
Khandyga Rus. Fed. 65 O3
Khanewal Pak. 89 H4
Khan Hung Vietnam see Soc Trăng
Khaniá Greece see Chania
Khānī Yek Iran 88 D4
Khanka, Lake China/Rus. Fed. 74 D3
Khanka, Ozero l. China/Rus. Fed. see Khanka, Lake
Khankendi Azer. see Xankändi
Khanna India 82 D3
Khannā, Qā' salt pan Jordan 85 C3
Khanpur Pak. 89 H4
Khanpur Pak. 89 H4
Khān Ruḥābah Iraq see Khān ar Raḥbah
Khansar Pak. 89 H4
Khān Shaykhūn Syria 85 C2
Khantayskoye, Ozero l. Rus. Fed. 64 K3
Khanthabouli Laos see Savannakhét
Khanty-Mansiysk Rus. Fed. 64 H3
Khān Yūnis Gaza 85 B4
Khanzi admin. dist. Botswana see Ghanzi
Khao Ang Rua Nai Wildlife Reserve nature res. Thai. 71 C4
Khao Banthat Wildlife Reserve nature res. Thai. 71 B6
Khao Chum Thong Thai. 71 B5
Khaoen Si Nakarin National Park Thai. 71 B4
Khao Laem, Ang Kep Nam Thai. 70 B4
Khao Laem National Park Thai. 70 B4
Khao Luang National Park Thai. 71 B5
Khao Pu-Khao Ya National Park Thai. 71 B6
Khao Soi Dao Wildlife Reserve nature res. Thai. 71 C4
Khao Sok National Park Thai. 71 B5
Khao Yai National Park Thai. 71 C4
Khaplu Pak. 80 E4
Khaptad National Park Nepal 82 E3
Kharabali Rus. Fed. 43 J7
Kharagpur Bihar India 83 F4
Kharagpur W. Bengal India 83 F5
Khārān r. Iran 87 I4
Kharari India see Abu Road
Kharda India 84 B2
Khardi India 82 C6
Khardong La pass India see Khardung La
Khardung La pass India 82 D2
Kharez Ilias Afgh. 89 F3
Kharfiyah Iraq 91 G5
Kharga Egypt see Al Khārijah
Kharga r. Rus. Fed. 74 D1
Khârga, El Wâḥât el oasis Egypt see Khārijah, Wāḥāt al
Kharga Oasis Egypt see Khārijah, Wāḥāt al
Kharg Islands Iran 88 C4
Khargon India 82 C5
Khari r. Rajasthan India 82 C4
Khari r. Rajasthan India 82 C4
Kharian Pak. 89 I3
Khariar India 84 D1
Khārijah, Wāḥāt al oasis Egypt 86 D5
Kharîm, Gebel hill Egypt see Kharīm, Jabal
Kharīm, Jabal hill Egypt 85 A4
Kharkhara r. India 82 E5
Kharkiv Ukr. 43 H6
Khar'kov Ukr. see Kharkiv
Khār Kūh mt. Iran 88 D4
Kharlovka Rus. Fed. 42 H1
Kharlu Rus. Fed. 44 Q6
Kharmanli Bulg. 59 K4
Kharoti reg. Afgh. 89 H3
Kharovsk Rus. Fed. 42 I4
Kharsia India 83 E5

▶Khartoum Sudan 86 D6
Capital of Sudan. 4th most populous city in Africa.

Kharwar reg. Afgh. 89 H3
Khasavyurt Rus. Fed. 91 G2
Khash Afgh. 89 F4
Khāsh Iran 89 F4
Khāsh, Dasht-e Afgh. 89 F4
Khashgort Rus. Fed. 41 T2
Khashm el Girba Sudan 86 E7
Khashm Şana' Saudi Arabia 90 E6
Khash Rūd r. Afgh. 89 F4
Khashuri Georgia 91 F2
Khasi Hills India 83 G4
Khaskovo Bulg. 59 K4
Khatanga Rus. Fed. 65 L2
Khatanga, Gulf of Rus. Fed. see Khatangskiy Zaliv
Khatangskiy Zaliv b. Rus. Fed. 65 L2
Khatayakha Rus. Fed. 42 M2
Khatinza Pass Pak. 89 H2
Khatmat al Malāha Oman 88 E5
Khatyrka Rus. Fed. 65 S3
Khāvāk, Khowtal-e Afgh. 89 H3
Khavda India 82 B5
Khayamnandi S. Africa 101 G6
Khaybar Saudi Arabia 86 E4
Khayelitsha S. Africa 100 D8
Khayrān, Ra's al pt Oman 88 E6
Khedrī Iran 88 E3
Khefa Israel see Haifa
Khehuene, Ponta pt Moz. 101 L2
Khemis Miliana Alg. 57 H5
Khemmarat Thai. 70 D3
Khenchela Alg. 58 B7
Khenifra Morocco 54 C5
Kherāmeh Iran 88 D4
Kherrata Alg. 57 I5
Kherreh Iran 88 D5
Khersan r. Iran 88 C4
Kherson Ukr. 59 O1
Kheta r. Rus. Fed. 65 L2
Kheyrābād Iran 88 D4
Khezerābād Iran 88 D2
Khiching India 83 F5
Khilok Rus. Fed. 73 K2
Khilok r. Rus. Fed. 73 J2
Khinganskiy Zapovednik nature res. Rus. Fed. 74 C2
Khinsar Pak. 89 H5
Khíos i. Greece see Chios
Khipro Pak. 89 H5
Khirbat Isrīyah Syria 85 C2
Khitai Dawan Aksai Chin 82 D2
Khiyāv Iran 88 B2
Khiytola Rus. Fed. 45 P6
Khlevnoye Rus. Fed. 43 H5
Khlong, Mae r. Thai. 71 C4
Khlong Saeng Wildlife Reserve nature res. Thai. 71 B5
Khlong Wang Chao National Park Thai. 70 B3
Khlung Thai. 71 C4
Khmel'nik Ukr. see Khmil'nyk
Khmel'nitskiy Ukr. see Khmel'nyts'kyy
Khmel'nyts'kyy Ukr. 43 E6
Khmer Republic country Asia see Cambodia
Khmil'nyk Ukr. 43 E6
Khoai, Hon i. Vietnam 71 D5
Khobda Kazakh. 80 A1
Khobi Georgia 91 F2
Khodā Āfarīd spring Iran 88 E3
Khodzha-Kala Turkm. see Hojagala
Khodzhambaz Turkm. see Hojambaz
Khodzhent Tajik. see Khŭjand
Khodzheyli Qoraqalpog'iston Respublikasi Uzbek. see Xo'jayli
Khojand Tajik. see Khŭjand
Khokhowe Pan salt pan Botswana 100 E3
Khokhropar Pak. 89 H5
Khoksar India 82 D2
Kholm Afgh. 89 G2
Kholm Poland see Chełm
Kholm Rus. Fed. 42 F4
Kholmsk Rus. Fed. 74 F3
Kholon Israel see Ḥolon
Khomas admin. reg. Namibia 100 C2
Khomas Highland hills Namibia 100 B2
Khomeyn Iran 88 C3
Khomeynīshahr Iran 88 C3
Khong, Mae Nam r. Asia 70 D4 see Mekong
Khonj Iran 88 D5
Khonj, Kūh-e mts Iran 88 D5
Khon Kaen Thai. 70 C3
Khon Kriel Cambodia see Phumĭ Kon Kriel
Khonsa India 83 H4
Khonuu Rus. Fed. 65 P3
Khoper r. Rus. Fed. 43 I6
Khor Rus. Fed. 74 D3
Khor r. Rus. Fed. 74 D3
Khorat Plateau Thai. 70 C3
Khorda India see Khurda
Khordha India see Khurda
Khoreyver Rus. Fed. 42 M2
Khorinsk Rus. Fed. 73 J2
Khorixas Namibia 99 B6
Khormūj, Kūh-e mt. Iran 88 C4
Khorog Tajik. see Khorugh
Khorol Rus. Fed. 74 D3
Khorol Ukr. 43 G6
Khoroslū Dāgh hills Iran 88 B2
Khorramābād Iran 88 C3
Khorramshahr Iran 88 C4
Khorugh Tajik. 89 H2
Khosheutovo Rus. Fed. 43 J7
Khōst reg. Afgh./Pak. 89 H3
Khōst Khōst 89 H3
Khosūyeh Iran 88 D4
Khotan China see Hotan
Khouribga Morocco 54 C5
Khovaling Tajik. 89 H2
Khowrjān Iran 88 D4
Khowrnag, Kūh-e mt. Iran 88 D3
Khreum Myanmar 70 A2
Khroma r. Rus. Fed. 65 P2
Khromtau Kazakh. 80 A1
Khrushchev Ukr. see Svitlovods'k
Khrysokhou Bay Cyprus see Chrysochou Bay
Khrystynivka Ukr. 43 F6
Khuar Pak. 89 I3
Khudumelapye Botswana 100 G2
Khudzhand Tajik. see Khŭjand
Khufaysah, Khashm al hill Saudi Arabia 88 B6
Khugiana Afgh. see Pirzada
Khuis Botswana 100 E4
Khŭjand Tajik. 80 C3
Khŭjayli Qoraqalpog'iston Respublikasi Uzbek. see Xo'jayli
Khŭjayli Uzbek. see Xo'jayli
Khu Khan Thai. 71 D4
Khulays Saudi Arabia 86 E5
Khulkhuta Rus. Fed. 43 J7
Khulm r. Afgh. 89 G2
Khulna Bangl. 83 G5
Khulo Georgia 91 F2
Khuma S. Africa 101 H4
Khŭm Batheay Cambodia 71 D5
Khunayzīr, Jabal al mts Syria 85 C2
Khūnīk Bālā Iran 88 E3
Khūnīnshahr Iran see Khorramshahr
Khunjerab Pass China/Pakistan 82 C1
Khunsar Iran 88 C3
Khun Yuam Thai. 70 B3
Khūr Iran 88 E3
Khūran sea chan. Iran 88 D5
Khurayṣ Saudi Arabia 86 G4
Khurd, Koh-i- mt. Afgh. 89 G3
Khurda India 84 E1
Khurdha India see Khurda
Khurja India 82 D3
Khurmalik Afgh. 89 F3
Khurmuli Rus. Fed. 74 E2
Khūrrāb Iran 88 D4
Khurz Iran 88 D3
Khushab Pak. 89 I3
Khushalgarh Pak. 89 H3
Khushshah, Wādī al watercourse Jordan/Saudi Arabia 85 C5
Khust Ukr. 43 D6
Khutse Game Reserve nature res. Botswana 100 G2
Khutsong S. Africa 101 H4
Khutu r. Rus. Fed. 74 E2
Khuzdar Pak. 89 G5
Khvāf Iran 89 F3
Khvāf reg. Iran 89 F3
Khvājeh Iran 88 B2
Khvalynsk Rus. Fed. 43 K5
Khvodrān Iran 88 D4
Khvord Nārvan Iran 88 E3
Khvormūj Iran 88 C4
Khvoy Iran 88 B2
Khvoynaya Rus. Fed. 42 G4
Khwaja Amran mt. Pak. 89 G4
Khwaja Muhammad Range mts Afgh. 89 H2
Khyber Pass Afgh./Pak. 89 H3
Kiama Australia 112 E5
Kiamichi r. U.S.A. 131 E5
Kiangsi prov. China see Jiangxi
Kiangsu prov. China see Jiangsu
Kiantajärvi l. Fin. 44 P4
Kīāseh Iran 88 D2
Kiatassuaq i. Greenland 119 M2
Kibaha Tanz. 99 D4
Kibali r. Dem. Rep. Congo 98 C3
Kibangou Congo 98 B4
Kibaya Tanz. 99 D4
Kiboga Uganda 98 D3
Kibombo Dem. Rep. Congo 98 C4
Kibondo Tanz. 98 D4
Kibre Mengist Eth. 97 G4
Kibris country Asia see Cyprus
Kibungo Rwanda 98 D4
Kičevo Macedonia 59 I4
Kichmengskiy Gorodok Rus. Fed. 42 J4
Kiçik Qafqaz mts Asia see Lesser Caucasus
Kicking Horse Pass Canada 120 G5
Kidal Mali 96 D3

Kolyma Range mts Rus. Fed. see Kolymskiy, Khrebet
Kolymskaya Nizmennost' lowland Rus. Fed. 65 Q3
Kolymskiy, Khrebet mts Rus. Fed. 65 R3
Kolyshley Rus. Fed. 43 J5
Kom mt. Bulg. 59 J3
Komadugu-gana watercourse Nigeria 96 E3
Komaggas S. Africa 100 C5
Komaio P.N.G. 69 K8
Komaki Japan 75 E6
Komandnaya, Gora mt. Rus. Fed. 74 E2
Komandorskiye Ostrova is Rus. Fed. 65 R4
Komárno Slovakia 47 Q7
Komati r. Swaziland 101 J3
Komatipoort S. Africa 101 J3
Komatsu Japan 75 E5
Komba i. Indon. 108 C1
Komga S. Africa 101 H7
Komintern Ukr. see Marhanets'
Kominternivs'ke Ukr. 59 N1
Komiža Croatia 58 G3
Komló Hungary 58 H1
Kommunarsk Ukr. see Alchevs'k
Komodo, Taman Nasional Indon. 108 B2
Kôm Ombo Egypt see Kawm Umbū
Komono Congo 98 B4
Komoran i. Indon. 69 J8
Komotini Greece 59 K4
Kompong Cham Cambodia see Kâmpóng Cham
Kompong Chhnang Cambodia see Kâmpóng Chhnăng
Kompong Kleang Cambodia see Kâmpóng Khleăng
Kompong Som Cambodia see Sihanoukville
Kompong Speu Cambodia see Kâmpóng Spœ
Kompong Thom Cambodia see Kâmpóng Thum
Komrat Moldova see Comrat
Komsberg mts S. Africa 100 E7
Komsomol Kazakh. see Karabalyk
Komsomolabad Tajik. see Komsomolobod
Komsomolets Kazakh. see Karabalyk
Komsomolets, Ostrov i. Rus. Fed. 64 K1
Komsomolobod Tajik. 89 H2
Komsomol's'k Ukr. 43 G6
Komsomol'skiy Chukotskiy Avtonomnyy Okrug Rus. Fed. 153 C2
Komsomol'skiy Khanty-Mansiyskiy Avtonomnyy Okrug Rus. Fed. see Yugorsk
Komsomol'skiy Respublika Kalmykiya - Khalm'g-Tangch Rus. Fed. 43 J7
Komsomol'sk-na-Amure Rus. Fed. 74 E2
Komsomol'skoye Kazakh. 80 B1
Komsomol'skoye Rus. Fed. 43 J6
Kömürlü Turkey 91 F2
Kon India 83 E4
Konacık Turkey 85 B1
Konada India 84 D2
Konarak India see Konarka
Konarka India 83 F6
Konch India 82 D4
Kondagaon India 84 D2
Kondinin Australia 109 B8
Kondinskoye Rus. Fed. see Oktyabr'skoye
Kondoa Tanz. 99 D4
Kondol' Rus. Fed. 43 J5
Kondopoga Rus. Fed. 42 G3
Kondoz Afgh. see Kunduz
Kondrovo Rus. Fed. 43 G5
Köneürgenç Turkm. 87 I1
Köneürgenç Turkm. see Köneürgenç
Kong Cameroon 96 E4
Kong, Kaôh i. Cambodia 71 C5
Kông, Tônlé r. Cambodia 71 D4
Kong, Xé r. Laos 70 D4
Kong Christian IX Land reg. Greenland 119 O3
Kong Christian X Land reg. Greenland 119 P2
Kongelab atoll Marshall Is see Rongelap
Kong Frederik IX Land reg. Greenland 119 M3
Kong Frederik VI Kyst coastal area Greenland 119 N3
Kongolo Dem. Rep. Congo 99 C4
Kongor Sudan 97 G4
Kong Oscars Fjord inlet Greenland 119 P2
Kongoussi Burkina 96 C3
Kongsberg Norway 45 F7
Kongsvinger Norway 45 H6
Kongur Shan mt. China 80 E4
Königsberg Rus. Fed. see Kaliningrad
Königsee Germany 53 L4
Königswinter Germany 53 H4
Königs Wusterhausen Germany 53 N2
Konimekh Uzbek. see Konimex
Konimex Uzbek. 89 G1
Konin Poland 47 Q4
Konjic Bos.-Herz. 58 G3
Konkiep watercourse Namibia 100 C5
Könnern Germany 53 L3
Konnevesi Fin. 44 O5
Konosha Rus. Fed. 42 I3
Konotop Ukr. 43 G6
Konpara India 83 E5
Kon Plông Vietnam 71 E4
Konqi He r. China 80 G3
Konso Eth. 98 D3
Konstantinograd Ukr. see Krasnohrad
Konstantinovka Rus. Fed. 74 B2
Konstantinovka Ukr. see Kostyantynivka
Konstantinovy Lázně Czech Rep. 53 M5
Konstanz Germany 47 L7
Kontha Myanmar 70 B2
Kontiolahti Fin. 44 P5
Konttila Fin. 44 O4
Kon Tum Vietnam 71 D4
Kon Tum, Cao Nguyên Vietnam 71 E4
Könugard Ukr. see Kiev
Konushin, Mys pt Rus. Fed. 42 I2
Konya Turkey 90 D3
Konz Germany 52 G5
Konzhakovskiy Kamen', Gora mt. Rus. Fed. 41 R4
Koocanusa, Lake resr Canada/U.S.A. 120 H5
Kooch Bihar India see Koch Bihar
Kookynie Australia 109 C7
Koolyanobbing Australia 109 B7
Koondrook Australia 112 B5
Koorawatha Australia 112 D5
Koordarrie Australia 108 A5
Kootenay r. Canada 120 G5
Kootenay Lake Canada 120 G5
Kootenay National Park Canada 120 G5
Kootjieskolk S. Africa 100 E6
Kópasker Iceland 44 [inset]
Kopbirlik Kazakh. 80 E2
Koper Slovenia 58 E2
Kopet Dag mts Iran/Turkm. 88 E2
Kopet-Dag, Khrebet mts Iran/Turkm. see Kopet Dag
Köpetdag Gershi mts Iran/Turkm. see Kopet Dag
Köping Sweden 45 J7
Köpmanholmen Sweden 44 K5
Kopong Botswana 101 G3
Koppal India 84 C3
Koppang Norway 45 G6
Kopparberg Sweden 45 I7
Koppeh Dāgh mts Iran/Turkm. see Kopet Dag
Köppel hill Germany 53 H4
Koppi r. Rus. Fed. 74 F2
Koppies S. Africa 101 H4
Koppieskraal Pan salt pan S. Africa 100 E4
Koprivnica Croatia 58 G1
Köprülü Turkey 85 A1
Köprülü Kanyon Milli Parkı nat. park Turkey 59 N6
Kopyl' Belarus see Kapyl'
Kora India 82 E4
Korablino Rus. Fed. 43 I5
K'orahē Eth. 98 E3
Korak Pak. 89 G5
Koramlik China 83 F1
Korangal India 84 C2
Korangi Pak. 89 G5
Korān va Monjan Afgh. 89 H2
Koraput India 84 D2
Korat Thai. see Nakhon Ratchasima
Koratla India 84 C2
Korba India 83 E5
Korbach Germany 53 I3
Korçë Albania 59 I4
Korčula Croatia 58 G3
Korčula i. Croatia 58 G3
Korčulanski Kanal sea chan. Croatia 58 G3
Korday Kazakh. 80 D3
Kord Küy Iran 88 D2
Kords reg. Iran 89 F5
Korea, North country Asia 75 B5
Korea, South country Asia 75 B5
Korea Bay g. China/N. Korea 75 B5
Korea Strait Japan/S. Korea 75 C6
Koregaon India 84 B2
Korenovsk Rus. Fed. 91 E1
Korenovskaya Rus. Fed. see Korenovsk
Korepino Rus. Fed. 41 R3
Korets' Ukr. 43 E6
Körfez Turkey 59 M4
Korff Ice Rise Antarctica 152 L1
Korfovskiy Rus. Fed. 74 D2
Korgalzhyn Kazakh. 80 D1
Korgen Norway 44 H3
Korhogo Côte d'Ivoire 96 C4
Koribundu Sierra Leone 96 B4
Kori Creek inlet India 82 B5
Korinthiakos Kolpos sea chan. Greece see Corinth, Gulf of
Korinthos Greece see Corinth
Kőris-hegy hill Hungary 58 G1
Koritnik mt. Albania 59 I3
Koritsa Albania see Korçë
Kōriyama Japan 75 F5
Korkuteli Turkey 59 N6
Korla China 80 G3
Kormakitis, Cape Cyprus 85 A2
Körmend Hungary 58 G1
Kornat nat. park Croatia 58 F3
Korneyevka Rus. Fed. 43 K6
Koro Côte d'Ivoire 96 C4
Koro i. Fiji 107 H3
Koro Mali 96 C3
Koroc r. Canada 123 I2
Köroğlu Dağları mts Turkey 59 O4
Köroğlu Tepesi mt. Turkey 90 D2
Korogwe Tanz. 99 D4
Koroneia, Limni l. Greece 59 J4
Korong Vale Australia 112 A6
Koronia, Limni l. Greece see Koroneia, Limni

▶Koror Palau 69 I5
Former capital of Palau.

Koro Sea b. Fiji 107 H3
Korosten' Ukr. 43 F6
Korostyshiv Ukr. 43 F6
Koro Toro Chad 97 E3
Korpilahti Fin. 44 N5
Korpo Fin. 45 L6
Korppoo Fin. see Korpo
Korsakov Rus. Fed. 74 F3
Korsnäs Fin. 44 L5
Korsør Denmark 45 G9
Korsun'-Shevchenkivs'kyy Ukr. 43 F6
Korsun'-Shevchenkovskiy Ukr. see Korsun'-Shevchenkivs'kyy
Korsze Poland 47 R3
Kortesjärvi Fin. 44 M5
Korti Sudan 86 D6
Kortkeros Rus. Fed. 42 K3
Kortrijk Belgium 52 D4
Korvala Fin. 44 O3
Koryakskaya, Sopka vol. Rus. Fed. 65 Q4
Koryakskoye Nagor'ye mts Rus. Fed. 65 S3
Koryazhma Rus. Fed. 42 J3
Koryŏng S. Korea 75 C6
Kos i. Greece 59 L6
Kosa Rus. Fed. 41 Q4
Kosam India 82 E4
Kosan N. Korea 75 B5
Kościan Poland 47 P4
Kosciusko, Mount Australia see Kosciuszko, Mount
Kosciuszko, Mount Australia 112 D6
Kosciuszko National Park Australia 112 D6
Köse Turkey 91 E2
Köseçobanlı Turkey 85 A1
Kosgi India 84 C2
Kosh-Agach Rus. Fed. 80 G2
Koshikijima-rettō is Japan 75 C7
Koshk Afgh. 89 F3
Koshk-e Kohneh Afgh. 89 F3
Koshki Rus. Fed. 43 K5
Kosi Bay S. Africa 101 K4
Košice Slovakia 43 D6
Kosigi India 84 C3
Koskullskulle Sweden 44 L3
Köslin Poland see Koszalin
Kosma r. Rus. Fed. 42 K2
Koson Uzbek. 89 G2
Kosŏng N. Korea 75 C5
Kosova prov. Europe see Kosovo

▶Kosovo country Europe 59 I3
World's newest independent country. Gained independence from Serbia in February 2008.

Kosovo-Metohija prov. Europe see Kosovo
Kosovska Mitrovica Kosovo see Mitrovicë
Kosrae atoll Micronesia 150 G5
Kosrap China 89 J2
Kösseine hill Germany 53 L5
Kosta-Khetagurovo Rus. Fed. see Nazran'
Kostanay Kazakh. 78 F1
Kostenets Bulg. 59 J3
Kosti Sudan 86 D7
Kostinbrod Bulg. 59 J3
Kostino Rus. Fed. 64 J3
Kostomuksha Rus. Fed. 44 Q4
Kostopil' Ukr. 43 E6
Kostopol' Ukr. see Kostopil'
Kostroma Rus. Fed. 42 I4
Kostrzyn Poland 47 O4
Kostyantynivka Ukr. 43 H6
Kostyukovichi Belarus see Kastsyukovichy
Kos'yu Rus. Fed. 41 R2
Koszalin Poland 47 P3
Kőszeg Hungary 58 G1
Kota Andhra Prad. India 84 D3
Kota Chhattisgarh India 83 E5
Kota Rajasthan India 82 C4
Kota Baharu Malaysia see Kota Bharu
Kotabaru Aceh Indon. 71 B7
Kotabaru Kalimantan Selatan Indon. 68 F7
Kota Bharu Malaysia 71 C6
Kotabumi Indon. 68 C7
Kot Addu Pak. 89 H4
Kota Kinabalu Sabah Malaysia 68 F5
Kotamobagu Indon. 69 G6
Kotaneelee Range mts Canada 120 E2
Kotaparh India 84 D2
Kotapinang Indon. 71 C7
Kotatengah Indon. 71 C7
Kota Tinggi Malaysia 71 C7
Kotcho r. Canada 120 F3
Kotcho Lake Canada 120 F3
Kot Diji Pak. 89 H5
Kotel'nich Rus. Fed. 42 K4
Kotel'nikovo Rus. Fed. 43 I7
Kotel'nyy, Ostrov i. Rus. Fed. 65 O2
Kotgar India 84 D2
Kotgarh India 82 D3
Kothagudem India see Kottagudem
Köthen (Anhalt) Germany 53 L3
Kotido Uganda 97 G4
Kotikovo Rus. Fed. 74 D3
Kot Imamgarh Pak. 89 H5
Kotka Fin. 45 O6
Kot Kapura India 82 C3
Kotkino Rus. Fed. 42 K2
Kotlas Rus. Fed. 42 J3
Kotli Pak. 89 I3
Kotlik U.S.A. 118 B3
Kötlutangi pt Iceland 44 [inset]
Kotly Rus. Fed. 45 P7
Kotorkoshi Nigeria 96 D3
Kotovo Rus. Fed. 43 J6
Kotovsk Rus. Fed. 43 I5
Kotra India 82 C4
Kotra Pak. 89 G4
Kotri r. India 84 D2
Kot Sarae Pak. 89 G6
Kottagudem India 84 D2
Kottarakara India 84 C4
Kottayam India 84 C4
Kotte Sri Lanka see Sri Jayewardenepura Kotte
Kotto r. Cent. Afr. Rep. 98 C3
Kotturu India 84 C3
Kotuy r. Rus. Fed. 65 L2
Kotzebue U.S.A. 118 B3
Kotzebue Sound sea chan. U.S.A. 118 B3
Kötzting Germany 53 M5
Kouango Cent. Afr. Rep. 98 C3
Koubia Guinea 96 B3
Kouchibouguac National Park Canada 123 I5
Koudougou Burkina 96 C3
Kouebokkeveld mts S. Africa 100 D7
Koufey Niger 96 E3
Koufonisi i. Greece 59 L7
Kougaberge mts S. Africa 100 F7
Koukourou r. Cent. Afr. Rep. 98 B3
Koulen Cambodia see Kulen
Koulikoro Mali 96 C3
Koumac New Caledonia 107 G4
Koumpentoum Senegal 96 B3
Koundâra Guinea 96 B3
Kountze U.S.A. 131 E6
Koupéla Burkina 96 C3
Kourou Fr. Guiana 143 H2
Kouroussa Guinea 96 C3
Kousséri Cameroon 97 E3
Koutiala Mali 96 C3
Kouvola Fin. 45 O6
Kovallberget Sweden 44 J4
Kovdor Rus. Fed. 44 Q3
Kovdozero, Ozero l. Rus. Fed. 44 R3
Kovel' Ukr. 43 E6
Kovernino Rus. Fed. 42 I4
Kovilpatti India 84 C4
Kovno Lith. see Kaunas
Kovriga, Gora hill Rus. Fed. 42 K2
Kovrov Rus. Fed. 42 I4
Kovylkino Rus. Fed. 43 I5
Kovzhskoye, Ozero l. Rus. Fed. 42 H3
Kowanyama Australia 110 C2
Kowloon H.K. China 77 [inset]
Kowloon Peak hill H.K. China 77 [inset]
Kowloon Peninsula H.K. China 77 [inset]
Kowŏn N. Korea 75 B5
Kōyama-misaki pt Japan 75 C6
Köyceğiz Turkey 59 M6
Koygorodok Rus. Fed. 42 K3
Koyna Reservoir India 84 B2
Köýtendag Turkm. 89 G2
Koyuk U.S.A. 118 B3
Koyukuk r. U.S.A. 118 C3
Koyulhisar Turkey 90 E2
Kozağacı Turkey see Günyüzü
Kō-zaki pt Japan 75 C6
Kozan Turkey 90 D3
Kozani Greece 59 I4
Kozara mts Bos.-Herz. 58 G2
Kozara nat. park Bos.-Herz. 58 G2
Kozarska Dubica Bos.-Herz. see Bosanska Dubica
Kozelets' Ukr. 43 F6
Kozel'sk Rus. Fed. 43 G5
Kozhikode India see Calicut
Kozhva Rus. Fed. 42 M2
Kozlu Turkey 59 N4
Koz'modem'yansk Rus. Fed. 42 J4
Kožuf mts Greece/Macedonia 59 J4
Kōzu-shima i. Japan 75 E6
Kozyatyn Ukr. 43 F6
Kpalimé Togo 96 D4
Kpandae Ghana 96 C4
Kpungan Pass India/Myanmar 70 B1
Kra, Isthmus of Thai. 71 B5
Krabi Thai. 71 B5
Kra Buri Thai. 71 B5
Krâchéh Cambodia 71 D4
Kraddsele Sweden 44 J4
Kragerø Norway 45 F7
Kraggenburg Neth. 52 F2
Kragujevac Serbia 59 I2
Krakatau vol. Indon. 68 D8
Krakau Poland see Kraków
Kraków Poland 47 Q5
Krakower See l. Germany 53 M1
Krâlănh Cambodia 71 C4
Kralendijk Neth. Antilles 137 K6
Kramators'k Ukr. 43 H6
Kramfors Sweden 44 J5
Krammer est. Neth. 52 E3
Kranidi Greece 59 J6
Kranj Slovenia 58 F1
Kranji Reservoir Sing. 71 [inset]
Kranskop S. Africa 101 J5
Krasavino Rus. Fed. 42 J3
Krasilov Ukr. see Krasyliv
Krasino Rus. Fed. 64 G2
Kraskino Rus. Fed. 74 C4
Krāslava Latvia 45 O9
Kraslice Czech Rep. 53 M4
Krasnaya Gorbatka Rus. Fed. 42 I5
Krasnaya Zarya Rus. Fed. 43 H5
Krasnoarmeysk Rus. Fed. 43 J6
Krasnoarmeysk Ukr. see Krasnoarmiys'k
Krasnoarmiys'k Ukr. 43 H6
Krasnoborsk Rus. Fed. 42 J3
Krasnodar Rus. Fed. 90 E1
Krasnodar Kray admin. div. Rus. Fed. see Krasnodarskiy Kray
Krasnodarskiy Kray admin. div. Rus. Fed. 90 E1
Krasnodon Ukr. 43 H6
Krasnogorodskoye Rus. Fed. 45 P8
Krasnogorsk Rus. Fed. 74 F2
Krasnogorskoye Rus. Fed. 42 L4
Krasnograd Ukr. see Krasnohrad
Krasnogvardeysk Uzbek. see Bulung'ur
Krasnogvardeyskoye Rus. Fed. 43 I7
Krasnohrad Ukr. 43 G6
Krasnohvardiys'ke Ukr. 43 G7
Krasnokamsk Rus. Fed. 41 R4
Krasnoperekops'k Ukr. 43 G7
Krasnopol'ye Rus. Fed. 74 F2
Krasnorechenskiy Rus. Fed. 74 D3
Krasnoslobodsk Rus. Fed. 43 I5
Krasnotur'insk Rus. Fed. 41 S4
Krasnoufimsk Rus. Fed. 41 R4
Krasnovishersk Rus. Fed. 41 R3
Krasnovodsk Turkm. see Türkmenbaşy
Krasnovodsk, Mys pt Turkm. 88 D2
Krasnovodskoye Plato plat. Turkm. 91 I2
Krasnowodsk Aylagy b. Turkm. see Türkmenbaşy Aýlagy
Krasnoyarovo Rus. Fed. 74 C2
Krasnoyarsk Rus. Fed. 64 K4
Krasnoyarskoye Vodokhranilishche resr Rus. Fed. 72 G2
Krasnoye Lipetskaya Oblast' Rus. Fed. 43 H5
Krasnoye Respublika Kalmykiya - Khalm'g-Tangch Rus. Fed. see Ulan Erge
Krasnoznamenskiy Kazakh. see Yegindykol'
Krasnoznamenskoye Kazakh. see Yegindykol'
Krasnyy Rus. Fed. 43 F5
Krasnyy Chikoy Rus. Fed. 73 J2
Krasnyye Baki Rus. Fed. 42 J4
Krasnyy Kamyshanik Rus. Fed. see Komsomol'skiy
Krasnyy Kholm Rus. Fed. 42 H4
Krasnyy Kut Rus. Fed. 43 J6
Krasnyy Luch Ukr. 43 H6
Krasnyy Lyman Ukr. 43 H6
Krasnyy Yar Rus. Fed. 43 K7
Krasyliv Ukr. 43 E6
Kratie Cambodia see Krâchéh
Kratke Range mts P.N.G. 69 L8
Kraulshavn Greenland see Nuussuaq
Krâvanh, Chuŏr Phnum mts Cambodia/Thai. see Cardamom Range
Kraynovka Rus. Fed. 91 G2
Krefeld Germany 52 G3
Kremenchug Ukr. see Kremenchuk
Kremenchugskoye Vodokhranilishche resr Ukr. see Kremenchuts'ka Vodoskhovyshche
Kremenchuk Ukr. 43 G6
Kremenchuts'ka Vodoskhovyshche resr Ukr. 43 G6
Křemešník hill Czech Rep. 47 O6
Kremges Ukr. see Svitlovods'k
Kremmidi, Akra pt Greece see Kremmydi, Akrotirio
Kremmydi, Akrotirio pt Greece 59 J6
Krems Austria see Krems an der Donau
Krems an der Donau Austria 47 O6
Kresta, Zaliv g. Rus. Fed. 65 T3
Kresttsy Rus. Fed. 42 G4
Kretinga Lith. 45 L9
Kreuzau Germany 52 G4
Kreuztal Germany 53 H4
Kreva Belarus 45 O9
Kribi Cameroon 96 D4
Krichev Belarus see Krychaw
Kriel S. Africa 101 I4
Krikellos Greece 59 I5
Kril'on, Mys c. Rus. Fed. 74 F3
Krishna India 84 C2
Krishna r. India 84 D2
Krishnanagar India 83 G5
Krishnaraja Sagara l. India 84 C3
Kristiania Norway see Oslo
Kristiansand Norway 45 E7
Kristianstad Sweden 45 I8
Kristiansund Norway 44 E5
Kristiinankaupunki Fin. see Kristinestad
Kristinehamn Sweden 45 I7
Kristinestad Fin. 44 L5
Kristinopol' Ukr. see Chervonohrad
Kriti i. Greece see Crete
Kritiko Pelagos sea Greece 59 K6
Krivoy Rog Ukr. see Kryvyy Rih
Križevci Croatia 58 G1
Krk i. Croatia 58 F2
Krkonošský narodní park nat. park Czech Rep./Poland 47 O5
Krokom Sweden 44 I5
Krokstadøra Norway 44 F5
Krokstranda Norway 44 I3
Krolevets' Ukr. 43 G6
Kronach Germany 53 L4
Krŏng Kaôh Kŏng Cambodia 71 C5
Kronoby Fin. 44 M5
Kronprins Christian Land reg. Greenland 153 I1
Kronprins Frederik Bjerge nunataks Greenland 119 O3
Kronshtadt Rus. Fed. 45 P7
Kronstadt Romania see Braşov
Kronstadt Rus. Fed. see Kronshtadt
Kronwa Myanmar 70 B4
Kroonstad S. Africa 101 H4
Kropotkin Rus. Fed. 91 F1
Kropstädt Germany 53 M3
Krosno Poland 43 D6
Krotoszyn Poland 47 P5
Kruger National Park S. Africa 101 J2
Kruglikovo Rus. Fed. 74 D2
Kruglyakov Rus. Fed. see Oktyabr'skiy
Krui Indon. 68 C8
Kruisfontein S. Africa 100 G8
Kruja Albania see Krujë
Krujë Albania 59 H4
Krumovgrad Bulg. 59 K4
Krungkao Thai. see Ayutthaya
Krung Thep Thai. see Bangkok
Krupa Bos.-Herz. see Bosanska Krupa
Krupa na Uni Bos.-Herz. see Bosanska Krupa
Krupki Belarus 43 F5
Krusenstern, Cape U.S.A. 118 B3
Kruševac Serbia 59 I3
Krušné hory mts Czech Rep. 53 M4
Kruzof Island U.S.A. 120 C3
Krychaw Belarus 43 F5
Krylov Seamount sea feature N. Atlantic Ocean 148 G4
Krym' pen. Ukr. see Crimea
Krymsk Rus. Fed. 90 E1
Krymskaya Rus. Fed. see Krymsk
Kryms'kyy Pivostriv pen. Ukr. see Crimea
Krystynopol Ukr. see Chervonohrad
Krytiko Pelagos sea Greece see Kritiko Pelagos
Kryvyy Rih Ukr. 43 G7
Ksabi Alg. 54 D6
Ksar Chellala Alg. 57 H6
Ksar el Boukhari Alg. 57 H6
Ksar el Kebir Morocco 57 D6
Ksar-es-Souk Morocco see Er Rachidia
Ksenofontova Rus. Fed. 41 R3
Kshirpai India 83 F5
Ksour Essaf Tunisia 58 D7
Kstovo Rus. Fed. 42 J4
Kū', Jabal al hill Saudi Arabia 86 G4
Kuah Malaysia 71 B6
Kuaidamao China see Tonghua
Kuala Belait Brunei 68 E6
Kuala Dungun Malaysia see Dungun
Kuala Kangsar Malaysia 71 C6
Kualakapuas Indon. 68 E7
Kuala Kerai Malaysia 71 C6
Kuala Lipis Malaysia 71 C6

▶Kuala Lumpur Malaysia 71 C7
Joint capital (with Putrajaya) of Malaysia.

Kuala Nerang Malaysia 71 C6
Kuala Pilah Malaysia 71 C7
Kuala Rompin Malaysia 71 C7
Kuala Selangor Malaysia 71 C7
Kualasimpang Indon. 71 B6
Kuala Terengganu Malaysia 71 C6
Kualatungal Indon. 68 C7
Kuamut Sabah Malaysia 68 F5
Kuandian China 74 B4
Kuantan Malaysia 71 C7
Kuba Azer. see Quba
Kuban' r. Rus. Fed. 43 H7
Kubār Syria 91 E4
Kubaybāt Syria 85 C2
Kubaysah Iraq 91 F4
Kubenskoye, Ozero l. Rus. Fed. 42 H4
Kubrat Bulg. 59 L3
Kubuang Indon. 68 F6
Kuchaman Road India 89 I5
Kuchema Rus. Fed. 42 I2
Kuching Sarawak Malaysia 68 E6
Kucing Sarawak Malaysia see Kuching
Kuçovë Albania 59 H4
Kuda India 82 B5
Kudal India 84 B3
Kudap Indon. 71 C7
Kudat Sabah Malaysia 68 F5
Kudligi India 84 C3
Kudremukh mt. India 84 B3
Kudus Indon. 68 E8
Kudymkar Rus. Fed. 41 Q4
Kueishan Tao i. Taiwan 77 I3
Kūfah Iraq 91 G4
Kufstein Austria 47 N7
Kugaaruk Canada 119 J3
Kugesi Rus. Fed. 42 J4
Kugka Lhai China 83 G3
Kugluktuk Canada 118 G3
Kugmallit Bay Canada 153 A2
Kūh, Ra's-al- pt Iran 88 E5
Kūhak Iran 89 F5
Kuhanbokano mt. China 83 E3
Kuhbier Germany 53 M1
Kūhdasht Iran 88 B3
Kūhīn Iran 88 C2
Kūhīrī Iran 89 F5
Kuhmo Fin. 44 P4
Kuhmoinen Fin. 45 N6
Kūhpāyeh mt. Iran 88 E4
Kūhrān, Kūh-e mt. Iran 88 E5
Kühren Germany 53 M3
Kui Buri Thai. 71 B4
Kuis Namibia 100 C3
Kuiseb watercourse Namibia 100 B2
Kuitan China 77 G4
Kuito Angola 99 B5
Kuitun China see Kuytun
Kuiu Island U.S.A. 120 C3
Kuivaniemi Fin. 44 N4
Kujang N. Korea 75 B5
Kuji Japan 75 F4
Kujū-san vol. Japan 75 C6
Kukālār, Kūh-e hill Iran 88 C4
Kukan Rus. Fed. 74 D2
Kukës Albania 59 I3
Kukesi Albania see Kukës
Kukmor Rus. Fed. 42 K4
Kukshi India 82 C5
Kukunuru India 84 D2
Kükürtli Turkm. 88 E2
Kūl r. Iran 88 D5
Kula Turkey 59 M5
Kulaisila India 83 F5
Kula Kangri mt. China/Bhutan 83 G3
Kulandy Kazakh. 80 A2
Kulaneh reg. Pak. 89 F5
Kular Rus. Fed. 65 O2
Kuldīga Latvia 45 L8
Kuldja China see Yining
Kul'dur Rus. Fed. 74 C2
Kule Botswana 100 E2
Kulebaki Rus. Fed. 43 I5
Kulen Cambodia 71 D4
Kulgera Australia 109 F6
Kulikovo Rus. Fed. 42 J3
Kulim Malaysia 71 C6
Kulin Australia 109 B8
Kulja Australia 109 B7
Kulkyne watercourse Australia 112 B3
Kullu India 82 D3
Kulmbach Germany 53 L4
Kŭlob Tajik. 89 H2
Kuloy Rus. Fed. 42 I3
Kuloy r. Rus. Fed. 42 I2
Kulp Turkey 91 F3
Kul'sary Kazakh. 78 E2
Külsheim Germany 53 J5
Kulu India see Kullu
Kulu Turkey 90 D3
Kulunda Rus. Fed. 72 D2
Kulundinskaya Step' plain Kazakh./Rus. Fed. 72 D2
Kulundinskoye, Ozero salt l. Rus. Fed. 72 D2
Kulusuk Greenland 119 O3
Kulwin Australia 111 C7
Kulyab Tajik. see Kŭlob
Kuma r. Rus. Fed. 43 J7
Kumagaya Japan 75 E5
Kumai, Teluk b. Indon. 68 E7
Kumalar Dağı mts Turkey 59 N5
Kumamoto Japan 75 C6
Kumano Japan 75 E6
Kumanovo Macedonia 59 I3
Kumara Rus. Fed. 74 B2
Kumasi Ghana 96 C4
Kumayri Armenia see Gyumri
Kumba Cameroon 96 D4
Kumbakonam India 84 C4
Kumbe Indon. 69 K8
Kümbet Turkey 59 N5
Kumbharli Ghat mt. India 84 B2
Kumbla India 84 B3
Kumchuru Botswana 100 F2
Kum-Dag Turkm. see Gumdag
Kumdah Saudi Arabia 86 G5
Kumel well Iran 88 D3
Kumeny Rus. Fed. 42 K4
Kumertau Rus. Fed. 64 G4
Kumgang-san mt. N. Korea 75 C5
Kumguri India 83 G4
Kumi S. Korea 75 C5
Kumi Uganda 97 G4
Kumla Sweden 45 I7
Kumlu Turkey 85 C1
Kummersdorf-Alexanderdorf Germany 53 N2
Kumo Nigeria 96 E3
Kŭmŏ-do i. S. Korea 75 B6
Kumon Range mts Myanmar 70 B1
Kumphawapi Thai. 70 C3
Kums Namibia 100 D5
Kumta India 84 B3

La Macarena, Parque Nacional nat. park Col. 142 D3
La Maddalena Sardinia Italy 58 C4
La Madeleine, Îles de is Canada 123 J5
La Madeleine, Monts de mts France 56 F3
Lamadian China 74 B3
Lamadianzi China see Lamadian
La Maiko, Parc National de nat. park Dem. Rep. Congo 98 C4
La Malbaie Canada 123 H5
Lamam Laos 70 D4
La Mancha Mex. 131 C7
La Mancha reg. Spain 57 E4
La Manche strait France/U.K. see English Channel
La Máquina Mex. 131 B6
Lamar CO U.S.A. 130 C4
Lamar MO U.S.A. 131 E4
Lamard Iran 88 D5
La Margeride, Monts de mts France 56 F4
La Marmora, Punta mt. Sardinia Italy 58 C5
La Marne au Rhin, Canal de France 52 G6
La Marque U.S.A. 131 E6
La Martre, Lac l. Canada 120 G2
Lamas r. Turkey 85 B1
La Mauricie, Parc National de nat. park Canada 123 G5
Lambaréné Gabon 98 B4
Lambasa Fiji see Labasa
Lambayeque Peru 142 C5
Lambay Island Ireland 51 G4
Lambert atoll Marshall Is see Ailinglaplap
▶Lambert Glacier Antarctica 152 E2
Largest series of glaciers in the world.
Lambert's Bay S. Africa 100 D7
Lambeth Canada 134 E2
Lambi India 82 C3
Lambourn Downs hills U.K. 49 F7
Lame Indon. 71 B7
La Medjerda, Monts de mts Alg. 58 B6
Lamego Port. 57 C3
Lamèque, Île i. Canada 123 I5
La Merced Arg. 144 C3
La Merced Peru 142 C6
Lameroo Australia 111 C7
La Mesa U.S.A. 128 E5
Lamesa U.S.A. 131 C5
Lamia Greece 59 J5
Lamington National Park Australia 112 F2
La Misión Mex. 128 E5
Lamma Island H.K. China 77 [inset]
Lammerlaw Range mts N.Z. 113 B7
Lammermuir Hills U.K. 50 G5
Lammhult Sweden 45 I8
Lammi Fin. 45 N6
Lamont CA U.S.A. 128 D4
Lamont WY U.S.A. 126 G4
La Montagne d'Ambre, Parc National de nat. park Madag. 99 E5
La Montaña de Covadonga, Parque Nacional de nat. park Spain see Los Picos de Europa, Parque Nacional de
La Mora Mex. 131 C7
La Morita Chihuahua Mex. 131 B6
La Morita Coahuila Mex. 131 C6
Lamotrek atoll Micronesia 69 L5
La Moure U.S.A. 130 D2
Lampang Thai. 70 B3
Lam Pao, Ang Kep Nam Thai. 70 C3
Lampasas U.S.A. 131 D6
Lampazos Mex. 131 C7
Lampedusa, Isola di i. Sicily Italy 58 E7
Lampeter U.K. 49 C6
Lamphun Thai. 70 B3
Lampsacus Turkey see Lâpseki
Lam Tin H.K. China 77 [inset]
Lamu Kenya 98 E4
Lamu Myanmar 70 A3
Lāna'i i. U.S.A. 127 [inset]
Lāna'i City U.S.A. 127 [inset]
La Nao, Cabo de c. Spain 57 G4
Lanao, Lake Phil. 69 G5
Lanark Canada 135 G1
Lanark U.K. 50 F5
Lanbi Kyun i. Myanmar 71 B5
Lancang China 76 C4
Lancang Jiang r. China 76 C2
Lancaster Canada 135 H1
Lancaster U.K. 48 E4
Lancaster CA U.S.A. 128 D4
Lancaster KY U.S.A. 134 C5
Lancaster MO U.S.A. 130 E3
Lancaster NH U.S.A. 135 J1
Lancaster OH U.S.A. 134 D4
Lancaster PA U.S.A. 135 G3
Lancaster SC U.S.A. 133 D5
Lancaster VA U.S.A. 135 G5
Lancaster WI U.S.A. 130 F3
Lancaster Canal U.K. 48 E5
Lancaster Sound strait Canada 119 J2
Lanchow China see Lanzhou
Landana Angola see Cacongo
Landau an der Isar Germany 53 M6
Landau in der Pfalz Germany 53 I5
Landeck Austria 47 M7
Lander watercourse Australia 108 E5
Lander U.S.A. 126 F4
Landesbergen Germany 53 J2
Landfall Island India 71 A4
Landhi Pak. 89 G5
Landis Canada 121 I4
Landor Australia 109 B6
Landsberg Poland see Gorzów Wielkopolski
Landsberg am Lech Germany 47 M6
Land's End pt U.K. 49 B8
Landshut Germany 53 M6
Landskrona Sweden 45 H9
Landstuhl Germany 53 H5
Land Wursten reg. Germany 53 I1
Lanesborough Ireland 51 E4
La'nga Co l. China 82 E3
Langao China 77 F1
Langar Afgh. 89 H3
Langberg mts S. Africa 100 F5
Langdon U.S.A. 130 D1
Langeac France 56 F4
Langeberg mts S. Africa 100 D7
Langeland i. Denmark 45 G9
Längelmäki Fin. 45 N6
Langelsheim Germany 53 K3
Langen Germany 53 I1
Langenburg Canada 121 K5
Langenhagen Germany 53 J2
Langenhahn Germany 53 H4
Langenlonsheim Germany 53 H5
Langenthal Switz. 56 H3
Langenweddingen Germany 53 L2
Langeoog Germany 53 H1
Langesund Norway 45 F7
Langfang China 73 L5
Langgapayung Indon. 71 B7
Langgar China 76 B2
Langgöns Germany 53 I4
Langjan Nature Reserve S. Africa 101 I2
Langjökull ice cap Iceland 44 [inset]
Langka Indon. 71 B6
Langkawi i. Malaysia 71 B6
Lang Kha Toek, Khao mt. Thai. 71 B5
Langklip S. Africa 100 E5
Langley Canada 120 F5
Langley U.S.A. 134 D5
Langlo Crossing Australia 111 D5
Langmusi China see Dagcanglhamo
Langong, Xé r. Laos 70 D3
Langøya i. Norway 44 I2
Langphu mt. China 83 F3
Langport U.K. 49 E7
Langqên Zangbo r. China 82 D3
Langqi China 77 H3
Langres France 56 G3
Langres, Plateau de France 56 G3
Langru China 82 D1
Langsa Indon. 71 B6
Langsa, Teluk b. Indon. 71 B6
Långsele Sweden 44 J5
Lang Sơn Vietnam 70 D2
Langtang National Park Nepal 83 F3
Langtao Myanmar 70 B1
Langting India 83 H4
Langtoft U.K. 48 G4
Langtry U.S.A. 131 C6
Languan China see Lantian
Languedoc reg. France 56 E5
Långvattnet Sweden 44 L4
Langwedel Germany 53 J2
Langxi China 77 H2
Langzhong China 76 E2
Lanigan Canada 121 J5
Lanín, Parque Nacional nat. park Arg. 144 B5
Lanín, Volcán vol. Arg./Chile 144 B5
Lanji India 82 E5
Lanka country Asia see Sri Lanka
Länkäran Azer. 91 H3
Lannion France 56 C2
Lanping China 76 C3
Lansån Sweden 44 M3
L'Anse U.S.A. 130 F2
Lanshan China 77 G3
▶Lansing U.S.A. 134 C2
Capital of Michigan.
Lanta, Ko i. Thai. 71 B6
Lantau Island H.K. China 77 [inset]
Lantau Peak hill H.K. China 77 [inset]
Lantian China 77 F1
Lanxi Heilong. China 74 B3
Lanxi Zhejiang China 77 H2
Lan Yü i. Taiwan 77 I4
Lanzarote i. Canary Is 96 B2
Lanzhou China 72 I5
Lanzijing China 74 A3
Laoag Phil. 69 G3
Laoang Phil. 69 H4
Laobie Shan mts China 76 C4
Laobukou China 77 F3
Lao Cai Vietnam 70 C2
Laodicea Syria see Latakia
Laodicea Turkey see Denizli
Laodicea ad Lycum Turkey see Denizli
Laodicea ad Mare Syria see Latakia
Laohekou China 77 F1
Laohupo China see Logpung
Laojie China see Yongping
Laojunmiao China see Yumen
La Okapi, Parc National de nat. park Dem. Rep. Congo 98 C3
Lao Ling mts China 74 B4
Laon France 52 D5
La Oroya Peru 142 C6
Laos country Asia 70 C3
Laotougou China 74 C4
Laotuding Shan hill China 74 B4
Laowohi pass India see Khardung La
Laoye Ling mts Heilongjiang/Jilin China 74 B4
Laoye Ling mts Heilongjiang/Jilin China 74 C4
Lapa Brazil 145 A4
La Palma i. Canary Is 96 B2
La Palma Panama 137 I7
La Palma U.S.A. 129 H5
La Palma del Condado Spain 57 C5
La Panza Range mts U.S.A. 128 C4
La Paragua Venez. 142 F2
La Parilla Mex. 131 B8
La Paya, Parque Nacional nat. park Col. 142 D3
La Paz Arg. 144 E4
▶La Paz Bol. 142 E7
Official capital of Bolivia.
La Paz Hond. 136 G6
La Paz Mex. 136 B4
La Pedrera Col. 142 E4
Lapeer U.S.A. 134 D2
La Pendjari, Parc National de nat. park Benin 96 D3
La Perla Mex. 131 B6
La Pérouse Strait Japan/Rus. Fed. 74 F3
La Pesca Mex. 131 D8
Lapinlahti Fin. 44 O5
Lapithos Cyprus 85 A2
Lap Lae Thai. 70 C3
La Plant U.S.A. 130 C2
La Plata Arg. 144 E4
La Plata MD U.S.A. 135 G4
La Plata MO U.S.A. 130 E3
La Plata, Isla i. Ecuador 142 B4
▶La Plata, Río de sea chan. Arg./Uruguay 144 E4
Part of the Río de la Plata - Paraná, 2nd longest river in South America, and 9th in the world.
La Plonge, Lac l. Canada 121 J4
Lapmežciems Latvia 45 M8
Lapominka Rus. Fed. 42 I2
La Porte U.S.A. 134 B3
Laporte U.S.A. 135 G3
Laporte, Mount Canada 120 E2
La Potherie, Lac l. Canada 123 G2
La Poza Grande Mex. 127 E8
Lappajärvi Fin. 44 M5
Lappajärvi l. Fin. 44 M5
Lappeenranta Fin. 45 P6
Lappersdorf Germany 53 M5
Lappi Fin. 45 L6
Lappland reg. Europe 44 K3
La Pryor U.S.A. 131 D6
Lâpseki Turkey 59 L4
Laptevo Rus. Fed. see Yasnogorsk
Laptev Sea Rus. Fed. 65 N2
Lapua Fin. 44 M5
Lapurdum France see Bayonne
La Purísima Mex. 127 E8
Laqiya Arbain well Sudan 86 C5
La Quiaca Arg. 144 C2
L'Aquila Italy 58 E3
La Quinta U.S.A. 128 E5
Lār Iran 88 D5
Larache Morocco 57 C6
Lārak i. Iran 88 E5
Laramie U.S.A. 126 G4
Laramie r. U.S.A. 126 G4
Laramie Mountains U.S.A. 126 G4
Laranda Turkey see Karaman
Laranjal Paulista Brazil 145 B3
Laranjeiras do Sul Brazil 144 F3
Laranjinha r. Brazil 145 A3
Larantuka Indon. 108 C2
Larat Indon. 108 E1
Larat i. Indon. 108 E1
Larba Alg. 57 H5
Lärbro Sweden 45 K8
L'Archipélago de Mingan, Réserve du Parc National de nat. park Canada 123 J4
L'Ardenne, Plateau de plat. Belgium see Ardennes
Laredo Spain 57 E2
Laredo U.S.A. 131 D7
La Reina Adelaida, Archipiélago de is Chile 144 B8
Largeau Chad see Faya
Largo U.S.A. 133 D7
Largs U.K. 50 E5
Lārī Iran 88 B2
L'Ariana Tunisia 58 D6
Larimore U.S.A. 130 D2
La Rioja Arg. 144 C3
La Rioja aut. comm. Spain 57 E2
Larisa Greece 59 J5
Larissa Greece see Larisa
Laristan reg. Iran 88 E5
Larkana Pak. 89 H5
Lark Harbour Canada 123 K4
Lar Koh mt. Afgh. 89 F3
Lark Passage Australia 110 D2
L'Arli, Parc National de nat. park Burkina 96 D3
Larnaca Cyprus 85 A2
Larnaka Cyprus see Larnaca
Larnaka Bay Cyprus 85 A2
Larnakos, Kolpos b. Cyprus see Larnaka Bay
Larne U.K. 51 G3
Larned U.S.A. 130 D4
La Robe Noire, Lac de l. Canada 123 J4
La Robla Spain 57 D2
La Roche-en-Ardenne Belgium 52 F4
La Rochelle France 56 D3
La Roche-sur-Yon France 56 D3
La Roda Spain 57 E4
La Romana Dom. Rep. 137 K5
La Ronge Canada 121 J4
La Ronge, Lac l. Canada 121 J4
La Rosa Mex. 131 C7
La Rosita Mex. 131 C6
Larrey Point Australia 108 B4
Larrimah Australia 108 F3
Lars Christensen Coast Antarctica 152 E2
Larsen Ice Shelf Antarctica 152 L2
Larsmo Fin. 44 M5
Larvik Norway 45 G7
Las Adjuntas, Presa de resr Mex. 131 D8
La Sal U.S.A. 129 I2
LaSalle Canada 135 I1
La Salle U.S.A. 122 C6
La Salonga Nord, Parc National de nat. park Dem. Rep. Congo 98 C4
La Sambre à l'Oise, Canal de France 52 D5
Las Animas U.S.A. 130 C4
Las Anod Somalia see Laascaanood
La Sarre Canada 122 F4
Las Avispas Mex. 127 F7
La Savonnière, Lac l. Canada 123 G3
La Scie Canada 123 L4
Las Cruces CA U.S.A. 128 C4
Las Cruces NM U.S.A. 127 G6
La Selle, Pic mt. Haiti 137 J5
La Serena Chile 144 B3
Las Esperanças Mex. 131 C7
La Seu d'Urgell Spain 57 G2
Las Flores Arg. 144 E5
Las Guacamatas, Cerro mt. Mex. 127 F7
Lāshār r. Iran 89 F5
Lashburn Canada 121 I4
Las Heras Arg. 144 C4
Lashio Myanmar 70 B2
Lashkar India 82 D4
Lashkar Gāh Afgh. 89 G4
Las Juntas Chile 144 C3
Las Lomitas Arg. 144 D2
Las Marismas marsh Spain 57 C5
Las Martinetas Arg. 144 C7
Las Mesteñas Mex. 131 B6
Las Minas, Cerro de mt. Hond. 136 G6
Las Nopaleras, Cerro mt. Mex. 131 C7
La Société, Archipel de is Fr. Polynesia see Society Islands
La Somme, Canal de France 52 C5
Las Palmas watercourse Mex. 128 E5
▶Las Palmas de Gran Canaria Canary Is 96 B2
Joint capital of the Canary Islands.
Las Petas Bol. 143 G7
La Spezia Italy 58 C2
Las Piedras, Río de r. Peru 142 E6
Las Plumas Arg. 144 C6
Laspur Pak. 89 I2
Lassance Brazil 145 B2
Lassen Peak vol. U.S.A. 128 C1
Lassen Volcanic National Park U.S.A. 128 C1
Las Tablas Panama 137 H7
Las Tablas de Daimiel, Parque Nacional de nat. park Spain 57 E4
Last Chance U.S.A. 130 C4
Las Termas Arg. 144 D3
Last Mountain Lake Canada 121 J5
Las Tórtolas, Cerro mt. Chile 144 C3
Lastoursville Gabon 98 B4
Lastovo i. Croatia 58 G3
Las Tres Vírgenes, Volcán vol. Mex. 127 E8
Lastrup Germany 53 H2
Las Tunas Cuba 137 I4
Las Varas Chihuahua Mex. 127 G7
Las Varas Nayarit Mex. 136 C4
Las Varillas Arg. 144 D4
Las Vegas NM U.S.A. 127 G6
Las Vegas NV U.S.A. 129 F3
Las Viajas, Isla de i. Peru 142 C6
Las Villuercas mt. Spain 57 D4
La Tabatière Canada 123 K4
Latacunga Ecuador 142 C4
Latady Island Antarctica 152 L2
Latakia Syria 85 B2
La Teste-de-Buch France 56 D4
Latham Australia 109 B7
Lathen Germany 53 H2
Latheron U.K. 50 F2
Lathi India 82 B4
Latho India 82 D2
Lathrop U.S.A. 128 C3
Latina Italy 58 E4
La Tortuga, Isla i. Venez. 142 E1
Latrobe U.S.A. 134 F3
Latrun West Bank 85 B4
Lattaquié Syria see Latakia
Lattrop Neth. 52 G2
La Tuque Canada 123 G5
Latur India 84 C2
Latvia country Europe 45 N8
Latvija country Europe see Latvia
Latviyskaya S.S.R. country Europe see Latvia
Lauca, Parque Nacional nat. park Chile 142 E7
Lauchhammer Germany 47 N5
Lauder U.K. 50 G5
Laudio Spain see Llodio
Lauenbrück Germany 53 J1
Lauenburg (Elbe) Germany 53 K1
Lauf an der Pegnitz Germany 53 L5
Laufen Switz. 56 H3
Lauge Koch Kyst reg. Greenland 119 L2
Laughlen, Mount Australia 109 F5
Laughlin Peak U.S.A. 127 G5
Lauka Estonia 45 M7
Launceston Australia 111 [inset]
Launceston U.K. 49 C8
Laune r. Ireland 51 C5
Launggyaung Myanmar 70 B1
Launglon Myanmar 71 B4
Launglon Bok Islands Myanmar 71 B4
La Unión Bol. 142 F7
Laura Australia 110 D2
Laurel DE U.S.A. 135 H4
Laurel MS U.S.A. 131 F6
Laurel MT U.S.A. 126 F3
Laureldale U.S.A. 135 H3
Laurel Hill hills U.S.A. 134 F4
Laurencekirk U.K. 50 G4
Laurieton Australia 112 F3
Laurinburg U.S.A. 133 E5
Lauru i. Solomon Is see Choiseul
Lausanne Switz. 56 H3
Laut i. Indon. 68 F7
Laut i. Indon. 71 E6
Lautem East Timor 108 D2
Lautersbach (Hessen) Germany 53 J4
Laut Kecil, Kepulauan is Indon. 68 F8
Lautoka Fiji 107 H3
Lauvuskylä Fin. 44 P5
Lauwersmeer l. Neth. 52 G1
Lava Beds National Monument nat. park U.S.A. 126 C4
Laval Canada 122 G5
Laval France 56 D2
La Vall d'Uixó Spain 57 F4
Lāvān i. Iran 88 D5
La Vanoise, Massif de mts France 56 H4
La Vanoise, Parc National de nat. park France 56 H4
Lavapié, Punta pt Chile 144 B5
Lāvar Iran 88 C4
Laveaga Peak U.S.A. 128 C3
La Vega Dom. Rep. 137 J5
Laverne U.S.A. 131 D4
Laverton Australia 109 C7
La Víbora Mex. 131 C7
La Vila Joíosa Spain see Villajoyosa-La Vila Joíosa
La Viña Peru 142 C5
Lavongal i. P.N.G. see New Hanover
Lavras Brazil 145 B3
Lavumisa Swaziland 101 J4
Lavushi-Manda National Park Zambia 99 D5
Lawa India 82 C4
Lawa Myanmar 70 B1
Lawa Pak. 89 H3
Lawashi r. Canada 122 E3
Law Dome ice feature Antarctica 152 F2
Lawit, Gunung mt. Malaysia 71 C6
Lawksawk Myanmar 70 B2
Lawn Hill National Park Australia 110 B3
La Woëvre, Plaine de plain France 52 F5
Lawra Ghana 96 C3
Lawrence IN U.S.A. 134 B4
Lawrence KS U.S.A. 130 E4
Lawrence MA U.S.A. 135 J2
Lawrenceburg IN U.S.A. 134 C4
Lawrenceburg KY U.S.A. 134 C4
Lawrenceburg TN U.S.A. 132 C5
Lawrenceville GA U.S.A. 133 D5
Lawrenceville IL U.S.A. 134 B4
Lawrenceville VA U.S.A. 135 G5
Lawrence Wells, Mount hill Australia 109 C6
Lawton U.S.A. 131 D5
Lawz, Jabal al mt. Saudi Arabia 90 D5
Laxå Sweden 45 I7
Laxey Isle of Man 48 C4
Laxgalts'ap Canada 120 D4
Lax Kw'alaams Canada 120 D4
Laxo U.K. 50 [inset]
Laya r. Rus. Fed. 42 M2
Laydennyy, Mys c. Rus. Fed. 42 J1
Laylá Saudi Arabia 86 G5
Layla salt pan Saudi Arabia 85 D4
Laysan Island U.S.A. 150 I4
Laytonville U.S.A. 128 B2
Layyah Pak. 89 H4
Laza Myanmar 70 B1
Lazarev Rus. Fed. 74 F1
Lazarevac Serbia 59 I2
Lázaro Cárdenas Mex. 136 D5
Lazcano Uruguay 144 F4
Lazdijai Lith. 45 M9
Lazikou China 76 D1
Lazo Primorskiy Kray Rus. Fed. 74 D4
Lazo Respublika Sakha (Yakutiya) Rus. Fed. 65 O3
Lead U.S.A. 130 C2
Leader Water r. U.K. 50 G5
Leadville Australia 112 D4
Leaf r. U.S.A. 131 F6
Leaf Bay Canada see Tasiujaq
Leaf Rapids Canada 121 K3
Leakey U.S.A. 131 D6
Leaksville U.S.A. see Eden
Leamington Canada 134 D2
Leamington Spa, Royal U.K. 49 F6
Leane, Lough l. Ireland 51 C5
Leap Ireland 51 C6
Leatherhead U.K. 49 G7
L'Eau Claire, Lac à l. Canada 122 G2
L'Eau Claire, Rivière à r. Canada 122 G2
L'Eau d'Heure l. Belgium 52 E4
Leavenworth IN U.S.A. 134 B4
Leavenworth KS U.S.A. 130 E4
Leavenworth WA U.S.A. 126 C3
Leavitt Peak U.S.A. 128 D2
Lebach Germany 52 G5
Lebanon country Asia 85 B2
Lebanon IN U.S.A. 134 B3
Lebanon KY U.S.A. 134 C5
Lebanon MO U.S.A. 130 E4
Lebanon NH U.S.A. 135 I2
Lebanon OH U.S.A. 134 C4
Lebanon OR U.S.A. 126 C3
Lebanon PA U.S.A. 135 G3
Lebanon TN U.S.A. 132 C4
Lebanon VA U.S.A. 134 D5
Lebanon Junction U.S.A. 134 C5
Lebanon Mountains Lebanon see Liban, Jebel
Lebbeke Belgium 52 E3
Lebec U.S.A. 128 D4
Lebedyan' Rus. Fed. 43 H5
Lebel-sur-Quévillon Canada 122 F4
Le Blanc France 56 E3
Lębork Poland 47 P3
Lebowakgomo S. Africa 101 I3
Lebrija Spain 57 C5
Łebsko, Jezioro lag. Poland 47 P3
Lebu Chile 144 B5
Lebyazh'ye Kazakh. see Akku
Lebyazh'ye Rus. Fed. 42 K4
Le Caire Egypt see Cairo
Le Cateau-Cambrésis France 52 D4
Le Catelet France 52 D4
Lecce Italy 58 H4
Lecco Italy 58 C2
Lech r. Austria/Germany 47 M7
Lechaina Greece 59 I6
Lechang China 77 G3
Le Chasseron mt. Switz. 56 H3
Le Chesne France 52 E5
Lechtaler Alpen mts Austria 47 M7
Leck Germany 47 L3
Lecompte U.S.A. 131 E6
Le Creusot France 56 G3
Le Crotoy France 52 B4
Lectoure France 56 E5
Ledang, Gunung mt. Malaysia 71 C7
Ledbury U.K. 49 E6
Ledesma Spain 57 D3
Ledmore U.K. 50 E2
Ledmozero Rus. Fed. 44 R4
Ledong Hainan China 70 E3
Ledong Hainan China 77 F5
Le Dorat France 56 E3
Leduc Canada 120 H4
Lee r. Ireland 51 D6
Lee IN U.S.A. 134 B3
Lee MA U.S.A. 135 I2
Leech Lake U.S.A. 130 E2
Leeds U.K. 48 F5
Leedstown U.K. 49 B8
Leek Neth. 52 G1
Leek U.K. 49 E5
Leende Neth. 52 F3
Leer (Ostfriesland) Germany 53 H1
Leesburg FL U.S.A. 133 D6
Leesburg GA U.S.A. 133 C6
Leesburg OH U.S.A. 134 D4
Leesburg VA U.S.A. 135 G4
Leese Germany 53 J2
Lee Steere Range hills Australia 109 C6
Leesville U.S.A. 131 E6
Leesville Lake OH U.S.A. 134 E3
Leesville Lake VA U.S.A. 134 F5
Leeton Australia 112 C5
Leeu-Gamka S. Africa 100 E7
Leeuwarden Neth. 52 F1
Leeuwin, Cape Australia 109 A8
Leeuwin-Naturaliste National Park Australia 109 A8
Lee Vining U.S.A. 128 D3
Leeward Islands Caribbean Sea 137 L5
Lefka Cyprus 85 A2
Lefkada Greece 59 I5
Lefkada i. Greece 59 I5
Lefkás Greece see Lefkada
Lefke Cyprus see Lefka
Lefkimmi Greece 59 I5
Lefkoniko Cyprus see Lefkonikon
Lefkonikon Cyprus 85 A2
Lefkoşa Cyprus see Nicosia
Lefkosia Cyprus see Nicosia
Lefroy r. Canada 123 H2
Lefroy, Lake salt flat Australia 109 C7
Legarde r. Canada 122 D4
Legaspi Phil. 69 G4
Legden Germany 52 H2
Legges Tor mt. Australia 111 [inset]
Leghorn Italy see Livorno
Legnago Italy 58 D2
Legnica Poland 47 P5
Le Grand U.S.A. 128 C3
Legune Australia 108 E3
Leh India 82 D2
Le Havre France 56 E2
Lehi U.S.A. 129 H1
Lehighton U.S.A. 135 H3
Lehmo Fin. 44 P5
Lehre Germany 53 K2
Lehrte Germany 53 J2
Lehtimäki Fin. 44 M5
Lehututu Botswana 100 E2
Leibnitz Austria 47 O7
Leicester U.K. 49 F6
Leichhardt r. Australia 106 B3
Leichhardt Falls Australia 110 B3
Leichhardt Range mts Australia 110 D4
Leiden Neth. 52 E2
Leie r. Belgium 52 D3
Leigh N.Z. 113 E3
Leigh U.K. 48 E5
Leighton Buzzard U.K. 49 G7
Leiktho Myanmar 70 B3
Leimen Germany 53 I5
Leine r. Germany 53 J2
Leinefelde Germany 53 K3
Leinster Australia 109 C6
Leinster reg. Ireland 51 F4
Leinster, Mount hill Ireland 51 F5
Leipsic U.S.A. 134 D3
Leipsoi i. Greece 59 L6
Leipzig Germany 53 M3
Leipzig-Halle airport Germany 53 M3
Leiranger Norway 44 I3
Leiria Port. 57 B4
Leirvik Norway 45 D7
Leishan China 77 F3
Leisler, Mount hill Australia 109 E5
Leisnig Germany 53 M3
Leitchfield U.S.A. 134 B5
Leith Hill hill U.K. 49 G7
Leiva, Cerro mt. Col. 142 D3
Leixlip Ireland 51 F4
Leiyang China 77 G3
Leizhou China 77 F4
Leizhou Bandao pen. China 77 F4
Leizhou Wan b. China 77 F4
Lek r. Neth. 52 E3
Leka Norway 44 G4
Lékana Congo 98 B4
Le Kef Tunisia 58 C6
Lekhainá Greece see Lechaina
Lekitobi Indon. 69 G7
Lekkersing S. Africa 100 C5
Lékoni Gabon 98 B4
Leksand Sweden 45 I6
Leksozero, Ozero l. Rus. Fed. 44 Q5
Lelai, Tanjung pt Indon. 69 H6
Leland U.S.A. 134 C1
Leli China see Tianlin
Lélouma Guinea 96 B3
Lelystad Neth. 52 F2
Le Maire, Estrecho de sea chan. Arg. 144 C9
Léman, Lac l. France/Switz. see Geneva, Lake
Le Mans France 56 E2
Le Mars U.S.A. 130 D3
Lemberg France 53 H5
Lemberg Ukr. see L'viv
Lembruch Germany 53 I2
Lemdiyya Alg. see Médéa
Leme Brazil 145 B3
Lemele Neth. 52 G2
Lemesos Cyprus see Limassol
Lemgo Germany 53 I2
Lemhi Range mts U.S.A. 126 E3
Lemi Fin. 45 O6
Lemieux Islands Canada 119 L3
Lemmenjoen kansallispuisto nat. park Fin. 44 N2
Lemmer Neth. 52 F2
Lemmon U.S.A. 130 C2
Lemmon, Mount U.S.A. 129 H5
Lemnos i. Greece see Limnos
Lemoncove U.S.A. 128 D3
Lemoore U.S.A. 128 D3
Le Moyne, Lac l. Canada 123 H2
Lemro r. Myanmar 70 A2
Lemtybozh Rus. Fed. 41 R3
Le Murge hills Italy 58 G4
Lemvig Denmark 45 F8
Lem"yu r. Rus. Fed. 42 M3
Lena r. Rus. Fed. 72 J1
Lena U.S.A. 134 A1
Lena, Mount U.S.A. 129 I1
Lenadoon Point Ireland 51 C3
Lenchung Tso salt l. China 83 E2
Lençóis Brazil 145 C1
Lençóis Maranhenses, Parque Nacional dos nat. park Brazil 143 J4
Lendeh Iran 88 C4
Lendery Rus. Fed. 44 Q5
Le Neubourg France 49 H9
Lengerich Germany 53 H2
Lenglong Ling mts China 72 I5
Lengshuijiang China 77 F3
Lengshuitan China 77 F3
Lenham U.K. 49 H7
Lenhovda Sweden 45 I8
Lenin Tajik. 89 H2
Lenin, Qullai mt. Kyrg./Tajik. see Lenin Peak
Lenina, Pik mt. Kyrg./Tajik. see Lenin Peak
Leninabad Tajik. see Khŭjand
Leninakan Armenia see Gyumri

Lenin Atyndagy Choku mt. Kyrg./Tajik. see Lenin Peak
Lenine Ukr. 90 D1
Leningrad Rus. Fed. see St Petersburg
Leningrad Tajik. 89 H2
Leningrad Oblast admin. div. Rus. Fed. see Leningradskaya Oblast'
Leningradskaya Rus. Fed. 43 H7
Leningradskaya Oblast' admin. div. Rus. Fed. 45 R7
Leningradskiy Rus. Fed. 65 S3
Leningradskiy Tajik. see Leningrad
Lenino Ukr. see Lenine
Leninobod Tajik. see Khŭjand
Lenin Peak Kyrg./Tajik. 89 I2
Leninsk Kazakh. see Baykonyr
Leninsk Rus. Fed. 43 J6
Leninskiy Rus. Fed. 43 H5
Leninsk-Kuznetskiy Rus. Fed. 64 J4
Leninskoye Kazakh. 43 K6
Leninskoye Kirovskaya Oblast' Rus. Fed. 42 J4
Leninskoye Yevreyskaya Avtonomnaya Oblast' Rus. Fed. 74 D3
Lenkoran' Azer. see Länkäran
Lenne r. Germany 53 H3
Lennoxville Canada 135 J1
Lenoir U.S.A. 132 D5
Lenore U.S.A. 134 D5
Lenore Lake Canada 121 J4
Lenox U.S.A. 135 I2
Lens France 52 C4
Lensk Rus. Fed. 65 M3
Lenti Hungary 58 G1
Lentini Sicily Italy 58 F6
Lenya Myanmar 71 B5
Lenzen Germany 53 L1
Léo Burkina 96 C3
Leoben Austria 47 O7
Leodhais, Eilean i. U.K. see Lewis, Isle of
Leominster U.K. 49 E6
Leominster U.S.A. 135 J2
León Mex. 136 D4
León Nicaragua 137 G6
León Spain 57 D2
Leon r. U.S.A. 131 D6
Leonardtown U.S.A. 135 G4
Leonardville Namibia 100 D2
Leongatha Australia 112 B7
Leonidi Peloponnisos Greece see Leonidio
Leonidio Greece 59 J6
Leonidovo Rus. Fed. 74 F2
Leonora Australia 109 C7
Leopold U.S.A. 134 E4
Leopold and Astrid Coast Antarctica see King Leopold and Queen Astrid Coast
Léopold II, Lac l. Dem. Rep. Congo see Mai-Ndombe, Lac
Leopoldina Brazil 145 C3
Leopoldo de Bulhões Brazil 145 A2
Léopoldville Dem. Rep. Congo see Kinshasa
Leoti U.S.A. 130 C4
Leoville Canada 121 J4
Lepalale S. Africa see Lephalale
Lepaya Latvia see Liepāja
Lepel' Belarus see Lyepyel'
Lepellé r. Canada 123 H1
Lephalala r. S. Africa 101 H2
Lephalale S. Africa 101 H2
Lephepe Botswana 101 G2
Lephoi S. Africa 101 G6
Leping China 77 H2
Lepontine, Alpi mts Italy/Switz. 58 C1
Leppävirta Fin. 44 O5
Lepreau, Point Canada 123 I5
Lepsa Kazakh. see Lepsy
Lepsy Kazakh. 80 E2
Le Puy France see Le Puy-en-Velay
Le Puy-en-Velay France 56 F4
Le Quesnoy France 52 D4
Lerala Botswana 101 H2
Leratswana S. Africa 101 H5
Léré Mali 96 C3
Lereh Indon. 69 J7
Leribe Lesotho see Hlotse
Lérida Col. 142 D4
Lérida Spain see Lleida
Lerik Azer. 91 H3
Lerma Spain 57 E2
Lermontov Rus. Fed. 91 F1
Lermontovka Rus. Fed. 74 D3
Lermontovskiy Rus. Fed. see Lermontov
Leros i. Greece 59 L6
Le Roy U.S.A. 135 G2
Le Roy, Lac l. Canada 122 G2
Lerum Sweden 45 H8
Lerwick U.K. 50 [inset]
Les Amirantes is Seychelles see Amirante Islands
Lesbos i. Greece 59 K5
Les Cayes Haiti 137 J5
Leshan China 76 D2
Leshukonskoye Rus. Fed. 42 J2
Lesi watercourse Sudan 97 F4
Leskhimstroy Ukr. see Syeverodonets'k
Leskovac Serbia 59 I3
Leslie U.S.A. 134 C2
Lesneven France 56 B2
Lesnoy Kirovskaya Oblast' Rus. Fed. 42 L4
Lesnoy Murmanskaya Oblast' Rus. Fed. see Umba
Lesnoye Rus. Fed. 42 G4
Lesogorsk Rus. Fed. 74 F2
Lesopil'noye Rus. Fed. 74 D3
Lesosibirsk Rus. Fed. 64 K4
Lesotho country Africa 101 I5
Lesozavodsk Rus. Fed. 74 D3
L'Espérance Rock i. Kermadec Is 107 I5
Les Pieux France 49 F9
Les Sables-d'Olonne France 56 D3
Lesse r. Belgium 52 E4
Lesser Antarctica reg. Antarctica see West Antarctica
Lesser Antilles is Caribbean Sea 137 K6
Lesser Caucasus mts Asia 91 F2
Lesser Himalaya mts India/Nepal 82 D3
Lesser Khingan Mountains China see Xiao Hinggan Ling
Lesser Slave Lake Canada 120 H4
Lesser Tunb i. The Gulf 88 D5
Lessines Belgium 52 D4
L'Est, Canal de France 52 G6
L'Est, Île de i. Canada 123 J5
L'Est, Pointe de pt Canada 123 J4
Lester U.S.A. 134 E5
Lestijärvi Fin. 44 N5
Les Vans France 56 G4
Lesvos i. Greece see Lesbos
Leszno Poland 47 P5
Letaba S. Africa 101 J2
Letchworth Garden City U.K. 49 G7
Le Télégraphe hill France 56 G3
Leteri India 82 D4
Letha Range mts Myanmar 70 A2
Lethbridge Alta Canada 121 H5
Lethbridge Nfld. and Lab. Canada 123 L4
Leti i. Indon. 108 D2
Leti, Kepulauan is Indon. 108 D2
Leticia Col. 142 E4
Letlhakeng Botswana 101 G3
Letnerechenskiy Rus. Fed. 42 G2
Letniy Navolok Rus. Fed. 42 H2
Le Touquet-Paris-Plage France 52 B4
Letpadan Myanmar 70 A3
Le Tréport France 52 B4
Letsitele S. Africa 101 J2
Letsopa S. Africa 101 G4
Letterkenny Ireland 51 E3
Letung Indon. 71 D7
Lëtzebuerg country Europe see Luxembourg
Letzlingen Germany 53 L2
Léua Angola 99 C5
Leucas Greece see Lefkada
Leucate, Étang de l. France 56 F5
Leuchars U.K. 50 G4
Leukas Greece see Lefkada
Leung Shuen Wan Chau i. H.K. China see High Island
Leunovo Rus. Fed. 42 I2
Leupp U.S.A. 129 H4
Leupung Indon. 71 A6
Leura Australia 110 E4
Leusden Neth. 52 F2
Leuser, Gunung mt. Indon. 71 B7
Leutershausen Germany 53 K5
Leuven Belgium 52 E4
Levadeia Sterea Ellada Greece see Livadeia
Levan U.S.A. 129 H2
Levanger Norway 44 G5
Levante, Riviera di coastal area Italy 58 C2
Levanto Italy 58 C2
Levashi Rus. Fed. 91 G2
Levelland U.S.A. 131 C5
Leven England U.K. 48 G5
Leven Scotland U.K. 50 G4
Leven, Loch l. U.K. 50 F4
Lévêque, Cape Australia 108 C4
Leverkusen Germany 52 G3
Lévézou mts France 56 F4
Levice Slovakia 47 Q6
Levin N.Z. 113 E5
Lévis Canada 123 H5
Levitha i. Greece 59 L6
Levittown NY U.S.A. 135 I3
Levittown PA U.S.A. 135 H3
Levkás i. Greece see Lefkada
Levkímmi Greece see Lefkimmi
Levskigrad Bulg. see Karlovo
Lev Tolstoy Rus. Fed. 43 H5
Lévy, Cap c. France 49 F9
Lewe Myanmar 70 B3
Lewerberg mt. S. Africa 100 C5
Lewes U.K. 49 H8
Lewes U.S.A. 135 H4
Lewis CO U.S.A. 129 I3
Lewis IN U.S.A. 134 B4
Lewis KS U.S.A. 130 D4
Lewis, Isle of i. U.K. 50 C2
Lewis, Lake salt flat Australia 108 F5
Lewisburg KY U.S.A. 134 B5
Lewisburg PA U.S.A. 135 G3
Lewisburg WV U.S.A. 134 E5
Lewis Cass, Mount Canada/U.S.A. 120 D3
Lewis Hills hill Canada 123 K4
Lewis Pass N.Z. 113 D6
Lewis Range hills Australia 108 E5
Lewis Range mts U.S.A. 126 E2
Lewis Smith, Lake U.S.A. 133 C5
Lewiston ID U.S.A. 126 D3
Lewiston ME U.S.A. 135 J1
Lewistown IL U.S.A. 130 F3
Lewistown MT U.S.A. 126 F3
Lewistown PA U.S.A. 135 G3
Lewisville U.S.A. 131 E5
Lexington KY U.S.A. 134 C4
Lexington MI U.S.A. 134 D2
Lexington NC U.S.A. 132 D5
Lexington NE U.S.A. 130 D3
Lexington TN U.S.A. 131 F5
Lexington VA U.S.A. 134 F5
Lexington Park U.S.A. 135 G4
Leyden Neth. see Leiden
Leye China 76 E3
Leyla Dāgh mt. Iran 88 B2
Leyte i. Phil. 69 G4
Lezha Albania see Lezhë
Lezhë Albania 59 H4
Lezhi China 76 E2
Lezhu China 77 G4
L'gov Rus. Fed. 43 G6
Lhagoi Kangri mt. China 83 F3
Lharigarbo China 83 G2
Lhasa China 83 G3
Lhasoi China 76 B2
Lhatog China 76 C2
Lhaviyani Atoll Maldives see Faadhippolhu Atoll
Lhazê Xizang China 76 B2
Lhazê Xizang China 83 F3
Lhazhong China 83 F3
Lhokkruet Indon. 71 A6
Lhokseumawe Indon. 71 B6
Lhoksukon Indon. 71 B6
Lhomar China 83 G3
Lhorong China 76 B2
▶Lhotse mt. China/Nepal 83 F4
4th highest mountain in the world and in Asia.
Lhozhag China 83 G3
Lhuntshi Bhutan 83 G4
Lhünzê China see Xingba
Lhünzhub China see Gaindainqoinkor
Liakoura mt. Greece 59 J5
Liancheng China see Guangnan
Liancourt France 52 C5
Liancourt Rocks i. Asia 75 C5
Liandu China see Lishui
Liangdang China 76 E1
Liangdaohe China 83 G3
Lianghe Chongqing China 77 F2
Lianghe Yunnan China 76 C3
Lianghekou Chongqing China see Lianghe
Lianghekou Gansu China 76 E1
Lianghekou Sichuan China 76 D2
Liangping China 76 E2
Liangshan China see Liangping
Liang Shan mt. Myanmar 70 B1
Liangshi China see Shaodong
Liangtian China 77 F4
Liangyuan China see Shangqiu
Liangzhou China see Wuwei
Liangzi Hu l. China 77 G2
Lianhe China see Qianjiang
Lianhua China 77 G3
Lianhua Shan mts China 77 G4
Lianjiang Fujian China 77 H3
Lianjiang Jiangxi China see Xingguo
Liannan China 77 G3
Lianping China 77 G3
Lianran China see Anning
Lianshan Guangdong China 77 G3
Lianshan Liaoning China 73 M4
Lianshui China 77 H1
Liant, Cape i. Thai. see Samae San, Ko
Liantang China see Nanchang
Lianxian China see Lianzhou
Lianyin China 74 A1
Lianyungang China 77 H1
Lianzhou Guangdong China 77 G3
Lianzhou Guangxi China see Hepu
Liaocheng China 73 L5
Liaodong Bandao pen. China 73 M4
Liaodong Wan b. China 73 M4
Liaogao China see Songtao
Liao He r. China 74 A4
Liaoning prov. China 74 A4
Liaoyang China 74 A4
Liaoyuan China 74 B4
Liaozhong China 74 A4
Liapades Greece 59 H5
Liard r. Canada 120 F2
Liard Highway Canada 120 F2
Liard Plateau Canada 120 E2
Liard River Canada 120 E3
Liari Pak. 89 G5
Liathach mt. U.K. 50 D3
Liban country Asia see Lebanon
Liban, Jebel mts Lebanon 85 C2
Libau Latvia see Liepāja
Libby U.S.A. 126 E2
Libenge Dem. Rep. Congo 98 B3
Liberal U.S.A. 131 C4
Liberdade Brazil 145 B3
Liberec Czech Rep. 47 O5
Liberia country Africa 96 C4
Liberia Costa Rica 137 G6
Liberty IN U.S.A. 134 C4
Liberty KY U.S.A. 134 C5
Liberty ME U.S.A. 135 K1
Liberty MO U.S.A. 130 E4
Liberty MS U.S.A. 131 F6
Liberty NY U.S.A. 135 H3
Liberty TX U.S.A. 131 E6
Liberty Lake U.S.A. 135 G4
Libin Belgium 52 F5
Libnī, Gebel hill Egypt see Libnī, Jabal
Libnī, Jabal hill Egypt 85 A4
Libo China 76 E3
Libobo, Tanjung pt Indon. 69 H7
Libode S. Africa 101 I6
Libong, Ko i. Thai. 71 B6
Libourne France 56 D4
Libral Well Australia 108 D5
Libre, Sierra mts Mex. 127 F7
▶Libreville Gabon 98 A3
Capital of Gabon.
▶Libya country Africa 97 E2
4th largest country in Africa.
Libyan Desert Egypt/Libya 86 C5
Libyan Plateau Egypt 90 B5
Licantén Chile 144 B4
Licata Sicily Italy 58 E6
Lice Turkey 91 F3
Lich Germany 53 I4
Lichas pen. Greece 59 J5
Licheng Guangxi China see Lipu
Licheng Jiangsu China see Jinhu
Lichfield U.K. 49 F6
Lichinga Moz. 99 D5
Lichte Germany 53 L4
Lichtenau Germany 53 I3
Lichtenburg S. Africa 101 H4
Lichtenfels Germany 53 L4
Lichtenvoorde Neth. 52 G3
Lichuan Hubei China 77 F2
Lichuan Jiangxi China 77 H3
Lida Belarus 45 N10
Liddel Water r. U.K. 50 G5
Lidfontein Namibia 100 D3
Lidköping Sweden 45 H7
Lidsjöberg Sweden 44 I4
Liebenau Germany 53 J2
Liebenburg Germany 53 K2
Liebenwalde Germany 53 N2
Liebig, Mount Australia 109 E5
Liechtenstein country Europe 56 I3
Liège Belgium 52 F4
Liegnitz Poland see Legnica
Lieksa Fin. 44 Q5
Lielupe r. Latvia 45 N8
Lielvārde Latvia 45 N8
Lienart Dem. Rep. Congo 98 C3
Lienchung i. Taiwan see Matsu Tao
Liên Nghia Vietnam 71 E5
Liên Sơn Vietnam 71 E4
Lienz Austria 47 N7
Liepāja Latvia 45 L8
Liepaya Latvia see Liepāja
Lier Belgium 52 E3
Lierre Belgium see Lier
Lieshout Neth. 52 F3
Lietuva country Europe see Lithuania
Liévin France 52 C4
Lièvre, Rivière du r. Canada 122 G5
Liezen Austria 47 O7
Liffey r. Ireland 51 F4
Lifford Ireland 51 E3
Lifi Mahuida mt. Arg. 144 C6
Lifou i. New Caledonia 107 G4
Lifu i. New Caledonia see Lifou
Līgatne Latvia 45 N8
Lightning Ridge Australia 112 C2
Ligny-en-Barrois France 52 F6
Ligonha r. Moz. 99 D5
Ligonier U.S.A. 134 C3
Ligui Mex. 127 F8
Ligure, Mar sea France/Italy see Ligurian Sea
Ligurian Sea France/Italy 58 C3
Ligurienne, Mer sea France/Italy see Ligurian Sea
Ligurta U.S.A. 129 F5
Lihir Group is P.N.G. 106 F2
Lihou Reef and Cays Australia 110 E3
Liivi laht b. Estonia/Latvia see Riga, Gulf of
Lijiang Yunnan China 76 D3
Lijiang Yunnan China see Yuanjiang
Lijiazhai China 77 G2
Lika reg. Croatia 58 F2
Likasi Dem. Rep. Congo 99 C5
Likati Dem. Rep. Congo 98 C3
Likely Canada 120 F4
Likhachevo Ukr. see Pervomays'kyy
Likhachyovo Ukr. see Pervomays'kyy
Likhapani India 83 H4
Likhás pen. Greece see Lichas
Likhoslavl' Rus. Fed. 42 G4
Liku Indon. 68 D6
Likurga Rus. Fed. 42 I4
L'Île-Rousse Corsica France 56 I5
Lilienthal Germany 53 I1
Liling China 77 G3
Lilla Pak. 89 I3
Lilla Edet Sweden 45 H7
Lille Belgium 52 E3
Lille France 52 D4
Lille (Lesquin) airport France 52 D4
Lille Bælt sea chan. Denmark see Little Belt
Lillebonne France 49 H9
Lillehammer Norway 45 G6
Lillers France 52 C4
Lillesand Norway 45 F7
Lillestrøm Norway 45 G7
Lilley U.S.A. 134 C2
Lillholmsjö Sweden 44 I5
Lillian, Point hill Australia 109 D6
Lillington U.S.A. 133 E5
Lillooet Canada 120 F5
Lillooet r. Canada 120 F5
Lillooet Range mts Canada 120 F5
▶Lilongwe Malawi 99 D5
Capital of Malawi.
Lilydale Australia 111 B7
▶Lima Peru 142 C6
Capital of Peru. 5th most populous city in South America.
Lima MT U.S.A. 126 E3
Lima NY U.S.A. 135 G2
Lima OH U.S.A. 134 C3
Lima Duarte Brazil 145 C3
Lima Islands China see Wanshan Qundao
Liman Rus. Fed. 43 J7
Limar Indon. 108 D1
Limassol Cyprus 85 A2
Limavady U.K. 51 F2
Limay r. Arg. 144 C5
Limbaži Latvia 45 N8
Limbunya Australia 108 E4
Limburg an der Lahn Germany 53 I4
Lim Chu Kang hill Sing. 71 [inset]
Lime Acres S. Africa 100 F5
Limeira Brazil 145 B3
Limerick Ireland 51 D5
Limestone Point Canada 121 L4
Limingen Norway 44 H4
Limingen l. Norway 44 H4
Limington U.S.A. 135 J2
Liminka Fin. 44 N4
Limmen Bight b. Australia 110 B2
Limnos i. Greece 59 K5
Limoeiro Brazil 143 K5
Limoges Canada 135 H1
Limoges France 56 E4
Limón Costa Rica see Puerto Limón
Limon U.S.A. 130 C4
Limonlu Turkey 85 B1
Limonum France see Poitiers
Limousin reg. France 56 E4
Limoux France 56 F5
Limpopo prov. S. Africa 101 I2
Limpopo r. S. Africa/Zimbabwe 101 K3
Limpopo National Park nat. park 101 J2
Limu China 77 F3
Līnah well Saudi Arabia 91 F5
Linakhamari Rus. Fed. 44 Q2
Lin'an China see Jianshui
Linares Chile 144 B5
Linares Mex. 131 D7
Linares Spain 57 E4
Lincang China 76 D4
Lincheng Hainan China see Lingao
Lincheng Hunan China see Huitong
Linchuan China see Fuzhou
Linck Nunataks nunataks Antarctica 152 K1
Lincoln Arg. 144 D4
Lincoln U.K. 48 G5
Lincoln CA U.S.A. 128 C2
Lincoln IL U.S.A. 130 F3
Lincoln MI U.S.A. 134 D1
▶Lincoln NE U.S.A. 130 D3
Capital of Nebraska.
Lincoln City IN U.S.A. 134 B4
Lincoln City OR U.S.A. 126 B3
Lincoln Island Paracel Is 68 E3
Lincoln National Park Australia 111 A7
Lincoln Sea Canada/Greenland 153 J1
Lincolnshire Wolds hills U.K. 48 G5
Lincolnton U.S.A. 133 D5
Linda, Serra hills Brazil 145 C1
Linda Creek watercourse Australia 110 B4
Lindau Germany 53 M2
Lindau (Bodensee) Germany 47 L7
Lindeman Group is Australia 110 E4
Linden Canada 120 H5
Linden Germany 53 I4
Linden Guyana 143 G2
Linden AL U.S.A. 133 C5
Linden MI U.S.A. 134 D2
Linden TN U.S.A. 132 C5
Linden TX U.S.A. 131 E5
Linden Grove U.S.A. 130 E2
Lindern (Oldenburg) Germany 53 H2
Lindesnes c. Norway 45 E7
Líndhos Greece see Lindos
Lindi r. Dem. Rep. Congo 98 C3
Lindi Tanz. 99 D4
Lindian China 74 B3
Lindisfarne i. U.K. see Holy Island
Lindley S. Africa 101 H4
Lindos Greece 55 J4
Lindos, Akra pt Notio Aigaio Greece see Gkinas, Akrotirio
Lindsay Canada 135 F1
Lindsay CA U.S.A. 128 D3
Lindsay MT U.S.A. 126 G3
Lindsborg U.S.A. 130 D4
Lindside U.S.A. 134 E5
Lindum U.K. see Lincoln
Line Islands Kiribati 151 J5
Linesville U.S.A. 134 E3
Linfen China 73 K5
Lingampet India 84 C2
Linganamakki Reservoir India 84 B3
Lingao China 77 F5
Lingayen Phil. 69 G3
Lingbi China 77 H1
Lingcheng Anhui China see Lingbi
Lingcheng Guangxi China see Lingshan
Lingcheng Hainan China see Lingshui
Lingchuan Guangxi China 77 F3
Lingchuan Shanxi China 77 G1
Lingelethu S. Africa 101 H7
Lingen (Ems) Germany 53 H2
Lingga, Kepulauan is Indon. 68 D7
Lingle U.S.A. 126 G4
Lingomo Dem. Rep. Congo 98 C3
Lingshan China 77 F4
Lingshui China 77 F5
Lingshui Wan b. China 77 F5
Lingsugur India 84 C2
Lingtai China 76 E1
Linguère Senegal 96 B3
Lingui China 77 F3
Lingxi China see Yongshun
Lingxian China see Yanling
Lingxiang China 77 G2
Lingyang China see Cili
Lingyun China 76 E3
Lingzi Tang reg. Aksai Chin 82 D2
Linhai China 77 I2
Linhares Brazil 145 C2
Linhe China 73 J4
Linhpa Myanmar 70 A1
Linjiang China 74 B4
Linjin China 77 F1
Linköping Sweden 45 I7
Linkou China 74 C3
Linli China 77 F2
Linlithgow U.K. 50 F5
Linn MO U.S.A. 130 F4
Linn TX U.S.A. 131 D7
Linn, Mount U.S.A. 128 B1
Linnansaaren kansallispuisto nat. park Fin. 44 P5
Linnhe, Loch inlet U.K. 50 D4
Linnich Germany 52 G4
Linosa, Isola di i. Sicily Italy 58 E7
Linpo Myanmar 70 B2
Linquan China 77 G1
Linru China see Ruzhou
Linruzhen China 77 G1
Lins Brazil 145 A3
Linshu China 77 H1
Linshui China 76 E2
Lintan China 76 D1
Lintao China 76 D1
Linton IN U.S.A. 134 B4
Linton ND U.S.A. 130 C2
Linwu China 77 G3
Linxi China 73 L4
Linxia China 76 D1
Linxiang China 77 G2
Linyi Shandong China 73 L5
Linyi Shandong China 77 H1
Linying China 77 G1
Linz Austria 47 O6
Lion, Golfe du g. France 56 F5
Lions, Gulf of France see Lion, Golfe du
Lions Bay Canada 120 F5
Lioua Chad 97 E3
Lipari Sicily Italy 58 F5
Lipari, Isole is Italy 58 F5
Lipetsk Rus. Fed. 43 H5
Lipin Bor Rus. Fed. 42 H3
Liping China 77 F3
Lipova Romania 59 I1
Lipovtsy Rus. Fed. 74 C3
Lippe r. Germany 53 G3
Lippstadt Germany 53 I3
Lipsoí i. Greece see Leipsoi
Lipti Lekh pass Nepal 82 E3
Liptrap, Cape Australia 112 B7
Lipu China 77 F3
Lira Uganda 98 D3
Liranga Congo 98 B4
Lircay Peru 142 D6
Lisala Dem. Rep. Congo 98 C3
L'Isalo, Massif de mts Madag. 99 E6
L'Isalo, Parc National de nat. park Madag. 99 E6
Lisbellaw U.K. 51 E3
Lisboa Port. see Lisbon
▶Lisbon Port. 57 B4
Capital of Portugal.
Lisbon ME U.S.A. 135 J1
Lisbon NH U.S.A. 135 J1
Lisbon OH U.S.A. 134 E3
Lisburn U.K. 51 F3
Liscannor Bay Ireland 51 C5
Lisdoonvarna Ireland 51 C4
Lishan Taiwan 77 I3
Lishe Jiang r. China 76 D3
Lishi Jiangxi China see Dingnan
Lishi Shanxi China 73 K5
Lishu China 74 B4
Lishui China 77 H2
Li Shui r. China 77 F2
Lisichansk Ukr. see Lysychans'k
Lisieux France 56 E2
Liskeard U.K. 49 C8
Liski Rus. Fed. 43 H6
L'Isle-Adam France 52 C5
Lismore Australia 112 F2
Lismore Ireland 51 E5
Lisnarrick U.K. 51 E3
Lisnaskea U.K. 51 E3
Liss mt. Saudi Arabia 85 D4
Lissa Poland see Leszno
Lister, Mount Antarctica 152 H1
Listowel Canada 134 E2
Listowel Ireland 51 C5
Lit Sweden 44 I5
Litang Guangxi China 77 F4
Litang Sichuan China 76 D2
Līṭānī, Nahr el r. Lebanon 85 B3
Litchfield CA U.S.A. 128 C1
Litchfield CT U.S.A. 135 I3
Litchfield IL U.S.A. 130 F4
Litchfield MI U.S.A. 134 C2
Litchfield MN U.S.A. 130 E2
Lit-et-Mixe France 56 D4
Lithgow Australia 112 E4
Lithino, Akra pt Kriti Greece see Lithino, Akrotirio
Lithino, Akrotirio pt Greece 59 K7
Lithuania country Europe 45 M9
Lititz U.S.A. 135 G3
Litoměřice Czech Rep. 47 O5
Litovko Rus. Fed. 74 D2
Litovskaya S.S.R. country Europe see Lithuania
Little r. U.S.A. 131 E6
Little Abaco i. Bahamas 133 E7
Little Abitibi r. Canada 122 E4
Little Abitibi Lake Canada 122 E4
Little Andaman i. India 71 A5
Little Bahama Bank sea feature Bahamas 133 E7
Little Barrier i. N.Z. 113 E3
Little Belt sea chan. Denmark 45 F9
Little Belt Mountains U.S.A. 126 F3
Little Bitter Lake Egypt 85 A4
Little Cayman i. Cayman Is 137 H5
Little Churchill r. Canada 121 M3
Little Chute U.S.A. 134 A1
Little Coco Island Cocos Is 71 A4
Little Colorado r. U.S.A. 129 H3
Little Creek Peak U.S.A. 129 G3
Little Current Canada 122 E5
Little Current r. Canada 122 D4
Little Desert National Park Australia 111 C8
Little Egg Harbor inlet U.S.A. 135 H4
Little Exuma i. Bahamas 133 F8
Little Falls U.S.A. 130 E2
Littlefield AZ U.S.A. 129 G3
Littlefield TX U.S.A. 131 C5
Little Fork r. U.S.A. 130 E1
Little Grand Rapids Canada 121 M4
Littlehampton U.K. 49 G8
Little Inagua Island Bahamas 133 F8
Little Karas Berg plat. Namibia 100 D4
Little Karoo plat. S. Africa 100 E7
Little Lake U.S.A. 128 E4
Little Mecatina Island Canada see Petit Mécatina, Île du
Little Minch sea chan. U.K. 50 B3
Little Missouri r. U.S.A. 130 C2
Little Namaqualand reg. S. Africa see Namaqualand
Little Nicobar i. India 71 A6
Little Ouse r. U.K. 49 H6
Little Pamir mts Asia 89 I2
Little Rancheria r. Canada 120 D2
Little Red River Canada 120 H3
▶Little Rock U.S.A. 131 E5
Capital of Arkansas.
Littlerock U.S.A. 128 E4
Little Sable Point U.S.A. 134 B2
Little Salmon Lake Canada 120 C2
Little Salt Lake U.S.A. 129 G3
Little Sandy Desert Australia 109 B5
Little San Salvador i. Bahamas 133 F7
Little Smoky Canada 120 G4
Little Tibet reg. India/Pak. see Ladakh
Littleton U.S.A. 126 G5
Little Valley U.S.A. 135 F2
Little Wind r. U.S.A. 126 F4
Litunde Moz. 99 D5
Liu'an China see Lu'an
Liuba China 76 E1
Liucheng China 77 F3
Liuchiu Yü i. Taiwan 77 I4
Liuchong He r. China 76 E3
Liuchow China see Liuzhou
Liuhe China 74 B4
Liuheng Dao i. China 77 I2
Liujiachang China 77 F2
Liujiaxia Shuiku resr China 76 D1
Liukesong China 74 B3
Liulin China see Jonê
Liupan Shan mts China 76 E1
Liupanshui China see Lupanshui
Liuquan China 77 H1
Liuwa Plain National Park Zambia 99 C5

Liuyang China 77 G2
Liuzhan China 74 B2
Liuzhou China 77 F3
Livadeia Greece 59 J5
Līvāni Latvia 45 O8
Live Oak U.S.A. 133 D6
Liveringa Australia 106 C3
Livermore CA U.S.A. 128 C3
Livermore KY U.S.A. 134 B5
Livermore, Mount U.S.A. 131 B6
Livermore Falls U.S.A. 135 J1
Liverpool Australia 112 E4
Liverpool Canada 123 I5
Liverpool U.K. 48 E5
Liverpool Bay Canada 118 E3
Liverpool Plains Australia 112 E3
Liverpool Range mts Australia 112 D3
Livia U.S.A. 134 B5
Livingston U.K. 50 F5
Livingston AL U.S.A. 131 F5
Livingston KY U.S.A. 134 C5
Livingston MT U.S.A. 126 F3
Livingston TN U.S.A. 134 C5
Livingston TX U.S.A. 131 E6
Livingston, Lake U.S.A. 131 E6
Livingstone Zambia 99 C5
Livingston Island Antarctica 152 L2
Livingston Manor U.S.A. 135 H3
Livno Bos.-Herz. 58 G3
Livny Rus. Fed. 43 H5
Livojoki r. Fin. 44 O4
Livonia MI U.S.A. 134 D2
Livonia NY U.S.A. 135 G2
Livorno Italy 58 D3
Livramento do Brumado Brazil 145 C1
Liwā Oman 88 E5
Liwā', Wādī al watercourse Syria 85 C3
Liwale Tanz. 99 D4
Lixian Gansu China 76 E1
Lixian Sichuan China 76 D2
Lixus Morocco see Larache
Liyang China see Hexian
Liyuan China see Sangzhi
Lizard U.K. 49 B9
Lizarda Brazil 143 I5
Lizard Point U.K. 49 B9
Lizarra Spain see Estella
Lizemores U.S.A. 134 E4
Liziping China 76 D2
Lizy-sur-Ourcq France 52 D5
Ljouwert Neth. see Leeuwarden

▶Ljubljana Slovenia 58 F1
Capital of Slovenia.

Ljugarn Sweden 45 K8
Ljungan r. Sweden 44 J5
Ljungaverk Sweden 44 J5
Ljungby Sweden 45 H8
Ljusdal Sweden 45 J6
Ljusnan r. Sweden 45 J6
Ljusne Sweden 45 J6
Llaima, Volcán vol. Chile 144 B5
Llanandras U.K. see Presteigne
Llanbadarn Fawr U.K. 49 C6
Llanbedr Pont Steffan U.K. see Lampeter
Llanbister U.K. 49 D6
Llandeilo U.K. 49 D7
Llandissilio U.K. 49 C7
Llandovery U.K. 49 D7
Llandrindod Wells U.K. 49 D6
Llandudno U.K. 48 D5
Llandysul U.K. 49 C6
Llanegwad U.K. 49 C7
Llanelli U.K. 49 C7
Llanfair Caereinion U.K. 49 D6
Llanfair-ym-Muallt U.K. see Builth Wells
Llangefni U.K. 48 C5
Llangollen U.K. 49 D6
Llangurig U.K. 49 D6
Llanllyfni U.K. 49 C5
Llannerch-y-medd U.K. 48 C5
Llannor U.K. 49 C6
Llano Mex. 127 F7
Llano U.S.A. 131 D6
Llano r. U.S.A. 131 D6
Llano Estacado plain U.S.A. 131 C5
Llanos plain Col./Venez. 142 E2
Llanquihue, Lago l. Chile 144 B6
Llanrhystud U.K. 49 C6
Llantrisant U.K. 49 D7
Llanuwchllyn U.K. 49 D6
Llanwnog U.K. 49 D6
Llanymddyfri U.K. see Llandovery
Llay U.K. 49 D5
Lleida Spain 57 G3
Llerena Spain 57 C4
Llíria Spain 57 F4
Llodio Spain 57 E2
Lloyd George, Mount Canada 120 E3
Lloyd Lake Canada 121 I3
Lloydminster Canada 121 I4
Llucmayor Spain see Llucmajor
Llucmajor Spain 57 H4

▶Llullaillaco, Volcán vol. Chile 144 C2
Highest active volcano in the world and South America.

Lô, Sông r. China/Vietnam 70 D2
Loa r. Chile 144 B2
Loa U.S.A. 129 H2
Loban' r. Rus. Fed. 42 K4
Lobatejo mt. Spain 57 D5
Lobatse Botswana 101 G3
Lobaye r. Cent. Afr. Rep. 98 B3
Löbejün Germany 53 L3
Löbenberg hill Germany 53 M3
Loberia Arg. 144 E5
Lobito Angola 99 B5
Lobos Arg. 144 E5
Lobos, Cabo c. Mex. 127 E7
Lobos, Isla i. Mex. 127 F8
Lobos de Tierra, Isla i. Peru 142 B5
Loburg Germany 53 M2
Lôc Binh Vietnam 70 D2
Lochaline U.K. 50 D4
Lo Chau H.K. China see Beaufort Island
Loch Baghasdail U.K. see Lochboisdale
Lochboisdale U.K. 50 B3
Lochcarron U.K. 50 D3
Lochearnhead U.K. 50 E4
Lochem Neth. 52 G2
Lochern National Park Australia 110 C5
Loches France 56 E3
Loch Garman Ireland see Wexford
Lochgelly U.K. 50 F4
Lochgilphead U.K. 50 D4
Lochinver U.K. 50 D2
Loch Lomond and Trossachs National Park U.K. 50 E4
Lochmaddy U.K. 50 B3
Lochnagar mt. U.K. 50 F4
Loch nam Madadh U.K. see Lochmaddy
Loch Raven Reservoir U.S.A. 135 G4
Lochy, Loch l. U.K. 50 E4
Lock Australia 111 A7
Lockerbie U.K. 50 F5
Lockhart Australia 112 C5
Lockhart U.S.A. 131 D6
Lock Haven U.S.A. 135 G3
Löcknitz r. Germany 53 L1
Lockport U.S.A. 135 F2
Lôc Ninh Vietnam 71 D5
Lod Israel 85 B4
Loddon r. Australia 112 A5
Lodève France 56 F5
Lodeynoye Pole Rus. Fed. 42 G3
Lodge, Mount Canada/U.S.A. 120 B3
Lodhikheda India 82 D5
Lodhran Pak. 89 H4
Lodi Italy 58 C2
Lodi CA U.S.A. 128 C2
Lodi OH U.S.A. 134 D3
Lødingen Norway 44 I2
Lodja Dem. Rep. Congo 98 C4
Lodomeria Rus. Fed. see Vladimir
Lodrani India 82 B5
Lodwar Kenya 98 D3
Łódź Poland 47 Q5
Loei Thai. 70 C3
Loeriesfontein S. Africa 100 D6
Lofoten is Norway 44 H2
Lofusa Sudan 97 G4
Log Rus. Fed. 43 I6
Loga Niger 96 D3
Logan IA U.S.A. 130 E3
Logan OH U.S.A. 134 D4
Logan UT U.S.A. 126 F4
Logan WV U.S.A. 134 E5

▶Logan, Mount Canada 120 A2
2nd highest mountain in North America.

Logan, Mount U.S.A. 126 C2
Logan Creek r. Australia 110 D4
Logan Lake Canada 120 F5
Logan Mountains Canada 120 D2
Logansport IN U.S.A. 134 B3
Logansport LA U.S.A. 131 E6
Logatec Slovenia 58 F2
Logpung China 76 D1
Logroño Spain 57 E2
Logtak Lake India 83 H4
Lohardaga India 83 F5
Loharu India 82 C3
Lohatlha S. Africa 100 F5
Lohawat India 82 C4
Lohfelden Germany 53 J3
Lohil r. China/India see Zayü Qu
Lohiniva Fin. 44 N3
Lohjanjärvi l. Fin. 45 M6
Löhne Germany 53 I2
Lohne (Oldenburg) Germany 53 I2
Lohtaja Fin. 44 M4
Loi, Nam r. Myanmar 70 C2
Loikaw Myanmar 70 B3
Loi Lan mt. Myanmar/Thai. 70 B3
Loi-lem Myanmar 70 B2
Loi Lun Myanmar 70 B2
Loimaa Fin. 45 M6
Loipyet Hills Myanmar 70 B1
Loire r. France 56 C3
Loi Sang mt. Myanmar 70 B2
L'Oise à l'Aisne, Canal de France 52 D5
Loi Song mt. Myanmar 70 B2
Loja Ecuador 142 C4
Loja Spain 57 D5
Lokan tekojärvi l. Fin. 44 O3
Lokchim r. Rus. Fed. 42 K3
Lokeren Belgium 52 E3
Lokgwabe Botswana 100 E3
Lokichar Kenya 78 C6
Lokichokio Kenya 98 D3
Lokilalaki, Gunung mt. Indon. 69 G7
Løkken Denmark 45 F8
Løkken Norway 44 F5
Loknya Rus. Fed. 42 F4
Lokoja Nigeria 96 D4
Lokolama Dem. Rep. Congo 98 B4
Lokossa Benin 96 D4
Lokot' Rus. Fed. 43 G5
Lol Sudan 97 F4
Lola Guinea 96 C4
Lola, Mount U.S.A. 128 C2
Loleta U.S.A. 128 A1
Lolland i. Denmark 45 G9
Lollondo Tanz. 98 D4
Lolo U.S.A. 126 E3
Loloda Indon. 69 H6
Lolo Pass U.S.A. 126 E3
Lolowau Indon. 71 B7
Lolwane S. Africa 100 F4
Lom Bulg. 59 J3
Lom Norway 45 F6
Loma U.S.A. 129 I2
Lomami r. Dem. Rep. Congo 98 C3
Lomar Pass Afgh. 89 G3
Lomas, Bahía de b. Chile 144 C8
Lomas de Zamora Arg. 144 E4
Lombarda, Serra hills Brazil 143 H3
Lomblen i. Indon. 108 C2
Lombok Indon. 108 B2
Lombok i. Indon. 108 B2
Lombok, Selat sea chan. Indon. 108 A2

▶Lomé Togo 96 D4
Capital of Togo.

Lomela Dem. Rep. Congo 98 C4
Lomela r. Dem. Rep. Congo 97 F5
Lomira U.S.A. 134 A2
Lomme France 52 C4
Lommel Belgium 52 F3
Lomond Canada 123 K4
Lomond, Loch l. U.K. 50 E4
Lomonosov Rus. Fed. 45 P7
Lomonosov Ridge sea feature Arctic Ocean 153 B1
Lomovoye Rus. Fed. 42 I2
Lomphat Cambodia see Lumphăt
Lompoc U.S.A. 128 C4
Lom Sak Thai. 70 C3
Łomża Poland 47 S4
Lơn, Hon i. Vietnam 71 E4
Lonar India 84 C2
Londa Bangl. 83 G5
Londa India 84 B3
Londinières France 52 B5
Londinium U.K. see London
Londoko Rus. Fed. 74 D2
London Canada 134 E2

▶London U.K. 49 G7
Capital of the United Kingdom and of England. 4th most populous city in Europe.

London KY U.S.A. 134 C5
London OH U.S.A. 134 D4
Londonderry U.K. 51 E3
Londonderry OH U.S.A. 134 D4
Londonderry VT U.S.A. 135 I2
Londonderry, Cape Australia 108 D3
Londrina Brazil 145 A3
Lone Pine U.S.A. 128 D3
Long Thai. 70 B3
Longa Angola 99 B5
Longa, Proliv sea chan. Rus. Fed. 65 S2
Long'an China 76 E4
Long Ashton U.K. 49 E7
Long Bay U.S.A. 133 E5
Longbeach N.Z. 113 C7
Long Beach U.S.A. 128 D5
Longbo China see Shuangpai
Long Branch U.S.A. 135 I3
Longchang China 76 E2
Longcheng Anhui China see Xiaoxian
Longcheng Guangdong China see Longmen
Longcheng Yunnan China see Chenggong
Longchuan China see Nanhua
Longchuan Jiang r. China 76 C4
Long Creek r. Canada 121 K5
Long Creek U.S.A. 126 D3
Long Eaton U.K. 49 F6
Longford Ireland 51 E4
Longgang Chongqing China see Dazu
Longgang Guangdong China 77 G4
Longhoughton U.K. 48 F3
Longhui China 77 F3
Longhurst, Mount Antarctica 152 H1
Long Island Bahamas 133 F8
Long Island N.S. Canada 123 I5
Long Island Nunavut Canada 122 F3
Long Island India 71 A4
Long Island P.N.G. 69 L8
Long Island U.S.A. 135 I3
Long Island Sound sea chan. U.S.A. 135 I3
Longjiang China 74 A3
Longjin China see Qingliu
Longju China 76 B2
Longlac Canada 122 D4
Long Lake l. Canada 122 D4
Long Lake U.S.A. 135 H2
Long Lake l. ME U.S.A. 132 G2
Long Lake l. MI U.S.A. 134 D1
Long Lake l. ND U.S.A. 130 C2
Long Lake l. NY U.S.A. 135 H1
Longli China 76 E3
Longlin China 76 E3
Longling China 76 C3
Longmeadow U.S.A. 135 I2
Long Melford U.K. 49 H6
Longmen Guangdong China 77 G4
Longmen Heilong. China 74 B2
Longmen Shan hill China 77 F1
Longmen Shan mts China 76 E1
Longming China 76 E4
Longmont U.S.A. 126 G4
Longnan China 76 E1
Longnan China 77 G3
Long Phu Vietnam 71 D5
Longping China see Luodian
Long Point Ont. Canada 134 E2
Long Point Man. Canada 121 L4
Long Point Ont. Canada 134 E2
Long Point N.Z. 113 B8
Long Point Bay Canada 134 E2
Long Prairie U.S.A. 130 E2
Long Preston U.K. 48 E4
Longquan Guizhou China see Danzhai
Longquan Guizhou China see Fenggang
Longquan Hunan China see Xintian
Longquan Xi r. China 77 I2
Long Range Mountains Nfld. and Lab. Canada 123 K4
Long Range Mountains Nfld. and Lab. Canada 123 K5
Longreach Australia 110 D4
Longriba China 76 D1
Longshan Guizhou China see Longli
Longshan Hunan China 77 F2
Longshan Yunnan China see Longling
Long Shan mts China 76 E1
Longsheng China 77 F3
Longs Peak U.S.A. 126 G4
Long Stratton U.K. 49 I6
Longtom Lake Canada 120 G1
Longtown U.K. 48 E3
Longue-Pointe-de-Mingan Canada 123 I4
Longueuil Canada 122 G5
Longuyon France 52 F5
Longvale U.S.A. 128 B2
Longview TX U.S.A. 131 E5
Longview WA U.S.A. 126 C3
Longwangmiao China 74 D3
Longwei Co l. China 83 G2
Longxi China 76 E1
Longxian Guangdong China see Wengyuan
Longxian Shaanxi China 76 E1
Longxingchang China see Wuyuan
Longxi Shan mt. China 77 H3
Longxu China see Cangwu
Long Xuyên Vietnam 71 D5
Longyan China 77 H3

▶Longyearbyen Svalbard 64 C2
Capital of Svalbard.

Longzhen China 74 B2
Longzhou China 76 E4
Longzhouping China see Changyang
Löningen Germany 53 H2
Lonoke U.S.A. 131 F5
Lönsboda Sweden 45 I8
Lons-le-Saunier France 56 G3
Lonton Myanmar 70 B1
Looc Phil. 69 G4
Loochoo Islands Japan see Ryukyu Islands
Loogootee U.S.A. 134 B4
Lookout, Cape Canada 122 E3
Lookout, Cape U.S.A. 133 E5
Lookout, Point Australia 112 F1
Lookout, Point U.S.A. 134 D1
Lookout Mountain U.S.A. 129 I4
Lookout Point Australia 109 B8
Loolmalasin vol. crater Tanz. 98 D4
Loon Canada 122 C4
Loon r. Canada 120 H3
Loongana Australia 109 D7
Loon Lake Canada 121 I4
Loop Head hd Ireland 51 C5
Lop China 82 E1
Lopasnya Rus. Fed. see Chekhov
Lopatina, Gora mt. Rus. Fed. 74 F2
Lop Buri Thai. 70 C4
Lopez Phil. 69 G4
Lopez, Cap c. Gabon 98 A4
Lop Nur salt flat China 80 H3
Lopphavet b. Norway 44 L1
Loptyuga Rus. Fed. 42 K3
Lora Pak. 89 G5
Lora r. Venez. 142 D2
Lora del Río Spain 57 D5
Lorain U.S.A. 134 D3
Loralai Pak. 89 H4
Loralai r. Pak. 89 H4
Loramie, Lake U.S.A. 134 C3
Lorca Spain 57 F5
Lorch Germany 53 H4
Lordegān Iran 88 C4
Lord Howe Atoll Solomon Is see Ontong Java Atoll
Lord Howe Island Australia 107 F5
Lord Howe Rise sea feature S. Pacific Ocean 150 G7
Lord Loughborough Island Myanmar 71 B5
Lordsburg U.S.A. 129 I5
Lore East Timor 108 D2
Lore Lindu, Taman Nasional Indon. 68 G7
Lorena Brazil 145 B3
Lorengau P.N.G. 69 L7
Lorentz, Taman Nasional Indon. 69 J7
Loreto Brazil 143 I5
Loreto Mex. 127 F8
Lorient France 56 C3
Lorillard r. Canada 121 N1
Loring U.S.A. 126 G2
Lorn, Firth of est. U.K. 50 D4
Lorne Australia 110 D5
Lorne watercourse Australia 110 B3
Lorrain, Plateau France 53 G6
Lorraine Australia 110 B3
Lorraine admin. reg. France 52 G6
Lorraine reg. France 52 F5
Lorsch Germany 53 I5
Lorup Germany 53 H2
Losal India 82 C4
Los Alamos CA U.S.A. 128 C4
Los Alamos NM U.S.A. 127 G6
Los Alerces, Parque Nacional nat. park Arg. 144 B6
Los Ángeles Chile 144 B5

▶Los Angeles U.S.A. 128 D4
3rd most populous city in North America.

Los Angeles Aqueduct canal U.S.A. 128 D4
Los Arabos Cuba 133 D8
Los Banos U.S.A. 128 C3
Los Blancos Arg. 144 D2
Los Canarreos, Archipiélago de is Cuba 137 H4
Los Cerritos watercourse Mex. 127 F8
Los Chonos, Archipiélago de is Chile 144 A6
Los Coronados, Islas is Mex. 128 E5
Los Desventurados, Islas de is S. Pacific Ocean 151 O7
Los Estados, Isla de i. Arg. 144 D8
Los Gigantes, Llanos de plain Mex. 131 B6
Los Glaciares, Parque Nacional nat. park Arg. 144 B8
Losheim Germany 52 G5
Los Hoyos Mex. 127 F7
Lošinj i. Croatia 58 F2
Los Jardines de la Reina, Archipiélago de is Cuba 137 I4
Los Juríes Arg. 144 D3
Los Katios, Parque Nacional nat. park Col. 137 I7
Loskop Dam S. Africa 101 I3
Los Lunas U.S.A. 127 G6
Los Menucos Arg. 144 C6
Los Mochis Mex. 127 F8
Los Molinos U.S.A. 128 B1
Losombo Dem. Rep. Congo 98 B3
Los Palacios Cuba 133 D8
Los Picos de Europa, Parque Nacional de nat. park Spain 57 D2
Los Remedios r. Mex. 131 B7
Los Roques, Islas is Venez. 142 E1
Losser Neth. 52 G2
Lossie r. U.K. 50 F3
Lossiemouth U.K. 50 F3
Lößnitz Germany 53 M4
Lost Creek KY U.S.A. 134 D5
Lost Creek WV U.S.A. 134 E4
Los Teques Venez. 142 E1
Los Testigos is Venez. 142 F1
Lost Hills U.S.A. 128 D4
Lost Trail Pass U.S.A. 126 E3
Lostwithiel U.K. 49 C8
Los Vidrios Mex. 129 G6
Los Vilos Chile 144 B4
Lot r. France 56 E4
Lota Chile 144 B5
Loṭfābād Turkm. 88 E2
Lothringen reg. France see Lorraine
Lotikipi Plain Kenya/Sudan 98 D3
Loto Dem. Rep. Congo 98 C4
Lotsane r. Botswana 101 I2
Lot's Wife i. Japan see Sōfu-gan
Lotta r. Fin./Rus. Fed. 44 Q2
also known as Lutto
Lotte Germany 53 H2
Louangnamtha Laos 70 C2
Louangphabang Laos 70 C3
Loubomo Congo 99 B4
Loudéac France 56 C2
Loudi China 77 F3
L'Ouest, Pointe de pt Canada 123 I4
Louga Senegal 96 B3
Loughborough U.K. 49 F6
Lougheed Island Canada 119 H2
Loughor r. U.K. 49 C7
Loughrea Ireland 51 D4
Loughton U.K. 49 H7
Louhans France 56 G3
Louisa KY U.S.A. 134 D4
Louisa VA U.S.A. 135 G4
Louisbourg Canada 123 K5
Louisburg Canada see Louisbourg
Louisburgh Ireland 51 C4
Louise Falls Canada 120 G2
Louis-Gentil Morocco see Youssoufia
Louisiade Archipelago is P.N.G. 110 F1
Louisiana U.S.A. 130 F4
Louisiana state U.S.A. 131 F6
Louis Trichardt S. Africa see Makhado
Louisville GA U.S.A. 133 D5
Louisville IL U.S.A. 130 F4
Louisville KY U.S.A. 134 C4
Louisville MS U.S.A. 131 F5
Louisville Ridge sea feature S. Pacific Ocean 150 I8
Louis-XIV, Pointe pt Canada 122 F3
Loukhi Rus. Fed. 44 R3
Loukoléla Congo 98 B4
Loukouo Congo 97 E5
Loulé Port. 57 B5
Loum Cameroon 96 D4
Louny Czech Rep. 47 N5
Loup r. U.S.A. 130 D3
Loups Marins, Lacs des lakes Canada 122 G2
Loups Marins, Petit lac des l. Canada 123 G2
Lourdes Canada 123 K4
Lourdes France 56 D5
Lourenço Marques Moz. see Maputo
Lousã Port. 57 B3
Loushan China 74 C3
Loushanguan China see Tongzi
Louth Australia 112 B3
Louth U.K. 48 G5
Loutra Aidipsou Greece 59 J5
Louvain Belgium see Leuven
Louviers France 52 B5
Louwater-Suid Namibia 100 C2
Louwsburg S. Africa 101 J4
Lövånger Sweden 44 L4
Lovat' r. Rus. Fed. 42 F4
Lovech Bulg. 59 K3
Lovell U.S.A. 135 J1
Lovelock U.S.A. 128 D1
Lovendegem Belgium 52 D3
Lovers' Leap mt. U.S.A. 134 E5
Loviisa Fin. 45 O6
Lovington U.S.A. 131 C5
Lovozero Rus. Fed. 42 G1
Lóvua Angola 99 C4
Lóvua Angola 99 C5
Low, Cape Canada 119 J3
Lowa Dem. Rep. Congo 98 C4
Lowa r. Dem. Rep. Congo 98 C4
Lowarai Pass Pak. 89 H3
Lowell IN U.S.A. 134 B3
Lowell MA U.S.A. 135 J2
Lower Arrow Lake Canada 120 G5
Lower California pen. Mex. see Baja California
Lower Glenelg National Park Australia 111 C8
Lower Granite Gorge U.S.A. 129 G4
Lower Hutt N.Z. 113 E5
Lower Laberge Canada 120 C2
Lower Lake U.S.A. 128 B2
Lower Lough Erne l. U.K. 51 E3
Lower Post Canada 120 D3
Lower Red Lake U.S.A. 130 E2
Lower Saxony land Germany see Niedersachsen
Lower Tunguska r. Rus. Fed. see Nizhnyaya Tunguska
Lower Zambezi National Park Zambia 99 C5
Lowestoft U.K. 49 I6
Łowicz Poland 47 Q4
Low Island Kiribati see Starbuck Island
Lowkhi Afgh. 89 F4
Lowther Hills U.K. 50 F5
Lowville U.S.A. 135 H2
Loxstedt Germany 53 I1
Loxton Australia 111 C7
Loyal, Loch l. U.K. 50 E2
Loyalsock Creek r. U.S.A. 135 G3
Loyalton U.S.A. 128 C2
Loyalty Islands New Caledonia see Loyauté, Îles
Loyang China see Luoyang
Loyauté, Îles is New Caledonia 107 G4
Loyev Belarus see Loyew
Loyew Belarus 43 F6
Lozère, Mont mt. France 56 F4
Loznica Serbia 59 H2
Lozova Ukr. 43 H6
Lozovaya Ukr. see Lozova
Lua r. Dem. Rep. Congo 98 B3
Luacano Angola 99 C5
Lu'an China 77 H2
Luân Châu Vietnam 70 C2
Luanchuan China 77 F1

▶Luanda Angola 99 B4
Capital of Angola.

Luang, Khao mt. Thai. 71 B5
Luang, Thale lag. Thai. 71 C6
Luang Namtha Laos see Louangnamtha
Luang Phrabang, Thiu Khao mts Laos/Thai. 70 C3
Luang Prabang Laos see Louangphabang
Luanhaizi China 76 B1
Luanshya Zambia 99 C5
Luanza Dem. Rep. Congo 99 C4
Luao Angola see Luau
Luarca Spain 57 C2
Luashi Dem. Rep. Congo 99 C5
Luau Angola 99 C5
Luba Equat. Guinea 96 D4
Lubaczów Poland 43 D6
Lubalo Angola 99 B4
Lubānas ezers l. Latvia 45 O8
Lubang Islands Phil. 68 F4
Lubango Angola 99 B5
Lubao Dem. Rep. Congo 99 C4
Lubartów Poland 43 D6
Lübbecke Germany 53 I2
Lubbeskolk salt pan S. Africa 100 D5
Lubbock U.S.A. 131 C5
Lübbow Germany 53 L2
Lübeck Germany 47 M4
Lubeck U.S.A. 134 E4
Lubefu Dem. Rep. Congo 99 C4
Lubei China 73 M4
Lüben Poland see Lubin
Lubersac France 56 E4
Lubin Poland 47 P5
Lublin Poland 43 D6
Lubnān country Asia see Lebanon
Lubnān, Jabal mts Lebanon see Liban, Jebel
Lubny Ukr. 43 G6
Lubok Antu Sarawak Malaysia 68 E6
Lübtheen Germany 53 L1
Lubudi Dem. Rep. Congo 99 C4
Lubuklinggau Indon. 68 C7
Lubukpakam Indon. 71 B7
Lubuksikaping Indon. 68 C6
Lubumbashi Dem. Rep. Congo 99 C5
Lubutu Dem. Rep. Congo 98 C4
Lübz Germany 53 M1
Lucala Angola 99 B4
Lucan Canada 134 E2
Lucan Ireland 51 F4
Lucania, Mount Canada 120 A2
Lucapa Angola 99 C4
Lucas U.S.A. 134 B5
Lucasville U.S.A. 134 D4
Lucca Italy 58 D3
Luce Bay U.K. 50 E6
Lucedale U.S.A. 131 F6
Lucélia Brazil 145 A3
Lucena Phil. 69 G4
Lucena Spain 57 D5
Lučenec Slovakia 47 Q6
Lucera Italy 58 F4
Lucerne Switz. 56 I3
Lucerne Valley U.S.A. 128 E4
Lucero Mex. 127 G7
Luchegorsk Rus. Fed. 74 D3
Lucheng Guangxi China see Luchuan
Lucheng Sichuan China see Kangding
Luchuan China 77 F4
Lüchun China 76 D4
Lucipara, Kepulauan is Indon. 69 H8
Łuck Ukr. see Luts'k
Luckeesarai India see Lakhisarai
Luckenwalde Germany 53 N2
Luckhoff S. Africa 100 G5
Lucknow Canada 134 E2
Lucknow India 82 E4
Lücongpo China 77 F2
Lucrecia, Cabo c. Cuba 137 I4
Lucusse Angola 99 C5
Lucy Creek Australia 110 B4
Lüda China see Dalian
Lüdenscheid Germany 53 H3
Lüderitz Namibia 100 B4
Ludewa Tanz. 99 D5
Ludhiana India 82 C3
Ludian China 76 D3
Luding China 76 D2
Ludington U.S.A. 134 B2
Ludlow U.K. 49 E6
Ludlow U.S.A. 128 E4
Ludogorie reg. Bulg. 59 L3
Ludowici U.S.A. 133 D6
Ludvika Sweden 45 I6
Ludwigsburg Germany 53 J6
Ludwigsfelde Germany 53 N2
Ludwigshafen am Rhein Germany 53 I5
Ludwigslust Germany 53 L1
Ludza Latvia 45 O8
Luebo Dem. Rep. Congo 99 C4
Luena Angola 99 B5
Luena Flats plain Zambia 99 C5
Lüeyang China 76 E1
Lufeng Guangdong China 77 G4
Lufeng Yunnan China 76 D3
Lufkin U.S.A. 131 E6
Lufu China see Shilin
Luga Rus. Fed. 45 P7
Luga r. Rus. Fed. 45 P7
Lugano Switz. 56 I3
Lugansk Ukr. see Luhans'k
Lugau Germany 53 M4
Lügde Germany 53 J3
Lugdunum France see Lyon
Lugg r. U.K. 49 E6
Luggudontsen mt. China 83 G3
Lugnaquilla hill Ireland 51 F5
Lugo Italy 58 D2
Lugo Spain 57 C2
Lugoj Romania 59 I2
Luhans'k Ukr. 43 H6
Luhe China 77 H1
Luhe r. Germany 53 K1
Luḥfī, Wādī watercourse Jordan 85 C3
Luhit r. China/India see Zayü Qu
Luhit r. India 83 H4
Luhua China see Heishui
Luhuo China 76 D2

Luhyny Ukr. 43 F6
Luia Angola 99 C4
Luiana Angola 99 C5
Luichow Peninsula China see Leizhou Bandao
Luik Belgium see Liège
Luimneach Ireland see Limerick
Luiro r. Fin. 44 O3
Luis Echeverría Álvarez Mex. 128 E5
Luitpold Coast Antarctica 152 A1
Luiza Dem. Rep. Congo 99 C4
Lujiang China 77 H2
Lüjing China 76 E1
Lukachek Rus. Fed. 74 D1
Lukapa Angola see Lucapa
Lukavac Bos.-Herz. 58 H2
Lukenga, Lac l. Dem. Rep. Congo 99 C4
Lukenie r. Dem. Rep. Congo 98 B4
Lukh r. Rus. Fed. 42 I4
Lukhovitsy Rus. Fed. 43 H5
Luk Keng H.K. China 77 [inset]
Lukou China see Zhuzhou
Lukovit Bulg. 59 K3
Łuków Poland 43 D6
Lukoyanov Rus. Fed. 43 J5
Lukusuzi National Park Zambia 99 D5
Luleå Sweden 44 M4
Luleälven r. Sweden 44 M4
Lüleburgaz Turkey 59 L4
Luliang China 76 D3
Lüliang Shan mts China 73 K5
Lulimba Dem. Rep. Congo 99 C4
Luling U.S.A. 131 D6
Lulonga r. Dem. Rep. Congo 98 B3
Luluabourg Dem. Rep. Congo see Kananga
Lülung China 83 F3
Lumachomo China 83 F3
Lumajang Indon. 68 E8
Lumajangdong Co salt l. China 82 E2
Lumbala Moxico Angola see Lumbala Kaquengue
Lumbala Moxico Angola see Lumbala N'guimbo
Lumbala Kaquengue Angola 99 C5
Lumbala N'guimbo Angola 99 C5
Lumberton U.S.A. 133 E5
Lumbini Nepal 83 E4
Lumbis Indon. 68 F6
Lumbrales Spain 57 C3
Lumezzane Italy 58 D2
Lumi P.N.G. 69 K7
Lumphăt Cambodia 71 D4
Lumpkin U.S.A. 133 C5
Lumsden Canada 121 J5
Lumsden N.Z. 113 B7
Lumut Malaysia 71 C6
Lumut, Tanjung pt Indon. 68 D7
Luna U.S.A. 129 I5
Lunan China see Shilin
Lunan Bay U.K. 50 G4
Lunan Lake Canada 121 M1
Lunan Shan mts China 76 D3
Luna Pier U.S.A. 134 D3
Lund Pak. 89 H5
Lund Sweden 45 H9
Lund NV U.S.A. 129 F2
Lund UT U.S.A. 129 G2
Lundar Canada 121 L5
Lundy U.K. 49 C7
Lune r. Germany 53 I1
Lune r. U.K. 48 E4
Lüneburg Germany 53 K1
Lüneburger Heide reg. Germany 53 K1
Lünen Germany 53 H3
Lunenburg U.S.A. 135 F5
Lunéville France 56 H2
Lunga r. Zambia 99 C5
Lungdo China 83 E2
Lunggar China 83 E3
Lung Kwu Chau i. H.K. China 77 [inset]
Lungleh India see Lunglei
Lunglei India 83 H5
Lungmari mt. China 83 F3
Lungmu Co salt l. China 82 E2
Lung-tzu Xizang China see Xingba
Lung-tzu Xizang China see Xingba
Lungwebungu r. Zambia 99 C5
Lunh Nepal 83 E3
Luni India 82 C4
Luni r. India 82 B4
Luni r. Pak. 89 H4
Luninets Belarus see Luninyets
Luning U.S.A. 128 D2
Luninyets Belarus 45 O10
Lunkaransar India 82 C3
Lunkha India 82 C3
Lünne Germany 53 H2
Lunsar Sierra Leone 96 B4
Lunsklip S. Africa 101 I3
Luntai China 80 F3
Luobei China 74 C3
Luobuzhuang China 80 G4
Luocheng Fujian China see Hui'an
Luocheng Guangxi China 77 F3
Luodian China 76 E3
Luoding China 77 F4
Luodou Sha i. China 77 F4
Luohe China 77 G1
Luo He r. China 77 G1
Luonan China 77 F1
Luoning China 77 F1
Luoping China 76 E3
Luotian China 77 G2
Luoto Fin. see Larsmo
Luoxiao Shan mts China 77 G3
Luoxiong China see Luoping
Luoyang Guangdong China see Boluo
Luoyang Henan China 77 G1
Luoyang Zhejiang China see Taishun
Luoyuan China 77 H3
Luozigou China 74 C4
Lupane Zimbabwe 99 C5
Lupanshui China 76 E3
L'Upemba, Parc National de nat. park Dem. Rep. Congo 99 C4
Lupeni Romania 59 J2
Lupilichi Moz. 99 D5
Lupton U.S.A. 129 I4
Luqiao China see Luding
Luqu China 76 D1
Lu Qu r. China see Tao He
Luquan China 70 C1
Luray U.S.A. 135 F4
Luremo Angola 99 B4
Lurgan U.K. 51 F3
Luring China see Oma
Lúrio Moz. 99 E5
Lurio r. Moz. 99 E5

▶Lusaka Zambia 99 C5
Capital of Zambia.

Lusambo Dem. Rep. Congo 99 C4
Lusancay Islands and Reefs P.N.G. 106 F2
Lusangi Dem. Rep. Congo 99 C4
Luseland Canada 121 I4
Lush, Mount hill Australia 108 D4
Lushi China 77 F1
Lushnja Albania see Lushnjë
Lushnjë Albania 59 H4
Lushui China see Luzhang
Lushuihe China 74 B4
Lüsi China 77 I1
Lusikisiki S. Africa 101 I6
Lusk U.S.A. 126 G4
Luso Angola see Luena
Lussvale Australia 112 C1
Lut, Bahrat salt l. Asia see Dead Sea
Lut, Dasht-e des. Iran 88 E4
Lü Tao i. Taiwan 77 I4
Lutetia France see Paris
Lüt-e Zangī Aḥmad des. Iran 88 E4
Luther U.S.A. 134 C1
Luther Lake Canada 134 E2
Lutherstadt Wittenberg Germany 53 M3
Luton U.K. 49 G7
Łutselk'e Canada 121 I2
Luts'k Ukr. 43 E6
Luttelgeest Neth. 52 F2
Luttenberg Neth. 52 G2
Lutto r. Fin./Rus. Fed. see Lotta
Lutz U.S.A. 133 D6
Lützelbach Germany 53 J5
Lützow-Holm Bay Antarctica 152 D2
Lutzputs S. Africa 100 E5
Lutzville S. Africa 100 D6
Luumäki Fin. 45 O6
Luuq Somalia 98 E3
Luverne AL U.S.A. 133 C6
Luverne MN U.S.A. 130 D3
Luvuei Angola 99 C5
Luvuvhu r. S. Africa 101 J2
Luwero Uganda 98 D3
Luwingu Zambia 99 C5
Luwuk Indon. 69 G7
Luxembourg country Europe 52 G5

▶Luxembourg Lux. 52 G5
Capital of Luxembourg.

Luxembourg country Europe see Luxembourg
Luxeuil-les-Bains France 56 H3
Luxi Hunan China see Wuxi
Luxi Yunnan China 76 C3
Luxi Yunnan China 76 D3
Luxolweni S. Africa 101 G6
Luxor Egypt 86 D4
Luyi China 77 G1
Luyksgestel Neth. 52 F3
Luza Rus. Fed. 42 J3
Luza r. Rus. Fed. 42 J3
Luza r. Rus. Fed. 42 M2
Luzern Switz. see Lucerne
Luzhai China 77 F3
Luzhang China 76 C3
Luzhi China 76 E3
Luzhou China 76 E2
Luziânia Brazil 145 B2
Luzon i. Phil. 69 G3
Luzon Strait Phil. 69 G2
Luzy France 56 F3
L'viv Ukr. 43 E6
L'vov Ukr. see L'viv
Lwów Ukr. see L'viv
Lyady Rus. Fed. 45 P7
Lyakhavichy Belarus 45 O10
Lyakhovichi Belarus see Lyakhavichy
Lyallpur Pak. see Faisalabad
Lyamtsa Rus. Fed. 42 H2
Lycia reg. Turkey 59 M6
Lyck Poland see Ełk
Lycksele Sweden 44 K4
Lycopolis Egypt see Asyūṭ
Lydd U.K. 49 H8
Lydda Israel see Lod
Lyddan Island Antarctica 152 B2
Lydia reg. Turkey 59 L5
Lydney U.K. 49 E7
Lyel'chytsy Belarus 43 F6
Lyell, Mount U.S.A. 128 D3
Lyell Brown, Mount hill Australia 109 E5
Lyell Island Canada 120 D4
Lyepyel' Belarus 45 P9
Lykens U.S.A. 135 G3
Lyman U.S.A. 126 F4
Lyme Bay U.K. 49 E8
Lyme Regis U.K. 49 E8
Lymington U.K. 49 F8
Lynchburg OH U.S.A. 134 D4
Lynchburg TN U.S.A. 132 C5
Lynchburg VA U.S.A. 134 F5
Lynchville U.S.A. 135 J1
Lyndhurst N.S.W. Australia 112 D4
Lyndhurst Qld Australia 110 D3
Lyndhurst S.A. Australia 111 B6
Lyndon Australia 109 A5
Lyndon r. Australia 109 A5
Lyndonville U.S.A. 135 I1
Lyne r. U.K. 48 D4
Lyness U.K. 50 F2
Lyngdal Norway 45 E7
Lynn U.K. see King's Lynn
Lynn IN U.S.A. 134 C3
Lynn MA U.S.A. 135 J2
Lynndyl U.S.A. 129 G2
Lynn Lake Canada 121 K3
Lynton U.K. 49 D7
Lynx Lake Canada 121 J2
Lyon France 56 G4
Lyon r. U.K. 50 F4
Lyon Mountain U.S.A. 135 I1
Lyons Australia 109 F7
Lyons France see Lyon
Lyons GA U.S.A. 133 D5
Lyons NY U.S.A. 135 G2
Lyons Falls U.S.A. 135 H2
Lyozna Belarus 43 F5
Lyra Reef P.N.G. 106 F2
Lys r. France 52 D4
Lysekil Sweden 45 G7
Lyskovo Rus. Fed. 42 J4
Ly Sơn, Đao i. Vietnam 70 E4
Lys'va Rus. Fed. 41 R4
Lysychans'k Ukr. 43 H6
Lysyye Gory Rus. Fed. 43 J6
Lytham St Anne's U.K. 48 D5
Lytton Canada 120 F5
Lyuban' Belarus 45 P10
Lyubertsy Rus. Fed. 41 N4
Lyubeshiv Ukr. 43 E6
Lyubim Rus. Fed. 42 I4
Lyubytino Rus. Fed. 42 G4
Lyudinovo Rus. Fed. 43 G5
Lyunda r. Rus. Fed. 42 J4
Lyzha r. Rus. Fed. 42 M2

M

Ma r. Myanmar 70 B2
Ma, Nam r. Laos 70 C2
Ma'agan Israel 85 B3
Maale Maldives see Male
Maale Atholhu atoll Maldives see Male Atoll
Maalhosmadulu Atholhu Uthuruburi atoll Maldives see North Maalhosmadulu Atoll
Maalhosmadulu Atoll Maldives 84 B5
Ma'ān Jordan 85 B4
Maan Turkey see Nusratiye
Maaninka Fin. 44 O5
Maaninkavaara Fin. 44 P3
Ma'anshan China 77 H2
Maardu Estonia 45 N7
Maarianhamina Fin. see Mariehamn
Ma'arrat an Nu'mān Syria 85 C2
Maarssen Neth. 52 F2
Maas r. Neth. 52 E3
also known as Meuse (Belgium/France)
Maaseik Belgium 52 F3
Maasin Phil. 69 G4
Maasmechelen Belgium 52 F4
Maas-Schwalm-Nette nat. park Germany/Neth. 52 F3
Maastricht Neth. 52 F4
Maaza Plateau Egypt 90 C6
Maba Guangdong China see Qujiang
Maba Jiangsu China 77 H1
Mabai China see Maguan
Mabalane Moz. 101 K2
Mabana Dem. Rep. Congo 98 C3
Mabaruma Guyana 142 G2
Mabein Myanmar 70 B2
Mabel Creek Australia 109 F7
Mabel Downs Australia 108 D4
Mabella Canada 122 C4
Mabel Lake Canada 120 G5
Maberly Canada 135 G1
Mabian China 76 D2
Mablethorpe U.K. 48 H5
Mabopane S. Africa 101 I3
Mabote Moz. 101 L2
Mabou Canada 123 J5
Mabrak, Jabal mt. Jordan 85 B4
Mabuasehube Game Reserve nature res. Botswana 100 F3
Mabule Botswana 100 G3
Mabutsane Botswana 100 F3
Macá, Monte mt. Chile 144 B7
Macadam Plains Australia 109 B6
Macaé Brazil 145 C3
Macajuba Brazil 145 C1
Macaloge Moz. 99 D5
MacAlpine Lake Canada 119 H3
Macamic Canada 122 F4
Macandze Moz. 101 K2
Macao China 77 G4
Macao aut. reg. China 77 G4
Macapá Brazil 143 H3
Macará Ecuador 142 C4
Macarani Brazil 145 C1
Macas Ecuador 142 C4
Macassar Indon. see Makassar
Macau Brazil 143 K5
Macau China see Macao
Macau aut. reg. China see Macao
Macaúba Brazil 143 H6
Macauley Island N.Z. 107 I5
Maccaretane Moz. 101 K3
Macclenny U.S.A. 133 D6
Macclesfield U.K. 48 E5
Macdiarmid Canada 122 C4
Macdonald, Lake salt flat Australia 109 E5
Macdonald Range hills Australia 108 D3
Macdonnell Ranges mts Australia 109 E5
MacDowell Lake Canada 121 M4
Macduff U.K. 50 G3
Macedo de Cavaleiros Port. 57 C3
Macedon mt. Australia 112 B6
Macedon country Europe see Macedonia
Macedonia country Europe 59 I4
Maceió Brazil 143 K5
Macenta Guinea 96 C4
Macerata Italy 58 E3
Macfarlane, Lake salt flat Australia 111 B7
Macgillycuddy's Reeks mts Ireland 51 C6
Machachi Ecuador 142 C4
Machaila Moz. 101 K2
Machakos Kenya 98 D4
Machala Ecuador 142 C4
Machali China see Madoi
Machanga Moz. 99 D6
Machar Marshes Sudan 86 D8
Machattie, Lake salt flat Australia 110 B5
Machatuine Moz. 101 K3
Machault France 52 E5
Machaze Moz. see Chitobe
Macheng China 77 G2
Macherla India 84 C2
Machhagan India 83 F5
Machias ME U.S.A. 132 H2
Machias NY U.S.A. 135 F2
Machilipatnam India 84 D2
Machiques Venez. 142 D1
Mach Kowr Iran 89 F5
Machrihanish U.K. 50 D5
Machu Picchu tourist site Peru 142 D6
Machynlleth U.K. 49 D6
Macia Moz. 101 K3
Macias Nguema i. Equat. Guinea see Bioco
Măcin Romania 59 M2
Macintyre r. Australia 112 E2
Macintyre Brook r. Australia 112 E2
Mack U.S.A. 129 I2
Maçka Turkey 91 E2
Mackay Australia 110 E4
MacKay r. Canada 121 I3
Mackay U.S.A. 126 E3
Mackay, Lake salt flat Australia 108 E5
MacKay Lake Canada 121 I2
Mackenzie r. Australia 110 E4
Mackenzie Canada 120 F4

▶Mackenzie r. Canada 120 F2
Part of the Mackenzie-Peace-Finlay, the 2nd longest river in North America.

Mackenzie Guyana see Linden
Mackenzie atoll Micronesia see Ulithi
Mackenzie Bay Antarctica 152 E2
Mackenzie Bay Canada 118 E3
Mackenzie Highway Canada 120 G2
Mackenzie King Island Canada 119 G2
Mackenzie Mountains Canada 120 C1

▶Mackenzie-Peace-Finlay r. Canada 118 E3
2nd longest river in North America

Mackillop, Lake salt flat Australia see Yamma Yamma, Lake
Mackintosh Range hills Australia 109 D6
Macklin Canada 121 I4
Macksville Australia 112 F3
Maclean Australia 112 F2
Maclear S. Africa 101 I6
MacLeod Canada see Fort Macleod
MacLeod, Lake imp. l. Australia 109 A6
Macmillan r. Canada 120 C2
Macmillan Pass Canada 120 D2
Macomb U.S.A. 130 F3
Macomer Sardinia Italy 58 C4
Mâcon France 56 G3
Macon GA U.S.A. 133 D5
Macon MO U.S.A. 130 E4
Macon MS U.S.A. 131 F5
Macon OH U.S.A. 134 D4
Macondo Angola 99 C5
Macoun Lake Canada 121 K3
Macpherson Robertson Land reg. Antarctica see Mac. Robertson Land
Macpherson's Strait India 71 A5
Macquarie r. Australia 112 C3
Macquarie, Lake b. Australia 112 E4

▶Macquarie Island S. Pacific Ocean 150 G9
Part of Australia. Most southerly point of Oceania.

Macquarie Marshes Australia 112 C3
Macquarie Mountain Australia 112 D4
Macquarie Ridge sea feature S. Pacific Ocean 150 G9
MacRitchie Reservoir Sing. 71 [inset]
Mac. Robertson Land reg. Antarctica 152 E2
Macroom Ireland 51 D6
Macumba Australia 111 A5
Macumba watercourse Australia 111 B5
Macuzari, Presa resr Mex. 127 F8
Mādabā Jordan 85 B4
Madadeni S. Africa 101 J4

▶Madagascar country Africa 99 E6
Largest island in Africa and 4th in the world.

Madagascar Basin sea feature Indian Ocean 149 L7
Madagascar Ridge sea feature Indian Ocean 149 K8
Madagasikara country Africa see Madagascar
Madakasira India 84 C3
Madama Niger 97 E2
Madan Bulg. 59 K4
Madanapalle India 84 C3
Madang P.N.G. 69 L8
Madaoua Niger 96 D3
Madaripur Bangl. 83 G5
Madau Turkm. see Madaw
Madaw Turkm. 88 D2
Madawaska Canada 135 G1
Madawaska r. Canada 135 G1
Madaya Myanmar 70 B2
Madded India 84 D2

▶Madeira r. Brazil 142 G4
4th longest river in South America.

▶Madeira terr. N. Atlantic Ocean 96 B1
Autonomous Region of Portugal.

Madeira, Arquipélago da terr. N. Atlantic Ocean see Madeira
Maden Turkey 91 E3
Madera Mex. 127 F7
Madera U.S.A. 128 C3
Madgaon India 84 B3
Madha India 84 B2
Madhavpur India 82 B5
Madhepura India 83 F4
Madhipura India see Madhepura
Madhubani India 83 F4
Madhya Pradesh state India 82 D5
Madibogo S. Africa 101 G4
Madidi r. Bol. 142 E6
Madikeri India 84 B3
Madikwe Game Reserve nature res. S. Africa 101 H3
Madill U.S.A. 131 D5
Madīnat ath Thawrah Syria 85 D2
Madingo-Kayes Congo 99 B4
Madingou Congo 99 B4
Madison FL U.S.A. 133 D6
Madison GA U.S.A. 133 D5
Madison IN U.S.A. 134 C4
Madison ME U.S.A. 135 K1
Madison NE U.S.A. 130 D3
Madison SD U.S.A. 130 D2
Madison VA U.S.A. 135 F4

▶Madison WI U.S.A. 130 F3
Capital of Wisconsin.

Madison WV U.S.A. 134 E4
Madison r. U.S.A. 126 F3
Madison Heights U.S.A. 134 F5
Madisonville KY U.S.A. 134 B5
Madisonville TX U.S.A. 131 E6
Madiun Indon. 68 E8
Madley, Mount hill Australia 109 C6
Madoc Canada 135 G1
Mado Gashi Kenya 98 D3
Madoi China 76 C1
Madona Latvia 45 O8
Madpura India 82 B4
Madra Dağı mts Turkey 59 L5
Madrakah Saudi Arabia 86 E5
Madrakah, Ra's c. Oman 87 I6
Madras India see Chennai
Madras state India see Tamil Nadu
Madras U.S.A. 126 C3
Madre, Laguna lag. Mex. 131 D7
Madre, Laguna lag. U.S.A. 131 D7
Madre de Dios r. Peru 142 E6
Madre de Dios, Isla i. Chile 144 A8
Madre del Sur, Sierra mts Mex. 136 D5
Madre Mountain U.S.A. 129 J4
Madre Occidental, Sierra mts Mex. 127 F7
Madre Oriental, Sierra mts Mex. 131 C7

▶Madrid Spain 57 E3
Capital of Spain. 5th most populous city in Europe.

Madridejos Spain 57 E4
Madruga Cuba 133 D8
Madugula India 84 D2
Madura i. Indon. 68 E8
Madura, Selat sea chan. Indon. 68 E8
Madurai India 84 C4
Madurantakam India 84 C3
Madvār, Kūh-e mt. Iran 88 D4
Madwas India 83 E4
Maé i. Vanuatu see Émaé
Maebashi Japan 75 E5
Mae Hong Son Thai. 70 B3
Mae Ping National Park Thai. 70 B3
Mae Ramat Thai. 70 B3
Mae Sai Thai. 70 B2
Mae Sariang Thai. 70 B3
Mae Sot Thai. 70 B3
Mae Suai Thai. 70 B3
Mae Tuen Wildlife Reserve nature res. Thai. 70 B3
Maevatanana Madag. 99 E5
Maéwo i. Vanuatu 107 G3
Mae Wong National Park Thai. 70 B4
Mae Yom National Park Thai. 70 C3
Mafeking Canada 121 K4
Mafeking S. Africa see Mafikeng
Mafeteng Lesotho 101 H5
Maffra Australia 112 C6
Mafia Island Tanz. 99 D4
Mafikeng S. Africa 101 G3
Mafinga Tanz. 99 D4
Mafra Brazil 145 A4
Mafraq Jordan see Al Mafraq
Magabeni S. Africa 101 J6
Magadan Rus. Fed. 65 Q4
Magadi Kenya 98 D4
Magaiza Moz. 101 K2
Magallanes Chile see Punta Arenas
Magallanes, Estrecho de Chile see Magellan, Strait of
Magangue Col. 142 D2
Mağara Dağı mt. Turkey 85 A1
Magaramkent Rus. Fed. 91 H2
Magaria Niger 96 D3
Magarida P.N.G. 110 E1
Magas Rus. Fed. 91 G2
Magazine Mountain hill U.S.A. 131 E5
Magdagachi Rus. Fed. 74 B1
Magdalena Bol. 142 F6
Magdalena r. Col. 142 D1
Magdalena Baja California Sur Mex. 127 E8
Magdalena Sonora Mex. 127 F7
Magdalena r. Mex. 127 F7
Magdalena, Bahía b. Mex. 136 B4
Magdalena, Isla i. Chile 144 B6
Magdeburg Germany 53 L2
Magdelaine Cays atoll Australia 110 E3
Magellan, Strait of Chile 144 B8
Magellan Seamounts sea feature N. Pacific Ocean 150 F4
Magenta, Lake salt flat Australia 109 B8
Magerøya i. Norway 44 N1
Maggiorasca, Monte mt. Italy 58 C2
Maggiore, Lago Italy see Maggiore, Lake
Maggiore, Lake Italy 58 C2
Maghâgha Egypt see Maghāghah
Maghāghah Egypt 90 C5
Maghama Mauritania 96 B3
Maghâra, Gebel hill Egypt see Maghārah, Jabal
Maghārah, Jabal hill Egypt 85 A4
Maghera U.K. 51 F3
Magherafelt U.K. 51 F3
Maghnia Alg. 57 F6
Maghor Afgh. 89 F3
Maghull U.K. 48 E5
Magilligan Point U.K. 51 F2
Magma U.S.A. 129 H5
Magna Grande mt. Sicily Italy 58 F6
Magnetic Island Australia 110 D3
Magnetic Passage Australia 110 D3
Magnetity Rus. Fed. 44 R2
Magnitogorsk Rus. Fed. 64 G4
Magnolia AR U.S.A. 131 E5
Magnolia MS U.S.A. 131 F6
Magny-en-Vexin France 52 B5
Mago Rus. Fed. 74 F1
Màgoé Moz. 99 D5
Magog Canada 135 I1
Mago National Park Eth. 98 D3
Magosa Cyprus see Famagusta
Magpie r. Canada 123 I4
Magpie, Lac l. Canada 123 I4
Magṭa' Laḥjar Mauritania 96 B3
Magu Tanz. 98 D4
Magu, Khrebet mts Rus. Fed. 74 E1
Maguan China 76 E4
Magude Moz. 101 K3
Magueyal Mex. 131 C7
Magura Bangl. 83 G5
Maguse Lake Canada 121 M2
Magway Myanmar see Magwe
Magwe Myanmar 70 A2
Magyar Köztársaság country Europe see Hungary
Magyichaung Myanmar 70 A2
Mahābād Iran 88 B2
Mahabharat Range mts Nepal 83 F4
Mahaboobnagar India see Mahbubnagar
Mahad India 84 B2
Mahadeo Hills India 82 D5
Mahaffey U.S.A. 135 F3
Mahajan India 82 C3
Mahajanga Madag. 99 E5
Mahakam r. Indon. 68 F7
Mahalapye Botswana 101 H2
Mahale Mountains National Park Tanz. 99 C4
Mahalevona Madag. 99 E5
Mahallāt Iran 88 C3
Māhān Iran 88 E4
Mahanadi r. India 84 E1
Mahanoro Madag. 99 E5
Maha Oya Sri Lanka 84 D5
Maharashtra state India 84 B2
Maha Sarakham Thai. 70 C3
Mahasham, Wâdi el watercourse Egypt see Muhashsham, Wādī al
Mahaxai Laos 70 D3
Mahbubabad India 84 D2
Mahbubnagar India 84 C2
Mahd adh Dhahab Saudi Arabia 86 F5
Mahdia Alg. 57 G6
Mahdia Guyana 143 G2
Mahdia Tunisia 58 D7
Mahe China 76 E1
Mahé i. Seychelles 149 L6
Mahendragiri mt. India 84 E2
Mahenge Tanz. 99 D4
Mahesana India 82 C5
Mahi r. India 82 C5
Mahia Peninsula N.Z. 113 F4
Mahilyow Belarus 43 F5
Mahim India 84 B2
Mah Jān Iran 88 D4
Mahlabatini S. Africa 101 J5
Mahlsdorf Germany 53 L2
Maḥmūdābād Iran 88 D2
Maḥmūd-e 'Erāqī Afgh. see Maḥmūd-e Rāqī
Maḥmūd-e Rāqī Afgh. 89 H3
Mahnomen U.S.A. 130 D2
Maho Sri Lanka 84 D5
Mahoba India 82 D4
Maholi India 82 E4
Mahón Spain 57 I4
Mahony Lake Canada 120 E1
Mahrauni India 82 D4
Mahrès Tunisia 58 D7
Māhrūd Iran 89 F3
Mahsana India see Mahesana
Mahudaung mts Myanmar 70 A2
Māhukona U.S.A. 127 [inset]
Mahur India 84 C2
Mahuva India 82 B5
Mahwa India 82 D4
Mahya Dağı mt. Turkey 59 L4
Mai i. Vanuatu see Émaé
Maiaia Moz. see Nacala
Maibang India 70 A1
Maicao Col. 142 D1
Maicasagi r. Canada 122 F4
Maicasagi, Lac l. Canada 122 F4
Maichen China 77 F4
Maidenhead U.K. 49 G7
Maidstone Canada 121 I4
Maidstone U.K. 49 H7
Maiduguri Nigeria 96 E3
Maiella, Parco Nazionale della nat. park Italy 58 F3
Mai Gudo mt. Eth. 98 D3
Maigue r. Ireland 51 D5
Maihar India 82 E4
Maiji Shan mt. China 76 E1
Maikala Range hills India 82 E5
Maiko r. Dem. Rep. Congo 98 C3
Mailan Hill mt. India 83 E5
Mailly-le-Camp France 52 E6
Mailsi Pak. 89 I4
Main r. Germany 53 I4
Main r. U.K. 51 F3
Main Brook Canada 123 L4
Mainburg Germany 53 L6
Main Channel lake channel Canada 134 E1
Maindargi India 84 C2
Mai-Ndombe, Lac l. Dem. Rep. Congo 98 B4
Main-Donau-Kanal canal Germany 53 K5
Maindong Xizang China see Coqên
Main Duck Island Canada 135 G2
Maine state U.S.A. 135 K1
Maine, Gulf of Canada/U.S.A. 135 K2
Mainé Hanari, Cerro hill Col. 142 D4
Maïné-Soroa Niger 96 E3
Maingkaing Myanmar 70 A1
Maingkwan Myanmar 70 B1
Maingy Island Myanmar 71 B4
Mainhardt Germany 53 J5
Mainkung China 76 C2
Mainland i. Scotland U.K. 50 F1
Mainland i. Scotland U.K. 50 [inset]
Mainleus Germany 53 L4
Mainoru Australia 108 F3

Mainpat reg. India 83 E5
Mainpuri India 82 D4
Main Range National Park Australia 112 F2
Maintenon France 52 B6
Maintirano Madag. 99 E5
Mainz Germany 53 I4
Maio i. Cape Verde 96 [inset]
Maipú Arg. 144 E5
Maiskhal Island Bangl. 83 G5
Maisons-Laffitte France 52 C6
Maitengwe Botswana 99 C6
Maitland N.S.W. Australia 112 E4
Maitland S.A. Australia 111 B7
Maitland r. Australia 108 B5
Maitri research station Antarctica 152 C2
Maiwo i. Vanuatu see Maéwo
Maiyu, Mount hill Australia 108 E4
Maíz, Islas del is Nicaragua 137 H6
Maizar Pak. 89 H3
Maizuru Japan 75 D6
Maja Jezercë mt. Albania 59 H3
Majdel Aanjar tourist site Lebanon 85 B3
Majene Indon. 68 F7
Majestic U.S.A. 134 D5
Majḩūd well Saudi Arabia 88 C6
Majī Eth. 98 D3
Majiang Guangxi China 77 F4
Majiang Guizhou China 76 E3
Majiazi China 74 B2
Majōl country N. Pacific Ocean see Marshall Islands
Major, Puig mt. Spain 57 H4
Majorca i. Spain 57 H4
Mājro atoll Marshall Is see Majuro
Majunga Madag. see Mahajanga
Majuro atoll Marshall Is 150 H5
Majwemasweu S. Africa 101 H5
Makabana Congo 98 B4
Makale Indon. 69 F7

▶Makalu mt. China/Nepal 83 F4
5th highest mountain in the world and in Asia.

Makalu Barun National Park Nepal 83 F4
Makanchi Kazakh. 80 F2
Makanpur India 82 E4
Makari Mountain National Park Tanz. see Mahale Mountains National Park
Makarov Rus. Fed. 74 F2
Makarov Basin sea feature Arctic Ocean 153 B1
Makarska Croatia 58 G3
Makarwal Pak. 89 H3
Makar'ye Rus. Fed. 42 K4
Makar'yev Rus. Fed. 42 I4
Makasar, Selat strait Indon. see Makassar, Selat
Makassar Indon. 68 F8
Makassar, Selat strait Indon. 68 F7
Makassar Strait Indon. see Makassar, Selat
Makat Kazakh. 78 E2
Makatini Flats lowland S. Africa 101 K4
Makedonija country Europe see Macedonia
Makeni Sierra Leone 96 B4
Makete Tanz. 99 D4
Makeyevka Ukr. see Makiyivka
Makgadikgadi depr. Botswana 99 C6
Makgadikgadi Pans National Park Botswana 99 C6
Makhachkala Rus. Fed. 91 G2
Makhad Pak. 89 H3
Makhado S. Africa 101 I2
Makhāzin, Kathīb al des. Egypt 85 A4
Makhâzin, Kathîb el des. Egypt see Makhāzin, Kathīb al
Makhazine, Barrage El dam Morocco 57 D6
Makhmūr Iraq 91 F4
Makhtal India 84 C2
Makin atoll Kiribati see Butaritari
Makindu Kenya 98 D4
Makinsk Kazakh. 79 G1
Makira i. Solomon Is see San Cristobal
Makiyivka Ukr. 43 H6
Makkah Saudi Arabia see Mecca
Makkovik Canada 123 K3
Makkovik, Cape Canada 123 K3
Makkum Neth. 52 F1
Makó Hungary 59 I1
Makokou Gabon 98 B3
Makopong Botswana 100 F3
Makotipoko Congo 97 E5
Makran reg. Iran/Pak. 89 F5
Makrana India 82 C4
Makran Coast Range mts Pak. 89 F5
Makri India 84 D2
Maksatikha Rus. Fed. 42 G4
Maksi India 82 D5
Maksimovka Rus. Fed. 74 E3
Maksotag Iran 89 F4
Maksudangarh India 82 D5
Mākū Iran 88 B2
Makunguwiro Tanz. 99 D5
Makurdi Nigeria 96 D4
Makwassie S. Africa 101 G4
Mal India 83 G4
Mala Ireland see Mallow
Mala i. Solomon Is see Malaita
Malå Sweden 44 K4
Mala, Punta pt Panama 137 H7
Malabar Coast India 84 B3

▶Malabo Equat. Guinea 96 D4
Capital of Equatorial Guinea.

Malaca Spain see Málaga
Malacca Malaysia see Melaka
Malacca, Strait of Indon./Malaysia 71 B6
Malad City U.S.A. 126 E4
Maladzyechna Belarus 45 O9
Malá Fatra nat. park Slovakia 47 Q6
Málaga Spain 57 D5
Malaga U.S.A. 131 B5
Malagasy Republic country Africa see Madagascar
Málainn Mhóir Ireland 51 D3
Malaita i. Solomon Is 107 G2
Malakal Sudan 86 D8
Malakanagiri India see Malkangiri
Malakheti Nepal 82 E3
Malakula i. Vanuatu 107 G3
Malan, Ras pt Pak. 89 G5
Malang Indon. 68 E8
Malangana Nepal see Malangwa
Malange Angola see Malanje
Malangwa Nepal 83 F4
Malanje Angola 99 B4
Malappuram India 84 C4
Mälaren l. Sweden 45 J7
Malargüe Arg. 144 C5
Malartic Canada 122 F4
Malaspina Glacier U.S.A. 120 A3
Malatya Turkey 90 E3
Malavalli India 84 C3
Malawi country Africa 99 D5
Malawi, Lake Africa see Nyasa, Lake
Malawi National Park Zambia see Nyika National Park
Malaya pen. Malaysia see Peninsular Malaysia
Malaya Pera Rus. Fed. 42 L2
Malaya Vishera Rus. Fed. 42 G4
Malaybalay Phil. 69 H5
Malāyer Iran 88 C3
Malay Peninsula Asia 71 B4
Malay Reef Australia 110 E3
Malaysia country Asia 68 D5
Malaysia, Semenanjung pen. Malaysia see Peninsular Malaysia
Malazgirt Turkey 91 F3
Malbon Australia 110 C4
Malbork Poland 47 Q3
Malborn Germany 52 G5
Malchin Germany 47 N4
Malcolm Australia 109 C7
Malcolm, Point Australia 109 C8
Malcolm Island Myanmar 71 B5
Maldegem Belgium 52 D3
Malden U.S.A. 131 F4
Malden Island Kiribati 151 J6
Maldives country Indian Ocean 81 D10
Maldon Australia 112 B6
Maldon U.K. 49 H7
Maldonado Uruguay 144 F4

▶Male Maldives 81 D11
Capital of the Maldives.

Maleas, Akra pt Peloponnisos Greece see Maleas, Akrotirio
Maleas, Akrotirio pt Greece 59 J6
Male Atoll Maldives 81 D11
Malebogo S. Africa 101 G5
Malegaon Mahar. India 84 B1
Malegaon Mahar. India 84 C2
Malé Karpaty hills Slovakia 47 P6
Malek Sīāh, Kūh-e mt. Afgh. 89 F4
Malele Dem. Rep. Congo 99 B4
Maler Kotla India 82 C3
Maleševske Planine mts Bulg./Macedonia 59 J4
Malgobek Rus. Fed. 91 G2
Malgomaj l. Sweden 44 J4
Malḩa, Naqb mt. Egypt see Mālihah, Naqb
Malhada Brazil 145 C1
Malheur r. U.S.A. 126 D3
Malheur Lake U.S.A. 126 D4
Mali country Africa 96 C3
Mali Dem. Rep. Congo 98 C4
Mali Guinea 96 B3
Maliana East Timor 108 D2
Malianjing China 80 I3
Mālihah, Naqb mt. Egypt 85 A5
Malik Naro mt. Pak. 89 F4
Mali Kyun i. Myanmar 71 B4
Malili Indon. 69 G7
Malin Ukr. see Malyn
Malindi Kenya 98 E4
Malines Belgium see Mechelen
Malin Head hd Ireland 51 E2
Malipo China 76 E4
Mali Raginac mt. Croatia 58 F2
Malita Phil. 69 H5
Malka r. Rus. Fed. 91 G2
Malkangiri India 84 D2
Malkapur India 84 B2
Malkara Turkey 59 L4
Mal'kavichy Belarus 45 O10
Malko Tŭrnovo Bulg. 59 L4
Mallacoota Australia 112 D6
Mallacoota Inlet b. Australia 112 D6
Mallaig U.K. 50 D4
Mallani reg. India 89 H5
Mallawī Egypt 90 C6
Mallee Cliffs National Park Australia 111 C7
Mallery Lake Canada 121 L1
Mallét Brazil 145 A4
Mallorca i. Spain see Majorca
Mallow Ireland 51 D5
Mallowa Well Australia 108 D5
Mallwyd U.K. 49 D6
Malm Norway 44 G4
Malmberget Sweden 44 L3
Malmédy Belgium 52 G4
Malmesbury S. Africa 100 D7
Malmesbury U.K. 49 E7
Malmö Sweden 45 H9
Malmyzh Rus. Fed. 42 K4
Maloca Brazil 143 G3
Malone U.S.A. 135 H1
Malonje mt. Tanz. 99 D4
Maloshuyka Rus. Fed. 42 H3
Malosmadulu Atoll Maldives see Maalhosmadulu Atoll
Måløy Norway 44 D6
Maloyaroslavets Rus. Fed. 43 H5
Malozemel'skaya Tundra lowland Rus. Fed. 42 K2
Malpelo, Isla de i. N. Pacific Ocean 137 H8
Malprabha r. India 84 C2
Malta country Europe 58 F7
Malta Latvia 45 O8
Malta ID U.S.A. 126 E4
Malta MT U.S.A. 126 G2
Malta Channel Italy/Malta 58 F6
Maltahöhe Namibia 100 C3
Maltby U.K. 48 F5
Maltby le Marsh U.K. 48 H5
Malton U.K. 48 G4
Maluku is Indon. see Moluccas
Maluku, Laut sea Indon. 69 H6
Ma'lūlā, Jabal mts Syria 85 C3
Malung Sweden 45 H6
Maluti Mountains Lesotho 101 I5
Malu'u Solomon Is 107 G2
Malvan India 84 B2
Malvasia Greece see Monemvasia
Malvern U.K. see Great Malvern
Malvern U.S.A. 131 E5
Malvérnia Moz. see Chicualacuala
Malvinas, Islas terr. S. Atlantic Ocean see Falkland Islands
Malyn Ukr. 43 F6
Malyy Anyuy r. Rus. Fed. 65 R3
Malyye Derbety Rus. Fed. 43 J7
Malyy Kavkaz mts Asia see Lesser Caucasus
Malyy Lyakhovskiy, Ostrov i. Rus. Fed. 65 P2
Malyy Uzen' r. Kazakh./Rus. Fed. 43 K6
Mamadysh Rus. Fed. 42 K5
Mamafubedu S. Africa 101 I4
Mamatān Nāvar l. Afgh. 89 G4
Mamba China 76 B2
Mambai Brazil 145 B1
Mambasa Dem. Rep. Congo 98 C3
Mamburao Phil. 69 G4
Mamelodi S. Africa 101 I3
Mamfe Cameroon 96 D4
Mamit India 83 H5
Mammoth U.S.A. 129 H5
Mammoth Cave National Park U.S.A. 134 B5
Mammoth Reservoir U.S.A. 128 D3
Mamonas Brazil 145 C1
Mamoré r. Bol./Brazil 142 E6
Mamou Guinea 96 B3
Mampikony Madag. 99 E5
Mampong Ghana 96 C4
Mamuju Indon. 68 F7
Mamuno Botswana 100 E2
Man Côte d'Ivoire 96 C4
Man India 84 B2
Man r. India 84 B2
Man U.S.A. 134 E5

▶Man, Isle of terr. Irish Sea 48 C4
United Kingdom Crown Dependency.

Manacapuru Brazil 142 F4
Manacor Spain 57 H4
Manado Indon. 69 G6

▶Managua Nicaragua 137 G6
Capital of Nicaragua.

Manakara Madag. 99 E6
Manakau mt. N.Z. 113 D6
Manākhah Yemen 86 F6

▶Manama Bahrain 88 C5
Capital of Bahrain.

Manamadurai India 84 C4
Mana Maroka National Park S. Africa 101 H5
Manamelkudi India 84 C4
Manam Island P.N.G. 69 L7
Mananara Avaratra Madag. 99 E5
Manangoora Australia 110 B3
Mananjary Madag. 99 E6
Manantali, Lac de l. Mali 96 B3
Manantenina Madag. 99 E6
Mana Pass China/India 82 D3
Mana Pools National Park Zimbabwe 99 C5

▶Manapouri, Lake N.Z. 113 A7
Deepest lake in Oceania.

Manasa India 82 C4
Manas He r. China 80 G2
Manas Hu l. China 80 G2
Manāṣīr reg. U.A.E. 88 D6

▶Manaslu mt. Nepal 83 F3
8th highest mountain in the world and in Asia.

Manassas U.S.A. 135 G4
Manastir Macedonia see Bitola
Manas Wildlife Sanctuary nature res. Bhutan 83 G4
Man-aung Myanmar 70 A3
Man-aung Kyun Myanmar 70 A3
Manaus Brazil 142 F4
Manavgat Turkey 90 C3
Manbazar India 83 F5
Manbij Syria 85 C1
Manby U.K. 48 H5
Mancelona U.S.A. 134 C1
Manchar India 84 B2
Manchester U.K. 48 E5
Manchester CT U.S.A. 135 I3
Manchester IA U.S.A. 130 F3
Manchester KY U.S.A. 134 D5
Manchester MD U.S.A. 135 G4
Manchester MI U.S.A. 134 C2
Manchester NH U.S.A. 135 J2
Manchester OH U.S.A. 134 D4
Manchester TN U.S.A. 132 C5
Manchester VT U.S.A. 135 I2
Mancılık Turkey 90 E3
Mand Pak. 89 F5
Mand, Rūd-e r. Iran 88 C4
Manda Tanz. 99 D4
Manda, Jebel mt. Sudan 97 F4
Manda, Parc National de nat. park Chad 97 E4
Mandabe Madag. 99 E6
Mandai Sing. 71 [inset]
Mandal Norway 45 E7

▶Mandala, Puncak mt. Indon. 69 K7
3rd highest mountain in Oceania.

Mandalay Myanmar 70 B2
Mandale Myanmar see Mandalay
Mandalgovĭ Mongolia 72 J3
Mandalī Iraq 91 G4
Mandal-Ovoo Mongolia 72 I4
Mandalt China 73 K4
Mandan U.S.A. 130 C2
Mandas Sardinia Italy 58 C5
Mandasa India 84 E2
Mandasor India see Mandsaur
Mandav Hills India 82 B5
Mandel Afgh. 89 F3
Mandera Kenya 98 E3
Manderfield U.S.A. 129 G2
Manderscheid Germany 52 G4
Mandeville Jamaica 137 I5
Mandeville N.Z. 113 B7
Mandha India 82 B4
Mandhoúdhíon Greece see Mantoudi
Mandi India 82 D3
Mandiana Guinea 96 C3
Mandi Burewala Pak. 89 I4
Mandié Moz. 99 D5
Mandini S. Africa 101 J5
Mandira Dam India 83 F5
Mandla India 82 E5
Mandleshwar India 82 C5
Mandrael India 82 D4
Mandritsara Madag. 99 E5
Mandsaur India 82 C4
Mandurah Australia 109 A8
Manduria Italy 58 G4
Mandvi India 82 B5
Mandya India 84 C3
Manerbio Italy 58 D2
Manevychi Ukr. 43 E6
Manfalūṭ Egypt 90 C6
Manfredonia Italy 58 F4
Manfredonia, Golfo di g. Italy 58 G4
Manga Brazil 145 C1
Manga Burkina 96 C3
Mangabeiras, Serra das hills Brazil 143 I6
Mangai Dem. Rep. Congo 98 B4
Mangaia i. Cook Is 151 J7
Mangakino N.Z. 113 E4
Mangalagiri India 84 D2
Mangaldai India 70 A1
Mangaldoi India see Mangaldai
Mangalia Romania 59 M3
Mangalmé Chad 97 E3
Mangalore India 84 B3
Mangaon India 84 B2
Mangareva Islands Fr. Polynesia see Gambier, Îles
Mangaung Free State S. Africa 101 H5
Mangaung Free State S. Africa see Bloemfontein
Mangawan India 83 E4
Ma'ngê China see Luqu
Mangea i. Cook Is see Mangaia
Mangghyshlaq Kazakh. see Mangystau
Mangghystaū Kazakh. see Mangystau
Mangghystaū admin. div. Kazakh. see Mangistauskaya Oblast'
Mangghyt Uzbek. see Mang'it
Manghit Uzbek. see Mang'it
Mangin Range mts Myanmar see Mingin Range
Mangistau Kazakh. see Mangystau
Mangistauskaya Oblast' admin. div. Kazakh. 91 I2
Mang'it Uzbek. 80 B3
Mangla Bangl. see Mongla
Mangla China see Guinan
Mangla Pak. 89 I3
Manglaqiongtuo China see Guinan
Mangnai China 80 H4
Mangnai Zhen China 80 H4
Mangochi Malawi 99 D5
Mangoky r. Madag. 99 E6
Mangole i. Indon. 69 H7
Mangoli India 84 B2
Mangotsfield U.K. 49 E7
Mangqystaū Shyghanaghy b. Kazakh. see Mangyshlakskiy Zaliv
Mangra China see Guinan
Mangrol India 82 B5
Mangrul India 84 C1
Mangshi China see Luxi
Mangualde Port. 57 C3
Manguéni, Plateau du Niger 96 E2
Mangui China 74 A2
Mangula Zimbabwe see Mhangura
Mangum U.S.A. 131 D5
Mangyshlak Kazakh. see Mangystau
Mangyshlak, Poluostrov pen. Kazakh. 91 H1
Mangyshlak Oblast admin. div. Kazakh. see Mangistauskaya Oblast'
Mangyshlakskaya Oblast' admin. div. Kazakh. see Mangistauskaya Oblast'
Mangyshlakskiy Zaliv b. Kazakh. 91 H1
Mangystau Kazakh. 91 H2
Manhā Brazil 145 B1
Manhattan U.S.A. 130 D4
Manhica Moz. 101 K3
Manhoca Moz. 101 K4
Manhuaçu Brazil 145 C3
Manhuaçu r. Brazil 145 C2
Mani China 83 F2
Mania r. Madag. 99 E5
Maniago Italy 58 E1
Manicouagan Canada 123 H4
Manicouagan r. Canada 123 H4
Manicouagan, Réservoir resr Canada 123 H4
Manic Trois, Réservoir resr Canada 123 H4
Manīfah Saudi Arabia 88 C5
Maniganggo China 76 C2
Manigotagan Canada 121 L5
Manihiki atoll Cook Is 150 J6
Maniitsoq Greenland 119 M3
Manikchhari Bangl. 83 H5
Manikgarh India see Rajura

▶Manila Phil. 69 G4
Capital of the Philippines.

Manila U.S.A. 126 F4
Manildra Australia 112 D4
Manilla Australia 112 E3
Maningrida Australia 108 F3
Manipur India see Imphal
Manipur state India 83 H4
Manisa Turkey 59 L5
Manistee U.S.A. 134 B1
Manistee r. U.S.A. 134 B1
Manistique U.S.A. 132 C2
Manitoba prov. Canada 121 L4
Manitoba, Lake Canada 121 L5
Manito Lake Canada 121 I4
Manitou Canada 121 L5
Manitou, Lake U.S.A. 134 B3
Manitou Beach U.S.A. 135 G2
Manitou Falls Canada 121 M5
Manitou Islands U.S.A. 134 B1
Manitoulin Island Canada 122 E5
Manitouwadge Canada 122 D4
Manitowoc U.S.A. 134 B1
Maniwaki Canada 122 G5
Manizales Col. 142 C2
Manja Madag. 99 E6
Manjarabad India 84 B3
Manjeri India 84 C4
Manjhand Pak. 89 H5
Manjhi India 83 F4
Manjra r. India 84 C2
Man Kabat Myanmar 70 B1
Mankaiana Swaziland see Mankayane
Mankato KS U.S.A. 130 D4
Mankato MN U.S.A. 130 E2
Mankayane Swaziland 101 J4
Mankera Pak. 89 H4
Mankono Côte d'Ivoire 96 C4
Mankota Canada 121 J5
Manlay Mongolia 72 J4
Manley Hot Springs U.S.A. 118 C3
Manmad India 84 B1
Mann r. Australia 108 F3
Mann, Mount Australia 109 E6
Manna Indon. 68 C7
Man Na Myanmar 70 B2
Mannahill Australia 111 B7
Mannar Sri Lanka 84 C4
Mannar, Gulf of India/Sri Lanka 84 C4
Manneru r. India 84 D3
Mannessier, Lac l. Canada 123 H3
Mannheim Germany 53 I5
Mannicolo Islands Solomon Is see Vanikoro Islands
Manning r. Australia 112 F3
Manning Canada 120 G3
Manning U.S.A. 133 D5
Mannington U.S.A. 134 E4
Manningtree U.K. 49 I7
Mann Ranges mts Australia 109 E6
Mannsville KY U.S.A. 134 C5
Mannsville NY U.S.A. 135 G2
Mannu, Capo c. Sardinia Italy 58 C4
Mannville Canada 121 I4
Man-of-War Rocks is U.S.A. see Gardner Pinnacles
Manoharpur India 82 D4
Manohar Thana India 82 D4
Manokotak U.S.A. 118 C4
Manokwari Indon. 69 I7
Manoron Myanmar 71 B5
Manosque France 56 G5
Manouane r. Canada 123 H4
Manouane, Lac l. Canada 123 H4
Man Pan Myanmar 70 B2
Manp'o N. Korea 74 B4
Manra i. Kiribati 107 I2
Manresa Spain 57 G3
Mansa Gujarat India 82 C5
Mansa Punjab India 82 C3
Mansa Zambia 99 C5
Mansa Konko Gambia 96 B3
Man Sam Myanmar 70 B2
Mansehra Pak. 87 L3
Mansel Island Canada 119 K3
Mansfield Australia 112 C6
Mansfield U.K. 49 F5
Mansfield LA U.S.A. 131 E5
Mansfield OH U.S.A. 134 D3
Mansfield PA U.S.A. 135 G3
Mansfield, Mount U.S.A. 135 I1
Man Si Myanmar 70 B1
Mansi Myanmar 70 A1
Manso r. Brazil see Mortes, Rio das
Manta Ecuador 142 B4
Mantaro r. Peru 142 D6
Manteca U.S.A. 128 C3
Mantena Brazil 145 C2
Manteo U.S.A. 132 F5
Mantes-la-Jolie France 52 B6
Mantiqueira, Serra da mts Brazil 145 B3
Manton U.S.A. 134 C1
Mantoudi Greece 59 J5
Mantova Italy see Mantua
Mäntsälä Fin. 45 N6
Mänttä Fin. 44 N5
Mantua Cuba 133 C8
Mantua Italy 58 D2
Mantuan Downs Australia 110 D5
Manturovo Rus. Fed. 42 J4
Mäntyharju Fin. 45 O6
Mäntyjärvi Fin. 44 O3
Manú Peru 142 D6
Manu, Parque Nacional nat. park Peru 142 D6
Manuae atoll Fr. Polynesia 151 J7
Manu'a Islands American Samoa 107 I3
Manuel Ribas Brazil 145 A4
Manuel Vitorino Brazil 145 C1
Manuelzinho Brazil 143 H5
Manui i. Indon. 69 G7
Manukau N.Z. 113 E3
Manukau Harbour N.Z. 113 E3
Manunda watercourse Australia 111 B7
Manusela, Taman Nasional Indon. 69 H7
Manus Island P.N.G. 69 L7
Manvi India 84 C3
Many U.S.A. 131 E6
Manyana Botswana 101 G3
Manyas Turkey 59 L4
Manyas Gölü l. Turkey see Kuş Gölü
Manych-Gudilo, Ozero l. Rus. Fed. 43 I7
Many Island Lake Canada 121 I5
Manyoni Tanz. 99 D4
Manzai Pak. 89 H3
Manzanares Spain 57 E4
Manzanillo Cuba 137 I4
Manzanillo Mex. 136 D5
Manzhouli China 73 L3
Manzini Swaziland 101 J4
Mao Chad 97 E3
Maó Spain see Mahón
Maoba Guizhou China 76 E3
Maoba Hubei China 77 F2
Maocifan China 77 G2
Mao'ergai China 76 D1
Maoke, Pegunungan mts Indon. 69 J7
Maokeng S. Africa 101 H4
Maokui Shan mt. China 74 A4
Maolin China 74 A4
Maoming China 77 F4
Ma On Shan hill H.K. China 77 [inset]
Maopi T'ou c. Taiwan 77 I4
Maopora i. Indon. 108 D1
Maotou Shan mt. China 76 D3
Mapai Moz. 101 J2
Mapam Yumco l. China 83 E3
Mapanza Zambia 99 C5
Maphodi S. Africa 101 G6
Mapimí Mex. 131 C7
Mapinhane Moz. 101 L2
Mapiri Bol. 142 E7
Maple r. MI U.S.A. 134 C2
Maple r. ND U.S.A. 130 D2
Maple Creek Canada 121 I5
Maple Heights U.S.A. 134 E3
Maple Peak U.S.A. 129 I5
Mapmakers Seamounts sea feature N. Pacific Ocean 150 H4
Mapoon Australia 110 C1
Mapor i. Indon. 71 D7
Mapoteng Lesotho 101 H5
Maprik P.N.G. 69 K7
Mapuera r. Brazil 143 G4
Mapulanguene Moz. 101 K3
Mapungubwe National Park S. Africa 101 I2

▶Maputo Moz. 101 K3
Capital of Mozambique.

Maputo prov. Moz. 101 K3
Maputo r. Moz./S. Africa 101 K4
Maputo, Baía de b. Moz. 101 K4
Maputsoe Lesotho 101 H5
Maqanshy Kazakh. see Makanchi
Maqar an Na'am well Iraq 91 F5
Maqat Kazakh. see Makat
Maqên China 76 D1
Maqên Kangri mt. China 76 C1
Maqnā Saudi Arabia 90 D5
Maqṭeïr reg. Mauritania 96 B2
Maqu China 76 D1
Ma Qu r. China see Yellow River
Maquan He r. China 83 F3
Maquela do Zombo Angola 99 B4
Maquinchao Arg. 144 C6
Mar r. Pak. 89 G5
Mar, Serra do mts Rio de Janeiro/São Paulo Brazil 145 B3
Mar, Serra do mts Rio Grande do Sul/Santa Catarina Brazil 145 A5
Mara r. Canada 121 I1
Mara India 83 E5
Mara S. Africa 101 I2
Maraã Brazil 142 E4
Marabá Brazil 143 I5
Maraboon, Lake resr Australia 110 E4
Maracá, Ilha de i. Brazil 143 H3
Maracaibo Venez. 142 D1
Maracaibo, Lago de Venez. see Maracaibo, Lake
Maracaibo, Lake Venez. 142 D2
Maracaju Brazil 144 E2
Maracaju, Serra de hills Brazil 144 E2
Maracanda Uzbek. see Samarqand
Maracás Brazil 145 C1
Maracás, Chapada de hills Brazil 145 C1
Maracay Venez. 142 E1
Marādah Libya 97 E2
Maradi Niger 96 D3
Marāgheh Iran 88 B2
Marahuaca, Cerro mt. Venez. 142 E3
Marajó, Baía de est. Brazil 143 I4
Marajó, Ilha de i. Brazil 143 H4
Marakele National Park S. Africa 101 H3
Maralal Kenya 98 D3
Maralbashi China see Bachu
Maralinga Australia 109 E7
Maralwexi China see Bachu
Maramasike i. Solomon Is 107 G2
Maramba Zambia see Livingstone
Marambio research station Antarctica 152 A2
Maran Malaysia 71 C7
Maran mt. Pak. 89 G4
Marana U.S.A. 129 H5
Marand Iran 88 B2
Marandellas Zimbabwe see Marondera
Marang Malaysia 71 C6
Marang Myanmar 71 B5
Maranhão r. Brazil 145 A1
Maranoa r. Australia 112 D1
Marañón r. Peru 142 D4
Marão Moz. 101 L3
Marão mt. Port. 57 C3
Mara Rosa Brazil 145 A1
Maraş Turkey see Kahramanmaraş
Marathon Canada 122 D4
Marathon FL U.S.A. 133 D7
Marathon NY U.S.A. 135 G2
Marathon TX U.S.A. 131 C6
Maratua i. Indon. 68 F6
Maraú Brazil 145 D1
Maravillas Creek watercourse U.S.A. 131 C6
Mārāzā Azer. 91 H2
Marbella Spain 57 D5
Marble Bar Australia 108 B5
Marble Canyon U.S.A. 129 H3
Marble Canyon gorge U.S.A. 129 H3
Marble Hall S. Africa 101 I3
Marble Hill U.S.A. 131 F4
Marble Island Canada 121 N2
Marbul Pass India 82 C2
Marburg S. Africa 101 J6
Marburg Slovenia see Maribor
Marburg an der Lahn Germany 53 I4
Marca, Ponta do pt Angola 99 B5
Marcali Hungary 58 G1
Marcelino Ramos Brazil 145 A4
March U.K. 49 H6
Marche reg. France 56 E3
Marche-en-Famenne Belgium 52 F4
Marchena Spain 57 D5
Marchinbar Island Australia 110 B1
Mar Chiquita, Laguna l. Arg. 144 D4

Marchtrenk Austria 47 O6
Marco U.S.A. 133 D7
Marcoing France 52 D4
Marcona Peru 142 C7
Marcopeet Islands Canada 122 F2
Marcus Baker, Mount U.S.A. 118 D3
Marcy, Mount U.S.A. 135 I1
Mardan Pak. 89 I3
Mar del Plata Arg. 144 E5
Mardīān Afgh. 89 G2
Mardin Turkey 91 F3
Maré i. New Caledonia 107 G4
Maree, Loch l. U.K. 50 D3
Mareh Iran 89 E5
Marengo IA U.S.A. 130 E3
Marengo IN U.S.A. 134 B4
Marevo Rus. Fed. 42 G4
Marfa U.S.A. 131 B6
Marganets Ukr. see Marhanets'
Margao India see Madgaon
Margaret r. Australia 108 D4
Margaret watercourse Australia 111 B6
Margaret, Mount hill Australia 108 B5
Margaret Lake Alta Canada 120 H3
Margaret Lake N.W.T. Canada 120 G1
Margaret River Australia 109 A8
Margaretville U.S.A. 135 H2
Margarita, Isla de i. Venez. 142 F1
Margaritovo Rus. Fed. 74 D4
Margate U.K. 49 I7
Margherita, Lake Eth. see Abaya, Lake

▶Margherita Peak
Dem. Rep. Congo/Uganda 98 C3
3rd highest mountain in Africa.

Marghilon Uzbek. see Marg'ilon
Marg'ilon Uzbek. 80 D3
Mārgo, Dasht-i des. Afgh. see Māragow, Dasht-e
Margog Caka l. China 83 F2
Mārgow, Dasht-e des. Afgh. 89 F4
Margraten Neth. 52 F4
Marguerite Canada 120 F4
Marguerite, Pic mt. Dem. Rep. Congo/Uganda see Margherita Peak
Marguerite Bay Antarctica 152 L2
Margyang China 83 G3
Marhaj Khalīl Iraq 91 G4
Marhanets' Ukr. 43 G7
Marhoum Alg. 54 D5
Mari Myanmar 70 B1
Maria atoll Fr. Polynesia 151 J7
María Elena Chile 144 C2
Maria Island Australia 110 A2
Maria Island Myanmar 71 B5
Maria Island National Park Australia 111 [inset]
Mariala National Park Australia 111 D5
Mariana Brazil 145 C3
Marianao Cuba 133 D8
Mariana Ridge sea feature N. Pacific Ocean 150 F4

▶Mariana Trench sea feature
N. Pacific Ocean 150 F5
Deepest trench in the world.

Mariani India 83 H4
Mariánica, Cordillera mts Spain see Morena, Sierra
Marian Lake Canada 120 G2
Marianna AR U.S.A. 131 F5
Marianna FL U.S.A. 133 C6
Mariano Machado Angola see Ganda
Mariánské Lázně Czech Rep. 53 M5
Marias r. U.S.A. 126 F3
Marías, Islas is Mex. 136 C4

▶Mariato, Punta pt Panama 137 H7
Most southerly point of North America.

Maria van Diemen, Cape N.Z. 113 D2
Ma'rib Yemen 86 G6
Maribor Slovenia 58 F1
Marica r. Bulg. see Maritsa
Maricopa AZ U.S.A. 129 G5
Maricopa CA U.S.A. 128 D4
Maricopa Mountains U.S.A. 129 G5
Maridi Sudan 97 F4
Marie Byrd Land reg. Antarctica 152 J1
Marie-Galante i. Guadeloupe 137 L5
Mariehamn Fin. 45 K6
Mariembero r. Brazil 145 A1
Marienbad Czech Rep. see Mariánské Lázně
Marienberg Germany 53 N4
Marienburg Poland see Malbork
Marienhafe Germany 53 H1
Mariental Namibia 100 C3
Marienwerder Poland see Kwidzyn
Mariestad Sweden 45 H7
Mariet r. Canada 122 F2
Marietta GA U.S.A. 133 C5
Marietta OH U.S.A. 134 E4
Marietta OK U.S.A. 131 D5
Marignane France 56 G5
Marii, Mys pt Rus. Fed. 66 G2
Mariinsk Rus. Fed. 64 J4
Mariinskiy Posad Rus. Fed. 42 J4
Marijampolė Lith. 45 M9
Marília Brazil 145 A3
Marillana Australia 108 B5
Marimba Angola 99 B4
Marín Spain 57 B2
Marina U.S.A. 128 C3
Marina di Gioiosa Ionica Italy 58 G5
Mar'ina Gorka Belarus see Mar"ina Horka
Mar"ina Horka Belarus 45 P10
Marinduque i. Phil. 69 G4
Marinette U.S.A. 134 B1
Maringá Brazil 145 A3
Maringa r. Dem. Rep. Congo 98 B3
Maringo U.S.A. 134 D3
Marinha Grande Port. 57 B4
Marion AL U.S.A. 133 C5
Marion AR U.S.A. 131 F5
Marion IL U.S.A. 130 F4
Marion IN U.S.A. 134 C3
Marion KS U.S.A. 130 D4
Marion MI U.S.A. 134 C1
Marion NY U.S.A. 135 G2
Marion OH U.S.A. 134 D3
Marion SC U.S.A. 133 E5
Marion VA U.S.A. 134 E5
Marion, Lake U.S.A. 133 D5
Marion Reef Australia 110 F3
Maripa Venez. 142 E2
Mariposa U.S.A. 128 D3
Marisa Indon. 69 G6
Mariscal José Félix Estigarribia Para. 144 D2
Maritime Alps mts France/Italy 56 H4
Maritime Kray admin. div. Rus. Fed. see Primorskiy Kray
Maritimes, Alpes mts France/Italy see Maritime Alps
Maritsa r. Bulg. 59 L4
also known as Evros (Greece), Marica (Bulgaria), Meriç (Turkey)
Marittime, Alpi mts France/Italy see Maritime Alps
Mariupol' Ukr. 43 H7
Mariusa nat. park Venez. 142 F2
Marīvān Iran 88 B3
Marjan Afgh. see Wazi Khwa
Marjayoûn Lebanon 85 B3
Marka Somalia 98 E3
Markala Mali 96 C3
Markam China 76 C2
Markaryd Sweden 45 H8
Markdale Canada 134 E1
Marken S. Africa 101 I2
Markermeer l. Neth. 52 F2
Market Deeping U.K. 49 G6
Market Drayton U.K. 49 E6
Market Harborough U.K. 49 G6
Markethill U.K. 51 F3
Market Weighton U.K. 48 G5
Markha r. Rus. Fed. 65 M3
Markham Canada 134 F2
Markit China 80 E4
Markkleeberg Germany 53 M3
Markleeville U.S.A. 128 D2
Marklohe Germany 53 J2
Markog Qu r. China 76 D1
Markounda Cent. Afr. Rep. 98 B3
Markovo Rus. Fed. 65 S3
Markranstädt Germany 53 M3
Marks Rus. Fed. 43 J6
Marks U.S.A. 131 F5
Marksville U.S.A. 131 E6
Marktheidenfeld Germany 53 J5
Marktredwitz Germany 53 M4
Marl Germany 52 H3
Marla Australia 109 F6
Marlborough Downs hills U.K. 49 F7
Marle France 52 D5
Marlette U.S.A. 134 D2
Marlin U.S.A. 131 D6
Marlinton U.S.A. 134 E4
Marlo Australia 112 D6
Marmagao India 84 B3
Marmande France 56 E4
Marmara, Sea of g. Turkey 59 M4
Marmara Denizi g. Turkey see Marmara, Sea of
Marmara Gölü l. Turkey 59 M5
Marmarica reg. Libya 90 B5
Marmaris Turkey 59 M6
Marmarth U.S.A. 130 C2
Marmet U.S.A. 134 E4
Marmion, Lake salt l. Australia 109 C7
Marmion Lake Canada 121 N5
Marmolada mt. Italy 58 D1
Marne r. France 52 C6
Marne-la-Vallée France 52 C6
Marnitz Germany 53 L1
Maroantsetra Madag. 99 E5
Maroc country Africa see Morocco
Marol Pak. 89 I4
Marol Pak. 82 D2
Maroldsweisach Germany 53 K4
Maromokotro mt. Madag. 99 E5
Marondera Zimbabwe 99 D5
Maroochydore Australia 112 F1
Maroonah Australia 109 A5
Maroon Peak U.S.A. 126 G5
Marosvásárhely Romania see Târgu Mureş
Maroua Cameroon 97 E3
Marovoay Madag. 99 E5
Marqādah Syria 91 F4
Mar Qu r. China see Markog Qu
Marquard S. Africa 101 H5
Marquesas Islands Fr. Polynesia 151 K6
Marquesas Keys is U.S.A. 133 D7
Marquês de Valença Brazil 145 C3
Marquette U.S.A. 132 C2
Marquez U.S.A. 131 D6
Marquion France 52 D4
Marquise France 52 B4
Marquises, Îles is Fr. Polynesia see Marquesas Islands
Marra Australia 112 A3
Marra r. Australia 112 C3
Marra, Jebel mt. Sudan 97 F3
Marra, Jebel Sudan 97 F3
Marracuene Moz. 101 K3
Marrakech Morocco 54 C5
Marrakesh Morocco see Marrakech
Marrangua, Lagoa l. Moz. 101 L3
Marrar Australia 112 C5
Marrawah Australia 111 [inset]
Marrawah Tas. Australia 111 [inset]
Marree Australia 111 B6
Marrowbone U.S.A. 134 C5
Marruecos country Africa see Morocco
Marrupa Moz. 99 D5
Marryat Australia 109 F6
Marsá al 'Alam Egypt 86 D4
Marsa 'Alam Egypt see Marsá al 'Alam
Marsa al Burayqah Libya 97 E1
Marsabit Kenya 98 D3
Marsala Sicily Italy 58 E6
Marsá Maṭrūḥ Egypt 90 B5
Marsberg Germany 53 I3
Marsciano Italy 58 E3
Marsden Australia 112 C4
Marsden Canada 121 I4
Marsdiep sea chan. Neth. 52 E2
Marseille France 56 G5
Marseilles France see Marseille
Marsfjället mt. Sweden 44 I4
Marshall watercourse Australia 110 B4
Marshall AR U.S.A. 131 E5
Marshall IL U.S.A. 134 B4
Marshall MI U.S.A. 134 C2
Marshall MN U.S.A. 130 E2
Marshall MO U.S.A. 130 E4
Marshall TX U.S.A. 131 E5
Marshall Islands country N. Pacific Ocean 150 H5
Marshalltown U.S.A. 130 E3
Marshfield MO U.S.A. 131 E4
Marshfield WI U.S.A. 130 F2
Marsh Harbour Bahamas 133 E7
Mars Hill U.S.A. 132 H2
Marsh Island U.S.A. 131 F6
Marsh Peak U.S.A. 129 I1
Marsh Point Canada 121 M3
Marsing U.S.A. 126 D4
Märsta Sweden 45 J7
Marsyaty Rus. Fed. 41 S3
Martaban, Gulf of g. Myanmar see Mottama, Gulf of
Martapura Indon. 68 E7
Marten River Canada 122 F5
Marte R. Gómez, Presa resr Mex. 131 D7
Martha's Vineyard i. U.S.A. 135 J3
Martigny Switz. 56 H3
Martim Vaz, Ilhas is S. Atlantic Ocean see Martin Vas, Ilhas
Martin r. Canada 120 F2
Martin Slovakia 47 Q6
Martin MI U.S.A. 134 C2
Martin SD U.S.A. 130 C3
Martinez Lake U.S.A. 129 F5
Martinho Campos Brazil 145 B2

▶Martinique terr. West Indies 137 L6
French Overseas Department.

Martinique Passage Dominica/Martinique 137 L5
Martin Peninsula Antarctica 152 K2
Martinsburg U.S.A. 135 G4
Martins Ferry U.S.A. 134 E3
Martinsville IL U.S.A. 134 B4
Martinsville IN U.S.A. 134 B4
Martinsville VA U.S.A. 134 F5

▶Martin Vas, Ilhas is S. Atlantic Ocean 148 G7
Most easterly point of South America.

Martin Vaz Islands S. Atlantic Ocean see Martin Vas, Ilhas
Martök Kazakh. see Martuk
Marton N.Z. 113 E5
Martorell Spain 57 G3
Martos Spain 57 E5
Martuk Kazakh. 78 E1
Martuni Armenia 91 G2
Maruf Afgh. 89 G4
Maruim Brazil 143 K6
Marukhis Ugheltekhili pass Georgia/Rus. Fed. 91 F2
Marulan Australia 112 D5
Marusthali reg. India 89 H5
Marvast Iran 88 D4
Marv Dasht Iran 88 D4
Marvejols France 56 F4
Marvine, Mount U.S.A. 129 H2
Marwayne Canada 121 I4
Mary r. Australia 108 E3
Mary Turkm. 89 F2
Maryborough Qld Australia 111 F5
Maryborough Vic. Australia 112 A6
Marydale S. Africa 100 F5
Mary Frances Lake Canada 121 J2
Mary Lake Canada 121 K2
Maryland state U.S.A. 135 G4
Maryport U.K. 48 D4
Mary's Harbour Canada 123 L3
Marysvale U.S.A. 129 G2
Marysville CA U.S.A. 128 C2
Marysville KS U.S.A. 130 D4
Marysville OH U.S.A. 134 D3
Maryvale N.T. Australia 109 F6
Maryvale Qld Australia 110 D3
Maryville MO U.S.A. 130 E3
Maryville TN U.S.A. 132 D5
Marzagão Brazil 145 A2
Marzahna Germany 53 M2
Masada tourist site Israel 85 B4
Masāhūn, Kūh-e mt. Iran 88 D4
Masai Steppe plain Tanz. 99 D4
Masaka Uganda 98 D4
Masakhane S. Africa 101 H6
Masalembu Besar i. Indon. 68 E8
Masallı Azer. 91 H3
Masan S. Korea 75 C6
Masasi Tanz. 99 D5
Masavi Bol. 142 F7
Masbate Phil. 69 G4
Masbate i. Phil. 69 G4
Mascara Alg. 57 G6
Mascarene Basin sea feature Indian Ocean 149 L7
Mascarene Plain sea feature Indian Ocean 149 L7
Mascarene Ridge sea feature Indian Ocean 149 L6
Mascote Brazil 145 D1
Masein Myanmar 70 A2
Masela Indon. 108 E2
Masela i. Indon. 108 E2

▶Maseru Lesotho 101 H5
Capital of Lesotho.

Mashai Lesotho 101 I5
Mashan China 77 F4
Masherbrum mt. Pak. 82 D2
Mashhad Iran 89 E2
Mashishing S. Africa 101 J3
Mashket r. Pak. 89 F5
Mashki Chah Pak. 89 F4
Masi Norway 44 M2
Masiáca Mex. 127 F8
Masibambane S. Africa 101 H6
Masīlah, Wādī al watercourse Yemen 86 H6
Masilo S. Africa 101 H5
Masi-Manimba Dem. Rep. Congo 99 B4
Masindi Uganda 98 D3
Masinyusane S. Africa 100 F6
Masira, Gulf of Oman see Maşīrah, Khalīj
Maşīrah, Jazīrat i. Oman 87 I5
Maşīrah, Khalīj b. Oman 87 I6
Masira Island Oman see Maşīrah, Jazīrat
Masjed Soleymān Iran 88 C4
Mask, Lough l. Ireland 51 C4
Maskūtān Iran 89 E5
Maslovo Rus. Fed. 41 S3
Masoala, Tanjona c. Madag. 99 F5
Mason MI U.S.A. 134 C2
Mason OH U.S.A. 134 C4
Mason TX U.S.A. 131 D6
Mason, Lake salt flat Australia 109 B6
Mason Bay N.Z. 113 A8
Mason City U.S.A. 130 E3
Masontown U.S.A. 134 F4
Masqaṭ Oman see Muscat
Masqaṭ reg. Oman see Muscat
'Masrūg well Oman 88 D6
Massa Italy 58 D2
Massachusetts state U.S.A. 135 I2
Massachusetts Bay U.S.A. 135 J2
Massadona U.S.A. 129 I1
Massafra Italy 58 G4
Massakory Chad 97 E3
Massa Marittimo Italy 58 D3
Massangena Moz. 99 D6
Massango Angola 99 B4
Massawa Eritrea 86 E6
Massawippi, Lac l. Canada 135 I1
Massena U.S.A. 135 H1
Massenya Chad 97 E3
Masset Canada 120 C4
Massieville U.S.A. 134 D4
Massif Central mts France 56 F4
Massilia France see Marseille
Massillon U.S.A. 134 E3
Massina Mali 96 C3
Massinga Moz. 101 L2
Massingir Moz. 101 K2
Massingir, Barragem de resr Moz. 101 K2
Masson Island Antarctica 152 F2
Mastchoh Tajik. 89 H2
Masterton N.Z. 113 E5
Masticho, Akra pt Voreio Aigaio Greece see Oura, Akrotirio
Mastung Pak. 78 F4
Mastūrah Saudi Arabia 86 E5
Masty Belarus 45 N10
Masuda Japan 75 C6
Masuku Gabon see Franceville
Masulipatam India see Machilipatnam
Masulipatnam India see Machilipatnam
Masuna i. American Samoa see Tutuila
Masvingo Zimbabwe 99 D6
Masvingo prov. Zimbabwe 101 J1
Maswa Tanz. 98 D4
Maswaar i. Indon. 69 I7
Maşyāf Syria 85 C2
Mat, Nam r. Laos 70 D3
Mata Myanmar 70 B1
Matabeleland South prov. Zimbabwe 101 I1
Matachewan Canada 122 E5
Matad Dornod Mongolia 73 L3
Matadi Dem. Rep. Congo 99 B4
Matador U.S.A. 131 C5
Matagalpa Nicaragua 137 G6
Matagami Canada 122 F4
Matagami, Lac l. Canada 122 F4
Matagorda Island U.S.A. 131 D6
Matak i. Indon. 71 D7
Matakana Island N.Z. 113 F3
Matala Angola 99 B5
Maṭāli', Jabal hill Saudi Arabia 91 F6
Matam Senegal 96 B3
Matamey Niger 96 D3
Matamoros U.S.A. 135 H3
Matamoros Coahuila Mex. 131 C7
Matamoros Tamaulipas Mex. 131 D7
Matandu r. Tanz. 99 D4
Matane Canada 123 I4
Matanzas Cuba 137 H4
Matapan, Cape pt Greece see Tainaro, Akrotirio
Matapédia, Lac l. Canada 123 I4
Maṭār well Saudi Arabia 88 B5
Matara Sri Lanka 84 D5
Mataram Indon. 108 B2
Matarani Peru 142 D7
Mataranka Australia 108 F3
Matarípe Brazil 145 D1
Mataró Spain 57 H3
Matasiri i. Indon. 68 F7
Matatiele S. Africa 101 I6
Matatila Reservoir India 82 D4
Mataura N.Z. 113 B8

▶Matā'utu Wallis and Futuna Is 107 I3
Capital of Wallis and Futuna Islands.

Mata-Utu Wallis and Futuna Is see Matā'utu
Matawai N.Z. 113 F4
Matay Kazakh. 80 E2
Matcha Tajik. see Mashchoh
Mat Con, Hon i. Vietnam 70 D3
Mategua Bol. 142 F6
Matehuala Mex. 131 C8
Matemanga Tanz. 99 D5
Matera Italy 58 G4
Mateur Tunisia 58 C6
Mathaji India 82 B4
Matheson Canada 122 E4
Mathews U.S.A. 135 G5
Mathis U.S.A. 131 D6
Mathoura Australia 112 B5
Mathura India 82 D4
Mati Phil. 69 H5
Matiali India 83 G4
Matias Cardoso Brazil 145 C1
Matías Romero Mex. 136 E5
Matimekosh Canada 123 I3
Matin India 83 E5
Matinenda Lake Canada 122 E5
Matizi China 76 D1
Matla r. India 83 G5
Matlabas r. S. Africa 101 H2
Matli Pak. 89 H5
Matlock U.K. 49 F5
Mato, Cerro mt. Venez. 142 E2
Matobo Hills Zimbabwe 99 C6
Mato Grosso Brazil 142 G7
Mato Grosso state Brazil 145 A1
Matopo Hills Zimbabwe see Matobo Hills
Matos Costa Brazil 145 A4
Matosinhos Port. 57 B3
Mato Verde Brazil 145 C1
Maṭraḥ Oman 88 E6
Matroosberg mt. S. Africa 100 D7
Matsesta Rus. Fed. 91 E2
Matsue Japan 75 D6
Matsumoto Japan 75 E5
Matsu Tao i. Taiwan 77 I3
Matsuyama Japan 75 D6
Mattagami r. Canada 122 E4
Mattamuskeet, Lake U.S.A. 132 E5
Mattawa Canada 122 F5
Matterhorn mt. Italy/Switz. 58 B2
Matterhorn mt. U.S.A. 126 E4
Matthew Town Bahamas 137 J4
Maṭṭī, Sabkhat salt pan Saudi Arabia 88 D6
Mattoon U.S.A. 130 F4
Matturai Sri Lanka see Matara
Matuku i. Fiji 107 H3
Matumbo Angola 99 B5
Maturín Venez. 142 F2
Matusadona National Park Zimbabwe 99 C5
Matwabeng S. Africa 101 H5
Maty Island P.N.G. see Wuvulu Island
Mau India see Maunath Bhanjan
Maúa Moz. 99 D5
Maubeuge France 52 D4
Maubin Myanmar 70 A3
Ma-ubin Myanmar 70 B1
Maubourguet France 56 E5
Mauchline U.K. 50 E5
Maudaha India 82 E4
Maude Australia 111 D7
Maud Seamount sea feature S. Atlantic Ocean 148 I10
Mau-é-ele Moz. see Marão
Maués Brazil 143 G4
Maughold Head hd Isle of Man 48 C4
Maug Islands N. Mariana Is 69 L2
Maui i. U.S.A. 127 [inset]
Maukkadaw Myanmar 70 A2
Maulbronn Germany 53 I6
Maule r. Chile 144 B5
Maulvi Bazar Bangl. see Moulvibazar
Maumee U.S.A. 134 D3
Maumee Bay U.S.A. 134 D3
Maumere Indon. 108 C2
Maumturk Mts hills Ireland 51 C4
Maun Botswana 99 C5
Mauna Kea vol. U.S.A. 127 [inset]
Mauna Loa vol. U.S.A. 127 [inset]
Maunath Bhanjan India 83 E4
Maunatlala Botswana 101 H2
Maungaturoto N.Z. 113 E3
Maungdaw Myanmar 70 A2
Maungmagan Islands Myanmar 71 B4
Maurepas, Lake U.S.A. 131 F6
Mauriac France 56 F4
Maurice country Indian Ocean see Mauritius
Maurice, Lake salt flat Australia 109 E7
Maurik Neth. 52 F3
Mauritania country Africa 96 B3
Mauritanie country Africa see Mauritania
Mauritius country Indian Ocean 149 L7
Maurs France 56 F4
Mauston U.S.A. 130 F3
Mava Dem. Rep. Congo 98 C3
Mavago Moz. 99 D5
Mavan, Kūh-e hill Iran 88 E3
Mavanza Moz. 101 L2
Mavinga Angola 99 C5
Mavrovo nat. park Macedonia 59 I4
Mavume Moz. 101 L2
Mavuya S. Africa 101 H6
Ma Wan i. H.K. China 77 [inset]
Māwān, Khashm hill Saudi Arabia 88 B6
Mawana India 82 D3
Mawanga Dem. Rep. Congo 99 B4
Ma Wang Dui tourist site China 77 G2
Mawei China 77 H3
Mawjib, Wādī al r. Jordan 85 B4
Mawkmai Myanmar 70 B2
Mawlaik Myanmar 70 A2
Mawlamyaing Myanmar 70 B3
Mawlamyine Myanmar see Mawlamyaing
Mawqaq Saudi Arabia 91 F6
Mawson research station Antarctica 152 E2
Mawson Coast Antarctica 152 E2
Mawson Escarpment Antarctica 152 E2
Mawson Peninsula Antarctica 152 H2
Maw Taung mt. Myanmar 71 B5
Mawza Yemen 86 F7
Maxán Arg. 144 C3
Maxhamish Lake Canada 120 F3
Maxia, Punta mt. Sardinia Italy 58 C5
Maxixe Moz. 101 L2
Maxmo Fin. 44 M5
May, Isle of i. U.K. 50 G4
Maya r. Rus. Fed. 65 O3
Mayaguana i. Bahamas 133 F8
Mayaguana Passage Bahamas 133 F8
Mayagüez Puerto Rico 137 K5
Mayahi Niger 96 D3
Mayak Rus. Fed. 74 E2
Mayakovskiy, Qullai mt. Tajik. 89 H2
Mayakovskogo, Pik mt. Tajik. see Mayakovskiy, Qullai
Mayama Congo 98 B4
Maya Mountains Belize/Guat. 136 G5
Mayan China see Mayanhe
Mayang China 77 F3
Mayanhe China 76 E1
Mayar hill U.K. 50 F4
Maybeury U.S.A. 134 E5
Maybole U.K. 50 E5
Maych'ew Eth. 98 D2
Maydān Shahr Afgh. see Meydān Shahr
Maydh Somalia 86 G7
Maydos Turkey see Eceabat
Mayen Germany 53 H4
Mayenne France 56 D2
Mayenne r. France 56 D3
Mayer U.S.A. 129 G4
Mayêr Kangri mt. China 83 F2
Mayersville U.S.A. 131 F5
Mayerthorpe Canada 120 H4
Mayfield N.Z. 113 C6
Mayi He r. China 74 C3
Maykop Rus. Fed. 91 F1
Maymanah Afgh. 89 G3
Mayna Respublika Khakasiya Rus. Fed. 72 H2
Mayna Ul'yanovskaya Oblast' Rus. Fed. 43 J5
Mayni India 84 B2
Maynooth Canada 135 G1
Mayo Canada 120 C2
Mayo U.S.A. 133 D6
Mayo Alim Cameroon 96 E4
Mayoko Congo 98 B4
Mayo Lake Canada 120 C2
Mayo Landing Canada see Mayo
Mayor, Puig mt. Spain see Major, Puig
Mayor Island N.Z. 113 F3
Mayor Pablo Lagerenza Para. 144 D1

▶Mayotte terr. Africa 99 E5
French Departmental Collectivity.

Mayskaya Amurskaya Oblast' Rus. Fed. 74 C1
Mayskiy Kabardino-Balkarskaya Respublika Rus. Fed. 91 G2
Mays Landing U.S.A. 135 H4
Mayson Lake Canada 121 J3
Maysville U.S.A. 134 D4
Mayumba Gabon 98 B4
Mayum La pass China 83 E3
Mayuram India 84 C4
Mayville MI U.S.A. 134 D2
Mayville ND U.S.A. 130 D2
Mayville NY U.S.A. 134 F2
Mayville WI U.S.A. 134 A2
Mazabuka Zambia 99 C5
Mazaca Turkey see Kayseri
Mazagan Morocco see El Jadida
Mazar China 82 D1
Mazar, Koh-i- mt. Afgh. 89 G3
Mazara, Val di valley Sicily Italy 58 E6
Mazara del Vallo Sicily Italy 58 E6
Mazār-e Sharīf Afgh. 89 G2
Mazārī' reg. U.A.E. 88 D6
Mazatán Mex. 127 F7
Mazatlán Mex. 136 C4
Mazatzal Peak U.S.A. 129 H4
Mazdaj Iran 91 H4
Mažeikiai Lith. 45 M8
Maẓhūr, 'Irq al des. Saudi Arabia 88 A5
Mazīm Oman 88 E6
Mazocahui Mex. 127 F7
Mazocruz Peru 142 E7
Mazomora Tanz. 99 D4
Mazu Dao i. Taiwan see Matsu Tao
Mazunga Zimbabwe 99 C6
Mazyr Belarus 43 F5
Mazzouna Tunisia 58 C7

▶Mbabane Swaziland 101 J4
Capital of Swaziland.

Mbahiakro Côte d'Ivoire 96 C4
Mbaïki Cent. Afr. Rep. 98 B3
Mbakaou, Lac de l. Cameroon 96 E4
Mbala Zambia 99 D4
Mbale Uganda 98 D3
Mbalmayo Cameroon 96 E4
Mbam r. Cameroon 96 E4
Mbandaka Dem. Rep. Congo 98 B4
M'banza Congo Angola 99 B4
Mbarara Uganda 97 G5
Mbari r. Cent. Afr. Rep. 98 C3
Mbaswana S. Africa 101 K4
Mbemkuru r. Tanz. 99 D4
Mbeya Tanz. 99 D4
Mbinga Tanz. 99 D5
Mbini Equat. Guinea 96 D4
Mbizi Zimbabwe 99 D6
Mboki Cent. Afr. Rep. 98 C3
Mbomo Congo 98 B3
Mbouda Cameroon 96 E4
Mbour Senegal 96 B3
Mbout Mauritania 96 B3
Mbozi Tanz. 99 D4
Mbrès Cent. Afr. Rep. 98 B3
Mbuji-Mayi Dem. Rep. Congo 99 C4
Mbulu Tanz. 98 D4
Mburucuyá Arg. 144 E3
McAdam Canada 123 I5
McAlester U.S.A. 131 E5
McAlister mt. Australia 112 D5
McAllen U.S.A. 131 D7
McArthur r. Australia 110 B2
McArthur U.S.A. 134 D4
McArthur Mills Canada 135 G1
McBain U.S.A. 134 C1
McBride Canada 120 F4
McCall U.S.A. 126 D3
McCamey U.S.A. 131 C6
McCammon U.S.A. 126 E4
McCauley Island Canada 120 D4
McClintock, Mount Antarctica 152 H1
McClintock Channel Canada 119 H2
McClintock Range hills Australia 108 D4
McClure, Lake U.S.A. 128 C3
McClure Strait Canada 118 G2
McClusky U.S.A. 130 C2
McComb U.S.A. 131 F6
McConaughy, Lake U.S.A. 130 C3
McConnellsburg U.S.A. 135 G4
McConnelsville U.S.A. 134 E4
McCook U.S.A. 130 C3
McCormick U.S.A. 133 D5
McCrea r. Canada 120 H2
McCreary Canada 121 L5
McDame Canada 120 D3
McDermitt U.S.A. 126 D4
McDonald Islands Indian Ocean 149 M9
McDonald Peak U.S.A. 126 E3
McDonough U.S.A. 133 C5
McDougall's Bay S. Africa 100 C5
McDowell Peak U.S.A. 129 H5
McFarland U.S.A. 128 D4
McGill U.S.A. 129 F2
McGivney Canada 123 I5
McGrath AK U.S.A. 118 C3
McGrath MN U.S.A. 130 E2

McGraw U.S.A. 135 G2
McGregor r. Canada 120 F4
McGregor S. Africa 100 D7
McGregor, Lake Canada 120 H5
McGregor Range hills Australia 111 C5
McGuire, Mount U.S.A. 126 E3
Mchinga Tanz. 99 D4
Mchinji Malawi 99 D5
McIlwraith Range hills Australia 110 C2
McInnes Lake Canada 121 M4
McIntosh U.S.A. 130 C2
McKay Range hills Australia 108 C5
McKean i. Kiribati 107 I2
McKee U.S.A. 134 C5
McKenzie r. U.S.A. 126 C3
McKinlay r. Australia 110 C4

▶McKinley, Mount U.S.A. 118 C3
Highest mountain in North America.

McKinney U.S.A. 131 D5
McKittrick U.S.A. 128 D4
McLaughlin U.S.A. 130 C2
McLeansboro U.S.A. 130 F4
McLennan Canada 120 G4
McLeod r. Canada 120 H4
McLeod Bay Canada 121 I2
McLeod Lake Canada 120 F4
McLoughlin, Mount U.S.A. 126 C4
McMillan, Lake U.S.A. 131 B5
McMinnville OR U.S.A. 126 C3
McMinnville TN U.S.A. 132 C5
McMurdo research station Antarctica 152 H1
McMurdo Sound b. Antarctica 152 H1
McNary U.S.A. 129 I4
McNaughton Lake Canada see Kinbasket Lake
McPherson U.S.A. 130 D4
McQuesten r. Canada 120 B2
McRae U.S.A. 133 D5
McTavish Arm b. Canada 120 G1
McVeytown U.S.A. 135 G3
McVicar Arm b. Canada 120 F1
Mdantsane S. Africa 101 H7
M'Daourouch Alg. 58 B6
M'Đrak Vietnam 71 E4
Mê, Hon i. Vietnam 70 D3
Mead, Lake resr U.S.A. 129 F3
Meade U.S.A. 131 C4
Meade r. U.S.A. 118 C2
Meadow Australia 109 A6
Meadow SD U.S.A. 130 C2
Meadow UT U.S.A. 129 G2
Meadow Lake Canada 121 I4
Meadville MS U.S.A. 131 F6
Meadville PA U.S.A. 134 E3
Meaford Canada 134 E1
Meaken-dake vol. Japan 74 G4
Mealhada Port. 57 B3
Mealy Mountains Canada 123 K3
Meandarra Australia 112 D1
Meander River Canada 120 G3
Meaux France 52 C6
Mecca Saudi Arabia 86 E5
Mecca CA U.S.A. 128 E5
Mecca OH U.S.A. 134 E3
Mechanic Falls U.S.A. 135 J1
Mechanicsville U.S.A. 135 G5
Mechelen Belgium 52 E3
Mechelen Neth. 52 F4
Mecherchar i. Palau see Eil Malk
Mecheria Alg. 54 D5
Mechernich Germany 52 G4
Mecitözü Turkey 90 D2
Meckenheim Germany 52 H4
Mecklenburger Bucht b. Germany 47 M3
Mecklenburg-Vorpommern land Germany 53 M1
Mecklenburg - West Pomerania land Germany see Mecklenburg-Vorpommern
Meda r. Australia 108 C4
Meda Port. 57 C3
Medak India 84 C2
Medan Indon. 71 B7
Medanosa, Punta pt Arg. 144 C7
Médanos de Coro, Parque Nacional nat. park Venez. 142 E1
Medawachchiya Sri Lanka 84 D4
Médéa Alg. 57 H5
Medebach Germany 53 I3
Medellín Col. 142 C2
Meden r. U.K. 48 G5
Medenine Tunisia 54 G5
Mederdra Mauritania 96 B3
Medford NY U.S.A. 135 I3
Medford OK U.S.A. 131 D4
Medford OR U.S.A. 126 C4
Medford WI U.S.A. 130 F2
Medgidia Romania 59 M2
Media U.S.A. 135 H4
Mediaş Romania 59 K1
Medicine Bow r. U.S.A. 126 G4
Medicine Bow Mountains U.S.A. 126 G4
Medicine Bow Peak U.S.A. 126 G4
Medicine Hat Canada 121 I5
Medicine Lake U.S.A. 126 G2
Medicine Lodge U.S.A. 131 D4
Medina Brazil 145 C2
Medina Saudi Arabia 86 E5
Medina ND U.S.A. 130 D2
Medina NY U.S.A. 135 F2
Medina OH U.S.A. 134 E3
Medinaceli Spain 57 E3
Medina del Campo Spain 57 D3
Medina de Rioseco Spain 57 D3
Medina Lake U.S.A. 131 D6
Medinipur India 83 F5
Mediolanum Italy see Milan
Mediterranean Sea 54 K5
Mednyy, Ostrov i. Rus. Fed. 150 H2
Médoc reg. France 56 D4
Mêdog China 76 B2
Medora U.S.A. 130 C2
Medstead Canada 121 I4
Meduro atoll Marshall Is see Majuro
Medvedevo Rus. Fed. 42 J4
Medveditsa r. Rus. Fed. 43 I6
Medvednica mts Croatia 58 F2
Medvezh'i, Ostrova is Rus. Fed. 65 R2
Medvezh'ya vol. Rus. Fed. 74 H3
Medvezh'ya, Gora mt. Rus. Fed. 74 E3
Medvezh'yegorsk Rus. Fed. 42 G3
Medway r. U.K. 49 H7
Meekatharra Australia 109 B6
Meeker CO U.S.A. 129 J1
Meeker OH U.S.A. 134 D3
Meelpaeg Reservoir Canada 123 K4
Meemu Atoll Maldives see Mulaku Atoll
Meerane Germany 53 M4
Meerlo Neth. 52 G3
Meerut India 82 D3
Mega Escarpment Eth./Kenya 98 D3
Megalopoli Greece 59 J6
Megamo Indon. 69 I7
Mégantic, Lac l. Canada 123 H5
Megara Greece 59 J5
Megezez mt. Eth. 98 D3

▶Meghalaya state India 83 G4
Highest mean annual rainfall in the world.

Meghasani mt. India 83 F5
Meghri Armenia 91 G3
Megin Turkm. 88 E2
Megisti i. Greece 59 M6
Megri Armenia see Meghri
Mehamn Norway 44 O1
Mehar Pak. 89 G5
Meharry, Mount Australia 109 B5
Mehbubnagar India see Mahbubnagar
Mehdia Tunisia see Mahdia
Meherpur Bangl. 83 G5
Meherrin U.S.A. 135 F5
Meherrin r. U.S.A. 135 G5
Mehlville U.S.A. 130 F4
Mehrakān salt marsh Iran 88 D5
Mehrān Hormozgan Iran 88 D5
Mehrān Īlām Iran 88 B3
Mehren Germany 52 G4
Mehriz Iran 88 D4
Mehsana India see Mahesana
Mehtar Lām Afgh. 89 H3
Meia Ponte r. Brazil 145 A2
Meicheng China see Minqing
Meiganga Cameroon 97 E4
Meighen Island Canada 119 I2
Meigu China 76 D2
Meihekou China 74 B4
Meikeng China 77 G3
Meikle r. Canada 120 G3
Meikle Says Law hill U.K. 50 G5
Meiktila Myanmar 70 A2
Meilin China see Ganxian
Meilleur r. Canada 120 E2
Meilu China 77 F4
Meine Germany 53 K2
Meinersen Germany 53 K2
Meiningen Germany 53 K4
Meishan Anhui China see Jinzhai
Meishan Sichuan China 76 D2
Meishan Shuiku resr China 77 G2
Meißen Germany 47 N5
Meister r. Canada 120 D2
Meitan China 76 E3
Meixi China 74 C3
Meixian China see Meizhou
Meixing China see Xiaojin
Meizhou China 77 H3
Mej r. India 82 D4
Mejicana mt. Arg. 144 C3
Mejillones Chile 144 B2
Mékambo Gabon 98 B3
Mek'elē Eth. 98 D2
Mekelle Eth. see Mek'elē
Mékhé Senegal 96 B3
Mekhtar Pak. 89 H4
Meknassy Tunisia 58 C7
Meknès Morocco 54 C5
Mekong r. Asia 70 D4
also known as Ménam Khong (Laos/Thailand)
Mekong, Mouths of the Vietnam 71 D5
Mekoryuk U.S.A. 118 B3
Melaka Malaysia 71 C7
Melanau, Gunung hill Indon. 71 E7
Melanesia is Pacific Ocean 150 G6
Melanesian Basin sea feature Pacific Ocean 150 G5

▶Melbourne Australia 112 B6
Capital of Victoria. 2nd most populous city in Oceania.

Melbourne U.S.A. 133 D6
Melby U.K. 50 [inset]
Meldorf Germany 47 L3

▶Melekeok Palau 69 I5
Capital of Palau.

Melekess Rus. Fed. see Dimitrovgrad
Melenki Rus. Fed. 43 I5
Melet Turkey see Mesudiye
Mélèzes, Rivière aux r. Canada 123 H2
Melfa U.S.A. 135 H5
Melfi Chad 97 E3
Melfi Italy 58 F4
Melfort Canada 121 J4
Melhus Norway 44 G5
Meliadine Lake Canada 121 M2
Melide Spain 57 C2

▶Melilla N. Africa 57 E6
Autonomous Community of Spain.

Melimoyu, Monte mt. Chile 144 B6
Meliskerke Neth. 52 D3
Melita Canada 121 K5
Melitene Turkey see Malatya
Melitopol' Ukr. 43 G7
Melk Austria 47 O6
Melka Guba Eth. 98 D3
Melksham U.K. 49 E7
Mellakoski Fin. 44 N3
Mellansel Sweden 44 K5
Melle Germany 53 I2
Mellerud Sweden 45 H7
Mellette U.S.A. 130 D2
Mellid Spain see Melide
Mellilia N. Africa see Melilla
Mellor Glacier Antarctica 152 E2
Mellrichstadt Germany 53 K4
Mellum i. Germany 53 I1
Melmoth S. Africa 101 J5
Mel'nichoye Rus. Fed. 74 D3
Melo Uruguay 144 F4
Meloco Moz. 99 D5
Melolo Indon. 108 C2
Melozitna r. U.S.A. 118 C3
Melrhir, Chott salt l. Alg. 54 F5
Melrose Australia 109 C6
Melrose U.K. 50 G5
Melrose U.S.A. 130 E2
Melsungen Germany 53 J3
Melton Australia 112 B6
Melton Mowbray U.K. 49 G6
Melun France 56 F2
Melville Canada 121 K5
Melville, Cape Australia 110 D2
Melville, Lake Canada 123 K3
Melville Bugt b. Greenland see Qimusseriarsuaq
Melville Island Australia 108 E2
Melville Island Canada 119 H2
Melville Peninsula Canada 119 J3
Melvin U.S.A. 134 A3
Melvin, Lough l. Ireland/U.K. 51 D3
Mêmar Co salt l. China 83 E2
Memba Moz. 99 E5
Memberamo r. Indon. 69 J7
Memel Lith. see Klaipėda
Memel S. Africa 101 I4
Memmelsdorf Germany 53 K5
Memmingen Germany 47 M7
Mempawah Indon. 68 D6
Memphis tourist site Egypt 90 C5
Memphis MI U.S.A. 134 D2
Memphis TN U.S.A. 131 F5
Memphis TX U.S.A. 131 C5
Memphrémagog, Lac l. Canada 135 I1
Mena Ukr. 43 G6
Mena U.S.A. 131 E5
Menado Indon. see Manado
Ménaka Mali 96 D3
Menard U.S.A. 131 D6
Menasha U.S.A. 134 A1
Mendanha Brazil 145 C2
Mendarik i. Indon. 71 D7
Mende France 56 F4
Mendefera Eritrea 86 E7
Mendeleyev Ridge sea feature Arctic Ocean 153 B1
Mendeleyevsk Rus. Fed. 42 L5
Mendenhall U.S.A. 131 F6
Mendenhall, Cape U.S.A. 118 B4
Mendenhall Glacier U.S.A. 120 C3
Méndez Mex. 131 D7
Mendī Eth. 98 D3
Mendi P.N.G. 69 K8
Mendip Hills U.K. 49 E7
Mendocino U.S.A. 128 B2
Mendocino, Cape U.S.A. 128 A1
Mendocino, Lake U.S.A. 128 B2
Mendooran Australia 112 D3
Mendota CA U.S.A. 128 C3
Mendota IL U.S.A. 130 F3
Mendoza Arg. 144 C4
Menemen Turkey 59 L5
Ménerville Alg. see Thenia
Mengban China 76 D4
Mengcheng China 77 H1
Menghai China 76 D4
Mengjin China 77 G1
Mengla China 76 D4
Menglang China see Lancang
Menglie China see Jiangcheng
Mengyang China see Mingshan
Mengzi China 76 D4
Menihek Canada 123 I3
Menihek Lakes Canada 123 I3
Menindee Australia 111 C7
Menindee, Lake Australia 111 C7
Ménistouc, Lac l. Canada 123 I3
Menkere Rus. Fed. 65 N3
Mennecy France 52 C6
Menominee U.S.A. 134 B1
Menomonee Falls U.S.A. 134 A2
Menomonie U.S.A. 130 F2
Menongue Angola 99 B5
Menorca i. Spain see Minorca
Mentawai, Kepulauan is Indon. 68 B7
Mentawai, Selat sea chan. Indon. 68 C7
Menteroda Germany 53 K3
Mentmore U.S.A. 129 I4
Menton France 56 H5
Mentone U.S.A. 131 C6
Menuf Egypt see Minūf
Menzel Bourguiba Tunisia 58 C6
Menzelet Barajı resr Turkey 90 E3
Menzelinsk Rus. Fed. 41 Q4
Menzel Temime Tunisia 58 D6
Menzies Australia 109 C7
Menzies, Mount Antarctica 152 E2
Meobbaai b. Namibia 100 B3
Meoqui Mex. 131 B6
Meppel Neth. 52 G2
Meppen Germany 53 H2
Mepuze Moz. 101 K2
Meqheleng S. Africa 101 H5
Mequon U.S.A. 134 B2
Merak Indon. 68 D8
Meråker Norway 44 G5
Merano Italy 58 D1
Meratswe r. Botswana 100 G2
Merauke Indon. 69 K8
Merca Somalia see Marka
Mercantour, Parc National du nat. park France 56 H4
Merced U.S.A. 128 C3
Merced r. U.S.A. 128 C3
Mercedes Arg. 144 E3
Mercedes Uruguay 144 E4
Mercer ME U.S.A. 135 K1
Mercer PA U.S.A. 134 E3
Mercer WI U.S.A. 130 F2
Mercês Brazil 145 C3
Mercury Islands N.Z. 113 E3
Mercy, Cape Canada 119 L3
Merdenik Turkey see Göle
Mere Belgium 52 D4
Mere U.K. 49 E7
Meredith U.S.A. 135 J2
Meredith, Lake U.S.A. 131 C5
Merefa Ukr. 43 H6
Merga Oasis Sudan 86 C6
Mergui Myanmar see Myeik
Mergui Archipelago is Myanmar 71 B5
Meriç r. Turkey 59 L4
also known as Evros (Greece), Marica, Maritsa (Bulgaria)
Mérida Mex. 136 G4
Mérida Spain 57 C4
Mérida Venez. 142 D2
Mérida, Cordillera de mts Venez. 142 D2
Meriden U.S.A. 135 I3
Meridian MS U.S.A. 131 F5
Meridian TX U.S.A. 131 D6
Mérignac France 56 D4
Merijärvi Fin. 44 N4
Merikarvia Fin. 45 L6
Merimbula Australia 112 D6
Merín, Laguna l. Brazil/Uruguay see Mirim, Lagoa
Meringur Australia 111 C7
Merir i. Palau 69 I6
Merjayoun Lebanon see Marjayoûn
Merkel U.S.A. 131 C5
Merluna Australia 110 C2
Mermaid Reef Australia 108 B4
Meron, Har mt. Israel 85 B3
Merowe Sudan 86 D6
Mêrqung Co l. China 83 F3
Merredin Australia 109 B7
Merrick hill U.K. 50 E5
Merrickville Canada 135 H1
Merrill MI U.S.A. 134 C2
Merrill WI U.S.A. 130 F2
Merrill, Mount Canada 120 E2
Merrillville U.S.A. 134 B3
Merriman U.S.A. 130 C3
Merritt Canada 120 F5
Merritt Island U.S.A. 133 D6
Merriwa Australia 112 E4
Merrygoen Australia 112 D3
Mersa Fatma Eritrea 86 F7
Mersa Maṭrûḥ Egypt see Marsá Maṭrūḥ
Mersch Lux. 52 G5
Merseburg (Saale) Germany 53 L3
Mersey est. U.K. 48 E5
Mersin Turkey 85 B1
Mersin prov. Turkey 85 A1
Mersing Malaysia 71 C7
Mērsrags Latvia 45 M8
Merta India 82 C4
Merthyr Tydfil U.K. 49 D7
Mértola Port. 57 C5
Mertz Glacier Antarctica 152 G2
Mertz Glacier Tongue Antarctica 152 G2
Mertzon U.S.A. 131 C6
Méru France 52 C5

▶Meru vol. Tanz. 98 D4
4th highest mountain, and highest active volcano, in Africa.

Merui Pak. 89 F4
Merv Turkm. see Mary
Merweville S. Africa 100 E7
Merzifon Turkey 90 D2
Merzig Germany 52 G5
Merz Peninsula Antarctica 152 L2
Mesa AZ U.S.A. 129 H5
Mesa NM U.S.A. 127 G6
Mesabi Range hills U.S.A. 130 E2
Mesagne Italy 58 G4
Mesa Negra mt. U.S.A. 129 J4
Mesara, Ormos b. Kriti Greece see Kolpos Messaras
Mesara, Ormos b. Kriti Greece see Kolpos Messaras
Mesa Verde National Park U.S.A. 129 I3
Meschede Germany 53 I3
Mese Myanmar 70 B3
Meselefors Sweden 44 J4
Mesgouez, Lac Canada 122 G4
Meshed Iran see Mashhad
Meshkān Iran 88 E2
Meshra'er Req Sudan 86 C8
Mesick U.S.A. 134 C1
Mesimeri Greece 59 J4
Mesolongi Greece 59 I5
Mesolóngion Greece see Mesolongi
Mesopotamia reg. Iraq 91 F4
Mesquita Brazil 145 C2
Mesquite NV U.S.A. 129 F3
Mesquite TX U.S.A. 131 D5
Mesquite Lake U.S.A. 129 F4
Messaad Alg. 54 E5
Messana Sicily Italy see Messina
Messina Sicily Italy 58 F5
Messina, Strait of Italy 58 F5
Messina, Stretta di Italy see Messina, Strait of
Messini Greece 59 J6
Messiniakos Kolpos b. Greece 59 J6
Mesta r. Bulg. 59 K4
Mesta r. Greece see Nestos
Mesta, Akrotirio pt Greece 59 K5
Mestghanem Alg. see Mostaganem
Mestlin Germany 53 L1
Meston, Akra pt Voreio Aigaio Greece see Mesta, Akrotirio
Mestre Italy 58 E2
Mesudiye Turkey 90 E2
Meta r. Col./Venez. 142 E2
Métabetchouan Canada 123 H4
Meta Incognita Peninsula Canada 119 L3
Metairie U.S.A. 131 F6
Metallifere, Colline mts Italy 58 D3
Metán Arg. 144 C3
Meteghan Canada 123 I5
Meteor Depth sea feature S. Atlantic Ocean 148 G9
Methoni Greece 59 I6
Methuen U.S.A. 135 J2
Methven U.K. 50 F4
Metionga Lake Canada 122 C4
Metković Croatia 58 G3
Metlaoui Tunisia 54 F5
Metoro Moz. 99 D5
Metro Indon. 68 D8
Metropolis U.S.A. 131 F4
Metsada tourist site Israel see Masada
Metter U.S.A. 133 D5
Mettet Belgium 52 E4
Mettingen Germany 53 H2
Mettler U.S.A. 128 D4
Mettur India 84 C4
Metu Eth. 98 D3
Metz France 52 G5
Metz U.S.A. 134 C3
Meulaboh Indon. 71 B6
Meureudu Indon. 71 B6
Meuse r. Belgium/France 52 F3
also known as Maas (Netherlands)
Meuselwitz Germany 53 M3
Mevagissey U.K. 49 C8
Mêwa China 76 D1
Mexia U.S.A. 131 D6
Mexiana, Ilha i. Brazil 143 I3
Mexicali Mex. 129 F5
Mexican Hat U.S.A. 129 I3
Mexicanos, Lago de los l. Mex. 127 G7
Mexican Water U.S.A. 129 I3

▶Mexico country Central America 136 D4
2nd most populous and 3rd largest country in North America.

México Mex. see Mexico City
Mexico ME U.S.A. 135 J1
Mexico MO U.S.A. 130 F4
Mexico NY U.S.A. 135 G2
Mexico, Gulf of Mex./U.S.A. 125 H6

▶Mexico City Mex. 136 E5
Capital of Mexico. Most populous city in North America, and 2nd in the world.

Meybod Iran 88 D3
Meydanī, Ra's-e pt Iran 88 E5
Meydān Shahr Afgh. 89 H3
Meyenburg Germany 53 M1
Meyersdale U.S.A. 134 F4
Meymeh Iran 88 C3
Meynypil'gyno Rus. Fed. 153 C2
Mezada tourist site Israel see Masada
Mezdra Bulg. 59 J3
Mezen' Rus. Fed. 42 J2
Mezen' r. Rus. Fed. 42 J2
Mézenc, Mont mt. France 56 G4
Mezenskaya Guba b. Rus. Fed. 42 I2
Mezhdurechensk Kemerovskaya Oblast' Rus. Fed. 72 F2
Mezhdurechensk Respublika Komi Rus. Fed. 42 K3
Mezhdurechnye Rus. Fed. see Shali
Mezhdusharskiy, Ostrov i. Rus. Fed. 64 G2
Mezitli Turkey 85 B1
Mezőtúr Hungary 59 I1
Mežvidi Latvia 45 O8
Mhàil, Rubh' a' pt U.K. 50 C5
Mhangura Zimbabwe 99 D5
Mhlume Swaziland 101 J4
Mhow India 82 C5
Mi r. Myanmar 83 H5
Miahuatlán Mex. 136 E5
Miajadas Spain 57 D4
Miaméré Cent. Afr. Rep. 98 B3
Miami AZ U.S.A. 129 H5

▶Miami FL U.S.A. 133 D7
5th most populous city in North America.

Miami OK U.S.A. 131 E4
Miami Beach U.S.A. 133 D7
Miancaowan China 76 C1
Mīāndehī Iran 88 E3
Mīāndowāb Iran 88 B2
Miandrivazo Madag. 99 E5
Mīāneh Iran 88 B2
Miang, Phu mt. Thai. 70 C3
Miani India 89 I4
Miani Hor b. Pak. 89 G5
Mianjoi Afgh. 89 G3
Mianning China 76 D2
Mianwali Pak. 89 H3
Mianxian China 76 E1
Mianyang Hubei China see Xiantao
Mianyang Shaanxi China see Mianxian
Mianyang Sichuan China 76 E2
Mianzhu China 76 E2
Miaoli Taiwan 77 I3
Miarinarivo Madag. 99 E5
Miarritze France see Biarritz
Miass Rus. Fed. 64 H4
Mica Creek Canada 120 G4
Mica Mountain U.S.A. 129 H5
Micang Shan mts China 76 E1
Michalovce Slovakia 43 D6
Michel Canada 121 I4
Michelau in Oberfranken Germany 53 L4
Michelson, Mount U.S.A. 118 D3
Michelstadt Germany 53 J5
Michendorf Germany 53 N2
Micheng China see Midu
Michigan state U.S.A. 134 C2

▶Michigan, Lake U.S.A. 134 B2
3rd largest lake in North America, and 5th in the world.

Michigan City U.S.A. 134 B3
Michinberi India 84 D2
Michipicoten Bay Canada 122 D5
Michipicoten Island Canada 122 D5
Michipicoten River Canada 122 D5
Michurin Bulg. see Tsarevo
Michurinsk Rus. Fed. 43 I5
Micronesia country N. Pacific Ocean see Micronesia, Federated States of
Micronesia is Pacific Ocean 150 F5
Micronesia, Federated States of country N. Pacific Ocean 150 G5
Midai i. Indon. 71 D7
Mid-Atlantic Ridge sea feature Atlantic Ocean 148 E4
Mid-Atlantic Ridge sea feature Atlantic Ocean 148 G8
Middelburg Neth. 52 D3
Middelburg E. Cape S. Africa 101 G6
Middelburg Mpumalanga S. Africa 101 I3
Middelfart Denmark 45 F9
Middelharnis Neth. 52 E3
Middelwit S. Africa 101 H3
Middle Alkali Lake U.S.A. 126 C4
Middle America Trench sea feature N. Pacific Ocean 151 N5
Middle Andaman i. India 71 A4
Middle Atlas mts Morocco see Moyen Atlas
Middle Bay Canada 123 K4
Middlebourne U.S.A. 134 E4
Middleburg U.S.A. 135 G3
Middleburgh U.S.A. 135 H2
Middlebury IN U.S.A. 134 C3
Middlebury VT U.S.A. 135 I1
Middle Caicos i. Turks and Caicos Is 133 G8
Middle Concho r. U.S.A. 131 C6
Middle Congo country Africa see Congo
Middle Island Thai. see Tasai, Ko
Middle Loup r. U.S.A. 130 D3
Middlemarch N.Z. 113 C7
Middlemount Australia 110 E4
Middle River U.S.A. 135 G4
Middlesbrough U.K. 48 F4
Middle Strait India see Andaman Strait
Middleton Australia 110 C4
Middleton Canada 123 I5
Middleton Island atoll American Samoa see Rose Island
Middletown CA U.S.A. 128 B2
Middletown CT U.S.A. 135 I3
Middletown NY U.S.A. 135 H3
Middletown VA U.S.A. 135 F4
Midelt Morocco 54 D5
Midhurst U.K. 49 G8
Midi, Canal du France 56 F5
Mid-Indian Basin sea feature Indian Ocean 149 N6
Mid-Indian Ridge sea feature Indian Ocean 149 M7
Midland Canada 135 F1
Midland CA U.S.A. 129 F5
Midland IN U.S.A. 134 B4
Midland MI U.S.A. 134 C2
Midland SD U.S.A. 130 C2
Midland TX U.S.A. 131 C5
Midleton Ireland 51 D6
Midnapore India see Medinipur
Midnapur India see Medinipur
Midongy Atsimo Madag. 99 E6
Mid-Pacific Mountains sea feature N. Pacific Ocean 150 G4
Midu China 76 D3
Miðvágur Faroe Is 44 [inset]
Midway Oman see Thamarīt

▶Midway Islands terr. N. Pacific Ocean 150 I4
United States Unincorporated Territory.

Midway Well Australia 109 C5
Midwest U.S.A. 126 G4
Midwest City U.S.A. 131 D5
Midwoud Neth. 52 F2
Midyat Turkey 91 F3
Midye Turkey see Kıyıköy
Mid Yell U.K. 50 [inset]
Midzhur mt. Bulg./Serbia 90 A2
Miehikkälä Fin. 45 O6
Miekojärvi l. Fin. 44 N3
Mielec Poland 43 D6
Mienhua Yü i. Taiwan 77 I3
Mieraslompolo Fin. 44 O2
Mierašluoppal Fin. see Mieraslompolo
Miercurea-Ciuc Romania 59 K1
Mieres Spain 57 D2
Mieres del Camín Spain see Mieres
Mī'ēso Eth. 98 E3
Mieste Germany 53 L2
Mifflinburg U.S.A. 135 G3
Mifflintown U.S.A. 135 G3
Migang Shan mt. China 76 E1
Migdol S. Africa 101 G4
Miging India 76 B3
Migriggyangzham Co l. China 83 G2
Miguel Auza Mex. 131 C7
Miguel Hidalgo, Presa resr Mex. 127 F8
Mihalıççık Turkey 59 N5
Mihara Japan 75 D6
Mihintale Sri Lanka 84 D4
Mihmandar Turkey 85 B1
Mijares r. Spain see Millárs
Mijdrecht Neth. 52 E2
Mikhaylov Rus. Fed. 43 H5
Mikhaylovgrad Bulg. see Montana
Mikhaylov Island Antarctica 152 E2
Mikhaylovka Amurskaya Oblast' Rus. Fed. 74 C2
Mikhaylovka Primorskiy Kray Rus. Fed. 74 D4
Mikhaylovka Tul'skaya Oblast' Rus. Fed. see Kimovsk
Mikhaylovka Volgogradskaya Oblast' Rus. Fed. 43 I6
Mikhaylovskiy Rus. Fed. 80 E1
Mikhaylovskoye Rus. Fed. see Shpakovskoye
Mikhrot Timna Israel 85 B5
Mikir Hills India 83 H4
Mikkeli Fin. 45 O6
Mikkelin mlk Fin. 45 O6
Mikkwa r. Canada 120 H3
Míkonos i. Greece see Mykonos
Mikoyan Armenia see Yeghegnadzor
Mikulkin, Mys c. Rus. Fed. 42 J2
Mikumi National Park Tanz. 99 D4
Mikun' Rus. Fed. 42 K3
Mikuni-sanmyaku mts Japan 75 E5
Mikura-jima i. Japan 75 E6
Milaca U.S.A. 130 E2
Miladhunmadulu Atoll Maldives 84 B5
Miladummadulu Atoll Maldives see Miladhunmadulu Atoll
Milan Italy 58 C2
Milan MI U.S.A. 134 D2
Milan MO U.S.A. 130 E3
Milan OH U.S.A. 134 D3
Milange Moz. 99 D5
Milano Italy see Milan
Milas Turkey 59 L6
Milazzo Sicily Italy 58 F5
Milazzo, Capo di c. Sicily Italy 58 F5
Milbank U.S.A. 130 D2
Milbridge U.S.A. 132 H2
Milde r. Germany 53 L2

Mildenhall U.K. 49 H6
Mildura Australia 111 C7
Mile China 76 D3
Mileiz, Wâdi el watercourse Egypt see Mulayz, Wādī al
Miles Australia 112 E1
Miles City U.S.A. 126 G3
Milestone Ireland 51 D5
Miletto, Monte mt. Italy 58 F4
Mileura Australia 109 B6
Milford Ireland 51 E2
Milford DE U.S.A. 135 H4
Milford IL U.S.A. 134 B3
Milford MA U.S.A. 135 J2
Milford MI U.S.A. 134 D2
Milford NE U.S.A. 130 D3
Milford NH U.S.A. 135 J2
Milford PA U.S.A. 135 H3
Milford UT U.S.A. 129 G2
Milford VA U.S.A. 135 G4
Milford Haven U.K. 49 B7
Milford Sound N.Z. 113 A7
Milford Sound inlet N.Z. 113 A7
Milgarra Australia 110 C3
Milḩ, Baḩr al l. Iraq see Razāzah, Buḩayrat ar
Miliana Alg. 57 H5
Milid Turkey see Malatya
Milikapiti Australia 108 E2
Miling Australia 109 B7
Milk r. U.S.A. 126 G2
Milk, Wadi el watercourse Sudan 86 D6
Mil'kovo Rus. Fed. 65 Q4
Millaa Millaa Australia 110 D3
Millárs r. Spain 57 F4
Millau France 56 F4
Millbrook Canada 135 F1
Mill Creek r. U.S.A. 128 B1
Milledgeville U.S.A. 133 D5
Mille Lacs lakes U.S.A. 130 E2
Mille Lacs, Lac des l. Canada 119 I5
Millen U.S.A. 133 D5
Millennium Island atoll Kiribati see Caroline Island
Miller U.S.A. 130 D2
Miller Lake Canada 134 E1
Millerovo Rus. Fed. 43 I6
Millersburg OH U.S.A. 134 E3
Millersburg PA U.S.A. 135 G3
Millers Creek U.S.A. 134 D5
Millersville U.S.A. 135 G4
Millerton Lake U.S.A. 128 D3
Millet Canada 120 H4
Milleur Point U.K. 50 D5
Mill Hall U.S.A. 135 G3
Millicent Australia 111 C8
Millington MI U.S.A. 134 D2
Millington TN U.S.A. 131 F5
Millinocket U.S.A. 132 G2
Mill Island Canada 119 K3
Millmerran Australia 112 E1
Millom U.K. 48 D4
Millport U.K. 50 E5
Millsboro U.S.A. 135 H4
Mills Creek watercourse Australia 110 C4
Mills Lake Canada 120 G2
Millstone KY U.S.A. 134 D5
Millstone WV U.S.A. 134 E4
Millstream-Chichester National Park Australia 108 B5
Millthorpe Australia 112 D4
Milltown Canada 123 I5
Milltown U.S.A. 126 E3
Milltown Malbay Ireland 51 C5
Millungera Australia 110 C3
Millville U.S.A. 135 H4
Millwood U.S.A. 134 B5
Millwood Lake U.S.A. 131 E5
Milly Milly Australia 109 B6
Milne Land i. Greenland see Ilimananngip Nunaa
Milner U.S.A. 129 J1
Milo r. Guinea 96 C3
Milogradovo Rus. Fed. 74 D4
Miloli'i U.S.A. 127 [inset]
Milos i. Greece 59 K6
Milparinka Australia 111 C6
Milpitas U.S.A. 128 C3
Milroy U.S.A. 135 G3
Milton N.Z. 113 B8
Milton DE U.S.A. 135 H4
Milton NH U.S.A. 135 J2
Milton WV U.S.A. 134 D4
Milton Keynes U.K. 49 G6
Miluo China 77 G2
Milverton Canada 134 E2
Milwaukee U.S.A. 134 B2

▶Milwaukee Deep sea feature Caribbean Sea 148 D4
Deepest point in the Puerto Rico Trench and in the Atlantic.

Mimbres watercourse U.S.A. 129 J5
Mimili Australia 109 F6
Mimisal India 84 C4
Mimizan France 56 D4
Mimongo Gabon 98 B4
Mimosa Rocks National Park Australia 112 E6
Mina Mex. 131 C7
Mina U.S.A. 128 D2
Mīnāb Iran 88 E5
Minaçu Brazil 145 A1
Minahasa, Semenanjung pen. Indon. 69 G6
Minahassa Peninsula Indon. see Minahasa, Semenanjung
Minaker Canada see Prophet River
Mīnakh Syria 85 C1
Minaki Canada 121 M5
Minamia Australia 108 F3
Minami-Daitō-jima i. Japan 73 O7
Minami-Iō-jima vol. Japan 69 K2
Min'an China see Longshan
Minaret of Jam tourist site Afgh. 89 G3
Minas Indon. 71 C7
Minas Uruguay 144 E4
Minas de Matahambre Cuba 133 D8
Minas Gerais state Brazil 145 B2
Minas Novas Brazil 145 C2
Minatitlán Mex. 136 F5
Minbu Myanmar 70 A2
Minbya Myanmar 70 A2
Minchinmávida vol. Chile 144 B6
Mindanao i. Phil. 69 H5
Mindanao Trench sea feature N. Pacific Ocean see Philippine Trench
Mindelo Cape Verde 96 [inset]
Minden Canada 135 F1
Minden Germany 53 I2
Minden LA U.S.A. 131 E5
Minden NE U.S.A. 124 H3
Minden NV U.S.A. 128 D2
Mindon Myanmar 70 A3
Mindoro i. Phil. 69 G4
Mindoro Strait Phil. 69 F4
Mindouli Congo 98 B4
Mine Head hd Ireland 51 E6
Minehead U.K. 49 D7
Mineola U.S.A. 135 I3
Mineral U.S.A. 135 G4
Mineral'nyye Vody Rus. Fed. 91 F1
Mineral Wells U.S.A. 131 D5
Mineralwells U.S.A. 134 E4
Minersville PA U.S.A. 135 G3
Minersville UT U.S.A. 129 G2
Minerva U.S.A. 134 E3
Minerva Reefs Fiji 107 I4
Minfeng China 83 E1
Minga Dem. Rep. Congo 99 C5
Mingäçevir Azer. 91 G2
Mingäçevir Su Anbarı resr Azer. 91 G2
Mingala Cent. Afr. Rep. 98 C3
Mingan, Îles de is Canada 123 J4
Mingan Archipelago National Park Reserve Canada see L'Archipélago de Mingan, Réserve du Parc National de
Mingbuloq Uzbek. 80 B3
Mingechaur Azer. see Mingäçevir
Mingechaurskoye Vodokhranilishche resr Azer. see Mingäçevir Su Anbarı
Mingenew Australia 109 A7
Mingfeng China see Yuan'an
Minggang China 77 G1
Mingguang China 77 H1
Mingin Range mts Myanmar 70 A2
Minglanilla Spain 57 F4
Mingoyo Tanz. 99 D5
Mingshan China 76 D2
Mingshui Gansu China 80 I3
Mingshui Heilong. China 74 B3
Mingteke China 82 C1
Mingulay i. U.K. 50 B4
Mingxi China 77 H3
Mingzhou China see Suide
Minhe China see Jinxian
Minhla Magwe Myanmar 70 A3
Minhla Pegu Myanmar 70 A3
Minho r. Port./Spain see Miño
Minicoy atoll India 84 B4
Minigwal, Lake salt flat Australia 109 C7
Minilya Australia 109 A5
Minilya r. Australia 109 A5
Minipi Lake Canada 123 J3
Miniss Lake Canada 121 N5
Minitonas Canada 121 K4
Minjian China see Mabian
Min Jiang r. Sichuan China 76 E2
Min Jiang r. China 77 H3
Minna Nigeria 96 D4
Minna Bluff pt Antarctica 152 H1
Minne Sweden 44 I5
Minneapolis KS U.S.A. 130 D4
Minneapolis MN U.S.A. 130 E2
Minnedosa Canada 121 L5
Minnehaha Springs U.S.A. 134 F4
Minneola U.S.A. 131 C4
Minnesota r. U.S.A. 130 E2
Minnesota state U.S.A. 130 E2
Minnewaukan U.S.A. 130 D1
Minnitaki Lake Canada 121 N5
Miño r. Port./Spain 57 B3
also known as Minho
Minorca i. Spain 57 H3
Minot U.S.A. 130 C1
Minqār, Ghadīr imp. l. Syria 85 C3
Minqing China 77 H3
Minquan China 77 G1
Min Shan mts China 76 D1
Minsin Myanmar 70 A1

▶Minsk Belarus 45 O10
Capital of Belarus.

Mińsk Mazowiecki Poland 47 R4
Minsterley U.K. 49 E6
Mintaka Pass China/Pakistan 82 C1
Minto, Lac l. Canada 122 G2
Minto, Mount Antarctica 152 H2
Minto Inlet Canada 118 G2
Minton Canada 121 J5
Mīnudasht Iran 88 D2
Minūf Egypt 90 C5
Minusinsk Rus. Fed. 72 G2
Minvoul Gabon 98 B3
Minxian China 76 E1
Minya Konka mt. China see Gongga Shan
Minywa Myanmar 70 A2
Minzong India 83 I4
Mio U.S.A. 134 C1
Miquelon Canada 122 F4
Miquelon i. St Pierre and Miquelon 123 K5
Mirabad Afgh. 89 F4
Mirabela Brazil 145 B2
Mirador, Parque Nacional de nat. park Brazil 143 I5
Mīrah, Wādī al watercourse Iraq/Saudi Arabia 91 F4
Miraí Brazil 145 C3
Miraj India 84 B2
Miramar Arg. 144 E5
Miramichi Canada 123 I5
Miramichi Bay Canada 123 I5
Mirampellou, Kolpos b. Greece 59 K7
Mirampelou, Kolpos b. Kriti Greece see Mirampellou, Kolpos
Miranda Brazil 144 E2
Miranda Moz. see Macaloge
Miranda U.S.A. 128 B1
Miranda, Lake salt flat Australia 109 C6
Miranda de Ebro Spain 57 E2
Mirandela Port. 57 C3
Mirandola Italy 58 D2
Mirante Brazil 145 C1
Mirante, Serra do hills Brazil 145 A3
Mirassol Brazil 145 A3
Mir-Bashir Azer. see Tärtär
Mirbāţ Oman 87 H6
Mirboo North Australia 112 C7
Mirepoix France 56 E5
Mirgarh Pak. 89 I4
Mirgorod Ukr. see Myrhorod
Miri Sarawak Malaysia 68 E6
Miri mt. Pak. 89 F4
Mirialguda India 84 C2
Miri Hills India 83 H4
Mirim, Lagoa l. Brazil/Uruguay 144 F4
Mirim, Lagoa do l. Brazil 145 A5
Mirintu watercourse Australia 112 A2
Mirjan India 84 B3
Mirny research station Antarctica 152 F2
Mirnyy Arkhangel'skaya Oblast' Rus. Fed. 42 I3
Mirnyy Respublika Sakha (Yakutiya) Rus. Fed. 65 M3
Mirond Lake Canada 121 K4
Mironovka Ukr. see Myronivka
Mirow Germany 53 M1
Mirpur Khas Pak. 89 H5
Mirpur Sakro Pak. 89 G5
Mirs Bay H.K. China 77 [inset]
Mirtoan Sea Greece see Myrtoo Pelagos
Mirtoö Pelagos sea Greece see Myrtoo Pelagos
Miryalaguda India see Mirialguda
Miryang S. Korea 75 C6
Mirzachirla Turkm. see Murzechirla
Mirzachul Uzbek. see Guliston
Mirzapur India 83 E4
Mirzawal India 82 C3
Misaw Lake Canada 121 K3
Miscou Island Canada 123 I5
Misehkow r. Canada 122 C4
Mīsh, Kūh-e hill Iran 88 E3
Misha India 71 A6
Mishāsh al Ashāwī well Saudi Arabia 88 C5
Mishāsh az Ẕuayyinī well Saudi Arabia 88 C5
Mishawaka U.S.A. 134 B3
Mishicot U.S.A. 134 B1
Mi-shima i. Japan 75 C6
Mishmi Hills India 83 H3
Mishvan' Rus. Fed. 42 L2
Misima Island P.N.G. 110 F1
Misis Dağ hills Turkey 85 B1
Miskin Oman 88 E6
Miskitos, Cayos is Nicaragua 137 H6
Miskolc Hungary 43 D6
Mismā, Tall al hill Jordan 85 C3
Misoöl i. Indon. 69 I7
Misquah Hills U.S.A. 130 F2
Misr country Africa see Egypt
Misraç Turkey see Kurtalan
Mişrātah Libya 97 E1
Missinaibi r. Canada 122 E4
Mission Beach Australia 110 D3
Mission Viejo U.S.A. 128 E5
Missisa r. Canada 122 D3
Missisa Lake Canada 122 D3
Missisicabi r. Canada 122 F4
Mississauga Canada 134 F2
Mississinewa Lake U.S.A. 134 C3

▶Mississippi r. U.S.A. 131 F6
4th longest river in North America, and a major part of the longest (Mississippi-Missouri).

Mississippi state U.S.A. 131 F5
Mississippi Delta U.S.A. 131 F6
Mississippi Lake Canada 135 G1

▶Mississippi-Missouri r. U.S.A. 125 I4
Longest river in North America, and 4th in the world.

Mississippi Sound sea chan. U.S.A. 131 F6
Missolonghi Greece see Mesolongi
Missoula U.S.A. 126 E3

▶Missouri r. U.S.A. 130 F4
3rd longest river in North America, and a major part of the longest (Mississippi-Missouri).

Missouri state U.S.A. 130 E4
Mistanipisipou r. Canada 123 J4
Mistassibi r. Canada 119 K5
Mistassini r. Canada 123 G4
Mistassini, Lac l. Canada 122 G4
Mistastin Lake Canada 123 J3
Mistelbach Austria 47 P6
Mistinibi, Lac l. Canada 123 J2
Mistissini Canada 122 G4
Misty Fiords National Monument Wilderness nat. park U.S.A. 120 D4
Misumba Dem. Rep. Congo 99 C4
Misuratah Libya see Mişrātah
Mitchell Australia 111 D5
Mitchell r. N.S.W. Australia 112 F2
Mitchell r. Qld Australia 110 C2
Mitchell r. Vic. Australia 112 C6
Mitchell Canada 134 E2
Mitchell IN U.S.A. 134 B4
Mitchell OR U.S.A. 126 C3
Mitchell SD U.S.A. 130 D3
Mitchell, Lake Australia 110 D3
Mitchell, Mount U.S.A. 132 D5
Mitchell and Alice Rivers National Park Australia 110 C2
Mitchell Island Cook Is see Nassau
Mitchell Island atoll Tuvalu see Nukulaelae
Mitchell Point Australia 108 E2
Mitchelstown Ireland 51 D5
Mīt Ghamr Egypt 90 C5
Mit Ghamr Egypt see Mīt Ghamr
Mithi Pak. 89 H5
Mithrau Pak. 89 H5
Mithri Pak. 89 G4
Mitilíni Greece see Mytilini
Mitkof Island U.S.A. 120 C3
Mito Japan 75 F5
Mitole Tanz. 99 D4
Mitre mt. N.Z. 113 E5
Mitre Island Solomon Is 107 H3
Mitrofanovka Rus. Fed. 43 H6
Mitrovica Kosovo see Mitrovicë
Mitrovicë Kosovo 59 I3
Mitsinjo Madag. 99 E5
Mits'iwa Eritrea see Massawa
Mitta Mitta Australia 112 C6
Mittellandkanal canal Germany 53 I2
Mitterteich Germany 53 M5
Mittimatalik Canada see Pond Inlet
Mittweida Germany 53 M4
Mitú Col. 142 D3
Mitumba, Chaîne des mts Dem. Rep. Congo 99 C5
Mitzic Gabon 98 B3
Miughalaigh i. U.K. see Mingulay
Miura Japan 75 E6
Mixian China see Xinmi
Miyake-jima i. Japan 75 E6
Miyako Japan 75 F5
Miyakonojō Japan 75 C7
Miyang China see Mile
Miyani India 82 B5
Miyazaki Japan 75 C7
Miyazu Japan 75 D6
Miyi China 76 D3
Miyoshi Japan 75 D6
Mīzāni Afgh. 89 G3
Mīzan Teferī Eth. 98 D3
Mizdah Libya 97 E1
Mizen Head hd Ireland 51 C6
Mizhhir"ya Ukr. 43 D6
Mizo Hills state India see Mizoram
Mizoram state India 83 H5
Mizpé Ramon Israel 85 B4
Mizusawa Japan 75 F5
Mjölby Sweden 45 I7
Mkata Tanz. 99 D4
Mkushi Zambia 99 C5
Mladá Boleslav Czech Rep. 47 O5
Mladenovac Serbia 59 I2
Mława Poland 47 R4
Mlilwane Nature Reserve Swaziland 101 J4
Mljet i. Croatia 58 G3
Mlungisi S. Africa 101 H6
Mmabatho S. Africa 101 G3
Mmamabula Botswana 101 H2
Mmathethe Botswana 101 G3
Mo Norway 45 D6
Moa i. Indon. 108 E2
Moab reg. Jordan 85 B4
Moab U.S.A. 129 I2
Moa Island Australia 110 C1
Moala i. Fiji 107 H3
Mo'alla Iran 88 D3
Moamba Moz. 101 K3
Moanda Gabon 98 B4
Moapa U.S.A. 129 F3
Moate Ireland 51 E4
Mobārakeh Iran 88 C3
Mobayembongo Dem. Rep. Congo see Mobayi-Mbongo
Mobayi-Mbongo Dem. Rep. Congo 98 C3
Moberly U.S.A. 130 E4
Moberly Lake Canada 120 F4
Mobha India 82 C5
Mobile AL U.S.A. 131 F6
Mobile AZ U.S.A. 129 G5
Mobile Bay U.S.A. 131 F6
Moble watercourse Australia 112 B1
Mobridge U.S.A. 130 C2
Mobutu, Lake Dem. Rep. Congo/Uganda see Albert, Lake
Mobutu Sese Seko, Lake Dem. Rep. Congo/Uganda see Albert, Lake
Moca Geçidi pass Turkey 85 A1
Moçambique country Africa see Mozambique
Moçambique Moz. 99 E5
Moçâmedes Angola see Namibe
Môc Châu Vietnam 70 D2
Mocha Yemen 86 F7
Mocha, Isla i. Chile 144 B5
Mochirma, Parque Nacional nat. park Venez. 142 F1
Mochudi Botswana 101 H3
Mochudi admin. dist. Botswana see Kgatleng
Mocimboa da Praia Moz. 99 E5
Möckern Germany 53 L2
Möckmühl Germany 53 J5
Mockträsk Sweden 44 L4
Mocoa Col. 142 C3
Mococa Brazil 145 B3
Mocoduene Moz. 101 L2
Mocorito Mex. 127 G8
Moctezuma Chihuahua Mex. 127 G7
Moctezuma San Luis Potosí Mex. 136 D4
Moctezuma Sonora Mex. 127 F7
Mocuba Moz. 99 D5
Mocun China 77 G4
Modan Indon. 69 I7
Modane France 56 H4
Modder r. S. Africa 101 G5
Modena Italy 58 D2
Modena U.S.A. 129 G3
Modesto U.S.A. 128 C3
Modesto Lake U.S.A. 128 C3
Modimolle S. Africa 101 I3
Modung China 76 C2
Moe Australia 112 C7
Moel Sych hill U.K. 49 D6
Moelv Norway 45 G6
Moen Norway 44 K2
Moenkopi U.S.A. 129 H3
Moenkopi Wash r. U.S.A. 129 H4
Moeraki Point N.Z. 113 C7
Moero, Lake Dem. Rep. Congo/Zambia see Mweru, Lake
Moers Germany 52 G3
Moffat U.K. 50 F5
Moga India 82 C3

▶Mogadishu Somalia 98 E3
Capital of Somalia.

Mogador Morocco see Essaouira
Mogadore Reservoir U.S.A. 134 E3
Moganyaka S. Africa 101 I3
Mogaung Myanmar 70 B1
Mogdy Rus. Fed. 74 D2
Mögelin Germany 53 M2
Mogilev Belarus see Mahilyow
Mogilev Podol'skiy Ukr. see Mohyliv Podil's'kyy
Mogi-Mirim Brazil 145 B3
Mogiquiçaba Brazil 145 D2
Mogocha Rus. Fed. 73 L2
Mogod mts Tunisia 58 C6
Mogoditshane Botswana 101 G3
Mogollon Mountains U.S.A. 129 I5
Mogollon Plateau U.S.A. 129 H4
Mogontiacum Germany see Mainz
Mogroum Chad 97 E3
Moguqi China 74 A3
Mogwadi S. Africa 101 I2
Mogwase S. Africa 101 H3
Mogzon Rus. Fed. 73 K2
Mohács Hungary 58 H2
Mohaka r. N.Z. 113 F4
Mohala India 84 D1
Mohale Dam Lesotho 101 I5
Mohale's Hoek Lesotho 101 H6
Mohall U.S.A. 130 C1
Mohammad Iran 88 E3
Mohammadia Alg. 57 G6
Mohan r. India/Nepal 82 E3
Mohana India 82 D4
Mohave, Lake U.S.A. 129 F4
Mohawk r. U.S.A. 135 I2
Mohawk Mountains U.S.A. 129 G5
Mohenjo Daro tourist site Pak. 89 H5
Moher, Cliffs of Ireland 51 C5
Mohill Ireland 51 E4
Möhne r. Germany 53 H3
Möhnetalsperre resr Germany 53 I3
Mohon Peak U.S.A. 129 G4
Mohoro Tanz. 99 D4
Mohyliv Podil's'kyy Ukr. 43 E6
Moi Norway 45 E7
Moijabana Botswana 101 H2
Moincêr China 82 E3
Moinda China 83 G3
Moine Moz. 101 K3
Moineşti Romania 59 L1
Mointy Kazakh. see Moyynty
Mo i Rana Norway 44 I3
Moirang India 76 B3
Mõisaküla Estonia 45 N7
Moisie Canada 123 I4
Moisie r. Canada 123 I4
Moissac France 56 E4
Mojave U.S.A. 128 D4
Mojave r. U.S.A. 128 E4
Mojave Desert U.S.A. 128 E4
Mojiang China 76 D4
Moji das Cruzes Brazil 145 B3
Mojos, Llanos de plain Bol. 142 E6
Moju r. Brazil 143 I4
Mokama India 83 F4
Mokau N.Z. 113 E4
Mokau r. N.Z. 113 E4
Mokelumne r. U.S.A. 128 C2
Mokelumne Aqueduct canal U.S.A. 128 C2
Mokhoabong Pass Lesotho 101 I5
Mokhotlong Lesotho 101 I5
Mokhtārān Iran 88 E3
Moknine Tunisia 58 D7
Mokohinau Islands N.Z. 113 E2
Mokokchung India 83 H4
Mokolo Cameroon 97 E3
Mokolo r. S. Africa 101 H2
Mokopane S. Africa 101 I3
Mokp'o S. Korea 75 B6
Mokrous Rus. Fed. 43 J6
Moksha r. Rus. Fed. 43 I5
Mokshan Rus. Fed. 43 J5
Möksy Fin. 44 N5
Mōktama Myanmar see Mottama
Mōktama, Gulf of g. Myanmar see Mottama, Gulf of
Mokundurra India see Mukandwara
Mokwa Nigeria 96 D4
Molatón mt. Spain 57 F4
Moldavia country Europe see Moldova
Moldavskaya S.S.R. country Europe see Moldova
Molde Norway 44 E5
Moldjord Norway 44 I3
Moldova country Europe 43 F7
Moldoveanu, Vârful mt. Romania 59 K2
Moldovei de Sud, Cîmpia plain Moldova 59 M1
Molega Lake Canada 123 I5
Molen r. S. Africa 101 I4
Mole National Park Ghana 96 C4
Molepolole Botswana 101 G3
Molėtai Lith. 45 N9
Molfetta Italy 58 G4
Molière Alg. see Bordj Bounaama
Molihong Shan mt. China see Morihong Shan
Molina de Aragón Spain 57 F3
Moline U.S.A. 131 D4
Molkom Sweden 45 H7
Mollagara Turkm. 88 D2
Mollakara Turkm. see Mollagara
Mol Len mt. India 83 H4
Möllenbeck Germany 53 N1
Mollendo Peru 142 D7
Mölln Germany 53 K1
Mölnlycke Sweden 45 H8
Molochnyy Rus. Fed. 44 R2
Molodechno Belarus see Maladzyechna
Molodezhnaya research station Antarctica 152 D2
Moloka'i i. U.S.A. 127 [inset]
Moloma r. Rus. Fed. 42 K4
Molong Australia 112 D4
Molopo watercourse Botswana/S. Africa 100 E5
Molotov Rus. Fed. see Perm'
Molotovsk Kyrg. see Kayyngdy
Molotovsk Arkhangel'skaya Oblast' Rus. Fed. see Severodvinsk
Molotovsk Kirovskaya Oblast' Rus. Fed. see Nolinsk
Moloundou Cameroon 97 E4
Molson Lake Canada 121 L4
Molu i. Indon. 69 I8
Moluccas is Indon. 69 H7
Molucca Sea sea Indon. see Maluku, Laut
Moma Moz. 99 D5
Moma r. Rus. Fed. 65 P3
Momba Australia 112 A3
Mombaça Brazil 143 K5
Mombasa Kenya 98 D4
Mombetsu Hokkaidō Japan see Monbetsu
Mombi New India 83 H4
Mombum Indon. 69 J8
Momchilgrad Bulg. 59 K4
Momence U.S.A. 134 B3
Momi, Ra's pt Yemen 87 H7
Mompós Col. 142 D2
Møn i. Denmark 45 H9
Mon India 83 H4
Mona terr. Irish Sea see Isle of Man
Mona U.S.A. 129 H2
Monaca U.S.A. 134 E3
Monach, Sound of sea chan. U.K. 50 B3
Monach Islands U.K. 50 B3
Monaco country Europe 56 H5
Monaco Basin sea feature N. Atlantic Ocean 148 G4
Monadhliath Mountains U.K. 50 E3
Monaghan Ireland 51 F3
Monahans U.S.A. 131 C6
Mona Passage Dom. Rep./Puerto Rico 137 K5
Monapo Moz. 99 E5
Monar, Loch l. U.K. 50 D3
Monarch Mountain Canada 120 E5
Monarch Pass U.S.A. 127 G5
Mona Reservoir U.S.A. 129 H2
Monashee Mountains Canada 120 G5
Monastir Macedonia see Bitola
Monastir Tunisia 58 D7
Monastyrishche Ukr. see Monastyryshche
Monastyryshche Ukr. 43 F6
Monbetsu Hokkaidō Japan 74 F3
Monbetsu Hokkaidō Japan 74 F4
Moncalieri Italy 58 B2
Monchegorsk Rus. Fed. 44 R3
Mönchengladbach Germany 52 G3
Monchique Port. 57 B5
Moncks Corner U.S.A. 133 D5
Monclova Mex. 131 C7
Moncouche, Lac l. Canada 123 H4
Moncton Canada 123 I5
Mondego r. Port. 57 B3
Mondlo S. Africa 101 J4
Mondo Chad 97 E3
Mondovì Italy 58 B2
Mondragone Italy 58 E4
Mondy Rus. Fed. 72 I2
Monemvasia Greece 59 J6
Monessen U.S.A. 134 F3
Moneta U.S.A. 126 G4
Moneygall Ireland 51 E5
Moneymore U.K. 51 F3
Monfalcone Italy 58 E2
Monfalut Egypt see Manfalūţ
Monforte de Lemos Spain 57 C2
Monga Dem. Rep. Congo 98 C3
Mongala r. Dem. Rep. Congo 98 B3
Mongar Bhutan 83 G4
Mongbwalu Dem. Rep. Congo 98 D3
Mông Cai Vietnam 70 D2
Mongers Lake salt flat Australia 109 B7
Mong Hang Myanmar 70 B2
Mong Hkan Myanmar 70 C2
Mong Hpayak Myanmar 70 B2
Mong Hsat Myanmar 70 B2
Mong Hsawk Myanmar 70 B2
Mong Hsu Myanmar 70 B2
Monghyr India see Munger
Mong Kung Myanmar 70 B2
Mong Kyawt Myanmar 70 B3
Mongla Bangl. 83 G5
Mong Lin Myanmar 70 C2
Mong Loi Myanmar 70 C2
Mong Long Myanmar 70 B2
Mong Nai Myanmar 70 B2
Mong Nawng Myanmar 70 B2
Mongo Chad 97 E3
Mongolia country Asia 72 I3
Mongol Uls country Asia see Mongolia
Mongonu Nigeria 96 E3
Mongora Pak. 89 I3
Mongour hill U.K. 50 G4
Mong Pan Myanmar 70 B2
Mong Ping Myanmar 70 B2
Mong Pu Myanmar 70 B2
Mong Pu-awn Myanmar 70 B2
Mong Si Myanmar 70 B2
Mongu Zambia 99 C5
Mong Un Myanmar 70 C2
Mong Yai Myanmar 70 B2
Mong Yang Myanmar 70 B2
Mong Yawn Myanmar 70 B2
Mong Yawng Myanmar 70 C2
Mönhaan Mongolia 73 K3
Mönh Hayrhan Uul mt. Mongolia 80 H2
Moniaive U.K. 50 F5
Monitor Mountain U.S.A. 128 E2
Monitor Range mts U.S.A. 128 E2
Monivea Ireland 51 D4
Monkey Bay Malawi 99 D5
Monkira Australia 110 C5
Monkton Canada 134 E2
Monmouth U.K. 49 E7
Monmouth U.S.A. 130 F3
Monmouth Mountain Canada 120 F5
Monnow r. U.K. 49 E7
Mono, Punta del pt Nicaragua 137 H6
Mono Lake U.S.A. 128 D2
Monolithos Greece 59 L6
Monomoy Point U.S.A. 135 J3
Monon U.S.A. 134 B3
Monopoli Italy 58 G4
Monreal del Campo Spain 57 F3
Monreale Sicily Italy 58 E5
Monroe IN U.S.A. 134 C3

Mühlhausen (Thüringen) Germany 53 K3
Mühlig-Hofmann Mountains Antarctica 152 C2
Muhos Fin. 44 N4
Muḩradah Syria 85 C2
Mui Bai Bung c. Vietnam see Mui Ca Mau
Mui Ba Lang An pt Vietnam 70 E4
Mui Ca Mau c. Vietnam 71 D5
Mui Đôc pt Vietnam 70 D3
Muié Angola 99 C5
Muineachán Ireland see Monaghan
Muir U.S.A. 134 C2
Muirkirk U.K. 50 E5
Muir of Ord U.K. 50 E3
Mui Ron hd Vietnam 70 D3
Muite Moz. 99 D5
Muji China 82 D1
Muju S. Korea 75 B5
Mukacheve Ukr. 43 D6
Mukachevo Ukr. see Mukacheve
Mukah Sarawak Malaysia 68 E6
Mukalla Yemen 86 G7
Mukandwara India 82 D4
Mukdahan Thai. 70 D3
Mukden China see Shenyang
Muketei r. Canada 122 D3
Mukhen Rus. Fed. 74 E2
Mukhino Rus. Fed. 74 B1
Mukhtuya Rus. Fed. see Lensk
Mukinbudin Australia 109 B7
Mu Ko Chang Marine National Park Thai. 71 C5
Mukojima-rettō is Japan 75 F8
Mukry Turkm. 89 G2
Muktsar India 82 C3
Mukutawa r. Canada 121 L4
Mukwonago U.S.A. 134 A2
Mula r. India 84 B2
Mulakatholhu atoll Maldives see Mulaku Atoll
Mulaku Atoll Maldives 81 D11
Mulan China 74 C3
Mulanje, Mount Malawi 99 D5
Mulapula, Lake salt flat Australia 111 B6
Mulatos Mex. 127 F7
Mulayḩ Saudi Arabia 88 B5
Mulayḩah, Jabal hill U.A.E. 88 D5
Mulayz, Wādī al watercourse Egypt 85 A4
Mulchatna r. U.S.A. 118 C3
Mulde r. Germany 53 M3
Mule Creek NM U.S.A. 129 I5
Mule Creek WY U.S.A. 126 G4
Mulegé Mex. 127 E8
Mules i. Indon. 108 C2
Muleshoe U.S.A. 131 C5
Mulga Park Australia 109 E6
Mulgathing Australia 109 F7
Mulhacén mt. Spain 57 E5
Mülhausen France see Mulhouse
Mülheim an der Ruhr Germany 52 G3
Mulhouse France 56 H3
Muli China 76 D3
Muli Rus. Fed. see Vysokogorniy
Mulia Indon. 69 J7
Muling Heilong. China 74 C3
Muling He r. China 74 D3
Mull i. U.K. 50 D4
Mull, Sound of sea chan. U.K. 50 C4
Mullaghcleevaun hill Ireland 51 F4
Mullaittivu Sri Lanka 84 D4
Mullaley Australia 112 D3
Mullengudgery Australia 112 C3
Mullens U.S.A. 134 E5
Muller watercourse Australia 108 F5
Muller, Pegunungan mts Indon. 68 E6
Mullett Lake U.S.A. 134 C1
Mullewa Australia 109 A7
Mullica r. U.S.A. 135 H4
Mullingar Ireland 51 E4
Mullion Creek Australia 112 D4
Mull of Galloway c. U.K. 50 E6
Mull of Kintyre hd U.K. 50 D5
Mull of Oa hd U.K. 50 C5
Mullumbimby Australia 112 F2
Mulobezi Zambia 99 C5
Mulshi Lake India 84 B2
Multai India 82 D5
Multan Pak. 89 H4
Multia Fin. 44 N5
Multien reg. France 52 C6
Mulug India 84 C2

▶Mumbai India 84 B2
2nd most populous city in Asia and 3rd in the world.

Mumbil Australia 112 D4
Mumbwa Zambia 99 C5
Muminabad Tajik. see Leningrad
Mŭ'minobod Tajik. see Leningrad
Mun, Mae Nam r. Thai. 70 D4
Muna i. Indon. 69 G8
Muna Mex. 136 G4
Muna r. Rus. Fed. 65 N3
Munabao Pak. 89 H5
Munaðarnes Iceland 44 [inset]
Münchberg Germany 53 L4
München Germany see Munich
München-Gladbach Germany see Mönchengladbach
Münchhausen Germany 53 I4
Muncho Lake Canada 120 E3
Muncie U.S.A. 134 C3
Muncoonie West, Lake salt flat Australia 110 B5
Muncy U.S.A. 135 G3
Munda Pak. 89 H4
Mundel Lake Sri Lanka 84 C5
Mundesley U.K. 49 I6
Mundford U.K. 49 H6
Mundiwindi Australia 109 C5
Mundra India 82 B5
Mundrabilla Australia 106 C5
Munds Park U.S.A. 129 H4
Mundubbera Australia 111 E5
Mundwa India 82 C4
Munfordville U.S.A. 134 C5
Mungallala Australia 111 D5
Mungana Australia 110 D3
Mungári Moz. 99 D5
Mungbere Dem. Rep. Congo 98 C3
Mungeli India 83 E5
Munger India 83 F4
Mu Nggava i. Solomon Is see Rennell
Mungindi Australia 112 D2
Mungla Bangl. see Mongla
Mungo Angola 99 B5
Mungo, Lake Australia 112 A4
Mungo National Park Australia 112 A4
Munich Germany 47 M6
Munising U.S.A. 132 C2
Munjpur India 82 B5
Munkács Ukr. see Mukacheve
Munkebakken Norway 44 P2
Munkedal Sweden 45 G7
Munkfors Sweden 45 H7
Munkhafaḑ al Qaţţārah depr. Egypt see Qattara Depression
Munku-Sardyk, Gora mt. Mongolia/Rus. Fed. 72 I2
Münnerstadt Germany 53 K4
Munnik S. Africa 101 I2
Munroe Lake Canada 121 L3
Munsan S. Korea 75 B5
Münster Hessen Germany 53 I5
Münster Niedersachsen Germany 53 K2
Münster Nordrhein-Westfalen Germany 53 H3
Munster reg. Ireland 51 D5
Münsterland reg. Germany 53 H3
Muntadgin Australia 109 B7
Muntervary hd Ireland 51 C6
Munyal-Par sea feature India see Bassas de Pedro Padua Bank
Munzur Vadisi Milli Parkı nat. park Turkey 55 L4
Muojärvi l. Fin. 44 P4
Mương Nhe Vietnam 70 C2
Muong Sai Laos see Oudômxai
Muonio Fin. 44 M3
Muonioälven r. Fin./Sweden 44 M3
Muonionjoki r. Fin./Sweden see Muonioälven
Mupa, Parque Nacional da nat. park Angola 99 B5
Muping China see Baoxing
Muqaynimah well Saudi Arabia 88 C6
Muqdisho Somalia see Mogadishu
Muquem Brazil 145 A1
Muqui Brazil 145 C3
Mur r. Austria 47 P7
also known as Mura (Croatia/Slovenia)
Mura r. Austria see Mur
Murai, Tanjong pt Sing. 71 [inset]
Murai Reservoir Sing. 71 [inset]
Murakami Japan 75 E5
Murallón, Cerro mt. Chile 144 B7
Muramvya Burundi 98 C4
Murashi Rus. Fed. 42 K4
Murat r. Turkey 91 E3
Muratlı Turkey 59 L4
Muraysah, Ra's al pt Libya 90 B5
Murchison watercourse Australia 109 A6
Murchison, Mount Antarctica 152 H2
Murchison, Mount hill Australia 109 B6
Murchison Falls National Park Uganda 98 D3
Murcia Spain 57 F5
Murcia aut. comm. Spain 57 F5
Murdo U.S.A. 130 C3
Murehwa Zimbabwe 99 D5
Mureşul r. Romania 59 I1
Muret France 56 E5
Murewa Zimbabwe see Murehwa
Murfreesboro AR U.S.A. 131 E5
Murfreesboro TN U.S.A. 132 C5
Murg r. Germany 53 I6
Murgab Tajik. see Murghob
Murgab Turkm. see Murgap
Murgab r. Turkm. see Murgap
Murgap Turkm. 89 F2
Murgap r. Turkm. 87 J2
Murgha Kibzai Pak. 89 H4
Murghob Tajik. 89 I2
Murgon Australia 111 E5
Murgoo Australia 109 B6
Muri India 83 F5
Muriaé Brazil 145 C3
Murid Pak. 89 G4
Muriege Angola 99 C4
Müritz l. Germany 53 M1
Müritz, Nationalpark nat. park Germany 53 N1
Murmansk Rus. Fed. 44 R2
Murmanskaya Oblast' admin. div. Rus. Fed. 44 S2
Murmanskiy Bereg coastal area Rus. Fed. 42 G1
Murmansk Oblast admin. div. Rus. Fed. see Murmanskaya Oblast'
Muro, Capo di c. Corsica France 56 I6
Murom Rus. Fed. 42 I5
Muroran Japan 74 F4
Muros Spain 57 B2
Muroto Japan 75 D6
Muroto-zaki pt Japan 75 D6
Murphy ID U.S.A. 126 D4
Murphy NC U.S.A. 133 D5
Murphysboro U.S.A. 130 F4
Murrah reg. Saudi Arabia 88 C6
Murrah al Kubrá, Al Buḩayrah al l. Egypt see Great Bitter Lake
Murrah aş Şughrá, Al Buḩayrah al l. Egypt see Little Bitter Lake
Murramarang National Park nat. park N.S.W. 112 I5
Murra Murra Australia 112 C2
Murrat el Kubra, Buheirat l. Egypt see Great Bitter Lake
Murrat el Sughra, Buheirat l. Egypt see Little Bitter Lake

▶Murray r. S.A. Australia 111 B7
3rd longest river in Oceania, and a major part of the longest (Murray-Darling).

Murray r. W.A. Australia 109 A8
Murray KY U.S.A. 131 F4
Murray UT U.S.A. 129 H1
Murray, Lake P.N.G. 69 K8
Murray, Lake U.S.A. 133 D5
Murray, Mount Canada 120 D2
Murray Bridge Australia 111 B7

▶Murray-Darling r. Australia 106 E5
Longest river in Oceania.

Murray Downs Australia 108 F5
Murray Range hills Australia 109 E6
Murraysburg S. Africa 100 F6
Murray Sunset National Park Australia 111 C7
Murrhardt Germany 53 J6
Murrieta U.S.A. 128 E5
Murringo Australia 112 D5
Murrisk reg. Ireland 51 C4
Murroogh Ireland 51 C4

▶Murrumbidgee r. Australia 112 A5
4th longest river in Oceania.

Murrumburrah Australia 112 D5
Murrurundi Australia 112 E3
Mursan India 82 D4
Murshidabad India 83 G4
Murska Sobota Slovenia 58 G1
Mürt Iran 89 F5
Murtoa Australia 111 C8
Murua i. P.N.G. see Woodlark Island
Murud India 84 B2
Murud, Gunung mt. Indon. 68 F6
Murunkan Sri Lanka 84 D4
Murupara N.Z. 113 F4
Mururoa atoll Fr. Polynesia 151 K7
Murviedro Spain see Sagunto
Murwara India 82 E5
Murwillumbah Australia 112 F2
Murzechirla Turkm. 89 F2
Murzūq Libya 97 E2
Mürzzuschlag Austria 47 O7
Muş Turkey 91 F3
Mūsā, Khowr-e b. Iran 88 C4
Musakhel Pak. 89 H4
Musala mt. Bulg. 59 J3
Musala i. Indon. 71 B7
Musan N. Korea 74 C4
Musandam Peninsula Oman/U.A.E. 88 E5
Mūsā Qal'eh, Rūd-e r. Afgh. 89 G3
Musay'īd Qatar see Umm Sa'id

▶Muscat Oman 88 E6
Capital of Oman.

Muscat reg. Oman 88 E5
Muscat and Oman country Asia see Oman
Muscatine U.S.A. 130 F3
Musgrave Australia 110 C2
Musgrave Harbour Canada 123 L4
Musgrave Ranges mts Australia 109 E6
Mushāsh al Kabid well Jordan 85 C5
Mushayyish, Wādī al watercourse Jordan 85 C4
Mushie Dem. Rep. Congo 98 B4
Mushkaf Pak. 89 G4
Music Mountain U.S.A. 129 G4
Musina S. Africa 101 J2
Musinia Peak U.S.A. 129 H2
Muskeg r. Canada 120 F2
Muskeget Channel U.S.A. 135 J3
Muskegon MI U.S.A. 132 C3
Muskegon MI U.S.A. 134 B2
Muskegon r. U.S.A. 134 B2
Muskegon Heights U.S.A. 134 B2
Muskeg River Canada 120 G4
Muskogee U.S.A. 131 E5
Muskoka, Lake Canada 134 F1
Muskrat Dam Lake Canada 121 N4
Musmar Sudan 86 E6
Musoma Tanz. 98 D4
Musquanousse, Lac l. Canada 123 J4
Musquaro, Lac l. Canada 123 J4
Mussau Island P.N.G. 69 L7
Musselburgh U.K. 50 F5
Musselkanaal Neth. 52 H2
Musselshell r. U.S.A. 126 G3
Mussende Angola 99 B5
Mustafakemalpaşa Turkey 59 M4
Mustjala Estonia 45 M7
Mustvee Estonia 45 O7
Musu-dan pt N. Korea 74 C4
Muswellbrook Australia 112 E4
Mūţ Egypt 86 C4
Mut Turkey 85 A1
Mutá, Ponta do pt Brazil 145 D1
Mutare Zimbabwe 99 D5
Mutayr reg. Saudi Arabia 88 B5
Mutina Italy see Modena
Muting Indon. 69 K8
Mutis Col. 142 C2
Mutnyy Materik Rus. Fed. 42 L2
Mutoko Zimbabwe 99 D5
Mutsamudu Comoros 99 E5
Mutsu Japan 74 F4
Muttaburra Australia 110 D4
Mutton Island Ireland 51 C5
Muttukuru India 84 D3
Muttupet India 84 C4
Mutum Brazil 145 C2
Mutunópolis Brazil 145 A1
Mutur Sri Lanka 84 D4
Mutusjärvi r. Fin. 44 O2
Muurola Fin. 44 N3
Mu Us Shamo des. China 73 J5
Muxaluando Angola 99 B4
Muxi China see Muchuan
Muxima Angola 99 B4
Muyezerskiy Rus. Fed. 44 R5
Muyinga Burundi 98 D4
Mŭynoq Uzbek. see Mo'ynoq
Muyumba Dem. Rep. Congo 99 C4
Muyunkum, Peski des. Kazakh. see Moyynkum, Peski
Muyuping China 77 F2
Muzaffarabad Pak. 89 I3
Muzaffargarh Pak. 89 H4
Muzaffarnagar India 82 D3
Muzaffarpur India 83 F4
Muzamane Moz. 101 K2
Muzhi Rus. Fed. 41 S2
Mūzīn Iran 89 F5
Muzon, Cape U.S.A. 120 C4
Múzquiz Mex. 131 C7
Muztag mt. China 82 E2
Muz Tag mt. China 83 F1
Muztagata mt. China 89 I2
Muztor Kyrg. see Toktogul
Mvadi Gabon 98 B3
Mvolo Sudan 97 F4
Mvuma Zimbabwe 99 D5
Mwanza Malawi 99 D5
Mwanza Tanz. 98 D4
Mweelrea hill Ireland 51 C4
Mweka Dem. Rep. Congo 99 C4
Mwene-Ditu Dem. Rep. Congo 99 C4
Mwenezi Zimbabwe 99 D6
Mwenga Dem. Rep. Congo 98 C4
Mweru, Lake Dem. Rep. Congo/Zambia 99 C4
Mweru Wantipa National Park Zambia 99 C4
Mwimba Dem. Rep. Congo 99 C4
Mwinilunga Zambia 99 C5
Myadaung Myanmar 70 B2
Myadzyel Belarus 45 O9
Myajlar India 82 B4
Myall Lakes National Park Australia 112 F4
Myanaung Myanmar 70 A3
Myanmar country Asia 70 A2
Myauk-U Myanmar see Mrauk-U
Myaungmya Myanmar 70 A3
Myawadi Thai. 70 B3
Mybster U.K. 50 F2
Myebon Myanmar 70 A2
Myede Myanmar see Aunglan
Myeik Myanmar 71 B4
Myingyan Myanmar 70 A2
Myinkyado Myanmar 70 B2
Myinmoletkat mt. Myanmar 71 B4
Myitkyina Myanmar 70 B1
Myitson Myanmar 70 B2
Myitta Myanmar 71 B4
Myittha Myanmar 70 B2
Mykolayiv Ukr. 59 O1
Mykonos i. Greece 59 K6
Myla Rus. Fed. 42 K2
Myla r. Rus. Fed. 42 K2
Mylae Sicily Italy see Milazzo
Mylasa Turkey see Milas
Mymensing Bangl. see Mymensingh
Mymensingh Bangl. 83 G4
Mynämäki Fin. 45 M6
Myŏnggan N. Korea 74 C4
Myory Belarus 45 O9
My Phước Vietnam 71 D5
Mýrdalsjökull ice cap Iceland 44 [inset]
Myre Norway 44 I2
Myrheden Sweden 44 L4
Myrhorod Ukr. 43 G6
Myrnam Canada 121 I4
Myronivka Ukr. 43 F6
Myrtle Beach U.S.A. 133 E5
Myrtleford Australia 112 C6
Myrtle Point U.S.A. 126 B4
Myrtoo Pelagos sea Greece 59 J6
Mys Articheskiy c. Rus. Fed. 153 E1
Mysia reg. Turkey 59 L5
Mys Lazareva Rus. Fed. see Lazarev
Myślibórz Poland 47 O4
My Son Sanctuary tourist site Vietnam 70 E4
Mysore India 84 C3
Mysore state India see Karnataka
Mys Shmidta Rus. Fed. 65 T3
Mysy Rus. Fed. 42 L3
My Tho Vietnam 71 D5
Mytikas mt. Greece see Olympus, Mount
Mytilene i. Greece see Lesbos
Mytilini Greece 59 L5
Mytilini Strait Greece/Turkey 59 L5
Mytishchi Rus. Fed. 42 H5
Myton U.S.A. 129 H1
Myyeldino Rus. Fed. 42 L3
Mzamomhle S. Africa 101 H6
Mže r. Czech Rep. 53 M5
Mzimba Malawi 99 D5
Mzuzu Malawi 99 D5

N

Naab r. Germany 53 M5
Nā'ālehu U.S.A. 127 [inset]
Naantali Fin. 45 M6
Naas Ireland 51 F4
Naba Myanmar 70 B1
Nababeep S. Africa 100 C5
Nababganj Bangl. see Nawabganj
Nabadwip India see Navadwip
Nabarangapur India 84 D2
Nabarangpur India see Nabarangapur
Nabari Japan 75 E6
Nabatîyé et Tahta Lebanon 85 B3
Nabatiyet et Tahta Lebanon see Nabatîyé et Tahta
Nabberu, Lake salt flat Australia 109 C6
Nabburg Germany 53 M5
Naberera Tanz. 99 D4
Naberezhnyye Chelny Rus. Fed. 41 Q4
Nabesna U.S.A. 120 A2
Nabeul Tunisia 58 D6
Nabha India 82 D3
Nabil'skiy Zaliv lag. Rus. Fed. 74 F2
Nabire Indon. 69 J7
Nabi Younés, Ras en pt Lebanon 85 B3
Nāblus West Bank 85 B3
Naboomspruit S. Africa 101 I3
Nabq Reserve nature res. Egypt 90 D5
Nābulus West Bank see Nāblus
Nacala Moz. 99 E5
Nachalovo Rus. Fed. 43 K7
Nachicapau, Lac l. Canada 123 I2
Nachingwea Tanz. 99 D5
Nachna India 82 B4
Nachuge India 71 A5
Nacimiento Reservoir U.S.A. 128 C4
Naco U.S.A. 127 F7
Nacogdoches U.S.A. 131 E6
Nada China see Danzhou
Nadaleen r. Canada 120 C2
Nådendal Fin. see Naantali
Nadezhdinskoye Rus. Fed. 74 D2
Nadiad India 82 C5
Nadol India 82 C4
Nador Morocco 57 E6
Nadqān, Qalamat well Saudi Arabia 88 C6
Nadūshan Iran 88 D3
Nadvirna Ukr. 43 E6
Nadvoitsy Rus. Fed. 42 G3
Nadvornaya Ukr. see Nadvirna
Nadym Rus. Fed. 64 I3
Næstved Denmark 45 G9
Nafarroa aut. comm. Spain see Navarra
Nafas, Ra's an mt. Egypt 85 B5
Nafḩa, Har hill Israel 85 B4
Nafpaktos Greece 59 I5
Nafplio Greece 59 J6
Naftalan Azer. 91 G2
Naft-e Safīd Iran 88 C4
Naft-e Shāh Iran see Naft Shahr
Naft Shahr Iran 88 B3
Nafūd ad Daḩl des. Saudi Arabia 88 B6
Nafūd al Ghuwayṭah des. Saudi Arabia 85 D5
Nafūd al Jur'ā des. Saudi Arabia 88 B5
Nafūd as Sirr des. Saudi Arabia 88 B5
Nafūd as Surrah des. Saudi Arabia 88 A6
Nafūd Qunayfidhah des. Saudi Arabia 88 B5
Nafūsah, Jabal hills Libya 96 E1
Nafy Saudi Arabia 86 F4
Nag, Co l. China 83 G2
Naga Phil. 69 G4
Nagagami r. Canada 122 D4
Nagagami Lake Canada 122 D4
Nagahama Japan 75 D6
Naga Hills India 83 H4
Naga Hills state India see Nagaland
Nagaland state India 83 H4
Nagamangala India 84 C3
Nagambie Australia 112 B6
Nagano Japan 75 E5
Nagaoka Japan 75 E5
Nagaon India 83 H4
Nagapatam India see Nagapattinam
Nagapattinam India 84 C4
Nagar Hima. Prad. India 87 M3
Nagar Karnataka India 84 B3
Nagaram India 84 D2
Nagari Hills India 84 C3
Nagarjuna Sagar Reservoir India 84 C2
Nagar Parkar Pak. 89 H5
Nagar Untari India 83 E4
Nagasaki Japan 75 C6
Nagato Japan 75 C6
Nagaur India 82 C4
Nagbhir India 84 C1
Nagda India 82 C5
Nageezi U.S.A. 129 J3
Nagercoil India 84 C4
Nagha Kalat Pak. 89 G5
Nag' Ḥammâdî Egypt see Naj' Ḥammādī
Nagina India 82 D3
Nagold r. Germany 53 I6
Nagong Chu r. China see Parlung Zangbo
Nagorno-Karabakh aut. reg. Azer. see Dağlıq Qarabağ
Nagornyy Karabakh aut. reg. Azer. see Dağlıq Qarabağ
Nagorsk Rus. Fed. 42 K4
Nagoya Japan 75 E6
Nagpur India 82 D5
Nagqu China 76 B2
Nag Qu r. China 76 B2
Nagurskoye Rus. Fed. 64 F1
Nagyatád Hungary 58 G1
Nagybecskerek Serbia see Zrenjanin
Nagyenyed Romania see Aiud
Nagykanizsa Hungary 58 G1
Nagyvárad Romania see Oradea
Naha Japan 73 N7
Nahan India 82 D3
Nahanni Butte Canada 120 F2
Nahanni National Park Reserve Canada 120 E2
Nahanni Range mts Canada 120 F2
Naharāyim Jordan 85 B3
Nahariyya Israel 85 B3
Nahāvand Iran 88 C3
Nahr Dijlah r. Asia 91 G5 see Tigris
Nahuel Huapi, Parque Nacional nat. park Arg. 144 B6
Nahunta U.S.A. 133 D6
Naica Mex. 131 B7
Nai Ga Myanmar 76 C3
Naij Tal China 83 H2
Naikliu Indon. 108 C2
Nain Canada 123 J2
Nā'īn Iran 88 D3
Nainital India 82 D3
Naini Tal India see Nainital
Nairn U.K. 50 F3
Nairn r. U.K. 50 F3

▶Nairobi Kenya 98 D4
Capital of Kenya.

Naissus Serbia see Niš
Naivasha Kenya 98 D4
Najaf Iraq 91 G5
Najafābād Iran 88 C3
Na'jān Saudi Arabia 88 B5
Najd reg. Saudi Arabia 86 F4
Nájera Spain 57 E2
Naj' Ḥammādī Egypt 86 D4
Naji China 74 A2
Najibabad India 82 D3
Najin N. Korea 74 C4
Najitun China see Naji
Najrān Saudi Arabia 86 F6
Nakadōri-shima i. Japan 75 C6
Na Kae Thai. 70 D3
Nakambé r. Burkina/Ghana see White Volta
Nakanbe r. Burkina/Ghana see White Volta
Nakanno Rus. Fed. 65 L3
Nakano-shima i. Japan 75 D5
Nakasongola Uganda 97 G4
Nakatsu Japan 75 C6
Nakatsugawa Japan 75 E6
Nakfa Eritrea 86 E6
Nakhichevan' Azer. see Naxçıvan
Nakhl Egypt 85 A5
Nakhodka Rus. Fed. 74 D4
Nakhola India 83 H4
Nakhon Nayok Thai. 71 C4
Nakhon Pathom Thai. 71 C4
Nakhon Phanom Thai. 70 D3
Nakhon Ratchasima Thai. 70 C4
Nakhon Sawan Thai. 70 C4
Nakhon Si Thammarat Thai. 71 B5
Nakhtarana India 82 B5
Nakina Canada 122 D4
Nakina r. Canada 120 C3
Naknek U.S.A. 118 C4
Nakonde Zambia 99 D4
Nakskov Denmark 45 G9
Naktong-gang r. S. Korea 75 C6
Nakuru Kenya 98 D4
Nakusp Canada 120 G5
Nal Pak. 89 G5
Nal r. Pak. 89 G5
Na-lang Myanmar 70 B2
Nalázi Moz. 101 K3
Nalbari India 83 G4
Nal'chik Rus. Fed. 91 F2
Naldurg India 84 C2
Nalgonda India 84 C2
Naliya India 82 B5
Nallamala Hills India 84 C3
Nallıhan Turkey 59 N4
Nālūt Libya 96 E1
Namaacha Moz. 101 K3
Namacurra Moz. 99 D5
Namadgi National Park Australia 112 D5
Namahadi S. Africa 101 I4
Namak, Daryācheh-ye salt flat Iran 88 C3
Namak, Kavīr-e salt flat Iran 88 E3
Namakkal India 84 C4
Namakwaland reg. Namibia see Great Namaqualand
Namakzar-e Shadad salt flat Iran 88 E4
Namaland reg. Namibia see Great Namaqualand
Namangan Uzbek. 80 D3
Namaqualand reg. Namibia see Great Namaqualand
Namaqualand reg. S. Africa 100 C5
Namaqua National Park S. Africa 100 C6
Namas Indon. 69 K8
Namatanai P.N.G. 106 F2
Nambour Australia 112 F1
Nambucca Heads Australia 112 F3
Nambung National Park Australia 109 A7
Năm Căn Vietnam 71 D5
Namcha Barwa mt. China see Namjagbarwa Feng
Namche Bazar Nepal 83 F4
Nam Co salt l. China 83 G3
Namdalen valley Norway 44 H4
Namdalseid Norway 44 G4
Nam Đinh Vietnam 70 D2
Namen Belgium see Namur
Nam-gang r. N. Korea 75 B5
Namhae-do i. S. Korea 75 B6
Namhsan Myanmar 70 B2
Namib Desert Namibia 100 B3
Namibe Angola 99 B5
Namibia country Africa 99 B6
Namibia Abyssal Plain sea feature N. Atlantic Ocean 148 I8
Namib-Naukluft Game Park nature res. Namibia 100 B3
Namie Japan 75 F5
Namīn Iran 91 H3
Namjagbarwa Feng mt. China 76 B2
Namlan Myanmar 70 B2
Namlang r. Myanmar 70 B2
Nam Loi r. China see Nanlei He
Nam Nao National Park Thai. 70 C3
Nam Ngum Reservoir Laos 70 C3
Namoi r. Australia 112 D3
Namonuito atoll Micronesia 69 L5
Nampa mt. Nepal 82 E3
Nampa U.S.A. 126 D4
Nampala Mali 96 C3
Nam Phong Thai. 70 C3
Namp'o N. Korea 75 B5
Nampula Moz. 99 D5
Namsai Myanmar 70 B1
Namsang Myanmar 70 B2
Namsen r. Norway 44 G4
Nam She Tsim hill H.K. China see Sharp Peak
Namsos Norway 44 G4
Namti Myanmar 70 B1
Namtok Myanmar 70 B3
Namtok Chattakan National Park Thai. 70 C3
Namton Myanmar 70 B2
Namtsy Rus. Fed. 65 N3
Namtu Myanmar 70 B2
Namu Canada 120 E5
Namuli, Monte mt. Moz. 99 D5
Namuno Moz. 99 D5
Namur Belgium 52 E4
Namutoni Namibia 99 B5
Namwŏn S. Korea 75 B6
Namya Ra Myanmar 70 B1
Namyit Island S. China Sea 68 E4
Nan Thai. 70 C3
Nana Bakassa Cent. Afr. Rep. 98 B3
Nanaimo Canada 120 F5
Nanam N. Korea 74 C4
Nan'an China 77 H3
Nanango Australia 112 F1
Nananib Plateau Namibia 100 C3
Nanao Japan 75 E5
Nanatsu-shima i. Japan 75 E5
Nanbai China see Zunyi
Nanbin China see Shizhu
Nanbu China 76 E2
Nancha China 74 C3
Nanchang Jiangxi China 77 G2
Nanchang Jiangxi China 77 G2
Nanchong China 76 E2
Nanchuan China 76 E2
Nancowry i. India 71 A6
Nancun China 77 G1
Nancy France 52 G6
Nancy (Essey) airport France 52 G6
Nanda Devi mt. India 82 E3
Nanda Kot mt. India 82 E3
Nandan China 76 E3
Nandapur India 84 D2
Nanded India 84 C2
Nander India see Nanded
Nandewar Range mts Australia 112 E3
Nandod India 84 B1
Nandurbar India 82 C5
Nandyal India 84 C3

Nanfeng Guangdong China 77 F4
Nanfeng Jiangxi China 77 H3
Nang China 76 B2
Nanga Eboko Cameroon 96 E4
▶Nanga Parbat mt. Pak. 82 C2
9th highest mountain in the world and in Asia.
Nangar National Park Australia 112 D4
Nangatayap Indon. 68 E7
Nangin Myanmar 71 B5
Nangnim-sanmaek mts N. Korea 75 B4
Nangqên China 76 C1
Nangulangwa Tanz. 99 D4
Nanguneri India 84 C4
Nanhua China 76 D3
Nanhui China 77 I2
Nanjian China 76 D3
Nanjiang China 76 E1
Nanjing China 77 H1
Nanji Shan i. China 77 I3
Nanka Jiang r. China 76 C4
Nankang China 77 G3
Nanking China see Nanjing
Nankova Angola 99 B5
Nanlei He r. China 76 C4
also known as Nam Loi (Myanmar)
Nanling China 77 H2
Nan Ling mts China 77 F3
Nanliu Jiang r. China 77 F4
Nanlong China see Nanbu
Nannilam India 84 C4
Nannine Australia 109 B6
Nanning China 77 F4
Nannup Australia 109 A8
Na Noi Thai. 70 C3
Nanortalik Greenland 119 N3
Nanouki atoll Kiribati see Nonouti
Nanouti atoll Kiribati see Nonouti
Nanpan Jiang r. China 76 E3
Nanping China 77 H3
Nanpu China see Pucheng
Nanri Dao i. China 77 H3
Nansei-shotō is Japan see Ryukyu Islands
Nansei-shotō Trench sea feature N. Pacific Ocean see Ryukyu Trench
Nansen Basin sea feature Arctic Ocean 153 H1
Nansen Sound sea chan. Canada 119 I1
Nan-sha Ch'ün-tao is S. China Sea see Spratly Islands
Nanshan Island S. China Sea 68 F4
Nansha Qundao is S. China Sea see Spratly Islands
Nansio Tanz. 98 D4
Nantes France 56 D3
Nantes à Brest, Canal de France 56 C3
Nanteuil-le-Haudouin France 52 C5
Nanthi Kadal lag. Sri Lanka 84 D4
Nanticoke Canada 134 E2
Nanticoke U.S.A. 135 H4
Nantong China 77 I2
Nantou China 77 [inset]
Nant'ou Taiwan 77 I4
Nantucket U.S.A. 135 J3
Nantucket Island U.S.A. 135 K3
Nantucket Sound g. U.S.A. 135 J3
Nantwich U.K. 49 E5
Nanumaga i. Tuvalu see Nanumanga
Nanumanga i. Tuvalu 107 H2
Nanumea atoll Tuvalu 107 H2
Nanuque Brazil 145 C2
Nanusa, Kepulauan is Indon. 69 H6
Nanxi China 76 E2
Nanxian China 77 G2
Nanxiong China 77 G3
Nanyang China 77 G1
Nanyuki Kenya 98 D4
Nanzhang China 77 F2
Nanzhao China see Zhao'an
Nanzhou China see Nanxian
Naococane, Lac l. Canada 123 H3
Naoero country S. Pacific Ocean see Nauru
Naogaon Bangl. 83 G4
Naoli He r. China 74 D3
Naomid, Dasht-e des. Afgh./Iran 89 F3
Naoshera India 82 C2
Napa U.S.A. 128 B2
Napaktulik Lake Canada 121 H1
Napanee Canada 135 G1
Napasoq Greenland 119 M3
Naperville U.S.A. 134 A3
Napier N.Z. 113 F4
Napier Range hills Australia 108 D4
Napierville Canada 135 I1
Naples Italy 58 F4
Naples FL U.S.A. 133 D7
Naples ME U.S.A. 135 J2
Naples TX U.S.A. 131 E5
Naples UT U.S.A. 129 I1
Napo China 76 E4
Napoleon IN U.S.A. 134 C4
Napoleon ND U.S.A. 130 D2
Napoleon OH U.S.A. 134 C3
Napoli Italy see Naples
Naqadeh Iran 88 B2
Nara India 82 B5
Nara Japan 75 D6
Nara Mali 96 C3
Narach Belarus 45 O9
Naracoorte Australia 111 C8
Naradhan Australia 112 C4
Narainpur India 84 D2
Naralua India 83 F4
Naranjal Ecuador 142 C4
Naranjo Mex. 127 F8
Narasapur India 84 D2
Narasaraopet India 84 D2
Narasinghapur India 84 E1
Narathiwat Thai. 71 C6
Nara Visa U.S.A. 131 C5
Narayanganj Bangl. 83 G5
Narayanganj India 82 E5
Narayangarh India 82 C4
Narbada r. India see Narmada
Narberth U.K. 49 C7
Narbo France see Narbonne
Narbonne France 56 F5
Narborough Island Galápagos Ecuador see Fernandina, Isla
Narcea r. Spain 57 C2
Narcondam Island India 71 A4
Nardò Italy 58 H4
Narechi r. Pak. 89 H4
Narembeen Australia 109 B8
Nares Abyssal Plain sea feature S. Atlantic Ocean 148 D4
Nares Deep sea feature N. Atlantic Ocean 148 D4
Nares Strait Canada/Greenland 119 K2
Naretha Australia 109 D7
Narew r. Poland 47 R4
Narib Namibia 100 C3
Narikel Jinjira i. Bangl. see St Martin's Island
Narimanov Rus. Fed. 43 J7
Narimskiy Khrebet mts Kazakh. see Narymskiy Khrebet
Narin Afgh. 89 H2
Narin reg. Afgh. 89 H2
Narince Turkey 90 E3
Narin Gol watercourse China 83 H1
Narizon, Punta pt Mex. 127 F8
Narkher India 82 D5
Narmada r. India 82 C5
Narman Turkey 91 F2
Narnaul India 82 D3
Narni Italy 58 E3
Narnia Italy see Narni
Narodnaya, Gora mt. Rus. Fed. 41 S3
Naro-Fominsk Rus. Fed. 43 H5
Narok Kenya 98 D4
Narooma Australia 112 E6
Narovchat Rus. Fed. 43 I5
Narowlya Belarus 43 F6
Närpes Fin. 44 L5
Narrabri Australia 112 D3
Narragansett Bay U.S.A. 135 J3
Narran r. Australia 112 C2
Narrandera Australia 112 C5
Narran Lake Australia 112 C2
Narrogin Australia 109 B8
Narromine Australia 112 D4
Narrows U.S.A. 134 E5
Narrowsburg U.S.A. 135 H3
Narsapur India 84 C2
Narsaq Greenland 119 N3
Narshingdi Bangl. see Narsingdi
Narsimhapur India see Narsinghpur
Narsingdi Bangl. 83 G5
Narsinghpur India 82 D5
Narsipatnam India 84 D2
Nartkala Rus. Fed. 91 F2
Naruto Japan 75 D6
Narva Estonia 45 P7
Narva Bay Estonia/Rus. Fed. 45 O7
Narva laht b. Estonia/Rus. Fed. see Narva Bay
Narva Reservoir resr Estonia/Rus. Fed. see Narvskoye Vodokhranilishche
Narva veehoidla resr Estonia/Rus. Fed. see Narvskoye Vodokhranilishche
Narvik Norway 44 J2
Narvskiy Zaliv b. Estonia/Rus. Fed. see Narva Bay
Narvskoye Vodokhranilishche resr Estonia/Rus. Fed. 45 P7
Narwana India 82 D3
Nar'yan-Mar Rus. Fed. 42 L2
Narymskiy Khrebet mts Kazakh. 80 F2
Naryn Kyrg. 80 E3
Näsåker Sweden 44 J5
Nashik India 84 B1
Nashua U.S.A. 135 J2
Nashville AR U.S.A. 131 E5
Nashville GA U.S.A. 133 D6
Nashville IN U.S.A. 134 B4
Nashville NC U.S.A. 132 E5
Nashville OH U.S.A. 134 D3
▶Nashville TN U.S.A. 132 C4
Capital of Tennessee.
Našib Syria 85 C3
Näsijärvi l. Fin. 45 M6
Nasik India see Nashik
Nasir Pak. 89 H4
Nasir Sudan 86 D8
Nasirabad Bangl. see Mymensingh
Nasirabad India 82 C4
Nāşirīyah Iraq 91 G5
Naskaupi r. Canada 123 J3
Naşr Egypt 90 C5
Nasratabad Iran see Zābol
Naşrīān-e Pā'īn Iran 88 B3
Nass r. Canada 120 D4
Nassau r. Australia 110 C2
▶Nassau Bahamas 133 E7
Capital of The Bahamas.
Nassau i. Cook Is 107 J3
Nassau U.S.A. 135 I2
Nassawadox U.S.A. 135 H5
Nasser, Lake resr Egypt 86 D5
Nässjö Sweden 45 I8
Nassuttooq inlet Greenland 119 M3
Nastapoca r. Canada 122 F2
Nastapoka Islands Canada 122 F2
Nasugbu Phil. 69 G4
Nasva Rus. Fed. 42 F4
Nata Botswana 99 C6
Natal Brazil 143 K5
Natal Indon. 68 B6
Natal prov. S. Africa see KwaZulu-Natal
Natal Basin sea feature Indian Ocean 149 K8
Naṭanz Iran 88 C3
Natashquan Canada 123 J4
Natashquan r. Canada 123 J4
Natchez U.S.A. 131 F6
Natchitoches U.S.A. 131 E6
Nathalia Australia 112 B6
Nathia Gali Pak. 89 I3
Nati, Punta pt Spain 57 H3
Natillas Mex. 131 C7
National City U.S.A. 128 E5
National West Coast Tourist Recreation Area park Namibia 100 B2
Natitingou Benin 96 D3
Natividad, Isla i. Mex. 127 E8
Natividade Brazil 143 I6
Natkyizin Myanmar 70 B4
Natla r. Canada 120 D2
Natmauk Myanmar 70 A2
Nator Bangl. see Natore
Nátora Mex. 127 F7
Natore Bangl. 83 G4
Natori Japan 75 F5
Natron, Lake salt l. Tanz. 98 D4
Nattai National Park Australia 112 E5
Nattalin Myanmar 70 A3
Nattaung mt. Myanmar 70 B3
Na'tū Iran 89 F3
Natuashish Nfld. and Lab. 123 J3
Natuna, Kepulauan is Indon. 71 D6
Natuna Besar i. Indon. 71 E6
Natural Bridges National Monument nat. park U.S.A. 129 H3
Naturaliste, Cape Australia 109 A8
Naturaliste Plateau sea feature Indian Ocean 149 P8
Naturita U.S.A. 129 I2
Nauchas Namibia 100 C2
Nau Co l. China 83 E2
Nauen Germany 53 M2
Naufragados, Ponta dos pt Brazil 145 A4
Naujoji Akmenė Lith. 45 M8
Naukh India 82 C4
Naukot Pak. 89 H5
Naumburg (Hessen) Germany 53 J3
Naumburg (Saale) Germany 53 L3
Naunglon Myanmar 70 B3
Naungpale Myanmar 70 B3
Naupada India 84 E2
Na'ūr Jordan 85 B4
Nauroz Kalat Pak. 89 G4
Naurskaya Rus. Fed. 91 G2
Nauru i. Nauru 107 G2
Nauru country S. Pacific Ocean 107 G2
Naustdal Norway 45 D6
Nauta Peru 142 D4
Nautaca Uzbek. see Qarshi
Naute Dam Namibia 100 C4
Nauzad Afgh. 89 G3
Nava Mex. 131 C6
Navadwip India 83 G5
Navahrudak Belarus 45 N10
Navajo Lake U.S.A. 129 J3
Navajo Mountain U.S.A. 129 H3
Navalmoral de la Mata Spain 57 D4
Navalvillar de Pela Spain 57 D4
Navan Ireland 51 F4
Navangar India see Jamnagar
Navapolatsk Belarus 45 P9
Nāvar, Dasht-e depr. Afgh. 89 G3
Navarin, Mys c. Rus. Fed. 65 S3
Navarra aut. comm. Spain 57 F2
Navarra, Comunidad Foral de aut. comm. Spain see Navarra
Navarre Australia 112 A6
Navarre aut. comm. Spain see Navarra
Navarro r. U.S.A. 128 B2
Navashino Rus. Fed. 42 I5
Navasota U.S.A. 131 D6
▶Navassa Island terr. West Indies 137 I5
United States Unincorporated Territory.
Naver r. U.K. 50 E2
Näverede Sweden 44 I5
Navi Mumbai Mahar. 87 L6
Navlakhi India 82 B5
Navlya Rus. Fed. 43 G5
Năvodari Romania 59 M2
Navoi Uzbek. see Navoiy
Navoiy Uzbek. 89 G1
Navojoa Mex. 127 F8
Navolato Mex. 136 C4
Návpaktos Greece see Nafpaktos
Návplion Greece see Nafplio
Navşar Turkey see Şemdinli
Navsari India 84 B1
Nawá Syria 85 C3
Nawabganj Bangl. 83 G4
Nawabshah Pak. 89 H5
Nawada India 83 F4
Nāwah Afgh. 89 G3
Nawalgarh India 82 C4
Nawanshahr India 82 D3
Nawan Shehar India see Nawanshahr
Nawar, Dasht-i depr. Afgh. see Nāvar, Dasht-e
Nawarangpur India see Nabarangapur
Nawngcho Myanmar see Nawnghkio
Nawnghkio Myanmar 70 B2
Nawng Hpa Myanmar 70 B2
Nawngleng Myanmar 70 B2
Nawoiy Uzbek. see Navoiy
Naxçıvan Azer. 91 G3
Naxos i. Greece 59 K6
Nayagarh India 84 E1
Nayak Afgh. 89 G3
Nayar Mex. 136 D4
Näy Band, Küh-e mt. Iran 88 E3
Nayong China 76 E3
Nayoro Japan 74 F3
▶Nay Pyi Taw Myanmar 70 B3
Joint capital (with Rangoon) of Myanmar.
Nazaré Brazil 145 D1
Nazareno Mex. 131 C7
Nazareth Israel 85 B3
Nazário Brazil 145 A2
Nazas Mex. 131 B7
Nazas r. Mex. 131 B7
Nazca Peru 142 D6
Nazca Ridge sea feature S. Pacific Ocean 151 O7
Nāzīl Iran 89 F4
Nazilli Turkey 59 M6
Nazimabad Pak. 89 G5
Nazımiye Turkey 91 E3
Nazir Hat Bangl. 83 G5
Nazko Canada 120 F4
Nazran' Rus. Fed. 91 G2
Nazrēt Eth. 98 D3
Nazwá Oman 88 E6
Ncojane Botswana 100 E2
N'dalatando Angola 99 B4
Ndélé Cent. Afr. Rep. 98 C3
Ndendé Gabon 98 B4
Ndende i. Solomon Is see Ndeni
Ndeni i. Solomon Is 107 G3
▶Ndjamena Chad 97 E3
Capital of Chad.
N'Djamena Chad see Ndjamena
Ndjouani i. Comoros see Nzwani
Ndoi i. Fiji see Doi
Ndola Zambia 99 C5
Nduke i. Solomon Is see Kolombangara
Ndwedwe S. Africa 101 J5
Ne, Hon i. Vietnam 70 D3
Neabul Creek r. Australia 112 C1
Neagh, Lough l. U.K. 51 F3
Neah Bay U.S.A. 126 B2
Neale, Lake salt flat Australia 109 E6
Nea Liosia Greece 59 J5
Neapoli Greece 59 J6
Neapolis Italy see Naples
Nea Roda Greece 59 J4
Neath U.K. 49 D7
Neath r. U.K. 49 D7
Nebbi Uganda 98 D3
Nebine Creek r. Australia 112 C2
Neblina, Pico da mt. Brazil 142 E3
Nebo Australia 110 E4
Nebo, Mount U.S.A. 129 H2
Nebolchi Rus. Fed. 42 G4
Nebraska state U.S.A. 130 C3
Nebraska City U.S.A. 130 E3
Nebrodi, Monti mts Sicily Italy 58 F6
Neches r. U.S.A. 131 E6
Nechisar National Park Eth. 98 D3
Nechranice, Vodní nádrž resr Czech Rep. 53 N4
Neckar r. Germany 53 I5
Neckarsulm Germany 53 J5
Necker Island U.S.A. 150 J4
Necochea Arg. 144 E5
Nederland country Europe see Netherlands
Nederlandse Antillen terr. West Indies see Netherlands Antilles
Neder Rijn r. Neth. 52 F3
Nedlouc, Lac l. Canada 123 G2
Nedluk Lake Canada see Nedlouc, Lac
Nêdong China see Zêtang
Nedre Soppero Sweden 44 L2
Nédroma Alg. 57 F6
Needle Mountain U.S.A. 126 F3
Needles U.S.A. 129 F4
Neemach India see Neemuch
Neemuch India 82 C4
Neenah U.S.A. 134 A1
Neepawa Canada 121 L5
Neergaard Lake Canada 119 J2
Neerijnen Neth. 52 F3
Neerpelt Belgium 52 F3
Neftçala Azer. 91 H3
Neftechala Azer. see Uzboy
Neftechala Azer. see Neftçala
Neftegorsk Sakhalinskaya Oblast' Rus. Fed. 74 F1
Neftegorsk Samarskaya Oblast' Rus. Fed. 43 K5
Neftekamsk Rus. Fed. 41 Q4
Neftekumsk Rus. Fed. 91 G1
Nefteyugansk Rus. Fed. 64 I3
Neftezavodsk Turkm. see Seýdi
Neftezavodsk Turkm. see Seýdi
Nefyn U.K. 49 C6
Nefza Tunisia 58 C6
Negage Angola 99 B4
Negār Iran 88 E4
Negara Indon. 108 A2
Negēlē Eth. 98 D3
Negev des. Israel 85 B4
Negomane Moz. 99 D5
Negombo Sri Lanka 84 C5
Negotino Macedonia 59 J4
Negra, Cordillera mts Peru 142 C5
Negra, Punta pt Peru 142 B5
Negra, Serra mts Brazil 145 C2
Negrais, Cape Myanmar 70 A4
Négrine Alg. 58 B7
Negro r. Arg. 144 D6
Negro r. Brazil 143 G7
Negro r. Brazil 145 A4
Negro r. S. America 142 G4
Negro, Cabo c. Morocco 57 D6
Negroponte i. Greece see Evvoia
Negros i. Phil. 69 G5
Negru Vodă, Podişul plat. Romania 59 M3
Nehbandān Iran 89 F4
Nehe China 74 B2
Neijiang China 76 E2
Neilburg Canada 121 I4
Neimenggu aut. reg. China see Nei Mongol Zizhiqu
Nei Mongol Zizhiqu aut. reg. China 74 A2
Neinstedt Germany 53 L3
Neiva Col. 142 C3
Neixiang China 77 F1
Nejanilini Lake Canada 121 L3
Nejd reg. Saudi Arabia see Najd
Neka Iran 88 D2
Nek'emtē Eth. 98 D3
Nekrasovskoye Rus. Fed. 42 I4
Neksø Denmark 45 I9
Nelang India 82 D3
Nelia Australia 110 C4
Nelidovo Rus. Fed. 42 G4
Neligh U.S.A. 130 D3
Nel'kan Rus. Fed. 65 P3
Nellore India 84 C3
Nelluz watercourse Turkey 85 D1
Nel'ma Rus. Fed. 74 E3
Nelson Canada 120 G5
Nelson r. Canada 121 M3
Nelson N.Z. 113 D5
Nelson U.K. 48 E5
Nelson U.S.A. 129 G4
Nelson, Cape Australia 111 C8
Nelson, Cape P.N.G. 69 L8
Nelson, Estrecho strait Chile 144 A8
Nelson Bay Australia 112 F4
Nelson Forks Canada 120 F3
Nelsonia U.S.A. 135 H5
Nelson Lakes National Park N.Z. 113 D6
Nelson Reservoir U.S.A. 126 G2
Nelspruit S. Africa 101 J3
Néma Mauritania 96 C3
Nema Rus. Fed. 42 K4
Neman r. Belarus/Lith. see Nyoman
Neman Rus. Fed. 45 M9
Nemausus France see Nîmes
Nemawar India 82 D5
Nemed Rus. Fed. 42 L3
Nementcha, Monts des mts Alg. 58 B7
Nemetocenna France see Arras
Nemetskiy, Mys c. Rus. Fed. 44 Q2
Nemirov Ukr. see Nemyriv
Nemiscau r. Canada 122 F4
Nemiscau, Lac l. Canada 122 F4
Nemor He r. China 74 B2
Nemours Alg. see Ghazaouet
Nemours France 56 F2
Nemrut Dağı mt. Turkey 91 F3
Nemunas r. Belarus/Lith. see Nyoman
Nemuro Japan 74 G4
Nemuro-kaikyō sea chan. Japan/Rus. Fed. 74 G4
Nemyriv Ukr. 43 F6
Nenagh Ireland 51 D5
Nenana U.S.A. 118 D3
Nene r. U.K. 49 H6
Nenjiang China 74 B2
Nen Jiang r. China 74 B3
Neosho U.S.A. 131 E4
Nepal country Asia 83 E3
Nepalganj Nepal 83 E3
Nepean Canada 135 H1
Nepean, Point Australia 112 B7
Nephi U.S.A. 129 H2
Nephin hill Ireland 51 C3
Nephin Beg Range hills Ireland 51 C3
Nepisiguit r. Canada 123 I5
Nepoko r. Dem. Rep. Congo 98 C3
Nérac France 56 E4
Nerang Australia 112 F1
Nera Tso l. China 83 H3
Nerchinsk Rus. Fed. 73 L2
Nerekhta Rus. Fed. 42 I4
Néret, Lac l. Canada 123 H3
Neretva r. Bos.-Herz./Croatia 58 G3
Nêri Pünco l. China 83 G3
Neriquinha Angola 99 C5
Neris r. Lith. 45 M9
also known as Viliya (Belarus/Lithuania)
Nerl' r. Rus. Fed. 42 H4
Nerópolis Brazil 145 A2
Neryungri Rus. Fed. 65 N4
Nes Neth. 52 F1
Nes Norway 45 F6
Nes' Rus. Fed. 42 J2
Nesbyen Norway 45 F6
Neskaupstaður Iceland 44 [inset]
Nesle France 52 C5
Nesna Norway 44 H3
Nesri India 84 B2
Ness r. U.K. 50 E3
Ness, Loch l. U.K. 50 E3
Ness City U.S.A. 130 D4
Nesse r. Germany 53 K4
Nesselrode, Mount Canada/U.S.A. 120 C3
Nestor Falls Canada 121 M5
Nestos r. Greece 59 K4
also known as Mesta
Nesvizh Belarus see Nyasvizh
Netanya Israel 85 B3
Netherlands country Europe 52 F2
▶Netherlands Antilles terr. West Indies 137 K6
Self-governing Netherlands Territory.
Netphen Germany 53 I4
Netrakona Bangl. 83 G4
Netrokona Bangl. see Netrakona
Nettilling Lake Canada 119 K3
Neubrandenburg Germany 53 N1
Neuburg an der Donau Germany 53 L6
Neuchâtel Switz. 56 H3
Neuchâtel, Lac de l. Switz. 56 H3
Neuendettelsau Germany 53 K5
Neuenhaus Germany 52 G2
Neuenkirchen Germany 53 J1
Neuenkirchen (Oldenburg) Germany 53 I2
Neufchâteau Belgium 52 F5
Neufchâteau France 56 G2
Neufchâtel-en-Bray France 52 B5
Neufchâtel-Hardelot France 52 B4
Neuharlingersiel Germany 53 H1
Neuhausen Rus. Fed. see Gur'yevsk
Neuhof Germany 53 J4
Neu Kaliß Germany 53 L1
Neukirchen Hessen Germany 53 J4
Neukirchen Sachsen Germany 53 M4
Neukuhren Rus. Fed. see Pionerskiy
Neumarkt in der Oberpfalz Germany 53 L5
Neumayer research station Antarctica 152 B2
Neumünster Germany 47 L3
Neunburg vorm Wald Germany 53 M5
Neunkirchen Austria 47 P7
Neunkirchen Germany 53 H5
Neuquén Arg. 144 C5
Neuruppin Germany 53 M2
Neu Sandez Poland see Nowy Sącz
Neuse r. U.S.A. 133 E5
Neusiedler See l. Austria/Hungary 47 P7
Neusiedler See Seewinkel, Nationalpark nat. park Austria 47 P7
Neuss Germany 52 G3
Neustadt (Wied) Germany 53 H4
Neustadt am Rübenberge Germany 53 J2
Neustadt an der Aisch Germany 53 K5
Neustadt an der Hardt Germany see Neustadt an der Weinstraße
Neustadt an der Waldnaab Germany 53 M5
Neustadt an der Weinstraße Germany 53 I5
Neustadt bei Coburg Germany 53 L4
Neustadt-Glewe Germany 53 L1
Neustrelitz Germany 53 N1
Neutraubling Germany 53 M6
Neuville-lès-Dieppe France 52 B5
Neuwied Germany 53 H4
Neu Wulmstorf Germany 53 J1
Nevada IA U.S.A. 130 E3
Nevada MO U.S.A. 130 E4
Nevada state U.S.A. 126 D5
Nevada, Sierra mts Spain 57 E5
Nevada, Sierra mts U.S.A. 128 C1
Nevada City U.S.A. 128 C2
Nevado, Cerro mt. Arg. 144 C5
Nevado, Sierra del mts Arg. 144 C5
Nevasa India 84 B2
Nevatim Israel 85 B4
Nevdubstroy Rus. Fed. see Kirovsk
Nevel' Rus. Fed. 42 F4
Nevel'sk Rus. Fed. 74 F3
Never Rus. Fed. 74 B1
Nevers France 56 F3
Nevertire Australia 112 C3
Nevesinje Bos.-Herz. 58 H3
Nevinnomyssk Rus. Fed. 91 F1
Nevşehir Turkey 90 D3
Nevskoye Rus. Fed. 74 D3
New r. CA U.S.A. 129 F5
New r. WV U.S.A. 134 E5
Newala Tanz. 99 D5
New Albany IN U.S.A. 134 C4
New Albany MS U.S.A. 131 F5
New Amsterdam Guyana 143 G2
New Amsterdam U.S.A. see New York
New Angledool Australia 112 C2
Newark DE U.S.A. 135 H4
Newark NJ U.S.A. 135 H3
Newark NY U.S.A. 135 G2
Newark OH U.S.A. 134 D3
Newark airport U.S.A. 132 F3
Newark Lake U.S.A. 129 F2
Newark-on-Trent U.K. 49 G5
New Bedford U.S.A. 135 J3
Newberg U.S.A. 126 C3
New Berlin U.S.A. 135 H2
New Bern U.S.A. 133 E5
Newberry IN U.S.A. 134 B4
Newberry MI U.S.A. 132 C2
Newberry SC U.S.A. 133 D5
Newberry National Volcanic Monument nat. park U.S.A. 126 C4
Newberry Springs U.S.A. 128 E4
New Bethlehem U.S.A. 134 F3
Newbiggin-by-the-Sea U.K. 48 F3
New Bight Bahamas 133 F7
New Bloomfield U.S.A. 135 G3
Newboro Canada 135 G1
New Boston OH U.S.A. 134 D4
New Boston TX U.S.A. 131 E5
New Braunfels U.S.A. 131 D6
Newbridge Ireland 51 F4
New Britain i. P.N.G. 69 L8
New Britain U.S.A. 135 I3
New Britain Trench sea feature S. Pacific Ocean 150 G6
New Brunswick prov. Canada 123 I5
New Brunswick U.S.A. 135 H3
New Buffalo U.S.A. 134 B3
Newburgh Canada 135 G1
Newburgh U.K. 50 G3
Newburgh U.S.A. 135 H3
Newbury U.K. 49 F7
Newburyport U.S.A. 135 J2
Newby Bridge U.K. 48 E4
▶New Caledonia terr. S. Pacific Ocean 107 G4
French Overseas Collectivity.
New Caledonia Trough sea feature Tasman Sea 150 G7
New Carlisle Canada 123 I4
Newcastle Australia 112 E4
Newcastle Canada 135 F2
Newcastle Ireland 51 F4
Newcastle S. Africa 101 I4
Newcastle U.K. 51 G3
New Castle CO U.S.A. 129 J2
New Castle IN U.S.A. 134 C4
New Castle KY U.S.A. 134 C4
New Castle PA U.S.A. 134 E3
Newcastle UT U.S.A. 129 G3
New Castle VA U.S.A. 134 E5
Newcastle WY U.S.A. 126 G4
Newcastle Emlyn U.K. 49 C6
Newcastle-under-Lyme U.K. 49 E5
Newcastle upon Tyne U.K. 48 F4
Newcastle Waters Australia 108 F4
Newcastle West Ireland 51 C5
Newchwang China see Yingkou
New City U.S.A. 135 I3
Newcomb U.S.A. 135 H2
New Concord U.S.A. 134 E4
New Cumberland U.S.A. 134 E3
New Cumnock U.K. 50 E5
New Deer U.K. 50 G3
▶New Delhi India 82 D3
Capital of India.
New Don Pedro Reservoir U.S.A. 128 C3
Newell U.S.A. 130 C2
Newell, Lake salt flat Australia 109 D6
Newell, Lake Canada 121 I5
New England National Park Australia 112 F3
New England Range mts Australia 112 E3
New England Seamounts sea feature N. Atlantic Ocean 148 E3
Newenham, Cape U.S.A. 118 B4
Newent U.K. 49 E7
New Era U.S.A. 134 B2
Newfane NY U.S.A. 135 F2
Newfane VT U.S.A. 135 I2
New Forest National Park nat. park England 49 F8
Newfoundland i. Canada 123 K4
Newfoundland prov. Canada see Newfoundland and Labrador
Newfoundland and Labrador prov. Canada 123 K3
Newfoundland Evaporation Basin salt l. U.S.A. 129 G1
New Galloway U.K. 50 E5
New Georgia i. Solomon Is 107 F2
New Georgia Islands Solomon Is 107 F2
New Georgia Sound sea chan. Solomon Is 107 F2
New Glasgow Canada 123 J5
▶New Guinea i. Indon./P.N.G. 69 K8
Largest island in Oceania, and 2nd in the world.

New Halfa Sudan 86 E6
New Hampshire state U.S.A. 135 J1
New Hampton U.S.A. 130 E3
New Hanover i. P.N.G. 106 F2
New Haven CT U.S.A. 135 I3
New Haven IN U.S.A. 134 C3
New Haven WV U.S.A. 134 E4
New Hebrides country S. Pacific Ocean see Vanuatu
New Hebrides Trench sea feature S. Pacific Ocean 150 H7
New Holstein U.S.A. 134 A2
New Iberia U.S.A. 131 F6
Newington S. Africa 101 J3
Newinn Ireland 51 E5
New Ireland i. P.N.G. 106 F2
New Jersey state U.S.A. 135 H4
New Kensington U.S.A. 134 F3
New Kent U.S.A. 135 G5
Newkirk U.S.A. 131 D4
New Lanark U.K. 50 F5
Newland Range hills Australia 109 C7
New Lexington U.S.A. 134 D4
New Liskeard Canada 122 F5
New London CT U.S.A. 135 I3
New London MO U.S.A. 130 F4
New Madrid U.S.A. 131 F4
Newman Australia 109 B5
Newman U.S.A. 128 C3
Newmarket Canada 134 F1
Newmarket Ireland 51 C5
Newmarket U.K. 49 H6
New Market U.S.A. 135 F4
Newmarket-on-Fergus Ireland 51 D5
New Martinsville U.S.A. 134 E4
New Meadows U.S.A. 126 D3
New Mexico state U.S.A. 127 G6
New Miami U.S.A. 134 C4
New Milford U.S.A. 135 H3
Newnan U.S.A. 133 C5
New Orleans U.S.A. 131 F6
New Paris IN U.S.A. 134 C3
New Paris OH U.S.A. 134 C4
New Philadelphia U.S.A. 134 E3
New Pitsligo U.K. 50 G3
New Plymouth N.Z. 113 E4
Newport Mayo Ireland 51 C4
Newport Tipperary Ireland 51 D5
Newport England U.K. 49 E6
Newport England U.K. 49 F8
Newport Wales U.K. 49 D7
Newport AR U.S.A. 131 F5
Newport IN U.S.A. 134 B4
Newport KY U.S.A. 134 C4
Newport MI U.S.A. 134 D3
Newport NH U.S.A. 135 I2
Newport NJ U.S.A. 135 H4
Newport OR U.S.A. 126 B3
Newport RI U.S.A. 135 J3
Newport VT U.S.A. 135 I1
Newport WA U.S.A. 126 D2
Newport Beach U.S.A. 128 E5
Newport News U.S.A. 135 G5
Newport Pagnell U.K. 49 G6
New Port Richey U.S.A. 133 D6
New Providence i. Bahamas 133 E7
Newquay U.K. 49 B8
New Roads U.S.A. 131 F6
New Rochelle U.S.A. 135 I3
New Rockford U.S.A. 130 D2
New Romney U.K. 49 H8
New Ross Ireland 51 F5
Newry Australia 108 E4
Newry U.K. 51 F3
New Siberia Islands Rus. Fed. 65 P2
New Smyrna Beach U.S.A. 133 D6
New South Wales state Australia 112 C4
New Stanton U.S.A. 134 F3
Newton U.K. 48 E5
Newton GA U.S.A. 133 C6
Newton IA U.S.A. 130 E3
Newton IL U.S.A. 130 F4
Newton KS U.S.A. 130 D4
Newton MA U.S.A. 135 J2
Newton MS U.S.A. 131 F5
Newton NC U.S.A. 132 D5
Newton NJ U.S.A. 135 H3
Newton TX U.S.A. 131 E6
Newton Abbot U.K. 49 D8
Newton Mearns U.K. 50 E5
Newton Stewart U.K. 50 E6
Newtown Ireland 51 D5
Newtown England U.K. 49 E6
Newtown Wales U.K. 49 D6
Newtown U.S.A. 134 C4
New Town U.S.A. 130 C1
Newtownabbey U.K. 51 G3
Newtownards U.K. 51 G3
Newtownbarry Ireland see Bunclody
Newtownbutler U.K. 51 E3
Newtown Mount Kennedy Ireland 51 F4
Newtown St Boswells U.K. 50 G5
Newtownstewart U.K. 51 E3
New Ulm U.S.A. 130 E2
Newville U.S.A. 135 G3
New World Island Canada 123 L4

▶New York U.S.A. 135 I3
2nd most populous city in North America, and 5th in the world.

New York state U.S.A. 135 H2

▶New Zealand country Oceania 113 D5
3rd largest and 3rd most populous country in Oceania.

Neya Rus. Fed. 42 I4
Ney Bīd Iran 88 E4
Neyrīz Iran 88 D4
Neyshābūr Iran 88 E2
Nezhin Ukr. see Nizhyn
Nezperce U.S.A. 126 D3
Ngabé Congo 98 B4
Nga Chong, Khao mt. Myanmar/Thai. 70 B4
Ngagahtawng Myanmar 76 C3
Ngagau mt. Tanz. 99 D4
Ngalu Indon. 108 C2
Ngamring China 83 F3
Ngangla Ringco salt l. China 83 E3
Nganglong Kangri mt. China 82 E2
Nganglong Kangri mts China 82 E2
Ngangzê Co salt l. China 83 F3
Ngangzê Shan mts China 83 F3
Ngân Sơn Vietnam 70 D2
Ngaoundal Cameroon 96 E4
Ngaoundéré Cameroon 97 E4
Ngape Myanmar 70 A2
Ngaputaw Myanmar 70 A3
Ngarrab China see Gyaca
Ngathainggyaung Myanmar 70 A3
Ngau i. Fiji see Gau
Ngawa China see Aba
Ngeaur i. Palau see Angaur
Ngeruangel i. Palau 69 I5
Ngga Pulu mt. Indon. see Jaya, Puncak
Ngiap r. Laos 70 C3
Ngilmina Indon. 108 D2
Ngiva Angola see Ondjiva
Ngo Congo 98 B4
Ngoako Ramalepe S. Africa see Duiwelskloof
Ngoin, Co salt l. China 83 G3
Ngok Linh mt. Vietnam 70 D4
Ngoko r. Cameroon/Congo 97 E4
Ngola Shankou pass China 76 C1
Ngom Qu r. China see Ji Qu
Ngong Shuen Chau pen. H.K. China see Stonecutters' Island
Ngoqumaima China 83 F2
Ngoring China 76 C1
Ngoring Hu l. China 76 C1
Ngourti Niger 96 E3
Nguigmi Niger 96 E3
Nguiu Australia 108 E2
Ngükang China 76 B2
Ngukurr Australia 108 F3
Ngulu atoll Micronesia 69 J5
Ngunza Angola see Sumbe
Ngunza-Kabolu Angola see Sumbe
Nguru Nigeria 96 E3
Ngwaketse admin. dist. Botswana see Southern
Ngwane country Africa see Swaziland
Ngwathe S. Africa 101 H4
Ngwavuma r. S. Africa/Swaziland 101 K4
Ngwelezana S. Africa 101 J5
Nhachengue Moz. 101 L2
Nhamalabué Moz. 99 D5
Nha Trang Vietnam 71 E4
Nhecolândia Brazil 143 G7
Nhill Australia 111 C8
Nhlangano Swaziland 101 J4
Nho Quan Vietnam 70 D2
Nhow i. Fiji see Gau
Nhulunbuy Australia 110 B2
Niacam Canada 121 J4
Niafounké Mali 96 C3
Niagara U.S.A. 132 C2
Niagara Falls Canada 134 F2
Niagara Falls U.S.A. 134 F2
Niagara-on-the-Lake Canada 134 F2
Niagzu Aksai Chin 82 D2
Niah Sarawak Malaysia 68 E6
Niakaramandougou Côte d'Ivoire 96 C4

▶Niamey Niger 96 D3
Capital of Niger.

Nīām Kand Iran 88 E5
Niampak Indon. 69 H6
Niangara Dem. Rep. Congo 98 C3
Niangay, Lac l. Mali 96 C3
Nianzishan China 74 A3
Nias i. Indon. 71 B7
Niassa, Lago l. Africa see Nyasa, Lake
Niaur i. Palau see Angaur
Nīāzābād Iran 89 F3
Nibil Well Australia 108 D5
Nīca Latvia 45 L8

▶Nicaragua country Central America 137 G6
5th largest country in North America.

Nicaragua, Lago de Nicaragua 137 G6
Nicastro Italy 58 G5
Nice France 56 H5
Nice U.S.A. 128 B2
Nicephorium Syria see Ar Raqqah
Niceville U.S.A. 133 C6
Nichicun, Lac l. Canada 123 H3
Nicholas Channel Bahamas/Cuba 133 D8
Nicholasville U.S.A. 134 C5
Nichols U.S.A. 134 A1
Nicholson r. Australia 110 B3
Nicholson Lake Canada 121 K2
Nicholson Range hills Australia 109 B6
Nicholville U.S.A. 135 H1
Nicobar Islands India 71 A5
Nicolaus U.S.A. 128 C2
Nicomedia Kocaeli Turkey see İzmit

▶Nicosia Cyprus 85 A2
Capital of Cyprus.

Nicoya, Península de pen. Costa Rica 137 G7
Nida Lith. 45 L9
Nidagunda India 84 C2
Nidd r. U.K. 48 F4
Nidda Germany 53 J4
Nidder r. Germany 53 I4
Nidzica Poland 47 R4
Niebüll Germany 47 L3
Nied r. France 52 G5
Niederanven Lux. 52 G5
Niederaula Germany 53 J4
Niedere Tauern mts Austria 47 N7
Niedersachsen land Germany 53 I2
Niedersächsisches Wattenmeer, Nationalpark nat. park Germany 52 G1
Niefang Equat. Guinea 96 E4
Niellé Côte d'Ivoire 96 C3
Nienburg (Weser) Germany 53 J2
Niers r. Germany 52 F3
Nierstein Germany 53 I5
Nieuwe-Niedorp Neth. 52 E2
Nieuwerkerk aan de IJssel Neth. 52 E3
Nieuw Nickerie Suriname 143 G2
Nieuwolda Neth. 52 G1
Nieuwoudtville S. Africa 100 D6
Nieuwpoort Belgium 52 C3
Nieuw-Vossemeer Neth. 52 E3
Niğde Turkey 90 D3
Niger country Africa 96 D3

▶Niger r. Africa 96 D4
3rd longest river in Africa.

Niger, Mouths of the Nigeria 96 D4
Niger Cone sea feature S. Atlantic Ocean 148 I5

▶Nigeria country Africa 96 D4
Most populous country in Africa, and 8th in the world.

Nighthawk Lake Canada 122 E4
Nigrita Greece 59 J4
Nihing Pak. 89 G4
Nihon country Asia see Japan
Niigata Japan 75 E5
Niihama Japan 75 D6
Ni'ihau i. U.S.A. 127 [inset]
Nii-jima i. Japan 75 E6
Niimi Japan 75 D6
Niitsu Japan 75 E5
Nijil, Wādī watercourse Jordan 85 B4
Nijkerk Neth. 52 F2
Nijmegen Neth. 52 F3
Nijverdal Neth. 52 G2
Nikel' Rus. Fed. 44 Q2
Nikki Benin 96 D4
Nikkō Kokuritsu-kōen nat. park Japan 75 E5
Nikolayev Ukr. see Mykolayiv
Nikolayevka Rus. Fed. 43 J5
Nikolayevsk Rus. Fed. 43 J6
Nikolayevskiy Rus. Fed. see Nikolayevsk
Nikolayevsk-na-Amure Rus. Fed. 74 F1
Nikol'sk Rus. Fed. 42 J4
Nikol'skiy Kazakh. see Satpayev
Nikol'skoye Kamchatskaya Oblast' Rus. Fed. 65 R4
Nikol'skoye Vologod. Obl. Rus. Fed. see Sheksna
Nikopol' Ukr. 43 G7
Niksar Turkey 90 E2
Nīkshahr Iran 89 F5
Nikšić Montenegro 58 H3
Nīkū Jahān Iran 89 F5
Nikumaroro atoll Kiribati 107 I2
Nikunau i. Kiribati 107 H2
Nīl, Bahr el r. Africa see Nile
Nilagiri India 83 F5
Niland U.S.A. 129 F5
Nilande Atoll Maldives see Nilandhoo Atoll
Nilandhe Atoll Maldives see Nilandhoo Atoll
Nilandhoo Atoll Maldives 81 D11
Nilang India see Nelang
Nilanga India 84 C2
Nilaveli Sri Lanka 84 D4

▶Nile r. Africa 90 C5
Longest river in the world.

Niles MI U.S.A. 134 B3
Niles OH U.S.A. 134 E3
Nilgiri Hills India 84 C4
Nīlī Dāykundī 89 G3
Nīl Kowtal Afgh. 89 G3
Nilphamari Bangl. 83 G4
Nilsiä Fin. 44 P5
Nimach India see Neemuch
Niman r. Rus. Fed. 74 D2
Nimba, Monts mts Africa see Nimba, Mount
Nimba, Mount Africa 96 C4
Nimbal India 84 B2
Nimberra Well Australia 109 C5
Nimelen r. Rus. Fed. 74 E1
Nîmes France 56 G5
Nimmitabel Australia 111 E8
Nimrod Glacier Antarctica 152 H1
Nimu India 82 D2
Nimule Sudan 97 G4
Nimwegen Neth. see Nijmegen
Nindigully Australia 112 D2
Nine Degree Channel India 84 B4
Nine Islands P.N.G. see Kilinailau Islands
Ninepin Group is H.K. China 77 [inset]
Ninetyeast Ridge sea feature Indian Ocean 149 N8
Ninety Mile Beach Australia 112 C7
Ninety Mile Beach N.Z. 113 D2
Nineveh U.S.A. 135 H2
Ning'an China 74 C3
Ningbo China 77 I2
Ningde China 77 H3
Ning'er China see Pu'er
Ningguo China 77 H2
Ninghai China 77 I2
Ninghsia Hui Autonomous Region aut. reg. China see Ningxia Huizu Zizhiqu
Ninghua China 77 H3
Ningjing India 83 H3
Ningjiang China see Songyuan
Ningjing Shan mts China 76 C2
Ninglang China 76 D3
Ningming China 76 E4
Ningnan China 76 D3
Ningqiang China 76 E1
Ningwu China 73 K5
Ningxia aut. reg. China see Ningxia Huizu Zizhiqu
Ningxia Huizu Zizhiqu aut. reg. China 76 E1
Ningxian China 73 J5
Ningxiang China 77 G2
Ningzhou China see Huaning
Ninh Binh Vietnam 70 D2
Ninh Hoa Vietnam 71 E4
Ninigo Group atolls P.N.G. 69 K7
Ninnis Glacier Antarctica 152 G2
Ninnis Glacier Tongue Antarctica 152 H2
Ninohe Japan 75 F4
Niobrara r. U.S.A. 130 D3
Niokolo Koba, Parc National du nat. park Senegal 96 B3
Niono Mali 96 C3
Nioro Mali 96 C3
Niort France 56 D3
Nipani India 84 B2
Nipawin Canada 121 J4
Niphad India 84 B1
Nipigon Canada 119 J5
Nipigon, Lake Canada 119 J5
Nipishish Lake Canada 123 J3
Nipissing, Lake Canada 122 F5
Nippon country Asia see Japan
Nippon Hai sea N. Pacific Ocean see Japan, Sea of
Nipton U.S.A. 129 F4
Niquelândia Brazil 145 A1
Nīr Ardabīl Iran 88 B2
Nīr Yazd Iran 88 D4
Nira r. India 84 B2
Nirji China 74 B2
Nirmal India 84 C2
Nirmali India 83 F4
Nirmal Range hills India 84 C2
Niš Serbia 59 I3
Nisa Port. 57 C4
Nisarpur India 84 B1
Niscemi Sicily Italy 58 F6
Nīshāpūr Iran see Neyshābūr
Nishino-shima vol. Japan 75 F8
Nishi-Sonogi-hantō pen. Japan 75 C6
Nisibis Turkey see Nusaybin
Nísiros i. Greece see Nisyros
Niskibi r. Canada 121 N3
Nisling r. Canada 120 B2
Nispen Neth. 52 E3
Nissan r. Sweden 45 H8
Nistru r. Ukr. 59 N1 see Dniester
Nisutlin r. Canada 120 C2
Nisyros i. Greece 59 L6
Niṭā Saudi Arabia 88 C5
Nitchequon Canada 123 H3
Nitendi i. Solomon Is see Ndeni
Niterói Brazil 145 C3
Nith r. U.K. 50 F5
Nitibe East Timor 108 D2
Niti Pass China/India 82 D3
Niti Shankou pass China/India see Niti Pass
Nitmiluk National Park Australia 108 F3
Nitra Slovakia 47 Q6
Nitro U.S.A. 134 E4
Niuafo'ou i. Tonga 107 I3
Niuatoputopu i. Tonga 107 I3

▶Niue terr. S. Pacific Ocean 107 J3
Self-governing New Zealand Overseas Territory.

Niujing China see Binchuan
Niulakita i. Tuvalu 107 H3
Niutao i. Tuvalu 107 H2
Niutoushan China 77 H2
Nivala Fin. 44 N5
Nive watercourse Australia 110 D5
Nivelles Belgium 52 E4
Niwai India 82 C4
Niwas India 82 E5
Nixia China see Sêrxü
Nixon U.S.A. 128 D2
Niya China see Minfeng
Niya He r. China 83 E1
Nizamabad India 84 C2
Nizam Sagar l. India 84 C2
Nizhnedevitsk Rus. Fed. 43 H6
Nizhnekamsk Rus. Fed. 42 K5
Nizhnekamskoye Vodokhranilishche resr Rus. Fed. 41 Q4
Nizhnekolymsk Rus. Fed. 65 R3
Nizhnetambovskoye Rus. Fed. 74 E2
Nizhneudinsk Rus. Fed. 72 H2
Nizhnevartovsk Rus. Fed. 64 I3
Nizhnevolzhsk Rus. Fed. see Narimanov
Nizhneyansk Rus. Fed. 65 O2
Nizhniy Baskunchak Rus. Fed. 43 J6
Nizhniye Kresty Rus. Fed. see Cherskiy
Nizhniy Lomov Rus. Fed. 43 I5
Nizhniy Novgorod Rus. Fed. 42 I4
Nizhniy Odes Rus. Fed. 42 L3
Nizhniy Pyandzh Tajik. see Panji Poyon
Nizhniy Tagil Rus. Fed. 41 R4
Nizhnyaya Mola Rus. Fed. 42 J2
Nizhnyaya Omra Rus. Fed. 42 L3
Nizhnyaya Pirenga, Ozero l. Rus. Fed. 44 R3
Nizhnyaya Tunguska r. Rus. Fed. 64 J3
Nizhnyaya Tura Rus. Fed. 41 R4
Nizhyn Ukr. 43 F6
Nizina r. U.S.A. 120 A2
Nizina Mazowiecka reg. Poland 47 R4
Nizip Turkey 85 C1
Nízke Tatry nat. park Slovakia 47 Q6
Nizwá Oman see Nazwá
Nizza France see Nice
Njallavarri mt. Norway 44 L2
Njavve Sweden 44 K3
Njazidja i. Comoros 99 E5
Njombe Tanz. 99 D4
Njurundabommen Sweden 44 J5
Nkambe Cameroon 96 E4
Nkandla S. Africa 101 J5
Nkawkaw Ghana 96 C4
Nkhata Bay Malawi 99 D5
Nkhotakota Malawi 99 D5
Nkondwe Tanz. 99 D4
Nkongsamba Cameroon 96 D4
Nkululeko S. Africa 101 H6
Nkwenkwezi S. Africa 101 H7
Noakhali Bangl. 83 G5
Noatak r. U.S.A. 118 B3
Nobber Ireland 51 F4
Nobeoka Japan 75 C6
Noblesville U.S.A. 134 B3
Noboribetsu Japan 74 F4
Noccundra Australia 111 C5
Nockatunga Australia 111 C5
Nocona U.S.A. 131 D5
Noel Kempff Mercado, Parque Nacional nat. park Bol. 142 F6
Noelville Canada 122 E5
Nogales Mex. 127 F7
Nogales U.S.A. 127 F7
Nōgata Japan 75 C6
Nogent-le-Rotrou France 56 E2
Nogent-sur-Oise France 52 C5
Noginsk Rus. Fed. 42 H5
Nogliki Rus. Fed. 74 F2
Nogoa r. Australia 110 E4
Nohar India 82 C3
Noheji Japan 74 F4
Nohfelden Germany 52 H5
Noida India 82 D3
Noirmoutier, Île de i. France 56 C3
Noirmoutier-en-l'Île France 56 C3
Noisseville France 52 G5
Nokhowch, Kūh-e mt. Iran 89 F5
Nōkis Uzbek. see Nukus
Nok Kundi Pak. 89 F4
Nokomis Canada 121 J5
Nokomis Lake Canada 121 K3
Nokou Chad 97 E3
Nokrek Peak India 83 G4
Nola Cent. Afr. Rep. 98 B3
Nolin River Lake U.S.A. 134 B5
Nolinsk Rus. Fed. 42 K4
No Mans Land i. U.S.A. 135 J3
Nome U.S.A. 118 B3
Nomgon Mongolia 72 J4
Nomhon China 80 I4
Nomoi Islands Micronesia see Mortlock Islands
Nomonde S. Africa 101 H6
Nomzha Rus. Fed. 42 I4
Nonacho Lake Canada 121 I2
Nondweni S. Africa 101 J5
Nong'an China 74 B3
Nông Hèt Laos 70 D3
Nonghui China see Guang'an
Nong Khai Thai. 70 C3
Nongoma S. Africa 101 J4
Nongstoin India 83 G4
Nonidas Namibia 100 B2
Nonni r. China see Nen Jiang
Nonning Australia 111 B7
Nonnweiler Germany 52 G5
Nonoava Mex. 127 G8
Nonouti atoll Kiribati 107 H2
Nonthaburi Thai. 71 C4
Nonzwakazi S. Africa 100 G6
Noolyeanna Lake salt flat Australia 111 B5
Noondie, Lake salt flat Australia 109 B7
Noonkanbah Australia 108 D4
Noonthorangee Range hills Australia 111 C6
Noorama Creek watercourse Australia 112 B1
Noordbeveland i. Neth. 52 D3
Noorderhaaks i. Neth. 52 E2
Noordoost Polder Neth. 52 F2
Noordwijk-Binnen Neth. 52 E2
Nootka Island Canada 120 E5
Nora r. Rus. Fed. 74 C2
Norak Tajik. 89 H2
Norak, Obanbori resr Tajik. 89 H2
Norala Phil. 69 G5
Noranda Canada 122 F4
Nor-Bayazet Armenia see Gavarr
Norberg Sweden 45 I6
Nord Greenland see Station Nord
Nord, Canal du France 52 D4
Nordaustlandet i. Svalbard 64 D2
Nordegg Canada 120 G4
Norden Germany 53 H1
Nordenshel'da, Arkhipelag is Rus. Fed. 64 K2
Nordenskjold Archipelago is Rus. Fed. see Nordenshel'da, Arkhipelag
Norderney Germany 53 H1
Norderstedt Germany 53 K1
Nordfjordeid Norway 44 D6
Nordfold Norway 44 I3
Nordfriesische Inseln Germany see North Frisian Islands
Nordhausen Germany 53 K3
Nordholz Germany 53 I1
Nordhorn Germany 52 H2
Nordkapp c. Norway see North Cape
Nordkinnhalvøya i. Norway 44 O1
Nordkjosbotn Norway 44 K2
Nordli Norway 44 H4
Nördlingen Germany 53 K6
Nordmaling Sweden 44 K5
Nord- og Østgrønland, Nationalparken i nat. park Greenland 119 O2

▶Nordøstrundingen c. Greenland 153 I1
Most easterly point of North America.

Nord-Ostsee-Kanal Germany see Kiel Canal
Norðoyar i. Faroe Is 40 E3
Nord-Pas-de-Calais admin. reg. France 52 C4
Nordpfälzer Bergland reg. Germany 53 H5
Nordre Strømfjord inlet Greenland see Nassuttooq
Nordrhein-Westfalen land Germany 53 H3
Nordvik Rus. Fed. 65 M2
Nore r. Ireland 51 F5
Nore, Pic de mt. France 56 F5
Noreg country Europe see Norway
Norfolk NE U.S.A. 130 D3
Norfolk NY U.S.A. 135 H1
Norfolk VA U.S.A. 135 G5

▶Norfolk Island terr. S. Pacific Ocean 107 G4
Territory of Australia.

Norfolk Island Ridge sea feature Tasman Sea 150 H7
Norfork Lake U.S.A. 131 E4
Norg Neth. 52 G1
Norge country Europe see Norway
Norheimsund Norway 45 E6
Noril'sk Rus. Fed. 64 J3
Norkyung China 83 G3
Norland Canada 135 F1
Norma Co l. China 83 G2
Norman U.S.A. 131 D5
Norman, Lake resr U.S.A. 132 D5
Normanby Island P.N.G. 110 E1
Normandes, Îles is English Chan. see Channel Islands
Normandia Brazil 143 G3
Normandie reg. France see Normandy
Normandie, Collines de hills France 56 D2
Normandy reg. France 56 D2
Normanton Australia 110 C3
Norquay Canada 121 K5
Ñorquinco Arg. 144 B6
Norra Kvarken strait Fin./Sweden 44 L5
Norra Storfjället mts Sweden 44 I4
Norrent-Fontes France 52 C4
Norris Lake U.S.A. 134 D5
Norristown U.S.A. 135 H3
Norrköping Sweden 45 J7
Norrtälje Sweden 45 K7
Norseman Australia 109 C8
Norsjö Sweden 44 K4
Norsk Rus. Fed. 74 C1
Norsup Vanuatu 107 G3
Norte, Punta pt Arg. 144 E5
Norte, Serra do hills Brazil 143 G6
Nortelândia Brazil 143 G6
Nörten-Hardenberg Germany 53 J3
North, Cape Antarctica 152 H2
North, Cape Canada 123 J5
Northallerton U.K. 48 F4
Northam Australia 109 B7
Northampton Australia 106 B4
Northampton U.K. 49 G6
Northampton MA U.S.A. 135 I2
Northampton PA U.S.A. 135 H3
North Andaman i. India 71 A4
North Anna r. U.S.A. 135 G5
North Arm b. Canada 120 H2
North Atlantic Ocean Atlantic Ocean 125 O4
North Augusta U.S.A. 133 D5
North Aulatsivik Island Canada 123 J2
North Australian Basin sea feature Indian Ocean 149 P6
North Baltimore U.S.A. 134 D3
North Battleford Canada 121 I4
North Bay Canada 122 F5
North Belcher Islands Canada 122 F2
North Berwick U.K. 50 G4
North Berwick U.S.A. 135 J2
North Bourke Australia 112 B3
North Branch U.S.A. 130 E2
North Caicos i. Turks and Caicos Is 133 G8
North Canton U.S.A. 134 E3
North Cape Canada 123 I5
North Cape Norway 44 N1
North Cape N.Z. 113 D2
North Cape U.S.A. 118 A4
North Caribou Lake Canada 121 N4
North Carolina state U.S.A. 132 E4
North Cascades National Park U.S.A. 126 C2
North Channel lake channel Canada 122 E5
North Channel U.K. 51 G2
North Charleston U.S.A. 133 E5
North Chicago U.S.A. 134 B2
Northcliffe Glacier Antarctica 152 F2
North Collins U.S.A. 135 F2
North Concho r. U.S.A. 131 C6
North Conway U.S.A. 135 J1
North Dakota state U.S.A. 130 C2
North Downs hills U.K. 49 G7
North East U.S.A. 134 F2
Northeast Foreland c. Greenland see Nordøstrundingen
North-East Frontier Agency state India see Arunachal Pradesh
Northeast Pacific Basin sea feature N. Pacific Ocean 151 J4
Northeast Point Bahamas 133 F8
Northeast Providence Channel Bahamas 133 E7
North Edwards U.S.A. 128 E4
Northeim Germany 53 J3
Northern prov. S. Africa see Limpopo
Northern Areas admin. div. Pak. 89 I2
Northern Cape prov. S. Africa 100 D5
Northern Donets r. Rus. Fed./Ukr. see Severskiy Donets
Northern Dvina r. Rus. Fed. see Severnaya Dvina
Northern Indian Lake Canada 121 L3
Northern Ireland prov. U.K. 51 F3
Northern Lau Group is Fiji 107 I3
Northern Light Lake Canada 122 C4

▶Northern Mariana Islands terr. N. Pacific Ocean 69 K3
United States Commonwealth.

Northern Rhodesia country Africa see Zambia
Northern Sporades is Greece see Voreies Sporades
Northern Territory admin. div. Australia 106 D3
Northern Transvaal prov. S. Africa see Limpopo
North Esk r. U.K. 50 G4
Northfield MN U.S.A. 130 E2
Northfield VT U.S.A. 135 I1
North Foreland c. U.K. 49 I7
North Fork U.S.A. 128 D3
North Fork Pass Canada 118 E3
North French r. Canada 122 E4
North Frisian Islands Germany 47 L3
North Geomagnetic Pole (2008) Arctic Ocean 119 K1
North Grimston U.K. 48 G4
North Haven U.S.A. 135 I3
North Head hd N.Z. 113 E3
North Henik Lake Canada 121 L2
North Hero U.S.A. 135 I1
North Horr Kenya 98 D3
North Island India 84 B4

▶North Island N.Z. 113 D4
3rd largest island in Oceania.

North Jadito Canyon gorge U.S.A. 129 H4
North Judson U.S.A. 134 B3
North Kingsville U.S.A. 134 E3
North Knife r. Canada 121 M3
North Knife Lake Canada 121 L3
North Korea country Asia 75 B5
North Lakhimpur India 83 H4
North Las Vegas U.S.A. 129 F3
North Little Rock U.S.A. 131 E5
North Loup r. U.S.A. 130 D3
North Luangwa National Park Zambia 99 D5

North Maalhosmadulu Atoll Maldives 84 B5
North Magnetic Pole (2008) Arctic Ocean 153 A1
North Malosmadulu Atoll Maldives see North Maalhosmadulu Atoll
North Mam Peak U.S.A. 129 J2
North Muskegon U.S.A. 134 B2
North Palisade mt. U.S.A. 128 D3
North Perry U.S.A. 134 E3
North Platte U.S.A. 130 C3
North Platte r. U.S.A. 130 C3
North Pole Arctic Ocean 153 I1
North Port U.S.A. 133 D7
North Reef Island India 71 A4
North Rhine - Westphalia land Germany see Nordrhein-Westfalen
North Rim U.S.A. 129 G3
North Rona i. U.K. see Rona
North Ronaldsay i. U.K. 50 G1
North Ronaldsay Firth sea chan. U.K. 50 G1
North Saskatchewan r. Canada 121 J4
North Schell Peak U.S.A. 129 F2
North Sea Europe 46 H2
North Seal r. Canada 121 L3
North Sentinel Island India 71 A5
North Shields U.K. 48 F3
North Shoal Lake Canada 121 L5
North Shoshone Peak U.S.A. 128 E2
North Siberian Lowland Rus. Fed. 64 L2
North Simlipal National Park India 83 F5
North Sinai governorate Egypt see Shamāl Sīnā'
North Slope plain U.S.A. 118 D3
North Somercotes U.K. 48 H5
North Spirit Lake Canada 121 M4
North Stradbroke Island Australia 112 F1
North Sunderland U.K. 48 F3
North Syracuse U.S.A. 135 G2
North Taranaki Bight b. N.Z. 113 E4
North Terre Haute U.S.A. 134 B4
Northton U.K. 50 B3
North Tonawanda U.S.A. 135 F2
North Trap reef N.Z. 113 A8
North Troy U.S.A. 135 I1
North Tyne r. U.K. 48 E4
North Uist i. U.K. 50 B3
Northumberland National Park U.K. 48 E3
Northumberland Strait Canada 123 I5
North Vancouver Canada 120 F5
North Vernon U.S.A. 134 C4
Northville U.S.A. 135 H2
North Wabasca Lake Canada 120 H3
North Walsham U.K. 49 I6
Northway Junction U.S.A. 120 A2
North West prov. S. Africa 100 G4
Northwest Atlantic Mid-Ocean Channel N. Atlantic Ocean 148 E1
North West Cape Australia 108 A5
North West Frontier prov. Pak. 89 H3
North West Nelson Forest Park nat. park N.Z. see Kahurangi National Park
Northwest Pacific Basin sea feature N. Pacific Ocean 150 G3
Northwest Providence Channel Bahamas 133 E7
North West River Canada 123 K3
Northwest Territories admin. div. Canada 120 J2
Northwich U.K. 48 E5
North Wildwood U.S.A. 135 H4
North Windham U.S.A. 135 J2
Northwind Ridge sea feature Arctic Ocean 153 B1
Northwood U.S.A. 135 J2
North York Canada 134 F2
North York Moors moorland U.K. 48 G4
North York Moors National Park U.K. 48 G4
Norton U.K. 48 G4
Norton KS U.S.A. 130 D4
Norton VA U.S.A. 134 D5
Norton VT U.S.A. 135 J1
Norton de Matos Angola see Balombo
Norton Shores U.S.A. 134 B2
Norton Sound sea chan. U.S.A. 118 B3
Nortonville U.S.A. 134 B5
Norvegia, Cape Antarctica 152 B2
Norwalk CT U.S.A. 135 I3
Norwalk OH U.S.A. 134 D3
Norway country Europe 44 E6
Norway U.S.A. 135 J1
Norway House Canada 121 L4
Norwegian Basin sea feature N. Atlantic Ocean 148 H1
Norwegian Bay Canada 119 I2
Norwegian Sea N. Atlantic Ocean 153 H2
Norwich Canada 134 E2
Norwich U.K. 49 I6
Norwich CT U.S.A. 135 I3
Norwich NY U.S.A. 135 H2
Norwood CO U.S.A. 129 I2
Norwood NY U.S.A. 135 H1
Norwood OH U.S.A. 134 C4
Nose Lake Canada 121 I1
Noshiro Japan 75 F4
Nosovaya Rus. Fed. 42 L1
Noşratābād Iran 89 E4
Noss, Isle of i. U.K. 50 [inset]
Nossebro Sweden 45 H7
Nossen Germany 53 N3
Nossob watercourse Africa 100 D2 also known as Nosop
Nossob watercourse Africa 100 D2 also known as Nossob
Notakwanon r. Canada 123 J2
Notch Peak U.S.A. 129 G2
Noteć r. Poland 47 O4
Notikewin r. Canada 120 G3
Noto, Golfo di g. Sicily Italy 58 F6
Notodden Norway 45 F7
Noto-hantō pen. Japan 75 E5
Notre-Dame, Monts mts Canada 123 H5
Notre Dame Bay Canada 123 L4
Notre-Dame-de-Koartac Canada see Quaqtaq
Nottawasaga Bay Canada 134 E1
Nottaway r. Canada 122 F4
Nottingham U.K. 49 F6
Nottingham Island Canada 119 K3
Nottoway r. U.S.A. 135 G5
Nottuln Germany 53 H3
Notukeu Creek r. Canada 121 J5
Nouabalé-Ndoki, Parc National nat. park Congo 98 B3
Nouâdhibou Mauritania 96 B2
Nouâdhibou, Râs c. Mauritania 96 B2

▶Nouakchott Mauritania 96 B3
Capital of Mauritania.

Nouâmghâr Mauritania 96 B3
Nouei Vietnam 70 D4

▶Nouméa New Caledonia 107 G4
Capital of New Caledonia.

Nouna Burkina 96 C3
Noupoort S. Africa 100 G6
Nousu Fin. 44 P3
Nouveau-Brunswick prov. Canada see New Brunswick
Nouveau-Comptoir Canada see Wemindji
Nouvelle Calédonie i. S. Pacific Ocean 107 G4
Nouvelle Calédonie terr. S. Pacific Ocean see New Caledonia
Nouvelle-France, Cap de c. Canada 119 K3
Nouvelles Hébrides country S. Pacific Ocean see Vanuatu
Nova América Brazil 145 A1
Nova Chaves Angola see Muconda
Nova Freixa Moz. see Cuamba
Nova Friburgo Brazil 145 C3
Nova Gaia Angola see Cambundi-Catembo
Nova Goa India see Panaji
Nova Gradiška Croatia 58 G2
Nova Iguaçu Brazil 145 C3
Nova Kakhovka Ukr. 59 O1
Nova Lima Brazil 145 C2
Nova Lisboa Angola see Huambo
Novalukoml' Belarus 43 F5
Nova Mambone Moz. 99 D6
Nova Nabúri Moz. 99 D5
Nova Odesa Ukr. 43 F7
Nova Paraiso Brazil 142 F3
Nova Pilão Arcado Brazil 143 J5
Nova Ponte Brazil 145 B2
Nova Ponte, Represa resr Brazil 145 B2
Novara Italy 58 C2
Nova Roma Brazil 145 B1
Nova Scotia prov. Canada 123 I6
Nova Sento Sé Brazil 143 J5
Novato U.S.A. 128 B2
Nova Trento Brazil 145 A4
Nova Venécia Brazil 145 C2
Nova Xavantino Brazil 143 H6
Novaya Kakhovka Ukr. see Nova Kakhovka
Novaya Kazanka Kazakh. 41 P6
Novaya Ladoga Rus. Fed. 42 G3
Novaya Lyalya Rus. Fed. 41 S4
Novaya Odessa Ukr. see Nova Odesa
Novaya Sibir', Ostrov i. Rus. Fed. 65 P2
Novaya Ussura Rus. Fed. 74 E2

▶Novaya Zemlya is Rus. Fed. 64 G2
3rd largest island in Europe.

Nova Zagora Bulg. 59 L3
Novelda Spain 57 F4
Nové Zámky Slovakia 47 Q7
Novgorod Rus. Fed. see Velikiy Novgorod
Novgorod-Severskiy Ukr. see Novhorod-Sivers'kyy
Novgorod-Volynskiy Ukr. see Novohrad-Volyns'kyy
Novhorod-Sivers'kyy Ukr. 43 G6
Novi Grad Bos.-Herz. see Bosanski Novi
Novi Iskŭr Bulg. 59 J3
Novikovo Rus. Fed. 74 F3
Novi Kritsim Bulg. see Stamboliyski
Novi Ligure Italy 58 C2
Novi Pazar Bulg. 59 L3
Novi Pazar Serbia 59 I3
Novi Sad Serbia 59 H2
Novo Acre Brazil 145 C1
Novoalekseyevka Kazakh. see Khobda
Novoaltaysk Rus. Fed. 72 E2
Novoanninskiy Rus. Fed. 43 I6
Novo Aripuanã Brazil 142 F5
Novoazovs'k Ukr. 43 H7
Novocheboksarsk Rus. Fed. 42 J4
Novocherkassk Rus. Fed. 43 I7
Novo Cruzeiro Brazil 145 C2
Novodugino Rus. Fed. 42 G5
Novodvinsk Rus. Fed. 42 I2
Novoekonomicheskoye Ukr. see Dymytrov
Novogeorgiyevka Rus. Fed. 74 B2
Novogrudok Belarus see Navahrudak
Novo Hamburgo Brazil 145 A5
Novohradské hory mts Czech Rep. 47 O6
Novohrad-Volyns'kyy Ukr. 43 E6
Novokhopersk Rus. Fed. 43 I6
Novokiyevskiy Uval Rus. Fed. 74 C2
Novokubansk Rus. Fed. 91 F1
Novokubanskiy Rus. Fed. see Novokubansk
Novokuybyshevsk Rus. Fed. 43 K5
Novokuznetsk Rus. Fed. 72 F2
Novolazarevskaya research station Antarctica 152 C2
Novolukoml' Belarus see Novalukoml'
Novo Mesto Slovenia 58 F2
Novomikhaylovskiy Rus. Fed. 90 E1
Novomoskovsk Rus. Fed. 43 H5
Novomoskovs'k Ukr. 43 G6
Novonikolayevsk Rus. Fed. see Novosibirsk
Novonikolayevskiy Rus. Fed. 43 I6
Novooleksiyivka Ukr. 43 G7
Novopashiyskiy Rus. Fed. see Gornozavodsk
Novopokrovka Rus. Fed. 74 D3
Novopokrovskaya Rus. Fed. 43 I7
Novopolotsk Belarus see Navapolatsk
Novopskov Ukr. 43 H6
Novo Redondo Angola see Sumbe
Novorossiyka Rus. Fed. 74 C1
Novorossiysk Rus. Fed. 90 E1
Novorybnaya Rus. Fed. 65 L2
Novorzhev Rus. Fed. 42 F4
Novoselovo Rus. Fed. 72 G1
Novoselskoye Rus. Fed. see Achkhoy-Martan
Novosel'ye Rus. Fed. 45 P7
Novosergiyevka Rus. Fed. 41 Q5
Novoshakhtinsk Rus. Fed. 43 H7
Novosheshminsk Rus. Fed. 42 K5
Novosibirsk Rus. Fed. 64 J4
Novosibirskiye Ostrova is Rus. Fed. see New Siberia Islands
Novosil' Rus. Fed. 43 H5
Novosokol'niki Rus. Fed. 42 F4
Novospasskoye Rus. Fed. 43 J5
Novotroyits'ke Ukr. 43 G7
Novoukrainka Ukr. see Novoukrayinka
Novoukrayinka Ukr. 43 F6
Novouzensk Rus. Fed. 43 K6
Novovolyns'k Ukr. 43 E6
Novovoronezh Rus. Fed. 43 H6
Novovoronezhskiy Rus. Fed. see Novovoronezh
Novovoskresenovka Rus. Fed. 74 B1
Novozybkov Rus. Fed. 43 F5
Nový Jičín Czech Rep. 47 P6
Novyy Afon Georgia see Akhali Ap'oni
Novyy Bor Rus. Fed. 42 L2
Novyy Donbass Ukr. see Dymytrov
Novyye Petushki Rus. Fed. see Petushki
Novyy Kholmogory Rus. Fed. see Archangel
Novyy Margelan Uzbek. see Farg'ona
Novyy Nekouz Rus. Fed. 42 H4
Novyy Oskol Rus. Fed. 43 H6
Novyy Port Rus. Fed. 64 I3
Novyy Urengoy Rus. Fed. 64 I3
Novyy Urgal Rus. Fed. 74 D2
Novyy Uzen' Kazakh. see Zhanaozen
Novyy Zay Rus. Fed. 42 L5
Now Iran 88 D4
Nowabganj Bangl. see Nawabganj
Nowata U.S.A. 131 E4
Nowdī Iran 88 C2
Nowgong India see Nagaon
Now Kharegan Iran 88 D2
Nowleye Lake Canada 121 K2
Nowogard Poland 47 O4
Noworadomsk Poland see Radomsko
Nowra Australia 112 E5
Nowrangapur India see Nabarangapur
Nowshera Pak. 89 I3
Nowyak Lake Canada 121 L2
Nowy Sącz Poland 47 R6
Nowy Targ Poland 47 R6
Noxen U.S.A. 135 G3
Noy, Xé r. Laos 70 D3
Noyabr'sk Rus. Fed. 64 I3
Noyes Island U.S.A. 120 C4
Noyon France 52 C5
Noyon Mongolia 80 J3
Nozizwe S. Africa 101 G6
Nqamakwe S. Africa 101 H7
Nqutu S. Africa 101 J5
Nsanje Malawi 99 D5
Nsombo Zambia 99 C5
Nsukka Nigeria 96 D4
Nsumbu National Park Zambia see Sumbu National Park
Ntambu Zambia 99 C5
Ntha S. Africa 101 H4
Ntoro, Kavo pt Greece 59 K5
Ntoum Gabon 98 A3
Ntungamo Uganda 98 D4
Nuanetsi Zimbabwe see Mwenezi
Nu'aym reg. Oman 88 D6
Nuba Mountains Sudan 86 D7
Nubian Desert Sudan 86 D5
Nudo Coropuna mt. Peru 142 D7
Nueces r. U.S.A. 131 D7
Nueltin Lake Canada 121 L2
Nueva Ciudad Guerrero Mex. 131 D7
Nueva Gerona Cuba 137 H4
Nueva Harberton Arg. 144 C8
Nueva Imperial Chile 144 B5
Nueva Loja Ecuador see Lago Agrio
Nueva Rosita Mex. 131 C7
Nueva San Salvador El Salvador 136 G6
Nueva Villa de Padilla Mex. 131 D7
Nueve de Julio Arg. see 9 de Julio
Nuevitas Cuba 137 I4
Nuevo, Golfo g. Arg. 144 D6
Nuevo Casas Grandes Mex. 127 G7
Nuevo Ideal Mex. 131 B7
Nuevo Laredo Mex. 131 D7
Nuevo León Mex. 129 F5
Nuevo León state Mex. 131 D7
Nuevo Rocafuerte Ecuador 142 C4
Nugaal watercourse Somalia 98 E3
Nugget Point N.Z. 113 B8
Nugur India 84 D2
Nuguria Islands P.N.G. 106 F2
Nuh, Ras pt Pak. 89 F5
Nuhaka N.Z. 113 F4
Nui atoll Tuvalu 107 H2
Nui Con Voi r. Vietnam see Red
Nuiqsut U.S.A. 118 C2
Nui Thanh Vietnam 70 E4
Nui Ti On mt. Vietnam 70 D4
Nujiang China 76 C2
Nu Jiang r. China/Myanmar see Salween
Nukey Bluff hill Australia 111 A7
Nukha Azer. see Şäki

▶Nuku'alofa Tonga 107 I4
Capital of Tonga.

Nukufetau atoll Tuvalu 107 H2
Nukuhiva i. Fr. Polynesia see Nuku Hiva
Nuku Hiva i. Fr. Polynesia 151 K6
Nukuhu P.N.G. 69 L8
Nukulaelae atoll Tuvalu 107 H2
Nukulailai atoll Tuvalu see Nukulaelae
Nukumanu Islands P.N.G. 107 F2
Nukunau i. Kiribati see Nikunau
Nukunono atoll Tokelau see Nukunonu
Nukunonu atoll Tokelau 107 I2
Nukus Uzbek. 80 A3
Nulato U.S.A. 118 C3
Nullagine Australia 108 C5
Nullarbor Australia 109 E7
Nullarbor National Park Australia 109 E7
Nullarbor Plain Australia 109 E7
Nullarbor Regional Reserve park Australia 109 E7
Nuluarniavik, Lac l. Canada 122 F2
Nulu'erhu Shan mts China 73 L4
Num i. Indon. 69 J7
Numalla, Lake salt flat Australia 112 B2
Numan Nigeria 98 B3
Numanuma P.N.G. 110 E1
Numazu Japan 75 E6
Numbulwar Australia 110 A2
Numedal valley Norway 45 F6
Numfoor i. Indon. 69 I7
Numin He r. China 74 B3
Numurkah Australia 112 B6
Nunaksaluk Island Canada 123 J3
Nunakuluut i. Greenland 119 N3
Nunap Isua c. Greenland see Farewell, Cape
Nunarsuit i. Greenland see Nunakuluut
Nunavik reg. Canada 122 G1
Nunavut admin. div. Canada 121 L2
Nunda U.S.A. 135 G2
Nundle Australia 112 E3
Nuneaton U.K. 49 F6
Nungba India 83 H4
Nungesser Lake Canada 121 M5
Nungnain Sum China 73 L3
Nunivak Island U.S.A. 118 B4
Nunkapasi India 84 E1
Nunkun mt. India 82 D2
Nunligran Rus. Fed. 65 T3
Nuñomoral Spain 57 C3
Nunspeet Neth. 52 F2
Nuojiang China see Tongjiang
Nuoro Sardinia Italy 58 C4
Nupani i. Solomon Is 107 G3
Nuqrah Saudi Arabia 86 F4
Nur r. Iran 88 D2
Nūrābād Iran 88 C4
Nurakita i. Tuvalu see Niulakita
Nurata Uzbek. see Nurota
Nur Dağları mts Turkey 85 B1
Nurek Tajik. see Norak
Nurek Reservoir Tajik. see Norak, Obanbori
Nurekskoye Vodokhranilishche resr Tajik. see Norak, Obanbori
Nuremberg Germany 53 L5
Nuri Mex. 127 F7
Nurla India 82 D2
Nurlat Rus. Fed. 43 K5
Nurmes Fin. 44 P5
Nurmo Fin. 44 M5
Nürnberg Germany see Nuremberg
Nurota Uzbek. 80 C3
Nurri, Mount hill Australia 112 C3
Nusawulan Indon. 69 I7
Nusaybin Turkey 91 F3
Nu Shan mts China 76 C3
Nushki Pak. 89 G4
Nusratiye Turkey 85 D1
Nutak Canada 123 J2
Nutarawit Lake Canada 121 L2
Nutrioso U.S.A. 129 I5
Nuttal Pak. 89 H4
Nutwood Downs Australia 108 F3
Nutzotin Mountains U.S.A. 120 A2

▶Nuuk Greenland 119 M3
Capital of Greenland.

Nuupas Fin. 44 O3
Nuussuaq Greenland 119 M2
Nuussuaq pen. Greenland 119 M2
Nuwaybi' al Muzayyinah Egypt 90 D5
Nuweiba el Muzeina Egypt see Nuwaybi' al Muzayyinah
Nuwerus S. Africa 100 D6
Nuweveldberge mts S. Africa 100 E7
Nuyts, Point Australia 109 B8
Nuyts Archipelago is Australia 109 F8
Nuzvid India 84 D2
Nwanedi Nature Reserve S. Africa 101 J2
Nxai Pan National Park Botswana 99 C5
Nyagan' Rus. Fed. 41 T3
Nyagquka China see Yajiang
Nyagrong China see Xinlong
Nyahururu Kenya 98 D3
Nyah West Australia 112 A5
Nyainqêntanglha Feng mt. China 83 G3
Nyainqêntanglha Shan mts China 83 G3
Nyainrong China 76 B1
Nyainronglung China see Nyainrong
Nyåker Sweden 44 K5
Nyakh Rus. Fed. see Nyagan'
Nyaksimvol' Rus. Fed. 41 S3
Nyala Sudan 97 F3
Nyalam China see Congdü
Nyalikungu Tanz. see Maswa
Nyamandhlovu Zimbabwe 99 C5
Nyamtumbo Tanz. 99 D5
Nyande Zimbabwe see Masvingo
Nyandoma Rus. Fed. 42 I3
Nyandomskiy Vozvyshennost' hills Rus. Fed. 42 H3
Nyanga Congo 98 B4
Nyanga Zimbabwe 99 D5
Nyangbo China 76 B2
Nyarling r. Canada 120 H2

▶Nyasa, Lake Africa 99 D4
3rd largest lake in Africa, and 9th in the world.

Nyasaland country Africa see Malawi
Nyashabozh Rus. Fed. 42 L2
Nyasvizh Belarus 45 O10
Nyaungdon Myanmar see Yandoon
Nyaunglebin Myanmar 70 B3
Nyborg Denmark 45 G9
Nyborg Norway 44 P1
Nybro Sweden 45 I8
Nyeboe Land reg. Greenland 119 M1
Nyêmo China 83 G3
Nyenchen Tanglha Range mts China see Nyainqêntanglha Shan
Nyeri Kenya 98 D4
Nyi, Co l. China 83 F2
Nyika National Park Zambia 99 D5
Nyima China 83 F3
Nyimba Zambia 99 D5
Nyingchi China 76 B2
Nyinma China see Maqu
Nyíregyháza Hungary 43 D7
Nyiru, Mount Kenya 98 D3
Nykarleby Fin. 44 M5
Nykøbing Denmark 45 G9
Nykøbing Sjælland Denmark 45 G9
Nyköping Sweden 45 J7
Nyland Sweden 44 J5
Nylsvley nature res. S. Africa 101 I3
Nymagee Australia 112 C4
Nymboida National Park Australia 112 F2
Nynäshamn Sweden 45 J7
Nyngan Australia 112 C3
Nyogzê China 83 E3
Nyoman r. Belarus/Lith. 45 M10 also known as Neman or Nemunas
Nyon Switz. 56 H3
Nyons France 56 G4
Nýřany Czech Rep. 53 N5
Nyrob Rus. Fed. 41 R3
Nysa Poland 47 P5
Nysh Rus. Fed. 74 F2
Nyssa U.S.A. 126 D4
Nystad Fin. see Uusikaupunki
Nytva Rus. Fed. 41 R4
Nyuksenitsa Rus. Fed. 42 J3
Nyunzu Dem. Rep. Congo 99 C4
Nyurba Rus. Fed. 65 M3
Nyyskiy Zaliv lag. Rus. Fed. 74 F1
Nzambi Congo 98 B4
Nzega Tanz. 99 D4
Nzérékoré Guinea 96 C4
N'zeto Angola 99 B4
Nzwani i. Comoros 99 E5

O

Oahe, Lake U.S.A. 130 C2
O'ahu i. U.S.A. 127 [inset]
Oaitupu i. Tuvalu see Vaitupu
Oak Bluffs U.S.A. 135 J3
Oak City U.S.A. 129 G2
Oak Creek U.S.A. 129 J1
Oakdale U.S.A. 131 E6
Oakes U.S.A. 130 D2
Oakey Australia 112 E1
Oak Grove KY U.S.A. 134 B5
Oak Grove LA U.S.A. 131 F5
Oak Grove MI U.S.A. 134 C1
Oakham U.K. 49 G6
Oak Harbor U.S.A. 134 D3
Oak Hill OH U.S.A. 134 D4
Oak Hill WV U.S.A. 134 E5
Oakhurst U.S.A. 128 D3
Oak Lake Canada 121 K5
Oakland CA U.S.A. 128 B3
Oakland MD U.S.A. 134 F4
Oakland ME U.S.A. 135 K1
Oakland NE U.S.A. 130 D3
Oakland OR U.S.A. 126 C4
Oakland airport U.S.A. 128 B3
Oakland City U.S.A. 134 B4
Oaklands Australia 112 C5
Oak Lawn U.S.A. 134 B3
Oakley U.S.A. 130 C4
Oakover r. Australia 108 C5
Oak Park IL U.S.A. 134 B3
Oak Park MI U.S.A. 134 C2
Oak Park Reservoir U.S.A. 129 I1
Oakridge U.S.A. 126 C4
Oak Ridge U.S.A. 132 C4
Oakvale Australia 111 C7
Oak View U.S.A. 128 D4
Oakville Canada 134 F2
Oakwood OH U.S.A. 134 C3
Oakwood TN U.S.A. 134 B5
Oamaru N.Z. 113 C7
Oaro N.Z. 113 D6
Oasis CA U.S.A. 128 E3
Oasis NV U.S.A. 126 E4
Oates Coast reg. Antarctica see Oates Land
Oates Land reg. Antarctica 152 H2
Oaxaca Mex. 136 E5
Oaxaca de Juárez Mex. see Oaxaca

▶Ob' r. Rus. Fed. 72 E2
Part of the Ob'-Irtysh, the 2nd longest river in Asia.

Ob, Gulf of sea chan. Rus. Fed. see Obskaya Guba
Oba Canada 122 D4
Oba i. Vanuatu see Aoba
Obala Cameroon 96 E4
Obama Japan 75 D6
Oban U.K. 50 D4
O Barco Spain 57 C2
Obbia Somalia see Hobyo
Obdorsk Rus. Fed. see Salekhard
Óbecse Serbia see Bečej
Obed Canada 120 G4
Oberaula Germany 53 J4
Oberdorla Germany 53 K3
Oberhausen Germany 52 G3
Oberlin KS U.S.A. 130 C4
Oberlin LA U.S.A. 131 E6
Oberlin OH U.S.A. 134 D3
Obermoschel Germany 53 H5
Oberon Australia 112 D4
Oberpfälzer Wald mts Germany 53 M5
Obersinn Germany 53 J4
Oberthulba Germany 53 J4
Obertshausen Germany 53 I4
Oberwälder Land reg. Germany 53 J3
Obi i. Indon. 69 H7
Óbidos Brazil 143 G4
Obihiro Japan 74 F4
Obil'noye Rus. Fed. 43 J7

▶Ob'-Irtysh r. Rus. Fed. 64 H3
2nd longest river in Asia, and 5th in the world.

Obluch'ye Rus. Fed. 74 C2
Obninsk Rus. Fed. 43 H5
Obo Cent. Afr. Rep. 98 C3
Obock Djibouti 86 F7
Ŏbŏk N. Korea 74 C4
Obokote Dem. Rep. Congo 98 C4
Obo Liang China 80 H4
Obouya Congo 98 B4
Oboyan' Rus. Fed. 43 H6
Obozerskiy Rus. Fed. 42 I3
Obregón, Presa resr Mex. 127 F8
Obrenovac Serbia 59 I2
Obruk Turkey 90 D3
Observatory Hill hill Australia 109 F7
Obshchiy Syrt hills Rus. Fed. 41 Q5
Obskaya Guba sea chan. Rus. Fed. 64 I3
Obuasi Ghana 96 C4
Ob"yachevo Rus. Fed. 42 K3
Ocala U.S.A. 133 D6
Ocampo Mex. 131 C7
Ocaña Col. 142 D2
Ocaña Spain 57 E4
Occidental, Cordillera mts Chile 142 E7
Occidental, Cordillera mts Col. 142 C3
Occidental, Cordillera mts Peru 142 D7
Oceana U.S.A. 134 E5
Ocean Cay i. Bahamas 133 E7
Ocean City MD U.S.A. 135 H4
Ocean City NJ U.S.A. 135 H4
Ocean Falls Canada 120 E4
Ocean Island Kiribati see Banaba
Ocean Island atoll U.S.A. see Kure Atoll
Oceanside U.S.A. 128 E5
Ocean Springs U.S.A. 131 F6
Ochakiv Ukr. 59 N1
Och'amch'ire Georgia 91 F2
Ocher Rus. Fed. 41 Q4
Ochiishi-misaki pt Japan 74 G4
Ochil Hills U.K. 50 F4
Ochrida, Lake Albania/Macedonia see Ohrid, Lake
Ochsenfurt Germany 53 K5
Ochtrup Germany 53 H2
Ocilla U.S.A. 133 D6
Ockelbo Sweden 45 J6
Ocolaşul Mare, Vârful mt. Romania 59 K1
Oconomowoc U.S.A. 134 A2
Oconto U.S.A. 134 B1
Octeville-sur-Mer France 49 H9
October Revolution Island Rus. Fed. see Oktyabr'skoy Revolyutsii, Ostrov
Ocussi enclave East Timor 108 D2
Ocussi-Ambeno enclave East Timor see Ocussi
Oda, Jebel mt. Sudan 86 E5
Ódáðahraun lava field Iceland 44 [inset]
Ŏdaejin N. Korea 74 C4
Odae-san National Park S. Korea 75 C5
Ōdate Japan 75 F4
Odawara Japan 75 E6
Odda Norway 45 E6
Odei r. Canada 121 L3
Odell U.S.A. 134 B3
Odem U.S.A. 131 D7
Odemira Port. 57 B5
Ödemiş Turkey 59 L5
Ödenburg Hungary see Sopron
Odense Denmark 45 G9
Odenwald reg. Germany 53 I5
Oder r. Germany 53 J3 also known as Odra (Poland)
Oderbucht b. Germany 47 O3
Oder-Havel-Kanal canal Germany 53 N2
Ödeshog Sweden 45 I7
Odessa Ukr. 59 N1
Odessa TX U.S.A. 131 C6
Odessa WA U.S.A. 126 D3
Odessus Bulg. see Varna
Odiel r. Spain 57 C5
Odienné Côte d'Ivoire 96 C4
Odintsovo Rus. Fed. 42 H5
Ŏdŏngk Cambodia 71 D5
Odra r. Germany/Pol. 47 Q6 also known as Oder (Germany)
Odzala, Parc National d' nat. park Congo 98 B3
Oea Libya see Tripoli
Oé-Cusse enclave East Timor see Ocussi
Oecussi enclave East Timor see Ocussi
Oeiras Brazil 143 J5
Oekussi enclave East Timor see Ocussi
Oelsnitz Germany 53 M4
Oenkerk Neth. 52 F1
Oenpelli Australia 108 F3
Oesel i. Estonia see Hiiumaa
Oeufs, Lac des l. Canada 123 G3
Of Turkey 91 F2
O'Fallon r. U.S.A. 126 G3
Ofanto r. Italy 58 G4
Ofaqim Israel 85 B4
Offa Nigeria 96 D4
Offenbach am Main Germany 53 I4
Offenburg Germany 47 K6
Oga Japan 75 E5
Ogadēn reg. Eth. 98 E3
Oga-hantō pen. Japan 75 E5
Ōgaki Japan 75 E6
Ogallala U.S.A. 130 C3
Ogasawara-shotō is Japan see Bonin Islands
Ogbomosho Nigeria 96 D4
Ogbomoso Nigeria see Ogbomosho
Ogden IA U.S.A. 130 E3
Ogden UT U.S.A. 126 F4
Ogden, Mount Canada 120 C3
Ogdensburg U.S.A. 135 H1
Ogidaki Canada 122 D5
Ogilvie r. Canada 118 E3
Ogilvie Mountains Canada 118 D3
Oglethorpe, Mount U.S.A. 133 C5
Oglio r. Italy 58 D2
Oglongi Rus. Fed. 74 E1
Ogmore Australia 110 E4
Ogoamas, Gunung mt. Indon. 69 G6
Ogodzha Rus. Fed. 74 D1
Ogoja Nigeria 96 D4
Ogoki r. Canada 122 D4
Ogoki Lake Canada 130 G1
Ogoki Reservoir Canada 122 C4
Ogoron Rus. Fed. 74 C1
Ogosta r. Bulg. 59 J3
Ogre Latvia 45 N8
Ogulin Croatia 58 F2
Ogurchinskiy, Ostrov i. Turkm. see Ogurjaly Adasy
Ogurjaly Adasy i. Turkm. 88 D2
Oğuzeli Turkey 85 C1
Ohai N.Z. 113 A7
Ohakune N.Z. 113 E4
Ohanet Alg. 96 D2
Ōhata Japan 74 F4

Ohcejohka Fin. see Utsjoki
O'Higgins (Chile) research station Antarctica 152 A2
O'Higgins, Lago l. Chile 144 B7
Ohio r. U.S.A. 134 A5
Ohio state U.S.A. 134 D3
Ohm r. Germany 53 I4
Ohrdruf Germany 53 K4
Ohře r. Czech Rep. 53 N4
Ohre r. Germany 53 L2
Ohrid Macedonia 59 I4
Ohrid, Lake Albania/Macedonia 59 I4
Ohridsko Ezero l. Albania/Macedonia see Ohrid, Lake
Ohrigstad S. Africa 101 J3
Öhringen Germany 53 J5
Ohrit, Liqeni i l. Albania/Macedonia see Ohrid, Lake
Ohura N.Z. 113 E4
Oich r. U.K. 50 E3
Oiga China 76 B2
Oignies France 52 C4
Oil City U.S.A. 134 F3
Oise r. France 52 C6
Ōita Japan 75 C6
Oiti mt. Greece 59 J5
Ojai U.S.A. 128 D4
Ojalava i. Samoa see 'Upolu
Ojinaga Mex. 131 B6
Ojiya Japan 75 E5
Ojo Caliente U.S.A. 127 G5
Ojo de Laguna Mex. 127 G7

▶Ojos del Salado, Nevado mt. Arg./Chile 144 C3
2nd highest mountain in South America.

Oka r. Rus. Fed. 43 I4
Oka r. Rus. Fed. 72 I1
Okahandja Namibia 100 C1
Okahukura N.Z. 113 E4
Okakarara Namibia 99 B6
Okak Islands Canada 123 J2
Okanagan Lake Canada 120 G5
Okanda Sri Lanka 84 D5
Okano r. Gabon 98 B4
Okanogan U.S.A. 126 D2
Okanogan r. U.S.A. 126 D2
Okara Pak. 89 I4
Okarem Turkm. see Ekerem
Okataina vol. N.Z. see Tarawera, Mount
Okaukuejo Namibia 99 B5
Okavango r. Africa 99 C5

▶Okavango Delta swamp Botswana 99 C5
Largest oasis in the world.

Okavango Swamps Botswana see Okavango Delta
Okaya Japan 75 E5
Okayama Japan 75 D6
Okazaki Japan 75 E6
Okeechobee U.S.A. 133 D7
Okeechobee, Lake U.S.A. 133 D7
Okeene U.S.A. 131 D4
Okefenokee Swamp U.S.A. 133 D6
Okehampton U.K. 49 C8
Okemah U.S.A. 131 D5
Oker r. Germany 53 K2
Okha India 82 B5
Okha Rus. Fed. 74 F1
Okha Rann marsh India 82 B5
Okhotsk Rus. Fed. 65 P4
Okhotsk, Sea of Japan/Rus. Fed. 74 G3
Okhotskoye More sea Japan/Rus. Fed. see Okhotsk, Sea of
Okhtyrka Ukr. 43 G6
Okinawa i. Japan 75 B8
Okinawa-guntō is Japan see Okinawa-shotō
Okinawa-shotō is Japan 75 B8
Okino-Daitō-jima i. Japan 73 O8
Okino-Tori-shima i. Japan 73 P8
Oki-shotō is Japan 73 O5
Oki-shotō is Japan 75 D5
Okkan Myanmar 70 A3
Oklahoma state U.S.A. 131 D5

▶Oklahoma City U.S.A. 131 D5
Capital of Oklahoma.

Okmulgee U.S.A. 131 D5
Okolona KY U.S.A. 134 C4
Okolona MS U.S.A. 131 F5
Okondja Gabon 98 B4
Okovskiy Les for. Rus. Fed. 42 G5
Okoyo Congo 98 B4
Øksfjord Norway 44 M1
Oktemberyan Armenia see Armavir
Oktwin Myanmar 70 B3
Oktyabr' Kazakh. see Kandyagash
Oktyabr'sk Kazakh. see Kandyagash
Oktyabr'skiy Belarus see Aktsyabrski
Oktyabr'skiy Amurskaya Oblast' Rus. Fed. 74 C1
Oktyabr'skiy Arkhangel'skaya Oblast' Rus. Fed. 42 I3
Oktyabr'skiy Kamchatskaya Oblast' Rus. Fed. 65 Q4
Oktyabr'skiy Respublika Bashkortostan Rus. Fed. 41 Q5
Oktyabr'skiy Volgogradskaya Oblast' Rus. Fed. 43 I7
Oktyabr'skoye Rus. Fed. 41 T3
Oktyabr'skoy Revolyutsii, Ostrov i. Rus. Fed. 65 K2
Okulovka Rus. Fed. 42 G4
Okushiri-tō i. Japan 74 E4
Okusi enclave East Timor see Ocussi
Okuta Nigeria 96 D4
Okwa watercourse Botswana 100 G1
Ólafsvík Iceland 44 [inset]
Olakkur India 84 C3
Olancha U.S.A. 128 D3
Olancha Peak U.S.A. 128 D3
Öland i. Sweden 45 J8
Olary Australia 111 C7
Olathe CO U.S.A. 129 J2
Olathe KS U.S.A. 130 E4
Olavarría Arg. 144 D5
Oława Poland 47 P5
Olbernhau Germany 53 N4
Olbia Sardinia Italy 58 C4
Old Bahama Channel Bahamas/Cuba 133 E8
Old Bastar India 84 D2
Oldcastle Ireland 51 E4
Old Cork Australia 110 C4
Old Crow Canada 118 E3
Oldeboorn Neth. see Aldeboarn
Oldenburg Germany 53 I1
Oldenburg in Holstein Germany 47 M3
Oldenzaal Neth. 52 G2
Olderdalen Norway 44 L2
Old Forge U.S.A. 135 H2
Old Gidgee Australia 109 B6
Oldham U.K. 48 E5
Old Harbor U.S.A. 118 C4
Old Head of Kinsale hd Ireland 51 D6
Oldman r. Canada 120 I5
Oldmeldrum U.K. 50 G3
Old Perlican Canada 123 L5
Old River U.S.A. 128 D4
Olds Canada 120 H5
Old Speck Mountain U.S.A. 135 J1
Old Station U.S.A. 128 C1
Old Wives Lake Canada 121 J5
Olean U.S.A. 135 F2
Olecko Poland 47 S3
Olekma r. Rus. Fed. 65 N3
Olekminsk Rus. Fed. 65 N3
Olekminskiy Stanovik mts Rus. Fed. 73 M2
Oleksandrivs'k Ukr. see Zaporizhzhya
Oleksandriya Ukr. 43 G6
Ølen Norway 45 D7
Olenegorsk Rus. Fed. 44 R2
Olenek Rus. Fed. 65 M3
Olenek r. Rus. Fed. 65 M2
Olenek Bay Rus. Fed. see Olenekskiy Zaliv
Olenekskiy Zaliv b. Rus. Fed. 65 N2
Olenino Rus. Fed. 42 G4
Olenitsa Rus. Fed. 42 G2
Olenivs'ki Kar"yery Ukr. see Dokuchayevs'k
Olenya Rus. Fed. see Olenegorsk
Oleshky Ukr. see Tsyurupyns'k
Olevs'k Ukr. 43 E6
Ol'ga Rus. Fed. 74 D4
Olga, Lac l. Canada 122 F4
Olga, Mount Australia 109 E6
Ol'ginsk Rus. Fed. 74 D1
Olginskoye Rus. Fed. see Kochubeyevskoye
Ölgiy Mongolia 80 G2
Olhão Port. 57 C5
Olia Chain mts Australia 109 E6
Olifants r. Moz./S. Africa 101 J3
also known as Elefantes
Olifants watercourse Namibia 100 D3
Olifants S. Africa 101 J2
Olifants r. W. Cape S. Africa 100 D6
Olifants r. W. Cape S. Africa 100 E7
Olifantshoek S. Africa 100 F4
Olifantsrivierberge mts S. Africa 100 D7
Olimarao atoll Micronesia 69 L5
Olimbos hill Cyprus see Olympos
Olimbos mt. Greece see Olympus, Mount
Olimpos Beydağları Milli Parkı nat. park Turkey 59 N6
Olinda Brazil 143 L5
Olinga Moz. 99 D5
Olio Australia 110 C4
Oliphants Drift S. Africa 101 H3
Olisipo Port. see Lisbon
Oliva Spain 57 F4
Oliva, Cordillera de mts Arg./Chile 144 C3
Olivares, Cerro de mt. Arg./Chile 144 C4
Olive Hill U.S.A. 134 D4
Olivehurst U.S.A. 128 C2
Oliveira dos Brejinhos Brazil 145 C1
Olivença Moz. see Lupilichi
Olivenza Spain 57 C4
Oliver Lake Canada 121 K3
Olivet MI U.S.A. 134 C2
Olivet SD U.S.A. 130 D3
Olivia U.S.A. 130 E2
Ol'khovka Rus. Fed. 43 J6
Ollagüe Chile 144 C2
Ollombo Congo 98 B4
Olmaliq Uzbek. 80 C3
Olmos Peru 142 C5
Olmütz Czech Rep. see Olomouc
Olney U.K. 49 G6
Olney IL U.S.A. 130 F4
Olney MD U.S.A. 135 G4
Olney TX U.S.A. 131 D5
Olofström Sweden 45 I8
Olomane r. Canada 123 J4
Olomouc Czech Rep. 47 P6
Olonets Rus. Fed. 42 G3
Olongapo Phil. 69 G4
Oloron-Ste-Marie France 56 D5
Olosenga atoll American Samoa see Swains Island
Olot Spain 57 H2
Olot Uzbek. 89 F2
Olovyannaya Rus. Fed. 73 L2
Oloy r. Rus. Fed. 65 Q3
Oloy, Qatorkŭhi mts Asia see Alai Range
Olpe Germany 53 H3
Olsztyn Poland 47 R4
Olt r. Romania 59 K3
Olten Switz. 56 H3
Oltenița Romania 59 L2
Oltu Turkey 91 F2
Oluan Pi c. Taiwan 77 I4
Ol'viopol' Ukr. see Pervomays'k
Olymbos hill Cyprus see Olympos

▶Olympia U.S.A. 126 C3
Capital of Washington state.

Olympic National Park U.S.A. 126 C3
Olympos hill Cyprus 85 A2
Olympos Greece see Olympus, Mount
Olympos mt. Greece see Olympus, Mount
Olympos nat. park Greece see Olympou, Ethnikos Drymos
Olympou, Ethnikos Drymos nat. park Greece 59 J4
Olympus, Mount Greece 59 J4
Olympus, Mount U.S.A. 126 C3
Olyutorskiy Rus. Fed. 65 R3
Olyutorskiy, Mys c. Rus. Fed. 65 S4
Olyutorskiy Zaliv b. Rus. Fed. 65 R4
Olzheras Rus. Fed. see Mezhdurechensk
Oma China 83 E2
Oma r. Rus. Fed. 42 J2
Omagh U.K. 51 E3
Omaha U.S.A. 130 E3
Omaheke admin. reg. Namibia 100 D2
Omal'skiy Khrebet mts Rus. Fed. 74 E1
Oman country Asia 87 I6
Oman, Gulf of Asia 88 E5
Omaruru Namibia 99 B6
Omate Peru 142 D7
Omaweneno Botswana 100 F3
Omba i. Vanuatu see Aoba
Ombai, Selat sea chan. Indon. 108 D2
Ombalantu Namibia see Uutapi
Omboué Gabon 98 A4
Ombu China 83 F3
Omdraaisvlei S. Africa 100 F6
Omdurman Sudan 86 D6
Omeo Australia 112 C6
Omer U.S.A. 134 D1
Ometepec Mex. 136 E5
Omgoy Wildlife Reserve nature res. Thai. 70 B3
Om Hajēr Eritrea 86 E7
Omīdīyeh Iran 88 C4
Omineca Mountains Canada 120 E3
Omitara Namibia 100 C2
Ōmiya Japan 75 E6
Ommaney, Cape U.S.A. 120 C3
Ommen Neth. 52 G2
Omolon Rus. Fed. 65 R3
Omo National Park Eth. 98 D3
Omsk Rus. Fed. 64 I4
Omsukchan Rus. Fed. 65 Q3
Ōmū Japan 74 F3
O-mu Myanmar 70 B2
Omu, Vârful mt. Romania 59 K2
Ōmura Japan 75 C6
Omutninsk Rus. Fed. 42 L4
Onaman Lake Canada 122 D4
Onamia U.S.A. 130 E2
Onancock U.S.A. 135 H5
Onangué, Lac l. Gabon 98 B4
Onaping Lake Canada 122 E5
Onatchiway, Lac l. Canada 123 H4
Onavas Mex. 127 F7
Onawa U.S.A. 130 D3
Onaway U.S.A. 134 C1
Onbingwin Myanmar 71 B4
Oncativo Arg. 144 D4
Onchan Isle of Man 48 C4
Oncócua Angola 99 B5
Öncül Turkey 85 D1
Ondal India see Andal
Ondangwa Namibia 99 B5
Onderstedorings S. Africa 100 E6
Ondjiva Angola 99 B5
Ondo Nigeria 96 D4
Öndörhaan Mongolia 73 K3
Öndörshil Mongolia 73 J3
Ondozero Rus. Fed. 42 G3
One Botswana 100 E2
One and a Half Degree Channel Maldives 81 D11
Onega Rus. Fed. 42 H3
Onega r. Rus. Fed. 42 H3
Onega, Lake l. Rus. Fed. see Onezhskoye Ozero

▶Onega, Lake Rus. Fed. 42 G3
3rd largest lake in Europe.

Onega Bay g. Rus. Fed. see Onezhskaya Guba
One Hundred and Fifty Mile House Canada see 150 Mile House
One Hundred Mile House Canada see 100 Mile House
Oneida NY U.S.A. 135 H2
Oneida TN U.S.A. 134 C5
Oneida Lake U.S.A. 135 H2
O'Neill U.S.A. 130 D3
Onekama U.S.A. 134 B1
Onekotan, Ostrov i. Rus. Fed. 65 Q5
Oneonta AL U.S.A. 133 C5
Oneonta NY U.S.A. 135 H2
Onești Romania 59 L1
Onezhskaya Guba g. Rus. Fed. 42 G2
Onezhskoye Ozero Rus. Fed. 41 N3
Onezhskoye Ozero l. Rus. Fed. see Onega, Lake
Ong r. India 84 D1
Onga Gabon 98 B4
Ongers watercourse S. Africa 100 F5
Ongiyn Gol r. Mongolia 80 J3
Ongjin N. Korea 75 B5
Ongole India 84 D3
Onida U.S.A. 130 C2
Onilahy r. Madag. 99 E6
Onistagane, Lac l. Canada 123 H4
Onitsha Nigeria 96 D4
Onjati Mountain Namibia 100 C2
Onjiva Angola see Ondjiva
Ono-i-Lau i. Fiji 107 I4
Onomichi Japan 75 D6
Onon atoll Micronesia see Namonuito
Onor, Gora mt. Rus. Fed. 74 F2
Onotoa atoll Kiribati 107 H2
Onseepkans S. Africa 100 D5
Onslow Australia 108 A5
Onslow Bay U.S.A. 133 E5
Onstwedde Neth. 52 H1
Ontake-san vol. Japan 75 E6
Ontario prov. Canada 134 E1
Ontario U.S.A. 128 E4
Ontario, Lake Canada/U.S.A. 135 G2
Ontong Java Atoll Solomon Is 107 F2
Onutu atoll Kiribati see Onotoa
Onverwacht Suriname 143 G2
Onyx U.S.A. 128 D4
Oodnadatta Australia 111 A5
Oodweyne Somalia 98 E3
Oolambeyan National Park nat. park N.S.W. 111 D7
Oolambeyan National Park nat. park N.S.W. 112 F5
Ooldea Australia 109 E7
Ooldea Range hills Australia 109 E7
Oologah Lake resr U.S.A. 131 E4
Ooratippra r. Australia 110 B4
Oos-Londen S. Africa see East London
Oostburg Neth. 52 D3
Oostende Belgium see Ostend
Oostendorp Neth. 52 F2
Oosterhout Neth. 52 E3
Oosterschelde est. Neth. 52 D3
Oosterwolde Neth. 52 G2
Oostvleteren Belgium 52 C4
Oost-Vlieland Neth. 52 F1
Ootacamund India see Udagamandalam
Ootsa Lake Canada 120 E4
Ootsa Lake l. Canada 120 E4
Opal Mex. 131 C7
Opala Dem. Rep. Congo 98 C4
Oparino Rus. Fed. 42 K4
Oparo i. Fr. Polynesia see Rapa
Opasatika r. Canada 122 E4
Opasatika Lake Canada 122 E4
Opasquia Canada 121 M4
Opataca, Lac l. Canada 122 G4
Opava Czech Rep. 47 P6
Opel hill Germany 53 H5
Opelika U.S.A. 133 C5
Opelousas U.S.A. 131 E6
Opeongo Lake Canada 122 F5
Opheim U.S.A. 126 G2
Opienge Dem. Rep. Congo 98 C3
Opinaca r. Canada 122 F3
Opinaca, Réservoir resr Canada 122 F3
Opinnagau r. Canada 122 E3
Opiscotéo, Lac l. Canada 123 H3
Op Luang National Park Thai. 70 B3
Opmeer Neth. 52 E2
Opochka Rus. Fed. 45 P8
Opocopa, Lac l. Canada 123 I3
Opodepe Mex. 136 B3
Opole Poland 47 P5
Oporto Port. 57 B3
Opotiki N.Z. 113 F4
Opp U.S.A. 133 C6
Oppdal Norway 44 F5
Oppeln Poland see Opole
Opportunity U.S.A. 126 D3
Opunake N.Z. 113 D4
Opuwo Namibia 99 B5
Oqsu r. Tajik. 89 I2
Oracle U.S.A. 129 H5
Oradea Romania 59 I1
Orahovac Kosovo see Rahovec
Orai India 82 D4
Oraibi U.S.A. 129 H4
Oraibi Wash watercourse U.S.A. 129 H4
Oral Kazakh. see Ural'sk
Oran Alg. 57 F6
Orán Arg. 144 D2
O Rang Cambodia 71 D4
Orang India 83 H4
Ŏrang N. Korea 74 C4
Orange Australia 112 D4
Orange France 56 G4
Orange r. Namibia/S. Africa 100 C5
Orange CA U.S.A. 128 E5
Orange MA U.S.A. 135 I2
Orange TX U.S.A. 131 E6
Orange VA U.S.A. 135 F4
Orange, Cabo c. Brazil 143 H3
Orangeburg U.S.A. 133 D5
Orange City U.S.A. 130 D3
Orange Cone sea feature S. Atlantic Ocean 148 I8
Orange Free State prov. S. Africa see Free State
Orangeville Canada 134 E2
Orange Walk Belize 136 G5
Oranienburg Germany 53 N2
Oranje r. Namibia/S. Africa see Orange
Oranje Gebergte hills Suriname 143 G3
Oranjemund Namibia 100 C5

▶Oranjestad Aruba 137 J6
Capital of Aruba.

Oranmore Ireland 51 D4
Orapa Botswana 99 C6
Orăștie Romania 59 J2
Orașul Stalin Romania see Brașov
Oravais Fin. 44 M5
Orba Co l. China 82 E2
Orbetello Italy 58 D3
Orbost Australia 112 D6
Orcadas research station S. Atlantic Ocean 152 A2
Orchard City U.S.A. 129 J2
Orchha India 82 D4
Orchila, Isla i. Venez. 142 E1
Orchy r. U.K. 50 D4
Orcutt U.S.A. 128 C4
Ord r. Australia 108 E3
Ord U.S.A. 130 D3
Ord, Mount hill Australia 108 D4
Órdenes Spain see Ordes
Orderville U.S.A. 129 G3
Ordes Spain 57 B2
Ordesa-Monte Perdido, Parque Nacional nat. park Spain 57 G2
Ord Mountain U.S.A. 128 E4
Ordos Nei Mongol China 73 K5
Ord River Dam Australia 108 E4
Ordu Hatay Turkey see Yayladağı
Ordu Ordu Turkey 90 E2
Ordubad Azer. 91 G3
Ordway U.S.A. 130 C4
Ordzhonikidze Rus. Fed. see Vladikavkaz
Ore Nigeria 96 D4
Oreana U.S.A. 128 D1
Örebro Sweden 45 I7
Oregon IL U.S.A. 130 F3
Oregon OH U.S.A. 134 D3
Oregon state U.S.A. 126 C4
Oregon City U.S.A. 126 C3
Orekhov Ukr. see Orikhiv
Orekhovo-Zuyevo Rus. Fed. 42 H5
Orel Rus. Fed. 43 H5
Orel, Gora mt. Rus. Fed. 74 E1
Orel', Ozero l. Rus. Fed. 74 E1
Orem U.S.A. 129 H1
Ore Mountains Czech Rep./Germany see Erzgebirge
Orenburg Rus. Fed. 64 G4
Orense Spain see Ourense
Oreor Palau see Koror
Orepuki N.Z. 113 A8
Öresund strait Denmark/Sweden 45 H9
Oretana, Cordillera mts Spain see Toledo, Montes de
Orewa N.Z. 113 E3
Oreye Belgium 52 F4
Orfanou, Kolpos b. Greece 59 J4
Orford Australia 111 [inset]
Orford U.K. 49 I6
Orford Ness hd U.K. 49 I6
Organabo Fr. Guiana 143 H2
Organ Pipe Cactus National Monument nat. park U.S.A. 129 G5
Orge r. France 52 C6
Orgūn Afgh. 89 H3
Orhaneli Turkey 59 M5
Orhangazi Turkey 59 M4
Orhon Gol r. Mongolia 80 J2
Orichi Rus. Fed. 42 K4
Oriental, Cordillera mts Bol. 142 E7
Oriental, Cordillera mts Col. 142 D2
Oriental, Cordillera mts Peru 142 E6
Orihuela Spain 57 F4
Orikhiv Ukr. 43 G7
Orillia Canada 134 F1
Orimattila Fin. 45 N6
Orin U.S.A. 126 G4
Orinoco r. Col./Venez. 142 F2
Orinoco Delta Venez. 142 F2
Orissa state India 84 E1
Orissaare Estonia 45 M7
Oristano Sardinia Italy 58 C5
Orivesi Fin. 45 N6
Orivesi l. Fin. 44 P5
Oriximiná Brazil 143 G4
Orizaba Mex. 136 E5

▶Orizaba, Pico de vol. Mex. 136 E5
Highest active volcano and 3rd highest mountain in North America.

Orizona Brazil 145 A2
Orkanger Norway 44 F5
Örkelljunga Sweden 45 H8
Orkla r. Norway 44 F5
Orkney S. Africa 101 H4
Orkney Islands is U.K. 50 F1
Orla U.S.A. 131 C6
Orland U.S.A. 128 B2
Orlândia Brazil 145 B3
Orlando U.S.A. 133 D6
Orland Park U.S.A. 134 B3
Orleaes Brazil 145 A5
Orléans France 56 E3
Orleans IN U.S.A. 134 B4
Orleans VT U.S.A. 135 I1
Orléans, Île d' i. Canada 123 H5
Orléansville Alg. see Chlef
Orlik Rus. Fed. 72 H2
Orlov Rus. Fed. 42 K4
Orlov Gay Rus. Fed. 43 K6
Orlovskiy Rus. Fed. 43 I7
Ormara Pak. 89 G5
Ormara, Ras hd Pak. 89 G5
Ormiston Canada 121 J5
Ormoc Phil. 69 G4
Ormskirk U.K. 48 E5
Ormstown Canada 135 I1
Ornach Pak. 89 G5
Ornain r. France 52 E6
Orne r. France 56 D2
Ørnes Norway 44 H3
Örnsköldsvik Sweden 44 K5
Orobie, Alpi mts Italy 58 C1
Orobo, Serra do hills Brazil 145 C1
Orodara Burkina 96 C3
Orofino U.S.A. 126 D3
Oro Grande U.S.A. 128 E4
Orogrande U.S.A. 127 G6
Orol Dengizi salt l. Kazakh./Uzbek. see Aral Sea
Oromocto Canada 123 I5
Oromocto Lake Canada 123 I5
Oron Israel 85 B4
Orona atoll Kiribati 107 I2
Orono U.S.A. 132 G2
Orontes r. Asia 90 E3 see 'Āṣī, Nahr al
Orontes r. Lebanon/Syria 85 C2
Oroqen Zizhiqi China see Alihe
Oroquieta Phil. 69 G5
Orós, Açude resr Brazil 143 K5
Orosei, Golfo di b. Sardinia Italy 58 C4
Orosháza Hungary 59 I1
Oroville U.S.A. 128 C2
Oroville, Lake U.S.A. 128 C2
Orqohan China 74 A2
Orr U.S.A. 130 E1
Orsa Sweden 45 I6
Orsha Belarus 43 F5
Orshanka Rus. Fed. 42 J4
Orsk Rus. Fed. 64 G4
Ørsta Norway 44 E5
Orta Toroslar plat. Turkey 85 A1
Ortegal, Cabo c. Spain 57 C2
Orthez France 56 D5
Ortigueira Spain 57 C2
Ortíz Mex. 127 F7
Ortles mt. Italy 58 D1
Orton U.K. 48 E4
Ortona Italy 58 F3
Ortonville U.S.A. 130 D2
Ortospana Afgh. see Kābul
Orulgan, Khrebet mts Rus. Fed. 65 N3
Orumbo Namibia 100 C2
Orūmīyeh Iran see Urmia
Oruro Bol. 142 E7
Orūzgān Afgh. 89 G3
Orvieto Italy 58 E3
Orville Coast Antarctica 152 L1
Orwell OH U.S.A. 134 E3
Orwell VT U.S.A. 135 I2
Oryol Rus. Fed. see Orel
Os Norway 44 G5
Osa Rus. Fed. 41 R4
Osa, Península de pen. Costa Rica 137 H7
Osage IA U.S.A. 130 E3
Osage WV U.S.A. 134 E4
Osage WY U.S.A. 126 G3
Ōsaka Japan 75 D6
Osakarovka Kazakh. 80 D1
Osawatomie U.S.A. 130 E4
Osborne U.S.A. 130 D4
Osby Sweden 45 H8
Osceola IA U.S.A. 130 E3
Osceola MO U.S.A. 130 E4
Osceola NE U.S.A. 130 D3
Oschatz Germany 53 N3
Oschersleben (Bode) Germany 53 L2
Oschiri Sardinia Italy 58 C4
Ösel i. Estonia see Hiiumaa
Osetr r. Rus. Fed. 43 H5
Ōse-zaki pt Japan 75 C6
Osgoode Canada 135 H1
Osgood Mountains U.S.A. 126 D4
Osh Kyrg. 80 D3
Oshakati Namibia 99 B5
Oshawa Canada 135 F2
Oshika-hantō pen. Japan 75 F5
Ō-shima i. Japan 74 E4
Ō-shima i. Japan 75 E6
Oshkosh NE U.S.A. 130 C3
Oshkosh WI U.S.A. 134 A1
Oshmyany Belarus see Ashmyany
Oshnovīyeh Iran 88 B2
Oshogbo Nigeria 96 D4
Oshtorān Kūh mt. Iran 88 C3
Oshwe Dem. Rep. Congo 98 B4
Osijek Croatia 58 H2
Osilinka r. Canada 120 E3
Osimo Italy 58 E3
Osipenko Ukr. see Berdyans'k
Osipovichi Belarus see Asipovichy
Osiyan India 82 C4
Osizweni S. Africa 101 J4
Osječenica mts Bos.-Herz. 58 G2
Ösjön l. Sweden 44 I5
Oskaloosa U.S.A. 130 E3
Oskarshamn Sweden 45 J8
Öskemen Kazakh. see Ust'-Kamenogorsk

▶Oslo Norway 45 G7
Capital of Norway.

Oslofjorden sea chan. Norway 45 G7
Osmanabad India 84 C2
Osmancık Turkey 90 D2
Osmaneli Turkey 59 M4
Osmaniye Turkey 90 E3
Osmannagar India 84 C2
Os'mino Rus. Fed. 45 P7
Osnabrück Germany 53 I2
Osnaburg atoll Fr. Polynesia see Mururoa
Osogbo Nigeria see Oshogbo
Osogovska Planina mts Bulg./Macedonia 59 J3
Osogovske Planine mts Bulg./Macedonia see Osogovska Planina
Osogovski Planini mts Bulg./Macedonia see Osogovska Planina
Osorno Chile 144 B6
Osorno Spain 57 D2
Osoyoos Canada 120 G5
Osøyri Norway 45 D6
Osprey Reef Australia 110 D2
Oss Neth. 52 F3
Ossa, Mount Australia 111 [inset]
Osseo U.S.A. 122 C5
Ossineke U.S.A. 134 D1
Ossining U.S.A. 135 I3
Ossipee U.S.A. 135 J2
Ossipee Lake U.S.A. 135 J2
Oßmannstedt Germany 53 L3
Ossokmanuan Lake Canada 123 I3
Ossora Rus. Fed. 65 R4
Ostashkov Rus. Fed. 42 G4
Ostbevern Germany 53 H2
Oste r. Germany 53 J1
Ostend Belgium 52 C3
Ostende Belgium see Ostend
Osterburg (Altmark) Germany 53 L2
Österbymo Sweden 45 I8
Österdalälven l. Sweden 45 H6
Østerdalen valley Norway 45 G5
Osterfeld Germany 53 L3
Osterholz-Scharmbeck Germany 53 I1
Osterode am Harz Germany 53 K3
Österreich country Europe see Austria
Östersund Sweden 44 I5
Osterwieck Germany 53 K3
Ostfriesische Inseln Germany see East Frisian Islands
Ostfriesland reg. Germany 53 H1
Östhammar Sweden 45 K6
Ostrava Czech Rep. 47 Q6
Ostróda Poland 47 Q4
Ostrogozhsk Rus. Fed. 43 H6
Ostrov Czech Rep. 53 M4
Ostrov Rus. Fed. 45 P8
Ostrovets Poland see Ostrowiec Świętokrzyski
Ostrovskoye Rus. Fed. 42 I4
Ostrov Vrangelya i. Rus. Fed. see Wrangel Island
Ostrów Poland see Ostrów Wielkopolski
Ostrowiec Poland see Ostrowiec Świętokrzyski
Ostrowiec Świętokrzyski Poland 43 D6
Ostrów Mazowiecka Poland 47 R4
Ostrowo Poland see Ostrów Wielkopolski
Ostrów Wielkopolski Poland 47 P5
O'Sullivan Lake Canada 122 D4
Osŭm r. Bulg. 59 K3
Ōsumi-shotō is Japan 75 C7
Osuna Spain 57 D5
Oswego KS U.S.A. 131 E4
Oswego NY U.S.A. 135 G2
Oswestry U.K. 49 D6
Otago Peninsula N.Z. 113 C7
Otahiti i. Fr. Polynesia see Tahiti
Otaki N.Z. 113 E5
Otanmäki Fin. 44 O4
Otaru Japan 74 F4
Otavi Namibia 99 B5
Ōtawara Japan 75 F5
Otdia atoll Marshall Is see Wotje
Otelnuc, Lac l. Canada 123 H2
Otematata N.Z. 113 C7
Otepää Estonia 45 O7
Otgon Tenger Uul mt. Mongolia 80 I2
Otinapa Mex. 131 B7
Otira N.Z. 113 C6
Otis U.S.A. 130 C3
Otish, Monts hills Canada 123 H4

Otjinene Namibia 99 B6
Otjiwarongo Namibia 99 B6
Otjozondjupa admin. reg. Namibia 100 C1
Otley U.K. 48 F5
Otorohanga N.Z. 113 E4
Otoskwin r. Canada 121 N5
Otpan, Gora hill Kazakh. 91 H1
Otpor Rus. Fed. see Zabaykal'sk
Otradnoye Rus. Fed. see Otradnyy
Otradnyy Rus. Fed. 43 K5
Otranto Italy 58 H4
Otranto, Strait of Albania/Italy 58 H4
Otrogovo Rus. Fed. see Stepnoye
Otrozhnyy Rus. Fed. 65 S3
Otsego Lake U.S.A. 135 H2
Ōtsu Japan 75 D6
Otta Norway 45 F6

▶Ottawa Canada 135 H1
Capital of Canada.

Ottawa r. Canada 122 G5
also known as Rivière des Outaouais
Ottawa IL U.S.A. 130 F3
Ottawa KS U.S.A. 130 E4
Ottawa OH U.S.A. 134 C3
Ottawa Islands Canada 122 E2
Otter r. U.K. 49 D8
Otterbein U.S.A. 134 B3
Otterburn U.K. 48 E3
Otter Rapids Canada 122 E4
Ottersberg Germany 53 J1
Ottignies Belgium 52 E4
Ottumwa U.S.A. 130 E3
Ottweiler Germany 53 H5
Otukpo Nigeria 96 D4
Oturkpo Nigeria see Otukpo
Otuzco Peru 142 C5
Otway, Cape Australia 112 A7
Otway National Park Australia 112 A7
Ouachita r. U.S.A. 131 E5
Ouachita, Lake U.S.A. 131 E5
Ouachita Mountains Arkansas/Oklahoma U.S.A. 131 E5
Ouadda Cent. Afr. Rep. 98 C3
Ouaddaï reg. Chad 97 F3

▶Ouagadougou Burkina 96 C3
Capital of Burkina.

Ouahigouya Burkina 96 C3
Ouahran Alg. see Oran
Ouaka r. Cent. Afr. Rep. 98 B3
Oualâta Mauritania 96 C3
Ouallam Niger 96 D3
Ouanda-Djailé Cent. Afr. Rep. 98 C3
Ouando Cent. Afr. Rep. 98 C3
Ouango Cent. Afr. Rep. 98 C3
Ouara r. Cent. Afr. Rep. 98 C3
Ouarâne reg. Mauritania 96 C2
Ouargaye Burkina 96 D3
Ouargla Alg. 54 F5
Ouarogou Burkina see Ouargaye
Ouarzazate Morocco 54 C5
Ouasiemsca r. Canada 123 G4
Oubangui r. Cent. Afr. Rep./Dem. Rep. Congo see Ubangi
Oubergpas pass S. Africa 100 G7
Oudenaarde Belgium 52 D4
Oudômxai Laos 70 C2
Oudtshoorn S. Africa 100 F7
Oud-Turnhout Belgium 52 E3
Oued Tlélat Alg. 57 F6
Oued Zem Morocco 54 C5
Oued Zénati Alg. 58 B6
Ouessant, Île d' i. France 56 B2
Ouesso Congo 98 B3
Ouezzane Morocco 57 D6
Oughter, Lough l. Ireland 51 E3
Ouguati Namibia 100 B1
Ouistreham France 49 G9
Oujda Morocco 57 F6
Oujeft Mauritania 96 B3
Oulainen Fin. 44 N4
Oulangan kansallispuisto nat. park Fin. 44 P3
Ouled Djellal Alg. 57 I6
Ouled Farès Alg. 57 G5
Ouled Naïl, Monts des mts Alg. 57 H6
Oulu Fin. 44 N4
Oulujärvi l. Fin. 44 O4
Oulujoki r. Fin. 44 N4
Oulunsalo Fin. 44 N4
Oulx Italy 58 B2
Oum-Chalouba Chad 97 F3
Oum el Bouaghi Alg. 58 B7
Oum-Hadjer Chad 97 E3
Ounasjoki r. Fin. 44 N3
Oundle U.K. 49 G6
Oungre Canada 121 K5
Ounianga Kébir Chad 97 F3
Oupeye Belgium 52 F4
Our r. Lux. 52 G5
Oura, Akrotirio pt Greece 59 L5
Ouray CO U.S.A. 129 J2
Ouray UT U.S.A. 129 I1
Ourcq r. France 52 D5
Ourense Spain 57 C2
Ouricurí Brazil 143 J5
Ourinhos Brazil 145 A3
Ouro r. Brazil 145 A1
Ouro Preto Brazil 145 C3
Ourthe r. Belgium 52 F4
Our Valley valley Germany/Lux. 52 G5
Ous Rus. Fed. 41 S3
Ouse r. England U.K. 48 G5
Ouse r. England U.K. 49 H8
Outaouais, Rivière des r. Canada 122 G5
see Ottawa
Outardes, Rivière aux r. Canada 123 H4
Outardes Quatre, Réservoir resr Canada 123 H4
Outer Hebrides is U.K. 50 B3
Outer Mongolia country Asia see Mongolia
Outer Santa Barbara Channel U.S.A. 128 D5
Outjo Namibia 99 B6
Outlook Canada 121 J5
Outokumpu Fin. 44 P5
Out Skerries is U.K. 50 [inset]
Ouvéa atoll New Caledonia 107 G4
Ouyanghai Shuiku resr China 77 G3
Ouyen Australia 111 C7
Ouzel r. U.K. 49 G6
Ovace, Punta d' mt. Corsica France 56 I6
Ovacık Turkey 85 A1
Ovada Italy 58 C2
Ovalle Chile 144 B4
Ovamboland reg. Namibia 99 B5
Ovan Gabon 98 B3
Ovar Port. 57 B3
Overath Germany 53 H4
Överkalix Sweden 44 M3
Overlander Roadhouse Australia 109 A6
Overland Park U.S.A. 130 E4
Overton U.S.A. 129 F3
Övertorneå Sweden 44 M3
Överum Sweden 45 J8
Overveen Neth. 52 E2
Ovid CO U.S.A. 130 C3
Ovid NY U.S.A. 135 G2
Oviedo Spain 57 D2
Øvre Anárjohka Nasjonalpark nat. park Norway 44 N2
Øvre Dividal Nasjonalpark nat. park Norway 44 K2
Øvre Rendal Norway 45 G6
Ovruch Ukr. 43 F6
Ovsyanka Rus. Fed. 74 B1
Owando Congo 98 B4
Owa Rafa i. Solomon Is see Santa Ana
Owasco Lake U.S.A. 135 G2
Owase Japan 75 E6
Owatonna U.S.A. 130 E2
Owbeh Afgh. 89 F3
Owego U.S.A. 135 G2
Owel, Lough l. Ireland 51 E4
Owen Island Myanmar 71 B5
Owenmore r. Ireland 51 C3
Owenreagh r. U.K. 51 E3
Owen River N.Z. 113 D5
Owens r. U.S.A. 128 E3
Owensboro U.S.A. 134 B5
Owen Sound Canada 134 E1
Owen Sound inlet Canada 134 E1
Owen Stanley Range mts P.N.G. 69 L8
Owenton U.S.A. 134 C4
Owerri Nigeria 96 D4
Owikeno Lake Canada 120 E5
Owingsville U.S.A. 134 D4
Owkal Afgh. 89 F3
Owl r. Canada 121 M3
Owl Creek Mountains U.S.A. 126 F4
Owo Nigeria 96 D4
Owosso U.S.A. 134 C2
Owyhee U.S.A. 126 D4
Owyhee r. U.S.A. 126 D4
Owyhee Mountains U.S.A. 126 D4
Öxarfjörður b. Iceland 44 [inset]
Oxbow Canada 121 K5
Ox Creek r. U.S.A. 130 C1
Oxelösund Sweden 45 J7
Oxford N.Z. 113 D6
Oxford U.K. 49 F7
Oxford IN U.S.A. 134 B3
Oxford MA U.S.A. 135 J2
Oxford MD U.S.A. 135 G4
Oxford MS U.S.A. 131 F5
Oxford NC U.S.A. 132 E4
Oxford NY U.S.A. 135 H2
Oxford OH U.S.A. 134 C4
Oxford House Canada 121 M4
Oxford Lake Canada 121 M4
Oxley Australia 112 B5
Oxleys Peak Australia 112 E3
Oxley Wild Rivers National Park Australia 112 F3
Ox Mountains hills Ireland 51 C4
Oxnard U.S.A. 128 D4
Oxtongue Lake Canada 135 F1
Oxus r. Asia see Amudar'ya
Øya Norway 44 H3
Oyama Japan 75 E5
Oyapock r. Brazil/Fr. Guiana 143 H3
Oyem Gabon 98 B3
Oyen Canada 121 I5
Oykel r. U.K. 50 E3
Oyo Nigeria 96 D4
Oyonnax France 56 G3
Oyster Rocks is India 84 B3
Oyten Germany 53 J1
Oytograk China 83 E1
Oyukludağı mt. Turkey 85 A1
Özalp Turkey 91 G3
Ozamiz Phil. 69 G5
Ozark AL U.S.A. 133 C6
Ozark AR U.S.A. 131 E5
Ozark MO U.S.A. 131 E4
Ozark Plateau U.S.A. 131 E4
Ozarks, Lake of the U.S.A. 130 E4
O'zbekiston country Asia see Uzbekistan
Özen Kazakh. see Kyzylsay
Ozernovskiy Rus. Fed. 65 Q4
Ozernyy Rus. Fed. 43 G5
Ozerpakh Rus. Fed. 74 F1
Ozersk Rus. Fed. 45 M9
Ozerskiy Rus. Fed. 74 F3
Ozery Rus. Fed. 43 H5
Ozeryane Rus. Fed. 74 C2
Ozieri Sardinia Italy 58 C4
Ozinki Rus. Fed. 43 K6
Oznachennoye Rus. Fed. see Sayanogorsk
Ozona U.S.A. 131 C6
Ozuki Japan 75 C6

P

Paamiut Greenland 119 N3
Pa-an Myanmar see Hpa-an
Paanopa i. Kiribati see Banaba
Paarl S. Africa 100 D7
Paatsjoki r. Europe see Patsoyoki
Paballelo S. Africa 100 E5
P'abal-li N. Korea 74 C4
Pabbay i. U.K. 50 B3
Pabianice Poland 47 Q5
Pabianitz Poland see Pabianice
Pabna Bangl. 83 G4
Pabradė Lith. 45 N9
Pab Range mts Pak. 89 G5
Pacaás Novos, Parque Nacional nat. park Brazil 142 F6
Pacaraimã, Serra mts S. America see Pakaraima Mountains
Pacasmayo Peru 142 C5
Pachagarh Bangl. see Panchagarh
Pacheco Chihuahua Mex. 127 F7
Pacheco Zacatecas Mex. 131 C7
Pachikha Rus. Fed. 42 J3
Pachino Sicily Italy 58 F6
Pachmarhi India 82 D5
Pachor India 82 D5
Pachora India 84 B1
Pachpadra India 82 C4
Pachuca Mex. 136 E4
Pachuca de Soto Mex. see Pachuca
Pacific-Antarctic Ridge sea feature S. Pacific Ocean 151 J9
Pacific Grove U.S.A. 128 C3

▶Pacific Ocean 150
Largest ocean in the world.

Pacific Rim National Park Canada 120 E5
Pacitan Indon. 68 E8
Packsaddle Australia 111 C6
Pacoval Brazil 143 H4
Pacuí r. Brazil 145 B2
Paczków Poland 47 P5
Padali Rus. Fed. see Amursk
Padampur India 82 C3
Padang Indon. 68 C7
Padang i. Indon. 71 C7
Padang Endau Malaysia 71 C7
Padangpanjang Indon. 68 C7
Padangsidimpuan Indon. 71 B7
Padany Rus. Fed. 42 G3
Padatha, Kūh-e mt. Iran 88 C3
Padaung Myanmar 70 A3
Padcaya Bol. 142 F8
Paddington Australia 112 B4
Paden City U.S.A. 134 E4
Paderborn Germany 53 I3
Paderborn/Lippstadt airport Germany 53 I3
Padeşu, Vârful mt. Romania 59 J2
Padibyu Myanmar 70 B2
Padilla Bol. 142 F7
Padjelanta nationalpark nat. park Sweden 44 J3
Padova Italy see Padua
Padrão, Ponta pt Angola 99 B4
Padrauna India 83 F4
Padre Island U.S.A. 131 D7
Padstow U.K. 49 C8
Padsvillye Belarus 45 O9
Padua India 84 D2
Padua Italy 58 D2
Paducah KY U.S.A. 131 F4
Paducah TX U.S.A. 131 C5
Padum India 82 D2
Paegam N. Korea 74 C4
Paektu-san mt. China/N. Korea see Baotou Shan
Paengnyŏng-do i. S. Korea 75 B5
Pafos Cyprus see Paphos
Pafuri Moz. 101 J2
Pag Croatia 58 F2
Pag i. Croatia 58 F2
Paga Indon. 108 C2
Pagadian Phil. 69 G5
Pagai Selatan i. Indon. 68 C7
Pagalu i. Equat. Guinea see Annobón
Pagan i. N. Mariana Is 69 L3
Pagasitikos Kolpos b. Greece 59 J5
Pagatan Indon. 68 F7
Page U.S.A. 129 H3
Paget, Mount S. Georgia 144 I8
Paget Cay reef Australia 110 F3
Pagon i. N. Mariana Is see Pagan
Pagosa Springs U.S.A. 127 G5
Pagqên China see Gadê
Pagwa River Canada 122 D4
Pagwi P.N.G. 69 K7
Pāhala U.S.A. 127 [inset]
Pahang r. Malaysia 71 C7
Pahlgam India 82 C2
Pāhoa U.S.A. 127 [inset]
Pahokee U.S.A. 133 D7
Pahra Kariz Afgh. 89 F3
Pahranagat Range mts U.S.A. 129 F3
Pahrump U.S.A. 129 F3
Pahuj r. India 82 D4
Pahute Mesa plat. U.S.A. 128 E3
Pai Thai. 70 B3
Paicines U.S.A. 128 C3
Paide Estonia 45 N7
Paignton U.K. 49 D8
Päijänne l. Fin. 45 N6
Paikü Co l. China 83 F3
Pailin Cambodia 71 C4
Pailolo Channel U.S.A. 127 [inset]
Paimio Fin. 45 M6
Painel Brazil 145 A4
Painesville U.S.A. 134 E3
Pains Brazil 145 B3
Painted Desert U.S.A. 129 H3
Painted Rock Dam U.S.A. 129 G5
Paint Hills Canada see Wemindji
Paint Rock U.S.A. 131 D6
Paintsville U.S.A. 134 D5
Paisley U.K. 50 E5
Paita Peru 142 B5
Paitou China 77 I2
Paiva Couceiro Angola see Quipungo
Paizhou China 77 G2
Pajala Sweden 44 M3
Paka Malaysia 71 C6
Pakala India 84 C3
Pakanbaru Indon. see Pekanbaru
Pakangyi Myanmar 70 A2
Pakaraima Mountains S. America 142 F3
Pakaur India 83 F4
Pakesley Canada 122 E5
Pakhachi Rus. Fed. 65 R3
Pakhoi China see Beihai
Paki Nigeria 96 D3

▶Pakistan country Asia 89 H4
4th most populous country in Asia, and 6th in the world.

Pakkat Indon. 71 B7
Paknampho Thai. see Nakhon Sawan
Pakokku Myanmar 70 A2
Pakowki Lake imp. l. Canada 121 I5
Pakpattan Pak. 89 I4
Pak Phanang Thai. 71 C5
Pak Phayun Thai. 71 C6
Pakruojis Lith. 45 M9
Paks Hungary 58 H1
Pakse Laos see Pakxé
Pak Tam Chung H.K. China 77 [inset]
Pak Thong Chai Thai. 70 C4
Pakur India see Pakaur
Pakxan Laos 70 C3
Pakxé Laos 70 D4
Pakxeng Laos 70 C2
Pala Chad 97 E4
Pala Myanmar 71 B4
Palaestinia reg. Asia see Palestine
Palaiochora Greece 59 J7
Palaiseau France 52 C6
Palakkad India see Palghat
Palakkat India see Palghat
Palamakoloi Botswana 100 F2
Palamau India see Palamu
Palamós Spain 57 H3
Palamu India 83 F5
Palana Rus. Fed. 65 Q4
Palandur India 84 D1
Palangān, Kūh-e mts Iran 89 F4
Palangkaraya Indon. 68 E7
Palani India 84 C4
Palanpur India 82 C4
Palantak Pak. 89 G5
Palapye Botswana 101 H2
Palatka Rus. Fed. 65 Q3
Palatka U.S.A. 133 D6
Palau country N. Pacific Ocean 69 I5
Palau Islands Palau 69 I5
Palauk Myanmar 71 B4
Palaw Myanmar 71 B4
Palawan i. Phil. 68 F5
Palawan Passage strait Phil. 68 F5
Palawan Trough sea feature N. Pacific Ocean 150 D5
Palayankottai India 84 C4
Palchal Lake India 84 D2
Paldiski Estonia 45 N7
Palekh Rus. Fed. 42 I4
Palembang Indon. 68 C7
Palena Chile 144 B6
Palencia Spain 57 D2
Palermo Sicily Italy 58 E5
Palestine reg. Asia 85 B3
Palestine U.S.A. 131 E6
Paletwa Myanmar 70 A2
Palezgir Chauki Pak. 89 H4
Palghat India 84 C4
Palgrave, Mount hill Australia 109 A5
Palhoca Brazil 145 A4
Pali Chhattisgarh India 84 D1
Pali Mahar. India 84 B2
Pali Rajasthan India 82 C4

▶Palikir Micronesia 150 G5
Capital of Micronesia.

Palinuro, Capo c. Italy 58 F4
Paliouri, Akra pt Greece see Paliouri, Akrotirio
Paliouri, Akra pt Greece see Paliouri, Akrotirio
Paliouri, Akrotirio pt Greece 59 J5
Palisade U.S.A. 129 I2
Paliseul Belgium 52 F5
Palitana India 82 B5
Palivere Estonia 45 M7
Palk Bay Sri Lanka 84 C4
Palkino Rus. Fed. 45 P8
Palkonda Range mts India 84 C3
Palk Strait India/Sri Lanka 84 C4
Palla Bianca mt. Austria/Italy see Weißkugel
Pallamallawa Australia 112 E2
Pallas Green New Ireland 51 D5
Pallasovka Rus. Fed. 43 J6
Pallas-Yllästunturin kansallispuisto nat. park Fin. 44 M2
Pallavaram India 84 D3
Palliser, Cape N.Z. 113 E5
Palliser, Îles is Fr. Polynesia 151 K7
Palliser Bay N.Z. 113 E5
Pallu India 82 C3
Palma r. Brazil 145 B1
Palma del Río Spain 57 D5
Palma de Mallorca Spain 57 H4
Palmaner India 84 C3
Palmares Brazil 143 K5
Palmares do Sul Brazil 145 A5
Palmas Brazil 145 A4
Palmas Tocantins 142 I6
Palmas, Cape Liberia 96 C4
Palm Bay U.S.A. 133 D7
Palmdale U.S.A. 128 D4
Palmeira Brazil 145 A4
Palmeira das Missões Brazil 144 F3
Palmeira dos Índios Brazil 143 K5
Palmeirais Brazil 143 J5
Palmeiras Brazil 145 C1
Palmeirinhas, Ponta das pt Angola 99 B4
Palmer research station Antarctica 152 L2
Palmer r. Australia 110 C3
Palmer watercourse Australia 109 F6
Palmer U.S.A. 118 D3
Palmer Land reg. Antarctica 152 L2
Palmerston N.T. Australia 108 E3
Palmerston N.T. Australia see Darwin
Palmerston Canada 134 E2
Palmerston atoll Cook Is 107 J3
Palmerston N.Z. 113 C7
Palmerston North N.Z. 113 E5
Palmerton U.S.A. 135 H3
Palmerville Australia 110 D2
Palmetto Point Bahamas 133 E7
Palmi Italy 58 F5
Palmira Col. 142 C3
Palmira Cuba 133 D8
Palm Springs U.S.A. 128 E5
Palmyra Syria see Tadmur
Palmyra MO U.S.A. 130 F4
Palmyra PA U.S.A. 135 G3
Palmyra VA U.S.A. 135 F5

▶Palmyra Atoll terr. N. Pacific Ocean 150 J5
United States Unincorporated Territory.

Palmyras Point India 83 F5
Palni Hills India 84 C4
Palo Alto U.S.A. 128 B3
Palo Blanco Mex. 131 C7
Palo Chino watercourse Mex. 127 E7
Palo Duro watercourse U.S.A. 131 C5
Paloich Sudan 86 D7
Palojärvi Fin. 44 M2
Palojoensuu Fin. 44 M2
Palomaa Fin. 44 O2
Palomar Mountain U.S.A. 128 E5
Paloncha India 84 D2
Palo Pinto U.S.A. 131 D5
Palopo Indon. 69 G7
Palos, Cabo de c. Spain 57 F5
Palo Verde U.S.A. 129 F5
Paltamo Fin. 44 O4
Palu Indon. 68 F7
Palu i. Indon. 108 C2
Palu Turkey 91 E3
Pal'vart Turkm. 89 G2
Palwal India 82 D3
Palwancha India see Paloncha
Palyeskaya Nizina marsh Belarus/Ukr. see Pripet Marshes

▶Pamana i. Indon. 108 C2
Most southerly point of Asia.

Pambarra Moz. 101 L1
Pambula Australia 112 D6
Pamidi India 84 C3
Pamiers France 56 E5
Pamir mts Asia 89 I2
Pamlico Sound sea chan. U.S.A. 133 E5
Pamouscachiou, Lac l. Canada 123 H4
Pampa U.S.A. 131 C5
Pampa de Infierno Arg. 144 D3
Pampas reg. Arg. 144 D5
Pampeluna Spain see Pamplona
Pamphylia reg. Turkey 59 N6
Pamplin U.S.A. 135 F5
Pamplona Col. 142 D2
Pamplona Spain 57 F2
Pampow Germany 53 L1
Pamukova Turkey 59 N4
Pamzal India 82 D2
Pana U.S.A. 130 F4
Panaca U.S.A. 129 F3
Panache, Lake Canada 122 E5
Panagyurishte Bulg. 59 K3
Panaitan i. Indon. 68 D8
Panaji India 84 B3
Panama country Central America 137 H7
Panamá Panama see Panama City
Panamá, Gulf of Panama 137 I7
Panama, Isthmus of Panama 137 I7
Panamá, Istmo de Panama see Panama, Isthmus of
Panama Canal Panama 137 I7

▶Panama City Panama 137 I7
Capital of Panama

Panama City U.S.A. 133 C6
Panamint Range mts U.S.A. 128 E3
Panamint Valley U.S.A. 128 E3
Panao Peru 142 C5
Panarea, Isola i. Italy 58 F5
Panarik Indon. 71 E7
Panay i. Phil. 69 G4
Panayarvi Natsional'nyy Park nat. park Rus. Fed. 44 Q3
Pancake Range mts U.S.A. 129 F2
Pančevo Serbia 59 I2
Panchagarh Bangl. 83 G4
Pancsova Serbia see Pančevo
Panda Moz. 101 L3
Pandan, Selat strait Sing. 71 [inset]
Pandan Reservoir Sing. 71 [inset]
Pandeiros r. Brazil 145 B1
Pandharpur India 84 B2
Pandy U.K. 49 E7
Paneas Syria see Bāniyās
Panevėžys Lith. 45 N9
Panfilov Kazakh. see Zharkent
Pang, Nam r. Myanmar 70 B2
Panghsang Myanmar 70 B2
Pangi Range mts Pak. 89 I3
Pangkalanbuun Indon. 68 E7
Pangkalansusu Indon. 71 B6
Pangkalpinang Indon. 68 D7
Pangkalsiang, Tanjung pt Indon. 69 G7
Panglang Myanmar 70 B1
Pangman Canada 121 J5
Pangnirtung Canada 119 L3
Pangody Rus. Fed. 64 I3
Pangong Tso salt l. China/India see Bangong Co
Pang Sida National Park Thai. 71 C4
Pang Sua, Sungai r. Sing. 71 [inset]
Pangtara Myanmar 76 C4
Pangu He r. China 74 B1
Panguitch U.S.A. 129 G3
Panhandle U.S.A. 131 C5
Panipat India 82 D3
Panir Pak. 89 G4
Panj Tajik. 89 H2
Panjāb Afgh. 89 G3
Panjakent Tajik. 89 G2
Panjang i. Indon. 71 E7
Panjang, Bukit Sing. 71 [inset]
Panjgur Pak. 89 G5
Panjim India see Panaji
Panji Poyon Tajik. 89 H2
Panjnad r. Pak. 89 H4
Panjshīr reg. Afgh. 89 H3
Pankakoski Fin. 44 Q5
Panlian China see Miyi
Panna India 82 E4
Panna reg. India 82 D4
Pannawonica Australia 108 B5
Pano Lefkara Cyprus 85 A2
Panorama Brazil 145 A3
Panormus Sicily Italy see Palermo
Panshi China 74 B4
Panshui China see Pu'an

▶Pantanal marsh Brazil 143 G7
Largest area of wetlands in the world.

Pantanal Matogrossense, Parque Nacional do nat. park Brazil 143 G7
Pantano U.S.A. 129 H6
Pantar i. Indon. 108 D2
Pantelaria Sicily Italy see Pantelleria
Pantelleria Sicily Italy 58 D6
Pantelleria, Isola di i. Sicily Italy 58 E6
Panth Myanmar 70 A2
Panther r. U.S.A. 134 B5
Panth Piploda India 82 C5
Panticapaeum Ukr. see Kerch
Pantonlabu Indon. 71 B6
Pánuco Sinaloa Mex. 131 B8
Pánuco Veracruz Mex. 136 E4
Panwari India 82 D4
Panxian China 76 E3
Panyu China 77 G4
Panzhihua China 76 D3
Panzi Dem. Rep. Congo 99 B4
Paola Italy 58 G5
Paola U.S.A. 130 E4
Paoli U.S.A. 134 B4
Paoua Cent. Afr. Rep. 98 B3
Paôy Pêt Cambodia 71 C4
Pápa Hungary 58 G1
Papa, Monte del mt. Italy 58 F4
Papagni r. India 84 C3
Pāpa'ikou U.S.A. 127 [inset]
Papakura N.Z. 113 E3
Papanasam India 84 C4
Papantla Mex. 136 E4
Paparoa National Park N.Z. 113 C6
Papa Stour i. U.K. 50 [inset]
Papa Westray i. U.K. 50 G1
Papay i. U.K. see Papa Westray

▶Papeete Fr. Polynesia 151 K7
Capital of French Polynesia.

Papenburg Germany 53 H1
Paphos Cyprus 85 A2
Paphus Cyprus see Paphos
Papillion U.S.A. 130 D3
Papoose Lake U.S.A. 129 F3
Pappenheim Germany 53 K6
Papua, Gulf of P.N.G. 69 K8

▶Papua New Guinea country Oceania 106 E2
2nd largest and 2nd most populous country in Oceania.

Pa Qal'eh Iran 88 D4
Par U.K. 49 C8
Pará r. Brazil 145 B2
Pará, Rio do r. Brazil 143 I4
Paraburdoo Australia 109 B5
Paracatu Brazil 145 B2
Paracatu r. Brazil 145 B2
Paracel Islands S. China Sea 68 E3
Parachilna Australia 111 B6
Parachute U.S.A. 129 I2
Paraćin Serbia 59 I3
Paracuru Brazil 143 K4
Pará de Minas Brazil 145 B2
Paradis Canada 122 F4
Paradise r. Canada 123 K3
Paradise U.S.A. 128 C2
Paradise Hill Canada 121 I4
Paradise Peak U.S.A. 128 E2
Paradise River Canada 123 K3
Paradwip India 83 F5
Paraetonium Egypt see Marsá Maṭrūḥ
Paragominas Brazil 143 I4
Paragould U.S.A. 131 F4
Paragua i. Phil. see Palawan
Paraguaçu Paulista Brazil 145 A3
Paraguay r. Arg./Para. 144 E3
Paraguay country S. America 144 E2
Paraíba do Sul r. Brazil 145 C3
Parainen Fin. see Pargas
Paraíso do Norte Brazil 143 I6
Paraisópolis Brazil 145 B3
Parak Iran 88 D5
Parakou Benin 96 D4
Paralakhemundi India 84 E2
Paralkot India 84 D2
Paramagudi India see Paramakkudi
Paramakkudi India 84 C4

▶Paramaribo Suriname 143 G2
Capital of Suriname.

Paramillo, Parque Nacional nat. park Col. 142 C2
Paramirim Brazil 145 C1
Paramo Frontino mt. Col. 142 C2
Paramus U.S.A. 135 H3
Paramushir, Ostrov i. Rus. Fed. 65 Q4
Paran watercourse Israel 85 B4
Paraná Arg. 144 D4
Paranã Brazil 145 B1
Paraná r. Brazil 145 A1
Paraná state Brazil 145 A4

▶Paraná r. S. America 144 E4
Part of the Río de la Plata - Paraná, 2nd longest river in South America.

Paraná, Serra do hills Brazil 145 B1
Paranaguá Brazil 145 A4
Paranaíba Brazil 145 A2
Paranaíba r. Brazil 145 A3
Paranapiacaba, Serra mts Brazil 145 A4
Paranavaí Brazil 144 F2
Parangi Aru r. Sri Lanka 84 D4
Parang Pass India 82 D2
Parângul Mare, Vârful mt. Romania 59 J2
Paranthan Sri Lanka 84 D4
Paraopeba Brazil 145 B2
Pārapāra Iraq 91 G4
Paraparaumu N.Z. 113 E5

Paras Mex. 131 D7
Paras Pak. 89 I3
Paraspori, Akra pt Greece see Paraspori, Akrotirio
Paraspori, Akrotirio pt Greece 59 L7
Parateca Brazil 145 C1
Paratinga Brazil 145 C1
Parāū, Kūh-e mt. Iraq 91 G4
Paraúna Brazil 145 A2
Parbhani India 84 C2
Parchim Germany 53 L1
Parding China 83 G2
Pardo r. Bahia Brazil 145 D1
Pardo r. Mato Grosso do Sul Brazil 144 F2
Pardo r. São Paulo Brazil 145 A3
Pardoo Australia 108 B5
Pardubice Czech Rep. 47 O5
Parece Vela i. Japan see Okino-Tori-shima
Parecis, Serra dos hills Brazil 142 F6
Pareh Iran 88 B2
Parenda India 84 B2
Parent Canada 122 G5
Parent, Lac l. Canada 122 F4
Pareora N.Z. 113 C7
Parepare Indon. 68 F7
Parga Greece 59 I5
Pargas Fin. 45 M6
Parghelia Italy 58 F5
Pargi India 84 C2
Paria, Gulf of Trin. and Tob./Venez. 137 L6
Paria, Península de pen. Venez. 142 F1
Paria Plateau U.S.A. 129 G3
Parikkala Fin. 45 P6
Parikud Islands India 84 E2
Parima, Serra mts Brazil 142 F3
Parima-Tapirapecó, Parque Nacional nat. park Venez. 142 F3
Parintins Brazil 143 G4
Paris Canada 134 E2

▶Paris France 52 C6
Capital of France. 3rd most populous city in Europe.

Paris IL U.S.A. 134 B4
Paris KY U.S.A. 134 C4
Paris MO U.S.A. 130 E4
Paris TN U.S.A. 131 F4
Paris TX U.S.A. 131 E5
Paris (Charles de Gaulle) airport France 52 C5
Paris (Orly) airport France 52 C6
Paris Crossing U.S.A. 134 C4
Parit Buntar Malaysia 71 C6
Pārīz Iran 88 D4
Pārk Iran 89 F5
Park U.K. 51 E3
Parkano Fin. 45 M5
Park City U.S.A. 134 B5
Parke Lake Canada 123 K3
Parker AZ U.S.A. 129 F4
Parker CO U.S.A. 126 G5
Parker Dam U.S.A. 129 F4
Parker Lake Canada 121 M2
Parker Range hills Australia 109 B8
Parkersburg U.S.A. 134 E4
Parkers Lake U.S.A. 134 C5
Parkes Australia 112 D4
Park Falls U.S.A. 130 F2
Park Forest U.S.A. 134 B3
Parkhar Tajik. see Farkhor
Parkhill Canada 134 E2
Park Rapids U.S.A. 130 E2
Parkutta Pak. 82 D2
Park Valley U.S.A. 126 E4
Parla Kimedi India see Paralakhemundi
Parlakimidi India see Paralakhemundi
Parli Vaijnath India 84 C2
Parlung Zangbo r. China 76 B2
Parma Italy 58 D2
Parma ID U.S.A. 126 D4
Parma OH U.S.A. 134 E3
Parnaíba Brazil 143 J4
Parnaíba r. Brazil 143 J4
Parnassos mt. Greece see Liakoura
Parnassos mt. Greece see Liakoura
Parnassus N.Z. 113 D6
Parner India 84 B2
Parnon mts Greece see Parnonas
Parnon mts Greece see Parnonas
Parnonas mts Greece 59 J6
Pärnu Estonia 45 N7
Pärnu-Jaagupi Estonia 45 N7
Paro Bhutan 83 G4
Paroikia Greece 59 K6
Parona Turkey see Fındık
Paroo watercourse Australia 112 A3
Paroo Channel watercourse Australia 112 A3
Paroo-Darling National Park nat. park N.S.W. 111 C6
Paroo-Darling National Park nat. park N.S.W. 112 E3
Paros Notio Aigaio Greece see Paroikia
Paros i. Greece 59 K6
Parowan U.S.A. 129 G3
Parral Chile 144 B5
Parramatta Australia 112 E4
Parramore Island U.S.A. 135 H5
Parras Mex. 131 C7
Parrett r. U.K. 49 D7
Parry, Cape Canada 153 A2
Parry, Kap c. Greenland see Kangaarsussuaq
Parry, Lac l. Canada 122 G2
Parry Bay Canada 119 J3
Parry Channel Canada 119 G2
Parry Islands Canada 119 G2
Parry Range hills Australia 108 A5
Parry Sound Canada 134 E1
Parsnip Peak U.S.A. 129 F2
Parsons KS U.S.A. 131 E4
Parsons WV U.S.A. 134 F4
Parsons Range hills Australia 108 F3
Partabgarh India 84 B2
Partabpur India 83 E5
Partenstein Germany 53 J4
Parthenay France 56 D3
Partizansk Rus. Fed. 74 D4
Partney U.K. 48 H5
Partridge r. Canada 122 E4
Partry Ireland 51 C4
Partry Mts hills Ireland 51 C4
Paru r. Brazil 143 H4
Pārūd Iran 89 F5
Paryang China 83 E3
Parys S. Africa 101 H4
Pasa Dağı mt. Turkey 90 D3
Pasadena CA U.S.A. 128 D4
Pasadena TX U.S.A. 131 E6
Pasado, Cabo c. Ecuador 142 B4
Pa Sang Thai. 70 B3
Pasawng Myanmar 70 B3
Pascagama r. Canada 122 G4
Pascagoula U.S.A. 131 F6
Pascagoula r. U.S.A. 131 F6
Paşcani Romania 59 L1
Pasco U.S.A. 126 D3
Pascoal, Monte hill Brazil 145 D2
Pascua, Isla de i. S. Pacific Ocean see Easter Island
Pas de Calais strait France/U.K. see Dover, Strait of
Pasewalk Germany 47 O4
Pasfield Lake Canada 121 J3
Pasha Rus. Fed. 42 G3
Pashih Haihsia sea chan. Phil./Taiwan see Bashi Channel
Pashkovo Rus. Fed. 74 C2
Pashkovskiy Rus. Fed. 43 H7
Pashtun Zarghun Afgh. 89 F3
Pashū'īyeh Iran 88 E4
Pasi Ga Myanmar 70 B1
Pasighat India 83 H3
Pasinler Turkey 91 F3
Pasir Gudang Malaysia 71 [inset]
Pasir Mas Malaysia 71 C6
Pasir Putih Malaysia 71 C6
Paskūh Iran 89 F5
Pasni Pak. 149 M4
Paso de los Toros Uruguay 144 E4
Paso de San Antonio Mex. 131 C6
Pasok Myanmar 70 A2
Paso Robles U.S.A. 128 C4
Pasquia Hills Canada 121 K4
Passaic U.S.A. 135 H3
Passa Tempo Brazil 145 B3
Passau Germany 47 N6
Passo del San Gotthardo Switz. see St Gotthard Pass
Passo Fundo Brazil 144 F3
Passos Brazil 145 B3
Passur r. Bangl. see Pusur
Passuri Nadi r. Bangl. see Pusur
Pastavy Belarus 45 O9
Pastaza r. Peru 142 C4
Pasto Col. 142 C3
Pastora Peak U.S.A. 129 I3
Pastos Bons Brazil 143 J5
Pasu Pak. 82 C1
Pasur Turkey see Kulp
Pasvalys Lith. 45 N8
Pasvikelva r. Europe see Patsoyoki
Patache, Punta pt Chile 144 B2
Patagonia reg. Arg. 144 B8
Pataliputra India see Patna
Patan Gujarat India see Somnath
Patan Gujarat India 82 C5
Patan Mahar. India 84 B2
Patan Nepal 83 F4
Patan Pak. 89 I3
Patandar, Koh-i- mt. Pak. 89 G5
Patavium Italy see Padua
Patea N.Z. 113 E4
Patea inlet N.Z. see Doubtful Sound
Pate Island Kenya 98 E4
Pateley Bridge U.K. 48 F4
Patensie S. Africa 100 G7
Patera India 82 D4
Paterson Australia 112 E4
Paterson r. Australia 112 C2
Paterson U.S.A. 135 H3
Paterson Range hills Australia 108 C5
Pathanamthitta India 84 C4
Pathankot India 82 C2
Pathari India 82 D5
Pathein Myanmar see Bassein
Pathfinder Reservoir U.S.A. 126 G4
Pathiu Thai. 71 B5
Pathum Thani Thai. 71 C4
Patía r. Col. 142 C3
Patiala India 82 D3
Patkai Bum mts India/Myanmar 83 H4
Patkaklik China 83 F1
Patmos i. Greece 59 L6
Patna India 83 F4
Patna Orissa India 83 F5
Patnagarh India 83 E5
Patnos Turkey 91 F3
Pato Branco Brazil 144 F3
Patoda India 84 B2
Patoka r. U.S.A. 134 B4
Patoka Lake U.S.A. 134 B4
Patos Albania 59 H4
Patos Brazil 143 K5
Patos, Lagoa dos l. Brazil 144 F4
Patos de Minas Brazil 145 B2
Patquía Arg. 144 C4
Patra Greece see Patras
Patrae Greece see Patras
Pátrai Greece see Patras
Patras Greece 59 I5
Patreksfjörður Iceland 44 [inset]
Patricio Lynch, Isla i. Chile 144 A7
Patrick Creek watercourse Australia 110 D4
Patrimônio Brazil 145 A2
Patrocínio Brazil 145 B2
Patrū Iran 89 E3
Patsoyoki r. Europe 44 Q2
Pattadakal tourist site India 84 B2
Pattani Thai. 71 C6
Pattaya Thai. 71 C4
Pattensen Germany 53 J2
Patterson CA U.S.A. 128 C3
Patterson LA U.S.A. 131 F6
Patterson, Mount Canada 120 C1
Patti India 83 E4
Pattijoki Fin. 44 N4
Pättikkä Fin. 44 L2
Patton U.S.A. 135 F3
Pattullo, Mount Canada 120 D3
Patu Brazil 143 K5
Patuakhali Bangl. 83 G5
Patuanak Canada 121 J4
Patuca, Punta pt Hond. 137 H5
Patur India 84 C1
Patuxent r. U.S.A. 135 G4
Patuxent Range mts Antarctica 152 L1
Patvinsuon kansallispuisto nat. park Fin. 44 Q5
Pau France 56 D5
Pauhunri mt. China/India 83 G4
Pauillac France 56 D4
Pauini Brazil 142 E5
Pauiní r. Brazil 142 E5
Pauk Myanmar 70 A2
Paukkaung Myanmar 70 A3
Paulatuk Canada 153 A2
Paulden U.S.A. 129 G4
Paulding U.S.A. 134 C3
Paulicéia Brazil 145 A3
Paulis Dem. Rep. Congo see Isiro
Paul Island Canada 123 J2
Paulo Afonso Brazil 143 K5
Paulo de Faria Brazil 145 A3
Paulpietersburg S. Africa 101 J4
Paul Roux S. Africa 101 H5
Pauls Valley U.S.A. 131 D5
Paumotu, Îles is Fr. Polynesia see Tuamotu Islands
Paung Myanmar 70 B3
Paungbyin Myanmar 70 A1
Paungde Myanmar 70 A3
Pauni India 84 C1
Pauri India 82 D3
Pavagada India 84 C3
Pavão Brazil 145 C2
Päveh Iran 88 B3
Pavia Italy 58 C2
Pāvilosta Latvia 45 L8
Pavino Rus. Fed. 42 J4
Pavlikeni Bulg. 59 K3
Pavlodar Kazakh. 80 E1
Pavlof Volcano U.S.A. 118 B4
Pavlograd Ukr. see Pavlohrad
Pavlohrad Ukr. 43 G6
Pavlovka Rus. Fed. 43 J5
Pavlovo Rus. Fed. 42 I5
Pavlovsk Altayskiy Kray Rus. Fed. 72 E2
Pavlovsk Voronezhskaya Oblast' Rus. Fed. 43 I6
Pavlovskaya Rus. Fed. 43 H7
Pawahku Myanmar 70 B1
Pawai India 82 E4
Pawnee U.S.A. 131 D4
Pawnee r. U.S.A. 130 D4
Pawnee City U.S.A. 130 D3
Paw Paw MI U.S.A. 134 C2
Paw Paw WV U.S.A. 135 F4
Pawtucket U.S.A. 135 J3
Pawut Myanmar 71 B4
Paxson U.S.A. 118 D3
Paxton U.S.A. 134 A3
Payakumbuh Indon. 68 C7
Paya Lebar Sing. 71 [inset]
Payette U.S.A. 126 D3
Pay-Khoy, Khrebet hills Rus. Fed. 64 H3
Payne Canada see Kangirsuk
Payne, Lac l. Canada 122 G2
Paynes Creek U.S.A. 128 C1
Payne's Find Australia 109 B7
Paynesville U.S.A. 130 E2
Paysandú Uruguay 144 E4
Pays de Bray reg. France 52 B5
Payshanba Uzbek. 89 G1
Payson U.S.A. 129 H4
Pazar Turkey 91 F2
Pazarcık Turkey 90 E3
Pazardzhik Bulg. 59 K3
Pazin Croatia 58 E2
Pe Myanmar 71 B4
Peabody KS U.S.A. 130 D4
Peabody MA U.S.A. 135 J2

▶Peace r. Canada 120 I3
Part of the Mackenzie-Peace-Finlay, the 2nd longest river in North America.

Peace Point Canada 121 H3
Peace River Canada 120 G3
Peach Creek U.S.A. 134 E5
Peach Springs U.S.A. 129 G4
Peacock Hills Canada 121 I1
Peak Charles hill Australia 109 C8
Peak Charles National Park Australia 109 C8
Peak District National Park U.K. 48 F5
Peake watercourse Australia 111 B6
Peaked Mountain hill U.S.A. 132 G2
Peak Hill N.S.W. Australia 112 D4
Peak Hill W.A. Australia 109 B6
Peale, Mount U.S.A. 129 I2
Peanut U.S.A. 128 B1
Pearce U.S.A. 129 I6
Pearce Point Australia 108 E3
Pearisburg U.S.A. 134 E5
Pearl r. U.S.A. 131 F6
Pearl Harbor inlet U.S.A. 127 [inset]
Pearsall U.S.A. 131 D6
Pearson U.S.A. 133 D6
Pearston S. Africa 101 G7
Peary Channel Canada 119 I2
Peary Land reg. Greenland 153 J1
Pease r. U.S.A. 131 D5
Peawanuck Canada 122 D3
Pebane Moz. 99 D5
Pebas Peru 142 D4
Peć Kosovo see Pejë
Peçanha Brazil 145 C2
Peças, Ilha das i. Brazil 145 A4
Pechenga Rus. Fed. 44 Q2
Pechora Rus. Fed. 42 M2
Pechora r. Rus. Fed. 42 L1
Pechora Sea Rus. Fed. see Pechorskoye More
Pechorskaya Guba b. Rus. Fed. 42 L1
Pechorskoye More sea Rus. Fed. 153 G2
Pechory Rus. Fed. 45 O8
Peck U.S.A. 134 D2
Pecos U.S.A. 131 C6
Pecos r. U.S.A. 131 C6
Pécs Hungary 58 H1
Pedda Vagu r. India 84 C2
Pedder, Lake Australia 111 [inset]
Peddie S. Africa 101 H7
Pedernales Dom. Rep. 137 J5
Pedersöre Fin. 44 M5
Pediaios r. Cyprus 85 A2
Pediva Angola 99 B5
Pedra Azul Brazil 145 C1
Pedra Preta, Serra da mts Brazil 145 A1
Pedras de Maria da Cruz Brazil 145 B1
Pedregulho Brazil 145 B3
Pedreiras Brazil 143 J4
Pedriceña Mex. 131 C7
Pedro, Point Sri Lanka 84 D4
Pedro Betancourt Cuba 133 D8
Pedro II, Ilha reg. Brazil/Venez. 142 E3
Pedro Juan Caballero Para. 144 E2
Peebles U.K. 50 F5
Peebles U.S.A. 134 D4
Pee Dee r. U.S.A. 133 E5
Peekskill U.S.A. 135 I3
Peel r. Australia 112 E3
Peel r. Canada 118 E3
Peel Isle of Man 48 C4
Peer Belgium 52 F3
Peera Peera Poolanna Lake salt flat Australia 111 B5
Peerless Lake Canada 120 H3
Peerless Lake l. Canada 120 H3
Peers Canada 120 G4
Peery Lake salt flat Australia 112 A3
Pegasus Bay N.Z. 113 D6
Pegnitz Germany 53 L5
Pegu Myanmar 70 B3
Pegu Yoma mts Myanmar 70 A3
Pegysh Rus. Fed. 42 K3
Pehuajó Arg. 144 D5
Peikang Taiwan 77 I4
Peine Chile 144 C2
Peine Germany 53 K2
Peint India 84 B1
Peipsi järv l. Estonia/Rus. Fed. see Peipus, Lake
Peipus, Lake Estonia/Rus. Fed. 45 O7
Peiraias Greece see Piraeus
Pei Shan mts China see Bei Shan
Peißen Germany 53 L3
Peixe Brazil 143 I6
Peixe r. Brazil 145 A1
Peixian Jiangsu China 77 H1
Peixian Jiangsu China see Pizhou
Peixoto de Azevedo Brazil 143 H6
Pejë Kosovo 59 I3
Pèk Laos see Phônsavan
Peka Lesotho 101 H5
Pekan Malaysia 71 C7
Pekanbaru Indon. 68 C6
Pekin U.S.A. 130 F3
Peking China see Beijing
Pekinga Benin 96 D3
Pelabohan Klang Malaysia see Pelabuhan Klang
Pelabuhan Klang Malaysia 71 C7
Pelagie, Isole is Sicily Italy 58 E7
Pelaihari Indon. 68 E7
Peleaga, Vârful mt. Romania 59 J2
Pelee Island Canada 134 D3
Pelee Point Canada 134 D3
Peles Rus. Fed. 42 K3
Pélican, Lac du l. Canada 123 G2
Pelican Lake Canada 121 K4
Pelican Lake U.S.A. 130 E1
Pelican Narrows Canada 121 K4
Pelkosenniemi Fin. 44 O3
Pella S. Africa 100 D5
Pellatt Lake Canada 121 I1
Pelleluhu Islands P.N.G. 69 K7
Pello Fin. 44 M3
Pelly r. Canada 120 C2
Pelly Crossing Canada 120 B2
Pelly Lake Canada 121 K1
Pelly Mountains Canada 120 C2
Peloponnese admin. reg. Greece 59 J6
Pelopónnesos admin. reg. Greece see Peloponnese
Peloponnisos admin. reg. Greece see Peloponnese
Pelotas Brazil 144 F4
Pelotas, Rio das r. Brazil 145 A4
Pelusium tourist site Egypt 85 A4
Pelusium, Bay of Egypt see Ţīnah, Khalīj aţ
Pemangkat Indon. 71 E7
Pematangsiantar Indon. 71 B7
Pemba Moz. 99 E5
Pemba Island Tanz. 99 D4
Pemberton Canada 120 F5
Pembina r. Canada 120 H4
Pembina r. U.S.A. 130 D1
Pembine U.S.A. 132 C2
Pembre Indon. 69 J8
Pembroke Canada 122 F5
Pembroke U.K. 49 C7
Pembroke U.S.A. 133 D5
Pembrokeshire Coast National Park U.K. 49 B7
Pen India 84 B2
Peña Cerredo mt. Spain see Torrecerredo
Peñalara mt. Spain 57 E3
Penamar Brazil 145 C1
Peña Nevada, Cerro mt. Mex. 136 E4
Penang Malaysia see George Town
Penang i. Malaysia see Pinang
Penápolis Brazil 145 A3
Peñaranda de Bracamonte Spain 57 D3
Penarie Australia 112 A5
Penarlâg U.K. see Hawarden
Peñarroya mt. Spain 57 F3
Peñarroya-Pueblonuevo Spain 57 D4
Penarth U.K. 49 D7
Peñas, Cabo de c. Spain 57 D2
Penas, Golfo de g. Chile 144 A7
Penasi, Pulau i. Indon. 71 A6
Peña Ubiña mt. Spain 57 D2
Pender U.S.A. 130 D3
Pendle Hill hill U.K. 48 E5
Pendleton U.S.A. 126 D3
Pendleton Bay Canada 120 E4
Pend Oreille r. U.S.A. 126 D2
Pend Oreille Lake U.S.A. 126 D2
Pendra India 83 E5
Penduv India 84 B2
Pendzhikent Tajik. see Panjakent
Penebangan i. Indon. 68 D7
Peneda Gerês, Parque Nacional da nat. park Port. 57 B3
Penetanguishene Canada 134 F1
Penfro U.K. see Pembroke
Peng'an China 76 E2
Penganga r. India 84 C2
Peng Chau i. H.K. China 77 [inset]
P'engchia Yü i. Taiwan 77 I3
Penge Dem. Rep. Congo 99 C4
Penge S. Africa 101 J3
P'enghu Ch'üntao is Taiwan 77 H4
P'enghu Liehtao is Taiwan see P'enghu Ch'üntao
P'enghu Tao i. Taiwan 77 H4
Peng Kang hill Sing. 71 [inset]
Penglaizhen China see Daying
Pengshan China 76 D2
Pengshui China 77 F2
Pengwa Myanmar 70 A2
Pengxi China 76 E2
Penha Brazil 145 A4
Penhoek Pass S. Africa 101 H6
Penhook U.S.A. 134 F5
Peniche Port. 57 B4
Penicuik U.K. 50 F5
Penig Germany 53 M4
Peninga Rus. Fed. 44 R5
Peninsular Malaysia Malaysia 71 D6
Penitente, Serra do hills Brazil 143 I5
Penn U.S.A. see Penn Hills
Pennell Coast Antarctica 152 H2
Penn Hills U.S.A. 134 F3
Pennine, Alpi mts Italy/Switz. 58 B2
Pennine Alps mts Italy/Switz. see Pennine, Alpi
Pennines hills U.K. 48 E4
Pennington Gap U.S.A. 134 D5
Pennsburg U.S.A. 135 H3
Penns Grove U.S.A. 135 H4
Pennsville U.S.A. 135 H4
Pennsylvania state U.S.A. 134 F3
Pennville U.S.A. 134 C3
Penn Yan U.S.A. 135 G2
Penny Icecap Canada 119 L3
Penny Point Antarctica 152 H1
Penola Australia 111 C8
Peñón Blanco Mex. 131 B7
Penong Australia 109 F7
Penonomé Panama 137 H7
Penrhyn atoll Cook Is 151 J6
Penrhyn Basin sea feature S. Pacific Ocean 151 J6
Penrith Australia 112 E4
Penrith U.K. 48 E4
Pensacola U.S.A. 133 C6
Pensacola Mountains Antarctica 152 L1
Pensi La pass India 82 D2
Pentadaktylos Range mts Cyprus 85 A2
Pentakota India 84 D2
Pentecost Island Vanuatu 107 G3
Pentecôte, Île i. Vanuatu see Pentecost Island
Penticton Canada 120 G5
Pentire Point U.K. 49 B8
Pentland Australia 110 D4
Pentland Firth sea chan. U.K. 50 F2
Pentland Hills U.K. 50 F5
Pentwater U.S.A. 134 B2
Penwegon Myanmar 70 B3
Pen-y-Bont ar Ogwr U.K. see Bridgend
Penygadair hill U.K. 49 D6
Penylan Lake Canada 121 J2
Penza Rus. Fed. 43 J5
Penzance U.K. 49 B8
Penzhinskaya Guba b. Rus. Fed. 65 R3
Peoria AZ U.S.A. 129 G5
Peoria IL U.S.A. 130 F3
Peotone U.S.A. 134 B3
Pequeña, Punta pt Mex. 127 E8
Pequop Mountains U.S.A. 129 F1
Peradeniya Sri Lanka 84 D5
Pera Head hd Australia 110 C2
Perak i. Malaysia 71 B6
Perales del Alfambra Spain 57 F3
Perambalur India 84 C4
Perämeren kansallispuisto nat. park Fin. 44 N4
Peräseinäjoki Fin. 44 M5
Percé Canada 123 I4
Percival Lakes salt flat Australia 108 D5
Percy U.S.A. 135 J1
Percy Isles Australia 110 E4
Percy Reach l. Canada 135 G1
Perdizes Brazil 145 B2
Perdu, Lac l. Canada 123 H4
Peregrebnoye Rus. Fed. 41 T3
Pereira Col. 142 C3
Pereira Barreto Brazil 145 A3
Pereira de Eça Angola see Ondjiva
Pere Marquette r. U.S.A. 134 B2
Peremul Par reef India 84 B4
Peremyshlyany Ukr. 43 E6
Perenjori Australia 109 B7
Pereslavl'-Zalesskiy Rus. Fed. 42 H4
Pereslavskiy Natsional'nyy Park nat. park Rus. Fed. 42 H4
Pereyaslavka Rus. Fed. 74 D3
Pereyaslav-Khmel'nitskiy Ukr. see Pereyaslav-Khmel'nyts'kyy
Pereyaslav-Khmel'nyts'kyy Ukr. 43 F6
Perforated Island Thai. see Bon, Ko
Pergamino Arg. 144 D4
Perhentian Besar, Pulau i. Malaysia 71 C6
Perho Fin. 44 N5
Péribonka, Lac l. Canada 123 H4
Perico Arg. 144 C2
Pericos Mex. 127 G8
Peridot U.S.A. 129 H5
Périgueux France 56 E4
Perijá, Parque Nacional nat. park Venez. 142 D2
Perija, Sierra de mts Venez. 142 D2
Periyar India see Erode
Perkasie U.S.A. 135 H3
Perlas, Punta de pt Nicaragua 137 H6
Perleberg Germany 53 L1
Perm' Rus. Fed. 41 R4
Permas Rus. Fed. 42 J4
Pernambuco Brazil see Recife
Pernambuco Plain sea feature S. Atlantic Ocean 148 G6
Pernatty Lagoon salt flat Australia 111 B6
Pernem India 84 B3
Pernik Bulg. 59 J3
Pernov Estonia see Pärnu
Perojpur Bangl. see Pirojpur
Peron Islands Australia 108 E3
Péronne France 52 C5
Perpignan France 56 F5
Perranporth U.K. 49 B8
Perrégaux Alg. see Mohammadia
Perris U.S.A. 128 E5
Perros-Guirec France 56 C2
Perrot, Île i. Canada 135 I1
Perry FL U.S.A. 133 D6
Perry GA U.S.A. 133 D5
Perry MI U.S.A. 134 C2
Perry OK U.S.A. 131 D4
Perry Lake U.S.A. 130 E4
Perryton U.S.A. 131 C4
Perryville AK U.S.A. 118 C4
Perryville MO U.S.A. 130 F4
Perseverancia Bol. 142 F6
Pershore U.K. 49 E6
Persia country Asia see Iran
Persian Gulf Asia see The Gulf
Pertek Turkey 91 E3

▶Perth Australia 109 A7
Capital of Western Australia. 4th most populous city in Oceania.

Perth Canada 135 G1
Perth U.K. 50 F4
Perth Amboy U.S.A. 135 H3
Perth-Andover Canada 123 I5
Perth Basin sea feature Indian Ocean 149 P7
Pertominsk Rus. Fed. 42 H2
Pertunmaa Fin. 45 O6
Pertusato, Capo c. Corsica France 56 I6
Peru atoll Kiribati see Beru

▶Peru country S. America 142 D6
3rd largest and 4th most populous country in South America.

Peru IL U.S.A. 130 F3
Peru IN U.S.A. 134 B3
Peru NY U.S.A. 135 I1
Peru-Chile Trench sea feature S. Pacific Ocean 151 O6
Perugia Italy 58 E3
Peruru India 84 C3
Perusia Italy see Perugia
Péruwelz Belgium 52 D4
Pervomaysk Rus. Fed. 43 I5
Pervomays'k Ukr. 43 F6
Pervomayskiy Kazakh. 80 F1
Pervomayskiy Arkhangel'skaya Oblast' Rus. Fed. see Novodvinsk
Pervomayskiy Tambovskaya Oblast' Rus. Fed. 43 I5
Pervomays'kyy Ukr. 43 H6
Pervorechenskiy Rus. Fed. 65 R3
Pesaro Italy 58 E3
Pescadores is Taiwan see P'enghu Ch'üntao
Pescara Italy 58 F3
Pescara r. Italy 58 F3
Peschanokopskoye Rus. Fed. 43 I7
Peschanoye Rus. Fed. see Yashkul'
Peschanyy, Mys pt Kazakh. 91 H2
Pesha r. Rus. Fed. 42 J2
Peshanjan Afgh. 89 F3
Peshawar Pak. 89 H3
Peshkopi Albania 59 I4
Peshtera Bulg. 59 K3
Peski Turkm. 89 F2
Peski Karakumy des. Turkm. see Karakum Desert
Peskovka Rus. Fed. 42 L4
Pesnica Slovenia 58 F1
Pessac France 56 D4
Pessin Germany 53 M2
Pestovo Rus. Fed. 42 G4
Pestravka Rus. Fed. 43 K5
Petah Tiqwa Israel 85 B3
Petäjävesi Fin. 44 N5
Petaling Jaya Malaysia 71 C7
Petalion, Kolpos sea chan. Greece 59 K5
Petaluma U.S.A. 128 B2
Pétange Lux. 52 F5
Petatlán Mex. 136 D5
Petauke Zambia 99 D5
Petenwell Lake U.S.A. 130 F2
Peterbell Canada 122 E4
Peterborough Australia 111 B7
Peterborough Canada 135 F1
Peterborough U.K. 49 G6
Peterborough U.S.A. 135 J2
Peterculter U.K. 50 G3
Peterhead U.K. 50 H3
Peter I Island Antarctica 152 K2
Peter I Øy i. Antarctica see Peter I Island
Peter Lake Canada 121 M2
Peterlee U.K. 48 F4
Petermann Bjerg nunatak Greenland 119 P2
Petermann Ranges mts Australia 109 E6
Peter Pond Lake Canada 121 I4
Peters, Lac l. Canada 123 H2
Petersberg Germany 53 J4
Petersburg AK U.S.A. 120 C3
Petersburg IL U.S.A. 130 F4
Petersburg IN U.S.A. 134 B4
Petersburg NY U.S.A. 135 I2
Petersburg VA U.S.A. 135 G5
Petersburg WV U.S.A. 134 F4
Petersfield U.K. 49 G7
Petershagen Germany 53 I2
Petersville U.S.A. 118 C3
Peter the Great Bay Rus. Fed. see Petra Velikogo, Zaliv
Peth India 84 B2
Petilia Policastro Italy 58 G5
Petit Atlas mts Morocco see Anti Atlas
Petitcodiac Canada 123 I5
Petitjean Morocco see Sidi Kacem
Petit Lac Manicouagan l. Canada 123 I3
Petit Mécatina r. Nfld. and Lab./Que. Canada 123 K4
Petit Mécatina, Île du i. Canada 123 K4
Petit Morin r. France 52 D6
Petitot r. Canada 120 F2
Petit St-Bernard, Col du pass France 56 H4

Point Lake Canada 120 H1
Point of Rocks U.S.A. 126 F4
Point Pelee National Park Canada 134 D3
Point Pleasant NJ U.S.A. 135 H3
Point Pleasant WV U.S.A. 134 D4
Poitiers France 56 E3
Poitou reg. France 56 E3
Poix-de-Picardie France 52 B5
Pojuca r. Brazil 145 D1
Pokaran India 82 B4
Pokataroo Australia 112 D2
Pokcha Rus. Fed. 41 R3
Pokhara Nepal 83 E3
Pokhran Landi Pak. 89 G5
Pokhvistnevo Rus. Fed. 41 Q5
Pok Liu Chau i. H.K. China see Lamma Island
Poko Dem. Rep. Congo 98 C3
Pokosnoye Rus. Fed. 72 I1
P'ok'r Kovkas mts Asia see Lesser Caucasus
Pokrovka Chitinskaya Oblast' Rus. Fed. 74 A1
Pokrovka Primorskiy Kray Rus. Fed. 74 C4
Pokrovsk Respublika Sakha (Yakutiya) Rus. Fed. 65 N3
Pokrovsk Saratovskaya Oblast' Rus. Fed. see Engel's
Pokrovskoye Rus. Fed. 43 H7
Pokshen'ga r. Rus. Fed. 42 J3
Pol India 82 C5
Pola Croatia see Pula
Polacca Wash watercourse U.S.A. 129 H4
Pola de Lena Spain 57 D2
Pola de Siero Spain 57 D2
Poland country Europe 40 J5
Poland NY U.S.A. 135 H2
Poland OH U.S.A. 134 E3
Polar Plateau Antarctica 152 A1
Polatlı Turkey 90 D3
Polatsk Belarus 45 P9
Polavaram India 84 D2
Polcirkeln Sweden 44 L3
Pol-e 'Alam Lowgar 89 H3
Pol-e Fāsā Iran 88 D4
Pol-e Khatum Iran 89 F2
Pol-e Khomrī Afgh. 89 H3
Pol-e Safid Iran 88 D2
Polessk Rus. Fed. 45 L9
Poles'ye marsh Belarus/Ukr. see Pripet Marshes
Polgahawela Sri Lanka 84 D5
Poli Cyprus see Polis
Políaigos i. Greece see Polyaigos
Police Poland 47 O4
Policoro Italy 58 G4
Poligny France 56 G3
Políkastron Greece see Polykastro
Polillo Islands Phil. 69 G3
Polis Cyprus 85 A2
Polis'ke Ukr. 43 F6
Polis'kyy Zapovidnyk nature res. Ukr. 43 F6
Politovo Rus. Fed. 42 K2
Políyiros Greece see Polygyros
Polkowice Poland 47 P5
Pollachi India 84 C4
Pollard Islands U.S.A. see Gardner Pinnacles
Polle Germany 53 J3
Pollino, Monte mt. Italy 58 G5
Pollino, Parco Nazionale del nat. park Italy 58 G5
Pollock Pines U.S.A. 128 C2
Pollock Reef Australia 109 C8
Polmak Norway 44 O1
Polnovat Rus. Fed. 41 T3
Polo Fin. 44 P4
Poloat atoll Micronesia see Puluwat
Pologi Ukr. see Polohy
Polohy Ukr. 43 H7
Polokwane S. Africa 101 I2
Polonne Ukr. 43 E6
Polonnoye Ukr. see Polonne
Polotsk Belarus see Polatsk
Polperro U.K. 49 C8
Polska country Europe see Poland
Polson U.S.A. 126 E3
Polta r. Rus. Fed. 42 I2
Poltava Ukr. 43 G6
Poltoratsk Turkm. see Aşgabat
Põltsamaa Estonia 45 N7
Polunochnoye Rus. Fed. 41 S3
Põlva Estonia 45 O7
Polvadera U.S.A. 127 G6
Polvijärvi Fin. 44 P5
Polyaigos i. Greece 59 K6
Polyanovgrad Bulg. see Karnobat
Polyarnyy Chukotskiy Avtonomnyy Okrug Rus. Fed. 65 S3
Polyarnyy Murmanskaya Oblast' Rus. Fed. 44 R2
Polyarnyye Zori Rus. Fed. 44 R3
Polyarnyy Ural mts Rus. Fed. 41 S2
Polygyros Greece 59 J4
Polykastro Greece 59 J4
Polynesia is Pacific Ocean 150 I6
Polynésie Française terr. S. Pacific Ocean see French Polynesia
Pom Indon. 69 J7
Pomarkku Fin. 45 M6
Pombal Pará Brazil 143 H4
Pombal Paraíba Brazil 143 K5
Pombal Port. 57 B4
Pomene Moz. 101 L2
Pomeranian Bay Poland 47 O3
Pomeroy S. Africa 101 J5
Pomeroy U.K. 51 F3
Pomeroy OH U.S.A. 134 D4
Pomeroy WA U.S.A. 126 D3
Pomezia Italy 58 E4
Pomfret S. Africa 100 F3
Pomona Namibia 100 B4
Pomona U.S.A. 128 E4
Pomorie Bulg. 59 L3
Pomorskie, Pojezierze reg. Poland 47 O4
Pomorskiy Bereg coastal area Rus. Fed. 42 G2
Pomorskiy Proliv sea chan. Rus. Fed. 42 K1
Pomos Point Cyprus 85 A2
Pomo Tso l. China see Puma Yumco
Pomou, Akra pt Cyprus see Pomos Point
Pomozdino Rus. Fed. 42 L3
Pompain China 76 B2
Pompano Beach U.S.A. 133 D7
Pompei Italy 58 F4
Pompéia Brazil 145 A3
Pompey France 52 G6
Pompeyevka Rus. Fed. 74 C2
Ponape atoll Micronesia see Pohnpei
Ponask Lake Canada 121 M4
Ponazyrevo Rus. Fed. 42 J4
Ponca City U.S.A. 131 D4
Ponce Puerto Rico 137 K5
Ponce de Leon Bay U.S.A. 133 D7
Poncheville, Lac l. Canada 122 F4
Pondicherry India see Puducherry
Pondicherry union terr. India see Puducherry
Pondichéry India see Puducherry
Pond Inlet Canada 153 K2
Ponds Bay Canada see Pond Inlet
Ponente, Riviera di coastal area Italy 58 B3
Poneto U.S.A. 134 C3
Ponferrada Spain 57 C2
Pongara, Pointe pt Gabon 98 A3
Pongaroa N.Z. 113 F5
Pongo watercourse Sudan 97 F4
Pongola r. S. Africa 101 K4
Pongolapoort Dam l. S. Africa 101 J4
Ponnagyun Myanmar 70 A2
Ponnaivar r. India 84 C4
Ponnampet India 84 B3
Ponnani India 84 B4
Ponnyadaung Range mts Myanmar 70 A2
Pono Indon. 69 I8
Ponoka Canada 120 H4
Ponoy r. Rus. Fed. 42 I2
Pons r. Canada 123 H2

▶Ponta Delgada Arquipélago dos Açores 148 G3
Capital of the Azores.

Ponta Grossa Brazil 145 A4
Pontal Brazil 145 A3
Pontalina Brazil 145 A2
Pont-à-Mousson France 52 G6
Ponta Porã Brazil 144 E2
Pontarfynach U.K. see Devil's Bridge
Pont-Audemer France 49 H9
Pontault-Combault France 52 C6
Pontax r. Canada 122 F4
Pontchartrain, Lake U.S.A. 131 F6
Pont-de-Loup Belgium 52 E4
Ponte Alta do Norte Brazil 143 I6
Ponte de Sor Port. 57 B4
Ponte Firme Brazil 145 B2
Pontefract U.K. 48 F5
Ponteix Canada 121 J5
Ponteland U.K. 48 F3
Ponte Nova Brazil 145 C3
Pontes-e-Lacerda Brazil 143 G7
Pontevedra Spain 57 B2
Ponthierville Dem. Rep. Congo see Ubundu
Pontiac IL U.S.A. 130 F3
Pontiac MI U.S.A. 134 D2
Pontiae is Italy see Ponziane, Isole
Pontianak Indon. 68 D7
Pontine Islands is Italy see Ponziane, Isole
Pont-l'Abbé France 56 B3
Pontoise France 52 C5
Ponton watercourse Australia 109 C7
Ponton Canada 121 L4
Pontotoc U.S.A. 131 F5
Pont-Ste-Maxence France 52 C5
Pontypool U.K. 49 D7
Pontypridd U.K. 49 D7
Ponza, Isola di i. Italy 58 E4
Ponziane, Isole is Italy 58 E4
Poochera Australia 109 F8
Poole U.K. 49 F8
Poole U.S.A. 134 B5
Poolowanna Lake salt flat Australia 111 B5
Poona India see Pune
Pooncarie Australia 111 C7
Poonch India see Punch
Poopelloe Lake salt l. Australia 112 B3
Poopó, Lago de l. Bol. 142 E7
Poor Knights Islands N.Z. 113 E2
Popayán Col. 142 C3
Poperinge Belgium 52 C4
Popigay r. Rus. Fed. 65 L2
Popiltah Australia 111 C7
Popilta Lake imp. l. Australia 111 C7
Poplar r. Canada 121 L4
Poplar U.S.A. 126 G2
Poplar Bluff U.S.A. 131 F4
Poplar Camp U.S.A. 134 E5
Poplarville U.S.A. 131 F6

▶Popocatépetl, Volcán vol. Mex. 136 E5
5th highest mountain in North America.

Popokabaka Dem. Rep. Congo 99 B4
Popondetta P.N.G. 69 L8
Popovichskaya Rus. Fed. see Kalininskaya
Popovo Bulg. 59 L3
Popovo Polje plain Bos.-Herz. 58 G3
Poppberg hill Germany 53 L5
Poppenberg hill Germany 53 K3
Poprad Slovakia 47 R6
Poquoson U.S.A. 135 G5
Porali r. Pak. 89 G5
Porangahau N.Z. 113 F5
Porangatu Brazil 145 A1
Porbandar India 82 B5
Porcher Island Canada 120 D4
Porcos r. Brazil 145 B1
Porcupine, Cape Canada 123 K3
Porcupine Abyssal Plain sea feature N. Atlantic Ocean 148 G2
Porcupine Gorge National Park Australia 110 D4
Porcupine Hills Canada 121 K4
Porcupine Mountains U.S.A. 130 F2
Poreč Croatia 58 E2
Porecatu Brazil 145 A3
Poretskoye Rus. Fed. 43 J5
Pori Fin. 45 L6
Porirua N.Z. 113 E5
Porkhov Rus. Fed. 45 P8
Porlamar Venez. 142 F1
Pormpuraaw Australia 110 C2
Pornic France 56 C3
Poronaysk Rus. Fed. 74 F2
Porong China 83 G3
Poros Greece 59 J6
Porosozero Rus. Fed. 42 G3
Porpoise Bay Antarctica 152 G2
Porsangerfjorden sea chan. Norway 44 N1
Porsangerhalvøya pen. Norway 44 N1
Porsgrunn Norway 45 F7
Porsuk r. Turkey 59 N5
Portadown U.K. 51 F3
Portaferry U.K. 51 G3
Portage MI U.S.A. 134 C2
Portage PA U.S.A. 135 F3
Portage WI U.S.A. 130 F3
Portage Lakes U.S.A. 134 E3
Portage la Prairie Canada 121 L5
Portal U.S.A. 130 C1
Port Alberni Canada 120 E5
Port Albert Australia 112 C7
Portalegre Port. 57 C4
Portales U.S.A. 131 C5
Port-Alfred Canada see La Baie
Port Alfred S. Africa 101 H7
Port Alice Canada 120 E5
Port Allegany U.S.A. 135 F3
Port Allen U.S.A. 131 F6
Port Alma Australia 110 E4
Port Angeles U.S.A. 126 C2
Port Antonio Jamaica 137 I5
Portarlington Ireland 51 E4
Port Arthur Australia 111 [inset]
Port Arthur U.S.A. 131 E6
Port Askaig U.K. 50 C5
Port Augusta Australia 111 B7

▶Port-au-Prince Haiti 137 J5
Capital of Haiti.

Port Austin U.S.A. 134 D1
Port aux Choix Canada 123 K4
Portavogie U.K. 51 G3
Port Beaufort S. Africa 100 E8
Port Blair India 71 A5
Port Bolster Canada 134 F1
Portbou Spain 57 H2
Port Burwell Canada 134 E2
Port Campbell Australia 112 A7
Port Campbell National Park Australia 112 A7
Port Carling Canada 134 F1
Port-Cartier Canada 123 I4
Port Chalmers N.Z. 113 C7
Port Charlotte U.S.A. 133 D7
Port Clements Canada 120 C4
Port Clinton U.S.A. 134 D3
Port Credit Canada 134 F2
Port-de-Paix Haiti 137 J5
Port Dickson Malaysia 71 C7
Port Douglas Australia 110 D3
Port Edward Canada 120 D4
Port Edward S. Africa 101 J6
Porteira Brazil 143 G4
Porteirinha Brazil 145 C1
Portel Brazil 143 H4
Port Elgin Canada 134 E1
Port Elizabeth S. Africa 101 G7
Port Ellen U.K. 50 C5
Port Erin Isle of Man 48 C4
Porter Lake N.W.T. Canada 121 J2
Porter Lake Sask. Canada 121 J3
Porter Landing Canada 120 D3
Porterville S. Africa 100 D7
Porterville U.S.A. 128 D3
Port Étienne Mauritania see Nouâdhibou
Port Everglades U.S.A. see Fort Lauderdale
Port Fitzroy N.Z. 113 E3
Port Francqui Dem. Rep. Congo see Ilebo
Port-Gentil Gabon 98 A4
Port Glasgow U.K. 50 E5
Port Harcourt Nigeria 96 D4
Port Harrison Canada see Inukjuak
Porthcawl U.K. 49 D7
Port Hedland Australia 108 B5
Port Henry U.S.A. 135 I1
Port Herald Malawi see Nsanje
Porthleven U.K. 49 B8
Porthmadog U.K. 49 C6
Port Hope Canada 135 F2
Port Hope Simpson Canada 123 L3
Port Hueneme U.S.A. 128 D4
Port Huron U.S.A. 134 D2
Portimão Port. 57 B5
Port Jackson Australia see Sydney
Port Jackson inlet Australia 112 E4
Port Keats Australia see Wadeye
Port Klang Malaysia see Pelabuhan Klang
Port Láirge Ireland see Waterford
Portland N.S.W. Australia 112 D4
Portland Vic. Australia 111 C8
Portland IN U.S.A. 134 C3
Portland ME U.S.A. 135 J2
Portland MI U.S.A. 134 C2
Portland OR U.S.A. 126 C3
Portland TN U.S.A. 134 B5
Portland, Isle of pen. U.K. 49 E8
Portland Bill hd U.K. see Bill of Portland
Portland Creek Pond l. Canada 123 K4
Portland Roads Australia 110 C2
Port-la-Nouvelle France 56 F5
Portlaoise Ireland 51 E4
Port Lavaca U.S.A. 131 D6
Portlaw Ireland 51 E5
Portlethen U.K. 50 G3
Port Lincoln Australia 111 A7
Port Loko Sierra Leone 96 B4

▶Port Louis Mauritius 149 L7
Capital of Mauritius.

Port-Lyautrey Morocco see Kénitra
Port Macquarie Australia 112 F3
Portmadoc U.K. see Porthmadog
Port McNeill Canada 120 E5
Port-Menier Canada 123 I4

▶Port Moresby P.N.G. 69 L8
Capital of Papua New Guinea.

Portnaguran U.K. 50 C2
Portnahaven U.K. 50 C5
Port nan Giúran U.K. see Portnaguran
Port Neill Australia 111 B7
Portneuf r. Canada 123 H4
Port Nis U.K. see Port of Ness
Port Nis Scotland U.K. see Port of Ness
Port Noarlunga Australia 111 B7
Port Nolloth S. Africa 100 C5
Port Norris U.S.A. 135 H4
Port-Nouveau-Québec Canada see Kangiqsualujjuaq
Porto Port. see Oporto
Porto Acre Brazil 142 E5
Porto Alegre Brazil 145 A5
Porto Alexandre Angola see Tombua
Porto Amboim Angola 99 B5
Porto Amélia Moz. see Pemba
Porto Artur Brazil 143 G6
Porto Belo Brazil 145 A4
Porto de Moz Brazil 143 H4
Porto de Santa Cruz Brazil 145 C1
Porto dos Gaúchos Óbidos Brazil 143 G6
Porto Esperança Brazil 143 G7
Porto Esperidião Brazil 143 G7
Portoferraio Italy 58 D3
Port of Ness U.K. 50 C2
Porto Franco Brazil 143 I5

▶Port of Spain Trin. and Tob. 137 L6
Capital of Trinidad and Tobago.

Porto Grande Brazil 143 H3
Portogruaro Italy 58 E2
Porto Jofre Brazil 143 G7
Portola U.S.A. 128 C2
Portomaggiore Italy 58 D2
Porto Mendes Brazil 144 F2
Porto Murtinho Brazil 144 E2
Porto Nacional Brazil 143 I6

▶Porto-Novo Benin 96 D4
Capital of Benin.

Porto Novo Cape Verde 96 [inset]
Porto Primavera, Represa resr Brazil 144 F2
Port Orchard U.S.A. 126 C3
Port Orford U.S.A. 126 B4
Porto Rico Angola 99 B4
Porto Santo, Ilha de i. Madeira 96 B1
Porto Seguro Brazil 145 D2
Porto Tolle Italy 58 E2
Porto Torres Sardinia Italy 58 C4
Porto União Brazil 145 A4
Porto-Vecchio Corsica France 56 I6
Porto Velho Brazil 142 F5
Portoviejo Ecuador 142 B4
Porto Wálter Brazil 142 D5
Portpatrick U.K. 50 D6
Port Perry Canada 135 F1
Port Phillip Bay Australia 112 B7
Port Pirie Australia 111 B7
Port Radium Canada see Echo Bay
Portreath U.K. 49 B8
Portree U.K. 50 C3
Port Rexton Canada 123 L4
Port Royal U.S.A. 135 G4
Port Royal Sound inlet U.S.A. 133 D5
Portrush U.K. 51 F2
Port Safaga Egypt see Būr Safājah
Port Said Egypt 85 A4
Port St Joe U.S.A. 133 C6
Port St Lucie City U.S.A. 133 D7
Port St Mary Isle of Man 48 C4
Portsalon Ireland 51 E2
Port Sanilac U.S.A. 134 D2
Port Severn Canada 134 F1
Port Shepstone S. Africa 101 J6
Port Simpson Canada see Lax Kw'alaams
Portsmouth U.K. 49 F8
Portsmouth NH U.S.A. 135 J2
Portsmouth OH U.S.A. 134 D4
Portsmouth VA U.S.A. 135 G5
Portsoy U.K. 50 G3
Port Stanley Falkland Is see Stanley
Port Stephens b. Australia 112 F4
Portstewart U.K. 51 F2
Port Sudan Sudan 86 E6
Port Swettenham Malaysia see Pelabuhan Klang
Port Talbot U.K. 49 D7
Porttipahdan tekojärvi l. Fin. 44 O2
Port Townsend U.S.A. 126 C2
Portugal country Europe 57 C4
Portugália Angola see Chitato
Portuguese East Africa country Africa see Mozambique
Portuguese Guinea country Africa see Guinea-Bissau
Portuguese Timor country Asia see East Timor
Portuguese West Africa country Africa see Angola
Portumna Ireland 51 D4
Portus Herculis Monoeci country Europe see Monaco
Port-Vendres France 56 F5

▶Port Vila Vanuatu 107 G3
Capital of Vanuatu.

Portville U.S.A. 135 F2
Port Vladimir Rus. Fed. 44 R2
Port Waikato N.Z. 113 E3
Port Washington U.S.A. 134 B2
Port William U.K. 50 E6
Porvenir Bol. 142 E6
Porvenir Chile 144 B8
Porvoo Fin. 45 N6
Posada Spain 57 D2
Posada de Llanera Spain see Posada
Posadas Arg. 144 E3
Posen Poland see Poznań
Posen U.S.A. 134 D1
Poseyville U.S.A. 134 B4
Poshekhon'ye Rus. Fed. 42 H4
Poshekhon'ye-Volodarsk Rus. Fed. see Poshekhon'ye
Posht-e Badam Iran 88 D3
Poshteh-ye Chaqvīr hill Iran 88 E4
Posht-e Kūh mts Iran 88 B3
Posht-e Rūd-e Zamindavar reg. Afgh. see Zamīndāvar
Posht Kūh hill Iran 88 C2
Posio Fin. 44 P3
Poso Indon. 69 G7
Posof Turkey 91 F2
Posŏng S. Korea 75 B6
Possession Island Namibia 100 B4
Pößneck Germany 53 L4
Post U.S.A. 131 C5
Postavy Belarus see Pastavy
Poste-de-la-Baleine Canada see Kuujjuarapik
Poste Weygand Alg. 96 D2
Postmasburg S. Africa 100 F5
Poston U.S.A. 129 F4
Postville Canada 123 K3
Postville U.S.A. 122 C6
Postysheve Ukr. see Krasnoarmiys'k
Pota Indon. 108 C2
Pótam Mex. 127 F8
Poté Brazil 145 C2
Poteau U.S.A. 131 E5
Potegaon India 84 D2
Potentia Italy see Potenza
Potenza Italy 58 F4
Poth U.S.A. 131 D6
P'ot'i Georgia 91 F2
Potikal India 84 D2
Potiraguá Brazil 145 D1
Potiskum Nigeria 96 E3
Potlatch U.S.A. 126 D3
Pot Mountain U.S.A. 126 E3
Po Toi i. H.K. China 77 [inset]
Potomac r. U.S.A. 135 G4
Potosí Bol. 142 E7
Potosi U.S.A. 130 F4
Potosi Mountain U.S.A. 129 F4
Potrerillos Chile 144 C3
Potrero del Llano Mex. 131 B6
Potsdam Germany 53 N2
Potsdam U.S.A. 135 H1
Potter U.S.A. 130 C3
Potterne U.K. 49 E7
Potters Bar U.K. 49 G7
Potter Valley U.S.A. 128 B2
Pottstown U.S.A. 135 H3
Pottsville U.S.A. 135 G3
Pottuvil Sri Lanka 84 D5
Potwar reg. Pak. 89 I3
Pouch Cove Canada 123 L5
Poughkeepsie U.S.A. 135 I3
Poulin de Courval, Lac l. Canada 123 H4
Poulton-le-Fylde U.K. 48 E5
Pouso Alegre Brazil 145 B3
Poŭthĭsăt Cambodia 71 C4
Poŭthĭsăt, Stœng r. Cambodia 71 D4
Považská Bystrica Slovakia 47 Q6
Povenets Rus. Fed. 42 G3
Poverty Bay N.Z. 113 F4
Povlen mt. Serbia 59 H2
Póvoa de Varzim Port. 57 B3
Povorino Rus. Fed. 43 I6
Povorotnyy, Mys hd Rus. Fed. 74 D4
Poway U.S.A. 128 E5
Powder r. U.S.A. 126 G3
Powder, South Fork r. U.S.A. 126 G4
Powder River U.S.A. 126 G4
Powell r. U.S.A. 134 D5
Powell, Lake resr U.S.A. 129 H3
Powell Lake Canada 120 E5
Powell Mountain U.S.A. 128 D2
Powell Point Bahamas 133 E7
Powell River Canada 120 E5
Powhatan AR U.S.A. 131 F4
Powhatan VA U.S.A. 135 G5
Powo China 76 C1
Pōwrize Turkm. 88 E2
Poxoréu Brazil 143 H7
Poyang China see Boyang
Poyang Hu l. China 77 H2
Poyan Reservoir Sing. 71 [inset]
Poyarkovo Rus. Fed. 74 C2
Pozantı Turkey 90 D3
Požarevac Serbia 59 I2
Poza Rica Mex. 136 E4
Pozdeyevka Rus. Fed. 74 C2
Požega Croatia 58 G2
Požega Serbia 59 I3
Pozharskoye Rus. Fed. 74 D3
Poznań Poland 47 P4
Pozoblanco Spain 57 D4
Pozo Colorado Para. 144 E2
Pozsony Slovakia see Bratislava
Pozzuoli Italy 58 F4
Prabumulih Indon. 68 C7
Prachatice Czech Rep. 47 O6
Prachi r. India 83 F6
Prachin Buri Thai. 71 C4
Prachuap Khiri Khan Thai. 71 B5
Prades France 56 F5
Prado Brazil 145 D2

▶Prague Czech Rep. 47 O5
Capital of the Czech Republic.

Praha Czech Rep. see Prague

▶Praia Cape Verde 96 [inset]
Capital of Cape Verde.

Praia do Bilene Moz. 101 K3
Prainha Brazil 143 H4
Prairie Australia 110 D4
Prairie r. U.S.A. 130 E2
Prairie Dog Town Fork r. U.S.A. 131 C5
Prairie du Chien U.S.A. 130 F3
Prairie River Canada 121 K4
Pram, Khao mt. Thai. 71 B5
Pran r. Thai. 71 C4
Pran Buri Thai. 71 B4
Prapat Indon. 71 B7
Prasonisi, Akra pt Notio Aigaio Greece see Prasonisi, Akrotirio
Prasonisi, Akrotirio pt Greece 59 L7
Prata Brazil 145 A2
Prata r. Brazil 145 A2
Prat de Llobregat Spain see El Prat de Llobregat
Prathes Thai country Asia see Thailand
Prato Italy 58 D3
Pratt U.S.A. 130 D4
Prattville U.S.A. 133 C5
Pravdinsk Rus. Fed. 45 L9
Praya Indon. 108 B2
Preah, Prêk r. Cambodia 71 D4
Preăh Vihéar Cambodia 71 D4
Preble U.S.A. 135 G2
Prechistoye Smolenskaya Oblast' Rus. Fed. 43 G5
Prechistoye Yaroslavskaya Oblast' Rus. Fed. 42 I4
Precipice National Park Australia 110 E5
Preeceville Canada 121 K5
Pregolya r. Rus. Fed. 45 L9
Preiļi Latvia 45 O8
Prelate Canada 121 I5
Premer Australia 112 D3
Prémery France 56 F3
Premnitz Germany 53 M2
Prentiss U.S.A. 131 F6
Prenzlau Germany 47 N4
Preparis Island Cocos Is 68 A4
Preparis North Channel Cocos Is 68 A4
Preparis South Channel Cocos Is 68 A4
Přerov Czech Rep. 47 P6
Presa San Antonio Mex. 131 C7
Prescelly Mts hills U.K. see Preseli, Mynydd
Prescott Canada 135 H1
Prescott AR U.S.A. 131 E5
Prescott AZ U.S.A. 129 G4
Prescott Valley U.S.A. 129 G4
Preseli, Mynydd hills U.K. 49 C7
Preševo Serbia 59 I3
Presidencia Roque Sáenz Peña Arg. 144 D3
Presidente Dutra Brazil 143 J5
Presidente Hermes Brazil 142 F6
Presidente Olegário Brazil 145 B2
Presidente Prudente Brazil 145 A3
Presidente Venceslau Brazil 145 A3
Presidio U.S.A. 131 B6
Preslav Bulg. see Veliki Preslav
Prešov Slovakia 43 D6
Prespa, Lake Europe 59 I4
Prespansko Ezero l. Europe see Prespa, Lake
Prespes nat. park Greece 59 I4
Prespës, Liqeni i l. Europe see Prespa, Lake
Presque Isle ME U.S.A. 132 G2
Presque Isle MI U.S.A. 134 D1
Pressburg Slovakia see Bratislava
Presteigne U.K. 49 D6
Preston U.K. 48 E5
Preston ID U.S.A. 126 F4
Preston MN U.S.A. 130 E3
Preston MO U.S.A. 130 E4
Preston, Cape Australia 108 B5
Prestonpans U.K. 50 G5
Prestonsburg U.S.A. 134 D5
Prestwick U.K. 50 E5
Preto r. Bahia Brazil 143 J6
Preto r. Minas Gerais Brazil 145 B2
Preto r. Brazil 145 D1

▶Pretoria S. Africa 101 I3
Official capital of South Africa.

Pretoria-Witwatersrand-Vereeniging prov. S. Africa see Gauteng
Pretzsch Germany 53 M3
Preussisch-Eylau Rus. Fed. see Bagrationovsk
Preußisch Stargard Poland see Starogard Gdański
Preveza Greece 59 I5
Prewitt U.S.A. 129 I4
Prey Vêng Cambodia 71 D5
Priaral'skiye Karakumy, Peski des. Kazakh. 80 B2
Priargunsk Rus. Fed. 73 L2
Pribilof Islands U.S.A. 118 A4
Priboj Serbia 59 H3
Price r. Australia 108 E3
Price NC U.S.A. 134 F5
Price UT U.S.A. 129 H2
Price r. U.S.A. 129 H2
Price Island Canada 120 D4
Prichard AL U.S.A. 131 F6
Prichard WV U.S.A. 134 D4
Pridorozhnoye Rus. Fed. see Khulkhuta
Priekule Latvia 45 L8
Priekuļi Latvia 45 N8
Priel'brus'ye, Natsional'nyy Park nat. park Rus. Fed. 43 I8
Prienai Lith. 45 M9
Prieska S. Africa 100 F5
Prievidza Slovakia 47 Q6
Prignitz reg. Germany 53 M1
Prijedor Bos.-Herz. 58 G2
Prijepolje Serbia 59 H3
Prikaspiyskaya Nizmennost' lowland Kazakh./Rus. Fed. see Caspian Lowland
Prilep Macedonia 59 I4
Priluki Ukr. see Pryluky
Přimda Czech Rep. 53 M5
Primero de Enero Cuba 133 E8
Primorsk Rus. Fed. 45 P6
Primorsk Ukr. see Prymors'k
Primorskiy Kray admin. div. Rus. Fed. 74 D3
Primorsko-Akhtarsk Rus. Fed. 43 H7
Primo Tapia Mex. 128 E5
Primrose Lake Canada 121 I4
Prims r. Germany 52 G5
Prince Albert Canada 121 J4
Prince Albert S. Africa 100 F7
Prince Albert Mountains Antarctica 152 H1
Prince Albert National Park Canada 121 J4
Prince Albert Peninsula Canada 118 G2
Prince Albert Road S. Africa 100 E7
Prince Alfred, Cape Canada 118 F2
Prince Alfred Hamlet S. Africa 100 D7
Prince Charles Island Canada 119 K3
Prince Charles Mountains Antarctica 152 E2
Prince Edward Island prov. Canada 123 J5

▶Prince Edward Islands Indian Ocean 149 K9
Part of South Africa.

Prince Edward Point Canada 135 G2
Prince Frederick U.S.A. 135 G4
Prince George Canada 120 F4
Prince Harald Coast Antarctica 152 D2
Prince of Wales, Cape U.S.A. 118 B3
Prince of Wales Island Australia 110 C1

Prince of Wales Island Canada 119 I2
Prince of Wales Island U.S.A. 120 C4
Prince of Wales Strait Canada 118 G2
Prince Patrick Island Canada 118 G2
Prince Regent Inlet sea chan. Canada 119 I2
Prince Rupert Canada 120 D4
Princess Anne U.S.A. 135 H4
Princess Astrid Coast Antarctica 152 C2
Princess Charlotte Bay Australia 110 C2
Princess Elizabeth Land reg. Antarctica 152 E2
Princess Mary Lake Canada 121 L1
Princess Ragnhild Coast Antarctica 152 C2
Princess Royal Island Canada 120 D4
Princeton Canada 120 F5
Princeton CA U.S.A. 128 B2
Princeton IL U.S.A. 130 F3
Princeton IN U.S.A. 134 B4
Princeton MO U.S.A. 130 E3
Princeton NJ U.S.A. 135 H3
Princeton WV U.S.A. 134 E5
Prince William Sound b. U.S.A. 118 D3
Príncipe i. São Tomé and Príncipe 96 D4
Prineville U.S.A. 126 C3
Prins Harald Kyst coastal area Antarctica see Prince Harald Coast
Prinzapolca Nicaragua 137 H6
Priozersk Rus. Fed. 45 Q6
Priozyorsk Rus. Fed. see Priozersk
Pripet r. Belarus/Ukr. 43 F6
also spelt Pryp"yat' (Ukraine) or Prypyats' (Belarus)
Pripet Marshes Belarus/Ukr. 43 E6
Prirechnyy Rus. Fed. 44 Q2

▶Prishtinë Kosovo 59 I3
Capital of Kosovo

Priština Kosovo see Prishtinë
Pritzier Germany 53 L1
Pritzwalk Germany 53 M1
Privas France 56 G4
Privlaka Croatia 58 F2
Privolzhsk Rus. Fed. 42 I4
Privolzhskaya Vozvyshennost' hills Rus. Fed. 43 J6
Privolzhskiy Rus. Fed. 43 J6
Privolzh'ye Rus. Fed. 43 K5
Priyutnoye Rus. Fed. 43 I7
Prizren Kosovo 59 I3
Probolinggo Indon. 68 E8
Probstzella Germany 53 L4
Probus U.K. 49 C8
Proddatur India 84 C3
Professor van Blommestein Meer resr Suriname 143 G3
Progreso Hond. see El Progreso
Progreso Mex. 131 C7
Progress Rus. Fed. 74 C2
Project City U.S.A. 126 C4
Prokhladnyy Rus. Fed. 91 G2
Prokop'yevsk Rus. Fed. 72 F2
Prokuplje Serbia 59 I3
Proletarsk Rus. Fed. 43 I7
Proletarskaya Rus. Fed. see Proletarsk
Prome Myanmar see Pyè
Promissão Brazil 145 A3
Promissão, Represa resr Brazil 145 A3
Prophet r. Canada 120 F3
Prophet River Canada 120 F3
Propriá Brazil 143 K6
Proskurov Ukr. see Khmel'nyts'kyy
Prosser U.S.A. 126 D3
Protem S. Africa 100 E8
Provadiya Bulg. 59 L3
Prøven Greenland see Kangersuatsiaq
Provence reg. France 56 G5
Providence KY U.S.A. 134 B5
Providence MD U.S.A. see Annapolis

▶Providence RI U.S.A. 135 J3
Capital of Rhode Island.

Providence, Cape N.Z. 113 A8
Providencia, Isla de i. Caribbean Sea 137 H6
Provideniya Rus. Fed. 65 T3
Provincetown U.S.A. 135 J2
Provo U.S.A. 129 H1
Provost Canada 121 I4
Prudentópolis Brazil 145 A4
Prudhoe Bay U.S.A. 118 D2
Prüm Germany 52 G4
Prüm r. Germany 52 G5
Prunelli-di-Fiumorbo Corsica France 56 I5
Pruntytown U.S.A. 134 E4
Prusa Turkey see Bursa
Prushkov Poland see Pruszków
Pruszków Poland 47 R4
Prut r. Europe 43 F7
Prydz Bay Antarctica 152 E2
Pryluky Ukr. 43 G6
Prymors'k Ukr. 43 H7
Prymors'ke Ukr. see Sartana
Pryp"yat' r. Belarus/Ukr. 43 F6 see Pripet
Prypyats' r. Belarus/Ukr. 41 L5 see Pripet
Przemyśl Poland 43 D6
Przheval'sk Kyrg. see Karakol
Psara i. Greece 59 K5
Pskov Rus. Fed. 45 P8
Pskov, Lake Estonia/Rus. Fed. 45 O7
Pskov Oblast admin. div. Rus. Fed. see Pskovskaya Oblast'
Pskovskaya Oblast' admin. div. Rus. Fed. 45 P8
Pskovskoye Ozero l. Estonia/Rus. Fed. see Pskov, Lake
Ptolemaïda Greece 59 I4
Ptolemais Israel see 'Akko
Ptuj Slovenia 58 F1
Pua Thai. 70 C3
Puaka hill Sing. 71 [inset]
Pu'an Guizhou China 76 E3
Pu'an Sichuan China 76 E2
Puan S. Korea 75 B6
Pucallpa Peru 142 D5
Pucheng Fujian China 77 H3
Pucheng Shaanxi China 77 F1
Puchezh Rus. Fed. 42 I4
Puch'ŏn S. Korea 75 B5
Puck Poland 47 Q3
Pudai watercourse Afgh. see Dor
Pūdanū Iran 88 D3
Pudasjärvi Fin. 44 O4
Pudimoe S. Africa 100 G4
Pudong Shanghai China 66 E4
Pudozh Rus. Fed. 42 H3
Pudsey U.K. 48 F5
Pudu China see Suizhou
Puduchcheri India see Puducherry
Puducherry India 84 C4
Puducherry union terr. India 84 C4
Pudukkottai India 84 C4
Puebla Baja California Mex. 129 F5
Puebla Puebla Mex. 136 E5
Puebla de Sanabria Spain 57 C2
Puebla de Zaragoza Mex. see Puebla
Pueblo U.S.A. 127 G5
Pueblo Yaqui Mex. 127 F8
Puelches Arg. 144 C5
Puelén Arg. 144 C5
Puente-Genil Spain 57 D5
Pu'er China 76 D4
Puerco watercourse U.S.A. 129 H4
Puerto Acosta Bol. 142 E7
Puerto Alegre Bol. 142 F6
Puerto Ángel Mex. 136 E5
Puerto Armuelles Panama 137 H7
Puerto Ayacucho Venez. 142 E2
Puerto Bahía Negra Para. see Bahía Negra
Puerto Baquerizo Moreno Galápagos Ecuador 142 [inset]
Puerto Barrios Guat. 136 G5
Puerto Cabello Venez. 142 E1
Puerto Cabezas Nicaragua 137 H6
Puerto Carreño Col. 142 E2
Puerto Casado Para. 144 E2
Puerto Cavinas Bol. 142 E6
Puerto Coig Arg. 144 C8
Puerto Cortés Mex. 136 B4
Puerto de Lobos Mex. 127 E7
Puerto Escondido Mex. 136 E5
Puerto Francisco de Orellana Orellana Ecuador see Coca
Puerto Francisco de Orellana Ecuador see Coca
Puerto Frey Bol. 142 F6
Puerto Génova Bol. 142 E6
Puerto Guarani Para. 144 E2
Puerto Heath Bol. 142 E6
Puerto Huitoto Col. 142 D3
Puerto Inírida Col. 142 E3
Puerto Isabel Bol. 143 G7
Puerto Leguízamo Col. 142 D4
Puerto Lempira Hond. 137 H5
Puerto Libertad Mex. 127 E7
Puerto Limón Costa Rica 137 H6
Puertollano Spain 57 D4
Puerto Lobos Arg. 144 C6
Puerto Madryn Arg. 144 C6
Puerto Maldonado Peru 142 E6
Puerto Máncora Peru 142 B4
Puerto México Mex. see Coatzacoalcos
Puerto Montt Chile 144 B6
Puerto Natales Chile 144 B8
Puerto Nuevo Col. 142 E2
Puerto Peñasco Mex. 127 E7
Puerto Pirámides Arg. 144 D6
Puerto Plata Dom. Rep. 137 J5
Puerto Portillo Peru 142 D5
Puerto Prado Peru 142 D6
Puerto Princesa Phil. 68 F5
Puerto Rico Arg. 144 E3
Puerto Rico Bol. 142 E6

▶Puerto Rico terr. West Indies 137 K5
United States Commonwealth.

▶Puerto Rico Trench sea feature Caribbean Sea 148 D4
Deepest trench in the Atlantic Ocean.

Puerto Santa Cruz Arg. 144 C8
Puerto Sastre Para. 144 E2
Puerto Saucedo Bol. 142 F6
Puerto Suárez Bol. 143 G7
Puerto Supe Peru 142 C6
Puerto Vallarta Mex. 136 C4
Puerto Victoria Peru 142 D5
Puerto Visser Arg. 144 C7
Puerto Yartou Chile 144 B8
Puerto Ybapobó Para. 144 E2
Pugachev Rus. Fed. 43 K5
Pugal India 82 C3
Puge China 76 D3
Pūhāl-e Khamīr, Kūh-e mts Iran 88 D5
Puhiwaero c. N.Z. see South West Cape
Puigmal mt. France/Spain 56 F5
Pui O Wan b. H.K. China 77 [inset]
Puji China see Puge
Pukaki, Lake N.Z. 113 C7
Pukapuka atoll Cook Is 107 J3
Pukaskwa National Park Canada 122 D4
Pukatawagan Canada 121 K4
Pukchin N. Korea 75 B4
Pukch'ŏng N. Korea 75 C4
Pukekohe N.Z. 113 E3
Puketeraki Range mts N.Z. 113 D6
Pukeuri Junction N.Z. 113 C7
Puksubaek-san mt. N. Korea 74 B4
Pula China see Nyingchi
Pula Croatia 58 E2
Pula Sardinia Italy 58 C5
Pulap atoll Micronesia 69 L5
Pulaski NY U.S.A. 135 G2
Pulaski VA U.S.A. 134 E5
Pulaski WI U.S.A. 134 A1
Pulau Simeulue, Suaka Margasatwa nature res. Indon. 71 A7
Pulheim Germany 52 G3
Pulicat Lake inlet India 84 D3
Pulivendla India 84 C3
Pulkkila Fin. 44 N4
Pullman U.S.A. 126 D3
Pulo Anna i. Palau 69 I6
Pulozero Rus. Fed. 44 R2
Púlpito, Punta pt Mex. 127 F8
Pulu China 82 E1
Pülümür Turkey 91 E3
Pulusuk atoll Micronesia 69 L5
Puluwat atoll Micronesia 69 L5
Pulwama India 89 I3
Pumasillo, Cerro mt. Peru 142 D6
Puma Yumco l. China 83 G3
Pumiao China see Yongning
Puná, Isla i. Ecuador 142 B4
Punakha Bhutan 83 G4
Punch India 82 C2
Punchaw Canada 120 F4
Punda Maria S. Africa 101 J2
Pundri India 82 D3
Pune India 84 B2
P'ungsan N. Korea 74 C4
Puning China 77 H4
Punjab state India 82 C3
Punjab prov. Pak. 89 H4
Punmah Glacier China/Pakistan 82 D2
Puno Peru 142 D7
Punta, Cerro de mt. Puerto Rico 137 K5
Punta Abreojos Mex. 127 E8
Punta Alta Arg. 144 D5
Punta Arenas Chile 144 B8
Punta Balestrieri mt. Italy 58 C4
Punta del Este Uruguay 144 F5
Punta Delgada Arg. 144 D6
Punta Gorda Belize 136 G5
Punta Gorda U.S.A. 133 D7
Punta Norte Arg. 144 D6
Punta Prieta Mex. 127 E7
Puntarenas Costa Rica 137 H6
Punxsutawney U.S.A. 135 F3
Puokio Fin. 44 O4
Puolanka Fin. 44 O4
Puqi China see Chibi
Pur r. Rus. Fed. 64 I3
Puracé, Volcán de vol. Col. 142 C3
Purcell U.S.A. 131 D5
Purcell Mountains Canada 120 G5
Purgatoire r. U.S.A. 130 C4
Puri India 84 E2
Purmerend Neth. 52 E2
Purna r. Mahar. India 82 D5
Purna r. Mahar. India 84 C2
Purnea India see Purnia
Purnia India 83 F4
Purnululu National Park Australia 108 E4
Pursat Cambodia see Poŭthĭsăt
Puruliya India 83 F5

▶Purus r. Peru 142 F4
3rd longest river in South America.

Puruvesi l. Fin. 44 P6
Purwodadi Indon. 68 E8
Puryŏng N. Korea 74 C4
Pusad India 84 C2
Pusan S. Korea 75 C6
Pusatlı Dağı mt. Turkey 85 A1
Pushchino Rus. Fed. 43 H5
Pushemskiy Rus. Fed. 42 J3
Pushkin Rus. Fed. 45 Q7
Pushkino Azer. see Biläsuvar
Pushkinskaya, Gora mt. Rus. Fed. 74 F3
Pushkinskiye Gory Rus. Fed. 45 P8
Pusht-i-Rud reg. Afgh. see Zamīndāvar
Pustoshka Rus. Fed. 42 F4
Pusur r. Bangl. 83 G5
Putahow Lake Canada 121 K3
Putain Indon. 108 D2
Putao Myanmar 70 B1
Puteoli Italy see Pozzuoli
Puthein Myanmar see Bassein
Putian China 77 H3
Puting China see De'an
Puting, Tanjung pt Indon. 68 E7
Putlitz Germany 53 M1
Putna r. Romania 59 L2
Putney U.S.A. 135 I2
Putoi i. H.K. China see Po Toi
Putorana, Gory mts Rus. Fed. 153 E2

▶Putrajaya Malaysia 71 C7
Joint capital (with Kuala Lumpur) of Malaysia.

Putre Chile 142 E7
Putsonderwater S. Africa 100 E5
Puttalam Sri Lanka 84 C4
Puttalam Lagoon Sri Lanka 84 C4
Puttelange-aux-Lacs France 52 G5
Putten Neth. 52 F2
Puttershoek Neth. 52 E3
Puttgarden Germany 47 M3
Putumayo r. Col. 142 D4
also known as Ica (Peru)
Putuo China see Shenjiamen
Puumala Fin. 45 P6
Pu'uwai U.S.A. 127 [inset]
Puvirnituq Canada 122 F1
Puyallup U.S.A. 126 C3
Puyang China 77 G1
Puy de Sancy mt. France 56 F4
Puyehue, Parque Nacional nat. park Chile 144 B6
Puysegur Point N.Z. 113 A8
Puzak, Hāmūn-e marsh Afgh. 89 F4
Puzla Rus. Fed. 42 L3
Pweto Dem. Rep. Congo 99 C4
Pwinbyu Myanmar 70 A2
Pwllheli U.K. 49 C6
Pyal'ma Rus. Fed. 42 G3
Pyalo Myanmar 70 A3
Pyamalaw r. Myanmar 70 A4
Pyandzh Tajik. see Panj
Pyaozero, Ozero l. Rus. Fed. 44 Q3
Pyaozerskiy Rus. Fed. 44 Q4
Pyapali India 84 C3
Pyapon Myanmar 70 A3
Pyasina r. Rus. Fed. 64 J2
Pyatigorsk Rus. Fed. 91 F1
Pyatikhatki Ukr. see P"yatykhatky
P"yatykhatky Ukr. 43 G6
Pyay Myanmar see Pyè
Pychas Rus. Fed. 42 L4
Pyè Myanmar 70 A3
Pye, Mount hill N.Z. 113 B8
Pyetrykaw Belarus 43 F5
Pygmalion Point India 71 A6
Pyhäjoki Fin. 44 N4
Pyhäjoki r. Fin. 44 N4
Pyhäntä Fin. 44 O4
Pyhäsalmi Fin. 44 N5
Pyhäselkä l. Fin. 44 P5
Pyi Myanmar see Pyè
Pyin Myanmar see Pyè
Pyingaing Myanmar 70 A2
Pyinmana Myanmar 70 B3
Pyin-U-Lwin Myanmar 70 B2
Pyle U.K. 49 D7
Pyl'karamo Rus. Fed. 64 J3
Pylos Greece 59 I6
Pymatuning Reservoir U.S.A. 134 E3
Pyŏktong N. Korea 74 B4
P'yŏnggang N. Korea 75 B5
P'yŏnghae S. Korea 75 C5
P'yŏngsong N. Korea 75 B5
P'yŏngt'aek S. Korea 75 B5

▶P'yŏngyang N. Korea 75 B5
Capital of North Korea.

Pyramid Hill Australia 112 B6
Pyramid Lake U.S.A. 128 D1
Pyramid Peak U.S.A. 129 J1
Pyramid Range mts U.S.A. 128 D2
Pyramids of Giza tourist site Egypt 90 C5
Pyrenees mts Europe 57 H2
Pyrénées mts Europe see Pyrenees
Pyrénées, Parc National des nat. park France/Spain 56 D5
Pyrgos Greece 59 I6
Pyryatyn Ukr. 43 G6
Pyrzyce Poland 47 O4
Pyshchug Rus. Fed. 42 J4
Pytalovo Rus. Fed. 45 O8
Pyxaria mt. Greece 59 J5

Q

Qaa Lebanon 85 C2
Qaanaaq Greenland see Thule
Qabātiya West Bank 85 B3
Qabnag China 76 B2
Qabqa China see Gonghe
Qacentina Alg. see Constantine
Qacha's Nek Lesotho 101 I6
Qādes Afgh. 89 F3
Qādisīyah, Sadd dam Iraq 91 F4
Qadisiyah Dam Iraq see Qādisīyah, Sadd
Qā'emābād Iran 89 F4
Qagan China 73 L3
Qagan Nur China 73 K4
Qagan Nur l. China 74 B3
Qagan Us Nei Mongol China 73 K4
Qagan Us Qinghai China see Dulan
Qagbasêrag China 76 B2
Qagca China 76 C1
Qagcaka China 83 E2
Qagchêng China see Xiangcheng
Qahremānshahr Iran see Kermānshāh
Qaidam He r. China 83 H1
Qaidam Pendi basin China 80 H4
Qainaqangma China 83 G2
Qaisar, Koh-i- mt. Afgh. see Qeyṣār, Kūh-e
Qakar China 82 E1
Qalā Diza Iraq 91 G3
Qalagai Afgh. 89 H3
Qala-i-Kang Afgh. see Kang
Qal'aikhum Tajik. 89 H2
Qala Jamal Afgh. 89 F3
Qalansīyah Yemen 87 H7
Qala Shinia Takht Afgh. 89 G3
Qalāt Afgh. see Kalāt
Qal'at al Ḥiṣn Syria 85 C2
Qal'at al Mu'aẓẓam Saudi Arabia 90 E6
Qal'at Bīshah Saudi Arabia 86 F5
Qal'at Muqaybirah, Jabal mt. Syria 85 D2
Qal'eh Dāgh mt. Iran 88 B2
Qal'eh Tirpul Afgh. 89 F3
Qal'eh-ye Bost Afgh. 89 G4
Qal'eh-ye Now Afgh. 89 F3
Qal'eh-ye Shūrak well Iran 88 E3
Qalhāt Oman 88 E6
Qalīb Bāqūr well Iraq 91 G5
Qalluviartuuq, Lac l. Canada 122 G2
Qalyūb Egypt see Qalyūb
Qalyūb Egypt 90 C5
Qamalung China 76 C1
Qamanirjuaq Lake Canada 121 M2
Qamanittuaq Canada see Baker Lake
Qamashi Uzbek. 89 G2
Qamata S. Africa 101 H6
Qamdo China 76 C2
Qandahar Afgh. see Kandahār
Qandarānbāshī, Kūh-e mt. Iran 88 B2
Qandyaghash Kazakh. see Kandyagash
Qangzê China 82 D3
Qapan Iran 88 D2
Qapshagay Kazakh. see Kapchagay
Qapshagay Bögeni resr Kazakh. see Kapchagayskoye Vodokhranilishche
Qapugtang China see Zadoi
Qaqortoq Greenland 119 N3
Qara Āghach r. Iran see Mand, Rūd-e
Qarabutaq Kazakh. see Karabutak
Qaraçala Azer. 88 C2
Qara Ertis r. China/Kazakh. see Ertix He
Qaraghandy Kazakh. see Karaganda
Qaraghayly Kazakh. see Karagayly
Qārah Egypt 90 B5
Qārah Saudi Arabia 91 F5
Qarah Bāgh Afgh. 89 H3
Qarak China 89 J2
Qaraqum des. Turkm. see Garagum
Qaraqum des. Turkm. see Karakum Desert
Qara Quzi Iran 88 D2
Qarasu Azer. 91 H2
Qara Ṣū Chāy r. Syria/Turkey see Karasu
Qara Tarai mt. Afgh. 89 G3
Qarataū Kazakh. see Karatau
Qarataū Zhotasy mts Kazakh. see Karatau, Khrebet
Qara Tikan Iran 88 C2
Qarazhal Kazakh. see Karazhal
Qardho Somalia 98 E3
Qareh Chāy r. Iran 88 C3
Qareh Sū r. Iran 88 B2
Qareh Tekān Iran 89 F2
Qarhan China 83 H1
Qarkilik China see Ruoqiang
Qarn al Kabsh, Jabal mt. Egypt 90 D5
Qarnayn i. U.A.E. 88 D5
Qarnein i. U.A.E. see Qarnayn
Qarn el Kabsh, Gebel mt. Egypt see Qarn al Kabsh, Jabal
Qarnobcho'l cho'li plain Uzbek. 89 G2
Qarokŭl l. Tajik. 89 I2
Qarqan China see Qiemo
Qarqan He r. China 80 G4
Qarqaraly Kazakh. see Karkaralinsk
Qarshi Uzbek. 89 G2
Qarshi cho'li plain Uzbek. 89 G2
Qarshi Chŭli plain Uzbek. see Qarshi cho'li
Qartaba Lebanon 85 B2
Qārūh, Jazīrat i. Kuwait 88 C4
Qārūn, Birkat l. Egypt 90 C5
Qârûn, Birket l. Egypt see Qārūn, Birkat
Qaryat al Gharab Iraq 91 G5
Qaryat al Ulyā Saudi Arabia 88 B5
Qasa Murg mts Afgh. 89 F3
Qāsemābād Iran 88 E3
Qash Qai reg. Iran 88 C4
Qasigiannguit Greenland 119 M3
Qaṣr al Azraq Jordan 85 C4
Qaṣr al Farāfirah Egypt 90 B6
Qaṣr al Kharānah Jordan 85 C4
Qaṣr al Khubbāz Iraq 91 F4
Qaṣr 'Amrah tourist site Jordan 85 C4
Qaṣr Burqu' tourist site Jordan 85 C3
Qaṣr-e Shīrīn Iran 88 B3
Qaṣr Farâfra Egypt see Qaṣr al Farāfirah
Qassimiut Greenland 119 N3
Qaṭanā Syria 85 C3
Qatar country Asia 88 C5
Qaṭmah Syria 85 C1
Qaṭrūyeh Iran 88 D4
Qaṭṭāfī, Wādī al watercourse Jordan 85 C4
Qaṭṭâra, Râs esc. Egypt see Qaṭṭārah, Ra's
Qattara Depression Egypt 90 B5
Qaṭṭārah, Ra's esc. Egypt 90 B5
Qaṭṭīnah, Buḥayrat resr Syria 85 C2
Qax Azer. 91 G2
Qāyen Iran 88 E3
Qaynar Kazakh. see Kaynar
Qayṣār Afgh. 89 G3
Qaysīyah, Qā' al imp. l. Jordan 85 C4
Qaysūm, Juzur is Egypt 90 D6
Qayyārah Iraq 91 F4
Qazangödağ mt. Armenia/Azer. 91 G3
Qazaq Shyghanaghy b. Kazakh. see Kazakhskiy Zaliv
Qazaqstan country Asia see Kazakhstan
Qazax Azer. 86 G1
Qazi Ahmad Pak. 89 H5
Qazımämmäd Azer. 91 H2
Qazvīn Iran 88 C2
Qeisûm, Gezâ'ir is Egypt see Qaysūm, Juzur
Qeisum Islands Egypt see Qaysūm, Juzur
Qena Egypt see Qinā
Qeqertarsuaq Greenland 119 M3
Qeqertarsuaq i. Greenland 119 M3
Qeqertarsuatsiaat Greenland 119 M3
Qeqertarsuup Tunua b. Greenland 119 M3
Qeshm Iran 88 E5
Qeydār Iran 88 C2
Qeydū Iran 88 C3
Qeyṣār, Kūh-e mt. Afgh. 89 G3
Qezel Owzan, Rūdkhāneh-ye r. Iran 88 C2
Qeẓi'ot Israel 85 B4
Qian'an China 74 B3
Qian Gorlos China see Qianguozhen
Qianguozhen China 74 B3
Qianjiang Chongqing China 77 F2
Qianjiang Hubei China 77 G2
Qianjin Heilong. China 74 D3
Qianjin Jilin China 74 C3
Qianning China 76 D2
Qianqihao China 74 A3
Qian Shan mts China 74 A4
Qianxi China 76 E3
Qiaocheng China see Bozhou
Qiaojia China 76 D3
Qiaoshan China see Huangling
Qiaowa China see Muli
Qiaowan China 80 I3
Qiaozhuang China see Qingchuan
Qibā' Saudi Arabia 91 G6
Qibing S. Africa 101 H5
Qichun China 77 G2
Qidong China 77 G3
Qidukou China 76 B1
Qiemo China 80 G4
Qijiang China 76 E2
Qijiaojing China 80 H3
Qikiqtarjuaq Canada 119 L3
Qila Ladgasht Pak. 89 F5
Qila Saifullah Pak. 89 H4
Qilian China 80 J4
Qilian Shan mts China 80 I4
Qillak i. Greenland 119 O3
Qiman Tag mts China 83 G1
Qimusseriarsuaq b. Greenland 119 L2
Qinā Egypt 86 D4
Qin'an China 76 E1
Qincheng China see Nanfeng
Qing'an China 74 B3
Qingchuan China 76 E1
Qingdao China 73 M5
Qinggang China 74 B3
Qinggil China see Qinghe
Qinghai prov. China 76 B1
Qinghai Hu salt l. China 80 J4
Qinghai Nanshan mts China 80 I4
Qinghe Heilong. China 74 C3
Qinghe Xinjiang China 80 H2
Qinghecheng China 74 B4
Qinghua China see Bo'ai
Qingjiang Jiangsu China see Huai'an
Qingjiang Jiangxi China see Zhangshu
Qing Jiang r. China 77 F2
Qingkou China see Ganyu
Qinglan China 77 F5
Qingliu China 77 H3
Qinglung China 83 G3
Qingpu China 77 I2
Qingquan China see Xishui
Qingshan China see Wudalianchi
Qingshui China 76 E1
Qingshuihe Nei Mongol China 73 K5
Qingshuihe Qinghai China 76 C1
Qingtian China 77 I2
Qingyang Anhui China 77 H2
Qingyang Gansu China 76 E1
Qingyang Jiangsu China see Sihong
Qingyuan Gansu China see Weiyuan
Qingyuan Guangdong China 77 G4
Qingyuan Guangxi China see Yizhou
Qingyuan Liaoning China 74 B4
Qingyuan Zhejiang China 77 H3
Qingzang Gaoyuan plat. China see Tibet, Plateau of
Qingzhen China 76 E3
Qinhuangdao China 73 L5
Qinjiang China see Shicheng
Qin Ling mts China 76 E1
Qinshui China 77 G1
Qinting China see Lianhua
Qinzhou China 77 F4
Qionghai China 77 F5
Qiongjiexue China see Qonggyai
Qionglai China 76 D2
Qionglai Shan mts China 76 D2
Qiongxi China see Hongyuan
Qiongzhong China 77 F5
Qiongzhou Haixia strait China see Hainan Strait
Qiqian China 74 A1
Qiqihar China 74 A3
Qīr Iran 88 D4
Qira China 82 E1
Qirâîya, Wâdi watercourse Egypt see Qurayyah, Wādī
Qiryat Israel 85 B3
Qiryat Shemona Israel 85 B3
Qishan China 76 E1
Qishon r. Israel 85 B3
Qitab ash Shāmah vol. crater Saudi Arabia 85 C4
Qitaihe China 74 C3
Qiubei China 76 E3
Qiujin China 77 G2
Qixing He r. China 74 D3
Qiyang China 77 F3
Qizhou Liedao i. China 77 F5
Qızılağac Körfäzi b. Azer. 88 C2
Qizil-Art, Aghbai pass Kyrg./Tajik. see Kyzylart Pass
Qizilqum des. Kazakh./Uzbek. see Kyzylkum Desert
Qizilrabot Tajik. 89 I2
Qogir Feng mt. China/Pakistan see K2
Qog Qi China see Sain Us
Qom Iran 88 C3
Qomdo China see Qumdo
Qomīsheh Iran see Shahrezā
Qomolangma Feng mt. China/Nepal see Everest, Mount
Qomsheh Iran see Shahrezā
Qonāq, Kūh-e hill Iran 88 C3
Qondūz Afgh. see Kunduz
Qonggyai China 83 G3
Qo'ng'irot Uzbek. 80 A3
Qong Muztag mt. China 83 E2
Qongrat Uzbek. see Qo'ng'irot
Qoornoq Greenland 119 M3
Qoqek China see Tacheng
Qo'qon Uzbek. 80 D3
Qorakŏ'l Uzbek. 89 F2
Qorghalzhyn Kazakh. see Korgalzhyn
Qornet es Saouda mt. Lebanon 85 C2
Qorovulbozor Uzbek. 89 G2
Qorowulbozor Uzbek. see Qorovulbozor
Qorveh Iran 88 B3
Qo'shrabot Uzbek. 89 G1
Qosh Tepe Iraq 91 F3
Qostanay Kazakh. see Kostanay
Qoubaiyat Lebanon 85 C2
Qowowuyag mt. China/Nepal see Cho Oyu
Qozideh Tajik. 89 H2
Quabbin Reservoir U.S.A. 135 I2
Quadra Island Canada 120 E5
Quadros, Lago dos l. Brazil 145 A5
Quaidabad Pak. 89 H3
Quail Mountains U.S.A. 128 E4
Quairading Australia 109 B8
Quakenbrück Germany 53 H2
Quakertown U.S.A. 135 H3
Quambatook Australia 112 A5
Quambone Australia 112 C3
Quamby Australia 110 C4
Quanah U.S.A. 131 D5
Quanbao Shan mt. China 77 F1
Quan Dao Hoang Sa is S. China Sea see Paracel Islands
Quân Đao Nam Du i. Vietnam 71 D5
Quan Dao Truong Sa is S. China Sea see Spratly Islands
Quang Ha Vietnam 70 D2
Quang Ngai Vietnam 70 E4
Quang Tri Vietnam 70 D3
Quan Hoa Vietnam 70 D2
Quan Long Vietnam see Ca Mau
Quannan China 77 G3
Quan Phu Quoc i. Vietnam see Phu Quôc, Đao
Quantock Hills U.K. 49 D7
Quanwan H.K. China see Tsuen Wan
Quanzhou Fujian China 77 H3
Quanzhou Guangxi China 77 F3
Qu'Appelle r. Canada 121 K5
Quaqtaq Canada 119 L3
Quarry Bay H.K. China 77 [inset]
Quartu Sant'Elena Sardinia Italy 58 C5
Quartzite Mountain U.S.A. 128 E3
Quartzsite U.S.A. 129 F5
Quba Azer. 91 H2
Quchan Iran 88 E2
Qudaym Syria 85 D2
Queanbeyan Australia 112 D5

▶Québec Canada 123 H5
Capital of Québec.

Québec prov. Canada 135 I1
Quebra Anzol r. Brazil 145 B2
Quedlinburg Germany 53 L3
Queen Adelaide Islands Chile see La Reina Adelaida, Archipiélago de
Queen Anne U.S.A. 135 H4
Queen Bess, Mount Canada 126 B2
Queen Charlotte Canada 120 C4
Queen Charlotte Islands Canada 120 C4
Queen Charlotte Sound sea chan. Canada 120 D5
Queen Charlotte Strait Canada 120 E5
Queen Creek U.S.A. 129 H5

Reisjärvi Fin. 44 N5
Reitz S. Africa 101 I4
Rekapalle India 84 D2
Reken Germany 52 H3
Reliance Canada 121 I2
Relizane Alg. 57 G6
Rellano Mex. 131 B7
Rellingen Germany 53 J1
Remagen Germany 53 H4
Remarkable, Mount hill Australia 111 B7
Remedios Cuba 133 E8
Remeshk Iran 88 E5
Remhoogte Pass Namibia 100 C2
Remi France see Reims
Remmel Mountain U.S.A. 126 C2
Remscheid Germany 53 H3
Rena Norway 45 G6
Renaix Belgium see Ronse
Renam Myanmar 76 C3
Renapur India 84 C2
Rendsburg Germany 47 L3
René-Levasseur, Île i. Canada 123 H4
Renews Canada 123 L5
Renfrew Canada 135 G1
Renfrew U.K. 50 E5
Rengali Reservoir India 83 F5
Rengat Indon. 68 C7
Rengo Chile 144 B4
Ren He r. China 77 F1
Renheji China 77 G2
Renhua China 77 G3
Reni Ukr. 59 M2
Renick U.S.A. 134 E5
Renland reg. Greenland see Tuttut Nunaat
Rennell i. Solomon Is 107 G3
Rennerod Germany 53 I4
Rennes France 56 D2
Rennick Glacier Antarctica 152 H2
Rennie Canada 121 M5
Reno r. Italy 58 E2
Reno U.S.A. 128 D2
Renovo U.S.A. 135 G3
Rensselaer U.S.A. 134 B3
Renswoude Neth. 52 F2
Renton U.S.A. 126 C3
Réo Burkina 96 C3
Reo Indon. 108 C2
Repalle India 84 D2
Repetek Turkm. 89 F2
Repetek Döwlet Gorugy nature res. Turkm. 89 F2
Repolka Rus. Fed. 45 P7
Republic U.S.A. 126 D2
Republican r. U.S.A. 130 D4

▶Republic of South Africa country Africa 100 F5
5th most populous country in Africa.

Repulse Bay b. Australia 110 E4
Repulse Bay Canada 119 J3
Requena Peru 142 D5
Requena Spain 57 F4
Reşadiye Turkey 90 E2
Reserva Brazil 145 A4
Reserve U.S.A. 129 I5
Reshi China 77 F2
Reshteh-ye Alborz mts Iran see Elburz Mountains
Resistencia Arg. 144 E3
Reşiţa Romania 59 I2
Resolute Canada 119 I2
Resolute Bay Nunavut Canada see Resolute
Resolution Island Canada 119 L3
Resolution Island N.Z. 113 A7
Resplendor Brazil 145 C2
Restigouche r. Canada 123 I5
Resülayn Turkey see Ceylanpınar
Retalhuleu Guat. 136 F6
Retezat, Parcul Naţional nat. park Romania 59 J2
Retford U.K. 48 G5
Rethel France 52 E5
Rethem (Aller) Germany 53 J2
Réthimnon Greece see Rethymno
Rethymno Greece 59 K7
Retreat Australia 110 C5
Reuden Germany 53 M2

▶Réunion terr. Indian Ocean 149 L7
French Overseas Department.

Reus Spain 57 G3
Reusam, Pulau i. Indon. 71 B7
Reutlingen Germany 47 L6
Reval Estonia see Tallinn
Revda Rus. Fed. 44 S3
Revel Estonia see Tallinn
Revel France 56 F5
Revelstoke Canada 120 G5
Revigny-sur-Ornain France 52 E6
Revillagigedo, Islas is Mex. 136 B5
Revillagigedo Island U.S.A. 120 D4
Revin France 52 E5
Revivim Israel 85 B4
Revolyutsii, Pik mt. Tajik. see Revolyutsiya, Qullai
Revolyutsiya, Qullai mt. Tajik. 89 I2
Rewa India 82 E4
Rewari India 82 D3
Rexburg U.S.A. 126 F4
Rexton Canada 123 I5
Reyes, Point U.S.A. 128 B2
Reyhanlı Turkey 85 C1
Reykir Iceland 44 [inset]
Reykjanes Ridge sea feature N. Atlantic Ocean 148 F2
Reykjanestá pt Iceland 44 [inset]

▶Reykjavík Iceland 44 [inset]
Capital of Iceland.

Reyneke, Ostrov i. Rus. Fed. 74 E1
Reynoldsburg U.S.A. 134 D4
Reynolds Range mts Australia 108 F5
Reynosa Mex. 131 D7
Rezā Iran 88 D3
Reẓā'īyeh Iran see Urmia
Reẓā'īyeh, Daryācheh-ye salt l. Iran see Urmia, Lake
Rēzekne Latvia 45 O8
Rezvān Iran 89 F4
Reẕvāndeh Iran see Reẕvānshahr
Reẕvānshahr Iran 88 C2
Rhaeader Gwy U.K. see Rhayader
Rhayader U.K. 49 D6
Rheda-Wiedenbrück Germany 53 I3
Rhede Germany 52 G3
Rhegium Italy see Reggio di Calabria
Rheims France see Reims
Rhein r. Germany 53 G3 see Rhine
Rheine Germany 53 H2
Rheinland-Pfalz land Germany 53 H5
Rheinsberg Germany 53 M1
Rheinstetten Germany 53 I6
Rhemilès well Alg. 96 C2
Rhin r. Germany 53 I6 see Rhine
Rhine r. Germany 53 G3
also spelt Rhein (Germany) or Rhin (France)
Rhinebeck U.S.A. 135 I3
Rhinelander U.S.A. 130 F2
Rhineland-Palatinate land Germany see Rheinland-Pfalz
Rhinkanal canal Germany 53 M2
Rhinow Germany 53 M2
Rhiwabon U.K. see Ruabon
Rho Italy 58 C2
Rhode Island state U.S.A. 135 J3
Rhodes Greece 59 M6
Rhodes i. Greece 59 M6
Rhodesia country Africa see Zimbabwe
Rhodes Peak U.S.A. 126 E3
Rhodope Mountains Bulg./Greece 59 J4
Rhodus i. Greece see Rhodes
Rhône r. France/Switz. 56 G5
Rhum i. U.K. see Rum
Rhuthun U.K. see Ruthin
Rhydaman U.K. see Ammanford
Rhyl U.K. 48 D5
Riachão Brazil 143 I5
Riacho Brazil 145 C2
Riacho de Santana Brazil 145 C1
Riacho dos Machados Brazil 145 C1
Rialma Brazil 145 A1
Rialto U.S.A. 128 E4
Riasi India 82 C2
Riau, Kepulauan is Indon. 68 C6
Ribadeo Spain 57 C2
Ribadesella Spain 57 D2
Ribas do Rio Pardo Brazil 144 F2
Ribat Afgh. 89 H2
Ribat-i-Shur waterhole Iran 88 E3
Ribáuè Moz. 99 D5
Ribble r. U.K. 48 E5
Ribblesdale valley U.K. 48 E4
Ribe Denmark 45 F9
Ribécourt-Dreslincourt France 52 C5
Ribeira r. Brazil 145 B4
Ribeirão Preto Brazil 145 B3
Ribemont France 52 D5
Ribérac France 56 E4
Riberalta Bol. 142 E6
Rîbniţa Moldova 43 F7
Ribnitz-Damgarten Germany 47 N3
Říčany Czech Rep. 47 O6
Rice U.S.A. 135 F5
Rice Lake Canada 135 F1
Richards Bay S. Africa 101 K5
Richards Inlet Antarctica 152 H1
Richards Island Canada 118 E3
Richardson r. Canada 121 I3
Richardson U.S.A. 131 D5
Richardson Island Canada 120 G1
Richardson Lakes U.S.A. 135 J1
Richardson Mountains Canada 118 E3
Richardson Mountains N.Z. 113 B7
Richfield U.S.A. 129 G2
Richfield Springs U.S.A. 135 H2
Richford NY U.S.A. 135 G2
Richford VT U.S.A. 135 I1
Richgrove U.S.A. 128 D4
Richland U.S.A. 126 D3
Richland Center U.S.A. 130 F3
Richmond N.S.W. Australia 112 E4
Richmond Qld Australia 110 C4
Richmond Canada 135 H1
Richmond N.Z. 113 D5
Richmond Kwazulu-Natal S. Africa 101 J5
Richmond N. Cape S. Africa 100 F6
Richmond U.K. 48 F4
Richmond CA U.S.A. 128 B3
Richmond IN U.S.A. 134 C4
Richmond KY U.S.A. 134 C5
Richmond MI U.S.A. 134 D2
Richmond MO U.S.A. 130 E4
Richmond TX U.S.A. 131 E6

▶Richmond VA U.S.A. 135 G5
Capital of Virginia.

Richmond Dale U.S.A. 134 D4
Richmond Hill U.S.A. 133 D6
Richmond Range hills Australia 112 F2
Richtersveld National Park S. Africa 100 C5
Richvale U.S.A. 128 C2
Richwood U.S.A. 134 E4
Rico U.S.A. 129 I3
Ricomagus France see Riom
Riddell Nunataks Antarctica 152 E2
Rideau Lakes Canada 135 G1
Ridge r. Canada 122 D4
Ridgecrest U.S.A. 128 E4
Ridge Farm U.S.A. 134 B4
Ridgeland MS U.S.A. 131 F5
Ridgeland SC U.S.A. 133 D5
Ridgetop U.S.A. 134 B5
Ridgetown Canada 134 E2
Ridgeway OH U.S.A. 134 D3
Ridgeway VA U.S.A. 134 F5
Ridgway CO U.S.A. 129 J2
Ridgway PA U.S.A. 135 F3
Riding Mountain National Park Canada 121 K5
Riecito Venez. 142 E1
Riemst Belgium 52 F4
Riesa Germany 53 N3
Riesco, Isla i. Chile 144 B8
Riet watercourse S. Africa 100 E6
Rietavas Lith. 45 L9
Rietfontein S. Africa 100 E4
Rieti Italy 58 E3
Rifā'ī, Tall mt. Jordan/Syria 85 C3
Rifeng China see Lichuan
Rifle U.S.A. 129 J2
Rifstangi pt Iceland 44 [inset]
Rift Valley Lakes National Park Eth. see Abijatta-Shalla National Park

▶Rīga Latvia 45 N8
Capital of Latvia.

Riga, Gulf of Estonia/Latvia 45 M8
Rigain Pünco l. China 83 F2
Rīgān Iran 88 E4
Rīgas jūras līcis b. Estonia/Latvia see Riga, Gulf of
Rigby U.S.A. 126 F4
Rīgestān reg. Afgh. see Registān
Rigolet Canada 123 K3
Rigside U.K. 50 F5
Riia laht b. Estonia/Latvia see Riga, Gulf of
Riihimäki Fin. 45 N6
Riiser-Larsen Ice Shelf Antarctica 152 B2
Riito Mex. 129 F5
Rijau Nigeria 96 D3
Rijeka Croatia 58 F2
Rikā, Wādī ar watercourse Saudi Arabia 88 B6
Rikitgaib Indon. 71 B6
Rikor India 76 B2
Rikuchū-kaigan Kokuritsu-kōen nat. park Japan 75 F5
Rikuzen-takata Japan 75 F5
Rila mts Bulg. 59 J3
Rila China 83 F3
Riley U.S.A. 126 D4
Rileyville U.S.A. 135 F4
Rillieux-la-Pape France 56 G4
Rillito U.S.A. 129 H5
Rimah, Wādī al watercourse Saudi Arabia 86 F4
Rimavská Sobota Slovakia 47 R6
Rimbey Canada 120 H4
Rimini Italy 58 E2
Rîmnicu Sărat Romania see Râmnicu Sărat
Rîmnicu Vîlcea Romania see Râmnicu Vâlcea
Rimouski Canada 123 H4
Rimpar Germany 53 J5
Rimsdale, Loch l. U.K. 50 E2
Rinbung China 83 G3
Rincão Brazil 145 A3
Rindal Norway 44 F5
Ringarooma Bay Australia 111 [inset]
Ringas India 82 C4
Ringe Germany 52 G2
Ringebu Norway 45 G6
Ringhkung Myanmar 70 B1
Ringkøbing Denmark 45 F8
Ringsend U.K. 51 F2
Ringsted Denmark 45 G9
Ringtor China 83 E3
Ringvassøya i. Norway 44 K2
Ringwood Australia 112 B6
Ringwood U.K. 49 F8
Rinjani, Gunung vol. Indon. 68 F8
Rinns Point U.K. 50 C5
Ringênzê China 83 G3
Rinteln Germany 53 J2
Río Abiseo, Parque Nacional nat. park Peru 142 C5
Rio Azul Brazil 145 A4
Riobamba Ecuador 142 C4
Rio Blanco U.S.A. 129 J2
Rio Bonito Brazil 145 C3
Rio Branco Brazil 142 E6
Rio Branco, Parque Nacional do nat. park Brazil 142 F3
Río Bravo, Parque Internacional del nat. park Mex. 131 C6
Rio Brilhante Brazil 144 F2
Rio Casca Brazil 145 C3
Rio Claro Brazil 145 B3
Río Colorado Arg. 144 D5
Río Cuarto Arg. 144 D4
Rio das Pedras Moz. 101 L2
Rio de Contas Brazil 145 C1

▶Rio de Janeiro Brazil 145 C3
Former capital of Brazil. 3rd most populous city in South America.

Rio de Janeiro state Brazil 145 C3

▶Río de la Plata-Paraná r. S. America 144 E4
2nd longest river in South America, and 9th in the world.

Rio Dell U.S.A. 128 A1
Rio do Sul Brazil 145 A4
Río Gallegos Arg. 144 C8
Río Grande Arg. 144 C8
Rio Grande Brazil 144 F4
Río Grande Mex. 131 C8
Rio Grande r. Mex./U.S.A. 127 G5
also known as Río Bravo del Norte
Rio Grande City U.S.A. 131 D7
Rio Grande do Sul state Brazil 145 A5
Rio Grande Rise sea feature S. Atlantic Ocean 148 F8
Ríohacha Col. 142 D1
Río Hondo, Embalse resr Arg. 144 C3
Rioja Peru 142 C5
Río Lagartos Mex. 133 B8
Rio Largo Brazil 143 K5
Riom France 56 F4
Rio Manso, Represa do resr Brazil 143 G6
Río Mulatos Bol. 142 E7
Río Muni reg. Equat. Guinea 96 E4
Río Negro, Embalse del resr Uruguay 144 E4
Rioni r. Georgia 91 F2
Rio Novo Brazil 145 C3
Rio Pardo de Minas Brazil 145 C1
Rio Preto Brazil 145 C3
Rio Preto, Serra do hills Brazil 145 B2
Rio Rancho U.S.A. 127 G6
Río Tigre Ecuador 142 C4
Riou Lake Canada 121 J3
Rio Verde Brazil 145 A2
Rio Verde de Mato Grosso Brazil 143 H7
Rio Vista U.S.A. 128 C2
Ripky Ukr. 43 F6
Ripley England U.K. 48 F4
Ripley England U.K. 49 F5
Ripley NY U.S.A. 134 F2
Ripley OH U.S.A. 134 D4
Ripley WV U.S.A. 134 E4
Ripoll Spain 57 H2
Ripon U.K. 48 F4
Ripon U.S.A. 128 C3
Ripu India 83 G4
Risca U.K. 49 D7
Rishiri-tō i. Japan 74 F3
Rishon LeẔiyyon Israel 85 B4
Rish Pish Iran 89 F5
Rising Sun IN U.S.A. 134 C4
Rising Sun MD U.S.A. 135 G4
Risle r. France 49 H9
Risør Norway 45 F7
Rissa Norway 44 F5
Ristiina Fin. 45 O6
Ristijärvi Fin. 44 P4
Ristikent Rus. Fed. 44 Q2
Risum China 82 D2
Ritchie S. Africa 100 G5
Ritchie's Archipelago is India 71 A4
Ritscher Upland mts Antarctica 152 B2
Ritsem Sweden 44 J3
Ritter, Mount U.S.A. 128 D3
Ritterhude Germany 53 I1
Ritzville U.S.A. 126 D3
Riu, Laem pt Thai. 71 B5
Riva del Garda Italy 58 D2
Rivas Nicaragua 137 G6
Rivera Arg. 144 D5
Rivera Uruguay 144 E4
River Cess Liberia 96 C4
Riverhead U.S.A. 135 I3
Riverhurst Canada 121 J5
Riverina Australia 109 C7
Riverina reg. Australia 112 B5
Riversdale S. Africa 100 E8
Riverside S. Africa 101 I6
Riverside U.S.A. 128 E5
Rivers Inlet Canada 120 E5
Riversleigh Australia 110 B3
Riverton N.Z. 113 B8
Riverton VA U.S.A. 135 F4
Riverton WY U.S.A. 126 F4
Riverview Canada 123 I5
Rivesaltes France 56 F5
Riviera Beach U.S.A. 133 D7
Rivière-du-Loup Canada 123 H5
Rivière-Pentecôte Canada 123 I4
Rivière-Pigou Canada 123 I4
Rivne Ukr. 43 E6
Rivungo Angola 99 C5
Riwaka N.Z. 113 D5
Riwoqê China see Racaka

▶Riyadh Saudi Arabia 86 G5
Capital of Saudi Arabia.

Riyan India 89 I5
Riza well Iran 88 D3
Rize Turkey 91 F2
Rizhao Shandong China see Donggang
Rizhao Shandong China 77 H1
Rizokarpaso Cyprus see Rizokarpason
Rizokarpason Cyprus 85 B2
Rīzū well Iran 88 E3
Rīzū'īyeh Iran 88 E4
Rjukan Norway 45 F7
Rjuvbrokkene mt. Norway 45 E7
Rkîz Mauritania 96 B3
Roa Norway 45 G6
Roachdale U.S.A. 134 B4
Roach Lake U.S.A. 129 F4
Roade U.K. 49 G6
Roads U.S.A. 134 D4

▶Road Town Virgin Is (U.K.) 137 L5
Capital of the British Virgin Islands.

Roan Fell hill U.K. 50 G5
Roan High Knob mt. U.S.A. 132 D4
Roanne France 56 G3
Roanoke IN U.S.A. 134 C3
Roanoke VA U.S.A. 134 F5
Roanoke r. U.S.A. 132 E4
Roanoke Rapids U.S.A. 132 E4
Roan Plateau U.S.A. 129 I2
Roaring Spring U.S.A. 135 F3
Roaringwater Bay Ireland 51 C6
Roatán Hond. 137 G5
Röbäck Sweden 44 L5
Robat r. Afgh. 89 F4
Robāţe Tork Iran 88 C3
Robāţ Karīm Iran 88 C3
Robāt-Sang Iran 88 E3
Robb Canada 120 G4
Robbins Island Australia 111 [inset]
Robbinsville U.S.A. 133 D5
Robe Australia 111 B8
Robe r. Australia 108 A5
Robe r. Ireland 51 C4
Röbel Germany 53 M1
Robert-Bourassa, Réservoir resr Canada 122 F3
Robert Glacier Antarctica 152 D2
Robert Lee U.S.A. 131 C6
Roberts U.S.A. 126 E4
Roberts, Mount Australia 112 F2
Robertsburg U.S.A. 134 E4
Roberts Butte mt. Antarctica 152 H2
Roberts Creek Mountain U.S.A. 128 E2
Robertsfors Sweden 44 L4
Robertsganj India 83 E4
Robertson S. Africa 100 D7
Robertson, Lac l. Canada 123 K4
Robertson Bay Antarctica 152 H2
Robertson Island Antarctica 152 A2
Robertson Range hills Australia 109 C5
Robertsport Liberia 96 B4
Roberval Canada 123 G4
Robhanais, Rubha hd U.K. see Butt of Lewis
Robin Hood's Bay U.K. 48 G4
Robin's Nest hill H.K. China 77 [inset]
Robinson Canada 120 C2
Robinson U.S.A. 134 B4
Robinson Range hills Australia 109 B6
Robinson River Australia 110 B3
Robles Pass U.S.A. 129 H5
Roblin Canada 121 K5
Robsart Canada 121 I5
Robson, Mount Canada 120 G4
Robstown U.S.A. 131 D7
Roby U.S.A. 131 C5
Roçadas Angola see Xangongo
Rocca Busambra mt. Sicily Italy 58 E6
Rocha Uruguay 144 F4
Rochdale U.K. 48 E5
Rochechouart France 56 E4
Rochefort Belgium 52 F4
Rochefort France 56 D4
Rochefort, Lac l. Canada 123 G2
Rochegda Rus. Fed. 42 I3
Rochester Australia 112 B6
Rochester U.K. 49 H7
Rochester IN U.S.A. 134 B3
Rochester MN U.S.A. 130 E2
Rochester NH U.S.A. 135 J2
Rochester NY U.S.A. 135 G2
Rochford U.K. 49 H7
Rochlitz Germany 53 M3
Roc'h Trévezel hill France 56 C2
Rock r. Canada 120 E2
Rockall i. N. Atlantic Ocean 40 D4
Rockall Bank sea feature N. Atlantic Ocean 148 G2
Rock Creek Canada 120 B1
Rock Creek U.S.A. 134 E3
Rock Creek r. U.S.A. 126 G2
Rockdale U.S.A. 131 D6
Rockefeller Plateau Antarctica 152 J1
Rockford AL U.S.A. 133 C5
Rockford IL U.S.A. 130 F3
Rockford MI U.S.A. 134 C2
Rockglen Canada 121 J5
Rockhampton Australia 110 E4
Rockhampton Downs Australia 108 F4
Rock Hill U.S.A. 133 D5
Rockingham Australia 109 A8
Rockingham U.S.A. 133 E5
Rockingham Bay Australia 110 D3
Rockinghorse Lake Canada 121 H1
Rock Island Canada 135 I1
Rock Island U.S.A. 130 F3
Rocklake U.S.A. 130 D1
Rockland MA U.S.A. 135 J2
Rockland ME U.S.A. 132 G2
Rocknest Lake Canada 120 H1
Rockport IN U.S.A. 134 B5
Rockport TX U.S.A. 131 D7
Rock Rapids U.S.A. 130 D3
Rock River U.S.A. 126 G4
Rock Sound Bahamas 133 E7
Rock Springs MT U.S.A. 126 G3
Rocksprings U.S.A. 131 C6
Rock Springs WY U.S.A. 126 F4
Rockstone Guyana 143 G2
Rockville CT U.S.A. 135 I3
Rockville IN U.S.A. 134 B4
Rockville MD U.S.A. 135 G4
Rockwell City U.S.A. 130 E3
Rockwood MI U.S.A. 134 D2
Rockwood PA U.S.A. 134 F4
Rockyford Canada 120 H5
Rocky Harbour Canada 123 K4
Rocky Hill U.S.A. 134 D4
Rocky Island Lake Canada 122 E5
Rocky Lane Canada 120 G3
Rocky Mount U.S.A. 134 F5
Rocky Mountain House Canada 120 H4
Rocky Mountain National Park U.S.A. 126 G4
Rocky Mountains Canada/U.S.A. 124 F3
Rocourt-St-Martin France 52 D5
Rocroi France 52 E5
Rodberg Norway 45 F6
Rødbyhavn Denmark 45 G9
Roddickton Canada 123 L4
Rodeio Brazil 145 A4
Rodel U.K. 50 C3
Roden Neth. 52 G1
Rödental Germany 53 L4
Rodeo Arg. 144 C4
Rodeo Mex. 131 B7
Rodeo U.S.A. 127 F7
Rodez France 56 F4
Rodhos i. Greece see Rhodes
Rodi i. Greece see Rhodes
Roding Germany 53 M5
Rodney, Cape U.S.A. 118 B3
Rodniki Rus. Fed. 42 I4
Rodolfo Sanchez Toboada Mex. 127 D7
Rodopi Planina mts Bulg./Greece see Rhodope Mountains
Rodos Greece see Rhodes
Rodos i. Greece see Rhodes
Rodosto Turkey see Tekirdağ
Rodrigues Island Mauritius 149 M7
Roe r. U.K. 51 F2
Roebourne Australia 108 B5
Roebuck Bay Australia 108 C4
Roedtan S. Africa 101 I3
Roe Plains Australia 109 D7
Roermond Neth. 52 F3
Roeselare Belgium 52 D4
Roes Welcome Sound sea chan. Canada 119 J3
Rogachev Belarus see Rahachow
Rogätz Germany 53 L2
Rogers U.S.A. 131 E4
Rogers, Mount U.S.A. 134 E5
Rogers City U.S.A. 134 D1
Rogers Lake U.S.A. 128 E4
Rogerson U.S.A. 126 E4
Rogersville U.S.A. 134 D5
Roggan r. Canada 122 F3
Roggan, Lac l. Canada 122 F3
Roggeveen Basin sea feature S. Pacific Ocean 151 O8
Roggeveld plat. S. Africa 100 E7
Roggeveldberge esc. S. Africa 100 E7
Roghadal U.K. see Rodel
Rognan Norway 44 I3
Rögnitz r. Germany 53 K1
Rogue r. U.S.A. 126 B4
Roha India 84 B2
Rohnert Park U.S.A. 128 B2
Rohrbach in Oberösterreich Austria 47 N6
Rohrbach-lès-Bitche France 53 H5
Rohri Sangar Pak. 89 H5
Rohtak India 82 D3
Roi Et Thai. 70 C3
Roi Georges, Îles du is Fr. Polynesia 151 K6
Rois-Bheinn hill U.K. 50 D4
Roisel France 52 D5
Roja Latvia 45 M8
Rojas Arg. 144 D4
Rokeby Australia 110 C2
Rokeby National Park Australia 110 C2
Rokiškis Lith. 45 N9
Roknäs Sweden 44 L4
Rokytne Ukr. 43 E6
Rolagang China 83 G2
Rola Kangri mt. China 83 G2
Rolândia Brazil 145 A3
Rolim de Moura Brazil 142 F6
Roll AZ U.S.A. 129 G5
Roll IN U.S.A. 134 C3
Rolla MO U.S.A. 130 F4
Rolla ND U.S.A. 130 D1
Rollag Norway 45 F6
Rolleston Australia 110 E5
Rolleville Bahamas 133 F8
Rolling Fork U.S.A. 131 F5
Rollins U.S.A. 126 E3
Roma Australia 111 E5
Roma Italy see Rome
Roma Lesotho 101 H5
Roma Sweden 45 K8
Romain, Cape U.S.A. 133 E5
Romaine r. Canada 123 J4
Roman Romania 59 L1
Română, Câmpia plain Romania 59 J2
Romanche Gap sea feature S. Atlantic Ocean 148 G6
Romanet, Lac l. Canada 123 I2
Romang, Pulau i. Indon. 108 D1
Romania country Europe 59 K2
Roman-Kosh mt. Ukr. 90 D1
Romano, Cape U.S.A. 133 D7
Romanovka Rus. Fed. 73 K2
Romans-sur-Isère France 56 G4
Romanzof, Cape U.S.A. 118 B3
Rombas France 52 G5
Romblon Phil. 69 G4

▶Rome Italy 58 E4
Capital of Italy.

Rome GA U.S.A. 133 C5
Rome ME U.S.A. 135 K1
Rome NY U.S.A. 135 H2
Rome TN U.S.A. 134 B5
Rome City U.S.A. 134 C3
Romeo U.S.A. 134 D2
Romford U.K. 49 H7
Romilly-sur-Seine France 56 F2
Romiton Uzbek. 89 G2
Romney U.S.A. 135 F4
Romney Marsh reg. U.K. 49 H7
Romny Ukr. 43 G6
Rømø i. Denmark 45 F9
Romodanovo Rus. Fed. 43 J5
Romorantin-Lanthenay France 56 E3
Rompin r. Malaysia 71 C7
Romsey U.K. 49 F8
Romulus U.S.A. 134 D2
Ron India 84 B3
Rona i. U.K. 50 D1
Ronas Hill hill U.K. 50 [inset]
Roncador, Serra do hills Brazil 143 H6
Roncador Reef Solomon Is 107 F2
Ronda Spain 57 D5
Ronda, Serranía de mts Spain 57 D5
Rondane Nasjonalpark nat. park Norway 45 F6
Rondon Brazil 144 F2
Rondonópolis Brazil 143 H7
Rondout Reservoir U.S.A. 135 H3
Rongcheng Anhui China see Qingyang
Rongcheng Guangxi China see Rongxian
Rongcheng Hubei China see Jianli
Rong Chu r. China 83 G3
Rongelap atoll Marshall Is 150 H5
Rongjiang Guizhou China 77 F3
Rongjiang Jiangxi China see Nankang
Rongjiawan China see Yueyang
Rongklang Range mts Myanmar 70 A2
Rongmei China see Hefeng
Rongshui China 77 F3
Rongwo China see Tongren
Rongxian China 77 F4
Rongyul China 76 C2
Rongzhag China see Danba
Rōnlap atoll Marshall Is see Rongelap
Rønne Denmark 45 I9
Ronneby Sweden 45 I8
Ronne Entrance strait Antarctica 152 L2
Ronne Ice Shelf Antarctica 152 L1
Ronnenberg Germany 53 J2
Ronse Belgium 52 D4
Roodeschool Neth. 52 G1
Rooke Island P.N.G. see Umboi
Roordahuizum Neth. see Reduzum
Roorkee India 82 D3
Roosendaal Neth. 52 E3
Roosevelt AZ U.S.A. 129 H5
Roosevelt UT U.S.A. 129 I1
Roosevelt, Mount Canada 120 E3
Roosevelt Island Antarctica 152 I1
Root r. Canada 120 F2
Root r. U.S.A. 130 F3
Ropar India see Rupnagar
Roper r. Australia 110 A2
Roper Bar Australia 108 F3
Roquefort France 56 D4
Roraima, Mount Guyana 142 F2
Rori India 82 C3
Rori Indon. 69 J7
Røros Norway 44 G5
Rørvik Norway 44 G4
Rosa, Punta pt Mex. 127 F8
Rosalia U.S.A. 126 D3
Rosamond U.S.A. 128 D4
Rosamond Lake U.S.A. 128 D4
Rosario Arg. 144 D4
Rosário Brazil 143 J4
Rosario Baja California Mex. 127 E7
Rosario Coahuila Mex. 131 C7
Rosario Sinaloa Mex. 136 C4
Rosario Sonora Mex. 127 F8
Rosario Zacatecas Mex. 131 C7
Rosario Venez. 142 D1
Rosário do Sul Brazil 144 F4
Rosário Oeste Brazil 143 G6

Rosarito Baja California Mex. 127 E7
Rosarito Baja California Mex. 128 E5
Rosarito Baja California Sur Mex. 127 F8
Rosarno Italy 58 F5
Roscoff France 56 C2
Roscommon Ireland 51 D4
Roscommon U.S.A. 134 C1
Roscrea Ireland 51 E5
Rose r. Australia 110 A2
Rose, Mount U.S.A. 128 D2
Rose Atoll American Samoa see Rose Island

▶Roseau Dominica 137 L5
Capital of Dominica.

Roseau U.S.A. 130 E1
Roseau r. U.S.A. 130 D1
Roseberth Australia 111 B5
Rose Blanche Canada 123 K5
Rosebud r. Canada 120 H5
Rosebud U.S.A. 126 G3
Roseburg U.S.A. 126 C4
Rose City U.S.A. 134 C1
Rosedale U.S.A. 131 F5
Rosedale Abbey U.K. 48 G4
Roseires Reservoir Sudan 86 D7
Rose Island atoll American Samoa 107 J3
Rosenberg U.S.A. 131 E6
Rosendal Norway 45 E7
Rosendal S. Africa 101 H5
Rosenheim Germany 47 N7
Rose Peak U.S.A. 129 I5
Rose Point Canada 120 D4
Roseto degli Abruzzi Italy 58 F3
Rosetown Canada 121 J5
Rosetta Egypt see Rashīd
Rose Valley Canada 121 K4
Roseville CA U.S.A. 128 C2
Roseville MI U.S.A. 134 D2
Roseville OH U.S.A. 134 D4
Rosewood Australia 112 F1
Roshchino Rus. Fed. 45 P6
Rosh Pinah Namibia 100 C4
Roshtkala Tajik. see Roshtqal'a
Roshtqal'a Tajik. 89 H2
Rosignano Marittimo Italy 58 D3
Roşiori de Vede Romania 59 K2
Roskilde Denmark 45 H9
Roskruge Mountains U.S.A. 129 H5
Roslavl' Rus. Fed. 43 G5
Roslyakovo Rus. Fed. 44 R2
Roslyatino Rus. Fed. 42 J4
Ross N.Z. 113 C6
Ross, Mount hill N.Z. 113 E5
Rossano Italy 58 G5
Rossan Point Ireland 51 D3
Ross Barnett Reservoir U.S.A. 131 F5
Ross Bay Junction Canada 123 I3
Rosscarbery Ireland 51 C6
Ross Dependency reg. Antarctica 152 I2
Rosseau, Lake Canada 134 F1
Rossel Island P.N.G. 110 F1
Ross Ice Shelf Antarctica 152 I1
Rossignol, Lac l. Canada 122 G3
Rössing Namibia 100 B2
Ross Island Antarctica 152 H1
Rossiyskaya Sovetskaya Federativnaya Sotsialisticheskaya Respublika country Asia/Europe see Russian Federation
Rossland Canada 120 G5
Rosslare Ireland 51 F5
Rosslare Harbour Ireland 51 F5
Roßlau Germany 53 M3
Rosso Mauritania 96 B3
Ross-on-Wye U.K. 49 E7
Rossony Belarus see Rasony
Rossosh' Rus. Fed. 43 H6
Ross River Canada 120 C2
Ross Sea Antarctica 152 H1
Roßtal Germany 53 K5
Røssvatnet l. Norway 44 I4
Rossville U.S.A. 134 B3
Roßwein Germany 53 N3
Rosswood Canada 120 D4
Rostāq Afgh. 89 H2
Rostāq Iran 88 D5
Rosthern Canada 121 J4
Rostock Germany 47 N3
Rostov Rus. Fed. 42 H4
Rostov-na-Donu Rus. Fed. 43 H7
Rostov-on-Don Rus. Fed. see Rostov-na-Donu
Rosvik Sweden 44 L4
Roswell U.S.A. 127 G6
Rota i. N. Mariana Is 69 L4
Rot am See Germany 53 K5
Rotch Island Kiribati see Tamana
Rote i. Indon. 108 C2
Rotenburg (Wümme) Germany 53 J1
Roth Germany 53 L5
Rothaargebirge hills Germany 53 I4
Rothbury U.K. 48 F3
Rothenburg ob der Tauber Germany 53 K5
Rother r. U.K. 49 G8
Rothera research station Antarctica 152 L2
Rotherham U.K. 48 F5
Rothes U.K. 50 F3
Rothesay U.K. 50 D5
Rothwell U.K. 49 G6
Roti Indon. 108 C2
Roti i. Indon. see Rote
Roto Australia 112 B4
Rotomagus France see Rouen
Rotomanu N.Z. 113 C6
Rotondo, Monte mt. Corsica France 56 I5
Rotorua N.Z. 113 F4
Rotorua, Lake N.Z. 113 F4
Röttenbach Germany 53 L5
Rottendorf Germany 53 K5
Rottenmann Austria 47 O7
Rotterdam Neth. 52 E3
Rottleberode Germany 53 K3
Rottnest Island Australia 109 A8
Rottumeroog i. Neth. 52 G1
Rottweil Germany 47 L6
Rotuma i. Fiji 107 H3
Rotung India 76 B2
Rötviken Sweden 44 I5
Rötz Germany 53 M5
Roubaix France 52 D4
Rouen France 52 B5
Rough River Lake U.S.A. 134 B5
Roulers Belgium see Roeselare
Roumania country Europe see Romania
Roundeyed Lake Canada 123 H3
Round Hill hill U.K. 48 F4
Round Mountain Australia 112 F3
Round Rock AZ U.S.A. 129 I3
Round Rock TX U.S.A. 131 D6
Roundup U.S.A. 126 F3
Rousay i. U.K. 50 F1
Rouses Point U.S.A. 135 I1
Rouxville S. Africa 101 H6
Rouyn-Noranda Canada 122 F4
Rovaniemi Fin. 44 N3
Roven'ki Rus. Fed. 43 H6
Rovereto Italy 58 D2
Rôviêng Tbong Cambodia 71 D4
Rovigo Italy 58 D2
Rovinj Croatia 58 E2
Rovno Ukr. see Rivne
Rovnoye Rus. Fed. 43 J6
Rovuma r. Moz./Tanz. see Ruvuma
Rowena Australia 112 D2
Rowley Island Canada 119 K3
Rowley Shoals sea feature Australia 108 B4
Równe Ukr. see Rivne
Roxas Mindoro Phil. 69 G4
Roxas Palawan Phil. 68 F4
Roxas Panay Phil. 69 G4
Roxboro U.S.A. 132 E4
Roxburgh N.Z. 113 B7
Roxburgh Island Cook Is see Rarotonga
Roxby Downs Australia 111 B6
Roxo, Cabo c. Senegal 96 B3
Roy MT U.S.A. 126 F3
Roy NM U.S.A. 127 G5
Royal Canal Ireland 51 E4
Royal Chitwan National Park Nepal 83 F4
Royale, Île i. Canada see Cape Breton Island
Royale, Isle i. U.S.A. 130 F1
Royal Natal National Park S. Africa 101 I5
Royal National Park Australia 112 E5
Royal Oak U.S.A. 134 D2
Royal Sukla Phanta Wildlife Reserve Nepal 82 E3
Royan France 56 D4
Roye France 52 C5
Roy Hill Australia 108 B5
Royston U.K. 49 G6
Rozdil'na Ukr. 59 N1
Rozivka Ukr. 43 H7
Rtishchevo Rus. Fed. 43 I5
Ruabon U.K. 49 D6
Ruaha National Park Tanz. 99 D4
Ruahine Range mts N.Z. 113 F5
Ruanda country Africa see Rwanda

▶Ruapehu, Mount vol. N.Z. 113 E4
Highest active volcano in Oceania.

Ruapuke Island N.Z. 113 B8
Ruatoria N.Z. 113 G3
Ruba Belarus 43 F5

▶Rub' al Khālī des. Saudi Arabia 86 G6
Largest uninterrupted stretch of sand in the world.

Rubaydā reg. Saudi Arabia 88 C5
Rubtsovsk Rus. Fed. 80 F1
Ruby U.S.A. 118 C3
Ruby Dome mt. U.S.A. 129 F1
Ruby Mountains U.S.A. 129 F1
Rubys Inn U.S.A. 129 G3
Ruby Valley U.S.A. 129 F1
Rucheng China 77 G3
Ruckersville U.S.A. 135 F4
Rudall River National Park Australia 108 C5
Rudarpur India 83 E4
Ruda Śląska Poland 47 Q5
Rudauli India 83 E4
Rūdbār Iran 88 C2
Rudkøbing Denmark 45 G9
Rudnaya Pristan' Rus. Fed. 74 D3
Rudnichnyy Rus. Fed. 42 L4
Rudnik Ingichka Uzbek. see Ingichka
Rudnya Smolenskaya Oblast' Rus. Fed. 43 F5
Rudnya Volgogradskaya Oblast' Rus. Fed. 43 J6
Rudnyy Kazakh. 78 F1
Rudolf, Lake salt l. Eth./Kenya see Turkana, Lake

▶Rudol'fa, Ostrov i. Rus. Fed. 64 G1
Most northerly point of Europe.

Rudolph Island Rus. Fed. see Rudol'fa, Ostrov
Rudolstadt Germany 53 L4
Rudong China 77 I1
Rūdsar Iran 88 C2
Rue France 52 B4
Rufiji r. Tanz. 99 D4
Rufino Arg. 144 D4
Rufisque Senegal 96 B3
Rufrufua Indon. 69 I7
Rufunsa Zambia 99 C5
Rugao China 77 I1
Rugby U.K. 49 F6
Rugby U.S.A. 130 C1
Rugeley U.K. 49 F6
Rügen i. Germany 47 N3
Rugged Mountain Canada 120 E5
Rügland Germany 53 K5
Ruḩayyat al Ḩamr'ā' waterhole Saudi Arabia 88 B5
Ruhengeri Rwanda 98 C4
Ruhnu i. Estonia 45 M8
Ruhr r. Germany 53 G3
Ruhuna National Park Sri Lanka 84 D5
Rui'an China 77 I3
Rui Barbosa Brazil 145 C1
Ruicheng China 77 F1
Ruijin China 77 G3
Ruili China 76 C3
Ruin Point Canada 121 P2
Ruipa Tanz. 99 D4
Ruiz Mex. 136 C4
Ruiz, Nevado del vol. Col. 142 C3
Rujaylah, Ḩarrat ar lava field Jordan 85 C3
Rūjiena Latvia 45 N8
Ruk is Micronesia see Chuuk
Rukanpur Pak. 89 I4
Rukumkot Nepal 83 E3
Rukwa, Lake Tanz. 99 D4
Rulin China see Chengbu
Rulong China see Xinlong
Rum i. U.K. 50 C4
Rum, Jebel mts Jordan see Ramm, Jabal
Ruma Serbia 59 H2
Rumāh Saudi Arabia 86 G4
Rumania country Europe see Romania
Rumbek Sudan 97 F4
Rumberpon i. Indon. 69 I7
Rum Cay i. Bahamas 133 F8
Rum Jungle Australia 108 E3
Rummānā hill Syria 85 D3
Rumphi Malawi 99 D5
Runan China 77 G1
Runaway, Cape N.Z. 113 F3
Runcorn U.K. 48 E5
Rundu Namibia 99 B5
Rundvik Sweden 44 K5
Rũng, Kaôh i. Cambodia 71 C5
Rungwa Tanz. 99 D4
Rungwa r. Tanz. 99 D4
Runheji China 77 H1
Runing China see Runan
Runton Range hills Australia 109 C5
Ruokolahti Fin. 45 P6
Ruoqiang China 80 G4
Rupa India 83 H4
Rupat i. Indon. 71 C7
Rupert r. Canada 122 F4
Rupert ID U.S.A. 126 E4
Rupert WV U.S.A. 134 E5
Rupert Bay Canada 122 F4
Rupert Coast Antarctica 152 J1
Rupert House Canada see Waskaganish
Rupnagar India 82 D3
Rupshu reg. India 82 D2
Ruqqād, Wādī ar watercourse Israel 85 B3
Rural Retreat U.S.A. 134 E5
Rusaddir N. Africa see Melilla
Rusape Zimbabwe 99 D5
Ruschuk Bulg. see Ruse
Ruse Bulg. 59 K3
Rusera India 83 F4
Rush U.S.A. 134 D4
Rush Creek r. U.S.A. 130 C4
Rushden U.K. 49 G6
Rushinga Zimbabwe 99 D5
Rushville IL U.S.A. 130 F3
Rushville IN U.S.A. 134 C4
Rushville NE U.S.A. 130 C3
Rushworth Australia 112 B6
Rusk U.S.A. 131 E6
Russell Man. Canada 121 K5
Russell Ont. Canada 135 H1
Russell N.Z. 113 E2
Russell KS U.S.A. 130 D4
Russell PA U.S.A. 134 F3
Russell Bay Antarctica 152 J2
Russell Lake Man. Canada 121 K3
Russell Lake N.W.T. Canada 120 H2
Russell Lake Sask. Canada 121 J3
Russell Range hills Australia 109 C8
Russell Springs U.S.A. 134 C5
Russellville AL U.S.A. 131 G5
Russellville AR U.S.A. 131 E5
Russellville KY U.S.A. 134 B5
Rüsselsheim Germany 53 I4
Russia country Asia/Europe see Russian Federation
Russian r. U.S.A. 128 B2

▶Russian Federation country Asia/Europe 64 I3
Largest country in the world, Europe and Asia. Most populous country in Europe, 5th in Asia and 9th in the world.

Russian Soviet Federal Socialist Republic country Asia/Europe see Russian Federation
Russkiy, Ostrov i. Rus. Fed. 74 C4
Russkiy Kameshkir Rus. Fed. 43 J5
Rust'avi Georgia 91 G2
Rustburg U.S.A. 134 F5
Rustenburg S. Africa 101 H3
Ruston U.S.A. 131 E5
Rutanzige, Lake Dem. Rep. Congo/Uganda see Edward, Lake
Ruteng Indon. 108 C2
Ruth U.S.A. 129 F2
Rüthen Germany 53 I3
Rutherglen Australia 112 C6
Ruther Glen U.S.A. 135 G5
Ruthin U.K. 49 D5
Ruthiyai India 82 D4
Ruth Reservoir U.S.A. 128 B1
Rutka r. Rus. Fed. 42 J4
Rutland U.S.A. 135 I2
Rutland Water resr U.K. 49 G6
Rutledge Lake Canada 121 I2
Rutog Xizang China 76 B2
Rutög China see Dêrub
Rutog Xizang China 83 F3
Rutul Rus. Fed. 91 G2
Ruukki Fin. 44 N4
Ruvuma r. Moz./Tanz. 99 E5
also known as Rovuma
Ruwayshid, Wādī watercourse Jordan 85 C3
Ruwayṭah, Wādī watercourse Jordan 85 C5
Ruweis U.A.E. 88 D5
Ruwenzori National Park Uganda see Queen Elizabeth National Park
Ruza Rus. Fed. 42 H5
Ruzayevka Kazakh. 78 F1
Ruzayevka Rus. Fed. 43 J5
Ruzhou China 77 G1
Ružomberok Slovakia 47 Q6
Rwanda country Africa 98 C4
Ryābād Iran 88 D2
Ryan, Loch b. U.K. 50 D5
Ryazan' Rus. Fed. 43 H5
Ryazhsk Rus. Fed. 43 I5
Rybachiy, Poluostrov pen. Rus. Fed. 44 R2
Rybach'ye Kyrg. see Balykchy
Rybinsk Rus. Fed. 42 H4

▶Rybinskoye Vodokhranilishche resr Rus. Fed. 42 H4
5th largest lake in Europe

Rybnik Poland 47 Q5
Rybnitsa Moldova see Rîbniţa
Rybnoye Rus. Fed. 43 H5
Rybreka Rus. Fed. 42 G3
Ryd Sweden 45 I8
Rydberg Peninsula Antarctica 152 L2
Ryde U.K. 49 F8
Rye U.K. 49 H8
Rye r. U.K. 48 G4
Rye Bay U.K. 49 H8
Ryegate U.S.A. 126 F3
Rye Patch Reservoir U.S.A. 128 D1
Rykovo Ukr. see Yenakiyeve
Ryl'sk Rus. Fed. 43 G6
Rylstone Australia 112 D4
Ryn-Peski des. Kazakh. 41 P6
Ryukyu Islands Japan 75 B8
Ryūkyū-rettō is Japan see Ryukyu Islands
Ryukyu Trench sea feature N. Pacific Ocean 150 E4
Rzeszów Poland 43 D6
Rzhaksa Rus. Fed. 43 I5
Rzhev Rus. Fed. 42 G4

S

Sa'ādah al Barṣā' pass Saudi Arabia 85 C5
Sa'ādatābād Iran 88 D4
Saal an der Donau Germany 53 L6
Saale r. Germany 53 L3
Saalfeld Germany 53 L4
Saanich Canada 120 F5
Saar land Germany see Saarland
Saar r. Germany 52 G5
Saarbrücken Germany 52 G5
Saaremaa i. Estonia 45 M7
Saarenkylä Fin. 44 N3
Saargau reg. Germany 52 G5
Saarijärvi Fin. 44 N5
Saari-Kämä Fin. 44 O3
Saarikoski Fin. 44 L2
Saaristomeren kansallispuisto nat. park Fin. see Skärgårdshavets nationalpark
Saarland land Germany 52 G5
Saarlouis Germany 52 G5
Saatlı Azer. 91 H3
Saatly Azer. see Saatlı
Sab'a Egypt see Saba'ah
Saba'ah Egypt 85 A4
Sab' Ābār Syria 85 C3
Šabac Serbia 59 H2
Sabadell Spain 57 H3
Sabae Japan 75 E6
Sabak Malaysia 71 C7
Sabalana i. Indon. 68 F8
Sabalana, Kepulauan is Indon. 68 F8
Sabana, Archipiélago de is Cuba 137 H4
Sabang Indon. 71 A6
Şabanözü Turkey 90 D2
Sabará Brazil 145 C2
Sabastiya West Bank 85 B3
Sab'atayn, Ramlat as des. Yemen 86 G6
Sabaudia Italy 58 E4
Sabaya Bol. 142 E7
Sabdê China 76 D2
Sabelo S. Africa 100 F6
Sāberi, Hāmūn-e marsh Afgh./Iran 89 F4
Şabḩā Jordan 85 C3
Sabhā Libya 97 E2
Şabḩā' Saudi Arabia 88 B6
Sabhrai India 82 B5
Sabi r. India 82 D3
Sabi r. Moz./Zimbabwe see Save
Sabie Moz. 101 K3
Sabie r. Moz./S. Africa 101 K3
Sabie S. Africa 101 J3
Sabina U.S.A. 134 D4
Sabinal Mex. 127 G7
Sabinal, Cayo i. Cuba 133 E8
Sabinas Mex. 131 C7
Sabinas r. Mex. 131 C7
Sabinas Hidalgo Mex. 131 C7
Sabine r. U.S.A. 131 E6
Sabine Lake U.S.A. 131 E6
Sabine Pass U.S.A. 131 E6
Sabini, Monti mts Italy 58 E3
Sabirabad Azer. 91 H2
Sabkhat al Bardawīl Reserve nature res. Egypt see Lake Bardawil Reserve
Sable, Cape Canada 123 I6
Sable, Cape U.S.A. 133 D7
Sable, Lac du l. Canada 123 I3
Sable Island Canada 123 K6
Sabon Kafi Niger 96 D3
Sabrina Coast Antarctica 152 F2
Sabugal Port. 57 C3
Sabzawar Afgh. see Shīndand
Sabzevār Iran 88 E2
Sabzvārān Iran see Jīroft
Sacalinul Mare, Insula i. Romania 59 M2
Sacaton U.S.A. 129 H5
Sac City U.S.A. 130 E3
Săcele Romania 59 K2
Sachigo r. Canada 121 N4
Sachigo Lake Canada 121 M4
Sachin India 82 C5
Sach'on S. Korea 75 C6
Sach Pass India 82 D2
Sachsen land Germany 53 N3
Sachsen-Anhalt land Germany 53 L2
Sachsenheim Germany 53 J6
Sachs Harbour Canada 118 F2
Sacirsuyu r. Syria/Turkey see Sājūr, Nahr
Sackpfeife hill Germany 53 I4
Sackville Canada 123 I5
Saco ME U.S.A. 135 J2
Saco MT U.S.A. 126 G2
Sacramento Brazil 145 B2

▶Sacramento U.S.A. 128 C2
Capital of California.

Sacramento r. U.S.A. 128 C2
Sacramento Mountains U.S.A. 127 G6
Sacramento Valley U.S.A. 128 B1
Sada S. Africa 101 H7
Sádaba Spain 57 F2
Sá da Bandeira Angola see Lubango
Şadad Syria 85 C2
Şa'dah Yemen 86 F6
Sadao Thai. 71 C6
Saddat al Hindīyah Iraq 91 G4
Saddleback Mesa mt. U.S.A. 131 C5
Saddle Hill hill Australia 110 D2
Saddle Peak hill India 71 A4
Sa Đec Vietnam 71 D5
Sadêng China 76 B2
Sadieville U.S.A. 134 C4
Sadīj watercourse Iran 88 E5
Sadiola Mali 96 B3
Sadiqabad Pak. 89 H4
Sad Istragh mt. Afgh./Pak. 89 I2
Sa'dīyah, Hawr as imp. l. Iraq 91 G4
Sa'diyat i. U.A.E. 88 D5
Sado r. Port. 57 B4
Sadoga-shima i. Japan 75 E5
Sadot Egypt see Sadūt
Sadovoye Rus. Fed. 43 J7
Sa Dragonera i. Spain 57 H4
Sadras India 84 D3
Sadūt Egypt 85 B4
Sadût Egypt see Sadūt
Sæby Denmark 45 G8
Saena Julia Italy see Siena
Safad Israel see Ẕefat
Safāshahr Iran 88 D4
Safayal Maqūf well Iraq 91 G5
Safed Khirs mts Afgh. 89 H2
Safed Koh mts Afgh. 89 G3
Safed Koh mts Afgh./Pak. 89 H3
Saffānīyah, Ra's as pt Saudi Arabia 88 C4
Säffle Sweden 45 H7
Safford U.S.A. 129 I5
Saffron Walden U.K. 49 H6
Safi Morocco 54 C5
Safīdār, Kūh-e mt. Iran 88 D4
Safīd Kūh mts Afgh. 89 F3
Safīd Kūh mts Afgh. see Safīd Kūh
Safīd Sagak Iran 89 F3
Safiras, Serra das mts Brazil 145 C2
Şāfītā Syria 85 C2
Safonovo Arkhangel'skaya Oblast' Rus. Fed. 42 K2
Safonovo Smolenskaya Oblast' Rus. Fed. 43 G5
Safrā' al Asyāḩ esc. Saudi Arabia 88 A5
Safrā' as Sark esc. Saudi Arabia 86 F4
Safranbolu Turkey 90 D2
Saga China 83 F3
Saga Japan 75 C6
Saga Kazakh. 80 B1
Sagaing Myanmar 70 A2
Sagami-nada g. Japan 75 E6
Sagamore U.S.A. 134 F3
Saganthit Kyun i. Myanmar 71 B4
Sagar Karnataka India 84 B3
Sagar Karnataka India 84 C2
Sagar Madh. Prad. India 82 D5
Sagaredzho Georgia see Sagarejo
Sagarejo Georgia 91 G2
Sagar Island India 83 G5
Sagarmatha National Park Nepal 83 F4
Sagastyr Rus. Fed. 65 N2
Sagavanirktok r. U.S.A. 118 D2
Sage U.S.A. 126 F4
Saggi, Har mt. Israel 85 B4
Saghand Iran 88 D3
Saginaw U.S.A. 134 D2
Saginaw Bay U.S.A. 134 D2
Saglek Bay Canada 123 J2
Saglouc Canada see Salluit
Sagone, Golfe de b. Corsica France 56 I5
Sagres Port. 57 B5
Sagthale India 82 C5
Saguache U.S.A. 127 G5
Sagua la Grande Cuba 137 H4
Saguaro Lake U.S.A. 129 H5
Saguaro National Park U.S.A. 129 H5
Saguenay r. Canada 123 H4
Sagunt Spain see Sagunto
Sagunto Spain 57 F4
Saguntum Spain see Sagunto
Sahagún Spain 57 D2
Sahand, Kūh-e mt. Iran 88 B2

▶Sahara des. Africa 96 D3
Largest desert in the world.

Şaḩara el Gharbîya des. Egypt see Western Desert
Şaḩara el Sharqîya des. Egypt see Eastern Desert
Saharan Atlas mts Alg. see Atlas Saharien
Saharanpur India 82 D3
Sahara Well Australia 108 C5
Saharsa India 83 F4
Sahaswan India 82 D3
Sahat, Kūh-e hill Iran 88 D3
Sahatwar India 83 F4
Şahbuz Azer. 91 G3
Sahdol India see Shahdol
Sahebganj India see Sahibganj
Sahebgunj India see Sahibganj
Saheira, Wâdi el watercourse Egypt see Suhaymī, Wādī as
Sahel reg. Africa 96 C3
Sahibganj India 83 F4
Sahiwal Pak. 89 I4
Sahlābād Iran 89 E3
Şaḩm Oman 88 E5
Şaḩneh Iran 88 B3
Şaḩrā al Ḩijārah reg. Iraq 91 G5
Sahuaripa Mex. 127 F7
Sahuayo Mex. 136 D4
Sahuteng China see Zadoi
Sa Huynh Vietnam 71 E4
Sahyadri mts India see Western Ghats
Sahyadriparvat Range hills India 84 B1
Sai r. India 83 E4
Sai Buri Thai. 71 C6
Saïda Alg. 57 G6
Saïda Lebanon see Sidon
Sai Dao Tai, Khao mt. Thai. 71 C4
Saïdia Morocco 57 E6
Sa'īdīyeh Iran see Solţānīyeh
Saidpur Bangl. 83 G4
Saiha India 83 H5
Saihan Tal China 73 K4
Saijō Japan 75 D6
Saikai Kokuritsu-kōen nat. park Japan 75 C6
Saiki Japan 75 C6
Sai Kung H.K. China 77 [inset]
Sailana India 82 C5
Saimaa l. Fin. 45 P6
Saimbeyli Turkey 90 E3
Saindak Pak. 89 F4
Sa'īndezh Iran 88 B2
Sa'īn Qal'eh Iran see Sa'īndezh
St Abb's Head hd U.K. 50 G5
St Agnes U.K. 49 B8
St Agnes i. U.K. 49 A9
St Alban's Canada 123 L5
St Albans U.K. 49 G7
St Albans VT U.S.A. 135 I1
St Albans WV U.S.A. 134 E4
St Alban's Head hd England U.K. see St Aldhelm's Head
St Albert Canada 120 H4
St Aldhelm's Head hd U.K. 49 E8
St-Amand-les-Eaux France 52 D4
St-Amand-Montrond France 56 F3
St-Amour France 56 G3
St-André, Cap pt Madag. see Vilanandro, Tanjona
St Andrews U.K. 50 G4
St Andrew Sound inlet U.S.A. 133 D6
St Anne U.S.A. 134 B3
St Ann's Bay Jamaica 137 I5
St Anthony Canada 123 L4
St Anthony U.S.A. 126 F4
St-Arnaud Alg. see El Eulma
St Arnaud Australia 112 A6
St Arnaud Range mts N.Z. 113 D6
St-Arnoult-en-Yvelines France 52 B6
St-Augustin Canada 123 K4
St Augustin r. Canada 123 K4
St Augustine U.S.A. 133 D6
St Austell U.K. 49 C8
St-Avertin France 56 E3
St-Avold France 52 G5
St Barbe Canada 123 K4

▶St-Barthélemy i. West Indies 137 L5
French Overseas Collectivity.

St Bees U.K. 48 D4
St Bees Head hd U.K. 48 D4
St Bride's Bay U.K. 49 B7
St-Brieuc France 56 C2
St Catharines Canada 134 F2
St Catherines Island U.S.A. 133 D6
St Catherine's Point U.K. 49 F8
St-Céré France 56 E4
St-Chamond France 56 G4
St Charles ID U.S.A. 126 F4
St Charles MD U.S.A. 135 G4
St Charles MI U.S.A. 134 C2
St Charles MO U.S.A. 130 F4
St-Chély-d'Apcher France 56 F4
St Christopher and Nevis country West Indies see St Kitts and Nevis
St Clair r. Canada/U.S.A. 134 D2
St Clair, Lake Canada/U.S.A. 134 D2
St-Claude France 56 G3
St Clears U.K. 49 C7
St Cloud U.S.A. 130 E2
St Croix r. U.S.A. 122 B5
St Croix Falls U.S.A. 130 E2
St David U.S.A. 129 H6
St David's Head hd U.K. 49 B7
St-Denis France 52 C6

▶St-Denis Réunion 149 L7
Capital of Réunion.

St-Denis-du-Sig Alg. see Sig
St-Dié France 56 H2
St-Dizier France 52 E6
St-Domingue country West Indies see Haiti
Sainte Anne Canada 121 L5
Ste-Anne, Lac l. Canada 123 I4
St Elias, Cape U.S.A. 118 D4

▶St Elias, Mount U.S.A. 120 A2
4th highest mountain in North America.

St Elias Mountains Canada 120 A2
Ste-Marguerite r. Canada 123 I4
Ste-Marie, Cap c. Madag. see Vohimena, Tanjona
Sainte-Marie, Île i. Madag. see Boraha, Nosy
Ste-Maxime France 56 H5
Sainte Rose du Lac Canada 121 L5
Saintes France 56 D4
Sainte Thérèse, Lac l. Canada 120 F1
St-Étienne France 56 G4
St-Étienne-du-Rouvray France 52 B5
St-Fabien Canada 123 H4
St-Félicien Canada 123 G4
Saintfield U.K. 51 G3
St-Florent Corsica France 56 I5
St-Florent-sur-Cher France 56 F3
St-Floris, Parc National nat. park Cent. Afr. Rep. 98 C3
St-Flour France 56 F4
St Francesville U.S.A. 131 F6
St Francis U.S.A. 130 C4
St Francis r. U.S.A. 131 F5
St Francis Isles Australia 109 F8
St-François r. Canada 123 G5
St-François, Lac l. Canada 123 H5
St-Gaudens France 56 E5
St George Australia 112 D2
St George r. Australia 110 D3
St George AK U.S.A. 118 B4
St George SC U.S.A. 133 D5
St George UT U.S.A. 129 G3
St George, Point U.S.A. 126 B4
St George Island U.S.A. 118 B4
St George Range hills Australia 108 D4
St-Georges Canada 123 H5

Sanggau Indon. 68 E6
Sangilen, Nagor'ye mts Rus. Fed. 80 I1
San Giovanni in Fiore Italy 58 G5
Sangir India 82 C5
Sangir i. Indon. 69 H6
Sangir, Kepulauan is Indon. 69 G6
Sangkapura Indon. 68 E8
Sangkulirang Indon. 68 F6
Sangli India 84 B2
Sangmai China see Dêrong
Sangmélima Cameroon 96 E4
Sangngagqoiling China 76 B2
Sango Zimbabwe 99 D6
Sangole India 84 B2
San Gorgonio Mountain U.S.A. 128 E4
Sangpi China see Xiangcheng
Sangre de Cristo Range mts U.S.A. 127 G5
Sangrur India 82 C3
Sangu r. Bangl. 83 G5
Sanguem India 84 B3
Sangutane r. Moz. 101 K3
Sangzhi China 77 F2
Sanhe China see Sandu
San Hipólito, Punta pt Mex. 127 E8
Sanhûr Egypt see Sanhûr
Sanhûr Egypt 90 C5
San Ignacio Beni Bol. 142 E6
San Ignacio Santa Cruz Bol. 142 F7
San Ignacio Baja California Mex. 127 E7
San Ignacio Durango Mex. 131 C7
San Ignacio Sonora Mex. 127 F7
San Ignacio Para. 144 E3
San Ignacio, Laguna l. Mex. 127 E8
Sanikiluaq Canada 122 F2
Sanin-kaigan Kokuritsu-kōen nat. park Japan 75 D6
San Jacinto U.S.A. 128 E5
San Jacinto Peak U.S.A. 128 E5
San Javier Bol. 142 F7
Sanjiang Guangdong China see Liannan
Sanjiang Guangxi China 77 F3
Sanjiang Guizhou China see Jinping
Sanjiangkou China 74 A4
Sanjiaocheng China see Haiyan
Sanjiaoping China 77 F2
Sanjō Japan 75 E5
San Joaquin r. U.S.A. 128 C2
San Joaquin Valley U.S.A. 128 C3
Sanjoli India 82 C5
San Jon U.S.A. 131 C5
San Jorge, Golfo de g. Arg. 144 C7
San Jorge, Golfo de g. Spain see Sant Jordi, Golf de
▶San José Costa Rica 137 H7
Capital of Costa Rica.
San Jose Phil. 69 G3
San Jose CA U.S.A. 128 C3
San Jose NM U.S.A. 127 G6
San Jose watercourse U.S.A. 129 J4
San José, Isla i. Mex. 136 B4
San José de Amacuro Venez. 142 F2
San José de Bavicora Mex. 127 G7
San Jose de Buenavista Phil. 69 G4
San José de Chiquitos Bol. 142 F7
San José de Comondú Mex. 127 F8
San José de Gracia Mex. 127 E8
San Joséde la Brecha Mex. 127 F8
San José del Cabo Mex. 136 C4
San José del Guaviare Col. 142 D3
San José de Mayo Uruguay 144 E4
San José de Raíces Mex. 131 C7
San Juan Arg. 144 C4
San Juan r. Costa Rica/Nicaragua 137 H6
San Juan mt. Cuba 133 D8
San Juan Mex. 127 G8
San Juan r. Mex. 131 D7
▶San Juan Puerto Rico 137 K5
Capital of Puerto Rico.
San Juan U.S.A. 129 J5
San Juan r. U.S.A. 129 H3
San Juan, Cabo c. Arg. 144 D8
San Juan, Cabo c. Equat. Guinea 96 D4
San Juan Bautista Para. 144 E3
San Juan Bautista de las Misiones Para. see San Juan Bautista
San Juan de Guadalupe Mex. 131 C7
San Juan de los Morros Venez. 142 E2
San Juan Mountains U.S.A. 129 J3
San Juan y Martínez Cuba 133 D8
San Julián Arg. 144 C7
San Justo Arg. 144 D4
Sankari Drug India 84 C4
Sankh r. India 81 F7
Sankhu India 82 C3
Sankra Chhattisgarh India 84 D1
Sankra Rajasthan India 82 B4
Sankt Augustin Germany 53 H4
Sankt Gallen Switz. 56 I3
Sankt-Peterburg Rus. Fed. see St Petersburg
Sankt Pölten Austria 47 O6
Sankt Veit an der Glan Austria 47 O7
Sankt Vith Belgium see St-Vith
Sankt Wendel Germany 53 H5
Sanku India 82 D2
Şanlıurfa Turkey 90 E3
Şanlıurfa prov. Turkey 85 D1
San Lorenzo Arg. 144 D4
San Lorenzo Beni Bol. 142 E7
San Lorenzo Tarija Bol. 142 F8
San Lorenzo Ecuador 142 C3
San Lorenzo mt. Spain 57 E2
San Lorenzo, Cerro mt. Arg./Chile 144 B7
San Lorenzo, Isla i. Mex. 127 E7
Sanlúcar de Barrameda Spain 57 C5
San Lucas Baja California Sur Mex. 127 E8
San Lucas Baja California Sur Mex. 136 C4
San Lucas, Serranía de mts Col. 142 D2
San Luis Arg. 144 C4
San Luis AZ U.S.A. 129 F5
San Luis AZ U.S.A. 129 H5
San Luis CO U.S.A. 131 B4
San Luís, Isla i. Mex. 127 E7
San Luisito Mex. 127 E7
San Luis Obispo U.S.A. 128 C4
San Luis Obispo Bay U.S.A. 128 C4
San Luis Potosí Mex. 136 D4
San Luis Reservoir U.S.A. 128 C3
San Luis Río Colorado Mex. 129 F5
San Manuel U.S.A. 129 H5
San Marcial, Punta pt Mex. 127 F8
San Marcos U.S.A. 131 D6
San Marcos, Isla i. Mex. 127 E8
San Marino country Europe 58 E3
▶San Marino San Marino 58 E3
Capital of San Marino.
San Martín research station Antarctica 152 L2
San Martín Catamarca Arg. 144 C3
San Martín Mendoza Arg. 144 C4
San Martín, Lago l. Arg./Chile 144 B7
San Martín de los Andes Arg. 144 B6
San Mateo U.S.A. 128 B3
San Mateo Mountains U.S.A. 129 J4
San Matías Bol. 143 G7
San Matías, Golfo g. Arg. 144 D6
Sanmen China 77 I2
Sanmen Wan b. China 77 I2
Sanmenxia China 77 F1
San Miguel El Salvador 136 G6
San Miguel U.S.A. 128 C4
San Miguel r. U.S.A. 129 I2
San Miguel de Huachi Bol. 142 E7
San Miguel de Tucumán Arg. 144 C3
San Miguel do Araguaia Brazil 145 A1
San Miguel Island U.S.A. 128 C4
Sanming China 77 H3
Sanndatti India 84 B3
Sanndraigh i. U.K. see Sandray
Sannicandro Garganico Italy 58 F4
San Nicolás Durango Mex. 131 B7
San Nicolás Tamaulipas Mex. 131 D7
San Nicolas Island U.S.A. 128 D5
Sannieshof S. Africa 101 G4
Sanniquellie Liberia 96 C4
Sanok Poland 43 D6
San Pablo Bol. 142 E8
San Pablo Phil. 69 G4
San Pablo de Manta Ecuador see Manta
San Pedro Arg. 144 D2
San Pedro Bol. 142 F7
San Pedro Chile 144 C2
San-Pédro Côte d'Ivoire 96 C4
San Pedro Baja California Sur Mex. 124 E7
San Pedro Chihuahua Mex. 127 G7
San Pedro Para. see San Pedro de Ycuamandyyú
San Pedro watercourse U.S.A. 129 H5
San Pedro, Sierra de mts Spain 57 C4
San Pedro Channel U.S.A. 128 D5
San Pedro de Arimena Col. 142 D3
San Pedro de Atacama Chile 144 C2
San Pedro de las Colonias Mex. 131 C7
San Pedro de Macorís Dom. Rep. 137 K5
San Pedro de Ycuamandyyú Para. 144 E2
San Pedro Martir, Parque Nacional nat. park Mex. 127 E7
San Pedro Sula Hond. 136 G5
San Pierre U.S.A. 134 B3
San Pietro, Isola di i. Sardinia Italy 58 C5
San Pitch r. U.S.A. 129 H2
Sanqaçal Azer. 91 H2
Sanquhar U.K. 50 F5
Sanquianga, Parque Nacional nat. park Col. 142 C3
San Quintín, Cabo c. Mex. 127 D7
San Rafael Arg. 144 C4
San Rafael CA U.S.A. 128 B3
San Rafael NM U.S.A. 129 J4
San Rafael r. U.S.A. 129 H2
San Rafael Knob mt. U.S.A. 129 H2
San Rafael Mountains U.S.A. 128 C4
San Ramón Bol. 142 F6
Sanrao China 77 H3
San Remo Italy 58 B3
San Roque Spain 57 B2
San Roque, Punta pt Mex. 127 E8
San Saba U.S.A. 131 D6
San Salvador i. Bahamas 133 F7
▶San Salvador El Salvador 136 G6
Capital of El Salvador.
San Salvador, Isla i. Galápagos Ecuador 142 [inset]
San Salvador de Jujuy Arg. 144 C2
Sansanné-Mango Togo 96 D3
San Sebastián Arg. 144 C8
San Sebastián Spain see Donostia-San Sebastián
San Sebastián de los Reyes Spain 57 E3
Sansepolcro Italy 58 E3
San Severo Italy 58 F4
San Simon U.S.A. 129 I5
Sanski Most Bos.-Herz. 58 G2
Sansoral Islands Palau see Sonsorol Islands
Sansui China 77 F3
Santa r. Peru 142 C5
Santa Ana Bol. 142 E7
Santa Ana El Salvador 136 G6
Santa Ana Mex. 127 F7
Santa Ana i. Solomon Is 107 G3
Santa Ana U.S.A. 128 E5
Santa Ana de Yacuma Bol. 142 E6
Santa Anna U.S.A. 131 D6
Santa Bárbara Brazil 145 C2
Santa Bárbara Cuba see La Demajagua
Santa Bárbara Mex. 131 B7
Santa Barbara U.S.A. 128 D4
Santa Bárbara, Ilha i. Brazil 145 D2
Santa Barbara Channel U.S.A. 128 C4
Santa Bárbara d'Oeste Brazil 145 B3
Santa Barbara Island U.S.A. 128 D5
Santa Catalina, Gulf of U.S.A. 128 E5
Santa Catalina, Isla i. Mex. 127 F8
Santa Catalina de Armada Spain 57 B2
Santa Catalina Island U.S.A. 128 D5
Santa Catarina state Brazil 145 A4
Santa Catarina Baja California Mex. 127 E7
Santa Catarina Nuevo León Mex. 131 C7
Santa Catarina, Ilha de i. Brazil 145 A4
Santa Clara Col. 142 E4
Santa Clara Cuba 137 I4
Santa Clara Mex. 131 B6
Santa Clara CA U.S.A. 128 C3
Santa Clara UT U.S.A. 129 G3
Santa Clarita U.S.A. 128 D4
Santa Clotilde Peru 142 D4
Santa Comba Angola see Waku-Kungo
Santa Croce, Capo c. Sicily Italy 58 F6
Santa Cruz Bol. 142 F7
Santa Cruz Brazil 143 K5
Santa Cruz Costa Rica 142 A1
Santa Cruz U.S.A. 128 B3
Santa Cruz watercourse U.S.A. 129 G5
Santa Cruz, Isla i. Galápagos Ecuador 142 [inset]
Santa Cruz, Isla i. Mex. 127 F8
Santa Cruz Cabrália Brazil 145 D2
Santa Cruz de Goiás Brazil 145 A2
Santa Cruz de la Palma Canary Is 96 B2
Santa Cruz del Sur Cuba 137 I4
Santa Cruz de Moya Spain 57 F4
▶Santa Cruz de Tenerife Canary Is 96 B2
Joint capital of the Canary Islands.
Santa Cruz do Sul Brazil 144 F3
Santa Cruz Island U.S.A. 128 D4
Santa Cruz Islands Solomon Is 107 G3
Santa Elena, Bahía de b. Ecuador 142 B4
Santa Elena, Cabo c. Costa Rica 137 G6
Santa Elena, Punta pt Ecuador 142 B4
Santa Eudóxia Brazil 145 B3
Santa Eufemia, Golfo di g. Italy 58 G5
Santa Fé Arg. 144 D4
Santa Fé Cuba 133 D8
▶Santa Fe U.S.A. 127 G6
Capital of New Mexico.
Santa Fé de Bogotá Col. see Bogotá
Santa Fé de Minas Brazil 145 B2
Santa Fé do Sul Brazil 145 A3
Santa Helena Brazil 143 I4
Santa Helena de Goiás Brazil 145 A2
Santai Sichuan China 76 E2
Santai Yunnan China 76 D3
Santa Inês Brazil 143 I4
Santa Inés, Isla i. Chile 152 L3
Santa Isabel Arg. 144 C5
Santa Isabel Equat. Guinea see Malabo
Santa Isabel i. Solomon Is 107 F2
Santa Juliana Brazil 145 B2
Santalpur India 82 B5
Santa Lucia Range mts U.S.A. 128 C3
Santa Margarita U.S.A. 128 C4
Santa Margarita, Isla i. Mex. 136 B4
Santa María Arg. 144 C3
Santa Maria Amazonas Brazil 143 G4
Santa Maria Rio Grande do Sul Brazil 144 F3
Santa Maria Cape Verde 96 [inset]
Santa María r. Mex. 127 G7
Santa María Peru 142 D4
Santa Maria U.S.A. 128 C4
Santa Maria r. U.S.A. 129 G4
Santa Maria, Cabo de c. Moz. 101 K4
Santa Maria, Cabo de c. Port. 57 C5
Santa Maria, Chapadão de hills Brazil 145 A1
Santa María, Isla i. Galápagos Ecuador 142 [inset]
Santa Maria, Serra de hills Brazil 145 B1
Santa Maria da Vitória Brazil 145 B1
Santa María de Cuevas Mex. 131 B7
Santa Maria do Suaçuí Brazil 145 C2
Santa María Island Vanuatu 107 G3
Santa Maria Madalena Brazil 145 C3
Santa Maria Mountains U.S.A. 129 G4
Santa Marta Col. 142 D1
Santa Marta, Cabo de c. Angola 99 B5
Santa Marta Grande, Cabo de c. Brazil 145 A5
Santa Maura i. Greece see Lefkada
Santa Monica U.S.A. 128 D4
Santa Monica, Pico mt. Mex. 127 E8
Santa Monica Bay U.S.A. 128 D5
Santan Indon. 68 F7
Santana Brazil 145 C1
Santana r. Brazil 145 A2
Santana do Araguaia Brazil 143 H5
Santander Spain 57 E2
Santa Nella U.S.A. 128 C3
Santanilla, Islas is Caribbean Sea see Cisne, Islas del
Santan Mountain hill U.S.A. 129 H5
Sant'Antioco Sardinia Italy 58 C5
Sant'Antioco, Isola di i. Sardinia Italy 58 C5
Sant Antoni de Portmany Spain 57 G4
Santapilly India 84 D2
Santaquin U.S.A. 129 H2
Santa Quitéria Brazil 143 J4
Santarém Brazil 143 H4
Santarém Port. 57 B4
Santa Rita Mex. 131 C7
Santa Rosa Arg. 144 D5
Santa Rosa Acre Brazil 142 D5
Santa Rosa Rio Grande do Sul Brazil 144 F3
Santa Rosa Mex. 131 C7
Santa Rosa CA U.S.A. 128 B2
Santa Rosa NM U.S.A. 127 G6
Santa Rosa de Copán Hond. 136 G6
Santa Rosa de la Roca Bol. 142 F7
Santa Rosa Island U.S.A. 128 C5
Santa Rosalía Mex. 127 E8
Santa Rosa Range mts U.S.A. 126 D4
Santa Rosa Wash watercourse U.S.A. 129 G5
Santa Sylvina Arg. 144 D3
Santa Teresa Australia 109 F6
Santa Teresa r. Brazil 145 A1
Santa Teresa Mex. 131 D7
Santa Vitória Brazil 145 A2
Santa Ynez r. U.S.A. 128 C4
Santa Ysabel i. Solomon Is see Santa Isabel
Santee U.S.A. 128 E5
Santee r. U.S.A. 133 E5
Santiago Brazil 144 F3
Santiago i. Cape Verde 96 [inset]
▶Santiago Chile 144 B4
Capital of Chile.
Santiago Dom. Rep. 137 J5
Santiago Panama 137 H7
Santiago Phil. 69 G3
Santiago de Compostela Spain 57 B2
Santiago de Cuba Cuba 137 I4
Santiago del Estero Arg. 144 D3
Santiago de los Caballeros Dom. Rep. see Santiago
Santiago de Veraguas Panama see Santiago
Santiaguillo, Laguna de l. Mex. 131 B7
Santianna Point Canada 121 P2
Santipur India see Shantipur
Sant Jordi, Golf de g. Spain 57 G3
Santo Amaro Brazil 145 D1
Santo Amaro de Campos Brazil 145 C3
Santo Anastácio Brazil 145 A3
Santo André Brazil 145 B3
Santo Angelo Brazil 144 F3
▶Santo Antão i. Cape Verde 96 [inset]
Most westerly point of Africa.
Santo Antônio Brazil 142 F4
Santo Antônio r. Brazil 145 C2
Santo António São Tomé and Príncipe 96 D4
Santo Antônio, Cabo c. Brazil 145 D1
Santo Antônio da Platina Brazil 145 A3
Santo Antônio de Jesus Brazil 145 D1
Santo Antônio do Içá Brazil 142 E4
Santo Corazón Bol. 143 G7
Santo Domingo Cuba 133 D8
▶Santo Domingo Dom. Rep. 137 K5
Capital of the Dominican Republic.
Santo Domingo Baja California Mex. 127 E7
Santo Domingo Baja California Sur Mex. 127 F8
Santo Domingo country West Indies see Dominican Republic
Santo Domingo de Guzmán Dom. Rep. see Santo Domingo
Santo Hipólito Brazil 145 B2
Santorini i. Greece 59 K6
Santos Brazil 145 B3
Santos Dumont Brazil 145 C3
Santos Plateau sea feature S. Atlantic Ocean 148 E7
Santo Tomás Mex. 127 E7
Santo Tomás Peru 142 D6
Santo Tomé Arg. 144 E3
Sanup Plateau U.S.A. 129 G3
San Valentín, Cerro mt. Chile 144 B7
San Vicente El Salvador 136 G6
San Vicente Mex. 127 D7
San Vicente de Baracaldo Spain see Barakaldo
San Vicente de Cañete Peru 142 C6
San Vincenzo Italy 58 D3
San Vito, Capo c. Sicily Italy 58 E5
Sanwer India 82 C5
Sanxia Shuiku resr China see Three Gorges Reservoir
Sanya China 77 F5
Sanyuan China 77 F1
S. A. Nyýazow Adyndaky Turkm. 89 F2
Sanza Pombo Angola 99 B4
Sao, Phou mt. Laos 70 C3
São Bernardo do Campo Brazil 145 B3
São Borja Brazil 144 E3
São Carlos Brazil 145 B3
São Domingos Brazil 145 B1
São Felipe, Serra de hills Brazil 145 B1
São Félix Bahia Brazil 145 D1
São Félix Mato Grosso Brazil 143 H6
São Félix Pará Brazil 143 H5
São Fidélis Brazil 145 C3
São Francisco Brazil 145 B1
▶São Francisco r. Brazil 145 C1
5th longest river in South America.
São Francisco, Ilha de i. Brazil 145 A4
São Francisco de Paula Brazil 145 A5
São Francisco de Sales Brazil 145 A2
São Francisco do Sul Brazil 145 A4
São Gabriel Brazil 144 F4
São Gonçalo Brazil 145 C3
São Gonçalo do Abaeté Brazil 145 B2
São Gonçalo do Sapucaí Brazil 145 B3
São Gotardo Brazil 145 B2
São João, Ilhas de is Brazil 143 J4
São João da Barra Brazil 145 C3
São João da Boa Vista Brazil 145 B3
São João da Madeira Port. 57 B3
São João da Ponte Brazil 145 B1
São João del Rei Brazil 145 B3
São João do Paraíso Brazil 145 C1
São Joaquim Brazil 145 A5
São Joaquim da Barra Brazil 145 B3
São José Amazonas Brazil 142 E4
São José Santa Catarina Brazil 145 A4
São José do Rio Preto Brazil 145 A3
São José dos Campos Brazil 145 B3
São José dos Pinhais Brazil 145 A4
São Leopoldo Brazil 145 A5
São Lourenço Brazil 145 B3
São Lourenço r. Brazil 143 G7
São Luís Brazil 143 J4
São Luís Brazil 143 G4
São Luís de Montes Belos Brazil 145 A2
São Manuel Brazil 145 A3
São Marcos r. Brazil 145 B2
São Mateus Brazil 145 D2
São Mateus do Sul Brazil 145 A4
São Miguel i. Arquipélago dos Açores 148 G3
São Miguel r. Brazil 145 B2
São Miguel do Tapuio Brazil 143 J5
Saône r. France 56 G4
Saoner India 82 D5
São Nicolau i. Cape Verde 96 [inset]
▶São Paulo Brazil 145 B3
Most populous city in South America and 4th in the world.
São Paulo state Brazil 145 A3
São Paulo de Olivença Brazil 142 E4
São Pedro da Aldeia Brazil 145 C3
São Pedro e São Paulo is N. Atlantic Ocean 148 G5
São Pires r. Brazil see Teles Pires
São Raimundo Nonato Brazil 143 J5
São Romão Amazonas Brazil 142 E5
São Romão Minas Gerais Brazil 145 B2
São Roque Brazil 145 B3
São Roque, Cabo de c. Brazil 143 K5
São Salvador Angola see M'banza Congo
São Salvador do Congo Angola see M'banza Congo
São Sebastião Brazil 145 B3
São Sebastião, Ilha do i. Brazil 145 B3
São Sebastião do Paraíso Brazil 145 B3
São Sebastião dos Poções Brazil 145 B1
São Simão Minas Gerais Brazil 143 H7
São Simão São Paulo Brazil 145 B3
São Simão, Barragem de resr Brazil 145 A2
São Tiago i. Cape Verde see Santiago
▶São Tomé São Tomé and Príncipe 96 D4
Capital of São Tomé and Príncipe.
São Tomé i. São Tomé and Príncipe 96 D4
São Tomé, Cabo de c. Brazil 145 C3
São Tomé, Pico de mt. São Tomé and Príncipe 96 D4
São Tomé and Príncipe country Africa 96 D4
Saoura, Oued watercourse Alg. 54 D6
São Vicente Brazil 145 B3
São Vicente i. Cape Verde 96 [inset]
São Vicente, Cabo de c. Port. 57 B5
Sapanca Turkey 59 N4
Sapaul India see Supaul
Şaphane Dağı mt. Turkey 59 N5
Sapo National Park Liberia 96 C4
Sapouy Burkina 96 C3
Sapozhok Rus. Fed. 43 I5
Sappa Creek r. U.S.A. 130 D3
Sapporo Japan 74 F4
Sapulpa U.S.A. 131 D4
Sapulut Sabah Malaysia 68 F6
Saputang China see Zadoi
Sāqī Iran 88 E3
Saqqez Iran 88 B2
Sarā Iran 88 B2
Sarāb Iran 88 B2
Sara Buri Thai. 71 C4
Saradiya India 82 B5
Saragossa Spain see Zaragoza
Saragt Turkm. 89 F2
Saraguro Ecuador 142 C4
Sarahs Turkm. see Saragt
Sarai Afgh. 89 G3
Sarai Sidhu Pak. 89 I4
▶Sarajevo Bos.-Herz. 58 H3
Capital of Bosnia-Herzegovina.
Sarakhs Iran 89 F2
Saraktash Rus. Fed. 64 G4
Saraland U.S.A. 131 F6
Saramati mt. India/Myanmar 70 A1
Saran' Kazakh. 80 D2
Saranac U.S.A. 134 C2
Saranac r. U.S.A. 135 I1
Saranac Lake U.S.A. 135 H1
Saranda Albania see Sarandë
Sarandë Albania 59 I5
Sarandib country Asia see Sri Lanka
Sarangani Islands Phil. 69 H5
Sarangpur India 82 D5
Saransk Rus. Fed. 43 J5
Sara Peak Nigeria 96 D4
Saraphi Thai. 70 B3
Sarapul Rus. Fed. 41 Q4
Sarāqib Syria 85 C2
Sarasota U.S.A. 133 D7
Saraswati r. India 89 H6
Sarata Ukr. 59 M1
Saratoga CA U.S.A. 128 B3
Saratoga WY U.S.A. 126 G4
Saratoga Springs U.S.A. 132 F3
Saratok Sarawak Malaysia 68 E6
Saratov Rus. Fed. 43 J6
Saratovskoye Vodokhranilishche resr Rus. Fed. 43 J5
Saratsina, Akrotirio pt Greece 59 K5
Saravan Iran 89 F5
Saray Turkey 59 L4
Sarayköy Turkey 59 M6
Sarayönü Turkey 90 D3
Sarbāz Iran 87 J4
Sarbāz reg. Iran 89 F5
Sarbhang Bhutan 83 G4
Sarbīsheh Iran 87 I3
Sarda r. Nepal 83 E3
Sard Āb Afgh. 89 H2
Sardarshahr India 82 C3
Sar Dasht Iran 88 B2
Sardegna i. Sardinia Italy see Sardinia
Sardica Bulg. see Sofia
Sardinia i. Sardinia Italy 58 C4
Sardis MS U.S.A. 131 F5
Sardis WV U.S.A. 134 E4
Sardis Lake resr U.S.A. 131 F5
Sar-e Būm Afgh. 89 G3
Sareks nationalpark nat. park Sweden 44 J3
Sarektjåkkå mt. Sweden 44 J3
Sar-e Pol Afgh. 89 G2
Sar-e Pol-e Zahāb Iran 88 B3
Sar Eskandar Iran see Hashtrud
Sare Yazd Iran 88 D4
Sargasso Sea N. Atlantic Ocean 151 P4
Sargodha Pak. 89 I3
Sarh Chad 97 E4
Sarhad reg. Iran 89 F4
Sārī Iran 88 D2
Saria i. Greece 59 L7
Sar-i-Bum Afgh. see Sar-e Būm
Sáric Mex. 127 F7
Sarigan i. N. Mariana Is 69 L3
Sarigh Jilganang Kol salt l. Aksai Chin 82 D2
Sarıgöl Turkey 59 M5
Sarıkamış Turkey 91 F2
Sarikei Sarawak Malaysia 68 E6
Sarikŭl, Qatorkŭhi mts China/Tajik. see Sarykol Range
Sarila India 82 D4
Sarina Australia 110 E4
Sarıoğlan Kayseri Turkey 90 D3
Sarıoğlan Konya Turkey see Belören
Sariqamish Kuli salt l. Turkm./Uzbek. see Sarykamyshskoye Ozero
Sarīr Tibesti des. Libya 97 E2
Sarita U.S.A. 131 D7
Sarıveliler Turkey 85 A1
Sariwŏn N. Korea 75 B5
Sarıyar Barajı resr Turkey 59 N5
Sarıyer Turkey 59 M4
Sarız Turkey 90 E3
Sark i. Channel Is 49 E9
Sarkand Kazakh. 80 E2
Şarkikaraağaç Turkey 59 N5
Şarkışla Turkey 90 E3
Şarköy Turkey 59 L4
Sarlath Range mts Afgh./Pak. 89 G4
Sarmi Indon. 69 J7
Särna Sweden 45 H6
Sarneh Iran 88 B3
Sarnen Switz. 56 I3
Sarni India see Amla
Sarnia Canada 134 D2
Sarny Ukr. 43 E6
Sarolangun Indon. 68 C7
Saroma-ko l. Japan 74 F3
Saronikos Kolpos g. Greece 59 J6
Saros Körfezi b. Turkey 59 L4
Sarova Rus. Fed. 43 I5
Sarowbī Afgh. 89 H3
Sarpa, Ozero l. Rus. Fed. 43 J6
Sarpan i. N. Mariana Is see Rota
Sarpsborg Norway 45 G7
Sarqant Kazakh. see Sarkand
Sarre r. France 52 H5
Sarrebourg France 52 H6
Sarreguemines France 52 H5
Sarria Spain 57 C2
Sarry France 52 E6
Sartana Ukr. 43 H7
Sartanahu Pak. 89 H5
Sartène Corsica France 56 I6
Sarthe r. France 56 D3
Sartu China see Daqing
Saruna Pak. 89 G5
Sarupsar India 82 C3
Şärur Azer. 91 G3
Saru Tara tourist site Afgh. 89 F4
Sarv Iran 88 D3
Sarvābād Iran 88 B3
Sárvár Hungary 58 G1
Sarwar India 82 C4
Sarygamysh Köli salt l. Turkm./Uzbek. see Sarykamyshskoye Ozero
Sary-Ishikotrau, Peski des. Kazakh. see Saryyesik-Atyrau, Peski
Sarykamyshskoye Ozero salt l. Turkm./Uzbek. 91 J2
Sarykol Range mts China/Tajik. 89 I2
Saryozek Kazakh. 80 E3
Saryshagan Kazakh. 80 D2
Sarysu watercourse Kazakh. 80 C2
Sarytash Kazakh. 91 H1
Sary-Tash Kyrg. 89 I2
Saryýazy Suw Howdany resr Turkm. 89 F2
Saryyesik-Atyrau, Peski des. Kazakh. 80 E2
Sarzha Kazakh. 91 H2
Sasar, Tanjung pt Indon. 108 B2
Sasaram India 83 F4
Sasebo Japan 75 C6
Saskatchewan prov. Canada 121 J4
Saskatchewan r. Canada 121 K4
Saskatoon Canada 121 J4
Saskylakh Rus. Fed. 65 M2
Saslaya mt. Nicaragua 137 H6
Sasoi r. India 82 B5
Sasolburg S. Africa 101 H4
Sasovo Rus. Fed. 43 I5
Sass r. Canada 120 H2
Sassandra Côte d'Ivoire 96 C4
Sassari Sardinia Italy 58 C4
Sassenberg Germany 53 I3
Sassnitz Germany 47 N3
Sass Town Liberia 96 C4
Sasykkol', Ozero l. Kazakh. 80 F2
Sasykoli Rus. Fed. 43 J7
Sasyqköl l. Kazakh. see Sasykkol', Ozero
Satahual i. Micronesia see Satawal
Sata-misaki c. Japan 75 C7
Satana India 84 B1
Satan Pass U.S.A. 129 I4
Satara India 84 B2
Satara S. Africa 101 J3
Satawal i. Micronesia 69 L5
Sätbaev Kazakh. see Satpayev
Satevó Mex. 131 B7
Satevo r. Mex. 127 G8
Satırlar Turkey see Yeşilova
Satkania Bangl. 83 H5
Satkhira Bangl. 83 G5
Satluj r. India/Pak. see Sutlej
Satmala Range hills India 84 C2
Satna India 82 E4
Satpayev Kazakh. 80 C2
Satpura Range mts India 82 C5
Satsuma-hantō pen. Japan 75 C7
Sattahip Thai. 71 C4
Satteldorf Germany 53 K5
Satthwa Myanmar 70 A3
Satu Mare Romania 43 D7
Satun Thai. 71 C6
Satwas India 82 D5
Sauceda Mountains U.S.A. 129 G5
Saucillo Mex. 131 B6
Sauda Norway 45 E7
Sauðárkrókur Iceland 44 [inset]
▶Saudi Arabia country Asia 86 F4
5th largest country in Asia.
Sauer r. France 53 I6
Saugatuck U.S.A. 134 B2
Saugeen r. Canada 134 E1
Sāūjbolāgh Iran see Mahābād
Sauk Center U.S.A. 130 E2
Saulieu France 56 G3
Saulnois reg. France 52 G6
Sault Sainte Marie Canada 122 D5
Sault Sainte Marie U.S.A. 132 C2
Saumalkol' Kazakh. 78 F1
Saumarez Reef Australia 110 F4
Saumlakki Indon. 108 E2
Saumur France 56 D3
Saunders, Mount hill Australia 108 E3
Saunders Coast Antarctica 152 J1
Saurimo Angola 99 C4
Sautar Angola 99 B5
Sauvolles, Lac l. Canada 123 G3
Sava r. Europe 58 I2
Savage River Australia 111 [inset]

Savai'i i. Samoa 107 I3
Savala r. Rus. Fed. 43 I6
Savalou Benin 96 D4
Savanat Iran see Eşţahbān
Savane r. Canada 123 H4
Savanna U.S.A. 130 F3
Savannah GA U.S.A. 133 D5
Savannah OH U.S.A. 134 D3
Savannah TN U.S.A. 131 F5
Savannah r. U.S.A. 133 D5
Savannah Sound Bahamas 133 E7
Savannakhét Laos 70 D3
Savanna-la-Mar Jamaica 137 I5
Savant Lake Canada 122 C4
Savant Lake l. Canada 122 C4
Savanur India 84 B3
Sävar Sweden 44 L5
Savaştepe Turkey 59 L5
Savè Benin 96 D4
Save r. Moz./Zimbabwe 99 D6
Sāveh Iran 88 C3
Saverne France 53 H6
Saverne, Col de pass France 53 H6
Saviaho Fin. 44 P5
Savinskiy Rus. Fed. 42 I3
Savitri r. India 84 B2
Savli India 82 C5
Savoie reg. France see Savoy
Savona Italy 58 C2
Savonlinna Fin. 44 P6
Savonranta Fin. 44 P5
Savoy reg. France 56 H3
Şavşat Turkey 91 F2
Sävsjö Sweden 45 I8
Savu i. Indon. 108 C2
Savukoski Fin. 44 P3
Savur Turkey 91 F3
Savu Sea Indon. see Sawu, Laut
Saw Myanmar 70 A2
Sawai Madhopur India 82 D4
Sawan Myanmar 70 B1
Sawar India 82 C4
Sawatch Range mts U.S.A. 126 G5
Sawel Mountain hill U.K. 51 E3
Sawi, Ao b. Thai. 71 B5
Sawn Myanmar 70 B2
Sawtell Australia 112 F3
Sawtooth Range mts U.S.A. 126 C2
Sawu Indon. 108 C2
Sawu i. Indon. see Savu
Sawu, Laut sea Indon. 108 C2
Sawye Myanmar 70 B2
Sawyer U.S.A. 134 B3
Saxilby U.K. 48 G5
Saxmundham U.K. 49 I6
Saxnäs Sweden 44 I4
Saxony land Germany see Sachsen
Saxony-Anhalt land Germany see Sachsen-Anhalt
Saxton U.S.A. 135 F3
Say Niger 96 D3
Sayabouri Laos see Xaignabouli
Sayak Kazakh. 80 E2
Sayanogorsk Rus. Fed. 72 G2
Sayano-Shushenskoye Vodokhranilishche resr Rus. Fed. 72 G2
Sayansk Rus. Fed. 72 I2
Sayaq Kazakh. see Sayak
Sayat Turkm. see Saýat
Saýat Turkm. 89 F2
Şaydā Lebanon see Sidon
Sāyen Iran 88 D4
Sayer Island Thai. see Similan, Ko
Sayghān Afgh. 89 G3
Sayhan-Ovoo Mongolia 72 I3
Şayḩūt Yemen 86 H6
Sayingpan China 76 D3
Saykhin Kazakh. 41 P6
Saylac Somalia 97 H3
Saylan country Asia see Sri Lanka
Saynshand Mongolia 73 K4
Sayoa mt. Spain see Saioa
Sayot Turkm. see Saýat
Şayqal, Baḩr imp. l. Syria 85 C3
Sayqyn Kazakh. see Saykhin
Sayre OK U.S.A. 131 D5
Sayre PA U.S.A. 135 G3
Sayreville U.S.A. 135 H3
Sayula Mex. 136 F5
Sayyod Turkm. see Saýat
Sazdy Kazakh. 43 K7
Sazin Pak. 89 I3
Sbaa Alg. 54 D6
Sbeitla Tunisia 58 C7
Scaddan Australia 109 C8
Scafell Pike hill U.K. 48 D4
Scalasaig U.K. 50 C4
Scalea Italy 58 F5
Scalloway U.K. 50 [inset]
Scalpaigh, Eilean i. U.K. see Scalpay
Scalpay i. U.K. 50 C3
Scapa Flow inlet U.K. 50 F2
Scarba i. U.K. 50 D4
Scarborough Canada 134 F2
Scarborough Trin. and Tob. 137 L6
Scarborough U.K. 48 G4
Scarborough Shoal sea feature S. China Sea 68 F3
Scariff Island Ireland 51 B6
Scarp i. U.K. 50 B2
Scarpanto i. Greece see Karpathos
Schaale r. Germany 53 K1
Schaalsee l. Germany 53 K1
Schaerbeek Belgium 52 E4
Schaffhausen Switz. 56 I3
Schafstädt Germany 53 L3
Schagen Neth. 52 E2
Schagerbrug Neth. 52 E2
Schakalskuppe Namibia 100 C4
Schärding Austria 47 N6
Scharendijke Neth. 52 D3
Scharteberg hill Germany 52 G4
Schaumburg U.S.A. 134 A2
Schebheim Germany 53 K5
Scheeßel Germany 53 J1
Schefferville Canada 123 I3
Scheibbs Austria 47 O6
Schelde r. Belgium see Scheldt
Scheldt r. Belgium 52 E3
Schell Creek Range mts U.S.A. 129 F2
Schellerten Germany 53 K2
Schellville U.S.A. 128 B2
Schenectady U.S.A. 135 I2
Schenefeld Germany 53 J1
Schermerhorn Neth. 52 E2
Schertz U.S.A. 131 D6
Schierling Germany 53 M6
Schiermonnikoog Neth. 52 G1
Schiermonnikoog i. Neth. 52 G1
Schiermonnikoog Nationaal Park nat. park Neth. 52 G1
Schiffdorf Germany 53 I1
Schinnen Neth. 52 F4
Schio Italy 58 D2
Schkeuditz Germany 53 M3
Schleiden Germany 52 G4
Schleiz Germany 53 L4
Schleswig Germany 47 L3
Schleswig-Holstein land Germany 53 K1
Schleswig-Holsteinisches Wattenmeer, Nationalpark nat. park Germany 47 L3
Schleusingen Germany 53 K4
Schlitz Germany 53 J4
Schloss Holte-Stukenbrock Germany 53 I3
Schloss Wartburg tourist site Germany 53 K3
Schlüchtern Germany 53 J4
Schlüsselfeld Germany 53 K5
Schmallenberg Germany 53 I3
Schmidt Island Rus. Fed. see Shmidta, Ostrov
Schmidt Peninsula Rus. Fed. see Shmidta, Poluostrov
Schneeberg Germany 53 M4
Schneidemühl Poland see Piła
Schneidlingen Germany 53 L3
Schneverdingen Germany 53 J1
Schoharie U.S.A. 135 H2
Schönebeck Germany 53 M1
Schönebeck (Elbe) Germany 53 L2
Schönefeld airport Germany 53 N2
Schöningen Germany 53 K2
Schöntal Germany 53 J5
Schoolcraft U.S.A. 134 C2
Schoonhoven Neth. 52 E3
Schopfloch Germany 53 K5
Schöppenstedt Germany 53 K2
Schortens Germany 53 H1
Schouten Island Australia 111 [inset]
Schouten Islands P.N.G. 69 K7
Schrankogel mt. Austria 47 M7
Schreiber Canada 122 D4
Schroon Lake U.S.A. 135 I2
Schröttersburg Poland see Płock
Schulenburg U.S.A. 131 D6
Schuler Canada 121 I5
Schull Ireland 51 C6
Schultz Lake Canada 121 L1
Schüttorf Germany 53 H2
Schuyler U.S.A. 130 D3
Schuyler Lake U.S.A. 135 H2
Schuylkill Haven U.S.A. 135 G3
Schwabach Germany 53 L5
Schwäbische Alb mts Germany 47 L7
Schwäbisch Gmünd Germany 53 J6
Schwäbisch Hall Germany 53 J5
Schwaförden Germany 53 I2
Schwalm r. Germany 53 J3
Schwalmstadt-Ziegenhain Germany 53 J4
Schwandorf Germany 53 M5
Schwaner, Pegunungan mts Indon. 68 E7
Schwanewede Germany 53 I1
Schwarmstedt Germany 53 J2
Schwarze Elster r. Germany 53 M3
Schwarzenbek Germany 53 K1
Schwarzenberg Germany 53 M4
Schwarzer Mann hill Germany 52 G4
Schwarzrand mts Namibia 100 C3
Schwarzwald mts Germany see Black Forest
Schwatka Mountains U.S.A. 118 C3
Schwaz Austria 47 M7
Schwedt an der Oder Germany 47 O4
Schwegenheim Germany 53 I5
Schweich Germany 52 G5
Schweinfurt Germany 53 K4
Schweinitz Germany 53 N3
Schweinrich Germany 53 M1
Schweiz country Europe see Switzerland
Schweizer-Reneke S. Africa 101 G4
Schwelm Germany 53 H3
Schwerin Germany 53 L1
Schweriner See l. Germany 53 L1
Schwetzingen Germany 53 I5
Schwyz Switz. 56 I3
Sciacca Sicily Italy 58 E6
Scicli Sicily Italy 58 F6
Science Hill U.S.A. 134 C5
Scilly, Île atoll Fr. Polynesia see Manuae
Scilly, Isles of U.K. 49 A9
Scioto r. U.S.A. 134 D4
Scipio U.S.A. 129 G2
Scobey U.S.A. 126 G2
Scodra Albania see Shkodër
Scofield Reservoir U.S.A. 129 H2
Scole U.K. 49 I6
Scone Australia 112 E4
Scone U.K. 50 F4
Scoresby Land reg. Greenland 119 P2
Scoresbysund Greenland see Ittoqqortoormiit
Scoresby Sund sea chan. Greenland see Kangertittivaq
Scorno, Punta dello pt Sardinia Italy see Caprara, Punta
Scorpion Bight b. Australia 109 D8
Scotia Ridge sea feature S. Atlantic Ocean 148 E9
Scotia Sea S. Atlantic Ocean 148 F9
Scotland Canada 134 E2
Scotland admin. div. U.K. 50 F3
Scotland U.S.A. 135 G4
Scotstown Canada 123 H5
Scott U.S.A. 134 C3
Scott, Cape Australia 108 E3
Scott, Cape Canada 120 D5
Scott, Mount hill U.S.A. 131 D5
Scott Base research station Antarctica 152 H1
Scottburgh S. Africa 101 J6
Scott City U.S.A. 130 C4
Scott Coast Antarctica 152 H1
Scott Glacier Antarctica 152 I1
Scott Island Antarctica 152 H2
Scott Islands Canada 120 D5
Scott Lake Canada 121 J3
Scott Mountains Antarctica 152 D2
Scott Reef Australia 108 C3
Scottsbluff U.S.A. 130 C3
Scottsboro U.S.A. 133 C5
Scottsburg U.S.A. 134 C4
Scottsville KY U.S.A. 134 B5
Scottsville VA U.S.A. 135 F5
Scourie U.K. 50 D2
Scousburgh U.K. 50 [inset]
Scrabster U.K. 50 F2
Scranton U.S.A. 135 H3
Scunthorpe U.K. 48 G5
Scuol Switz. 56 J3
Scupi Macedonia see Skopje
Scutari Albania see Shkodër
Scutari, Lake Albania/Montenegro 59 H3
Seaboard U.S.A. 135 G5
Seabrook, Lake salt flat Australia 109 B7
Seaford U.K. 49 H8
Seaforth Canada 134 E2
Seal r. Canada 121 M3
Seal, Cape S. Africa 100 F8
Sea Lake Australia 111 C7
Seal Lake Canada 123 J3
Sealy U.S.A. 131 D6
Seaman U.S.A. 134 D4
Seaman Range mts U.S.A. 129 F3
Seamer U.K. 48 G4
Searchlight U.S.A. 129 F4
Searcy U.S.A. 131 F5
Searles Lake U.S.A. 128 E4
Seaside CA U.S.A. 127 C5
Seaside OR U.S.A. 126 C3
Seaside Park U.S.A. 135 H4
Seattle U.S.A. 126 C3
Seaview Range mts Australia 110 D3
Seba Indon. 108 C2
Sebago Lake U.S.A. 135 J2
Sebastea Turkey see Sivas
Sebastian U.S.A. 133 D7
Sebastián Vizcaíno, Bahía b. Mex. 127 E7
Sebasticook r. U.S.A. 135 K1
Sebasticook Lake U.S.A. 135 K1
Sebastopol Ukr. see Sevastopol'
Sebastopol U.S.A. 128 B2
Sebatik i. Indon. 68 F6
Sebba Burkina 96 D3
Seben Turkey 59 N4
Sebenico Croatia see Šibenik
Sebeş Romania 59 J2
Sebewaing U.S.A. 134 D2
Sebezh Rus. Fed. 45 P8
Şebinkarahisar Turkey 90 E2
Sebree U.S.A. 134 B5
Sebring U.S.A. 133 D7
Sebrovo Rus. Fed. 43 I6
Sebta N. Africa see Ceuta
Sebuku i. Indon. 68 F7
Sechelt Canada 120 F5
Sechenovo Rus. Fed. 43 J5
Sechura Peru 142 B5
Sechura, Bahía de b. Peru 142 B5
Seckach Germany 53 J5
Second Mesa U.S.A. 129 H4
Secretary Island N.Z. 113 A7
Secunda S. Africa 101 I4
Secunderabad India 84 C2
Sedalia U.S.A. 130 E4
Sedam India 84 C2
Sedan France 52 E5
Sedan U.S.A. 131 D4
Sedan Dip Australia 110 C3
Seddon N.Z. 113 E5
Seddonville N.Z. 113 C5
Sedeh Iran 88 E3
Sederot Israel 85 B4
Sedlčany Czech Rep. 47 O6
Sedlets Poland see Siedlce
Sedom Israel 85 B4
Sedona U.S.A. 129 H4
Sédrata Alg. 58 B6
Šeduva Lith. 45 M9
Seedorf Germany 53 K1
Seehausen Germany 53 L2
Seehausen (Altmark) Germany 53 L2
Seeheim Namibia 100 C4
Seeheim-Jugenheim Germany 53 I5
Seelig, Mount Antarctica 152 K1
Seelze Germany 53 J2
Seenu Atoll Maldives see Addu Atoll
Sées France 56 E2
Seesen Germany 53 K3
Seevetal Germany 53 K1
Sefadu Sierra Leone 96 B4
Sefare Botswana 101 H2
Seferihisar Turkey 59 L5
Sefīd, Kūh-e mt. Iran 88 C3
Sefophe Botswana 101 H2
Segalstad Norway 45 G6
Segamat Malaysia 71 C7
Ségbana Benin 96 D3
Segeletz Germany 53 M2
Segezha Rus. Fed. 42 G3
Seghnān Afgh. 89 H2
Segontia U.K. see Caernarfon
Segontium U.K. see Caernarfon
Segorbe Spain 57 F4
Ségou Mali 96 C3
Segovia r. Hond./Nicaragua see Coco
Segovia Spain 57 D3
Segozerskoye, Ozero resr Rus. Fed. 42 G3
Seguam Island U.S.A. 118 A4
Séguédine Niger 96 E2
Séguéla Côte d'Ivoire 96 C4
Seguin U.S.A. 131 D6
Segura r. Spain 57 F4
Segura, Sierra de mts Spain 57 E5
Sehithwa Botswana 99 C6
Sehlabathebe National Park Lesotho 101 I5
Sehore India 82 D5
Sehwan Pak. 89 G5
Seibert U.S.A. 130 C4
Seignelay r. Canada 123 H4
Seikphyu Myanmar 70 A2
Seiland i. Norway 44 M1
Seille r. France 52 G5
Seinäjoki Fin. 44 M5
Seine r. Canada 121 N5
Seine r. France 52 A5
Seine, Baie de b. France 56 D2
Seine, Val de valley France 56 F2
Seistan reg. Iran see Sīstān
Sejny Poland 45 M9
Sekayu Indon. 68 C7
Seke China see Sêrtar
Sekoma Botswana 100 F3
Sekondi Ghana 96 C4
Sek'ot'a Eth. 98 D2
Sekura Indon. 71 E7
Şela Rus. Fed. see Shali
Selama Malaysia 71 C6
Selaru i. Indon. 108 E2
Selassi Indon. 69 I7
Selatan, Tanjung pt Indon. 68 E7
Selat Makassar strait Indon. see Makassar, Selat
Selatpanjang Indon. 71 C7
Selawik U.S.A. 118 B3
Selb Germany 53 M4
Selbekken Norway 44 F5
Selbu Norway 44 G5
Selby U.K. 48 F5
Selby U.S.A. 130 C2
Selbyville U.S.A. 135 H4
Selden U.S.A. 130 C4
Selebi-Phikwe Botswana 99 C6
Selebi-Pikwe Botswana see Selebi-Phikwe
Selemdzha r. Rus. Fed. 74 C1
Selemdzhinsk Rus. Fed. 74 C1
Selemdzhinskiy Khrebet mts Rus. Fed. 74 D1
Selendi Turkey 59 M5
▶Selenga r. Mongolia/Rus. Fed. 72 J2
Part of the Yenisey-Angara-Selenga, 3rd longest river in Asia.
Also known as Selenga Mörön.
Selenga Mörön r. Mongolia/Rus. Fed. see Selenga
Seletar Sing. 71 [inset]
Seletar Reservoir Sing. 71 [inset]
Selety r. Kazakh. see Sileti
Seletyteniz, Ozero salt l. Kazakh. see Siletiteniz, Ozero
Seleucia Turkey see Silifke
Seleucia Pieria Turkey see Samandağı
Selfridge U.S.A. 130 C2
Sel'gon Stantsiya Rus. Fed. 74 D2
Selib Rus. Fed. 42 K3
Sélibabi Mauritania 96 B3
Selibe-Phikwe Botswana see Selebi-Phikwe
Seligenstadt Germany 53 I4
Seliger, Ozero l. Rus. Fed. 42 G4
Seligman U.S.A. 129 G4
Selikhino Rus. Fed. 74 E2
Selîma Oasis Sudan 86 C5
Selimiye Turkey 59 L6
Selinsgrove U.S.A. 135 G3
Selizharovo Rus. Fed. 42 G4
Seljord Norway 45 F7
Selkirk Canada 121 L5
Selkirk U.K. 50 G5
Selkirk Mountains Canada 120 G4
Sellafield U.K. 48 D4
Sellersburg U.S.A. 134 C4
Sellore Island Myanmar see Saganthit Kyun
Sells U.S.A. 129 H6
Selm Germany 53 H3
Selma AL U.S.A. 133 C5
Selma CA U.S.A. 128 D3
Selmer U.S.A. 131 F5
Selous, Mount Canada 120 C2
Selseleh-ye Pīr Shūrān mts Iran 89 F4
Selsey Bill hd U.K. 49 G8
Sel'tso Rus. Fed. 43 G5
Selty Rus. Fed. 42 L4
Selu i. Indon. 108 E1
Seluan i. Indon. 71 D6
Selvas reg. Brazil 142 D5
Selvin U.S.A. 134 B4
Selway r. U.S.A. 126 E3
Selwyn Lake Canada 121 J2
Selwyn Mountains Canada 120 D1
Selwyn Range hills Australia 110 B4
Selz r. Germany 53 I5
Semarang Indon. 68 E8
Semau i. Indon. 108 C2
Sembawang Sing. 71 [inset]
Sembé Congo 98 B3
Şemdinli Turkey 91 G3
Semendire Serbia see Smederevo
Semenivka Ukr. 43 G5
Semenov Rus. Fed. 42 J4
Semenovka Ukr. see Semenivka
Semey Kazakh. see Semipalatinsk
Semidi Islands U.S.A. 118 C4
Semikarakorsk Rus. Fed. 43 I7
Semiluki Rus. Fed. 43 H6
Seminoe Reservoir U.S.A. 126 G4
Seminole U.S.A. 131 C5
Semipalatinsk Kazakh. 80 F1
Semirara Islands Phil. 69 G4
Semīrom Iran 88 C4
Sem Kolodezey Ukr. see Lenine
Semnān Iran 88 D3
Semnān va Dāmghān reg. Iran 88 D3
Semois r. Belgium/France 52 E5
Semois, Vallée de la valley Belgium/France 52 E5
Semyonovskoye Arkhangel'skaya Oblast' Rus. Fed. see Bereznik
Semyonovskoye Kostromskaya Oblast' Rus. Fed. see Ostrovskoye
Sena Bol. 142 E6
Sena Madureira Brazil 142 E5
Senanga Zambia 99 C5
Sendai Kagoshima Japan 75 C7
Sendai Miyagi Japan 75 F5
Sêndo China 76 B2
Senebui, Tanjung pt Indon. 71 C7
Seneca KS U.S.A. 130 D4
Seneca OR U.S.A. 126 D3
Seneca Lake U.S.A. 135 G2
Seneca Rocks U.S.A. 134 F4
Senecaville Lake U.S.A. 134 E4
Senegal country Africa 96 B3
Sénégal r. Mauritania/Senegal 96 B3
Seney U.S.A. 130 G2
Senftenberg Germany 47 O5
Senga Hill Zambia 99 D4
Sengerema Tanz. 98 D4
Sengeyskiy, Ostrov i. Rus. Fed. 42 K1
Sengiley Rus. Fed. 43 K5
Sengirli, Mys pt Kazakh. see Syngyrli, Mys
Senhor do Bonfim Brazil 143 J6
Senigallia Italy 58 E3
Senj Croatia 58 F2
Senja i. Norway 44 J2
Sen'kina Rus. Fed. 42 K2
Şenköy Turkey 85 C1
Senlac S. Africa 100 F3
Senlin Shan mt. China 74 C4
Senlis France 52 C5
Senmonorom Cambodia 71 D4
Sennar Sudan 86 D7
Sennen U.K. 49 B8
Senneterre Canada 122 F4
Senqu r. Lesotho 101 H6
Sens France 56 F2
Sensuntepeque El Salvador 136 G6
Senta Serbia 59 I2
Senthal India 82 D3
Sentinel U.S.A. 129 G5
Sentinel Peak Canada 120 F4
Sentosa i. Sing. 71 [inset]
Senwabarwana S. Africa 101 I2
Şenyurt Turkey 91 F3
Seo de Urgell Spain see La Seu d'Urgell
Seonath r. India 84 D1
Seoni India 82 D5
Seorinarayan India 83 E5
▶Seoul S. Korea 75 B5
Capital of South Korea.
Separation Well Australia 108 C5
Sepik r. P.N.G. 69 K7
Sep'o N. Korea 75 B5
Sepon India 83 H4
Seppa India 83 H4
Sept-Îles Canada 123 I4
Sequoia National Park U.S.A. 128 D3
Serafimovich Rus. Fed. 43 I6
Sêraitang China see Baima
Seram i. Indon. 69 H7
Seram, Laut sea Indon. 69 I7
Serang Indon. 68 D8
Serangoon Harbour b. Sing. 71 [inset]
Serapi, Gunung hill Indon. 71 E7
Serapong, Mount hill Sing. 71 [inset]
Serasan i. Indon. 71 E7
Serasan, Selat sea chan. Indon. 71 E7
Seraya i. Indon. 71 E7
Serbâl, Gebel mt. Egypt see Sirbāl, Jabal
▶Serbia country Europe 59 I3
Formerly known as Yugoslavia and as Serbia and Montenegro. Up to 1993 included Bosnia-Herzegovina, Croatia, Macedonia, Montenegro and Slovenia. Became independent from Montenegro in June 2006. Kosovo declared independence in February 2008.
Sêrbug Co l. China 83 G2
Sêrca China 76 B2
Serchhip India 83 H5
Serdar Turkm. 88 E2
Serdica Bulg. see Sofia
Serdo Eth. 98 E2
Serdoba r. Rus. Fed. 43 J5
Serdobsk Rus. Fed. 43 J5
Serebryansk Kazakh. 80 F2
Seredka Rus. Fed. 45 P7
Şereflikoçhisar Turkey 90 D3
Seremban Malaysia 71 C7
Serengeti National Park Tanz. 98 D4
Serenje Zambia 99 D5
Serezha r. Rus. Fed. 42 I5
Sergach Rus. Fed. 42 J5
Sergeyevka Rus. Fed. 74 B2
Sergiyev Posad Rus. Fed. 42 H4
Sergo Ukr. see Stakhanov
Serh China 80 I4
Serhetabat Turkm. 89 F3
Serifos i. Greece 59 K6
Sérigny r. Canada 123 H3
Sérigny, Lac l. Canada 123 H3
Serik Turkey 90 C3
Seringapatam Reef Australia 108 C3
Sêrkang China see Nyainrong
Sermata i. Indon. 108 E2
Sermata, Kepulauan is Indon. 108 E2
Sermersuaq glacier Greenland 119 M2
Sermilik inlet Greenland 119 O3
Sernovodsk Rus. Fed. 43 K5
Sernur Rus. Fed. 42 K4
Sernyy Zavod Turkm. see Kükürtli
Seronga Botswana 99 C5
Serov Rus. Fed. 41 S4
Serowe Botswana 101 H2
Serpa Port. 57 C5
Serpa Pinto Angola see Menongue
Serpentine Lakes salt flat Australia 109 E7
Serpukhov Rus. Fed. 43 H5
Serra Brazil 145 C3
Serra Alta Brazil 145 A4
Serrachis r. Cyprus 85 A2
Serra da Bocaina, Parque Nacional da nat. park Brazil 145 B3
Serra da Canastra, Parque Nacional da nat. park Brazil 145 B3
Serra da Mesa, Represa resr Brazil 145 A1
Serra das Araras Brazil 145 B1
Serra do Divisor, Parque Nacional da nat. park Brazil 142 D5
Sérrai Greece see Serres
Serranía de la Neblina, Parque Nacional nat. park Venez. 142 E3
Serraria, Ilha i. Brazil see Queimada, Ilha
Serra Talhada Brazil 143 K5
Serre r. France 52 D5
Serres Greece 59 J4
Serrinha Brazil 143 K6
Sêrro Brazil 145 C2
Sers Tunisia 58 C6
Sertanópolis Brazil 145 A3
Sertãozinho Brazil 145 B3
Sêrtar China 76 D1
Sertavul Geçidi pass Turkey 85 A1
Sertolovo Rus. Fed. 45 Q6
Seruai Indon. 71 B6
Serui Indon. 69 J7
Serule Botswana 99 C6
Seruna India 82 C3
Sêrwolungwa China 76 B1
Sêrxü China 76 C1
Seryshevo Rus. Fed. 74 C2
Seseganaga Lake Canada 122 C4
Sese Islands Uganda 98 D4
Sesel country Indian Ocean see Seychelles
Sesfontein Namibia 99 B5
Seshachalam Hills India 84 C3
Sesheke Zambia 99 C5
Sesostris Bank sea feature India 84 A3
Ses Salines, Cap de c. Spain 57 H4
Sestri Levante Italy 58 C2
Sestroretsk Rus. Fed. 45 P6
Set, Phou mt. Laos 70 D4
Sète France 56 F5
Sete Lagoas Brazil 145 B2
Setermoen Norway 44 K2
Setesdal valley Norway 45 E7
Seti r. Nepal 82 E3
Sétif Alg. 54 F4
Seto Japan 75 E6
Seto-naikai sea Japan 73 O6
Seto-naikai Kokuritsu-kōen nat. park Japan 75 D6
Setsan Myanmar 70 A3
Settat Morocco 54 C5
Settepani, Monte mt. Italy 58 C2
Settle U.K. 48 E4
Setúbal Port. 57 B4
Setúbal, Baía de b. Port. 57 B4
Seul, Lac l. Canada 121 M5
Sevan Armenia 91 G2
Sevan, Lake Armenia 91 G2
Sevan, Ozero l. Armenia see Sevan, Lake
Sevana Lich l. Armenia see Sevan, Lake
Sevastopol' Ukr. 90 D1
Seven Islands Canada see Sept-Îles
Seven Islands Bay Canada 123 J2
Sevenoaks U.K. 49 H7
Seventy Mile House Canada see 70 Mile House
Sévérac-le-Château France 56 F4
Severn r. Australia 112 E2
Severn r. Canada 122 D3
Severn S. Africa 100 F4
Severn r. U.K. 49 E7
also known as Hafren
Severnaya Dvina r. Rus. Fed. 42 I2
Severnaya Sos'va r. Rus. Fed. 41 T3
Severnaya Zemlya is Rus. Fed. 65 L1
Severn Lake Canada 121 N4
Severnoye Rus. Fed. 41 Q5
Severnyy Nenetskiy Avtonomnyy Okrug Rus. Fed. 42 K1
Severnyy Respublika Komi Rus. Fed. 64 H3
Severobaykal'sk Rus. Fed. 73 J1
Severo-Baykal'skoye Nagor'ye mts Rus. Fed. 65 M4
Severodonetsk Ukr. see Syeverodonets'k
Severodvinsk Rus. Fed. 42 H2
Severo-Kuril'sk Rus. Fed. 65 Q4
Severomorsk Rus. Fed. 44 R2
Severoonezhsk Rus. Fed. 42 H3
Severo-Sibirskaya Nizmennost' lowland Rus. Fed. see North Siberian Lowland
Severoural'sk Rus. Fed. 41 R3
Severo-Yeniseyskiy Rus. Fed. 64 K3
Severskaya Rus. Fed. 90 E1
Severskiy Donets r. Rus. Fed./Ukr. 43 I7
also known as Northern Donets, Sivers'kyy Donets'
Sevier U.S.A. 129 G2
Sevier r. U.S.A. 129 G2
Sevier Desert U.S.A. 129 G2
Sevier Lake U.S.A. 129 G2
Sevierville U.S.A. 132 D5
Sevilla Col. 142 C3
Sevilla Spain see Seville
Seville Spain 57 D5
Sevlyush Ukr. see Vynohradiv
Sewani India 82 C3
Seward AK U.S.A. 118 D3
Seward NE U.S.A. 130 D3
Seward Mountains Antarctica 152 L2
Seward Peninsula U.S.A. 118 B3
Sexi Spain see Almuñécar
Sexsmith Canada 120 G4
Sextín Mex. 131 B7
Seyah Band Koh mts Afgh. 89 F3
Seyakha Rus. Fed. 153 F2
Seychelles country Indian Ocean 149 L6
Seydi Turkm. 89 F2
Seydişehir Turkey 90 C3
Seyðisfjörður Iceland 44 [inset]
Seyhan Turkey see Adana
Seyhan r. Turkey 85 B1
Seyitgazi Turkey 59 N5
Seym r. Rus. Fed./Ukr. 43 G6
Seymchan Rus. Fed. 65 Q3
Seymour Australia 112 B6
Seymour S. Africa 101 H7
Seymour IN U.S.A. 134 C4
Seymour TX U.S.A. 131 D5
Seymour Inlet Canada 120 E5
Seymour Range mts Australia 109 F6
Seypan i. N. Mariana Is see Saipan
Seyyedābād Afgh. 89 H3
Sézanne France 52 D6
Sfakia Kriti Greece see Chora Sfakion
Sfântu Gheorghe Romania 59 K2
Sfax Tunisia 58 D7
Sfikia, Limni resr Greece see Sfikias, Limni
Sfikias, Limni resr Greece 59 J4
Sfîntu Gheorghe Romania see Sfântu Gheorghe
Sgiersch Poland see Zgierz
's-Graveland Neth. 52 F2
's-Gravenhage Neth. see The Hague
Sgurr Alasdair hill U.K. 50 C3
Sgurr Dhomhnuill hill U.K. 50 D4
Sgurr Mòr mt. U.K. 50 D3
Sgurr na Ciche mt. U.K. 50 D3
Shaanxi prov. China 76 F1
Shaartuz Tajik. see Shahrtuz
Shaban Pak. 89 G4
Shabani Zimbabwe see Zvishavane

Shabeelle, Webi r. Ethiopia/Somalia see Shebelē Wenz, Wabē
Shabestar Iran 88 B2
Shabībī, Jabal ash mt. Jordan 85 B5
Shabla, Nos pt Bulg. 59 M3
Shabogamo Lake Canada 123 I3
Shabunda Dem. Rep. Congo 98 C4
Shache China 80 E4
Shackleton Coast Antarctica 152 H1
Shackleton Glacier Antarctica 152 I1
Shackleton Ice Shelf Antarctica 152 F2
Shackleton Range mts Antarctica 152 A1
Shadaogou China 77 F2
Shadaw Myanmar 70 B3
Shādegān Iran 88 C4
Shadihar Pak. 89 G4
Shady Grove U.S.A. 126 C4
Shady Spring U.S.A. 134 E5
Shafer, Lake U.S.A. 134 B3
Shafer Peak Antarctica 152 H2
Shafter U.S.A. 128 D4
Shaftesbury U.K. 49 E7
Shagamu r. Canada 122 D3
Shagedu China 73 K5
Shageluk U.S.A. 118 C3
Shaghyray Üstirti plat. Kazakh. see Shagyray, Plato
Shagonar Rus. Fed. 80 H1
Shag Point N.Z. 113 C7
Shag Rocks is S. Georgia 144 H8
Shagyray, Plato plat. Kazakh. 80 A2
Shahabad Karnataka India 84 C2
Shahabad Rajasthan India 82 D4
Shahabad Uttar Prad. India 82 E4
Shāhābād Iran see Eslāmābād-e Gharb
Shah Alam Malaysia 71 C7
Shah Bandar Pak. 89 G5
Shahdād Iran 88 E4
Shahdol India 82 E5
Shahe China 77 F2
Shahejie China see Jiujiang
Shahezhen China see Jiujiang
Shah Fuladi mt. Afgh. 89 G3
Shahid, Ras pt Pak. 89 F5
Shāhīn Dezh Iran see Sa'īndezh
Shah Ismail Afgh. 89 G4
Shahjahanpur India 82 D4
Shāh Jehān, Kūh-e mts Iran 88 E2
Shāh Jūy Afgh. 89 G3
Shāh Kūh mt. Iran 88 E4
Shāhpūr Iran see Salmās
Shahrak Afgh. 89 G3
Shahrakht Iran 89 F3
Shahr-e Bābak Iran 88 D4
Shahr-e Kord Iran 88 C3
Shahr-e Ṣafā Afgh. 89 G4
Shahrezā Iran 88 C3
Shahrig Pak. 89 G4
Shahrisabz Uzbek. 89 G2
Shahriston Tajik. 89 H2
Shahr Rey Iran 88 C3
Shahr Sultan Pak. 89 H4
Shahrtuz Tajik. 89 H2
Shāhrūd Iran see Emāmrūd
Shāhrūd, Rūdkhāneh-ye r. Iran 88 C2
Shahrud Bustam reg. Iran 88 D3
Shāh Savārān, Kūh-e mts Iran 88 E4
Shāh Taqī Iran see Emām Taqī
Shaighalu Pak. 89 H4
Shaikh Husain mt. Pak. 89 G4
Shaikhpura India see Sheikhpura
Shā'īr, Jabal mts Syria 85 C2
Sha'īra, Gebel mt. Egypt see Sha'īrah, Jabal
Sha'īrah, Jabal mt. Egypt 85 B5
Shaj'ah, Jabal hill Saudi Arabia 88 C5
Shajapur India 82 D5
Shajianzi China 74 B4
Shakaville S. Africa 101 J5
Shakh Tajik. see Shoh
Shakhbuz Azer. see Şahbuz
Shākhen Iran 89 E3
Shakhovskaya Rus. Fed. 42 G4
Shakhrisabz Uzbek. see Shahrisabz
Shakhristan Tajik. see Shahriston
Shakhtinsk Kazakh. 80 D2
Shakhty Respublika Buryatiya Rus. Fed. see Gusinoozersk
Shakhty Rostovskaya Oblast' Rus. Fed. 43 I7
Shakhun'ya Rus. Fed. 42 J4
Shaki Nigeria 96 D4
Shakotan-hantō pen. Japan 74 F4
Shalakusha Rus. Fed. 42 I3
Shalang China 77 F4
Shali Rus. Fed. 91 G2
Shaliuhe China see Gangca
Shalkar India 82 D3
Shalkar Kazakh. 80 A2
Shalkarteniz, Solonchak salt marsh Kazakh. 80 B2
Shalqar Kazakh. see Shalkar
Shaluli Shan mts China 76 C2
Shaluni mt. India 83 I3
Shama r. Tanz. 99 D4
Shamâl Sînâ' governorate Egypt see Shamāl Sīnā'
Shamāl Sīnā' governorate Egypt 85 A4
Shamalzā'ī Afgh. 89 G4
Shāmat al Akbād des. Saudi Arabia 91 F5
Shamattawa Canada 121 N4
Shamattawa r. Canada 122 D3
Shambār Iran 88 C3
Shamgong Bhutan see Shemgang
Shamīl Iran 88 E5
Shāmīyah des. Iraq/Syria 85 D2
Shamkhor Azer. see Şämkir
Shamrock U.S.A. 131 C5
Shancheng Fujian China see Taining
Shancheng Shandong China see Shanxian
Shand Afgh. 89 F4
Shandan China 80 J4
Shandong prov. China 77 H1
Shandong Bandao pen. China 73 M5
Shandur Pass Pak. 89 I2
Shangchao China 77 F3
Shangcheng China 77 G2
Shangchuan Dao i. China 77 G4
Shangdu China 73 K4
Shangganling China 74 C3

▶Shanghai China 77 I2
4th most populous city in Asia and 7th in the world.

Shanghai municipality China 77 I2
Shangji China see Xichuan
Shangjie China see Yangbi
Shangjin China 77 F1
Shangluo China 77 F1
Shangmei China see Xinhua
Shangnan China 77 F1
Shangpa China see Fugong
Shangpai China see Feixi
Shangpaihe China see Feixi
Shangqiu Henan China 77 G1
Shangqiu Henan China see Suiyang
Shangrao China 77 H2
Shangshui China 77 G1
Shangyou China 77 G3
Shangyou Shuiku resr China 80 F3
Shangyu China 77 I2
Shangzhi China 74 B3
Shangzhou Shaanxi China see Shangluo
Shangzhou Shaanxi China see Shangluo
Shanhe China see Zhengning
Shanhetun China 74 B3
Shankou China 77 F4
Shanlaragh Ireland 51 C6
Shannon airport Ireland 51 D5
Shannon est. Ireland 51 D5
Shannon r. Ireland 51 D5
Shannon, Mouth of the Ireland 51 C5
Shannon National Park Australia 109 B8
Shannon Ø i. Greenland 153 I1
Shan Plateau Myanmar 70 B2
Shansi prov. China see Shanxi
Shan Teng hill H.K. China see Victoria Peak
Shantipur India 83 G5
Shantou China 77 H4
Shantung prov. China see Shandong
Shanwei China 77 G4
Shanxi prov. China 77 F1
Shanxian China 77 H1
Shanyang China 77 F1
Shaodong China 77 F3
Shaoguan China 77 G3
Shaowu China 77 H3
Shaoxing China 77 I2
Shaoyang China 77 F3
Shap U.K. 48 E4
Shapa China 77 F4
Shaping China see Ebian
Shapinsay i. U.K. 50 G1
Shapkina r. Rus. Fed. 42 L2
Shapshal'skiy Khrebet mts Rus. Fed. 80 G1
Shaqrā' Saudi Arabia 86 G4
Shār, Jabal mt. Saudi Arabia 90 D6
Sharaf well Iraq 91 F5
Sharan Paktīkā 89 H3
Sharan Jogizai Pak. 89 H4
Shārb Māh Iran 88 E4
Shardara Kazakh. 80 C3
Shardara, Step' plain Kazakh. see Chardara, Step'
Shari r. Cameroon/Chad see Chari
Shārī, Buḩayrat imp. l. Iraq 91 G4
Shari-dake vol. Japan 74 G4
Sharīfah Syria 85 C2
Sharjah U.A.E. 88 D5
Sharka-leb La pass China 83 G3
Sharkawshchyna Belarus 45 O9
Shark Bay Australia 109 A6
Shark Reef Australia 110 D2
Sharlyk Rus. Fed. 41 Q5
Sharm ash Shaykh Egypt 90 D6
Sharm el Sheikh Egypt see Sharm ash Shaykh
Sharon U.S.A. 134 E3
Sharon Springs U.S.A. 130 C4
Sharpe Lake Canada 121 M4
Sharp Peak hill H.K. China 77 [inset]
Sharqat Iraq see Ash Sharqāţ
Sharqī, Jabal ash mts Lebanon/Syria 85 B3
Sharqiy Ustyurt Chink esc. Uzbek. 80 A3
Sharur Azer. see Şärur
Shar'ya Rus. Fed. 42 J4
Shashe r. Botswana/Zimbabwe 99 C6
Shashemenē Eth. 98 D3
Shashi China see Jingzhou
Shasta U.S.A. 128 B1
Shasta, Mount vol. U.S.A. 126 C4
Shasta Lake U.S.A. 128 B1
Shatilki Belarus see Svyetlahorsk
Sha Tin H.K. China 77 [inset]
Shatki Rus. Fed. 43 J5
Shaṭnat as Salmās, Wādī watercourse Syria 85 D2
Sha Tong Hau Shan H.K. China see Bluff Island
Shatoy Rus. Fed. 91 G2
Shatsk Rus. Fed. 43 I5
Shaṭṭ al 'Arab r. Iran/Iraq 91 H5
Shatura Rus. Fed. 43 H5
Shaubak Jordan see Ash Shawbak
Shaunavon Canada 121 I5
Shaver Lake U.S.A. 128 D3
Shaw r. Australia 108 B5
Shawangunk Mountains hills U.S.A. 135 H3
Shawano U.S.A. 134 A1
Shawano Lake U.S.A. 134 A1
Shawinigan Canada 123 G5
Shawnee OK U.S.A. 131 D5
Shawnee WY U.S.A. 126 G4
Shawneetown U.S.A. 130 F4
Shaxian China 77 H3
Shay Gap (abandoned) Australia 108 C5
Shaykh, Jabal ash mt. Lebanon/Syria see Hermon, Mount
Shaykh Miskīn Syria 85 C3
Shayṭūr Iran 88 D4
Shāzand Iran 88 C3
Shaẕāẕ, Jabal mt. Saudi Arabia 91 F6
Shazud Tajik. 89 I2
Shchekino Rus. Fed. 43 H5
Shchel'yayur Rus. Fed. 42 L2
Shcherbakov Rus. Fed. see Rybinsk
Shchigry Rus. Fed. 43 H6
Shchors Ukr. 43 F6
Shchuchin Belarus see Shchuchyn
Shchuchyn Belarus 45 N10
Shebalino Rus. Fed. 80 G1
Shebekino Rus. Fed. 43 H6

▶Shebelē Wenz, Wabē r. Ethiopia/Somalia 98 E3
5th longest river in Africa.

Sheberghān Afgh. 89 G2
Sheboygan U.S.A. 134 B2
Shebshi Mountains Nigeria 96 E4
Shebunino Rus. Fed. 74 F3
Shediac Canada 123 I5
Shedin Peak Canada 120 E4
Shedok Rus. Fed. 91 F1
Sheelin, Lough l. Ireland 51 E4
Sheep Haven b. Ireland 51 E2
Sheepmoor S. Africa 101 J4
Sheep Mountain U.S.A. 129 J2
Sheep Peak U.S.A. 129 F3
Sheep's Head hd Ireland see Muntervary
Sheerness U.K. 49 H7
Sheet Harbour Canada 123 J5
Shefar'am Israel 85 B3
Sheffield N.Z. 113 D6
Sheffield U.K. 48 F5
Sheffield AL U.S.A. 133 C5
Sheffield PA U.S.A. 134 F3
Sheffield TX U.S.A. 131 C6
Sheffield Lake Canada 123 K4
Shegah Afgh. 89 G4
Shegmas Rus. Fed. 42 K2
Shehong China 76 E2
Sheikh, Jebel esh mt. Lebanon/Syria see Hermon, Mount
Sheikhpura India 83 F4
Sheikhupura Pak. 89 I4
Shekak r. Canada 122 D4
Shekār Āb Iran 88 D3
Shekhawati reg. India 89 I5
Shekhem West Bank see Nāblus
Shekhpura India see Sheikhpura
Sheki Azer. see Şäki
Shekka Ch'ün-Tao H.K. China see Soko Islands
Shek Kwu Chau i. H.K. China 77 [inset]
Shekou China 77 [inset]
Sheksna Rus. Fed. 42 H4
Sheksninskoye Vodokhranilishche resr Rus. Fed. 42 H4
Shek Uk Shan mt. H.K. China 77 [inset]
Shela China 76 B2
Shelagskiy, Mys pt Rus. Fed. 65 S2
Shelbina U.S.A. 130 E4
Shelburn U.S.A. 134 B4
Shelburne N.S. Canada 123 I6
Shelburne Ont. Canada 134 E1
Shelburne Bay Australia 110 C1
Shelby MI U.S.A. 134 B2
Shelby MS U.S.A. 131 F5
Shelby MT U.S.A. 126 F2
Shelby NC U.S.A. 133 D5
Shelbyville IL U.S.A. 130 F4
Shelbyville IN U.S.A. 134 C4
Shelbyville KY U.S.A. 134 C4
Shelbyville TN U.S.A. 132 C5
Sheldon IA U.S.A. 130 E3
Sheldon IL U.S.A. 134 B3
Sheldrake Canada 123 I4
Shelek Kazakh. see Chilik
Shelikhova, Zaliv g. Rus. Fed. 65 Q3
Shelikof Strait U.S.A. 118 C4
Shell U.S.A. 130 B2
Shellbrook Canada 121 J4
Shelley U.S.A. 126 E4
Shellharbour Australia 112 E5
Shell Lake Canada 121 J4
Shell Lake U.S.A. 130 F2
Shell Mountain U.S.A. 128 B1
Shelter Bay Canada see Port-Cartier
Shelter Island U.S.A. 135 I3
Shelter Point N.Z. 113 B8
Shelton U.S.A. 126 C3
Shemakha Azer. see Şamaxı
Shemgang Bhutan 83 G4
Shemordan Rus. Fed. 42 K4
Shenandoah IA U.S.A. 130 E3
Shenandoah PA U.S.A. 135 G3
Shenandoah Mountains U.S.A. 134 F4
Shenandoah National Park U.S.A. 135 F4
Shendam Nigeria 96 D4
Shending Shan hill China 74 D3
Shengena mt. Tanz. 99 D4
Shengli China 77 G2
Shengli Feng mt. China/Kyrg. see Pobeda Peak
Shengping China 74 B3
Shengrenjian China see Pinglu
Shengsi China 77 I2
Shengsi Liedao is China 77 I2
Shenjiamen China 77 I2
Shen Khan Bandar Afgh. 89 H2
Shenkursk Rus. Fed. 42 I3
Shenmu China 73 K5
Shennong Ding mt. China 77 F2
Shennongjia China 77 F2
Shenqiu China 77 G1
Shenshu China 74 C3
Shensi prov. China see Shaanxi
Shentala Rus. Fed. 43 K5
Shenton, Mount hill Australia 109 C7
Shenyang China 74 A4
Shenzhen China 77 G4
Shenzhen Wan b. H.K. China see Deep Bay
Sheopur India 82 D4
Shepetivka Ukr. 43 E6
Shepetovka Ukr. see Shepetivka
Shepherd Islands Vanuatu 107 G3
Shepherdsville U.S.A. 134 C5
Shepparton Australia 112 B6
Sheppey, Isle of i. U.K. 49 H7
Sheqi China 77 G1
Sherabad Uzbek. see Sherobod
Sherborne U.K. 49 E8
Sherbro Island Sierra Leone 96 B4
Sherbrooke Canada 123 H5
Sherburne U.S.A. 135 H2
Shercock Ireland 51 F4
Shereiq Sudan 86 D6
Shergaon India 83 H4
Shergarh India 82 C4
Sheridan AR U.S.A. 131 E5
Sheridan WY U.S.A. 126 G3
Sheringham U.K. 49 I6
Sherman U.S.A. 131 D5
Sherman Mountain U.S.A. 129 F1
Sherobod Uzbek. 89 G2
Sherpur Dhaka Bangl. 83 G4
Sherpur Rajshahi Bangl. 83 G4
Sherridon Canada 121 K4
's-Hertogenbosch Neth. 52 F3
Sherwood Forest reg. U.K. 49 F5
Sherwood Lake Canada 121 K2
Sheslay Canada 120 D3
Sheslay r. Canada 120 C3
Shethanei Lake Canada 121 L3
Shetland Islands is U.K. 50 [inset]
Shetpe Kazakh. 78 E2
Sheung Shui H.K. China 77 [inset]
Sheung Sze Mun sea chan. H.K. China 77 [inset]
Shevchenko Kazakh. see Aktau
Shevli r. Rus. Fed. 74 D1
Shexian China 77 H2
Sheyang China 77 I1
Sheyenne r. U.S.A. 130 D2
Shey Phoksundo National Park Nepal 83 E3
Shiant Islands U.K. 50 C3
Shiashkotan, Ostrov i. Rus. Fed. 65 Q5
Shibām Yemen 86 G6
Shibar, Kowtal-e Afgh. 89 H3
Shibata Japan 75 E5
Shibazhan China 74 B1
Shibh Jazīrat Sīnā' pen. Egypt see Sinai
Shibīn al Kawm Egypt 90 C5
Shibîn el Kôm Egypt see Shibīn al Kawm
Shibogama Lake Canada 122 C3
Shibotsu-jima i. Rus. Fed. see Zelenyy, Ostrov
Shicheng Fujian China see Zhouning
Shicheng Jiangxi China 77 H3
Shidād al Mismā' hill Saudi Arabia 85 D4
Shidao China 73 M5
Shidian China 76 C3
Shiel, Loch l. U.K. 50 D4
Shield, Cape Australia 110 B2
Shīeli Kazakh. see Chiili
Shifa, Jabal ash mts Saudi Arabia 90 D5
Shifang China 76 E2
Shigatse China see Xigazê
Shiḩān mt. Jordan 85 B4
Shihezi China 80 G3
Shihkiachwang China see Shijiazhuang
Shijiao China see Fogang
Shijiazhuang China 73 K5
Shijiu Hu l. China 77 H2
Shijiusuo China see Rizhao
Shikag Lake Canada 122 C4
Shikar r. Pak. 89 F4
Shikarpur Pak. 89 H5
Shikengkong mt. China 77 G3
Shikhany Rus. Fed. 43 J5
Shikohabad India 82 D4
Shikoku i. Japan 75 D6
Shikoku-sanchi mts Japan 75 D6
Shikotan, Ostrov i. Rus. Fed. 74 G4
Shikotan-tō i. Rus. Fed. see Shikotan, Ostrov
Shikotsu-Tōya Kokuritsu-kōen nat. park Japan 74 F4
Shildon U.K. 48 F4
Shilega Rus. Fed. 42 J2
Shiliguri India 83 G4
Shilin China 76 D3
Shilipu China 77 G2
Shiliu China see Changjiang
Shilla mt. India 82 D2
Shillelagh Ireland 51 F5
Shillo r. Israel 85 B3
Shillong India 83 G4
Shilovo Rus. Fed. 43 I5
Shimada Japan 75 E6
Shimanovsk Rus. Fed. 74 B1
Shimbiris mt. Somalia 98 E2
Shimen Gansu China 76 D1
Shimen Hunan China 77 F2
Shimen Yunnan China see Yunlong
Shimla India 82 D3
Shimoga India 84 B3
Shimokita-hantō pen. Japan 74 F4
Shimoni Kenya 99 D4
Shimonoseki Japan 75 C6
Shimsk Rus. Fed. 42 F4
Shin, Loch l. U.K. 50 E2
Shināfīyah Iraq see Ash Shanāfīyah
Shinan China see Xingye
Shīndand Afgh. 89 F3
Shingbwiyang Myanmar 70 B1
Shing-gai Myanmar 70 B1
Shinghshal Pass Pak. 89 I2
Shingletown U.S.A. 128 C1
Shingū Japan 75 E6
Shingwedzi S. Africa 101 J2
Shingwedzi r. S. Africa 101 J2
Shīnkāy Afgh. 89 G4
Shīnkay Ghar Afgh. 89 H3
Shinnston U.S.A. 134 E4
Shinshār Syria 85 C2
Shinyanga Tanz. 98 D4
Shiocton U.S.A. 134 A1
Shiogama Japan 75 F5
Shiono-misaki c. Japan 75 D6
Shipai China 77 H2
Shiping China 76 D4
Shipki Pass China/India 82 D3
Shipman U.S.A. 135 F5
Shippegan Island Canada 123 I5
Shippensburg U.S.A. 135 G3
Shiprock U.S.A. 129 I3
Shiprock Peak U.S.A. 129 I3
Shipu China 77 I2
Shipunovo Rus. Fed. 72 E2
Shiqian China 77 F3
Shiqiao China see Panyu
Shiqizhen China see Zhongshan
Shiquan China 77 F1
Shiquanhe Xizang China see Ali
Shiquanhe Xizang China see Gar
Shiquan Shuiku resr China 77 F1
Shira Rus. Fed. 72 F2
Shīrābād Iran 88 C2
Shirakawa-go and Gokayama tourist site Japan 75 E5
Shirane-san vol. Japan 75 E5
Shirase Coast Antarctica 152 J1
Shirase Glacier Antarctica 152 D2
Shīrāz Iran 88 D4
Shire r. Malawi 99 D5
Shireza Pak. 89 G5
Shirīn Tagāb Afgh. 89 G2
Shiriya-zaki c. Japan 74 F4
Shirkala reg. Kazakh. 80 A2
Shīr Kūh mt. Iran 88 D4
Shiroro Reservoir Nigeria 96 D3
Shirpur India 82 C5
Shirten Holoy Gobi des. China 80 I3
Shīrvān Iran 88 E2
Shisanzhan China 74 B2
Shishaldin Volcano U.S.A. 118 B4
Shisha Pangma mt. China see Xixabangma Feng
Shishou China 77 G2
Shitan China 77 G3
Shitang China 77 I2
Shithāthah Iraq 91 F4
Shiv India 82 B4
Shiveluch, Sopka vol. Rus. Fed. 65 R4
Shivpuri India 82 D4
Shivwits U.S.A. 129 G3
Shivwits Plateau U.S.A. 129 G3
Shiwan Dashan mts China 76 E4
Shiwa Ngandu Zambia 99 D5
Shixing China 77 G3
Shiyan China 77 F1
Shizhu China 77 F2
Shizilu China see Junan
Shizipu China 77 H2
Shizong China 76 D3
Shizuishan China 72 J5
Shizuoka Japan 75 E6

▶Shkhara mt. Georgia/Rus. Fed. 91 F2
3rd highest mountain in Europe.

Shklov Belarus see Shklow
Shklow Belarus 43 F5
Shkodër Albania 59 H3
Shkodra Albania see Shkodër
Shkodrës, Liqeni i l. Albania/Montenegro see Scutari, Lake
Shmidta, Ostrov i. Rus. Fed. 64 K1
Shmidta, Poluostrov pen. Rus. Fed. 74 F1
Shoal Lake Canada 121 K5
Shoals U.S.A. 134 B4
Shōbara Japan 75 D6
Shoh Tajik. 89 H2
Shohi Pass Pak. see Tal Pass
Shokanbetsu-dake mt. Japan 74 F4
Sholakkorgan Kazakh. 80 C3
Sholapur India see Solapur
Sholaqorghan Kazakh. see Sholakkorgan
Shomba r. Rus. Fed. 44 R4
Shomvukva Rus. Fed. 42 K3
Shona Ridge sea feature S. Atlantic Ocean 148 I9
Shonzha Kazakh. see Chundzha
Shor India 82 D2
Shorap Pak. 89 G5
Shorapur India 84 C2
Shorawak reg. Afgh. 89 G4
Sho'rchi Uzbek. 89 G2
Shorewood IL U.S.A. 134 A3
Shorewood WI U.S.A. 134 B2
Shorkot Pak. 89 I4
Shorkozakhly, Solonchak salt flat Turkm. 91 J2
Shoshone CA U.S.A. 128 E4
Shoshone ID U.S.A. 126 E4
Shoshone r. U.S.A. 126 F3
Shoshone Mountains U.S.A. 128 E2
Shoshone Peak U.S.A. 128 E3
Shoshong Botswana 101 H2
Shoshoni U.S.A. 126 F4
Shostka Ukr. 43 G6
Shotor Khūn Afgh. 89 G3
Shouyang Shan mt. China 77 F1
Showak Sudan 86 E7
Show Low U.S.A. 129 H4
Shoyna Rus. Fed. 42 J2
Shpakovskoye Rus. Fed. 91 F1
Shpola Ukr. 43 F6
Shqipëria country Europe see Albania
Shreve U.S.A. 134 D3
Shreveport U.S.A. 131 E5
Shrewsbury U.K. 49 E6
Shri Lanka country Asia see Sri Lanka
Shri Mohangarh India 82 B4
Shrirampur India 83 G5
Shu Kazakh. 80 D3
Shū r. Kazakh./Kyrg. see Chu
Shu'ab, Ra's pt Yemen 87 H7
Shuajingsi China 76 D1
Shuangbai China 76 D3
Shuangcheng Fujian China see Zherong
Shuangcheng Heilong. China 74 B3
Shuanghe China 77 G2
Shuanghechang China 76 E2
Shuanghedagang China 74 C2
Shuangjiang Guizhou China see Jiangkou
Shuangjiang Hunan China see Tongdao
Shuangjiang Yunnan China see Eshan
Shuangliao China 74 A4
Shuangliu China 76 D2
Shuangpai China 77 F3
Shuangshipu China see Fengxian
Shuangxi China see Shunchang
Shuangyang China 74 B4
Shuangyashan China 74 C3
Shubarkuduk Kazakh. 80 A2
Shubayh well Saudi Arabia 85 D4
Shugozero Rus. Fed. 42 G4
Shuicheng China see Lupanshui
Shuidong China see Dianbai
Shuijing China 76 E1
Shuikou China 77 F3
Shuikouguan China 76 E4
Shuikoushan China 77 G3
Shuiluocheng China see Zhuanglang
Shuizhai China see Wuhua
Shulan China 74 B3
Shumagin Islands U.S.A. 118 B4
Shumba Zimbabwe 99 C5
Shumen Bulg. 59 L3
Shumerlya Rus. Fed. 42 J5
Shumilina Belarus 43 F5
Shumyachi Rus. Fed. 43 G5
Shunchang China 77 H3
Shuncheng China 74 A4
Shunde China 77 G4
Shuoxian China see Shuozhou
Shuozhou China 73 K5
Shuqrah Yemen 86 G7
Shūr r. Iran 88 D4
Shūr r. Iran 89 F3
Shūr watercourse Iran 88 D5
Shur watercourse Iran 88 E3
Shūr, Rūd-e watercourse Iran 88 E4
Shūr Āb watercourse Iran 88 D4
Shūrjestān Iran 88 D4
Shūrū Iran 89 F4
Shuryshkarskiy Sor, Ozero l. Rus. Fed. 41 T2
Shūsh Iran 88 C3
Shusha Azer. see Şuşa
Shushtar Iran 88 C3
Shutfah, Qalamat well Saudi Arabia 88 D6
Shuwaysh, Tall ash hill Jordan 85 C4
Shuya Ivanovskaya Oblast' Rus. Fed. 42 I4
Shuya Respublika Kareliya Rus. Fed. 42 G3
Shuyskoye Rus. Fed. 42 I4
Shwebo Myanmar 70 A2
Shwedwin Myanmar 70 A1
Shwegun Myanmar 70 B3
Shwegyin Myanmar 70 B3
Shweudaung mt. Myanmar 70 B2
Shyghanaq Kazakh. see Chiganak
Shymkent Kazakh. 80 C3
Shyok India 82 D2
Shypuvate Ukr. 43 H6
Shyroke Ukr. 43 G7
Sia Indon. 69 I8
Siabu Indon. 71 B7
Siahan Range mts Pak. 89 F5
Sīah Chashmeh Iran 88 B2
Siahgird Afgh. 89 G2
Siah Koh mts Afgh. 89 G3
Sialkot Pak. 89 I3
Siam country Asia see Thailand
Sian China see Xi'an
Sian Rus. Fed. 74 B1
Siang r. India see Brahmaputra
Siantan i. Indon. 71 D7
Siargao i. Phil. 69 H5
Siau i. Indon. 69 H6
Šiauliai Lith. 45 M9
Siazan' Azer. see Siyäzän
Si Bai, Lam r. Thai. 70 D4
Sibasa S. Africa 101 J2
Sibayi, Lake S. Africa 101 K4
Sibda China 76 C2
Šibenik Croatia 58 F3
Siberia reg. Rus. Fed. 65 M3
Siberut i. Indon. 68 B7
Siberut, Selat sea chan. Indon. 68 B7
Sibi Pak. 89 G4
Sibidiri P.N.G. 69 K8
Sibigo Indon. 71 A7
Sibiloi National Park Kenya 98 D3
Sibir' reg. Rus. Fed. see Siberia
Sibiti Congo 98 B4
Sibiu Romania 59 K2
Sibley U.S.A. 130 E3
Siboa Indon. 69 G6
Sibolga Indon. 71 B7
Siborongborong Indon. 71 B7
Sibsagar India 83 H4
Sibu Sarawak Malaysia 68 E6
Sibut Cent. Afr. Rep. 98 B3
Sibuyan i. Phil. 69 G4
Sibuyan Sea Phil. 69 G4
Sicamous Canada 120 G5
Sicca Veneria Tunisia see Le Kef
Siccus watercourse Australia 111 B6
Sicheng Anhui China see Sixian
Sicheng Guangxi China see Lingyun
Sichon Thai. 71 B5
Sichuan prov. China 76 D2
Sichuan Pendi basin China 76 E2
Sicié, Cap c. France 56 G5
Sicilia i. Italy see Sicily
Sicilian Channel Italy/Tunisia 58 E6
Sicily i. Italy 58 F5
Sicuani Peru 142 D6
Siddhapur India 82 C5
Siddipet India 84 C2
Sideros, Akra pt Kriti Greece see Sideros, Akrotirio
Sideros, Akrotirio pt Greece 59 L7
Sidesaviwa S. Africa 100 F7
Sidhauli India 82 E4
Sidhi India 83 E4
Sidhpur India see Siddhapur
Sidi Aïssa Alg. 57 H6
Sidi Ali Alg. 57 G5
Sīdī Barrānī Egypt 90 B5
Sidi Bel Abbès Alg. 57 F6
Sidi Bennour Morocco 54 C5
Sidi Bou Sa'īd Tunisia see Sidi Bouzid
Sidi Bouzid Tunisia 58 C7
Sidi el Barrâni Egypt see Sīdī Barrānī
Sidi El Hani, Sebkhet de salt pan Tunisia 58 D7
Sidi Ifni Morocco 96 B2
Sidi Kacem Morocco 54 C5
Sidikalang Indon. 71 B7
Sidi Khaled Alg. 54 E5
Sid Lake Canada 121 J2
Sidlaw Hills U.K. 50 F4
Sidley, Mount Antarctica 152 J1
Sidli India 83 G4
Sidmouth U.K. 49 D8
Sidney IA U.S.A. 130 E3
Sidney MT U.S.A. 126 G3
Sidney NE U.S.A. 130 C3
Sidney OH U.S.A. 134 C3
Sidney Lanier, Lake U.S.A. 133 D5
Sidoktaya Myanmar 70 A2
Sidon Lebanon 85 B3
Sidr Egypt see Sudr
Siedlce Poland 43 D5
Sieg r. Germany 53 H4
Siegen Germany 53 I4
Siĕmréab Cambodia 71 C4

225

Sofrana *i.* Greece 59 L6
Softa Kalesi *tourist site* Turkey 85 A1
Sōfu-gan *i.* Japan 75 F7
Sog China 76 B2
Soğanlı Dağları *mts* Turkey 91 E2
Sogda Rus. Fed. 74 D2
Sögel Germany 53 H2
Sogma China 82 E2
Søgne Norway 45 E7
Sognefjorden *inlet* Norway 45 D6
Sogruma China 76 D1
Söğüt Turkey 59 N4
Söğüt Dağı *mts* Turkey 59 M6
Soh Iran 88 C3
Sohâg Egypt *see* Sūhāj
Sohagpur India 82 D5
Soham U.K. 49 H6
Sohan *r.* Pak. 89 H3
Sohano P.N.G. 106 F2
Sohar Oman *see* Şuḩār
Sohawal India 82 E4
Sohela India 83 E5
Sohng Gwe, Khao *hill* Myanmar/Thai. 71 B4
Sŏho-ri N. Korea 75 C4
Sohŭksan-do *i.* S. Korea 75 B6
Soignies Belgium 52 E4
Soila China 76 C2
Soini Fin. 44 N5
Soissons France 52 D5
Sojat India 82 C4
Sojat Road India 82 C4
Sok *r.* Rus. Fed. 43 K5
Sokal' Ukr. 43 E6
Sokch'o S. Korea 75 C5
Söke Turkey 59 L6
Sokhor, Gora *mt.* Rus. Fed. 72 J2
Sokhumi Georgia 91 F2
Sokiryany Ukr. *see* Sokyryany
Sokodé Togo 96 D4
Soko Islands *H.K.* China 77 [inset]
Sokol Rus. Fed. 42 I4
Sokolo Mali 96 C3
Sokolov Czech Rep. 53 M4
Sokoto Nigeria 96 D3
Sokoto *r.* Nigeria 96 D3
Sokyryany Ukr. 43 E6
Sola Cuba 133 E8
Sola *i.* Tonga *see* Ata
Solan India 82 D3
Solana Beach U.S.A. 128 E5
Solander Island N.Z. 113 A8
Solapur India 84 B2
Soldotna U.S.A. 118 C3
Soledad U.S.A. 128 C3
Soledade Brazil 144 F3
Solenoye Rus. Fed. 43 I7
Solfjellsjøen Norway 44 H3
Solginskiy Rus. Fed. 42 I3
Solhan Turkey 91 F3
Soligalich Rus. Fed. 42 I4
Soligorsk Belarus *see* Salihorsk
Solihull U.K. 49 F6
Solikamsk Rus. Fed. 41 R4
Sol'-Iletsk Rus. Fed. 64 G4
Solimões *r.* S. America *see* Amazon
Solingen Germany 52 H3
Solitaire Namibia 100 B2
Sol-Karmala Rus. Fed. *see* Severnoye
Şollar Azer. 91 H2
Sollefteå Sweden 44 J5
Söllichau Germany 53 M3
Solling *hills* Germany 53 J3
Sollstedt Germany 53 K3
Sollum, Gulf of Egypt *see* Sallum, Khalīj as
Solms Germany 53 I4
Solnechnogorsk Rus. Fed. 42 H4
Solnechnyy *Amurskaya Oblast'* Rus. Fed. 74 A1
Solnechnyy *Khabarovskiy Kray* Rus. Fed. 74 E2
Solok Indon. 68 C7
Solomon U.S.A. 129 I5
Solomon, North Fork *r.* U.S.A. 130 D4

▶Solomon Islands *country* S. Pacific Ocean 107 G2
4th largest and 5th most populous country in Oceania.

Solomon Sea S. Pacific Ocean 106 F2
Solon U.S.A. 135 K1
Solon Springs U.S.A. 130 F2
Solor *i.* Indon. 108 C2
Solor, Kepulauan *is* Indon. 108 C2
Solothurn Switz. 56 H3
Solovetskiye Ostrova *is* Rus. Fed. 42 G2
Solov'yevsk Rus. Fed. 74 B1
Šolta *i.* Croatia 58 G3
Solṭānābād *Kermān* Iran 88 E4
Solṭānābād *Khorāsān* Iran 89 E3
Solṭānābād Iran 88 C3
Solṭānīyeh Iran 88 C2
Soltau Germany 53 J2
Sol'tsy Rus. Fed. 42 F4
Solvay U.S.A. 135 G2
Sölvesborg Sweden 45 I8
Solway Firth *est.* U.K. 50 F6
Solwezi Zambia 99 C5
Soma Turkey 59 L5
Somain France 52 D4
Somalia *country* Africa 98 E3
Somali Basin *sea feature* Indian Ocean 149 L6
Somali Republic *country* Africa *see* Somalia
Sombo Angola 99 C4
Sombor Serbia 59 F4
Sombrero Channel India 71 A6
Sombrio, Lago do *l.* Brazil 145 A5
Somero Fin. 45 M6
Somerset *KY* U.S.A. 134 C5
Somerset *MI* U.S.A. 134 C2
Somerset *OH* U.S.A. 134 D4
Somerset *PA* U.S.A. 134 F4
Somerset, Lake Australia 112 F1
Somerset East S. Africa 101 G7
Somerset Island Canada 119 I2
Somerset Reservoir U.S.A. 135 I2
Somerset West S. Africa 100 D8
Somersworth U.S.A. 135 J2
Somerton U.S.A. 129 F5
Somerville *NJ* U.S.A. 135 H3
Somerville *TN* U.S.A. 131 F5
Someydeh Iran 88 B3
Somme *r.* France 52 B4
Sommen *l.* Sweden 45 I7
Sömmerda Germany 53 L3
Sommet, Lac du *l.* Canada 123 H3
Somnath India 82 B5
Somutu Myanmar 70 B1
Son *r.* India 83 F4
Sonag China *see* Zêkog
Sonapur India 84 D1
Sonar *r.* India 82 D4
Sŏnbong N. Korea 74 C4
Sŏnch'ŏn N. Korea 75 B5
Sønderborg Denmark 45 F9
Sondershausen Germany 53 K3
Søndre Strømfjord Greenland *see* Kangerlussuaq
Søndre Strømfjord *inlet* Greenland *see* Kangerlussuaq
Sondrio Italy 58 C1
Sonepat India *see* Sonipat
Sonepur India *see* Sonapur
Songbai China *see* Shennongjia
Songbu China 77 G2
Sông Câu Vietnam 71 E4
Songcheng China *see* Xiapu
Sông Đa, Hô *resr* Vietnam 70 D2
Songea Tanz. 99 D5
Songhua Hu *resr* China 74 B4
Songhua Jiang *r. Heilongjiang/Jilin* China 74 D3
Songhua Jiang *r. Jilin* China *see* Di'er Songhua Jiang
Songjiang China 77 I2
Songjianghe China 74 B4
Sŏngjin N. Korea *see* Kimch'aek
Songkan China 76 E2
Songkhla Thai. 71 C6
Songling China *see* Ta'erqi
Songlong Myanmar 70 B2
Sŏngnam S. Korea 75 B5
Songnim N. Korea 75 B5
Songo Angola 99 B4
Songo Moz. 99 D5
Songpan China 76 D1
Songshan China *see* Ziyun
Song Shan *mt.* China 77 G1
Songtao China 77 F2
Songxi China 77 H3
Songxian China 77 G1
Songyuan *Fujian* China *see* Songxi
Songyuan *Jilin* China 74 B3
Songzi China 77 F2
Sơn Hai Vietnam 71 E5
Sonid Youqi China *see* Saihan Tal
Sonid Zuoqi China *see* Mandalt
Sonipat India 82 D3
Sonkajärvi Fin. 44 O5
Sonkovo Rus. Fed. 42 H4
Sơn La Vietnam 70 C2
Sonmiani Pak. 89 G5
Sonmiani Bay Pak. 89 G5
Sonneberg Germany 53 L4
Sono *r. Minas Gerais* Brazil 145 B2
Sono *r. Tocantins* Brazil 143 I5
Sonoma U.S.A. 128 B2
Sonoma Peak U.S.A. 128 E1
Sonora *r.* Mex. 127 F7
Sonora *state* Mex. 127 F7
Sonora *CA* U.S.A. 128 C3
Sonora *KY* U.S.A. 134 C5
Sonora *TX* U.S.A. 131 C6
Sonoran Desert U.S.A. 129 G5
Sonoran Desert National Monument *nat. park* U.S.A. 127 E6
Sonqor Iran 88 B3
Sonsonate El Salvador 136 G6
Sonsorol Islands Palau 69 I5
Sơn Tây Vietnam 70 D2
Sonwabile S. Africa 101 I6
Soochow China *see* Suzhou
Soomaaliya *country* Africa *see* Somalia
Sopi, Tanjung *pt* Indon. 69 H6
Sopo *watercourse* Sudan 97 F4
Sopot Bulg. 59 K3
Sopot Poland 47 Q3
Sop Prap Thai. 70 B3
Sopron Hungary 58 G1
Sopur India 82 C2
Sora Italy 58 E4
Sorab India 84 B3
Sorada India 84 E2
Söråker Sweden 44 J5
Sŏrak-san *mt.* S. Korea 75 C5
Sorak-san National Park S. Korea 75 C5
Sorel Canada 123 G5
Soreq *r.* Israel 85 B4
Sorgun Turkey 90 D3
Sorgun *r.* Turkey 85 B1
Soria Spain 57 E3
Sorkh, Kūh-e *mts* Iran 88 D3
Sorkhān Iran 88 E4
Sorkheh Iran 88 D3
Sørli Norway 44 H4
Soro India 83 F5
Soroca Moldova 43 F6
Sorocaba Brazil 145 B3
Soroki Moldova *see* Soroca
Sorol *atoll* Micronesia 69 K5
Sorong Indon. 69 I7
Soroti Uganda 98 D3
Sørøya *i.* Norway 44 M1
Sorraia *r.* Port. 57 B4
Sørreisa Norway 44 K2
Sorrento Italy 58 F4
Sorsele Sweden 44 J4
Sorsogon Phil. 69 G4
Sortavala Rus. Fed. 44 Q6
Sortland Norway 44 I2
Sortopolovskaya Rus. Fed. 42 K3
Sorvizhi Rus. Fed. 42 K4
Sōsan S. Korea 75 B5
Sosenskiy Rus. Fed. 43 G5
Soshanguve S. Africa 101 I3
Sosna *r.* Rus. Fed. 43 H5
Sosneado *mt.* Arg. 144 C4
Sosnogorsk Rus. Fed. 42 L3
Sosnovka *Arkhangel'skaya Oblast'* Rus. Fed. 42 J3
Sosnovka *Kaliningradskaya Oblast'* Rus. Fed. 41 K5
Sosnovka *Murmanskaya Oblast'* Rus. Fed. 42 I2
Sosnovka *Tambovskaya Oblast'* Rus. Fed. 43 I5
Sosnovo Rus. Fed. 45 Q6
Sosnovo-Ozerskoye Rus. Fed. 73 K2
Sosnovyy Rus. Fed. 44 R4
Sosnovyy Bor Rus. Fed. 45 P7
Sosnowiec Poland 47 Q5
Sosnowitz Poland *see* Sosnowiec
Sos'va *Khanty-Mansiyskiy Avtonomnyy Okrug* Rus. Fed. 41 S3
Sos'va *Sverdlovskaya Oblast'* Rus. Fed. 41 S4
Sotang China 76 B2
Sotara, Volcán *vol.* Col. 142 C3
Sotkamo Fin. 44 P4
Sotteville-lès-Rouen France 52 B5
Souanké Congo 98 B3
Soubré Côte d'Ivoire 96 C4
Souderton U.S.A. 135 H3
Soufflenheim France 53 H6
Soufli Greece 59 L4
Soufrière St Lucia 137 L6
Soufrière *vol.* St Vincent 137 L6
Sougueur Alg. 57 G6
Souillac France 56 E4
Souilly France 52 F5
Souk Ahras Alg. 58 B6
Souk el Arbaâ du Rharb Morocco 54 C5
Sŏul S. Korea *see* Seoul
Soulac-sur-Mer France 56 D4
Soulom France 56 D5
Sounding Creek *r.* Canada 121 I4
Souni Cyprus 85 A2
Soûr Lebanon *see* Tyre
Soure Brazil 143 I4
Sour el Ghozlane Alg. 57 H5
Souris Canada 121 K5
Souris *r.* Canada 121 L5
Souriya *country* Asia *see* Syria
Sousa Brazil 143 K5
Sousa Lara Angola *see* Bocoio
Sousse Tunisia 58 D7
Soustons France 56 D5

▶South Africa, Republic of *country* Africa 100 F5
5th most populous country in Africa.

Southampton Canada 134 E1
Southampton U.K. 49 F8
Southampton U.S.A. 135 I3
Southampton, Cape Canada 119 J3
Southampton Island Canada 119 J3
South Andaman *i.* India 71 A5
South Anna *r.* U.S.A. 135 G5
South Anston U.K. 48 F5
South Aulatsivik Island Canada 123 J2
South Australia *state* Australia 106 D5
South Australian Basin *sea feature* Indian Ocean 149 P8
Southaven U.S.A. 131 F5
South Baldy *mt.* U.S.A. 127 G6
South Bank U.K. 48 F4
South Bass Island U.S.A. 134 D3
South Bend *IN* U.S.A. 134 B3
South Bend *WA* U.S.A. 126 C3
South Bluff *pt* Bahamas 133 F8
South Boston U.S.A. 135 F5
South Brook Canada 123 K4
South Cape *pt* U.S.A. *see* Ka Lae
South Carolina *state* U.S.A. 133 D5
South Charleston *OH* U.S.A. 134 D4
South Charleston *WV* U.S.A. 134 E4
South China Sea N. Pacific Ocean 68 F4
South Coast Town Australia *see* Gold Coast
South Dakota *state* U.S.A. 130 C2
South Downs *hills* U.K. 49 G8
South-East *admin. dist.* Botswana 101 G3
South East Cape Australia 111 [inset]
Southeast Cape U.S.A. 118 B3
Southeast Indian Ridge *sea feature* Indian Ocean 149 N8
South East Isles Australia 109 C8
Southeast Pacific Basin *sea feature* S. Pacific Ocean 151 M10
South East Point Australia 112 C7
Southend Canada 121 K3
Southend U.K. 50 D5
Southend-on-Sea U.K. 49 H7
Southern *admin. dist.* Botswana 100 G3
Southern Alps *mts* N.Z. 113 C6
Southern Cross Australia 109 B7
Southern Indian Lake Canada 121 L3
Southern Lau Group *is* Fiji 107 I3
Southern National Park Sudan 97 F4
Southern Ocean 152 C2
Southern Pines U.S.A. 133 E5
Southern Rhodesia *country* Africa *see* Zimbabwe
Southern Uplands *hills* U.K. 50 E5
South Esk *r.* U.K. 50 F4
South Esk Tableland *reg.* Australia 108 D4
Southey Canada 121 J5
Southfield U.S.A. 134 D2
South Fiji Basin *sea feature* S. Pacific Ocean 150 H7
South Fork U.S.A. 128 B1
South Geomagnetic Pole (2008) Antarctica 152 F1
South Georgia *i.* S. Atlantic Ocean 144 I8

▶South Georgia and the South Sandwich Islands *terr.* S. Atlantic Ocean 144 I8
United Kingdom Overseas Territory

South Harris *pen.* U.K. 50 B3
South Haven U.S.A. 134 B2
South Henik Lake Canada 121 L2
South Hill U.S.A. 135 F5
South Honshu Ridge *sea feature* N. Pacific Ocean 150 F3
South Indian Lake Canada 121 L3
South Island India 84 B4

▶South Island N.Z. 113 D7
2nd largest island in Oceania.

South Junction Canada 121 M5
South Korea *country* Asia 75 B5
South Lake Tahoe U.S.A. 128 C2
South Luangwa National Park Zambia 99 D5
South Magnetic Pole (2008) Antarctica 152 G2
South Mills U.S.A. 135 G5
Southminster U.K. 49 H7
South Mountains *hills* U.S.A. 135 G4
South New Berlin U.S.A. 135 H2
South Orkney Islands S. Atlantic Ocean 148 F10
South Paris U.S.A. 135 J1
South Platte *r.* U.S.A. 130 C3
South Point Bahamas 133 F8
South Pole Antarctica 152 C1
Southport *Qld* Australia 112 F1
Southport *Tas.* Australia 111 [inset]
Southport U.K. 48 D5
Southport U.S.A. 135 G2
South Portland U.S.A. 135 J2
South Ronaldsay *i.* U.K. 50 G2
South Royalton U.S.A. 135 I2
South Salt Lake U.S.A. 129 H1
South Sand Bluff *pt* S. Africa 101 J6

▶South Sandwich Islands S. Atlantic Ocean 148 G9
United Kingdom Overseas Territory.

South Sandwich Trench *sea feature* S. Atlantic Ocean 148 G9
South San Francisco U.S.A. 128 B3
South Saskatchewan *r.* Canada 121 J4
South Seal *r.* Canada 121 L3
South Shetland Islands Antarctica 152 A2
South Shetland Trough *sea feature* S. Atlantic Ocean 152 L2
South Shields U.K. 48 F3
South Sinai *governorate* Egypt *see* Janūb Sīnā'
South Solomon Trench *sea feature* S. Pacific Ocean 150 G6
South Taranaki Bight *b.* N.Z. 113 E4
South Tasman Rise *sea feature* Southern Ocean 150 F9
South Tent *mt.* U.S.A. 129 H2
South Tons *r.* India 83 E4
South Twin Island Canada 122 F3
South Tyne *r.* U.K. 48 E4
South Uist *i.* U.K. 50 B3
South Wellesley Islands Australia 110 B3
South-West Africa *country* Africa *see* Namibia
South West Cape N.Z. 113 A8
South West Entrance *sea chan.* P.N.G. 110 E1
Southwest Indian Ridge *sea feature* Indian Ocean 149 K8
South West National Park Australia 111 [inset]
Southwest Pacific Basin *sea feature* S. Pacific Ocean 150 I8
Southwest Peru Ridge *sea feature* S. Pacific Ocean *see* Nazca Ridge
South West Rocks Australia 112 F3
South Whitley U.S.A. 134 C3
South Wichita *r.* U.S.A. 131 D5
South Windham U.S.A. 135 J2
Southwold U.K. 49 I6
Southwood National Park Australia 112 E1
Soutpansberg *mts* S. Africa 101 I2
Souttouf, Adrar *mts* W. Sahara 96 B2
Soverato Italy 58 G5
Sovetsk *Kaliningradskaya Oblast'* Rus. Fed. 45 L9
Sovetsk *Kirovskaya Oblast'* Rus. Fed. 42 K4
Sovetskaya Gavan' Rus. Fed. 74 F2
Sovetskiy *Khanty-Mansiyskiy Avtonomnyy Okrug* Rus. Fed. 41 S3
Sovetskiy *Leningradskaya Oblast'* Rus. Fed. 45 P6
Sovetskiy *Respublika Mariy El* Rus. Fed. 42 K4
Sovetskoye *Chechenskaya Respublika* Rus. Fed. *see* Shatoy
Sovetskoye *Stavropol'skiy Kray* Rus. Fed. *see* Zelenokumsk
Sovyets'kyy Ukr. 90 D1
Sowa China 76 C2
Soweto S. Africa 101 H4
So'x Tajik. 89 H2
Sōya-kaikyō *strait* Japan/Rus. Fed. *see* La Pérouse Strait
Sōya-misaki *c.* Japan 74 F3
Soyana *r.* Rus. Fed. 42 I2
Soyma *r.* Rus. Fed. 42 K2
Soyopa Mex. 127 F7
Sozh *r.* Europe 43 F6
Sozopol Bulg. 59 L3
Spa Belgium 52 F4

▶Spain *country* Europe 57 E3
4th largest country in Europe.

Spalato Croatia *see* Split
Spalatum Croatia *see* Split
Spalding U.K. 49 G6
Spanish Canada 122 E5
Spanish Fork U.S.A. 129 H1
Spanish Guinea *country* Africa *see* Equatorial Guinea
Spanish Netherlands *country* Europe *see* Belgium
Spanish Sahara *terr.* Africa *see* Western Sahara
Spanish Town Jamaica 137 I5
Sparks U.S.A. 128 D2
Sparta Greece *see* Sparti
Sparta *GA* U.S.A. 133 D5
Sparta *KY* U.S.A. 134 C4
Sparta *MI* U.S.A. 134 C2
Sparta *NC* U.S.A. 134 E5
Sparta *TN* U.S.A. 132 C5
Spartanburg U.S.A. 133 D5
Sparti Greece 59 J6
Spartivento, Capo *c.* Italy 58 G6
Spas-Demensk Rus. Fed. 43 G5
Spas-Klepiki Rus. Fed. 43 I5
Spassk-Dal'niy Rus. Fed. 74 D3
Spassk-Ryazanskiy Rus. Fed. 43 I5
Spatha, Akra *pt Kriti* Greece *see* Spatha, Akrotirio
Spatha, Akrotirio *pt* Greece 59 J7
Spearman U.S.A. 131 C4
Speedway U.S.A. 134 B4
Spence Bay Canada *see* Taloyoak
Spencer *IA* U.S.A. 130 E3
Spencer *ID* U.S.A. 126 E3
Spencer *IN* U.S.A. 134 B4
Spencer *NE* U.S.A. 130 D3
Spencer *WV* U.S.A. 134 E4
Spencer, Cape U.S.A. 120 B3
Spencer Bay Namibia 100 B3
Spencer Gulf *est.* Australia 111 B7
Spencer Range *hills* Australia 108 E3
Spennymoor U.K. 48 F4
Sperrin Mountains *hills* U.K. 51 E3
Sperryville U.S.A. 135 F4
Spessart *reg.* Germany 53 J5
Spétsai *i.* Greece *see* Spetses
Spetses *i.* Greece 59 J6
Spey *r.* U.K. 50 F3
Speyer Germany 53 I5
Spezand Pak. 89 G4
Spice Islands Indon. *see* Moluccas
Spijk Neth. 52 G1
Spijkenisse Neth. 52 E3
Spilimbergo Italy 58 E1
Spilsby U.K. 48 H5
Spīn Būldak Afgh. 89 G4
Spintangi Pak. 89 H4
Spirit Lake U.S.A. 130 E3
Spirit River Canada 120 G4
Spirovo Rus. Fed. 42 G4
Spišská Nová Ves Slovakia 43 D6
Spiti *r.* India 82 D3

▶Spitsbergen *i.* Svalbard 64 C2
5th largest island in Europe.

Spittal an der Drau Austria 47 N7
Spitzbergen *i.* Svalbard *see* Spitsbergen
Split Croatia 58 G3
Split Lake Canada 121 L3
Split Lake *l.* Canada 121 L3
Spokane U.S.A. 126 D3
Spoletium Italy *see* Spoleto
Spoleto Italy 58 E3
Spōng Cambodia 71 D4
Spoon *r.* U.S.A. 130 F3
Spooner U.S.A. 130 F2
Spornitz Germany 53 L1
Spotsylvania U.S.A. 135 G4
Spotted Horse U.S.A. 126 G3
Spranger, Mount Canada 120 F4
Spratly Islands S. China Sea 68 E4
Spray U.S.A. 126 D3
Spree *r.* Germany 47 N4
Sprimont Belgium 52 F4
Springbok S. Africa 100 C5
Springdale Canada 123 L4
Springdale U.S.A. 134 C4
Springe Germany 53 J2
Springer U.S.A. 127 G5
Springerville U.S.A. 129 I4
Springfield *CO* U.S.A. 130 C4

▶Springfield *IL* U.S.A. 130 F4
Capital of Illinois.

Springfield *KY* U.S.A. 134 C5
Springfield *MA* U.S.A. 135 I2
Springfield *MO* U.S.A. 131 E4
Springfield *OH* U.S.A. 134 D4
Springfield *OR* U.S.A. 126 C3
Springfield *TN* U.S.A. 134 B5
Springfield *VT* U.S.A. 135 I2
Springfield *WV* U.S.A. 135 F4
Springfontein S. Africa 101 G6
Spring Glen U.S.A. 129 H2
Spring Grove U.S.A. 134 A2
Springhill Canada 123 I5
Spring Hill U.S.A. 133 D6
Springhouse Canada 120 F5
Spring Mountains U.S.A. 129 F3
Springs Junction N.Z. 113 D6
Springsure Australia 110 E5
Spring Valley *MN* U.S.A. 130 E3
Spring Valley *NY* U.S.A. 135 H3
Springview U.S.A. 130 D3
Springville *CA* U.S.A. 128 D3
Springville *NY* U.S.A. 135 F2
Springville *PA* U.S.A. 135 H3
Springville *UT* U.S.A. 129 H1
Sprowston U.K. 49 I6
Spruce Grove Canada 120 H4
Spruce Knob *mt.* U.S.A. 132 E4
Spruce Mountain *CO* U.S.A. 129 I2
Spruce Mountain *NV* U.S.A. 129 F1
Spurn Head *hd* U.K. 48 H5
Spuzzum Canada 120 F5
Squam Lake U.S.A. 135 J2
Square Lake U.S.A. 123 H5
Squillace, Golfo di *g.* Italy 58 G5
Squires, Mount *hill* Australia 109 D6
Srbija *country* Europe *see* Serbia
Srbinje Bos.-Herz. *see* Foča
Srê Âmběl Cambodia 71 C5
Srebrenica *Republika Srpska* 59 H2
Sredets *Burgas* Bulg. 59 L3
Sredets *Sofiya-Grad* Bulg. *see* Sofia
Sredinnyy Khrebet *mts* Rus. Fed. 65 Q4
Sredna Gora *mts* Bulg. 59 J3
Srednekolymsk Rus. Fed. 65 Q3
Sredne-Russkaya Vozvyshennost' *hills* Rus. Fed. *see* Central Russian Upland
Sredne-Sibirskoye Ploskogor'ye *plat.* Rus. Fed. *see* Central Siberian Plateau
Sredneye Kuyto, Ozero *l.* Rus. Fed. 44 Q4
Sredniy Ural *mts* Rus. Fed. 41 R4
Srednogorie Bulg. 59 K3
Srednyaya Akhtuba Rus. Fed. 43 J6
Sreepur Bangl. *see* Sripur
Sre Khtum Cambodia 71 D4
Srê Noy Cambodia 71 D4
Sretensk Rus. Fed. 73 L2
Sri Aman *Sarawak* Malaysia 68 E6
Sriharikota Island India 84 D3

▶Sri Jayewardenepura Kotte Sri Lanka 84 C5
Capital of Sri Lanka.

Srikakulam India 84 E2
Sri Kalahasti India 84 C3
Sri Lanka *country* Asia 84 D5
Srinagar India 82 C2
Sri Pada *mt.* Sri Lanka *see* Adam's Peak
Sripur Bangl. 83 G4
Srirangam India 84 C4
Sri Thep *tourist site* Thai. 70 C3
Srivardhan India 84 B2
Staaten *r.* Australia 110 C3
Staaten River National Park Australia 110 C3
Stabroek Guyana *see* Georgetown
Stade Germany 53 J1
Staden Belgium 52 D4
Stadskanaal Neth. 52 G2
Stadtallendorf Germany 53 J4
Stadthagen Germany 53 J2
Stadtilm Germany 53 L4
Stadtlohn Germany 52 G3
Stadtoldendorf Germany 53 J3
Stadtroda Germany 53 L4
Staffa *i.* U.K. 50 C4
Staffelberg *hill* Germany 53 L4
Staffelstein Germany 53 K4
Stafford U.K. 49 E6
Stafford U.S.A. 135 G4
Stafford Creek Bahamas 133 E7
Stafford Springs U.S.A. 135 I3
Stagg Lake Canada 120 H2
Staicele Latvia 45 N8
Staines U.K. 49 G7
Stakhanov Ukr. 43 H6
Stakhanovo Rus. Fed. *see* Zhukovskiy
Stalbridge U.K. 49 E8
Stalham U.K. 49 I6
Stalin Bulg. *see* Varna
Stalinabad Tajik. *see* Dushanbe
Stalingrad Rus. Fed. *see* Volgograd
Staliniri Georgia *see* Ts'khinvali
Stalino Ukr. *see* Donets'k
Stalinogorsk Rus. Fed. *see* Novomoskovsk
Stalinogród Poland *see* Katowice
Stalinsk Rus. Fed. *see* Novokuznetsk
Stalowa Wola Poland 43 D6
Stamboliyski Bulg. 59 K3
Stamford Australia 110 C4
Stamford U.K. 49 G6
Stamford *CT* U.S.A. 135 I3
Stamford *NY* U.S.A. 135 H2
Stampalia *i.* Greece *see* Astypalaia
Stampriet Namibia 100 D3
Stamsund Norway 44 H2
Stanardsville U.S.A. 135 F4
Stanberry U.S.A. 130 E3
Stancomb-Wills Glacier Antarctica 152 B1
Standard Canada 120 H5
Standdaarbuiten Neth. 52 E3
Standerton S. Africa 101 I4
Standish U.S.A. 134 D2
Stanfield U.S.A. 129 H5
Stanford *KY* U.S.A. 134 C5
Stanford *MT* U.S.A. 126 F3
Stanger S. Africa 101 J5
Stanislaus *r.* U.S.A. 128 C3
Stanislav Ukr. *see* Ivano-Frankivs'k
Stanke Dimitrov Bulg. *see* Dupnitsa
Staňkov Czech Rep. 53 N5
Stanley Australia 111 [inset]
Stanley *H.K.* China 77 [inset]

▶Stanley Falkland Is 144 E8
Capital of the Falkland Islands.

Stanley U.K. 48 F4
Stanley *ID* U.S.A. 126 E3
Stanley *KY* U.S.A. 134 B5
Stanley *ND* U.S.A. 130 C1
Stanley *VA* U.S.A. 135 F4
Stanley, Mount *hill N.T.* Australia 108 E5
Stanley, Mount *hill Tas.* Australia 111 [inset]
Stanley, Mount Dem. Rep. Congo/Uganda *see* Margherita Peak
Stanleyville Dem. Rep. Congo *see* Kisangani
Stann Creek Belize *see* Dangriga
Stannington U.K. 48 F3
Stanovoye Rus. Fed. 43 H5
Stanovoye Nagor'ye *mts* Rus. Fed. 73 L1
Stanovoy Khrebet *mts* Rus. Fed. 65 N4
Stansmore Range *hills* Australia 108 E5
Stanthorpe Australia 112 E2
Stanton U.K. 49 H6
Stanton *KY* U.S.A. 134 D5
Stanton *MI* U.S.A. 134 C2
Stanton *ND* U.S.A. 130 C2
Stanton *TX* U.S.A. 131 C5
Stapleton U.S.A. 130 C3
Starachowice Poland 47 R5
Stara Planina *mts* Bulg./Serbia *see* Balkan Mountains
Staraya Russa Rus. Fed. 42 F4
Stara Zagora Bulg. 59 K3
Starbuck Island Kiribati 151 J6
Star City U.S.A. 134 B3
Starcke National Park Australia 110 D2
Stargard in Pommern Poland *see* Stargard Szczeciński
Stargard Szczeciński Poland 47 O4
Staritsa Rus. Fed. 42 G4
Starke U.S.A. 133 D6
Starkville U.S.A. 131 F5
Star Lake U.S.A. 135 H1
Starnberger See *l.* Germany 47 M7
Starobel'sk Ukr. *see* Starobil's'k
Starobil's'k Ukr. 43 H6
Starogard Gdański Poland 47 Q4
Starokonstantinov Ukr. *see* Starokostyantyniv
Starokostyantyniv Ukr. 43 E6
Starominskaya Rus. Fed. 43 H7
Staroshcherbinovskaya Rus. Fed. 43 H7
Star Peak U.S.A. 128 D1
Start Point U.K. 49 D8
Starve Island Kiribati *see* Starbuck Island
Staryya Darohi Belarus 43 F5
Staryye Dorogi Belarus *see* Staryya Darohi
Staryy Kayak Rus. Fed. 65 L2
Staryy Oskol Rus. Fed. 43 H6
Staßfurt Germany 53 L3
State College U.S.A. 135 G3
State Line U.S.A. 131 F6

Svay Chék Cambodia 71 C4
Svay Riĕng Cambodia 71 D5
Svecha Rus. Fed. 42 J4
Sveg Sweden 45 I5
Sveķi Latvia 45 O8
Svelgen Norway 44 D6
Svellingen Norway 44 F5
Švenčionėliai Lith. 45 N9
Švenčionys Lith. 45 O9
Svendborg Denmark 45 G9
Svensbu Norway 44 K2
Svenstavik Sweden 44 I5
Sverdlovsk Rus. Fed. see Yekaterinburg
Sverdlovs'k Ukr. 43 H6
Sverdrup Islands Canada 119 I2
Sverige country Europe see Sweden
Sveti Nikole Macedonia 59 I4
Svetlaya Rus. Fed. 74 E3
Svetlogorsk Belarus see Svyetlahorsk
Svetlogorsk Kaliningradskaya Oblast' Rus. Fed. 45 L9
Svetlogorsk Krasnoyarskiy Kray Rus. Fed. 64 J3
Svetlograd Rus. Fed. 91 F1
Svetlovodsk Ukr. see Svitlovods'k
Svetlyy Kaliningradskaya Oblast' Rus. Fed. 45 L9
Svetlyy Orenburgskaya Oblast' Rus. Fed. 80 B1
Svetlyy Yar Rus. Fed. 43 J6
Svetogorsk Rus. Fed. 45 P6
Svíahnúkar vol. Iceland 44 [inset]
Svilaja mts Croatia 58 G3
Svilengrad Bulg. 59 L4
Svinecea Mare, Vârful mt. Romania 59 J2
Svir Belarus 45 O9
Svir' r. Rus. Fed. 42 G3
Svishtov Bulg. 59 K3
Svitava r. Czech Rep. 47 P6
Svitavy Czech Rep. 47 P6
Svitlovods'k Ukr. 43 G6
Sviyaga r. Rus. Fed. 42 K5
Svizzer, Parc Naziunal Switz. 58 D1
Svizzera country Europe see Switzerland
Svobodnyy Rus. Fed. 74 C2
Svolvær Norway 44 I2
Svrljiške Planine mts Serbia 59 J3
Svyatoy Nos, Mys c. Rus. Fed. 42 K2
Svyetlahorsk Belarus 43 F5
Swadlincote U.K. 49 F6
Swaffham U.K. 49 H6
Swain Reefs Australia 110 F4
Swainsboro U.S.A. 133 D5
Swains Island atoll American Samoa 107 I3
Swakop watercourse Namibia 100 B2
Swakopmund Namibia 100 B2
Swale r. U.K. 48 F4
Swallow Islands Solomon Is 107 G3
Swamihalli India 84 C3
Swampy r. Canada 123 J4
Swan r. Australia 109 A7
Swan r. Man./Sask. Canada 121 K4
Swan r. Ont. Canada 122 E3
Swanage U.K. 49 F8
Swandale U.S.A. 134 E4
Swan Hill Australia 112 A5
Swan Hills Canada 120 H4
Swan Lake B.C. Canada 120 D4
Swan Lake Man. Canada 121 K4
Swanley U.K. 49 H7
Swanquarter U.S.A. 133 E5
Swan Reach Australia 111 B7
Swan River Canada 121 K4
Swansea U.K. 49 D7
Swansea Bay U.K. 49 D7
Swanton CA U.S.A. 128 B3
Swanton VT U.S.A. 135 I1
Swartbergpas pass S. Africa 100 F7
Swart Nossob watercourse Namibia see Black Nossob
Swartruggens S. Africa 101 H3
Swartz Creek U.S.A. 134 D2
Swasey Peak U.S.A. 129 G2
Swat Kohistan reg. Pak. 89 I3
Swatow China see Shantou
Swayzee U.S.A. 134 C3
Swaziland country Africa 101 J4

▶Sweden country Europe 44 I5
5th largest country in Europe.

Sweet Home U.S.A. 126 C3
Sweet Springs U.S.A. 134 E5
Sweetwater U.S.A. 131 C5
Sweetwater r. U.S.A. 126 G4
Swellendam S. Africa 100 E8
Świdnica Poland 47 P5
Świdwin Poland 47 O4
Świebodzin Poland 47 O4
Świecie Poland 47 Q4
Swift Current Canada 121 J5
Swiftcurrent Creek r. Canada 121 J5
Swilly r. Ireland 51 E3
Swilly, Lough inlet Ireland 51 E2
Swindon U.K. 49 F7
Swinford Ireland 51 D4
Świnoujście Poland 47 O4
Swinton U.K. 50 G5
Swiss Confederation country Europe see Switzerland
Switzerland country Europe 56 I3
Swords Ireland 51 F4
Swords Range hills Australia 110 C4
Syamozero, Ozero l. Rus. Fed. 42 G3
Syamzha Rus. Fed. 42 I3
Syang Nepal 83 E3
Syas'troy Rus. Fed. 42 G3
Sychevka Rus. Fed. 42 G5
Sydenham atoll Kiribati see Nonouti

▶Sydney Australia 112 E4
Capital of New South Wales. Most populous city in Oceania.

Sydney Canada 123 J5
Sydney Island Kiribati see Manra
Sydney Lake Canada 121 M5
Sydney Mines Canada 123 J5
Syedra tourist site Turkey 85 A1
Syeverodonets'k Ukr. 43 H6
Syke Germany 53 I2
Sykesville U.S.A. 135 F3
Syktyvkar Rus. Fed. 42 K3
Sylarna mt. Norway/Sweden 44 H5
Sylhet Bangl. 83 G4
Syloga Rus. Fed. 42 I3
Sylt i. Germany 47 L3
Sylva U.S.A. 133 D5
Sylvania GA U.S.A. 133 D5
Sylvania OH U.S.A. 134 D3
Sylvan Lake Canada 120 H4
Sylvester U.S.A. 133 D6
Sylvester, Lake salt flat Australia 110 A3
Sylvia, Mount Canada 120 E3
Symerton U.S.A. 134 A3
Symi i. Greece 59 L6
Synel'nykove Ukr. 43 G6
Syngyrli, Mys pt Kazakh. 91 I2
Synya Rus. Fed. 41 R2
Syowa research station Antarctica 152 D2
Syracusae Sicily Italy see Syracuse
Syracuse Sicily Italy 58 F6
Syracuse KS U.S.A. 130 C4
Syracuse NY U.S.A. 135 G2
Syrdar'ya r. Asia 80 C3
Syrdar'ya Uzbek. see Sirdaryo
Syrdaryinskiy Uzbek. see Sirdaryo
Syria country Asia 90 E4
Syriam Myanmar see Thanlyin
Syrian Desert Asia 90 E4
Syrna i. Greece 59 L6
Syros i. Greece 59 K6
Syrskiy Rus. Fed. 43 H5
Sysmä Fin. 45 N6
Sysola r. Rus. Fed. 42 K3
Syumsi Rus. Fed. 42 K4
Syurkum Rus. Fed. 74 F2
Syurkum, Mys pt Rus. Fed. 74 F2
Syzran' Rus. Fed. 43 K5
Szabadka Serbia see Subotica
Szczecin Poland 47 O4
Szczecinek Poland 47 P4
Szczytno Poland 47 R4
Szechwan prov. China see Sichuan
Szeged Hungary 59 I1
Székesfehérvár Hungary 58 H1
Szekszárd Hungary 58 H1
Szentes Hungary 59 I1
Szentgotthárd Hungary 58 G1
Szigetvár Hungary 58 G1
Szolnok Hungary 59 I1
Szombathely Hungary 58 G1
Sztálinváros Hungary see Dunaújváros

T

Taagga Duudka reg. Somalia 98 E3
Tābah Saudi Arabia 86 F4
Tabajara Brazil 142 F5
Tabakhmela Georgia see Kazret'i
Tabalo P.N.G. 69 L7
Tabanan Indon. 108 A2
Tabankulu S. Africa 101 I6
Ţabaqah Ar Raqqah Syria 85 D2
Ţabaqah Ar Raqqah Syria see Madīnat ath Thawrah
Tabar Islands P.N.G. 106 F2
Tabarka Tunisia 58 C6
Ţabas Iran 89 F3
Tabāsin Iran 88 E4
Tābask, Kūh-e mt. Iran 88 C4
Tabatinga Amazonas Brazil 142 E4
Tabatinga São Paulo Brazil 145 A3
Tabatinga, Serra da hills Brazil 143 J6
Tabatsquri, Tba l. Georgia 91 F2
Tabayin Myanmar 70 A2
Tabbita Australia 112 B5
Tabelbala Alg. 54 D6
Taber Canada 121 H5
Tabet, Nam r. Myanmar 70 B1
Tabia Tsaka salt l. China 83 F3
Tabiteuea atoll Kiribati 107 H2
Tabivere Estonia 45 O7
Table Cape N.Z. 113 F4
Table Mountain Nature Reserve S. Africa 100 D8
Tabligbo Togo 96 D4
Tábor Czech Rep. 47 O6
Tabora Tanz. 99 D4
Tabou Côte d'Ivoire 96 C4
Tabrīz Iran 88 B2
Tabuaeran atoll Kiribati 151 J5
Tabūk Saudi Arabia 90 E5
Tabulam Australia 112 F2
Tabuyung Indon. 71 B7
Tabwémasana, Mount Vanuatu 107 G3
Täby Sweden 45 K7
Tacalé Brazil 143 H3
Tacheng China 80 F2
Tachie Canada 120 E4
Tachov Czech Rep. 53 M5
Tacloban Phil. 69 H4
Tacna Peru 142 D7
Tacoma U.S.A. 126 C3
Taco Pozo Arg. 144 D3
Tacuarembó Uruguay 144 E4
Tacupeto Mex. 127 F7
Tadcaster U.K. 48 F5
Tademaït, Plateau du Alg. 54 E6
Tadin New Caledonia 107 G4
Tadjikistan country Asia see Tajikistan
Tadjourah Djibouti 86 F7
Tadmur Syria 85 D2
Tadohae Haesang National Park S. Korea 75 B6
Tadoule Lake Canada 121 L3
Tadoussac Canada 123 H4
Tadpatri India 84 C3
Tadwale India 84 C2
Tadzhikskaya S.S.R. country Asia see Tajikistan
T'aean Haean National Park S. Korea 75 B5
Taech'ŏng-do i. S. Korea 75 B5
Taedasa-do N. Korea 75 B5
Taedong-man b. N. Korea 75 B5
Taegu S. Korea 75 C6
Taehan-min'guk country Asia see South Korea
Taehŭksan-kundo is S. Korea 75 B6
Taejŏn S. Korea 75 B5
Taejŏng S. Korea 75 B6
T'aepaek S. Korea 75 C5
Ta'erqi China 73 M3
Taf r. U.K. 49 C7
Tafahi i. Tonga 107 I3
Tafalla Spain 57 F2
Tafeng China see Lanshan
Tafila Jordan see Aţ Ţafīlah
Tafí Viejo Arg. 144 C3
Tafresh Iran 88 C3
Taft Iran 88 D4
Taft U.S.A. 128 D4
Taftān, Kūh-e mt. Iran 89 F4
Taftanāz Syria 85 C2
Tafwap India 71 A6
Taganrog Rus. Fed. 43 H7
Taganrog, Gulf of Rus. Fed./Ukr. 43 H7
Taganrogskiy Zaliv b. Rus. Fed./Ukr. see Taganrog, Gulf of
Tagarev, Gora mt. Iran/Turkm. 88 E2
Tagarkaty, Pereval pass Tajik. 89 I2
Tagaung Myanmar 70 B2
Tagchagpu Ri mt. China 83 E2
Tagdempt Alg. see Tiaret
Taghmon Ireland 51 F5
Tagish Canada 120 C2
Tagtabazar Turkm. 89 F3
Tagula P.N.G. 110 F1
Tagula Island P.N.G. 110 F1
Tagus r. Port. 57 B4
also known as Tajo (Portugal) or Tejo (Spain)
Taha China 74 B3
Tahaetkun Mountain Canada 120 G5
Tahan, Gunung mt. Malaysia 71 C6
Tahanroz'ka Zatoka b. Rus. Fed./Ukr. see Taganrog, Gulf of
Tahat, Mont mt. Alg. 96 D2
Tahaurawe i. U.S.A. see Kaho'olawe
Tahe China 74 B1
Taheke N.Z. 113 D2
Tahiti i. Fr. Polynesia 151 K7
Tahlab r. Iran/Pak. 89 F4
Tahlab, Dasht-i- plain Pak. 89 F4
Tahlequah U.S.A. 131 E5
Tahltan Canada 120 D3
Tahoe, Lake U.S.A. 128 C2
Tahoe Lake Canada 119 H3
Tahoe Vista U.S.A. 128 C2
Tahoka U.S.A. 131 C5
Tahoua Niger 96 D3
Tahrūd Iran 88 E4
Tahrūd r. Iran 88 E4
Tahtsa Peak Canada 120 E4
Tahulandang i. Indon. 69 H6
Tahuna Indon. 69 H6
Taï, Parc National de nat. park Côte d'Ivoire 96 C4
Tai'an China 73 L5
Taibai China 76 E1
Taibai Shan mt. China 76 E1
Taibei Taiwan see T'aipei
Taibus Qi China see Baochang
T'aichung Taiwan 77 I3
Taidong Taiwan see T'aitung
Taigong China see Taijiang
Taihang Shan mts Hebei China 73 K5
Taihang Shan mts China 73 K5
Taihape N.Z. 113 E4
Taihe Jiangxi China 77 G3
Taihe Sichuan China see Shehong
Taihezhen China see Shehong
Tai Ho Wan H.K. China 77 [inset]
Taihu China 77 H2
Tai Hu l. China 77 I2
Taijiang China 77 F3
Taikang China 74 B3
Tailai China 74 A3
Tai Lam Chung Shui Tong resr H.K. China 77 [inset]
Tailem Bend Australia 111 B7
Tai Long Wan b. H.K. China 77 [inset]
Taimani reg. Afgh. 89 F3
Tai Mo Shan hill H.K. China 77 [inset]
Tain U.K. 50 F2
T'ainan Taiwan 77 I4
T'ainan Taiwan see Hsinying
Tainaro, Akra pt Greece see Tainaro, Akrotirio
Tainaro, Akrotirio pt Greece 59 J6
Taining China 77 H3
Tai O H.K. China 77 [inset]
Taiobeiras Brazil 145 C1
Tai Pang Wan b. H.K. China see Mirs Bay

▶T'aipei Taiwan 77 I3
Capital of Taiwan.

Taiping Guangdong China see Shixing
Taiping Guangxi China see Chongzuo
Taiping Guangxi China 77 F4
Taiping Malaysia 71 C6
Taipingchuan China 74 A3
Tai Po H.K. China 77 [inset]
Tai Po Hoi b. H.K. China see Tolo Harbour
Tai Poutini National Park N.Z. see Westland National Park
Tairbeart U.K. see Tarbert
Tai Rom Yen National Park Thai. 71 B5
Tairuq Iran 88 B3
Tais P.N.G. 69 K8
Taishan China 77 G4
Taishun China 77 H3
Tai Siu Mo To is H.K. China see The Brothers
Taissy France 52 E5
Taitao, Península de pen. Chile 144 B7
Tai Tapu N.Z. 113 D6
Tai To Yan mt. H.K. China 77 [inset]
T'aitung Taiwan 77 I4
Tai Tung Shan hill H.K. China see Sunset Peak
Taivalkoski Fin. 44 P4
Taivaskero hill Fin. 44 N2
Taiwan country Asia 77 I4
T'aiwan Haihsia strait China/Taiwan see Taiwan Strait
Taiwan Haixia strait China/Taiwan see Taiwan Strait
Taiwan Shan mts Taiwan see Chungyang Shanmo
Taiwan Strait China/Taiwan 77 H4
Taixian China see Jiangyan
Taixing China 77 I1
Taiyuan China 73 K5
Tai Yue Shan i. H.K. China see Lantau Island
Taizhao China 76 B2
Taizhong Taiwan see T'aichung
Taizhong Taiwan see Fengyüan
Taizhou Jiangsu China 77 H1
Taizhou Zhejiang China 77 I2
Taizhou Liedao i. China 77 I2
Taizhou Wan b. China 77 I2
Taizi He r. China 74 B4
Ta'izz Yemen 86 F7
Tājābād Iran 88 E4
Tajal Pak. 89 H5
Tajamulco, Volcán de vol. Guat. 136 F5
Tajerouine Tunisia 58 C7
Tajikistan country Asia 89 H2
Tajitos Mex. 127 E7
Tajo r. Port. 57 C4 see Tagus
Tajrīsh Iran 88 C3
Tak Thai. 70 B3
Takāb Iran 88 B2
Takabba Kenya 98 E3
Takahashi Japan 75 D6
Takamatsu Japan 75 D6
Takaoka Japan 75 E5
Takapuna N.Z. 113 E3
Ta karpo China 83 G4
Takatokwane Botswana 100 G3
Takatshwaane Botswana 100 E2
Takatsuki-yama mt. Japan 75 D6
Takayama Japan 75 E5
Tak Bai Thai. 71 C6
Takefu Japan 75 E6
Takengon Indon. 71 B6
Takeo Cambodia see Takêv
Take-shima i. Asia see Liancourt Rocks
Takestān Iran 88 C2
Takêv Cambodia 71 D5
Takhemaret Alg. 57 G6
Takhini Hotspring Canada 120 C2
Ta Khli Thai. 70 C4
Ta Khmau Cambodia 71 D5
Takhta-Bazar Turkm. see Tagtabazar
Takht Apān, Kūh-e mt. Iran 88 C3
Takhteh Iran 88 D4
Takhteh Pol Afgh. 89 G4
Takht-e Soleymān mt. Iran 88 C2
Takht-e Soleymān tourist site Iran 88 B2
Takht-i-Bahi tourist site Pak. 89 H3
Takht-i-Sulaiman mt. Pak. 89 H4
Takijuq Lake Canada see Napaktulik Lake
Takingeun Indon. see Takengon
Takinoue Japan 74 F3
Takla Lake Canada 120 E4
Takla Landing Canada 120 E4
Takla Makan des. China see Taklimakan Desert
Taklimakan Desert China 82 E1
Taklimakan Shamo des. China see Taklimakan Desert
Takpa Shiri mt. China 76 B2
Taku Canada 120 C3
Takum Nigeria 96 D4
Takuu Islands P.N.G. 107 F2
Talachyn Belarus 43 F5
Talaja India 82 C5
Talakan Amurskaya Oblast' Rus. Fed. 74 C2
Talakan Khabarovskiy Kray Rus. Fed. 74 D2
Talandzha Rus. Fed. 74 C2
Talangbatu Indon. 68 D7
Talara Peru 142 B4
Talar-i-Band mts Pak. see Makran Coast Range
Talas Kyrg. 80 D3
Talas Ala-Too mts Kyrg. 80 D3
Talas Range mts Kyrg. see Talas Ala-Too
Talasskiy Alatau, Khrebet mts Kyrg. see Talas Ala-Too
Ţal'at Mūsá mt. Lebanon/Syria 85 C2
Talaud, Kepulauan is Indon. 69 H6
Talavera de la Reina Spain 57 D4
Talawgyi Myanmar 70 B1
Talaya Rus. Fed. 65 Q3
Talbehat India 82 D4
Talbīsah Syria 85 C2
Talbot, Mount hill Australia 109 D6
Talbotton U.S.A. 133 C5
Talbragar r. Australia 112 D4
Talca Chile 144 B5
Talcahuano Chile 144 B5
Taldan Rus. Fed. 74 B1
Taldom Rus. Fed. 42 H4
Taldykorgan Kazakh. 80 E3
Taldy-Kurgan Kazakh. see Taldykorgan
Taldyqorghan Kazakh. see Taldykorgan
Tālesh Iran see Hashtpar
Talgarth U.K. 49 D7
Talguppa India 84 B3
Talia Australia 111 A7
Taliabu i. Indon. 69 G7
Talikota India 84 C2
Talimardzhan Uzbek. see Tollimarjon
Talin Hiag China 74 B3
Taliparamba India 84 B3
Talisay Phil. 69 G4
Taliş Dağları mts Azer./Iran 88 C2
Talitsa Rus. Fed. 42 J4
Taliwang Indon. 108 B2
Talkeetna U.S.A. 118 C3
Talkeetna Mountains U.S.A. 118 D3
Talkh Āb Iran 88 E3
Tallacootra, Lake salt flat Australia 109 F7
Talladega U.S.A. 133 C5

▶Tallahassee U.S.A. 133 C6
Capital of Florida.

Tall al Aḥmar Syria 85 D1
Tall Baydar Syria 91 F3
Tall-e Ḥalāl Iran 88 D4

▶Tallinn Estonia 45 N7
Capital of Estonia.

Tall Kalakh Syria 85 C2
Tall Kayf Iraq 91 F3
Tall Kūjik Syria 91 F3
Tallow Ireland 51 D5
Tallulah U.S.A. 131 F5
Tall 'Uwaynāt Iraq 91 F3
Tallymerjen Uzbek. see Tollimarjon
Talmont-St-Hilaire France 56 D3
Tal'ne Ukr. 43 F6
Tal'noye Ukr. see Tal'ne
Taloda India 82 C5
Talodi Sudan 86 D7
Taloga U.S.A. 131 D4
Talon, Lac l. Canada 123 I3
Ta-long Myanmar 70 B2
Tāloqān Afgh. 89 H2
Talos Dome ice feature Antarctica 152 H2
Ta Loung San mt. Laos 70 C2
Talovaya Rus. Fed. 43 I6
Taloyoak Canada 119 I3
Tal Pass Pak. 89 I3
Talsi Latvia 45 M8
Tal Sīyāh Iran 89 F4
Taltal Chile 144 B3
Taltson r. Canada 121 H2
Talu China 76 B2
Talvik Norway 44 M1
Talwood Australia 112 D2
Talyshskiye Gory mts Azer./Iran see Taliş Dağları
Talyy Rus. Fed. 42 L2
Tamala Australia 109 A6
Tamala Rus. Fed. 43 I5
Tamale Ghana 96 C4
Tamana i. Kiribati 107 H2
Taman Negara National Park Malaysia 71 C6
Tamano Japan 75 D6
Tamanrasset Alg. 96 D2
Tamanthi Myanmar 70 A1
Tamaqua U.S.A. 135 H3
Tamar India 83 F5
Tamar Syria see Tadmur
Tamar r. U.K. 49 C8
Tamarugal, Pampa de plain Chile 142 E7
Tamasane Botswana 101 H2
Tamatave Madag. see Toamasina
Tamaulipas state Mex. 131 D7
Tambacounda Senegal 96 B3
Tambaqui Brazil 142 F5
Tambar Springs Australia 112 D3
Tambelan, Kepulauan is Indon. 71 D7
Tambelan Besar i. Indon. 71 D7
Tambo r. Australia 112 C6
Tambohorano Madag. 99 E5

▶Tambora, Gunung vol. Indon. 108 B2
Deadliest recorded volcanic eruption (1815).

Tamboritha mt. Australia 112 C6
Tambov Rus. Fed. 43 I5
Tambovka Rus. Fed. 74 C2
Tambura Sudan 97 F4
Tamburi Brazil 145 C1
Tâmchekkeţ Mauritania 96 B3
Tamdybulak Uzbek. see Tomdibuloq
Tâmega r. Port. 57 B3
Tamenghest Alg. see Tamanrasset
Tamenglong India 83 H4
Tamerza Tunisia 58 B7
Tamgak, Adrar mt. Niger 96 D3
Tamgué, Massif du mt. Guinea 96 B3
Tamiahua, Laguna de lag. Mex. 136 E4
Tamiang, Ujung pt Indon. 71 B6
Tamil Nadu state India 84 C4
Tamitsa Rus. Fed. 42 H2
Ţāmīyah Egypt see Ţāmīyah
Ţāmīyah Egypt 90 C5
Tamkuhi India 83 F4
Tam Ky Vietnam 70 E4
Tammarvi r. Canada 121 K1
Tammerfors Fin. see Tampere
Tammisaari Fin. see Ekenäs
Tampa U.S.A. 133 D7
Tampa Bay U.S.A. 133 D7
Tampere Fin. 45 M6
Tampico Mex. 136 E4
Tampin Malaysia 71 C7
Tampines Sing. 71 [inset]
Tamsagbulag Mongolia 73 L3
Tamsweg Austria 47 N7
Tamu Myanmar 70 A1
Tamworth Australia 112 E3
Tamworth U.K. 49 F6
Tana r. Fin./Norway see Tenojoki
Tana r. Kenya 98 E4
Tana Madag. see Antananarivo
Tana i. Vanuatu see Tanna
Tana, Lake Eth. 98 D2
Tanabe Japan 75 D6
Tanabi Brazil 145 A3
Tana Bru Norway 44 P1
Tanada Lake U.S.A. 120 A2
Tanafjorden inlet Norway 44 P1
Tanah, Tanjung pt Indon. 68 D8
T'ana Hāyk' l. Eth. see Tana, Lake
Tanahgrogot Indon. 68 F7
Tanah Merah Malaysia 71 C6
Tanahputih Indon. 71 C7
Tanakeke i. Indon. 68 F8
Tanami Australia 108 E4
Tanami Desert Australia 108 E4
Tân An Vietnam 71 D5
Tanana r. U.S.A. 120 A2
Tananarive Madag. see Antananarivo
Tanandava Madag. 99 E6
Tancheng China see Pingtan
Tanch'ŏn N. Korea 75 C4
Tanda Côte d'Ivoire 96 C4
Tanda Uttar Prad. India 82 D3
Tanda Uttar Prad. India 83 E4
Tandag Phil. 69 H5
Ţăndărei Romania 59 L2
Tandaué Angola 99 B5
Tandi India 82 D2
Tandil Arg. 144 E5
Tando Adam Pak. 89 H5
Tando Allahyar Pak. 89 H5
Tando Bago Pak. 89 H5
Tandou Lake imp. l. Australia 111 C7
Tandragee U.K. 51 F3
Tandur India 84 C2
Tanduri Pak. 89 G4
Tanega-shima i. Japan 75 C7
Tanen Taunggyi mts Thai. 70 B3
Tanezrouft reg. Alg./Mali 96 C2
Ţanf, Jabal aţ hill Syria 85 D3
Tang, Ra's-e pt Iran 89 E5
Tanga Tanz. 99 D4
Tangail Bangl. 83 G4
Tanga Islands P.N.G. 106 F2
Tanganyika country Africa see Tanzania

▶Tanganyika, Lake Africa 99 C4
Deepest and 2nd largest lake in Africa, and 6th largest in the world.

Tangará Brazil 145 A4
Tangasseri India 84 C4
Tangdan China 76 D3
Tangeli Iran 88 D2
Tanger Morocco see Tangier
Tangerhütte Germany 53 L2
Tangermünde Germany 53 L2
Tang-e Sarkheh Iran 89 E5
Tanggor China 76 D1
Tanggulashan China 76 B1
Tanggula Shan mt. China 83 G2
Tanggula Shan mts China 83 G2
Tanggula Shankou pass China 83 G2
Tangguo China 83 F3
Tanghe China 77 G1
Tangier Morocco 57 D6
Tangiers Morocco see Tangier
Tang La pass China 83 G4
Tangla India 83 G4
Tanglag China 76 C1
Tanglin Sing. 71 [inset]
Tangmai China 76 B2
Tangnag China 76 D1
Tangorin Australia 110 D4
Tangra Yumco salt l. China 83 F3
Tangse Indon. 71 A6
Tangshan Guizhou China see Shiqian
Tangshan Hebei China 73 L5
Tangte mt. Myanmar 70 B2
Tangtse India see Tanktse
Tangwan China 77 F3
Tangwanghe China 74 C2
Tangyuan China 74 C3
Tangyung Tso salt l. China 83 F3
Tanhaçu Brazil 145 C1
Tanhua Fin. 44 O3
Tani Cambodia 71 D5
Taniantaweng Shan mts China 76 B2
Tanimbar, Kepulauan is Indon. 108 E1
Taninthari Myanmar see Tenasserim
Tanintharyi Myanmar see Tenasserim
Tanintharyi Myanmar see Tenasserim
Tanjah Morocco see Tangier
Tanjay Phil. 69 G5
Tanjore India see Thanjavur
Tanjung Indon. 68 F7
Tanjungbalai Indon. 71 B7
Tanjungkarang-Telukbetung Indon. see Bandar Lampung
Tanjungpandan Indon. 68 D7
Tanjungpinang Indon. 71 D7
Tanjungpura Indon. 71 B7
Tanjung Puting, Taman Nasional Indon. 68 E7
Tanjungredeb Indon. 68 F6
Tanjungselor Indon. 68 F6
Tankse India see Tanktse
Tanktse India 82 D2
Tankwa-Karoo National Park S. Africa 100 D7
Tanna i. Vanuatu 107 G3
Tannadice U.K. 50 G4
Tännäs Sweden 44 H5
Tanner, Mount Canada 120 G5
Tannu-Ola, Khrebet mts Rus. Fed. 80 H1
Tanot India 82 B4
Tanout Niger 96 D3
Tansen Nepal 83 E4
Tanshui Taiwan 77 I3
Ţanţā Egypt 90 C5
Ţanta Egypt see Ţanţā
Tan-Tan Morocco 96 B2
Tantu China 74 A3
Tanuku India 84 D2
Tanumbirini Australia 108 F4
Tanumshede Sweden 45 G7
Tanzania country Africa 99 D4
Tanzilla r. Canada 120 D3
Tao, Ko i. Thai. 71 B5
Tao'an China see Taonan
Taobh Tuath U.K. see Northton
Taocheng China see Daxin
Tao He r. China 76 D1
Taohong China see Longhui
Taohuajiang China see Taojiang
Taohuaping China see Longhui
Taojiang China 77 G2
Taolanaro Madag. see Tôlañaro
Taonan China 74 A3
Taongi atoll Marshall Is 150 H5
Taos U.S.A. 127 G5
Taounate Morocco 54 D5
Taourirt Morocco 54 D5
Taoxi China 77 H3
Taoyang China see Lintao
Taoyuan China 77 F2
T'aoyüan Taiwan 77 I3
Tapa Estonia 45 N7
Tapachula Mex. 136 F6
Tapah Malaysia 71 C6
Tapajós r. Brazil 143 H4
Tapaktuan Indon. 71 B7
Tapauá Brazil 142 F5
Tapauá r. Brazil 142 F5
Taperoá Brazil 145 D1
Tapi r. India 82 C5
Tapiau Rus. Fed. see Gvardeysk
Tapis, Gunung mt. Malaysia 71 C6
Tapisuelas Mex. 127 F8
Taplejung Nepal 83 F4
Tap Mun Chau i. H.K. China 77 [inset]
Ta-pom Myanmar 70 B2
Tappahannock U.S.A. 135 G5
Tappeh, Kūh-e hill Iran 88 C3
Taprobane country Asia see Sri Lanka
Tapuaenuku mt. N.Z. 113 D5

Tapulonanjing mt. Indon. 71 B7
Tapurucuara Brazil 142 E4
Taputeouea atoll Kiribati see Tabiteuea
Ţaqţaq Iraq 91 G4
Taquara Brazil 145 A5
Taquari Rio Grande do Sul Brazil 145 A5
Taquarí r. Brazil 143 G7
Taquaritinga Brazil 145 A3
Tar r. Ireland 51 E5
Tara Australia 112 E1
Ţarābulus Lebanon see Tripoli
Ţarābulus Libya see Tripoli
Tarahuwan India 82 E4
Tarai reg. India 83 G4
Tarakan Indon. 68 F6
Tarakan i. Indon. 68 F6
Tarakki reg. Afgh. 89 G3
Taraklı Turkey 59 N4
Taran, Mys pt Rus. Fed. 45 K9
Tarana Australia 112 D4
Taranagar India 82 C3
Taranaki, Mount vol. N.Z. 113 E4
Tarancón Spain 57 E3
Tarangambadi India 84 C4
Tarangire National Park Tanz. 98 D4
Taranto Italy 58 G4
Taranto, Golfo di g. Italy 58 G4
Taranto, Gulf of Italy see Taranto, Golfo di
Tarapoto Peru 142 C5
Tarapur India 84 B2
Tararua Range mts N.Z. 113 E5
Tarascon-sur-Ariège France 56 E5
Tarasovskiy Rus. Fed. 43 I6
Tarauacá Brazil 142 D5
Tarauacá r. Brazil 142 E5
Tarawera N.Z. 113 F4
Tarawera, Mount vol. N.Z. 113 F4
Taraz Kazakh. 80 D3
Tarazona Spain 57 F3
Tarazona de la Mancha Spain 57 F4
Tarbagatay, Khrebet mts Kazakh. 80 F2
Tarbat Ness pt U.K. 50 F3
Tarbert Ireland 51 C5
Tarbert Scotland U.K. 50 C3
Tarbert Scotland U.K. 50 D5
Tarbes France 56 E5
Tarboro U.S.A. 132 E5
Tarcoola Australia 109 F7
Tarcoon Australia 112 C3
Tarcoonyinna watercourse Australia 109 F6
Tarcutta Australia 112 C5
Tardoki-Yani, Gora mt. Rus. Fed. 74 E2
Taree Australia 112 F3
Tarella Australia 111 C6
Tarentum Italy see Taranto
Ţarfā', Baţn aţ depr. Saudi Arabia 88 C6
Tarfaya Morocco 96 B2
Targa well Niger 96 D3
Targan China see Talin Hiag
Targhee Pass U.S.A. 126 F3
Târgovişte Romania 59 K2
Targuist Morocco 57 D6
Târgu Jiu Romania 59 J2
Târgu Mureş Romania 59 K1
Târgu Neamţ Romania 59 L1
Târgu Secuiesc Romania 59 L1
Targyailing China 83 F3
Tari P.N.G. 69 K8
Tariat Mongolia 80 I2
Tarif U.A.E. 88 D5
Tarifa Spain 57 D5
Tarifa, Punta de pt Spain 57 D5
Tarija Bol. 142 F8
Tarikere India 84 B3
Tariku r. Indon. 69 J7
Tarīm Yemen 86 G6
Tarim Basin China 80 F4
Tarime Tanz. 98 D4
Tarim He r. China 80 G3
Tarim Pendi basin China see Tarim Basin
Tarīn Kowt Afgh. 89 G3
Taritatu r. Indon. 69 J7
Tarka r. S. Africa 101 G7
Tarkastad S. Africa 101 H7
Tarkio U.S.A. 130 E3
Tarko-Sale Rus. Fed. 64 I3
Tarkwa Ghana 96 C4
Tarlac Phil. 69 G3
Tarlo River National Park Australia 112 D5
Tarma Peru 142 C6
Tarmstedt Germany 53 J1
Tarn r. France 56 E4
Tärnaby Sweden 44 I4
Tarnak r. Afgh. 89 G4
Târnăveni Romania 59 K1
Tarnobrzeg Poland 43 D6
Tarnogskiy Gorodok Rus. Fed. 42 I3
Tarnopol Ukr. see Ternopil'
Tarnów Poland 43 D6
Tarnowitz Poland see Tarnowskie Góry
Tarnowskie Góry Poland 47 Q5
Taro Co salt l. China 83 E3
Ţārom Iran 88 D4
Taroom Australia 111 E5
Taroudannt Morocco 54 C5
Tarpaulin Swamp Australia 110 B3
Tarq Iran 88 C3
Tarquinia Italy 58 D3
Tarquinii Italy see Tarquinia
Tarrabool Lake salt flat Australia 110 A3
Tarraco Spain see Tarragona
Tarrafal Cape Verde 96 [inset]
Tarragona Spain 57 G3
Tårrajaur Sweden 44 K3
Tarran Hills hill Australia 112 C4
Tarrant Point Australia 110 B3
Tàrrega Spain 57 G3
Tarrong China see Nyêmo
Tarso Emissi mt. Chad 97 E2
Tarsus Turkey 85 B1
Tart China 83 H1
Tärtär Azer. 91 G2
Tartu Estonia 45 O7
Ţarţūs Syria 85 B2
Tarumovka Rus. Fed. 91 G1
Tarung Hka r. Myanmar 70 B1
Tarutao, Ko i. Thai. 71 B6
Tarutao National Park Thai. 71 B6
Tarutung Indon. 71 B7
Tarvisium Italy see Treviso
Tarz Iran 88 E4
Tasai, Ko i. Thai. 71 B5
Taschereau Canada 122 F4
Taseko Mountain Canada 120 F5
Tashauz Turkm. see Daşoguz
Tashi Chho Bhutan see Thimphu
Tashigang Bhutan 83 G4
Tashino Rus. Fed. see Pervomaysk
Tashir Armenia 91 G2
Tashk, Daryācheh-ye l. Iran 88 D4
Tashkent Toshkent Uzbek. see Toshkent
Tāshqurghān Afgh. see Kholm
Tashtagol Rus. Fed. 72 F2
Tashtyp Rus. Fed. 72 F2
Tasialujjuaq, Lac l. Canada 123 G2
Tasiat, Lac l. Canada 122 G2
Tasiilap Karra c. Greenland 119 O3
Tasiilaq Greenland see Ammassalik
Tasīl Syria 85 B3
Tasiujaq Canada 123 H2
Tasiusaq Greenland 119 M2
Taşkent Turkey 85 A1
Tasker Niger 96 E3
Taskesken Kazakh. 80 F2
Taşköprü Turkey 90 D2
Tasman Abyssal Plain sea feature Tasman Sea 150 G8
Tasman Basin sea feature Tasman Sea 150 G8
Tasman Bay N.Z. 113 D5

►Tasmania state Australia 111 [inset]
4th largest island in Oceania.

Tasman Islands P.N.G. see Nukumanu Islands
Tasman Mountains N.Z. 113 D5
Tasman Peninsula Australia 111 [inset]
Tasman Sea S. Pacific Ocean 106 H6
Taşova Turkey 90 E2
Tassara Niger 96 D3
Tassialouc, Lac l. Canada 122 G2
Tassili du Hoggar plat. Alg. 96 D2
Tassili n'Ajjer plat. Alg. 96 D2
Tasty Kazakh. 80 C3
Taşucu Turkey 85 A1
Tas-Yuryakh Rus. Fed. 65 M3
Tata Morocco 54 C6
Tatabánya Hungary 58 H1
Tatamailau, Foho mt. East Timor 108 D2
Tataouine Tunisia 54 G5
Tatarbunary Ukr. 59 M2
Tatarsk Rus. Fed. 64 I4
Tatarskiy Proliv strait Rus. Fed. 74 F2
Tatar Strait Rus. Fed. see Tatarskiy Proliv
Tate r. Australia 110 C3
Tateyama Japan 75 E6
Tathlina Lake Canada 120 G2
Tathlīth Saudi Arabia 86 F6
Tathlīth, Wādī watercourse Saudi Arabia 86 F5
Tathra Australia 112 D6
Tatinnai Lake Canada 121 L2
Tatishchevo Rus. Fed. 43 J6
Tatkon Myanmar 70 B2
Tatla Lake Canada 120 E5
Tatla Lake l. Canada 120 E5
Tatlayoko Lake Canada 120 E5
Tatnam, Cape Canada 121 N3
Tatra Mountains Poland/Slovakia 47 Q6
Tatry mts Poland/Slovakia see Tatra Mountains
Tatrzański Park Narodowy nat. park Poland 47 Q6
Tatshenshini-Alsek Provincial Wilderness Park Canada 120 B3
Tatsinskiy Rus. Fed. 43 I6
Tatuí Brazil 145 B3
Tatuk Mountain Canada 120 E4
Tatum U.S.A. 131 C5
Tatvan Turkey 91 F3
Tau Norway 45 D7
Taua Brazil 143 J5
Tauapeçaçu Brazil 142 F4
Taubaté Brazil 145 B3
Tauber r. Germany 53 J5
Tauberbischofsheim Germany 53 J5
Taucha Germany 53 M3
Taufstein hill Germany 53 J4
Taukum, Peski des. Kazakh. 80 D3
Taumarunui N.Z. 113 E4
Taumaturgo Brazil 142 D5
Taung S. Africa 100 G4
Taungdwingyi Myanmar 70 A2
Taunggyi Myanmar 70 B2
Taunglau Myanmar 70 B2
Taung-ngu Myanmar 70 B3
Taungnyo Range mts Myanmar 70 B3
Taungtha Myanmar 70 A2
Taungup Myanmar 76 B5
Taunton U.K. 49 D7
Taunton U.S.A. 135 J3
Taunus hills Germany 53 H4
Taupo N.Z. 113 F4
Taupo, Lake N.Z. 113 E4
Tauragė Lith. 45 M9
Tauranga N.Z. 113 F3
Taurasia Italy see Turin
Taureau, Réservoir resr Canada 122 G5
Taurianova Italy 58 G5
Tauroa Point N.Z. 113 D2
Taurus Mountains Turkey 85 A1
Taute r. France 49 F9
Tauz Azer. see Tovuz
Tavas Turkey 59 M6
Tavastehus Fin. see Hämeenlinna
Taverham U.K. 49 I6
Taveuni i. Fiji 107 I3
Tavildara Tajik. 89 H2
Tavira Port. 57 C5
Tavistock Canada 134 E2
Tavistock U.K. 49 C8
Tavoy Myanmar 71 B4
Tavoy r. mouth Myanmar 71 B4
Tavoy Island Myanmar see Mali Kyun
Tavoy Point Myanmar 71 B4
Tavşanlı Turkey 59 M5
Taw r. U.K. 49 C7
Tawang India 83 G4
Tawas City U.S.A. 134 D1
Tawau Sabah Malaysia 68 F6
Tawè Myanmar see Tavoy
Tawe r. U.K. 49 D7
Ţawī Ḩafīr well U.A.E. 88 D5
Ţawī Murra well U.A.E. 88 D5
Tawmaw Myanmar 70 B1
Tawu Taiwan 77 I4
Taxkorgan China 80 E4
Tay r. Canada 120 C2
Tay r. U.K. 50 F4
Tay, Firth of est. U.K. 50 F4
Tay, Lake salt flat Australia 109 C8
Tay, Loch l. U.K. 50 E4
Tayandu, Kepulauan is Indon. 69 I8
Taybola Rus. Fed. 44 R2
Taycheedah U.S.A. 134 A2
Tayinloan U.K. 50 D5
Taylor Canada 120 F3
Taylor AK U.S.A. 118 B3
Taylor MI U.S.A. 134 D2
Taylor NE U.S.A. 130 D3
Taylor TX U.S.A. 131 D6
Taylor, Mount U.S.A. 129 J4
Taylorsville U.S.A. 134 C4
Taylorville U.S.A. 130 F4
Taymā' Saudi Arabia 90 E6
Taymura r. Rus. Fed. 65 K3
Taymyr, Ozero l. Rus. Fed. 65 L2
Taymyr, Poluostrov pen. Rus. Fed. see Taymyr Peninsula
Taymyr Peninsula Rus. Fed. 64 J2
Tây Ninh Vietnam 71 D5
Taypak Kazakh. 41 Q6
Taypaq Kazakh. see Taypak
Tayshet Rus. Fed. 72 H1
Taytay Phil. 68 F4
Tayuan China 74 B2
Tayyebād Iran 89 F3
Taz r. Rus. Fed. 64 I3
Taza Morocco 54 D5
Tāza Khurmātū Iraq 91 G4
Taze Myanmar 70 A2
Tazewell TN U.S.A. 134 D5
Tazewell VA U.S.A. 134 E5
Tazin r. Canada 121 I2
Tazin Lake Canada 121 I3
Tāzirbū Libya 97 F2
Tazmalt Alg. 57 I5
Tazovskaya Guba sea chan. Rus. Fed. 64 I3
Tbessa Alg. see Tébessa

►T'bilisi Georgia 91 G2
Capital of Georgia.

Tbilisskaya Rus. Fed. 43 I7
Tchabal Mbabo mt. Cameroon 96 E4
Tchad country Africa see Chad
Tchamba Togo 96 D4
Tchibanga Gabon 98 B4
Tchigaï, Plateau du Niger 97 E2
Tchin-Tabaradene Niger 96 D3
Tcholliré Cameroon 97 E4
Tchula U.S.A. 131 F5
Tczew Poland 47 Q3
Te, Prêk r. Cambodia 71 D4
Teague, Lake salt flat Australia 109 C6
Te Anau N.Z. 113 A7
Te Anau, Lake N.Z. 113 A7
Teapa Mex. 136 F5
Te Araroa N.Z. 113 G3
Teate Italy see Chieti
Te Awamutu N.Z. 113 E4
Teba Indon. 69 J7
Tébarat Niger 96 D3
Tebas Indon. 71 E7
Tebay U.K. 48 E4
Tebesjuak Lake Canada 121 L2
Tébessa Alg. 58 C7
Tébessa, Monts de mts Alg. 58 C7
Tebingtinggi Indon. 71 B7
Téboursouk Tunisia 58 C6
Téboursouk Tunisia 58 C6
Tebulos Mt'a Georgia/Rus. Fed. 91 G2
Tecate Mex. 128 E5
Tece Turkey 85 B1
Techiman Ghana 96 C4
Tecka Arg. 144 B6
Tecklenburger Land reg. Germany 53 H2
Tecoripa Mex. 127 F7
Técpan Mex. 136 D5
Tecuala Mex. 136 C4
Tecuci Romania 59 L2
Tecumseh MI U.S.A. 134 D3
Tecumseh NE U.S.A. 130 D3
Tedzhen Turkm. see Tejen
Teec Nos Pos U.S.A. 129 I3
Tees r. U.K. 48 F4
Teeswater Canada 134 E1
Tefé r. Brazil 142 F4
Tefenni Turkey 59 M6
Tegal Indon. 68 D8
Tegel airport Germany 53 N2
Tegid, Llyn l. Wales U.K. see Bala Lake

►Tegucigalpa Hond. 137 G6
Capital of Honduras.

Teguidda-n-Tessoumt Niger 96 D3
Tehachapi U.S.A. 128 D4
Tehachapi Mountains U.S.A. 128 D4
Tehachapi Pass U.S.A. 128 D4
Tehek Lake Canada 121 M1
Teheran Iran see Tehrān
Tehery Lake Canada 121 M1
Téhini Côte d'Ivoire 96 C4

►Tehrān Iran 88 C3
Capital of Iran.

Tehri India see Tikamgarh
Tehuacán Mex. 136 E5
Tehuantepec, Gulf of Mex. 136 F5
Tehuantepec, Istmo de isthmus Mex. 136 F5
Teide, Pico del vol. Canary Is 96 B2
Teifi r. U.K. 49 C6
Teignmouth U.K. 49 D8
Teixeira de Sousa Angola see Luau
Teixeiras Brazil 145 C3
Teixeira Soares Brazil 145 A4
Tejakula Indon. 108 A2
Tejen Turkm. 89 F2
Tejo r. Port. 57 B4 see Tagus
Tejon Pass U.S.A. 128 D4
Tekapo, Lake N.Z. 113 C6
Tekax Mex. 136 G4
Tekeli Kazakh. 80 E3
Tekes China 80 F3
Tekiliktag mt. China 82 E1
Tekin Rus. Fed. 74 D2
Tekirdağ Turkey 59 L4
Tekka India 84 D2
Tekkali India 84 E2
Teknaf Bangl. 83 H5
Tekong Kechil, Pulau i. Sing. 71 [inset]
Te Kuiti N.Z. 113 E4
Tel r. India 84 D1
Télagh Alg. 57 F6
Telanaipura Indon. see Jambi
Tel Ashqelon tourist site Israel 85 B4
Télataï Mali 96 D3
Tel Aviv-Yafo Israel 85 B3
Telč Czech Rep. 47 O6
Telchac Puerto Mex. 136 G4
Telekhany Belarus see Tsyelyakhany
Telêmaco Borba Brazil 145 A4
Teleorman r. Romania 59 K3
Telertheba, Djebel mt. Alg. 96 D2
Telescope Peak U.S.A. 128 E3
Teles Pires r. Brazil 143 G5
Telford U.K. 49 E6
Telgte Germany 53 H3
Télimélé Guinea 96 B3
Teljo, Jebel mt. Sudan 86 C7
Telkwa Canada 120 E4
Tell Atlas mts Alg. see Atlas Tellien
Tell City U.S.A. 134 B5
Teller U.S.A. 118 B3
Tell es Sultan West Bank see Jericho
Tellicherry India 84 B4
Tellin Belgium 52 F4
Telloh Iraq 91 G5
Telluride U.S.A. 129 J3
Tel'novskiy Rus. Fed. 74 F2
Telok Anson Malaysia see Teluk Intan
Telo Martius France see Toulon
Telpoziz, Gora mt. Rus. Fed. 41 R3
Telsen Arg. 144 C6
Telšiai Lith. 45 M9
Teltow Germany 53 N2
Teluk Anson Malaysia see Teluk Intan
Telukbetung Indon. see Bandar Lampung
Teluk Cenderawasih, Taman Nasional Indon. 69 I7
Teluk Intan Malaysia 71 C6
Temagami Lake Canada 122 F5
Temanggung Indon. 68 E8
Têmarxung China 83 G2
Temba S. Africa 101 I3
Tembagapura Indon. 69 J7
Tembenchi r. Rus. Fed. 65 K3
Tembilahan Indon. 68 C7
Tembisa S. Africa 101 I4
Tembo Aluma Angola 99 B4
Teme r. U.K. 49 E6
Temecula U.S.A. 128 E5
Temerloh Malaysia see Temerluh
Temerluh Malaysia 71 C7
Teminabuan Indon. 69 I7
Temirtau Kazakh. 80 D1
Témiscamie r. Canada 123 G4
Témiscamie, Lac l. Canada 123 G4
Témiscaming Canada 122 F5
Témiscamingue, Lac l. Canada 122 F5
Témiscouata, Lac l. Canada 123 H5
Temmes Fin. 44 N4
Temnikov Rus. Fed. 43 I5
Temora Australia 112 C5
Temósachic Mex. 127 G7
Tempe U.S.A. 129 H5
Tempe Downs Australia 109 F6
Tempelhof airport Germany 53 N2
Temple MI U.S.A. 134 C1
Temple TX U.S.A. 131 D6
Temple Bar U.K. 49 C6
Temple Dera Pak. 89 H4
Templemore Ireland 51 E5
Temple Sowerby U.K. 48 E4
Templeton watercourse Australia 110 B4
Templin Germany 53 N1
Tempué Angola 99 B5
Temryuk Rus. Fed. 90 E1
Temryukskiy Zaliv b. Rus. Fed. 43 H7
Temuco Chile 144 B5
Temuka N.Z. 113 C7
Temuli China see Butuo
Tena Ecuador 142 C4
Tenabo Mex. 136 F4
Tenabo, Mount U.S.A. 128 E1
Tenali India 84 D2
Tenasserim Myanmar 71 B4
Tenasserim r. Myanmar 71 B4
Tenbury Wells U.K. 49 E6
Tenby U.K. 49 C7
Tendaho Eth. 98 E2
Tende, Col de pass France/Italy 56 H4
Ten Degree Channel India 71 A5
Tendō Japan 75 F5
Tenedos i. Turkey see Bozcaada
Ténenkou Mali 96 C3
Ténéré reg. Niger 96 D2
Ténéré du Tafassâsset des. Niger 96 E2
Tenerife i. Canary Is 96 B2
Ténès Alg. 57 G5
Teng, Nam r. Myanmar 70 B3
Tengah, Kepulauan is Indon. 68 F8
Tengah, Sungai r. Sing. 71 [inset]
Tengcheng China see Tengxian
Tengchong China 76 C3
Tengeh Reservoir Sing. 71 [inset]
Tengger Shamo des. China 72 I5
Tenggul i. Malaysia 71 C6
Tengiz, Ozero salt l. Kazakh. 80 C1
Tengqiao China 77 F5
Tengréla Côte d'Ivoire 96 C3
Ten'gushevo Rus. Fed. 43 I5
Tengxian China 77 F4
Teni India see Theni
Teniente Jubany research station Antarctica see Jubany
Tenille U.S.A. 133 D6
Tenke Dem. Rep. Congo 99 C5
Tenkeli Rus. Fed. 65 P2
Tenkodogo Burkina 96 C3
Ten Mile Lake salt flat Australia 109 C6
Ten Mile Lake Canada 123 K4
Tennant Creek Australia 108 F4
Tennessee r. U.S.A. 131 F4
Tennessee state U.S.A. 134 C5
Tennessee Pass U.S.A. 126 G5
Tennevoll Norway 44 J2
Tenojoki r. Fin./Norway 44 P1
Tenosique Mex. 136 F5
Tenteno Indon. 69 G7
Tenterden U.K. 49 H7
Tenterfield Australia 112 F2
Ten Thousand Islands U.S.A. 133 D7
Tentudia mt. Spain 57 C4
Tentulia Bangl. see Tetulia
Teodoro Sampaio Brazil 144 F2
Teófilo Otôni Brazil 145 C2
Tepa Indon. 108 E1
Tepache Mex. 127 F7
Te Paki N.Z. 113 D2
Tepatitlán Mex. 136 D4
Tepehuanes Mex. 131 B7
Tepeköy Turkey see Karakoçan
Tepelenë Albania 59 I4
Tepelská vrchovina hills Czech Rep. 53 M5
Tepequem, Serra mts Brazil 137 L8
Tepic Mex. 136 D4
Te Pirita N.Z. 113 C6
Teplá r. Czech Rep. 53 M4
Teplice Czech Rep. 47 N5
Teplogorka Rus. Fed. 42 L3
Teploozersk Rus. Fed. 74 C2
Teploye Rus. Fed. 43 H5
Teploye Ozero Rus. Fed. see Teploozersk
Tepoca, Cabo c. Mex. 127 E7
Tepopa, Punta pt Mex. 127 E7
Tequila Mex. 136 D4
Téra Niger 96 D3
Teramo Italy 58 E3
Terang Australia 112 A7
Ter Apel Neth. 52 H2
Teratani r. Pak. 89 H4
Tercan Turkey 91 F3
Terebovlya Ukr. 43 E6
Terekty Kazakh. 80 G2
Teresa Cristina Brazil 145 A4
Tereshka r. Rus. Fed. 43 J6
Teresina Brazil 143 J5
Teresina de Goias Brazil 145 B1
Teresita Col. 142 E3
Teresópolis Brazil 145 C3
Teressa Island India 71 A5
Terezinha Brazil 143 H3
Tergeste Italy see Trieste
Tergnier France 52 D5
Teriberka Rus. Fed. 44 S2
Termez Uzbek. see Termiz
Termini Imerese Sicily Italy 58 E6
Términos, Laguna de lag. Mex. 136 F5
Termit-Kaoboul Niger 96 E3
Termiz Uzbek. 89 G2
Termo U.S.A. 128 C1
Termoli Italy 58 F4
Termonde Belgium see Dendermonde
Tern r. U.K. 49 E6
Ternate Indon. 69 H6
Terneuzen Neth. 52 D3
Terney Rus. Fed. 74 E3
Terni Italy 58 E3
Ternopil' Ukr. 43 E6
Ternopol' Ukr. see Ternopil'
Terpeniya, Mys c. Rus. Fed. 74 G2
Terpeniya, Zaliv g. Rus. Fed. 74 F2
Terra Alta U.S.A. 134 F4
Terra Bella U.S.A. 128 D4
Terrace Canada 120 D4
Terrace Bay Canada 122 D4
Terra Firma S. Africa 100 F3
Terråk Norway 44 H4
Terralba Sardinia Italy 58 C5
Terra Nova Bay Antarctica 152 H1
Terra Nova National Park Canada 123 L4
Terrebonne Bay U.S.A. 131 F6
Terre Haute U.S.A. 134 B4
Terre-Neuve prov. Canada see Newfoundland and Labrador
Terre-Neuve-et-Labrador prov. Canada see Newfoundland and Labrador
Terres Australes et Antarctiques Françaises terr. Indian Ocean see French Southern and Antarctic Lands
Terry U.S.A. 126 G3
Terschelling i. Neth. 52 F1
Terskiy Bereg coastal area Rus. Fed. 42 H2
Tertenia Sardinia Italy 58 C5
Terter Azer. see Tärtär
Teruel Spain 57 F3
Tervola Fin. 44 N3
Tes Mongolia 80 I2
Tešanj Bos.-Herz. 58 G2
Teseney Eritrea 86 E6
Tesha r. Rus. Fed. 43 I5
Teshekpuk Lake U.S.A. 118 C2
Teshio Japan 74 F3
Teshio-gawa r. Japan 74 F3
Teslin Canada 120 C2
Teslin r. Canada 120 C2
Teslin Lake Canada 120 C2
Tesouras r. Brazil 145 A1
Tessalit Mali 96 D2
Tessaoua Niger 96 D3
Tessolo Moz. 101 L1
Test r. U.K. 49 F8
Testour Tunisia 58 C6
Tetachuck Lake Canada 120 E4
Tetas, Punta pt Chile 144 B2
Tete Moz. 99 D5
Te Teko N.Z. 113 F4
Teteriv r. Ukr. 43 F6
Teterow Germany 47 N4
Tetiyev Ukr. see Tetiyiv
Tetiyiv Ukr. 43 F6
Tetlin U.S.A. 120 A2
Tetlin Lake U.S.A. 120 A2
Tetney U.K. 48 G5
Teton r. U.S.A. 126 F3
Tétouan Morocco 57 D6
Tetovo Macedonia 59 I3
Tetuán Morocco see Tétouan
Tetulia Bangl. 83 G4
Tetulia sea chan. Bangl. 83 G5
Tetyukhe Rus. Fed. see Dal'negorsk
Tetyukhe-Pristan' Rus. Fed. see Rudnaya Pristan'
Tetyushi Rus. Fed. 43 K5
Teuco r. Arg. 144 D2
Teufelsbach Namibia 100 C2
Teunom Indon. 71 A6
Teunom r. Indon. 71 A6
Teutoburger Wald hills Germany 53 I2
Teuva Fin. 44 L5
Tevere r. Italy see Tiber
Teverya Israel see Tiberias
Teviot r. U.K. 50 G5
Te Waewae Bay N.Z. 113 A8
Te Waipounamu i. N.Z. see South Island
Tewane Botswana 101 H2
Tewantin Australia 111 F5
Tewkesbury U.K. 49 E7
Têwo China 76 D1
Texarkana AR U.S.A. 131 E5
Texarkana TX U.S.A. 131 E5
Texas Australia 112 E2
Texas state U.S.A. 131 D6
Texel i. Neth. 52 E1
Texhoma U.S.A. 131 C4
Texoma, Lake U.S.A. 131 D5
Teyateyaneng Lesotho 101 H5
Teykovo Rus. Fed. 42 I4
Teza r. Rus. Fed. 42 I4
Tezpur India 83 H4
Tezu India 83 I4
Tha, Nam r. Laos 70 C2
Thaa Atoll Maldives see Kolhumadulu Atoll
Tha-anne r. Canada 121 M2
Thabana-Ntlenyana mt. Lesotho 101 I5
Thaba Nchu S. Africa 101 H5
Thaba Putsoa mt. Lesotho 101 H5
Thaba-Tseka Lesotho 101 I5
Thabazimbi S. Africa 101 H3
Thab Lan National Park Thai. 71 C4
Tha Bo Laos 70 C3
Thabong S. Africa 101 H4
Thabyedaung Myanmar 76 C4
Thade r. Myanmar 70 A3
Thagyettaw Myanmar 71 B4
Tha Hin Thai. see Lop Buri
Thai Binh Vietnam 70 D2
Thailand country Asia 70 C4
Thailand, Gulf of Asia 71 C5
Thai Muang Thai. 71 B5
Thai Nguyên Vietnam 70 D2
Thaj Saudi Arabia 88 C5
Thakèk Laos 70 D3
Thakurgaon Bangl. 83 G4
Thakurtola India 82 E5
Thal Germany 53 K4
Thala Tunisia 58 C7
Thalang Thai. 71 B5
Thalassery India see Tellicherry
Thal Desert Pak. 89 H4
Thale (Harz) Germany 53 L3
Thaliparamba India see Taliparamba
Thallon Australia 112 D2
Thalo Pak. 89 G4
Thamaga Botswana 101 G3
Thamar, Jabal mt. Yemen 86 G7
Thamarīt Oman 87 H6
Thame r. U.K. 49 F7
Thames r. Ont. Canada 125 K3
Thames r. Ont. Canada 134 D2
Thames N.Z. 113 E3
Thames est. U.K. 49 H7
Thames r. U.K. 49 H7
Thamesford Canada 134 E2
Thana India see Thane
Thanatpin Myanmar 70 B3
Thandwè Myanmar 70 A3
Thane India 84 B2
Thanet, Isle of pen. U.K. 49 I7
Thangoo Australia 108 C4
Thangra India 82 D2
Thanh Hoa Vietnam 70 D3
Thanjavur India 84 C4
Than Kyun i. Myanmar 71 B5
Thanlwin r. China/Myanmar see Salween
Thanlyin Myanmar 70 B3
Thaolintoa Lake Canada 121 L2
Tha Pla Thai. 70 C3
Thap Put Thai. 71 B5
Thapsacus Syria see Dibsī
Thap Sakae Thai. 71 B5
Tharabwin Myanmar 71 B4
Tharad India 82 B4
Thar Desert India/Pak. 89 H5
Thargomindah Australia 112 A1
Tharrawaw Myanmar 70 A3
Tharthār, Buḩayrat ath l. Iraq 91 F4
Tharwāniyyah U.A.E. 88 D6
Thasos i. Greece 59 K4
Thatcher U.S.A. 129 I5
Thât Khê Vietnam 70 D2
Thaton Myanmar 70 B3
Thatta Pak. 89 G5
Thaungdut Myanmar 70 A1
Tha Uthen Thai. 70 D3
Thayawthadangyi Kyun i. Myanmar 71 B4
Thayetmyo Myanmar 70 A3
Thazi Magwe Myanmar 70 A3
Thazi Mandalay Myanmar 83 I5
The Aldermen Islands N.Z. 113 F3
Theba U.S.A. 129 G5
The Bahamas country West Indies 133 E7
Thebes Greece see Thiva
The Bluff Bahamas 133 E7
The Broads nat. park U.K. 49 I6
The Brothers is H.K. China 77 [inset]
The Calvados Chain is P.N.G. 110 F1
The Cheviot hill U.K. 48 E3
The Dalles U.S.A. 126 C3
Thedford U.S.A. 130 C3
The Entrance Australia 112 E4
The Faither stack U.K. 50 [inset]
The Fens reg. U.K. 49 G6
The Gambia country Africa 96 B3
Thegon Myanmar 70 A3
The Grampians mts Australia 111 C8

The Great Oasis oasis Egypt see Khārijah, Wāḥāt al
The Grenadines is St Vincent 137 L6
The Gulf Asia 88 C4

▶The Hague Neth. 52 E2
Seat of government of the Netherlands.

The Hunters Hills N.Z. 113 C7
Thekulthili Lake Canada 121 I2
The Lakes National Park Australia 112 C6
Thelon r. Canada 121 L1
The Lynd Junction Australia 110 D3
Themar Germany 53 K4
Thembalihle S. Africa 101 I4
The Minch sea chan. U.K. 50 C2
The Naze c. Norway see Lindesnes
The Needles stack U.K. 49 F8
Theni India 84 C4
Thenia Alg. 57 H5
Theniet El Had Alg. 57 H6
The North Sound sea chan. U.K. 50 G1
Theodore Australia 110 E5
Theodore Canada 121 K5
Theodore Roosevelt Lake U.S.A. 129 H5
Theodore Roosevelt National Park U.S.A. 130 C2
Theodosia Ukr. see Feodosiya
The Old Man of Coniston hill U.K. 48 D4
The Paps hill Ireland 51 C5
The Pas Canada 121 K4
The Pilot mt. Australia 112 D6
Thera i. Greece see Santorini
Thérain r. France 52 C5
Theresa U.S.A. 135 H1
Thermaïkos Kolpos g. Greece 59 J4
Thermopolis U.S.A. 126 F4
The Rock Australia 112 C5
Thérouanne France 52 C4
The Salt Lake salt flat Australia 111 C6

▶The Settlement Christmas I. 68 D9
Capital of Christmas Island.

The Skaw spit Denmark see Grenen
The Skelligs is Ireland 51 B6
The Slot sea chan. Solomon Is see New Georgia Sound
The Solent strait U.K. 49 F8
Thessalon Canada 122 E5
Thessalonica Greece see Thessaloniki
Thessaloniki Greece 59 J4
The Storr hill U.K. 50 C3
Thet r. U.K. 49 H6
The Terraces hills Australia 109 C7
Thetford U.K. 49 H6
Thetford Mines Canada 123 H5
Thetkethaung r. Myanmar 70 A4
The Triangle mts Myanmar 70 B1
The Trossachs hills U.K. 50 E4
The Twins Australia 111 A6
Theva-i-Ra reef Fiji see Ceva-i-Ra

▶The Valley Anguilla 137 L5
Capital of Anguilla.

Thevenard Island Australia 108 A5
Thévenet, Lac l. Canada 123 H2
Theveste Alg. see Tébessa
The Wash b. U.K. 49 H6
The Weald reg. U.K. 49 H7
The Woodlands U.S.A. 131 E6
Thibodaux U.S.A. 131 F6
Thicket Portage Canada 121 L4
Thief River Falls U.S.A. 130 D1
Thiel Neth. see Tiel
Thiel Mountains Antarctica 152 K1
Thielsen, Mount U.S.A. 126 C4
Thielt Belgium see Tielt
Thiérache reg. France 52 D5
Thiers France 56 F4
Thiès Senegal 96 B3
Thika Kenya 98 D4
Thiladhunmathi Atoll Maldives 84 B5
Thiladunmathi Atoll Maldives see Thiladhunmathi Atoll
Thimbu Bhutan see Thimphu

▶Thimphu Bhutan 83 G4
Capital of Bhutan.

Thionville France 52 G5
Thira i. Greece see Santorini
Thirsk U.K. 48 F4
Thirty Mile Lake Canada 121 L2
Thiruvananthapuram India see Trivandrum
Thiruvannamalai India see Tiruvannamalai
Thiruvarur India 84 C4
Thiruvattiyur India see Tiruvottiyur
Thisted Denmark 45 F8
Thistle Creek Canada 120 B2
Thistle Lake Canada 121 I1
Thityabin Myanmar 70 A2
Thiu Khao Luang Phrabang mts Laos/Thai. see Luang Phrabang, Thiu Khao
Thiva Greece 59 J5
Thívai Greece see Thiva
Thlewiaza r. Canada 121 M2
Thoa r. Canada 121 I2
Thô Chu, Đao i. Vietnam 71 C5
Thoen Thai. 76 C5
Thoeng Thai. 70 C3
Thohoyandou S. Africa 101 J2
Tholen Neth. 52 E3
Tholen i. Neth. 52 E3
Tholey Germany 52 H5
Thomas Hill Reservoir U.S.A. 130 E4
Thomas Hubbard, Cape Canada 119 I1
Thomaston CT U.S.A. 135 I3
Thomaston GA U.S.A. 133 C5
Thomastown Ireland 51 E5
Thomasville AL U.S.A. 133 C6
Thomasville GA U.S.A. 133 D6
Thommen Belgium 52 G4
Thompson Canada 121 L4
Thompson r. Canada 120 F5
Thompson U.S.A. 129 I2
Thompson r. U.S.A. 124 I4
Thompson Falls U.S.A. 126 E3
Thompson Peak U.S.A. 127 G6
Thompson's Falls Kenya see Nyahururu
Thompson Sound Canada 120 E5
Thomson U.S.A. 133 D5
Thon Buri Thai. 71 C4
Thonokied Lake Canada 121 I1
Thoothukudi India see Tuticorin
Thoreau U.S.A. 129 I4
Thorn Neth. 52 F3
Thorn Poland see Toruń
Thornaby-on-Tees U.K. 48 F4
Thornapple r. U.S.A. 134 C2
Thornbury U.K. 49 E7
Thorne U.K. 48 G5
Thorne U.S.A. 128 D2
Thornton r. Australia 110 B3
Thorold Canada 134 F2
Thorshavnfjella reg. Antarctica see Thorshavnheiane
Thorshavnheiane reg. Antarctica 152 C2
Thota-ea-Moli Lesotho 101 H5
Thôt Nôt Vietnam 71 D5
Thouars France 56 D3
Thoubal India 83 H4
Thourout Belgium see Torhout
Thousand Islands Canada/U.S.A. 135 G1
Thousand Lake Mountain U.S.A. 129 H2
Thousand Oaks U.S.A. 128 D4
Thousandsticks U.S.A. 134 D5
Thrace reg. Europe 59 L4
Thraki reg. Europe see Thrace
Thrakiko Pelagos sea Greece 59 K4
Three Gorges Reservoir China 77 F2
Three Hills Canada 120 H5
Three Hummock Island Australia 111 [inset]
Three Kings Islands N.Z. 113 D2
Three Oaks U.S.A. 134 B3
Three Pagodas Pass Myanmar/Thai. 70 B4
Three Points, Cape Ghana 96 C4
Three Rivers U.S.A. 134 C3
Three Sisters mt. U.S.A. 126 C3
Three Springs Australia 109 A7
Thrissur India see Trichur
Throckmorton U.S.A. 131 D5
Throssell, Lake salt flat Australia 109 D6
Throssel Range hills Australia 108 C5
Thrushton National Park Australia 112 C1
Thư Ba Vietnam 71 D5
Thubun Lakes Canada 121 I2
Thu Dâu Môt Vietnam 71 D5
Thuddungra Australia 112 D5
Thu Đuc Vietnam 71 D5
Thuin Belgium 52 E4
Thul Pak. 89 H4
Thulaythawāt Gharbī, Jabal hill Syria 85 D2
Thule Greenland 119 L2
Thun Switz. 56 H3
Thunder Bay Canada 119 J5
Thunder Bay b. U.S.A. 134 D1
Thunder Creek r. Canada 121 J5
Thüngen Germany 53 J5
Thung Salaeng Luang National Park Thai. 70 C3
Thung Song Thai. 71 B5
Thung Yai Naresuan Wildlife Reserve nature res. Thai. 70 B4
Thüringen land Germany 53 K3
Thüringer Becken reg. Germany 53 L3
Thüringer Wald mts Germany 53 K4
Thuringia land Germany see Thüringen
Thuringian Forest mts Germany see Thüringer Wald
Thurles Ireland 51 E5
Thurn, Pass Austria 47 N7
Thursday Island Australia 110 C1
Thurso U.K. 50 F2
Thurso r. U.K. 50 F2
Thurston Island Antarctica 152 K2
Thurston Peninsula i. Antarctica see Thurston Island
Thüster Berg hill Germany 53 J2
Thuthukudi India see Tuticorin
Thwaite U.K. 48 E4
Thwaites Glacier Tongue Antarctica 152 K1
Thyatira Turkey see Akhisar
Thyborøn Denmark 45 F8
Thymerais reg. France 52 B6
Tianchang China 77 H1
Tiancheng China see Chongyang
Tianchi China see Lezhi
Tiandeng China 76 E4
Tiandong China 76 E4
T'ianet'i Georgia 91 G2
Tianfanjie China 77 H2
Tianjin China 73 L5
Tianjin municipality China 73 L5
Tianjun China 80 I4
Tianlin China 76 E3
Tianma China see Changshan
Tianmen China 77 G2
Tianqiaoling China 74 C4
Tianquan China 76 D2
Tianshan China 73 M4
Tian Shan mts China/Kyrg. see Tien Shan
Tianshui China 76 E1
Tianshuihai Aksai Chin 82 D2
Tiantai China 77 I2
Tiantang China see Yuexi
Tianyang China 76 E4
Tianzhou China see Tianyang
Tianzhu Gansu China 72 I5
Tianzhu Guizhou China 77 F3
Tiaret Alg. 57 G6
Tiassalé Côte d'Ivoire 96 C4
Tibagi Brazil 145 A4
Tibal, Wādī watercourse Iraq 91 F4
Tibati Cameroon 96 E4
Tibba Pak. 89 H4
Tibé, Pic de mt. Guinea 96 C4
Tiber r. Italy 58 E4
Tiberias Israel 85 B3
Tiberias, Lake Israel see Galilee, Sea of
Tiber Reservoir U.S.A. 126 F2
Tibesti mts Chad 97 E2
Tibet aut. reg. China see Xizang Zizhiqu
Tibet, Plateau of China 83 F2
Tibi India 89 I4
Tibooburra Australia 111 C6
Tibrikot Nepal 83 E3
Tibro Sweden 45 I7
Tibur Italy see Tivoli
Tiburón, Isla i. Mex. 127 E7
Ticehurst U.K. 49 H7
Tichborne Canada 135 G1
Tichégami r. Canada 123 G4
Tichît Mauritania 96 C3
Tichla W. Sahara 96 B2
Ticinum Italy see Pavia
Ticonderoga U.S.A. 135 I2
Ticul Mex. 136 G4
Tidaholm Sweden 45 H7
Tiddim Myanmar 70 A2
Tiden India 71 A6
Tidjikja Mauritania 96 B3
Tiefa Liaoning China see Diaobingshan
Tiel Neth. 52 F3
Tieli China 74 B3
Tieling China 74 A4
Tielongtan Aksai Chin 82 D2
Tielt Belgium 52 D4
Tienen Belgium 52 E4
Tien Shan mts China/Kyrg. 72 D4
Tientsin municipality China see Tianjin
Tiên Yên Vietnam 70 D2
Tierp Sweden 45 J6
Tierra Amarilla U.S.A. 127 G5

▶Tierra del Fuego, Isla Grande de i. Arg./Chile 144 C8
Largest island in South America.

Tierra del Fuego, Parque Nacional nat. park Arg. 144 C8
Tiétar r. Spain 57 D4
Tiétar, Valle de valley Spain 57 D3
Tietê r. Brazil 145 A3
Tieyon Australia 109 F6
Tiffin U.S.A. 134 D3
Tiflis Georgia see T'bilisi
Tifton U.S.A. 133 D6
Tiga Reservoir Nigeria 96 D3
Tigen Kazakh. 91 H1
Tigh Āb Iran 89 F5
Tigheciului, Dealurile hills Moldova 59 M2
Tighina Moldova 59 M1
Tigiria India 84 E1
Tignère Cameroon 96 E4
Tignish Canada 123 I5
Tigranocerta Turkey see Siirt
Tigre r. Venez. 142 F2
Tigris r. Asia 91 G5
also known as Dicle (Turkey) or Nahr Dijlah (Iraq/Syria)
Tigrovaya Balka Zapovednik nature res. Tajik. 89 H2
Tiguidit, Falaise de esc. Niger 96 D3
Tīh, Gebel el plat. Egypt see Tīh, Jabal at
Tīh, Jabal at plat. Egypt 85 A5
Tijuana Mex. 128 E5
Tikamgarh India 82 D4
Tikanlik China 80 G3
Tikhoretsk Rus. Fed. 43 I7
Tikhvin Rus. Fed. 42 G4
Tikhvinskaya Gryada ridge Rus. Fed. 42 G4
Tiki Basin sea feature S. Pacific Ocean 151 L7
Tikokino N.Z. 113 F4
Tikopia i. Solomon Is 107 G3
Tikrīt Iraq 91 F4
Tikse India 82 D2
Tikshozero, Ozero l. Rus. Fed. 44 R3
Tiksi Rus. Fed. 65 N2
Tiladummati Atoll Maldives see Thiladhunmathi Atoll
Tilaiya Reservoir India 83 F4
Tilbeşar Ovasi plain Turkey 85 C1
Tilbooroo Australia 112 B1
Tilburg Neth. 52 F3
Tilbury Canada 134 D2
Tilbury U.K. 49 H7
Tilcara Arg. 144 C2
Tilcha Creek watercourse Australia 111 C6
Tilden U.S.A. 131 D6
Tilemsès Niger 96 D3
Tilemsi, Vallée du watercourse Mali 96 D3
Tilhar India 82 D4
Tilimsen Alg. see Tlemcen
Tilin Myanmar 70 A2
Tillabéri Niger 96 D3
Tillamook U.S.A. 126 C3
Tillanchong Island India 71 A5
Tillia Niger 96 D3
Tillicoultry U.K. 50 F4
Tillsonburg Canada 134 E2
Tillyfourie U.K. 50 G3
Tilonia India 89 I5
Tilos i. Greece 59 L6
Tilothu India 83 F4
Tilpa Australia 112 B3
Tilsit Rus. Fed. see Sovetsk
Tilt r. U.K. 50 F4
Tilton IL U.S.A. 134 B3
Tilton NH U.S.A. 135 J2
Tim Rus. Fed. 43 H6
Ţimā Egypt 86 D4
Timah, Bukit hill Sing. 71 [inset]
Timakara i. India 84 B4
Timanskiy Kryazh ridge Rus. Fed. 42 K2
Timar Turkey 91 F3
Timaru N.Z. 113 C7
Timashevsk Rus. Fed. 43 H7
Timashevskaya Rus. Fed. see Timashevsk
Timbedgha Mauritania 96 C3
Timber Creek Australia 106 D3
Timber Mountain U.S.A. 128 E3
Timberville U.S.A. 135 F4
Timbuktu Mali 96 C3
Timétrine reg. Mali 96 C3
Timiaouine Alg. 96 D2
Timimoun Alg. 54 E6
Timirist, Râs pt Mauritania 96 B3
Timiskaming, Lake Canada see Témiscamingue, Lac
Timişoara Romania 59 I2
Timmins Canada 122 E4
Timms Hill hill U.S.A. 130 F2
Timon Brazil 143 J5
Timor i. Indon. 108 D2
Timor-Leste country Asia see East Timor
Timor Loro Sae country Asia see East Timor
Timor Sea Australia/Indon. 106 C3
Timor Timur country Asia see East Timor
Timperley Range hills Australia 109 C6
Timrå Sweden 44 J5
Tīn, Ra's at pt Libya 90 A4
Ţīna, Khalīg el b. Egypt see Ţīnah, Khalīj aţ
Tīnah Syria 85 D1
Ţīnah, Khalīj aţ b. Egypt 85 A4
Tin Can Bay Australia 111 F5
Tindivanam India 84 C3
Tindouf Alg. 54 C6
Ti-n-Essako Mali 96 D3
Tinggi i. Malaysia 71 D7
Tingha Australia 112 E2
Tingis Morocco see Tangier
Tingo María Peru 142 C5
Tingréla Côte d'Ivoire see Tengréla
Tingsryd Sweden 45 I8
Tingvoll Norway 44 F5
Tingwall U.K. 50 F1
Tingzhou China see Changting
Tinharé, Ilha de i. Brazil 145 D1
Tinh Gia Vietnam 70 D3
Tinian i. N. Mariana Is 69 L4
Tini Heke is N.Z. see Snares Islands
Tinnelvelly India see Tirunelveli
Tinogasta Arg. 144 C3
Tinos Greece 59 K6
Tinos i. Greece 59 K6
Tinqueux France 52 D5
Tinrhert, Hamada de Alg. 96 D2
Tinsukia India 83 H4
Tintagel U.K. 49 C8
Ţînţâne Mauritania 96 B3
Tintina Arg. 144 D3
Tintinara Australia 111 C7
Tioga U.S.A. 130 C1
Tioman i. Malaysia 71 D7
Tionesta U.S.A. 134 F3
Tionesta Lake U.S.A. 134 F3
Tipasa Alg. 57 H5
Tiphsah Syria see Dibsī
Tipperary Ireland 51 D5
Tipton CA U.S.A. 128 D3
Tipton IA U.S.A. 130 F3
Tipton IN U.S.A. 134 B3
Tipton MO U.S.A. 130 E4
Tipton, Mount U.S.A. 129 F4
Tiptop U.S.A. 134 E5
Tip Top Hill hill Canada 122 D4
Tiptree U.K. 49 H7
Tiptur India 84 C3
Tipturi India see Tiptur
Tiracambu, Serra do hills Brazil 143 I4
Tirah reg. Pak. 89 H3

▶Tirana Albania 59 H4
Capital of Albania.

Tiranë Albania see Tirana
Tirano Italy 58 D1
Tirari Desert Australia 111 B5
Tiraspol Moldova 59 M1
Tiraz Mountains Namibia 100 C4
Tire Turkey 59 L5
Tirebolu Turkey 91 E2
Tiree i. U.K. 50 C4
Tîrgovişte Romania see Târgovişte
Tîrgu Jiu Romania see Târgu Jiu
Tîrgu Mureş Romania see Târgu Mureş
Tîrgu Neamţ Romania see Târgu Neamţ
Tîrgu Secuiesc Romania see Târgu Secuiesc
Tiri Pak. 89 G4
Tirich Mir mt. Pak. 89 H2
Tirlemont Belgium see Tienen
Tirna r. India 84 C2
Tîrnăveni Romania see Târnăveni
Tírnavos Greece see Tyrnavos
Tiros Brazil 145 B2
Tirourda, Col de pass Alg. 57 I5
Tirreno, Mare sea France/Italy see Tyrrhenian Sea
Tirso r. Sardinia Italy 58 C5
Tirthahalli India 84 B3
Tiruchchendur India 84 C4
Tiruchchirappalli India 84 C4
Tiruchengodu India 84 C4
Tirunelveli India 84 C4
Tirupati India 84 C3
Tiruppattur Tamil Nadu India 84 C3
Tiruppattur Tamil Nadu India 84 C4
Tiruppur India 84 C4
Tiruttani India 84 C3
Tirutturaippundi India 84 C4
Tiruvallur India 84 C3
Tiruvannamalai India 84 C3
Tiruvottiyur India 84 D3
Tiru Well Australia 108 D5
Tisa r. Serbia 59 I2
also known as Tisza (Hungary), Tysa (Ukraine)
Tisdale Canada 121 J4
Tishomingo U.S.A. 131 D5
Ţīsīyah Syria 85 C3
Tissemsilt Alg. 57 G6
Tisza r. Serbia see Tisa
Titalya Bangl. see Tetulia
Titan Dome ice feature Antarctica 152 H1
Titao Burkina 96 C3
Tit-Ary Rus. Fed. 65 N2
Titawin Morocco see Tétouan
Titicaca, Lago Bol./Peru see Titicaca, Lake

▶Titicaca, Lake Bol./Peru 142 E7
Largest lake in South America.

Titi Islands N.Z. 113 A8
Tititea mt. N.Z. see Aspiring, Mount
Titlagarh India 84 D1
Titograd Montenegro see Podgorica
Titova Mitrovica Kosovo see Mitrovicë
Titovo Užice Serbia see Užice
Titovo Velenje Slovenia see Velenje
Titov Veles Macedonia see Veles
Titov Vrbas Serbia see Vrbas
Ti Tree Australia 108 F5
Titu Romania 59 K2
Titusville FL U.S.A. 133 D6
Titusville PA U.S.A. 134 F3
Tiu Chung Chau i. H.K. China 77 [inset]
Tiumpain, Rubha an hd U.K. see Tiumpan Head
Tiumpan Head hd U.K. 50 C2
Tiva watercourse Kenya 98 D4
Tivari India 82 C4
Tiverton Canada 134 E1
Tiverton U.K. 49 D8
Tivoli Italy 58 E4
Ţīwī Oman 88 E6
Ti-ywa Myanmar 71 B4
Tizi El Arba hill Alg. 57 H5
Tizimín Mex. 136 G4
Tizi N'Kouilal pass Alg. 57 I5
Tizi Ouzou Alg. 57 I5
Tiznap He r. China 82 D1
Tiznit Morocco 96 C2
Tiztoutine Morocco 57 E6
Tjaneni Swaziland 101 J3
Tjappsåive Sweden 44 K4
Tjeukemeer l. Neth. 52 F2
Tjirebon Indon. see Cirebon
Tjolotjo Zimbabwe see Tsholotsho
Tjorhom Norway 45 E7
Tkibuli Georgia see Tqibuli
Tlahualilo Mex. 131 C7
Tlaxcala Mex. 136 E5
Tl'ell Canada 120 D4
Tlemcen Alg. 57 F6
Tlhakalatlou S. Africa 100 F5
Tlholong S. Africa 101 I5
Tlokweng Botswana 101 G3
Tlyarata Rus. Fed. 91 G2
To r. Myanmar 70 B3
Toad r. Canada 120 E3
Toad River Canada 120 E3
Toamasina Madag. 99 E5
Toana mts U.S.A. 129 F1
Toano U.S.A. 135 G5
Toa Payoh Sing. 71 [inset]
Toba China 76 C2
Toba, Danau l. Indon. 71 B7
Toba, Lake Indon. see Toba, Danau
Toba and Kakar Ranges mts Pak. 89 G4
Toba Gargaji Pak. 89 I4
Tobago i. Trin. and Tob. 137 L6
Tobelo Indon. 69 H6
Tobercurry Ireland 51 D3
Tobermorey Australia 110 B4
Tobermory Australia 112 A1
Tobermory Canada 134 E1
Tobermory U.K. 50 C4
Tobi i. Palau 69 I6
Tobin, Lake salt flat Australia 108 D5
Tobin, Mount U.S.A. 128 E1
Tobin Lake Canada 121 K4
Tobin Lake l. Canada 121 K4
Tobi-shima i. Japan 75 E5
Tobol r. Kazakh./Rus. Fed. 78 F1
Tobol'sk Rus. Fed. 64 H4
Tobruk Libya see Tubruq
Tobseda Rus. Fed. 42 L1
Tobyl r. Kazakh./Rus. Fed. see Tobol
Tobysh r. Rus. Fed. 42 K2
Tocache Nuevo Peru 142 C5
Tocantinópolis Brazil 143 I5
Tocantins r. Brazil 145 A1
Tocantins state Brazil 145 A1
Tocantinzinha r. Brazil 145 A1
Toccoa U.S.A. 133 D5
Tochi r. Pak. 89 H3
Töcksfors Sweden 45 G7
Tocopilla Chile 144 B2
Tocumwal Australia 112 B5
Tod, Mount Canada 120 G5
Todd watercourse Australia 110 A5
Todi Italy 58 E3
Todoga-saki pt Japan 75 F5
Todos Santos Mex. 136 B4
Toe Head hd U.K. 50 B3
Tofino Canada 120 E5
Toft U.K. 50 [inset]
Tofua i. Tonga 107 I3
Togatax China 82 E2
Togian i. Indon. 69 G7
Togian, Kepulauan is Indon. 69 G7
Togliatti Rus. Fed. see Tol'yatti
Togo country Africa 96 D4
Togtoh China 73 K4
Togton He r. China 83 H2
Togton Heyan China see Tanggulashan
Tohatchi U.S.A. 129 I4
Toholampi Fin. 44 N5
Toiba China 83 G3
Toibalewe India 71 A5
Toijala Fin. 45 M6
Toili Indon. 69 G7
Toi-misaki pt Japan 75 C7
Toivakka Fin. 44 O5
Toiyabe Range mts U.S.A. 128 E2
Tojikiston country Asia see Tajikistan
Tok U.S.A. 120 A2
Tokar Sudan 86 E6
Tokara-rettō is Japan 75 C7
Tokarevka Rus. Fed. 43 I6
Tokat Turkey 90 E2
Tŏkchŏk-to i. S. Korea 75 B5
Tokdo i. Asia see Liancourt Rocks

▶Tokelau terr. S. Pacific Ocean 107 I2
New Zealand Overseas Territory.

Tokmak Kyrg. see Tokmok
Tokmak Ukr. 43 G7
Tokmok Kyrg. 80 E3
Tokomaru Bay N.Z. 113 G4
Tokoroa N.Z. 113 E4
Tokoza S. Africa 101 I4
Toksun China 80 G3
Tok-to i. Asia see Liancourt Rocks
Toktogul Kyrg. 80 D3
Tokto-ri i. Asia see Liancourt Rocks
Tokur Rus. Fed. 74 D1
Tokushima Japan 75 D6
Tokuyama Japan 75 C6

▶Tōkyō Japan 75 E6
Capital of Japan. Most populous city in the world and in Asia.

Tokzār Afgh. 89 G3
Tolaga Bay N.Z. 113 G4
Tôlañaro Madag. 99 E6
Tolbo Mongolia 80 H2
Tolbukhin Bulg. see Dobrich
Tolbuzino Rus. Fed. 74 B1
Toledo Brazil 144 F2
Toledo Spain 57 D4
Toledo IA U.S.A. 130 E3
Toledo OH U.S.A. 134 D3
Toledo OR U.S.A. 126 C3
Toledo, Montes de mts Spain 57 D4
Toledo Bend Reservoir U.S.A. 131 E6
Toletum Spain see Toledo
Toliara Madag. 99 E6
Tolitoli Indon. 69 G6
Tol'ka Rus. Fed. 64 J3
Tolleson U.S.A. 129 G5
Tollimarjon Uzbek. 89 G2
Tolmachevo Rus. Fed. 45 P7
Tolo Dem. Rep. Congo 98 B4
Tolo Channel H.K. China 77 [inset]
Tolochin Belarus see Talachyn
Tolo Harbour b. H.K. China 77 [inset]
Tolosa France see Toulouse
Tolosa Spain 57 E2
Toluca Mex. 136 E5
Toluca de Lerdo Mex. see Toluca
To-lun Nei Mongol China see Dolonnur
Tol'yatti Rus. Fed. 43 K5
Tom' r. Rus. Fed. 74 B2
Tomah U.S.A. 130 F3
Tomakomai Japan 74 F4
Tomales U.S.A. 128 B2
Tomali Indon. 69 G7
Tomamae Japan 74 F3
Tomanivi mt. Fiji 107 H3
Tomar Brazil 142 F4
Tomar Port. 57 B4
Tomari Rus. Fed. 74 F3
Tomarza Turkey 90 D3
Tomaszów Lubelski Poland 43 D6
Tomaszów Mazowiecki Poland 47 R5
Tomatin U.K. 50 F3
Tomatlán Mex. 136 C5
Tomazina Brazil 145 A3
Tombador, Serra do hills Brazil 143 G6
Tombigbee r. U.S.A. 133 C6
Tomboco Angola 99 B4
Tombouctou Mali see Timbuktu
Tombstone U.S.A. 127 F7
Tombua Angola 99 B5
Tom Burke S. Africa 101 H2
Tomdibuloq Uzbek. 80 B3
Tome Moz. 101 L2
Tomelilla Sweden 45 H9
Tomelloso Spain 57 E4
Tomi Romania see Constanţa
Tomingley Australia 112 D4
Tomini, Teluk g. Indon. 69 G7
Tominian Mali 96 C3
Tomintoul U.K. 50 F3
Tomislavgrad Bos.-Herz. 58 G3
Tomkinson Ranges mts Australia 109 E6
Tømmerneset Norway 44 I3
Tommot Rus. Fed. 65 N4
Tomo r. Col. 142 E2
Tomóchic Mex. 127 G7
Tomortei China 73 K4
Tompkinsville U.S.A. 134 C5
Tom Price Australia 108 B5
Tomra China 83 F3
Tomsk Rus. Fed. 64 J4
Toms River U.S.A. 135 H4
Tomtabacken hill Sweden 45 I8
Tomtor Rus. Fed. 65 P3
Tomur Feng mt. China/Kyrg. see Pobeda Peak
Tomuzlovka r. Rus. Fed. 43 J7
Tom White, Mount U.S.A. 118 D3
Tonalá Mex. 136 F5
Tonantins Brazil 142 E4
Tonb-e Bozorg, Jazīreh-ye i. The Gulf see Greater Tunb
Tonb-e Kūchek, Jazīreh-ye i. The Gulf see Lesser Tunb
Tonbridge U.K. 49 H7
Tondano Indon. 69 G6
Tønder Denmark 45 F9
Tondi India 84 C4
Tone r. U.K. 49 E7
Toney Mountain Antarctica 152 K1
Tonga country S. Pacific Ocean 107 I4
Tongaat S. Africa 101 J5
Tongariro National Park N.Z. 113 E4
Tongatapu Group is Tonga 107 I4

▶Tonga Trench sea feature S. Pacific Ocean 150 I7
2nd deepest trench in the world.

Tongbai Shan mts China 77 G1
Tongcheng China 77 H2
T'ongch'ŏn N. Korea 75 B5
Tongchuan Shaanxi China 77 F1
Tongchuan Sichuan China see Santai
Tongdao China 77 F3
Tongde China 76 D1
Tongduch'ŏn S. Korea 75 B5
Tongeren Belgium 52 F4
Tonggu China 77 G2
Tonggu Zui pt China 77 F5
Tonghae S. Korea 75 C5
Tonghai China 76 D3
Tonghe China 74 C3
Tonghua Jilin China 74 B4
Tonghua Jilin China 74 B4
Tongi Bangl. see Tungi
Tongjiang Heilong. China 74 D3
Tongjiang Sichuan China 76 E2
Tongking, Gulf of China/Vietnam 70 E2
Tongle China see Leye
Tongliang China 76 E2
Tongliao China 73 M4
Tongling China 77 H2
Tonglu China 77 H2
Tongo Australia 112 A3
Tongo Lake salt flat Australia 112 A3
Tongren Guizhou China 77 F3
Tongren Qinghai China 76 D1
Tongres Belgium see Tongeren
Tongsa Bhutan 83 G4

Tongshan Jiangsu China see Xuzhou
Tongshi Hainan China see Wuzhishan
Tongta Myanmar 70 B2
Tongtian He r. Qinghai China 76 B1
Tongtian He r. Qinghai China 76 C1 see Yangtze
Tongue U.K. 50 E2
Tongue r. U.S.A. 126 G3
Tongue of the Ocean sea chan. Bahamas 133 E7
Tongxin China 72 J5
T'ongyŏng S. Korea 75 C6
Tongzi China 76 E2
Tónichi Mex. 127 F7
Tonk India 82 C4
Tonkābon Iran 88 C2
Tonkin reg. Vietnam 70 D2
Tônle Repou r. Laos 71 D4
Tônlé Sab l. Cambodia see Tonle Sap

▶Tonle Sap l. Cambodia 71 C4
Largest lake in southeast Asia.

Tonopah AZ U.S.A. 129 G5
Tonopah NV U.S.A. 128 E2
Tønsberg Norway 45 G7
Tonstad Norway 45 E7
Tonto Creek watercourse U.S.A. 129 H5
Tonvarjeh Iran 88 E3
Tonzang Myanmar 70 A2
Tonzi Myanmar 70 A1
Toobeah Australia 112 D2
Toobli Liberia 96 C4
Tooele U.S.A. 129 G1
Toogoolawah Australia 112 F1
Tooma r. Australia 112 D6
Toompine Australia 112 B1
Toora Australia 112 C7
Tooraweenah Australia 112 D3
Toorberg mt. S. Africa 100 G7
Toowoomba Australia 112 E1
Tooxin Somalia 98 F2
Top Afgh. 89 H3
Top Boğazı Geçidi pass Turkey 85 C1

▶Topeka U.S.A. 130 E4
Capital of Kansas.

Topia Mex. 127 G8
Töplitz Germany 53 M2
Topoľčany Slovakia 47 Q6
Topolobampo Mex. 127 F8
Topolovgrad Bulg. 59 L3
Topozero, Ozero l. Rus. Fed. 44 R4
Topsfield U.S.A. 132 H2
Tor Eth. 97 G4
Tor Baldak mt. Afgh. 89 G4
Torbalı Turkey 59 L5
Torbat-e Heydarīyeh Iran 88 E3
Torbat-e Jām Iran 89 F3
Torbay Bay Australia 109 B8
Torbert, Mount U.S.A. 118 C3
Torbeyevo Rus. Fed. 43 I5
Torch r. Canada 121 K4
Tordesillas Spain 57 D3
Tordesilos Spain 57 F3
Töre Sweden 44 M4
Torelló Spain 57 H2
Torenberg hill Neth. 52 F2
Toretam Kazakh. see Baykonyr
Torgau Germany 53 M3
Torghay Kazakh. see Turgay
Torgun r. Rus. Fed. 43 J6
Torhout Belgium 52 D3
Torino Italy see Turin
Tori-shima i. Japan 75 F7
Torit Sudan 97 G4
Torkamān Iran 88 B2
Torkovichi Rus. Fed. 42 F4
Tornado Mountain Canada 120 H5
Torneå Fin. see Tornio
Torneälven r. Sweden 44 N4
Torneträsk l. Sweden 44 K2
Torngat, Monts mts Canada see Torngat Mountains
Torngat Mountains Canada 123 I2
Tornio Fin. 44 N4
Toro Spain 57 D3
Toro, Pico del mt. Mex. 131 C7
Torom Rus. Fed. 74 D1

▶Toronto Canada 134 F2
Capital of Ontario.

Toro Peak U.S.A. 128 E5
Toropets Rus. Fed. 42 F4
Tororo Uganda 98 D3
Toros Dağları mts Turkey see Taurus Mountains
Torphins U.K. 50 G3
Torquay Australia 112 B7
Torquay U.K. 49 D8
Torrance U.S.A. 128 D5
Torrão Port. 57 B4
Torre mt. Port. 57 C3
Torreblanca Spain 57 G3
Torre Blanco, Cerro mt. Mex. 127 E6
Torrecerredo mt. Spain 57 D2
Torre del Greco Italy 58 F4
Torre de Moncorvo Port. 57 C3
Torrelavega Spain 57 D2
Torremolinos Spain 57 D5

▶Torrens, Lake imp. l. Australia 111 B6
2nd largest lake in Oceania.

Torrens Creek Australia 110 D4
Torrent Spain 57 F4
Torrente Spain see Torrent
Torreón Mex. 131 C7
Torres Brazil 145 A5
Torres Mex. 127 F7
Torres del Paine, Parque Nacional nat. park Chile 144 B8
Torres Islands Vanuatu 107 G3
Torres Novas Port. 57 B4
Torres Strait Australia 106 E2
Torres Vedras Port. 57 B4
Torrevieja Spain 57 F5
Torrey U.S.A. 129 H2
Torridge r. U.K. 49 C8
Torridon, Loch b. U.K. 50 D3
Torrijos Spain 57 D4
Torrington Australia 112 E2
Torrington CT U.S.A. 132 F3
Torrington WY U.S.A. 126 G4
Torsby Sweden 45 H6

▶Tórshavn Faroe Is 44 [inset]
Capital of the Faroe Islands.

Tortilla Flat U.S.A. 129 H5
To'rtko'l Uzbek. 80 B3
Törtköl Uzbek. see To'rtko'l
Tortoli Sardinia Italy 58 C5
Tortona Italy 58 C2
Tortosa Spain 57 G3
Tortum Turkey 91 F2
Ţorūd Iran 88 D3
Torugart, Pereval pass China/Kyrg. see Turugart Pass
Torul Turkey 91 E2
Toruń Poland 47 Q4
Tory Island Ireland 51 D2
Tory Sound sea chan. Ireland 51 D2
Torzhok Rus. Fed. 42 G4
Tosa Japan 75 D6
Tosbotn Norway 44 H4
Tosca S. Africa 100 F3
Toscano, Arcipelago is Italy 58 C3
Tosham India 82 C3
Tōshima-yama mt. Japan 75 F4

▶Toshkent Uzbek. 80 C3
Capital of Uzbekistan.

Tosno Rus. Fed. 42 F4
Toson Hu l. China 83 I1
Tostado Arg. 144 D3
Tostedt Germany 53 J1
Tosya Turkey 90 D2
Totapola mt. Sri Lanka 84 D5
Tôtes France 52 B5
Tot'ma Rus. Fed. 42 I4
Totness Suriname 143 G2
Tottenham Australia 112 C4
Totton U.K. 49 F8
Tottori Japan 75 D6
Touba Côte d'Ivoire 96 C4
Touba Senegal 96 B3
Toubkal, Jbel mt. Morocco 54 C5
Toubkal, Parc National du nat. park Morocco 54 C5
Touboro Cameroon 97 E4
Tougan Burkina 96 C3
Touggourt Alg. 54 F5
Tougué Guinea 96 B3
Touil Mauritania 96 B3
Toul France 52 F6
Touliu Taiwan 77 I4
Toulon France 56 G5
Toulon U.S.A. 130 F3
Toulouse France 56 E5
Toumodi Côte d'Ivoire 96 C4
Toupai China 77 F3
Tourane Vietnam see Đa Nẵng
Tourcoing France 52 D4
Tourgis Lake Canada 121 J1
Tourlaville France 49 F9
Tournai Belgium 52 D4
Tournon-sur-Rhône France 56 G4
Tournus France 56 G3
Touros Brazil 143 K5
Tours France 56 E3
Tousside, Pic mt. Chad 97 E2
Toussoro, Mont mt. Cent. Afr. Rep. 98 C3
Toutai China 74 B3
Touwsrivier S. Africa 100 E7
Toužim Czech Rep. 53 M4
Tovarkovo Rus. Fed. 43 G5
Tovil'-Dora Tajik. see Tavildara
Tovuz Azer. 91 G2
Towada Japan 74 F4
Towak Mountain hill U.S.A. 118 B3
Towanda U.S.A. 135 G3
Towaoc U.S.A. 129 I3
Towcester U.K. 49 G6
Tower Ireland 51 D6
Towner U.S.A. 130 C1
Townes Pass U.S.A. 128 E3
Townsend U.S.A. 126 F3
Townsend, Mount Australia 112 D6
Townshend Island Australia 110 E4
Townsville Australia 110 D3
Towot Sudan 97 G4
Towr Kham Afgh. 89 H3
Towson U.S.A. 135 G4
Towyn U.K. see Tywyn
Toy U.S.A. 128 D1
Toyah U.S.A. 131 C6
Toyama Japan 75 E5
Toyama-wan b. Japan 75 E5
Toyohashi Japan 75 E6
Toyokawa Japan 75 E6
Toyonaka Japan 75 D6
Toyooka Japan 75 D6
Toyota Japan 75 E6
Tozanlı Turkey see Almus
Tozê Kangri mt. China 83 E2
Tozeur Tunisia 54 F5
Tozi, Mount U.S.A. 118 C3
Tqibuli Georgia 91 F2
Traben Germany 52 H5
Trâblous Lebanon see Tripoli
Trabotivište Macedonia 59 J4
Trabzon Turkey 91 E2
Tracy CA U.S.A. 128 C3
Tracy MN U.S.A. 130 E2
Trading r. Canada 122 C4
Traer U.S.A. 130 E3
Trafalgar U.S.A. 134 B4
Trafalgar, Cabo c. Spain 57 C5
Traffic Mountain Canada 120 D2
Trail Canada 120 G5
Tràille, Rubha na pt U.K. 50 D5
Traill Island Greenland see Traill Ø
Traill Ø i. Greenland 119 P2
Trainor Lake Canada 120 F2
Trajectum Neth. see Utrecht
Trakai Lith. 45 N9
Tra Khuc, Sông r. Vietnam 70 E4
Trakiya reg. Europe see Thrace
Trakt Rus. Fed. 42 K3
Trakya reg. Europe see Thrace
Tralee Ireland 51 C5
Tralee Bay Ireland 51 C5
Trá Li Ireland see Tralee
Tramandai Brazil 145 A5
Tramán Tepuí mt. Venez. 142 F2
Trá Mhór Ireland see Tramore
Tramore Ireland 51 E5
Tranås Sweden 45 I7
Trancas Arg. 144 C3
Trancoso Brazil 145 D2
Tranemo Sweden 45 H8
Tranent U.K. 50 G5
Trang Thai. 71 B6
Trangan i. Indon. 108 F1
Trangie Australia 112 C4
Trân Ninh, Cao Nguyên Laos 70 C3
Transantarctic Mountains Antarctica 152 H2
Trans Canada Highway Canada 121 H5
Transylvanian Alps mts Romania 59 J2
Transylvanian Basin plat. Romania 59 K1
Trapani Sicily Italy 58 E5
Trapezus Turkey see Trabzon
Trapper Peak U.S.A. 126 E3
Trappes France 52 C6
Traralgon Australia 112 C7
Trashigang Bhutan see Tashigang
Trasimeno, Lago l. Italy 58 E3
Trasvase, Canal de Spain 57 E4
Trat Thai. 71 C4
Traunsee l. Austria 47 N7
Traunstein Germany 47 N7
Travellers Lake imp. l. Australia 111 C7
Travers, Mount N.Z. 113 D6
Traverse City U.S.A. 134 C1
Tra Vinh Vietnam 71 D5
Travnik Bos.-Herz. 58 G2
Trbovlje Slovenia 58 F1
Tre, Hon i. Vietnam 71 E4
Treasury Islands Solomon Is 106 F2
Trebbin Germany 53 N2
Trebević nat. park Bos.-Herz. 58 H3
Třebíč Czech Rep. 47 O6
Trebinje Bos.-Herz. 58 H3
Trebišov Slovakia 43 D6
Trebizond Turkey see Trabzon
Trebnje Slovenia 58 F2
Trebur Germany 53 I5
Tree Island India 84 B4
Trefaldwyn U.K. see Montgomery
Treffurt Germany 53 K3
Treffynnon U.K. see Holywell
Trefyclawdd U.K. see Knighton
Trefynwy U.K. see Monmouth
Tregosse Islets and Reefs Australia 110 E3
Treinta y Tres Uruguay 144 F4
Trelew Arg. 144 C6
Trelleborg Sweden 45 H9
Trélon France 52 E4
Tremblant, Mont hill Canada 122 G5
Trembleur Lake Canada 120 E4
Tremiti, Isole is Italy 58 F3
Tremont U.S.A. 135 G3
Tremonton U.S.A. 126 E4
Tremp Spain 57 G2
Trenance U.K. 49 B8
Trenary U.S.A. 132 C2
Trenche r. Canada 123 G5
Trenčín Slovakia 47 Q6
Trendelburg Germany 53 J3
Trêng Cambodia 71 C4
Trenque Lauquén Arg. 144 D5
Trent Italy see Trento
Trent r. U.K. 49 G5
Trento Italy 58 D1
Trenton Canada 135 G1
Trenton FL U.S.A. 133 D6
Trenton GA U.S.A. 133 C5
Trenton KY U.S.A. 134 B5
Trenton MO U.S.A. 130 E3
Trenton NC U.S.A. 133 E5
Trenton NE U.S.A. 130 C3

▶Trenton NJ U.S.A. 135 H3
Capital of New Jersey.

Treorchy U.K. 49 D7
Trepassey Canada 123 L5
Tres Arroyos Arg. 144 D5
Tresco i. U.K. 49 A9
Três Corações Brazil 145 B3
Tres Esquinas Col. 142 C3
Tres Forcas, Cabo c. Morocco see Trois Fourches, Cap des
Três Lagoas Brazil 145 A3
Três Marias, Represa resr Brazil 145 B2
Tres Picachos, Sierra mts Mex. 127 G7
Tres Picos, Cerro mt. Arg. 144 D5
Três Pontas Brazil 145 B3
Tres Puntas, Cabo c. Arg. 144 C7
Três Rios Brazil 145 C3
Tretten Norway 45 G6
Tretyy Severnyy Rus. Fed. see 3-y Severnyy
Treuchtlingen Germany 53 K6
Treuenbrietzen Germany 53 M2
Treungen Norway 45 F7
Treves Germany see Trier
Treviglio Italy 58 C2
Treviso Italy 58 E2
Trevose Head hd U.K. 49 B8
Tri An, Hô resr Vietnam 71 D5
Triánda Greece see Trianta
Triangle U.S.A. 135 G4
Trianta Greece 59 M6
Tribal Areas admin. div. Pak. 89 H3
Tri Brata, Gora hill Rus. Fed. 74 F1
Tribune U.S.A. 130 C4
Tricase Italy 58 H5
Trichinopoly India see Tiruchchirappalli
Trichur India 84 C4
Tricot France 52 C5
Trida Australia 112 B4
Tridentum Italy see Trento
Trier Germany 52 G5
Trieste Italy 58 E2
Trieste, Golfo di g. Europe see Trieste, Gulf of
Trieste, Gulf of Europe 58 E2
Triglav mt. Slovenia 58 E1
Triglavski narodni park nat. park Slovenia 58 E1
Trikala Greece 59 I5
Tríkkala Greece see Trikala

▶Trikora, Puncak mt. Indon. 69 J7
2nd highest mountain in Oceania.

Trim Ireland 51 F4
Trincomalee Sri Lanka 84 D4
Trindade Brazil 145 A2
Trindade, Ilha da i. S. Atlantic Ocean 148 G7
Trinidad Bol. 142 F6
Trinidad Cuba 137 I4
Trinidad i. Trin. and Tob. 137 L6
Trinidad Uruguay 144 E4
Trinidad U.S.A. 127 G5
Trinidad country West Indies see Trinidad and Tobago
Trinidad and Tobago country West Indies 137 L6
Trinity U.S.A. 131 E6
Trinity r. CA U.S.A. 128 B1
Trinity r. TX U.S.A. 131 E6
Trinity Bay Canada 123 L5
Trinity Islands U.S.A. 118 C4
Trinity Range mts U.S.A. 128 D1
Trinkat Island India 71 A5
Trionto, Capo c. Italy 58 G5
Tripa r. Indon. 71 B7
Tripkau Germany 53 L1
Tripoli Greece 59 J6
Tripoli Lebanon 85 B2

▶Tripoli Libya 97 E1
Capital of Libya.

Trípolis Greece see Tripoli
Tripolis Lebanon see Tripoli
Tripunittura India 84 C4
Tripura state India 83 G5

▶Tristan da Cunha i. S. Atlantic Ocean 148 H8
Dependency of St Helena.

Trisul mt. India 82 D3
Triton Canada 123 L4
Triton Island atoll Paracel Is 68 E3
Trittau Germany 53 K1
Trittenheim Germany 52 G5
Trivandrum India 84 C4
Trivento Italy 58 F4
Trnava Slovakia 47 P6
Trobriand Islands P.N.G. 106 F2
Trochu Canada 120 H5
Trofors Norway 44 H4
Trogir Croatia 58 G3
Troia Italy 58 F4
Troisdorf Germany 53 H4
Trois Fourches, Cap des c. Morocco 57 E6
Trois-Ponts Belgium 52 F4
Trois-Rivières Canada 123 G5
Troitsko-Pechorsk Rus. Fed. 41 R3
Troitskoye Altayskiy Kray Rus. Fed. 72 E2
Troitskoye Khabarovskiy Kray Rus. Fed. 74 E2
Troitskoye Respublika Kalmykiya - Khalm'g-Tangch Rus. Fed. 43 J7
Troll research stn 152 B2
Trollhättan Sweden 45 H7
Trombetas r. Brazil 143 G4
Tromelin, Île i. Indian Ocean 149 L7
Tromelin Island Micronesia see Fais
Tromen, Volcán vol. Arg. 144 B5
Tromie r. U.K. 50 E3
Trompsburg S. Africa 101 G6
Tromsø Norway 44 K2
Trona U.S.A. 128 E4
Tronador, Monte mt. Arg. 144 B6
Trondheim Norway 44 G5
Trondheimsfjorden sea chan. Norway 44 F5
Trongsa Bhutan see Tongsa
Troödos, Mount Cyprus 85 A2
Troödos Mountains Cyprus 85 A2
Troon U.K. 50 E5
Tropeiros, Serra dos hills Brazil 145 B1
Tropic U.S.A. 129 G3
Tropic of Cancer 131 B8
Tropic of Capricorn 110 G4
Trosh Rus. Fed. 42 L2
Trostan hill U.K. 51 F2
Trout r. B.C. Canada 120 E3
Trout r. N.W.T. Canada 120 G2
Trout Lake Alta Canada 120 H3
Trout Lake N.W.T. Canada 120 F2
Trout Lake l. N.W.T. Canada 120 F2
Trout Lake l. Ont. Canada 121 M5
Trout Peak U.S.A. 126 F3
Trout Run U.S.A. 135 G3
Trouville-sur-Mer France 49 H9
Trowbridge U.K. 49 E7
Troy tourist site Turkey 59 L5
Troy AL U.S.A. 133 C6
Troy KS U.S.A. 130 E4
Troy MI U.S.A. 134 D2
Troy MO U.S.A. 130 F4
Troy MT U.S.A. 126 E2
Troy NH U.S.A. 135 I2
Troy NY U.S.A. 135 I2
Troy OH U.S.A. 134 C3
Troy PA U.S.A. 135 G3
Troyan Bulg. 59 K3
Troyes France 56 G2
Troy Lake U.S.A. 128 E4
Troy Peak U.S.A. 129 F2
Trstenik Serbia 59 I3
Truc Giang Vietnam see Bên Tre
Trucial Coast country Asia see United Arab Emirates
Trucial States country Asia see United Arab Emirates
Trud Rus. Fed. 42 G4
Trufanovo Rus. Fed. 42 J2
Trujillo Hond. 137 G5
Trujillo Peru 142 C5
Trujillo Spain 57 D4
Trujillo Venez. 142 D2
Trujillo, Monte mt. Dom. Rep. see Duarte, Pico
Truk is Micronesia see Chuuk
Trulben Germany 53 H5
Trumbull, Mount U.S.A. 129 G3
Trumon Indon. 71 B7
Trundle Australia 112 C4
Trưng Hiệp Vietnam 70 D4
Trung Khanh Vietnam 70 D2
Truong Sa is S. China Sea see Spratly Islands
Truro Canada 123 J5
Truro U.K. 49 B8
Truskmore hill Ireland 51 D3
Trutch Canada 120 F3
Truth or Consequences U.S.A. 127 G6
Trutnov Czech Rep. 47 O5
Truuli Peak U.S.A. 118 C4
Truva tourist site Turkey see Troy
Trypiti, Akra pt Kriti Greece see Trypiti, Akrotirio
Trypiti, Akrotirio pt Greece 59 K7
Trysil Norway 45 H6
Trzebiatów Poland 47 O3
Tsagaannuur Mongolia 80 G2
Tsagaan-Uul Mongolia 80 I2
Tsagan Aman Rus. Fed. 43 J7
Tsagan-Nur Rus. Fed. 43 J7
Tsaidam Basin China see Qaidam Pendi
Tsaka La pass China/India 82 D2
Tsalenjikha Georgia 91 F2
Tsaratanana, Massif du mts Madag. 99 E5
Tsarevo Bulg. 59 L3
Tsaris Mountains Namibia 100 C3
Tsaritsyn Rus. Fed. see Volgograd
Tsaukaib Namibia 100 B4
Tsavo East National Park Kenya 98 D4
Tsavo West National Park Africa 98 D3
Tsefat Israel see Ẕefat
Tselinograd Kazakh. see Astana
Tsenhermandal Mongolia 73 J3
Tsenogora Rus. Fed. 42 J2
Tses Namibia 100 D3
Tsetseg Mongolia 80 H2
Tsetseng Botswana 100 F2
Tsetserleg Arhangay Mongolia 80 J2
Tsetserleg Mongolia 80 I2
Tshabong Botswana 100 F4
Tshad country Africa see Chad
Tshane Botswana 100 E3
Tshela Dem. Rep. Congo 99 B4
Tshibala Dem. Rep. Congo 99 C4
Tshikapa Dem. Rep. Congo 99 C4
Tshing S. Africa 101 H4
Tshipise S. Africa 101 J2
Tshitanzu Dem. Rep. Congo 99 C4
Tshofa Dem. Rep. Congo 99 C4
Tshokwane S. Africa 101 J3
Tsholotsho Zimbabwe 99 C5
Tshootsha Botswana 100 E2
Tshuapa r. Dem. Rep. Congo 97 F5
Tshwane S. Africa see Pretoria
Tsil'ma r. Rus. Fed. 42 K2
Tsimlyansk Rus. Fed. 43 I7
Tsimlyanskoye Vodokhranilishche resr Rus. Fed. 43 I7
Tsimmermanovka Rus. Fed. 74 E2
Tsinan China see Jinan
Tsineng S. Africa 100 F4
Tsinghai prov. China see Qinghai
Tsing Shan Wan H.K. China see Castle Peak Bay
Tsingtao China see Qingdao
Tsing Yi i. H.K. China 77 [inset]
Tsining China see Jining
Tsiombe Madag. 99 E6
Tsiroanomandidy Madag. 99 E5
Tsitsihar China see Qiqihar
Tsitsikamma Forest and Coastal National Park S. Africa 100 F8
Tsitsutl Peak Canada 120 E4
Tsivil'sk Rus. Fed. 42 J5
Tskhaltubo Georgia see Tsqaltubo
Ts'khinvali Georgia 91 F2
Tsna r. Rus. Fed. 43 I5
Tsnori Georgia 91 G2
Tsokar Chumo l. India 82 D2
Tsolo S. Africa 101 I6
Tsomo S. Africa 101 H7
Tsona China see Cona
Tsqaltubo Georgia 91 F2
Tsu Japan 75 E6
Tsuchiura Japan 75 F5
Tsuen Wan H.K. China 77 [inset]
Tsugarū-kaikyō strait Japan 74 F4
Tsugaru Strait Japan see Tsugarū-kaikyō
Tsumeb Namibia 99 B5
Tsumis Park Namibia 100 C2
Tsumkwe Namibia 99 C5
Tsuruga Japan 75 E6
Tsurugi-san mt. Japan 75 D6
Tsurukhaytuy Rus. Fed. see Priargunsk
Tsuruoka Japan 75 E5
Tsushima is Japan 75 C6
Tsushima-kaikyō strait Japan/S. Korea see Korea Strait
Tsuyama Japan 75 D6
Tswaane Botswana 100 E2
Tswaraganang S. Africa 101 G5
Tswelelang S. Africa 101 G4
Tsyelyakhany Belarus 45 N10
Tsyp-Navolok Rus. Fed. 44 R2
Tsyurupyns'k Ukr. 59 O1
Tthenaagoo Canada see Nahanni Butte
Tua Dem. Rep. Congo 98 B4
Tual Indon. 69 I8
Tuam Ireland 51 D4
Tuamotu, Archipel des is Fr. Polynesia see Tuamotu Islands
Tuamotu Islands Fr. Polynesia 151 K6
Tuân Giao Vietnam 70 C2
Tuangku i. Indon. 71 B7
Tuapse Rus. Fed. 90 E1
Tuas Sing. 71 [inset]
Tuath, Loch a' b. U.K. 50 C2
Tuba City U.S.A. 129 H3
Tubarão Brazil 145 A5
Tubarjal Saudi Arabia 85 D4
Tübingen Germany 47 L6
Tubmanburg Liberia 96 B4
Tubruq Libya 90 A4
Tubuai i. Fr. Polynesia 151 K7
Tubuai Islands Fr. Polynesia 151 J7
Tucano Brazil 143 K6
Tucavaca Bol. 143 G7
Tüchen Germany 53 M1
Tuchheim Germany 53 M2
Tuchitua Canada 120 D2
Tuchodi r. Canada 120 F3
Tuckerton U.S.A. 135 H4
Tucopia i. Solomon Is see Tikopia
Tucson U.S.A. 129 H5
Tucson Mountains U.S.A. 129 H5
Tuctuc r. Canada 123 I2
Tucumán Arg. see San Miguel de Tucumán
Tucumcari U.S.A. 131 C5
Tucupita Venez. 142 F2
Tucuruí Brazil 143 I4
Tucuruí, Represa resr Brazil 143 I4
Tudela Spain 57 F2
Tuder Italy see Todi
Tüdevtey Mongolia 80 I2
Tuela r. Port. 57 C3
Tuen Mun H.K. China 77 [inset]
Tuensang India 83 H4
Tufts Abyssal Plain sea feature N. Pacific Ocean 151 K2
Tugela r. S. Africa 101 J5
Tuglung China 76 B2
Tuguegarao Phil. 69 G3
Tugur Rus. Fed. 74 E1
Tuhemberua Indon. 71 B7
Tujiabu China see Yongxiu
Tukangbesi, Kepulauan is Indon. 69 G8
Tukarak Island Canada 122 F2
Ţukhmān, Banī reg. Saudi Arabia 88 C6
Tukituki r. N.Z. 113 F4
Tuktoyaktuk Canada 118 E3
Tuktut Nogait National Park Canada 118 F3
Tukums Latvia 45 M8
Tukuringra, Khrebet mts Rus. Fed. 74 B1
Tukuyu Tanz. 99 D4
Tula Rus. Fed. 43 H5
Tulach Mhór Ireland see Tullamore
Tulagt Ar Gol r. China 83 H1
Tulak Afgh. 89 F3
Tulameen Canada 120 F5
Tula Mountains Antarctica 152 D2
Tulancingo Mex. 136 E4
Tulare U.S.A. 128 D3
Tulare Lake Bed U.S.A. 128 D4
Tularosa Mountains U.S.A. 129 I5
Tulasi mt. India 84 D2
Tulbagh S. Africa 100 D7
Tulcán Ecuador 142 C3
Tulcea Romania 59 M2
Tule r. U.S.A. 131 C5
Tuléar Madag. see Toliara
Tulemalu Lake Canada 121 L2
Tulia U.S.A. 131 C5
Tulihe China 74 A2
Tulita Canada 120 E1
Tulkarem West Bank see Ţūlkarm
Ţūlkarm West Bank 85 B3
Tulla Ireland 51 D5
Tullahoma U.S.A. 132 C5
Tullamore Australia 112 C4
Tullamore Ireland 51 E4
Tulle France 56 E4
Tulleråsen Sweden 44 I5
Tullibigeal Australia 112 C4
Tullow Ireland 51 F5
Tully Australia 110 D3
Tully r. Australia 110 D3
Tully U.K. 51 E3
Tulos Rus. Fed. 44 Q5
Tulqarem West Bank see Ţūlkarm
Tulsa U.S.A. 131 E4
Tulsipur Nepal 83 E3
Tuluá Col. 142 C3
Tuluksak U.S.A. 153 B2
Tulūl al Ashāqif hills Jordan 85 C3
Tulun Rus. Fed. 72 I2
Tulu-Tuloi, Serra hills Brazil 142 F3
Tulu Welel mt. Eth. 98 D3
Tuma Rus. Fed. 43 I5
Tumaco Col. 142 C3
Tumahole S. Africa 101 H4
Tumain China 83 G2
Tumannyy Rus. Fed. 44 S2
Tumasik Sing. see Singapore
Tumba Dem. Rep. Congo 98 C4
Tumba Sweden 45 J7
Tumba, Lac l. Dem. Rep. Congo 98 B4
Tumbarumba Australia 112 D5
Tumbes Peru 142 B4
Tumbler Ridge Canada 120 F4
Tumby Bay Australia 111 B7
Tumcha r. Fin./Rus. Fed. 44 Q3
also known as Tuntsajoki
Tumen Jilin China 74 C4
Tumen Shaanxi China 77 F1
Tumereng Guyana 142 F2
Tumindao i. Phil. 68 F6
Tumiritinga Brazil 145 C2
Tumkur India 84 C3
Tummel r. U.K. 50 F4
Tummel, Loch l. U.K. 50 F4
Tumnin r. Rus. Fed. 74 F2
Tump Pak. 89 F5
Tumpat Malaysia 71 C6
Tumpôr, Phnum mt. Cambodia 71 C4
Tumshuk Uzbek. 89 G2
Tumu Ghana 96 C3
Tumucumaque, Serra hills Brazil 143 G3
Tumudibandh India 84 D2
Tumut Australia 112 D5
Tuna India 82 B5
Ţunb al Kubrá i. The Gulf see Greater Tunb
Ţunb aş Şughrá i. The Gulf see Lesser Tunb
Tunbridge Wells, Royal U.K. 49 H7
Tunceli Turkey 91 E3
Tunchang China 77 F5
Tuncurry Australia 112 F4
Tundun-Wada Nigeria 96 D3
Tunduru Tanz. 99 D5
Tunes Tunisia see Tunis
Tunga Nigeria 96 D4
Tungabhadra Reservoir India 84 C3
Tungi Bangl. 83 G5
Tung Lung Island H.K. China 77 [inset]
Tungnaá r. Iceland 44 [inset]
Tungor Rus. Fed. 74 F1

Ure r. U.K. 48 F4
Ureki Georgia 91 F2
Uren' Rus. Fed. 42 J4
Urengoy Rus. Fed. 64 I3
Uréparapara i. Vanuatu 107 G3
Urewera National Park N.Z. 113 F4
Urfa Turkey see Şanlıurfa
Urfa prov. Turkey see Şanlıurfa
Urga Mongolia see Ulan Bator
Urgal r. Rus. Fed. 74 D2
Urganch Uzbek. 80 B3
Urgench Uzbek. see Urganch
Ürgüp Turkey 90 D3
Urgut Uzbek. 89 G2
Urho China 80 G2
Urho Kekkosen kansallispuisto nat. park Fin. 44 O2
Urie r. U.K. 50 G3
Uril Rus. Fed. 74 C2
Urisino Australia 112 A2
Urjala Fin. 45 M6
Urk Neth. 52 F2
Urkan Rus. Fed. 74 B1
Urkan r. Rus. Fed. 74 B1
Urla Turkey 59 L5
Urlingford Ireland 51 E5
Urluk Rus. Fed. 73 J2
Urmā aş Şughrá Syria 85 C1
Urmai China 83 F3
Urmia Iran 88 B2
Urmia, Lake salt l. Iran 88 B2
Urmston Road sea chan. H.K. China 77 [inset]
Uromi Nigeria 96 D4
Uroševac Kosovo see Ferijaz
Urosozero Rus. Fed. 42 G3
Ŭroteppa Tajik. 89 H2
Urru Co salt l. China 83 F3
Urt Moron China 80 H4
Uruáchic Mex. 124 F6
Uruaçu Brazil 145 A1
Uruana Brazil 145 A1
Uruapan Baja California Mex. 127 D7
Uruapan Michoacán Mex. 136 D5
Urubamba r. Peru 142 D6
Urucara Brazil 143 G4
Urucu r. Brazil 142 F4
Uruçuca Brazil 145 D1
Uruçuí Brazil 143 J5
Uruçuí, Serra do hills Brazil 143 I5
Urucuia Brazil 145 B2
Urucurituba Brazil 143 G4
Uruguai r. Arg./Uruguay see Uruguay
Uruguaiana Brazil 144 E3
Uruguay r. Arg./Uruguay 144 E4
also known as Uruguai
Uruguay country S. America 144 E4
Uruhe China 74 B2
Urumchi China see Ürümqi
Ürümqi China 80 G3
Urundi country Africa see Burundi
Urup, Ostrov i. Rus. Fed. 73 S3
Urusha Rus. Fed. 74 A1
Urutaí Brazil 145 A2
Uryl' Kazakh. 80 G2
Uryupino Rus. Fed. 73 M2
Uryupinsk Rus. Fed. 43 I6
Ürzhar Kazakh. see Urdzhar
Urzhum Rus. Fed. 42 K4
Urziceni Romania 59 L2
Usa Japan 75 C6
Usa r. Rus. Fed. 42 M2
Uşak Turkey 59 M5
Usakos Namibia 100 B1
Usarp Mountains Antarctica 152 H2
Usborne, Mount hill Falkland Is 144 E8
Ushakova, Ostrov i. Rus. Fed. 64 I1
Ushant i. France see Ouessant, Île d'
Usharal Kazakh. see Ucharal
Ush-Bel'dyr Rus. Fed. 72 H2
Ushtobe Kazakh. 80 E2
Ush-Tyube Kazakh. see Ushtobe
Ushuaia Arg. 144 C8
Ushumun Rus. Fed. 74 B1
Usingen Germany 53 I4
Usinsk Rus. Fed. 41 R2
Usk U.K. 49 E7
Usk r. U.K. 49 E7
Uskhodni Belarus 45 O10
Uskoplje Bos.-Herz. see Gornji Vakuf
Üsküdar Turkey 59 M4
Uslar Germany 53 J3
Usman' Rus. Fed. 43 H5
Usmanabad India see Osmanabad
Usmas ezers l. Latvia 45 M8
Usogorsk Rus. Fed. 42 K3
Usol'ye-Sibirskoye Rus. Fed. 72 I2
Uspenovka Rus. Fed. 74 B1
Ussel France 56 F4
Ussuri r. China/Rus. Fed. 74 D2
Ussuriysk Rus. Fed. 74 C4
Ust'-Abakanskoye Rus. Fed. see Abakan
Usta Muhammad Pak. 89 H4
Ust'-Balyk Rus. Fed. see Nefteyugansk
Ust'-Donetskiy Rus. Fed. 43 I7
Ust'-Dzheguta Rus. Fed. 91 F1
Ust'-Dzhegutinskaya Rus. Fed. see Ust'-Dzheguta
Ustica, Isola di i. Sicily Italy 58 E5
Ust'-Ilimsk Rus. Fed. 65 L4
Ust'-Ilimskiy Vodokhranilishche resr Rus. Fed. 65 L4
Ust'-Ilych Rus. Fed. 41 R3
Ústí nad Labem Czech Rep. 47 O5
Ustinov Rus. Fed. see Izhevsk
Üstirt plat. Kazakh./Uzbek. see Ustyurt Plateau
Ustka Poland 47 P3
Ust'-Kamchatsk Rus. Fed. 65 R4
Ust'-Kamenogorsk Kazakh. 80 F2
Ust'-Kan Rus. Fed. 80 F1
Ust'-Koksa Rus. Fed. 80 G1
Ust'-Kulom Rus. Fed. 42 L3
Ust'-Kut Rus. Fed. 65 L4
Ust'-Kuyga Rus. Fed. 65 O2
Ust'-Labinsk Rus. Fed. 91 E1
Ust'-Labinskaya Rus. Fed. see Ust'-Labinsk
Ust'-Lyzha Rus. Fed. 42 M2
Ust'-Maya Rus. Fed. 65 O3
Ust'-Nera Rus. Fed. 65 P3
Ust'-Ocheya Rus. Fed. 42 K3
Ust'-Olenek Rus. Fed. 65 M2
Ust'-Omchug Rus. Fed. 65 P3
Ust'-Ordynskiy Rus. Fed. 72 I2
Ust'-Penzhino Rus. Fed. see Kamenskoye
Ust'-Port Rus. Fed. 64 J3
Ustrem Rus. Fed. 41 T3
Ust'-Tsil'ma Rus. Fed. 42 L2
Ust'-Uda Rus. Fed. 72 I2
Ust'-Umalta Rus. Fed. 74 D2
Ust'-Undurga Rus. Fed. 73 L2
Ust'-Ura Rus. Fed. 42 J3
Ust'-Urgal Rus. Fed. 74 D2
Ust'-Usa Rus. Fed. 42 M2
Ust'-Vayen'ga Rus. Fed. 42 I3
Ust'-Voya Rus. Fed. 41 R3
Ust'-Vyyskaya Rus. Fed. 42 J3
Ust'ya r. Rus. Fed. 42 I3
Ust'ye Rus. Fed. 42 H4
Ustyurt, Plato plat. Kazakh./Uzbek. see Ustyurt Plateau
Ustyurt Plateau Kazakh./Uzbek. 78 E2
Ustyurt Platosi plat. Kazakh./Uzbek. see Ustyurt Plateau
Ustyuzhna Rus. Fed. 42 H4
Usulután El Salvador 136 G6
Usumbura Burundi see Bujumbura
Usvyaty Rus. Fed. 42 F5
Utah state U.S.A. 126 F5
Utah Lake U.S.A. 129 H1
Utajärvi Fin. 44 O4
Utashinai Rus. Fed. see Yuzhno-Kuril'sk
'Utaybah, Buḩayrat al imp. l. Syria 85 C3
Utena Lith. 45 N9
Uterlai India 82 B4
Uthai Thani Thai. 70 C4
Uthal Pak. 89 G5
'Uthmānīyah Syria 85 C2
Utiariti Brazil 143 G6
Utica NY U.S.A. 135 H2
Utica OH U.S.A. 134 D3
Utiel Spain 57 F4
Utikuma Lake Canada 120 H4
Utlwanang S. Africa 101 G4
Utrecht Neth. 52 F2
Utrecht S. Africa 101 J4
Utrera Spain 57 D5
Utsjoki Fin. 44 O2
Utsunomiya Japan 75 E5
Utta Rus. Fed. 43 J7
Uttaradit Thai. 70 C3
Uttarakhand state India see Uttaranchal
Uttaranchal state India 82 D3
Uttarkashi India 82 D3
Uttar Kashi India see Uttarkashi
Uttar Pradesh state India 82 D4
Uttoxeter U.K. 49 F6
Uttranchal state India see Uttaranchal
Utubulak China 80 G2
Utupua i. Solomon Is 107 G3
Uummannaq Greenland see Dundas
Uummannaq Fjord inlet Greenland 153 J2
Uummannarsuaq c. Greenland see Farewell, Cape
Uurainen Fin. 44 N5
Uusikaarlepyy Fin. see Nykarleby
Uusikaupunki Fin. 45 L6
Uutapi Namibia 99 B5
Uva Rus. Fed. 42 L4
Uvalde U.S.A. 131 D6
Uval Karabaur hills Kazakh./Uzbek. 91 I2
Uval Muzbel' hills Kazakh. 91 I2
Uvarovo Rus. Fed. 43 I6
Uvéa atoll New Caledonia see Ouvéa
Uvinza Tanz. 99 D4
Uvs Nuur salt l. Mongolia 80 H1
Uwajima Japan 75 D6
'Uwayrid, Ḩarrat al lava field Saudi Arabia 86 A4
Uwaysiţ well Saudi Arabia 85 D4
Uweinat, Jebel mt. Sudan 86 C5
Uwi i. Indon. 71 D7
Uxbridge Canada 134 F1
Uxbridge U.K. 49 G7
Uxin Qi China see Dabqig
Uyaly Kazakh. 80 B3
Uyar Rus. Fed. 72 G1
Uyo Nigeria 96 D4
Uyu Chaung r. Myanmar 70 A1
Uyuni Bol. 142 E8
Uyuni, Salar de salt flat Bol. 142 E8
Uza r. Rus. Fed. 43 J5
Uzbekistan country Asia 80 B3
Ŭzbekiston country Asia see Uzbekistan
Uzbekskaya S.S.R. country Asia see Uzbekistan
Uzbek S.S.R. country Asia see Uzbekistan
Uzboy Azer. 91 H3
Uzboý Turkm. 88 D2
Uzen' Kazakh. see Kyzylsay
Uzhgorod Ukr. see Uzhhorod
Uzhhorod Ukr. 43 D6
Užhorod Ukr. see Uzhhorod
Užice Serbia 59 H3
Uzlovaya Rus. Fed. 43 H5
Üzümlü Turkey 59 M6
Uzun Uzbek. 89 H2
Uzunköprü Turkey 59 L4
Uzynkair Kazakh. 80 B3

V

Vaaf Atoll Maldives see Felidhu Atoll
Vaajakoski Fin. 44 N5
Vaal r. S. Africa 101 F5
Vaala Fin. 44 O4
Vaalbos National Park S. Africa 100 G5
Vaal Dam S. Africa 101 I4
Vaalwater S. Africa 101 I3
Vaasa Fin. 44 L5
Vaavu Atoll Maldives see Felidhu Atoll
Vác Hungary 47 Q7
Vacaria Brazil 145 A5
Vacaria, Campo da plain Brazil 145 A5
Vacaville U.S.A. 128 C2
Vachon r. Canada 123 H1
Vad Rus. Fed. 42 J5
Vad r. Rus. Fed. 43 I5
Vada India 84 B2
Vadla Norway 45 E7
Vadodara India 82 C5
Vadsø Norway 44 P1

▶Vaduz Liechtenstein 56 I3
Capital of Liechtenstein.

Værøy i. Norway 44 H3
Vaga r. Rus. Fed. 42 I3
Vågåmo Norway 45 F6
Vaganski Vrh mt. Croatia 58 F2
Vágar i. Faroe Is 44 [inset]
Vägsele Sweden 44 K4
Vágur Faroe Is 44 [inset]
Váh r. Slovakia 47 Q7
Vähäkyrö Fin. 44 M5

▶Vaiaku Tuvalu 107 H2
Capital of Tuvalu, on Funafuti atoll.

Vaida Estonia 45 N7
Vaiden U.S.A. 131 F5
Vail U.S.A. 124 F4
Vailly-sur-Aisne France 52 D5
Vaitupu i. Tuvalu 107 H2
Vajrakarur India see Kanur
Vakhsh Tajik. 89 H2
Vakhsh r. Tajik. 89 H2
Vakhstroy Tajik. see Vakhsh
Vakīlābād Iran 88 E4
Valbo Sweden 45 J6
Valcheta Arg. 144 C6
Valdai Hills Rus. Fed. see Valdayskaya Vozvyshennost'
Valday Rus. Fed. 42 G4
Valdayskaya Vozvyshennost' hills Rus. Fed. 42 G4
Valdecañas, Embalse de resr Spain 57 D4
Valdemārpils Latvia 45 M8
Valdemarsvik Sweden 45 J7
Valdepeñas Spain 57 E4
Val-de-Reuil France 52 B5
Valdés, Península pen. Arg. 144 D6
Valdez U.S.A. 118 D3
Valdivia Chile 144 B5
Val-d'Or Canada 122 F4
Valdosta U.S.A. 133 D6
Valdres valley Norway 45 F6
Vale Georgia 91 F2
Vale U.S.A. 126 D3
Valemount Canada 120 G4
Valença Brazil 145 D1
Valence France 56 G4
Valencia Spain 57 F4
València Spain see Valencia
Valencia reg. Spain 57 F4
Valencia Venez. 142 E1
Valencia, Golfo de g. Spain 57 G4
Valencia de Don Juan Spain 57 D2
Valencia Island Ireland 51 B6
Valenciennes France 52 D4
Valensole, Plateau de France 56 H5
Valentia Spain see Valencia
Valentin Rus. Fed. 74 D4
Valentine U.S.A. 130 C3
Våler Norway 45 G6
Valera Venez. 142 D2
Vale Verde Brazil 145 D2
Val Grande, Parco Nazionale della nat. park Italy 58 C1
Valjevo Serbia 59 H2
Valka Latvia 45 O8
Valkeakoski Fin. 45 N6
Valkenswaard Neth. 52 F3
Valky Ukr. 43 G6
Valkyrie Dome ice feature Antarctica 152 D1
Valladolid Mex. 136 G4
Valladolid Spain 57 D3
Vallard, Lac l. Canada 123 H3
Valle Norway 45 E7
Vallecillos Mex. 131 D7
Vallecito Reservoir U.S.A. 129 J3
Valle de la Pascua Venez. 142 E2
Valledupar Col. 142 D1
Vallée-Jonction Canada 123 H5
Valle Fértil, Sierra de mts Arg. 144 C4
Valle Grande Bol. 142 F7
Valle Hermoso Mex. 131 D7
Vallejo U.S.A. 128 B2
Vallenar Chile 144 B3

▶Valletta Malta 58 F7
Capital of Malta.

Valley r. Canada 121 L5
Valley U.K. 48 C5
Valley City U.S.A. 130 D2
Valleyview Canada 120 G4
Valls Spain 57 G3
Val Marie Canada 121 J5
Valmiera Latvia 45 N8
Valmy U.S.A. 128 E1
Valnera mt. Spain 57 E2
Valognes France 49 F9
Valona Albania see Vlorë
Valozhyn Belarus 45 O9
Val-Paradis Canada 122 F4
Valparai India 84 C4
Valparaíso Chile 144 B4
Valparaiso U.S.A. 134 B3
Valpoi India 84 B3
Valréas France 56 G4
Vals, Tanjung c. Indon. 69 J8
Valsad India 84 B1
Valspan S. Africa 100 G4
Val'tevo Rus. Fed. 42 J2
Valtimo Fin. 44 P5
Valuyevka Rus. Fed. 43 I7
Valuyki Rus. Fed. 43 H6
Vammala Fin. 45 M6
Van Turkey 91 F3
Van, Lake salt l. Turkey 91 F3
Vanadzor Armenia 91 G2
Van Buren AR U.S.A. 131 E5
Van Buren MO U.S.A. 131 F4
Van Buren OH U.S.A. see Kettering
Vanceburg U.S.A. 134 D4
Vanch Tajik. see Vanj
Vancleve U.S.A. 134 D5
Vancouver Canada 120 F5
Vancouver U.S.A. 126 C3
Vancouver, Mount Canada/U.S.A. 120 B2
Vancouver Island Canada 120 E5
Vanda Fin. see Vantaa
Vandalia IL U.S.A. 130 F4
Vandalia OH U.S.A. 134 C4
Vandekerckhove Lake Canada 121 K3
Vanderbijlpark S. Africa 101 H4
Vanderbilt U.S.A. 134 C1
Vandergrift U.S.A. 134 F3
Vanderhoof Canada 120 E4
Vanderkloof Dam resr S. Africa 100 G6
Vanderlin Island Australia 110 B2
Vanderwagen U.S.A. 129 I4
Van Diemen, Cape N.T. Australia 108 E2
Van Diemen, Cape Qld Australia 110 B3
Van Diemen Gulf Australia 108 F2
Van Diemen's Land state Australia see Tasmania
Vändra Estonia 45 N7
Väner, Lake Sweden see Vänern

▶Vänern l. Sweden 45 H7
4th largest lake in Europe.

Vänersborg Sweden 45 H7
Vangaindrano Madag. 99 E6
Van Gia Vietnam 71 E4
Van Gölü salt l. Turkey see Van, Lake
Van Horn U.S.A. 127 G7
Vanikoro Islands Solomon Is 107 G3
Vanimo P.N.G. 69 K7
Vanino Rus. Fed. 74 F2
Vanivilasa Sagara resr India 84 C3
Vaniyambadi India 84 C3
Vanj Tajik. 89 H2
Vännäs Sweden 44 K5
Vannes France 56 C3
Vannes, Lac l. Canada 123 I3
Vannovka Kazakh. see Turar Ryskulov
Vannøya i. Norway 44 K1
Van Rees, Pegunungan mts Indon. 69 J7
Vanrhynsdorp S. Africa 100 D6
Vansant U.S.A. 134 D5
Vansbro Sweden 45 I6
Vansittart Island Canada 119 J3
Van Starkenborgh Kanaal canal Neth. 52 G1
Vantaa Fin. 45 N6
Van Truer Tableland reg. Australia 109 C6
Vanua Lava i. Vanuatu 107 G3
Vanua Levu i. Fiji 107 H3
Vanuatu country S. Pacific Ocean 107 G3
Van Wert U.S.A. 134 C3
Vanwyksvlei S. Africa 100 E6
Vanwyksvlei l. S. Africa 100 E6
Văn Yên Vietnam 70 D2
Van Zylsrus S. Africa 100 F4
Varadero Cuba 133 D8
Varahi India 82 B5
Varakļāni Latvia 45 O8
Varalé Côte d'Ivoire 96 C4
Varāmīn Iran 88 C3
Varanasi India 83 E4
Varandey Rus. Fed. 42 M1
Varangerfjorden sea chan. Norway 44 P1
Varangerhalvøya pen. Norway 41 L1
Varangerhalvøya pen. Norway 44 P1
Varaždin Croatia 58 G1
Varberg Sweden 45 H8
Vardar r. Macedonia 59 J4
Varde Denmark 45 F9
Vardenis Armenia 91 G2
Vardø Norway 44 Q1
Varel Germany 53 I1
Varėna Lith. 45 N9
Varese Italy 58 C2
Varfolomeyevka Rus. Fed. 74 D3
Vårgårda Sweden 45 H7
Varginha Brazil 145 B3
Varik Neth. 52 F3
Varillas Chile 144 B2
Varkana Iran see Gorgān
Varkaus Fin. 44 O5
Varna Bulg. 59 L3
Värnamo Sweden 45 I8
Värnäs Sweden 45 H6
Varnavino Rus. Fed. 42 J4
Várnjárg pen. Norway see Varangerhalvøya
Varpaisjärvi Fin. 44 O5
Várpalota Hungary 58 H1
Varsaj Afgh. 89 H2
Varsh, Ozero l. Rus. Fed. 42 J2
Varto Turkey 91 F3
Várzea da Palma Brazil 145 B2
Vasa Fin. see Vaasa
Vasai India 84 B2
Vashka r. Rus. Fed. 42 J2
Vasht Iran see Khāsh
Vasilkov Ukr. see Vasyl'kiv
Vasknarva Estonia 45 O7
Vaslui Romania 59 L1
Vassar U.S.A. 134 D2
Vas-Soproni-síkság hills Hungary 58 G1
Vastan Turkey see Gevaş
Västerås Sweden 45 J7
Västerdalälven r. Sweden 45 I6
Västerfjäll Sweden 44 J3
Västerhaninge Sweden 45 K7
Västervik Sweden 45 J8
Vasto Italy 58 F3
Vasyl'kiv Ukr. 43 F6
Vatan France 56 E3
Vaté i. Vanuatu see Éfaté
Vatersay i. U.K. 50 B4
Vathar India 84 B2
Vathí Greece see Vathy
Vathy Greece 59 L6

▶Vatican City Europe 58 E4
Independent papal state, the smallest country in the world.

Vaticano, Città del Europe see Vatican City
Vatnajökull ice cap Iceland 44 [inset]
Vatoa i. Fiji 107 I3
Vatra Dornei Romania 59 K1
Vätter, Lake Sweden see Vättern
Vättern l. Sweden 45 I7
Vaughn U.S.A. 127 G6
Vaupés r. Col. 142 E3
Vauquelin r. Canada 122 F3
Vauvert France 56 G5
Vauxhall Canada 121 H5
Vavatenina Madag. 99 E5
Vava'u Group is Tonga 107 I3
Vavitao i. Fr. Polynesia see Raivavae
Vavoua Côte d'Ivoire 96 C4
Vavozh Rus. Fed. 42 K4
Vavuniya Sri Lanka 84 D4
Vawkavysk Belarus 45 N10
Växjö Sweden 45 I8
Vay, Đao i. Vietnam 71 C5
Vayenga Rus. Fed. see Severomorsk
Vazante Brazil 145 B2
Vazáš Sweden see Vittangi
Veaikevárri Sweden see Svappavaara
Veal Vêng Cambodia 71 C4
Vecht r. Neth. 52 G2
also known as Vechte (Germany)
Vechta Germany 53 I2
Vechte r. Germany 52 G2
also known as Vecht (Netherlands)
Veckerhagen (Reinhardshagen) Germany 53 J3
Vedaranniyam India 84 C4
Vedasandur India 84 C4
Veddige Sweden 45 H8
Vedea r. Romania 59 K3
Veedersburg U.S.A. 134 B3
Veendam Neth. 52 G1
Veenendaal Neth. 52 F2
Vega i. Norway 44 G4
Vega U.S.A. 131 C5
Vegreville Canada 121 H4
Vehari Pak. 89 I4
Vehkalahti Fin. 45 O6
Vehoa Pak. 89 H4
Veinticinco de Mayo Buenos Aires Arg. see 25 de Mayo
Veinticinco de Mayo La Pampa Arg. see 25 de Mayo
Veirwaro Pak. 89 H5
Veitshöchheim Germany 53 J5
Vejle Denmark 45 F9
Vekil'bazar Turkm. see Wekilbazar
Velbert Germany 52 H3
Velbŭzhdki Prokhod pass Bulg./Macedonia 59 J3
Velddrif S. Africa 100 D7
Velebit mts Croatia 58 F2
Velen Germany 52 G3
Velenje Slovenia 58 F1
Veles Macedonia 59 I4
Vélez-Málaga Spain 57 D5
Vélez-Rubio Spain 57 E5
Velhas r. Brazil 145 B2
Velibaba Turkey see Aras
Velika Gorica Croatia 58 G2
Velika Plana Serbia 59 I2
Velikaya r. Rus. Fed. 42 K4
Velikaya r. Rus. Fed. 45 P8
Velikaya r. Rus. Fed. 65 S3
Velikaya Kema Rus. Fed. 74 E3
Veliki Preslav Bulg. 59 L3
Velikiye Luki Rus. Fed. 42 F4
Velikiy Novgorod Rus. Fed. 42 F4
Velikiy Ustyug Rus. Fed. 42 J3
Velikonda Range hills India 84 C3
Veliko Tŭrnovo Bulg. 59 K3
Velikoye Rus. Fed. 42 H4
Velikoye, Ozero l. Rus. Fed. 43 I5
Veli Lošinj Croatia 58 F2
Velizh Rus. Fed. 42 F5
Vella Lavella i. Solomon Is 107 F2
Vellar r. India 84 C4
Vellberg Germany 53 J5
Vellmar Germany 53 J3
Vellore India 84 C3
Velpke Germany 53 K2
Vel'sk Rus. Fed. 42 I3
Velsuna Italy see Orvieto
Velten Germany 53 N2
Veluwezoom, Nationaal Park nat. park Neth. 52 F2
Velykyy Tokmak Ukr. see Tokmak
Vel'yu r. Rus. Fed. 42 L3
Vemalwada India 84 C2
Vema Seamount sea feature S. Atlantic Ocean 148 I8
Vema Trench sea feature Indian Ocean 149 M6
Vempalle India 84 C3
Venado Tuerto Arg. 144 D4
Venafro Italy 58 F4
Venceslau Bráz Brazil 145 A3
Vendinga Rus. Fed. 42 J3
Vendôme France 56 E3
Venegas Mex. 131 C8
Venetia Italy see Venice
Venetie Landing U.S.A. 118 D3
Venev Rus. Fed. 43 H5
Venezia Italy see Venice
Venezia, Golfo di g. Europe see Venice, Gulf of

▶Venezuela country S. America 142 E2
5th most populous country in South America.

Venezuela, Golfo de g. Venez. 142 D1
Venezuelan Basin sea feature S. Atlantic Ocean 148 D4
Vengurla India 84 B3
Veniaminof Volcano U.S.A. 118 C4
Venice Italy 58 E2
Venice U.S.A. 133 D7
Venice, Gulf of Europe 58 E2
Vénissieux France 56 G4
Venkatapalem India 84 D2
Venkatapuram India 84 D2
Venlo Neth. 52 G3
Vennesla Norway 45 E7
Venray Neth. 52 F3
Venta r. Latvia/Lith. 45 M8
Venta Lith. 45 M8
Ventersburg S. Africa 101 H5
Ventersdorp S. Africa 101 H4
Venterstad S. Africa 101 G6
Ventnor U.K. 49 F8
Ventotene, Isola i. Italy 58 E4
Ventoux, Mont mt. France 56 G4
Ventspils Latvia 45 L8
Ventura U.S.A. 128 D4
Venus Bay Australia 112 B7
Venustiano Carranza Mex. 131 C7
Venustiano Carranza, Presa resr Mex. 131 C7
Vera Arg. 144 D3
Vera Spain 57 F5
Vera Cruz Brazil 145 A3
Veracruz Mex. 136 E5
Vera Cruz Mex. see Veracruz
Veraval India 82 B5
Verbania Italy 58 C2
Vercelli Italy 58 C2
Vercors reg. France 56 G4
Verdalsøra Norway 44 G5
Verde r. Goiás Brazil 145 A2
Verde r. Goiás Brazil 145 B2
Verde r. Minas Gerais Brazil 145 A2
Verde r. Mex. 127 G8
Verde r. U.S.A. 129 H5
Verden (Aller) Germany 53 J2
Verde Pequeno r. Brazil 145 C1
Verdi U.S.A. 128 D2
Verdon r. France 56 G5
Verdun France 52 F5
Vereeniging S. Africa 101 H4
Vereshchagino Rus. Fed. 41 Q4
Vergennes U.S.A. 135 I1
Véria Greece see Veroia
Verín Spain 57 C3
Veríssimo Brazil 145 A2
Verkhneimbatsk Rus. Fed. 64 J3
Verkhnekolvinsk Rus. Fed. 42 M2
Verkhnespasskoye Rus. Fed. 42 J4
Verkhnetulomskiy Rus. Fed. 44 Q2
Verkhnetulomskoye Vodokhranilishche res. Rus. Fed. 44 Q2
Verkhnevilyuysk Rus. Fed. 65 N3
Verkhneye Kuyto, Ozero l. Rus. Fed. 44 Q4
Verkhnezeysk Rus. Fed. 73 N2
Verkhniy Vyalozerskiy Rus. Fed. 42 G2
Verkhnyaya Khava Rus. Fed. 43 H6
Verkhnyaya Salda Rus. Fed. 41 S4
Verkhnyaya Tunguska r. Rus. Fed. see Angara
Verkhnyaya Tura Rus. Fed. 41 R4
Verkhoshizhem'ye Rus. Fed. 42 K4
Verkhovazh'ye Rus. Fed. 42 I3
Verkhov'ye Rus. Fed. 43 H5
Verkhoyansk Rus. Fed. 65 O3
Verkhoyanskiy Khrebet mts Rus. Fed. 65 N2
Vermand France 52 D5
Vermelho r. Brazil 145 A1
Vermilion Canada 121 I4
Vermilion Bay U.S.A. 131 F6
Vermilion Cliffs AZ U.S.A. 129 G3
Vermilion Cliffs UT U.S.A. 129 G3
Vermilion Cliffs National Monument nat. park U.S.A. 129 H3
Vermilion Lake U.S.A. 130 E2
Vermillion U.S.A. 130 D3
Vermillion Bay Canada 121 M5
Vermont state U.S.A. 135 I1
Vernadsky research station Antarctica 152 L2
Vernal U.S.A. 129 I1
Verner Canada 122 E5
Verneuk Pan salt pan S. Africa 100 E5
Vernon Canada 120 G5
Vernon France 52 B5
Vernon AL U.S.A. 131 F5
Vernon IN U.S.A. 134 C4
Vernon TX U.S.A. 131 D5
Vernon UT U.S.A. 129 G1
Vernon Islands Australia 108 E3
Vernoye Rus. Fed. 74 C2
Vernyy Kazakh. see Almaty
Vero Beach U.S.A. 133 D7
Veroia Greece 59 J4
Verona Italy 58 D2
Verona U.S.A. 134 F4
Versailles France 52 C6
Versailles IN U.S.A. 134 C4
Versailles KY U.S.A. 134 C4
Versailles OH U.S.A. 134 C3
Versec Serbia see Vršac
Versmold Germany 53 I2
Vert, Île i. Canada 123 H4
Vertou France 56 D3
Verulam S. Africa 101 J5
Verulamium U.K. see St Albans
Verviers Belgium 52 F4
Vervins France 52 D5
Verwood Canada 121 J5
Verzy France 52 E5
Vescovato Corsica France 56 I5
Vesele Ukr. 43 G7
Veselyy Rus. Fed. 43 I7
Veselyy Yar Rus. Fed. 74 D4
Veshenskaya Rus. Fed. 43 I6
Vesle r. France 52 D5
Veslyana r. Rus. Fed. 42 L3
Vesontio France see Besançon
Vesoul France 56 H3
Vessem Neth. 52 F3
Vesterålen is Norway 44 H2
Vesterålsfjorden sea chan. Norway 44 H2
Vestertana Norway 44 O1
Vestfjorddalen valley Norway 45 F7
Vestfjorden sea chan. Norway 44 H3
Véstia Brazil 145 A3
Vestmanna Faroe Is 44 [inset]
Vestmannaeyjar Iceland 44 [inset]
Vestmannaeyjar is Iceland 44 [inset]
Vestnes Norway 44 E5
Vesturhorn hd Iceland 44 [inset]
Vesuvio vol. Italy see Vesuvius
Vesuvius vol. Italy 58 F4
Ves'yegonsk Rus. Fed. 42 H4
Veszprém Hungary 58 G1
Veteli Fin. 44 M5
Veteran Canada 121 I4
Vetlanda Sweden 45 I8
Vetluga Rus. Fed. 42 J4
Vetluga r. Rus. Fed. 42 J4
Vetluzhskiy Kostromskaya Oblast' Rus. Fed. 42 J4
Vetluzhskiy Nizhegorodskaya Oblast' Rus. Fed. 42 J4
Vettore, Monte mt. Italy 58 E3
Veurne Belgium 52 C3

Vevay U.S.A. 134 C4
Vevey Switz. 56 H3
Vexin Normand reg. France 52 B5
Veyo U.S.A. 129 G3
Vézère r. France 56 E4
Vezirköprü Turkey 90 D2
Vialar Alg. see Tissemsilt
Viamao Brazil 145 A5
Viana *Espírito Santo* Brazil 145 C3
Viana *Maranhão* Brazil 143 J4
Viana do Castelo Port. 57 B3
Vianen Neth. 52 F3
Viangchan Laos see Vientiane
Viangphoukha Laos 70 C2
Viannos Greece 59 K7
Vianópolis Brazil 145 A2
Viareggio Italy 58 D3
Viborg Denmark 45 F8
Viborg Rus. Fed. see Vyborg
Vibo Valentia Italy 58 G5
Vic Spain 57 H3
Vicam Mex. 127 F8
Vicecomodoro Marambio research station Antarctica see Marambio
Vicente, Point U.S.A. 128 D5
Vicente Guerrero Mex. 127 D7
Vicenza Italy 58 D2
Vich Spain see Vic
Vichada r. Col. 142 E3
Vichadero Uruguay 144 F4
Vichy France 56 F3
Vicksburg *AZ* U.S.A. 129 G5
Vicksburg *MS* U.S.A. 131 F5
Viçosa Brazil 145 C3
Victor, Mount Antarctica 152 D2
Victor Harbor Australia 111 B7
Victoria Arg. 144 D4
Victoria r. Australia 108 E3
Victoria state Australia 112 B6
▶Victoria Canada 120 F5
Capital of British Columbia.
Victoria Chile 144 B5
Victoria Malaysia see Labuan
Victoria Malta 58 F6
▶Victoria Seychelles 149 L6
Capital of the Seychelles.
Victoria *TX* U.S.A. 131 D6
Victoria *VA* U.S.A. 135 F5
Victoria prov. Zimbabwe see Masvingo
▶Victoria, Lake Africa 98 D4
Largest lake in Africa, and 3rd in the world.
Victoria, Lake Australia 111 C7
Victoria, Mount Fiji see Tomanivi
Victoria, Mount Myanmar 70 A2
Victoria, Mount P.N.G. 69 L8
Victoria and Albert Mountains Canada 119 K2
Victoria Falls Zambia/Zimbabwe 99 C5
Victoria Harbour sea chan. H.K. China see Hong Kong Harbour
▶Victoria Island Canada 118 H2
3rd largest island in North America, and 9th in the world.
Victoria Land coastal area Antarctica 152 H2
Victoria Peak Belize 136 G5
Victoria Peak hill H.K. China 77 [inset]
Victoria Range mts N.Z. 113 D6
Victoria River Downs Australia 108 E4
Victoriaville Canada 123 H5
Victoria West S. Africa 100 F6
Victorica Arg. 144 C5
Victorville U.S.A. 128 E4
Victory Downs Australia 109 F6
Vidalia U.S.A. 131 F6
Vidal Junction U.S.A. 129 F4
Videle Romania 59 K2
Vidisha India 82 D5
Vidlin U.K. 50 [inset]
Vidlitsa Rus. Fed. 42 G3
Viechtach Germany 53 M5
Viedma Arg. 144 D6
Viedma, Lago l. Arg. 144 B7
Viejo, Cerro mt. Mex. 127 E7
Vielank Germany 53 L1
Vielsalm Belgium 52 F4
Vienenburg Germany 53 K3
▶Vienna Austria 47 P6
Capital of Austria.
Vienna *MO* U.S.A. 130 F4
Vienna *WV* U.S.A. 134 E4
Vienne France 56 G4
Vienne r. France 56 E3
▶Vientiane Laos 70 C3
Capital of Laos.
Vieques i. Puerto Rico 137 K5
Vieremä Fin. 44 O5
Viersen Germany 52 G3
Vierzon France 56 F3
Viesca Mex. 131 C7
Viesīte Latvia 45 N8
Vieste Italy 58 G4
Vietas Sweden 44 K3
Viêt Nam country Asia see Vietnam
Vietnam country Asia 70 D3
Viêt Quang Vietnam 70 D2
Viêt Tri Vietnam 70 D2
Vieux Comptoir, Lac du l. Canada 122 F3
Vieux-Fort Canada 123 K4
Vieux Poste, Pointe du pt Canada 123 J4
Vigan Phil. 69 G3
Vigevano Italy 58 C2
Vigia Brazil 143 I4
Vignacourt France 52 C4
Vignemale mt. France 54 D3
Vignola Italy 58 D2
Vigo Spain 57 B2
Vihanti Fin. 44 N4
Vihti Fin. 45 N6
Viipuri Rus. Fed. see Vyborg
Viitasaari Fin. 44 N5
Vijayadurg India 84 B2
Vijayanagaram India see Vizianagaram
Vijayapati India 84 C4
Vijayawada India 84 D2
Vík Iceland 44 [inset]
Vikajärvi Fin. 44 O3
Vikeke East Timor see Viqueque
Viking Canada 121 I4
Vikna i. Norway 44 G4
Vikøyri Norway 45 E6
Vila Vanuatu see Port Vila
Vila Alferes Chamusca Moz. see Guija
Vila Bittencourt Brazil 142 E4
Vila Bugaço Angola see Camanongue
Vila Cabral Moz. see Lichinga
Vila da Ponte Angola see Kuvango
Vila de Aljustrel Angola see Cangamba
Vila de Almoster Angola see Chiange
Vila de João Belo Moz. see Xai-Xai
Vila de María Arg. 144 D3
Vila de Trego Morais Moz. see Chókwé
Vila Fontes Moz. see Caia
Vila Franca de Xira Port. 57 B4
Vilagarcía de Arousa Spain 57 B2
Vila Gomes da Costa Moz. 101 K3
Vilalba Spain 57 C2
Vila Luísa Moz. see Marracuene
Vila Marechal Carmona Angola see Uíge
Vila Miranda Moz. see Macaloge
Vilanandro, Tanjona pt Madag. 99 E5
Vilanculos Moz. 101 L1
Vila Nova de Gaia Port. 57 B3
Vilanova i la Geltrú Spain 57 G3
Vila Pery Moz. see Chimoio
Vila Real Port. 57 C3
Vilar Formoso Port. 57 C3
Vila Salazar Angola see N'dalatando
Vila Salazar Zimbabwe see Sango
Vila Teixeira de Sousa Angola see Luau
Vila Velha Brazil 145 C3
Vilcabamba, Cordillera mts Peru 142 D6
Vil'cheka, Zemlya i. Rus. Fed. 64 H1
Viled' r. Rus. Fed. 42 J3
Vileyka Belarus see Vilyeyka
Vil'gort Rus. Fed. 42 K3
Vilhelmina Sweden 44 J4
Vilhena Brazil 142 F6
Viliya r. Lith. see Neris
Viljandi Estonia 45 N7
Viljoenskroon S. Africa 101 H4
Vilkaviškis Lith. 45 M9
Vilkija Lith. 45 M9
Vil'kitskogo, Proliv strait Rus. Fed. 65 K2
Vilkovo Ukr. see Vylkove
Villa Abecia Bol. 142 E8
Villa Ahumada Mex. 127 G7
Villa Ángela Arg. 144 D3
Villa Bella Bol. 142 E6
Villa Bens Morocco see Tarfaya
Villablino Spain 57 C2
Villacañas Spain 57 E4
Villach Austria 47 N7
Villacidro *Sardinia* Italy 58 C5
Villa Cisneros W. Sahara see Ad Dakhla
Villa Constitución Mex. see Ciudad Constitución
Villa Dolores Arg. 144 C4
Villagarcía de Arosa Spain see Vilagarcía de Arousa
Villagrán Mex. 131 D7
Villaguay Arg. 144 E4
Villahermosa Mex. 136 F5
Villa Insurgentes Mex. 127 F8
Villajoyosa Spain see Villajoyosa-La Vila Joíosa
Villajoyosa-La Vila Joíosa Spain 57 F4
Villaldama Mex. 131 C7
Villa Mainero Mex. 131 D7
Villa María Arg. 144 D4
Villa Montes Bol. 142 F8
Villa Nora S. Africa 101 I2
Villanueva de la Serena Spain 57 D4
Villanueva de los Infantes Spain 57 E4
Villanueva-y-Geltrú Spain see Vilanova i la Geltrú
Villa Ocampo Arg. 144 E3
Villa Ocampo Mex. 131 B7
Villa Ojo de Agua Arg. 144 D3
Villaputzu *Sardinia* Italy 58 C5
Villa Regina Arg. 144 C5
Villarrica Para. 144 E3
Villarrica, Lago l. Chile 144 B5
Villarrica, Parque Nacional nat. park Chile 144 B5
Villarrobledo Spain 57 E4
Villas U.S.A. 135 H4
Villasalazar Zimbabwe see Sango
Villa San Giovanni Italy 58 F5
Villa Sanjurjo Morocco see Al Hoceima
Villa San Martin Arg. 144 D3
Villa Unión Arg. 144 C3
Villa Unión *Coahuila* Mex. 131 C6
Villa Unión *Durango* Mex. 131 B8
Villa Unión *Sinaloa* Mex. 136 C4
Villa Valeria Arg. 144 D4
Villavicencio Col. 142 D3
Villazon Bol. 142 E8
Villefranche-sur-Saône France 56 G4
Ville-Marie Canada see Montréal
Villena Spain 57 F4
Villeneuve-sur-Lot France 56 E4
Villeneuve-sur-Yonne France 56 F2
Villers-Cotterêts France 52 D5
Villers-sur-Mer France 49 G9
Villerupt France 52 F5
Villeurbanne France 56 G4
Villiers S. Africa 101 I4
Villingen Germany 47 L6
Villuppuram India see Villupuram
Villupuram India 84 C4
Vilna Canada 121 I4
Vilna Lith. see Vilnius
▶Vilnius Lith. 45 N9
Capital of Lithuania.
Vil'nyans'k Ukr. 43 G7
Vilppula Fin. 44 N5
Vils r. Germany 53 L5
Vils r. Germany 53 N6
Vilvoorde Belgium 52 E4
Vilyeyka Belarus 45 O9
Vilyuy r. Rus. Fed. 65 N3
Vilyuyskoye Vodokhranilishche resr Rus. Fed. 65 M3
Vimmerby Sweden 45 I8
Vimy France 52 C4
Vina r. Cameroon 97 E4
Vina U.S.A. 128 B2
Viña del Mar Chile 144 B4
Vinalhaven Island U.S.A. 132 G2
Vinaròs Spain 57 G3
Vinaroz Spain see Vinaròs
Vincelotte, Lac l. Canada 123 G3
Vincennes U.S.A. 134 B4
Vincennes Bay Antarctica 152 F2
Vinchina Arg. 144 C3
Vindelälven r. Sweden 44 K5
Vindeln Sweden 44 K4
Vindhya Range hills India 82 C5
Vindobona Austria see Vienna
Vine Grove U.S.A. 134 C5
Vineland U.S.A. 135 H4
Vinh Vietnam 70 D3
Vinh Loc Vietnam 70 D2
Vinh Long Vietnam 71 D5
Vinh Thực, Đao i. Vietnam 70 D2
Vinita U.S.A. 131 E4
Vinjhan India 82 B5
Vinland i. Canada see Newfoundland
Vinnitsa Ukr. see Vinnytsya
Vinnytsya Ukr. 43 F6
Vinogradov Ukr. see Vynohradiv
▶Vinson Massif mt. Antarctica 152 L1
Highest mountain in Antarctica.
Vinstra Norway 45 F6
Vinton U.S.A. 130 E3
Vinukonda India 84 C2
Violeta Cuba see Primero de Enero
Vipperow Germany 53 M1
Viqueque East Timor 108 D2
Virac Phil. 69 G4
Viramgam India 82 C5
Viranşehir Turkey 91 E3
Virawah Pak. 89 H5
Virchow, Mount hill Australia 108 B5
Virdel India 82 C5
Virden Canada 121 K5
Virden U.S.A. 129 I5
Vire France 56 D2
Virei Angola 99 B5
Virgem da Lapa Brazil 145 C2
Virgilina U.S.A. 135 F5
Virgin r. U.S.A. 129 F3
Virginia Ireland 51 E4
Virginia S. Africa 101 H5
Virginia U.S.A. 130 F4
Virginia state U.S.A. 134 F5
Virginia Beach U.S.A. 135 H5
Virginia City *MT* U.S.A. 126 F3
Virginia City *NV* U.S.A. 128 D2
Virginia Falls Canada 120 E2
▶Virgin Islands (U.K.) terr. West Indies 137 L5
United Kingdom Overseas Territory.
▶Virgin Islands (U.S.A.) terr. West Indies 137 L5
United States Unincorporated Territory.
Virgin Mountains U.S.A. 129 F3
Virginópolis Brazil 145 C2
Virkkala Fin. 45 N6
Virôchey Cambodia 71 D4
Viroqua U.S.A. 130 F3
Virovitica Croatia 58 G2
Virrat Fin. 44 M5
Virton Belgium 52 F5
Virtsu Estonia 45 M7
Virudhunagar India 84 C4
Virudunagar India see Virudhunagar
Virunga, Parc National des nat. park Dem. Rep. Congo 98 C4
Vis i. Croatia 58 G3
Visaginas Lith. 45 O9
Visakhapatnam India see Vishakhapatnam
Visalia U.S.A. 128 D3
Visapur India 84 B2
Visayan Sea Phil. 69 G4
Visbek Germany 53 I2
Visby Sweden 45 K8
Viscount Melville Sound sea chan. Canada 119 G2
Visé Belgium 52 F4
Viseu Brazil 143 I4
Viseu Port. 57 C3
Vishakhapatnam India 84 D2
Vishera r. Rus. Fed. 41 R4
Vishera r. Rus. Fed. 42 L3
Višķi Latvia 45 O8
Visnagar India 82 C5
Viso, Monte mt. Italy 58 B2
Visoko Bos.-Herz. 58 H3
Visp Switz. 56 H3
Visselhövede Germany 53 J2
Vista U.S.A. 128 E5
Vista Lake U.S.A. 128 D4
Vistonida, Limni lag. Greece 59 K4
Vistula r. Poland 47 Q3
Vitebsk Belarus see Vitsyebsk
Viterbo Italy 58 E3
Vitichi Bol. 142 E8
Vitigudino Spain 57 C3
Viti Levu i. Fiji 107 H3
Vitimskoye Ploskogor'ye plat. Rus. Fed. 73 K2
Vitória Brazil 145 C3
Vitória da Conquista Brazil 145 C1
Vitoria-Gasteiz Spain 57 E2
Vitória Seamount sea feature S. Atlantic Ocean 148 F7
Vitré France 56 D2
Vitry-en-Artois France 52 C4
Vitry-le-François France 52 E6
Vitsyebsk Belarus 43 F5
Vittangi Sweden 44 L3
Vittel France 56 G2
Vittoria *Sicily* Italy 58 F6
Vittorio Veneto Italy 58 E2
Viveiro Spain 57 C2
Vivero Spain see Viveiro
Vivo S. Africa 101 I2
Vizagapatam India see Vishakhapatnam
Vizcaíno, Desierto de des. Mex. 127 E8
Vizcaíno, Sierra mts Mex. 127 E8
Vize Turkey 59 L4
Vize, Ostrov i. Rus. Fed. 64 I2
Vizhas r. Rus. Fed. 42 J2
Vizianagaram India 84 D2
Vizinga Rus. Fed. 42 K3
Vlaardingen Neth. 52 E3
Vlădeasa, Vârful mt. Romania 59 J1
Vladikavkaz Rus. Fed. 91 G2
Vladimir *Primorskiy Kray* Rus. Fed. 74 D4
Vladimir *Vladimirskaya Oblast'* Rus. Fed. 42 I4
Vladimiro-Aleksandrovskoye Rus. Fed. 74 D4
Vladimir-Volynskiy Ukr. see Volodymyr-Volyns'kyy
Vladivostok Rus. Fed. 74 C4
Vlakte S. Africa 101 I3
Vlasotince Serbia 59 J3
Vlas'yevo Rus. Fed. 74 F1
Vlieland i. Neth. 52 E1
Vlissingen Neth. 52 D3
Vlora Albania see Vlorë
Vlorë Albania 59 H4
Vlotho Germany 53 I2
Vlotslavsk Poland see Włocławek
Vltava r. Czech Rep. 47 O5
Vobkent Uzbek. 89 G1
Vöcklabruck Austria 47 N6
Vodlozero, Ozero l. Rus. Fed. 42 H3
Voe U.K. 50 [inset]
Voerendaal Neth. 52 F4
Vogelkop Peninsula Indon. see Doberai, Jazirah
Vogelsberg hills Germany 53 I4
Voghera Italy 58 C2
Vohburg an der Donau Germany 53 L6
Vohémar Madag. see Iharaña
Vohenstrauß Germany 53 M5
Vohibinany Madag. see Ampasimanolotra
Vohimarina Madag. see Iharaña
Vohimena, Tanjona c. Madag. 99 E6
Vohipeno Madag. 99 E6
Vöhl Germany 53 I3
Võhma Estonia 45 N7
Voinjama Liberia 96 C4
Vojens Denmark 45 F9
Vojvodina prov. Serbia 59 H2
Vokhma Rus. Fed. 42 J4
Voknavolok Rus. Fed. 44 Q4
Vol' r. Rus. Fed. 42 L3
Volcano Bay Japan see Uchiura-wan
▶Volcano Islands Japan 69 K2
Part of Japan.
Volda Norway 44 E5
Vol'dino Rus. Fed. 42 L3
Volendam Neth. 52 F2
Volga Rus. Fed. 42 H4
▶Volga r. Rus. Fed. 43 J7
Longest river in Europe.
Volga Upland hills Rus. Fed. see Privolzhskaya Vozvyshennost'
Volgodonsk Rus. Fed. 43 I7
Volgograd Rus. Fed. 43 J6
Volgogradskoye Vodokhranilishche resr Rus. Fed. 43 J6
Völkermarkt Austria 47 O7
Volkhov Rus. Fed. 42 G4
Volkhov r. Rus. Fed. 42 G3
Völklingen Germany 52 G5
Volkovysk Belarus see Vawkavysk
Volksrust S. Africa 101 I4
Vol'no-Nadezhdinskoye Rus. Fed. 74 C4
Volnovakha Ukr. 43 H7
Vol'nyansk Ukr. see Vil'nyans'k
Volochanka Rus. Fed. 64 K2
Volochisk Ukr. see Volochys'k
Volochys'k Ukr. 43 E6
Volodars'ke Ukr. 43 H7
Volodarskoye Kazakh. see Saumalkol'
Volodymyr-Volyns'kyy Ukr. 43 E6
Vologda Rus. Fed. 42 H4
Volokolamsk Rus. Fed. 42 G4
Volokovaya Rus. Fed. 42 K2
Volos Greece 59 J5
Volosovo Rus. Fed. 45 P7
Volot Rus. Fed. 42 F4
Volovo Rus. Fed. 43 H5
Volozhin Belarus see Valozhyn
Volsinii Italy see Orvieto
Vol'sk Rus. Fed. 43 J5
▶Volta, Lake resr Ghana 96 D4
4th largest lake in Africa.
Volta Blanche r. Burkina/Ghana see White Volta
Voltaire, Cape Australia 108 D3
Volta Redonda Brazil 145 B3
Volturno r. Italy 58 E4
Volubilis tourist site Morocco 54 C5
Volvi, Limni l. Greece 59 J4
Volzhsk Rus. Fed. 42 K5
Volzhskiy *Samarskaya Oblast'* Rus. Fed. 43 K5
Volzhskiy *Volgogradskaya Oblast'* Rus. Fed. 43 J6
Vondanka Rus. Fed. 42 J4
Vontimitta India 84 C3
Vopnafjörður Iceland 44 [inset]
Vopnafjörður b. Iceland 44 [inset]
Vörå Fin. 44 M5
Voranava Belarus 45 N9
Voreies Sporades is Greece 59 J5
Voreioi Sporades is Greece see Voreies Sporades
Voríai Sporádhes is Greece see Voreies Sporades
Voring Plateau sea feature N. Atlantic Ocean 148 I1
Vorjing mt. India 83 H3
Vorkuta Rus. Fed. 64 H3
Vormsi i. Estonia 45 M7
Vorona r. Rus. Fed. 43 I6
Voronezh Rus. Fed. 43 H6
Voronezh r. Rus. Fed. 43 H6
Voronov, Mys pt Rus. Fed. 42 I2
Vorontsovo-Aleksandrovskoye Rus. Fed. see Zelenokumsk
Voroshilov Rus. Fed. see Ussuriysk
Voroshilovgrad Ukr. see Luhans'k
Voroshilovsk Rus. Fed. see Stavropol'
Voroshilovsk Ukr. see Alchevs'k
Vorotynets Rus. Fed. 42 J4
Vorozhba Ukr. 43 G6
Vorpommersche Boddenlandschaft, Nationalpark nat. park Germany 47 N3
Vorskla r. Rus. Fed. 43 G6
Võrtsjärv l. Estonia 45 N7
Võru Estonia 45 O8
Vorukh Tajik. 89 H2
Vosburg S. Africa 100 F6
Vose Tajik. 89 H2
Vosges mts France 56 H3
Voskresensk Rus. Fed. 43 H5
Voskresenskoye Rus. Fed. 42 H4
Voss Norway 45 E6
Vostochno-Sakhalinskiy Gory mts Rus. Fed. 74 F2
Vostochno-Sibirskoye More sea Rus. Fed. see East Siberian Sea
Vostochnyy *Kirovskaya Oblast'* Rus. Fed. 42 L4
Vostochnyy *Sakhalinskaya Oblast'* Rus. Fed. 74 F2
Vostochnyy Sayan mts Rus. Fed. 72 G2
▶Vostok research station Antarctica 152 F1
Lowest recorded screen temperature in the world.
Vostok *Primorskiy Kray* Rus. Fed. 74 D3
Vostok *Sakhalinskaya Oblast'* Rus. Fed. see Neftegorsk
Vostok Island Kiribati 151 J6
Vostroye Rus. Fed. 42 J3
Votkinsk Rus. Fed. 41 Q4
Votkinskoye Vodokhranilishche resr Rus. Fed. 41 R4
Votuporanga Brazil 145 A3
Vouziers France 52 E5
Voves France 56 E2
Voyageurs National Park U.S.A. 130 E1
Voynitsa Rus. Fed. 44 Q4
Võyri Fin. see Vörå
Voyvozh Rus. Fed. 42 L3
Vozhayel' Rus. Fed. 42 J4
Vozhe, Ozero l. Rus. Fed. 42 H3
Vozhega Rus. Fed. 42 I3
Vozhgaly Rus. Fed. 42 K4
Voznesens'k Ukr. 43 F7
Vozonin Trough sea feature Arctic Ocean 153 F1
Vozrozhdenya Island i. Uzbek. 80 A3
Vozzhayevka Rus. Fed. 74 C2
Vrangel' Rus. Fed. 74 D4
Vrangelya, Mys pt Rus. Fed. 74 E1
Vranje Serbia 59 I3
Vratnik pass Bulg. 59 L3
Vratsa Bulg. 59 J3
Vrbas Serbia 59 H2
Vrede S. Africa 101 I4
Vredefort S. Africa 101 H4
Vredenburg S. Africa 100 C7
Vredendal S. Africa 100 D6
Vresse Belgium 52 E5
Vriddhachalam India 84 C4
Vries Neth. 52 G1
Vrigstad Sweden 45 I8
Vršac Serbia 59 I2
Vryburg S. Africa 100 G4
Vryheid S. Africa 101 J4
Vsevidof, Mount vol. U.S.A. 118 B4
Vsevolozhsk Rus. Fed. 42 F3
Vu Ban Vietnam 70 D2
Vučitrn Kosovo see Vushtrri
Vukovar Croatia 59 H2
Vuktyl' Rus. Fed. 41 R3
Vukuzakhe S. Africa 101 I4
Vulcan Canada 120 H5
Vulcan Island P.N.G. see Manam Island
Vulcano, Isola i. Italy 58 F5
Vu Liêt Vietnam 70 D3
Vulture Mountains U.S.A. 129 G5
Vung Tau Vietnam 71 D5
Vuohijärvi Fin. 45 O6
Vuolijoki Fin. 44 O4
Vuollerim Sweden 44 L3
Vuostimo Fin. 44 O3
Vurnary Rus. Fed. 42 J5
Vushtrri Kosovo 59 I3
Vvedenovka Rus. Fed. 74 C2
Vyara India 82 C5
Vyarkhowye Belarus see Ruba
Vyatka Rus. Fed. see Kirov
Vyatka r. Rus. Fed. 42 K5
Vyatskiye Polyany Rus. Fed. 42 K4
Vyazemskiy Rus. Fed. 74 D3
Vyaz'ma Rus. Fed. 43 G5
Vyazniki Rus. Fed. 42 I4
Vyazovka Rus. Fed. 43 J5
Vyborg Rus. Fed. 45 P6
Vychegda r. Rus. Fed. 42 J3
Vychegodskiy Rus. Fed. 42 J3
Vyerkhnyadzvinsk Belarus 45 O9
Vyetryna Belarus 45 P9
Vygozero, Ozero l. Rus. Fed. 42 G3
Vyksa Rus. Fed. 43 I5
Vylkove Ukr. 59 M2
Vym' r. Rus. Fed. 42 K3
Vynohradiv Ukr. 43 D6
Vypin Island India 84 C4
Vypolzovo Rus. Fed. 42 G4
Vyritsa Rus. Fed. 45 Q7
Vyrnwy, Lake U.K. 49 D6
Vyselki Rus. Fed. 43 H7
Vysha Rus. Fed. 43 I5
Vyshhorod Ukr. 43 F6
Vyshnevolotskaya Gryada ridge Rus. Fed. 42 G4
Vyshniy-Volochek Rus. Fed. 42 G4
Vyškov Czech Rep. 47 P6
Vysokaya Gora Rus. Fed. 42 K5
Vysokogorniy Rus. Fed. 74 E2
Vystupovychi Ukr. 43 F6
Vytegra Rus. Fed. 42 H3
Vyya r. Rus. Fed. 42 J3
Vyžuona r. Lith. 45 N9

W

Wa Ghana 96 C3
Waal r. Neth. 52 E3
Waalwijk Neth. 52 F3
Waat Sudan 86 D8
Wabag P.N.G. 69 K8
Wabakimi Lake Canada 122 C4
Wabasca r. Canada 120 H3
Wabasca-Desmarais Canada 120 H4
Wabash U.S.A. 134 C3
Wabash r. U.S.A. 134 A5
Wabasha U.S.A. 130 E2
Wabassi r. Canada 122 D4
Wabatongushi Lake Canada 122 D4
Wabē Gestro r. Eth. 78 D6
Wabē Shebelē Wenz r. Eth. 98 E3
Wabigoon Lake Canada 121 M5
Wabowden Canada 121 L4
Wabrah well Saudi Arabia 88 B5
Wabu China 77 H1
Wabuk Point Canada 122 D3
Wabush Canada 123 I3
Waccasassa Bay U.S.A. 133 D6
Wächtersbach Germany 53 J4
Waco Canada 123 I4
Waco U.S.A. 131 D6
Waconda Lake U.S.A. 130 D4
Wadbilliga National Park Australia 112 D6
Waddān Libya 55 H6
Waddell Dam U.S.A. 129 G5
Waddeneilanden Neth. 52 E1
Waddenzee sea chan. Neth. 52 E2
Waddington, Mount Canada 120 E5
Waddinxveen Neth. 52 E2
Wadebridge U.K. 49 C8
Wadena Canada 121 K5
Wadena U.S.A. 130 E2
Wadern Germany 52 G5
Wadesville U.S.A. 134 B4
Wadeye Australia 108 E3
Wadgassen Germany 52 G5
Wadh Pak. 89 G5
Wadhwan India see Surendranagar
Wadi India 84 C2
Wādī as Sīr Jordan 85 B4
Wadi Halfa Sudan 86 D5
Wad Medani Sudan 86 D7
Wad Rawa Sudan 86 D6
Wadsworth U.S.A. 128 D2
Waenhuiskrans S. Africa 100 E8
Wafangdian China 73 M5
Wafra Kuwait see Al Wafrah
Wagenfeld Germany 53 I2
Wagenhoff Germany 53 K2
Wagga Wagga Australia 112 C5
Wagner U.S.A. 130 D3
Wagoner U.S.A. 131 E4
Wagon Mound U.S.A. 127 G5
Wah Pak. 89 I3
Wahai Indon. 69 H7
Wāḥāt Jālū Libya 97 F2
Wahemen, Lac l. Canada 123 H3
Wahiawā U.S.A. 127 [inset]
Wahlhausen Germany 53 J3
Wahpeton U.S.A. 130 D2
Wahran Alg. see Oran
Wah Wah Mountains U.S.A. 129 G2
Wai India 84 B2
Waialua U.S.A. 127 [inset]
Waiau N.Z. see Franz Josef Glacier
Waiau r. N.Z. 113 D6
Waiblingen Germany 53 J6
Waidhofen an der Ybbs Austria 47 O7
Waigeo i. Indon. 69 I7
Waiheke Island N.Z. 113 E3
Waikabubak Indon. 108 B2
Waikaia r. N.Z. 113 B7
Waikari N.Z. 113 D6
Waikerie Australia 111 B7
Waikouaiti N.Z. 113 C7
Wailuku U.S.A. 127 [inset]
Waimangaroa N.Z. 113 C5
Waimarama N.Z. 113 F4
Waimate N.Z. 113 C7
Waimea U.S.A. 127 [inset]
Wainganga r. India 84 C2
Waingapu Indon. 108 C2
Wainhouse Corner U.K. 49 C8
Waini Point Guyana 143 G2
Wainwright Canada 121 I4
Wainwright U.S.A. 118 C2
Waiouru N.Z. 113 E4
Waipahi N.Z. 113 B8
Waipaoa r. N.Z. 113 F4
Waipara N.Z. 113 D6
Waipawa N.Z. 113 F4
Waipukurau N.Z. 113 F4
Wairarapa, Lake N.Z. 113 E5
Wairau r. N.Z. 113 E5
Wairoa N.Z. 113 F4
Wairoa r. N.Z. 113 F4
Waitahanui N.Z. 113 F4
Waitahuna N.Z. 113 B7
Waitakaruru N.Z. 113 E3
Waitaki r. N.Z. 113 C7
Waitangi N.Z. 107 I6
Waite River Australia 108 F5
Waiuku N.Z. 113 E3
Waiwera South N.Z. 113 B8
Waiyang China 77 H3
Wajima Japan 75 E5
Wajir Kenya 98 E3
Waka Indon. 108 C2
Wakasa-wan b. Japan 75 D6
Wakatipu, Lake N.Z. 113 B7
Wakaw Canada 121 J4
Wakayama Japan 75 D6
Wake Atoll terr. N. Pacific Ocean see Wake Island
WaKeeney U.S.A. 130 D4
Wakefield N.Z. 113 D5
Wakefield U.K. 48 F5

Wakefield MI U.S.A. 130 F2
Wakefield RI U.S.A. 135 J3
Wakefield VA U.S.A. 135 G5

▶Wake Island terr. N. Pacific Ocean 150 H4
United States Unincorporated Territory.

Wakema Myanmar 70 A3
Wakhan reg. Afgh. 89 I2
Wakkanai Japan 74 F3
Wakkerstroom S. Africa 101 J4
Wakool Australia 112 B5
Wakool r. Australia 112 A5
Wakuach, Lac l. Canada 123 I3
Waku-Kungo Angola 99 B5
Wałbrzych Poland 47 P5
Walcha Australia 112 E3
Walcott U.S.A. 126 G4
Walcourt Belgium 52 E4
Wałcz Poland 47 P4
Waldburg Range mts Australia 109 B6
Walden U.S.A. 135 H3
Waldenbuch Germany 53 J6
Waldenburg Poland see Wałbrzych
Waldkraiburg Germany 47 N6
Waldo U.S.A. 134 D3
Waldoboro U.S.A. 135 K1
Waldorf U.S.A. 135 G4
Waldport U.S.A. 126 B3
Waldron U.S.A. 131 E5
Waldron, Cape Antarctica 152 F2
Walebing Australia 109 B7
Walêg China 76 D2
Wales admin. div. U.K. 49 D6
Walgaon India 82 D5
Walgett Australia 112 D3
Walgreen Coast Antarctica 152 K1
Walhalla MI U.S.A. 134 B2
Walhalla ND U.S.A. 130 D1
Walikale Dem. Rep. Congo 97 F5
Walingai P.N.G. 69 L8
Walker r. Australia 110 A2
Walker watercourse Australia 109 F6
Walker MI U.S.A. 134 C2
Walker MN U.S.A. 130 E2
Walker r. U.S.A. 128 D2
Walker Bay S. Africa 100 D8
Walker Creek r. Australia 110 C3
Walker Lake Canada 121 L4
Walker Lake U.S.A. 128 D2
Walker Pass U.S.A. 128 D4
Walkersville U.S.A. 135 G4
Walkerton Canada 134 E1
Walkerton U.S.A. 134 B3
Wall, Mount hill Australia 108 B5
Wallaby Island Australia 110 C2
Wallace ID U.S.A. 126 D3
Wallace NC U.S.A. 133 E5
Wallace VA U.S.A. 134 D5
Wallaceburg Canada 134 D2
Wallal Downs Australia 108 C4
Wallangarra Australia 112 E2
Wallaroo Australia 111 B7
Wallasey U.K. 48 D5
Walla Walla Australia 112 C5
Walla Walla U.S.A. 126 D3
Walldürn Germany 53 J5
Wallekraal S. Africa 100 C6
Wallendbeen Australia 112 D5
Wallingford U.K. 49 F7
Wallis, Îles is Wallis and Futuna Is 107 I3

▶Wallis and Futuna Islands terr. S. Pacific Ocean 107 I3
French Overseas Collectivity.

Wallis et Futuna, Îles terr. S. Pacific Ocean see Wallis and Futuna Islands
Wallis Islands Wallis and Futuna Is see Wallis, Îles
Wallis Lake inlet Australia 112 F4
Wallops Island U.S.A. 135 H5
Wallowa Mountains U.S.A. 126 D3
Walls U.K. 50 [inset]
Walls of Jerusalem National Park Australia 111 [inset]
Wallumbilla Australia 111 E5
Walmsley Lake Canada 121 I2
Walney, Isle of i. U.K. 48 D4
Walnut Creek U.S.A. 128 B3
Walnut Grove U.S.A. 128 C2
Walnut Ridge U.S.A. 131 F4
Walong India 83 I3
Walpole U.S.A. 135 I2
Walsall U.K. 49 F6
Walsenburg U.S.A. 127 G5
Walsh U.S.A. 131 C4
Walsrode Germany 53 J2
Waltair India 84 D2
Walterboro U.S.A. 133 D5
Walters U.S.A. 131 D5
Walter's Range hills Australia 112 B2
Walthall U.S.A. 131 F5
Waltham U.S.A. 135 J2
Walton IN U.S.A. 134 B3
Walton KY U.S.A. 134 C4
Walton NY U.S.A. 135 H2
Walton WV U.S.A. 134 E4
Walvisbaai Namibia see Walvis Bay
Walvisbaai b. Namibia see Walvis Bay
Walvis Bay Namibia 100 B2
Walvis Bay b. Namibia 100 B2
Walvis Ridge sea feature S. Atlantic Ocean 148 H8
Wama Afgh. 89 H3
Wamba Équateur Dem. Rep. Congo 97 F5
Wamba Orientale Dem. Rep. Congo 98 C3
Wamba Nigeria 96 D4
Wampum U.S.A. 134 E3
Wampusirpi Hond. 137 H5
Wamsutter U.S.A. 126 G4
Wana Pak. 89 H3
Wanaaring Australia 112 B2
Wanaka N.Z. 113 B7
Wanaka, Lake N.Z. 113 B7
Wan'an China 77 G3
Wanapitei Lake Canada 122 E5
Wanbi Australia 111 C7
Wanbrow, Cape N.Z. 113 C7
Wanda Shan mts China 74 D3
Wandering River Canada 121 H4
Wandersleben Germany 53 K4
Wandlitz Germany 53 N2
Wando S. Korea 75 B6
Wandoan Australia 111 E5
Wanganui N.Z. 113 E4
Wanganui r. N.Z. 113 E4
Wangaratta Australia 112 C6
Wangcang China 76 E1
Wangda China see Zogang
Wangdain China 83 G3
Wangdi Phodrang Bhutan 83 G4
Wanggamet, Gunung mt. Indon. 108 C2
Wanggao China 77 F3
Wang Gaxun China 83 I1
Wangguan China 76 E1
Wangiwangi i. Indon. 69 G8
Wangkui China 74 B3
Wangmo China 76 E3
Wangqing China 74 C4
Wangwu Shan mts China 77 F1
Wangying China see Huaiyin
Wanham Canada 120 G4
Wan Hsa-la Myanmar 70 B2
Wanie-Rukula Dem. Rep. Congo 98 C3
Wankaner India 82 B5
Wankie Zimbabwe see Hwange
Wanlaweyn Somalia 98 E3
Wanna Germany 53 I1
Wanna Lakes salt flat Australia 109 E7
Wannian China 77 H2
Wanning China 77 F5
Wanroij Neth. 52 F3
Wanshan China 77 F3
Wanshan Qundao is China 77 G4
Wansheng China 76 E2
Wanshengchang China see Wansheng
Wantage U.K. 49 F7
Wanxian Chongqing China 77 F2
Wanxian Chongqing China see Shahe
Wanyuan China 77 F1
Wanzai China 77 G2
Wanze Belgium 52 F4
Wapakoneta U.S.A. 134 C3
Wapawekka Lake Canada 121 J4
Wapello U.S.A. 130 F3
Wapikaimaski Lake Canada 122 C4
Wapikopa Lake Canada 122 C3
Wapiti r. Canada 120 G4
Wapusk National Park Canada 121 M3
Waqên China 76 D1
Waqf aş Şawwān, Jibāl hills Jordan 85 C4
War U.S.A. 134 E5
Warab Sudan 86 C8
Warangal India 84 C2
Waranga Reservoir Australia 112 B6
Waratah Bay Australia 112 B7
Warbreccan Australia 110 C5
Warburg Germany 53 J3
Warburton Australia 109 D6
Warburton watercourse Australia 111 B5
Warburton Bay Canada 121 I2
Warche r. Belgium 52 F4
Ward, Mount N.Z. 113 B6
Warden S. Africa 101 I4
Wardenburg Germany 53 I1
Wardha India 84 C1
Wardha r. India 84 C2
Ward Hill hill U.K. 50 F2
Ward Hunt, Cape P.N.G. 69 L8
Ware Canada 120 E3
Ware U.S.A. 135 I2
Wareham U.K. 49 E8
Waremme Belgium 52 F4
Waren Germany 53 M1
Warendorf Germany 53 H3
Warginburra Peninsula Australia 110 E4
Wargla Alg. see Ouargla
Warialda Australia 112 E2
Warin Chamrap Thai. 70 D4
Warkum Neth. see Workum
Warkworth U.K. 48 F3
Warli China see Walêg
Warloy-Baillon France 52 C4
Warman Canada 121 J4
Warmbad Namibia 100 D5
Warmbad S. Africa 101 I3
Warmbaths S. Africa see Warmbad
Warminster U.K. 49 E7
Warminster U.S.A. 135 H3
Warmond Neth. 52 E2
Warm Springs NV U.S.A. 128 E2
Warm Springs VA U.S.A. 134 F4
Warmwaterberg mts S. Africa 100 E7
Warner Canada 121 H5
Warner Lakes U.S.A. 126 D4
Warner Mountains U.S.A. 126 C4
Warnes Bol. 142 F7
Warning, Mount Australia 112 F2
Waronda India 84 C2
Warora India 84 C1
Warra Australia 112 E1
Warragamba Reservoir Australia 112 E5
Warragul Australia 112 B7
Warrambool r. Australia 112 C3
Warrandirinna, Lake salt flat Australia 111 B5
Warrandyte Australia 112 B6
Warrawagine Australia 108 C5
Warrego r. Australia 112 B3
Warrego Range hills Australia 110 D5
Warren Australia 112 C3
Warren AR U.S.A. 131 E5
Warren MI U.S.A. 134 D2
Warren MN U.S.A. 130 D1
Warren OH U.S.A. 134 E3
Warren PA U.S.A. 134 F3
Warren Hastings Island Palau see Merir
Warren Island U.S.A. 120 C4
Warrenpoint U.K. 51 F3
Warrensburg MO U.S.A. 130 E4
Warrensburg NY U.S.A. 135 I2
Warrenton S. Africa 100 G5
Warrenton GA U.S.A. 133 D5
Warrenton MO U.S.A. 130 F4
Warrenton VA U.S.A. 135 G4
Warri Nigeria 96 D4
Warriners Creek watercourse Australia 111 B6
Warrington N.Z. 113 C7
Warrington U.K. 48 E5
Warrington U.S.A. 133 C6
Warrnambool Australia 111 C8
Warroad U.S.A. 130 E1
Warrumbungle National Park Australia 112 D3

▶Warsaw Poland 47 R4
Capital of Poland.

Warsaw IN U.S.A. 134 C3
Warsaw KY U.S.A. 134 C4
Warsaw MO U.S.A. 130 E4
Warsaw NY U.S.A. 135 F2
Warsaw VA U.S.A. 135 G5
Warshiikh Somalia 98 E3
Warstein Germany 53 I3
Warszawa Poland see Warsaw
Warta r. Poland 47 O4
Warwick Australia 112 F2
Warwick U.K. 49 F6
Warwick U.S.A. 135 J3
Warzhong China 76 D2
Wasaga Beach Canada 134 E1
Wasatch Range mts U.S.A. 126 F5
Wasbank S. Africa 101 J5
Wasco U.S.A. 128 D4
Washburn ND U.S.A. 130 C2
Washburn WI U.S.A. 130 F2
Washim India 84 C1

▶Washington DC U.S.A. 135 G4
Capital of the United States of America.

Washington GA U.S.A. 133 D5
Washington IA U.S.A. 130 F3
Washington IN U.S.A. 134 B4
Washington MO U.S.A. 130 F4
Washington NC U.S.A. 132 E5
Washington NJ U.S.A. 135 H3
Washington PA U.S.A. 134 E3
Washington UT U.S.A. 129 G3
Washington state U.S.A. 126 C3
Washington, Cape Antarctica 152 H2
Washington, Mount U.S.A. 135 J1
Washington Court House U.S.A. 134 D4
Washington Island U.S.A. 132 C2
Washington Land reg. Greenland 119 L2
Washir Afgh. 89 F3
Washita r. U.S.A. 131 D5
Washpool National Park Australia 112 F2
Washtucna U.S.A. 126 D3
Washuk Pak. 89 G5
Wasi India 84 B2
Wasī' Saudi Arabia 88 B5
Wasī' well Saudi Arabia 88 C6
Waskaganish Canada 122 F4
Waskagheganish Canada see Waskaganish
Waskaiowaka Lake Canada 121 L3
Waskey, Mount U.S.A. 118 C4
Wassenaar Neth. 52 E2
Wasser Namibia 100 D4
Wasserkuppe hill Germany 53 J4
Wassertrüdingen Germany 53 K5
Wassuk Range mts U.S.A. 128 D2
Wasua P.N.G. 69 K8
Wasum P.N.G. 69 L8
Waswanipi r. Canada 122 F4
Waswanipi, Lac l. Canada 122 F4
Watam P.N.G. 69 K7
Watampone Indon. 69 G7
Watapi Lake Canada 121 I4
Watarrka National Park Australia 109 E6
Watenstadt-Salzgitter Germany see Salzgitter
Waterbury CT U.S.A. 135 I3
Waterbury VT U.S.A. 135 I1
Waterbury Lake Canada 121 J3
Water Cays i. Bahamas 133 E8
Waterdown Canada 134 F2
Wateree r. U.S.A. 133 D5
Waterfall U.S.A. 120 C4
Waterford Ireland 51 E5
Waterford PA U.S.A. 134 F3
Waterford WI U.S.A. 134 A2
Waterford Harbour Ireland 51 F5
Watergrasshill Ireland 51 D5
Waterhen Lake Canada 121 L4
Waterloo Australia 108 E4
Waterloo Belgium 52 E4
Waterloo Ont. Canada 134 E2
Waterloo Que. Canada 135 I1
Waterloo IA U.S.A. 130 E3
Waterloo IL U.S.A. 130 F4
Waterloo NY U.S.A. 135 G2
Waterlooville U.K. 49 F8
Waterton Lakes National Park Canada 120 H5
Watertown NY U.S.A. 135 H2
Watertown SD U.S.A. 130 D2
Watertown WI U.S.A. 130 F3
Waterval Boven S. Africa 101 J3
Water Valley U.S.A. 131 F5
Waterville ME U.S.A. 135 K1
Waterville WA U.S.A. 126 C3
Watford Canada 134 E2
Watford U.K. 49 G7
Watford City U.S.A. 130 C2
Wathaman r. Canada 121 K3
Wathaman Lake Canada 121 K3
Watheroo National Park Australia 109 A7
Wathlingen Germany 53 K2
Watino Canada 120 G4
Watīr, Wādī watercourse Egypt 85 B5
Watkins Glen U.S.A. 135 G2
Watling Island Bahamas see San Salvador
Watmuri Indon. 108 E1
Watonga U.S.A. 131 D5
Watrous Canada 121 J5
Watrous U.S.A. 127 G6
Watseka U.S.A. 134 B3
Watsi Kengo Dem. Rep. Congo 97 F5
Watson r. Australia 110 C2
Watson Canada 121 J4
Watson Lake Canada 120 D2
Watsontown U.S.A. 135 G3
Watsonville U.S.A. 128 C3
Watten U.K. 50 F2
Watterson Lake Canada 121 L2
Watton U.K. 49 H6
Watts Bar Lake resr U.S.A. 132 C5
Wattsburg U.S.A. 134 F2
Watubela, Kepulauan is Indon. 69 I7
Wau P.N.G. 69 L8
Wau Sudan 86 C8
Waubay Lake U.S.A. 130 D2
Wauchope N.S.W. Australia 112 F3
Wauchope N.T. Australia 108 F5
Waukaringa (abandoned) Australia 111 B7
Waukarlycarly, Lake salt flat Australia 108 C5
Waukegan U.S.A. 134 B2
Waukesha U.S.A. 134 A2
Waupaca U.S.A. 130 F2
Waupun U.S.A. 130 F3
Waurika U.S.A. 131 D5
Wausau U.S.A. 130 F2
Wausaukee U.S.A. 132 C2
Wauseon U.S.A. 134 C3
Wautoma U.S.A. 130 F2
Wave Hill Australia 108 E4
Waveney r. U.K. 49 I6
Waverly IA U.S.A. 130 E3
Waverly NY U.S.A. 135 G2
Waverly OH U.S.A. 134 D4
Waverly TN U.S.A. 132 C4
Waverly VA U.S.A. 135 G5
Wavre Belgium 52 E4
Waw Myanmar 70 B3
Wawa Canada 122 D5
Wawalalindu Indon. 69 G7
Wāw al Kabīr Libya 97 E2
Wawasee, Lake U.S.A. 134 C3
Wawo Indon. 69 G7
Waxahachie U.S.A. 131 D5
Waxü China 76 D1
Waxxari China 80 G4
Way, Lake salt flat Australia 109 C6
Waycross U.S.A. 133 D6
Wayland KY U.S.A. 134 D5
Wayland MI U.S.A. 134 C2
Wayne NE U.S.A. 130 D3
Wayne WV U.S.A. 134 D4
Waynesboro GA U.S.A. 133 D5
Waynesboro MS U.S.A. 131 F6
Waynesboro TN U.S.A. 132 C5
Waynesboro VA U.S.A. 135 F4
Waynesburg U.S.A. 134 E4
Waynesville MO U.S.A. 130 E4
Waynesville NC U.S.A. 132 D5
Waynoka U.S.A. 131 D4
Waza, Parc National de nat. park Cameroon 97 E3
Wāzah Khwāh Afgh. see Wazi Khwa
Wazi Khwa Afgh. 89 H3
Wazirabad Pak. 89 I3
W du Niger, Parcs Nationaux du nat. park Niger 96 D3
We, Pulau i. Indon. 71 A6
Weagamow Lake Canada 121 N4
Weam P.N.G. 69 K8
Wear r. U.K. 48 F4
Weare U.S.A. 135 J2
Weatherford U.S.A. 131 D5
Weaver Lake Canada 121 L4
Weaverville U.S.A. 126 C4
Webb, Mount hill Australia 108 E5
Webequie Canada 122 D3
Weber, Mount Canada 120 D4
Weber Basin sea feature Laut Banda 150 E6
Webster IN U.S.A. 134 C4
Webster MA U.S.A. 135 J2
Webster SD U.S.A. 130 D2
Webster City U.S.A. 130 E3
Webster Springs U.S.A. 134 E4
Wecho Lake Canada 120 H2
Wedau P.N.G. 110 E1
Weddell Abyssal Plain sea feature Southern Ocean 152 A2
Weddell Island Falkland Is 144 D8
Weddell Sea Antarctica 152 A2
Wedderburn Australia 112 A6
Weddin Mountains National Park Australia 112 D4
Wedel (Holstein) Germany 53 J1
Wedge Mountain Canada 120 F5
Wedowee U.S.A. 133 C5
Weedville U.S.A. 135 F3
Weenen S. Africa 101 J5
Weener Germany 53 H1
Weert Neth. 52 F3
Weethalle Australia 112 C4
Wee Waa Australia 112 D3
Wegberg Germany 52 G3
Węgorzewo Poland 47 R3
Weichang China 73 L4
Weida Germany 53 M4
Weidenberg Germany 53 L5
Weiden in der Oberpfalz Germany 53 M5
Weidongmen China see Qianjin
Weifang China 73 L5
Weihai China 73 M5
Wei He r. Shaanxi China 76 F1
Wei He r. China 77 G1
Weilburg Germany 53 I4
Weilmoringle Australia 112 C2
Weimar Germany 53 L4
Weinan China 77 F1
Weinheim Germany 53 I5
Weining China 76 E3
Weinsberg Germany 53 J5
Weipa Australia 110 C2
Weiqu China see Chang'an
Weir r. Australia 112 D2
Weir River Canada 121 M3
Weirton U.S.A. 134 E3
Weiser U.S.A. 126 D3
Weishan China 76 D3
Weishan Hu l. China 77 H1
Weishi China 77 G1
Weiße Elster r. Germany 53 L3
Weißenburg in Bayern Germany 53 K5
Weißenfels Germany 53 L3
Weißkugel mt. Austria/Italy 47 M7
Weissrand Mountains Namibia 100 D3
Weiterstadt Germany 53 I5
Weitzel Lake Canada 121 J3
Weixi China 76 C3
Weixin China 76 E3
Weiya China 80 H3
Weiyuan Gansu China 76 E1
Weiyuan Sichuan China 76 E2
Weiyuan Yunnan China see Jinggu
Weiyuan Jiang r. China 76 D4
Weiz Austria 47 O7
Weizhou China see Wenchuan
Weizhou Dao i. China 77 F4
Wejherowo Poland 47 Q3
Wekilbazar Turkm. 89 F2
Wekusko Canada 121 L4
Wekusko Lake Canada 121 L4
Wekweêtì Canada 120 H1
Welatam Myanmar 70 B1
Welbourn Hill Australia 109 F6
Welch U.S.A. 134 E5
Weld U.S.A. 135 J1
Weldiya Eth. 98 D2
Welford National Park Australia 110 C5
Welk'ītē Eth. 98 D3
Welkom S. Africa 101 H4
Welland Canada 134 F2
Welland r. U.K. 49 G6
Welland Canal Canada 134 F2
Wellesley Canada 134 E2
Wellesley Islands Australia 110 B3
Wellesley Lake Canada 120 B2
Wellfleet U.S.A. 135 J3
Wellin Belgium 52 F4
Wellingborough U.K. 49 G6
Wellington Australia 112 D4
Wellington Canada 135 G2

▶Wellington N.Z. 113 E5
Capital of New Zealand.

Wellington S. Africa 100 D7
Wellington England U.K. 49 D8
Wellington England U.K. 49 E6
Wellington CO U.S.A. 126 G4
Wellington IL U.S.A. 134 B3
Wellington KS U.S.A. 131 D4
Wellington NV U.S.A. 128 D2
Wellington OH U.S.A. 134 D3
Wellington TX U.S.A. 131 C5
Wellington UT U.S.A. 129 H2
Wellington, Isla i. Chile 144 B7
Wellington Range hills N.T. Australia 108 F3
Wellington Range hills W.A. Australia 109 C6
Wells Canada 120 F4
Wells U.K. 49 E7
Wells U.S.A. 126 E4
Wells, Lake salt flat Australia 109 C6
Wellsboro U.S.A. 135 G3
Wellsburg U.S.A. 134 E3
Wellsford N.Z. 113 E3
Wells-next-the-Sea U.K. 49 H6
Wellston U.S.A. 134 C1
Wellsville U.S.A. 135 G2
Wellton U.S.A. 129 F5
Wels Austria 47 O6
Welshpool U.K. 49 D6
Welsickendorf Germany 53 N3
Welwitschia Namibia see Khorixas
Welwyn Garden City U.K. 49 G7
Welzheim Germany 53 J6
Wem U.K. 49 E6
Wembesi S. Africa 101 I5
Wembley Canada 120 G4
Wemindji Canada 122 F3
Wenatchee U.S.A. 126 C3
Wenatchee Mountains U.S.A. 126 C3
Wenbu China see Nyima
Wenchang Hainan China 77 F5
Wenchang Sichuan China see Zitong
Wenchow China see Wenzhou
Wenchuan China 76 D2
Wendelstein Germany 53 L5
Wenden Germany 53 H4
Wenden Latvia see Cēsis
Wenden U.S.A. 129 G5
Wendover U.S.A. 129 F1
Weng'an China 76 E3
Wengshui China 76 C2
Wengyuan China 77 G3
Wenhua China see Weishan
Wenlan China see Mengzi
Wenling China 77 I2
Wenlock r. Australia 110 C2
Wenping China see Ludian
Wenquan Guizhou China 76 E2
Wenquan Henan China see Wenxian
Wenquan Hubei China see Yingshan

▶Wenquan Qinghai China 83 G2
Highest settlement in the world.

Wenquan Xinjiang China 80 F3
Wenshan China 76 E4
Wenshui China 76 E2
Wensum r. U.K. 49 I6
Wentorf bei Hamburg Germany 53 K1
Wentworth Australia 111 C7
Wenxi China 77 F1
Wenxian Gansu China 76 E1
Wenxian Henan China 77 G1
Wenxing China see Xiangyin
Wenzhou China 77 I3
Wenzlow Germany 53 M2
Wepener S. Africa 101 H5
Wer India 82 D4
Werben (Elbe) Germany 53 L2
Werda Botswana 100 F3
Werdau Germany 53 M4
Werdër Eth. 98 E3
Werder Germany 53 M2
Werdohl Germany 53 H3
Werl Germany 53 H3
Wernberg-Köblitz Germany 53 M5
Werne Germany 53 H3
Wernecke Mountains Canada 120 B1
Wernigerode Germany 53 K3
Werra r. Germany 53 J3
Werris Creek Australia 112 E3
Wertheim Germany 53 J5
Wervik Belgium 52 D4
Wesel Germany 52 G3
Wesel-Datteln-Kanal canal Germany 52 G3
Wesenberg Germany 53 M1
Wesendorf Germany 53 K2
Weser r. Germany 53 I1
Weser sea chan. Germany 53 I1
Wesergebirge hills Germany 53 I2
Weslaco U.S.A. 131 D7
Weslemkoon Lake Canada 135 G1
Wesleyville Canada 123 L4
Wessel, Cape Australia 110 B1
Wessel Islands Australia 110 B1
Wesselsbron S. Africa 101 H4
Wesselton S. Africa 101 I4
Wessington Springs U.S.A. 130 D2
Westall, Point Australia 109 F8
West Allis U.S.A. 134 A2
West Antarctica reg. Antarctica 152 J1
West Australian Basin sea feature Indian Ocean 149 O7

▶West Bank terr. Asia 85 B3
Territory occupied by Israel.

West Bay Canada 123 K3
West Bay inlet U.S.A. 133 C6
West Bend U.S.A. 134 A2
West Bengal state India 83 F5
West Branch U.S.A. 134 C1
West Bromwich U.K. 49 F6
Westbrook U.S.A. 135 J2
West Burke U.S.A. 135 J1
West Burra i. U.K. see Burra
Westbury U.K. 49 E7
West Caicos i. Turks and Caicos Is 133 F8
West Cape Howe Australia 109 B8
West Caroline Basin sea feature N. Pacific Ocean 150 F5
West Chester U.S.A. 135 H4
Westcliffe U.S.A. 127 G5
West Coast National Park S. Africa 100 D7
West End Bahamas 133 E7
Westerburg Germany 53 H4
Westerholt Germany 53 H1
Westerland Germany 47 L3
Westerlo Belgium 52 E3
Westerly U.S.A. 135 J3
Western r. Canada 121 J1
Western Australia state Australia 109 C6
Western Cape prov. S. Africa 100 E7
Western Desert Egypt 90 C6
Western Dvina r. Europe see Zapadnaya Dvina
Western Ghats mts India 84 B3
Western Port b. Australia 112 B7

▶Western Sahara terr. Africa 96 B2
Disputed territory (Morocco).

Western Samoa country S. Pacific Ocean see Samoa
Western Sayan Mountains reg. Rus. Fed. see Zapadnyy Sayan
Westerschelde est. Neth. 52 D3
Westerstede Germany 53 H1
Westerville U.S.A. 134 D3
Westerwald hills Germany 53 H4
West Falkland i. Falkland Is 144 D8
West Fargo U.S.A. 130 D2
West Fayu atoll Micronesia 69 L5
Westfield IN U.S.A. 134 B3
Westfield MA U.S.A. 135 I2
Westfield NY U.S.A. 134 F2
Westfield PA U.S.A. 135 G3
West Frisian Islands Neth. see Waddeneilanden
Westgat sea chan. Neth. 52 G1
Westgate Australia 112 C1
West Glacier U.S.A. 126 E2
West Grand Lake U.S.A. 132 H2
West Hartford U.S.A. 135 I3
Westhausen Germany 53 K6
West Haven U.S.A. 135 I3
Westhill U.K. 50 G3
Westhope U.S.A. 130 C1
West Ice Shelf Antarctica 152 E2
West Indies is Caribbean Sea 137 J4
West Island India 71 A4
Westkapelle Neth. 52 D3
West Kazakhstan Oblast admin. div. Kazakh. see Zapadnyy Kazakhstan
West Kingston U.S.A. 135 J3
West Lafayette U.S.A. 134 B3
West Lamma Channel H.K. China 77 [inset]
Westland Australia 110 C4
Westland National Park N.Z. 113 C6
Westleigh S. Africa 101 H4
Westleton U.K. 49 I6
West Liberty U.S.A. 134 D5
West Linton U.K. 50 F5
West Loch Roag b. U.K. 50 C2
Westlock Canada 120 H4
West Lorne Canada 134 E2
West Lunga National Park Zambia 99 C5
West MacDonnell National Park Australia 109 F5
West Malaysia pen. Malaysia see Peninsular Malaysia
Westmalle Belgium 52 E3
Westmar Australia 112 D1
West Mariana Basin sea feature N. Pacific Ocean 150 F4
West Memphis U.S.A. 131 F5
Westminster U.S.A. 135 G4
Westmoreland Australia 110 B3
Westmoreland U.S.A. 134 B5
Westmorland U.S.A. 129 F5
Weston OH U.S.A. 134 D3
Weston WV U.S.A. 134 E4
Weston-super-Mare U.K. 49 E7
West Palm Beach U.S.A. 133 D7
West Plains U.S.A. 131 F4
West Point pt Australia 111 [inset]
West Point CA U.S.A. 128 C2
West Point KY U.S.A. 134 C5
West Point MS U.S.A. 131 F5
West Point NE U.S.A. 130 D3
West Point VA U.S.A. 135 G5
West Point Lake resr U.S.A. 133 C5
Westport Canada 135 G1
Westport Ireland 51 C4
Westport N.Z. 113 C5
Westport CA U.S.A. 128 B2
Westport KY U.S.A. 134 C4
Westport NY U.S.A. 135 I1
Westray Canada 121 K4

Westray i. U.K. 50 F1
Westray Firth sea chan. U.K. 50 F1
Westree Canada 122 E5
West Rutland U.S.A. 135 I2
West Salem U.S.A. 134 D3
West Siberian Plain Rus. Fed. 64 J3
West-Skylge Neth. see West-Terschelling
West Stewartstown U.S.A. 135 J1
West-Terschelling Neth. 52 F1
West Topsham U.S.A. 135 I1
West Union IA U.S.A. 130 F3
West Union IL U.S.A. 134 B4
West Union OH U.S.A. 134 D4
West Union WV U.S.A. 134 E4
West Valley City U.S.A. 129 H1
Westville U.S.A. 134 B3
West Virginia state U.S.A. 134 E4
Westwood U.S.A. 128 C1
West Wyalong Australia 112 C4
West York U.S.A. 135 G4
Westzaan Neth. 52 E2
Wetar i. Indon. 108 D1
Wetar, Selat sea chan. Indon. 108 D2
Wetaskiwin Canada 120 H4
Wete Tanz. 99 D4
Wetter r. Germany 53 I4
Wettin Germany 53 L3
Wetumpka U.S.A. 133 C5
Wetwun Myanmar 70 B2
Wetzlar Germany 53 I4
Wewahitchka U.S.A. 133 C6
Wewak P.N.G. 69 K7
Wewoka U.S.A. 131 D5
Wexford Ireland 51 F5
Wexford Harbour b. Ireland 51 F5
Weyakwin Canada 121 J4
Weybridge U.K. 49 G7
Weyburn Canada 121 K5
Weyhe Germany 53 I2
Weymouth U.K. 49 E8
Weymouth U.S.A. 135 J2
Wezep Neth. 52 G2
Whakaari i. N.Z. 113 F3
Whakatane N.Z. 113 F3
Whalan Creek r. Australia 112 D2
Whale r. Canada see La Baleine, Rivière à
Whalsay i. U.K. 50 [inset]
Whampoa China see Huangpu
Whangamata N.Z. 113 E3
Whanganui National Park N.Z. 113 E4
Whangarei N.Z. 113 E2
Whapmagoostui Canada 122 F3
Wharfe r. U.K. 48 F5
Wharfedale valley U.K. 48 F4
Wharton U.S.A. 131 D6
Wharton Lake Canada 121 L1
Whatî Canada 120 G2
Wheatland IN U.S.A. 134 B4
Wheatland WY U.S.A. 126 G4
Wheaton IL U.S.A. 134 A3
Wheaton MN U.S.A. 130 D2
Wheaton-Glenmont U.S.A. 135 G4
Wheeler U.S.A. 131 C5
Wheeler Lake Canada 120 H2
Wheeler Lake resr U.S.A. 133 C5
Wheeler Peak NM U.S.A. 127 G5
Wheeler Peak NV U.S.A. 129 F2
Wheelersburg U.S.A. 134 D4
Wheeling U.S.A. 134 E3
Whernside hill U.K. 48 E4
Whinham, Mount Australia 109 E6
Whiskey Jack Lake Canada 121 K3
Whitburn U.K. 50 F5
Whitby Canada 135 F2
Whitby U.K. 48 G4
Whitchurch U.K. 49 E6
Whitchurch-Stouffville Canada 134 F2
White r. Canada 122 D4
White r. Canada/U.S.A. 120 B2
White r. AR U.S.A. 125 I5
White r. AR U.S.A. 131 F5
White r. CO U.S.A. 129 I1
White r. IN U.S.A. 134 B4
White r. MI U.S.A. 134 B2
White r. NV U.S.A. 129 F3
White r. SD U.S.A. 130 D3
White r. VT U.S.A. 135 I2
White watercourse U.S.A. 129 H5
White, Lake salt flat Australia 108 E5
White Bay Canada 123 K4
White Butte mt. U.S.A. 130 C2
White Canyon U.S.A. 129 H3
White Cloud U.S.A. 134 C2
Whitecourt Canada 120 H4
Whiteface Mountain U.S.A. 135 I1
Whitefield U.S.A. 135 J1
Whitefish r. Canada 120 E1
Whitefish U.S.A. 126 E2
Whitefish Bay U.S.A. 134 B1
Whitefish Lake Canada 121 J2
Whitefish Point U.S.A. 132 C2
Whitehall Ireland 51 E5
Whitehall U.K. 50 G1
Whitehall NY U.S.A. 135 I2
Whitehall WI U.S.A. 130 F2
Whitehaven U.K. 48 D4
Whitehead U.K. 51 G3
White Hill hill Canada 123 J5
Whitehill U.K. 49 G7

▶Whitehorse Canada 120 C2
Capital of Yukon Territory.

White Horse U.S.A. 129 J4
White Horse, Vale of valley U.K. 49 F7
White Horse Pass U.S.A. 129 F1
White House U.S.A. 134 B5
White Island Antarctica 152 D2
White Island N.Z. see Whakaari
White Lake Ont. Canada 122 D4
White Lake Ont. Canada 135 G1
White Lake LA U.S.A. 131 E6
White Lake MI U.S.A. 134 B2
Whitemark Australia 111 [inset]
White Mountain Peak U.S.A. 128 D3
White Mountains U.S.A. 135 J1
White Mountains National Park Australia 110 D4
Whitemouth Lake Canada 121 M5
Whitemud r. Canada 120 G3
White Nile r. Sudan/Uganda 86 D6
also known as Bahr el Abiad or Bahr el Jebel
White Nossob watercourse Namibia 100 D2
White Oak U.S.A. 134 D5
White Otter Lake Canada 121 N5
White Pass Canada/U.S.A. 120 C3
White Pine Range mts U.S.A. 129 F2
White Plains U.S.A. 135 I3
White River Canada 122 D4
Whiteriver U.S.A. 129 I5
White River U.S.A. 130 C3
White River Valley U.S.A. 129 F2
White Rock Peak U.S.A. 129 F2
White Russia country Europe see Belarus
Whitesail Lake Canada 120 E4
White Salmon U.S.A. 126 C3
Whitesand r. Canada 120 H2
White Sands National Monument nat. park U.S.A. 127 G6
Whitesburg U.S.A. 134 D5
White Sea Rus. Fed. 42 H2
White Stone U.S.A. 135 G5
White Sulphur Springs MT U.S.A. 126 F3
White Sulphur Springs WV U.S.A. 134 E5
Whitesville U.S.A. 134 E5
Whiteville U.S.A. 133 E5
White Volta r. Burkina/Ghana 96 C4
also known as Nakambé or Nakanbe or Volta Blanche
Whitewater U.S.A. 129 I2
Whitewater Baldy mt. U.S.A. 129 I5
Whitewater Lake Canada 122 C4
Whitewood Australia 110 C4
Whitewood Canada 121 K5
Whitfield U.K. 49 I7
Whithorn U.K. 50 E6
Whitianga N.Z. 113 E3
Whitland U.K. 49 C7
Whitley Bay U.K. 48 F3
Whitmore Mountains Antarctica 152 K1
Whitney Canada 135 F1
Whitney, Mount U.S.A. 128 D3
Whitney Point U.S.A. 135 H2
Whitstable U.K. 49 I7
Whitsunday Group is Australia 110 E4
Whitsunday Island National Park Australia 110 E4
Whitsun Island Vanuatu see Pentecost Island
Whittemore U.S.A. 134 D1
Whittlesea Australia 112 B6
Whittlesey U.K. 49 G6
Whitton Australia 112 C5
Wholdaia Lake Canada 121 J2
Why U.S.A. 129 G5
Whyalla Australia 111 B7
Wiang Sa Thai. 70 C3
Wiarton Canada 134 E1
Wibaux U.S.A. 126 G3
Wichelen Belgium 52 D3
Wichita U.S.A. 130 D4
Wichita r. U.S.A. 131 D5
Wichita Falls U.S.A. 131 D5
Wichita Mountains U.S.A. 131 D5
Wick U.K. 50 F2
Wick r. U.K. 50 F2
Wickenburg U.S.A. 129 G5
Wickes U.S.A. 131 E5
Wickford U.K. 49 H7
Wickham r. Australia 108 E4
Wickham, Cape Australia 111 [inset]
Wickham, Mount hill Australia 108 E4
Wickliffe U.S.A. 131 F4
Wicklow Ireland 51 F5
Wicklow Head hd Ireland 51 G5
Wicklow Mountains Ireland 51 F5
Wicklow Mountains National Park Ireland 51 F4
Widerøe, Mount Antarctica 152 C2
Widerøefjellet mt. Antarctica see Widerøe, Mount
Widgeegoara watercourse Australia 112 B1
Widgiemooltha Australia 109 C7
Widnes U.K. 48 E5
Wi-do i. S. Korea 75 B6
Wied r. Germany 53 H4
Wiehengebirge hills Germany 53 I2
Wiehl Germany 53 H4
Wielkopolskie, Pojezierze reg. Poland 47 O4
Wielkopolski Park Narodowy nat. park Poland 47 P4
Wieluń Poland 47 Q5
Wien Austria see Vienna
Wiener Neustadt Austria 47 P7
Wierden Neth. 52 G2
Wieren Germany 53 K2
Wieringerwerf Neth. 52 F2
Wiesbaden Germany 53 I4
Wiesenfelden Germany 53 M5
Wiesentheid Germany 53 K5
Wiesloch Germany 53 I5
Wiesmoor Germany 53 H1
Wietze Germany 53 J2
Wietzendorf Germany 53 J2
Wieżyca hill Poland 47 Q3
Wigan U.K. 48 E5
Wiggins U.S.A. 131 F6
Wight, Isle of i. England U.K. 49 F8
Wigierski Park Narodowy nat. park Poland 45 M9
Wignes Lake Canada 121 J2
Wigston U.K. 49 F6
Wigton U.K. 48 D4
Wigtown U.K. 50 E6
Wigtown Bay U.K. 50 E6
Wijchen Neth. 52 F3
Wijhe Neth. 52 G2
Wilberforce, Cape Australia 110 B1
Wilbur U.S.A. 126 D3
Wilburton U.S.A. 131 E5
Wilcannia Australia 112 A3
Wilcox U.S.A. 135 F3
Wilczek Land i. Rus. Fed. see Vil'cheka, Zemlya
Wildberg Germany 53 M2
Wildcat Peak U.S.A. 128 E2
Wild Coast S. Africa 101 I6
Wilderness National Park S. Africa 100 F8
Wildeshausen Germany 53 I2
Wild Horse Hill mt. U.S.A. 130 C3
Wildspitze mt. Austria 47 M7
Wildwood FL U.S.A. 133 D6
Wildwood NJ U.S.A. 135 H4
Wilge r. S. Africa 101 I4
Wilge r. S. Africa 101 I3
Wilgena Australia 109 F7

▶Wilhelm, Mount P.N.G. 69 L8
5th highest mountain in Oceania.

Wilhelm II Land reg. Antarctica see Kaiser Wilhelm II Land
Wilhelmina Gebergte mts Suriname 143 G3
Wilhelmina Kanaal canal Neth. 52 F3
Wilhelmshaven Germany 53 I1
Wilhelmstal Namibia 100 C1
Wilkes-Barre U.S.A. 135 H3
Wilkesboro U.S.A. 132 D4
Wilkes Coast Antarctica 152 G2
Wilkes Land reg. Antarctica 152 G2
Wilkie Canada 121 I4
Wilkins Coast Antarctica 152 L2
Wilkins Ice Shelf Antarctica 152 L2
Wilkinson Lakes salt flat Australia 109 F7
Will, Mount Canada 120 D3
Willand U.K. 49 D8
Willandra Billabong watercourse Australia 112 B4
Willandra National Park Australia 112 B4
Willapa Bay U.S.A. 126 B3
Willard Mex. 127 F7
Willard NM U.S.A. 127 G6
Willard OH U.S.A. 134 D3
Willcox U.S.A. 129 I5
Willcox Playa salt flat U.S.A. 129 I5
Willebadessen Germany 53 J3
Willebroek Belgium 52 E3

▶Willemstad Neth. Antilles 137 K6
Capital of the Netherlands Antilles.

Willeroo Australia 108 E3
Willette U.S.A. 134 C5
William, Mount Australia 111 C8
William Creek Australia 111 B6
William Lake Canada 121 L4
Williams AZ U.S.A. 129 G4
Williams CA U.S.A. 128 B2
Williamsburg KY U.S.A. 134 C5
Williamsburg OH U.S.A. 134 C4
Williamsburg VA U.S.A. 135 G5
Williams Lake Canada 120 F4
William Smith, Cap c. Canada 123 I1
Williamson NY U.S.A. 135 G2
Williamson WV U.S.A. 134 D5
Williamsport IN U.S.A. 134 B3
Williamsport PA U.S.A. 135 G3
Williamston U.S.A. 132 E5
Williamstown KY U.S.A. 134 C4
Williamstown NJ U.S.A. 135 H4
Willimantic U.S.A. 135 I3
Willis Group atolls Australia 110 E3
Williston S. Africa 100 E6
Williston ND U.S.A. 130 C1
Williston SC U.S.A. 133 D5
Williston Lake Canada 120 F4
Williton U.K. 49 D7
Willits U.S.A. 128 B2
Willmar U.S.A. 130 E2
Willoughby, Lake U.S.A. 135 I1
Willow Beach U.S.A. 129 F4
Willow Bunch Canada 121 J5
Willow Hill U.S.A. 135 G3
Willow Lake Canada 120 G2
Willowlake r. Canada 120 F2
Willowmore S. Africa 100 F7
Willowra Australia 108 F5
Willows U.S.A. 128 B2
Willow Springs U.S.A. 131 F4
Willowvale S. Africa 101 I7
Wills, Lake salt flat Australia 108 E5
Wilma U.S.A. 133 C6
Wilmington DE U.S.A. 135 H4
Wilmington NC U.S.A. 133 E5
Wilmington OH U.S.A. 134 D4
Wilmore U.S.A. 134 C5
Wilmslow U.K. 48 E5
Wilno Lith. see Vilnius
Wilnsdorf Germany 53 I4
Wilpattu National Park Sri Lanka 84 D4
Wilseder Berg hill Germany 53 J1
Wilson watercourse Australia 111 C5
Wilson atoll Micronesia see Ifalik
Wilson KS U.S.A. 130 D4
Wilson NC U.S.A. 132 E5
Wilson NY U.S.A. 135 F2
Wilson, Mount CO U.S.A. 129 J3
Wilson, Mount NV U.S.A. 129 F2
Wilson, Mount OR U.S.A. 126 C3
Wilsonia U.S.A. 128 D3
Wilson's Promontory pen. Australia 112 C7
Wilson's Promontory National Park Australia 112 C7
Wilsum Germany 52 G2
Wilton r. Australia 108 F3
Wilton U.S.A. 135 J1
Wiltz Lux. 52 F5
Wiluna Australia 109 C6
Wimereux France 52 B4
Wina r. Cameroon see Vina
Winamac U.S.A. 134 B3
Winbin watercourse Australia 111 D5
Winburg S. Africa 101 H5
Wincanton U.K. 49 E7
Winchester Canada 135 H1
Winchester U.K. 49 F7
Winchester IN U.S.A. 134 C3
Winchester KY U.S.A. 134 C5
Winchester NH U.S.A. 135 I2
Winchester TN U.S.A. 133 C5
Winchester VA U.S.A. 135 F4
Wind r. Canada 120 C1
Wind r. U.S.A. 126 F4
Windau Latvia see Ventspils
Windber U.S.A. 135 F3
Wind Cave National Park U.S.A. 130 C3
Windermere U.K. 48 E4
Windermere l. U.K. 48 E4
Windham U.S.A. 120 C3

▶Windhoek Namibia 100 C2
Capital of Namibia.

Windigo Lake Canada 121 N4
Windlestraw Law hill U.K. 50 G5
Wind Mountain U.S.A. 127 G6
Windom U.S.A. 130 E3
Windom Peak U.S.A. 129 J3
Windorah Australia 110 C5
Window Rock U.S.A. 129 I4
Wind Point U.S.A. 134 B2
Wind River Range mts U.S.A. 126 F4
Windrush r. U.K. 49 F7
Windsbach Germany 53 K5
Windsor Australia 112 E4
Windsor N.S. Canada 123 I5
Windsor Ont. Canada 134 D2
Windsor U.K. 49 G7
Windsor NC U.S.A. 132 E4
Windsor NY U.S.A. 135 H2
Windsor VA U.S.A. 135 G5
Windsor VT U.S.A. 135 I2
Windsor Locks U.S.A. 135 I3
Windward Islands Caribbean Sea 137 L5
Windward Passage Cuba/Haiti 137 J5
Windy U.S.A. 118 D3
Winefred Lake Canada 121 I4
Winfield KS U.S.A. 131 D4
Winfield WV U.S.A. 134 E4
Wingate U.K. 48 F4
Wingen Australia 112 E3
Wingene Belgium 52 D3
Wingen-sur-Moder France 53 H6
Wingham Australia 112 F3
Wingham Canada 134 E2
Winisk r. Canada 122 D3
Winisk (abandoned) Canada 122 D3
Winisk Lake Canada 122 D3
Winkana Myanmar 70 B4
Winkelman U.S.A. 129 H5
Winkler Canada 121 L5
Winlock U.S.A. 126 C3
Winneba Ghana 96 C4
Winnebago, Lake U.S.A. 134 A1
Winnecke Creek watercourse Australia 108 E4
Winnemucca U.S.A. 128 E1
Winnemucca Lake U.S.A. 128 D1
Winner U.S.A. 130 C3
Winnett U.S.A. 126 F3
Winnfield U.S.A. 131 E6
Winnibigoshish, Lake U.S.A. 130 E2
Winnie U.S.A. 131 E6
Winning Australia 109 A5

▶Winnipeg Canada 121 L5
Capital of Manitoba.

Winnipeg r. Canada 121 L5
Winnipeg, Lake Canada 121 L5
Winnipegosis Canada 121 L5
Winnipegosis, Lake Canada 121 K4
Winnipesaukee, Lake U.S.A. 135 J2
Winona AZ U.S.A. 129 H4
Winona MN U.S.A. 130 F2
Winona MO U.S.A. 131 F4
Winona MS U.S.A. 131 F5
Winschoten Neth. 52 H1
Winsen (Aller) Germany 53 J2
Winsen (Luhe) Germany 53 K1
Winsford U.K. 48 E5
Winslow AZ U.S.A. 129 H4
Winslow ME U.S.A. 135 K1
Winsop, Tanjung pt Indon. 69 I7
Winsted U.S.A. 135 I3
Winston-Salem U.S.A. 132 D4
Winterberg Germany 53 I3
Winter Haven U.S.A. 133 D6
Winters CA U.S.A. 128 C2
Winters TX U.S.A. 131 D6
Wintersville U.S.A. 134 E3
Winterswijk Neth. 52 G3
Winterthur Switz. 56 I3
Winterton S. Africa 101 I5
Winthrop U.S.A. 135 K1
Winton Australia 110 C4
Winton N.Z. 113 B8
Winton U.S.A. 132 E4
Winwick U.K. 49 G6
Wirral pen. U.K. 48 D5
Wirrulla Australia 111 A7
Wisbech U.K. 49 H6
Wiscasset U.S.A. 135 K1
Wisconsin r. U.S.A. 130 F3
Wisconsin state U.S.A. 134 A1
Wisconsin Rapids U.S.A. 130 F2
Wise U.S.A. 134 D5
Wiseman U.S.A. 118 C3
Wishaw U.K. 50 F5
Wisher U.S.A. 130 D2
Wisil Dabarow Somalia 98 E3
Wisła r. Poland see Vistula
Wismar Germany 47 M4
Wistaria Canada 120 E4
Witbank S. Africa 101 I3
Witbooisvlei Namibia 100 D3
Witham U.K. 49 H7
Witham r. U.K. 49 H6
Witherbee U.S.A. 135 I1
Withernsea U.K. 48 H5
Witjira National Park Australia 111 A5
Witmarsum Neth. 52 F1
Witney U.K. 49 F7
Witrivier S. Africa 101 J3
Witry-lès-Reims France 52 E5
Witteberg mts S. Africa 101 H6
Wittenberg Germany see Lutherstadt Wittenberg
Wittenberge Germany 53 L2
Wittenburg Germany 53 L1
Wittingen Germany 53 K2
Wittlich Germany 52 G5
Wittmund Germany 53 H1
Wittstock Germany 53 M1
Witu Islands P.N.G. 69 L7
Witvlei Namibia 100 D2
Witzenhausen Germany 53 J3
Wivenhoe, Lake Australia 112 F1
Władysławowo Poland 47 Q3
Włocławek Poland 47 Q4
Wobkent Uzbek. see Vobkent
Wodonga Australia 112 C6
Wœrth France 53 H6
Wohlthat Mountains Antarctica 152 C2
Woippy France 52 G5
Wōjjā atoll Marshall Is see Wotje
Wokam i. Indon. 69 I8
Woken He r. China 74 C3
Wokha India 83 H4
Woking U.K. 49 G7
Wokingham watercourse Australia 110 C4
Wokingham U.K. 49 G7
Woko National Park Australia 112 E3
Wolcott IN U.S.A. 134 B3
Wolcott NY U.S.A. 135 G2
Woldegk Germany 53 N1
Wolea atoll Micronesia see Woleai
Woleai atoll Micronesia 69 K5
Wolf r. Canada 120 C2
Wolf r. TN U.S.A. 131 F5
Wolf r. WI U.S.A. 130 F2
Wolf Creek MT U.S.A. 126 E3
Wolf Creek OR U.S.A. 126 C4
Wolf Creek Pass U.S.A. 127 G5
Wolfen Germany 53 M3
Wolfenbüttel Germany 53 K2
Wolfhagen Germany 53 J3
Wolf Lake Canada 120 D2
Wolf Point U.S.A. 126 G2
Wolfsberg Austria 47 O7
Wolfsburg Germany 53 K2
Wolfstein Germany 53 H5
Wolfville Canada 123 I5
Wolgast Germany 47 N3
Wolin Poland 47 O4
Wollaston Lake Canada 121 K3
Wollaston Lake l. Canada 121 K3
Wollaston Peninsula Canada 118 G3
Wollemi National Park Australia 112 E4
Wollongong Australia 112 E5
Wolmaransstad S. Africa 101 G4
Wolmirstedt Germany 53 L2
Wolong Reserve nature res. China 76 D2
Wolseley Australia 111 C8
Wolseley S. Africa 100 D7
Wolsey U.S.A. 130 D2
Wolsingham U.K. 48 F4
Wolvega Neth. 52 G2
Wolvegea Neth. see Wolvega
Wolverhampton U.K. 49 E6
Wolverine U.S.A. 134 C1
Wommelgem Belgium 52 E3
Womrather Höhe hill Germany 53 H5
Wonarah Australia 110 B3
Wonay, Kowtal-e Afgh. 89 H3
Wondai Australia 111 E5
Wongalarroo Lake salt l. Australia 112 B3
Wongarbon Australia 112 D4
Wong Chuk Hang H.K. China 77 [inset]
Wong Leng hill H.K. China 77 [inset]
Wong Wan Chau H.K. China see Double Island
Wŏnju S. Korea 75 B5
Wonowon Canada 120 F3
Wŏnsan N. Korea 75 B5
Wonthaggi Australia 112 B7
Wonyulgunna, Mount hill Australia 109 B6
Woocalla Australia 111 B6
Wood, Mount Canada 120 A2
Woodbine GA U.S.A. 133 D6
Woodbine NJ U.S.A. 135 H4
Woodbridge U.K. 49 I6
Woodbridge U.S.A. 135 G4
Wood Buffalo National Park Canada 120 H3
Woodburn U.S.A. 126 C3
Woodbury NJ U.S.A. 135 H4
Woodbury TN U.S.A. 131 G5
Wooded Bluff hd Australia 112 F2
Wood Lake Canada 121 K4
Woodlake U.S.A. 128 D3
Woodland CA U.S.A. 128 C2
Woodland PA U.S.A. 135 F3
Woodland WA U.S.A. 126 C3
Woodlands Sing. 71 [inset]
Woodlark Island P.N.G. 106 F2
Woodridge Canada 121 L5
Woodroffe watercourse Australia 110 B4
Woodroffe, Mount Australia 109 E6
Woodruff UT U.S.A. 126 F4
Woodruff WI U.S.A. 130 F2
Woods, Lake salt flat Australia 108 F4
Woods, Lake of the Canada/U.S.A. 125 I2
Woodsfield U.S.A. 134 E4
Woodside Australia 112 C7
Woodstock N.B. Canada 123 I5
Woodstock Ont. Canada 134 E2
Woodstock IL U.S.A. 130 F3
Woodstock VA U.S.A. 135 F4
Woodstock VT U.S.A. 135 I2
Woodsville U.S.A. 135 I1
Woodville Canada 135 F1
Woodville MS U.S.A. 131 F6
Woodville OH U.S.A. 134 D3
Woodville TX U.S.A. 131 E6
Woodward U.S.A. 131 D4
Woody U.S.A. 128 D4
Wooler U.K. 48 E3
Woolgoolga Australia 112 F3
Wooli Australia 112 F2
Woollard, Mount Antarctica 152 K1
Woollett, Lac l. Canada 122 G4
Woolyeenyer Hill hill Australia 109 C8
Woomera Australia 111 B6
Woomera Prohibited Area Australia 109 F7
Woonsocket RI U.S.A. 135 J2
Woonsocket SD U.S.A. 130 D2
Woorabinda Australia 110 E5
Wooramel r. Australia 109 A6
Wooster U.S.A. 134 E3
Worbis Germany 53 K3
Worbody Point Australia 110 C2
Worcester S. Africa 100 D7
Worcester U.K. 49 E6
Worcester MA U.S.A. 135 J2
Worcester NY U.S.A. 135 H2
Wörgl Austria 47 N7
Workai i. Indon. 69 I8
Workington U.K. 48 D4
Worksop U.K. 48 F5
Workum Neth. 52 F2
Worland U.S.A. 126 G3
Wörlitz Germany 53 M3
Wormerveer Neth. 52 E2
Worms Germany 53 I5
Worms Head hd U.K. 49 C7
Wortel Namibia 100 C2
Wörth am Rhein Germany 53 I5
Worthing U.K. 49 G8
Worthington IN U.S.A. 134 B4
Worthington MN U.S.A. 130 E3
Wotje atoll Marshall Is 150 H5
Wotu Indon. 69 G7
Woudrichem Neth. 52 E3
Woustviller France 52 H5
Wowoni i. Indon. 69 G7
Wozrojdeniye Oroli i. Uzbek. see Vozrozhdenya Island
Wrangel Island Rus. Fed. 65 T2
Wrangell Island U.S.A. 120 C3
Wrangell Mountains U.S.A. 153 B3
Wrangell-St Elias National Park and Preserve U.S.A. 120 A2
Wrath, Cape U.K. 50 D2
Wray U.S.A. 130 C3
Wreake r. U.K. 49 F6
Wreck Point S. Africa 100 C5
Wreck Reef Australia 110 F4
Wrecsam U.K. see Wrexham
Wrestedt Germany 53 K2
Wrexham U.K. 49 E5
Wrightmyo India 71 A5
Wrightson, Mount U.S.A. 127 F7
Wrightwood U.S.A. 128 E4
Wrigley Canada 120 F2
Wrigley U.S.A. 134 D4
Wrigley Gulf Antarctica 152 J2
Wrocław Poland 47 P5
Września Poland 47 P4
Wu'an China see Changtai
Wubin Australia 109 B7
Wuchang Heilong. China 74 B3
Wuchang Hubei China see Jiangxia
Wuchow China see Wuzhou
Wuchuan Guangdong China see Meilu
Wuchuan Guizhou China 76 E2
Wudalianchi China 74 B2
Wuḍām 'Alwā Oman 88 E6
Wudang Shan mt. China 77 F1
Wudaoliang China 76 B1
Wuding China 76 D3
Wudinna Australia 109 F8
Wufeng Hubei China 77 F2
Wufeng Yunnan China see Zhenxiong
Wugang China 77 F3
Wuhai China 72 J5
Wuhan China 77 G2
Wuhe China 77 H1
Wuhu China 77 H2
Wuhua China 77 G4
Wuhubei China 77 H2
Wüjang China 82 D2
Wu Jiang r. China 76 E2
Wujin Jiangsu China see Changzhou
Wujin Sichuan China see Xinjin
Wukari Nigeria 96 D4
Wulang China 76 B2
Wuli China 76 B1
Wulian Feng mts China 76 D2
Wuliang Shan mts China 76 D3
Wuliaru i. Indon. 108 E1
Wuli Jiang r. China 77 F4
Wuling Shan mts China 77 F2
Wulong China 76 E2
Wulongji China see Huaibin
Wulur Indon. 108 E1
Wumeng Shan mts China 76 D3
Wuming China 77 F4
Wümme r. Germany 53 I1
Wundwin Myanmar 70 B2
Wungda China 76 D2
Wuning China 77 G2
Wünnenberg Germany 53 I3
Wunnummin Lake Canada 119 J4
Wunsiedel Germany 53 M4
Wunstorf Germany 53 J2
Wupatki National Monument nat. park U.S.A. 129 H4
Wuping China 77 H3
Wuppertal Germany 53 H3
Wuppertal S. Africa 100 D7
Wuqi China 73 J5
Wuqia China 80 D4
Wuquan China see Wuyang
Wuranga Australia 109 B7
Wurno Nigeria 96 D3
Würzburg Germany 53 J5
Wurzen Germany 53 M3
Wushan Chongqing China 77 F2
Wushan Gansu China 76 E1
Wu Shan mts China 77 F2
Wushi Guangdong China 77 F4
Wushi Xinjiang China 80 E3
Wüstegarten hill Germany 53 J3
Wusuli Jiang r. China/Rus. Fed. see Ussuri
Wuvulu Island P.N.G. 69 K7
Wuwei China 72 I5
Wuxi Chongqing China 77 F2
Wuxi Hunan China 77 F2
Wuxi Hunan China see Qiyang
Wuxi Jiangsu China 77 I2
Wuxia China see Wushan
Wuxian China see Suzhou
Wuxing China see Huzhou
Wuxu China 77 F4
Wuxuan China 77 F4
Wuxue China 77 G2
Wuyang Guizhou China see Zhenyuan
Wuyang Henan China 77 G1
Wuyang Zhejiang China see Wuyi
Wuyi China 77 H2
Wuyiling China 74 C2
Wuyi Shan mts China 77 H3
Wuyuan Jiangxi China 77 H2
Wuyuan Nei Mongol China 73 J4
Wuyuan Zhejiang China see Haiyan
Wuyun China see Jinyun
Wuzhishan China 77 F5
Wuzhi Shan mts China 77 F5

Wuzhong China 72 J5
Wuzhou China 77 F4
Wyalkatchem Australia 109 B7
Wyalong Australia 112 C4
Wyandra Australia 112 B1
Wyangala Reservoir Australia 112 D4
Wyara, Lake salt flat Australia 112 B2
Wycheproof Australia 112 A6
Wylliesburg U.S.A. 135 F5
Wyloo Australia 108 B5
Wylye r. U.K. 49 F7
Wymondham U.K. 49 I6
Wymore U.S.A. 130 D3
Wynbring Australia 109 F7
Wyndham Australia 108 E3
Wyndham-Werribee Australia 112 B6
Wynne U.S.A. 131 F5
Wynyard Canada 121 J5
Wyola Lake salt flat Australia 109 E7
Wyoming U.S.A. 134 C2
Wyoming state U.S.A. 126 G4
Wyoming Peak U.S.A. 126 F4
Wyoming Range mts U.S.A. 126 F4
Wyong Australia 112 E4
Wyperfeld National Park Australia 111 C7
Wysox U.S.A. 135 G3
Wyszków Poland 47 R4
Wythall U.K. 49 F6
Wytheville U.S.A. 134 E5
Wytmarsum Neth. see Witmarsum

X

Xaafuun Somalia 98 F2
▶Xaafuun, Raas pt Somalia 86 H7
Most easterly point of Africa.
Xabyaisamba China 76 C2
Xaçmaz Azer. 91 H2
Xago China 83 G3
Xagquka China 76 B2
Xaidulla China 82 D1
Xaignabouli Laos 70 C3
Xaignabouri Laos see Xaignabouli
Xainza China 83 G3
Xai-Xai Moz. 101 K3
Xalapa Mex. see Jalapa
Xambioa Brazil 143 I5
Xam Nua Laos 70 D2
Xá-Muteba Angola 99 B4
Xan r. Laos 70 C3
Xanagas Botswana 100 E2
Xangda China see Nangqên
Xangdin Hural China 73 K4
Xangdoring China 83 E2
Xangongo Angola 99 B5
Xankändi Azer. 91 G3
Xanlar Azer. 91 G2
Xanthi Greece 59 K4
Xarag China 83 I1
Xarardheere Somalia 98 E3
Xàtiva Spain 57 F4
Xavantes, Serra dos hills Brazil 143 I6
Xaxa China 83 E2
Xayar China 80 F3
Xela Guat. see Quetzaltenango
Xelva Spain see Chelva
Xenia U.S.A. 134 D4
Xero Potamos r. Cyprus see Xeros
Xeros r. Cyprus 85 A2
Xhora S. Africa see Elliotdale
Xiabole Shan mt. China 74 B2
Xiachuan Dao i. China 77 G4
Xiaguan China see Dali
Xiahe China 76 D1
Xiamen China 77 H3
Xi'an China 77 F1
Xianfeng China 77 F2
Xiangcheng Sichuan China 76 C2
Xiangcheng Yunnan China see Xiangyun
Xiangfan China 77 G1
Xiangfeng China see Laifeng
Xianggang H.K. China see Hong Kong
Xianggang Tebie Xingzhengqu aut. reg. China see Hong Kong
Xianggelila China 76 C3
Xiangjiang China see Huichang
Xiangkou China see Wulong
Xiangning China 73 K5
Xiangquan He r. China see Langqên Zangbo
Xiangride China 83 I2
Xiangshan China see Menghai
Xiangshui China 77 H1
Xiangshuiba China 77 F3
Xiangtan China 77 G3
Xiangxiang China 77 G3
Xiangyang China see Xiangfan
Xiangyang Hu l. China 83 G2
Xiangyin China 77 G2
Xiangyun China 76 D3
Xianju China 77 I2
Xianning China 77 G2
Xiannümiao China see Jiangdu
Xianshui He r. China 76 D2
Xiantao China 77 G2
Xianxia Ling mts China 77 H3
Xianyang China 77 F1
Xiaocaohu China 80 G3
Xiaodong China 77 F4
Xiaodongliang China 76 C1
Xiao'ergou China 74 A2
Xiaogan China 77 G2
Xiaogang China see Dongxiang
Xiao Hinggan Ling mts China 74 B2
Xiaojin China 76 D2
Xiaonanchuan China 83 H2
Xiaosanjiang China 77 G3
Xiaoshan China 77 I2
Xiao Shan mts China 77 F1
Xiaoshi China see Benxi
Xiao Surmang China 76 C1
Xiaotao China 77 H3
Xiaoxi China see Pinghe
Xiaoxian China 77 H1
Xiaoxiang Ling mts China 76 D2
Xiaoxita China see Yiling
Xiapu China 77 I3
Xiaqiong China see Batang
Xiashan China see Zhanjiang
Xiayang China see Yanling
Xiayanjing China see Yanjing
Xiayingpan Guizhou China see Lupanshui
Xiayingpan Guizhou China see Luzhi
Xiayukou China 77 F1
Xiazhuang China see Linshu
Xibdê China 76 C2
Xibing China 77 H3
Xibu China see Dongshan
Xichang China 76 D3
Xichou China 76 E4
Xichuan China 77 F1
Xide China 76 D2
Xidu China see Hengyang
Xiemahe' China 77 F2
Xieng Khouang Laos see Phônsavan
Xiêng Lam Vietnam 70 D3
Xieyang Dao i. China 77 F4
Xifeng Guizhou China 76 E3
Xifeng Liaoning China 74 B4
Xifengzhen China see Qingyang
Xigazê China 83 G3
Xihan Shui r. China 76 E1
Xi He r. China 76 E2
Xi Jiang r. China 77 G4
Xijir China 83 G2
Xijir Ulan Hu salt l. China 83 G2
Xiliao He r. China 74 A4
Xilin China 76 E3
Xilinhot China 73 L4
Ximiao China 80 J3
Xin'an Anhui China see Lai'an
Xin'an Guizhou China see Anlong
Xin'an Henan China 77 G1
Xin'anjiang China 77 H2
Xin'anjiang Shuiku resr China 77 H2
Xinavane Moz. 101 K3
Xin Barag Zuoqi China see Amgalang
Xincai China 77 G1
Xinchang Jiangxi China see Yifeng
Xinchang Zhejiang China 77 I2
Xincheng Fujian China see Gutian
Xincheng Guangdong China see Xinxing
Xincheng Guangxi China 77 F3
Xincheng Sichuan China see Zhaojue
Xincun China see Dongchuan
Xindi Guangxi China 77 F4
Xindi Hubei China see Honghu
Xindian China 74 B3
Xindu Guangxi China 77 F4
Xindu Sichuan China see Luhuo
Xindu Sichuan China 76 E2
Xinduqiao China 76 D2
Xinfeng Guangdong China 77 G3
Xinfeng Jiangxi China 77 G3
Xinfengjiang Shuiku resr China 77 G4
Xing'an Guangxi China 77 F3
Xingan China 77 G3
Xing'an Shaanxi China see Ankang
Xingba China 76 B2
Xingguo Gansu China see Qin'an
Xingguo Hubei China see Yangxin
Xingguo Jiangxi China 77 G3
Xinghai China 80 I4
Xinghua China 77 H1
Xinghua Wan b. China 77 H3
Xingkai China 74 D3
Xingkai Hu l. China/Rus. Fed. see Khanka, Lake
Xinglong China 74 B2
Xinglongzhen Gansu China 76 E1
Xinglongzhen Heilong. China 74 B3
Xingning Guangdong China 77 G3
Xingning Hunan China 77 G3
Xingou China 77 G2
Xingping China 77 F1
Xingqêngoin China 76 D2
Xingren China 76 E3
Xingsagoinba China 76 D1
Xingshan Guizhou China see Majiang
Xingshan Hubei China 77 F2
Xingtai China 73 K5
Xingu r. Brazil 143 H4
Xingu, Parque Indígena do res. Brazil 143 H6
Xinguara Brazil 143 H5
Xingye China 77 F4
Xingyi China 76 E3
Xinhua Guangdong China see Huadu
Xinhua Hunan China 77 F3
Xinhua Yunnan China see Qiaojia
Xinhua Yunnan China see Funing
Xinhuang China 77 F3
Xinhui China 77 G4
Xining China 72 I5
Xinjian China 77 G2
Xinjiang China 77 F1
Xinjiang aut. reg. China see Xinjiang Uygur Zizhiqu
Xinjiangkou China see Songzi
Xinjiang Uygur Zizhiqu aut. reg. China 82 E1
Xinjie Qinghai China 76 D1
Xinjie Yunnan China 76 C3
Xinjie Yunnan China 76 D4
Xinjin China 76 D2
Xinjing China see Jingxi
Xinkai He r. China 74 A4
Xinling China see Badong
Xinlitun China 74 B2
Xinlong China 76 D2
Xinmi China 77 G1
Xinmin China 74 B2
Xinning Gansu China see Ningxian
Xinning Hunan China 77 F3
Xinning Jiangxi China see Wuning
Xinning Sichuan China see Kaijiang
Xinping China 76 D3
Xinqiao China 77 G1
Xinqing China 74 C2
Xinquan China 77 H3
Xinshan China see Anyuan
Xinshiba China see Ganluo
Xinsi China 76 E1
Xintai China 73 L5
Xintanpu China 77 G2
Xintian China 77 G3
Xinxiang China 77 G1
Xinxing China 77 G4
Xinyang Henan China 77 G1
Xinyang Henan China see Pingqiao
Xinye China 77 G1
Xinyi Guangdong China 77 F4
Xinyi Jiangsu China 77 H1
Xinying China 77 F5
Xinying Taiwan see Hsinying
Xinyu China 77 G3
Xinyuan Qinghai China see Tianjun
Xinyuan Xinjiang China 80 F3
Xinzhangfang China 74 A2
Xinzhou Guangxi China see Longlin
Xinzhou Hubei China 77 G2
Xinzhou Shanxi China 73 K5
Xinzhu Taiwan see Hsinchu
Xinzo de Limia Spain 57 C2
Xiongshan China see Zhenghe
Xiongshi China see Guixi
Xiongzhou China see Nanxiong
Xiping Henan China 77 F1
Xiping Henan China 77 G1
Xiqing Shan mts China 76 D1
Xique Xique Brazil 143 J6
Xisa China see Xichou
Xisha Qundao is S. China Sea see Paracel Islands
Xishuangbanna reg. China 76 D4
Xishui Guizhou China 76 E2
Xishui Hubei China 77 G2
Xitianmu Shan mt. China 77 H2
Xiugu China see Jinxi
Xi Ujimqin Qi China see Bayan Ul Hot
Xiuning China 77 H2
Xiushan Chongqing China 77 F2
Xiushan Yunnan China see Tonghai
Xiushui China 77 G2
Xiuwen China 76 E3
Xiuwu China 77 G1
Xiuying China 77 F4
Xiwu China 76 C1
Xixabangma Feng mt. China 83 F3
Xixia China 77 F1
Xixiang China 76 E1
Xixiu China see Anshun
Xixón Spain see Gijón-Xixón
Xiyang Dao i. China 77 I3
Xiyang Jiang r. China 76 E3
Xizang aut. reg. China see Xizang Zizhiqu
Xizang Gaoyuan plat. China see Tibet, Plateau of
Xizang Zizhiqu aut. reg. China 83 G3
Xo'japiryox tog'i mt. Uzbek. 89 G2
Xo'jayli Uzbek. 80 A3
Xorkol China 80 H4
Xuancheng China 77 H2
Xuan'en China 77 F2
Xuanhua China 73 L4
Xuân Lôc Vietnam 71 D5
Xuanwei China 76 E3
Xuanzhou China see Xuancheng
Xuchang China 77 G1
Xucheng China see Xuwen
Xuddur Somalia 98 E3
Xuefeng China see Mingxi
Xuefeng Shan mts China 77 F3
Xue Shan mts China 76 C3
Xugui China 80 I4
Xuguit Qi China see Yakeshi
Xujiang China see Guangchang
Xümatang China 76 C1
Xunde Qundao is Paracel Is see Amphitrite Group
Xungba China see Xangdoring
Xungmai China 83 G3
Xunhe China 74 B2
Xun He r. China 74 C2
Xun Jiang r. China 77 F4
Xunwu China 77 G3
Xunyi China 77 F1
Xúquer, Riu r. Spain 57 F4
Xuru Co salt l. China 83 F3
Xuwen China 68 E2
Xuyi China 77 H1
Xuyong China 76 E2
Xuzhou China 77 H1

Y

Ya'an China 76 D2
Yabanabat Turkey see Kızılcahamam
Yabēlo Eth. 98 D3
Yablonovyy Khrebet mts Rus. Fed. 73 J2
Yabrīn reg. Saudi Arabia 88 C6
Yabuli China 74 C3
Yacha China see Baisha
Yacheng China 77 F5
Yachi He r. China 76 E3
Yacuma r. Bol. 142 E6
Yadgir India 84 C2
Yadrin Rus. Fed. 42 J5
Yaeyama-rettō is Japan 73 M8
Yafa Israel see Tel Aviv-Yafo
Yagaba Ghana 96 C3
Yagan China 72 I4
Yağda Turkey see Erdemli
Yaghan Basin sea feature S. Atlantic Ocean 148 D9
Yagman Turkm. 88 D2
Yagodnoye Rus. Fed. 65 P3
Yagodnyy Rus. Fed. 74 E2
Yagoua Cameroon 97 E3
Yagra China 83 E3
Yagradagzê Shan mt. China 76 B1
Yaguajay Cuba 133 E8
Yaha Thai. 71 C6
Yahk Canada 120 G5
Yahualica Mex. 136 D4
Yahyalı Turkey 55 L4
Yai Myanmar see Ye
Yai, Khao mt. Thai. 71 B4
Yaizu Japan 75 E6
Yajiang China 76 D2
Yakacık Turkey 85 C1
Yakeshi China 73 M3
Yakhab waterhole Iran 88 E3
Yakhehal Afgh. 89 G4
Yakima U.S.A. 126 C3
Yakima r. U.S.A. 126 D3
Yakmach Pak. 89 F4
Yako Burkina 96 C3
Yakovlevka Rus. Fed. 74 D3
Yaku-shima i. Japan 75 C7
Yakutat U.S.A. 120 B3
Yakutat Bay U.S.A. 120 A3
Yakutsk Rus. Fed. 65 N3
Yakymivka Ukr. 43 G7
Yala Thai. 71 C6
Yalai China 83 F3
Yala National Park Sri Lanka see Ruhuna National Park
Yalan Dünya Mağarası tourist site Turkey 85 A1
Yale Canada 120 F5
Yale U.S.A. 134 D2
Yalgoo Australia 109 B7
Yalleroi Australia 110 D5
Yaloké Cent. Afr. Rep. 98 B3
Yalova Turkey 59 M4
Yalta Ukr. 90 D1
Yalu Jiang r. China/N. Korea 74 B4
Yalujiang Kou r. mouth China/N. Korea 75 B5
Yalvaç Turkey 59 N5
Yamagata Japan 75 F5
Yamaguchi Japan 75 C6
Yamal, Poluostrov pen. Rus. Fed. see Yamal Peninsula
Yam-Alin', Khrebet mts Rus. Fed. 74 D1
Yamal Peninsula Rus. Fed. 64 H2
Yamanie Falls National Park Australia 110 D3
Yamba Australia 112 F2
Yamba Lake Canada 121 I1
Yambarran Range hills Australia 108 E3
Yambi, Mesa de hills Col. 142 D3
Yambio Sudan 97 F4
Yambol Bulg. 59 L3
Yamdena i. Indon. 108 E1
Yamethin Myanmar 70 B2
▶Yamin, Puncak mt. Indon. 69 J7
4th highest mountain in Oceania.
Yamkanmardi India 84 B2
Yamkhad Syria see Aleppo
Yamm Rus. Fed. 45 P7
Yamma Yamma, Lake salt flat Australia 111 C5
▶Yamoussoukro Côte d'Ivoire 96 C4
Capital of Côte d'Ivoire.
Yampa r. U.S.A. 129 I1
Yampil' Ukr. 43 F6
Yampol' Ukr. see Yampil'
Yamuna r. India 82 E4
Yamunanagar India 82 D3
Yamzho Yumco l. China 83 G3
Yana r. Rus. Fed. 65 O2
Yanam India 84 D2
Yan'an China 73 J5
Yanaoca Peru 142 D6
Yanaon India see Yanam
Yanaul Rus. Fed. 41 Q4
Yanbu' al Baḩr Saudi Arabia 86 E5
Yanceyville U.S.A. 132 E4
Yancheng Henan China 77 G1
Yancheng Jiangsu China 77 I1
Yanchep Australia 109 A7
Yanco Australia 112 C5
Yanco Creek r. Australia 112 B5
Yanco Glen Australia 111 C6
Yanda watercourse Australia 112 B3
Yandama Creek watercourse Australia 111 C6
Yandao China see Yingjing
Yandoon Myanmar 70 A3
Yandun China 80 H3
Yanfolila Mali 96 C3
Ya'ngamdo China 76 B2
Yangbi China 76 C3
Yangcheng Guangdong China see Yangshan
Yangcheng Shanxi China 77 G1
Yangchuan China see Suiyang
Yangchun China 77 F4
Yangcun China 77 G4
Yangdok N. Korea 75 B5
Yang Hu l. China 83 F2
Yangi Nishon Uzbek. 89 G2
Yangī Qal'ah Afgh. 89 H2
Yangiqishloq Uzbek. 80 C3
Yangirabot Uzbek. 89 G1
Yangiyo'l Uzbek. 80 C3
Yangjiajiang China 77 G2
Yangjiang China 77 F4
Yangming China see Heping
Yangôn Myanmar see Rangoon
Yangping China 77 F2
Yangquan China 73 K5
Yangshan China 77 G3
Yang Talat Thai. 70 C3
Yangtouyan China 76 D3
▶Yangtze r. China 76 E2
Longest river in Asia and 3rd in the world. Also known as Chang Jiang or Jinsha Jiang or Tongtian He or Yangtze Kiang or Zhi Qu.
Yangtze Kiang r. China see Yangtze
Yangudi Rassa National Park Eth. 98 E2
Yangweigang China 77 H1
Yangxi China 77 F4
Yangxian China 76 E1
Yangxin China 77 G2
Yangyang S. Korea 75 C5
Yangzhou Jiangsu China 77 H1
Yangzhou Shaanxi China see Yangxian
Yanhe China 77 F2
Yanhuqu China 83 E2
Yanishpole Rus. Fed. 42 G3
Yanis"yarvi, Ozero l. Rus. Fed. 44 Q5
Yanji China 74 C4
Yanjiang China see Ziyang
Yanjin Henan China 77 G1
Yanjin Yunnan China 76 E2
Yanjing Sichuan China see Yanyuan
Yanjing Xizang China 76 C2
Yanjing Yunnan China see Yanjin
Yankara National Park Nigeria 96 E4
Yankton U.S.A. 130 D3
Yanling Hunan China 77 G3
Yanling Sichuan China see Weiyuan
Yannina Greece see Ioannina
Yano-Indigirskaya Nizmennost' lowland Rus. Fed. 65 P2
Yanovski, Mount U.S.A. 120 C3
Yanrey r. Australia 109 A5
Yanshan Jiangxi China 77 H2
Yanshan Yunnan China 76 E4
Yanshi China 77 G1
Yanshiping China 76 B1
Yanskiy Zaliv g. Rus. Fed. 65 O2
Yantabulla Australia 112 B2
Yantai China 73 M5
Yanting China 76 E2
Yantongshan China 74 B4
Yantou China 77 I2
Yanwa China 76 C3
Yany-Kurgan Kazakh. see Zhanakorgan
Yanyuan China 76 D3
Yao Chad 97 E3
Yao'an China 76 D3
Yaodu China see Dongzhi
Yaoli China 77 H2
▶Yaoundé Cameroon 96 E4
Capital of Cameroon.
Yaoxian Shaanxi China see Yaozhou
Yaoxiaoling China 74 B2
Yao Yai, Ko i. Thai. 71 B6
Yaozhou China 77 F1
Yap i. Micronesia 69 J5
Yapen i. Indon. 69 J7
Yappar r. Australia 110 C3
Yap Trench sea feature N. Pacific Ocean 150 F5
Yaqui r. Mex. 127 F8
Yar Rus. Fed. 42 L4
Yaradzha Turkm. see Ýarajy
Ýarajy Turkm. 88 E2
Yaraka Australia 110 D5
Yarangüme Turkey see Tavas
Yaransk Rus. Fed. 42 J4
Yardea Australia 111 A7
Yardımcı Burnu pt Turkey 59 N6
Yardımlı Azer. 91 H3
Yardymly Azer. see Yardımlı
Yare r. U.K. 49 I6
Yarega Rus. Fed. 42 L3
▶Yaren Nauru 107 G2
Capital of Nauru.
Yarensk Rus. Fed. 42 K3
Yariga-take mt. Japan 75 E5
Yarīm Yemen 86 F7
Yarımca Turkey see Körfez
Yarkand China see Shache
Yarkant China see Shache
Yarkant He r. China 80 E4
Yarker Canada 135 G1
Yarkhun r. Pak. 89 I2
Yarlung Zangbo r. China 76 B2 see Brahmaputra
Yarmouth Canada 123 I6
Yarmouth England U.K. 49 F8
Yarmouth England U.K. see Great Yarmouth
Yarmouth U.S.A. 135 J2
Yarmuk r. Asia 85 B3
Yarnell U.S.A. 129 G4
Yaroslavl' Rus. Fed. 42 H4
Yaroslavskiy Rus. Fed. 74 D3
Yarra r. Australia 112 B6
Yarra Junction Australia 112 B6
Yarram Australia 112 C7
Yarraman Australia 112 E1
Yarrawonga Australia 112 B6
Yarra Yarra Lakes salt flat Australia 109 A7
Yarronvale Australia 112 B1
Yarrowmere Australia 110 D4
Yartö Tra La pass China 83 H3
Yartsevo Krasnoyarskiy Kray Rus. Fed. 64 J3
Yartsevo Smolenskaya Oblast' Rus. Fed. 43 G5
Yarumal Col. 142 C2
Yarwa China 76 C2
Yarzhong China 76 C2
Yaş Romania see Iaşi
Yasawa Group is Fiji 107 H3
Yashilkŭl l. Tajik. 89 I2
Yashkul' Rus. Fed. 43 J7
Yasin Pak. 82 C1
Yasnogorsk Rus. Fed. 43 H5
Yasnyy Rus. Fed. 74 C1
Yasothon Thai. 70 D4
Yass Australia 112 D5
Yass r. Australia 112 D5
Yassı Burnu c. Cyprus see Plakoti, Cape
Yāsūj Iran 88 C4
Yasuní, Parque Nacional nat. park Ecuador 142 C4
Yatağan Turkey 59 M6
Yaté New Caledonia 107 G4
Yates r. Canada 120 H2
Yates Center U.S.A. 130 E4
Yathkyed Lake Canada 121 L2
Yatsushiro Japan 75 C6
Yaṭṭa West Bank 85 B4
Yatton U.K. 49 E7
Yauca Peru 142 D7
Yau Tong b. H.K. China 77 [inset]
Yavan Tajik. see Yovon
Yavari r. Brazil/Peru 142 E4
also known as Javari (Brazil/Peru)
Yávaros Mex. 127 F8
Yavatmal India 84 C1
Yavi Turkey 91 F3
Yaví, Cerro mt. Venez. 142 E2
Yavoriv Ukr. 43 D6
Yavuzlu Turkey 85 C1
Yawatongguzlangar China 83 E1
Yaw Chaung r. Myanmar 76 B4
Yaxian China see Sanya
Yay Myanmar see Ye
Yayladağı Turkey 85 C2
Yazd Iran 88 D4
Yazdān Iran 89 F3
Yazd-e Khväst Iran 88 D4
Yazıhan Turkey 90 E3
Yazoo City U.S.A. 131 F5
Y Bala U.K. see Bala
Yding Skovhøj hill Denmark 47 L3
Ydra i. Greece 59 J6
Y Drenewydd U.K. see Newtown
Ye Myanmar 70 B4
Yea Australia 112 B6
Yealmpton U.K. 49 D8
Yebawmi Myanmar 70 A1
Yebbi-Bou Chad 97 E2
Yecheng China 80 E4
Yécora Mex. 127 F7
Yedashe Myanmar 70 B3
Yedatore India 84 C3
Yedi Burun Başı pt Turkey 59 M6
Yeeda River Australia 108 C4
Yefremov Rus. Fed. 43 H5
Yêgainnyin China see Henan
Yeghegnadzor Armenia 91 G3
Yegindykol' Kazakh. 80 C1
Yegorlykskaya Rus. Fed. 43 I7
Yegorova, Mys pt Rus. Fed. 74 E3
Yegor'yevsk Rus. Fed. 43 H5
Yei Sudan 97 G4
Yei r. Sudan 97 G4
Yeji China 77 G2
Yejiaji China see Yeji
Yekaterinburg Rus. Fed. 64 H4
Yekaterinodar Rus. Fed. see Krasnodar
Yekaterinoslav Ukr. see Dnipropetrovs'k
Yekaterinoslavka Rus. Fed. 74 C2
Yekhegnadzor Armenia see Yeghegnadzor
Ye Kyun i. Myanmar 70 A3
Yelabuga Khabarovskiy Kray Rus. Fed. 74 D2
Yelabuga Respublika Tatarstan Rus. Fed. 42 K5
Yelan' Rus. Fed. 43 I6
Yelan' r. Rus. Fed. 43 I6
Yelandur India 84 C3
Yelantsy Rus. Fed. 72 J2
Yelarbon Australia 112 E2
Yelbarsli Turkm. 89 F2
Yelenovskiye Kar'yery Ukr. see Dokuchayevs'k
Yelets Rus. Fed. 43 H5
Yélimané Mali 96 B3
Yelizavetgrad Ukr. see Kirovohrad
Yelkhovka Rus. Fed. 43 K5
Yell i. U.K. 50 [inset]
Yellabina Regional Reserve nature res. Australia 109 F7
Yellandu India 84 D2
Yellapur India 84 B3
Yellowhead Pass Canada 120 G4
▶Yellowknife Canada 120 H2
Capital of the Northwest Territories.
Yellowknife r. Canada 120 H2
Yellow Mountain hill Australia 112 C4
▶Yellow r. China 77 G1
4th longest river in Asia, and 7th in the world.
Yellow Sea N. Pacific Ocean 73 N5
Yellowstone r. U.S.A. 130 C2
Yellowstone Lake U.S.A. 126 F3
Yellowstone National Park U.S.A. 126 F3
Yell Sound strait U.K. 50 [inset]
Yeloten Turkm. see Ýolöten
Yelovo Rus. Fed. 41 Q4
Yel'sk Belarus 43 F6
Yelva r. Rus. Fed. 42 K3
Yematan China 76 C1
Yemen country Asia 86 G6
Yemetsk Rus. Fed. 42 I3
Yemişenbükü Turkey see Taşova
Yemmiganur India see Emmiganuru
Yemtsa Rus. Fed. 42 I3
Yemva Rus. Fed. 42 K3
Yena Rus. Fed. 44 Q3
Yenagoa Nigeria 96 D4
Yenakiieve Ukr. 43 H6
Yenakiyevo Ukr. see Yenakiieve
Yenangyat Myanmar 70 A2
Yenangyaung Myanmar 70 A2
Yenanma Myanmar 70 A3
Yenda Australia 112 C5
Yêndum China see Zhag'yab
Yengisar China 80 E4
Yengo National Park Australia 112 E4
Yenice Turkey 59 L5
Yenidamlar Turkey see Demirtaş
Yenihan Turkey see Yıldızeli
Yenije-i-Vardar Greece see Giannitsa
Yenişehir Greece see Larisa
Yenişehir Turkey 59 M4
▶Yenisey r. Rus. Fed. 64 J2
Part of the Yenisey-Angara-Selenga, 3rd longest river in Asia.
▶Yenisey-Angara-Selenga r. Rus. Fed. 64 J2
3rd longest river in Asia, and 6th in the world.
Yeniseysk Rus. Fed. 64 K4
Yeniseyskiy Kryazh ridge Rus. Fed. 64 K4
Yeniseyskiy Zaliv inlet Rus. Fed. 153 F2
Yeniyol Turkey see Borçka
Yên Minh Vietnam 70 D2
Yenotayevka Rus. Fed. 43 J7
Yeola India 84 B1
Yeo Lake salt flat Australia 109 D6
Yeotmal India see Yavatmal
Yeoval Australia 112 D4
Yeovil U.K. 49 E8
Yeo Yeo r. Australia see Bland
Yeppoon Australia 110 E4
Yeraliyev Kazakh. see Kuryk
Yerbent Turkm. 88 E2
Yerbogachen Rus. Fed. 65 L3
Yercaud India 84 C4
▶Yerevan Armenia 91 G2
Capital of Armenia.